The
Occupational
Therapy
Manager

5th Edition

W9-AHH-970

Edited by Karen Jacobs, EdD, OTR/L, CPE, FAOTA,
and Guy L. McCormack, PhD, OTR/L, FAOTA

AOTA PRESS
The American
Occupational Therapy
Association, Inc.

AOTA Centennial Vision

We envision that occupational therapy is a powerful, widely recognized, science-driven, and evidence-based profession with a globally connected and diverse workforce meeting society's occupational needs.

Mission Statement

The American Occupational Therapy Association advances the quality, availability, use, and support of occupational therapy through standard-setting, advocacy, education, and research on behalf of its members and the public.

AOTA Staff

Frederick P. Somers, *Executive Director*
Christopher M. Bluhm, *Chief Operating Officer*

Chris Davis, *Director, AOTA Press*
Ashley Hofmann, *Development/Production Editor*
Victoria Davis, *Production Editor/Editorial Assistant*

Beth Ledford, *Director of Marketing*
Emily Zhang, *Technology Marketing Specialist*
Jennifer Folden, *Marketing Specialist*

American Occupational Therapy Association, Inc.
4720 Montgomery Lane
Bethesda, MD 20814
Phone: 301-652-AOTA (2682)
TDD: 800-377-8555
Fax: 301-652-7711
www.aota.org

© 2011 by the American Occupational Therapy Association, Inc. All rights reserved.
No part of this book may be reproduced in whole or in part by any means without permission. Printed in the United States of America.

Disclaimers

This publication is designed to provide accurate and authoritative information in regard to the subject matter covered. It is sold or distributed with the understanding that the publisher is not engaged in rendering legal, accounting, or other professional service. If legal advice or other expert assistance is required, the services of a competent professional person should be sought.
—*From the Declaration of Principles jointly adopted by the American Bar Association and a Committee of Publishers and Associations*

It is the objective of the American Occupational Therapy Association to be a forum for free expression and interchange of ideas. The opinions expressed by the contributors to this work are their own and not necessarily those of the American Occupational Therapy Association.

ISBN: 978-56900-273-5

Library of Congress Control Number: 2009912738

Cover Artwork "Comfort Zone" by Ruth Palmer. Copyright © 2007, by Ruth Palmer. Used with permission.
Cover Design by Debra Naylor, Naylor Design, Inc., Washington, DC
Composition by Maryland Composition, Laurel, MD
Printed by Automated Graphic Systems, Inc., White Plains, MD

Contents

Figures, Tables, Exhibits, and Appendixes

Figures

Tables

Exhibits

Appendixes

Contributors

Beatriz C. Abreu, PhD, OTR, FAOTA
Clinical Professor
Division of Rehabilitation Sciences
School of Health Professions
University of Texas Medical Branch at Galveston

Lynne Cord Barnes, OT, MA, FACHE, FAOTA
Vice President, Clinical Operations
Carle Foundation Hospital
Urbana, IL

Lea C. Brandt, OTD, OTR/L
MHPC OTA Program Director
Clinical Assistant Professor
School of Health Professions
Faculty, Center for Health Ethics
University of Missouri–Columbia

Brent Braveman, PhD, OTR/L, FAOTA
Clinical Professor of Occupational Therapy
Department of Occupational Therapy
University of Illinois–Chicago

Pei-Fen J. Chang, PhD, OTR
Assistant Professor
School of Occupational Therapy
Texas Woman's University–Houston Center

Richard Y. Cheng, JD, OTR
General Counsel and Vice President of Medical Appeals
Century Rehabilitation, Inc.
Baton Rouge, LA

Denise Chisholm, PhD, OTR/L, FAOTA
Associate Professor and Vice Chairperson
University of Pittsburgh
Pittsburgh

Penelope Moyers Cleveland, EdD, OTR/L, BCMH, FAOTA
Dean of the Heinretta Schmoll School of Health
St. Catherine University
St. Paul, MN

Donna M. Costa, DHS, OTR/L, FAOTA
Professor and Director of OTD Program
Division of Occupational Therapy
University of Utah
Salt Lake City

Thomas H. Dillon, EdD, OTR/L
Dean of Graduate and Professional Studies
Associate Professor of Occupational Therapy
University of Findlay
Findlay, OH

Joy Doll, OTD, OTR/L
Assistant Professor of Occupational Therapy
Creighton University
Omaha, NE

Melanie T. Ellexson, DHSc, MBA, OTR/L, FAOTA
Associate Professor of Occupational Therapy
College of Health and Human Services
Governors State University
University Park, IL

Cynthia F. Epstein, MA, OTR, FAOTA
Executive Director
OT Consultants, Inc.
Somerset, NJ

Rebecca Estes, PhD, OTR, ATP
Associate Professor and Chairperson of Occupational Therapy
University of South Alabama
Mobile

Steven C. Eyler, MS, OTR/L
Director of Rehabilitation Therapies
Fletcher Allen Health Care
Burlington, VT

Thomas F. Fisher, PhD, OTR/L, CCM, FAOTA
Associate Professor and Chairperson
Department of Occupational Therapy
School of Health and Rehabilitation Sciences
Indiana University–Purdue University at Indianapolis

Joanne J. Foss, PhD, OTR/L
Associate Dean of Student and Academic Affairs
College of Public Health and Health Professions
Program Director, Master's in Occupational Therapy
Department of Occupational Therapy
University of Florida
Gainesville

Gordon Muir Giles, PhD, OTR/L, FAOTA
Professor
Samuel Merritt University
Oakland, CA
Director of Neurobehavioral Services
Crestwood Behavioral Health, Inc.
Sacramento, CA

Neil Harvison, PhD, OTR/L
Director of Accreditation and Academic Affairs
American Occupational Therapy Association
Bethesda, MD

Jim Hinojosa, PhD, OT, FAOTA
Professor, Department of Occupational Therapy
The Steinhardt School of Culture, Education, and Human
    Development
New York University
New York

Wendy Holmes, PhD, OTR/L
Associate Professor of Occupational Therapy
Eastern Washington University
Cheney

Karen Jacobs, EdD, OTR/L, CPE, FAOTA
Clinical Professor and Program Director
Department of Occupational Therapy
Boston University
Boston

Evelyn G. Jaffe, MPH, OTR/L, FAOTA
Professor Alumnus
Samuel Merritt University
Oakland, CA

Allison Kabel, PhD
Assistant Professor, School of Health Professions, Health
    Science Program and Department of Occupational
    Therapy and Occupational Science
University of Missouri
Columbia

Kristie Horner Kapusta, MS, OT/L
Occupational Therapist
Underhill, VT

Barbara L. Kornblau, JD, OTR, FAOTA
Dean, School of Health Professions and Studies
Univeristy of Michigan–Flint

Paula Kramer, PhD, OTR/L, FAOTA
Chairperson and Professor of Occupational Therapy
University of the Sciences
Philadelphia

Amy Lamb, OTD, OTR/L
Chairperson, American Occupational Therapy
    Political Action Committee
Bethesda, MD

Jeffrey D. Loveland, OTD, OTR/L
Associate Professor and Director, Occupational Therapy
    Program
James Madison University
Harrisonburg, VA

Guy L. McCormack, PhD, OTR/L, FAOTA
Professor of Occupational Therapy
Samuel Merritt University
Oakland, CA

Melissa Meier, OTD, OTR
Occupational Therapy Doctoral Student, Creighton
    University
Omaha, NE
On rotation with Federal Affairs Division, American
    Occupational Therapy Association
Bethesda, MD

Christina Metzler
Chief Public Affairs Officer
American Occupational Therapy Association
Bethesda, MD

Marie J. Morreale, OTR/L, CHT
Adjunct Faculty
Rockland Community College
State University of New York
Suffern

Amy Paul-Ward, PhD, OT
Associate Professor, Department of Occupational Therapy
College of Nursing and Health Sciences
Modesto Maidique Campus
Miami, FL

Pat Precin, MS, OTR/L, LP
Assistant Professor of Occupational Therapy
New York Institute of Technology
Old Westbury

Shawn Phipps, MS, OTR/L
President, Occupational Therapy Association of California
Manager, California Children's Services Medical Therapy
    Program
Los Angeles County Department of Public Health
Clinical Specialist, Rancho Los Amigos National
    Rehabilitation Center

Tammy Richmond, MS, OTR/L
Chief Operating Officer
Ultimate Rehab, LLC
Los Angeles

Charlotte Royeen, PhD, OTR, FAOTA
Dean of the Edward and Margaret Doisy College of
    Health Sciences
Professor in Occupational Science and Occupational
    Therapy
St. Louis University
St. Louis, MO

Marjorie E. Scaffa, PhD, OTR, FAOTA
Professor of Occupational Therapy
University of South Alabama
Mobile

Karen Sladyk, PhD, OTR, FAOTA
Professor of Occupational Therapy
Bay Path College
Longmeadow, MA

Deborah Yarett Slater, MS, OT/L, FAOTA
Staff Liaison to the Ethics Commission
Staff Liaison to the Special Interest Sections
American Occupational Therapy Association
Bethesda, MD

Diane L. Smith, PhD, OTR/L, FAOTA
Assistant Professor and Chairperson, Department of
Occupational Therapy
University of Missouri
Columbia

Jeff Snodgrass, PhD, MPH, OTR/L
Program Director and Associate Professor
Occupational Therapy Program
Milligan College
Milligan College, TN

Randy Strickland, EdD, OTR/L, FAOTA
Senior Vice President for Academic Affairs and Professor
    of Occupational Therapy
Spalding University
Louisville, KY

V. Judith Thomas
Senior Policy Manager, Division of Public Affairs
American Occupational Therapy Association
Bethesda, MD

Jon M. Thompson, PhD
Professor and Director, Health Services Administration
    Program
James Madison University
Harrisonburg, VA

Lori Vaughn, OTD, OTR/L
Program Director and Assistant Professor of
    Occupational Therapy
Bay Path College
Longmeadow, MA

Chuck Willmarth
Director, State Affairs and Reimbursement
American Occupational Therapy Association
Bethesda, MD

Lesly S. Wilson, PhD, OTR/L
Assistant Research Professor
University of South Carolina
School of Medicine, Department of Pediatrics
Center for Disability Resources–TECS
Columbia

About the Editors

Karen Jacobs, EdD, OTR/L, CPE, FAOTA, is a clinical professor and program director of online postprofessional occupational therapy programs in the Department of Occupational Therapy at Boston University. She is also past president and past vice president of AOTA. She is the founding editor of the interdisciplinary and international journal *Work: A Journal of Prevention, Assessment, and Rehabilitation* (IOS Press, The Netherlands). She earned a doctoral degree at the University of Massachusetts, a master of science in occupational therapy at Boston University, and a bachelor of arts at Washington University in St. Louis, Missouri.

Guy L. McCormack, PhD, OTR/L, FAOTA, is a professor of occupational therapy at Samuel Merritt University in Oakland, California, on special assignment to develop a doctoral program. He was previously clinical professor and chairperson of the Department of Occupational Therapy at the University of Missouri–Columbia. He earned a doctoral degree at Saybrook University in San Francisco, a master of science degree at Ohio State University, and a bachelor of science degree at the University of Puget Sound in Tacoma, Washington.

Preface

With the ongoing changes driven by health care reform, never before has the occupational therapy manager's role been so crucial to advocating for the profession as well as sustaining the day-to-day functions of clinical practice. Occupational therapy practitioners will need to take on broader leadership roles to advance the profession both in the continuum of care and at government and regulatory levels. *The Occupational Therapy Manager, 5th Edition* is a well-timed resource to support practitioners in the important work that they do.

The recent economic climate has challenged private practices, school systems, large organizations, and other health care–related businesses and programs to become more cost-conscious while continuing to provide clients with the necessary therapy services they need. New health care legislation threatens to reduce profit margins in some areas, furthering the need for greater efficiency and good management. Occupational therapy practitioners who have leadership and management skills will be in more demand than ever before.

The Occupational Manager acknowledges that occupational therapy leaders exist across all practice areas and at all levels, and its 37 new and updated chapters aim to guide and develop your leadership, management, and clinical skills, preparing you for expanding opportunities in your career and supporting the growth of occupational therapy.

At the heart of *The Occupational Therapy Manager* is encouragement of students, practitioners, and managers to provide the best occupational therapy services possible. To do this, occupational therapy students and professionals need to understand the role of occupational therapy management (Part I); know how to run a business, department, or program (Part II); become leaders (Part III); maintain strict standards of evidence when determining interventions (Part IV); understand public policy and ensure the highest level of professional standards (Part V); and properly guide the next generation of occupational therapy practitioners and leaders (Part VI).

The Occupational Therapy Manager has been a best-seller for decades and today remains the most comprehensive management-based text on the market for occupational therapy.

—*Frederick P. Somers*
Executive Director
American Occupational Therapy Association
Bethesda, MD

Introduction

The Occupational Therapy Manager has been a best-seller throughout its previous four editions and is the leading publication on management and leadership for occupational therapy practitioners and students. This newly updated and expanded edition aims to be the most comprehensive, up-to-date, and relevant management text in the field of occupational therapy.

"Part I: Defining and Rethinking Management" highlights the ways to conceptualize the role of the manager in the context of its historical development. Management has evolved from the time of the factories of Industrial Revolution in the 19th century through the hierarchical corporate styles of the 20th century to the more linear decision making in the modern global economy. Chapter authors argue that the skill sets needed to be an effective manager today are not dissimilar to the skills one needs to be an effect practitioner. "Evolution of Occupational Therapy Delivery Systems" (Chapter 3) describes how policy and social movements influence practice—a topic particularly relevant in light of the recent U.S. health care reform. Other chapters range from the more theoretical foundations (Chapter 4, "Dynamical Systems Theory in Occupational Therapy Management") to the more grounded systems of occupation-based practice (Chapter 5, "Occupational-Based Practice in Management") that can be immediately applied in daily occupational therapy practice.

"Part II: Strategic Planning" deals with the nuts and bolts of management, addressing the science of management through such topics as strategic planning (Chapter 6), financial planning (Chapter 7), and marketing professional services (Chapter 8), among many other important topics.

"Part III: Leading and Organizing" discusses the essential elements of what one might call the *art of management*. Here, authors examine various aspects of leadership, such as leadership development (Chapter 18), inspiring and motivating others (Chapters 15 and 19), and mentoring (Chapter 16). The basics of good management are reviewed from an occupational therapy perspective, including techniques for communicating in the workplace (Chapter 12) and dealing with personnel issues (Chapter 13). Authors also explore exciting new opportunities for occupational therapy management and leadership in areas of emerging practices (Chapter 21) and cultivating community outreach efforts into international collaboration (Chapter 17).

"Part IV: Controlling Outcomes" returns to the core of occupational therapy practice, that is, how one controls outcomes through evidence-based management approaches. Chapters discuss what constitutes evidence-based practice (Chapter 22) and current methods of documentation (Chapter 24), reimbursement (Chapter 25), evaluation of the efficacy of occupational therapy services (Chapter 26), and strategies for managing change (Chapter 27).

"Part V: Public Policy, Professional Standards, and Collaboration" provide useful information about policy and standards, guiding managers and practitioners in serving clients in ways that align with laws, ethics, and best practices. Although the standards of today may not be the standards of tomorrow, each chapter provides online resources and other methods of obtaining the latest information on standards that help to maintain a high level of compliance.

The final section, "Part VI: Supervision," addresses special supervision issues for occupational therapists and occupational therapy assistants, as well as management of fieldwork education.

Although practical for occupational therapy practitioners, managers, and leaders, *The Occupational Therapy Manager* is also a textbook. Students and educators will find case examples illustrating issues in at Levels I and II fieldwork, as well as for first-time and experienced managers that highlight contexts and scenarios in which the chapter material could apply. Learning objectives and key terms guide reading; multiple-choice questions assist in the review of material; learning activities provide opportunities to further explore particular topics; and evidence tables provide numerous useful resources in a well-organized, easy-to-use format.

Individual chapters refer to and align with the *Occupational Therapy Practice Framework: Domain and Process, 2nd Edition* (American Occupational Therapy Association [AOTA], 2008). The appendixes at the end of this book include AOTA official documents, Accreditation Council for Occupational Therapy Education® standards addressed by each individual chapter, and answers to the multiple-choice questions.

This new edition of *The Occupational Therapy Manager* has assembled a diverse set of chapters from a well-qualified group of scholars and practitioners who are indeed leaders in occupational therapy. We hope you agree that it is best text available to support occupational therapy managers as we move toward the profession's *Centennial Vision* (AOTA, 2007) and helping our clients in "Living Life To Its Fullest™" (Moyers Cleveland, 2008).

—Karen Jacobs, EdD, OTR/L, CPE, FAOTA,
and Guy L. McCormack, PhD, OTR/L, FAOTA

REFERENCES

American Occupational Therapy Association. (2007). AOTA's *Centennial Vision* and executive summary. *American Journal of Occupational Therapy, 61,* 613–614.

American Occupational Therapy Association. (2008). Occupational therapy practice framework: Domain and process (2nd ed.). *American Journal of Occupational Therapy, 62,* 625–883.

Moyers Cleveland, P. (2008). Be unreasonable. Knock on the big doors. Knock loudly [Presidential Address]. *American Journal of Occupational Therapy, 62,* 737–742.

Part I

Defining and Rethinking Management

1

Historical and Current Perspectives on Management

Guy L. McCormack, PhD, OTR/L, FAOTA

❖ Key Terms and Concepts

Bureaucracy. A system of classical management and organizational design that promoted specialization in jobs and positions of authority. Bureaucracy provided a system of rules, hierarchical structure, impersonal superior–subordinate relationships, and excessive red tape.

Hawthorne studies. Famous studies conducted between 1924 and 1933 at the Western Electric plant to determine the effects of the environment and work conditions on productivity. The study suggested that group dynamics and special attention paid to workers had a greater effect on productivity than external variables such as room illumination.

Human relations movement. Movement that grew out of a reaction to the shortcomings of classical scientific manage-

ment. It began in the 1920s and emphasized behavioral theory and the human aspects of productivity in the organization.

Intrapreneurial. Creating another service or product line within an organization to improve customer service or the performance of that product line.

Maslow's hierarchy of needs. A motivational theory by psychologist Abraham Maslow (1908–1970) that postulates that people in the workplace are motivated by a desire to satisfy a set of internal needs.

Scientific management. A classical system of management attributed to mechanical engineer Fredrick Taylor (1856–1915) that used time and motion studies and piece rate as a system to improve worker productivity.

❖ Learning Objectives

After completing this chapter, you should be able to do the following:

- Identify the primary characteristics, strengths, and weaknesses of scientific management.
- Describe the characteristics, strengths, and weaknesses of bureaucracy.
- Identify the major characteristics of the human relations movement, and compare and contrast them with those of scientific management.

- Identify the primary lessons learned from the Hawthorne studies.
- Describe the main concepts that history has contributed to management theory as it is perceived today.

In the United States, persons 25–54 years of age spend 8.7 hours per day on work-related activities (U.S. Bureau of Labor Statistics, 2009). Work experiences and positions become a record of one's accomplishments and provide lasting memories that convey meaning and a sense of achievement. Like their clients, occupational therapy practitioners are motivated by the desire to perform occupations that are important to them. The occupation of work is a gateway to connect with the world. In making

this connection, occupational therapy managers help practitioners discover sources of motivation, accomplishment, and personal meaning.

Philosopher George Santayana (1905) once wrote, "He who neglects history will be condemned to repeat it" (p. 284). This chapter reviews the historical roots of management and identifies current perspectives on management as it is practiced today. By looking at the past, occupational therapy managers can develop plans for the future that attempt to avoid past mistakes. A review of history illuminates the influences that have left a lasting imprint on today's management practices. It allows the occupational therapy manager to sort out what has worked and what has not worked in the past. It also allows the manager to apply best practices to promoting job satisfaction in the workplace; meeting the health care industry's demands for efficiency, safety, and cost containment (Karpf, 2006); and, most importantly, serving clients effectively. The occupational therapy manager should be familiar with the history of management and the theories that set the stage for the systems used today.

A BRIEF HISTORY OF MANAGEMENT

Systems of management were developed in ancient civilizations, including those of China, Egypt, Greece, Rome, and Java (Schermerborn, Hunt, & Asborn, 1994). Each society created management systems to meet its own practical needs, such as to obtain and protect natural resources (e.g., water supply); to create better systems for farming or for the practice of religion; to expand territory; and, most importantly, to maintain borders. In ancient times, the development of management systems contributed to the rise of great civilizations. For example, the Roman army used complex systems of management to mount military campaigns. The Chinese developed a system to manage large populations of workers to carry out public projects such as building the Great Wall and to protect their boundaries from the Mongols. The Chinese invented written exams to determine the best individuals for certain jobs and to guide promotion in public administration; during the same era in Europe, selection for a job was based primarily on birthright.

By the early 1900s, the United States and Europe had taken different paths to management. This was the beginning of the Industrial Revolution, which emphasized building railroads and large business organizations such as the steel industry. Until the Industrial Revolution, the United States had primarily been an agricultural society, and many people wanted to return to a more simple existence. In response to the Industrial Revolution, the Art and Crafts Movement evolved. The industrial might of the United States rested on harnessing vast natural resources, and the focus was directed toward accomplishing the individual task and fitting the best worker to that task (Davis, Hellervik, Skull, Gebelein, & Sheard, 1992). During the same period, Europeans were concerned mainly with developing better methods of managing people and production. As a result of the diverging paths, the United States focused on a system of management known as *scientific management*, whereas in Europe, the focus was on the *science of administration* (Bovee, Thill, Wood, & Dovel, 1993). The sections that follow discuss the lessons of both schools of thought.

SCIENTIFIC MANAGEMENT

Scientific management was an outgrowth of the effects of industrialization and is also referred to as the *classi-cal management perspective.* Frederick W. Taylor (1856–1915), a machinist and industrial engineer from Philadelphia, became known as the father of scientific management (Schermerborn et al., 1994). Taylor observed that employees worked at less than full capacity because they were concerned about being laid off when the job was completed. Taylor also observed that management did not clearly delineate tasks and paid little attention to matching the skills of employees to their assigned tasks. To address this problem, Taylor created a scientific analysis of tasks, called *time and motion studies,* that examined the physical requirements and movements needed to complete a particular work task. Taylor showed in various studies that he could systematically increase a worker's productivity through better body mechanics, economy of motion, and monetary incentives. The analysis of jobs gave rise to the *task concept*—that is, what is to be done, how it is to be done, and exactly when it is to be completed. Work incentives were typically financial rewards and coercion (Hodgetts, 1992; Taylor, 1911).

Taylor was very pragmatic. He did not believe that gainful occupations should be based on personal opinion and guesswork; he believed in proven fact. He found that standardized tools and procedures improved work performance and prevented injury and that periods of rest are necessary for increased productivity. He also believed that money was a significant incentive to workers (Schermerborn et al., 1994; Taylor, 1911). The same principles are accepted today in the science of human engineering called *ergonomics* or *human factors* (Bovee et al., 1993).

Worker Efficiency

Henry Ford (1863–1947), who invented the Model T, has long been associated with American ingenuity. The managerial approach used by Henry Ford is typical of the efficiency practices used in scientific management. He started the Ford Motor Company in 1903, and by 1908, the Model T was designed for affordability for the middle class. Using the principles of scientific management, Ford produced many cars at low cost. Ford's factory was conceived around the concept of efficiency: Each worker performed one task of the assembly line over and over again, and other workers down the line contributed their section of the assembly. By 1925, at the peak of the car's popularity, Model Ts were rolling off Ford's assembly lines at the rate of one every 5 seconds (Wren, 2005). Ford's mechanization of the plant had some adverse effects on the workers, however. The workers become disgruntled with the repetition of the same task day in and day out and the low wages they earned from piece-work assembly. The harder Ford pushed his workers to increase production speed, the less happy the worker became. In 1913, the turnover rate was 380%, and Ford had to hire more employees than he ostensibly needed to keep the assembly line moving and to keep up with consumer demand.

Monetary Motivation

Mechanical engineer Henry L. Gantt (1861–1919) redesigned Taylor's incentive system. He discovered that the differential rate system had a negative impact on motivation. Gantt developed a incentive system in which workers who finished the day's workload would earn a 50-cent bonus. In addition, the supervisor also earned a bonus for each worker who exceeded the daily workload. This incentive plan motivated the supervisors to do a better job at training their employees (Cross, Feather, & Lynch, 1994). To add more incentive, the worker's productivity was displayed on bar graphs so all of the workers could compare their productivity. Black bars were used on days the worker met the standard, and red bars were used when he or she fell below the standard level of production. Gantt is responsible for developing a charting system known as the *Gantt chart* that is still used throughout the world (Bovee et al., 1993).

Process Efficiency

Frank B. and Lillian M. Gilbreth (1868–1924 and 1878–1972) were a husband-and-wife team who collaborated to study work fatigue and motion (*motion studies* is the term used for time-and-motion studies) and looked at ways of protecting the individual worker from fatigue. To the Gilbreths, the goal was to help workers reach their full potential as human beings. They tried to find the most economical motions for each task in order to upgrade performance and reduce fatigue.

As a young man, Frank Gilbreth worked as a bricklayer (Bovee et al., 1993; Pearce & Robinson, 1994). He observed that the bricklayers who were training him used a variety of motions to complete their tasks, and he later used time-and-motion studies to analyze the most efficient method to lay bricks. Gilbreth was able to reduce the bricklaying process by 16 motions and invented an adjustable stand—an adaptive device—to hold bricks so workers would not have to bend over so often to pick up bricks. The Gilbreths had 12 children and claimed to have used scientific management to efficiently organize tasks in their daily living skills such as preparing dinner, folding laundry, and cleaning the house (Bovee et al., 1993).

Discussion of Scientific Management

Although scientific management neglected job satisfaction in its emphasis on job tasks, the piece-rate system and scientific selection of best workers are still in use today (Nadler & Nadler, 1998; Szilagyi & Wallace, 1990). Occupational therapy uses some of Taylor's principles when conducting a task analysis; to modify a task, the occupational therapy practitioner considers areas of occupation, the performance skills needed, the performance patterns of behavior related to the task that are habitual or routine, context, activity demands, and client factors that take into account the task's mental and physiologic demands. After analyzing these factors, the practitioner determines specific strategies to influence the desired outcomes, assessment data, and evidence. In occupational therapy, however, task analysis has a much more holistic focus because it takes into account the meaning and value the activity has to the client (Christiansen & Baum, 1997). The purpose of a time-and-motion study is to eliminate inefficiencies and wasted effort, whereas the purpose of the activity analysis is to set up an occupation that is goal-directed, purposeful, restorative, or designed to prevent or reverse dysfunction. Occupational therapy practitioners use scientific management principles when they teach work simplification and use ergonomics to make adaptations that improve the work site. For example, practitioners working in sheltered workshops often perform time-and-motion studies on small assembly jobs to be performed by individuals with physical and cognitive challenges (Covey & Merrill, 2006).

ADMINISTRATIVE MANAGEMENT

Henri Fayol (1841–1925) was a French engineer who was influential throughout Europe and the United States. He developed a systematic method of management that examined the organization from the top down (Bovee et al., 1993; Fayol, 1929; Turban & Meredith, 1991). Fayol stressed the functional aspects of the organizational structure. According to Fayol, business activities are composed of basic functions, such as technical activities, including production and manufacturing, and commercial activities, such as buying and selling or exchanging. With respect to the management function, Fayol identified *planning* (developing a course of action), *organizing* (mobilizing human resources and materials), *commanding* (directing employees), *coordinating* (integrating activities toward a common goal), and *controlling* (following up to make sure the goals are carried out).

Fayol contributed to the formal organizational structure and communication processes in the workplace. Fayol believed that sound management was the key to success in the workplace. From this basic insight, he drew up a list of 14 principles of management and insisted that management was a skill that could be taught once its underlying principles were revealed (Fayol, 1929; Szilagyi & Wallace, 1990).

Human Relations

Social worker Mary Parker Follett (1868–1933) built on classical management approaches and introduced concepts of human relations that further developed the emerging behavioral science approaches to management. Follett believed that a worker became a whole person through group process. She also believed that human beings developed through their relationships that evolved within the organization. Follett is credited with the belief that management is "the art of getting things done through people" (Tonn, 2003, p. 53). She believed that the distinction between managers (order givers) and subordinates (order takers) obscured this natural partnership. She advocated for the power of the group in enabling individuals to combine their diverse talents to make something bigger than each could do alone. Moreover, Follett's democratic approach to management addressed the effects of the context, the environment, economics, and biological factors. Follett took a new approach to working relationships within the organization and between organizations. (Graham, 1995).

Informal Organizations

Business executive Chester I. Barnard (1886–1961) was opposed to some of the practices of classical management theory and set out to improve management of human activity by examining the underlying informal interpersonal relationships that exist within the organization (McMahon & Carr, 1999). Barnard used his extensive reading in sociology and philosophy to formulate theories about strategic management.

Barnard's major contribution is the recognition of the "informal organization" in management theory. According to Barnard, communication among people in an organization contributed to a more vibrant workplace. He believed that people come together in formal organizations to accomplish goals that they could not achieve in isolation. Barnard saw the underlying humanistic elements of the organization as dynamic and the organizational structure as static. He was concerned with systems of good communication and providing essential services to employees. In order to accomplish the organization's goals, Barnard emphasized work satisfaction and attention to workers' individual needs. According to Barnard, an organization could operate efficiently and survive only when its goals are kept in balance with its aims, and the needs of the individuals working within the system are recognized. Barnard established that people work in stable and mutually beneficial relationships in the workplace: He observed that people naturally come together in informal groups or cliques, and he believed organizations could use these informal groups effectively to accomplish the managers' objectives.

Barnard also observed that employees performed certain duties without questioning their manager's authority; he called this the employee's *zone of indifference*. The more activities that fell within employees' zone of indifference, the better the organization functioned. Barnard also believed that executives had a responsibility to foster a sense of moral purpose in their employees. Bernard encouraged employees to think beyond their own self-interests and to make a commitment to provide a service to society. In this concept of the "greater good," Barnard saw the organization as a collaborative group of individuals working together for a common cause. This philosophical view set the stage for current thinking in management (McMahon & Carr, 1999).

Bureaucracy

Max Weber (1864–1920) was a German sociologist who conducted a systematic study of the social changes brought on by the Industrial Revolution (Bovee et al., 1993). Weber observed that large-scale organizations were on the rise and that the business world was moving away from charismatic leaders and family-based systems and toward macrocosmic organizations. Weber considered *bureaucracy* to be the ideal organizational structure; offices and management positions are arranged in a hierarchy of authority, activities and objectives are rationally thought out, and divisions of labor are explicitly spelled out.

According to Weber, technical competence is highly valued and performance evaluations should be based entirely on merit. Weber proposed that the authority to manage is implicit in the position held by the person, not by the person who holds the position. Bureaucracy encourages *compartmentalization*; work tasks are divided into specialized jobs that emphasize mastery of a narrow job skill.

To its credit, bureaucratic management clearly advanced the formation of huge corporations (Pearce & Robinson, 1994). But bureaucracy created an inflexible and impersonal work environment. For instance, senior workers or managers were encouraged to maintain an impersonal and formal relationship with subordinates. The bureaucratic system favored managers because it emphasized position protection, politics, and preservation of authority (Covey & Merrill, 2006; Pearce & Robinson, 1994). Critics of bureaucracy also have associated it with "red tape" and the need to involve multiple layers of authority in accomplishing a simple task (Gabarro, 1992; Manning & Huddock, 1995). In addition, strict rules can limit productivity and cause what is called *trained incapacity* by specifying only the minimum requirements. Bureaucracies are closed systems, with little transparency and a focus on the internal workings of the organization rather than the outside influences created by the surrounding environment. A truly bureaucratic system is not readily responsive to change; current management thought values innovation and flexibility as much as efficiency and predictability.

HUMAN RELATIONS MOVEMENT AND MOTIVATIONAL THEORY

By the 1920s, many large organizations had adopted the approaches of classical scientific management. Henry Ford had not only altered the industrial landscape with the introduction of the assembly line, even hospital organizations were not spared of studies to improve workflow and efficiency. Pamela B. Blake, manager of a central sterile supply department in a large hospital in New York City, studied the operating room preparatory area to determine how long employees took to set up for a medical procedure to identify ways to save critical time during surgery (Hodgetts, 1992).

During this period, the humanistic movement was taking place, occupational therapy had become an official profession in 1917, and large occupational therapy departments were being developed to care for people with mental health issues and infectious diseases like tuberculosis (Quiroga, 1995). Hugo Munsterberg (1863–1916), the founder of industrial psychology, made recommendations for motivating employees, finding the best person for the job through psychological testing, and creating better psychological conditions for workers (Schermerborn et al., 1994).

Influence of the Work Environment

Between 1924 and 1933, a series of studies was conducted to investigate the effects of work environment on productivity. The most famous of these studies were the illumination studies, designed to see if better lighting had an impact on the productivity of workers. Elton Mayo (1880–1949) was invited to consult on the illumination project, which was already underway outside Chicago at the Hawthorne Plant of Western Electric. The study used a control group and an experimental group of women who assembled telephone relay equipment. The experimental group was exposed to increases and decreases in illumination as they assembled equipment. The control group performed the same job, but the source of lighting was constant. The researchers were surprised to discover that when they increased the lighting in the experimental group workroom, the output of both the experimental and control groups increased. Conversely, when the researchers lowered the lighting, both groups continued to improve their productivity (Mondy, Holmes, & Flippo, 1995). The researchers were confused and disappointed; they believed that they failed to find any relationship between illumination and productivity.

A second set of studies was conducted on worker fatigue as the employees assembled relays in a controlled work environment. The researchers once again found that productivity rose without a clear correlation to the physical conditions being changed to influence productivity. Mayo and his colleagues finally concluded that the "social relationship" accounted for the increase in productivity; the employees received special attention that improved their performance, and the subtle changes in the environment were insignificant. This phenomenon is known as the *Hawthorne effect* and is a variable taken into account in randomized controlled studies (Pearce & Robinson, 1994).

The Hawthorne studies allowed managers to shift their attention away from planning physical work and monetary incentives and toward studying the significance of the social setting in the workplace. The human relations movement used this evidence to convince managers to act more collaboratively with subordinates and to encourage good social environments as well as technical knowledge of the job (Bovee et al., 1993; Schermerborn et al., 1994).

Hierarchy of Needs

Abraham Maslow (1908–1970) was an educator, plant manager, and psychologist during his prolific career (Turban & Meredith, 1991). Maslow was interested in what motivates workers and proposed the *hierarchy of needs* theory. According to this theory, people are motivated by the need to satisfy a sequence of human needs, including physiological, safety, social, esteem, and self-actualization needs (Maslow, 1954). According to this theory, once people satisfy their more basic needs, they strive to meet increasingly advanced needs (e.g., self-actualization). Maslow's contribution to the human relations movement was to clarify the importance of intrinsic factors other than financial incentives as sources of motivation. Today, many other factors are believed to contribute to increases and decreases in motivation.

Two-Factor Theory of Motivation

Other theorists and researchers followed in Maslow's footsteps. In 1968, psychologist Fredrick Herzberg (1923–2000) introduced a theory of motivation called the *two-factor* or *motivation-hygiene* theory. Similar to Maslow's needs theory (Szilagyi & Wallace, 1990), Herzberg's theory has been widely applied by managers interested in motivation. Herzberg used qualitative research to explore the *content*, or experiences of the job, and the *context*, or factors surrounding the job. In essence, the research revealed two distinct types of motivational factors: *satisfiers*, or motivators, and *dissatisfiers*, or hygiene factors (Herzberg, Mausner, & Snyderman, 1959). Herzberg's method of putting weighted value on the context of the job and on its intrinsic factors, which include achievement, the work itself, level of responsibility, and personal growth and development, is used today to help to build job satisfaction (Schermerborn et al., 1994; Szelagyi & Wallace, 1990).

McGregor's Theories of Motivation

Douglas M. McGregor (1906–1964) was a professor, college president, and consultant who specialized in psychology. Using social science theory, McGregor developed Theory X and Theory Y to depict two extreme examples of ways in which a manager could view employees. *Theory X* represents a classical management view that employees are lazy; dislike work; and must be coerced to perform, controlled to eliminate waste, or threatened with punishment to increase their daily performance. The theory describes the average employee as wanting to be directed, avoiding responsibility, and having little ambition. In short, Theory X suggests that human beings naturally resist the occupation of work (McGregor, 1960).

In contrast, Theory Y proposed an entirely different set of assumptions. *Theory Y* suggested that the occupation of work is as natural as rest and play, consistent with the holistic philosophy of occupational therapy. Theory Y suggested that people do not inherently dislike the occupation of work and are willing to seek out responsibility, with the capacity to exercise a relatively high degree of imagination, ingenuity, and creativity to provide a solution. Furthermore, people exercise self-direction and self-control in the service of the organization if the objectives are in their zone of indifference. Theory Y takes a more positive view of the employee's intellectual capacity, which is believed to be only partially used in the workplace (McGregor, 1960).

Theory X and Theory Y uncovered diametrically opposing philosophies of how to manage employees. Theory X is more consistent with the classical scientific managers' philosophy, whereas Theory Y supports the tenets of the human relations theory of collaboration, participation, and concern for worker morale.

Discussion of the Human Relations Movement

The human relations movement brought the behavioral and humanistic factors of management to the forefront (Szilagyi & Wallace, 1990). Studies investigating interpersonal factors such as attention and informal group relationships in the workplace established that job satisfaction comes from intrinsic factors, such as trust, that go a long way in affecting people's behavior in the workplace (Covey & Merrill, 2006, p. 266).

BEHAVIORAL SCIENCE MOVEMENT

In the 1950s, the human relations movement began to fade because it did not produce empirical evidence that work productivity and job satisfaction were strongly correlated (O'Donnell, 1997). Organizations wanted more empirical evidence to understand work performance, and the behavioral science movement was conceived (Mondy et al., 1995). The behavioral science movement is the scientific study of human behavior in organizations to help managers be more effective. Although better research methodology has been applied by a variety of disciplines to study organizational behavior, few ironclad theories for managing people have resulted. Evidence shows that it is often beneficial to redesign routine jobs to allow a broader range of roles for employees. In addition, managers must be aware of the informal groups and the culture of an organization, especially if they are trying to produce change (Kotter & Rathgeber, 2005).

Groupthink

Group decision strategies sometimes cause a phenomenon called *groupthink*. According to Janis (1972), when the thinking processes of group members become too homologous or homogeneous, decision making is compromised. Groups whose members think too much alike may develop an illusion of invulnerability and ignore threats and opportunities in the environment. Groups can begin to believe that they have the only answer and begin to cast moralistic judgment on groups that have a diverging opinion. Groupthink can lead group members to reinforce stereotypic perceptions, fall prey to group pressure for compliance, and engage in self-censorship by not expressing alternative opinions—what Janis called *unanimity* (the false assumption that those who remain silent are in agreement with the group's decision). Perhaps the most destructive outcome of groupthink is when group members "protect" the leader or key members of the group from information that might shatter the complacency of the group.

The Pareto Principle

In 1906, an Italian economist named Vilfredo Pareto reported that in Switzerland, 80% of the wealth was held by 20% of the families. From this observation, Joseph M. Juran (1904–2008), who wrote about quality control, popularized the principle sometimes called the *Pareto Principle*, or the *80–20 Rule*, or the "vital few and trivial many" (Envision Software, n.d.; Godfrey, 1998). The Pareto Principle has been applied to a wide variety of management and marketing schemes. Generally speaking, it holds that 80% of phenomena stem from 20% of causes. For example, 80% of client complaints are caused by 20% of employees, and 80% of marketing profit is generated by 20% of the marketing schemes.

The value of the Pareto Principle for the occupational therapy manager is to focus on which 20% of effort produces 80% of results. If one can identify and expand the 20%, it can improve the operation of the clinic or program. For example, if 80% of reimbursement comes from 20% of the occupational therapy practitioners, those individuals should be rewarded on a merit system. The manager might analyze how the 20% do their documentation and billing and teach that method to the other 80% to improve efficiency. Although some claim the Pareto Principle is testable, it has not been examined through empirical research, and one should not depend on it to be true all the time; it is helpful, however, as a general decision-making guideline.

The Peter Principle

In 1969, Laurence J. Peter and Raymond Hull introduced the concept that in a hierarchy, employees tend to rise to their level of incompetence; this has become known as the *Peter Principle*. In most organizations, employees are promoted up the hierarchy so long as they work competently. Sooner or later, they are promoted to a position at which they are no longer competent, and there they remain, having reached their career ceiling in the organization. The employee's incompetence is not necessarily the result of the position being more difficult; the job simply requires different skill sets from the job in which the employee previously excelled. For example, an occupational therapist who is an excellent practitioner may earn a promotion to a middle management position, or a teacher may be promoted to the chair or program director, at which point the skill sets that earned his or her promotion no longer apply to the duties needed for the new position. As organizations have become aware of the impact of the Peter Principle, they have implemented continuing competency training, mentoring, and coaching to help employees obtain the skill sets they need to be successful in each new position (Covey & Merrill, 2006; Lazear, 2000; Peter & Hull, 1969).

CONTEMPORARY MANAGEMENT THEORY

Current perspectives on management theory that deserve some discussion are the systems approach, the contingency approach, and the learning organization.

Systems Approach

The *systems approach* departs from the segmented and hierarchical view of management and views the organization as a unified, purposeful system composed of parts that are all intimately related. This approach gives occupational therapy managers a way of looking at the organization as a whole and as a part of the larger, external environment. Systems managers make decisions only after they have explored the impact these decisions may have on practitioners, clients, and other departments within the organization. Effective communication is essential not only within their own department, but with other employees and departments and even representatives of other organizations.

Systems managers grasp the importance of the interconnectivity among working relationships in advancing their efforts within and beyond their organization. The occupational therapy department is a subsystem that interrelates with other subsystems of the whole organization. The term *synergy* means that the whole is greater than the sum of its parts; synergy results when separate departments collaborate and interact and, as a result, are more productive than if each were to act in isolation. Each department or unit has a boundary that separates it from its environment. In a closed system, the system boundary is inflexible and impervious; the systems manager fosters an open system, in which the boundary is more flexible and porous, to maximize the effectiveness of the organization. For example, more organizations are "going green," meaning they are taking a responsibility for how their activities affect the natural environment.

Two other concepts—flow and feedback—are essential to an understanding of the systems approach. *Flow* pertains to the movement of information, materials, and human effort from the time they enter the system from the environment as "inputs" and undergo transformation processes within the system (e.g., clients become rehabilitated within acute rehabilitation units through adaptation) to the time they exit the system as "outputs" (e.g., clients are better able to carry out activities of daily living). *Feedback* is central to system controls; as the various operations of the system go forward, information is fed back to the appropriate people in the organization through communication systems so that the work or productivity can be assessed and corrected in a feedback loop.

The systems approach enables the occupational therapy manager to pay attention to the dynamic and interrelated nature of an organization and the continuous interactions of the management role. The systems approach provides a framework for planning actions and anticipating both immediate and far-reaching consequences and for understanding unanticipated consequences as they develop within the entire organization.

Contingency Approach

The best description for the *contingency approach* is "it all depends, on what it depends on, and on in what way does it depends" (Thompson, 2003, p. 203). When faced with difficult questions, the manager using the contingency approach seeks to determine the predictable relationships among situations, actions, and outcomes and to apply the best strategy available. The contingency approach, also called the *situational approach,* was developed by professional groups who tried to apply the best available information (including computer-generated data) to make managerial decisions. Advocates of the contingency approach argue that outcomes differ because situations differ; it is the manager's task to identify which technique will, in a particular situation, under particular circumstances, and at a particular time, best achieve the management goals.

For example, an occupational therapy manager wants to implement a new service for outpatients in a rural community as an extension of a hospital-based program. Implementing the new outpatient goals is contingent on the manager recruiting new occupational therapy assistants who are committed to delivering treatment plans that were developed by occupational therapists. The occupational therapists would need to coach and provide periodic supervision to the occupational therapy assistants to ensure the plans are followed through to completion.

Learning Organization

The learning organization is based on systems theory and the study of natural biological systems (Crist, 1996). According to advocates of the learning organization, the world is an inextricably connected system in which everything can affect everything else. Just as microscopic systems continue to grow, evolve, and learn, human organizations can emphasize a continuous generation and exchange of new ideas. Applying the learning organization requires a mental shift away from the linear and sequential, clockwork system to a more complex, adaptive system. The organizational design of the learning community is flat rather than a top-to-bottom, hierarchical chain of command. There is transparency in the information held by people in management positions, and lines of communication are bidirectional (Crist, 1996; Hesselbein, Goldsmith, & Beckhard, 1997).

The learning organization embraces egalitarian thought; all members of the learning community are treated as equals and are seen as having something to offer the organization. Unlike Taylor's perception of classical management, employees are seen as seeking lasting and deep relationships in the working environment (Hesselbein et al., 1997; Nadler & Nadler, 1998). The element of trust is essential for employees to feel safe in sharing their knowledge in the workplace.

FUTURE TRENDS IN OCCUPATIONAL THERAPY MANAGEMENT

This chapter has reviewed historical theories of management and the evolution of modern organizations. The occupational therapy manager can draw from history to learn the best practices for organizing people and behavior. History has shown that organizations and styles of management reflect the needs of society. The new organization defines itself as an open system; has a strong sense of mission, purpose, and core values; and is driven by shared information and technology (Sandstrom, Lohman, & Bramble, 2002).

The health care industry typically follows the management trends of the corporate world. For example, many health care organizations are moving away from disconnected strategic and financial planning toward more integrated decision making and allocation of resources. The occupational therapy manager can draw from management theory in placing a greater emphasis on strategic planning, mission, and goals for the greater good of the organization. The occupational therapy manager must be skilled with group decision strategies and advocate continuing education and continuing competency to maintain licensed and certified practitioners in the workplace. The manager should be capable of seeking grant funding and other resources of funding for practitioner training and retraining as deemed necessity (Hesselbein et al., 1997). The occupational therapy manager will coordinate with open organizational systems that are nimble and able to react quickly to changing trends. In addition, incentives-based planning and budgeting will become an increasingly popular way to allocate resources according to performance capacity and efficiency.

In the academic setting, students are the customers, and budget allocations are determined by success in student recruitment, enrollment projections, enrollment management, and use of allocated space. During the periods when enrollment projections are up, occupational therapy programs are considered to be "cash cows," meaning they bring in revenue for the college or university. Departments are looked at as units that possess a certain allocation of square footage of space, equipment, and potential for growth. If a department underachieves in respect to its enrollment projections and other factors such as reducing attrition, educating students who are employable in the job market, or poor performance on national exams, the administration may decide to take away space and resources and reallocate them to another department that is meeting or exceeding the expectations. This is an example of incentives-based planning and budgeting, which is the hard reality of a college or university campus being accountable to the taxpayers or alumni (Hearn, Lewis, Kallen, Holdsworth, & Jones, 2006).

Putting It All Into Perspective

In recent years, the role of the occupational therapy manager has changed. As previously mentioned, the occupational therapy manager should be aware of both the formal and the informal systems in an organization. The formal organization usually has an organizational structure with published rules and policies. According to Covey and Merrill (2006), organizations built on trust need fewer rules and policies. Some policies help the occupational therapy

manager make decisions and deal with issues that require support from administration. For example, the human resource manager can assist with discipline issues for employees or family medical leave policies.

The Hawthorne studies revealed that employees form groups with informal rules that influence work behavior. We have learned that social relationships brings meaning to the workplace. The social relationships of employees influence quotas and productivity (Bovee et al., 1993). Peer pressure is applied to those who do not abide by the rules of the informal system—a type of system that is prevalent in the health care industry. For example, the occupational therapy practitioner must devote time to documentation, in-services, rounds, and interactions with family members. Many times, practitioners who work overtime settle into a norm of work behavior that is acceptable to the peers in the setting—such work behavior becomes expected.

Large-scale conglomerate health care organizations are increasing in numbers in large part because small, private, stand-alone organizations can no longer provide comprehensive services and financially compete. Occupational therapy managers may work in smaller community-based clinics in which interdisciplinary teams work in specialized units or groups. As the economy forces health care organizations to down-size or merge with larger consortiums, middle-management positions often are eliminated unless the manager makes the services an essential to the organization.

The demand for occupational therapy practitioners will continue to grow and produce changing workforce demands (Carrasco, 2009). Due to the shortages of qualified health professionals and the effects of globalization, occupational therapy managers must contend with an increasing pace of change in the workplace. Future employees will require more supervision; they will seek out opportunities for personal growth and will expect more benefits, accelerated opportunities for advancement, and mentoring relationships with their managers (Strauss & Howe, 2000). Given the continuous changes in economic and political forces, the occupational therapy manager must adapt, use technology and innovation, and instill tolerance of change (Hamm, 2009). Organizations in the future will downplay the concepts of job obedience, allegiance, and diligence. Employees will expect to be managed with a participatory approach to the decision-making process. Every member of the organization will be expected to have knowledge of the marketplace within and beyond the boundaries of the organization. Trust will be essential because intellectual property will be shared and protected. New health care organizations will allow "intrapreneurial" opportunities for reasonably autonomous enterprises to operate within the larger corporate structure (Covey & Merrill, 2006).

The occupational therapy manager will see a paradigmatic shift from a paperwork form of technology, where treatment plans and documentation are manually stored in a file cabinet, to a high-technology model based on computer use and retrieval. Occupational therapy managers and program directors in the near future will participate in virtual organizations, where staff members may work in various locations using e-mail, videoconferencing, and conference calls to conduct business, and students will work from home on computer terminals to complete assignments and see lectures online. Some practitioners may screen clients or consult via telehealth or telecommunication networks. A client will be viewed on a monitor, and an attendant aide may carry out and follow up on treatment plans. Grand rounds may be viewed on a monitor several hundred miles away or across the globe (Hesselbein et al., 1997; Karpf, 2006).

Conclusion

Managers always have been concerned with organizing people for work, but the Industrial Revolution created the need for more structure in the workplace. History has shown that organizations and styles of management meet the needs of the time. Today's occupational therapy manager is faced with different challenges than the manager of the past.

The occupational therapy manager is challenged to maintain morale and improve efficiency while allowing employees to participate in decision making and sustaining their motivation. History has shown that coercion and punishment do not work as motivators for productivity (Szilagyi & Wallace, 1990); likewise, time-and-motion studies, monetary incentives alone, and authoritative relationships with subordinates do not enhance productivity. Recent evidence-based practice has shown that elements important to productivity and job satisfaction include recognition by peers, a sense of achievement, advancement or promotion, status, a supervisor who is competent, the job itself, coworker interpersonal relationships, opportunities for personal development, fringe benefits, and a safe and attractive work environment (Braveman, 2006; Gabarro, 1992).

The role of the occupational therapy manager will continue to be influenced by outside forces, such as changes in state and federal legislation. The "formula-driven" reimbursement system, fee-for-service regulations, prospective payment systems, and capitated contracts will continue to add stress to the workplace. Rigid organizational systems can dampen the motivation for planning, organizing, coordinating, and controlling to the extent that the system does not allow the flexible application of new management theory.

The occupational therapy manager needs to be interested in managing for a changing society, but certain fundamentals will remain: The manager must exhibit a sense of confidence in self and in others. The manager must always be a practitioner at heart so he or she can enable others to grow, to see the alternatives, and to overcome barriers. The manager must be a champion of change with a vision beyond the organization to survey what is happening in the world while keeping his or her feet planted firmly on the ground. Lastly, the occupational therapy manager must be an energizing force, demonstrating passion for the profession and influencing others to find excitement in their own success.

Case Examples

Level I Fieldwork

A seasoned practitioner, L, is a fieldwork educator for a college student on her first rotation in Level I fieldwork in acute rehabilitation at a teaching hospital. The student is on grand rounds with the medical staff; she frequently pulls out her cell phone and appears to be text messaging while the physician is examining a patient at the bedside. L, realizing that the student is inclined to maintain connectivity with her peers, tells her it is not acceptable to text message during rounds because this learning experience requires her full attention, and she will be required to report to the other staff a summary of the patient's examination. The student was given the opportunity to text message during her breaks.

Level II Fieldwork

R, a young fieldwork supervisor, had been in practice only 2 years. She was supervising a nontraditional student, an older woman who was starting a second career. R was not comfortable in her supervising role; there were times when the fieldwork student would come in late or ask to leave early to tend to her children. A younger Level II fieldwork student from another program also doing a rotation under her supervision thought R was giving the nontraditional student preferential treatment and privileges. R commits to using best practices with both students, adhering to the policies within the organizational structure.

First-Time Manager

C was asked to be the supervisor of a unit of 4 occupational therapists and 3 occupational therapy assistants. The morale and motivation of the unit were at an all-time low. Using the five strategies to motivate people, C recognized achievement, held meetings to discuss the work itself and how it could be improved, shared responsibility, and helped staff set goals for themselves. C arranged for therapists from a clinic across town to come to staff meetings to share strategies they had used to improve reimbursement.

(continued)

Case Examples *(cont.)*

MANAGER

In an academic program, the physical therapy and occupational therapy departments were traditionally compartmentalized. The physical therapy department started a doctoral program, and it had a larger enrollment, more faculty, and a well-established research agenda. The occupational therapy department recently converted to the entry-level master's degree, had fewer students (24–26) and faculty, and was just developing its research agenda. The occupational therapy program had two clinics, a pediatric and adult clinic, with more referrals than they could take. The physical therapy program did not have a clinic per se but saw patients for research purposes. A collaborative agreement was reached to offer occupational therapy and physical therapy students a joint clinic where the larger space could be shared during scheduled clinic hours and students could share space and do collaborative cotreatments.

❖ Learning Activities

1. Interview an occupational therapy manager, and shadow him or her on a typical workday. Write a brief job description specifying each of his or her duties.
2. Review the historical occupational therapy literature on the development of the profession during the Industrial Revolution. Describe why the craft movement was related to the Industrial Revolution.
3. Imagine you have been appointed to manage a brand new occupational therapy department in a large teaching hospital that provides both acute care and rehabilitation. Using the approaches to management discussed in this chapter, describe what your approach to management would be and why.
4. You have been funded to develop a community sheltered workshop for clients who are developmentally challenged. You have been given subcontracts from a local toy company to do some small assembly projects, and the product schedule is time sensitive. Describe how you would set up the project and how you would implement incentives and production expectations and, at the same time, make the prevocational experience therapeutic.
5. Interview an occupational therapy manager and practitioner and ask them their views on the AOTA *Centennial Vision* (AOTA, 2007). Conduct the interview, and compare and contrast their views in the context of their two different positions.

✓ Multiple-Choice Questions

1. What is the purpose of surveying the history of management?
   a. To determine how occupational therapy can operate like a business using strategies described in industry.
   b. To find historical correlations to occupational therapy.
   c. To avoid mistakes made in the past, understand how management has been shaped, and apply the best practices.
   d. To compare scientific management strategies to today's cost containment methods.
2. Who is credited with the four roles of the manager—planning, organizing, coordinating, and controlling?
   a. Henry Ford.
   b. Frederick Taylor.
   c. Max Weber.
   d. Henri Fayol.
3. What system of management was adopted in the United States in response to the Industrial Revolution?
   a. Science of administration.
   b. Scientific management.
   c. Human relations movement.
   d. Socialism.
4. Frederick Taylor developed a system of management that can best be described as which of the following?
   a. A system mainly concerned with better methods of managing people.
   b. A system that studied fatigue and motions to complete a task.
   c. A system built on 14 principles of management.
   d. Time-and-motion studies, task concept, and work incentives.
5. Henry Ford used Frederick Taylor's methods of management to revolutionize the automotive industry with the inception of the assembly line. What was the main criticism of Ford's management methods?
   a. Ford allowed people to select any color car they wanted, as long as it was black.
   b. People got tired of performing the same task over and over again.
   c. It was difficult to make friends at work due to turnover.
   d. There were not sufficient studies of consumer demands.

6. Frank and Lillian Gilbreth are credited with conducting time and motion studies for which primary purpose?
   a. To help workers gain more income on piece rate.
   b. To determine how many materials are needed to lay bricks.
   c. To help workers reach their full potential and reduce fatigue.
   d. To explore the psychosocial elements of work.
7. One of the greatest criticisms of scientific management is which of the following?
   a. It focused on the group process of management.
   b. It provided a system of incentives for employees.
   c. It centered on production and the informal group process.
   d. It did not address the humanistic factor.
8. Henri Fayol stressed the organizational structure of management. Which functions of management did he identify?
   a. Planning, production, cooperation.
   b. Planning, organizing, coordinating, controlling.
   c. Controlling, budgeting, morale, coordinating.
   d. Coordinating, planning, supervision, directing.
9. Henri Fayol identified 14 principles of management. Which of the following best describes the concept of centralization?
   a. Increasing the role of subordinates in decision making.
   b. Only one manager should control operations using one plan.
   c. Decreasing the role of subordinates in decision making.
   d. The line of authority of an organization.
10. Mary Parker Follett and Chester Barnard had a similar belief about management. Which best describes their similar belief?
    a. Workers are driven by their independence and individual drives.
    b. Human beings grow when they come together in formal organizations.
    c. Workers achieve more when they are rewarded for individual accomplishments.
    d. The worker is motivated more by the organization's goals, and personal goals are less significant.
11. Max Weber outlined what he saw as the ideal organization, called *bureaucracy*. What is the most positive outcome of bureaucracy as Max Weber described it?
    a. The idea of compartmentalization enabled workers to build small departments that were efficient yet isolated from the larger units.
    b. The more narrow and specialized job descriptions enabled people to work well within the chain of command.
    c. The layers of authority enabled better documentation because all work plans had to be submitted in triplicate.
    d. The bureaucracies advanced the formation of huge corporations to foster growth of the economy.
12. What is the essential lesson of the Hawthorne studies?
    a. Changes in the environment, such as better lighting, advance production quotas.
    b. The physical conditions in a production plant are less important than the attention paid to workers and the social relationships.
    c. A controlled work environment that restricts social relationships promotes more focus on the production elements of the job.
    d. The Hawthorne effect has been duplicated to use as a strategy to control people for research projects.
13. Which is the essential lesson of Abraham Maslow's hierarchy of needs?
    a. The physiological needs are of less importance than building self-esteem.
    b. It clarified the importance of intrinsic factors and a sequence of human needs.
    c. Workers do not need food and shelter if the organization provides a free lunch and a roof over their heads.
    d. No one reaches a level of self-actualization.
14. According to Douglas McGregor, there are two views of workers. Which statement does *not* reflect McGregor's theory?
    a. Theory X suggests that human beings naturally resist the occupation of work.
    b. Theory X suggests that people need to be coerced to work.
    c. Theory Y suggests that work is as natural as work and play.
    d. Theory Y suggests that imagination and responsibility are not a natural part of work ability.
15. The behavioral science movement is best described by which of the following?
    a. The scientific study of organizations that can be used to control human behavior.
    b. The use of scientific management to induce work behaviors for profit.
    c. The scientific study of human behavior in organizations.
    d. The use of scientific methods of behavioral modification to promote subconscious motivations to work with less fatigue.
16. Groupthink is best described by which of the following?
    a. Thinking out of the box in group process to produce individual thought process.
    b. Using group process to induce people to think all alike.
    c. The process of involving people in one unit of thought.
    d. A phenomenon that occurs when people working together become homogeneous in their decision-making processes.

17. Which best describes the Pareto Principle?
    a. People who are large in stature and good communicators often rise to the top of an organization.
    b. The "trivial many" take over an organization because the "vital few" cannot compete.
    c. Approximately 80% of phenomena stem from 20% of causes.
    d. Approximately 20% of production results from 80% of the incompetence of an organization.
18. The Peter Principle in an organization is best described by which of the following?
    a. In a hierarchy, employees tend to rise to their level of incompetence if they don't keep up training.
    b. There is a "glass ceiling" that prevents female employees from rising to upper management.
    c. If a person performs extremely well on one job, he or she can do any other job well.
    d. The incompetent worker is often promoted so he or she moves out of the ranks of competent workers.
19. In some health care and educational organizations, space, human resources, and the equipment budget are allocated according to the performance capacity of the unit. What is this system called?
    a. Competency-based planning.
    b. Contingency planning and budgeting.
    c. Management by "cash cow" incentives.
    d. Incentives-based planning and budgeting.
20. The systems approach to management has all of the following characteristics *except*:
    a. A view of the organization from a holistic perspective.
    b. A view of the organization as a unified system with all parts intimately related.
    c. A view of the organization in compartments with a segmented line of authority to the top.
    d. An integrative view of the organization that pulls resources and energy from routinized systems that form a foundation for the organization.

References

American Occupational Therapy Association. (2007). AOTA's *Centennial Vision* and executive summary. *American Journal of Occupational Therapy, 61,* 613–614.

Bovee, C. L., Thill, J. V., Wood, M. B., & Dovel, G. P. (1993). *Management.* New York: McGraw-Hill.

Braveman, B. (2006). *Leading and managing occupational therapy services.* Philadelphia: F. A. Davis.

Carrasco, R. C. (2009). Reflections on out-of-the-box employment. *OT Practice, 14*(20), 10–15.

Christiansen, C., & Baum, C. (1997). *Occupational therapy: Enabling function and well being.* Thorofare, NJ: Slack.

Covey, S. M. R., & Merrill, R. R. (2006). *The speed of trust: One thing that changes everything.* New York: Free Press.

Crist, P. (1996). Organizational effectiveness. In *Occupational therapy manager* (rev. ed., pp. 163–190). Bethesda, MD: American Occupational Therapy Association.

Cross, A. F., Feather, J. J., & Lynch, R. L. (1994). *Corporate renaissance: The art of re-engineering.* Cambridge, MA: Blackwell.

Davis, B. L., Hellervik, L. W., Skull, C. J., Gebelein, S. H., & Sheard, J. L. (1992). *Thinking strategically.* Minneapolis, MN: Personnel Decisions.

Duncan, J. W. (1989). *Great ideas in management.* San Francisco: Jossey-Bass.

Envision Software. (n.d.). *Pareto Principle or the 80/20 rule: The inception of the Pareto Principle.* Retrieved December 23, 2008, from http://www.envisionsoftware.com/Management/Pareto_Principle.html

Fayol, H. (1929). *General and industrial management* (J. A. Conbrough, Trans.). Geneva, Switzerland: International Management Institute.

Gabarro, J. J. (1992). *Managing people and organizations.* Boston: Harvard Business School.

Godfrey, A. B. (1998). *Juran's quality handbook.* New York: McGraw Hill.

Graham, P. (1995). *Mary P. Follett: Prophet of management.* Cambridge, MA: Harvard Business School.

Hamm, S. (2009, January 12). Is Silicon Valley losing its magic? *Business Week,* pp. 28–31.

Hearn, J. C., Lewis, D. R., Kallen, L., Holdsworth, J. M., & Jones, L. M. (2006). Incentives for managing change. *Journal of Higher Education, 77,* 287–316.

Herzberg, F., Mausner, B., & Snyderman, B. (1959). *The motivation to work* (2nd ed.). New York: Wiley.

Hesselbein, F., Goldsmith, M., & Beckhard, R. (Eds.). (1997). *The organization of the future.* San Francisco: Jossey-Bass.

Hodgetts, R. M. (1992). *Organizational behavior: Theory and practice.* New York: Macmillan.

Janis, J. L. (1972). *Victims of groupthink.* Boston: Houghton Mifflin.

Karpf, M. (2006). Moving to an integrated clinical enterprise: The emergence of UK healthcare. *Academic Medicine, 81,* 713–720.

Kotter, J., & Rathgeber, H. (2005). *Our iceberg is melting: Changing and success under any conditions.* New York: St. Martin's Press.

Lazear, E. P. (2000). *The Peter Principle: Promotions and declining productivity.* Stanford, CA: Hoover Institution and Graduate School of Business, Stanford University. Retrieved December 11, 2009, from http://www-siepr.stanford.edu/Papers/pdf/00-04.pdf

Manning, M., & Haddock, P. (1995). *Leadership skills for women.* Menlo Park, CA: Crisp Publications.

Maslow, A. H. (1954). *Motivation and personality.* New York: Harper & Row.

McGregor, D. (1960). *The human side of enterprise.* New York: McGraw-Hill.

McMahon, D., & Carr, J. C. (1999). The contributions of Chester Barnard to strategic management. *Journal of Management History, 5*(5), 228–240.

Mitchell, C., & Burick, T. (1985). *The right moves: Succeeding in a man's world without a Harvard MBA.* New York: Macmillan.

Mondy, W., Holmes, R. E., & Flippo, E. B. (1995). *Management concepts and practices.* Boston: Allyn & Bacon.

Nadler, D. A., & Nadler, M. B. (1998). *Champions of change.* San Francisco: Jossey-Bass.

O'Donnell, M. (1997). Health impact of workplace health promotion programs and methodological quality of the research literature. *Art of Health Promotion, 1,* 1–8.

Pearce, J. A., & Robinson, R. B. (1994). *Strategic management: Formation, implementation, and control.* Burr Ridge, IL: Irwin.

Peter, L. J., & Hull, R. (1969). *The Peter Principle: Why things always go wrong.* New York: William Morrow.

Quiroga, V. A. M. (1995). *Occupational therapy: The first 30 years.* Bethesda, MD: AOTA Press.

Sandstrom, R. W., Lohman, H. L., & Bramble, D. (2002). *Health services: Policy and systems for therapists.* Upper Saddle River, NJ: Prentice Hall.

Santayana, G. (1905). *Life of reason, reason in common sense.* New York: Scribner's.

Schermerborn, J. R., Hunt, F. G., & Asborn, R. N. (1994). *Managing organizational behavior* (5th ed.). New York: Wiley.

Strauss, W., & Howe, N. (2000). *Millennials rising: The next great generation.* New York: Vintage Books.

Szilagyi, A. D., & Wallace, M. J. (1990). *Organizational behavior and performance.* New York: HarperCollins.

Taylor, F. W. (1911). *The principles of scientific management.* New York: Harper & Row.

Tonn, J. (2003). *Mary P. Follett: Creating democracy and transforming management.* New Haven, CT: Yale University Press.

Thompson, J. D. (2003). *Organizations in action: Social sciences basics of administrative theory.* New Brunswick, NJ: Transaction.

Turban, E., & Meredith, J. R. (1991). *Management science* (5th ed.). Boston: Richard P. Irwin.

Wren, D. A. (2005). *The history of management.* Hoboken, NJ: Wiley.

U.S. Bureau of Labor Statistics. (2009). *American time-use survey.* Retrieved December 14, 2009, from www.bls.gov/tus/charts

APPENDIX 1.A. HISTORY EVIDENCE TABLE

Topic	Subtopic	Evidence
Historic influences on management	Scientific management	Fayol, H. (1929). *General and industrial management.* (J. A. Conbrough, Trans.). Geneva, Switzerland: International Management Institution. Taylor, F. W. (1911). *The principles of scientific management.* New York: Harper & Row. Wren, D. A. (2005). *The history of management.* Hoboken, NJ: John Wiley.
Motivating employees	Strategies for motivation	Covey, S. M. R., & Merrill, R. R. (2006). *The speed of trust: One thing that changes everything.* New York: Free Press. Duncan, J. W. (1989). *Great ideas in management.* San Francisco: Jossey-Bass. Herzberg, F., Mausner, B., & Snyderman, B. (1959). *The motivation to work* (2nd ed.). New York: Wiley. McGregor, D. (1960). *The human side of enterprise.* New York: McGraw-Hill.
Planning	Strategic planning	Davis, B. L., Hellervik, L. W., Skull, C. J., Gebelein, S. H., & Sheard, J. L. (1992). *Thinking strategically.* Minneapolis: Personnel Decisions. Kotter, J., & Rathgeber, H. (2005). *Our iceberg is melting: Changing and success under any conditions.* New York: St. Martin's Press. Nadler, D. A., & Nadler, M. B. (1998). *Champions of change.* San Francisco: Jossey-Bass. Pearce, J. A., & Robinson, R. B. (1994). *Strategic management: Formation, implementation, and control.* Burr Ridge, IL: Irwin.
Leadership	Gender stereotype	Manning, M., & Haddock, P. (1995). *Leadership skills for women.* Menlo Park, CA: Crisp Publications. Mitchell, C., & Burick, T. (1985). *The right moves: Succeeding in a man's world without a Harvard MBA.* New York: Macmillan.
Supervision and management	Applied techniques for everyday management	Braveman, B. (2006). *Leading and managing occupational therapy services.* Philadelphia: F. A. Davis. Gabarro, J. J. (1992). *Managing people and organizations.* Boston: Harvard Business School. Mondy, W., Holmes, R. E., & Flippo, E. B. (1995). *Management concepts and practices.* Boston: Allyn & Bacon.

2

Common Skill Sets for Occupational Therapy Managers and Practitioners

Guy L. McCormack, PhD, OTR/L, FAOTA

❖ Key Terms and Concepts

Hard skills. Linear competencies that tend to be quantitative and measurable.

Interactive leaders. Leaders who use a management style that promotes open communication and group consensus when making decisions.

Multitasking. Concurrently executing two or more functions.

Role delineation. In the workplace, the identification of tasks and duties to be performed by specific individuals on the basis of their credentials, duties, and skills.

Skill sets. Special competencies in performance or in a particular context.

Soft skills. Spatial competencies that tend to be qualitative and not easy to measure. Soft skills are more intuitive and oriented to interpersonal communication.

Transactional leadership. Management style similar to mentoring that enables others to contribute to their own development and professional growth.

❖ Learning Objectives

After completing this chapter, you should be able to do the following:

- Compare and contrast the roles of occupational therapy manager and occupational therapy practitioner.
- Recognize commonalities between the skill sets of the occupational therapy manager and the occupational therapy practitioner.

- Describe the contextual factors of occupational therapy management and clinical practice.
- Describe the characteristics of interactive and transitional management styles.

Skill sets include behaviors, manual skills, management skills, clinical skills, and psychological skills that are typically associated with an accomplished manager or practitioner. All occupational therapy practitioners are managers and all managers are clinicians, but occupational therapy managers have certain responsibilities and roles that are unique to their position, as do occupational therapy practitioners. Occupational therapy practitioners and occupational therapy managers, however, have more in common than most people realize.

In this chapter, *skill set* refers to the developed or acquired ability to perform something with competence, either man-

ually or intellectually. The skill sets associated with the occupational therapy manager and the occupational therapy practitioner are very similar; the context in which the skill sets are performed, however, can change the meaning and purpose of activity. Both the occupational therapy manager and the occupational therapy practitioner work within a context that influences their perception of the skill set. This chapter illustrates the similarities of the skill sets performed by occupational therapy managers and practitioners and describes the ways context influences these skill sets.

To provide a basis to compare the role of manager and practitioner, I conducted a systematic analysis of the following occupational therapy textbooks and official documents:

- The *Occupational Therapy Practice Framework: Domain and Process 2nd Edition* (American Occupational Therapy Association [AOTA], 2008)
- The American Council on Occupational Therapy Education (ACOTE, 2006) *Guidelines for an Accredited Educational Program for the Occupational Therapist*
- *The Guide to Occupational Therapy Practice* (Moyers, 1999)
- AOTA (2005) *Standards of Practice for Occupational Therapy*
- *Willard and Spackman's Occupational Therapy* (Crepeau, Cohn, & Schell, 2003)
- *Occupational Therapy: Enabling Function and Well-Being* (Christiansen & Baum, 1997).

These documents and textbooks provide guidelines for entry-level competencies for occupational therapists and occupational therapy assistants and define the skill sets of managers and practitioners.

Table 2.1 lists common skill sets in the first column in alphabetical order and indicates which pertain to occupational therapy practitioners exclusively, to occupational therapy managers exclusively, or to both. The table clearly shows that the roles of the manager and the practitioner blend more than discriminate. Out of the 195 skill sets identified, only 23 might be described as roles performed exclusively by occupational therapy practitioners. Conversely, only four can be exclusively associated with the role of the occupational therapy manager. A blank skill set chart appears in Appendix 2.B for personal use.

The meaning of the skill set changes according to role, however. For example, the term *caregiver* is associated with the clinical role, but managers may also perform clinical duties and see themselves in the caregiver role. Clearly, skill sets such as therapeutic use of self, activity analysis, and occupation-based practice fall within the realm of the occupational therapy practitioner. The term *administration* is clearly linked to the occupational therapy manager. However, it is evident that both the occupational therapy practitioner and the occupational therapy manager perform the majority of the skill sets in some capacity or context. Therefore, the occupational therapy manager is often a practitioner, and the practitioner must possess many of the skill sets commonly associated with the role of a manager.

The list in Table 2.1 may not include all of the skill sets required to perform the role of manager or practitioner, but it is sufficient to illustrate the considerable overlap between the two roles. Both roles involve working closely with people to enable them to perform occupation-based activities. Inherent in both positions is the need to make timely and informed decisions based on the best available evidence. It is typical for both the manager and the practitioner to involve subordinates or clients in the decision-making process. Both professionals are concerned with accomplishing goals through collaboration with other people. To accomplish goals, both should be good listeners and good communicators. Both must have an appreciation for people and the capacity to build trust, maintain integrity, and achieve results.

For example, the occupational therapy practitioner performs a number of tasks that require management ability. Throughout the course of the day, the practitioner must engage in planning to accomplish the daily role of performing therapy. Planning may take the form of ordering the right equipment, working out the logistics of treating clients in different locations, collaborating with professionals from other disciplines, attending meetings, and allowing time for documentation. Practitioners set goals, manage time, oversee assistants and coworkers, make important clinical decisions, and control outcomes; these roles are implicitly and explicitly management roles as well.

THE HUMAN FACTOR

Human beings bring complexity to the context of occupational therapy. Both the occupational therapy practitioner and the occupational therapy manager must have strong skill sets in dealing with the human factor. They must engage in planning, organizing, coordinating, controlling resources, and assuming leadership roles that involve people. Although their job descriptions are somewhat different, the human factor issues overlap considerably (Blair, n.d.-a, n.d.-b).

The practitioner strives to maintain a client-centered approach to get therapeutic work done. Similarly, the manager depends on maintaining good working relationships with staff to get administrative work done. Each client the occupational therapy practitioner sees presents with a different constellation of health-related challenges, and the manager may be simultaneously struggling to meet quotas and depends on staff to act cooperatively, quickly, and rationally. The human factor plays a huge part in promoting compliance with a treatment plan or implementing an administrative policy.

The occupational therapy practitioner may direct their focus on soft skills such as signs and symptoms of clients' medical diagnosis, their inherent strengths and weaknesses, their personal characteristics or physical attributes that influence the treatment, or the course of recovery. The occupational therapy manager must employ hard skills such as using data and spreadsheets to plan for daily staffing issues when occupational therapy practitioners are unable to work; coordinate services with other disciplines; monitor practitioners' use of the department's resources, including clinical supplies, equipment, and budget time for documentation; and review data that demonstrates measurable outcomes of the interventions.

People do not behave the same way every day, and things happen to people in their personal lives in the evening or between appointments that have an impact on their performance. They depend on intrinsic rewards and motivation to get through the daily activities of work, play, and

Table 2.1. Occupational Therapy Skill Sets—Scored

Skill set	Performed exclusively by occupational therapy practitioners	Performed exclusively by occupational therapy managers	Performed by both
Accommodations (many types)			X
Accountability			X
Acknowledging strengths			X
Action plans			X
Activities of daily living	X		
Activity analysis	X		
Activity demands			X
Adaptation (outcomes)			X
Adaptation of environment			X
Adaptation of performance skills	X		
Adjunctive methods	X		
Administration			X
Advocacy (political)			X
Aligning goals with the mission statement		X	
Allocation of resources		X	
Analytical problem solver			X
Annual performance assessment		X	
Appeal for reimbursement			X
Application of physical agent modalities	X		
Assertiveness			X
Assessment			X
Assistive technology	X		
Attends rounds and meetings			X
Author			X
Basic assessment			X
Basic life skills manager	X		
Behavior manager			X
Budget manager			X
Caregiver	X		
Charismatic motivator			X
Charting			X
Client-centered approach	X		
Clinical judgment			X
Clinical reasoning			X
Coach			X
Code of ethics			X
Cognitive restructuring	X		
Collaboration			X
Collecting data			X
Collecting evidence			X
Communication			X

(continued)

Table 2.1. Occupational Therapy Skill Sets—Scored *(cont.)*

Skill set	Performed exclusively by occupational therapy practitioners	Performed exclusively by occupational therapy managers	Performed by both
Compassion			X
Compensation			X
Computer skills			X
Conflict resolution		X	
Consultation			X
Consumer advocacy	X		
Context (cultural)			X
Continuing competence			X
Continuous quality improvement			X
Core values			X
Cost containment			X
Course of treatment	X		
Crafts person	X		
Critique of research studies			X
Cultural competency			X
Current policy awareness			X
Decision making			X
Delegation			X
Delivery of services			X
Descriptive research			X
Designing lifestyles	X		
Diagnosis	X		
Directing			X
Discharge planning	X		
Discontinuation reports			X
Discrimination (sensory)	X		
Disease/disability prevention	X		
Dispute resolution		X	
Documentation			X
Domestic violence	X		
Dressing skills	X		
Driving (adaptive)	X		
Early intervention	X		
Educational activity			X
Educator			X
Empathetic			X
Enabling activity	X		
Engagement in occupation			X
Endurance			X
Energy conservation	X		
Energy expenditure			X
Entrepreneur			X

Table 2.1. Occupational Therapy Skill Sets—Scored *(cont.)*

Skill set	Performed exclusively by occupational therapy practitioners	Performed exclusively by occupational therapy managers	Performed by both
Environmental context			X
Environmental factors			X
Environmental modification			X
Ergonomics	X		
Ethical behavior			X
Evaluation			X
Evidence-based practice			X
Explanation of services			X
Feedback			X
Feeding and swallowing	X		
Fieldwork educator			X
Fiscal planning		X	
Flexible			X
Focus group			X
Follow-up			X
Frames of reference			X
Functional activities	X		
Grading activities	X		
Grant writing			X
Group process			X
Guidance			X
Habit training	X		
Health care professional			X
Health educator			X
Health promotion			X
Home health	X		
Improvement measures			X
Independence promoter			X
Information retrieval			X
Interdisciplinary			X
Interpersonal skills			X
Interventions			X
Interviewing			X
Instrumental activities of daily living	X		
Job analysis			X
Job description			X
Judgment (clinical)			X
Knowledge (clinical)			X
Language skills			X
Leadership			X
Learning development	X		

(continued)

Table 2.1. Occupational Therapy Skill Sets—Scored *(cont.)*

Skill set	Performed exclusively by occupational therapy practitioners	Performed exclusively by occupational therapy managers	Performed by both
Legislation awareness			X
Leisure			X
Life balance			X
Lifestyle redesign	X		
Long-term plan			X
Maintain records			X
Management			X
Marketing			X
Measurement			X
Meetings (attends/conducts)			X
Mentoring			X
Models behavior			X
Monitoring			X
Narrative reasoning			X
Normative reports			X
Observation skills			X
Occupational performance			X
Occupational profile			X
Occupation-based approach			X
Orientation skills			X
Outcome studies			X
Passive range of motion	X		
Peer review			X
Performance patterns	X		
Performance skills	X		
Play	X		
Physical capacity evaluation	X		
Policy management		X	
Politician			X
Pragmatic reasoning			X
Prevention			X
Process skills			X
Problem solver			X
Productivity			X
Progressive disciplinary action		X	
Public policy		X	
Qualitative researcher			X
Quality assurance			X
Quality controller			X
Reasoning			X
Referral manager			X
Remediation expert	X		

Table 2.1. Occupational Therapy Skill Sets—Scored *(cont.)*

Skill set	Performed exclusively by occupational therapy practitioners	Performed exclusively by occupational therapy managers	Performed by both
Risk taker			X
Safety manager			X
Satisfaction employer			X
Scheduler			X
Selection process			X
Self-assessment			X
Self-efficacy improver			X
Staff development		X	
Staffing			X
Strategic planning		X	
Stress manager			X
Substance abuse manager			X
Supervision			X
Task analysis	X		
Task group organizer			X
Teacher			X
Test giver			X
Therapeutic relationship builder	X		
Time manager			X
Tolerance builder			X
Trainer			X
Values clarification			X
Virtual reality			X
Vocational exploration	X		
Wellness expert	X		
Work conditioner			X
Work performance evaluation			X
Work simplification expert			X
Workers' compensation			X

leisure. Using the early studies by Herzberg, Mausner, and Snyderman (1959) and contemporary views of motivation, both the occupational therapy manager and the occupational therapy practitioner can use five strategies to motivate people (Blair, n.d.-b):

1. *Achievement* involves setting targets that, when reached, bring a sense of accomplishment. If the targets are set too high, the client or staff member will fail to achieve the goal. If the target behavior is too easy, he or she will feel no sense of accomplishment. Occupational therapy practitioners grade activities, breaking them down into stages; managers similarly give employees a series of achievable targets and then challenge them to stretch just a little more after each target is accomplished.

2. *Recognition* is another strong motivator. When a client is given verbal encouragement for accomplishing targeted daily living skills or an employee is praised for a job well done, he or she feels appreciated. When a client or employee fails to meet the goal, it is important that he or she be told in a constructive fashion what needs to be improved and what is expected of him or her in the future.

3. *The work itself* for both client and employee should be challenging and interesting. The element of challenge provokes the client's or employee's interest, which in turn raises his or her attention or arousal level. The challenge for the occupational therapy practitioner and

manager is to find ways to make boring tasks interesting or to change the context in which the task is performed.

4. *Responsibility* is a motivator with a lasting effect. Delegating a client or an employee the responsibility and trust to perform something on his or her own requires good judgment to match the existing skill sets to the difficulty of the target goal. Responsibility is very empowering and can have long-term positive effects in therapy and in managing employees.

5. *Advancement* for the client has to do with achieving the goals of therapy and obtaining greater independence. For the employee, it may stem from receiving promotions, salary incentives, or new job prospects. Advancement reinforces the feeling that one is learning and improving onself or one's quality of life (Covey & Merrill, 2006).

SKILL SETS THAT DIFFERENTIATE THE ROLE OF MANAGER

Fayol (1929) introduced the four functions—planning, organizing, coordinating, and controlling—believed to be the keystones to management. (The term *controlling* does not mean micromanaging but rather managing expenses and minimizing waste.) In today's health care environment, however, the occupational therapy manager finds it difficult to balance and accomplish all four of these essential functions on a daily basis. Few managers have the time to be thoughtful and reflective in planning, and few have the ability to supervise outcomes with clocklike precision. The current views of scholars who study management suggest that the daily activities of the manager are anything but systematic and routine (Pfeffer & Sutton, 2006; Safian, 2009). It is estimated that the average manager is swamped by trivialities and spends only 9 minutes or so on any activity (Smolowitz, 1994).

Mintzberg (1977) analyzed the manager role through qualitative data sets such as detailed diaries, ethnographic observations, and in-depth interviews and found that managers work at an unrelenting pace and that their daily activities are characterized by spontaneity, brevity, many interruptions, multitasking, and discontinuity. In fact, the managers of today are oriented more toward action than reflection. Planning is often done in real time as job demands require change to keep up with the needs of the marketplace. Therefore, for many managers, planning is done in the context of the daily routine, and decisions are made based on experience and available data.

Most managers prefer to gather information via electronic media, brief meetings with staff, and phone conversations rather than documents. In fact, managers spend an average of 66% to 80% of their time engaging in oral communication (Solomon, 1988). E-mail in particular has given managers a quick method of communicating with staff and obtaining immediate feedback and follow-up information.

Occupational therapy managers need to constantly increase their capabilities, and they need to encourage practitioners to do the same. According to Covey and Merrill (2006), managers often learn and work at what they called the "margin of ignorance"; just when managers begin to master a skill set, a new learning challenge becomes apparent. In addition, Covey and Merrill advised managers to "feed strengths and starve weaknesses" (p. 104); managers who dwell on their weakness will not inspire peers, subordinates, or clients to follow their example. However, managers can make their weaknesses irrelevant by working effectively with others to compensate and by working through their strengths. For instance, if a manager does not like to work with numbers and budgets, he or she can delegate these tasks to free up time to perform the skill sets that got him or her recognized as a manager in the first place.

According to management guru Peter F. Drucker (1999), organizations should be transparent. Managers should articulate a purpose that is clear to and shared by all constituents. If the occupational therapy manager makes it clear that the department is devoted to delivering compassionate and efficient care, for example, everyone will focus on delivering such care.

The issue of trust has become essential both in management and in the delivery of services (Covey & Merrill, 2006). Managers who are planning and responding to change need to develop a context of trust among workers and clients. By working in a context of trust, the manager is free to make spontaneous decisions based on "soft data" such as intuition and word of mouth and to address problems as they arise, whereas hard data derived from market surveys and data sets such as the stock market may satisfy the analytical decision maker.

There is the perception among students, practitioners, and new managers that the effective manager or practitioner has regular duties to perform that are focused on supervision or direct client care (Kielhofner, 2009; Sladyk, 1997). However, the reality is that managers and practitioners attend meetings, meet regularly with coworkers and potential clients, and absorb and control incoming information on a continuum.

There is also a myth that upper management encourages competition among managers, which is good for business (Pfeffer & Sutton, 2006). For example, competition among the managers of occupational therapy, physical therapy, and speech communication may raise the efficiency of the departments, but the interpersonal relationships (i.e., soft skills in the area of communication) and multidisciplinary services to the client would be neglected. Instead, collaboration (the pooling of resources) and cooperation (working together) among managers and practitioners creates better business and services. Current management thinking indicates that organizations function better when resources and knowledge are shared and individuals work as a team, which requires soft skills that value social interactions for better communication rather than competition (Smolowitz, 1994).

TECHNOLOGY SKILLS

The increasing reliance on electronic devices in health care provision will challenge occupational therapy managers and practitioners to stay current with technology used to communicate, maintain records, document, and attend meetings or in-services while retaining the focus on client-centered interventions. For instance, the manager may use a personal digital assistant to check appointments, plan board meetings using calendar software, send text messages to a colleague at a business meeting, or talk on a mobile phone while waiting for a client or colleague. Practitioners may have a notebook computer nearby for getting quick information about durable medical equipment, listen to music on an iPod while performing manual range of motion, get paged on a device they carry, or hear a speaker call out their name to answer the phone while with a client in the clinic. Some practitioners use a camera phone or video recorder to record images of a client's wound and send them to another health care professional via the Internet to receive a consultation.

The occupational therapy manager must take care to avoid the following pitfalls of using electronic devices:

- Technology must be used with respect for privacy and confidentiality. Employers are coming under litigation because of employees sharing information via e-mail that is confidential or in violation of privacy regulations (Hill, 2000).
- Good managers or practitioners must be able to perform more than one task at a time to be effective in their daily routines. But they must resist the temptation to multitask that comes with many electronic devices. Unfortunately, the idea that one gets more accomplished when one multitasks is an illusion. Rubinstein, Meyer, and Evans (2001) studied patterns in the amounts of time lost when people repeatedly switched between two tasks of varying complexity and familiarity. In four experiments, participants switched between different tasks such as solving math problems or classifying geometric objects. The researchers measured participants' speed of performance as a function of whether the successive tasks were successful. The measurements revealed that for all types of tasks, participants lost time when they had to switch from one task to another, and time costs increased with the complexity of the tasks. Thus, the practitioner may want to be cautioned against multitasking.
- Electronic devices facilitate communication in some ways but, when used while with a client, also can inhibit social interaction (Sherry, 2001). Both the manager and the practitioner depend on social interaction and trust to get work done (Nielson, 2003).
- All professionals should avoid multitasking behaviors that pose a safety threat, such as talking on the phone while operating mechanical equipment or text messaging while driving a vehicle.

EFFECTS OF GENDER ON THERAPEUTIC AND MANAGEMENT ROLES

Many people believe that gender plays a role in the development of skill sets. Early in our growth and development, people are influenced by parents and others to assume male and female behaviors. Neuroscience shows that gender is defined by many biological characteristics and distinct differences (dimorphisms) that can be found in male and female brains that have been acquired during human evolution (Bear, Connors, & Paradiso, 2007).

Approximately 95.7% of occupational therapy practitioners are women (Fisher & Keehn, 2007). Because occupational therapy practitioners and managers are predominantly women, it is useful to understand stereotypes and discuss the advantages and disadvantages that gender bring to the workplace. There is no question that women are well suited for management roles (Amatucci & Sohl, 2004; Manning & Haddock, 1995). However, the management literature suggests that there is a "gender divide" between women and men in management style. The research has shown that women tend to be satisfied with less optimal outcomes and do not aggressively seek more favorable conditions for themselves when compared to men (Amatucci, Swartz, & Coleman, 2008). In negotiation, women strive for a more collaborative, win–win situation, whereas men tend to view negotiation as a rational, competitive game and are highly protective of their interests (Kray & Thompson, 2007).

Some women may be more accommodating than men to the needs of others, and it pays off when more people are involved in the decision-making process. Women who are interactive or participatory managers find that they are more likely to be supported when backup systems are needed for support, such as when staff are ill or absent from work. However, interactive or participatory management has some disadvantages in that it takes more time to get buy in and ideas from staff members. Interactive management also requires that the manager give up some control. Managers who share power and information may be perceived as needing approval or wanting to be liked by their subordinates.

By allowing more people to participate in the decision-making process, there may be turf conflicts over issues such as space if employees disagree. In some health care settings, staff members are limited in decision-making roles by licensure, scope of practice parameters, professional credentials, or level of work experience. In addition, shared power allows for the possibility that people will reject or openly disagree with the manager or challenge his or her authority (Grady, 2003).

EFFECTS OF GENERATION ON THERAPEUTIC AND MANAGERIAL ROLES

Many occupational therapy students enter their professional course of study with preconceived ideas and expectations about the role of occupational therapy practitioner.

There may be a "generation gap" between the student's perceptions of a professional career and behavior and those of college and university faculty of the Generation X and Baby Boomer generations. This gap may create discord between generations, and occupational therapy managers must be prepared to address it constructively to maximize the skill sets of this generation.

Students of the so-called Millennial generation (also referred to as Generation Y) have been described as bright, hopeful, and idealistic (Pletka, 2007). This generation is considered to be impatient because they were raised in a world dominated by technology and instant information access. The Millennials have been given ample material opportunities and a high level of support by their parents. This generation has been raised in an enriched environment and had exposure to multimedia-improved speed of learning (Glennon, 2009). Many Millennials are well informed and know that occupational therapy is among the fastest growing professions and may exceed the forecasts of the U.S. Bureau of Labor Statistics (2008).

At the risk of perpetuating stereotypes, the literature suggests that the Millennial generation have good self-esteem and believe that they can do anything they set their minds to accomplish; they are also fragile and respond negatively to criticism that is not constructive. At times their interpersonal skills may appear to be blunt and unpolished. The Millennials are often image-driven in their appearance; for example, they may sport tattoos, skin piercing, or unusual hair color and styles.

Baby Boomers (born between 1946 and 1965) and Generation Xers (born between 1965 and 1980) may consider the Millennials to have been overprotected and lack practicality (Glennon, 2009; Pletka, 2007). On the positive side, the Millennials are more tolerant of multicultural diversity and sexual orientation. As a group, they are more efficient in multitasking; they do things faster and better and are willing to volunteer for community projects, but they need to learn to slow down when working with elderly clients or populations with special needs (Glennon, 2009). The Millennials are technologically connected and may need to be warned against text messaging in class or at meetings.

Many occupational therapy students who will enter the workforce in the near future have values and perceptions different from those of Baby Boomers or Generation Xers. Management styles that depend on organizational structure and hierarchy may be a mismatch for the Millennials, who want to be involved in the decision-making process but may get bored with the consensus-building behavior of the Baby Boomer generation (Glennon, 2009). The Millennials will benefit from more of a mentoring relationship and shared responsibility to foster their connectedness.

The Millennials may have an idealistic image of being an occupational therapy practitioner. Most occupational therapy students entering the workforce visualize themselves in a one-on-one, client-centered caregiving role in which they spend the entire day in a helping relationship. This vision is consistent with the role described in textbooks in which the occupational therapy practitioner is depicted as enabling people to perform the day-to-day activities that are important to them (Christiansen & Baum, 1997). Thus, occupational therapy is a good fit for the Millennials.

Conclusion

The skill sets of a competent practitioner are similar to those of a manager. Occupational therapy professionals in both roles must be able to manage people, plan effectively, control resources, and organize time. The occupational therapy practitioner who does not have these skill sets will have difficulty surviving the rigors of today's health care environment. The occupational therapy manager is a facilitator who plans, organizes, coordinates, and takes control. He or she may have little time for the things that brought him or her into the field of occupational therapy in the first place, but being able to accomplish personal and professional goals is a major advantage in becoming a manager. The skill set of a manager involves the ability to endure long hours, enforce regulations, set policies, undergo high stress, and pay constant attention to detail.

Case Examples

LEVEL I FIELDWORK

For her Level I fieldwork assignment, S was assigned to a locked unit in a minimum-security mental health facility for residents who have a criminal background. The student was frightened to go to the facility and talked to the academic fieldwork coordinator about being reassigned to a pediatric facility. The coordinator assured the student that there would be ample security and that the residents were not known to be dangerous. To allay S's fears, they invited the therapist who was to supervise her to lunch to discuss the assignment goals and expectations of the facility. S felt more comfortable on the first day on the locked unit.

LEVEL II FIELDWORK

P, a Level II fieldwork student who had a pattern of being late for class and turning in assignments late, was reported to the academic fieldwork coordinator for being late for therapy sessions on an acute care hospital unit. The coordinator counseled P, and the fieldwork educator wrote a learning contract stating that he had to be on

(continued)

Case Examples *(cont.)*

time and prepared. The contract was part of a progressive disciplinary action plan that P read and agreed to. P was late for treatment sessions two more times. Because the academic fieldwork coordinator had documentation in P's file, he was counseled out of the occupational therapy program and changed his major field of study.

FIRST-TIME MANAGER

R was newly appointed to supervise a unit that served clients with burns and other traumatic injuries. A therapist working on the unit allowed her basic life support (BLS) certification to expire. R, faced with her first supervisory challenge, was uncomfortable confronting the therapist because she had been employed at the facility longer and had service awards and advanced expertise. R consulted with the human resources person and set up a meeting for the three of them. At the meeting, R reviewed the

hospital policy on BLS certification, and the human resource person reiterated the terms of the policy. The therapist was put on administrative leave for 2 days with pay and thereafter without pay until she took the training and showed evidence that she had completed BLS training and certification.

MANAGER

Because of a shortage of qualified occupational therapy practitioners, F hired three new therapists who had just completed their second Level II fieldwork rotation to fill vacancies in a skilled nursing facility (SNF). The new therapists were members of the Millennial generation and had good ideas and technical skills, but they seemed to be impatient with the pace at which the SNF operated. To better match the needs of the SNF with the abilities of the young therapists, F set up weekly mentoring groups and used more participatory and transformational leadership with the young therapists.

❖ Learning Activities

1. Shadow an executive or administrator, and record his or her activities for a typical workday.
2. Shadow an occupational therapy practitioner for a typical workday, and record how many tasks are administrative in nature.
3. Give the list of skill sets in Appendix 2.B to a manager and practitioner, and ask him or her to check off which he or she most typically uses on an average day.
4. Write a list of the skill sets you like and dislike using in your current job. Analyze the list, and set out to reduce the dislikes.

✓ Multiple-Choice Questions

1. Which of the following is a basic argument put forth in this chapter?
   a. The skill sets for the manager and the practitioner are distinctly different.
   b. The practitioner is not qualified to perform management duties.
   c. Managers are promoted to a position of authority not because they are good practitioners, but because they are good communicators.
   d. All occupational therapists are managers, and all managers are practitioners.
2. What expectation is required of both the occupational therapy manager and occupational therapy practitioner?
   a. To be efficient despite one's concern for client-centered therapy.
   b. To put reimbursement at the forefront and modulate client factors to satisfy the administration.
   c. To be able to multitask effectively.
   d. To use e-mail and text messaging as the primary mode of communication.

3. A *skill set* as defined in this chapter is which of the following?
   a. A developed or acquired ability to perform something (task or occupation) with competence, either manually or intellectually.
   b. A technique that is learned quickly to accomplish a task of short duration.
   c. A manual dexterity skill that can be timed to show superior motor performance.
   d. A combination of subcortical responses that are reflexive in nature and require little reflection.
4. Technology has altered the manager's and practitioner's role or performance in what way?
   a. It enables them to communicate with friends and family while on the job seeing clients.
   b. It enables them to perform several tasks in a shorter period of time.
   c. It facilitates documentation and deserves reimbursement for service.
   d. It really has not improved performance and has created a decline in productivity.

5. The manager and practitioner focus on getting work done to meet the demands of clients and the health care system. Which is an element that should not be neglected while getting work done?
   a. Answering e-mail and the cell phone while at work.
   b. Striving for efficiency at the cost of human relations.
   c. Establishing a formal work relationship and chain of command.
   d. The human factor.

6. Both the manager and the practitioner can motivate better performance if they attend to which set of strategies?
   a. Happy hour after work, flow charts, time-and-motion studies, forming subgroups.
   b. Achievement, recognition, the work itself, responsibility, and advancement.
   c. Giving monetary raises, giving extended vacation, monitoring paperwork, writing strategic plans.
   d. Extending the lunch hour, reducing referrals, delegating to occupational therapy assistants, offering a sign-on bonus.

7. Each generation of new practitioners is characterized by certain traits or qualities. Which are typical of the Millennial generation?
   a. Value on tradition, intolerance of other lifestyle perspectives.
   b. High achievement, egocentricity, unconventionality.
   c. Technological savvy, multitasking, impatience.
   d. Low performance, lack of sociability.

8. Based on the reported characteristics and understanding of the Millennial generation, what are the best management strategies for successful work interactions?
   a. Tell them to "suck it up" and work like their parents did.
   b. Have them hand over their cell phones so they can't text their friends and parents.
   c. Provide mentoring, constructive feedback in communicating, and opportunities to participate in decisions.
   d. Use consensus building and force them to write treatment plans in longhand.

9. Which vision do occupational therapy students typically have of the role of practitioner?
   a. Receiving high status in health care.
   b. Being a traveling therapist with a lavish sign-on bonus and perks.
   c. Being able to keep a close relationship with their parents and working less than 6 hours a day.
   d. Being in the caregiving role during the entire workday.

10. There are several myths about the role of a manager. Which of the following is *not* true?
    a. Managers prefer electronic media to obtain information.
    b. Managers spend most of their time in oral communication.
    c. Managers are preoccupied with controlling their subordinates.
    d. The element of trust enables the manager to make timely decisions.

11. Studies show that there is a gender divide in leadership style, and women occupy most management roles in occupational therapy. How might women be at a disadvantage in management situations?
    a. Women tend to be authoritative in their work relationships.
    b. During negotiation, women strive for more of a collaborative outcome and settle for less.
    c. Women are fearful of conflict.
    d. Women do not give up power when advanced to management position.

12. When comparing the most common skill sets of managers and practitioners, which are exclusively concerned with the role of the practitioner?
    a. Supervision, documentation, budgeting.
    b. Cost containment, interpersonal skills, scheduling.
    c. Mentoring, accounting, cost containment.
    d. Caregiving, therapeutic use of self, task analysis.

13. Which is an enduring myth about the role of manager?
    a. The manager organizes to maintain performance for only short periods of time.
    b. The manager needs to think globally.
    c. The manager has time to be reflective in planning.
    d. The manager is oriented toward action rather than reflection.

14. When managers are forced to make quick decisions based on soft data, what element needs to exist in the organization to allow for rapid changes?
    a. Good salary.
    b. Generous benefit package.
    c. Trust.
    d. Authority and power.

15. The skill sets of the practitioner and the manager may change according to which factor?
    a. The environment may alter the skill set.
    b. The presence of high-level management.
    c. The presence of client factors.
    d. The context of the situation.

16. All of the following skill sets fall within the purview of the practitioner *except*
    a. Therapeutic relationship builder.
    b. Politician.
    c. Activity analysis.
    d. Occupation-based approach.

17. The performance of adjunctive methods in therapy is
    a. Exclusively within the skill set of the manager.
    b. More important to the physical therapist.
    c. More typical of the role or skill set of the practitioner.
    d. More typical of nursing.

18. The line between the manager's role and the role of the practitioner is
    a. Clearly delineated.
    b. Somewhat delineated.
    c. There is little comparison between roles.
    d. Quite blurred.

19. The main advantage of becoming a manager is to
    a. Achieve prestige, power, and authority.
    b. Enforce regulations and policies.
    c. Be able to accomplish personal and professional goals.
    d. Be able to gain satisfaction by being in a position of authority.

20. In the context of the manager, the term *controlling* implies which of the following?
    a. Applying micromanagement skills to carefully see that work gets done correctly.
    b. Influencing the lighting and organization of the clinical space to increase motivation to work.
    c. Maintaining reasonable cost containment and efficiency to improve performance.
    d. Being in a position to set goals and federal reimbursement criteria.

References

Amatucci, F. M., & Sohl, J. E. (2004). Women entrepreneurs securing business angel financing: Tales from the field. *Venture Capital, 6*(2/3), 181–196.

Amatucci, F. M., Swartz, E., & Coleman, S. (2008, June). *Testing the "women don't ask" hypothesis: A qualitative study of contract negotiation in the private equity investment process.* Paper presented at the 2008 International Council for Small Business World Conference, Halifax, Nova Scotia, Canada. Retrieved August 28, 2009, from http://www.smu.ca/events/icsb/proceedings/creao17f.html

American Council on Occupational Therapy Education. (2006). *ACOTE manual.* Retrieved December 2, 2009, from http://www.aota.org/Educate/Accredit/Policies.aspx

American Occupational Therapy Association. (2005). Standards of practice for occupational therapy practice. *American Journal of Occupational Therapy, 59,* 663–665.

American Occupational Therapy Association. (2008). Occupational therapy practice framework: Domain and process (2nd ed.). *American Journal of Occupational Therapy, 62,* 625–683.

Bear, M. F., Connors, B. W., & Paradiso, M. A. (2007). *Neuroscience: Exploring the brain.* Baltimore: Lippincott Williams and Wilkins.

Blair, G. M. (n.d.-a). *Conversation as communication.* Retrieved December 14, 2008, from http://www.see.ed.ac.uk/~gerard/Management/art7.html

Blair, G. M. (n.d.-b). *The human factor.* Retrieved December 14, 2008, from http://www.see.ed.ac.uk/~gerard/Management/art6.html

Christiansen, C., & Baum, C. (1997). *Occupational therapy: Enabling function and well-being* (2nd ed.). Thorofare, NJ: Slack.

Covey, S. R., & Merrill, R. R. (2006). *The speed of trust: The one thing that changes everything.* New York: Free Press.

Crepeau, E. B., Cohn, E. S., & Schell, B. A. B. (2003). *Willard and Spackman's occupational therapy* (10th ed.). Baltimore: Lippincott Williams & Wilkins.

Drucker, P. (1999, March–April). Managing oneself. *Harvard Business Review.*

Fayol, H. (1929). *General and industrial management* (J. A. Conbrough, Trans.). Geneva, Switzerland: International Management Institute.

Fisher, G., & Keehn, M. (2007). *Workforce needs and issues in occupational therapy and physical therapy.* Chicago: Midwest Center for Health Workforce Studies.

Glennon, T. L. (2009, March). Millennials in the workforce: Implications for managers. *Administration and Management Special Interest Section Quarterly,* pp. 1–3.

Grady, A. P. (2003). From management to leadership. In G. McCormack, E. G. Jaffe, & M. Goodman-Lavey (Eds.), *The occupational therapy manager* (4th ed., pp. 311–347). Bethesda, MD: AOTA Press.

Herzberg, F., Mausner, B., & Snyderman, B. (1959). *The motivation to work* (2nd ed.). New York: Wiley.

Hill, D. B. (2000). Getting a lock on patient confidentiality with e-mail encryption. *Family Practice Management.* Retrieved March 7, 2009, from http://www.aafp.org/fpm/20001000/37gett.html

Kray, L. J., & Thompson, L. (2007). Gender stereotypes and negotiation performance: A review of theory and research. In B. Straw & R. Kramer (Eds.), *Research in Organizational Behavioral Series, 26,* 103–182.

Kielhofner, G. (2009). *Conceptual foundations of occupational therapy practice* (4th ed.). Philadelphia: F. A. Davis.

Manning, M., & Haddock, P. (1995). *Leadership skills for women.* Menlo Park, CA: Crisp Publications.

Mintzberg, M. (1977). Folklore and fact. *Harvard Business Review, 66,* 32–35.

Moyers, P. A. (1999). The guide to occupational therapy practice (Special Issue). *American Journal of Occupational Therapy, 53*(3).

Nielson, C. (2003). Communication in the workplace. In G. McCormack, E. G. Jaffe, & M. Goodman-Lavey (Eds.), *The occupational therapy manager* (4th ed., pp. 289–308). Bethesda, MD: AOTA Press.

Pfeffer, J., & Sutton, R. (2006). *Hard facts, dangerous half-truths, and total nonsense: Profiting from evidence-based management.* Boston: Harvard Business School Press.

Pletka, R. (2007). *Educating the net generation: How to engage students in the 21st century.* Santa Monica, CA: Santa Monica Press.

Rubinstein, J. S., Meyer, D. E., & Evans, J. E. (2001). Executive control of cognitive processes in task switching. *Journal of Experimental Psychology: Human Perception and Performance, 27*(4), 44–55.

Safian, R. (2009). The world's most innovative companies. *Fast Company, 133,* 52–99.

Sladyk, K. (1997). *OT student primer: A guide to college success.* Thorofare, NJ: Slack.

Sherry, J. L. (2001). The effects of violent video games on aggression: A meta-analysis. *Human Communication Research, 27,* 409–431.

Smolowitz, I. E. (1994). A dozen enduring myths about management. *Business Horizons, 37*(3), 40–43.

Solomon, I. (1988). Value profiles of male and female entrepreneurs. *International Small Business Journal, 6*(3), 24–33.

U.S. Bureau of Labor Statistics. (2008). *Occupational outlook handbook 2008–09.* Retrieved on November 10, 2009, from http://www.bls.gov/oco/ocos078.htm

APPENDIX 2.A. SKILL SET EVIDENCE TABLE

Topic	Evidence
The human factor	Blair, G. M. (n.d.). *The human factor.* Retrieved December 14, 2008, from http://www.see.ed.ac.uk/~gerard/Management/art6.html
Millennials' viewpoint on work	Glennon, T. L. (2009, March). Millennials in the workforce: Implications for managers. *Administration and Management Special Interest Section Quarterly*, pp. 1–3. Pletka, R. (2007). *Educating the net generation: How to engage students in the 21st century.* Santa Monica, CA: Santa Monica Press. Sherry, J. L. (2001). The effects of violent video games on aggression: A meta-analysis. *Human Communication Research, 27*, 409–431.
Approaches to management	Amatucci, F. M., & Sohl, J. E. (2004). Women entrepreneurs securing business angel financing: Tales from the field. *Venture Capital, 6*(2/3), 181–196. Amatucci, F. M., Swartz, E., & Coleman, S. (2008, June). *Testing the "women don't ask" hypothesis: A qualitative study of contract negotiation in the private equity investment process.* Paper presented at the 2008 International Council for Small Business World Conference, Halifax, Nova Scotia, Canada. Retrieved August 28, 2009, from http://www.smu.ca/events/icsb/proceedings/creao17f.html Covey, S. R., & Merrill, R. R. (2006). *The speed of trust: The one thing that changes everything.* New York: Free Press. Drucker, P. (1999, March–April). Managing oneself. *Harvard Business Review.* Kray, L. J., & Thompson, L. (2007). Gender stereotypes and negotiation performance: A review of theory and research. *Research in Organizational Behavioral Series, 26*, 103–182.

Appendix 2.B. Occupational Therapy Skill Sets—Unscored

Skill set	Performed exclusively by occupational therapy practitioners	Performed exclusively by occupational therapy managers	Performed by both
Accommodations (many types)			
Accountability			
Acknowledging strengths			
Action plans			
Activities of daily living			
Activity analysis			
Activity demands			
Adaptation (outcomes)			
Adaptation of environment			
Adaptation of performance skills			
Adjunctive methods			
Administration			
Advocacy (political)			
Aligning goals with the mission statement			
Allocation of resources			
Analytical problem solver			
Annual performance assessment			
Appeal for reimbursement			
Application of physical agent modalities			
Assertiveness			
Assessment			
Assistive technology			
Attends rounds and meetings			
Author			
Basic assessment			
Basic life skills manager			
Behavior manager			
Budget manager			
Caregiver			
Charismatic motivator			
Charting			
Client-centered approach			
Clinical judgment			
Clinical reasoning			
Coach			
Code of ethics			

(continued)

APPENDIX 2.B. OCCUPATIONAL THERAPY SKILL SETS—UNSCORED *(cont.)*

Skill set	Performed exclusively by occupational therapy practitioners	Performed exclusively by occupational therapy managers	Performed by both
Cognitive restructuring			
Collaboration			
Collecting data			
Collecting evidence			
Communication			
Compassion			
Compensation			
Computer skills			
Conflict resolution			
Consultation			
Consumer advocacy			
Context (cultural)			
Continuing competence			
Continuous quality improvement			
Core vales			
Cost containment			
Course of treatment			
Crafts person			
Critique of research studies			
Cultural competency			
Current policy awareness			
Decision making			
Delegation			
Delivery of services			
Descriptive research			
Designing lifestyles			
Diagnosis			
Directing			
Discharge planning			
Discontinuation reports			
Discrimination (sensory)			
Disease/disability prevention			
Dispute resolution			
Documentation			
Domestic violence			
Dressing skills			
Driving (adaptive)			
Early intervention			
Educational activity			
Educator			
Empathetic			

APPENDIX 2.B. OCCUPATIONAL THERAPY SKILL SETS — UNSCORED *(cont.)*

Skill set	Performed exclusively by occupational therapy practitioners	Performed exclusively by occupational therapy managers	Performed by both
Enabling activity			
Engagement in occupation			
Endurance			
Energy conservation			
Energy expenditure			
Entrepreneur			
Environmental context			
Environmental factors			
Environmental modification			
Ergonomics			
Ethical behavior			
Evaluation			
Evidence-based practice			
Explanation of services			
Feedback			
Feeding and swallowing			
Fieldwork educator			
Fiscal planning			
Flexible			
Focus group			
Follow-up			
Frames of reference			
Functional activities			
Grading activities			
Grant writing			
Group process			
Guidance			
Habit training			
Health care professional			
Health educator			
Health promotion			
Home health			
Improvement measures			
Independence promoter			
Information retrieval			
Interdisciplinary			
Interpersonal skills			
Interventions			
Interviewing			
Instrumental activities of daily living			
Job analysis			

(continued)

APPENDIX 2.B. OCCUPATIONAL THERAPY SKILL SETS—UNSCORED *(cont.)*

Skill set	Performed exclusively by occupational therapy practitioners	Performed exclusively by occupational therapy managers	Performed by both
Job description			
Judgment (clinical)			
Knowledge (clinical)			
Language skills			
Leadership			
Learning development			
Legislation awareness			
Leisure			
Life balance			
Lifestyle redesign			
Long-term plan			
Maintain records			
Management			
Marketing			
Measurement			
Meetings (attends/conducts)			
Mentoring			
Models behavior			
Monitoring			
Narrative reasoning			
Normative reports			
Observation skills			
Occupational performance			
Occupational profile			
Occupation-based approach			
Orientation skills			
Outcome studies			
Passive range of motion			
Peer review			
Performance patterns			
Performance skills			
Play			
Physical capacity evaluation			
Policy management			
Politician			
Pragmatic reasoning			
Prevention			
Process skills			
Problem solver			
Productivity			
Progressive disciplinary action			

APPENDIX 2.B. OCCUPATIONAL THERAPY SKILL SETS—UNSCORED *(cont.)*

Skill set	Performed exclusively by occupational therapy practitioners	Performed exclusively by occupational therapy managers	Performed by both
Public policy			
Qualitative researcher			
Quality assurance			
Quality controller			
Reasoning			
Referral manager			
Remediation expert			
Risk taker			
Safety manager			
Satisfaction employer			
Scheduler			
Selection process			
Self-assessment			
Self-efficacy improver			
Staff development			
Staffing			
Strategic planning			
Stress manager			
Substance abuse manager			
Supervision			
Task analysis			
Task group organizer			
Teacher			
Test giver			
Therapeutic relationship builder			
Time manager			
Tolerance builder			
Trainer			
Values clarification			
Virtual reality			
Vocational exploration			
Wellness expert			
Work conditioner			
Work performance evaluation			
Work simplification expert			
Workers' compensation			

3

Evolution of Occupational Therapy Delivery Systems

Karen Jacobs, EdD, OTR/L, CPE, FAOTA

❖ Key Terms and Concepts

Health maintenance organization (HMO). "A prepaid organized delivery system where the organization and the primary care physicians assume some financial risk for the care provided to its enrolled members" (Weiner & de Lissovoy, 1993, p. 96).

Indemnity policies. The standard fee-for-service insurance policies provided by employers, organizations, or individuals. Usually the most expensive type, this insurance covers service from any provider.

Managed care. A term used for all kinds of integrated delivery systems, in contrast to unmanaged, fee-for-service care. Also, "the entire range of utilization control tools that are applied to manage the practices of physicians and

others, regardless of the setting in which they practice" (Weiner & de Lissovoy, 1993, p. 97).

Point-of-service (POS) plan. An open-access plan similar to an HMO that provides limited coverage for self-referral outside the network (Andersen, Rice, & Kominski, 2001).

Preferred-provider organization (PPO). An entity that "acts as a broker between the purchaser of care and the provider. . . . Consumers have the option of using the 'preferred' providers available within the plan, or not" (Weiner & de Lissovoy, 1993, p. 99).

Utilization review. The review of cases after health care services are conducted.

❖ Learning Objectives

After completing this chapter, you should be able to do the following:

- Describe how health care is delivered in the United States.
- Describe the evolution of occupational therapy in the U.S. health care system.
- List three basic models of integrated delivery systems.

- List two health care cost-containment strategies used since the 1980s.
- Discuss two strategies to ensure the role of occupational therapy in the future health care environment.

Occupational therapy services are affected by the health care system's vulnerabilities and strengths. Health care costs rose from $27.1 billion in 1960 to $2.2 trillion in 2007 (Wilson, 2009), but the U.S. population is not receiving the appropriate health care value for the money spent (McCanne, 2004). In 2000, the World Health Or-

ganization (WHO) rated the United States first in health care spending per capita but 37th in its overall health system performance, below most other industrialized nations (WHO, 2000). Because of the health care industry's rising costs, growing emphasis on outcomes and accountability, lack of services to meet specific needs, imbalance in services

The author acknowledges the contributions of Boston University master of science in occupational therapy students S. Aldama, L. Byrne, C. Cabral, K. Carlin, J. Davis, S. DeNatale, D. Dewhurst, L. Ferraro, R. Fischer, S. Fulkerson, C. Giovannini, S. Gupta, A. Halverson, K. Hanauer, K. Henneman, L. Hess, M. Huang, S. H. Jung, N. Keshavjee, M. Krol, C. Macock, G. Mangini, B. Nichols, P. Nova, A. O'Malley, C. Peters, A. Regan, A. Savage, E. Sliwinski, M. Stoer, C. VanSweden, B. Von Bargen, E. Waugh-Quasebarth, and S. Weissman.

available to different populations, and advances in medical technology, the government and the public have begun to scrutinize industry practices.

In March 2010, President Barack Obama signed into law historic health care reform. "The Patient Protection and Affordable Care Act requires most U.S. citizens and legal immigrants to have healthcare coverage and will create a national exchange allowing people to shop for health insurance plans and providing subsides to low-income people" (Lowe, 2010, p. 14). In addition, insurance companies no longer will be allowed to deny coverage to children with preexisting conditions, children will be able to remain on parents' insurance policies until they reach 26 years of age, and Medicare recipients who fall into a specific coverage gap will receive a $250 rebate (Lowe, 2010).

Provisions that expand home- and community-based services may affect occupational therapy practitioners' work settings. The new provisions aim to allow persons with disabilities to live at home and participate in their communities instead of requiring them to live in institutional facilities in order to receive services (Emmons, 2010).

The new Community First Choice Option is expected to contribute to the expansion of home- and community-based services by allowing state Medicaid plans to choose these services for Medicaid-eligible persons with disabilities with incomes up to 150% of the federal poverty level who would otherwise require institutional care. "To encourage states to choose this option, states that opt in will receive an additional 6% added to the federal government's share of Medicaid costs for 5 years" (Emmons, 2010). These items become effective October 1, 2011.

Reform also extends the Money Follows the Person demonstration grants until September 2016, which "provide funding to state Medicaid programs for moving Medicaid recipients who have resided in inpatient facilities into community-based settings" (Emmons, 2010).

To better understand the debate and decision-making process that brought about health care reform, it is important to understand the history of the U.S. health care system. This chapter explores the evolution of the U.S. health care system and its effect on the delivery of occupational therapy services.

THE FEDERAL GOVERNMENT'S ROLE IN THE HEALTH CARE SYSTEM

Right-to-Health Concept and Ethics

The basis for much of the government's involvement in health care is the concept of the right to health. Although the *Congressional Record* refers to this concept as early as 1796 (Baum, 1992), it came to full attention in 1944 in President Franklin D. Roosevelt's Economic Bill of Rights, in which he proclaimed "the right to adequate needed care and the opportunity to achieve and enjoy good health," equating the right to health care with the most fundamental social and political rights guaranteed to every citizen (B. Chapman & Talmedge, 1971, p. 35).

Very few political leaders would publicly declare that they do not support a right to health care. However, many politicians debate this right on a daily basis as the government allocates funds. The right to health care, which would guarantee equal access to "basic and adequate health care"—a standard package including preventive, primary, reproductive, and long-term care; most types of acute care; and mental health services—would demand huge financial resources (A. R. Chapman, 1993, p. vi).

The right-to-health concept is ultimately a matter of ethics. In fact, this issue is one of many pressing moral concerns relevant to health care today (see Chapter 30 for a more complete discussion of this topic). Occupational therapy practitioners who enter management are likely to encounter related ethical dilemmas in their work. They need to develop an understanding of potential conflicts and ways of maintaining their personal ethics while successfully carrying out their roles. Goals such as independence, self-determination, and competency—all seen in the practice of occupational therapy—are all based on values and morals (Bloom, 1994).

Historically, the federal government has been locked into the role of providing assistance, not control. Since the mid-1940s, the federal government has made many significant contributions to the evolving health care system. The following summary of major historical events offers a perspective on these contributions.

Construction of Health Care Facilities

Minimal hospital construction occurred in the United States until after World War II. In 1944, the American Hospital Association (AHA) and the U.S. Public Health Service organized a commission on hospital care to determine the need for new hospital facilities. The work of the commission was reflected in the Hospital Survey and Construction Act of 1946, Title VI of the Public Health Service Act. Popularly known as the Hill–Burton Act, this legislation helped states determine their need for hospitals and other health care facilities and provided grants for construction projects. Over the next two decades, Congress extended and amended the Hill–Burton Act frequently, expanding its programs to cover diagnostic and treatment centers, chronic disease hospitals, rehabilitation facilities, and nursing homes. In 1964 and again in 1970, Congress earmarked funds for modernization of these health care facilities.

In 1963, the Mental Retardation Facilities Construction Act and the Community Mental Health Centers Act (P.L. 88–164) were passed to provide funding for the construction of facilities for people with cognitive disabilities and community-based mental health centers. Extensions and amendments to this federal legislation continued into the early 1980s.

The Hill–Burton Act was greatly modified in the National Health Planning and Resources Development Act of 1974 (P.L. 93–641). This legislation was especially critical in modernizing health care facilities. Many of the facilities built between 1946 and 1974 were struggling to survive, and too few health professionals were available to staff them. Also, some health facilities were obsolete, requiring nearly $20 billion a year for modernization. By the early 1970s, the federal government began to recognize the need for systems of control and meaningful plans for the construction and staffing of health care facilities.

Human Resources Legislation

Since the mid-1950s, the federal government has had an important role in financing human resources for health care. Its first peacetime legislation to support training of health care professionals was the Health Amendments Act of 1956 (P.L. 84–911), benefiting public health personnel and professional and practical nurses. In 1958, Congress established a program of formula grants to schools of public health. Soon to follow was a program of project grants for these and other schools training public health personnel.

The first construction grants for teaching facilities came in 1963, in the Health Professions Educational Assistance Act (P.L. 88–128). Schools of medicine, dentistry, pharmacy, podiatry, nursing, and public health were the eligible recipients. This act also made student loan funds available in medicine, osteopathy, and dentistry. In 1964, the Nurse Training Act (P.L. 88–581) provided separate funds for nursing school construction, set aside funds to expand educational training programs in nursing, and established nursing student loan programs. The Health Professions Educational Assistance Amendments of 1965 (P.L. 89–290) authorized grants to improve the quality of schools of medicine, dentistry, osteopathy, optometry, and podiatry. The amendments also made scholarship funds available to those schools and to schools of pharmacy.

The first federal funds for the support of occupational therapy education came in 1966 with the Allied Health Professions Personnel Training Act (P.L. 89–751). This legislation authorized the award of construction and improvement grants to training centers for allied health professions. It also made advanced traineeships available to allied health professionals. The Health Manpower Act of 1968 (P.L. 90–490) extended most of the programs for health and allied health professionals, including those for occupational therapy personnel.

Legislation supporting training in various ways continued into the 1970s (e.g., Health Training Improvement Act of 1970 [P.L. 91–519], Comprehensive Health Manpower Training Act of 1971 [P.L. 92–157], Nurse Training Act of 1975 [P.L. 94–63]). In the late 1970s and the 1980s, however, the federal government began to limit moneys for traineeships. In 1980, the training money for the Allied Health Professions Personnel Training Act was eliminated from the federal budget. From the late 1980s to the early 1990s, the government published several reports that documented a shortage of allied health professionals.

In 1990, moneys for the Allied Health Professions Personnel Training Act were returned to the federal budget (Elwood, 1991).

Health Resources Planning in Recent Administrations

By the early 1970s, the federal government was acutely aware of the need to control health care costs. Several major pieces of legislation addressed that need. A 1972 amendment to the Social Security Act (P.L. 92–336) created professional standards review organizations. Under this plan, associations of physicians reviewed professionals' activities and institutions' services to monitor and control both cost and quality of care. The law made it possible to give hospital utilization review committees the responsibility for carrying out these functions. Also in 1972, Congress enacted legislation giving the secretary of state the authority to establish limitations on Medicare reimbursements for routine services provided under Part A of Medicare (Hospital Insurance).

Two years later, Congress passed the National Health Planning and Resources Development Act (P.L. 93–641) to ensure the development of both a national health policy and effective state and area programs for health planning and resource allocation. Under the provisions of this act, each state is divided into health service areas, and health systems agencies are designated to administer them. The agencies have three purposes:

1. To improve the health of area residents;
2. To increase the accessibility, acceptability, continuity, and quality of health services; and
3. To restrain costs and prevent duplication of health services.

In 1982, Congress enacted the Tax Equity and Fiscal Responsibility Act (P.L. 97–248), which, among other provisions, extended the 1972 limits on reimbursements under Medicare to cover ancillary and rehabilitation services, including occupational therapy.

In April 1983, President Ronald Reagan signed the Social Security Amendments into law (P.L. 98–21). These amendments contained a congressional mandate to alter the way in which health care was subsidized and delivered. The intent of the legislation was to impose further constraints on the level of federal spending for Medicare benefits, particularly for inpatient hospital care. The law fundamentally changed the formula for disbursing health care dollars. For decades, health care had relied almost exclusively on a hospital-based delivery system: On the basis of a financial formula, the payer (the federal government, an insurance company, or an individual) reimbursed hospitals for the cost of the services provided. Under the Medicare prospective payment system (PPS) created by the Social Security Amendments of 1983, the Health Care Financing Administration established a nationwide schedule defining the payment the government would make for each inpatient stay by a Medicare beneficiary. The level of payment per case is determined by about 500 descriptive categories called *diagnosis-related groups* (DRGs; *The DRG Handbook*, 1994).

The PPS has had a profound effect on the development of the health care industry by reducing emphasis on inpatient services and expanding outpatient and community programs. Changes have occurred within both Medicare Part A (hospital insurance) and Medicare Part B (supplementary medical insurance), some of which directly affect occupational therapy. In 1986, Congress enacted legislation expanding Medicare coverage of occupational therapy services under Part B to include "services furnished in a skilled-nursing facility (when Part A coverage has been exhausted), in a clinic, [in a] rehabilitation agency, [in a] public health agency, or by an independently practicing therapist" (Social Security Administration, 1994, p. 94).

Although some health care legislation was passed during the administration of President Bill Clinton (1993–2001), First Lady Hillary Clinton's unsuccessful attempt at health care reform probably garnered the most attention. The Clinton health care plan of 1993 aimed to provide universal health care through a national plan but failed because of opposition in Congress and from lobbyists representing the American Medical Association and private health insurance companies. In 1997, along with a bipartisan team, Hillary Clinton again had a hand in health care reform by successfully supporting the State Children's Health Insurance Program (SCHIP; P.L. 105–33). SCHIP is a state and federally funded program that covers uninsured children (and sometimes adults) in families with incomes that are too high to qualify them for Medicaid. Similar to Medicaid, each state can design its own program under loose federal guidelines (Centers for Medicare and Medicaid Services, 1997). SCHIP helped provide health care to 5 million uninsured children (White House, 2009b).

In 1993, Clinton signed the Family and Medical Leave Act of 1993 (P.L. 103–3), which allows employees to take up to 12 weeks of unpaid, job-protected leave to recover from a serious health condition or to care for a child or sick family member (U.S. Department of Labor, 2009). The Clinton administration enacted the Health Insurance Portability and Accountability Act (known by its acronym, HIPAA; P.L. 104–191) in 1996, which assures citizens insurance coverage during times of employment change or loss, gives small businesses insurance options, and protects Americans' privacy rights regarding their medical records (White House, 2009b). In 1997, President Clinton worked toward reforming Medicare through the Balanced Budget Act (P.L. 105–33), which extended the Medicare Trust Fund to 2025 (it was previously due to run out of money in 1999) and addressed the growing problem of health care fraud (White House, 2009b). Clinton was also responsible for passing mental health parity provisions, which help ensure that citizens with mental health conditions receive proper care (White House, 2009b).

As his first term came to a close, President George W. Bush signed the Medicare Prescription Drug, Improvement, and Modernization Act of 2003 (P.L. 108–173), Medicare Part D. It allowed for prescription drugs to be covered, usually for a monthly premium, for individuals who receive Medicare benefits. Along with Medicare Part D came implementation of health savings accounts (HSAs), tax-free accounts that allow individuals to set aside money for potential health expenses (National Conference of State Legislatures, 2009). As of 2008, more than 6.1 million people were enrolled in a high-deductible insurance plan with an HSA. One criticism of this type of plan is that it benefits mostly higher-income households and those who are able to afford high-deductible insurance plans.

On November 4, 2008, Barack Obama was elected as the 44th president of the United States. President Obama's administration promoted health care reform to better suit the needs of Americans by finding a middle ground between government-run and privatized health care. The goal of the Patient Protection and Affordable Care Act (P.L. 111–148, 2010, see also Chapter 28) is for all Americans to have affordable, accessible health care that builds on existing health care plans. To achieve this goal, the administration intends to invest in electronic health information technology systems that will abolish paper claims, saving time and money. It also plans to improve access to prevention programs that have been proved to increase health, increase competition in the drug and insurance company forum, and reduce the costs of catastrophic illnesses for employers and their employees. However, it is too early to tell what health care reform will mean to occupational therapy, particularly because the rule-making process will take years to complete.

HEALTH CARE DELIVERY SYSTEMS

When people think of a hospital today, they envision a sophisticated facility providing technically advanced procedures to support life and a healthful status. Hospitals, however, were not medically oriented until after the turn of the century. Until then, they were facilities for people who were indigent, and the majority of health care was delivered at home. From the early 1900s until the early 1970s, most health care was provided and delivered in two facilities, the physician's office and the hospital. Nursing homes were mostly for custodial management, and today's concept of home health care was in its early development.

Modern health care organizations are the result of scientific developments and changes in society and federal legislation. The current system includes government, nonprofit, and for-profit facilities (Table 3.1).

Vertically Organized Hospitals

Alternative methods of delivering health care services at less cost than hospital services have existed for years. Hospitals were initially reluctant to support these systems because

Table 3.1. Health Care Organizations

Type of Organization	General Description
Federal government	Hospitals serving disabled veterans Hospitals serving the armed forces and the Coast Guard Indian Health Service Public Health Service hospitals and clinics (including a leprosarium) Medical facilities associated with prisons
State government	Infirmaries associated with prisons and reformatories Hospitals for people with mental illness State medical school hospitals and clinics
Local government	City hospitals and clinics County hospitals and public health clinics Rehabilitation facilities
Nonprofit organization	Charity hospitals Community hospitals Health maintenance organizations (HMOs) Home health facilities Hospices Industrial hospitals and clinics Preferred-provider organizations (PPOs) Private teaching hospitals Religious hospitals Specialty hospitals Surgical centers Wellness centers
For-profit organization	Facilities owned by individuals or groups for the care of their own patients or clients Investor-owned facilities (hospitals, laboratories, nursing homes, surgical centers, rehabilitation facilities, home health facilities, HMOs, PPOs, and hospices), including corporations and management corporations Walk-in medical clinics

under the former payment structure, hospitals were paid directly for their services. The set fees under the PPS now make it economically advantageous for hospitals to move clients with long-term problems out of acute care beds into another type of health care setting as quickly as possible. Instead of staying in the hospital, clients are transferred to home health care, nursing facilities, hospices, designated subacute care beds, designated rehabilitation beds, designated psychiatric beds, outpatient surgery, day treatment for elderly people, or outpatient programs. This system has expanded both the importance and the use of the rehabilitation fields, including occupational therapy, and has allowed hospitals to support these fields. Thus, most hospitals are now organized in a vertical system.

The vertical organization serves the hospital system well. Clients can be readmitted for necessary procedures, and the hospital is able to keep clients in its market by placing them in affiliated systems. This very skillful economic strategy has also created the greatest opportunity in history for rehabilitation. For nearly every one of a hospital's vertical programs to be effective, the programs require the rehabilitation professions' skills. The challenge to these professions is to provide the human resources to staff the programs. Should occupational therapy not have enough personnel, other professions will expand their roles to fill the need.

Health Networks

In today's changing society and economy, the free-standing hospital has become financially vulnerable. Concern about this vulnerability has led to the formation of large health networks linking individual facilities that engage in only one of several related corporate activities. Either a multihospital system or a diversified single-hospital system is created when two or more facilities are owned, leased, sponsored, or contract managed by a central organization. A network is created when some combination of hospitals, physicians, other providers, insurers, and community agencies work together to coordinate and deliver services (AHA, 2009). Since the 1970s, many types of multiinstitutional systems have developed, each with distinct ownership and governance. They have six features in common:

1. Strong financial and organizational management
2. A well-developed market strategy
3. Built-in referral strategies to keep their use high
4. A broad geographic approach
5. An expansive model of service delivery, from primary to restorative care, including home health services, ambulatory services, and skilled nursing facilities
6. Shared services for purchasing, billing, maintenance, and marketing.

The trend toward large corporate systems taking over facilities with fewer than 100 beds continues into the 21st century. In a 2007 survey, the AHA (2009) found that 63% of all hospital systems were for-profit, multi-institutional systems. They also found that 4,202 (74%) of the 5,708 hospitals in the United States were part of either a system or a network (AHA, 2009).

Alternative or Integrated Delivery Systems

Alternative or integrated delivery systems have evolved with the rise of vertically organized hospitals and are now among the most widespread health care delivery systems. Integrated delivery systems "usually involve a significant degree of integration between payer [the insurance company] and provider [the physician or hospital]" (Weiner & de Lissovoy, 1993, p. 94) and depend on managed care. Some use the term *managed care* as a synonym for all kinds of integrated delivery systems, contrasting these systems with unmanaged, fee-for-service care. More recently, however, the term frequently has denoted "the entire range of utilization control tools that are applied to manage the practices of physicians and others, regardless of the setting in which they practice" (Weiner & de Lissovoy, 1993, p. 97). *Utilization review* involves "evaluation of the necessity, appropriateness, and efficiency of the use of health care services, procedures, and facilities" and has become "one of the primary tools utilized by health plans to control over-utilization, reduce costs, and manage care" (Pohly, 2007). The types of controls used to manage care may include "preadmission certification, mandatory second opinion before surgery, certification of treatment plans for discretionary nonemergency services (such as mental health care), primary care physician gatekeepers, and non-physician case managers to monitor the care of particular patients" (Weiner & de Lissovoy, 1993, p. 97). In addition to utilization review, managed care systems cut costs through the practice of "gatekeeping," or requiring a primary care provider to authorize referrals to subspecialists and health and rehabilitation professionals and by encouraging or requiring their enrollees to use selected providers (Pati, Shea, Rabinowitz, & Carrasquillo, 2005).

The three major types of integrated delivery systems operating in today's health market are HMOs, PPOs, and POS plans. Occupational therapy services often covered by HMOs, PPOs, and POS plans include developmental screening, training in stress management, arthritis programs, ergonomic consultations, functional capacity evaluations, and hand-related services. Some integrated delivery services require home health rehabilitation services, and many practitioners are eager to develop contractual relationships with these insurance systems to provide those services. Figure 3.1 shows the types of delivery systems from least restrictive to most restrictive managed care.

The concept of managed care has proved successful in containing costs. Subsequently, many variants of managed care have evolved as large health care organizations and insurance companies compete in the marketplace for new

members. As of 2005, only 3% of covered American employees were enrolled in conventional, nonmanaged insurance programs (Sultz & Young, 2009). The conventional insurance policies are often referred to as *indemnity policies* and cover care on a fee-for-service basis. Indemnity policies are often more expensive for the client than enrollment in a managed care system.

Health Maintenance Organizations

HealthLeaders–Interstudy (2009) defined the *HMO* as "a prepaid health system providing care to members through specific health care providers often determined by the HMO." HMOs are a "traditional form of managed care" and typically require clients to contact a primary care physician before receiving specialty care (Andersen et al., 2001, p. 390). The member must also receive services only from a professional who works within the insurance company's network, referred to as an *in-network provider*.

Physicians can contract with an HMO in several different ways. In a closed-panel HMO, physicians are allowed to treat only clients who are subscribers to that HMO. The closed-panel HMO either contracts exclusively with a single group practice (group model) or employs individual physicians (staff model). These plans are often viewed as restrictive because clients are not permitted to choose a doctor outside the HMO. Closed-panel access offers no coverage for self-referral outside the network.

In contrast, open-panel HMOs avoid these restrictions. In open-panel HMOs, network association and independent practice association models permit HMOs to contract with multiple medical groups or individual physicians, respectively. In these cases, physicians are permitted to contract with more than one HMO and may treat clients who are not enrolled in the HMO. Open-panel access covers self-referral outside the network.

There are a number of forms of prepayment available in this HMO model. In a *fee-for-service* payment scheme, a fixed amount of money (*capitation*) is granted to a physician for each member enrolled. "The provider receives the payment whether or not services are used [by that member]" (Sultz & Young, 2009, p. 242). In a *withhold scheme*, physicians are provided with a target sum for their services. If the physician meets that monetary target, the physician receives the allocated funds. If the physician exceeds that target, monetary penalties are enacted.

Point-of-Service Plans

POS plans were developed in the 1980s to provide for more client choice in care when enrolled in HMO programs. They are similar to open-panel HMOs, but these plans permit limited coverage on a self-referral basis for services by physicians outside the network (Andersen et al., 2001). POS plans can have a varied billing system in which clients who work through a primary care physician pay the lowest copayments and copayments increase when the client self-refers within the network or receives services from

---

Least Restrictive Managed Care

Point-of-service (POS)
↓
Preferred-provider organization (PPO)
↓
*Independent practice association (HMO)
↓
*Network model (HMO)
↓
†Group model (HMO)
↓
†Staff model (HMO)

Most Restrictive Managed Care

Figure 3.1. Degree of restriction in managed care.

Note. * = Open-panel (access); coverage for self-referral outside the network. † = Closed-panel (access); no coverage for self-referral outside the network.

a physician outside the network. A POS plan "offers the consumer a choice of options at the time he or she seeks services (rather than at the time they choose to enroll in a health plan)" (Weiner & de Lissovoy, 1993, p. 99).

Preferred-Provider Organizations

PPOs are less restrictive than traditional HMOs because subscribers can self-refer to specialists and are not required to consult with a primary care physician before receiving specialty care (Andersen et al., 2001). Consumers can use either the "preferred" providers available within the plan or other providers (Weiner & de Lissovoy, 1993).

PPOs contract with physicians and groups, although clients are not required to use the doctors within the group. The physicians in a PPO agree to follow "utilization management guidelines" (Andersen et al., 2001) set forth by the PPO to control costs and ensure quality. "Physicians are also reimbursed at a discounted rate for their services on a fee for service basis and are ensured a certain volume of clients that are enrolled in the PPO without the financial risks associated with HMOs" (Sultz & Young, 2009, p. 243).

Clients pay less if they use physicians within the PPO network; however, they generally receive some coverage for services provided by physicians who are not preferred providers. According to the *PPO Directory and Performance Report 2.0* (InterStudy, 2001), the number of PPOs in the United States increased from 571 to 1,037 between 1990 and 1998. By 2001, 98.4 million Americans were enrolled in PPOs. According to the American Association of Preferred Provider Organizations (2009), 193 million Americans, or 69% of insured Americans, received their health care through a PPO in 2009.

Care for the Uninsured Population

Despite the large number of people enrolled in each of these health insurance programs, many Americans remain uninsured. By 2007, nearly 46 million Americans, or 18% of the population under age 65, were without health insurance, an increase of almost 8 million since 2000 (DeNavas-Walt, Proctor, & Smith, 2008; U. S. Bureau of the Census, 2001). This group includes all ages, incomes, geographic settings, races, and ethnic groups. Children and people in the lower- and middle-income brackets are less likely to have health insurance than older and wealthier people (U.S. Bureau of the Census, 2001). Many people without insurance either self-pay for health care or look to other organizations, such as public health organizations, to provide services.

Lack of insurance places the health of these individuals at risk. They receive less preventive care, are diagnosed at later stages of disease, receive less therapeutic care, and have higher mortality rates. It also creates additional costs for the nation; the United States spends nearly $100 billion per year to provide health services to the uninsured, often for diseases that could have been prevented or treated

more efficiently with earlier detection (National Coalition on Healthcare, 2009a).

Public Health Organizations

The American Public Health Association (APHA), a voluntary organization of public health professionals, actively serves the public, its members, and the public health profession through its scientific and practice programs, public health standards, publications, educational services, and advocacy efforts (APHA, 2009). Members of the APHA work in public health systems at the local, state, national, and international levels. The backbone of these systems at the national level is the U.S. Public Health Service, which now comprises eight agencies: the Agency for Healthcare Research and Quality, the Agency for Toxic Substances and Disease Registry, the Centers for Disease Control and Prevention (CDC), the Food and Drug Administration, the Health Resources and Services Administration, the Indian Health Service, the National Institutes of Health (NIH), and the Substance Abuse and Mental Health Services Administration.

For occupational therapists and support personnel, the public health system represents a critical link to people who, because of their location or inability to pay, do not use a private health system. Public health is primarily concerned with preventing disease by coordinating public programs, but it is also increasingly providing medical care to individual clients through neighborhood health centers.

The U.S. Public Health Service is responsible for several programs of great interest to occupational therapists. Voluntary organizations and foundations supplement these efforts with a multitude of programs and services.

State Health Insurance Programs

Although at this time the nation has not adopted a public health care model, some states have established universal health insurance programs. Massachusetts was the first state to approve legislation to require all adult residents to purchase health insurance or face legal consequences, and the state has made a commitment to provide affordable health insurance for all citizens. Uninsured people earning less than the federal poverty threshold are able to purchase subsidized policies with no premiums. Those earning between poverty level and three times that amount are able to purchase subsidized policies with premiums based on their ability to pay (Commonwealth of Massachusetts, n.d.).

MassHealth covers most of the nonelderly people in the state's Medicaid program. It was designed to reduce the number of uninsured and the cost of their care and to get federal funding into existing state health programs. Commonwealth Care is a newly created health insurance program for low- to moderate-income Massachusetts residents who do not have health insurance. Members get free to low-cost health care through managed care plans. When the law was implemented in 2006, an estimated 6% of the population in Massachusetts was uninsured. Within one year, the number of Massachusetts residents covered by MassHealth and Commonwealth Care increased by 122,000, nearly one-third of the people previously estimated to be uninsured (Raymond, 2007).

TRENDS IN OCCUPATIONAL THERAPY SERVICE DELIVERY

Workforce Trends

The practice of occupational therapy has been shaped by the government's influence on delivery systems, and trends in the supply and distribution of practicing occupational therapists reflect that influence. Between 1970 and 1984, the occupational therapy workforce increased by 41,000, more than doubling its previous numbers (American Occupational Therapy Association [AOTA], Ad Hoc Commission on Occupational Therapy Manpower, 1983–1984, p. 17). During the 1970s, the growth rate of occupational therapists entering the field was 9%–10% per year. In the mid-1980s, it slowed to 5% as the number of graduates from occupational therapy education programs stabilized.

The 1990s saw the growth rate rise to an average of 7%, influenced by an increase in the number of occupational therapists trained outside the United States (M. Hecker, director, Membership Department, AOTA, personal communication, December 1995). From 1995 through 2001, 20,552 new occupational therapy assistants and 38,004 new occupational therapists obtained certification (J. Jennings, administrative assistant, Membership Department, AOTA, personal communication, February 12, 2002). In 2006, the U.S. Bureau of Labor Statistics (BLS; 2009) recorded 104,500 working occupational therapists and estimated that that number would increase 26% to 133,300 by the year 2018.

Most occupational therapists work for a single employer; however, self-employment has increased since 2000. From 2000 to 2006, the proportion of occupational therapists who were self-employed and doing contract work increased from 19% to 25% (AOTA, 2006); these therapists "treat clients referred by other health professionals and provide consultation to health care facilities" (BLS, 2007b). Of these therapists, 12% reported that they were self-employed on a full-time basis and 13% on a part-time basis (AOTA, 2006). Since 2000, the number of occupational therapy assistants who are self-employed full-time or part-time has more than doubled (AOTA, 2006).

In the past, rehabilitation organizations and professionals expected payment from medical insurance providers. This practice will continue to be true for chronic medical problems causing disability. However, other disabling conditions as the result of work, home, and automobile accidents are covered by liability insurance. The insurance industry has recognized the cost–benefit potential of comprehensive models of rehabilitation that help a person acquire skills to function at a community level and become employed. This recognition has been the impetus for occupational therapists to move out of hospitals and other medical settings and provide their services in a variety of environments. The percentage of occupational therapists working in community-based settings is increasing, especially in settings such as home health agencies, outpatient clinics, private practice, school systems, and skilled nursing and intermediate care facilities (Scaffa, 2001).

In 2007, the minimum required entry-level degree for an occupational therapist was raised from a bachelor of science to a master of science degree, partially in order to maintain the profession's competitive edge in the job market. As of 2007, there were 124 master of science programs, 66 of which offered combined bachelor of science and master of science degrees, and five programs offered entry-level doctorate of occupational therapy degrees (AOTA, 2009c).

Current Practice Settings

The growth in the number of occupational therapists and occupational therapy assistants has been accompanied by changes in the distribution of practitioners across practice settings. Table 3.2 presents data on occupational therapists and occupational therapy assistants in various employment settings at 4- or 5-year intervals from 1973 through 2000. In particular, the data on occupational therapists reveal major increases in the percentage of occupational therapists working in school systems between 1997 and 2000. In 2000, nearly a quarter of all occupational therapists were working in schools. This number most likely reflects an increase in the school-age population and the enactment of the Individuals With Disabilities Education Act (IDEA) in June 1997, which mandated service delivery in the schools. The number of occupational therapists working in schools is expected to continue to increase as services for children with disabilities are expanded and the prevalence of children with sensory disorders increases (BLS, 2007b). Occupational therapists will be called on to help children with disabilities develop specific skills to enter special education programs or inclusion classrooms (BLS, 2007b).

In addition, the data indicate an emergence of occupational therapists in the general hospital settings of neonatal intensive care units, early intervention centers, psychiatric units, and rehabilitation units, as well as in physicians' offices and retirement or senior centers. Health management organizations have maintained a relatively stable percentage of occupational therapists. However, moderate to major decreases occurred in the percentages of occupational therapists employed in college or university settings, community mental health centers, correctional institutions, day care centers and programs, psychiatric hospitals, rehabilitation hospitals and centers, residential care facilities, and vocational or prevocational programs (BLS, 2009). These decreases were likely due to cuts in funding.

Many similarities occurred between distribution patterns of occupational therapists across practice settings and those of occupational therapy assistants. Table 3.3 shows the distribution of occupational therapists and occupational therapy assistants across acute care, skilled nursing, school, and rehabilitation settings.

Table 3.2. Primary Employment Settings of Occupational Therapists and Occupational Therapy Assistants, 1973–2000

% Registered Occupational Therapists							Primary Employment Setting	% Certified Occupational Therapy Assistants						
1973	1977	1982	1986	1990	1997	2000		1973	1977	1982	1986	1990	1997	2000
1.4	1.2	0.8	0.7	0.6	0.8	0.9	College, 2-year	0.8	0.9	0.6	0.8	0.9	1.9	2.5
5.6	4.9	4.1	3.1	3.4	3.3	5.6	College/university, 4-year	0.7	0.6	0.09	0.3	0.3	0.0	0.0
4.2	4.3	2.4	1.6	1.1	0.5	0.9	Community mental health center/program	4.0	3.5	3.1	3.8	1.7	0.4	0.8
—	—	—	—	—	0.3	0.4	Community residential care facility	—	—	—	—	—	1.5	0.8
—	—	—	—	—	1.1	1.7	Comprehensive outpatient rehab facility		—	—	—	—	—	1.5
0.2	0.2	0.1	0.1	—	—	—	Correctional institution	0.3	0.2	0.1	0.2	—	—	—
1.4	1.1	1.0	1.1	0.9	—	—	Day care center/program	1.2	2.4	2.0	4.3	1.7	—	—
—	—	—	—	—	0.1	0.3	Day care program—adult	—	—	—	—	—	0.4	0.0
—	—	—	—	—	0.3	0.6	Day care program—pediatric	—	—	—	—	—	0.4	1.2
—	—	—	—	—	0.4	0.5	Day treatment	—	—	—	—	—	0.4	0.4
—	—	—	—	—	2.2	3.7	Early intervention program	—	—	—	—	—	1.1	2.5
—	—	—	—	—	1.1	1.0	Freestanding—behavioral health	—	—	—	—	—	1.5	2.1
0.9	2.2	3.8	4.6	3.6	4.5	3.9	Freestanding—home health agency	0.2	0.4	0.8	1.2	1.5	1.9	0.8
—	—	—	—	—	1.1	0.3	Freestanding—intermediate nursing facility	—	—	—	—	—	1.5	1.2
—	—	—	—	—	16.3	7.7	Freestanding—skilled nursing facility	—	—	—	—	—	34.7	25.2
—	—	—	—	—	5.2	2.0	Freestanding—subacute nursing facility	—	—	—	—	—	6.8	7.0
—	—	2.5	2.4	3.7	—	—	Freestanding—outpatient clinic	—	—	1.7	0.9	2.2	—	—
—	—	—	—	—	3.9	3.8	Freestanding—rehabilitation hospital	—	—	—	—	—	2.3	1.7
—	—	—	—	—	2.2	2.0	Freestanding—rehabilitation hospital outpatient services/department	—	—	—	—	—	0.4	0.0

(continued)

Table 3.2. Primary Employment Settings of Occupational Therapists and Occupational Therapy Assistants, 1973–2000 *(cont.)*

% Registered Occupational Therapists							Primary Employment Setting	% Certified Occupational Therapy Assistants						
1973	1977	1982	1986	1990	1997	2000		1973	1977	1982	1986	1990	1997	2000
—	—	—	—	—	6.4	6.5	General hospital—acute	—	—	—	—	—	4.9	2.5
—	—	—	—	—	2.3	2.2	General hospital—behavioral health	—	—	—	—	—	2.3	1.7
—	—	0.0	0.1	0.0	0.0	0.1	General hospital—hospice	—	—	—	—	—	0.0	0.0
—	—	—	—	0.7	0.9	0.4	General hospital—neonatal intensive care unit	—	—	—	—	0.1	0.0	0.0
—	—	—	—	—	6.1	5.6	General hospital—outpatient services	—	—	—	—	—	2.3	2.5
—	—	—	—	—	0.1	0.5	General hospital—partial hospitalization unit	—	—	—	—	—	0.0	0.4
—	—	—	—	—	0.3	1.2	General hospital—pediatric unit	—	—	—	—	—	0.0	0.4
—	—	—	—	3.5	—	—	General hospital—psychiatric unit	—	—	—	—	4.0	—	—
—	—	—	4.2	5.3	4.7	5.1	General hospital—rehabilitation unit	—	—	—	4.5	5.5	5.7	6.6
—	—	—	—	—	2.1	2.1	General hospital—skilled nursing unit	—	—	—	—	—	2.3	2.9
—	—	—	—	—	1.1	0.8	General hospita—subacute unit	—	—	—	—	—	3.9	2.1
20.5	19.8	25.3	22.0	15.9	—	—	General hospital—all other	15.1	12.7	17.8	14.1	9.4	—	—
—	—	—	—	—	—	—	Group home	—	—	—	—	—	0.8	0.4
—	—	—	—	—	2.7	1.6	Hospital-based home health care	—	—	—	—	—	0.8	0.8
0.3	0.2	0.2	0.3	0.4	0.2	0.2	HMO (including PPO/IPA; staff model)	0.7	0.3	0.3	0.2	0.1	0.0	0.2
—	—	—	—	—	0.2	0.3	Independent living center	—	—	—	—	—	0.0	0.4
—	—	—	—	—	0.6	1.0	Industrial rehab/work programs	—	—	—	—	—	0.0	0.8
—	—	—	—	—	0.2	1.1	Mobile treatment team/home care	—	—	—	—	—	0.0	0.0

Table 3.2. Primary Employment Settings of Occupational Therapists and Occupational Therapy Assistants, 1973–2000 *(cont.)*

% Registered Occupational Therapists							Primary Employment Setting	% Certified Occupational Therapy Assistants						
1973	1977	1982	1986	1990	1997	2000		1973	1977	1982	1986	1990	1997	2000
—	—	—	—	—	0.0	0.0	Partial hospitalization program (community based, not outpatient)	—	—	—	—	—	0.0	0.0
2.9	2.0	1.6	1.7	1.7	—	—	Pediatric hospital	1.5	1.2	0.8	0.4	0.7	—	—
—	—	—	1.1	1.2	0.5	0.8	Physician's office	—	—	—	0.2	0.3	0.0	0.4
—	—	0.7	0.5	0.8	—	—	Private industry	1.0	0.5	0.7	—	—	—	—
1.3	2.1	3.5	6.0	7.7	3.9	5.5	Private practice (offfice based)	0.3	0.4	1.2	1.9	2.7	1.5	4.5
13.8	11.2	7.4	6.9	4.6	—	—	Psychiatric hospital	22.6	14.3	9.7	8.1	6.6	—	—
1.6	1.5	0.8	0.9	0.9	0.1	0.3	Public health agency	0.5	0.5	0.3	0.4	0.6	0.4	0.0
—	—	—	—	—	2.1	2.8	Rehabilitation agency/clinic	—	—	—	—	—	1.1	1.2
13.4	10.9	8.9	10.5	11.4	—	—	Rehabilitation hospital/center	9.5	11.0	8.4	8.4	10.9	—	—
0.3	0.3	0.4	0.2	0.2	—	—	Research facility	0.2	0.3	0.1	0.0	0.2	—	—
—	4.4	4.2	3.3	2.7	—	—	Residential care facility, including group home, independent living center	—	8.5	7.6.	7.5	5.9	—	—
—	—	—	—	—	0.2	0.2	Retirement/ assisted living	—	—	—	—	—	0.8	0.0
—	—	—	0.2	0.2	—	—	Retirement or senior center	—	—	—	1.1	0.8	—	—
11.0	14.0	18.3	17.0	18.6	18.1	24.9	School system (including private schools)	3.6	6.2	11.3	14.4	17.0	15.1	22.3
—	—	—	—	—	0.2	0.0	Senior center	—	—	—	—	—	0.4	0.0
0.7	0.7	0.7	0.4	0.4	0.1	0.0	Sheltered workshop	1.4	0.9	1.9	1.6	1.6	0.8	0.8
6.2	7.9	6.0	5.8	6.4	—	—	Skilled nursing home/intermediate care facility	22.8	26.1	22.5	20.1	20.1	—	—
—	—	—	—	—	0.0	0.0	Supervised housing	—	—	—	—	—	0.0	0.0
—	—	—	—	—	0.0	0.0	Supported employment	—	—	—	—	—	0.0	0.0
—	—	—	—	—	0.1	0.2	Transitional program	—	—	—	—	—	0.4	0.4
0.7	0.5	—	—	—	—	—	Vocational or prevocational program	—	—	—	1.6	0.8	—	—

(continued)

Table 3.2. Primary Employment Settings of Occupational Therapists and Occupational Therapy Assistants, 1973–2000 *(cont.)*

% Registered Occupational Therapists							Primary Employment Setting	% Certified Occupational Therapy Assistants						
1973	1977	1982	1986	1990	1997	2000		1973	1977	1982	1986	1990	1997	2000
—	1.7	1.7	1.4	1.0	0.2	0.3	Voluntary agency (e.g., Easter Seals, United Cerebral Palsy)	—	0.4	1.2	1.2	1.1	0.4	0.8
14.2	9.4	5.4	3.2	2.5	1.3	1.7	Other	14.7	9.3	6.7	2.3	2.3	0.8	1.7
99.9	100.0	99.8	100.0	99.9	—	—	**Total**	100.1	100.1	100.0	100.0	99.8	—	—

Note. Missing data are due to changing employment categories on the various administrations of the surveys. Recoding of additional settings from the "Other" category to existing alternatives may explain the decline in that category. For this reason, small differences in the percentages over time should be interpreted with care. The percentages contained in this report, with the exception of the demographic and educational information, represent only the individuals who responded to the AOTA Member Data Survey. They do not include the occupational therapy personnel who chose not to answer and return the survey.

Source. Adapted from *1990 Member Data Survey* and *2000 Member Data Survey* by American Occupational Therapy Association, Member Services, 1990 and 2000, Rockville (1990)/Bethesda (2000), MD: Author.

Top Emerging Practice Areas

According to Johansson (2000), the top emerging practice areas within occupational therapy include

- Ergonomics consulting,
- Driver rehabilitation and training,
- Design and accessibility consulting and home modification,
- Low-vision services,
- Private practice community health services,
- Technology and assistive device development and consulting,
- Health and wellness consulting,
- Welfare-to-work services (collaborating with recipients of financial assistance to identify suitable and satisfying work placements),
- Ticket-to-work services (providing employment support services to Supplemental Security Income and Social Security Disability Insurance beneficiaries), and
- Services addressing the psychosocial needs of children and youths.

By participating in emerging practice areas, occupational therapy practitioners hope to better the health and well-being of a wide range of populations through participation in meaningful occupations, and they are beginning to capitalize on trends in emerging practice areas as they turn ideas into successful businesses.

Specialty and Board Certification

Within these emerging areas of practice, an increasing number of occupational therapists are pursuing specialty or board certification. At present, AOTA board certifications are available in gerontology, mental health, pediatrics, and physical rehabilitation. Specialty certifications include driving and community mobility; environmental modification; feeding, eating, and swallowing; and low vision (AOTA, 2009d). Standards for these certifications were established in 2003 and vary depending on whether occupational therapists are obtaining specialty certification or board certification. To receive specialty certification, occupational therapists must complete 6 months of practice within that area of specialty and must undergo a portfolio review. Board certification requires 5 years of practice and a review through self-study (Glantz & Moyers, 2003). These certifications allow occupational therapists to receive recognition for ongoing professional development in addition to providing the opportunity for advancement and, in some cases, an increase in salary (LaGrossa, 2008).

FUTURE TRENDS IN OCCUPATIONAL THERAPY SERVICE DELIVERY

The health care system is at a crossroads. The public is demanding accountability for the outcomes of health care. With the election of President Obama in 2009 as a recession was taking hold, the health care system will certainly change. It is unknown whether change will take place incrementally through the expansion of current programs or drastically through a complete system redesign. Where do the system and occupational therapy go from here? The following sections describe current trends and projected outcomes, as well as possible roles and opportunities for occupational therapists and occupational therapy assistants.

Growing Elderly Population

As the current population ages, occupational therapy practitioners will continue providing programs to increase independence and maintain function in the elderly population, thus decreasing the costs of long-term health management. In 2005, 35 million Americans made up the population 65 years or older; this number is expected to double by 2030 (CDC, 2007).

Table 3.3. Primary Work Settings of 2007 Occupational Therapist and Occupational Therapy Assistant Practice Analysis Validation Survey Respondents

	Acute Care	Skilled Nursing Facility	School System	Rehabilitation Facility
Occupational therapist	13%	21%	23%	24%
Occupational therapy assistant	—	50%	16%	17%

Note. Data collected by the National Board Certification for Occupational Therapy (2007).

BLS (2007b) has predicted that the growing elderly population will continue to drive the growth of the profession in upcoming years. This increase in the elder population, coupled with expected medical advances extending the average life span, will increase the demand for occupational therapy services. As Baby Boomers age into retirement, they will want to "age in place"—that is, to stay in their own homes—a relatively new phenomenon for elder care. Occupational therapy practitioners will be called on to do whatever they can to allow people to transition from independence to interdependence (Brachtesende, 2005).

Increase in Chronic Conditions

Chronic disease is responsible for 70% of deaths in the United States each year. As a result of chronic, disabling conditions (e.g., heart disease, cancer, diabetes), 1 out of every 10 Americans may experience major limitations in everyday functioning (National Center for Chronic Disease Prevention and Health Promotion, 2008). Cardiovascular disease and cancer are the leading killers, causing two-thirds of deaths from chronic disease. Treatment of these diseases accounts for "75% of the $1 trillion spent on health care each year" (CDC, 2008). The incidence of stroke and heart disease is expected to increase in the near future, which would increase the demands for occupational therapists working in medical and rehabilitation settings (CDC & NIH, 2010).

Rehabilitation for traumatic brain injury (TBI) requires occupational therapy intervention. Each year, an estimated 1.4 million Americans sustain a TBI. Of these, 50,000 die, 235,000 are hospitalized, and 1.1 million are treated and released from an emergency department. A total of 5.3 million Americans currently experience a long-term disability resulting from a TBI. The estimated annual cost of direct medical care (acute care and rehabilitation service) and other indirect costs (e.g., lack of workplace productivity) for all Americans who sustained a TBI was $60 billion in 2000 (National Center for Injury Prevention and Control, 2007).

Occupational therapy practitioners have become more active in the workplace because of the increased incidence of cumulative trauma disorders (e.g., carpal tunnel syndrome) and chronic back problems. In 2008, BLS estimated that musculoskeletal disorders accounted for 29% of all workplace injuries resulting in missed days of work in 2007.

Military Personnel, Veterans, and Their Families

The role of occupational therapy with military personnel, veterans, and their families continues to unfold as the wars in Iraq and Afghanistan continue. Occupational therapy practitioners are encountering new challenges related to the large numbers of veterans returning with severe combat wounds, both physical and psychological in nature. Occupational therapists are expected to play a large role in the assessment and treatment of TBI and posttraumatic stress disorder (Nanof, 2007). According to Nanof (2007), "the needs of military veterans will remain a prevailing issue confronting both the military and civilian health care system" (p. 6). Occupational therapy practitioners must educate stakeholders about the unique role of occupational therapy related to rehabilitation and reintegration of wounded veterans into society so they can fully resume valued life roles.

Continuing Emphasis on Cost Containment

Health care expenditures have continued to rise each year, even following the advent of managed care (see Table 3.4 and Figures 3.2a and 3.2b). From 2000 to 2008, the cost of medical care items increased by almost 40%, whereas the cost of all items included in the consumer price index increased by about 20% (Crawford & Katz, 2008). Although the disparity between the rise in medical care costs and the cost of all expenditures decreased in the late 1990s, it began to slowly increase again in the early 2000s (Andersen et al., 2001; Crawford & Katz, 2008). From 1960 to 2008, expenditures for health care rose from 5% of GDP to 17% (Centers for Medicare & Medicaid Services, 2007; National Coalition on Health Care, 2009b). Some have predicted that health care spending will increase to 20% of the GDP by 2017 (Keehan et al., 2008).

The competitive market guarantees that costs will continue to be the topic of debate in health care delivery. On a daily basis, occupational therapy managers and occupational therapists must be cognizant of the cost considerations for clients as well as insurance companies and employers. Consumers and insurers will continue to scrutinize the diagnoses rendered, the treatments and evaluations provided, the clients to whom they are provided, the settings in which they are provided, the duration of treatments, and the effectiveness of treatments in bringing about functional performance. They will be asking the question, What can be expected from this expenditure? As discussed earlier in this chapter, spiraling costs have generated many cost-containment practices, including

- Alternatives to inpatient care such as ambulatory or outpatient care;
- Self-insurance (reserving funds for future *losses* instead of *purchasing insurance*);
- Greater emphasis on utilization review (i.e., independent review of providers' performance to validate quality of care);
- Adherence to diagnosis-related groups;
- Elimination of redundancy in services;
- Formation of medical service alliances;
- Mergers of insurance providers, hospitals, and health care organizations;
- Utilization control tools;
- Shorter lengths of stay and more delivery of services outside the hospital; and
- Strategies to maximize the number of interventions per hour, such as overlapping several clients' treatments and mixing group and individual treatment sessions (Freda, 1998).

These cost-containment practices—managed care, in particular—are having a profound effect on organizational structures and, in turn, on clinical practice. To contain costs and compete successfully for managed care contracts, provider organizations are compressing their structures, cutting their staffs, and reorganizing their way of doing business.

Increased Reliance on Case Managers

Case managers emerged in the mid-1990s and have become a central force in the delivery of health care services. Case management is a strategy to contain health care costs and distribute funds and resources appropriately. The external case manager, an employee of a managed care company, acts as a "gatekeeper" to manage costs, especially in the most expensive cases. The external case manager is expected to control the cost and length of services in the context of the most appropriate outcome (Fisher, 1995). The internal case manager functions as a liaison between clinical staff members and the external case manager. This person is usually a clinician and, frequently, a practitioner providing services to the client whose case he or she is managing. Case managers are central to the care delivery process and "serve as a patient advocate and resource as well as providing critical information and recommendations to the rest of the care team: physicians, surgeons, nurses, administrators, benefits coordinators, employers and family caregivers" (Case Management Society of America, 2008).

External case managers, not physicians or clinicians, are deciding how much of a specific service a client will receive. Occupational therapy managers and therapists must thoroughly document the need for their services, as they may find themselves negotiating with and justifying these services to external case managers. Moreover, case man-

Table 3.4. National Health Expenditures, 1960–2007

	Total				Private Funds			Government Funds		
Year	GDP ($ billion)	Amount ($ billion)	Per Capita	% of GNP	Amount ($ billion)	Per Capita	% of Total	Amount ($ billion)	Per Capita	% of Total
2007	13,808	2,241.2	7,421	16.2	1,205.5	3,991	53.8	1,035.7	3,429	46.2
2006	13,178	2,112.7	7,062	16.0	1,139.7	3,810	53.9	973.0	3,252	46.1
2005	12,422	1,980.6	6,687	15.9	1,081.6	3,652	54.6	899.0	3,035	45.4
2004	11,686	1,854.8	6,319	15.9	1,014.9	3,458	54.7	839.9	2,861	45.3
2003	10,961	1,734.9	5,967	15.8	956.0	3,288	55.1	779.0	2,679	44.9
2002	10,470	1,602.3	5,560	15.3	880.7	3,056	55.0	721.6	2,504	45.0
2001	10,122	1,469.4	5,149	14.5	807.0	2,828	54.9	662.4	2,321	45.1
2000	9,817	1,353.2	4,789	13.8	756.4	2,677	55.9	596.8	2,112	44.1
1999	9,268	1,265.2	4,522	13.7	709.1	2,534	56.1	556.0	1,987	43.9
1998	8,747	1,190.1	4,296	13.6	662.0	2,390	55.6	528.0	1,906	44.4
1997	8,304	1,124.8	4,102	13.5	613.5	2,237	54.5	511.4	1,865	45.5
1993	6,657	912.5	3,468	13.7	512.3	1,947	56.1	400.2	1,521	43.9
1990	5,803	714.1	2,814	12.3	427.4	1,684	59.8	286.8	1,130	40.2
1980	2,790	253.4	1,100	9.1	147.0	638	58.0	106.3	462	42.0
1970	1,039	74.9	356	7.2	46.8	222	62.4	28.1	134	37.6
1960	526	27.5	148	5.2	20.7	111	74.3	6.8	36	24.7

Note. GDP = gross domestic product; GNP = gross national product. Numbers and percentages may not add to totals because of rounding. Dollar amounts shown are in current dollars.

Source. Adapted from "Table 1: National Health Expenditures Aggregate, Per Capita Amounts, Percent Distribution, and Average Annual Percent Growth, by Source of Funds: Selected Calendar Years 1960–2007," Centers for Medicare and Medicaid Services, 2008, Washington, DC: Author. Retrieved October 8, 2009, from http://www.cms.hhs.gov/NationalHealthExpendData/downloads/tables.pdf

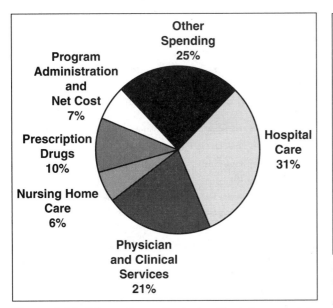

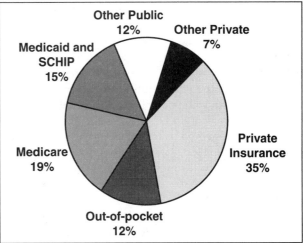

Figure 3.2A. Where the nation's health dollars went in 2007.

Note. "Other Spending" includes dental services, other professional services, home health, durable medical products, over-the-counter medicines and sundries, public health, other personal health care, research, and structures and equipment.

Source. The Nation's Health Dollar, Calendar Year 2007: Where It Came From, Where it Went, by Centers for Medicare and Medicaid Services, Office of the Actuary, National Health Statistics Group, 2008, Washington, DC: Author. Retrieved October 8, 2009, from http://www.cms.hhs.gov/NationalHealthExpendData/downloads/PieChartSources-Expenditures2007.pdf

Figure 3.2B. Where the nation's health dollars came from in 2007.

Note. "Other Public" includes programs such as workers' compensation, public health activity, Department of Defense, Department of Veterans Affairs, Indian Health Service, state and local government hospital subsidies, and school health. "Other Private" includes industrial in-plant, privately funded construction, and nonpatient revenues, including philanthropy.

Source. The Nation's Health Dollar, Calendar Year 2007: Where It Came From, Where it Went, by Centers for Medicare and Medicaid Services, Office of the Actuary, National Health Statistics Group, 2008, Washington, DC: Author. Retrieved October 8, 2009, from http://www.cms.hhs.gov/NationalHealthExpendData/downloads/PieChartSources-Expenditures2007.pdf

agers require frequent progress reports for their clients to evaluate client progress toward goals. In many situations, case managers authorize only a few sessions at a time to ensure appropriate utilization of resources. Occupational therapists must learn to work with case managers to ensure that their clients receive necessary care.

Use of Less Expensive Aides and Technicians

The American Occupational Therapy Association (2004) has called for careful collaboration among personnel and appropriate supervision by occupational therapists and occupational therapy assistants to ensure effective delivery of occupational therapy services. From 2006 to 2016, the number of occupational therapy assistants and aides is expected to increase at a greater rate than the number of occupational therapists (BLS, 2007a, 2007b). To control costs, organizations are asking occupational therapy assistants to take on more responsibilities. Because of the increase in nonprofessional staff members, professional staff members are doing more supervising than before; in some settings, occupational therapists provide off-site supervision while an occupational therapy assistant carries out the intervention. The more widespread use of aides and

technicians is requiring occupational therapy managers and therapists to develop statements of appropriate competencies, improve the orientation given to new personnel, and plan and carry out inservice training for support personnel already on the job. Occupational therapists must enhance their competence in supervision, particularly their ability to recognize when they should intervene in treatment or reassess a client's condition.

Because of the heightened expectations for productivity, therapists are busier than ever before. It is imperative that occupational therapists receive support—in both time and funding—from their employers to pursue their professional development. This will increase the accountability and quality of occupational therapy services provided and in turn will help clients achieve their desired outcomes more efficiently (Moyers, 2003).

Increasing Expectations for Documentation

With a growing emphasis on eliminating unnecessary costs, reimbursement agencies have imposed greater expectations for documentation. According to AOTA (2010), "an occupational therapist completes and documents occupational therapy evaluation results." Toto (2006) emphasized the importance of consulting the guidelines for documentation that are specific to each state.

President Obama has proposed several initiatives aimed at modernizing America's health care system, one of which focuses on the transition to an electronic documentation system. The incorporation of information technology into health care documentation will increase practitioners' accountability for client documentation and provide a timely and consistent method of information sharing among all stakeholders.

Fragmentation will continue to be a concern when the medical and rehabilitative needs of clients are being met at different sites (Sultz & Young, 2009), and system operators working toward integrating client diagnostic, treatment, and outcome information from different sites will face multiple challenges regarding client confidentiality and safe electronic transfer of information. Nevertheless, the role of advanced technology in increasing efficiency, ensuring accountability, and eliminating costs associated with errors in documentation is recognized by all who hold a stake in the future of the American health care system (Sultz & Young, 2009).

Continuing Developments in Technology
The rehabilitation field is benefiting from major technological advances. For example, the use of interactive driving simulators that assess the driving abilities of people with impairments (e.g., from stroke, aging) together with adaptive driving equipment has become marketable. The use of computer applications such as telemedicine, telehealth, telerehabilitation; environmental adaptations; and implanted computers to control motions and bodily functions will continue to increase.

Technology also has a profound impact on the delivery of occupational therapy services. For example, the use of electronic medical records has drastically increased in the past decade (Burt, Hing, & Woodwell, 2005; Hsiao et al., 2008). The private–public corporation National eHealth Collaborative is committed to promoting access to and efficiency of health care through technology. Occupational therapy managers and occupational therapists must stay informed about and be involved in research that links technology to occupational performance in order to best serve their clients.

Increased Emphasis on Wellness
With the cost-containment mandate for the health care industry, the philosophy of wellness is becoming increasingly important to all in the health care equation: consumers, providers, and the federal government. If people stay well, everyone benefits. This emphasis is consistent with occupational therapy's goal of optimal function in occupational performance areas. All people, with and without disabilities, can benefit from the promotion of health and wellness. Those with disabilities can learn how to live healthy lifestyles within the context of their disability. Those cur-

rently without disabilities benefit from increased education and resources for maintaining health and preventing disease or disability. Through the establishment of wellness promotion programs, occupational therapists can empower people to participate more fully in their society and important life roles (Hildenbrand & Froehlich, 2002).

ENSURING THE ROLE OF OCCUPATIONAL THERAPY IN THE FUTURE HEALTH CARE ENVIRONMENT
Today, the future looks bright for occupational therapy. In 2008, Shatkin ranked the profession 18th in his book *150 Best Recession-Proof Jobs*. The number of occupational therapy job listings on the job search engine SimplyHired.com increased 658% from June 2007 to December 2008. In 2009, *U.S. News and World Report* included occupational therapy on its list of "30 Best Careers for 2009" (Wolgemuth, 2008) based on job outlook, average job satisfaction, difficulty of training, prestige, and pay.

Positioning the Profession
Occupational therapy service delivery and methods of payment will continue to evolve with the health care system. Occupational therapy practitioners and other health care professionals are competing to provide the best and most cost-effective outcomes. Occupational therapy managers and practitioners must prove that their products are both essential and cost-effective to the hospital, the physician, the client, and business and industry. Improving participation in daily life activities, which has long been the mission of occupational therapy, is now being used by other professionals in the documentation they submit to receive third-party payment. Thus, occupational therapists must better explain what the profession involves and pinpoint their area of expertise so that their services continue to be used. Otherwise, consumers may look to other, more cost-effective—but not necessarily superior—sources of care.

The value of occupational therapy services must be skillfully marketed (see Chapter 8). Describing occupational therapy services in terms of products—for example, as driving programs, work evaluations, seating and mobility clinics, and life skills programs—will make the services easier for consumers to understand.

Promoting Public Policy
Increasing the public's awareness of the varied and valuable services of occupational therapy is a responsibility of every individual in the profession of occupational therapy. Educating the government is equally important. One way to increase government awareness is to contact legislators about any state or federal bills that will affect the delivery of occupational therapy and to include an explanation of the mission of occupational therapy and the importance of including occupational therapy in any comprehensive health care plan. According to AOTA (2008), "This is an exciting time of change, and if we voice the value of the work that we do as professionals in the field of occupational therapy,

we can enact reform that is in our interest." See Exhibit 3.1 for an example of a letter to a legislator asking for support on a federal bill to repeal the Medicare caps on outpatient rehabilitation.

AOTA's position on health care reform is as follows:

AOTA's Position:

". . . There is a need for reform in the American health care system to address problems including coverage for the uninsured, access to care, quality, cost growth, and workforce shortages. As the professional association representing the interests of more than 140,000 occupational therapy practitioners and students, AOTA believes that a national debate and discussion about health care is needed.

AOTA's Concerns:
- Health care must have a proactive, prevention focus.
- Health care must address the whole person across the life span and across needs for acute and chronic care.
- Mental health and substance abuse parity must be included for all.
- The provision of health care services should be integrated across facilities, communities, and set-

---

EXHIBIT 3.1. SAMPLE TEXT OF A LETTER TO A MEMBER OF CONGRESS

Dear Senator:

As a resident of Massachusetts and an occupational therapist, I am writing to request your support for bill S. 46, the Medicare Access to Rehabilitation Services Act of 2009, to repeal the Medicare outpatient rehabilitation therapy caps. The bill was introduced by Sen. John Ensign and is cosponsored by Sen. Daniel Akaka, Sen. Benjamin Cardin, Sen. Robert Casey, Sen. Susan Collins, Sen. Richard Durbin, Sen. Lindsey Graham, Sen. Tom Harkin, Sen. Patrick Leahy, Sen. Blanche Lincoln, Sen. Arlen Specter, Sen. Debbie Stabenow, and Sen. Sheldon Whitehouse.

Since the therapy caps were imposed by the Balanced Budget Act of 1997, a series of exception processes have prevented the caps from affecting the care of older adults receiving rehabilitation therapy services through Medicare. However, unless Congress repeals the act altogether or further extends the exception process, the therapy caps will take effect on January 1, 2010. This means that once the $1,840 cap for occupational therapy and the $1,840 cap for speech and physical therapy combined have been reached, the client will be responsible for 100% of the remaining cost of therapy, a significant financial burden.

Older adults experience a variety of age-related conditions such as osteoporosis, hip fractures and corrective surgeries, stroke, Parkinson's disease, visual impairments, cardiopulmonary disorders, cancer, dementia, and Alzheimer's disease that warrant therapeutic services. With rehabilitative therapies, including occupational therapy, physical therapy, and speech–language pathology, many of these disorders can be managed so that the individual can continue to function in daily life.

Occupational therapists provide restorative, compensatory, and preventive forms of therapy. We help individuals regain the abilities to participate in their necessary and desired activities, or we adapt and modify their activities so that they are able to participate with their current level of ability. Participating in preferred activities and remaining a contributing member of their families and communities support the overall health and well-being of older adults. This promotion of health and well-being prevents further decline in function and may reduce the number of times these individuals return to the health care system.

An older adult's care plan should be directed by their functional gains and remaining therapeutic needs rather than an arbitrary amount of money established by the cap. Although some disorders may be successfully treated with a few visits to therapy and the training of a caregiver or family member in strategies to use in the home and community, other disorders require a longer duration of therapy provided by skilled and trained professionals. For example, I treated a man in his 70s who suffered a stroke 9 years ago. Through the course of treatment, he went from being completely dependent on his wife to being independent with the use of adaptive equipment and compensatory strategies. He was still able to make functional gains 9 years after his stroke. With the therapy caps in place, this man, and many others like him, would not have received continued therapy by trained professionals 9 years after the onset of his condition. In our current health care system, often therapy comes to an end and recovery ceases when funding runs out, not when the individual has achieved his or her potential.

Repealing the Medicare caps is a first step in providing the older adults of our nation with quality care. Please support the Medicare Access to Rehabilitation Services Act of 2009. Thank you for your consideration and kind attention to this issue. I look forward to hearing from you.

Respectfully,

tings, including services where people live, work, and participate in society.

- Access to quality, affordable care for all should be the goal of reform.
- Ensuring access to supportive services for people with disabilities or chronic conditions is essential to promoting independence, productivity, and quality of life.
- Investments are needed in our health care education system to ensure availability of qualified professionals like occupational therapy practitioners to meet growing needs.
- Occupational therapy should be covered to provide preventive services, rehabilitation and habilitation, community and facility services, and any other approach where evidence shows that occupational therapy improves quality of life.
- Use of health information technology must be maximized to improve the efficiency and effectiveness of care.

Enacting meaningful reform requires a bipartisan approach that has the vision and commitment to invest in a system of health care even if it may cost more in the present to provide savings and improved outcomes through efficiency and quality in the future. Any health care reform must more equally and equitably distribute the costs and benefits of quality health care to all who need it for the benefit of individuals and society (AOTA, 2009a).

Unfortunately, some managed care organizations and health insurers attempt to save money by engaging in discriminatory practices that deny consumers rightful access to a variety of health professionals, including occupational therapists. Fortunately, some proposals for health care reform would broaden managed care coverage in both enrollment and service, and all reforms should prohibit arbitrary exclusion of entire classes or types of professionals from provider panels and networks. Reforms should also require managed care organizations to meet specific criteria to ensure a sufficient number, mix, and distribution of health care providers within their networks to meet the diverse needs of consumers and to give consumers the option of choosing certain specialists as their gatekeepers within the health plan (Somers & Browne, 1994, p. 3).

Conclusion

This chapter explored the U.S. health care system and its effect on the evolution of occupational therapy delivery. Society is demanding accountability for its health care dollars, and the services occupational therapy practitioners offer are gaining increased recognition. Readers are encouraged to keep up with health care reform through AOTA's Federal Affairs Department and other resources.

Case Examples

Level I Fieldwork

Steve was assigned to an adult day treatment program for his Level I fieldwork placement. He was not being supervised by an occupational therapist; instead, he was being supervised by a recreational therapist. As the weeks progressed, he noticed that clients were sitting in front of the TV for hours during the day. Clients were complaining of low back pain, neck pain, and difficulty sleeping at night. He wondered if there was a role for occupational therapy and what occupational therapists could do. He consulted the recreational therapist and asked him what could be done, and the recreational therapist suggested stopping the activity. Steve wondered if there was a way to meet this client need (watching TV) while ensuring health and wellness. He read about ergonomics in one of his textbooks and thought there could be a way to use ergonomics to enable occupational performance.

Level II Fieldwork

Michael was in the 7th week of his second Level II fieldwork placement at Healthy Hips Outpatient Rehabilitation Clinic for orthopedic conditions. He enjoyed working with other rehabilitation professionals but was frustrated by the productivity expectations and demands of the facility. He longed to be able to provide comprehensive services in a more natural context. Michael was beginning to search for jobs and was feeling overwhelmed by the process. He saw many opportunities where occupational therapy could expand and hoped to start his own business. He wanted to find an entry-level position that was compatible with his interests and experience and that would allow him to fulfill his potential and succeed in professional endeavors.

Case Examples *(cont.)*

FIRST-TIME MANAGER

Mary was a first-time manager of an inpatient rehabilitation facility that provided occupational therapy, physical therapy, and speech–language pathology. She just came home energized from the AOTA Conference & Expo, where the president of AOTA had given an inspiring keynote address. Mary wanted to integrate emerging fields of occupational therapy practice into her unit. She had a limited budget; however, the facility was part of an HMO that could have additional resources. She was also dealing with conflict among her staff about what consti-

tutes best practice. She hoped that by integrating these new ideas of practice, she could help facilitate a cohesive vision among her staff.

MANAGER

Alicia was the manager of the third-ranked subacute hospital in a large metropolitan area. She wanted to increase her hospital's standing and decided to plan inservices to increase her occupational therapists' knowledge of emerging areas of practice. After discussion with her staff and research on growing areas of practice, she determined that her staff needed further education in the following areas: technology training, ergonomics consulting, and the needs of the growing elderly population.

❖ Learning Activities

1. Write a letter to the editor of a major newspaper, such as the *Boston Globe, Boston Herald, The New York Times,* or *The Wall Street Journal,* or your hometown newspaper that focuses on an article published in the newspaper. Please select an article that is not an editorial. The topic of the article should be on global social issues and prevailing health and welfare needs, or current policy issues and the social, economic, political, geographic, and demographic factors that influence the various contexts for practice of occupational therapy.

2. Write a letter to your federal or state senator or representative urging him or her to support important legislation related to occupational thearpy. See the AOTA Web site (www.aota.org) for national and state legislative initiatives. Please check www.congress.com for information on your federal legislator and legislative issues. For specific state issues, contact your state occupational therapy association. Please make sure that the legislation you have chosen to write about is current and probably dead (i.e., bills that have been voted down, missed a transmittal deadline, or canceled). Please also feel free to ask a legislator to submit (i.e., sponsor) a bill on a topic.

3. Obtain a copy of your health insurance. Answer the questions at the end of this learning activity based on the following scenario: Imagine you are Rose, an undergraduate student 21 years of age who suffered a head injury during break. Rose is on the lacrosse team and is also a work-study student. After the injury, she now has short-term memory problems and loss of appetite and

reports feeling depressed. She has decreased coordination, mild left-side weakness, and mild expressive aphasia (i.e., word-finding ability). However, she is determined to get back into full participation at school, and with her physician's agreement, she begins the semester.

Using short answers, respond to the following questions:

- What is the annual cost of Rose's policy? What would be the additional annual cost if she had a spouse?
- What is the percentage of covered medical expenses incurred for inpatient hospital special services such as x-rays, anesthesia, and use of an operating room?
- What is the percentage of covered medical expenses per surgical procedure per policy year?
- What is Rose's copayment for preferred-provider physician office visits? If Rose had a nonpreferred chiropractic office visit, what percentage would the insurance plan pay?
- How much does Rose have to pay for generic prescription drugs? How much does she have to pay for brand-name prescription drugs?
- Rose's physician recommends mental health services to take place at least weekly for the next 2 months. What does her insurance cover?
- Suppose Rose needed a nutritional consultation, occupational therapy, physical therapy, and speech–language consultation. Which of these are covered by her plan, and how much does she pay?
- Identify two strengths and two weaknesses of this health insurance plan.

✓ Multiple-Choice Questions

1. The right-to-health concept is ultimately a matter of
   a. Economics.
   b. Politics.
   c. Ethics.
   d. Religion.

2. In what year did the Allied Health Professions Personnel Training Act establish the first federal funds for support of occupational therapy education?
   a. 1956.
   b. 1966.
   c. 1976.
   d. 1986.

3. The Medicare prospective payment system (PPS) has had a profound effect on the development of the health care industry by
   a. Reducing emphasis on inpatient services.
   b. Reducing outpatient programs.
   c. Reducing community programs.
   d. Increasing emphasis on inpatient services.

4. The Health Insurance Portability and Accountability Act (HIPAA) assures
   a. Citizens' insurance coverage during times of employment change or loss.
   b. Small businesses' insurance options.
   c. Protection of citizens' privacy rights regarding their medical records.
   d. All the above.

5. The Medicare Prescription Drug Improvement and Modernization Act of 2003 is
   a. Medicare Part A.
   b. Medicare Part B.
   c. Medicare Part C.
   d. Medicare Part D.

6. The three major types of integrated delivery systems operating in today's health care market are
   a. HMOs, PPOs, and POS plans.
   b. HMOs, PPOs, and indemnity plans.
   c. HMOs, indemnity plans, and POS plans.
   d. Indemnity plans, PPOs, and POS plans.

7. In a closed-panel HMO, which is true?
   a. Physicians are allowed to treat only clients who are subscribers to that HMO.
   b. The HMO does not contract exclusively with a single group practice (group model).
   c. The HMO allows the client to choose a doctor outside of the HMO.
   d. The HMO does not contract exclusively with individual physicians (staff model).

8. The least restrictive managed care model is
   a. Staff models (HMO).
   b. PPO.
   c. POS plan.
   d. Network models (HMO).

9. The most restrictive managed care model is
   a. Staff model (HMO).
   b. PPO.
   c. POS plan.
   d. Network model (HMO).

10. The evaluation of the necessity, appropriateness, and efficiency of the use of health care services, procedures, and facilities is called
    a. Diagnosis-related groups.
    b. Utilization review.
    c. Gatekeeping.
    d. Managed care.

11. In 2007, 46 million people in the United States did not have health insurance. Although this group includes all ages, incomes, geographic settings, races, and ethnic groups, which population is less likely to have health insurance than older and wealthier people?
    a. Children.
    b. People in the lower-income bracket.
    c. People in the middle-income bracket.
    d. All of the above.

12. Between 1970 and 1984, the number of practicing occupational therapists doubled because
    a. Occupational therapy became a glamorous profession.
    b. Schools of occupational therapy closed down.
    c. Federal legislation encouraged the growth of the profession to address a shortage of allied health personnel.
    d. None of the above.

13. At present, AOTA board certification is available in
    a. Gerontology.
    b. Ergonomics.
    c. Environmental modification.
    d. Low vision.

14. Occupational therapy services will be needed for which of the following increasing populations?
    a. Elderly population.
    b. Clients with chronic conditions.
    c. Military personnel, veterans, and their families.
    d. All of the above.

15. Spiraling health care costs have generated proposals for health care reform and many containment practices, including
    a. Alternatives to inpatient care such as ambulatory or outpatient care.
    b. Formation of medical service alliances.
    c. Elimination of redundancy in services.
    d. All of the above.

16. At present, U.S. health care moneys are generated by
    a. Business and industry.
    b. Third-party payers and government subsidies.
    c. Private fundraising and individuals.
    d. All the above.
17. In 2007, what percentage of U.S. health dollars were spent on hospital care?
    a. 21%.
    b. 25%.
    c. 31%.
    d. 35%.
18. In 2007, what percentage of U.S. health dollars came from Medicare?
    a. 7%.
    b. 12%.
    c. 19%.
    d. 35%.
19. In competing for health care dollars, occupational therapists must market their areas of expertise and, in particular, specify how the profession
    a. Grew from its origins in mental health care.
    b. Improves participation in daily life activities.
    c. Documents its services.
    d. Calls for health care reform.
20. AOTA's position on health care reform describes the following concerns:
    a. Health care must have a proactive, prevention focus.
    b. Health care must address the whole person across the life span and his or her needs for acute and chronic care.
    c. Mental health and substance abuse parity must be included for all.
    d. All of the above.

References

American Occupational Therapy Association. (1990). *1990 member data survey.* Rockville, MD: Author.

American Occupational Therapy Association. (2000). *2000 member data survey.* Rockville, MD: Author.

American Association of Preferred Provider Organizations. (2009). *PPO resources.* Retrieved February 24, 2009, from http://www.aappo.org/index.cfm?pageid=10

American Hospital Association. (2009). *Fast facts on U.S. hospitals.* Retrieved February 4, 2009, from http://www.aha.org/aha/resource-center/Statistics-and-Studies/fast-facts.html

American Occupational Therapy Association. (2006). *Occupational therapy salaries and job opportunities continue to improve: 2006 AOTA workforce compensation survey.* Retrieved February 1, 2009, from http://otjoblink.org/docs/otsalary06.pdf

American Occupational Therapy Association. (2008). *Healthcare reform is your future: AOTA is the voice for your future.* Retrieved February 21, 2009, from http://www.aota.org/news/advocacynews/health-reform.aspx

American Occupational Therapy Association. (2009a). *Board certification and specialty certification.* Retrieved February 12, 2009, from http://www.aota.org/Practitioners/ProfDev/Certification.aspx

American Occupational Therapy Association. (2009b). Guidelines for supervision, roles, and responsibilities during the delivery of occupational therapy services. *American Journal of Occupational Therapy, 63,* 797–803.

American Occupational Therapy Association (2009c, June 9). *Health care reform.* Retrieved August 28, 2009, from http://vocusgr.vocus.com/GRSPACE2/WebPublish/Controller.aspx?SiteName=AOTA&Definition=ViewIssue&IssueID=6069#Position

American Occupational Therapy Association. (2009d). *Schools.* Retrieved March 8, 2009, from http://www.aota.org/Students/Schools.aspx

American Occupational Therapy Association. (2010). Standards of practice for occupational therapy. *American Journal of Occupational Therapy, 64.*

American Occupational Therapy Association, Ad Hoc Commission on Occupational Therapy Manpower. (1983–1984). *Occupational therapy manpower: A plan for progress.* Rockville, MD: Author.

American Public Health Association. (2009). *About us.* Retrieved February 24, 2009, from http://www.apha.org/about/

Andersen, R. M., Rice, T. H., & Kominski, G. F. (2001). *Changing the U.S. health care system* (2nd ed.). San Francisco: Jossey-Bass.

Baum, C. M. (1992). The evolution of the U.S. health care system. In J. Bair & M. Gray (Eds.), *The occupational therapy manager* (pp. 1–25). Rockville, MD: American Occupational Therapy Association.

Blendon, R. J., Brodie, M., Benson, J. M., Altman, D. E., Levitt, L., Hoff, T., et al. (1998). Understanding the managed care backlash. *Health Affairs, 17*(4), 80–94.

Bloom, G. (1994). Ethics. In K. Jacobs & M. Logigian (Eds.), *Functions of a manager in occupational therapy* (pp. 51–66). Thorofare, NJ: Slack.

Brachtesende, A. (2005). The turnaround is here! *OT Practice, 23,* 13–19.

Burt, C. W., Hing, E., & Woodwell, D. (2005). *Electronic medical record use by office based physicians: United States, 2005.* Retrieved February 5, 2009, from http://www.cdc.gov/nchs/products/pubs/pubd/hestats/electronic/electronic.htm

Case Management Society of America. (2008). *About case management and CMSA.* Retrieved March 27, 2009, from http://www.cmsa.org/PolicyMaker/tabid/62/Default.aspx

Centers for Disease Control and Prevention. (2007*). Improving the health of older Americans: A CDC priority.* Retrieved February 3, 2009, from http://www.cdc.gov/nccdphp/publications/cdnr/pdf/CDNR.June.2007.pdf

Centers for Disease Control and Prevention. (2008). *Chronic disease overview*. Retrieved November 20, 2009, from http://www.cdc.gov/NCCdphp/overview.htm

Centers for Disease Control and Prevention, & National Institutes of Health. (2010). *Healthy people 2010: Heart disease and stroke*. Retrieved August 2, 2010, from http://www .healthypeople.gov/document/html/volume1/12heart.htm

Centers for Medicare and Medicaid Services. (1997). *State Children's Health Insurance Program*. Retrieved February 17, 2009, from http://www.cms.hhs.gov/home/schip.asp

Centers for Medicare and Medicaid Services. (2007). *National health expenditure Web tables*. Retrieved February 16, 2009, from http://www.cms.hhs.gov/NationalHealthExpendData/downloads/tables.pdf

Centers for Medicare and Medicaid Services. (2008). *The nation's health dollar: Where it came from, where it went*. Retrieved February 16, 2009, from http://www.cms.hhs.gov/NationalHealthExpendData/downloads/PieChartSourcesExpenditures2007.pdf

Chapman, A. R. (1993). *Exploring a human rights approach to health care reform*. Washington, DC: American Association for the Advancement of Science.

Chapman, B., & Talmedge, J. (1971). The evolution of the right to health concept in the United States. *The Pharos, 34*, 30–51.

Commonwealth of Massachusetts. (n.d.). *Chapter 58 of the acts of 2006: An act providing access to affordable, quality, accountable health care*. Retrieved February 21, 2009, from http://www.mass.gov/legis/laws/seslaw06/sl060058.htm

Crawford, M., & Katz, S. (2008). *CPI detailed report: Data for December 2008*. Retrieved February 16, 2009, from http://www.bls.gov/cpi/cpid0812.pdf

DeNavas-Walt, C. B., Proctor, B. D., & Smith, J. C. (2008). *Income, poverty, and health insurance coverage in the United States: 2007*. Retrieved February 16, 2009, from http://www.census.gov/prod/2008pubs/p60-235.pdf

The DRG handbook: Comparative clinical and financial standards. (1994). Baltimore and Cleveland, OH: HCIA and Ernst & Young.

Elwood, T. (1991). A view from Washington. *Journal of Allied Health, 20*, 47–62.

Emmons, N. (2010). OTs step up in health care reform. *Today in OT*. Retrieved June 26, 2010, from http://news.todayinot.com/article/20100621/TODAYINOT010101/100615003

Fisher, T. (1995). *The case manager in case management*. Unpublished manuscript, Columbia Healthcare.

Freda, M. (1998). Facility-based practice settings. In M. C. Neistadt & E. B. Crepeau (Eds.), *Willard and Spackman's occupational therapy* (9th ed., pp. 803–817). Philadelphia: Lippincott Williams & Wilkins.

Glantz, C. H., & Moyers P. A. (2003, September 8). New AOTA specialties board and programs established. *OT Practice, 8*, 11.

HealthLeaders–Interstudy. (2009). *Health maintenance organizations (HMOs): 1990–2007*. Retrieved February 24, 2009, from http://www.census.gov/compendia/statab/tables/09s0144.pdf

Hildenbrand, W., & Froehlich, K. (2002). Promoting health: Historical roots, renewed vision. *OT Practice, 7*, 10–15.

Hsiao, C. J., Burt, C. W., Rechtsteiner, E., Hing, E., Woodwell, D. A., & Sisk, J. E. (2008). *Preliminary estimates of electronic medical records use by office-based physicians: United States*. Retrieved February 5, 2009, from http://www.cdc.gov/nchs/products/pubs/pubd/hestats/physicians08/physicians08.htm

InterStudy. (2001). *PPO directory and performance report*. St. Paul, MN: InterStudy Publications.

Johansson, C. (2000). *Top 10 emerging practice areas to watch in the new millennium*. Retrieved November 20, 2009, from http://www.aota.org//nonmembers/area1/links/link61.asp

Keehan, S., Sisko, A., Truffer, C., Smith, S., Cowan, C., Poisal, J., et al. (2008). Health spending projections through 2017: The baby-boom generation is coming to Medicare. *Health Affairs, 27*, 145–155.

LaGrossa, J. (2008). *AOTA Board and Specialty Certification: Why and how*. Retrieved November 20, 2009, from http://community.advanceweb.com/blogs/ot_1/archive/2008/10/11/aota-board-specialty-certification-why-how.aspx

Lowe, L. (2010) Inside health care reform. *Today in PT*. Retrieved July 19, 2010, from http://news.todayinpt.com/article/20100510/TODAYINPT0301/100525005

McCanne, D. (2004). A national health insurance program for the United States. *Public Library of Science Medicine, 1*, 115–118.

Moyers, P. (2003). Employer support: A creative partnership. *OT Practice, 8*, 10.

Nanof, T. (2007). OT's role with wounded vets. *OT Practice, 12*(17), 6.

National Board Certification for Occupational Therapy. (2007). *Executive summary report*. Gaithersburg, MD: Author.

National Center for Chronic Disease Prevention and Health Promotion. (2008). *Chronic disease prevention and health promotion*. Retrieved February 3, 2009, from http://cdc.gov/nccdphp/2008/index.htm

National Center for Injury Prevention and Control. (2007). *Traumatic brain injury overview*. Retrieved October 8, 2009, from http://www.cdc.gov/ncipc/tbi/Overview.htm

National Coalition on Healthcare. (2009a). *Facts on health insurance coverage*. Retrieved February 17, 2009, from http://www.nchc.org/facts/coverage.shtml

National Coalition on Healthcare. (2009b). *Health insurance costs*. Retrieved February 16, 2009, from http://www.nchc.org/facts/cost.shtml

National Conference of State Legislatures. (2009). *State legislation and actions on health savings accounts (HSAs) and consumer-directed health plans, 2004–2008*. Retrieved February 10, 2009, from http://www.ncsl.org/programs/health/hsa.htm

Pati, S., Shea, S., Rabinowitz, D., & Carrasquillo, O. (2005). Health expenditures for privately insured adults enrolled in managed care gatekeeping vs. indemnity plans. *American Journal of Public Health, 95*, 286–291.

Patient Protection and Affordable Care Act, Pub. L. 111–114, 119 Stat. 124 (2010).

Pohly, P. (2007). *Glossary of terms in managed healthcare*. Retrieved February 21, 2009, from http://www.pohly.com/terms_u.html

Public Health Service Act of 1944, Pub. L. 78–410, Ch. 373, 58 Stat. 682 (1944).

Raymond, A. G. (2007). *The 2006 Massachusetts health care reform law: Progress and challenges after one year of implementation*. Retrieved February 21, 2009, from http://masshealthpolicyforum.brandeis.edu/publications/pdfs/31-May07/MassHealthCareReformProgess%20Report.pdf

Scaffa, M. (Ed.). (2001). *Occupational therapy in community-based practice settings*. Philadelphia: F. A. Davis.

Schneider, E. C., Zaslavsky, A. M., & Epstein, A. M. (2002). Racial disparities in the quality of care for enrollees in Medicare-managed care. *JAMA, 287*, 1288–1294.

Shatkin, L. (2008). *150 best recession-proof jobs*. Indianapolis, IN: Jist Publishing.

Social Security Administration. (1994). *Social Security bulletin, annual statistical supplement*. Washington, DC: U.S. Government Printing Office.

Somers, F., & Browne, S. (1994). *Key health care reform issues for 1995 state legislative sessions*. Rockville, MD: American Occupational Therapy Association.

Sultz, H. A., & Young, K. M. (2009). *Health care USA: Understanding its organization and delivery* (6th ed.). Sudbury, MA: Jones & Bartlett.

Toto, P. (2006). Documentation. *OT Practice, 11*(9), 22.

U.S. Bureau of the Census. (2001). *Statistical abstract of the United States* (121st ed.). Washington, DC: U.S. Government Printing Office.

U.S. Bureau of the Census. (2008). *Income, poverty, and health insurance coverage in the United States: 2007*. Washington, DC: U.S. Government Printing Office.

U.S. Bureau of Labor Statistics. (2007a). *Occupational therapist assistants and aides*. Retrieved March 1, 2009, from http://www.bls.gov/oco/ocos166.htm

U.S. Bureau of Labor Statistics. (2007b). *Occupational therapists*. Retrieved March 1, 2009, from http://www.bls.gov/oco/ocos078.htm

U.S. Bureau of Labor Statistics. (2008). *Nonfatal occupational injuries and illnesses requiring days away from work, 2007*. Retrieved February 3, 2009, from http://www.bls.gov/news.release/osh2.nr0.htm

U.S. Bureau of Labor Statistics. (2009). *Occupational therapists*. Retrieved November 21, 2009, from http://www.bls.gov/oco/ocos078.htm

U.S. Department of Labor. (2009). *Employment Standards Administration*. Retrieved February 17, 2009, from http://www.dol.gov/esa/whd/fmla/

Weiner, J. P., & de Lissovoy, G. (1993). Razing a tower of Babel: A taxonomy for managed care and health insurance plans. *Journal of Health Politics, Policy, and Law, 18*, 75–103.

White House. (2009a). *The agenda: Health care*. Retrieved on February 18, 2009, from http://www.whitehouse.gov/agenda/health_care/

White House. (2009b). *The Clinton–Gore Administration*. (2009). Retrieved February 17, 2009, from http://clinton5.nara.gov/WH/Accomplishments/eightyears-07.html

Wilson, K. (2009). *Health care costs 101*. Retrieved November 20, 2009, from http://www.chcf.org/topics/healthinsurance/index.cfm?itemID=133630

Wolgemuth, L. (2008). 30 best careers for 2009. *U.S. News and World Report*. Retrieved November 20, 2009, from http://www.usnews.com/money/careers/articles/2008/12/11/the-30-best-careers-for-2009.html

World Health Organization. (2000). *The World Health Report 2000*. Retrieved November 20, 2009, from http://www.who.int/whr/2000/en/

APPENDIX 3.A. DELIVERY SYSTEMS EVIDENCE TABLE

Topic	Evidence
Cost containment	Crawford, M., & Katz, S. (2008). *CPI detailed report: Data for December 2008.* Retrieved February 16, 2009, from http://www.bls.gov/cpi/cpid0812.pdf Hildenbrand, W., & Froehlich, K. (2002). Promoting health: Historical roots, renewed vision. *OT Practice, 7,* 10–15. Keehan, S., Sisko, A., Truffer, C., Smith, S., Cowan, C., Poisal, J., et al. (2008). Health spending projections through 2017: The baby-boom generation is coming to Medicare. *Health Affairs, 27,* 145–155.
Managed care	Blendon, R. J., Brodie, M., Benson, J. M., Altman, D. E., Levitt, L., Hoff, T., et al. (1998). Understanding the managed care backlash. *Health Affairs, 17*(4), 80–94. Schneider, E. C., Zaslavsky, A. M., & Epstein, A. M. (2002). Racial disparities in the quality of care for enrollees in Medicare-managed care. *JAMA, 287,* 1288–1294.

4

Dynamical Systems Theory in Occupational Therapy Management

Charlotte Royeen, PhD, OTR, FAOTA

❖ Key Terms and Concepts

Adaptive systems. Systems that are able to change in response to events or stimuli.

Chaos science. Knowledge and understanding based upon principles of chaos theory, including emergent systems, self-organization, and nonlinearity.

Complexity science. Knowledge and understanding that transcend linear systems to include a multifaceted worldview.

Dynamical systems theory (DNS). Analysis of systems or organizations that change.

Emergent behavior. When a system begins to organize itself, particular or systematic behaviors become manifest, which may indicate a new level or stage of organization.

Linear model. A linear model is based upon the assumption that for every change in a variable (x), there is an equal and proportionate change in variable (y), and this relationship can be plotted as a straight line, or a linear model. Western civilization operates very much on a linear model.

Network. An organization of connections in a manner or pattern that allows for coupling or communication across, between, and among parts of the organization.

Nonlinear model. When a change in variable x has unequal and disproportionate changes in variable y, one has a nonlinear model. That is, the relationship between variables cannot be symbolized using a straight line. Examples of nonlinear models may include a u-shaped curve, a j-shaped curve, or no discernable pattern of relationships.

Open systems. These systems are open to input from other systems; they are not closed and self-contained. Open systems, therefore, are susceptible to input or affect from other systems.

System. An organization of how parts are put together to operate.

❖ Learning Objectives

After completing this chapter, you should be able to do the following:

- Define and illustrate basic concepts in dynamical systems theory (DNS).
- Apply examples from dynamical systems theory to occupational therapy practice.
- Reflect on your own skills and abilities using a DNS perspective.
- Reflect on how virtues play a role in DNS-based occupational therapy management.

The "new science" (Battram, 1998) of dynamical systems theory (DNS) has much to offer the field of occupational therapy. This chapter uses the term *DNS* because it is most consistent with the wide literature on this topic. This science can help occupational therapy managers guide their teams toward openness, purposefulness, multidimensionality, and self-organizing properties (Luebben & Royeen, 2006). In every organization, we need to look internally, to see one another as critical resources on this voyage of discovery. We need to learn how to engage the creativity that exists everywhere in our organizations. There are no recipes or formulas, no checklists of expert advice that describe "reality." If context is as crucial as the science explains, then nothing really transfers; everything is always new and different and unique to each of us. We must engage with each other, experiment to find what works for us, and support one another as the true inventors that we are (Wheatley, 1999, p. 9). This aptly applies to occupational therapy management because each day we are presented with new and challenging tasks with fewer resources and less time. We are challenged to bring out the best in all in order to ensure that we practice well and serve clients and their families. We can only make it fit the place and time by interacting with each other and focusing upon the context of the setting.

As long as humans have existed, they have formed groups. In group settings, there are typically goals that need to be accomplished. Facilitation of work toward group goals is a task that is usually directed, facilitated, or orchestrated by a person called a *manager*. In early times, the manager might have been known as a tribal leader. In modern times, such persons may have different labels depending on the context in which the group occurs. For example, in a church setting, it might be the minister or pastor. In a classroom, it might be the teacher. Those who work in occupational therapy call such people the occupational therapy supervisor or manager. This chapter takes a careful look at the person who facilitates, directs, or orchestrates in occupational therapy settings—that is, the occupational therapy manager—using a particular worldview based on dynamical systems theory and the related concepts of chaos theory and complexity theory.

What Is Management?

It is difficult to separate out management (the process or the system) from the context in which it occurs (the environment); typically, one looks at management in its context or environmental setting (Pitts, 1980). For the purposes of this chapter, however, I will focus primarily on the occupational therapy management process, independent of site or setting. In addition, some authors, such as Osborn and Hunt (2007), have defined management and leadership in similar ways. It is beyond the scope of this chapter to address leadership (see Part III for more details on leadership), and the reader is referred to the leadership chapter for more on leadership in occupational therapy.

Management is a process of how one works with others in order to achieve desired goals or stated outcomes. Systems and systems analyses are widely used in management (Alexander, 1972). In a management textbook, Certo and Certo (2009) provided classic views of the roles and functions of a manager:

- "The role of managers is to guide organizations toward goal accomplishment" through the process of "planning, organizing, influencing and controlling" (p. 7).

- "Effectiveness . . . refers to the management's use of organizational resources in meeting organizational goals" (p. 11).
- "A management skill is the ability to carry out the process of reaching organizational goals by working with and through people and other organizational resources" (p. 13).

The manager's job description is changing (Robbins & Coulter, 2009). The methods of accomplishing the desired goals are probably what is changing most, for the basic definition of a manager by Certo and Certo (2009) still holds. Overall, management has moved from a *hierarchical* process—that is, a top-down model with formally designated leaders—to a *heterarchical* process—that is, a bottom-up model that attempts to better use input from all levels of the organization across specific functions or roles (network management), in which leaders may emerge during the execution of the task or process. Ecological research has revealed that bottom-up control yields greater stability and dynamic response (Shastri & Diwekar, 2006). In addition, technological change such as e-mail has radically altered management practices (Royeen, 2005). Further, globalization across almost all aspects of the U.S. economy means that organizations interact in tremendously more complex environments.

This level of complexity in management is well beyond that which existed in the past. The need to be responsive to constant change in a global environment means that we all now live with "future shock," or the perception that there is too much change in too short a period of time. In his 1970 book *Future Shock*, Alvin Toffler predicted that intense and prolonged change would disconnect people, leaving them disoriented and stressed. The skills a manager most needs to work effectively in this environment are presented in Table 4.1.

How does one operationalize these skills to be effective? That is an art of management practice, which is not dissimilar to the art of clinical practice; one uses many of these same skills as a clinician. Thus, occupational therapy management is not a distinctly different function from clinical occupational therapy (see Chapter 5). It is, rather, a different process of putting the skills together while interacting with various groups across unique environments.

In the past, most managers operated in a linear model of understanding the world and the workplace. The assumption underpinning the linear model is as follows: For every increase in x, there is a corresponding increase in y. Some things in the world do operate using this principle, of course. To illustrate, if you change your thermostat setting (x), there is typically a corresponding and proportionate change in temperature of the room (y). Or if you eat more calories (x), there is a corresponding and proportionate gain in weight (y). These examples reflect a linear model of cause and effect that has predictable, corresponding, and proportionate increases in y based on changes in x. This

Table 4.1. Management Skills Needed in Current Management Venues

Skill	Definition
Delegating	Ability to assign others to perform tasks
Communicating	Ability to send and receive verbal and nonverbal information in multiple formats such as person-to-person, e-mail, letter, and so forth
Critical thinking	Ability to think critically and in depth and to recognize problems and patterns for decision making
Organizing workloads	Ability to orchestrate who performs what tasks and activities
Organizing use of time	Ability to use temporal and sequentially ordered processes to accomplish what needs to get done
Role delineation	Ability to clearly define and communicate roles, functions, or tasks one is to perform
Creating trust	Ability to foster a feeling of confidence, a vision, and a bond of belief
Transparency	In management, the ability to communicate openly to constituents how decisions are made and how things operate

is a pervasive belief in Western civilization, yet it is rarely clearly acknowledged.

A linear worldview guides the actions of many managers. But in the highly complex and ever-changing modern environment, innovation and success in management are better served by a nonlinear worldview that better fits the postindustrial age of information management. Such a worldview is based on the concept of *dynamical systems*.

WHAT IS DYNAMICAL SYSTEMS THEORY?

Dynamics refers to change. More precisely, it involves a set of rules describing how a state or condition changes over time (Royeen & Luebben, 2003, p. 71). Dynamical systems theory is part of what many consider to be "the new science" that is based upon chaos, complexity, and dynamical systems called *DNS* (Hunt & Ropo, 2003). DNS is used in management theory to account for the wide-ranging factors managers must consider in leading their teams (Tse & Robb, 1994). According to Wheatley (1999), "The systematic nature of life—the vast webs of interconnection so well-described in the new science—has become part of our modern consciousness" (p. ix). *Chaos theory* developed as a mathematical model to describe states in which small changes in initial conditions had large effects in outcomes. *Complexity theory* typically encompasses chaos theory and

refers to the multifaceted situation wherein multiple variables contribute to a system in change. *Chaos* is actually a very precise mathematical description of the state of a condition of a system and is distinctly different from the common term in everyday language of chaos—or lack of order.

DNS is considered to be a third scientific discipline; the first discipline is experimentation, and the second is regression-based work, both of which are predicated on linear models. The third discipline encompasses computer modeling, grounded theory, and case study (Hunt & Ropo, 2003), none of which is based on linear models. Methods of analysis used in this discipline are presented in Table 4.2.

DNS originated in the basic sciences (Robbins & Coulter, 2009), most notably chemistry (Ilya Prigogine) and meteorology (Edward Lorenz), but it has been adapted for and readily adopted by many fields. Two seminal works brought this information to many: *Leadership and the New Science: Discovering Order in a Chaotic World*, by Wheatley (1999), and *The Fifth Discipline Fieldbook*, by Senge, Ross, Smith, Roberts, and Kleiner (1994). In occupational therapy, Kielhofner developed much of his theoretical work based on open systems, or systems that continually interact with the environment and change and adapt in response to it (Robbins & Coulter, 2009), and in more recent years he has changed his theory to include DNS. Early references to

Table 4.2. Nonlinear Methods of Analysis in Dynamical Systems Theory

Method of analysis	Definition
Embeddedness	Examination of what is within the existing "scene," similar to figure ground perception of visual tasks, only having to do with issues, problems, or actions set within a system
Temporal interconnectedness	Connections among the past, the present, and the future
Context shapes process	Influence of the environment on the course of action
Holistic vs. linear processes	Use of broader and multiple viewpoints to provide a systems view in which everything is considered in relationship or context; linear processes, by definition and function, follow one line of single viewpoints
Linking of processes to explanation of outcome	Rejection of the assumption that anything can exist or operate interdependently from the setting and related variables (epitomized by John Donne's phrase "No man is an island")

Source. Hunt & Ropo, 2003.

DNS in the occupational therapy literature appeared in two chapters by Gray, Kennedy, and Zemke (1996a, 1996b) in *Occupational Science: The Evolving Discipline* (Zemke & Clark, 1996). Royeen and Luebben (2003) annotated leading articles related to chaos theory in 2002, and in 2003, Royeen's Eleanor Clarke Slagle Lecture presented concepts related to chaos theory for occupational therapy.

In dynamical systems theory, when we are talking about systems, we are commonly referring to open systems (Robbins & Coulter, 2009, p. 35). A hallmark of open systems is that they are not self-contained (Robbins & Coulter, 2009, p. 36) and can, therefore, be affected by external stimuli.

WHAT IS COMPLEXITY THEORY, AND HOW IS IT RELATED?

In this chapter, as recommended by Battram (1998), I will use biological metaphors (rather than machine metaphors) as the starting point to describe DNS: "Metaphors help us to link ideas in new ways so that new knowledge can emerge. They are a wonderful way of using language to engage with complexity" (Battram, 1998, p. 56). Complexity theory, based upon nonlinear dynamics and chaos theory,

is linked to both biological and organizational adaptation and evolution (Schneider & Somers, 2006).

HOW DO MANAGEMENT AND DNS GO TOGETHER?

According to Lichtenstein (2000), concepts from nonlinear dynamic systems and complex systems can be used as examples or metaphors to understand how dynamic systems operate in management. This section presents the principles of DNS (summarized in Table 4.3) and provides illustrative examples in occupational therapy theory and practice.

Sensitivity to Initial Conditions

In Edward Lorenz's original theoretical work in meteorology, he mused, and others modeled using computers, that a butterfly flapping its wings in Tokyo—an "initial condition"—might account for a hurricane eventually ending offshore in Florida (Eoyang, 1997). This illustrated the concept of *sensitivity* to initial conditions. The concept refers to the finding that certain systems are highly dependent upon the state or conditions in which they first exist, whereas other systems or conditions may not be particularly vulner-

Table 4.3. Principles of Dynamical Systems Theory

Principle	Definition	Example
Sensitivity to initial conditions	Disproportionate effects of events during initial conditions on eventual outcomes	Melting of the glaciers is causing worldwide flooding and raising level of the ocean, creating an eventual effect on weather and climate across the globe
Co-effects and interrelationships	Effects of one variable or factor on another; neither is independent	Over the years, the Colorado River has cut out rock to form the Grand Canyon
Self-organizing systems	Systems that, left on their own, form some sort of organization	Watch a group of children play on a playground: They self-organize into some sort of network
Perturbations and bifurcations	Splits in paths or disturbances that impinge on a system.	The alarm ringing while you are asleep is a perturbation to your sleep cycle
Fractals	Self-referential parts of a repeated pattern	Parts of a snowflake that mimic the whole snowflake
Boundaries	The area in which two separate systems meet	Lines in a coloring book that distinguish one part from another
Transforming feedback loops	Communication events in which the communication across boundaries changes one or both systems defined by the boundaries	Interactions among staff and administration ranging from casual water-cooler talk to formal evaluation
Holism	Concept of the whole person, where no part, segment, or component is considered in isolation from any other	Participation in occupation in context
Dynamical systems theory	Systems or organizations that change	Systems in the state of change or flux
Adaptive systems	Systems that are able to change in response to events or stimuli	Ability of an occupational therapy staff member to change behavior on the basis of supervisor feedback
Complexity science	The knowledge and understanding that transcends linear systems to include a multifaceted worldview	A student or practitioner using an academic or scientific reference that recognizes the multifaceted view of the world

able or affected by variables from initial conditions. What this really means for occupational therapy managers is that a relatively small event or cause can have a tremendous effect and that the outcome or effect can be disproportionate to the input. (Again, this is not a linear model!)

Example A

Going into the occupational therapy clinic each day with a genuine "hello" to one and all may not seem like a major event or a complex process. Yet one cannot overestimate how this simple act may affect others. The act is setting the initial condition of a positive environment, thus predisposing all to have good feelings. These good feelings may then influence interpersonal interactions between clients and staff. Thus, a simple hello may have positive, reverberating consequences within the system.

Example B

Two B students did their Level I fieldwork with the same supervisor and setting. One had performed 180 hours of clinical work before entering the occupational therapy educational program, whereas the other had no prior clinical experience. The fieldwork setting was fast paced and very complex. The experienced student, not having to learn everything at once, could successfully link past and present for better performance. The other student had never seen a client previously and was overwhelmed by the noise, physical context, and pace of the clinical setting. The experienced student's initial condition on beginning the fieldwork experience was more conducive to success than that of the other student. Consequently, one student passed, and the other did not.

Coeffects and Interrelationships

The phrase "no man is an island," from metaphysical poet John Donne's *Devotions Upon Emergent Occasions, Meditation XVII*, reflects the reality that no person can exist independently of others. The principle of coeffects and interrelationships builds on this concept in an exponential manner, that is, the effects are not additive but multiplicative. *Coeffects* and *interrelationships* refer to the integral interconnections between parts of a system or between systems.

Example C

Occupational therapy theory, as established by its early founders, holds that participation in occupation shapes the brain and results in the state of health or wellness. Conversely, the early founders also assumed that the brain shapes or directs occupation. Since the founding of occupational therapy, neuroscience or neurology has been a key course in the curriculum. These disciplines are interrelated; the term *neuro-occupation* has recently been coined (Padilla & Peyton, 1997) to reflect the coeffects of one system on the other and the interrelationships between the brain and occupation.

Example D

An occupational therapist does not live in an emotional vacuum independent of the client. In fact, the empathetic occupational therapist or master practitioner typically tries to match the emotional tone of the client. Such actions reflect the implicit understanding that the therapist's mood can affect his or her client and that the client's mood can affect his or her therapist. There is an interrelationship in the psychosocial interactions between the two individuals.

Self-Organizing or Complex Adaptive Systems

Biology research reveals that the more complex a system is, the less stable it is (Rozdilsky, Stone, & Solow, 2004). In a healthy system, there is a dynamic balance between change and stability. Neither extreme stability nor extreme change is desirable: *Extreme change* is the state of chaos; *extreme stability* is, in fact, the state of death. The healthy system is constantly *self-organizing*, or spontaneously creating a new structure for itself, to accommodate change and move toward stability. Thus, a healthy system is always balancing between the two extremes through iterative processes of input, throughput, and output. *Input* refers to what goes into the system. *Throughput* refers to what is going through the system. *Output* is what comes out of the system. Self-organization is thought to be ubiquitous in organizational behavior (Guastello & Bond, 2007).

In self-organizing systems, it has been theorized that pushing the control downward assists in control or management (Lichtenstein, 2000). *Pushing control downward* refers to facilitating decision making and resource allocation to lower levels of organizational hierarchy. Also, *order*—that is, predictability and stereotypical behavior—is thought to emerge from self-organization (Battram, 1998). Order is predictability and stereotypical behavior (Battram, 1998, p. 141). *Self-organizing systems* are self-guided, meaning that external forces are not the primary control mechanism. Self-organized systems organize nonhierarchically and demonstrate emergent behavior (Royeen, 2003).

Example E

Ruth is an 88-year-old woman recently relocated from an independent living apartment in Tennessee to one in a facility in southern Illinois. The move from beautiful mountains in eastern Tennessee to relatively flat farmland in Illinois was disorienting, but especially disruptive was a fall on a concrete step outside her apartment the first night she was there. After visiting an emergency room and verifying that no bones were broken, the facility loaned her a standard-size wheelchair, but she needed assistance to move around in it—at 5 ft 1 in. and 131 lb, she was unable to propel it herself. Her physician provided a prescription for a wheelchair due to left side hip pain and bruising, and a wheelchair that was sized for her allowed her self-organization to emerge. Rather than being bound to whatever place in the apartment she had been "wheeled to," with the properly fitting wheelchair she was able to propel herself around the apartment. Within 3 days she was independent in toileting and dressing as her self-care system emerged with the assistance of a properly fitting wheelchair.

Example F

In her previous home, Ruth had kept her crossword puzzles, writing materials, and TV remote in a stand next to her favorite chair. In her new apartment, her favorite chair was no longer in the room with a TV, and the stand was given away because of lack of space. Yet Ruth re-created the same system in the new setting with no facilitation by the occupational therapist. She now sits primarily on a couch instead of her "old" favorite chair and places her crossword puzzles, writing materials, and TV remote on the end table to the left of the couch. She has adapted to the changed environment and self-organized a system for managing the tools that are part of her favorite occupations—solving crossword puzzles, writing, and watching TV. The occupational therapist did not do this for her—the pattern emerged on its own as she adapted to the new apartment. She became a model of a self-correcting system and independently achieved this.

Perturbations and Bifurcations

In self-organizing systems, a *perturbation* is a "disturbance" (Bondavalli, Favilla, & Bodini, 2009); any internal or external mechanism that causes a change in the functioning of a system as a result of internal or external mechanisms is a perturbation to that system. In other words, perturbations affect the system and force it to change in some way. *Bifurcations*, or a splitting of a dynamical system into two distinct pathways, can be one result of how a system self-organizes in response to a perturbation. Instead of a single system, the split or bifurcation results in two systems or two distinct paths taken by a single system.

Example G

Ruth's accidental fall significantly bruised her left hip, a serious perturbation, or challenge to her system. The result was a bifurcation in her movement patterns: She could no longer bear weight on the left leg, so independent ambulation (one pathway) was not possible until her hip healed. Instead, she used a wheelchair (another pathway) for mobility until her hip could heal enough for her to bear weight and resume independent ambulation.

Example H

Ruth's relocation, a perturbation, required her to change banks. She confronted the bifurcation of options in banking—continue with traditional statements and checking, or join an online checking option that paid significant interest on balances up to a certain limit. In this case, the path to take was clear—she enrolled in the online banking service that paid interest and allowed family members to monitor her financial transactions.

Fractals

Generally, fractals, also known as *self-similarities,* are characteristic of self-organizing systems (Schneider & Somers, 2006). Originally identified in geometric shapes, *fractals* are shapes whose parts mimic the shape of the whole. In occupational therapy, fractals or self-similarities take the form of behavioral patterns whose parts repeat themselves.

Example I

Ruth, at age 88, experienced ongoing tension between autonomy and dependence as her body inevitably declined with age, and this tension played out repeatedly in bifurcations such as walking versus wheelchair mobility, traditional banking versus online banking, and eating in the dining room versus having meals delivered to her room. Each bifurcation represents a repeated scenario of the conflict between dependence and autonomy and may be considered a fractal, or similar patterns across behaviors.

Example J

As her children were growing up, Ruth always hosted holiday celebrations at her house with special food. There was no way she could comfortably move her wheelchair around her children's houses. So how could they accomplish some semblance of a holiday celebration in her one-bedroom apartment? In essence, she and her family created a fractal version of Easter holiday at her place. Her children cooked dinner early and took it over to Ruth's apartment to eat. The celebration of eating together with family in a different setting is a fractal that connected the present with the past and maintained family ties.

Boundaries

The area between two parts of a system is a *boundary;* it is the area of distinction where the differences between the two systems meet (Eoyang, 1996). The condition or state within that boundary area influences the actions of the system. When boundaries are clear and distinct, the area in between them is subject to great stress or clashing of the distinct boundaries. When boundaries are indistinct, it is not clear when one part of the system ends and another begins (Eoyang, 1997). An example of a distinct boundary might be a coastline that separates water from land. An indistinct boundary might be the overlap of roles in management across vice presidents in a hospital or clinical setting. According to current organization theory, modern organizations have evolved from bureaucracies with clear and distinct boundaries to fluid structures with fluid boundaries (Schneider & Somers, 2006). In fact, sometimes one cannot identify boundaries at all across systems such as certain nations, multinational companies, or local government organizations (Battram, 1998).

Example K

For those of you who have worked with, studied, or read about eating disorders in young women, one of the theories in that area is illustrative. Much of the theory about eating disorders in young women is that there is not a clear boundary (indistinct) between the ego identities of the young woman and her mother. The lack of clear boundary or ego differentiation results in confusion. Thus, to cope with the confusion, the only control the young woman is able to operationalize is to exercise control over her eating habits.

Example L

In occupational therapy education, many faculty have casually discussed and popular media has covered the phenomenon of the so-called "helicopter parents," who are so enmeshed in their child's life that faculty interact with the parent, and not the student, on many issues. Helicopter parents do not have distinct boundaries of scope of responsibility with their children. Those students of the Millennial generation may not concur with this example, but as a dean, I see that it is a shared perception held by many educators.

Transforming Feedback Loops

Transforming feedback loops involves communication across a boundary from one part of a system to another that results in communication and interaction across a boundary within a complex system (Eoyang, 1996). Information is shared between the systems, and the difference between the two systems is used as a creative tension driving progress toward a mutual goal. When information is shared across systems and across boundaries, it changes one or both systems.

Example M

As Ruth recovered from her fall, she was discouraged with how slowly she progressed. She worked with an occupational therapist toward the mutual goal of establishing increasing independence for Ruth by improving transfers from the wheelchair to the car, to bed, or to sitting. As they worked, the therapist observed Ruth's improvement, but Ruth could not. So each day, after Ruth completed a transfer, the therapist told her how well she was doing and specifically how much improvement she had observed (e.g., increased weight bearing, number of steps in transfer). Ruth repeatedly expressed how important this transformative feedback was to her, because she did not see the improvement unless the therapist pointed it out. As Ruth became able to note improvement, it increased her motivation and, in turn, improved her mood. Likewise, the therapist was transformed by the feeling of being able to help Ruth improve. Both Ruth and the occupational therapist were changed by this transforming feedback loop.

Example N

In management, the performance review, or the system of evaluating and providing feedback to employees, is ideally a transforming feedback loop. That is, the information provided by the supervisor to the employee should assist the employee in performing his or her job responsibilities better and more effectively. The feedback provided by the employee to the supervisor can help the supervisor develop better ways of managing and operating the department. In this case, each system—supervisor and employee—is changed by the information shared between the systems.

Holism

Holism, in reference to DNS, refers to the relationship of networks to each other in a system. In this sense, holism may be defined as relationships of networks within an entity, or the "existence of multiple links between elements of the system" (Waliszewski, Molski, & Konarski, 1998, p. 71).

Example O

Occupational therapists use the biopsychosocial model of care rather than a medical model of care, meaning that they are concerned with all three systems of an individual (biological, psychological, and social) and not just the disease or pathology they might present. This holistic perspective places occupational therapy squarely in DNS!

Example P

Another concept in occupational therapy theory—person, environment, and occupational fit—relates to the intersection of each of these systems with the other. Good occupational therapy practice addresses all of these networks simultaneously.

TRANSLATION OF THEORY TO PRACTICE IN OCCUPATIONAL THERAPY MANAGEMENT

In spite of the current focus in the occupational therapy field on evidence-based practice, there are other ways of knowing how to act or interact in this world: Basing one's actions on a set of concepts such as dynamical systems theory provides one with a theoretical frame of reference to use in making decisions as a manager (e.g., see Lichtenstein, 2000). This theoretical reference may be more consistent with the occupational therapist's use of conditional reasoning, whereas use of evidence-based practice is more consistent with procedural reasoning. When occupational therapy managers use a delineation of core values to guide their organization and their management, that process uses a DNS frame of reference. Conversely, when managers use an organizational chart to guide their work, they are using a more linear, classical method of scientific management.

Using DNS as a frame of reference, I propose that we rename management in occupational therapy as *facilitation of change*. Such facilitation is what we do as clinicians and is, in fact, what we do as managers as well. Renaming and reframing occupational therapy management in this manner highlights its similarities with clinical practice. In addition to working with an individual client to foster change, occupational therapy managers also work with groups or systems to foster change.

In a DNS approach to occupational therapy management, good management is more a method or an approach than a set of techniques or protocols. It is the process of creating, reinforcing, and valuing relationships within the contextual setting that is the hallmark of DNS theory in management. Certain behaviors may be called "virtues" in that they are inherently ways to foster relationships. These behaviors are easily recognized and are listed in Table 4.4. Again, the behaviors presented in Table 4.4 are similar to those involved in occupational therapy practice. Thus, from this perspective, the transition to occupational therapy management is a natural flow from clinical practice.

In addition to adopting the behaviors presented in Table 4.4, an occupational therapy manager operating from a DNS frame of reference adopts the following eight action steps:

1. Take time to reflect and discern patterns. For example, one could use statistics to recognize patterns, such as that a particular therapist is using sick leave at a rate seven times the average.
2. Use the clinical reasoning skills you learned in school and in practice. Procedural reasoning is used when following standard or accepted protocols. Conditional reasoning involves taking people factors into consideration for any task or assignment—in other words, thinking through not just the steps and actions of a process, but

also considering the psychosocial aspects of the people who would be interacting to carry it out. Finally, narrative reasoning is the "story" or "play" constructed to explain the scenario or situation.
3. Constantly formulate theory based on your observations and interpretations. For example, if an employee is out sick at a rate seven times the norm, one might hypothesize that there is a medical condition underlying these occurrences.
4. Accommodate the use of tools or measurement systems based in linearity, given that so much of the world is operating on linear models, but recognize the inherent limitations of linear-based systems (such as a rating scale in performance review of personnel) when operating using DNS.
5. Use the tacit knowledge and understanding of why occupational therapy is so different from almost every other form of therapy and most other professions. Occupational therapy, in working with the person in context, is inherently working with an open system in context, a hallmark of DNS.
6. Practice management with the understanding that predictability is limited. Uncertainty and surprise are the norm. Thus, when things do not go as planned, one must not get flustered and upset but rather accept this as part of the normal processes of an emergent system and "goes with the flow."
7. Be wary of recipes, checklists, guidebooks, and so forth. Good management practice involves use of judgment and intuitive action.
8. Value and foster working or collaborative relationships as the "glue" of the entire system.

SELF-ASSESSMENT

Table 4.5 presents a self-assessment tool that poses questions related to the virtues of a DNS-oriented manager (from Royeen, 2006, based on Telford & Gostick, 2005). This self-assessment is designed to foster self-reflection, a constant input for an open system—your mind. Answering the questions posed in Table 4.5 can help you develop your management-oriented clinical reasoning from a DNS frame of reference.

CONCLUSION

Chaos is necessary to the development of a creative new order (Wheatley, 1999, p. 13). Chaos, as a part of DNS, is important to effective management in the modern age. To think that one controls anything, let alone other people, is a serious misconception. But occupational therapy managers can effect change through the use of virtuous behaviors, thus participating in, but not controlling, their environments (Eoyang, 1999). This chapter offers beginning steps in using DNS in occupational therapy management. DNS is a good fit for the way occupational therapists work.

Table 4.4. Virtues (or Manager Behaviors) That Reflect a Dynamical Systems Theory Frame of Reference

Behavior	Definition
Consulting	Checking with others for their input and suggestions or viewpoints
Encouraging	Spurring others on with verbal or nonverbal communication designed to increase their performance
Monitoring	Overseeing or checking in on others to judge how effectively and efficiently they are carrying out activities
Planning	Thinking through how to accomplish a task or activity
Recognizing	Making sense of out of relationships between variables and outcomes
Risking	Proceeding with an action plan that may or may not lead to a successful outcome
Supporting	Providing physical, emotional, or other type of assistance for others to accomplish a successful outcome

Source. Modern Concepts and Skills Management (11th ed.), by S. C. Certo & S. T. Certo, 2009, Upper Saddle River, NJ: Prentice Hall.

Table 4.5. Self-Assessment Questions to Foster Reflection in DNS Management

Question for reflection	Answers characteristic of DNS managers	Answers characteristic of traditional managers
Am I sensitive to the little things that others value?	Pays attention to the feelings, moods, and needs of others	Does not attend to the needs of others; is more self-centered
When others see gray, do I try and see black and white?	Discerns the extremes within a pattern; sees pattern recognition	Unable to clearly see patterns to abstract key pieces of information
Do I admit mistakes when they are made?	Admits when a mistake has been made	Does not admit when a mistake has been made; often tries to blame others
Do I foster a culture of trust?	Facilitates trust among staff and management	Does not facilitate trust or teamwork; pits staff against each other
Do I keep my word?	Actions match rhetoric	Actions do not match rhetoric
Do I care about the greater good?	Actions reflect concern for the larger organization and what is good for it	Actions that reflect concern for self-interest or parochial interests
Am I modest but honest?	Critically self-assesses strengths and acknowledges them	Unable or unwilling to identify strengths and abilities
Am I willing to be publicly monitored?	Achieves transparency; is open about information regarding actions taken	Is not transparent in actions or decision making
Do I maintain the course for the greater good?	Designs actions designed to meet the needs of the greater good	Designs actions that are self-serving or limited in whose needs are met
How do I try to improve my integrity?	Strives to do better; is responsive to other's needs; provide honest commentary	Maintains the status quo

Case Examples

LEVEL I FIELDWORK

In Level I fieldwork, G noticed an occupational therapy manager doing a 360° evaluation review with the staff. (In a *360° evaluation review*, the supervisor gives feedback to the employee, and the employee gives feedback to the supervisor.) This approach illustrates using DNS in management because it allows for facilitation of feedback from one open system (i.e., the therapist) with another (i.e., the manager). It could be considered to be a transforming feedback loop when each participant takes feedback from the other under consideration and reflection.

LEVEL II FIELDWORK

In R's Level II fieldwork setting, an advisory board of community members was convened to advise the program how best to work with the community. In the 2-hour meeting, the occupational therapy program manager spoke for 1½ hours, leaving only 30 minutes for community members to provide input. Such an approach reflects a very hierarchical structure with limited opportunity for true engagement across all parties involved. Such an approach is not consistent with a DNS approach to management.

FIRST-TIME MANAGER

An occupational therapy aide was late for many therapy sessions. In a traditional management approach, the aide would be written up for late arrival and would have a corrective plan of action written for remediation. Using a DNS approach, the supervisor would meet with the aide to explore (a) why she was late, (b) was she aware that she was late? (c) ways to assure timeliness, and (d) how to collaborate on a plan of action to ensure timely arrival for all sessions. In the DNS approach, interaction across the two systems allows for better collaboration and resolution.

MANAGER

The occupational therapy manager has just been informed that she has to cut 5% of operational costs from the budget for the upcoming year. Using a traditional approach, the manager would evenly cut 5% across all aspects of the budget—a proportional or linear approach to problem solving. Using a DNS approach, the manager would meet with all staff and therapists to identify that 5% of the budget must be cut and solicit input from all of them as to how to accomplish this.

❖Learning Activities

1. Contrast a hierarchically oriented occupational therapy management system with a dynamical systems oriented occupational therapy management system.
2. Reflect on your own leadership and interpersonal style. Compare and contrast the linear model of management with a DNS-based model. Which management frame of reference fits you best, and why?
3. Think about the last time you observed an occupational therapy "management moment"—that is, how work was accomplished through the relationship with others either in the clinic or in the classroom. Identify behaviors that orchestrated the management you observed to be effective. Do the behaviors fit with the DNS approach? Why or why not?
4. In a dictionary, look up the words in the key terms and concepts at the beginning of this chapter. How are dictionary definitions the same as or different from definitions presented in this chapter?
5. Search for the term *fractals* on the Internet to see the images of many examples in nature. Explore the visually beautiful world presented as you investigate fractals. How would you describe them as a system?

✓ Multiple-Choice Questions

1. Overall, on what is DNS based?
   a. Reductionism
   b. Linearity
   c. Hierarchy
   d. Chaos and complexity
2. As used in this chapter, one concept included in dynamical systems theory is
   a. Linearity
   b. Reductionism
   c. Transforming feedback loops
   d. Hierarchy
3. Which definition of management is consistent with a DNS approach?
   a. How one works with others
   b. Directing others to do something
   c. Telling others what to do
   d. Assigning work tasks
4. Which component of occupational therapy best reflects the DNS concept of holism?
   a. The people
   b. The environment
   c. The task
   d. All of the above
5. Why is management more difficult now than in the past?
   a. Globalization and technological innovation
   b. Training of personnel
   c. More MBAs in the field
   d. None of the above
6. The linear model of management is based on
   a. DNS
   b. Open feedback systems
   c. Metaphors
   d. Proportionate cause and effect
7. The term *dynamical* refers to which of the following?
   a. Impressiveness
   b. Change
   c. Stability
   d. Personality
8. If the first discipline is experimentation and the second discipline is regression-based work, what is the third discipline?
   a. Dynamical systems theory
   b. Management
   c. Open feedback systems
   d. None of the above
9. Who among the following is credited with being the founder of DNS theory?
   a. Robbins and Coulter
   b. Gray, Kennedy, and Zemke
   c. Lorenz
   d. Kielhofner
10. What is a common characteristic of an open system?
    a. Interaction with the environment
    b. No interaction with the environment
    c. Independence from the environment
    d. None of the above
11. In the description of dynamical systems, which creature is metaphorically linked with sensitivity to initial conditions?
    a. Moth
    b. Larvae
    c. Butterfly
    d. Skunk
12. The phrase "No man is an island comes" from
    a. Donne
    b. Royeen
    c. Kielhofner
    d. Zemke
13. The ultimate form of stability is
    a. DNS
    b. Birth
    c. Death
    d. Life

14. According to the chapter, the term *perturbations* is most closely linked to
    a. Distances
    b. Anger
    c. Change
    d. Systems
15. Self-similarity is a characteristic of
    a. Perturbations
    b. Open feedback systems
    c. Fractals
    d. Holism
16. If boundaries are too distinct, what might result?
    a. Lack of clarity
    b. Stress
    c. Multinational coalitions
    d. Confusion
17. When information is shared between two systems, it is called
    a. A bifurcation
    b. A fractal
    c. Linearity
    d. An open system
18. In DNS, the concept of holism is defined as
    a. Perturbations
    b. Bifurcations
    c. Relationships of networks
    d. Hierarchy of networks
19. Based upon this chapter, of the following, what does use of a protocol reflect?
    a. Efficiency
    b. Good practice
    c. DNS
    d. Linear approach
20. In DNS, predictability is considered to be
    a. Limited
    b. Bounded
    c. Perturbed
    d. Open

References

Alexander, M. J. (1972). Managerial information channels: A systems model. *Journal of Business Communication, 9*(4), 5–11.

Battram, A. (1998). *Navigating complexity.* London: Industrial Society.

Bondavalli, C., Favilla, S., & Bodini, A. (2009). Quantitative versus qualitative modeling: A complementary approach in ecosystem study. *Computational Biology and Chemistry, 33,* 22–28.

Certo, S. C., & Certo, S. T. (2009). *Modern management: Concepts and skills* (11th ed.). Upper Saddle River, NJ: Prentice Hall.

Eoyang, G. H. (1996). Complex? Yes! Adaptive? Well, maybe . . . *Interactions, 3*(1), 31–37.

Eoyang, G. H. (1997). *Coping with chaos: Seven simple tools.* Circle Pines, MN: Lagumo.

Eoyang, G. (1999). *Coping with chaos: Seven simple tools.* Cheyenne, WY: Lagumo.

Gray, J. M., Kennedy, B. L., & Zemke, R. (1996a). Application of dynamic systems theory to occupation. In R. Zemke & F. Clark (Eds.), *Occupational science: The evolving discipline* (pp. 309–324). Philadelphia: F. A. Davis.

Gray, J. M., Kennedy, B. L., & Zemke, R. (1996b). Dynamic systems theory: An overview. In R. Zemke & F. Clark (Eds.), *Occupational science: The evolving discipline* (pp. 297–308). Philadelphia: F. A. Davis.

Guastello, S. J., & Bond, R. W. (2007). The emergence of leadership in coordination-intensive groups. *Nonlinear Dynamics, Psychology, and Life Sciences, 11*(1), 91–117.

Hunt, J. G., & Ropo, A. (2003). Longitudinal organizational research and the third scientific discipline. *Group and Organization Management, 28,* 315–340.

Lichtenstein, B. B. (2000). Self-organized transitions: A pattern amid the chaos of transformative change. *Academy of Management Executive, 14*(4), 128–141.

Luebben, A. J., & Royeen, C. B. (2006). Leadership in a complex world: Surfing the edge of chaos. In *86th Annual American Occupational Therapy Conference Program* [electronic version]. Bethesda, MD: AOTA Press.

Osborn, R. N., & Hunt, J. G. (2007). Leadership and the choice of order: Complexity and hierarchical perspectives near the edge of chaos. *Leadership Quarterly, 18,* 319–340.

Padilla, R., & Peyton, C. (1997). Neuro-occupation. In C. B. Royeen (Ed.), *Neuroscience and occupation: Links to practice* (p. 1–31). Bethesda, MD: American Occupational Therapy Association.

Pitts, R. A. (1980). Toward a contingency theory of multibusiness organization design. *Academy of Management Review, 5,* 203–210.

Robbins, S. P., & Coulter, M. (2009). *Management* (10th ed.). Upper Saddle River, NJ: Prentice Hall.

Royeen, C. B. (2003). 2003 Eleanor Clarke Slagle Lecture— Chaotic occupational therapy: Collective wisdom for a complex profession. *American Journal of Occupational Therapy, 57,* 609–624.

Royeen, C. B. (2005). E-management: A survival guide. *Academic Leader, 21*(10), 2–9.

Royeen, C. B. (2006, April). Striving for integrity in research, teaching, and service. *Academic Leader,* pp. 22–24.

Royeen, C. B., & Luebben, A. J. (2003). Annotated bibliography of chaos for occupational therapy. *Occupational Therapy in Health Care, 16,* 63–80.

Rozdilsky, I. D., Stone, L., & Solow, A. (2003). The effects of interaction compartments on stability for competitive systems. *Journal of Theoretical Biology, 227,* 277–282.

Schneider, M., & Somers, M. (2006). Organizations as complex adaptive systems: Implications of complexity theory for leadership research. *Leadership Quarterly, 17,* 351–365.

Senge, P., Ross, R., Smith, B., Roberts, C., & Kleiner, A. (1994). *The fifth discipline fieldbook.* New York: Doubleday.

Shastri, Y., & Diwekar, U. (2006). Sustainable ecosystem management using optimal control theory: Part 1. *Journal of Theoretical Biology, 241,* 506–521.

Telford, D., & Gostick, A. (2005). The real power of integrity. *Electric Light and Power, 83*(5), 38.

Toffler, A. (1970). *Future shock.* New York: Random House.

Tse, N. S. F., & Robb, F. F. (1994). Dynamical systems theory applied to management accounting: Chaos in cost behavior in a standard costing system setting. *Transactions of the Institute of Measurement and Control, 16,* 269–279.

Waliszewki, P., Molski, M., & Konarski, J. (1998). On the holistic approach in cellular and cancer biology: Nonlinearity, complexity, and quasi-determinism of the dynamic cellular network. *Journal of Surgical Oncology, 68*(2), 70–78.

Wheatley, M. J. (1999). *Leadership and the new science: Discovering order in a chaotic world.* San Francisco: Berrett-Koehler.

Zemke, R., & Clark, F. (1996). *Occupational science: The evolving discipline.* Philadelphia: F. A. Davis.

5

Occupation-Based Practice in Management

Denise Chisholm, PhD, OTR/L, FAOTA

❖ Key Terms and Concepts

Client-centered practice. "An approach to service which embraces a philosophy of, respect for, and partnership with, people receiving services" (Law, Baptiste, & Mills, 1995, p. 253).

Occupation. "Activities that people engage in throughout their daily lives to fulfill their time and give life meaning. Occupations involve mental abilities and skills and may or may not have an observable physical dimension" (Hinojosa & Kramer, 1997, p. 865). "Activities . . . of everyday life, named, organized, and given value and meaning by individuals and a culture. Occupation is everything people to do to occupy themselves . . . enjoying life . . . and contributing to the social and economic fabric of their communities" (Law, Polatajko, Baptiste, & Townsend, 1997, p. 32).

Occupation-based interventions. "A type of occupational therapy intervention—a client-centered intervention in which the occupational therapy practitioner and client collaboratively select and design activities that have specific relevance or meaning to the client and support the client's interests, needs, health, and participation in daily life" (American Occupational Therapy Association [AOTA], 2008, p. 672).

Occupation-based practice. Services that include understanding the client as an occupational being, evaluating occupational performance, and using treatment activities that are less simulated and more similar to what they would be in the client's own context (Ward, Mitchell, & Price, 2007).

❖ Learning Objectives

After completing this chapter, you should be able to do the following:

- Describe occupation-based practice.
- Analyze the services an occupational therapy department provides in relationship to occupation-based practice.
- Identify circumstances and conditions that facilitate or limit the occupational therapy staff's ability to provide occupation-based services.

- Apply the principles of occupation-based practice to management.
- Identify resources that support the use of occupation-based practice.

Occupational therapy is unique in its focus on occupational performance. Occupational therapy practitioners enable clients to achieve their goals by helping clients overcome problems that limit their ability to perform the activities that fulfill their time and give their lives meaning (Hinojosa & Kramer, 1997). If practitioners stay true to the unique focus of the profession, their services reflect occupation-based practice. Occupational therapy managers need to ensure that their staff is providing occupation-based ser-

vices. To do so, managers need to analyze services, identify occupation-based practice opportunities and obstacles, and develop a plan of action that uses resources effectively to transform obstacles into occupation-based practice opportunities. Managers can incorporate the principles of occupation-based practice in their staff management strategies. This chapter contains practical information that occupational therapy managers can use to support and guide occupation-based practice.

1

PRINCIPLES OF OCCUPATION-BASED PRACTICE

Occupation-based practice requires occupational therapy practitioners "to know (a) what people do in their lives, (b) what motivates them, and (c) how their personal characteristics combine with the situations in which occupations are undertaken to influence successful performance" (Baum, 2000, p. 13). The client's needs and goals are the central feature of the occupational therapy process. The practitioner using a client-centered approach tailors the evaluation (occupational profile and analysis of occupational performance) and intervention (plan, implementation, and review) to the experiences, values, priorities, and desired outcomes of the client. The following concepts of client-centered practice are common to all models of client-centered, patient-centered, and family-centered care (Law, Baptiste, & Mills, 1995):

- Respect for clients and their choices;
- Recognition that clients are ultimately accountable for their decisions regarding services;
- Communication with clients using a person-centered approach;
- Client involvement in all aspects of services;
- Flexible and individualized services;
- Empowerment of clients to solve problems; and
- Focus of services on the dynamic interaction among the person, the environment, and the person's preferred occupations.

Incorporating these concepts into occupational therapy services forms the foundation for occupation-based practice.

The Canadian Occupational Performance Measure (COPM; Law et al., 2005) is a measure of a client's self-perception of occupational performance problems. The COPM is a semistructured interview tool that is used to identify and prioritize problem areas in occupational performance and rate the client's perceived performance of and satisfaction with the priority problem areas. The COPM can be included in client services regardless of client disability, age, or developmental stage and can detect change in a client's self-perception over time. To fulfill the intent of the COPM, it should be administered at the beginning of occupational therapy services and again during the course of services at appropriate intervals determined by the client and practitioner. The COPM can be administered to the members of a client's social environment (e.g., family member, caregiver), which is especially beneficial if the client is unable to be a respondent in the interview process. Additionally, the therapist may choose to interview the client and one or more of the client's significant others to compare multiple perspectives. Because of its value as an outcome measure, the COPM is best used in its entirety.

The practitioner also can use a client-centered interview to identify and prioritize problem areas of occupational performance. The client-centered interview is a strategy for obtaining information about the client's needs, wants, and expectations related to his or her occupational performance (Chisholm, Dolhi, & Schrieber, 2004). Exhibit 5.1 lists the steps of the client-centered interview process for gathering this information.

The identification of occupations the client needs, wants, and is expected to perform is based on the client's interpretation and perception. No category is considered more important than any other unless the client distinguishes it as more important. In general, *needs* are activities a person feels obligated or compelled to perform; *wants* are activities a person desires to perform; and *expectations* are activities that other people anticipate a person to perform. It is common and acceptable for a client to identify the same occupation in more than one category. Occupations identified more than once may be of greater priority than others.

As a reminder, the practitioner needs to orient the client to occupational therapy and must make sure that the client understands the definition of occupation from an occupa-

---

EXHIBIT 5.1. FORMAT FOR CLIENT-CENTERED INTERVIEW

Step 1. Consider the occupations you perform during a typical day. Provide 3–5 responses to the following:

Occupations I **need** to do:

1.
2.
3.
4.
5.

Occupations I **want** to do:

1.
2.
3.
4.
5.

Occupations I am **expected** to do:

1.
2.
3.
4.
5.

Step 2. Circle the 5 most important occupations.

tional therapy perspective before conducting the interview. Similar to the COPM, it may be beneficial to include the client's family members, caregivers, and/or significant others in the client-centered interview process. When using the client-centered interview with someone other than the client, the person is asked to consider the occupations that the client performs during a typical day and to identify the occupations he or she believes the client needs, wants, and is expected to do.

The COPM and client-centered interview are not meant to replace other assessments. These tools and strategies identify occupational performance problems and integrate a client-centered approach. Once problem areas are identified, the occupational therapist should observe the client's performance of desired occupations. The effectiveness of performance skills and patterns and the influence of contextual factors can be determined through observation of actual performance, and the occupational therapist should select assessments that measure occupational performance, such as the Performance Assessment of Self-Care Skills (PASS; Rogers & Holm, 1994). The PASS is a performance-based observational tool that yields summary scores for independence, safety, and adequacy of performance of particular self-care tasks. Tasks are presented in a standardized manner, which includes the verbal instructions and the placement of task objects, and different protocols for use in the home environment and in an occupational therapy clinic are included. In addition to occupation-based performance instruments, tools that evaluate select performance skills, performance patterns, contexts, activity demands, and client factors also may be used in the evaluation process.

Client-centered intervention is a hallmark of occupation-based practice. Occupational therapy practitioners can use an intervention continuum approach to determine whether the methods, activities, and interventions facilitate the client's engagement in occupation (Chisholm et al., 2004). The intervention continuum includes the range of occupational therapy interventions, including preparatory methods, purposeful activity, and occupation-based intervention (AOTA, 2008). Table 5.1 outlines the intervention continuum.

The categories of the intervention continuum progress left to right, with the aim of maximizing the inclusion of occupation-based interventions. Although the categories are presented in a sequence (i.e., preparatory methods are followed by purposeful activity, then occupation-based intervention), the client does not need to engage in interventions in this order. Additionally, a specific intervention (e.g., donning a sweater) may reflect more than one category of intervention in the continuum. For example, if the client is "practicing" donning and doffing a sweater in the occupational therapy clinic, it would best reflect a purposeful activity, whereas if the client was donning a sweater during his or her morning self-care routine, it would be an occupation-based intervention.

Based on the client's needs and interests, it may be appropriate to omit select categories of intervention, vary the sequence, and/or return to categories. Furthermore, all categories may not be included in a single intervention session or even in the client's intervention program. The intervention continuum is a guide for promoting the inclusion of occupation-based intervention. All interventions, regardless of the category they represent, should support

Table 5.1. Intervention Continuum

	Preparatory methods	Purposeful activity	Occupation-based intervention
Description	"Methods and techniques that prepare the client for occupational performance. Used in preparation for or concurrently with purposeful and occupation-based activities" (AOTA, 2008, p. 674).	"A goal-directed behavior or activity within a therapeutically designed context that leads to an occupation or occupations. Specifically selected activities that allow the client to develop skills that enhance occupational engagement" (AOTA, 2008, p. 674).	"A type of occupational therapy intervention—a client-centered intervention in which the occupational therapy practitioner and client collaboratively select and design activities that have specific relevance or meaning to the client and support the client's interests, needs, health, and participation in daily life" (AOTA, 2008, p. 672).
Examples	Physical agent modalities, passive/active range of motion, exercise, massage, splinting, sensory input, education, etc.	Practice . . . making a sandwich, dressing, cleaning windows, shooting a basketball, crafts, bean bag toss, turning the pages of a book, role play activities, money transactions, relaxation techniques, etc.	Laundering own clothes, copying a desired recipe from a magazine, writing in personal journal, telephoning a friend, typing own résumé, sewing a button on own shirt, baking cookies for family, purchasing items from the gift shop, transferring from own wheelchair to own car, playing checkers with family member, cleaning sink area after performing morning grooming tasks, etc.

the occupations the client needs to do, wants to do, and is expected to do. Planning and implementing intervention sessions that include occupation-based interventions often take more thought and time than preparatory and purposeful activity interventions; however, when managers support, facilitate, and require their staff to focus services on the client's occupations, occupation-based practice is the standard of practice of the department.

ANALYZING OCCUPATIONAL THERAPY SERVICES

To support, facilitate, and require occupation-based services, the manager needs to first determine whether the current services reflect occupation-based practice. Analyzing services is a critical first step. The analysis is best completed not solely by the manager or one staff member but rather with all staff members (occupational therapists, occupational therapy assistants, and technicians) engaged in the analysis process. Students completing their fieldwork experience with the department also should be included in the analysis process because they bring fresh perspective and innovative ideas in addition to their education.

Engaging everyone in the process fosters a more in-depth analysis of occupational therapy services. The staff and students also can enhance their practical understanding of occupation-based practice and evaluate the services they provide to their clients. Chisholm et al. (2004) identified a "practice analysis" for the individual practitioner. A similar process can be used to analyze occupational therapy services at the departmental level. As with any analysis, the first few steps require collection of data about the setting, clients and their problem areas, and interventions.

The first step is to identify the demographic and clinical characteristics of the practice setting and client population: type of setting (e.g., acute care, rehabilitation, school), diagnoses or conditions of clients, gender and age distribution, typical occupational roles of clients, average frequency and duration of services, typical discharge destination, and reimbursement sources. Step 2 includes identifying typical problem areas of the clients. The domains and items within the domains described in the *Occupational Therapy Practice Framework, 2nd Edition* (*Framework–II*; AOTA, 2008) can be used to identify and categorize problem areas.

Step 3 addresses intervention. Using the list of problem areas identified in Step 2, examples of interventions typically used to address the identified problem occupations, client factors, performance skills, performance patterns, and/or contexts and environments are identified. In Step 4, the data collected in the previous steps are examined using the intervention continuum (i.e., preparatory methods, purposeful activity, and occupation-based intervention). This step requires reviewing the interventions identified in Step 3 and organizing them by the type of intervention each represents in the real-life clinical situation of the department. Once interventions are organized by type, examine the distribution. Are the interventions evenly dis-

tributed? Do the majority of interventions represent one particular type of intervention—that is, are they preparatory methods, purposeful activities, or occupation-based interventions?

Step 5 requires identifying the range of interventions that could be used in the clinical practice of the department. The type of practice setting and client population(s) may restrict or promote the use of certain types of interventions. The intent, however, is to challenge the usual care provided by the department and to stretch the staff's innovative thinking. Using the common problem areas identified in Step 2, interventions are identified across the continuum that are used or could be used to better individualize care and direct occupational therapy services toward the inclusion of occupation-based interventions that reflect the clients' preferred and meaningful occupations.

The final step, Step 6, extends beyond the direct services provided by the department. Two lists are generated in Step 6—a list of circumstances and conditions that support the staff in providing occupation-based interventions and a list of issues that limit the staff in providing occupation-based interventions. These issues relate to the context and environment, including the facility and clinic space, materials, people, administration, temporal factors, processes, and culture. Exhibit 5.2 outlines the steps of the department practice analysis.

Completing a departmental practice analysis will lay the foundation to ensure that the services provided reflect occupation-based practice. The practice analysis is dynamic and should be reviewed and updated at least annually as a quality improvement activity. Departments, programs, and services grow and change; the needs of each are different, based on many factors. Analyzing a department's practice regularly assists the manager in proactively facilitating the advancement of services rather than being reactive after the

---

EXHIBIT 5.2. DEPARTMENT PRACTICE ANALYSIS

Step 1. Identify the demographic characteristics of the practice setting and client population.

Step 2. Identify typical problem areas of the client population.

Step 3. Identify example interventions typically used to address the problem areas of the client population (see Step 2).

Step 4. Categorize the interventions (see Step 3) using the intervention continuum.

Step 5. Identify intervention options across the intervention continuum that could be used to address the problem areas of the client population (see Step 2).

Step 6. Identify the circumstances and conditions that support occupation-based practice and those that limit occupation-based practice.

changes have already occurred. The departmental practice analysis can be modified and used as a management tool for monitoring the services and performance of staff members. The steps can be modified to address the interventions provided by an individual practitioner. The analysis can be conducted as a self-reflective exercise and/or as observation of performance. Additionally, the lists generated by the individual practitioner in Step 6 can be used as a catalyst for a practical discussion addressing strategies for enhancing performance and proposing change to facilitate the expansion of occupation-based practice at the individual and departmental levels.

OCCUPATION-BASED PRACTICE CONSIDERATIONS

The objective is to provide occupation-based services— that is, services that focus on occupation throughout the occupational therapy process. As previously addressed, the circumstances and conditions within the context and environment either can facilitate or limit the use of occupation-based practice. The manager needs to have a working knowledge of these circumstances and conditions to know how they positively or negatively influence the provision of services, and to develop and implement strategies to maximize the circumstances and conditions that facilitate occupation-based practice and moderate those that limit its use. Step 6 of the departmental practice analysis can assist the manager in recognizing the issues. Being able to name and describe the issue is essential in determining whether the issue, or a certain aspect of the issue, facilitates or limits occupation-based services. Once a circumstance is identified as limiting the use of occupation, then a plan can be developed that outlines a sequence of actions to alter the characteristics of the circumstance toward facilitating and maximizing the use of occupation. As with any well-thought-out action plan, someone needs not only to supervise the implementation of the sequential actions but also to monitor the outcomes. The manager does not need to be the person who directly performs the supervision and monitoring, but he or she needs to ensure that they are completed. Remember, similar to gathering the data in Step 6 of the practice analysis, it is equally beneficial to engage all staff members (i.e., occupational therapists, occupational therapy assistants, technicians) and students in the analysis of the facility and clinic context and environment.

The following sections address the facility and clinic context and environment factors of people, space, materials, administration, temporal factors, processes, and culture.

People

Look around the department and facility. Who are the people you see, and what is their relationship with the department and its staff members? The presence of these people, the relationships among them, and the expectations they have of occupational therapy services are important for the manager to recognize and address. These people include other health care professionals (e.g., phy-

sicians, nursing personnel, other therapy staff), clerical and maintenance staff, facility administrators, clients and their significant others (e.g., spouses, parents, children, friends, caregivers), and occupational therapy practitioners and students. Do they understand the unique focus of occupational therapy and its relevance to the services they receive, provide, or oversee? It is the responsibility of all occupational therapy practitioners—not just managers—to ensure that the people who come in contact with the department, no matter how indirect or brief the relationship, understand that the focus of occupational therapy services is on *occupations* that is, the "activities that people engage in throughout their daily lives to fulfill their time and give life meaning" (Hinojosa & Kramer, 1997, p. 865). Managers need to support their staff's efforts in educating and demonstrating how occupation is central to occupational therapy services. Supportive activities, including a journal club, case presentations, and individual and group discussions, can educate others about occupation-based practice and demonstrate its significance to the people connected with the department.

Access, read, summarize, and present evidence that supports occupation-based practice. Many occupational therapy practitioners are not comfortable using or educating others about the evidence that supports occupational therapy practice. As with the acquisition of any skill, the more a person practices a skill, the more advanced skill performance becomes. Managers need to facilitate the development of staff's evidence-based practice skills.

Establish a department journal club in which members read and analyze occupational therapy–related journal articles. The journal club can include all staff members and students, or it can be divided by specific diagnostic categories (e.g., stroke, brain injury, developmental disabilities) or practice setting (e.g., acute care, rehabilitation, school based). Use the journal club as an opportunity for building the evidence-based skills of the staff. Club members should not merely read and repeat what the author reports but rather use teaching techniques to address unfamiliar study designs, statistical analyses, outcome measures, and so on. Foster a supportive environment where learning is the goal and collaborative problem solving is encouraged. Students can be significant contributors and facilitators to this process because they are familiar with the most current evidence resources.

Set reasonable expectations for meetings. Consider meeting once per month, every 6 weeks, or even a few weeks after the most recent edition of a professional journal is received. Create an evidence-based library that is relevant to the practice of the department. Share the evidence that supports occupational therapy services with relevant people, such as physicians and other health professionals. In addition to providing them with the article, summarize it and include in the summary its relevance to your shared client population. Arrange for a staff member or pair of staff members to provide a staff development session on the evidence related to a specific topic. The evidence also can be summarized into a user-friendly 1-page handout for clients and their families. These evidence-based activities are effective learning assignments for students during fieldwork experiences. They are occupation-based assignments because they are meaningful for the student and the department.

Include case presentations and discussions in departmental meetings, or schedule them as a separate educational session. Be sure to focus the presentation and discussion on occupation. How did the occupational therapy evaluation (i.e., occupational profile and analysis of occupational performance) address areas of occupation? Identify methods for directing more time and effort during the evaluation to the occupations the client wants, needs, and is expected to do; determine the occupations the client can do and has done; and identify those factors that act as supports or barriers to the client's occupational performance. Use the intervention continuum to categorize the interventions the practitioner is using or plans to include in the intervention program.

- Do the interventions span all of the categories of the continuum (i.e., preparatory methods, purposeful activities, occupation-based interventions)?
- Do the interventions support the client's meaningful daily occupations?
- If preparatory methods and purposeful activities are requisite given the client's diagnosis and level of functioning, are the interventions organized in the plan so that they sequentially progress toward the inclusion of occupation-based interventions?
- Is the practitioner educating the client on the relationship between the interventions and his or her daily occupations?
- Does the practitioner reinforce that relationship during each therapy session?

The intent is not to negate the proposed or current intervention plan but rather to use the department's resources by having the staff brainstorm ideas and contribute alternatives that will ultimately enhance occupation-based services. The manager's role is to model behavior that creates a supportive learning environment in which ideas are generated and respected to facilitate the professional development of all members of the department. The student programs of many departments require a case presentation as a learning assignment for fieldwork students. Structure the case presentation format so that it reflects occupation-based practice.

It does not matter who the person is or what the service is; when people understand the service and how it will benefit them, they are more likely to be satisfied customers. Occupational therapy managers (and practitioners) should want clients to be satisfied customers. They want clients to understand how the occupation-based interventions they engage in will facilitate their ability to engage in the mean-

ingful occupations that they include in their daily routine. Occupational therapy practitioners should reinforce the connection between the client's daily occupations and the interventions included in the occupational therapy intervention program in each and every session. Clients should not be left to wonder why they are doing a certain intervention or how it relates to their health and wellness. They need to have as many choices as possible regarding the interventions they receive, and practitioners need to incorporate clients' choices in the intervention program.

The manager, in collaboration with the staff, should establish a client-centered approach as a standard of practice in the department. Use of a client-centered approach can be included as an item for measuring a practitioner's performance. Additionally, the staff should be encouraged to share all levels of evidence with clients. Have professional magazines (e.g., *OT Practice*) and journals (e.g., *American Journal of Occupational Therapy*) available in client waiting areas. Clients and their significant others are interested in the services they are receiving. Browsing through a magazine or journal can help people understand the breadth and depth of occupational therapy services.

Practitioners and students often look to other people as the reason for any misunderstanding or lack of awareness regarding occupational therapy services. However, occupational therapy practitioners and students often minimize the value and power of occupation as a therapeutic intervention. From the materials used in intervention sessions to the practitioner's or student's definition of occupation and explanation of occupation-based practice, everything they do and say should emphasize occupations and the relevance they have to an individual's health and wellness. Managers must challenge staff members to critically assess themselves and their colleagues by asking the following questions (Chisholm et al., 2004):

- Do they understand occupational therapy's unique focus?
- Do they have their own user-friendly style for describing occupational therapy's domain and process to others—their clients, colleagues, and administrators?
- Do they support occupation-based practice in what they say and do?
- Do they use and discuss the evidence for occupation-based practice?
- Are they occupation-based practitioners?

Managers also need to critically assess themselves to determine whether they are effective role models for their staff. Do they focus on and facilitate the use of occupation as a practitioner and a manager?

Space

People perform their daily occupations in a wide range of natural and built environments. For clients and staff to focus on and maximize the use of occupations, the spaces services are provided in need to be as similar as possible to the client's own context. Because the "real world" offers a wide range of natural and built environments, it is ideal for facilities and clinics to offer a broad range of environmental options.

First, examine the clinic space of your department. Describe the size, furniture, layout, functional utility (for both staff and clients), flow (especially during heavy traffic hours), aesthetic design, acoustic qualities, accessibility or user-friendliness (again, for both staff and clients), and flexibility. The manager and staff need to thoroughly evaluate how the department space is being used. Does the space offer opportunities for clients to engage in a range of occupations? For example, does the space support interventions related to the occupations of dressing, feeding, functional mobility, meal preparation and cleanup, health management and maintenance, rest, informal personal education participation, job performance, play and/or exploration and participation, and social participation? Would minor changes to the layout improve the functional utility, flow, or accessibility of the clinic space? Would practical adaptations allow for greater inclusion of occupation-based interventions? Find out how clients and staff, including students, feel when they are in the space. Does it allow for effective communication between clients and staff for both public and private evaluations and interventions?

Next, examine the space outside the clinic and department. Consider the space inside and outside of the facility. An obvious option for engaging in occupation-based interventions is the client's room. However, consider the other spaces where people engage in occupations—lounges, vending machine and public telephone areas, gift shops, cafeterias, public bathrooms, green space outside the building, and so forth. Challenge usual care—can the staff identify and use spaces in and around the facility that would allow for increased inclusion of occupation-based interventions? Maximize the clinic space—use furniture that is found in real-world environments (e.g., a sofa, a recliner, a double bed, conventional table and chairs), and arrange it to look like a natural living space. Identify the space needs of the department and possible solutions. Make the department space needs and solution options known to the most appropriate administrator, and persevere in your reasonable requests. As with any analysis, the manager should include the staff and students in the department space examination process. The viewpoints and creative ideas of many people are beneficial in identifying alternative options for the use of space.

Materials

The department practice analysis can assist in determining the materials needed to provide occupation-based services. Step 1 of the occupation-based analysis helps the manager identify and describe the population of clients being served. Once the occupational needs of the population are determined (Step 2; see Exhibit 5.2), the range of typical intervention options can be identified (Steps 2–5; see

Exhibit 5.2). A list of required equipment and supplies can be generated for each intervention. The materials needed for occupation-based interventions and purposeful activities are more likely to be available in people's homes and for purchase in local retail stores than the materials for preparatory methods. Examples of these materials include dishes, pots and pans, watering cans, magazines, sewing kits, banking forms, job applications, newspapers, and crafts. Additionally, clients often have their own materials for occupation-based interventions (e.g., hygiene supplies, clothing, leisure activities, mail items).

Create a list of the equipment and supplies in the department. This exercise is a great student project that can help orient students to the department. Often the list that is generated includes equipment and supplies that the staff forgot were available in the occupational therapy department. It also offers an opportunity for reorganization of the equipment and supplies for more efficient access and use. Explore whether the equipment and supplies are associated with preparatory methods (e.g., therapy putty, cuff weights, education handouts, visual perception worksheets, massage gel, therapy balls, peg boards) or are used to engage in occupations (e.g., coins and money wrappers, envelopes, coupon flyers, gift paper and boxes, recipe cards, cooking utensils, towels, bed linens, mop and broom, vacuum cleaner, pill bottles).

Be creative in obtaining the equipment and supplies that your department needs to provide occupation-based services. Contact the facility volunteer office, maintenance department, and service groups and organizations to assist you in obtaining the real-world materials needed for clients to engage in their preferred and meaningful occupations. The staff (and clients) can gather materials on an ongoing basis—mail advertisements, coupon flyers, catalogs, coins, household items, gardening tools, board games, wrapping paper, greeting cards, and so forth. Sometimes people associate the cost of an item with its perceived value—that is, they believe that if a piece of equipment or supply is ordered from a therapy catalog at a high cost, then it must have a high therapeutic value. The materials people use in their everyday lives, however, have even greater therapeutic value because they will ultimately be the items clients use when therapy services are no longer needed or provided. Practitioners need to remember that the materials they use when engaging in their daily occupations are the same types of materials that clients use, so an occupation-based practice clinic is filled with real-world materials.

Administration

There are administrators inside and outside of the occupational therapy department. The manager of the department is considered an administrator but also likely reports to administrators of the facility. The manager needs to expect department staff to perform occupation-based services while also advocating their use with the facility administrators. The interests of the department and occupational therapy services need to be effectively represented. If a representative from occupational therapy is not at the table when administrative decisions are being made, the department's needs and the focus of services may be easily overlooked.

The unique focus of occupational therapy's skilled services needs to be the central theme conveyed by the department representative. He or she needs to describe and illustrate occupation-based services, highlight the outcomes, and provide administrators with evidence that supports the inclusion of occupation-based services to enhance the quality of care and client outcomes. The manager may or may not always be the department representative. However, the manager must ensure not only that the department is represented on committees and at meetings but also that the representative effectively communicates the relevance and meaning of occupation-based practice. The manager can direct a department project to measure and examine the clients' outcomes (e.g., occupational performance, client satisfaction, role competence). The results can be shared with the facility administrators, and opportunities for presenting and/or publishing the findings can be explored.

Temporal Factors

Managers commonly hear occupational therapy practitioners identify lack of time as a reason for not providing occupation-based services. Yes, it does take time to find out what occupations the client wants, needs, and is expected to do; evaluate what the client can do; and provide interventions that facilitate the client's engagement in occupations related to health and participation. And yes, occupation-based interventions typically take longer to implement as they are activities with a beginning, a middle, and an end that have relevance and meaning to the client and support the client's interests, needs, health, and participation in daily life. It typically takes longer to change bed linens and load the dishwasher than it does to ambulate across the clinic room and do resistive upper-extremity exercises. But occupation-based interventions reflect the meaningful occupations the client needs to do, wants to do, or is expected to do after occupational therapy services are discontinued. So yes, occupational therapy practitioners should provide services that reflect occupation-based practice because although they may take increased time to implement, they are more meaningful.

The manager can guide the staff in critically thinking about how they as individual practitioners use their time and also how they as a department or group use their time. Review the evaluation process. Do the occupational therapists use an occupation-based approach—that is, do they evaluate occupational performance by observing the client performing activities relevant to desired occupations, noting the effectiveness of performance skills? Or do the occupational therapists use the session to evaluate the wide range of performance skills and then determine which occupations the skill deficits likely affect? Focusing on the

performance of occupations in the most natural setting, followed by evaluating only the performance skills that are restricting occupational performance, can streamline the evaluation process and also ensures that occupation is central in the evaluation process. Additionally, actively engaging the client throughout the occupational therapy process promotes a focus on what is important to him or her and can expedite clinical reasoning when planning and implementing interventions. Whether to include an intervention option in the session or program is easily determined by its relevance to the client's priority occupations.

Using the departmental practice analysis, the manager (and staff) can determine the typical occupations of the department's clients. Once identified, the materials needed to implement them can be determined, and the equipment and supplies can be organized for easy access and use. The development of intervention kits is one time-saving suggestion. Individual intervention kits can be created that include all of the materials needed so the practitioner can spend time implementing the intervention instead of gathering the materials. Depending on the practice setting, group interventions can be developed to address the needs of homogenous clients. Similar to the individual intervention kit, the materials needed to conduct the group intervention can be organized and available for immediate use. Yes, it does take time to develop and assemble the individual and group intervention kits. However, the department's intervention resources can be developed over time. The manager may consider having each staff member sign up to compile the "occupation-based kit of the month." The practitioner develops the idea and presents it to the staff for feedback. Once the idea, materials, and method of implementation are refined, the kits can be assembled. Intervention kits are a great occupation-based student assignment because they are both meaningful to the student's learning and useful to the department. The manager also needs to use all levels of occupational therapy personnel prudently, including him- or herself as manager, occupational therapists, occupational therapy assistants, and aides and technicians. Department staff should be assigned tasks based on the skill level required.

Processes

Managers are well aware of the many department and facility processes. Examples of processes include caseload assignments, productivity standards, documentation, and reimbursement. The manager who has occupation-based practice as a central theme when considering the development, implementation, and monitoring of policies and procedures is more likely to have a department staff of occupation-based practitioners and to implement procedures that assist the staff in providing occupation-based services.

Scheduling of clients can be an issue. Do practitioners have flexibility in scheduling their clients—that is, can they schedule clients who have similar occupational performance needs during the same session? An advantage to this approach is that clients are able to interact with other clients who are experiencing similar challenges. Depending on the practice setting and reimbursement regulations, including group interventions in the clients' therapy programs can be considered. Group interventions can be designed to complement individual interventions. Practitioners also should consider the coordination of their clients' therapy services. That is, if a client requires preparatory methods that are included in his or her services by another therapy provider (e.g., physical therapy), coordinate the schedule so that the client receives occupational therapy after the other service. Thus, they have already received preparatory methods of intervention and are prepared at the start of the occupational therapy session to engage in purposeful activities and occupation-based interventions.

The manager should critically analyze the frequency and duration patterns of services. Are clients getting the amount of services they need by the appropriate occupational therapy practitioner? Also, the manager should analyze the content of the session. Are the interventions occupation-based? Do they reflect the unique contribution of occupational therapy services? If an observer (e.g., a third-party payer representative) were watching the session to determine payment, would he or she view the interventions as representing daily occupations or as being duplicative of other services (e.g., preparatory methods)? Does the length of the session correspond with the usual time for performing the occupation it is targeting? Administering an occupation-based intervention in one unit of time (15 minutes) would be difficult to do because the majority of daily occupations take longer than 15 minutes to perform. Additionally, because intervention sessions include training and monitoring of performance, the time to perform the occupation-based intervention is usually extended.

Evidence-based clinical protocols can be developed to ensure that occupational therapy services employ cutting-edge rehabilitation practices that focus on clients' meaningful occupations. Clinical protocols are not clinical pathways or a "cookbook approach" to therapy; they are general guidelines based on the evidence that are flexible enough to allow for client-centered modification while structured enough to ensure that therapy is consistent across facilities. The process for developing clinical protocols starts with searching, examining, and synthesizing available literature related to the specific clinical population. The synthesis guides the formation of therapy protocols that incorporate research-derived best practices tailored to meet the specific needs of the clinical population. The therapy protocols target the most commonly affected occupational performance problems of the clinical population. Each clinical protocol specifies (1) the assessment tools to measure the occupational performance problem, (2) interventions to address the problem, (3) how the interventions should be conducted, and (4) the expected clinical outcomes. The use of clinical protocols can ensure best practice occupational therapy services for a population and consistent services for multiple facilities.

Once the clinical protocols are put into practice, the next step is to examine the outcomes. When therapy is standardized, the manager can determine whether differences in outcomes were the result of differences in the intervention or due to differences in other factors. Additionally, a multidisciplinary committee can develop evidence-based clinical protocols across rehabilitation services.

The manager needs to ensure not only that occupation-based services are being provided but also that the staff's documentation reflects occupation-based services. Documentation includes data that can be used for many purposes, including client care, interdisciplinary communication, program evaluation, clinical outcomes, reimbursement, regulatory agency requirements, and legal deliberations. Does the documentation generated by the department staff represent occupation-based practice? Review the documentation outlines, forms, and/or screens. Does the terminology support occupation-based practice? Is "occupation" included in the report, and if so, is it included on the first page, embedded in another section, used only to identify the client's worker role, or briefly addressed on the last page?

The language included in the *Framework–II* (AOTA, 2008) reflects occupational therapy's unique focus. Managers should use the *Framework* as a resource when developing or updating documentation forms or reports. There is an extensive list of life activities that people engage in outlined in the areas of occupation. Within each area of occupation (i.e., activities of daily living [ADLs], instrumental activities of daily living [IADLs], rest and sleep, education, work, play, leisure, social participation), there are a number of activities or occupations. For example, shopping is one of 12 occupations in the IADL category, and the occupation of shopping includes preparing shopping lists; selecting, purchasing, and transporting items; selecting methods of payment; and completing money transactions. Meaningful occupations included in the client's daily routine need to be highlighted in occupational therapy documentation. If "occupations" are concealed in the document, there is no guarantee that the reader will find them; if the document emphasizes performance skills and client factors such as body functions, then the reader will likely perceive that those are the primary focus of occupational therapy services.

Because occupations are performed in contexts and environments, sufficient attention needs to be devoted to the cultural, personal, temporal, virtual, physical, and social "conditions within and surrounding the client that influence performance" (AOTA, 2008, p. 645). *Performance patterns*—that is, the patterns of behavior or the habits, routines, rituals, and roles related to performance—also should be addressed in occupational therapy documentation. Occupation and the contexts and environments, patterns, skills, and factors related to performance should be included in documentation; however, occupation should be central to all reports. If occupation, the unique focus of occupational therapy services, isn't prominent in the document, then the reader will likely not acknowledge it. When the uniqueness of a skilled service is overlooked or discounted, it is likely that the value of the service is diminished. And when a service isn't valued, it is typically not required or reimbursed. Review and analysis of documentation forms can be a valuable learning assignment for fieldwork students. They bring a fresh viewpoint to the analysis process and can creatively assist the department in identifying formats that highlight occupation more effectively. In turn, the manager and staff should be receptive to the student's feedback and suggestions.

Culture

Managers (and practitioners) need to understand, appreciate, and accept the influence of culture in organizations. *Culture* consists of the "customs, beliefs, activity patterns, behavior standards, and expectations accepted by the society of which the person is a member" (AOTA, 1994, p. 1054). There are many levels to the "society" in which occupational therapists are members or workers. The health care system can be viewed as a society, as well as the facility and the department. In addition to organizational societies, practitioners have to understand, appreciate, and accept the diverse cultures of clients. Managers need to consider how each society views occupation-based practice, and asking the following questions can help clarify matters of culture:

- Do members of the department promote, support, and provide occupation-based services? Do members view them as valuable?
- Do members identify and adhere to occupation-based practice as a behavior standard?
- How do members of the facility view occupation-based services?
- How is occupation-based practice addressed in policies of the health care system?
- The primary role of health care organizations is to serve the health needs of the individuals and families of the community. Does the organization view occupation-based practice as necessary to meeting health needs?

If any of the societies in which practitioners work (i.e., department, facility or organization, health care system) does not value occupation-based services, or if the degree of value is questionable, managers (and practitioners) need to have a strategic objective to increase the significance of occupation within the society. The strategy needs to focus on attaining a working knowledge of the systems of the department, facility and organization, and health care system and being knowledgeable about alternative systems for each. Identify connections between the culture and use of occupation as a therapeutic focal point, and capitalize on the connections to blend occupation into the cultural beliefs, standards, and expectations.

Managers also need to recognize that organizational systems change, sometimes gradually and other times in a quick, stark manner. Because organizational change, especially in health care, is a certainty today, the task of understanding, appreciating, and accepting the influence of culture in organizations is an ongoing challenge. Therefore, managers cannot afford to be complacent; the occupational therapy manager needs to be forward thinking in making sure that services that include understanding the client as an occupational being, evaluating occupational performance, and using treatment activities that are less simulated and more similar to what they would be in the client's own context (Ward et al., 2007) have a valued role within the culture of health care organizations.

Circumstances and conditions that affect the use of occupation-based practice are a given. The issues identified in this section are not meant to be all inclusive but rather are intended to provide an overview of the typical circumstances and conditions that arise in practice settings. The challenge for the manager is to determine whether the situation (or an aspect of the situation) is currently facilitating or limiting services that focus on occupation. In general, the situations are continually changing, so the manager needs to routinely assess the environment to determine current issues and their impact on occupation-based services. When a situation limits the use of occupation, the manager, in collaboration with the staff, needs to identify opportunities for transforming the circumstance or condition to endorse and advance the use of occupation-based services. The transition process requires the use of problem-solving techniques—that is, identifying the best option from all possible options, implementing the chosen option, and then evaluating the outcome. If the outcome does not achieve the desired response, the manager needs to revisit the possible options to determine the current best option to implement. It is a trial-and-error process. Managers need to recognize that change usually does not occur quickly and that perseverance and adaptation are critical elements of transforming obstacles into opportunities.

OCCUPATION-BASED STAFF MANAGEMENT

Occupational therapy managers often apply their clinical practice skills to their management responsibilities. Ideally, the occupational therapy manager's clinical practice skills include knowledge and proficiency as an occupation-based practitioner. As with the principles of many clinical practice skills, the principles of occupation-based practice can be applied to management, specifically the management of staff. Baum (2000) described the requirements of occupation-based practice for the occupational therapy practitioner as "knowing what people do in their lives, what motivates them, and how their personal characteristics combine with the situations in which occupations are undertaken to influence successful performance" (p. 13). The occupational therapy practitioner's "people" are clients. Similarly, the occupational therapy manager's "people" or clients are the occupational therapy staff they manage. An effective manager knows what his or her staff members do in their lives, what motivates them, and how each staff member's personal characteristics combine with the situations to influence successful performance. The needs and goals of the staff are one of the central features of the management process. Comparable to the practitioner using a client-centered approach, the manager using a "staff-centered" approach tailors the process to the experiences, values, priorities, and desired outcomes of the staff. The occupation-based manager needs to consider the concepts of client-centered practice (Law et al., 1995) and appropriately integrate them into their management approach. That is, managers need to

- Respect staff and their work-related choices;
- Recognize that staff are ultimately accountable for their work decisions;
- Communicate with staff using a person-centered approach;
- Facilitate staff involvement in all aspects of department management;
- Provide flexible and individualized management;
- Empower staff to solve problems; and
- Focus management on the dynamic interaction among the staff member, his or her work environment, and his or her preferred and required work occupations.

The occupational therapy manager needs to balance use of a client-centered approach with his or her staff with fulfillment of responsibilities to the facility administration.

The client-centered interview outlined in Exhibit 5.1 can be adapted for use as a staff management strategy. The occupation-based manager can include a "staff-centered interview" in job performance reviews. Exhibit 5.3 outlines steps of the staff-centered interview process for obtaining information about the staff member's needs, wants, and expectations related to his or her job performance. This strategy can assist the manager in developing an action plan in collaboration with the staff member. The manager conducts the interview using theoretical and practical effective communication and interview techniques, including preparation of the person (staff member) and setting; attending and nurturing actions; listening and observation skills; and paraphrasing, questioning, and providing feedback (Denton, 1987).

A job performance review typically includes an analysis of the staff member's clinical practice. Similar to the analysis of occupational therapy services described previously in this chapter, the occupational therapy manager can focus on the use of occupation when analyzing the individual staff member's clinical performance. The analysis can be multifaceted, including a self-appraisal by the staff member, one or more peer appraisals, and a supervisor or manager appraisal. The data for the analysis are preferably collected throughout the review process period (typically 1 year) to obtain a balanced view of the staff member's clinical performance. The analysis should include the services that the staff member provides or participates in across the occupational therapy process: evaluation (occupational profile and analysis of occupational performance), intervention (plan,

---

EXHIBIT 5.3. STAFF-CENTERED INTERVIEW

Step 1. Provide 3–5 responses to the following:

Work-related occupations I **need** to do:

1.

2.

3.

4.

5.

Work-related occupations I **want** to do:

1.

2.

3.

4.

5.

Work-related occupations I am **expected** to do:

1.

2.

3.

4.

5.

Step 2. Circle the 5 most important work-related occupations.

---

implementation, and review), and outcomes. The intervention continuum can be used to analyze the degree to which services focus on occupation.

The manager can observe and appraise an evaluation session conducted by a staff member (occupational therapist). The appraisal can include identifying aspects of the session that address the client's engagement in meaningful occupations. For example, does the occupational therapist include a client-centered interview in the evaluation session? And how does the occupational therapist use the information when collaborating with the client to determine the intervention plan?

The manager also can observe and appraise an intervention session implemented by a staff member (occupational therapist or occupational therapy assistant) and categorize and examine the occupational therapy interventions administered using the intervention continuum. Are the interventions preparatory methods, purposeful activity, and/or occupation-based interventions? Do the interventions support the client's engagement in his or her preferred, meaningful occupations? The analysis can include suggestions for increasing the use of occupation-based interventions and enhancing the relationship between the client's personal occupations and the interventions.

An appraisal of the staff member's documentation also should be included in the job performance review. Similar to the observed performance, written performance can be appraised by the staff member, peers, and the supervisor or manager. Within the constraints of the documentation forms and processes, how and to what extent does the staff member address the client's engagement in preferred, meaningful occupations? Does the report of the evaluation tools administered, the intervention plan (objectives and measurable goals) developed, and the interventions included in the client's occupational therapy program emphasize occupation?

The job performance review also can include an opportunity for staff members to identify circumstances and conditions within the context of the department, facility, and community that facilitate or limit their ability to provide occupation-based services. It is beneficial for the manager not only to solicit a list of perceived problems but also to request potential solutions for transitioning the issue to an opportunity to promote occupation-based practice. When occupational therapy managers use occupation-based strategies, they are modeling a staff-centered management style that fosters respect and a two-way dialogue, supports empowerment, and embraces occupational therapy's unique focus on occupational performance.

EVIDENCE FOR OCCUPATION-BASED PRACTICE

Health care professionals are challenged to provide evidence that supports the effectiveness of their services. Occupational therapy practitioners need to provide evidence that engagement in occupation-based interventions promotes increased health and participation in life. In 2000, Margo B. Holm closed her Eleanor Clarke Slagle Lecture asking occupational therapy practitioners, "If in the year 2010 you stand accused of practicing occupational therapy based on research, will there be enough evidence to convict you?" (p. 584).

The good news is that the year 2010 is now, and the body of empirical evidence that supports the unique contribution of occupation therapy services continues to expand. Not only do occupational therapists need to provide occupation-based services, but they also need to provide pragmatic evidence that supports the effectiveness of occupation-based practice. Previously in this chapter, the manager was encouraged to establish a department journal club or clubs and an evidence-based library that is relevant to the practice of the department. It is beneficial for the occupational therapy manager to establish a system that requires practitioners (and students) to find, read, and interpret the available evidence. The essential element in ensuring the success of the system is that it be conducted in a supportive, shared learning environment. The learning environment needs not only to promote the acquisition of

knowledge for the good of the individual practitioner but also to determine the applicability of the evidence to clinical practice.

Literature should be gathered from all available electronic resources (e.g., OT Search, Medline, Cochrane Database) using keywords such as *occupation-based intervention, occupation, purposeful activity,* and *added purpose.* Articles also can be retrieved from the recent editions of professional journals. The following list is not meant to be all inclusive but is intended to provide a sample of professional journals:

- *American Journal of Geriatric Psychiatry*
- *American Journal of Occupational Therapy*
- *Archives of Physical Medicine and Rehabilitation*
- *Australian Journal of Occupational Therapy*
- *British Journal of Occupational Therapy*
- *Canadian Journal of Occupational Therapy*
- *Clinical Rehabilitation*
- *Disability and Rehabilitation*
- *International Journal of Rehabilitation Research*
- *JAMA*
- *Journal of Gerontology*
- *Occupational Therapy in Geriatrics*
- *Occupational Therapy in Health Care*
- *Occupational Therapy in Mental Health*
- *Occupational Therapy International*
- *OTJR: Occupation, Participation and Health*
- *Physical and Occupational Therapy in Pediatrics*
- *Stroke.*

The intervention continuum (occupation-based intervention, purposeful activity, and preparatory methods) can be used to categorize the type of intervention being investigated.

Appendix 5.A provides an overview of some of the evidence that addresses occupation-based practice. At least one of the interventions described in each article reflects occupation-based practice, as determined by comparing the described intervention with the definitions of purposeful activity and occupation-based intervention in the *Framework–II* (AOTA, 2008). *Occupation-based intervention* is defined as "a client-centered intervention in which the occupational therapy practitioner and client collaboratively select and design activities that have specific relevance or meaning to the client and support the client's interests, needs, health, and participation in daily life" (AOTA, 2008, p. 672). *Purposeful activity* is defined as "a goal-directed behavior or activity within a therapeutically designed context that leads to an occupation or occupations. Specifically selected activities that allow the client to develop skills that enhance occupational engagement" (AOTA, 2008, p. 674).

SUMMARY

The occupational therapy manager must ensure that the services that his or her staff provides reflect occupation-based practice. To do so, the manager must understand the principles of occupation-based practice as well as analyze current services to determine whether they focus on occupational performance and identify strategies for supporting and maximizing the focus on occupation throughout the occupational therapy process. The analysis process should occur at least annually and include all staff members, including students. In-depth analysis results in identifying circumstances and conditions within the context and environment that either facilitate or limit the use of occupation-based practice. People, space, materials, administration, temporal factors, processes, and culture each have the potential of being an obstacle for occupation-based practice. With an understanding of the practical issues that positively or negatively affect the provision of services, the occupational therapy manager can better identify and implement strategies to change obstacles into opportunities for facilitating occupation-based services.

Case Examples

LEVEL I FIELDWORK

Jennifer was in her third term of a master's of occupational therapy program. Her Level I fieldwork experience was in a community-based adult day care program for older adults and adults with functional limitations, and she was excited to begin applying what she had been learning in her coursework to services with real-life clients.

One of the required assignments for the theory and practice course was to formulate and implement an occupation-based intervention session with a group of clients to address areas of occupational performance relevant to their needs and goals. Jennifer attended 4 days of fieldwork, observing the clients during their participation in the day care program. The program included current events, physical exercise, games, crafts, music activities, and meal and snack times. Everyone participated in the same activities. Jennifer observed that in each session, there were clients who were passive observers rather than actively engaged in the activity and that the staff members often "did for" the client; that is, they performed the majority of the game or craft steps for the client. Jennifer also observed the following:

- The current events activity included a staff member reading sections of the daily newspaper to the clients.
- The physical exercise session consisted of the clients watching and trying to follow an exercise video.
- The game options were cards and board games.
- Crafts included painting, making tissue flowers, and making holiday decorations for the facility bulletin boards.
- The staff prepared, set up, and served the clients their meals and snacks. The facility had a kitchen, dining area, and outdoor courtyard area and a wide range of supplies.

Jennifer's supervisor said that she could design any group she chose and use any of the available supplies. If she needed additional materials or supplies, she could discuss it with the supervisor to determine whether the budget could support their purchase. Jennifer designed a group that addressed the occupation of meal preparation. One week prior to the group, Jennifer planned to give the clients a choice of three snacks (fruit salad, trail mix bars, vegetables and dip) and solicit snack ideas. The clients would make their snack choice as a group. The two snack options not chosen and the additional snack ideas would be used for future groups. Jennifer chose snack options that each required multiple steps that could be graded to meet the range of occupational performance strengths and limitations of the group of clients. Jennifer included the set-up and clean-up tasks as part of the group activity. Although the clients would perform all the steps and tasks, Jennifer would direct and facilitate the meal preparation intervention.

LEVEL II FIELDWORK

Kevin's first Level II fieldwork experience was in an outpatient clinic with a primary caseload of clients with upper extremity injuries and conditions. His supervisor was an occupational therapist with 20 years of experience who also was credentialed as a certified hand therapist.

The first few days of Kevin's fieldwork were spent in clinic orientation activities and observing his supervisor conduct evaluations and provide interventions, as well as general observation of the clinic. Kevin was required to complete a daily journal of his observations and experiences to serve as a basis for dialogue during his weekly meeting with his supervisor. In preparation for his first supervision meeting, he reviewed his journal entries. After reviewing the entries, Kevin noticed a lack of focus on occupation in the services at the facility. He had the opportunity to indirectly observe the physical therapy practitioners, and based on his observation, he felt that the physical therapy and occupational therapy services were essentially the same, except that his occupational therapy supervisor focused only on the upper extremity.

Kevin discussed the challenge of including occupation-based interventions in the practice setting with his supervisor. He asked if he could focus on occupation-based practice in his fieldwork assignments and suggested the following assignments: (1) an in-service for the occupational therapy staff on the literature on the use of occupation-based interventions for clients with upper-extremity injuries and conditions, (2) a case pre-

(continued)

sentation of a client's services focusing on occupation across the occupational therapy process, and (3) an analysis of the clinical setting's space and materials using the intervention continuum with strategies for maximizing occupation-based interventions for clients with upper-extremity injuries and conditions.

First-Time Manager

Mark had been an occupational therapist for 3 years at a large medical center. The occupational therapy director recently attended an administration meeting where she learned of the medical center's intent to establish a program specializing in cardiac rehabilitation. The director approached Mark about applying for the available position as the manager of the new program. Although Mark was confident in his knowledge and skills as an occupation-based practitioner and less confident in his skills as a manager, he believed he had knowledge and skills applicable to the position and that this opportunity would promote his own professional development. He applied for and was promoted to the manager position. The targeted opening date for the cardiac care program was in 6 months.

Mark attended his first development meeting for the cardiac care program. The administrator gave an overview of the coordination of services for the program and noted that there may be an overlap of services between disciplines. He provided a few examples, including multiple disciplines addressing exercise, stress management, and nutrition in their intervention plan and programs. He also said that not all clients may need all services; for example, only select clients may require self-care training. He instructed all members of the interdisciplinary team to consider their role in cardiac rehabilitation and to write a proposal for their discipline that included a description of services, including the unique characteristics and type (i.e., direct individual intervention, group intervention, consultation); staffing patterns, including staff levels and qualifications and number of personnel; reimbursement considerations; space requirements for the delivery of services; an itemized list of equipment and supplies with associated costs; and proposed methods for evaluating the program outcomes.

Mark wrote a proposal for occupational therapy services in cardiac rehabilitation that described a client-centered, occupation-based evaluation and intervention program. Mark's proposal included a summary of the evidence supporting occupation-based services and the association with cardiac rehabilitation outcomes; an outline of the space and material requirements for providing occupation-based services; and described the relationship between occupational performance and medical necessity for reimbursement. Additionally, Mark's proposed method for evaluating the program directly linked to supporting the client's health and participation in life through engagement in occupation.

Manager

Joan had been an occupational therapist for 7 years with a rehabilitation company specializing in contract occupational therapy services that had contracts with many facilities across a wide range of practice settings. She accepted a transfer to be the manager of occupational therapy services in a subacute and long-term-care facility the company had recently contracted with.

Joan knew that her first tasks were to familiarize herself with the facility procedures, administrative responsibilities, and the staff's performance. After 1 month of working with the staff and observing and reviewing their performance, Joan noted the following:

- The goals established during the evaluation process focused on performance skill impairments and client factors but were not linked to the client's desired occupations. A few of the goals were related to contexts and environments, but none of the goals were related to performance patterns.
- The department had kitchen and laundry areas; however, they were infrequently used in client care.
- Two of the occupational therapy assistants seemed to include more occupation-based interventions addressing IADLs and work and leisure activities in their services than the other staff members. Additionally, they conducted intervention sessions in spaces outside of the clinic (e.g., facility chapel, dining room, gift shop, public areas, outdoor courtyard).
- All of the staff members were meeting their productivity standards and adhered to the facility policies and procedures regarding documentation and services. All had consistently received satisfactory performance reviews from the previous manager.

Joan felt that the occupational therapy services provided met at least minimum standards but that they could be enhanced to better reflect occupation-based practice. Joan implemented a department practice analysis that engaged all of the staff members and scheduled a monthly occupation-based educational meeting. The educational meetings included the establishment of a department journal club. The article selection criteria included occupation-based practice with the purpose of creating evidence-based protocols and an evidence-based library relevant to the practice of the department. Case presentations and discussions were included in the meeting schedule. Joan encouraged the occupational therapy assistants to conduct the first case presentation focusing on practical strategies to maximize the use of occupation in the facility. With input from the staff, Joan revised the job performance review process to focus on the use of occupation.

❖ Learning Activities

1. Analyze an evaluation or reevaluation session—It could be a session you observe someone else carry out or a session that you plan and/or implement. Consider the following in your analysis: Does the occupational therapist begin with an explanation of occupational therapy and its unique focus on meaningful occupation? Are relevant examples of occupations included in the explanation? Are data relevant to the client's occupational profile obtained? Outline the methods used during the evaluation to assess the client, the context, the occupation or activity, and the occupational performance. Is a client-centered evaluation tool or interview included? If so, what information is obtained? Classify the methods by the aspect of occupational therapy's domain they best represent. How do the evaluation methods support the client's roles and desired occupations? Identify other evaluation methods and/or specific assessment tools that measure the client's occupational performance of his or her desired occupations. What circumstances and conditions support and limit the therapist's ability to focus on occupation in the evaluation session?

2. Analyze an intervention session—It could be a session you observe someone else carry out or a session that you plan and/or implement. Identify the occupational profile information of the client, and list the interventions included in the session. Categorize each intervention using the intervention continuum. Consider the following in your analysis: Do the interventions relate appropriately and effectively to the client's occupational profile? How do the interventions support the client's roles and desired occupations? Identify other purposeful activities and occupation-based interventions that support the client's occupational performance of his or her desired occupations. What circumstances and conditions support and limit the inclusion of occupation-based interventions in the session?

3. Analyze a documentation report—It could be an evaluation report, an intervention session report, a progress report, a reevaluation report, an intervention plan, or a discharge summary report. The analysis also can be completed using a documentation form or electronic screens versus a completed report for a specific client. Consider the following in your analysis: Does the terminology support occupation-based practice? Does the terminology reflect the *Occupational Therapy Practice Framework* (AOTA, 2008)—that is, areas of occupation, client factors, performance skills, performance patterns, context and environment, activity demands, and occupational profile? Where is "occupation" addressed on the form or in the report? Is it specifically labeled, and are a range of occupations addressed in the report? If so, is it on the first page or embedded elsewhere in the documentation form or report? How much space is dedicated to each aspect of occupational therapy's domain? How can the documentation be enhanced to better reflect occupation-based practice?

4. Analyze an occupational therapy setting—It could be a clinic, a classroom, or a laboratory environment. Consider the following in your analysis: Describe the physical (i.e., natural and built nonhuman spaces) and social (i.e., presence, relationships, and expectations of persons) environments of the clinic. Make a list of the objects (i.e., equipment, materials, and supplies) in the environment. Identify and describe cultural and temporal contextual factors of the clinic. Classify the evaluation equipment and materials by the aspect of occupational therapy's domain they best represent. Categorize the intervention equipment, materials, and supplies using the intervention continuum. What is the distribution? How do the available evaluation equipment and materials sufficiently support analysis of the client population's performance of preferred and meaningful occupations? Are the available evaluation equipment and materials used by the occupational therapists in daily practice? How do the available equipment, materials, and supplies support occupation-based interventions? Are they used by the occupational therapy practitioners for intervention implementation in daily practice? When you enter the clinic on a working day, do you see clients engaged in occupation-based interventions? What contextual circumstances and conditions (i.e., physical, social, cultural, temporal) support occupation-based practice in the clinic? What circumstances and conditions (i.e., physical, social, cultural, temporal) limit occupation-based practice in the evaluation session? Identify five ways to enhance the focus of occupation in the clinic context.

5. Plan (and implement) an occupation-based event to celebrate Occupational Therapy Month (April). Consider the following as you plan the event: How do the activities included in the event reflect occupational therapy's unique focus on occupation? Does the event include practical education of how engaging in occupations structures everyday life and contributes to health and well-being? If information related to performance skills and client factors is addressed, does it also include their relationship to areas of occupation, performance patterns, and context and environment? Analyze the event and its activities through the view of someone unfamiliar with occupational therapy. Would a person easily see how the components of the event reflect activities that people engage in throughout their daily lives? Describe three occupation-based activities that could be included in an occupational therapy month.

✓ Multiple-Choice Questions

1. An occupational therapist completes an initial evaluation with a client who has had a cerebrovascular accident. The client's roles include maintaining the home environment and working as a cook in a local restaurant. The occupational therapist designs an intervention that includes having the client plan and perform hot and cold meal preparation and clean-up tasks in the clinic kitchen. This intervention best represents which one of the following concepts of client-centered practice?
   a. Communicate with clients using a person-centered approach.
   b. Respect clients and their choices.
   c. Focus services on the dynamic interaction among the person, their environment, and their preferred occupations.
   d. Empower clients to solve problems.

2. An occupational therapist is completing an initial evaluation with a client with Alzheimer's disease. The therapist conducts a client-centered interview with the client's daughter, who is the primary caregiver. This interview integrates the concepts of which assessment tool?
   a. Functional Independence Measure (FIM).
   b. Kohlman Evaluation of Living Skills (KELS).
   c. Allen Cognitive Level Screen (ACLS).
   d. Canadian Occupational Performance Measure (COPM).

3. The client-centered interview requires the client to consider the occupations performed during a typical day and identify those that he or she needs, wants, and is expected to do and to prioritize the 5 most important occupations. What does the practitioner need to do prior to conducting the interview?
   a. Orient the client to occupational therapy and define IADLs.
   b. Orient the client to occupational therapy, and make sure the he or she understands the definition of *occupation* from an occupational therapy perspective.
   c. Have the client describe his or her personal performance patterns and their physical and social environments.
   d. Ask the client to identify a family member, caregiver, or significant other to include in the interview process.

4. The intervention continuum includes preparatory methods, purposeful activity, and occupation-based intervention. An occupational therapist is evaluating a client with a traumatic brain injury. During the client-centered interview, the client identified being able to perform grocery shopping as a priority occupation that she needs and is expected to do. Which of the following *best* reflects an occupation-based intervention the therapist may include in the client's intervention plan?
   a. Going to the facility gift shop and purchasing a card for a friend.
   b. Practicing writing a check to pay for a sample utility bill.
   c. Selecting the appropriate bills and coins to pay the amount on a sample grocery receipt.
   d. Navigating a course in the clinic that simulates potential environmental obstacles in a grocery store.

5. The occupational therapy manager is reviewing an occupational therapy practitioner's documentation to determine the degree of occupation-based services provided. Which of the following descriptions *do not* reflect an occupation-based intervention?
   a. Using an adaptive pen to copy a recipe from a magazine to give to a friend.
   b. Completing morning dressing and hygiene activities using adaptive equipment and minimal assistance from the therapist.
   c. Receiving a resting hand splint to provide support and proper positioning during sleep.
   d. With moderate assistance from the therapist, client establishes a sequence of self-care and relaxation activities for sleep and identifies a method for measuring the degree of success on a daily basis.

6. The practice analysis process identified by Chisholm et al. (2004) can be used to analyze occupational therapy services at the department level. The first step of the process is to identify the demographic characteristics of the practice setting and client population. The final step in the practice analysis process extends beyond the direct services of the department. Which of the following is the last step in the practice analysis process?
   a. Identifying the typical problem areas of the clients.
   b. Identifying circumstances and conditions that support the staff in providing occupation-based interventions and creating a list of issues that limit staff in providing occupation-based interventions.
   c. Identifying examples of interventions typically used to address problem occupations, client factors, performance skills, performance patterns, or contexts and environments.
   d. Identifying the range of interventions that could be used in the clinical practice of the department to address the typical problem areas of the clients.

7. Which of the following best reflects who should complete the practice analysis?
   a. The manager of occupational therapy services.
   b. The occupational therapist with the most years of experience.
   c. All staff members, with the exception of technicians and fieldwork students.
   d. All staff members, including fieldwork students.

8. People perform their daily occupations in a wide range of natural and built environments. The occupational therapy manager asks the staff to identify the department's space needs and possible solutions to improve it. Which of the following suggestions from the staff represents a space consideration that allows for the least inclusion of occupation-based interventions?

    a. Requesting the purchase of a bedside table and a wheelchair-accessible cutout table.

    b. Obtaining approval to use the courtyard picnic area from 1 to 4 p.m.

    c. Requesting the purchase of a double bed and conventional table and chairs.

    d. Rearranging the clinic furniture to look like a home bedroom.

9. A Level I occupational therapy student observes an evaluation of a client with a hand injury. The supervisor has the student generate a list of potential interventions and the supplies needed to implement each intervention. Which of the following lists of supplies best represent those used in an occupation-based intervention?

    a. Education handouts for adaptive strategies to perform home management tasks.

    b. Fork, knife, and therapy putty.

    c. Mail items, envelope opener, coupon section of the newspaper, and scissors.

    d. Cuff weights, graded pinch pegs, and elevated dowel rod.

10. The manager wants to support the practitioners' efforts in educating and demonstrating to others how occupation is central to occupational therapy services. Which of the following activities could the manager encourage the staff to participate in to educate others about occupation-based practice?

    a. Establish a department journal club that meets monthly.

    b. Create an evidence-based library focusing on topics relevant to the practice of the department.

    c. Schedule a case presentation to share the evidence with other health professionals.

    d. All of the above.

11. Occupational therapy practitioners identify time as a reason for not providing occupation-based services. The manager guides the staff in critically thinking about how they use their time. Which of the following activities do not support occupation-based services?

    a. Evaluating occupational performance by observing the client performing activities relevant to desired occupations.

    b. Evaluating performance skills and then determining which occupations the skill deficits likely affect.

    c. Including an intervention in a session or program on the basis of its relevance to the client's priority occupations.

    d. Having each student who is completing a fieldwork experience within the department develop and assemble an individual or group intervention kit.

12. The manager needs to ensure that occupation-based services are being provided as well as that the staff's documentation reflects occupation-based services. Which statement below best reflects occupation-based practice on a documentation form?

    a. A section on the first page for a comprehensive list of range-of-motion and muscle-strength measurements.

    b. A section on the first page with dressing, bathing, eating, and functional mobility activities.

    c. A section on the first page with areas of occupation, including ADLs, IADLs, rest and sleep, education, work, play, leisure, and social participation activities.

    d. A section on the last page to identify the client's reported priority occupations.

13. Managers and practitioners need to understand, appreciate, and accept the influence of culture in organizations. There is a change of the administrator at a facility who schedules a planning meeting to discuss the development of a new program at the facility. The list of planning committee members does not include a representative from the department of occupational therapy. Which of the following statements reflects the best option for the manager to transition the situation to endorse and advance the use of occupation-based services?

    a. Request a meeting with the administrator to obtain an understanding of the administrator's viewpoint and to discuss the significance of occupation-based services for the facility and the new program.

    b. After the planning meeting, ask one of the committee members what was discussed in order to identify opportunities for occupation-based services for the new program.

    c. Send a representative from the department of occupational therapy to the meeting to ensure that occupation-based services are included in the new program.

    d. Request a meeting with the administrator to obtain an understanding of the why the administrator did not include a representative from occupational therapy on the planning committee and why he or she does not value occupation-based services.

14. The needs and goals of the staff are one of the central features to the management process. A manager can include a "staff-centered interview" in the job performance review process. Which of the following concepts is best supported by the inclusion of a staff-centered interview?

a. Managers need to facilitate staff being involved in all aspects of department management.

b. Managers need to focus management on the dynamic interaction among the staff member, their work environment, and their preferred and required work occupations.

c. Managers need to provide flexible and individualized management.

d. Managers need to communicate with staff using a person-centered approach.

15. Not only do practitioners need to provide occupation-based services, they also must provide pragmatic evidence that supports the effectiveness of occupation-based practice. Literature should be gathered from all available electronic resources using relevant keywords. Which of the following keywords is not appropriate to use when searching for literature relevant to occupation-based practice?

a. Purposeful activity.

b. Occupation.

c. Added-purpose.

d. Performance skills.

16. The definitions of purposeful activity and occupation-based intervention in the *Framework–II* (AOTA, 2008) can be used to determine whether an intervention included in a study reflects occupation-based practice. Which of the following interventions is appropriate to include in an evidence-based practice chart that addresses occupation-based practice?

a. Participation in routine morning occupations versus dysfunctional behaviors with a positive reinforcement for participation.

b. Above-head arm stretches and below-waist arm stretches.

c. Arm movements simulating dunking a small, spongy ball into a basketball hoop.

d. Moving arm while imagining picking up a pencil from a pencil holder and pretending to write name.

17. During a performance review, the manager observes an occupational therapy assistant administering intervention sessions with clients who had hip replacement surgery. The manager observes that the COTA includes the same type of interventions in each session: upper-extremity exercise, practice of transfers, review of hip precautions, and education for use of adaptive equipment. Which of the following strategies would best show the OTA how to include occupation-based interventions in his or her services?

a. Have the OTA complete a review of the literature related to occupation-based practice for clients who have had hip replacement surgery.

b. Provide the OTA with a list of occupation-based interventions to use with clients who have had hip replacement surgery.

c. Have the OTA complete a self-reflective exercise that includes defining the problem area of a client and identifying the interventions included during the client's intervention session, categorizing the interventions using the intervention continuum, and identifying intervention options across the continuum that could be used to address the client's problems areas.

d. Have the OTA complete a self-reflective exercise identifying the circumstances and conditions that support and limit occupation-based practice.

18. The manager of an outpatient clinic with a primary caseload of clients with upper-extremity orthopedic conditions wants to enhance the provision of occupation-based services. Which of the following strategies would be most beneficial for the manager to implement?

a. Scheduling an education session for the staff on the components and benefits of occupation-based services for clients with upper-extremity orthopedic conditions.

b. Including a client-centered interview as the standard of care; that is, the interview will be administered as part of the evaluation and reviewed and revised during the intervention program.

c. Including case presentations and discussions in departmental meetings that focus on the use of occupation and opportunities for enhancing occupation-based services.

d. All of the above.

19. A manager overhears a client saying to a family member, "I don't know why I have to cook muffins in the OT kitchen. I don't even like muffins." The manager shares the situation during a departmental meeting to facilitate a discussion best related to which of the following issues?

a. Materials needed for occupation-based interventions and purposeful activities are more likely to be available in people's homes and for purchase in local retail stores than the materials for preparatory methods.

b. Clients need to understand how the interventions they engage in will facilitate their ability to engage in meaningful occupations that they include in their daily routine and the connection between the client's daily occupations and the interventions.

c. Maximizing the clinic space to reflect that of "real-world" environments and arranging it to look like a natural living space.

d. Clients and their significant others are interested in the services they are receiving so practitioners should share all levels of evidence with clients and their family members.

20. The occupational therapy department at a local medical center has recently established a fieldwork program. The manager wants to include student assignments that will enhance the department's occupation-

based services and are meaningful for the student. The manager asks the practitioners to generate a list of potential student assignments. Which of the following assignments best support occupation-based practice?

a. A department scavenger hunt that requires the student to locate and identify clinic spaces and materials, to categorize them using the language of the *Framework–II* (AOTA, 2008), such as categorizing evaluation items by domain and intervention items by type of intervention.

b. Leading one or more department journal club sessions, which would include selecting a recent article relevant to occupation-based practice and to the clinic population or practice setting; facilitating the discussion; creating a user-friendly 1-page handout for clients and families; and adding the article and materials to the department's evidence-based library.

c. Researching, developing, and presenting an education session on one or more evaluation tools that support occupation-based practice and are applicable to the population and practice setting of the department.

d. All of the above.

References

American Occupational Therapy Association. (1994). Uniform terminology for occupational therapy (3rd ed.). *American Journal of Occupational Therapy, 48,* 1047–1054.

American Occupational Therapy Association. (2008). Occupational therapy practice framework: Domain and process (2nd ed.). *American Journal of Occupational Therapy, 62,* 625–683.

Bakshi, R., Bhambhani, Y., & Madill, H. (1991). The effects of task preference on performance during purposeful and nonpurposeful activities. *American Journal of Occupational Therapy, 45,* 912–916.

Baum, C. (2000, January 3). Occupation-based practice: Reinventing ourselves for the new millennium. *OT Practice, 5*(1), 12–15.

Bazyk, S., & Bazyk, J. (2009). Meaning of occupation-based groups for low-income urban youths attending after-school care. *American Journal of Occupational Therapy, 63,* 69–80.

Bickles, M. B., DeLoache, S. N., Dicer, J. R., & Miller, S. C. (2001). Effectiveness of experiential and verbal occupational therapy groups in a community mental health setting. *Occupational Therapy in Mental Health, 17,* 51–72.

Bloch, M. W., Smith, D. A., & Nelson, D. L. (1989). Heart rate, activity, duration, and affect in added-purpose versus single-purpose jumping activities. *American Journal of Occupational Therapy, 43,* 25–30.

Chan, J., & Spencer, J. (2004). Adaptation to hand injury: An evolving experience. *American Journal of Occupational Therapy, 58,* 128–139.

Chisholm, D., Dolhi, C., & Schreiber, J. (2004). *Occupational therapy intervention resource manual: A guide for occupation-based practice.* Clifton Park, NY: Delmar Learning.

Clark, F., Azen, S. P., Carlson, M., Mandel, D., LaBree, L., Hay, J., et al. (2001). Embedding health-promoting changes into the daily lives of independent-living older adults: Long-term follow-up of occupational therapy intervention. *Journal of Gerontology, 56B,* P60–P63.

Clark, F., Azen, S. P., Zemke, R., Jackson, J., Carlson, M., Mandel, D., et al. (1997). Occupational therapy for independent-living older adults. *JAMA, 278,* 1321–582.

Denton, P. L. (1987). *Psychiatric occupational therapy: A workbook of practical skills* (pp. 1–40). Boston: Little, Brown.

Eakman, A. M., & Nelson, D. L. (2001). The effect of hands-on occupation on recall memory in men with traumatic brain injuries. *Occupational Therapy Journal of Research, 21,* 109–114.

Earley, D., & Shannon, M. (2006). The use of occupation-based treatment with a person who has shoulder adhesive capsulitis: A case report. *American Journal of Occupational Therapy, 60,* 397–403.

Fasoli, S. E., Trombly, C. A., Tickle-Degnen, L., & Verfaellie, M. H. (2002). Context and goal-directed movement: The effect of materials-based occupation. *OTJR: Occupation, Participation and Health, 22,* 119–128.

Ferguson, J. M., & Trombly, C. A. (1997). The effect of added-purpose and meaningful occupation on motor learning. *American Journal of Occupational Therapy, 51,* 508–515.

Fleming, J. M., Lucas, S. E., & Lightbody, S. (2006). Using occupation to facilitate self-awareness in people who have acquired brain injury: A pilot study. *Canadian Journal of Occupational Therapy, 73,* 44–55.

Frank, G., Fishman, M., Crowley, C., Blair, B., Murphy, S. T., Montoya, J. A., et al. (2001). The new stories/new cultures after-school enrichment program: A direct cultural intervention. *American Journal of Occupational Therapy, 55,* 501–508.

Hartman, B. A., Miller, B. K., & Nelson, D. L. (2000). The effects of hands-on occupation versus demonstration on children's recall memory. *American Journal of Occupational Therapy, 54,* 477–483.

Hinojosa, J., & Kramer, P. (1997). Fundamental concepts of occupational therapy: Occupation, purposeful activity, and function [Statement]. *American Journal of Occupational Therapy, 51,* 864–866.

Holm, M. B. (2000). Eleanor Clarke Slagle Lecture—Our mandate for the new millennium: Evidence-based practice. *American Journal of Occupational Therapy, 54,* 575–585.

Holm, M. B., Santangelo, M. A., Fromuth, D. J., Brown, S. O., & Walter, H. (2000). Effectiveness of everyday occupations for changing client behaviors in a community living arrangement. *American Journal of Occupational Therapy, 54,* 361–371.

Ivanoff, S. D., Sonn, U., & Svensson, E. (2002). A health education program for elderly persons with visual impairments and perceived security in performance of daily occupations: A randomized study. *American Journal of Occupational Therapy, 56,* 322–330.

Jackson, J. P., & Schkade, J. K. (2001). Occupational adaptation model versus biomechanical-rehabilitation model in the treatment of patients with hip fracture. *American Journal of Occupational Therapy, 55,* 531–537.

Kellegrew, D. H. (1998). Creating opportunities for occupation: An intervention to promote the self-care independence of young children with special needs. *American Journal of Occupational Therapy, 52,* 457–465.

Kircher, M. A. (1984). Motivation as a factor of perceived exertion in purposeful versus nonpurposeful activity. *American Journal of Occupational Therapy, 38,* 165–170.

Lam, W., Wong, K. W., Fulks, M.-A., & Holsti, L. (2008). Obsessional slowness: A case study. *Canadian Journal of Occupational Therapy, 75,* 249–254.

Lang, E. M., Nelson, D. L., & Bush, M. A. (1992). Comparison of performance in materials-based occupation, imagery-based occupation, and rote exercise in nursing home residents. *American Journal of Occupational Therapy, 46,* 607–611.

Law, M., Baptiste, S., Carswell, A., McColl, M. A., Polatajko, H., & Pollock, N. (2005). *Canadian Occupational Performance Measure* (4th ed.). Ottawa, Ontario: CAOT Publications ACE.

Law, M., Baptiste, S., & Mills, J. (1995). Client-centered practice: What does it mean and does it make a difference? *Canadian Journal of Occupational Therapy, 62,* 250–257.

Law, M., Polatajko, H., Baptiste, W., & Townsend, E. (1997). Core concepts of occupational therapy. In E. Townsend (Ed.), *Enabling occupation: An occupational therapy perspective* (pp. 29–56). Ottawa, Ontario: Canadian Association of Occupational Therapists.

Mastos, M., Miller, K., Eliasson, A. C., & Imms, C. (2007). Goal-directed training: Linking theories of treatment to clinical practice for improved functional activities in daily life. *Clinical Rehabilitation, 21,* 47–55.

Melchert-McKearnan, K., Deitz, J., Engel, J. M., & White, O. (2000). Children with burn injuries: Purposeful activity versus rote exercise. *American Journal of Occupational Therapy, 54,* 381–390.

Miller, L., & Nelson, D. L. (1987). Dual-purpose activity versus single-purpose activity in terms of duration on task, exertion level, and affect. *Occupational Therapy in Mental Health, 7,* 55–67.

Mountain, G., Mozley, C., Craig, C., & Ball, L. (2008). Occupational therapy led health promotion for older people: Feasibility of the Lifestyle Matters programme. *British Journal of Occupational Therapy, 71,* 406–413.

Mullins, C. S., Nelson, D. L., & Smith, D. A. (1987). Exercise through dual-purpose activity in the institutionalized elderly. *Physical and Occupational Therapy in Geriatrics, 5,* 29–39.

Nagel, M. J., & Rice, M. S. (2001). Cross-transfer effects in the upper extremity during an occupationally embedded exercise. *American Journal of Occupational Therapy, 55,* 317–323.

Nelson, D. L., Konosky, K., Fleharty, K., Webb, R., Newer, K., Hazboun, V. P., et al. (1996). The effects of an occupationally embedded exercise on bilaterally assisted supination in persons with hemiplegia. *American Journal of Occupational Therapy, 50,* 639–646.

Olsen, L. (2006). When a mother is depressed: Supporting her capacity to participate in co-occupation with her babe—A case study. *Occupational Therapy in Mental Health, 22,* 135–152.

Ownsworth, T., Fleming, J., Shum, D., Kuipers, P., & Strong, J. (2007). Comparison of individual, group and combined intervention formats in a randomized controlled trial for facilitating goal attainment and improving psychosocial function following acquired brain injury. *Journal of Rehabilitation Medicine, 40,* 81–88.

Paquette, S. (2008). Return to work with chronic low back pain: Using an evidence-based approach along with the occupational therapy framework. *Work, 31,* 63–71.

Phipps, S., & Richardson, P. (2007). Occupational therapy outcomes for clients with traumatic brain injury and stroke using the Canadian Occupational Performance Measure. *American Journal of Occupational Therapy, 61,* 328–334.

Price, P., & Miner, S. (2007). Occupation emerges in the process of therapy. *American Journal of Occupational Therapy, 61,* 441–450.

Quake-Rapp, C., Miller, B., Ananthan, G., & Chiu, E.-C. (2008). Direct observation as a means of assessing frequency of maladaptive behavior in youths with severe emotional and behavioral disorder. *American Occupational Therapy Association, 62,* 206–211.

Rebeiro, K. L., & Cook, J. V. (1999). Opportunity not prescription: An exploratory study of the experience of occupational engagement. *Canadian Journal of Occupational Therapy, 66,* 176–187.

Rebeiro, K. L., Day, D. G., Semeniuk, B., O'Brien, M. C., & Wilson, B. (2001). Northern Initiative for Social Action: An occupation-based mental health program. *American Journal of Occupational Therapy, 55,* 493–500.

Rexroth, P., Fisher, A. G., Merritt, B. K., & Gliner, J. (2005). ADL differences in individuals with unilateral hemispheric stroke. *Canadian Journal of Occupational Therapy, 72,* 212–221.

Rogers, J. C., & Holm, M. B. (1994). *Performance Assessment of Self-Care Skills (PASS)* (Version 3.1). Unpublished manuscript.

Rogers, J. C., Holm, M. B., Burgio, L. D., Granieri, E., Hsu, C., Hardin, J. M., et al. (1999). Improving morning care routines of nursing home residents with dementia. *Journal of the American Geriatrics Society, 47,* 1049–1057.

Ross, L. M., & Nelson, D. L. (2000). Comparing materials-based occupation, imagery-based occupation, and rote movement through kinematic analysis of reach. *Occupational Therapy Journal of Research, 20,* 45–60.

Sakemiller, L. M., & Nelson, D. L. (1998). Eliciting functional extension in prone through the use of a game [Case Report]. *American Journal of Occupational Therapy, 52,* 150–157.

Schmidt, C. L., & Nelson, D. L. (1996). A comparison of three occupation forms in rehabilitation patients receiving upper extremity strengthening. *Occupational Therapy Journal of Research, 16,* 200–215.

Sietsema, J. M., Nelson, D. L., Mulder, R. M., Mervau-Scheidel, D., & White, B. E. (1993). The use of a game to promote arm reach in persons with traumatic brain injury. *American Journal of Occupational Therapy, 47,* 19–24.

Steinbeck, T. M. (1986). Purposeful activity and performance. *American Journal of Occupational Therapy, 40,* 529–534.

Tham, K., Ginsburg, E., Fisher, A. G., & Tegnér, R. (2001). Training to improve awareness of disabilities in clients with unilateral neglect. *American Journal of Occupational Therapy, 55,* 46–54.

Thibodeaux, C. S., & Ludwig, F. M. (1988). Intrinsic motivation in product-oriented and non-product-oriented activities. *American Journal of Occupational Therapy, 42,* 169–175.

Thomas, J. J., Vander Wyk, S., & Boyer, J. (1999). Contrasting occupational forms: Effects on performance and affect in patients undergoing Phase II cardiac rehabilitation. *Occupational Therapy Journal of Research, 19,* 187–202.

Venable, E., Hanson, C., Shechtman, O., & Dasler, P. (2000). The effects of exercise on occupational functioning in the well elderly. *Physical and Occupational Therapy in Geriatrics, 17,* 20–42.

Ward, K., Mitchell, J., & Price, P. (2007). Occupation-based practice and its relationship to social and occupational participation in adults with spinal cord injury. *OTJR: Occupation, Participation and Health, 27*(4), 149–156.

Wu, C., Trombly, C. A., & Lin, K. (1994). The relationship between occupational form and occupational performance: A kinematic perspective. *American Journal of Occupational Therapy, 48,* 679–687.

Yoder, R. M., Nelson, D. L., & Smith, D. A. (1989). Added-purpose versus rote exercise in female nursing home residents. *American Journal of Occupational Therapy, 43,* 581–586.

Zimmerer-Branum, S., & Nelson, D. L. (1995). Occupationally embedded exercise versus rote exercise: A choice between occupation forms by elderly nursing home residents. *American Journal of Occupational Therapy, 49,* 397–402.

Additional Resources on Occupation-Based Practice

Canadian Association of Occupational Therapists. (2002). *Enabling occupation: An occupational therapy perspective* (rev. ed.). Ottawa, Ontario: Author. An introduction to "core concepts and processes that demonstrate the important contributions of occupational therapy to the everyday lives of Canadians and others around the world" (p. 1).

Chisholm, D., Dolhi, C., & Schreiber, J. (2004). *Occupational therapy intervention resource manual: A guide for occupation-based practice.* Clifton Park, NY: Delmar Learning. A "manual designed as a workbook to strengthen your understanding of occupation as the hallmark of occupational therapy intervention and to assist . . . in determining how intervention grounded in occupation may best integrated into your clinical practice" (p. viii).

Crist, P. A., Royeen, C. B., & Schkade, J. K. (Eds.). (2000). *Infusing occupation into practice* (2nd ed.). Bethesda, MD: American Occupational Therapy Association. Resource that provides "information and discussion regarding the practical application of various emerging approaches to occupation and the science of occupation" (p. vii).

Fazio, L. S. (2008). *Developing occupation-centered programs for the community.* Upper Saddle River, NJ: Prentice Hall. "A practice guide to mark the way for the return of occupational therapy to community practice. . . . This book will guide you in the introductory process of developing occupation-centered community programming" (p. xiii).

Hasselkus, B. R. (2002). *The meaning of everyday occupation.* Thorofare, NJ: Slack. Discussion of "meaning and everyday occupation. . . . Throughout the book, verbatim quotations from occupational therapists are used to illustrate and exemplify the concepts being presented and discussed" (pp. xi, xii).

Hinojosa, J., & Blount, M. (Eds.). (2009). *The texture of life: Purposeful activities in occupational therapy practice* (3rd ed.). Bethesda, MD: AOTA Press. "A major change in our profession is that occupational therapists and occupational therapy assistants have endorsed the use of the term *occupation*" (p. xxvii).

Holst, C., & Vogt, D. (1999). *Empowering occupational therapy.* Columbia, MO: TheraPower. "A simple system to make client-centered occupation-based treatment efficient, enjoyable and easy" with more than "100 occupation-based activities organized into treatment categories" (http://therapower.com).

Law, M. (Ed.). (1998). *Client-centered occupational therapy.* Thorofare, NJ: Slack. Discussion of "information and ideas to assist occupational therapists in meeting the challenge of practicing in a client-centered manner" (p. xv).

Law, M., Baum, C. M., & Baptiste, S. (2002). *Occupation-based practice: Fostering performance and participation.* Thorofare, NJ: Slack. Resource that is "a partner for individual occupational therapists, regardless of practice focus or primary role, in their exploration of developing an occupation-focused practice style based upon the complex relationships between the individuals, the environments in which they function, and the occupations with which they become involved" (p. 1).

Letts, L., Rigby, P., & Stewart, D. (Eds.). (2003). *Using environments to enable occupational performance.* Thorofare, NJ: Slack. Discussion of "how environments can be used by occupational therapists to enable occupational performance. Environments are broadly defined to include physical, social, cultural, and institutional components" (p. xv).

Pierce, D. (2003). *Occupation by design: Building therapeutic power.* Philadelphia: F. A. Davis. Synthesis of "theory and research on occupation and activity . . . [and includes] an explanation of how each described aspect of occupation can be used in practice" (p. xi).

Sumsion, T. (Ed.). (1999). *Client-centered practice in occupational therapy: A guide to implementation.* London: Churchill Livingstone. Resource to continue "the development of [client-centered practice] by combining information about the theoretical and practical aspects of client-centered practice. . . . Therapists . . . will find helpful information in this book that will remove barriers to the implementation of client-centered practice and strengthen their commitment to this approach for the benefit of their clients" (p. xi).

Velde, B., & Fidler, G. (2002). *Lifestyle performance: A model for engaging the power of occupation.* Thorofare, NJ: Slack. Resources that empowers "therapists to use the [Lifestyle Performance] model and to learn new ways of being client-centered" (p. xix).

Appendix 5.A. Occupation-Based Practice Evidence Table

Study	Purpose of Study	Population	Intervention(s)
Bakshi, Bhambhani, & Madill, 1991	To examine the role of preference in purposeful and nonpurposeful conditions	20 healthy college-age women	Selection of purposeful activities (i.e., craft with an end product) and nonpurposeful activities (i.e., repetitive movement pattern without an end product)
Bazyk & Bazyk, 2009	To describe the meaning of occupational therapy groups focusing on occupational engagement, group process, and social–emotional learning	70 children attending an inner-city faith-based after-school program	Health Occupations for Positive Emotions (HOPE): 9-week group intervention with 3 segments—introductory conversation time, participation in a structured leisure occupation, and closure discussion
Bickles, DeLoache, Dicer, & Miller, 2001	To examine the effectiveness of occupation-based verbal therapy and occupation-based experiential therapy in facilitating performance of daily life skills	14 adults in a community mental health day support program	Experiential group intervention to perform money management tasks (e.g., counting change, making change, simple budgeting); life skill of money management was chosen by group members
Bloch, Smith, & Nelson, 1989 (extension of Kircher, 1984)	To determine whether purposeful activity provides intrinsic motivation to exercise performance	30 healthy college-age women	Jump rope exercise vs. no-rope exercise
Chan & Spencer, 2004	To examine similarities and differences in physical recovery and psychosocial adaptation, engagement in occupations and relationships, perceived outcomes and expectations, and adaptive issues and strategies	5 adults with acute hand injuries	Usual care occupational therapy intervention protocols for nerve injuries, tendon injuries, or fracture
Clark et al., 1997	To evaluate the effectiveness of preventive occupational therapy services	361 older adults living in the community	Occupational therapy intervention addressing home and community safety, transportation use, joint protection, adaptive equipment, energy conservation, exercise, and nutrition vs. social program focused on activities designed to encourage social intervention vs. no intervention
Clark et al., 2001 (follow-up of Clark et al., 1997)	To explore the long-term effects of occupational therapy	285 older adults living in the community	Occupational therapy intervention addressing home and community safety, transportation use, joint protection, adaptive equipment, energy conservation, exercise, and nutrition vs. social program focused on activities designed to encourage social intervention vs. no intervention

Appendix 5.A. Occupation-Based Practice Evidence Table (cont.)

Study	Purpose of Study	Population	Intervention(s)
Eakman & Nelson, 2001	To compare hands-on occupation with verbal training only for recall	20 men with closed-head injuries	Making meatballs according to a multistep process (i.e., verbal instruction and manipulation of utensils and ingredients) vs. verbal instruction and reading the steps of making meatballs
Earley & Shannon, 2006	To illustrate occupational therapy intervention using Trombly's occupation-as-means as the framework for occupation-based intervention	A 53-year-old woman diagnosed with shoulder adhesive capsulitis	Compensatory occupation techniques, preparatory methods, and purposeful activities
Fasoli, Trombly, Tickle-Degnen, & Verfaellie, 2002	To investigate whether materials-based occupation elicited significantly better movement than imagery-based occupation	5 adults with left cerebrovascular accident and 5 healthy adults	Functional tasks (e.g., slicing bread) under four conditions: materials-based condition (needed tools and objects available for task completion) and three imagery-based conditions (either the tool or object of the tool's action was present, or participant was asked to simulate the task without objects)
Ferguson & Trombly, 1997	To examine the effects of both added-purpose and meaningful occupation on motor learning	20 healthy college-age adults	Practicing note patterns using an electric keyboard to produce a musical tune vs. practicing note patterns using an electric keyboard without producing a tune
Fleming, Lucas, & Lightbody, 2006	To investigate the effect of an occupation-based intervention program on self-awareness and emotional status	4 men with impaired self-awareness following acquired brain injury	A 10-week individualized program focusing on the performance of occupations (e.g., writing a job application, budgeting, using a diary and computer to compensate for memory problems, preparing a hot meal safely, performing housework duties)
Frank et al., 2001	To describe the organization, curriculum, and outcomes of New Stories/New Cultures, an activity-based program for after-school enrichment	200 5th-grade and 6th-grade students in 5 schools in low-income neighborhoods	A 12-week program focusing on media-related activities that are among the most relevant and valued occupations of U.S. children and teens
Hartman, Miller, & Nelson, 2000	To compare hands-on learning and demonstration teaching methods	73 healthy children in 3rd grade	Making a model of a volcano vs. observing someone making a model of a volcano
Holm, Santangelo, Fromuth, Brown, & Walter, 2000	To examine the effects of three occupation-based interventions on reducing the frequency of dysfunctional behaviors	2 young women residing in a community residential facility	Everyday occupations at school and sheltered workshop in conjunction with behavior modification program; participation in routine morning activities of daily living; and participation in routine afternoon and evening activities of daily living

(continued)

APPENDIX 5.A. OCCUPATION-BASED PRACTICE EVIDENCE TABLE *(cont.)*

Study	Purpose of Study	Population	Intervention(s)
Ivanoff, Sonn, & Svensson, 2002	To investigate the impact of a health education program on perceived security in the performance of daily occupations	253 older adults with age-related macular degeneration	Group interventions; information and skills training based on occupational categories (i.e., self-care, meals, communication, orientation and mobility, food preparation, shopping, financial management, cleaning)
Jackson & Schkade, 2001	To compare the effectiveness of the occupational adaptation frame of reference with the biomechanical–rehabilitation model	40 adults post hip fracture	Client-chosen tasks vs. facility protocol exercises and activities
Kellegrew, 1998	To explore the relationship between opportunities for occupation and skill performance	3 caregivers of children with disabilities	Caregiver education and caregiver performance of targeted self-care intervention with child vs. no intervention
Kircher, 1984	To determine whether purposeful activity provides intrinsic motivation to exercise performance	26 healthy women	Jump rope exercise vs. no-rope exercise
Lam, Wong, Fulks, & Holsti, 2008	To examine whether a behavioral intervention would reduce the time taken for functional daily occupations	An adolescent boy with obsessional slowness	Intermittent (2–3 times/week), short-term (4 weeks), occupation-based intervention using pacing and prompting
Lang, Nelson, & Bush, 1992	To compare materials-based occupation, imagery-based occupation, and rote exercise	15 older-adult nursing home residents	Materials-based occupation of kicking a balloon; imagery-based occupation of kicking foot while imaging kicking a balloon; rote exercise of kicking foot
Mastos, Miller, Eliasson, & Imms, 2007	To examine the principles of an activity-based approach (i.e., goal-directed training)	2 women with acquired brain injury	Self-care tasks: eating and tying hair into a ponytail
Melchert-McKearnan, Deitz, Engel, & White, 2000	To compare measures of pain when engaged in a purposeful activity vs. rote exercise	2 boys	Repetitions of movements within a set range-of-motion goal while playing a preferred play activity vs. repetitions of movements within a set range-of-motion goal
Miller & Nelson, 1987	To examine the performance and affective meanings of individuals engaged in 2 different activities (single purpose and dual purpose)	30 healthy college-age women	Stirring for the single purpose of exercise vs. stirring for the dual purposes of exercise and mixing cookie batter
Mountain, Mozley, Craig, & Ball, 2008	To determine whether an occupation-based health-promoting intervention for community-living older people could be delivered successfully and to provide information to guide a future trial of clinical effectiveness	28 older adults living in the community	Lifestyle Matters groups: 1 group session/week for 8 months and 1 monthly individual session; sessions include health-promoting interventions with identification of participants' own goals and their empowerment through sharing the strengths and skills possessed by group members

APPENDIX 5.A. OCCUPATION-BASED PRACTICE EVIDENCE TABLE *(cont.)*

Study	Purpose of Study	Population	Intervention(s)
Mullins, Nelson, & Smith, 1987	To examine elderly nursing home residents' preference when presented with two kinds of exercise (dual-purpose craft-and-exercise activity and single-purpose exercise)	28 older-adult nursing home residents	Making a wall hanging using a stencil and a stencil roller vs. shoulder flexion exercise
Nagel & Rice, 2001	To explore cross-transfer effects during an occupationally embedded task that involved learning a fine motor skill	48 healthy college-age adults	Training to perform toy maze, an instruction sheet, verbal instruction, and daily practice schedule vs. no materials or instruction
Nelson et al., 1996	To compare the effect of an occupationally embedded exercise with a rote exercise	26 adults with cerebrovascular accident	Arm exercise while playing a dice game vs. arm exercise
Olson, 2006	To provide an example of mother–infant occupation-based intervention during a short-term psychiatric hospitalization through home-based occupation-based intervention	1 woman with a 9-month old child	Home-based parent–child interventions; activities related to mother–child co-occupations, including feeding, indoor and outdoor play, behavior management, and effectively managing symptoms of depression
Ownsworth, Fleming, Shum, Kuipers, & Strong, 2007	To compare individual, group, and combined intervention formats for improving goal attainment and psychosocial function	35 adults with acquired brain injury	Group-based intervention led by a psychologist that targeted development of metacognitive skills (self-awareness and use of compensatory strategies) through group-based psychoeducation, peer and facilitator feedback, and goal setting; individualized occupation-based support led by an occupational therapist focused on client-centered goals and associated occupational activities considered important and meaningful to the individual; combined group and individualized support intervention designed to promote the development of metacognitive skills through activities in both the group context and the participant's home and community environment with the involvement of social supports
Paquette, 2008	To describe the occupational therapy framework with an evidence-based approach and an occupation-based intervention for returning to work and maintaining work status	Workers with chronic low back pain	Graduated return-to-work program using regular and modified duties

(continued)

APPENDIX 5.A. OCCUPATION-BASED PRACTICE EVIDENCE TABLE *(cont.)*

Study	Purpose of Study	Population	Intervention(s)
Phipps & Richardson, 2007	To determine whether people who received outpatient occupational therapy reported increased levels of performance and satisfaction with daily life activities	155 adults (38 with traumatic brain injury, 117 with cerebrovascular accident)	Outpatient occupational therapy focused on restoring functional abilities in occupational performance areas that the client identified as higher in importance and lower in performance and satisfaction; various intervention approaches included functional training in self-care, home management, community reintegration, vocational skills, academic skills, and leisure skills
Price & Miner, 2007	To demonstrate how occupation, as an idea, emerged in the therapeutic process as it interacted with the forms of intervention and how occupation has aspects of both doing and becoming	A 3-year-old girl with possible Asperger syndrome	Multiple therapeutic strategies to address goals of going to preschool and becoming a friend
Quake-Rapp, Miller, Ananthan, & Chiu, 2008	To identify the incidence of maladaptive behavior in youths enrolled in community living and support training programs	30 children and adolescents with behavioral disorders	Three naturalistic group settings—art (engagement in a structured project with sequential steps to complete a creative work), bowling (community outing to a local bowling alley), and Junior Adventure (community field trips)
Rebeiro & Cook, 1999	To explore the meaning of occupational engagement	8 women consumers of mental health services	Women's Group (outpatient women's mental health group) for support and resolution of issues, and cooperative participation in an occupation-based project (quilt)
Rebeiro, Day, Semeniuk, O'Brien, & Wilson, 2001	To evaluate an evolving, occupation-based, consumer-run mental health initiative	38 adult consumers of mental health services	Northern Initiative for Social Action—a safe and supportive work environment to permit regaining confidence and skills, to provide opportunities for participation in personally meaningful and socially valued occupations, and to support and empower members to become contributing members of society
Rexroth, Fisher, Merritt, & Gliner, 2005	To determine whether people with a cerebrovascular accident differ in their abilities to perform ADL tasks and actions as affected by their gender, age, and side of the lesion	3,878 adults with a left or right cerebrovascular accident	Occupation-based intervention focusing on the use of intact ADL skills to compensate for ADL skill deficits
Rogers et al., 1999	To examine the effectiveness of behavioral rehabilitation intervention for improving the performance of morning care ADLs	84 nursing home residents with probable or possible Alzheimer's disease	Individualized behavioral rehabilitation intervention designed to identify and elicit retained ADL skills (skill elicitation and habit training)

APPENDIX 5.A. OCCUPATION-BASED PRACTICE EVIDENCE TABLE (cont.)

Study	Purpose of Study	Population	Intervention(s)
Ross & Nelson, 2000 (extension of Wu, Trombly, & Lin, 1994)	To compare the kinematics of reach in materials-based occupational embedded movement, imagery-based occupationally embedded movement, and rote movement	60 healthy college-age women	Pick up a pencil from a pencil holder and prepare to write one's own name vs. pretend to pick up a pencil from a pencil holder and prepare to write one's own name vs. arm reach movement
Sakemiller & Nelson, 1998	To examine whether play elicits therapeutic patterns of movement	2 girls with hypotonic cerebral palsy	Facilitation of vertical neck and back extension with performance of participant-identified favorite game vs. facilitation of vertical neck and back extension without performance of game
Schmidt & Nelson, 1996	To examine the performance differences in altruistic occupationally embedded exercise, occupationally embedded exercise, and rote exercise	19 adults receiving occupational therapy to address upper-extremity strengthening	Sanding a board that would eventually become part of a rocking horse that would be given to the pediatrics ward of a participating hospital; sanding a board that would eventually be made into a shelf for use somewhere in the institution; sanding a board for exercise
Sietsema, Nelson, Mulder, Mervau-Scheidel, & White, 1993	To compare the movements elicited by occupationally embedded intervention with those elicited by rote exercise	20 adults with traumatic brain injury	Play Simon™ vs. leaning forward and reaching
Steinbeck, 1986	To examine whether the presence of a purpose or a goal would have an effect on the number of times an individual would repeat a desired motion before reaching a point of perceived exertion	15 healthy women, 15 healthy men	Woodworking activity (constructing a game) using a pedal-powered drill press vs. pedaling while depressing a lever; playing a game (squeezing a rubber bulb to keep a ping-pong ball suspended in air) vs. squeezing a rubber bulb
Tham, Ginsburg, Fisher, & Tegnér, 2001	To evaluate the effect of an intervention program focused on improving the awareness of disabilities	4 women with right cerebrovascular accident	Traditional occupational therapy (i.e., training in self-care activities focusing on the use of available abilities and adaptation of task demands and contexts) plus disability awareness training vs. traditional occupational therapy
Thibodeaux & Ludwig, 1988	To examine purposeful activity as an intrinsic motivator	15 healthy women	Sanding a cutting board they could keep vs. sanding a piece of wood they could not keep
Thomas, Vander Wyk, & Boyer, 1999	To examine performance differences during materials-based, imagery-based, and rote exercise–based occupational forms	15 adults undergoing outpatient Phase II cardiac rehabilitation	Hip abduction movement while performance a ball-kicking game vs. hip abduction movement while imagining performance of a ball-kicking game vs. hip abduction movement

(continued)

APPENDIX 5.A. OCCUPATION-BASED PRACTICE EVIDENCE TABLE *(cont.)*

Study	Purpose of Study	Population	Intervention(s)
Venable, Hanson, Shechtman, & Dasler, 2000	To examine the relationship between the occupation of exercise, functional abilities, and volition	48 adults living in the community	Social and craft activities (e.g., ceramics, Grandmother's Club, Bridge Club, quilting, and Senior Luncheon/Lecture series) vs. social and craft activities plus individual exercise vs. exercise or dance class
Ward, Mitchell, & Price, 2007	To explore social and occupation participation and the occupation-based approaches most helpful in achieving outcomes	3 adults with spinal cord injury living in the community	Services from an occupation-based occupational therapist
Wu, Trombly, & Lin, 1994	To examine the effect of occupational form on reaching performance through kinematic analysis	37 healthy college-age women	Pick up a pencil and prepare to write one's own name vs. pretend to pick up a pencil and prepare to write one's own name
Yoder, Nelson, & Smith, 1989 (extension of Miller & Nelson, 1987)	To examine the performance and affective meanings of individuals engaged in 2 different activities (single purpose and dual purpose)	30 older women residing in nursing homes	Stirring for the single purpose of exercise vs. stirring for the dual purposes of exercise and mixing cookie batter
Zimmerer-Branum & Nelson, 1995	To examine preferences when presented with an occupationally embedded exercise vs. a rote exercise	52 older adults residing in nursing homes	Unilateral dunking of a small, spongy ball into a basketball hoop vs. moving the arm above the head in a simulation of the dunking exercise

Part II

Strategic Planning

6
Strategic Planning

Randy Strickland, EdD, OTR/L, FAOTA

❖ Key Terms and Concepts

Mission. An organization's core, underlying purpose, or basis for its existence, focus, and actions.

Scenario development. Formulation of possible options or outcomes with varied levels of desirability or likelihood of occurring in the future of an organization or system.

Strategic planning. The process of ensuring that an organization's current purpose, aspirations, goals, activities, and strategies are connected to plans that maximize its performance and support its mission.

Strategy. A selected approach or activity that enables the achievement of organizational objectives and goals.

SWOT analysis. A specific step in the strategic planning process that identifies and analyzes an organization's internal environment (strengths and weaknesses) and external environment (opportunities and threats) that impart sustainability or growth.

Top-down approach. Management style in which decisions are made in the upper levels of an organization without the input and participation of staff from throughout the organization.

Vision. The ideal state or ultimate level of achievement to which an organization aspires.

❖ Learning Objectives

After completing this chapter, you should be able to do the following:

1. Understand the key parts of strategic planning for an organization.
2. Identify the current or possible future application of strategic planning processes in your work or professional environment.
3. Use the *S*trengths, *W*eaknesses, *O*pportunities, *T*hreats (SWOT) analysis and scenario development processes as a basis for organization or program understanding and planning.
4. Describe the possible leadership roles of the occupational therapy practitioner in strategic planning in both the work and related professional settings.
5. Implement the process for strategic planning in various settings.
6. Apply the strategic planning process to the Accreditation Council for Occupational Therapy Education (ACOTE; 2007) standards for the assistant and therapist levels as related to "context of service delivery" (Standard B.6) and "management of occupational therapy services" (Standard B.7).

Strategic planning is the process of ensuring that an organization's current purpose, aspirations, goals, activities, and strategies connect to plans and support its mission. As a management tool or approach, strategic planning has been formally used by many for-profit and not-for-profit organizations for many years. An organization's process for strategic planning is influenced by its culture, leaders, size, activities, mission, and often the organization's currently felt degree of urgency for change. The advent of business competitors or a shift in the marketplace may significantly emphasize the need for a more responsive, focused, and comprehensive strategic plan. But ultimately, the ability of a system—be it a large or small unit (e.g., occupational therapy department) in an organization, hospital, school system, community agency, private practice, or college or university—to meet its goals and objectives begins, ends, and starts again with the development, implementation, and outcomes of the strategic plan.

Strategic planning, at its optimum level, is dynamic, and the resulting organizational strategic plan includes a snapshot in time of the organization's internal and external environments, coupled with the identification of goals and strategies leading to the ongoing fulfillment of the organization's mission and its quest for its ideal state or vision. Essentially, the completed strategic plan is regularly evaluated on the basis of the organization's mission, vision, and current and future operating goals and priorities. The strategic plan provides a template for organizational action and resource allocation; it further ensures the agency's competitiveness, viability, and linkage with the community.

Broad participation in the strategic planning process by stakeholders or membership groups throughout the organization and the broader community is critical. Active participation and input help ensure the plan's relevance to the organization's mission. Occupational therapy practitioners employed in or affiliated with a particular system should be aware of the organization's overall strategic plan. In addition, the involvement of occupational therapy staff in strategic planning at the unit level increases the potential significance of the occupational therapy unit and its recognized value to the overall organizational strategic plan.

This chapter provides an overview of the strategic planning process and the ways occupational therapy participation can assist in the process. Occupational therapy practitioners can help ensure that, regardless of the service delivery system, their consumers' occupational needs and challenges, as well as strategies supportive of or specific to occupational therapy, are given due consideration and attention in the overall organizational plan.

RELEVANCE OF STRATEGIC PLANNING

Programs for individuals in health, educational, and social agencies are a major part of the United States's heavily invested service-based economy. Awareness of the current environment, including its economic, political, cultural, social, and technological factors, is essential in planning and providing needed services for consumers of occupational therapy services (Boshoff, 2003). Of particular note, the containment of health care, education, and human services costs and access have been major concerns for several decades and are highly prevalent now. As occupational therapy practitioners look toward the future, analysis of the current service delivery environment is of paramount importance. Occupational therapists' roles as essential service providers, consultants, administrators, and community leaders require that they possess an understanding of their employing organization and its needs and opportunities that extends far beyond the discipline-specific theoretical or procedural knowledge and skills. They must recognize the relationship (in terms of purpose, activities, and costs and revenues) between their specific service delivery unit and the overall organization. Additionally, occupational therapy programs and related client services are influenced by local, regional, and national factors.

KEY CONCEPTS IN STRATEGIC PLANNING

As one considers the process of strategic planning, it is necessary to carefully analyze the term *strategy*, which may be defined as the methods selected to achieve a given goal or objective. Typically, a strategy is chosen because there is a reasonable degree of trust in its effectiveness and reliability in accomplishing a particular goal. The selection of a strategy also clearly signals which options or approaches were not chosen and identifies an organization's direction and possible allocation of its fiscal and human resources (Harpst, 2008). One concept of strategic planning emphasizes the linking of strategies with goals and objectives. Strategic goals and corresponding strategies anchored by the organization's mission enhance the probable success of the plan for a particular agency or unit within an agency. Many occupational therapy service and education programs have their own strategic plan that reflects the larger organizational plan. For example, all accredited occupational therapy educational programs are required, as a portion of their accrediting standards, to have a unit-specific strategic plan as a complement to the broader strategic plan of the college or university (ACOTE, 2008, Standard A.5.1).

The major components of any strategic plan include mission, vision, stakeholder participation, environmental analysis, SWOT analysis, identification of possible scenarios, prioritization and selection of strategic goals, and determination of evaluation criteria. The following sections discuss each of these components in turn.

Mission

As any organization begins the process of strategic planning (whether initially or to revise or update an existing strategic plan), a logical start is a close examination of the organization's mission. The mission is a description, typically concise and carefully crafted, that defines the basic purpose or focus of the organization or agency. An organization's mission statement provides a benchmark that grounds all of its subsequent activities and objectives. Typically, the mission statement remains stable over time. For instance, the mission of an occupational therapy pediatric private practice during its 10-plus-year existence was the provision of community-based occupational therapy sessions for children with a primary focus on needs not met through the public school system.

Vision

The vision statement provides a description of the aspirations or the ideal state desired for the organization. The vision encapsulates the highest level of achievement and validation of the organization and its mission. The American Occupational Therapy Association (AOTA) sought broad input from both the profession and society for many years in the development of its *Centennial Vision* statement: "We envision that occupational therapy is a powerful, widely recognized, science-driven, and evidence-based profession with a globally connected and diverse workforce meeting society's occupational needs" (AOTA, 2007, p. 613). This statement provides a far-reaching aspiration for the profession (Skoufalos, 2005). Similarly, the occupational therapy pediatric private practice previously described (in the section on mission) developed a vision stating, "We strive to ensure that children and their families can achieve maximum participation in their lives, particularly in their homes and communities." This vision statement offers a direction far beyond the services mandated for children who are served in the public school setting under federal law.

Stakeholder Participation

Ideally, the initiation of the strategic planning process involves participants from throughout an agency, with representation from all departments, including occupational therapy. Administrators and staff members from throughout an organization have valued and varied perspectives that inform and enhance the strategic planning process. Likewise, consideration and solicitation of the viewpoints of groups and individuals in the community beyond the organization are essential in ensuring that the strategic planning process is connected to wider community concerns and needs. Seeking input and participation from a diverse group of internal and external stakeholder groups is likely to produce a better deliberated and more connected and timely strategic plan (Horton & Hall, 2008).

Environmental Analysis

The strategic plan provides one basis for allocating resources required to address designated strategic priorities and initiatives. (Generally, ongoing organizational operations are not included in the strategic plan.) The end result of strategic planning cannot occur in a vacuum and must reflect a thoughtful and systematic analysis of the organization's internal and external environments. Environmental analysis provides an assessment of quantitative data as well as impressions and observations for a better understanding of the context for strategic discussions.

SWOT Analysis

Perhaps the most clear-cut and readily recognized approach used in assessing the environment is a SWOT analysis. A SWOT analysis is an assessment of the strengths (S), weaknesses (W), opportunities (O), and threats (T) for a particular organization or unit. Strengths and weaknesses are assessed on the basis of an internal analysis of the organization's current status. The identification of opportunities and threats is based on an examination of external factors that may influence the organization's viability and sustainability. Care should be exercised when conducting a SWOT analysis to ensure that the internal analysis (strengths and weaknesses) is differentiated from the external analysis (opportunities and threats; Formisano, 2004; Grace, 2008). A thoughtfully completed SWOT analysis provides the basis for determining future options for the organization.

Identification of Possible Scenarios

Scenarios are possibilities that might occur for a specific organization based on how the internal (strengths and weaknesses) and external (opportunities and threats) factors play out. Scenario identification is a bit like the development of a playbook in sports; the organization projects which plays or strategies might be the most beneficial, given the potential influence of identified internal and external factors. The organization weighs which scenarios are most likely to occur (Begun, Hamilton, & Kaissi, 2005) and develops strategies linked to likely or desired outcomes that position the organization for future change, development, and opportunity. Proactive strategy selection can be oriented toward risk reduction or program enhancement.

Prioritization and Selection of Strategic Goals

Once an organization determines its strategic focus, potential goals and objectives can be formulated, prioritized, and selected. Generally, selection of five or fewer goals allows for organizational focus, in-depth strategy development, and clear management criteria (Ginter & Swayne, 2006). In turn, the strategic plan provides the framework for the identification and selection of strategies that enable goal attainment and support the organization's mission and vision.

Determination of Evaluation Criteria

Any measure of a strategic plan's success must be based on the development of objective criteria or metrics. Plan evaluation occurs throughout the life of a strategic plan; typically, strategic plans focus on a 3- to 5-year period. Ongoing review and periodic formal assessment of a plan's success are necessary to allow for any needed adjustments or modifications. Indeed, early attainment of a plan's objectives or significant difficulty in meeting the stated outcomes may result in changes as necessary. It is important for the strategic plan to have measurable and clearly understood outcome measures and for accountability for these outcomes to be designated to staff or units within an organization.

LINKING STRATEGIC PLANNING TO EVIDENCE-BASED PRACTICE

The strategic planning process begins with assessment and concludes with reassessment. Ongoing evaluation of the results achieved by the organization in regard to its strategic plan makes the strategic planning process dynamic and real. A schematic view of the strategic planning process is provided in Figure 6.1. Strategic planning is akin to basic concepts in evidence-based practice and ensures that decisions and the desired outcome are based on considerations of all available supporting data. A thoughtfully developed strategic plan begins with an objective assessment of the organization's internal and external environment linked to the organization's mission and vision.

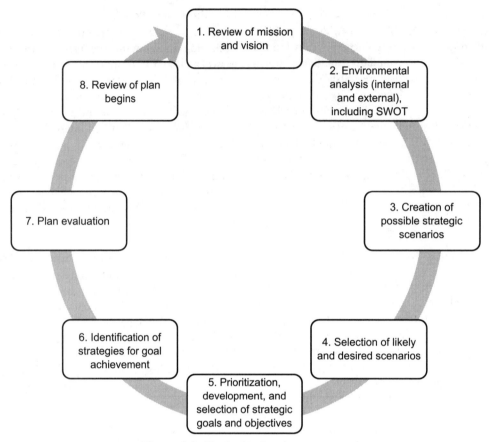

Figure 6.1. Strategic planning process.

LEADERSHIP OPPORTUNITIES

Individuals, at times, may believe that leadership rests only with a formal organizational position or role, such as department head, supervisor, or president. However, this chapter, as well as others throughout this book, suggests that all individuals employed in an organization have a responsibility to assume both formal and informal leadership roles in their daily practice. The occupational therapy practitioner is responsible for managing the delivery of occupational therapy services, whether on an individual basis or on behalf of other staff and students. The promotion of occupational therapy and the meeting of client needs are best supported by occupational therapy practitioners who are actively involved in the leadership and management of their primary work organization.

Additionally, occupational therapy practitioners can significantly maximize the contributions of their profession by assuming leadership roles in professional organizations such as AOTA, state and local occupational therapy associations, and other nonprofit and for-profit organizations. The strategic planning process provides an obvious stage for members of our profession to promote the expansion of occupational therapy and enhance the organization's overall achievement of its mission and strategic goals.

SAMPLE STRATEGIC PLAN

The following sample strategic plan outlines the results of all the major components in the strategic planning process. The plan is an adaptation of the strategic plan of Kosair Charities enTECH, an assistive technology agency that is a division of Spalding University and the Auerbach School of Occupational Therapy in Louisville, Kentucky. The agency is named for Kosair Charities, a significant community benefactor foundation for children and, specifically, the agency.

Agency Overview

Enabling Technologies of Kentuckiana (enTECH) began operations in 1987 as the Disabled Citizens Computer Center. The center changed its name to Enabling Technologies of Kentuckiana in 1994 to more accurately represent the organization's overall mission. enTECH is one of 12 charter members of a national organization, the Alliance for Technology Access. Since its inception, enTECH's goal has been to increase awareness, understanding, and implementation of technology to assist people with disabilities; enTECH provides consultations, demonstrations, training, and information sharing.

Although technology is constantly changing, the focus of enTECH remains to promote and foster independence and the potential of all persons by providing creative technology solutions. enTECH embraces the opportunity to work with persons of all ages, genders, races, and disabilities for full participation in life activities. Current agency staffing includes an occupational therapist, speech–language pathologist, community outreach coordinator, assistive technology assistant, and billing coordinator. Per diem occupational therapists also are employed by the organization. Additionally, there is an active occupational therapy fieldwork program (Levels I and II) for both the technical and professional levels.

Strategic Plan

The staff, including the lead occupational therapist, developed a strategic plan for enTECH (Strickland, 2009). This abbreviated sample of the plan is limited in scope; a strategic plan is typically much longer and more detailed (see Table 6.1).

Vision

The organizational vision is based on the concept of enabling full participation in life. Success in modern society is based on knowledge, and advancement occurs within contexts rich in technology, multiplicity, and access. Nearly 20% of the U.S. population consists of individuals with various disabilities. Alternative technologies and access to the various aspects of the technological world are of vital importance to ensure that all members of society are in-

Table 6.1. Outline of Sample Strategic Plan

Goal	Strategic objectives	Strategy
Strengthen and sustain partnerships with other community organizations in the area of assistive technology programming	Create at least three new relationships, including connections for the advancement of social justice for individuals with disabilities	Build capacity through the development of contractual agreements for providing services in the following: • An agency serving adults with developmental and physical disabilities • A residential organization that provides services for severely traumatized children who may be victims of sexual, physical, or emotional abuse • A private school serving students with learning difficulties in a nongraded elementary through secondary setting
Create an environment for learning that supports academic excellence and distinctiveness	Provide current fieldwork educators in other settings with opportunities for assistive technology resource use	• Develop Web-based seminars and learning modules for low-cost assistive technology solutions • Market educational program to regional occupational therapy schools for establishing Level I and II fieldwork agreements
Expand the community's awareness of technologies and services that increase an individual's performance in everyday living	Advance knowledge, skill, and ability to provide service and outreach for older adults and other disability groups who are underserved	• Participate in community health and wellness fairs • Enable organizational staff to serve on community boards • Conduct monthly community seminars that are promoted through the metropolitan government's office of elderly and disabled services
Develop external funding through grants and partnerships	Develop funding through workshop offerings, growing revenues by 10%	• Enter contractual agreements with at least 3 rural school districts in the local region that include training • Respond to requests for proposals from at least 2 community foundations • Establish training contract with a local private preschool for children with visual impairments to develop a model classroom
Communicate enTECH initiatives that integrate core messages to the larger community about our mission and vision	Appoint an advisory board of community leaders from the educational, disability, and rehabilitation communities in the metropolitan area	• Conduct at least 2 board meetings per year focused on outcomes and community capacity building

Advance the national recognition and reputation of the Center for Human Potential through publication and presentation of service provision and research initiatives	Link the strategic plan and mission of the university and the Center for Human Potential with individual staff development work plans	• Identify staff to work on specific initiatives:
		  – Speech–language pathology—school contracts
		  – Occupational therapy—early intervention assistive technology programming and service contracts
		  – Community coordinator—monthly trainings

Note. Copyright © Laura Strickland. Reprinted with permission.

cluded within its framework. An educational environment welcoming everyone to participate in programming will expand the diversity of the community and promote justice for many who otherwise might be excluded. enTECH is positioned to be locally and nationally recognized as a "Center for Human Potential," which reflects enTECH's vision to create opportunities for clients to be independent and empowered in their daily lives.

Mission

enTECH's mission is to provide services to consumers with the aim of providing creative technology solutions to enhance their participation in everyday life activities and to advance assistive technology educational opportunities for current and future practitioners.

Environmental and SWOT Analysis

The environmental analysis considered both the internal and external factors affecting enTECH's current and future operations. Program strengths included excellent staff credentials and competencies in assistive technology, highly favorable consumer outcomes and feedback, state-of-the-art lab demonstration areas, and a history of procurement of grant funding. Billable hours had steadily increased, and stable financial state and community foundation support for operations was significant. Three program weaknesses were identified: (1) Program scope and populations served were wide ranging and on occasion challenged the range of required staff expertise, (2) added staff was difficult to support given load and referral fluctuations, and (3) contributions to the university's overall overhead costs could affect the operating margin. External threats and opportunities were also evident: Although no other programs like enTECH existed in the Louisville metropolitan region, two other technology centers were located in other parts of the state. A further comprehensive investigation of how the center's services varied and the unique programming provided by enTECH was needed, particularly with state, federal, and third-party funding at possible risk of reduction.

Selected Strategic Goals, Objectives, and Strategies

enTECH's strategic goals, objectives, and strategies were developed on the basis of the mission, vision, and environmental and SWOT analysis described in this section. They are provided in Table 6.1 in the scorecard format (Wicks & St. Clair, 2007).

ENHANCING THE EFFECTIVENESS OF STRATEGIC PLANNING

The strategic plan provides a template for an organization's course over a possible 3- to 5-year period. Given the rapidly changing service delivery environments in which occupational therapists and occupational therapy assistants are employed, it is necessary to frequently assess an organization's direction and purpose. The strategic plan, in and of itself, is only a projection of what might be. Organizational leaders and participants from throughout the organization, including occupational therapy staff, should evaluate the fit between the strategic plan and the organization's mission and current operations on, at minimum, an annual basis. The strategic plan is a bit like a photograph, which depicts an image at a particular point in time. Like the subject of the photograph, the organization or unit continues to change and evolve as time progresses, and one should not consider the plan to be a finite or finished document. Rather, the plan provides a direction for an organization and its members.

Current practices indicate that the participation of individuals from throughout an organization in its management (vs. a top-down approach) clearly enhances the likelihood of organizational success. Consequently, a process as important as strategic planning benefits greatly from the buy-in and support of participants throughout the organization. Similarly, external stakeholder groups for whom an organization may exist to serve or from whom the organization requires support should be included in the process. What is essential in strategic planning is providing the opportunity of voice for all individuals who are a part of or influenced by the strategic plan. Always, the organization's mission should remain a focal point for any evaluation of the plan's merit, relevance, and success.

CONCLUSION

The key concepts of strategic planning require that an organization or unit carefully consider its purpose, review its internal and external environments, complete the SWOT analysis, develop strategic goals, and select strategies based on a careful consideration of all available data. The evaluation process of the strategic plan's success is very similar to the occupational therapy process in service provision. This planning success and relevance are significantly enhanced by the widespread participation of participants throughout the organization and communication with significant stakeholder groups outside the organization. A carefully constructed, flexible strategic plan creatively positions the unit or organization to withstand future challenges, meet its mission, and strive toward its vision.

Case Examples

LEVEL I FIELDWORK

As part of her Level I fieldwork placement, Rachel observed a community focus group for families of individuals with special needs and later discussed with her manager the implications for occupational therapy and broader public policy. During her university-based supervision seminar, Rachel presented an analysis of the feedback from the focus group and described the parameters for future direct-client services and population-based programming. After further discussion with students and faculty in her seminar group, Rachel was able to recommend proposed intervention services to her manager at the fieldwork site.

LEVEL II FIELDWORK

Joe did his Level II fieldwork in a large community hospital that had inpatient and outpatient rehabilitation facilities, a home health agency, and acute care. The hospital system's strategic plan included a public relations goal related to health and wellness for the entire community. Joe, as part of the development of strategies for this goal, was asked to represent the rehabilitation department in the development of rehabilitation-related community wellness activities that could be incorporated into the strategic plan. Joe looked for linkage between the ongoing daily activities and purpose of the rehabilitation department, specifically occupational therapy, and the public relations goal. The completed strategic plan incorporated wellness activities, including those with a rehabilitation focus, and thus Joe's contributions, including the development of an older adult wellness education module, helped the overall organization develop a strategic plan more relevant to community needs.

FIRST-TIME MANAGER

An occupational therapy service unit in a 195-bed skilled nursing facility (SNF) was staffed by two occupational therapy assistants; a staff occupational therapist; a Level II fieldwork student; and Jane, a recently promoted occupational therapy manager. In preparation for the development of the facility's strategic plan, the SNF administrator requested that each of the unit heads participate in the weekly department head meeting and present a SWOT analysis for his or her respective unit.

Over an extended series of brown bag lunch meetings, Jane led her staff in developing their own list of the unit's strengths and weaknesses from the internal perspective.

As they began to identify possible external opportunities and threats, differing ideas arose regarding new programmatic opportunities. The staff's knowledge of probable payment options for several new ventures was weak, so the fieldwork student volunteered to examine Medicare payment regulations, including the fiscal intermediary interpretive guidelines, and share the results. Compilation of this data led Jane to develop and administer a brief survey to similar occupational therapy units in the area and to confer with her state occupational therapy association for added data and sharing of possible resources. Jane's own development as a manager was supported by the SWOT process and interaction with staff. Jane shared the completed SWOT analysis with the administrator and other department heads, and ultimately the facility's strategic plan incorporated a strategic goal that included occupational therapy concerns and opportunities for two new programs and increased revenue (5% over the current fiscal year budget).

MANAGER

A health agency in a metropolitan community had a major objective addressing affordable community housing for individuals, including homeless individuals and families, older adults, and economically disadvantaged groups. In 2009, the federal government's economic development stimulus program provided funds for housing. Martha, an experienced occupational therapy manager from the agency, participated in a community task force to develop a strategic plan for the use of stimulus funding to promote the agency's housing objective. Martha's practice expertise was in the area of aging in place for seniors and the provision of community-based housing options for persons with developmental disabilities. With the task force, she focused on developing policy and funding criteria that ensured that underrepresented groups were included in the programs. Martha's leadership role in a broader community initiative allowed the resulting plan to more effectively meet community needs and used the occupational therapy skill set and knowledge of this experienced manager.

❖ Learning Activities

1. Identify a mission and vision statement for an occupational therapy–related nonprofit agency. Develop a possible SWOT analysis for the organization.

2. Using on a fieldwork experience, develop two to three strategic scenarios for the occupational therapy program to be presented in a 10-minute presentation to a simulated Board of Trustees (fellow classmates or colleagues).

3. Develop mission and vision statements for a proposed community organization.

4. From an Internet search, identify an organization's strategic plan and analyze that plan, particularly for evidence of member or stakeholder input.

✓ Multiple-Choice Questions

1. Strategic planning is best described as a
   a. Precise daily operations schedule
   b. Budget model
   c. Template for organizational action
   d. Allocation formula for staffing

2. The provision of occupational therapy services is most challenged by
   a. Lack of evidence-based practice
   b. Cost containment issues
   c. Insufficient supply of qualified workers
   d. Technology-related costs

3. The vision statement within the strategic plan identifies the organization's
   a. Strategy for success
   b. Most favored goal
   c. Primary purpose
   d. Aspired position

4. The foundation of any strategic plan is its
   a. Mission
   b. Vision
   c. Strategy
   d. Objectives

5. Assessment of the internal environment occurs by identifying
   a. Opportunities
   b. Threats
   c. Stakeholders
   d. Strengths

6. A completed SWOT analysis provides the basis for
   a. Evaluation criteria
   b. Possible scenarios
   c. Specific goals
   d. Predictable growth

7. Final scenario selection best predicts the
   a. Identification of goals
   b. Allocation of funding
   c. Expansion of mission
   d. Plan's success

8. A limitation of the strategic planning process is its
   a. Dynamic nature
   b. Small number of plan goals
   c. Reliance on broad input
   d. Ever-evolving plan currency

9. Strategy success and its measurement are best implemented by the
   a. Organizational president
   b. Responsible staff or unit
   c. Stakeholders
   d. Planning director

10. One key outcome of an organization's management of the planning process is
    a. Creation of positions
    b. Acceptance of consensus
    c. Allocation of resources
    d. Budget expansion

11. A step in the strategic planning process that identifies and examines an organization's internal and external environments is best described as
    a. Strategy development
    b. SWOT analysis
    c. Scenario expansion
    d. Vision clarification

12. An external condition providing potential obstacles for an organization is best described as a
    a. Scenario
    b. Threat
    c. Strategy
    d. Weakness

13. An external condition providing potential for organizational sustainability and growth is best described as a(n)
    a. Strength
    b. Vision
    c. Mission
    d. Opportunity

14. Methods selected to achieve goals and objectives are
    a. Action plans
    b. Strengths
    c. Strategies
    d. Scenarios
15. Stakeholder groups of an organization important in the planning process most likely include
    a. Employees, consumers, and supporting organizations
    b. Policy makers, service providers, and payer sources
    c. Consultants and external standard-setting agencies
    d. Focus groups, survey consultants, and practitioners
16. A template for an organization's course over a possible period of 3–5 years is its
    a. Mission statement
    b. Vision statement
    c. Strategy analysis
    d. Strategic plan
17. In response to the rapidly changing service delivery environment, organizations must frequently
    a. Revisit their payer source mix
    b. Assess their direction and purpose
    c. Revise goals and objectives
    d. Review employee performance
18. Individuals involved in an organization's strategic planning process should include
    a. Executives and managers within the organization
    b. Employees and administration
    c. Administrators and consumers
    d. All who are influenced by it
19. Strategic planning would be the least effective in an organization that has
    a. Cost containment concerns
    b. Environmental challenges
    c. Absence of identified mission
    d. Decreased morale among staff
20. The key strategic planning role for the entry-level practitioner (i.e., new graduate) is
    a. Developing unit budget for the new plan
    b. Networking with the broader community leaders
    c. Participating in identifying new initiatives
    d. Assigning strategies to staff for implementation

References

Accreditation Council for Occupational Therapy Education. (2007). Accreditation standards for a master's-degree-level educational program for the occupational therapist. *American Journal of Occupational Therapy, 61,* 652–661.

Accreditation Council for Occupational Therapy Education. (2008). *Accreditation Council for Occupational Therapy Education standards and interpretive guidelines.* Retrieved April 1, 2009, from www.aota.org/Educate/Accredit/StandardsReview/guide/42369.aspx

American Occupational Therapy Association. (2007). AOTA's *Centennial Vision* and executive summary. *American Journal of Occupational Therapy, 61,* 613–614.

Begun, J. W., Hamilton, J. A, & Kaissi, A. A. (2005). An exploratory study of healthcare planning in two metropolitan areas. *Journal of Healthcare Management, 50,* 264–274.

Boshoff, K. (2003). Utilisation of strategic analysis and planning by occupational therapy services. *Australian Occupational Therapy Journal, 50,* 252–258.

Formisano, R. A. (2004). *Manager's guide to strategy.* New York: McGraw-Hill.

Ginter, P. M., & Swayne, L. E. (2006). Moving toward strategic planning unique to health care. *Frontiers of Health Services Management, 23*(2), 33–37.

Grace, P. (2008). Strategic planning design and implementation. *OT Practice, 13*(19), CE1–CE7.

Harpst, G. (2008). *Six disciplines execution revolution.* Findlay, OH: Six Disciplines Publishing.

Horton, A., & Hall, J. (2008). Redesigning occupational therapy service provision to increase efficiency, effectiveness, and stakeholder satisfaction. *British Journal of Occupational Therapy, 71,* 161–164.

Skoufalos, M. (2005). *Changing the game: The future of OT: One man's vision.* Retrieved February 23, 2009, from www.therapytimes.com/0815OTGAME

Strickland, L. S. (2009). *enTech strategic plan.* Louisville, KY: Auerbach School of Occupational Therapy, Spalding University.

Wicks, A. M., & St. Clair, L. (2007). Competing values in healthcare: Balancing the (un)balanced scorecard. *Journal of Healthcare Management, 52,* 309–324.

Appendix 6.A. Strategic Planning Evidence Table

Topic	Evidence
Strategic planning concepts	Formisano, R. A. (2004). *Manager's guide to strategy.* New York: McGraw-Hill.
Mission and vision statements as organizational anchors	Boshoff, K. (2003). Utilisation of strategic analysis and planning by occupational therapy services. *Australian Occupational Therapy Journal, 50,* 252–258. Grace, P. (2008). Strategic planning design and implementation. *OT Practice, 13*(19), CE1–CE7. Horton, A., & Hall, J. (2008). Redesigning occupational therapy service provision to increase efficiency, effectiveness, and stakeholder satisfaction. *British Journal of Occupational Therapy, 71,* 161–164.
Scenario development	Grace, P. (2008). Strategic planning design and implementation. *OT Practice, 13*(19), CE1–CE7. Harpst, G. (2008). *Six disciplines execution revolution.* Findlay, OH: Six Disciplines Publishing.
SWOT analysis	Grace, P. (2008). Strategic planning design and implementation. *OT Practice, 13*(19), CE1–CE7.
Selection of goals, objectives, and strategies	Harpst, G. (2008). *Six disciplines execution revolution.* Findlay, OH: Six Disciplines Publishing.
Evaluation of strategic planning	Grace, P. (2008). Strategic planning design and implementation. *OT Practice, 13*(19), CE1–CE7. Wicks, A. M., & St. Clair, L. (2007). Competing values in healthcare: Balancing the (un)balanced scorecard. *Journal of Healthcare Management, 52,* 309–324.

7

Financial Planning and Budgeting

Melanie T. Ellexson, DHSc, MBA, OTR/L, FAOTA

❖ Key Terms and Concepts

Accounts payable. Involve the purchase of goods and services on credit.

Accounts receivable. Claims resulting from the delivery of goods or services on credit.

Balance sheet. Reports the amount of assets, liabilities, and owners' or stockholders' equity at a specified moment.

Breakeven. The point in units or sales where the amount of revenue is equal to the total expenses of a business or program.

Budgeting. Understanding how much money a business or program has and where it goes, followed by planning how to best allocate those funds.

Capital expenditure. Payment by a business for basic assets (e.g., property, fixtures, machinery), but not for day-to-day operations (e.g., payroll, inventory, maintenance, advertising).

Cash flow. The movement of money into and out of a business that determines its solvency.

Depreciation. A noncash expense that reduces the value of an asset as a result of wear and tear, age, or decreased utility.

Direct costs. Those costs that can be directly assigned to an activity with relative ease and a high degree of accuracy.

Expenses. Costs incurred to earn revenues, costs used up or expiring during an accounting period, and costs for which the future value cannot be measured.

Fixed costs. Costs required to produce a product or service that are not dependent on the quantity of services provided (e.g., rent for office space).

Income statement. Reports revenues, expenses, gains, losses, and net income during an indicated period of time.

Indirect costs. Expenses of doing business that are not readily identified with a particular project function or activity but are necessary for the general operation of the business.

Operating costs. Expenses arising during the normal course of running a business (e.g., office electrical bill).

Overhead costs. Indirect recurring costs of running a business that are not directly linked to the goods or service produced and sold (e.g., rent, utilities, advertising).

Passthrough taxation. Method in which business owners pay income tax on the basis of an organization's earnings rather than the business. (Sole proprietorships and partnerships pay through this method.)

Revenue. Total income, cash and noncash, received from a business before any expenses are paid.

Variable costs. Cost associated with producing each additional unit of goods or services.

Working capital. Current assets minus current liabilities.

❖ Learning Objectives

After completing this chapter, you should be able to do the following:

- Understand accounting basics in order to manage cash flow, improve profitability, develop a budget, and manage risk.
- Understand the different budget constraints and financial considerations when delivering services in for-profit and not-for-profit programs.
- Establish the cost of a program and determine funding necessary for viability.
- Recognize the advantages of the various types of business structure when developing programs and practices.
- Identify multiple funding sources and understand their unique function and structure.

The face of health care is changing, and reform measures will affect the financial future of the occupational therapy profession. Occupational therapy managers of existing programs within facilities or those managing community programs and private practices will need to manage resources and service delivery using sound business principles. New and existing business ventures will need to build the cost of developing, implementing, and maintaining electronic health care records into their budgets. The occupational therapy provider will be required to use proven disease management programs based on sound evidence. They may be challenged to collect and report measures of health care cost and quality beyond the traditional outcome measures. Occupational therapy managers may be involved in establishing performance thresholds that will ensure appropriate payment to meet budget demands (Obama for America, 2009).

Christina A. Metzler, chief public affairs officer of the American Occupational Therapy Association (AOTA), has stated, "Health care reform as a top priority is both a boon and a threat to occupational therapy at the same time." She indicated that there will be "significant changes to service delivery and payment, while creating new opportunities for the delivery of occupational therapy services to more individuals" (AOTA, 2008). Change requires planning and planning must include astute, accurate, and strategic budgeting and financial planning.

STRATEGIC PLANNING

Financial planning and budgeting are building blocks within a business's strategic plan. Financial ideas influence how your program or practice develops. What you must pay for (costs/expenses) and that what you are reimbursed for your services (income/revenue) directly affect your practice's strategy, direction, and decision making. When beginning programs and businesses, *financial strategic planning* means carefully assessing your start-up abilities, beginning operations, and projections for future viability within the organization and community. Hospital management literature provides an example of financial planning in the strategic planning process and provides a guide to the budgeting process.

UNDERSTANDING THE BASICS OF ACCOUNTING

In order to be a good financial planner, you must understand the language. Accounting, like occupational therapy, has a language of its own. Those of you working in a larger health care system will be working with the chief financial officer (CFO), who can guide you through this process. If you are developing your own program or business, you should hire an accountant or financial advisor to help in setting up your systems for accounting and keeping records. Regardless of the circumstances, it is important for a successful manager to understand several basic concepts of accounting: tracking accounts payable and receivable, monitoring cash flow, developing a budget, and managing risk for profitability.

Tracking Accounts Payable and Receivable

Accounts payable are bills, credit card balances, and loan obligations. The amounts that your clients, insurance companies, federal or state funding programs, and others owe you are the *accounts receivable*. There are two basic ways of recording expenses and income received. The *cash basis* method of accounting requires that your record your income when the "cash" is actually received. Cash may be in the form of checks, credit card charges, and electronic transfer of funds or currency. Likewise, expenses are recorded when you actually make the payment. This is a less complicated method of accounting for receivables or payables.

The method of accounting that records income and expense at the time they are incurred is called *accrual-based* accounting. This method is more complex and requires very careful monitoring because the expenses have been incurred but the payment is not in hand. This method is frequently used by larger hospitals and health care systems because payment by third-party payers and federal and state funding programs may take a long time. This method allows those organizations to have a more complete understanding of what they are earning and whether they are meeting budget projections.

Monitoring Cash Flow

Cash flow is the term used to describe the movement of actual income and expenses in and out of your program or business over a period of time. Remember, cash is the money that is in hand or in the bank. It is not equipment or accounts receivable. It is what you have readily available to pay salaries, rent, and monthly expenses (New York State Society of Certified Public Accountants, 2009). Cash inflow is what you receive from your clients, third-party payers, and lenders or investors every month. Cash outflow consists of salaries, rent, supply and utility bills, and other expenses you pay on a regular basis (Small Business Notes, 2009b). If the cash you have coming in is greater than that which is going out, you have a *positive cash flow*. If the opposite is true, you have a *negative cash flow*. A major goal of any new business or program is not necessarily to be profitable immediately but rather to have a positive cash flow to support current operations. This requires careful planning to ensure from the beginning a client base that has the ability to pay you on a timely basis.

To manage cash flow, the manager must gain an understanding of three more accounting basics: (a) capital expenditures, (b) fixed expenses, and (c) variable expenses. *Capital expenditure* refers to items you own, or will own in time, that you will deduct or depreciate according to schedules provided by the Internal Revenue Service (IRS). These expenditures include office equipment, therapy equipment, a business vehicle, computer software, or other tangible business items having a useful life of greater than 1 year and costing more than $1,000.

Fixed expenses are those that remain constant from month to month and do not change with volume or activity. Fixed expenses, often referred to as *overhead*, usually involve a contract or legal obligation fixing the terms for monthly payments within given time frames (Small Business Notes, 2009b). Examples are rent, lease of equipment, utilities, employee wages and benefits, and business loan payments. Fixed expenses must be carefully planned and monitored because they can make or break a new or continuing program or business.

Variable expenses change with the volume of service provided. Variable expenses include postage, telephone use, marketing brochures, advertising, and office and clinical supplies. You must keep careful watch on these expenses because your ability to control variable expenses can directly affect your profit. Variable expenses must be consistent with the volume of business you produce. Exhibit 7.1 shows a sample cash flow worksheet that managers can use to monitor cash flow.

Exhibit 7.1. Cash Flow Worksheet

Cash Flow Worksheet

For the period from _____ to _____

Cash and cash equivalents: Beginning of period _____
Cash flow from operating activities _____

Net income _____
(Adjustment to net income to produce net cash flow from operating activities)
- Depreciation expense _____
- Net change to accounts receivable _____
- Net change to accounts payable _____
Total adjustments to operating income _____

Net cash flow provided by operating activities _____

Cash flows from investing activities _____
- Purchase of new computer _____
- Purchase of new activity equipment _____

Net cash used in investing activities _____

Net cash flows from financing activities _____
- Increase in short-term debt _____
- Redemption of long-term debt _____

Total cash flow _____
- Cash at the beginning of the period _____
- Cash at the end of the period _____

All of these expenses are generally tax deductible. You should keep good records and review these costs regularly to better understand how your profit is made and where costs can be controlled. Good cash management means the following:

- Knowing when, where, and how your cash needs will occur;
- Knowing what the best sources are for meeting additional cash needs; and
- Being prepared to meet these needs when they occur by keeping good relationships with bankers and other creditors (Small Business Notes, 2009b).

Good business practice requires developing a *cash flow projection*. Managers should have both a short-term (weekly, monthly) cash flow projection and a long-term cash flow projection (3–5 years) to help in developing strategies for sustaining the program or business. Short-term cash flow projections help determine your cash position—what you can invest in short-term (money market, CD) investment accounts—and to estimate working capital requirements. *Working capital* is liquid assets (cash, accounts receivable, inventory) divided by short-term obligations such as accounts payable and salaries. The purpose of long-term cash flow projections is to support your strategic planning and estimates of borrowing requirements and ability to make payments (Small Business Notes, 2009b).

Developing a Budget

A budget is a forecast of revenue and expenditures. It most commonly covers a 12-month fiscal year. At the end of the fiscal year, you can compare your budgeted income and expenses to the actual performance of your business or program; additional monthly comparisons of income and expenses to budget will help you be sure you are on target. You may need to reduce expenses if you are off the projected mark for revenue.

One of the first steps in developing a budget is to establish your fiscal year. Programs embedded in larger organizations will use the fiscal year established for the organization. If you need to determine a fiscal year, you may choose to start with the month you start your business. For example, if you expect your first clients beginning in September, your fiscal year could run from September through August of the following year. If you are relying on government funding, you may choose a fiscal year ending June 30 so your budget corresponds with the major funding cycle of the government. Your accountant will advise you regarding your choice of a fiscal year.

Basic Budget Concepts

Basic budget concepts include revenue, total costs, and profit. It is very important to estimate anticipated units of service by payer source (revenue) as accurately as possible. During your first year, this will be a gradually increasing sum as your business becomes more established.

You will be able to look at your revenue history as a guide for continuing programs and for years subsequent to your first year. After you have determined your estimated units of revenue, you can calculate the related fixed and variable costs necessary to reach your budget goals (Gay, Lesbian, and Straight Education Network [GLSEN], 2000).

Profit should be large enough to make a return on your cash investment and a return on your work. For example, if you can expect a 7% return on monies invested outside of the business, then you should expect at least that much return on what you invest in the business. In targeting profits, you also want a fair return on your labor; your salary should reflect fair market value for your work. The basic budgeting equation is

$$\text{Revenue} - \text{Total Costs} = \text{Profits}$$

Managers of continuing programs or businesses will look to previous years' units of service and costs to forecast the future year's budget, making adjustments for price increases, inflation, and salary or wage increases. In starting a new venture, you will have to rely on your experience and knowledge of the health care industry in your geographic area to determine potential demand for your services. An accountant or business advisor may be helpful in projecting realistic numbers, but they may not be familiar with your specific area of health care. As the manager or owner, you are responsible for knowing about the market for your services.

To create a budget, you must determine how much profit you want to earn in your fiscal year. Occupational therapy programs within larger organizations, both nonprofit and for-profit, may be given an expected profit margin. *Nonprofit* does not mean that programs do not have to make money; they need to be profitable to support future programs and to help the organization grow.

In general, your budget will include the following:

- Revenues needed for operations,
- Cash required for labor and supplies,
- Total start-up costs,
- Day-to-day maintenance costs, and
- Expected profit.

Operating Costs

The next step in the budget process is to develop operating costs, including fixed and variable costs. Your capital equipment expense is depreciated according to IRS rules previously discussed. Purchasing capital equipment is an important step in the budgeting process, and timing is an important consideration; *capital equipment* is defined in accounting terms as any single piece of equipment that you use to provide a service or use to sell, store, or deliver merchandise. Salaries, benefits, and cost of supplies and equipment will require the most attention of most managers; Table 7.1 lists other operating costs that also must be considered (GLSEN, 2000).

The income statement, often referred to as the *profit-and-loss statement*, gives a complete financial overview by categorizing your revenue and expenses and is one of the best ways to look at a business or program's profitability (Table 7.2). If you are just starting your business or program, you will not yet have historical business financial data to report.

Labor is the largest operating expense in health care organizations. The first step in determining your personnel budget is to calculate the number of units of service that each occupational therapy practitioner is expected to produce on a daily basis and then establish the number of full-time equivalent (FTE) employees you will need to produce the units of service you have projected. FTE is the amount

Table 7.1. Operating Costs

Category	Amount ($)
General Fixed Expenses	
Rent	24,000
Utilities	6,000
Depreciation	4,000
Insurance	4,300
Loan repayments	13,900
Accounting service and fees	2,500
Clinical salaries and wages	85,000
Clerical salaries and wages	28,000
Benefits	12,000
Office supplies	1,900
Business license	300
Cleaning service	4,700
Telephone and telecommunication	7,600
Total	**194,200**
Variable Expenses	
Marketing	3,600
Temp wages	20,000
Medical and clinical supplies	5,000
Maintenance and repairs	700
Education	2,500
Travel	1,000
Total	**32,800**
General Purchase Expenses	
Office equipment	2,000
Clinic equipment	7,000
Business van	34,000
Other	1,000
Total	**44,000**

Table 7.2. Income Statement

Category	Amount ($)
Income	
Gross income from services or products	291,200
Less bad debt	1,456
Net income	289,744
Operating cost expense	227,000
Gross profit	**62,744**
Operating Costs	
General Fixed Expenses	
Rent	24,000
Utilities	6,000
Depreciation	4,000
Insurance	4,300
Loan repayments	13,900
Accounting service and fees	2,500
Clinical salaries and wages	85,000
Clerical salaries and wages	28,000
Benefits	12,000
Office supplies	1,900
Business license	300
Cleaning service	4,700
Telephone and telecommunication	7,600
General Variable Expenses	
Marketing	3,600
Temp wages	20,000
Medical and clinical supplies	5,000
Maintenance and repairs	700
Education	2,500
Travel	1,000
Total expenses	**227,000**
Net income before taxes	**62,744**
Provision for taxes on income	**12,548**
Net income after taxes (profit)	**50,196**

of work one full-time employee is expected to complete in a normal 8-hour day, 5 days a week for 52 weeks—that is, over the course of 2,080 work hours per year (Fogel, 2000). Many practitioners work part-time, 10-hour days, and/or weekend hours. Although you will need to consider these variances, your should base your FTE count on your projected units of service.

For example, two FTEs could produce 160 units per week, or 2 units per hour, during a start-up operation. This reflects a 50% productivity rate, which may be acceptable in the beginning of an operation when staff are involved in set-up and marketing, but would not be acceptable once operations are fully under way. Productivity standards vary from popula-

tion to population and from setting to setting. Most practices use a 75% to 90% productivity standard. At 75%, one FTE would deliver 24 units of service (6 hours) per day. This might be the expectation for an acute care hospital–based program in which set-up in the client's room and unanticipated interruptions might affect productivity. At 90% productivity, one FTE would deliver about 29 units of service, or just over 7 hours per day. This might be the expectation in a busy outpatient service where clients require fewer set-ups and are better able to participate in their rehabilitation.

In determining a program's productivity rate, consider what activities each staff member is able to perform, the nature of the program, the documentation requirements, the physical layout of the service delivery area, and the availability of shared equipment. There may be additional considerations based on the nature of the program or practice. Once you have developed your productivity standards, you can establish a staffing plan detailing how many and what kinds of personnel you will need. Your plan should be based on the FTE needs of your program and should cover all hours of operation. Once the plan is established, you may seek full- or part-time staff to fill your needs. It is important to establish the staffing plan based on the needs of the department or program and not on the needs of individuals who are working in the facility or those who may be seeking employment. Although it is important to consider the needs of your personnel, staffing on the basis of individuals' needs may interfere with productivity and have a negative impact on the bottom line. See Exhibit 7.2 for examples of typical staffing patterns and plans.

EXHIBIT 7.2. EXAMPLES OF STAFFING PATTERNS AND PLANS

Staffing by Type of Personnel, Outpatient Clinic

Manager	1.0 FTE
Occupational therapist	3.0 FTE
Occupational therapy assistant	2.0 FTE
Aide	1.0 FTE
Total	**7.0 FTE**

Staffing by Program, Hospital or Health Care System

Manager	1.0 FTE
Rehabilitation unit	4.0 FTE
Outpatient, main campus	3.0 FTE
Outpatient, community site	2.5 FTE
Acute care	3.5 FTE
Psychiatry unit	1.0 FTE
Neonatology service	1.5 FTE
Intensive care unit	1.0 FTE
Total	**17.5 FTE**

Note. FTE = full-time equivalent.

Employee benefits are an operating cost that must be considered in the budget. Benefit costs vary based on the size of a business. Employees of small businesses have access to fewer benefits than do employees of large businesses. Small and large businesses continue to provide benefits to their employees, but at a declining rate. The cost of health insurance for employees has increased in recent years (Popkin, 2005), and now, more than ever, health and other related benefits are an important budgetary consideration.

The general cost of benefits ranges between 20% and 40% of salaries, depending on the mix of mandatory and voluntary benefits available to each category of employee. Mandatory benefits, which include workers' compensation benefits, may vary by state or local law. Voluntary benefits might include general health insurance, dental insurance, prescription drug program coverage, accidental death and dismemberment insurance, long-term disability insurance, vision insurance, employee assistance programs, dependent care flexible spending accounts, and short-term disability insurance, as well as a number of other options (Society for Human Resource Management, 2009). Benefits have become a major consideration in potential employees' choice of employment and for retention of staff.

In cost–benefit analysis, used to compare different courses of action, a dollar value is assigned to both the expenditure and its results. A cost–benefit analysis is a simple tool and a great way to analyze actions for small businesses and large corporations alike. Web sites such as InfoTech Research (www.infotech.com) offer free tools to perform a cost–benefit analysis for your program.

Direct use supplies are a variable operating expense that must be considered as a direct cost of doing business. They are tied directly to your budget projection for units of service. Direct supply use must be managed carefully to avoid unnecessary expenditure. Reusable versus disposable products, multiuser workstations, and electronic reporting are just a few of the ways to control these costs.

Setting the Budget Pattern

Managers need to analyze and develop realistic productivity standards as part of the budgeting process. The first step is to determine the workload for the department or program. Workload can be calculated by number of visits or units of service produced in a given time period, generally 15 minutes. Medicare has a more complicated formula, the resource-based relative value scale, that may be used to determine productivity and related costs. The relative value unit (RVU) is the common scale by which practically all physician-driven Medicare services are measured. Medicare's Central Management System (www.medicare.gov) and most other insurers use RVU values to determine the reimbursement rate for services after incorporating geographic and other factors (Health Resources and Services Administration, n.d.; Shackelford, 1999). Measuring productivity using RVUs is a more complex system of management. (For those needing further information, see the Health Resources and Services Administration's [n.d.] online report on trends in physician productivity or Medicare's Web site [www.medicare.gov].)

For purposes of this chapter, the simpler unit-of-service method is used to determine staffing needs. Historical data should be used, when available, to project what the workload will be for the year. For new programs, begin by budgeting for a relatively lower number of visits or units and gradually build over time, called a *growth pattern* (see Table 7.3 and Figure 7.1).

Some practices experience peaks and valleys that follow a seasonal pattern. For example, a pediatric practice may see more children in the summer when school is not in session than they do when children can receive services at school. Programs that depend on referrals from outside sources, such as physicians or case managers, may find themselves very busy during the winter and summer holidays but experience a slowdown in the months following the holidays; referral sources may work diligently to get clients into services before vacation and then need to review old cases and investigate new cases after the holiday, causing a delay in the referral process. These and other factors may necessitate budgeting using a seasonal projection (Table 7.3). Many occupational therapy departments and programs, however, find that a straight-line pattern, in which expenses are spread relatively evenly over the course of the fiscal year, works best for budgeting (Table 7.3, Figure 7.1).

Managing Risk for Profitability

The goal of any business venture is for sufficient cash flow (income) to meet fixed and variable expenses and gradually

Table 7.3. Budgeting Patterns

	July	Aug	Sept	Oct	Nov	Dec	Jan	Feb	Mar	April	May	June
Revenue	$21	$26	$30	$36	$39	$44	$49	$53	$57	$58	$61	$63
Fixed expense	$25	$25	$25	$25	$25	$25	$25	$25	$33*	$33	$33	$33
Variable expense	$2	$2.5	$3	$3.5	$3.8	$4	$5	$5	$5.5	$6	$6	$6
Revenue	$60	$60	$65	$68	$70	$70	$65	$60	$60	$65	$70	$65
Fixed expense	$30	$30	$30	$30	$30	$30	$30	$30	$30	$30	$30	$30
Variable expense	$8	$8	$9	$10	$12	$12	$9	$8	$8	$9	$12	$9

*Denotes hiring of .5 FTE.

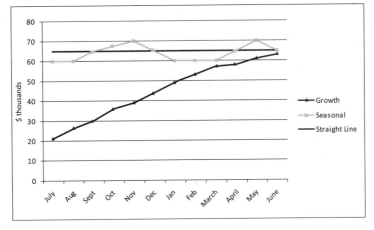

Figure 7.1 Budgeting patterns.

exceed these expenses to gain a profit. The point at which a program meets its fixed and variable expenses is called the *breakeven point* (see Table 7.4); at this point, the program is neither making nor losing money. To determine how many units of service (e.g., 15-minute periods) must be delivered to break even, first calculate the unit contribution margin, which is the charge per unit minus the variable expense per unit. Then divide fixed costs by the unit contribution margin to yield the number of units needed to break even. The following formula expresses this process:

Fixed Costs ÷ Unit Contribution Margin = Number of Units Needed to Break Even

For example, for a program with fixed costs of $194,200 per year, a reimbursement rate of $35 per unit of service, and a variable cost per unit of $4,

$194,200 ÷ ($35 − $4) = 6,264 units

Thus, the number of units required to cover expenses for the first year of operation is 6,264. If units of service provided are spread evenly over a 52-week work year, 30 hours, or 120 units of service, must be delivered, billed, and collected each week to break even (Small Business Notes, 2009a), as follows:

6,264 units per year ÷ 52 weeks = 120 units per week ÷ 4 units per hour = 30 hours per week

Table 7.4. Breakeven Analysis Summary

Category	Amount
Variable cost	$4 per unit
Fixed cost	$194,200
Expected sales	8,320 units
Price	$35 per unit
Total revenue	$291,200
Total variable costs	$33,280
Profit	$63,720

For new programs and services, units of service provided typically are lower at start-up and gradually increase as business volume increases. For the first year, and perhaps for a few subsequent years as the business grows, you should plan for those increases while still projecting an annual budgeted number of service units, called *revenue projection*. An individual who works a full day, usually 8 hours, is considered FTE. If two FTEs produce an average of 160 units per week for a total of 8,320 units for the year, the business has the potential of making a good profit in the first year.

Another way to improve cash flow is to carefully monitor accounts receivable and accounts payable. Investing in billing software and/or administrative staff with coding knowledge is critical to any rehabilitation program or business. Careful recordkeeping of incoming money and outgoing expenses is very important in controlling cash flow. Building and maintaining a *cash reserve*, or emergency fund equivalent to 3 to 6 months of fixed and variable expenses, should be a goal of any new business. Cash reserves may be needed for nonroutine expenditures such as a major repair, a capital expenditure, or another unplanned expense.

Managing your cash flow means making your money work for you. Once you have established reserve accounts, you should invest any monies not needed for daily operations in investment funds. Your financial advisor can assist in making these decisions (Small Business Administration [SBA], 1991). The bottom line on the best way to be profitable is to manage cash flow by collecting revenue, controlling costs, building reserves, and investing for the future.

DEVELOPING START-UP AND OPERATING COSTS FOR NEW PROGRAMS AND BUSINESSES

With a basic understanding of financial management, you can begin to determine how much and what information you will need to complete the financial components of your new business plan. You need to determine what it will cost to implement the plan you have developed for your program or business. The two categories of expense that should be calculated are start-up and operating costs. Start-up costs include one-time costs such as office furniture, signage, and major equipment; operating costs include rent, salaries, and utilities.

All business ventures are different, and cash needs may be different at the various stages of development. It is critical to know up front whether you will have enough money to start your program or business venture. When identifying these costs, you may want to determine which costs are essential and which may be optional (SBA, 2009). An effective way to calculate start-up costs is to use a worksheet listing fixed and variable expenses and one-time capital equipment purchases. Capital equipment has an extended life, so it is properly considered a fixed asset (Entrepreneur Network, 2009). Institutions use different amounts to capitalize equipment costs within the organization; check with your CFO or accountant to verify the amount you may use to designate capital equipment for your program or business (see Table 7.5).

Once you have determined how much money you will need and when you will need the cash in hand, you can research different types of funding. Where and how you look for money will depend on the type of program or business you are starting. If your program is part of a larger organization, you may ask the organization's administration or board of directors for funds.

The SBA makes loans to small businesses and start-up businesses. Most SBA loans are administered by local banks. You will normally deal with your local bank throughout the process. For start-up loans, the SBA generally requires that you supply one-third of the money you need for starting the business. The rest of the money must be guaranteed by business or personal assets. You can visit the SBA Web site at www.sba.gov/index.html.

Funding sources may include personal loans you make to the business or money that comes from friends or family. It is imperative that both you and your investors know the risks and can afford a loss if your business is not successful. The SBA recommends that you never take money from someone without first doing the legal work necessary to establish the terms of the loan. An appropriate professional must handle these investments in your business. The SBA warns business developers never to spend money they do not have in hand: Even if potential investors commit funds to your business, these investments can fall though (Berry, 2009).

Grants may be a source of start-up monies for certain types of health care programs, particularly community-based programs and those having educational or training components. New programs in established nonprofit health care organizations are frequently eligible for this type of funding. Unfortunately, many grants require programs and services to be nonprofit to qualify. If you're starting a for-profit business or program that will serve an underserved population or fill an established community need, however, you may be eligible for start-up funds through some federal, state, local, or private funding sources. Such funds are available, particularly for programs or service delivery that is unique and/or in emerging areas of practice (U.S. Department of Health and Human Services, 2003).

Determining the business structure for your operation requires decisions about the tax and legal criteria of your business in order to meet federal, state, and local laws. Business structures may differ depending on their size, ownership, control, taxes, and risks.

A business or program has two main tax options. A *for-profit* tax status means that the business or program provides goods and services with the goal of making money for the owners or stakeholders. A *nonprofit* or *not-for-profit* tax status means that goods and services are provided to individuals or populations, but shareholders or trustees do not financially benefit. The organization must retain money earned and use it for expenses, operations, and programs.

Legal structure determines the how your business will legally be organized and defines the ownership, relationship between owners, the type of business, and the management of the business. There are four common types of legal structure: (1) sole proprietorships, (2) partnerships, (3) corporations, and (4) limited liability companies (Quick MBA, 2007).

A *sole proprietorship*, in which the owner is the business, is the most common form of legal structure for small companies. The simplicity of the organization is an advantage of this type of structure; however, the owner is fully liable for all risk.

Table 7.5. Start-Up Costs

Category	Amount ($)
Start-up Expenses	
Legal	1,000
Office supplies	2,500
Brochures/business cards	3,000
Clinical supplies	5,000
Consultants	10,000
Insurance	500
Rent	2,100
Research and development	1,000
Expensed equipment	27,000
Other	2,000
Total start-up expenses	**54,100**
Start-up Assets Needed	
Cash balance on starting date	52,000
Other short-term assets	10,000
Total short-term assets	62,000
Long-term assets	0
Total assets	62,000
Total requirements	**116,100**

A *partnership* may be categorized as general or limited. A *general partnership* is an association among two or more people. The partners are personally liable for the debts of the business and are subject to passthrough taxation. A *limited partnership* is made up of two levels of partners in which the general partners are personally liable for the debts of the business while the limited partners have only invested in the business and only risk the capital that they have invested.

A *corporation* is the most common form of larger business and is a separate entity that limits the liability of its shareholders. Corporations generally have management or operational staff separate from the owners. The *limited liability company (LLC)* is a newer form of legal structure that allows owners the personal liability protection of the corporation, passthrough taxation, and operational flexibility of a partnership or sole proprietorship (Quick-MBA, 2007).

Conclusion

Occupational therapy managers, entrepreneurs, and intrapreneurs must change to meet the changing demands of the health care system. All require a foundational knowledge in accounting, financial planning, budgeting, and the financial aspects of human resource management. This chapter provides an introduction to the skills necessary to be a financially successful manager in an ever-changing system of care. Accounting basics are presented to help in the management of cash flow, improve profitability, develop a budget, and manage risk. Multiple funding sources are presented to provide an understanding of the unique and different structures available. Budget projections and productivity are discussed to help establish the cost of a program and to determine funding necessary for a viable program. And financial problem solving is presented to stimulate critical thinking and to encourage the use of evidence to support sound business decisions.

Case Examples

Note. Financial planning and budgeting does not apply to the work in which Level I and Level II Fieldwork students engage in during fieldwork. However, the following case studies will help the occupational therapy student prepare for future management opportunities.

First-Time Manager: Case 1

The occupational therapy department in a rural hospital is required to practice *zero-based budgeting*, which means that each year the department will develop a budget based upon the budget year projections and supported by past practices and experiences. The occupational therapy manager must determine staffing needs for the budget year according to the projected number and mix of admissions and the productivity expected by the department.

The occupational therapy manager is new to the organization, and this is her first management position. She goes back to her occupational therapy management course materials and finds a discussion of budget principles with the following example: Last year there were 8,250 admissions for the year, consisting of 1,500 labor and delivery admissions, with 115 infants admitted to the neonatal intensive care unit; 1,900 orthopedic admissions; 3,800 general admissions, including multiple system problems, cardiac care, and oncology; 435 inpatient rehabilitation admissions; and 500 pediatric admissions. The occupational therapy department services all areas except labor and delivery. Last year the occupational therapy department provided:

Service	Units of Occupational Therapy	Number of Individuals Served
Neonatal intensive care	1,350	90 (78%)
Orthopedics	16,200	1,800 (95%)
General admissions	13,300	2,660 (70%)
Rehabilitation unit	31,320	435 (100%)
Pediatrics	6,375	425 (85%)
Total	**68,545**	**5,410**

The occupational therapy department provided service 255 days during the last budget year and provided an average of 212 units of service per day. The productivity rate is 75% of an 8-hour day for all services except the rehabilitation unit, in which the productivity rate is 85%.

Service	Units of Occupational Therapy	Productivity	Average Units Per Day	FTEs Needed
NICU	1,350	75%	5.3	0.2
Orthopedics	16,200	75%	64.0	2.7
General Admits	13,300	75%	52.0	2.2
Rehab. Unit	31,320	85%	123.0	4.6
Pediatrics	6,375	75%	25.0	1.0
	68,545/ units /year		269 units/ day	10.7 FTEs

Note. FTE = full time equivalent employees.

(continued)

Case Examples *(cont.)*

The department had 10.7 full time equivalent employees (FTEs) to cover the needs of the department during this last budget year.

Using this example as a guide, the new occupational therapy manager realizes that she will have to consider any special requirements for the staff, the portability (movement between programs) of staff, coverage for vacations, and any weekend work. These considerations may suggest that some staff work part-time or that she should develop a registry for occupational therapy practitioners who want to work on an as-needed basis to cover weekends, vacations, and sick leave. The new occupational therapy manager goes to the administration and obtains the projected admission information and begins by determining the number of evaluations that the occupational therapy department is expected to perform in the coming year. She then begins to determine the mix of occupational therapists and occupational therapy assistants she will need.

First-Time Manager: Case 2

An occupational therapy practitioner is just completing his first year of running a pediatric outpatient clinic. Up to this point, the practitioner has been able to cover expenses using the funds on hand and the monies collected from services. The occupational therapy practitioner recognizes that this is not a good business practice and that a plan for moving money into and out of the business is needed.

It is time to project what the cash in and out of the business will look like for the second year of business. The occupational therapy practitioner has an accountant who is available for consultation, and he calls for an appointment.

The accountant helps the occupational therapy practitioner to set up a cash flow statement that evaluates the accounts receivable, inventory of supplies, current assets, accounts to pay cash flow into or out of the business from investments, and borrowing. Here is the cash flow statement for the pediatric clinic for the second year of operation.

Statement of Cash Flows
1/1/08 to 12/31/08

Cash flow from operating activities		
Net income		$134,000
Adjustments to reconcile net income to net cash		
Accounts receivable decrease	$10,000	
Prepaid expense increase	($6,000)	
Accounts payable increase	$35,000	
Depreciation	$21,000	
		$60,000
Net cash provided from operating activities		$194,000
Investing activities		
Supply sales	($70,000)	
Treatment	($200,000)	
Equipment purchase	($68,000)	($338,000)

Financing activities		
Dividend payment to shareholders	($18,000)	
Borrowed funds	$150,000	$132,000
Net decrease in cash		($12,000)
Cash January 1, 2008		$49,000
Cash Decememeber 31, 2008		$37,000

The occupational therapy practitioner is now better able to estimate any borrowing requirements and the clinic's ability to make timely payments.

Manager: Case 3

The occupational therapy manager of acute care occupational therapy services at a community hospital is told by the hospital administrator that they have decided to open a 20-bed inpatient rehabilitation unit. The administrator asks her to prepare a start-up budget for occupational therapy services on this unit.

One of the first things the manager does is ask about the projected admissions for the first year. This information will help her to determine labor costs, supplies, and equipment, and to request the space necessary for treatment. Once she has an idea of patient admissions, she can project the workload for the occupational therapy practitioners on the unit. The manager knows that in inpatient rehabilitation, the "3-hour" rule frequently translates into 90 minutes of direct service (6 15-minute units) of occupational therapy per client per day. To meet Medicare and accrediting agency standards, occupational therapy services are generally available 7 days a week on this type of unit. All of these requirements are considerations in determining the number and type of full-time equivalent employees she will put into a start-up budget.

Next, the occupational therapy manager makes an appointment with the hospital's CFO to determine the occupational therapy program's contribution to overhead costs. This revenue will be expensed for space and administrative services such as housekeeping, laundry, payroll, information technology, security, human resources, and other nonrevenue-producing departments that support the program. This amount may be shared by all disciplines on the team or be broken out by each specific discipline. The CFO will be able to help her with this information.

Discussions with the medical staff and other team members regarding the mix of anticipated diagnoses will be necessary to determine the type and amount of medical supply items necessary for start-up. The space allocated for evaluation and intervention will provide some guidance in determining what and how much equipment will be needed. The occupational therapy manager talks with the other rehabilitation managers to determine whether sharing larger equipment is appropriate. The occupational therapy manager knows that having the evidence to support the numbers and requests will be an important part of this opportunity. Research supporting specific assessments, equipment, or even levels of productivity will be very important to obtaining the start-up dollars necessary for a successful new program.

Manager: Case 4

The occupational therapist in a large nonprofit, community-based health care system is interested in developing a wellness program for the seniors in the community served by the medical community. She has completed a needs assessment of the community and determined that there is need for and interest in this type of programming for this population within the community. Th health care system has a fitness center that is open to the community. The center has a pool for recreational swimming, exercise equipment, a running track, and showers. The center also sponsors some class activities such as Tai Chi and weight training.

The administration gives approval to explore the possibility of developing this program but cautions the occupational therapist that it must be self-supporting. The occupational therapist begins researching how much wellness programs in surrounding areas charge. She also talks with the system's Giving Foundation to see whether it has any funds available for this program. A search for granting organizations interested in senior wellness programs offers another opportunity to secure funding. Due to her diligent and careful research, the occupational therapist can create a realistic plan to fund the program.

❖ Learning Activities

1. It is anticipated that your unit will admit an average of 20 patients per month for the first year and have an average daily census of 7 patients for the first 2 months, 9 patients for months 3–6, 12 patients for months 7–10, and 15 patients for the last 2 months of the year. Your program contribution will be 40% of $180,000 annually. You need to determine the average salary for various occupational therapy personnel in your area and use product catalogues to estimate the cost of supplies and equipment. You also may need to budget for consultants to teach staff about specific rehabilitation documentation, FIM™ scores, and other knowledge specific to inpatient rehabilitation. Develop a start-up budget using the form below.

2. Use the example in Case 1 to develop the number of FTE employees needed for a program in your area. You may use actual services and numbers. Although this is an exercise in calculations, it provides an opportunity for discussions about meeting the needs of 7-days-per-week service, registry opportunities, use of contract personnel, and how to provide safe and ethical coverage when staff shortages exist.

3. Contact a local lender to learn the rules for applying for small business loans. Discuss when small business loans might be appropriate for the type of program in Case 4.

4. Find grant organizations that might be interested in funding the type of program in Case 4. If your university has a giving foundation, talk with the officers of the foundation to learn about charitable giving.

Start-up Budget	Cost ($)
Personnel (prior to admission of clients)	
Computer, phone, fax machine	
Office supplies	
Brochures, business cards	
Clinical supplies	
Consultants	
Program contribution to overhead	
Clinic equipment	
Office furniture	
Other	
Total requirements	

✓ Multiple-Choice Questions

1. A *general partnership* is a legal structure that has
   a. More than one person involved in the management of a business.
   b. Two or more owners.
   c. One partner who manages the business and others who have only invested in the business.
   d. Stockholders.

2. All of the following are characteristics of not-for-profit organizations that distinguish them from business organizations except
   a. Ability to impose taxes on citizens.
   b. Contributions by resource providers who do not expect a return on investment.
   c. Operating purposes other than to earn a profit.
   d. Absence of ownership interests.

3. If the cash you have coming into a business is greater than that going out of the business, you have
   a. Profitability.
   b. Loss.
   c. Positive cash flow.
   d. Negative cash flow.

4. The financial statement that reports the revenues and expenses for a period of time such as a year or a month is the
   a. Balance sheet.
   b. Income statement.
   c. Statement of cash flows.
   d. Budget.

5. The financial statement that reports the assets, liabilities, and stockholders' (or owner's) equity at specific date is the
   a. Balance sheet.
   b. Income statement.
   c. Statement of cash flows.
   d. Budget.

6. Financial strategic planning for beginning programs and businesses means
   a. Assessment of start-up abilities.
   b. Hiring an accountant.
   c. Getting a small business loan from the bank.
   d. Doing a needs assessment.

7. You are setting up an account to handle your bills, credit card balances, and loan obligations. What is this type of account called?
   a. Cash flow.
   b. Accrual account.
   c. Accounts payable.
   d. Capital expenditure.

8. Expenses that remain constant from month to month and do not change with volume or activity are called
   a. Small business.
   b. Fixed.
   c. Variable.
   d. Flexible.

9. Good cash management means
   a. Knowing when, where, and how your cash needs will occur.
   b. Making sure that you have 6 months' reserve cash on hand.
   c. Keeping enough cash to cover the payroll in your checking account.
   d. Establishing credit so that you can acquire cash if you need it.

10. The U.S. Small Business Administration makes loans to small businesses and start-up businesses. These loans are administered by
    a. Federal government.
    b. State government.
    c. Local banks.
    d. Small Business Association.

11. Purchase expense refers to
    a. Expense that remains constant from one month to another.
    b. Expense that changes with the volume of service you provide.
    c. Items you own that will depreciate.
    d. Items you own that will appreciate.

12. Knowing when, where, and how your cash needs will occur is a principle of
    a. Good cash management.
    b. Federal tax law.
    c. Banking regulations.
    d. Variable expense control.

13. The point at which you meet fixed and variable costs is called
    a. Annual borrowing.
    b. Cost accounting.
    c. Short-term cash flow.
    d. Breakeven point.

14. Basic budget concepts are
    a. Capital expense, variable expense, and fixed expense.
    b. Revenue, total costs, and profit.
    c. Salaries, equipment, and overhead.
    d. Projected units of service and cost of producing a unit.

15. A not-for profit organization
    a. Must always spend less than they budget each year.
    b. Must reinvest all excess revenue in the organization.
    c. Cannot charge for their services or products.
    d. Is always subsidized by government agencies.

16. General fixed expenses include
    a. Clinical salaries and wages.
    b. Marketing.
    c. Maintenance and repairs.
    d. Education.

17. Breakeven is calculated by finding where
    a. All expenses can be paid each month.
    b. Revenue and fixed costs meet.
    c. Total costs and total revenue meet.
    d. The owner can draw a salary.
18. Full-time equivalent (FTE) refers to
    a. Each person who works for a company.
    b. Someone who works more than 30 hours a week.
    c. An individual who works more than 9 months in 1 year.
    d. The individuals who fill a full-time position.

19. A forecast of your revenue and expenditures is called
    a. The budget.
    b. Start-up costs.
    c. Gross income.
    d. Cash flow.
20. The key to profitability is
    a. Filling all staff positions.
    b. Managing supplies.
    c. Managing cash flow.
    d. Doing the work yourself.

References

American Occupational Therapy Association. (2008, December 17). *Health care reform is your future: AOTA is the voice for your future.* Retrieved March 17, 2009, from www.aota.org/news/advocacynews/healthreform.aspx

Berry, T. (2009). *How to get your business funded.* Retrieved March 14, 2009, from http://articles.bplans.com/starting-a-business/how-to-get-your-business-funded

Entrepreneur Network. (2009). *Capital equipment.* Retrieved January 14, 2010, from http://search.entrepreneur.com/googlesearchresults.php?q=www.entrepreneur.com%2Fencyclopedia%2Fterm+82028.html&cx=01357410517232325703311%3Axhkof7qpqpa&cof=FORID%3A9#848

Fogel, P. A. (2000). Achieving superior productivity. *Healthcare Financial Management.* Retrieved May 16, 2009, from http://findarticles.com/p/articles/mi_m3257/is_8_54/ai_64459012/?tag=content;col1

Gay, Lesbian and Straight Education Network. (2000). *How do we prepare a budget?* Retrieved March 4, 2009, from http://www.glsen.org/cgi-bin/iowa/all/news/record/36.htm

Health Resources and Services Administration. (n.d.). *Physician supply and demand: Projections to 2020.* Retrieved May 16, 2009, from http://bhpr.hrsa.gov/healthworkforce/reports/physician-supplydemand/trendsinphysicianproductivity.htm

Obama for America. (2009). *Barack Obama and Joe Biden's plan to lower health care costs and ensure affordable, accessible health coverage for all.* Retrieved March 17, 2009, from http://www.barackobama.com/pdf/issues/HealthCareFullPlan.pdf

New York State Society of Certified Public Accountants. (2009). *Accounting terminology guide.* Retrieved March 6, 2009, from www.nysscpa.org/prof_library/guide.htm

Popkin, J. S. (2005). Cost of employee benefits in small and large businesses. *Small Business Research Summary.* Retrieved June 23, 2009, from http://www.sba.gov/advo/research/rs262tot.pdf

QuickMBA. (2007). *Law and business.* Retrieved February 10, 2010 from http://www.quickmba.com/law/org

Shackelford, L. J. (1999). Measuring productivity using RBRVS cost accounting: Resource-based relative value scale. *Healthcare Financial Management.* Retrieved May 16, 2009, from http://findarticles.com/p/articles/mi_m3257/is_1_53/ai_53635418/pg_2/?tag=content;col1

Small Business Administration. (1991). *Financial management series: Budgeting for the small business.* Retrieved April 1, 2009, from www.sba.gov/idc/groups/public/documents/sba_homepage/pub_fm8t.txt

Small Business Administration. (2009). *Start-up costs.* Retrieved January 14, 2010, from http://www.sba.gov/smallbusinessplanner/start/financestartup/SERV_SBPLANNER_MANAGE_STARTUP_.html

Small Business Notes. (2009a). *Calculating break-even units.* Retrieved March 11, 2009, from http://www.sba.gov/smallbusinessplanner/start/financestartup/SERV_BREAKEVEN.html

Small Business Notes. (2009b). *Cash flow projections.* Retrieved March 11, 2009, from www.smallbusinessnotes.com/operating/finmgmt.financialsmts/cashprojection/html

Society for Human Resource Management. (2009). *Cost of health care benchmarking study: 2009 executive summary.* Retrieved January 14, 2010, from http://www.shrm.org/Research/SurveyFindings/Articles/Documents/2009%20Health%20Care%20Report_FULL_FINAL_sm.pdf

U.S. Department of Health and Human Services. (2003). *NIH policy statement.* Retrieved March 14, 2009, from http://grants.nih.gov/grants/policy/nihgps_2003/NIHGPS_Part3.htm

8

Marketing Occupational Therapy

Tammy Richmond, MS, OTR/L

❖ Key Terms and Concepts

Environmental assessment. "Evaluation of all forces and changes affecting the organization's ability to conduct business effectively within the market" (Kotler, Armstrong, & Cummingham, 2000, p. 100).

Marketing. The process of identifying and communicating to consumers through a set of strategies and techniques intended to attract, persuade, and maintain them as purchasers of services and products (Gandolf & Hirsch, n.d.-d).

Marketing research. The systematic gathering of data to use in understanding customers, markets, and marketing effectiveness (Kotler, 2003).

Organizational assessment. "An organization's evaluation of its effectiveness relative to the client population, the community, and the health care system" (Shoemaker & Wheeler, 1996, p. 108).

Outcome marketing. The use of evidence-based service or product outcomes to promote the results of processes or efforts.

Packaging. The way a service or product appears from the outside or in the eyes of the customer.

People. In marketing, the people internal and external to a business who are responsible for every element of implementing the marketing strategies.

Place. The physical or virtual location where a service is obtained or a product is purchased.

Positioning. Communication of the ways a service or product is a better value than similar services or products in the marketplace.

Price. "The amount of money charged for a product or service or the sum of the values that consumers exchange for the benefits of having and using the product or service" (Kotler et al., 2000, p. 421).

Product. Anything that can be used or consumed to satisfy a market's need or want.

Promotion. Methods of communicating with customers about services and products.

Social media. Virtual content technologies or social networks intended to communicate with, influence, and interact with peers and the global public.

Target market. The segment of the market with similar and measurable characteristics and needs that an organization desires to influence.

❖ Learning Objectives

After completing this chapter, you should be able to do the following:

- Define *marketing* and describe its objectives.
- Define *target market*.
- Define the 4 steps in market management.
- Describe the 7 *P*s of marketing mix.
- Describe marketing analysis through market assessments.
- Identify the components of a marketing plan, and name the 4 steps in creating a marketing plan.

- Describe outcome measurements.
- Describe marketing trends and technologies.
- Describe the use of social media and marketing channels.
- Define *outcome marketing*.

Health care professionals in private practice were legally prohibited from advertising or marketing their services until the landmark 1977 U.S. Supreme court case *Bates v. State Bar of Arizona* (Gandolf & Hirsch, n.d.-a). The decision opened up opportunities for all medical providers to market to their clients and potential clients. However, continued health care regulations, such as the Stark Law and the Health Insurance Portability and Accountability Act of 1996 (HIPAA), quickly quieted many marketing efforts as once again the ethical and legal implications of soliciting services for the benefit of attracting health care recipients became a moral debate. The reluctance to appear unethical or greedy and the cloudy legal interpretations of health care privacy and marketing regulations continue to discourage health care professionals from fully realizing and implementing sound marketing strategies and communicating the benefits of their services and products.

Consumers, however, are eager for health care information and seek it out in astounding numbers. According to Pew Internet and American Life Project research findings in 2009, 74% of U.S. adults used the Internet, and 8 in 10 looked for health information online—about 8 million people per day (Fox, 2009). Furthermore, 75% of these "online patients" had a chronic medical problem, and 57% reported that they went online to seek information about a health condition before going to their physician (Fox, 2009).

Today's health care consumers are savvy and equipped with information, want value for their time and money, and expect results. Occupational therapists must reach a broad audience and compete with multiple choices and shrinking financial means. To be competitive and financially sustainable, occupational therapists must become knowledgeable and skilled in marketing their services.

Marketing Fundamentals

Marketing is the process of identifying and communicating with consumers through a set of strategies and techniques intended to attract, persuade, and maintain the consumers as purchasers of services and products (Gandolf & Hirsch, n.d.-d). In occupational therapy, marketing facilitates the identification and development of a unique therapy product, service, or program that will meet the personal expectations and values of a particular group of consumers. The product or service must be made visible and easily accessible to the consumer through various types of communication strategies. Unlike other industries, marketing health care services also involves informing and influencing third-party payers to establish service contracts and reimbursement for the therapy services and products provided to the consumer.

The objectives of marketing efforts include

- Meeting the social, managerial, financial, and operational objectives of the organization
- Identifying and meeting consumer needs and wants

- Creating awareness of the service or product and increasing accessibility to the consumer
- Developing standards and policies that ensure the quality of clinical services and programs
- Promoting goodwill between the organization and the community, referral sources, clients, and payers
- Building consumers' loyalty and meeting their needs on the basis of value and satisfaction.

Market

A *market* consists of all the potential consumers sharing a particular need or want who are willing and able to engage in an exchange such as money or barter to fill the need or want (Kotler et al., 2000). For health care providers, the market includes anyone who will participate in, use, contract for, or pay for products or services. Instead of attempting to appeal to a market base that is too large and varied, successful organizations customize the marketing of products or services to the selected target markets they wish to influence. *Target markets* are segments of a market with similar demographics, measurable needs, money to buy the service or product, decision-making power, and easy access to the product or service. In occupational therapy, a target market has three main categories: (1) clients and potential clients, (2) referral sources, and (3) payers (Richmond & Powers, 2009). Table 8.1 lists examples of each of the three types of target market for different occupational therapy specialties.

A thorough understanding of the target market and the organization's relationship to it is necessary to develop marketing strategies that will result in profits. Each target market requires a different marketing mix based on its specific characteristics.

Marketing Mix

The *marketing mix* (or *promotional mix*) includes the essential communication strategies for achieving marketing objectives. A comprehensive marketing plan typically uses multiple marketing strategies to be effective. Traditionally, elements of the marketing mix have been called the four *P*s: *product, price, place,* and *promotion.* Recently, marketing experts have added three more *P*s: *positioning, packaging,* and *people* (Gandolf & Hirsch, n.d.-c). Each of these elements is described in the following sections.

Product

A *product* is "anything that can be offered to a market for attention, acquisition, use, or consumption and that might satisfy a need or want" (Kotler & Armstrong, 1991, p. 639). In occupational therapy, *product* includes services and programs. In promoting a product, it is important to be able to describe the product in terms of its features and value. For the consumer to purchase a product, it has to do several things: fill a need, appeal to the target market, have value and purpose, and provide advantages over another similar product. For example, an occupational therapist

Table 8.1. Examples of Potential Target Markets for Occupational Therapy Specialties

Client condition	Referral source	Payer
Orthopedic injuries	Physicians	Managed care
Neurological disorders	Home health agencies	Organizations
Hand injuries	Case managers	Workers' compensation
Seniors	Adult children	Medicare
Pediatrics	School system	State funds
Athletes	Friends or family	Cash
Mentally challenged	Professionals	Insurance plans
High-risk adolescents	Chambers of commerce	Charities
Corporations	Churches	Private donations
High schools	Provider networks	Legal sponsors
Area businesses	Legal professionals	Trust funds
Injured workers	Insurance	Federal grants
Persons with chronic diseases	Alternative practitioners	Private grants
Spas	Office staff	Private parties
Low-vision populations	Departments of motor vehicles	Local government
Assisted living centers	Clinical managers	Member networks
Community centers	Business owners	Foundations

Source. From *Business Fundamentals for the Rehabilitation Professional,* 2nd ed. (p. 84), by T. Richmond and D. Powers, 2009, Thorofare, NJ: Slack. Reprinted with permission.

developed a women's health program for postmenopausal women that included interventions for incontinence and pelvic floor pain, biofeedback, fitness and nutrition instruction, and educational materials. The promotional materials highlighted the product's (i.e., the program's) benefits and advantages and explained what needs it satisfied for the target market.

Price

Price is the amount of money charged for a product or service or the sum of the values that consumers exchange for the benefits of having and using the product or service (Kotler et al., 2000). Usually, price is the monetary exchange between the buyer (the client) and the seller (the occupational therapist). In some cases, the price or pricing components of occupational therapy services are governed by regulatory bodies and already are established—for example, the Medicare reimbursement fee schedule. In other situations, the occupational therapy practitioner establishes a price, such as determining the cash price of attending an onsite, 8-week Pilates class to work on body posture or a cash price for a hand soft splint not covered by the insurance policy. Pricing takes into account the following:

- Overhead costs per hour of providing the service or producing the product
- Fair market value of other similar services or products
- Fee options (e.g., costs for offering use of credit cards, payment extensions)
- Sales taxes

- Typical third-party payer rates or contracted payment rates per billable hour
- Amount needed to maintain customer service (administrative costs)
- The consumer's perception of value versus costs (Richmond & Powers, 2004).

The goal of pricing is to cover operational costs and make a profit. Pricing never should be thought of as static; constant changes in the marketplace warrant revisiting the issue of pricing often. Many businesses have sliding fees or give discounts to meet the changing financial environment. Occupational therapists in a contracted relationship with a payer must make sure they are charging the payer for all the billable time and supplies they use and providing the billing codes that are accepted. Nonbillable items, such as therapy products like resistance bands or soft splints, should be billed to the client (see Chapter 25) at prices based on the considerations previously described. Therapists starting a new program, class, or other support service should make sure their pricing is aligned with similar services within the organization and the immediate community.

Place

Place is the physical location where services, products, or programs are provided. Related issues include who will provide the services and where consumers will come in contact with the services or products, such as the Internet or phone book. Location is often a very important element of the decision-making process for customers, so promotional materials should supply them with exact addresses, landmarks, small maps or map links, parking information, and other helpful transportation information to promote easy accessibility. Putting a map on the back of the prescription pads given to referral sources or including a link to www.mapquest.com on the practice Web site is user friendly and promotes good customer service.

Promotion

Marketing is typically thought of as promotion. *Promotion* is communication of information to potential consumers about the service's or product's benefits, place, and price. The ultimate goals of marketing promotion are to create consumer awareness and persuade them to purchase. Successful promotional campaigns integrate several types of marketing promotions over a designated period and constantly monitor the target market to respond quickly to any new trends, changes, and needs.

Promotional strategies should inform target markets about convenience, costs, product comparison, the organization's ability (skills or specialties of staff), and accessibility. Such strategies should use a clear and simple image that demonstrates a value-added experience. Market branding through the use of slogans, tag lines, logos, colors, and other persuasive techniques also provides promotional advantages. For example, when a consumer sees a folded pink ribbon, he or she automatically thinks of breast cancer awareness without having to be told with words. In occupational therapy, the American Occupational Therapy Association's (AOTA's) slogan *Occupational Therapy: Living Life To Its Fullest™* is an example of effectiveness in creating product awareness. *Slogans* are short and memorable phrases that draw attention to the product or, in this case, service. The words *occupational therapy* alone do not immediately provoke visions of what occupational therapy is or what it can do. *Occupational Therapy: Living Life To Its Fullest* facilitates an idea of a health service that is all encompassing. Promotional strategies can be delineated into four categories: advertising, sales promotion, public relations, and personal selling (Exhibit 8.1 lists examples of each).

EXHIBIT 8.1. EXAMPLES OF PROMOTIONAL STRATEGIES

Advertising	Gift certificate	TV or radio guest appearance
Ad	Free demonstration	Involvement in community
Brochure	Free sample	Alliance formation
Flier	Phone hold messaging	Donation to charity
Direct mail	Treats at the reception window	Donation to fundraiser
Business card	Holiday gift	
Prescription pad	Trade show giveaway	**Personal Selling**
Booklet		Thank you card
Calendar	**Public Relations**	Birthday card
Promotional gift	News release	Request for referrals
Telemarketing	Study or survey	Lunch or meet with referral source
E-mail postcard	Case study	Seasonal greetings or gift
Fax broadcasting	Article writing	Treat or promotional gift
Postcard	Letter to the editor	Leaving article on table
Newsletter	Column writing	Message board
Insert	Testimonial	Referral board
TV ad	Guest lecture	Picture board
Radio ad	Seminar	Gift certificate
Internet ad	Health fair	Business card
Poster	Volunteering	Flier
	Media kit mailing	Brochure
Sales Promotion	Association membership	Networking
Patient referral incentive	Networking group membership	Volunteer
Open house	Focus group	Resource
Sweepstakes	Hosting meeting or seminar	Web site
Office giveaway	Lunch and learn	E-mail address
Free assessment	Open house	Cell phone or pager
Discount	Power breakfast	Fax
Coupon	Happy hour	Mailing or billing inserts

Advertising is generally accomplished via paid media. Business cards, brochures, and ad placements in magazines or on a Web site are examples of advertising. Advertising is regulated by several federal and states laws, as well as the *Occupational Therapy Code of Ethics and Ethics Standards* (AOTA, 2010) and state occupational therapy licensing regulations. Occupational therapy practitioners should become familiar with these guidelines before generating advertisements. For example, the statements you make in advertisements cannot be misleading or untruthful; you cannot state "We accept all insurance types" when you do not have contracts with all of the area insurance companies.

Sales promotion is "any initiative or incentive undertaken by an organization to promote an increase in sales, usage, or trial of a product or service" (Marketing Teacher n.d.). Often the incentives have value to the consumer, such as coupons, free assessments, discounts, product demonstration, or free samples. Conducting free health screenings at a practice or business is an example of a sales promotion that can lead to an increase in new referrals or increase in awareness and value to your organization's target markets.

Public relations consists of "the methods and activities employed to establish and promote a favorable relationship with the public" (*American Heritage Dictionary*, n.d.). Disseminating news releases, writing articles, donating to charities, and sponsoring a 5K race are all examples in which you create an image or opinion of your organization. Publicity efforts are most viable when they are visible to the target market you wish to influence. If your target market is children with autism, getting involved in local fundraising and support events for autism shows your passion, dedication, and advocacy for the consumers you want to attract.

Personal selling is the most effective and can be the least expensive type of promotion. It can occur through either face-to-face communication or word-of-mouth referral. Consumers value the opinions of others, especially if the opinion is from someone they trust, such as a close friend, or a source they consider trustworthy, such as a medical Web site. Customer service is very important to the success of personal selling; as a general rule, a pleased consumer tells three other people, who in turn continue to promote the benefits of a product or service. Because many health care providers are uncomfortable with self-promoting to consumers, Web sites and networking are excellent personal selling strategies that have a higher level of comfort. In addition, professional contacts are a way to share information and gain support and referrals. Affiliated partnerships and strategic alliances with area agencies such as the chamber of commerce may offer benefits such as Web site links, networking meetings, and health fairs.

Positioning

Positioning involves conveying how a service or product is a better value than similar services or products in the marketplace. When developing a marketing strategy, you need to closely evaluate the competition and compare product advantages and disadvantages. Positioning also depends on what your customers think about the service or product and whether and what they tell other people about your service or product. You can simply ask your present clients what key words or phrases they would use to describe you and your services to a friend or doctor. Positive testimonials are a great promotional tool to include in marketing materials, Web sites, and social media marketing. Then select one or two attributes to use on your marketing materials that best highlights your practice's unique position, such as "conveniently open 6 days a week" or "staff is always friendly and informative."

Packaging

Packaging can be thought of as the first impression someone gets when they come into contact with the occupational therapy practitioner or organization. Packaging was added to the marketing mix when marketing experts realized how important the element of initial impression is to consumers' decision making when purchasing a service or product. The first impression starts from the moment a member of your target market sees or hears you or another staff member. The first impression should inspire confidence and comfort in the customer about you and your products and services. For example, your practice should strive to have the ambience of a day spa with courteous staff and a very organized front reception area.

People

In fulfilling marketing tasks and responsibilities, people are as important as the message. Every employee of your practice or program is vital to the success of your marketing efforts. The organizational assessment or SWOT (*s*trengths, *w*eaknesses, *o*pportunities, and *t*hreats) analysis is used to define the organization's strategic overall vision, mission, and goals, which then provide people with the tools to carry out your marketing strategies. Your organization's marketing department or outside marketing expertise may be needed to implement the more specialized aspects of the marketing plan.

Market Management

Market management involves the practical application of marketing techniques, functions, and activities to achieve organizational objectives (Kotler & Keller, 2006). Market management is the systematic approach used to identify, persuade, and secure a target market for value and profit. Several different marketing approaches or management frameworks can result in marketing success for occupational therapy organizations (see Appendix 8.A); which marketing approach to use depends on the organization's philosophy and strategic goals. Presently, health care marketing has no established standards (Thomas, 2008); health care marketing seems to lend itself to the experiential and relationship marketing approaches because the services and products are mostly personalized, are interactive, and have a built-in relationship component in the necessary interaction between practitioner and consumer.

The classic purchase model was defined by the traditional media perspective and involved three stages: awareness, consideration, and purchase. The now-prevalent use of the Internet to communicate and gather information has expanded the consideration stage of the purchase model to include user-generated feedback after a purchase influencing the next consumer's decision (Evans, 2008). For example, when consumers purchase a product online, they often are asked to rate the buying experience and the actual service and product after they receive it. Numerous social media channels such as blogs (discussed in more detail later in this chapter) allow consumers to share their opinions with countless others, giving electronic "word-of-mouth" selling a greater impact than ever before. Thus, potential clients of occupational therapy services and products have tremendous power to either enhance or detract from the business relationship implemented in your marketing approach. Occupational therapists therefore must know as much as possible about their target markets and how to best manage them. There are four steps in market management: analysis, planning, implementation, and monitoring.

Market Analysis

Market analysis is the use of assessment techniques to understand customers, markets, and marketing effectiveness (Kotler, 2003). This most critical step in market management is also the most time consuming. Gathering, organizing, and assessing information during the analysis phase establishes the key elements of the marketing plan. The goals of market analysis are to

- Identify current trends, opportunities, and threats
- Assess consumer needs and demands

- Identify target markets
- Identify and compare competition and position in market
- Develop and enhance products and services.

Market analysis should answer the following questions:

- What are the emerging trends?
- Who is my target market, and why would they be interested in my service or product?
- How do I build a lifelong relationship with my target market?
- What is special about my service or product?
- Who is my competition?
- What are the opportunities for and threats to my service or product?
- How do I promote my strengths or selling points?

There are two analytic approaches to completing market analysis: organizational and environmental assessment. The organizational assessment addresses the internal and external SWOT factors within the organization, and the environmental assessment evaluates the relationship between the organization and the industry and target markets. Together, the organizational and environmental assessments provide the information you need to make effective marketing decisions regarding your target market, products, and competition (see Figure 8.1).

Organizational Assessment

An *organizational assessment* is a systematic review by an organization of its activities that allows it to identify its strengths and weaknesses and to plan activities and efforts for improvement (Levinson, 2002). This assessment can be accomplished by using the SWOT analysis format to identify the strengths, weaknesses, opportunities, and threats represented by various internal and external operational factors; Figure 8.2 provides a template for recording each

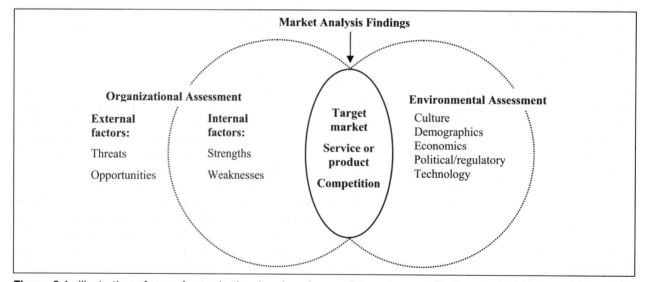

Figure 8.1. Illustration of use of organizational and environmental assessment findings in decisions regarding target market, services and products, and competition.

Internal issues	Strengths	Weaknesses	External issues	Opportunities	Threats
Staffing			Patient populations		
Customer service			Competition		
Programs			Regulations		
Quality assurance			Technology		
Risk management			Health care trends		
Other			Other		

Figure 8.2. Sample template for recording findings of the SWOT (strengths, weakness, opportunities, and threats) analysis.

element of this analysis (Aldag & Stearns, 1987; Fahey & Randall, 1994; also see Chapter 6). Internal issues address the basic operations of the occupational therapy organization such as customer service, staffing, and program development. External issues include current patient populations, competition, and other factors that directly influence present organizational operations.

Defining the strengths, weaknesses, opportunities, and threats of internal and external operational factors allows the organization to achieve a clear representation of its own emerging trends and changes. Sources of information to inform the SWOT analysis process include

- Operational documentation
- Outcome measurements
- Interviews with staff members
- Risk management program findings
- Medical records
- Product and service data
- Information from regulatory bodies
- Internet research.

Environmental Assessment

Environmental assessment is the evaluation of all forces and changes outside of the organization that affect its ability to conduct business effectively in its chosen market (Kotler et al., 2000). In the environmental assessment, the organization seeks to identify emerging trends and changes as they affect its relationship to its market and to define and explain the buying behaviors of the target market. The most important environmental factors include sociocultural trends, demographic information, economics, political and regulatory issues, and new technologies. The following paragraphs discuss each of these trends.

Identifying *sociocultural trends* involves tracking the ways such factors as language, education, religion, values, attitudes, superstitions, material culture, technology, social groups and organizations, and business customs and practices affect the behavior of the target market. This analysis assists you in selecting the marketing mix that will best deliver marketing messages that appeal to your target market's interests and needs. In particular, it will help you answer the overall question, Does the marketing mix I use communicate most effectively with my target market of

people with the type of illness, injury, or health care need who would be attracted to and benefit from my service or product? For example, an occupational therapy practice that serves a Latino pediatric population with juvenile diabetes should consider creating multilingual educational games or similar materials to promote healthy eating habits that include applicable cultural food choices and functional exercises that simulate cultural sports interests.

Demographic information such as population, age, housing, sex, ethnicity, educational level, buying income, and growth and labor force projections easily can be found on the Internet or in libraries and provides vital analytical support to the marketing plan. This information can assist you in determining your target markets and the products and services the target markets will purchase or engage in. For example, an occupational therapist seeking to implement a new elder fall prevention program consulted population age data to ascertain whether there were enough individuals older than the age of 65 living within a 5-mile radius of the program and income data to ascertain that these individuals were able to afford or willing to pay cash for the program.

Economics deals with the management of the income and resources of an organization, government, business, community, or household. Changes in the larger economic system, such as government spending or financial markets, influence consumer confidence and spending patterns. For example, an economic downturn undermines the ability of individuals and businesses to spend money on items they consider nonessential. In such a climate, an occupational therapy practice can post educational information and health self-assessments in its areas of service specialties to help those who investigate their health care problem online assess whether to spend scarce resources on a service, product, or program.

Political and regulatory issues constitute an important environmental factor because occupational therapy practice is heavily influenced by state and federal legislative rules and guidelines. Products and services developed for target markets must comply with occupational therapy standards of practice; the professional code of ethics; reimbursement and regulatory laws; and even local, state, and federal business and tax laws. State and national professional organizations are a valuable resource of information on political and regulatory issues. Additionally, reimbursement strategies also may fall under regulatory or paying agency limitations. Understanding the political and regulatory parameters of products, pricing, and promotional strategies is essential to marketing implementation. For example, many insurance policies do not pay for soft splints and therapy supplies, so it is vital that you create an alternative purchasing option such as payment by cash or credit card with pricing that is affordable for your target market.

The explosion of *new technologies* such as personal computers, handheld devices, and assistive technologies has already significantly affected health care. As consumers demand real-time communication and treatment strategies to manage their health at home, the Internet and other social media are becoming vital tools in marketing promotions. Telemedicine and health monitoring programs are examples of integrated service technologies that are emerging as important service applications.

Planning

The second step in market management is the development of the marketing plan. Developing a marketing plan, like a strategic plan or business plan, involves gathering information about the organization and its services or products and developing objectives and strategies for the organization's marketing activities. The marketing plan contains the following components:

- *Company description*—the who, what, where, when, and how of the company, department, agency, organization. The consumer should be able to identify immediately whether or not specific types of services are provided within an environment that they would want to participate in. The company description created for the business plan can be used in the marketing plan.
- *Mission statement*—a 25-or-fewer-word statement about the organization's goals or objectives, also found in the business plan. The marketing strategies must support the mission statement and vice versa. The mission statement or parts of it can be used in marketing materials to highlight the philosophy and value the organization intends to live up to.
- *Description of the target market*—behaviors, demographics, buying habits, and trends in the target market. This information should support the service's or product's fit to the target market's needs and desires. An accurate view of the target market can help the organization build a long-lasting, trust-based relationship with these clients.
- *Description of the products and services to be offered*—identification of the characteristics of services and products that fit the needs and common characteristics of the target market. For example, an occupational therapist wanting to provide consultation services in home modification needs to identify what these services include, such as onsite home assessment, owner health and functional assessment, home safety assessment, and enhanced design modifications. Customers want to

know exactly what the service is and how it can benefit them personally, and this information should be used on promotional materials.

- *Identification of the competition*—identification and SWOT analysis of the top competitors to define your advantages (strengths) and opportunities you can promote through your marketing mix. Your marketing should emphasize your advantages over your competition.
- *Marketing objectives*—identification of exactly what one is attempting to achieve through your marketing efforts. You can use these objectives to create monitoring or tracking measurements. For example, an occupational therapist's marketing goal is to add 10 orthopedic physician referrals to her active referral list in 1 month. The marketing strategies she implements need to be customized for and implemented directly with the 10 identified referral sources.
- *Marketing strategies*—promotion strategies based on your market analysis for the specific service or product and the target market. Some strategies will be appropriate for all three types of target market—clients and potential clients, referral sources, and payers.
- *Action plan*—a written document that lists target markets, your marketing strategies, your timeline, and the people who will perform the marketing activities. Short- and long-term goals should be listed for all three types of target market; these goals should be "SMARTER": that is, *s*pecific, *m*easurable, *a*ttainable, *t*imebound, *e*nthusiastic, and *r*ewarding (Sohnen-Moe, 2001).
- *Monitoring strategies* (discussed later in this section).

Implementation

Implementation is the action function or organized process of carrying out the marketing plan. In the business world, it is called the *marketing campaign*. Implementation involves the following action elements:

- *Identify the people and the experience.* Marketing actually begins the moment you schedule your first client or communicate with your target markets. Customer service through every staff member or point of contact is a form of personal selling. Every aspect of service or product delivery requires that four "people" goals are met: listen and clarify, respond with respect, deliver and support, and satisfy and survey. The first impression of your communication, the message, and the environment in which it is conveyed or in which the consumer participates becomes part of the consideration phase of relationship building. Marketing strategies beyond personal selling need to be performed by individuals or outside experts who understand the value factors and uniqueness of your relationship to each target market. Establish what and how each of your target markets wants to be communicated with. Your consumers need to perceive you as the expert and the experience or relationship as honest and trustworthy.

- *Identify short- and long-term marketing goals.* Develop a marketing goal worksheet with goals specific to each strategy and to each target market that can realistically be reached daily, weekly, monthly, quarterly, biannually, and annually. For example, a goal for the first 6 months of a new practice might be to create a Web site that makes the intake and other handouts and documentation available online. When consumers visit the Web site, they can take the opportunity to view and "experience" the other services and value-added features of the practice, such as relevant research articles or a monthly newsletter with healthy recipes.
- *Identify the marketing budget.* Marketing budgets depend on the organization's ability to raise or set aside business capital. A general rule is to set aside 4% of the expected gross income from your service or product for marketing (Braveman, 2006). Marketing strategies do not have to be expensive; creative thinking and organizational input can produce more for less. Estimate the cost of the various marketing materials such as business cards, letterhead, prescription pads, and so forth before moving forward to your marketing mix.
- *Select the marketing mix (strategies).* Each target market needs its own marketing mix, client mix, referral mix, and payer mix. Determining which promotional strategies to implement depends on finances, time, and personnel power; Exhibits 8.1 and 8.2 provide examples of such strategies. For each identified target market and marketing mix, write out your strategy, the monthly or yearly costs, the materials required, and the people who will implement them.
- *Create a timeline.* Determine a start date, a monitoring schedule, and an ending date, if applicable, for each marketing strategy. Adhere to your campaign calendar with the same discipline as you schedule your clients.

EXHIBIT 8.2. EXAMPLES OF TARGET MARKET STRATEGIES FOR CLIENTS, REFERRAL SOURCES, AND PAYERS

Clients or potential clients	Referral sources	Payers
Develop a company Web site	Distribute literature	Send publicity materials on specialty services, specialty staff, and outcomes and testimonial letters from referrals
Distribute educational handouts	Distribute prescription pads with menu of services to select from	Provide evidence-based service handouts
Send direct e-mail, newsletters, and in-house promotions	Send direct e-mail or fax of progress notes or outcome measurements	Send direct e-mail or fax of quality assurance policies and procedures, client surveys, chart review systems, client safety or risk management programs, treatment protocols, or resumes of treating therapists
Establish a reward referrals program	Ask referral source to come speak, contribute to newsletter, or promote service in newsletter, written materials, or Web site	Send publicity materials about outcome measurements, such as cost-effectiveness or decrease in client visits
Have employees wear logo or message clothing	Survey on "How are we doing?" and "How can we improve?"	Keep in constant communication about updates, support literature, and staff training topics
Create a customer advisory board	Ask physician to be on advisory panel for Web site or to respond to customer advisory board	Fax copy of advisory boards and topics covered
Offer free health screenings	Offer health screenings at referral location	Ask for any promotional materials that the payer may provide
Join or network with local agencies, organizations, business groups, or focus groups	Ask to see if referral source would like to cosponsor a seminar or teaching or networking event	Fax event materials to payers to keep them updated on public relations efforts
Write for professional journals, local papers, and health-related Web sites	Give articles or publicity materials to referral source to read or place in waiting room	Fax copies of publicity materials
Offer boutique services, such as water, fruit, retail products, vending machines, cash services	Promote the new "healing" environment by hosting a "private open house"	Send pictures and invitations or press releases of all improvements or updates

Monitoring

Monitoring and assessing the marketing strategies allows an organization to redirect its marketing efforts if necessary. Gandolf and Hirsch (n.d.-b) suggested asking these seven questions:

1. *Are you using evidence-based marketing approaches?* Such approaches include proved marketing strategies, a written marketing plan, and measurement of results. Write out specific survey-type questions for each strategy, such as "Did my referral source send 10 new clients to me in the 30 days after I implemented a communication routine of faxing evaluations, weekly progress reports and measurements, and monthly summaries as he or she requested?" or "Did our booth at the chamber of commerce networking evening last night generate eight new contacts for potential new contracts or follow-up meetings?"

2. *When is the last time you changed your marketing plan?* Marketing has to be dynamic and to change as frequent monitoring results suggest.

3. *Do you have clear and specific goals?* Marketing goals need to measure exactly what you need to demonstrate success, such as making a profit or meeting overall strategic goals. A goal of "adding new clients" may not be specific enough when your goal is to meet the return on investment in 3 months; goals should state what, how, how many, where, when, and why. For example, an occupational therapist hosted a free health screening in his clinic for balance and posture available to anyone in the community and paid for an advertisement in the local paper about an 8-week fall prevention class. He would need to enlist 15 class participants to cover the expenses for the health screening and the ad.

4. *Is the budget right?* The budget includes both material costs and people costs. People costs are where many marketing efforts fall short; staffing per hour to carry out a marketing strategy or to perform the new service or product has a price that needs to be assessed over time as pricing and reimbursement change.

5. *Are your internal, external, and doctor referral programs working together?* Table 8.1 shows how marketing strategies can work across all the target market groups simultaneously. Continuously survey the effectiveness of each strategy by developing a rating scale for use by all involved in marketing efforts. Conduct customer satisfaction surveys with each client at the end of the therapy session or on discharge. Ask specific questions about clients' experience with the service or product.

6. *How do you measure response and return on investment?* Establishing tracking documentation or systems will help you measure your marketing strategy success. Excel worksheets or online surveys are easy ways to customize, organize, and analyze your marketing monitoring data. For example, free giveaways have no real return on investment except to generate good public relations. However, providing an incentive such as a T-shirt or monthly newsletter to referral sources has a cost, and results can be measured in terms of new customers and new client testimonials highlighted on your Web site.

7. *Does your marketing message clearly highlight the advantages or uniqueness of your practice?* Not reaching your marketing response goals or return on investment can suggest that your marketing message is not clearly conveying the benefits or value of your services or products. Reassess your marketing materials or types of marketing strategies to ensure that you are emphasizing exactly how, what, and why a consumer should participate in or obtain your services.

MARKETING SUCCESS

Marketing success is dependent on two important elements: (1) reaching your specific marketing goals, which include sound financial or reimbursement models, and (2) pursuing service or practice growth opportunities. Health care is unique among market sectors in that the provider often charges a third party for services rendered and collects payment that may not be equal to what is charged. Multiple payer types and policies such as insurance companies and federal governmental insurance programs add layers of complication to the process of being paid for services and products provided. Regardless of who or how your payer target market reimburses for services, it is vital to actively pursue payment on a timely basis.

Kotler (2003) defined *marketing success* through four basic growth opportunity frameworks: (1) selling more current products to current customers, (2) selling new products to current customers, (3) selling more current products to new customers, and (4) selling new products to new customers. SWOT analysis can be used to continuously analyze current services and products and current customers to find unmet needs, ways to attract new clients, and untapped organizational assets. For example, an occupational therapist created a support group for stroke survivors. Through a monthly program survey, the therapist learned that many group members desired to learn more about nutrition. During the organizational assessment, the therapist identified a dietitian, and together they developed small cooking workshops for the group. This therapist created a way to sell more products to the current customers.

MARKETING TECHNOLOGIES AND TRENDS

The Internet will continue to grow in importance as a source of health care information. The advancement of technologies through the growth and convergence of devices such as the personal computer and smart phones, as well as technologies like blogging and instant messaging, have changed the way industries do business and market their services. Health care providers have been slow to take advantage of new technologies because they can be costly, complicated, and time consuming to integrate into the medical model, which involves huge amounts of documentation and information storing. Furthermore, health care is heavily regulated and has an overarching requirement to protect privacy. Consumers demand easy accessibility and immediate attention, however, and despite their reluctance, occupational therapy practitioners will have to meet these demands or lose their consumers to other vendors of health care products and services. Occupational therapists should give serious consideration to marketing their services using social media and outcome marketing.

Social Media

The Internet, once thought of merely as a source of worldwide information and news, has evolved into a "social web"—that is, a combination of video, audio, and messaging social networks (Evans, 2008). An estimated 3.5 billion electronic word-of-mouth conversations occur each day, and about 2 of 3 make a reference to a service or product (Evans, 2008). Marketers have coined the term *social media* to refer to the many online delivery channels, such as

- *Multimedia channels*, including blogs; microblogs; podcasts; and photo, audio, and video sharing
- *Social platforms*, including personal and business networks such as MySpace and Facebook and message boards and forums
- *Social interactions*, including location-based services such as event guides and e-mails, RSS (really simple syndication) feeds, SMS (short message service) text messaging, and mobile communication (Evans, 2008).

Social media allows the mass consumer to view, participate in, and influence outcomes in a collective and collaborative process. As stated previously, this tremendous increase in online presence has lengthened the consideration phase of the buying habit; people can read about and review services and products even before purchasing them.

The online presence of health care became best known through WebMD (www.webmd.com), a traditional business-to-business marketing site containing medical news and informational topics targeted separately to practitioners and consumers. To meet new consumers' demands and user trends, WebMD now includes many social media channels such as forums and mobile communications. The emerging push for universal electronic health records and database storage for personal medical records to trim costs and increase efficiency provides further incentive for the medical community to join the social web or potentially lose access to government insurance programs and payer reimbursement.

Occupational therapy practitioners and work settings are not exempt from the powerful influence of the Internet and social media for marketing their services. The first step is to develop a Web site. Your Web site needs to be informative and user friendly, promote your expertise, and answer as many of your target market's potential questions as possible. (See Appendix 8.B for a list of Web sites that have these characteristics.) Effective Web sites include the following:

- Services, programs, and products
- Staff and staff specialties
- Location and directions
- FAQs (frequently asked questions)
- Printable forms, research articles, and newsletters
- Consumer and referral testimonials
- Value-added links (e.g., if your practice specializes in pediatrics, you may have a link to the American Academy of Pediatrics), medical library, and health care news
- Insurance or payment information
- A design that is well-organized, easy to navigate, and includes pictures and interactive media
- Contact information
- Additional content such as community events, jobs, customer service surveys, blogs, and video.

The goal of your Web site is to be visible to any and all customers and target markets, convey the expertise of staff and services, cultivate a sense of professionalism and interactive communication, and communicate an overall sense of listening and caring (i.e., relationship). Your Web site should complement your other marketing strategies and materials.

Outcome Marketing

The value of occupational therapy services and products can best be communicated through outcome marketing. *Outcome marketing* is the use of evidence-based service or product outcomes or measurements to promote the results of processes or efforts. Its goal is to establish an interactive, personalized, and engaging relationship with the target market through the user's experience with your services or product. The outcomes communicated should match the desired outcomes of your target markets.

The market analysis can be used in creating your outcome marketing strategies. For example, an occupational therapist obtained grant funding to develop a 6-month, twice-weekly stroke recovery program. The market analysis indicated that physicians saw a need for occupational therapy treatment for clients with depression, isolation, and functional loss following inpatient treatment for stroke. The organizational assessment of the health care delivery system indicated that many clients with mild to moderate deficits who could obtain home health services were sent home after 14 days of hospitalization with unresolved independent activity of daily living issues. A grant-funding source had been created to pay for community outreach services left unavailable through the existing medical model. In the marketing materials for the program, the occupational therapist communicated the gap in care as well as the desired outcomes of the following target markets (Levinson, 2008):

- *Stroke survivors*—increased socialization skills, increased participation in family and community activities, effective health-monitoring techniques, increased safety at home, increased emotional support

- *Treating physicians and health care delivery system*—cost-effectiveness by treating clients outside the hospital, protection of their reputation
- *Funding source*—the opportunity to help others access opportunities and increase quality of life.

These desired outcomes typically reflect occupational therapy contextual or performance goals. The therapist incorporated into her marketing mix descriptions of the experience of the service, opportunity for relationships, and outcomes that can be achieved through the program. Communicating progress in meeting these desired outcomes to clients, referring physicians, and the funding source throughout the program was vital to keeping clients participating for 6 months, the physicians referring more clients to the program, and the funding source renewing the grant.

Summary

Marketing is the process of identifying and communicating with consumers through a set of strategies and techniques intended to attract, persuade, and maintain them as purchasers of services and products (Gandolf & Hirsch, n.d.-d). In the health care market, the occupational therapist plays the role of seller, and numerous individuals or agencies acts as buyer, including clients, third-party payers, and private businesses. Target markets are segments of buyers with similar and measurable characteristics and needs an organization desires to influence. The organization influences the target market through market management.

Market management consists of analysis, planning, implementation, and monitoring. Market analysis includes an organizational analysis to identify its strengths and weaknesses and to plan activities for improvement (Levinson, 2002), and the environmental assessment examines the forces and changes affecting the organization's ability to conduct business effectively within the market (Kotler et al., 2000). The functional outcomes of the assessments are the identification of emerging trends, target markets, unique products or services, and competition. The marketing plan is the tool developed to coordinate and implement strategies based on the information gathered during the market analysis.

Marketing strategies relate to the 7 *P*s of marketing: product, place, price, promotion, positioning, packaging, and people. The marketing mix consists of various elements of the 7 *P*s customized to each of the target markets you have identified as benefiting from your services. Implementation of the marketing plan involves five steps: establishing the people and the experience, identifying short- and long-term marketing goals, identifying the marketing budget, selecting a marketing mix for each target market, and creating a timeline. Outcome measurement, the last step in market management, requires establishing a systematic approach to collecting data following implementation of the marketing strategies in a given time frame. The results provide useful information for adjusting marketing strategies in response to target market trends and changes. To be successful in today's consumer-driven environment, occupational therapy practitioners must understand and become comfortable and skilled in social marketing and other market approaches.

Case Examples

Level I Fieldwork

Helen was assigned to a private practice hand therapy clinic for her Level I fieldwork requirement. Her supervising occupational therapist specialized in ergonomics and workplace environmental adaptation. He asked Helen to go with him to observe an onsite assessment at a die tool assembly company that was a new client of his practice. The supervisor asked Helen to make a list of possible marketing materials that could be given to the new company owner to promote further business.

Helen conducted a market analysis on the die tool assembly company with an online search in order to better understand the general operations of the company and types of work and work positions of its employees. After developing a sense for what the company and its employees' demands and needs might be, Helen gathered samples of all the marketing materials belonging to the

hand therapy practice. She identified and listed the following:

- Company's brochure
- Company's educational pamphlet of common worksite injuries and prevention strategies
- Company's flyer of the "lunch and learn" educational lectures for employers and employees on various workplace injury prevention strategies and practical worksite adaptations
- Company's CD-ROM "Worksite Assessments and Solutions," which depicted a real case example of a therapist conducting an assessment and planning and implementing worksite interventions as well as a client's testimonial.

Level II Fieldwork

Ron, an occupational therapy student doing his Level II fieldwork assignment, was assigned the project of devel-

(continued)

Case Examples *(cont.)*

oping a new program flyer for pregnant mothers with carpal tunnel syndrome. The ultimate marketing goal was to enroll pregnant mothers in a 4-week educational program on how to prevent and treat carpal tunnel syndrome, to begin in 1 month.

Ron decided to conduct a market analysis on the existing appropriate clientele for the program by developing a written survey to be completed by women presently receiving occupational therapy for carpal tunnel syndrome. Ron's goal was to determine the best date and time to conduct the program and to facilitate feedback on common concerns pregnant women have surrounding their injury. The survey asked the recipients to answer general questions about times and dates and specific questions regarding what daily tasks or roles they found to be difficult to perform with their injury. The supervisor approved Ron's survey and gave Ron 2 weeks to plan, conduct, and gather the survey results. After 2 weeks, Ron analyzed the survey replies and met with the supervisor to discuss the results. Ron then developed a program flyer containing the program's name, date, location, time, a brief description of the 4-week program's topics and goals and the program's expected results.

First-Time Manager

Shane, a first-time occupational therapy manager working in a group home for teenagers with behavioral disorders, decided to develop a 12-week occupational therapy expressive arts program. He wrote a one-page proposal to present to the director of the group home in hopes of convincing her that the program would provide valuable outcomes for this population and was worth investing money and resources to implement.

Shane conducted a market analysis on his target market—teenagers with behavioral disorders—and his selected program services—expressive arts programs—looking for evidence-based support and benefits through peer-reviewed articles and expert testimonials. He inves-

tigated other expressive arts programs and interviewed several other practitioners who worked with his target market. Shane also conducted an organizational assessment at his work setting. He performed a SWOT analysis and identified internal and external factors that supported the organization's benefit from implementing this type of program. After completing his market research and overall analysis, Shane developed a proposal stating the program's name, the results of the research that supported the program, the program's goals and benefits, the dates and times the program should take place, costs of conducting the program, and the estimated return on investment.

Manager

Rhonda, an experienced occupational therapy manager in an outpatient clinic, was asked by the clinic's marketing department to participate in a videocast to promote a newly developed fall prevention program for older individuals that would be posted on the clinic's new Web site. Rhonda was allotted 60 seconds in which to present the service, price, place, packaging (who, what, when, how), and unique value or benefits of the program.

Rhonda decided to conduct a market analysis online, looking at interactive media such as podcasts and videocasts of online companies to acquaint herself with this form of media and see what appealed to her. Rhonda also met with her facility's marketing department to find out who the audience would be, how the videocast would be marketed or distributed, and any other internal or external factors that would affect what she could promote. After gathering her market research notes, Rhonda decided that a personal story of a past elderly client who had participated in occupational therapy services related to a recent fall would be the most appealing approach to the videocast. Rhonda developed a 60-second audio script between her and her client to be accompanied with video demonstrating various therapy interventions for balance and fall prevention. Items detailing the time and place of the program were flashed at the bottom of the screen instead of stated.

❖ Learning Activities

1. Collect 5 different local and national newspapers. Find and identify a health care trend or story in which occupational therapy services could be useful or a new occupational therapy service or product could satisfy a need. Perform an environmental assessment on the need or service.

2. In a present fieldwork assignment, affiliation, or volunteer or work environment, identify 3 target markets, and write a small descriptive paragraph about each of them.

3. Visit the health care Web sites www.webmd.com and www.revolutionhealth.com. Find and identify each

company's mission and marketing strategies or marketing content.

4. Visit the American Occupational Therapy Association at www.aota.com, and locate 3 marketing promotions that you could use to tell a client or potential client or referral source about occupational therapy.

5. Gather 5 examples of marketing promotion materials, such as a brochure, business card, Web site, menu, booklet, advertisement, or newsletter. Write a comparison of the value, 7 Ps, accessibility, and quality of services or benefits portrayed in the material.

✓ Multiple-Choice Questions

1. Which is *not* true about consumers today?
   a. More than 50% of adults go online for health care information.
   b. Consumers still call their physician first when they have a health care concern.
   c. Eight million people look up health care–related issues online daily.
   d. Consumers expect value for their time and money.
2. Marketing objectives include which of the following?
   a. Solicit certified and licensed personnel.
   b. Meet short- and long-term strategic goals.
   c. Promote the disadvantages of your competitors.
   d. None of the above.
3. Which of the following is an example of a target market?
   a. Chamber of commerce.
   b. Blue Cross insurance company.
   c. Children with attention-deficit/hyperactivity disorder.
   d. All of the above.
4. A consumer expects a product or service to do which of the following?
   a. Outlast the similar product they have at home.
   b. Come with a lifetime warranty.
   c. Have personal value and purpose.
   d. Be able to be used by everyone in the family.
5. The pricing of a product or service varies according to which of the following factors?
   a. Overhead costs.
   b. Fair market value.
   c. Contracted rate with an insurance company.
   d. All of the above.
6. Which of the following promotions is the most cost-effective?
   a. Public relations.
   b. Sales promotions.
   c. Advertising.
   d. Personal selling.
7. Which of the following is an example of a sales promotion?
   a. Offering free health screenings.
   b. Placing an advertisement in the phone book.
   c. Giving a talk about your clinic service at the school.
   d. Meeting with the referring physician.

8. Which of the following is the best way to allow consumers to "experience" the service or product?
   a. Give free therapy sessions.
   b. Develop a Web site that allows consumers to interact with your service or product.
   c. Tell consumers about the service or product in a monthly newsletter.
   d. None of the above.
9. Which of the following best describes *packaging* of a service or product?
   a. The content of your brochure.
   b. The type of wrapping the therapy supplies come in.
   c. How you describe your service or product to others.
   d. The consumer's initial impression of your service or product.
10. In what order are the steps in market management properly conducted?
    a. Analysis, planning, implementation, monitoring.
    b. Planning, analysis, implemention, monitoring.
    c. Monitoring, analysis, planning, implementation.
    d. Planning, monitoring, implementation, analysis.
11. The SWOT analysis is an assessment tool that evaluates which of the following?
    a. Internal and external factors of an organization.
    b. Emerging opportunities.
    c. Possible factors that can negatively affect a service or product.
    d. All of the above.
12. The environmental assessment should evaluate all of the following *except* the
    a. Buying habits of your target markets.
    b. Lack of sufficient qualified personnel to provide the service.
    c. Scope of practice.
    d. Role of mobile devices in marketing your services.
13. A marketing plan needs to include which of the following components?
    a. Company description, target markets, marketing strategies.
    b. Description of services and products, action plan, monitoring measurements.
    c. Advantages over competition, timeline, costs of each marketing strategy.
    d. All of the above.

14. Which of the following is true about implementing a marketing plan?
    a. You need to make your employees a sales tool.
    b. You customize the marketing mix to each target market.
    c. You avoid telling consumers which insurance companies you contract with.
    d. a and b.

15. Which of the following is a characteristic of the social media?
    a. Not a good way to market to mass markets.
    b. Most costly type of marketing strategy.
    c. Different from traditional media in their use of a collaborative process among users.
    d. Cannot demonstrate value.

16. Which is an advantage of the social media?
    a. You can reach more consumers all of the time.
    b. You have the opportunity to attract new clients every day.
    c. It is the most effective means of word-of-mouth selling.
    d. All of the above.

17. Relationship marketing does which of the following?
    a. Gives consumers a personalized relationship with the service or product.
    b. Interferes with operations because consumers become too demanding.

    c. Allows informed decision making in purchasing new services or products.
    d. Both a and c.

18. Which of the following outcomes best represents marketing success?
    a. All your consumer surveys give you positive ratings.
    b. You stay within your marketing budget.
    c. You establish your value and your consumers' trust, promoting repeat business.
    d. You are easily accessible and noticeable from the street.

19. Which of the following statements is *not* true about the value of networking or collaboration?
    a. You risk losing business to your colleagues.
    b. You benefit from joint resources and advantages.
    c. You establish good public relations in your community.
    d. You promote your services and products through additional marketing channels.

20. The advantages of outcome marketing in health care include which of the following?
    a. It demonstrates value through objective measurements.
    b. It can build the confidence of your referral sources in you.
    c. It can promote your unique value to the payer.
    d. All of the above.

References

Aldag, R. J., & Stearns, T. M. (1987). *Management*. Cincinnati, OH: South-Western Publishing.

The American Heritage dictionary of the English language (4th ed.). (n.d.). Public relations. Retrieved June 4, 2009, from http://dictionary.classic.reference.com/browse/public relations

American Occupational Therapy Association. (2010). Occupational therapy code of ethics and ethics standards. *American Journal of Occupational Therapy, 64*.

Bates v. State Bar of Arizona. 433 U.S. 350 (1977).

Braveman, B. (2006). Marketing occupational therapy services. In B. Braveman (Ed.), *Leading and managing occupational therapy services: An evidence based approach* (pp. 333–346). Philadelphia: F. A. Davis.

Creveling, C., Hambleton, L., & McCarthy, B. (2006). *Six Sigma for marketing processes*. Boston: Prentice Hall.

Evans, D. (2008). *Social media marketing: An hour a day*. Indianapolis, IN: Wiley.

Fahey, L., & Randall, R. M. (Eds.). (1994). *The portable MBA in strategy*. New York: Wiley.

Fox, S. (2009, March 6). Researching and reviewing doctors online. *Pew Internet and American Life Project*. Retrieved March 20, 2009, from http://www.pewinternet.org/Commentary/2009/March/2--Researching-(and-Reviewing)-Doctors-Online.aspx

Gandolf, S., & Hirsch, L. (n.d.-a). Physician marketing made ethical and effective. *Healthcare Success Strategies*. Retrieved February 7, 2009, from http://www.healthcaresuccess.com/articles/ethical-marketing.html

Gandolf, S., & Hirsch, L. (n.d.-b). Planning for success in physical therapy practice marketing and advertising. *Healthcare Success Strategies*. Retrieved February 7, 2009, from http://www.healthcaresuccess.com/specialty/physical-therapy.html

Gandolf, S., & Hirsch, L. (n.d.-c). The 7 Ps of marketing. *Healthcare Success Strategies*. Retrieved February 7, 2009, from http://www.healthcaresuccess.com/articles/the-7-ps-of-marketing.html

Gandolf, S., & Hirsch, L. (n.d.-d). What is marketing? *Healthcare Success Strategies*. Retrieved February 7, 2009, from http://www.healthcaresuccess.com/articles/what-is-marketing.html

Health Insurance Portability and Accountability Act of 1996, Pub. L. 104–191.

Iacobucci, D., & Calder, D. (2003). *Kellogg on integrated marketing*. Hoboken, NJ: Wiley.

Kotler, P. (2003). *Marketing insights from A to Z: 80 concepts every manager needs to know*. Hoboken, NJ: Wiley.

Kotler, P., & Armstrong, G. (1991). *Principles of marketing* (5th ed.). Englewood Cliffs, NJ: Prentice Hall.

Kotler, P., Armstrong, G., & Cunningham, P. (2000). *Principles of marketing* (5th Canadian ed.). Upper Saddle River, NJ: Prentice Hall.

Kotler, P., & Keller, K. (2006). *A framework for marketing management.* Upper Saddle River, NJ: Prentice Hall.

Lendermen, M. (2006). *Experience the message: How experiential marketing is changing the brand world.* New York: Carroll & Graf.

Levinson, H. (2002). *Organizational assessment: A step-by-step guide to effective consulting.* Washington, DC: American Psychological Association.

Levinson, J. (2008). *Startup guide to guerrilla marketing.* Irvine, CA: Entrepreneur Media.

Marketing Teacher. (n.d.). *Sales promotion: What is sales promotion?* Retrieved February 6, 2010, from http://www.marketingteacher.com/Lessons/lesson_sales_promotion.htm

Richmond, T., & Powers, D. (2004). *Business fundamentals for the rehabilitation professional.* Thorofare, NJ: Slack.

Richmond, T., & Powers, D. (2009). *Business fundamentals for the rehabilitation professional* (2nd ed.). Thorofare, NJ: Slack.

Scott, D. (2007). *The new rules of marketing and PR: How to use news releases, blogs, podcasting, viral marketing, and online media to reach buyers directly.* Hoboken, NJ: Wiley.

Shoemaker, T., & Wheeler, C. (1996). Marketing. In M. Johnshon (Ed.), *The occupational therapy manager* (rev. ed., pp. 101–116). Bethesda, MD: American Occupational Therapy Association.

Sohnen-Moe, C. M. (2001). *Business mastery: A guide for creating a fulfilling, thriving business and keeping it successful* (4th ed.). Tucson, AZ: Sohnen-Moe Associates.

Stark Law (1989). Social Security Act, §1877, 42 CFR §411.350–§411.389.

Thomas, R. (2008). *Health services marketing.* New York: Springer.

Appendix 8.A. Marketing Evidence Table

Topic	Subtopics	Evidence
Strategy marketing, business-to-business marketing	Communicating common approaches to manage risk, making data-driven decisions, enhancing communication to drive sales, focusing on the full range of contact with consumers as it unfolds	FedEx; Coca Cola; airlines, and most other big, established brands, both national and international Creveling, C., Hambleton, L., & McCarthy, B. (2006). *Six Sigma for marketing processes.* Boston: Prentice Hall. Iacobucci, D., & Calder, D. (2003). *Kellogg on integrated marketing.* Hoboken, NJ: Wiley.
Database marketing	Continuously collecting data on consumers to create or adapt present services or products to meet consumers' needs and habits	Starbucks, Toyota, Apple, Sony, banks, grocery chains, book stores Kotler, P. (2003). *Marketing insights from A to Z: 80 concepts every manager needs to know.* Hoboken, NJ: Wiley.
Experiential marketing	Providing interactive experiences with products or services both in person and online to encourage purchase and loyalty	Disney, Niketown, Hard Rock Café Evans, D. (2008). *Social media marketing: An hour a day.* Indianapolis, IN: Wiley. Lendermen, M. (2006). *Experience the message: How experiential marketing is changing the brand world.* New York: Carroll & Graf. Thomas, R. (2008). *Health services marketing.* New York: Springer.
Image and emotional marketing	Developing marketing messages that touch emotions deeply, such as personal stories	Car insurance, home improvement stores, Super Bowl commercials Kotler, P. (2003). *Marketing insights from A to Z: 80 concepts every manager needs to know.* Hoboken, NJ: Wiley.
Relationship marketing	Customizing products to customers' preferences, pricing based on relationship with customer, personalizing product design, direct marketing to customer	Shoe companies such as Nike, Adidas, and Keds; M&Ms Scott, D. (2007). *The new rules of marketing and PR: How to use news releases, blogs, podcasting, viral marketing, and online media to reach buyers directly.* Hoboken, NJ: Wiley. Thomas, R. (2008). *Health services marketing.* New York: Springer.

Appendix 8.B. Online Marketing Resources

- **American Occupational Therapy Association:** www.aota.org (emerging practice areas, evidence-based practice issues and articles)
- **Bureau of Labor Statistics:** www.bls.gov (provides labor statistics)
- **Centers for Disease Control and Prevention:** www.cdc.gov (disease, health, and related topics)
- **Examples of effective Web sites:** www.wellspringtherapy.com, www.emergeachildsplace.com, and www.therapeuticassociates.com
- **Free Library:** www.thefreelibrary.com (free, current news and information on customizing your Web site or newsletter)
- **GovSpot:** www.govspot.com (government research on markets, market trends, statistics)
- **National Technical Information Services:** www.ntis.gov (government-funded scientific, technical, engineering, and business-related information)
- **Newswire.com:** www.newswire.com (popular news releases, videos, press releases, and search engines)
- **Pew Research Center:** www.pewresearch.org (public opinion polling and research on issues, attitudes, and trends shaping America and the world)
- **PR Web:** www.prweb.com (tool to send your own news releases)
- **SCORE:** www.score.org (counseling services for small businesses)
- **Survey Monkey:** www.surveymonkey.com (tool to create your own surveys)
- **U.S. Census Bureau:** www.census.gov (economic, demographic, social statistics)
- **U.S. Government:** www.usa.gov (links to government analysis and statistics)

9

Starting a New Program, Business, or Practice

Gordon Muir Giles, PhD, OTR/L, FAOTA

❖ Key Terms and Concepts

Business plan. A formal statement of a set of business development goals and a plan for reaching those goals with key requirements and outcomes.

Initial program proposal. Formal description of the practical application of the visionary goal in a specific context and applied to a specific population. The program proposal should include the resources required (including facilities), specify management and staffing, and provide an estimate of expenses and revenues. It is circulated to key decision makers. Approval of the program proposal leads to the development of a business plan.

Market analysis. A documented investigation of a market that is used to inform business planning activities. The market analysis examines the number of potential consumers, discusses the potential growth rate of the market for the service, describes the strengths and weaknesses of the program or service in comparison with the competition, and details marketing strategies.

Staffing pattern. Number of staff needed in particular job categories in relation to the type of service provided, number of clients served (census), and the clients' need for service.

Visionary goals. Excellence in whatever domain an individual or company chooses to pursue. Visionary goals are challenging and meaningful for the person, for a group of individuals, for a company, or for society as a whole.

❖ Learning Objectives

After completing this chapter, you should be able to do the following:

- Describe how to communicate the vision for a program.
- Describe how to write a program proposal.
- Describe how to write a business plan for program development.

- Describe key elements of a staffing pattern.
- Explain how the program's location and facilities can affect its success.

The American Occupational Therapy Association's (AOTA's) *Centennial Vision* for the occupational therapy profession sees occupational therapy practitioners as a leading force in 21st-century health care (AOTA, 2007). Making the *Centennial Vision* a reality requires that occupational therapy practitioners and students understand the changing demographic; value environments; and embrace new markets and emerging needs, practice areas, and models of service delivery (AOTA, 2007). Occupational therapy practitioners and students are innovators and have a passion for serving the needs of others, particularly underserved populations, such as children and youths with mental health disorders; homeless persons with chronic mental illnesses; or older populations as they seek to maintain health, wellness, and participation (AOTA, 2008; Hardeman, 2007). Employment in occupational therapy is expected to grow at a much higher rate than overall employment. Occupational therapy employment is projected to rise 23% from 99,000 in 2006 to 122,000 in 2016 (U.S. Bureau of Labor Statistics, 2009). As the Baby Boom generation ages, a large population cohort will enter an age range with increased vulnerability to the chronic health conditions (e.g., cerebrovascular accident, orthopedic conditions, dementia). Demographic changes, changes in expectations for services, and a focus on wellness and "aging in place" are anticipated to drive an increased need for occupational therapy services. The school-age population also is expected to increase in size. Changes in the overall economy lead to contractions in some service sectors and the potential for growth in others; for example, the reduction in the number of skilled nursing facility positions for occupational therapy practitioners that followed the Balanced Budget Act of 1997 resulted in increased numbers of school- and community-based occupational therapy services. Taken together, these forces will lead to an expanding and changing occupational therapy profession.

Occupational therapy practitioners are involved in developing both occupational therapy services and interdisciplinary services (Hardeman, 2007). Occupational therapists work as independent contractors, manage specialty private clinics, run businesses, and develop programs within larger corporate entities (Glennon, 2007; Hardeman, 2007). Despite the wide variety of clients served, program types, reimbursement sources, and contexts and environments, there are important commonalities in the requirements of program, business, or practice development. Central to most successful start-ups is one person or a group of people with a vision of what can be done to provide a novel service, assist people in a new way, or address an unmet need. A successful program harnesses the commitment and energy of practitioners doing what they love to do (Allen, 2009; Hardeman, 2007). This chapter describes ways in which a visionary goal may be developed into a program proposal and follows the major headings of a hypothetical business plan.

DEVELOPMENT OF A VISIONARY GOAL

The vision for a new program may come from many sources: Some practitioners are driven by a desire to control their own destiny or to increase work independence or flexibility or have "the heart of an entrepreneur" (Hardeman, 2007). Some practitioners, through continuing education or experience, develop skills that are marketable. For other practitioners, it is a commitment to an idea, practice area, or type of intervention and a desire to benefit a population that leads them to program development.

Alternatively, observation of referral patterns at a setting may indicate a sufficient number of individuals in a population to justify program development. There may be a call for a proposal from a public or private agency, such as when federal, state, or private charitable organizations request applications for funds to serve a specific purpose. Or an individual, group of individuals, institution, or agency may wish to develop a program and may investigate the need for a service in the community.

Practitioners opening their own business will be influenced by their financial situation and tolerance of risk. A part-time after-school clinic run out of converted garage space in a person's home involves less risk than quitting a job (with paid leave, benefits, and regular paycheck) and investing his or her life savings to open a freestanding work hardening clinic. But whatever type of program is envisioned, it should be undertaken with serious planning: Every business needs a business plan.

Going from the visionary goal to a functioning program is a long and often arduous process. Program development is usually a team undertaking, as typically a single individual does not have all the requisite knowledge and resources. Even individuals developing a private practice need to call on multiple resources and do a considerable amount of research before start-up. There are many ways to obtain valuable free assistance. Both the Small Business Administration (SBA; www.sba.gov) and America's Small Business Development Center (www.asbdc-us.org) provide many helpful Web-based resources, including sample business plans. Free information is available from the Web site of the Service Corps of Retired Executives (SCORE), which also provides free in-person mentoring through 370 offices nationwide (www.score.org). Seeking advice and performing a needs assessment (reviewed in the next section) can serve the dual purpose of involving key stakeholders early in the process and increasing the chances that the visionary goal will have wide-based support. Additionally, interested outside agencies (e.g., foundations) should be involved at an early stage. For example, in developing a hospital-based outpatient traumatic brain injury program, the rehabilitation manager may wish to involve staff practitioners from each discipline, referring physicians, the facilities manager, and representatives of consumer advocacy and service agencies.

PROGRAM PROPOSAL

Early in the development process, practitioners should consult with someone who is knowledgeable about the process of writing proposals. Proposals that have been successful within the same corporation or with the same funding agency may be used as a model. The initial proposal serves a multitude of functions but should be brief—no more than one to two single-spaced pages. If the program is to be developed as part of an existing institution or business, the initial proposal needs to demonstrate that the proposed program is consistent with the goals and culture of the existing entity. If the proposed program represents a departure from prior endeavors, the initial proposal should describe how the new program would complement previously existing services. For example, in developing a skilled nursing facility (SNF)–based program for persons with severe and chronic mental illness and medical comorbidity for a company specializing in long-term psychiatric services, it was necessary to show how a medically oriented service could maintain clients within the continuum of care, therefore providing a new, enhanced revenue stream plus an additional service important to key referral agencies.

The initial program proposal describes the population served, the program's goals and objectives, and the services to be provided and should report the outcome of the needs assessment. For the purposes of developing a program, a needs assessment establishes the potential demand for a product or service within a target population. Needs assessments vary in how elaborate they are and how many sources of information are tapped (Finlayson, 2007). At minimum, a needs assessment should include an estimate of the number of clients who would make use of the service and the length of treatment. In addition to determining the customer base, the needs assessment assists in determining which proposed services to change, which ones to incorporate, and which to eliminate. Although a needs assessment is desirable as part of program development, it also should be thought of as a continuous process, with every client or potential client as a potential program development resource to assist in establishing what clients want and expect of the program.

Once the need is described and is seen as adequate to support the program's targeted outcomes, the proposal should list the benefits to the population served and to the parent organization. Resources required, including facilities, management, and staffing, and an estimate of expenses and revenues should be included. The temptation to go into too much detail should be resisted; at this point, it is necessary only to get the approval of key decision makers to proceed with further investigation and obtain the resources necessary to develop a business plan. The initial proposal should be circulated to potential stakeholders for input. Favorable reception to the initial proposal should initiate the development of the business plan, which describes the proposed program in more detail and provides a more detailed blueprint for how to proceed with program development (Abrams, 2000).

DEVELOPMENT OF A BUSINESS PLAN

A business plan is a planning and decision-making tool. There is no set format for a business plan and its content is determined by the visionary goals and the needs of various audiences. A business plan should contain whatever information is needed to decide whether or not to pursue a visionary goal. Business plans may have an internal or external focus or both. *Externally focused* plans target goals that are important to external stakeholders, often financial stakeholders. They typically have detailed information about the individuals or team and how the visionary goal can be achieved. *Internally focused business* plans usually describe the development of a new product or service and how the new visionary goal will help meet the organization's overall goals. See Appendix 9.B for a sample outline of a business plan.

Background and Trends of the Service Sector

Nature of the Service Sector

The program developer should analyze the potential customer population and the service environment, including the nature of the problem to be addressed, and current service delivery models. Many sources of information are available in developing this background information, including epidemiological databases and population projections, literature reviews, business trends, prior referral patterns, information about competitors, and requests from referral agencies.

Identifying the Problem

The program developer needs to describe the nature of the problem or resource deficit to be addressed by the proposed program. This should be a succinct description of the problem that states the unmet need in the community. Clearly articulating the problem or deficit will assist in communication with stakeholders and convey the importance of the visionary goal.

Market Factors and Future Trends

It is important to note whether the population to be treated in the program is expanding (e.g., persons over 65 years of age, persons with an autism spectrum disorder) or contracting (e.g., persons with AIDS dementia syndrome). Changes in the health care market are often the result of the evolution of service delivery models and changes in reimbursement (e.g., changes in intermediary rules). For example, Alzheimer's programs have largely moved from SNFs to residential care facilities (RCFs) because of changes in funding and the development of new service delivery models. Consultation and service delivery in RCFs in areas such as wellness, activities programs, fall prevention, and environmental modification are an emerging practice area.

Services

Description of Services

The program developer should know the population to be served, the types of problem to be addressed, and the nature of the services to be delivered. There should be a clear definition of the service user and the treatment criteria—for example, whether the service will be inpatient or outpatient, what therapeutic disciplines will deliver services, how many hours of treatment will be provided per day, and how many times per week services will be provided. The target population should be defined as specifically as possible with inclusionary and exclusionary criteria.

Unique Program Services or Features

The program developer should consider the unique characteristics of the program under development and focus on factors that make it superior to other available programs. For example, the program may offer a unique service delivery model or represent evidence-based practice. A computer search and review of the literature using an appropriate database (e.g., PubMed, CINAHL) will locate reports on model programs and practice and treatment guidelines. Commercial search engines (e.g., Google) provide useful Web sites, and reference can be made to AOTA materials and AOTA's OT Connections listservs.

Intervention programs already in operation with a similar focus provide a resource for the program developer. Observing other programs can highlight both advantages and disadvantages of various approaches (e.g., physical plant, staffing, organizational structure). Building on the strong points of existing programs and evidence-based practice allows the clinician to develop an appropriate service model.

Market Analysis

Target Market and Characteristics

The market analysis estimates the total population of potential program users in the market area. The market analysis addresses the question of whether there are sufficient individuals in an area who can travel to the program, who need the program, and who represent sufficient revenue to support the program. When many people need the program, it is easier to find clients, and they do not have to travel a long way. The market analysis addresses whether the program will be covered by insurance and, if so, what type of insurance the population to be served has and at what level the insurance reimburses. If a program will not be covered by insurance, the market analysis addresses whether potential clients have sufficient funds and are willing to expend them to purchase the service (this also can be part of the needs assessment).

How the program is structured will determine the number of new clients needed to support it. A long-term 30-bed program for persons with severe chronic mental health disorders and medical co-morbidity with an average length of stay of 9 months will need an average of 40 admissions a year to stay viable; an admission rate above that will represent program growth. A practitioner in an orthopedic program with an average of 4–5 visits and 75% productivity will require 7 new clients per week (see "Staffing" section later in this chapter).

Competitors: Comparing Strengths and Weaknesses

The number of potential clients is only part of the information needed to estimate the potential utilization of the program; it is also important to estimate potential market share. Most programs have some type of competitor (even if the "competitor" is no intervention). A strengths, weaknesses, opportunities, and threats (SWOT) analysis may prove helpful in comparing relative strengths and weaknesses of the new program vis-à-vis competitors (Abrams, 2000). Strengths and weaknesses relate to characteristics of the program; opportunities and threats describe market factors (Lesonsky, 2007). A SWOT analysis is a useful tool to use throughout the life of a program (see Chapter 8 for more information).

Practitioners should determine the "selling points" of the program. What advantages does the new program offer over the programs to which clients are currently referred? Cost is an important determinant of choice of program, but it often is not the decisive factor: Many individuals pay more for perceived quality or may not consider cost at all if the payment will be covered by insurance. What added feature sets the new program apart? For example, developers of an SNF-based subacute rehabilitation program contacted discharge planners at local hospitals and emphasized the availability of admission and services 7 days per week, intravenous therapy, and total parenteral nutrition as factors that set it apart from its competitors.

Marketing

Promotion

The program developer must determine how the new program is to be promoted. *Promotion* involves disseminating information about a service, product, or company. Promotion involves understanding the needs of potential users of the product or service and communicating how the service will meet those needs (Robinson, Herz, & Brennan, 2009). AOTA promotes the profession of occupational therapy to the community at large, and part of the drive of the *Centennial Vision* was to advance a simple, clear, and compelling public image of the profession. Similarly, creating a "positioning statement" for a new service can help developers rapidly communicate their visionary goals (Lesonsky, 2007). Most programs developed by occupational therapy practitioners are directed toward a limited market, and promotion efforts should be highly focused toward specific populations. Many free or low-cost ways to promote the new service are available, such as listing it on special interest Web sites, maintaining a Web site, disseminating press releases or newsletters, and making presentations (personal selling) to interested community groups (Opila-Lehman, 2002). For example, rehabilitative services may be promoted in retirement communities, clubs, and organizations where individuals may need services themselves or know others who need services.

Developing a Marketing Strategy

The development of a marketing strategy is described in more detail in Chapter 8 and is briefly reviewed here. The marketing strategy is influenced by the program developers' knowledge of pre-established relationships and referral patterns in the community. Whereas promotion is used to "create the customer" (i.e., have customers recognize their need for the services provided), marketing is used to find, keep, and satisfy the customer. Providing client-centered care is central to developing a great reputation and is free, focused marketing. Individuals who refer clients for services (e.g., hospital or insurance case managers) need a reason to change established referral patterns, and the program developers need to introduce the new program to potential referrers. The needs assessment will have drawn attention to aspects of the service or program that have special value to potential referral sources. For example, accommodating clients at the last minute or rushing reports for someone who needs a rapid turnaround may help a service stand apart (Hardeman, 2007). Planning an open house for potential referrers to see the program's facilities and to meet the staff is helpful in increasing the referrers' comfort with the services offered. Indirect messages also may be very important in determining referrals; in addition to a focus on the quality of the therapeutic services provided, other factors that may influence program acceptance include whether or not the facility is clean and well-decorated and whether there is a courteous and professional staff (Leslie, 2005).

Once a program has begun to receive referrals, the referral source should be treated as a valuable resource. Referrers want to know that the clients they are sending to the program are obtaining timely and appropriate care (Hardeman, 2007). Within the constraints established by privacy requirements, the new program can provide outcome information to the referral agency (e.g., aggregate data regarding length of stay, gains in function, discharge destinations). *Networking* means connecting, online or in person, to share ideas and to discuss business opportunities. Depending on the program's market niche, venues for networking may include government agencies, chambers of commerce, business clubs, conferences, community benefit organizations, and competitors.

Management and Ownership

A company's external or internal audience of investors or managers wants to know that expertise will be available to open the program. It is important that the individuals listed as key personnel have the time and commitment to ensure the program's success. Gaps in expertise can be filled by the use of consultants in such areas as clinical issues, operations, administration, regulatory issues, financial issues, marketing, and reimbursement. Some programs are practical only with certain key posts filled, and a plan should be established to ensure that appropriate individuals are recruited for these positions.

Staffing

Staffing Patterns

The need for particular staffing levels and staff qualifications and experience will vary with *medical acuity* (defined as medical complexity and level of service), the severity of the client's condition, and type of services (e.g., is an SNF subacute unit going to accept clients with complex orthopedic or neurological conditions?). The number of occupational therapist, occupational therapy assistant, and aide staff and the mix of these staff also depend on client condition and program model, as well as applicable regulations. Programs in which the occupational therapist provides direct therapy services have a different staffing mix than those in which the occupational therapist assesses the client and then develops a plan for implementation by non-therapy personnel (e.g., a board-and-care home for persons with intellectual disability).

The program model and staff responsibilities are important factors in assessing the number of staff required. *Nonproductive time* is the term used to describe the time during which staff are not generating revenue in a fee-for-service model. Some models include nonproductive time for staff meetings, family meetings, documentation, scheduling, student supervision, and other non–direct-

care activities. Some models of service are communication intensive (usually programs with a need for coordination of services) and therefore have more nonproductive time. Knowing how many hours of therapy are needed is important in developing a staffing pattern. In an Alzheimer's disease day program (where there is a daily rate and services are not charged by the module), maintaining the program's routine of activities (e.g., lunch, activities program, nutrition breaks) and managing behaviors are as important as providing therapy, so it is important to know which staff are going to help with meals, when staff are going to take breaks, and when meetings are to occur. In a SNF, more therapy hours may be required for morning activities of daily living. Outlining staffing structure for a typical day and a typical week assists in assessing the need for staff.

Figure 9.1 presents data from a spreadsheet showing a simplified rehabilitation therapy staffing pattern for a subacute unit in an SNF. A module is a 15-minute period of direct therapy service. Staffing patterns differ based on medical acuity diagnosis and severity of condition; for example, persons with cerebrovascular accident may require extensive intervention from three therapy disciplines, whereas clients with knee replacement will require more physical therapy than occupational therapy and no speech therapy. Assumptions regarding therapy utilization per client are based on a mix of client condition and need for specific therapeutic services (hours of therapy needed depend on client utilization of individual disciplines, and reimbursement varies according to Medicare's Resource Utilization Group levels and minutes of service provided during reference periods).

In Figure 9.1, therapy staff hours increase predictably as the client census increases. The minimum requirement for 12-bed occupancy in the unit is one therapist in each discipline. However, if the census falls to seven clients or fewer, less than a full-time therapist is required in each discipline. Use of therapy aides and assistants reduces costs but should be determined on the basis of client complexity and regulatory requirements for the supervision of aides. Once salaries are averaged across hours for each staff qualification level, an average salary expense can be calculated. With the average salary cost per discipline established, the cost of staff per client day based on census and complexity mix can be estimated. Using this method, estimates of therapy labor costs for the program can be made. Similar staffing patterns can be developed for nursing, clerical, and ancillary labor. Estimation of cost will assist in determining how much the program will need to charge for the service (see "Finances" section later in this chapter).

Staff Recruitment

If the program is being developed within an existing corporation, then existing staff in the organization may begin the program However, in many circumstances, new staff will need to be recruited. Consideration should be given to the professional qualifications and personality characteristics of

ASSUMPTIONS	MODULES
PT = 4.0 MODS/REHAB PATIENT	4.0
OT = 3.0 MODS/REHAB PATIENT	3.0
ST = 2.0 MODS/REHAB PATIENT	2.0
PRODUCTIVITY - 75%	75%

Rehab Census	# of mods	# of hours	PT hours	PTA hours	PT Aide	Total	HPPD
20	80	26.67	11	8	8	27	1.35
19	76	25.33	9	8	8	25	1.32
18	72	24.00	8	8	8	24	1.33
17	68	22.67	8	8	7	23	1.35
16	64	21.33	8	8	5	21	1.31
15	60	20.00	8	8	4	20	1.33
14	56	18.67	8	5	6	19	1.36
13	52	17.33	8	5	4	17	1.31
12	48	16.00	8	0	8	16	1.33
11	44	14.67	8	0	7	15	1.36
10	40	13.33	8	0	5	13	1.30
9	36	12.00	7	0	5	12	1.33
8	32	10.67	5	0	5	10	1.25
7	28	9.33	5	0	4	9	1.29

Rehab Census	# of mods	# of hours	OT Hours	OTA	OT Aide	Total	HPPD
20	60	20.00	8	8	4	20	1.00
19	57	19.00	8	7	4	19	1.00
18	54	18.00	8	7	3	18	1.00
17	51	17.00	8	6	3	17	1.00
16	48	16.00	8	5	3	16	1.00
15	45	15.00	8	7	0	15	1.00
14	42	14.00	8	6	0	14	1.00
13	39	13.00	8	5	0	13	1.00
12	36	12.00	8	4	0	12	1.00
11	33	11.00	8	3	0	11	1.00
10	30	10.00	8	2	0	10	1.00
9	27	9.00	8	1	0	9	1.00
8	24	8.00	8	0	0	8	1.00
7	21	7.00	7	0	0	7	1.00

Figure 9.1 Rehab staffing patterns.

individuals recruited for a start-up program. For example, is there evidence that candidates are self-starters? Are they flexible in approaching problems? Do they embrace ambiguous situations and task demands? New programs often go through periods when it is necessary to work under less-than-ideal conditions. In a new program, frequent (3- to 6-month) reviews of the entire program model and changes in staff responsibilities may continue for 2 to 3 years or even longer as the program changes and develops and new organizational needs emerge. Individuals who enjoy the excitement of a start-up program may not enjoy the more routine aspects of service provision. Managers should keep in mind that staff turnover routinely occurs at a rate of 30% per year (Rollins, Salyers, Tsai, & Lydick, 2009), and in some settings turnover rates in excess of 100% over 2 years are not unheard of (Castle, 2006; Rollins et al., 2009; Woltmann

Rehab Census	# of mods	# of hours	ST hours		ST Aide	Total	HPPD
20	40	13.33	8		5	13	0.65
19	38	12.67	8		4	12	0.63
18	36	12.00	8		3	11	0.61
17	34	11.33	8		3	11	0.65
16	32	10.67	8		2	10	0.63
15	30	10.00	8		0	8	0.53
14	28	9.33	8		0	8	0.57
13	26	8.67	8		0	8	0.62
12	24	8.00	8		0	8	0.67
11	22	7.33	7		0	7	0.64
10	20	6.67	7		0	7	0.70
9	18	6.00	6		0	6	0.67
8	16	5.33	5		0	5	0.63
7	14	4.67	5		0	5	0.71

Note. HPPD = hours per patient day; MODS = modules; OT = occupational therapist; OTA = occupational therapy assistant; PT = physical therapist; PTA = physical therapy assistant; ST = speech therapist. The number of modules per day is derived from number of beds multiplied by utilization assumptions. To derive the number of hours required, the number of modules is divided by three (75% productivity estimate). The staffing pattern is derived by estimates of appropriate staff mix allowing for complexity of client condition and supervision requirements and totaling the necessary number of hours. Hours per patient day are derived from dividing total hours by census. As a check on accuracy, HPPD must total the number of modules per client plus nonproductive time (actual staff hours per patient day). The staffing projections can be used to demonstrate when staff hours need to be added or subtracted as the census changes. Contributed by Araceli D. Antonio, RN, MSN, nursing consultant, Antonio and Associates. Reprinted with permission.

Figure 9.1 Rehab staffing patterns *(cont.)*.

et al., 2008). There can be advantages to recruiting personnel with limited experience (e.g., new graduates), because such individuals may have fewer assumptions that are unhelpful in a novel service model (Robinson, et al., 2009). A supervisor should consider whether prospective staff match the characteristics of the staff and are a good fit with the established work group and program culture (Want, 2006). The roles and responsibilities of staff should be defined as clearly as possible in written job descriptions.

Availability of staff for hire may vary depending on location, number of training programs in the area, and number of new graduates entering the profession. The program's ability to attract staff may depend on personal connections, the reputation of the company in which the program is being developed, or the desirability of the service sector (e.g., at various times and geographic areas, acute rehabilitation and pediatrics may be regarded as more desirable practice areas).

Staff recruitment can be costly and time consuming. Various methods can be used to recruit staff, including advertising through newspapers and professional publications, Internet job listings, listings maintained by state and local organizations (e.g., psychiatric occupational therapy interest groups), and word of mouth; contacting schools in the local area; or using professional recruiters. As in other types of marketing, emphasis should be given to the selling points of the position (i.e., factors likely to attract appropriately experienced and qualified therapists). For example,

potential recruits may question whether a new program is stable, so recruitment should emphasize that the company is well-established or that participation in a start-up may offer many opportunities for personal and professional development.

Average regional salary levels can be obtained from professional membership organizations (e.g., AOTA) and discipline-specific publications (e.g., AOTA's *OT Practice* periodically offers salary surveys in different geographic areas) and from the U.S. Bureau of Labor Statistics. Salary levels are affected by many factors such as specialized training, experience, and expertise. Salary structures may be predetermined in already existing organization.

Training

Occupational therapy practitioners are required to maintain professional competency for the National Board for Certification in Occupational Therapy and state licensure boards. This section relates to program-specific training needs. For individual practitioners in a small clinic, continuing education and credentialing help establish the practitioner's reputation and can help the practitioner expand into new areas of service (Hardeman, 2007). Clinics offering evidence-based practices have the additional requirement of obtaining staff who have the requisite skills, or employers must be prepared to train staff to meet the clinic's requirements. Fidelity to the evidence-based practice is affected by turnover and having to assist new staff in developing competence in the evidence-based practice area (Rollins et al., 2009; Woltmann et al., 2008). The extent of staff training needs depends on the individual's qualifications and experience and the degree of specialization of the service.

Over much of the past 20 years, many occupational therapy training programs have taught occupational therapists to expect to practice in a fee-for-service, individual therapy model, and older practice arenas such as mental health have been deemphasized. With the rapid pace of change in the health care environment, practitioners are working in more varied service structures, including industry, wellness, and case management services. For individuals who have not worked in these arenas, the practices and expectations may be different from the practices they were taught in school, necessitating program-specific training.

Training requirements may include the content of therapy, the goals of the program, and the program philosophy. It is important to have written policies and procedures available to staff. Early in the development process, individuals need to be trained in basic practices. Once these practices are established, new staff can learn by on-the-job training with experienced staff. Ongoing training can occur at regular times during the week at times when others meet client needs.

Finances

The program developer should define the financial background and the financial performance expectations of the program. The basic financial concepts covered in this section are described in detail in texts on how to start a business (Abrams, 2000; Lesonsky, 2007; O'Donnell, 1991; Richmond & Powers, 2010).

Financial projections are based on assumptions formed from available information about the market, the client base, payer sources, and the competition. For example, is the program expected to be viable immediately, or in 1 to 2 years? It is important not to underestimate risk or make assumptions too optimistic. If the program does not meet the initial projections, confidence in the overall endeavor may be undermined. Projections should be conservative and build in an allowance for unforeseen circumstances (in a start-up, a general rule is that things cost twice as much and take twice as long as might be expected; Allen, 2009). For a private practitioner especially, it is important to establish how the start-up period of limited income and significant expenditure is to be managed (see Table 9.1). If money is going to be borrowed from a bank, how it is to be repaid?

It is possible to estimate one-time start-up costs for building alterations, renovations, and equipment and a staffing structure with salary and benefits (usually about 20% of sala-

Table 9.1. Start-Up Costs Worksheet

Item	Detail	Estimated Cost
Advertising	Graphic artist, Web site set-up, signs, open house, printing and postage for mailing brochures	$10,000
Remodeling	Remodeling to create an accessible bathroom with shower and tub. Hookup for kitchen stove and sink in the therapy room.	$35,000
Decorating	New lighting fixtures, wall paint, reception desk, waiting-area chairs, coffee table, side table, lamps, re-carpeting with carpet tiles in reception area, laminated wood-patterned flooring in therapy room	$25,000
Allocated costs	Insurance (i.e., property, professional liability), utilities, telephone, rent management fee (billing done by the SNF), costs paid by the SNF and allocated to the new program costs as a percentage of the square feet occupied by the new program, housekeeping, linen service, building and yard maintenance	$6,000
Licenses and permits	Building permit, approval from Office of Statewide Health Planning and Development	$4,000
Equipment	Two therapy wall-mounted matt tables, parallel bars, weights, pulleys, exercise bike, treadmill, hydroculator, ultrasound therapy Hilo table, computer cognitive testing and retaining software, shower chair, tub bench, stove, stairs, refrigerator, microwave, cognitive tests, copier	$40,000
Supplies	Computer, printer, phones, fax machine, forms, therapy supplies (e.g., kitchen supplies, Theraband feeding and dressing aids)	$5,000
Recruitment (staff)		$5,000
Unanticipated expenses		$10,000

Note. This worksheet relates to a subacute outpatient program being added to a SNF. The SNF has in-house therapies and is targeting residents of local assisted living facilities that do not have in-house therapy. Remodeling costs are for converting a ground-floor office suite into an outpatient rehabilitation clinic with independent access that does not go through an inpatient area and making a bathroom accessible with a tub for tub transfers. $140,000 amortized over 4 years = $35,000 per year and requires $2,916 per month to be generated to cover start-up expenses. The revenue generated by 39 hours of therapy per month needs to be allocated to repaying start-up costs.

ries). *Direct expenses* (i.e., labor and materials consumed in the provision of the service itself) should be listed separately from *indirect expenses* (i.e., rent, heating, lighting, housekeeping, telephone services, maintenance costs), and *fixed costs* (costs that do not change in line with service volume—e.g., rent, telephone, copier rental) and *variable costs* (costs that vary with service volume) also should be specified. Finally, the plan lists anticipated charges for services based on costs and other factors such as estimates of utilization and customary charges in the community.

Many institutions will want to see 2-year and 5-year financial projections for the program. Important milestones are the *breakeven point*, or the point at which the costs of providing services are the same as the revenues for the services (see Appendix 9.C), and the *payback period*, or the length of time needed to recuperate start-up costs. For example, a $100,000 investment that returned $20,000 per year in profit would have a 5-year payback period. If it is determined that a program can never be cost-effective, the plan should describe sources of additional funding.

Facilities

The facilities in which a program is housed are often a key factor in whether or not a program is successful. The extent to which the location and the nature of the facilities affect the ease of service provision depends on the type of service, client variables, and problems treated.

Location

Potential consumers' willingness to travel to a health care provider is influenced by many factors. If individuals are to attend regularly scheduled appointments, then getting to the point of service must be practical for them. Some facilities or programs provide transportation to increase the access of potential users of the service. Others programs locate in an area close to the population to be serviced or to public transportation.

Licensing

Numerous federal, state, and local laws regulate the services that occupational therapy practitioners provide. Federal or state requirements for access and egress, living space, and bathroom access must also be met. Local governments, occupational health agencies, and fire safety departments also have requirements. Typically, in addition to a business license from the local municipality, the state department of health or department of social services licenses the business services provided by occupational therapists in rehabilitation clinics, SNFs, and hospitals (occupational therapy practitioners themselves are licensed by state boards). Reimbursement agencies such as the Centers for Medicare and Medicaid Services may have very specific rules for reimbursement such that facilities must be certified to receive reimbursement through these programs. State governments maintain Web sites to assist with identifying pertinent regulations, and the SBA maintains a clearinghouse Web site at www.SBA.gov/hotlist/default.cfm.

Building and Space Requirements

Facilities need to both meet the physical requirements of clients (e.g., enough space for the number of clients using wheelchairs) and facilitate the provision of services. Structure should follow function. Appropriate facilities can be important in maintaining the health and welfare of staff and clients.

Equipment and Supplies

In planning a program, equipment requirements can be divided into "needs" and "wants." Different programs need different types of equipment. Certain types of equipment are required to provide services for all or almost all clients, and other types are required for only a small proportion of clients served. How many clients can be treated because of the availability of the proposed equipment? How many clients will not be accepted for treatment because of its absence? How many additional modules of service can be provided with the equipment? What is the expected payback period?

Capital equipment usually costs more than $500 and may include computer equipment, refrigerators, office furniture, wheelchairs, therapy tables, mats, equipment for modalities, and expensive testing equipment. This type of equipment is itemized and needs to be listed in an appendix of the business plan. It is helpful to collect catalogues and establish relationships with local vendors. Less costly equipment, such as tools, kitchen items, or a heat gun, are not itemized, and an overall sum for the purchase of all such items is determined. Supplies are items that that are consumed in their use, such as splinting materials, coloring books, and cooking supplies.

In some insurance systems, some supplies may be charged to the individual clients and others are not reimbursed and are a cost of providing services. A system needs to be put in place for tracking items so that billable items can be billed out and items to be kept on hand are available.

Program Evaluation

In defining a program, it is important to define the expected outcomes (Valluzzi, 2002), how the program is to be evaluated, and what indicators are to be used. One set of indicators relates to the safety and effectiveness of services rendered to clients as measured by standardized functional measures, rapidity of discharge to a lower level of care, and reduced recidivism. Another set of indicators are related to revenues and whether the program is on budget and meeting financial projections. Follow-up evaluations may include objective measures of outcome appropriate for the client population; client satisfaction surveys provide another set of important indicators (Forer, 1996).

There are often at least two customers in health care: the end user or client and the third-party payer or funding agency. Goals and quality indicators are likely to be different for each of these customers. The client is most likely to be concerned with the quality and convenience of the service. The third-party payer may be interested in cost containment and avoiding the utilization of more expensive acute services.

Risks

The program developer should consider the risks of entering the service area. Risks include inevitable risks, potential risks, and worst-case risks (Abrams, 2000; Allen, 2009). *Inevitable risks* include the financial loss associated with start-up, *potential risks* include not meeting client projections, and *worst-case risks* include failure to obtain clients or catastrophic outcomes for clients.

PROGRAM DEVELOPMENT WITHIN AN ESTABLISHED CONTEXT

Corporate culture relates to the internalized values, beliefs, and expectations for behavior within a business (Want, 2006). *Culture* refers to an organization's values, beliefs, and behaviors. Corporate culture is concerned with beliefs and values that people use to interpret experiences and behave with work colleagues and with consumers. Culture becomes operationalized when it modifies employees' behaviors, influencing both what is done and how it is done. Cultural values also extend to treatment models in terms of both the considerations given to the provision of services and the expectations for client behavior (Spencer, Young, Rintala, & Bates, 1994).

Introduction of a new program model within an existing staff or corporate culture when it does not conform to corporate or staff values presents considerable difficulty (Want, 2006). The importance of culture in health care service delivery is suggested by the superiority of specialized versus generalized units in the treatment of a number of diagnostic groups. For example, a rehabilitative culture may help staff internalize a model of disability and rehabilitation that facilitates communication of important postinjury values and principles to clients and families. In SNFs, culture change has come to mean the adoption of a client-centered or "green" alternative to services (e.g., the Eden alternative; Baker, 2007). Staff training and highly repetitive mechanisms for communicating the new cultural values are required for culture change. As elsewhere, having core staff members share a visionionary goal of what can be accomplished and benchmarks for change are essential.

PRIVATE PRACTICE AND SMALL BUSINESS

Many individuals' vision of their career includes being an entrepreneur (e.g., a business owner). Private practice has many advantages for some individuals: schedule flexibility, being one's own boss, and potentially increased income. Many of the issues for program development generally apply to private practice. Does the practitioner have the expertise and experience necessary to treat the clients? Does he or she have established networks that will provide client referrals? If not, where will clients come from? How will the practitioner determine pricing, and how will his or her services fare against those of any competitors? Are an office and equipment available? Have appropriate insurance and permits been obtained? How much money is available to pay the bills and expenditures associated with the business before the business generates enough revenue to pay a salary? If the practitioner is going to bill insurance companies, has he or she considered cash flow projections?

CONCLUSION

Program development is exciting because it provides occupational therapy practitioners with the opportunity to create a career based on an important personal vision. But it also requires personal and professional self-examination, adaptability, and the ability to tolerate risk. With the rate of change in health care showing no sign of slowing, program development is likely to be an area in which occupational therapy practitioners can make an important contribution for the foreseeable future.

Case Examples

LEVEL I FIELDWORK

During a Level I fieldwork assignment at a dementia care program in an RCF, the occupational therapist supervisor asked a student intern to perform a literature search of evidence-based approaches to reducing behavior problems in persons with Alzheimer's disease and other dementias. The intern used a range of indexing services (e.g., PubMed, OT Seeker) as well as the Cochrane Database of Systematic Reviews. The Cochrane Data base yielded three relevant systematic reviews. Using PubMed, the student intern searched for the terms *behavior therapy* and *dementia* and included the limits of humans, English, clinical trials, reviews and meta-analyses, locating 183 articles of poten-tial interest. After reviewing the abstracts, the student intern selected 29 articles published since 2005 for retrieval. Using OT Seeker, the student intern searched using the terms *Alzheimer's disease* and *behavioral interventions* and found 65 articles. The intern retrieved the 10 most interesting nonduplicate articles. Together the intern and the therapist tabulated the interventions for consideration by the clinical team at the dementia care program.

LEVEL II FIELDWORK

During a Level II internship at a subacute rehabilitation program in a SNF that uses in-house therapy staff, the

(continued)

Case Examples *(cont.)*

rehabilitation census was noted to have been 75%–80% occupancy for the prior 4 months. This percentage was considered low because the census had been running at 98% for the previous 8 months. In conjunction with the facility administrator, the occupational therapist and rehabilitation director decided to survey all discharge planners who had referred clients in the prior 18 months and to run a focus group made up of key local hospital case managers. The Level II student was given the responsibility of reviewing client admission records to identify the key case managers at local facilities and to draft a letter to them that informed them about the focus group and that the rehabilitation director would be calling to invite them in person. The Level II student also assisted in the logistics of planning the focus group. Then, using information from the focus group, the student developed a survey instrument to be sent to all the discharge planners who had referred patients to the facility. The survey was simultaneously used as an information-gathering and marketing tool.

FIRST-TIME MANAGER

An occupational therapist was working as a first-time manager of a 30-bed residential facility for young homeless persons with substance abuse problems. The facility was part of a large not-for-profit chain of facilities providing similar grant-funded programming in the metropolitan area. The program had been previously run by a psychologist and had been using a psychodynamic model that relied on psychology interns. When the psychologist and the interns left the program, the remaining staff lacked any commitment to the service model and found themselves often at a loss as to how to help the residents. The previous year, staff turnover for the residential care providers was 150%. Following an evidence-based literature review, the occupational therapist manager began discussing dialectical behavior therapy as a potential evidence-based intervention for the facility to adopt. The occupational therapy manager researched the cost of the initial training for staff and began discussing the idea with the not-for-profit corporate management. The manager was put in touch with the grant writer for the not-for-profit and together they submitted a training grant to a local foundation that underwrote training for key staff in the program in dialectical behavior therapy.

MANAGER

Ann Edwards, MOT, OTR/L, worked in a hospital outpatient clinic at a prestigious hospital with many professionals as clients. During her years at the site, she developed a reputation in the local community for providing cognitive rehabilitative services for persons with stroke and traumatic brain injury. Ms. Edwards also had an interest in caregiver training and cognitive and emotional support services for persons with various types of dementia.

Ms. Edwards noticed that few therapists practiced in this area and that there was significant demand for them, particularly among younger stroke survivors who were not yet ready to leave the workforce. She also noticed significant demand for support services for persons with early dementia. Ms. Edwards decided to develop a private practice focusing on these areas. After talking about it with her family, she decided that her current position was too demanding for her to be able to continue while simultaneously developing her practice. She decided to go to clients' homes so she will have little overhead cost and the knowledge that she can work per diem for an agency if things are slow.

Due to Ms. Edwards's contact with local physicians and therapists, it took her less than 6 months before she had more work than she could handle and was considering recruiting a partner.

SUGGESTED WEB SITES

- **U.S. Small Business Administration:** www.sba.gov/
- **America's Small Business Development Center:** www.asbdc-us.org
- **SCORE Counselors to America's Small Business:** www.score.org
- **U.S. Department of Labor, Bureau of Labor Statistics:** www.bls.gov/

❖ Learning Activities

1. Examine the vignettes at the end of the chapter (Appendix 9.D). What key principle derived from the chapter does each vignette exemplify?

2. Develop a staffing pattern for a 6-bed interdisciplinary rehabilitation program for persons with traumatic brain injury in a freestanding acute rehabilitation hospital. What categories of staff will you need? How much staff time will you need for each discipline (including nursing)? How much management and support staff time will you need?

3. For the same program, what are your admission requirements? What standard equipment will you need? What specialized equipment will you need?

4. Think of a program development idea (e.g., a living skills program for at-risk youths in a continuation high school, a hippotherapy program for children with multiple disabilities). Search the Internet to define referral criteria and model program features.

5. Develop a low-cost marketing strategy for (a) a wellness program for community-dwelling seniors and (b) a writing skills program for grade-school students.

6. You have developed a program to support independent living for marginally housed persons with chronic mental illness and co-occuring substance abuse. Potential clients live in shelters or single-room-occupancy hotels. You have obtained state and county grant funds to finance your services. You have established the components of your program as (a) an individual goal-setting and assessment phase, (b) a group treatment phase, and (c) a follow-up support phase. Define the staff for whom you have grant funding, and establish a time vs. census matrix that determines the number of clients you can support and for how long in each phase of your program.

✓ Multiple-Choice Questions

1. Which of the following trends is expected to increase demand for occupational therapy over the next 5 to 10 years?
   a. An increase in the number of people over age 65.
   b. An increased percentage of the population with chronic medical illness.
   c. Evolving expectations of those requiring services.
   d. All of the above.

2. A market analysis is
   a. A formal statement of a set of business development goals and a plan for reaching those goals with key requirements and outcomes.
   b. A documented investigation of supply and demand in a service sector that is used to inform business planning activities.
   c. Formal operationalization of the visionary goal.
   d. None of the above.

3. What statement below *best* describes persons who should develop a business plan?
   a. Persons considering going into private practice.
   b. Persons developing a new program within an established institution.
   c. A group of therapists planning on establishing a new clinic.
   d. Any persons embarking on a new program or business venture.

4. A needs assessment should be performed
   a. Because it gives clients an opportunity to state whether they are satisfied with current services.
   b. Because clients have a realistic expectation that they are asked about their wants and needs.
   c. Because it is important to find out about potential clients of the proposed service and what they would want and/or need from the potential services.
   d. None of the above.

5. When is the *best* to perform a needs assessment?
   a. Before a program is initiated.
   b. Before a program is initiated and as a continuing part of programmatic data collection.
   c. Annually.
   d. None of the above.

6. Methods that might be included in a program development needs assessment include
   a. Surveys.
   b. Interviews.
   c. Focus groups.
   d. All of the above.

7. It is important to establish market trends in establishing a new program to
   a. Establish how changes in the population to be served and service availability will affect the program.

b. Determine the needs of the target population.

c. Ensure that the population served is happy with the program's offerings.

d. None of the above.

8. A SWOT analysis should be performed

a. Because it gives clients an opportunity to state whether they are satisfied, worried, offended, or tired of the current services.

b. Because clients have a realistic expectation that they will be asked about their wants and needs.

c. Because it is important to find out about potential clients of the program or service and what they would want and/or need from a potential service.

d. To assess strengths, weaknesses, opportunities, and threats to the service or program.

9. A SWOT analysis should be performed

a. Before a program is initiated.

b. Before initiating a program and as a continuing part of assessing market conditions.

c. Annually.

d. None of the above.

10. Networking involves connecting with others and should include opportunities to interact

a. With others at conferences.

b. At meetings of local chambers of commerce and relevant community benefit organizations.

c. With competitors at various venues.

d. All of the above.

11. In establishing a staffing pattern, which of the following is important in decision making?

a. Census.

b. Severity of clients' condition.

c. Diagnosis and need for specific therapy.

d. All of the above.

12. A principle advantage of recruiting new graduates in a start-up service or program is that new graduates

a. Are less expensive.

b. Have fewer habits and expectations that may not be useful in a start-up situation and that need to be unlearned.

c. Have new skill sets.

d. May be willing to work longer hours, which may be necessary in a start-up situation.

13. A cost that does not change depending on client census—such as rent, property tax, insurance, or interest expense—is called a

a. Fixed cost.

b. Variable cost.

c. Direct cost.

d. Indirect cost.

14. The cost of labor or material that changes according to the change in the census is called a

a. Fixed cost.

b. Variable cost.

c. Direct cost.

d. Breakeven point.

15. Which of the following two costs will increase as census increases?

a. Fixed costs and variable costs.

b. Variable costs and direct costs.

c. Direct costs and fixed costs.

d. Indirect costs and fixed costs.

16. Expenses related to the principal activity of the business (e.g., therapy equipment consumed in the process of therapy, therapy labor costs) are called

a. Fixed costs.

b. Variable costs.

c. Direct costs.

d. Indirect costs.

17. Expenses such as marketing activities and administration activities are called

a. Fixed costs.

b. Variable costs.

c. Direct costs.

d. Indirect costs.

18. The term *corporate culture* refers to

a. Tolerance of diversity within a corporation.

b. Personnel policies and procedures and how employees are treated.

c. Corporate values and beliefs that influence what staff do and how they do it.

d. All of the above.

19. The *breakeven point* is

a. The point at which expenses and revenue are equal.

b. The time required for the return on an investment (i.e., to "repay" the original investment).

c. The time it takes to pay back investors.

d. None of the above.

20. The *payback period* for a service or program refers to

a. The period required for the return on an investment (i.e., to "repay" the sum of the original investment).

b. The point at which costs or expenses and revenue are equal.

c. The time it takes to pay back investors.

d. None of the above.

References

Abrams, R. (2000). *The successful business plan: Secrets and strategies* (3rd ed.). Palo Alto, CA: Running "R" Media.

Allen, M. (2009). *Visionary business: An entrepreneur's guide to success* (rev. ed.). Novato, CA: New World Library.

American Occupational Therapy Association. (2007). AOTA *Centennial Vision* and executive summary. *American Journal of Occupational Therapy, 61,* 613–614.

American Occupational Therapy Association. (2008). Occupational therapy practice framework: Domain and process (2nd ed.). *American Journal of Occupational Therapy, 62,* 625–683.

Baker, B. (2007). *Old age in a new age: The promise of transformative nursing homes.* Nashville, TN: Vanderbilt University Press.

Balanced Budget Act of 1997, Pub. L. 105–33, 111, Stat. 251.

Castle, N. G. (2006). Measuring staff turnover in nursing homes. *The Gerontologist, 46*(2), 210–219.

Finlayson, M. (2007). Community-based practice: Assessing community needs and strengths. [electronic version]. *OT Practice, 12*(5), 29–31.

Forer, S. (1996). *Outcome management and program evaluation made easy: A toolkit for occupational therapy practitioners.* Bethesda, MD: American Occupational Therapy Association.

Glennon, T. J. (2007). Putting on your business hat [electronic version]. *OT Practice, 12*(3), 23–25.

Hardeman, L. (2007). The heart of an entrepreneur [electronic version]. *OT Practice, 12*(1), 13–15.

Leslie, C. A. (2005). Entrepreneurial resource [electronic version]. *OT Practice, 10*(15), 10.

Lesonsky, R. (2007). *Start your own business: The only startup book you will ever need.* Irvine, CA: Entrepreneur Press.

O'Donnell, M. (1991). *Writing business plans that get results: A step-by-step guide.* Lincolnwood, IL: Contemporary Books.

Opila-Lehman, J. (2002). Marketing 101. *OT Practice, 7*(1), 18–21.

Perinchief, J. M. (2003). Documentation and management of occupational therapy services. In E. B. Crepeau, E. S. Cohn, & B. A. B. Schell (Eds.), *Willard and Spackman's occupational therapy* (10th ed., pp. 897–905). Philadelphia: Lippincott Williams & Wilkins.

Richmond, T., & Powers, D. (2010). *Business fundamentals* (2nd ed.). Thorofare, NJ: Slack.

Robinson, M., Herz, N. B., & Brennan, C. (2009). Program development and beyond: Creating a sustainable program. *OT Practice, 14*(15), CE1–CE8.

Rollins, A. L., Salyers, M. P., Tsai, J., & Lydick, J. M. (2009). Staff turnover in statewide implementation of ACT: Relationship with ACT fidelity and other team characteristics. *Administrative Policy and Mental Health.* doi: 10.1007/s10488-009-0257-4

Spencer, J., Young, M. E., Rintala, D., & Bates, S. (1994). Socialization to the culture of a rehabilitation hospital: An ethnographic study. *American Journal of Occupational Therapy, 49,* 53–62.

U.S. Bureau of Labor Statistics. (2009). *Occupational employment and wages, May 2008.* Retrieved January 1, 2010, from http://data.bls.gov/cgi-bin/print.pl/oes/current/oes291122.htm

Valluzzi, J. L. (2002). Evaluating and monitoring community based programs. *OT Practice, 7*(3), 10–13.

Want, J. H. (2006). *Corporate culture: Illuminating the black hole.* New York: St. Martin's Press.

Woltmann, E. M., Whitley, R., McHugo, G. J., Brunette, M., Torrey, W. C., Coots, L., et al. (2008). The role of staff turnover in the implementation of evidence-based practices in mental health care. *Psychiatric Services, 59,* 732–737.

Appendix 9.A. Program Development Evidence Table

Topic	Evidence
Visionary goals	Allen, M. (2009). *Visionary business: An entrepreneur's guide to success* (rev. ed.). Novato, CA: New World Library. Lesonsky, R. (2007). *Start your own business: The only startup book you will ever need.* Irvine, CA: Entrepreneur Press.
Business plan	Abrams, R. (2000). *The successful business plan: Secrets and strategies* (3rd ed.). Palo Alto, CA: Running "R" Media. Lesonsky, R. (2007). *Start your own business: The only startup book you will ever need.* Irvine, CA: Entrepreneur Press.
Staffing structure	Perinchief, J. M. (2003). Documentation and management of occupational therapy services In E. B. Crepeau, E. S. Cohn, & B. A. B. Schell (Eds.), *Willard and Spackman's occupational therapy* (10th ed., pp. 897–905). Philadelphia: Lippincott Williams & Wilkins.
Corporate culture	Want, J. H. (2006). *Corporate culture: Illuminating the black hole.* New York: St. Martin's Press.
Culture change	Baker, B. (2007). *Old age in a new age: The promise of transformative nursing homes.* Nashville, TN: Vanderbilt University Press.

APPENDIX 9.B. OUTLINE OF A BUSINESS PLAN

Executive Summary

1. Background and trends of the service sector
   a. Nature of the service sector
   b. Problem statement
   c. Market factors and future trends
2. Services
   a. Description of services
   b. Unique program services or features
3. Market analysis
   a. Target market and characteristics
   b. Competitors: Comparing strengths and weaknesses
4. Marketing
   a. Promotion
   b. Marketing strategy
5. Management and ownership
   a. Key players' qualifications and experience
   b. Administrative personnel
   c. Professional support
   d. Ownership
   e. Directors/advisors/community representation
6. Staffing
   a. Staffing patterns
   b. Staff recruitment and salaries
   c. Staff training
7. Finances
   a. Funding requests/investments
   b. Financial statements
   c. Expenses
   d. Revenues
   e. Financial projections
   f. Assumptions
8. Facilities
   a. Location
   b. Licensing
   c. Building and space requirements
   d. Equipment and supplies
9. Program evaluation
10. Risks

APPENDIX 9.C. DERIVING THE BREAKEVEN POINT

The *breakeven point* is reached when fixed costs and variable costs equal revenue. First, monthly fixed costs are established. Fixed costs are those that do not vary from month to month and include rents, telephone, copier rental, and so forth (Perinchief, 2003). For illustration, the fixed cost for operation of the new subacute rehabilitation program in a skilled nursing facility is determined to be $15,000 per month. This is the amount that needs to be covered whether or not clients are admitted.

Second, overall profit margin should be established by determining the cost of labor per hour of therapy plus any supplies used during therapy (variable costs). If the actual cost of therapy is $75 per hour (including nonproductive time), and for an hour of therapy the program bills $150, the overall profit margin is 50% (half of the $150 revenue is variable cost, so half is profit).

Dividing the fixed cost of services ($15,000) by the profit margin per hour of therapy ($75) gives a result of 200 billable hours. Thus, the program has to bill $30,000 dollars in services (200 hours at $150 per hour) to break even (i.e., cover fixed costs of $15,000 and variable costs). Revenues over $30,000 are 50% cost and 50% profit.

Appendix 9.D. Start-Up Program Vignettes

Program Vignette 1: Regional Medical and Psychiatric Comorbidity Program in a Locked Skilled Nursing Facility[1]

Visionary goals:

Creating a program dedicated to the treatment of individuals who have medical and psychiatric comorbidity and located in a locked skilled nursing facility (SNF). Treatment goals vary by client. Some clients are rehabilitation candidates and are able to move to a lower level of care such as a board-and-care home, and other clients are unmanageable in a nonspecialized setting and need long-term support.

Program benefits (how the proposed program will benefit the clients, organization, community, and other key players):

Clients who have medical and psychiatric needs are often difficult to manage in standard treatment programs and, as a result, often occupy acute hospital beds long after their need for medically intensive services has ended. The program is based on a non-aversive treatment model, which provides psychiatric services at the rate and intensity that clients can tolerate (Giles & Manchester, 2006; Giles, Wager, Fong, & Waraich, 2005). The program developed within the context of a corporation providing psychiatric programs, including long-term care, psychiatric rehabilitation, and board-and-care. Clients often fail at these programs due to concurrent medical conditions that result in frequent acute hospitalizations and negative client outcomes. The addition of comorbidity services allowed the corporation to provide a greater range and continuity of services to county mental health departments. A needs assessment directed at community stakeholders had identified services for persons with psychiatric and medical comorbidity as an unmet need.

Define service user:

Clients have medical and psychiatric disorders that require specialized services (e.g., concurrent schizophrenia and COPD, insulin-dependent diabetes and bipolar disorder) that cannot be managed in a nonspecialized program. Clients can be adults of any age but are typically over 40 years of age, with the majority in their 50s to 70s.

Marketing:

The clinical director and administrator met with county mental health directors and senior county placement personnel. The management team met with county mental health and aging and adult service managers

to introduce the new service. Key players with referral agencies were invited for facility tours. Soon after the program opened, some difficult clients were accepted into the program, and their outcome was aggressively managed. Professional staff presented at state and national conferences, consulted on difficult-to-manage patients at county hospitals, and served as consultant for county mental health departments.

Facilities:

The program was initially housed in a 32-bed distinct unit within a 180-bed, locked SNF. The program has gradually expanded to 120 beds and currently represents the majority of the SNF's business.

Staffing qualifications and numbers:

Licensed and certified nursing–staff levels were set at a level typically found in a subacute program (i.e., 5.0 nursing hours per patient day). In addition, 4 occupational therapists and 4 occupational therapy assistants were recruited to provide services for 36 clients. The clinical director and external consultants provided training.

Start-up funding needs:

The additional staff costs and allocation of beds for the new clients resulted in the SNF making an overall loss, so corporate commitment to accept significant financial losses in the facility for the first 18 months was required. The break-even point for the facility was achieved at 24 months of the new programs operations. Currently, the facility generates a small percentage profit, but the cost of services provided at the facility is high so the facility gross is large.

Implementation and timelines:

The clinical director was hired 4 months prior to opening the program to oversee program development and physical plant changes. Significant program and staffing reorganizations repeatedly occurred in the first 6 years of operation. Organizational structure and census has been stable for the past 3 years.

Program development insights:

The program was developed in an already functioning SNF. The organizational structure frequently changed (i.e., every 12 to 18 months) in response to changes in census and client referral patterns. Staff's expectations about how clients "should" behave derived from prior experience in regular SNF were largely unhelpful, so maintaining the nonaversive culture has required continuous staff training, supervision, and support.

---

[1]Vignette 1 provided by the author of this chapter.

PROGRAM VIGNETTE 2: FORENSIC TREATMENT SERVICES FOR MENTAL HEALTH CLIENTS[2]

Visionary goals:

To provide offenders with mental illness with an integrated service agency focusing on issues of occupational justice, including stabilized housing, substance abuse management, and management of mental health symptomatology; to reduce jail recidivism; and to increase client autonomy, focus on strengths, and emphasize wellness and hope.

How new service augments or differs from other available services:

The service (Citywide Case Management Forensics Program) specifically targets individuals with mental health and substance abuse disorders who are cycling through the criminal justice system and who have not previously been identified as in need of mental health services.

Program benefits (how the proposed program will benefit the clients, organization, community, and other key players):

Outcome goals are a 35% reduction of days in jail, decreased numbers of arrests and parole revocations, reduced criminal justice costs, reduction in the rate of violent crimes, less depressive symptoms, reduction in self-reported use of drugs, and increased ratings on quality-of-life and health status measures on a standardized recovery rating measure (Milestones of Recovery Scale [MORS; Pilon & Ragins, n.d.]). The program is conducted in the same space as Citywide Case Management and allows the organization to service another section of its core client population.

Services:

The type and range of services offered includes: linkage from jail or prison (clients are enrolled while still in jail), court advocacy, intensive case management, individual psychotherapy, a wide range of groups (e.g., symptom management, support, substance abuse, money management, leisure groups; medication monitoring; Wellness Recovery Action Plan groups), outreach, after-hours crisis intervention, prevocational and vocational services, linkages to housing or residential programs and gender-specific services, and financial benefits counseling. An occupational therapist was recruited to develop the group program, lead groups, and develop prevocational and vocational programs.

Frequency and intensity:

There are from 25 to 60 users a day, totaling 150 clients enrolled. Clients may come daily Monday to Saturday and attend up to four groups per day. Individuals may receive services for an indefinite period.

Facilities and operations:

The program is located in a downtown office building in an area of low-income housing and residential hotels, and it is secured. Clinical staff members function as gatekeepers to en-

sure individuals entering the program are displaying appropriate behavioral control and are not obviously under the influence of illicit substances or alcohol. Facilities include a café, art area, food bank, library and computer room, food preparation area, two group rooms, 12 interview rooms, and staff offices.

Funding types and sources:

Initially the program was funded through California Board of Corrections "Mentally Ill Offender Grant." Forty counties applied for the grant, and 17 were funded. Now the program is a community-based organization with a contract with the city and county of San Francisco.

Ongoing development issues:

Initially the program used a psychoeducational model focusing on abstinence. There was a decline in attendance; clients appeared to disengage from the staff and one another. Staff began to be reluctant to lead groups because the interactions and relationships between staff and clients were not positive (clients who were using drugs believed that they had to lie to staff about their use). After 1 year of operation, the program model was changed to a harm-reduction process group model (i.e., evidence-based interventions to reduce the negative consequences of drug use), which resulted in improved client and staff morale. Additionally, the program moved toward the incorporation of the other evidence-based practice models of forensic intensive case management, supported employment, and dialectical behavior therapy. Staff described the positive aspects of working in a start-up program as having one's own vision actualized, working as part of a team, and having the ability to modify things that are not effective. Negative aspects included that there is always more work to be done, the need to continue to do things that do not work until the program can be changed, and staff turnover and the sense of loss that goes with it. Other negative aspects included wanting to be able to carry out more one-on-one assessments and interventions.

Program development insights:

It is imperative that the team at the agency facilitates a collaborative relationship between the mental health system and the criminal justice system. It is important to recognize how different the two systems are in their values, expectations, and approaches to clients. Key individuals that agency needs to work with in the criminal justice system include judge, district attorney, public defender, and probation and parole officers. Additionally San Francisco County has a "mental health court" that specifically addresses clients with behavioral health needs and the agency has a central role in the operation of this court.

PROGRAM VIGNETTE 3: STUDENT CLINIC IN ENTRY-LEVEL GRADUATE OCCUPATIONAL THERAPY PROGRAM[3]

Several years ago, a free occupational therapy clinic was developed to augment the training of entry-level graduate oc-

[2]Vignette 2 contributed by **Gregory Jarasitis, MOT, OTR/L.** Printed with permission.

[3]Contributed by **Kate Hayner, EdD, OTR/L,** Associate Professor and Chairperson, Samuel Merritt University. Printed with permission.

cupational therapy (MOT) students by providing real-life skills in client evaluation and treatment. The clinic is supervised by faculty and staffed by students as part of their course work. Additionally, the clinic offers occupational therapy service to the community in an inner-city environment.

Program benefits (how the proposed program will benefit clients, the organization, the community, and other key players):
On a "student climate" survey, students indicated a desire for more clinical exposure. Participation in the new student clinic was intended to allow students to use interview skills; apply theoretical approaches to treatment and evaluation tools and methods; learn documentation skills; learn practical ethics; and experience writing home treatment programs. The student clinic increases the visibility of the university in the community by way of service announcements, newspaper pieces, and press releases, and provides faculty a clinical practice setting. Initially, administration needed to be convinced of the benefits of a student clinic. Administration was concerned with liability issues, start-up costs, and the availability of faculty to operate the clinic.

Services:
A children's clinic operates in the fall semester and an adult clinic operates in the spring semester. The admission criteria for treatment for potential clients are: (a) physical or developmental disability (pediatrics only), (b) medical stability, (c) physician's order for occupational therapy, and (d) ability to get to the clinic (free parking provided). Services are offered once per week for 1 hour over a 12-week period. Individuals could return to the clinic in consecutive years as space permits.

Market:
As the only free occupational therapy student–operated clinic in Northern California, a client's financial resources are not a barrier to treatment. Occupational therapists can refer clients who may continue to benefit from therapy but whose funded services are exhausted. Referrals to this program also can come from physicians, university's Web site, press releases, and word of mouth from the local therapy community. Because the clinic is free, it was assumed that recruitment of clients would not be an issue. However, clients have been difficult to recruit over the years, so additional measures were implemented (see below) to ensure enough clients so that pairs of students could be assigned to a client.

How recruitment was resolved:
Initially, recruitment was done by visiting area hospitals and SNFs. Now, postcards are sent to all prior clients who faculty believe would still gain from treatment. Faculty put out a press release, put a notification on the main page of the university Web site and sent fliers to area facilities to post for clients. Faculty developed ongoing relationships with physicians who recognize the value of free therapy and refer clients to the clinic and have visited area stroke groups to inform clients about the student clinic.

Facilities and operations:
The clinic is located in a wheelchair-accessible clinical classroom suite that includes private treatment areas, a pediatric room with a two-way mirror, and an adjacent lounge for parents to wait while the child is being treated. Faculty members supervise all treatments.

Funding types and sources:
The university provides faculty salaries, treatment facilities, and parking reimbursement for clients. Most of the materials and supplies required for the clinic were previously being used to teach students and therefore did not represent an additional cost to the university. Some clients required a specific occupational therapy service such as splint fabrication or cooking skills retraining that have additional materials costs associated with them. The MOT departmental budget now allows for these direct costs.

Implementation and timelines:
One semester unit was funded so a faculty member could write up the proposal. The proposal was reviewed by the department chairperson, followed by the academic vice president, the university president, and the university's Board of Regents. The clinic was approved and began the next semester and has been in operation since.

PROGRAM VIGNETTE 4: PEDIATRIC SENSORY INTEGRATION HOME CLINIC[4]

Visionary goal:
To provide full-time pediatric services in a home clinic for children with a sensory processing disorder.

Program goals and objectives:
To provide direct intervention to children who have difficulty processing sensory information to improve function at home, in school, and in the community. To educate families regarding the sensory, motor, behavioral, emotional, educational, and social implications of this disorder and to educate parents about how to manage the child's difficulties.

Service:
Clients accepted for treatment are toddlers to teens. The typical presenting problems of children are difficulty with fine and gross motor skills; organizational skills; writing and drawing; self-regulation; attention; transitioning; handling frustration; problem-solving; school performance; and processing certain sounds, types of touch, or textures of foods. Parents may describe their children as clumsy, awkward, or poorly coordinated; socially isolated; getting along better with adults and younger children than with peers; prone to "meltdowns"; anxious; difficult; fidgety or always in motion; inflexible; and having poor self-esteem. Children who have severe musculoskeletal involvement or

---

[4]Vignette 4 contributed by **Nan Arkwright, MOT, OTR,** in private pediatric practice specializing in sensory processing disorder. Printed with permission.

who are severely emotionally and behaviorally disregulated are not accepted for treatment because they cannot be accommodated in the location. Hours of service take place on Saturdays and weekdays. Average treatment duration lasts 1 to 2 years, 1 to 2 times per week. A summer intensive program is offered for families interested in treatment 5 days a week for 8 to 10 weeks.

Market:

The practice is situated in a relatively affluent suburban area. No market research or market development activities were carried out. After 10 years of the program being in place, current referrals come from behavioral pediatricians, neuropsychologists, psychologists, speech–language pathologists, marriage and family therapists, educators, other professionals working with families, tutors or educational therapists, online groups, the program's Web site, clients who refer friends, home school communities, presentations to groups and schools in the community, and other occupational therapists.

Facilities and operations:

Children are treated in the practitioner's home, using garage space that was converted into a clinic. The business is a sole proprietorship and requires a city business license and the city's permission to have an educational practice taking place in the home.

Expenses:

Yearly business expenses include professional and general liability insurance, disability insurance, health insurance, membership in professional organizations, licensing, equipment, supplies, maintenance costs, continuing education, and promotional materials. Initial major equipment purchases included a computer and printer, video camera, mats, ceiling hooks and chains, and suspended equipment. Examples of supplies needed include workbooks, stickers, toys, balls, art supplies, and puzzles. Equipment and supplies continue to be purchased for specific clients' needs and as new materials become available.

Revenues:

All clients' parents either pay privately or prepare the insurance company paperwork. Insurance companies typically do not pay for occupational therapy for children with developmental delays or sensory issues, but they may pay for therapy to address weakness or poor coordination. The practitioner charges at the lower end of the local market rate due to low overhead. Running the business out of the home allows for a home-office tax write-off.

The practitioner's first formal instruction in sensory processing disorder occurred at occupational therapy school. A research project carried out at the MOT program was developed into a publication for occupational therapists, teachers, and parents on sensory integration. The practitioner is certified to administer the sensory integration and praxis test.

Program development insights:

- *Creating a Web site:* The practitioner created a simple Web site that provides users with an overview of the program's services and a questionnaire listing some of the symptoms that may indicate a need for an evaluation by an occupational therapist. It is the equivalent of handing out a business card to thousands of people.
- *Training other professionals:* Professionals in other disciplines enjoy learning about services that occupational therapy practitioners can offer and their referrals lead to more clients getting the support they need. Using tools such as videos, hands-on materials, checklists, work samples, and handouts, the practitioner presented information designed to help a wide variety of professionals determine appropriate candidates for occupational therapy.
- *Joining or creating a professional group:* Networking, collaborating, and learning from other disciplines are some of the benefits of being in a professional group. The practitioner has appreciated being able to consult with members of other disciplines to ask questions about referring, get advice on handling a behavior, and determine how two or more disciplines can work together to support a client. In return, the practitioner shares her experiences, knowledge, and recommendations with them.
- *Speaking to groups:* Many groups are interested in learning about occupational therapy services, and referrals often result from a presentation that addresses the group's needs. The practitioner found that just as word-of-mouth referrals happen among individuals, word-of-mouth invitations to speak happen among groups. Groups often extend an invitation to speak regularly.
- *Partnering with the community:* Being a resource for the community can be a rewarding experience as well as a way to educate it about occupational therapy services. For example, the practitioner collaborated with a preschool that wanted recommendations for enhancing what they do from environmental and sensory perspectives. Interactions with staff and families gave the practitioner the opportunity to share information about her services as well as educate the staff or families about the importance of considering environmental and sensory factors that affect a child.

References

Giles, G. M., & Manchester, D. (2006). Two approaches to behavior disorder after traumatic brain injury. *Journal of Head Trauma Rehabilitation, 21*(2), 168–178.

Giles, G. M., Wager, J., Fong, L., & Waraich, B. S. (2005). Twenty-month effectiveness of a non-aversive, long-term, low-cost programme for persons with persisting neurobehavioural disability. *Brain Injury, 19*(10), 753–764.

Pilon, D., & Ragins, M. *Milestones of Recovery Scale (MORS).* Retrieved June 6, 2009, from http://www.cmhda.org/committees/documents/ASOC_handouts_(2-14-07)_Milestones_of_Recovery_Paper_(Dave_Pilon).pdf

APPENDIX 9.E. START-UP COSTS WORKSHEET

Item	Detail	Estimated Cost

10
Entrepreneurship

Lori Vaughn, OTD, OTR/L, and
Karen Sladyk, PhD, OTR, FAOTA

❖ Key Terms and Concepts

Conflict of interest. Occurs when the professional responsibilities of a practitioner providing occupational therapy services or in a position of trust are compromised by private interests (American Occupational Therapy Association, 2006).

Distinctiveness. Differentiation; development of a unique identity (Shepherd & Haynie, 2009).

Entrepreneur. An individual who organizes a business venture, manages its operation, and assumes the risks associated with the business (Ryan, 2000).

Entrepreneurial culture. Societal attitude of acceptance toward business enterprise that supports and enables entrepreneurship (Morrison, 2000).

Entrepreneurship. Process of creating new enterprise (Mazzarol, Volery, Doss, & Thein, 1999).

❖ Learning Objectives

After completing this chapter, you should be able to do the following:

- Understand the role of entrepreneurship.
- Identify the characteristics of entrepreneurs.
- Identify barriers to and benefits of entrepreneurship.
- Identify potential occupational therapy and non–occupational therapy entrepreneurial opportunities.

- Understand the process of transforming ideas into action.
- Describe the future of occupational therapy entrepreneurship.

Occupational therapy is a diverse, growing, forward-looking profession. Practitioners have the opportunity to work in a broad spectrum of settings and apply unique characteristics and skills to their practice. Characteristics that have been used to describe occupational therapy practitioners, such as *dynamic, creative, energetic,* and *problem solvers,* also can be ascribed to those innovative individuals who undertake the challenge to manage and operate their own businesses—entrepreneurs. This chapter explores entrepreneurship, including the role of entrepreneurs, characteristics of entrepreneurs, benefits and barriers of being an entrepreneur, suggestions for moving from ideas to action, and opportunities for the future.

Unfortunately, very little research has been targeted at entrepreneurship in occupational therapy or any other rehabilitation service. Even in the discipline of entrepreneurship, scholars complain of the lack of research in theory and practice (Gartner, 2001; Low, 2001; Ucbasaran, Westhead, & Wright, 2001). This chapter borrows information from many disciplines, mostly business, and applies that knowledge to occupational therapy.

ROLE OF ENTREPRENEURS

An entrepreneur acts on a new idea, venture, opportunity, or enterprise, whether for personal profit or for a social good, as in a nonprofit organization. The word *entrepreneur* has a long history in Europe; it is believed to have been coined in France in the early 1800s to describe a person mediating between capital resources and labor, or "middleman" (Deakins & Freel, 2009). Although there have been many uses of the word, the key concept in today's use of the term involves acting on a new, creative idea; Kirzner

(1997) described the entrepreneur as having "creative alertness," or the ability to spot opportunity based on available information.

In countries with capital-focused economies, entrepreneurs are often the backbone of the economy. In spite of the belief that large corporations account for the bulk of the U.S. economy, it is small business that carries the most weight and responsibility. The Small Business Administration (2009) reported that 60% to 80% of net new employment in the United States between 1992 and 2008 was created by small businesses. In addition, small businesses have been responsible for the greatest net job growth in the years following recessions (Wadhwa, Aggarwal, Holly, & Salkever, 2009). New innovations carry the United States into the future, and often these innovations are the enterprise of a single individual or small business.

Several factors contribute to individuals' entrepreneurial aspirations. For some, entrepreneurship provides the opportunity to pursue a dream. For others, it serves as an alternative to traditional salaried job experiences that may have been lost, restructured, or eliminated or that are unsatisfying. Although some people seek to become entrepreneurs, for many others, it happens by chance and as a result of opportunity (Wadhwa et al., 2009). Regardless of how an entrepreneur is "born," there is a heavy self-imposed burden on the individual, who usually sets high personal and professional goals. Many entrepreneurs state that they are most involved in life when they are involved in developing and acting on their ideas. That spirit of growing new ideas is central to the motivation of the entrepreneur. Overcoming the challenges of a new venture and making the opportunity successful are the main goals of the entrepreneur.

Entrepreneurs often see opportunities before others do or are in positions where they can quickly take advantage of new markets. They see *niche markets*, or groups that have special needs and interests. These markets often are willing to pay for services or products. The key is providing the services or products at a price the market is willing or even excited to pay.

Many occupational therapists and occupational therapy assistants are successful business owners or leaders of nonprofit agencies. Many more develop new products, ideas, or ventures as they begin their entrepreneurship journey. Professional conferences typically feature occupational therapy practitioners willing to share their business journey, some specifically in occupational therapy and others in areas outside of traditional practice. What makes occupational therapy entrepreneurs unique is their understanding of the skills of living, which, of course, are applicable in every possible business or nonprofit discipline. Occupational therapists have begun home health, marketing, lobbying, consulting, and private practice ventures, and business opportunities have increased since 2000 (American Occupational Therapy Association [AOTA], 2006). According to AOTA's (2006) *Workforce and Compensation Survey*, approximately 12% of occupational therapy practitioners are self-employed or contract employees, and an additional 13% have this arrangement at least part-time.

CHARACTERISTICS OF ENTREPRENEURS

The drive to become an entrepreneur facilitates the development of self-identity and satisfies an individual's innate need for *self-distinctiveness*, or the ability to develop a sense of self that is differentiated from others (Shepherd & Haynie, 2009). This trait is important in new ventures because business owners want to differentiate themselves and their businesses from the competition. Distinction is one factor that helps a business succeed in a competitive environment (Ames & Runko, 2005; Shepherd & Haynie, 2009). Social relationships and peer interactions have been associated with engagement in entrepreneurial activities in the literature (Bernheim, 1994; Giannetti & Simonov, 2009). Through engagement with entrepreneurial-minded peers, individuals learn ways to run a business and develop social networks.

Personal and professional traits and characteristics influence the outcome of each business venture (Holmes & Scaffa, 2009). In a study of occupational therapists working in emerging practice settings, Holmes and Scaffa (2009) identified several characteristics associated with competent entrepreneurial and leadership skills. The characteristics rated as having the greatest importance included self-direction, adaptability, ability to function outside the medical model, self-confidence, perseverance, and flexibility. In a study conducted by the Kauffman Foundation of Entrepreneurship, business owners identified similar traits as being essential to success, including a strong work ethic, perseverance, a positive attitude, fortitude, and a readiness to assume business risk (Wadhwa et al., 2009). An entrepreneur has not only the ability to identify and seize opportunity but also a willingness to disrupt the status quo (Thompson, 1999). Entrepreneurs not only think outside the box, but also develop new and innovative ways to use the box.

Historically, theories on the influence of experience and education on entrepreneurship have fluctuated. Some researchers have suggested that a minimum of 10 years of education or experience is necessary in a specific field before an individual can contribute substantially to that field; Simonton (1999), for example, believed that adequate knowledge is necessary to make discipline-specific discoveries. Other researchers have suggested that the more experience or education a person has in a given field, the less entrepreneurial he or she is likely to become; the assumption is that extensive training and experience can impede the creative process through the development of a mechanized process of problem solving. Highly trained individuals tend to rely on tried-and-true approaches to challenges rather than looking for new and innovative approaches (Feldman, 1999; McLaughlin, 2001). Current research has revealed that entrepreneurs in the late 20th and early 21st century are more educated than their earlier counterparts, largely because of the technological knowledge necessary for current business practices (Baumol, Schilling, & Wolff, 2009).

On the basis of a review of research related to entrepreneurial achievement, Miner (2000) proposed a four-way psychological typology to predict an individual's capacity for venture growth and success. All four types have been associated with both the ability to grow an existing business and the propensity to initiate a business venture. The typologies are (1) personal achievers, (2) real managers, (3) expert idea generators, and (4) empathic super-salespersons. According to Miner, each typology is associated with specific traits:

1. *Personal achievers* often have Type A personalities, are motivated, set long-range goals, are committed to their projects, and have a strong belief that they can control their futures.
2. *Real managers* like power and competition. They strive for distinction and enjoy the managerial aspects of business ownership.
3. *Expert idea generators* are inventors. They are innovative, creative, and typically very intelligent. Although they are comfortable with idea generation, they are not comfortable with risk taking.
4. *Empathic super-salespersons* tend to be social and supportive. Because they are empathic and motivated to care for others, helping professionals tend to fall into this category of entrepreneurship. The business venture is supported by the empathic caregiving, which motivates the customer to continue using the good or service provided (Miner, 2000).

Benefits of and Barriers to Entrepreneurship

Although research in the area of occupational therapy and entrepreneurship is sparse, the literatures of other health care disciplines, particularly nursing, are replete with entrepreneurship research. Studies by Leong (2004) and Wilson, Averis, and Walsh (2003) identified several benefits of entrepreneurship in the health care arena, including flexible hours, improved client satisfaction and outcomes, autonomy, and quality of care. Many entrepreneurs cite these nonfinancial benefits to self-employment; however, financial benefits are not always noted. Empirical evidence suggests that self-employment results in lower initial earnings and lower growth potential for entrepreneurs than skill-matched colleagues in traditional paid employment (Hamilton, 2000). It is important for potential entrepreneurs to weigh the potential risks and rewards of any business venture.

Several barriers also have been reported in the research, including challenges in obtaining referrals, the expense and challenges of reimbursement, and the perception and attitude of other health care providers regarding private practitioners (Leong, 2004; Wilson et al., 2003). Personal barriers reported include the challenge of reconciling the desire to help people with the need to make money; a lack of knowledge regarding how to begin a business venture, obtain necessary financing, and navigate legal documentation; and limited managerial experience (Elango, Hunter, & Winchell, 2007). Many of these challenges can be generalized to entrepreneurs in other health care professions, including occupational therapy.

According to a study conducted by the Kauffman Foundation (Wadhwa et al., 2009), entrepreneurs perceive several barriers to starting their own business. Reported personal barriers include the amount of time and effort necessary to begin a business, lack of financing, and limited business experience. Business owners surveyed also reported several factors they perceived to be potential barriers for others, including an inability or unwillingness to take risks; the high levels of time and effort required; challenges in raising capital; limited knowledge of business management, markets, and industry; and pressure from family members to maintain steady employment (Wadhwa et al., 2009).

Identifying Occupational Therapy Entrepreneurship Activities

There are many ways in which an occupational therapist can begin a new business venture. Therapists may decide to become a private practitioner and operate an occupational therapy–related business, to begin a health-related practice using skills acquired as an occupational therapist, or to begin a business unrelated to occupational therapy or the health care professions.

Changes in health care practices have led practitioners to expand service delivery into new and evolving areas of practice (Holmes & Scaffa, 2009; Johnson, Koenig, Piersol, Santalucia, & Wachter-Schutz, 2006). These emerging practice areas often are based in the community, which provides a rich landscape for entrepreneurial endeavors. AOTA (n.d.) identified as children and youth services; health and wellness; productive aging; rehabilitation, disability, and participation; and work and industry as emerging community-based practice areas (see Chapter 21 of this volume).

When a practitioner decides to begin a business using his or her skills in occupational therapy, it is essential to check the licensure laws, state regulations, and other legislative issues to ensure that the business and marketing efforts fall within the parameters of acceptable practice (Leslie, 2007; Maliszewski, 2003; see Part V of this volume). In addition, practitioners must disclose financial interests in occupational therapy–related services that might be interpreted as a conflict of interest (Austin, 2006). For example, if a practitioner holds a financial interest in a medical supply business, that interest should be disclosed if the therapist recommends medical supplies to clients.

As the presence of community-based, private practice, and other nontraditional practice settings increases, opportunities for clinical education in these settings also expand.

Students completing fieldwork affiliations in these settings have the opportunity to develop not only clinical skills but also managerial, leadership, administration, and marketing skills. This is a mutually beneficial arrangement, as it also affords clinicians the opportunity to learn current practice trends, interventions, and assessments (Doubt, Paterson, & O'Riordan, 2004).

Finally, entrepreneurship enables practitioners to transform their interests into businesses that fit their own lifestyles. The same passion for an interest can be used to develop a business into a full-time career. The creative spirit that brings a person to occupational therapy is easily transferred to new, dynamic, and creative ideas. Many resources are available in local libraries, bookstores, and business organizations to assist the budding occupational therapy entrepreneur.

TRANSFORMING IDEAS INTO ACTION

Incubating an Idea

Because occupational therapy addresses every aspect of life, ideas for entrepreneurial occupational therapy ventures can address anything in life. The world is our platter! It is best to start with something smaller than the world, however. Initial steps begin with daydreaming. Practitioners can ask themselves, "I wonder what would happen if I pursued this possibility?" "Do other people need this service?" "How can this aid be produced?"

Two good ways of facilitating the early incubation stage are to doodle on large sheets of paper and keep a notebook of ideas. Practitioners should preserve these early pieces of "art" because they may need to review early ideas when their concept takes a different track later on. New entrepreneurs should talk to people they trust, being careful not to give away their idea to someone who has the resources to run with it faster than they can. They should consider the time they have to devote to the idea and the potential long-term results if the business is wildly successful or fails without warning. It is also a good idea to do a thorough self-assessment to identify strengths and weaknesses. Tools such as AOTA's *Professional Development Tool* have been recommended (Hardeman, 2007). Self-assessments help practitioners ensure that congruence exists between their entrepreneurial dream and the reality of their personal and professional competencies and learning styles (AOTA, 2003).

Developing a Business Plan

Every entrepreneurship idea should have a business plan (Pinson, 2008). An entrepreneurial venture is any cutting edge idea taken from concept to fruition. It does not have to be a formal business; individual, unpaid, nonprofit, and for-profit concepts all qualify. The best plan for filling a need or niche market may not be a formal business. A for-profit business needs to be formal, of course, but even volunteer or nonprofit entrepreneurship ideas should be run formally to protect the people involved, the clients served,

the core idea, and the community at large. Everything you need to get started in the management of a new idea is in this book (see Part II of this volume).

Books are available on how to develop a well-thought-out plan over 6 weeks (Abrams, 2004), a day (Abrams, 2009), or even an hour (Fullen & Podmoroff, 2006); one even suggests "winging it" as you go (Spors, 2008). Without a business plan, every entrepreneur risks getting lost along the way because it is easy to get carried away by the excitement of the idea. When the entrepreneur wonders what the next priority is or is feeling overwhelmed, he or she can return to the business plan to stay on track or rewrite the plan to follow a new track.

Knowledge of how to run a business is not instinctive; it is learned. Before beginning a business, entrepreneurs should participate in learning opportunities whenever possible. Business leaders often lead seminars or offer informational sessions. Countless books, videos, and webinars are available to budding entrepreneurs, and the Small Business Administration provides information and resources to new ventures (Hardeman, 2007).

The risk level of financial resources to begin an entrepreneurial project ranges from low to high. Many entrepreneurs begin small, with their own savings. Others seek local bank loans, and still others seek investors or venture capitalists. The more people are involved in funding your business, the more people will have control over what you do. But having others involved means that more experience is available to support the plan. The local bookstore is a source of books on finding financial support, and local business organizations provide networking opportunities with local funding sources. Once the business plan and funding are in place, the venture can move forward.

THE FUTURE OF OCCUPATIONAL THERAPY ENTREPRENEURSHIP

Changing demographics provide numerous opportunities for occupational therapy entrepreneurs. The approximately 78 million members of the Baby Boom generation are becoming the largest population of senior citizens in U.S. history (Levy & Weitz, 2004). This aging population will produce an increased need for health care services. In addition, they have higher education levels, more socioeconomic resources, busier lifestyles, and a greater interest in preventive health care than previous generations, and historically they have been willing to access and use less traditional health care services (Levy & Weitz, 2004). These are all areas in which occupational therapy entrepreneurs can seize opportunity.

As the field of occupational therapy continues to grow, opportunities for occupational therapists to work in private ventures also are anticipated to grow (AOTA, 2006). Despite this expansion into new and developing practice areas, there is little knowledge or consistency regarding how to measure entrepreneurial competence (Foto, 1998). Competence in all realms of practice is a professional obligation and is essential for client protection and advancement of the profession (Foto, 1998). Because entrepreneurship is a viable career path for practitioners, specific standards of practice and methods of ensuring professional competence are recommended (Foto, 1998). A wide range of skills are necessary for competence in self-employment; in addition to the skills necessary for practice, entrepreneurial practitioners must have financial, marketing, sales, organizational, leadership, team-building, and management skills (Foto, 1998).

Entrepreneurship must be fostered not only within the occupational therapy profession but also within the global and cultural community. The beliefs, values, and attitudes of a society can promote or inhibit the development of an entrepreneurial culture (Morrison, 2000). A reciprocal relationship exists in cultures and communities that support entrepreneurship. There are many ways in which communities have an impact on business ventures; community members identify the needs of residents, define the types of business that can be established, support or oppose goods or services, and influence available resources. Communities and cultures that support entrepreneurship benefit from entrepreneurship through improved educational opportunities, access to necessary goods and services, and support for communities during times of economic downturn (Morrison, 2000). Throughout history, entrepreneurs have been agents of change. Occupational therapy practitioners should advocate at the federal, state, and local levels to promote entrepreneurial endeavors.

Case Examples

FIELDWORK STUDENT ENTREPRENEURS

Kim, Matt, and Diane met for coffee on a Friday afternoon after completing their first week of Level II fieldwork at three different sites. All were excited but exhausted by the wealth of information they had learned in just 1 week. The conversation turned to homework and what they needed to review before they returned Monday morning. Kim needed to review her anatomy, and Matt needed to look specifically at orthopedic issues. Diane was on a mental health fieldwork and needed to review cognitive levels and the effect on functioning at each level. All planned on poring over their class notes to find what they needed. "Too bad there is not a single 'cheat sheet' for each of our topics so we could attach it to our clipboards at work," Diane stated, and thus an entrepreneurial idea was launched. All three made a wish list of cheat sheets, and they assigned the topics to each other and to friends also out on fieldwork.

In a week, 10 cheat sheets were ready for the laminating machine, and each participant received one complete set. Then other students saw the sets and wanted them, too. Kim, Matt, and Diane were now in the 4th week of fieldwork, and the workload was becoming much more demanding. They decided to devote their full energies to fieldwork but did not want to see their idea die. They handed their product off to the Student Occupational Therapy Association at their school, which developed the project into a nationwide annual fundraiser.

FIRST-TIME ENTREPRENEUR

When Lisa, a mental health occupational therapist, came down with a viral infection that led to a vestibular balance condition, she became frustrated at the lack of services available to treat her problem. She knew from school that vestibular problems responded well to occupational therapy services, so she went back to her books to see if she could treat herself. With time, study, and experimentation, she overcame her issues. She began taking continuing education classes at national conferences on vestibular issues and connected with an occupational therapist who specialized in this area in another state and who offered her mentorship and externship opportunities. Then, when talking with local doctors from an ear clinic about her training, they asked if she would consider working part-time as a contract therapist in their ear clinic addressing balance in their patients.

Lisa began by investigating state laws on independently practicing therapists and registered her business with the state. She next contacted the doctors in the ear clinic and negotiated a referral system, space in the office, funding, and payment. She would work in the clinic as a contract service and the office would handle all the billing and appointment services, but she could leave the contract or bill herself if her service grew and she provided 6 months notice to the cancel the agreement. She began by having two appointments available each day after she completed her full-time work. Her part-time revenue allowed her to enjoy her skiing hobby on weekends.

EXPERIENCED ENTREPRENEURS

Lee and Jeff, both occupational therapists, met at work while they were working for the same traveling contract service company. They both loved to travel, and each had already worked in six different states. Their common interests led to a lunchtime discussion of a client who had

(continued)

Case Examples *(cont.)*

asked about support services available to people with disabilities who wanted to travel. After investigating the local options for the clients, Lee and Jeff formed a company to escort clients on travel vacations at the client's own pace.

Lee and Jeff knew that the population of people with disabilities who enjoyed travel and had the resources to do so was small, and they were not interested in traveling full-time with clients, so they designed the company around this specific niche market. They would accept clients during their vacations or during the break between their 13-week contracts with their full-time employer. If the company grew faster than they could manage, they would hire therapists they trusted on an as-needed basis.

Lee and Jeff developed a pay schedule and an hour-per-day sample formula for a variety of disabilities with which they were both comfortable assisting. The client would pay the day rate plus cover the cost of the therapist's trip. Lee and Jeff developed print advertising for the specialty newspapers typically found in organic food stores, assuming that clients who preferred this type of grocery and health care product store might be interested in their services. In addition, they volunteered to write monthly columns for the newspapers in exchange for reduced ad rates; their columns were so unique that sister papers across the nation picked them up.

Both Lee and Jeff set a limit of four trips a year, and they easily met this goal. When they were unable to meet a client's need, they used referrals to help connect the person to the needed program. When they stopped traveling full-time as therapists, they planned to develop the business into a national network of therapists.

❖ Learning Activities

1. Research your local community. Identify specific cultural groups, health care practices, regional resources, and any other information that might be helpful. On the basis of your research, identify a gap that might be addressed by occupational therapy. Answer the following questions:
   a. How would you address the gap?
   b. What role could an occupational therapist play in addressing the gap?
   c. What type of business might be developed to close the gap?
   d. Who would be the target audience for the business?

2. Assemble a focus group within your school, workplace, or community. Discuss any issues, concerns, challenges, or strengths about that setting. Write down any themes that come up in the discussion. On the basis of the issues discussed, come up with at least one way to address the needs that is not already in place. Design a brochure or other marketing materials. Reassemble the focus group and try to "sell" your idea.

3. Interview local business owners to get their stories. What factors helped them to be successful? What characteristics do they deem necessary to become an entrepreneur? What was the most challenging? What was the most fun? What would they do differently if they had to set up their business all over again? How did they finance their business? What advice would they offer to new business owners? After your interviews, do a personal self-assessment. In what ways are you similar to or different than successful business owners? What personal qualities do you have that might promote or inhibit your business success?

4. Develop a "Business on the Go" that can be operated from your vehicle. For example, one woman operates a traveling hair salon. She travels to clients' houses with all of the materials (except the sink) she needs to wash, dry, cut, color, and curl hair. Everything she needs fits into travel cases. Think of an appropriate occupational therapy–related business that you could operate from your vehicle. What needs would your business address? Who would your target population be? What supplies or materials would you need? Think of a catchy name for your business. Develop marketing materials to advertise your business.

5. Regarding the business you developed in Learning Activity 4, develop a "quick pitch" to sell your idea. Think of the acquaintances you encounter in the community—at church, at the grocery store, at the bank, and in the elevator—as potential investors in your business. Come up with a 30-second pitch to sell your business to these investors. Highlight the key selling points that make your idea or business unique. Remember, you want them to be as excited as you are, so give your pitch some punch!

✓ Multiple-Choice Questions

1. According to the Small Business Administration, what percentage of net new employment in the United States between 1992 and 2008 was created by small businesses?
   a. 30% to 50%.
   b. 40% to 60%.
   c. 50% to 70%.
   d. 60% to 80%.

2. An entrepreneur acts on a new
   a. Idea.
   b. Venture.
   c. Opportunity.
   d. All of the above.

3. Entrepreneurship can
   a. Provide the opportunity to pursue a dream.
   b. Serve as an alternative to traditional salaried job experiences lost to restructuring or elimination.
   c. Serve as an alternative to unsatisfying job experiences.
   d. All of the above.

4. An entrepreneur is concerned mainly about
   a. Personal profit.
   b. Venture profit.
   c. Social, nonprofit.
   d. Any success to match the mission.

5. The four psychological typologies identified by Miner (2000) are associated with which of the following?
   a. The ability to grow an existing business and the propensity to initiate a business venture.
   b. The ability to make a profit and manage a business.
   c. The ability to incubate an idea and develop a product.
   d. The ability to develop and implement a business plan.

6. The term *entrepreneur* originally was developed in France and meant
   a. Venture capitalist.
   b. Middleman.
   c. Tax avoider.
   d. Grand developer.

7. Which of the following typology classifications applies to individuals with a Type A personality, high motivation, commitment to projects, and a strong belief that they can control their futures?
   a. Real managers.
   b. Expert idea generators.
   c. Personal achievers.
   d. Empathic super-salespersons.

8. Kirzner (1997) believed that entrepreneurs spot opportunities for development on the basis of which of the following?
   a. Creative alertness.
   b. Research skills targeted at development.
   c. Ability to "read" others in the field.
   d. Good timing and luck.

9. According to the AOTA 2006 *Workforce and Compensation Survey*, what percentage of occupational therapy practitioners are self-employed or contract employees (not including part-time)?
   a. Approximately 7%.
   b. Approximately 12%.
   c. Approximately 23%.
   d. Approximately 37%.

10. *Niche markets* are
    a. Groups of special-needs populations.
    b. Large populations that corporations avoid because of low incomes.
    c. Difficult-to-find people because of their lifestyles.
    d. Groups of typical people in middle-class communities.

11. Occupational therapy practitioners can be entrepreneurs in which of the following ways?
    a. Operate an occupational therapy–related business.
    b. Operate a health-related practice.
    c. Operate a non-health-related practice.
    d. All of the above.

12. A key entrepreneur concept is
    a. Developing a long-term financial plan to sell the concept to high-paying corporations.
    b. Always including a social component to the business plan.
    c. Providing a product or service at a price the market is willing to pay.
    d. Finding the maximum income group before launching the product.

13. If a practitioner decides to begin a business using his or her skills in occupational therapy, it is essential that the practitioner does which of the following to ensure that the business falls within the parameters of acceptable practice?
    a. Check with the American Occupational Therapy Association.
    b. Check the licensure laws, state regulations, and other legislative issues.
    c. Check with the National Board for Certification in Occupational Therapy.
    d. All of the above.

14. Which of the following applies to research in theory and models of entrepreneurship?
    a. It comes primarily from the business disciplines.
    b. It is sorely lacking, according to experts in the area.
    c. It can be better developed through self-help books.
    d. It is well developed because of its long history.

15. A factor that helps a business succeed in a competitive environment is
    a. Competency.
    b. Distinctiveness.
    c. Supportiveness.
    d. Engagement.
16. Formal business plans are needed for
    a. Volunteer programs.
    b. Nonprofit program development.
    c. For-profit business ventures.
    d. All the above.
17. According to the most recent theories and research on entrepreneurship, which of the following statements is true?
    a. At least 10 years of education and experience in a field are necessary to contribute to that field.
    b. The more experience or education a person has in a given field, the less entrepreneurial he or she is likely to become.
    c. Extensive training and experience can impede the creative process.
    d. Entrepreneurs are more educated due in large part to the technological knowledge necessary for business.

18. Entrepreneurs are a central foundation of
    a. Large corporate companies.
    b. Capital-centered economies.
    c. Socialist-centered economies.
    d. Government-centered health research programs.
19. With regard to initial earnings and growth potential, empirical evidence suggests that self-employment results in which of the following when compared to skill-matched colleagues in traditional paid employment?
    a. Higher earnings and higher growth potential.
    b. Lower earnings and higher growth potential.
    c. Higher earnings and lower growth potential.
    d. Lower earnings and lower growth potential.
20. Incubating an idea for an entrepreneurial venture is an important step in developing a
    a. Business plan.
    b. Venture capital plan.
    c. Timeline to development.
    d. Funding plan.

References

Abrams, R. (2004). *Six week start-up.* Palo Alto, CA: Planning Shop.

Abrams, R. (2009). *Business plan in a day.* Palo Alto, CA: Planning Shop.

American Occupational Therapy Association. (2003). *AOTA professional development tool.* Bethesda, MD: Author. Retrieved January 25, 2010, from http://www1.aota.org/pdt/p1.htm

American Occupational Therapy Association. (2006). *Occupational therapy salaries and job opportunities continue to improve: 2006 AOTA workforce and compensation survey.* Retrieved January 30, 2010, from http://www.aota.org/Students/Prospective/Outlook/38230.aspx

American Occupational Therapy Association. (n.d.). *Emerging practice areas.* Retrieved January 25, 2010, from http://www.aota.org/Practitioners/PracticeAreas/Emerging.aspx

Ames, M., & Runko, M. A. (2005). Predicting entrepreneurship from ideation and divergent thinking. *Creativity and Innovation Management, 14,* 311–315.

Austin, D. (2006). *The American Occupational Therapy Association advisory opinion for the Ethics Commission: Ethical considerations when occupational therapists engage in business transactions with clients.* Retrieved January 25, 2010, from http://www.aota.org/Practitioners/Ethics/Advisory/36187.aspx

Baumol, W. J., Schilling, M. A., & Wolff, E. N. (2009). The superstar inventors and entrepreneurs: How were they educated? *Journal of Economics and Management Strategy, 18,* 711–728.

Bernheim, B. D. (1994). A theory of conformity. *Journal of Political Economy, 102,* 841–877.

Deakins, D., & Freel, M. (2009). *Entrepreneurship and small firms* (5th ed.). Maidenhead, UK: McGraw Hill Education.

Doubt, L., Paterson, M., & O'Riordan, A. (2004). Clinical education in private practice: An interdisciplinary project. *Journal of Allied Health, 33,* 47–50.

Elango, B., Hunter, G. L., & Winchell, M. (2007). Barriers to nurse entrepreneurship: A study of the process model of entrepreneurship. *Journal of the American Academy of Nurse Practitioners, 19,* 198–204.

Feldman, D. H. (1999). The development of creativity. In R. J. Sternberg (Ed.), *Handbook of creativity* (pp. 169–186). Cambridge, MA: Cambridge University Press.

Finnegan, M. (1997). Marketing occupational therapy: Can we do it? *British Journal of Therapy and Rehabilitation, 4*(4), 195–199.

Foto, M. (1998). Competence and the occupational therapy entrepreneur. *American Journal of Occupational Therapy, 52,* 765–769.

Fullen, S., & Podmoroff, D. (2006). *How to write a great business plan for your small business in 60 minutes or less.* Ocala, FL: Atlantic Publishing.

Ganesan, R., Kaur, D., & Maheshwari, R. C. (2002). Women entrepreneurs: Problems and prospects. *Journal of Entrepreneurship, 11*(1), 75–93.

Gartner, W. B. (2001). Is there an elephant in entrepreneurship? Blind assumptions in theory development. *Entrepreneurship Theory and Practice, 25*(4), 27–39.

Giannetti, M., & Simonov, A. (2009). Social interactions and entrepreneurial activity. *Journal of Economics and Management Strategy, 18,* 665–709.

Glancey, K. (1998). Determinants of growth and profitability in small entrepreneurial firms. *International Journal of Entrepreneurial Behaviour and Research, 4*(1), 18–27.

Glennon, T. J. (2007). Pediatric private practice: Perks and pitfalls. *Administration and Management Special Interest Section Quarterly, 23*(2), 1–4.

Gompers, P. A., Lerner, J., & Scharfstein, D. S. (2005). Entrepreneurial spawning: Public corporations and the formation of new ventures, 1986–1999. *Journal of Finance, 60,* 577–614.

Hamilton, B. H. (2000). Does entrepreneurship pay? An empirical analysis of the returns to self-employment. *Journal of Political Economy, 108,* 604–631.

Hardeman, L. (2007). The heart of an entrepreneur. *OT Practice, 12*(1), 13–15.

Holmes, W. M., & Scaffa, M. E. (2009). An exploratory study of competencies for emerging practice in occupational therapy. *Journal of Allied Health, 38,* 81–90.

Johnson, C. R., Koenig, K. P., Piersol, C. V., Santalucia, S. E., & Wachter-Schutz, W. (2006). Level I fieldwork today: A study of contexts and perceptions. *American Journal of Occupational Therapy, 60,* 275–287.

Kirzner, I. M. (1997). Entrepreneurial discovery and the competitive market process: An Austrian approach. *Journal of Economic Literature, 35*(1), 60–85.

Leong, S. L. J. (2004). Clinical nurse specialist entrepreneurship. *Internet Journal of Advanced Nursing Practice, 7*(1), 4–10.

Leslie, C. A. (2007). Taking it to the streets: Unconventional, entrepreneurial ways to market community-based practice. *OT Practice, 12*(7), 20–23.

Levy, M., & Weitz, B. A. (2004). *Retailing management.* Boston: McGraw-Hill/Irwin.

Low, M. B. (2001). The adolescence of entrepreneurial research: A specification of purpose. *Entrepreneurship Theory and Practice, 25*(4), 17–25.

Maliszewski, S. (2003). Walking a fine line: Being in practice requires business and legislative savvy. *Advance for Directors in Rehabilitation, 12*(7), 11–12, 14.

Mazzarol, T., Volery, T., Doss, N., & Thein, V. (1999). Factors influencing small business start-ups: A comparison with previous research. *International Journal of Entrepreneurial Behaviour and Research, 5*(2), 48–63.

McLaughlin, N. (2001). Optimal marginality: Innovation and orthodoxy in Fromm's revision of psychoanalysis. *Sociological Quarterly, 42,* 271–288.

Miner, J. B. (2000). Testing a psychological typology of entrepreneurs using business founders. *Journal of Applied Behavioral Science, 36*(1), 43–69.

Morris, A., Conrad-Reingold, M. J., & Sabata, D. (2006). Home modification entrepreneurs. *Home and Community Health Special Interest Section Quarterly, 13*(3), 1–3.

Morrison, A. (2000). Entrepreneurship: What triggers it? *International Journal of Entrepreneurial Behaviour and Research, 6*(2), 59–71.

Pinson, L. (2008). *Anatomy of a business plan: The step-by-step guide to building a business and securing your company's future.* Tustin, CA: Out of Your Mind and Into the Marketplace Publishing.

Ryan, V. (2000, April 10). Commerce: Anatomy of an entrepreneur. *Telephony.* Retrieved January 25, 2010, from http://find.galegroup.com.ezproxy.bu.edu/gtx/start.do?prodId=AONE&userGroupName=mlin_b_bumml

Shepherd, D., & Haynie, J. M. (2009). Birds of a feather don't always flock together: Identity management in entrepreneurship. *Journal of Business Venturing, 24,* 316–337.

Simonton, D. K. (1999). Creativity as blind variation and selective retention: Is the creative process Darwinian? *Psychological Inquiry, 10,* 309–328.

Small Business Administration. (2009). *The small business economy: A report to the President.* Retrieved June 24, 2010, from http://www.sba.gov/advo/research/sb_econ2009.pdf

Spors, K. K. (2008, February 17). The 100-page start-up plan: Don't bother. *Wall Street Journal.* Retrieved January 25, 2010, from http://online.wsj.com/article/SB120320971126773975.html

Stafford, J. E. (2004). The ABCs of beginning a private practice. *Sensory Integration Special Interest Section Quarterly, 27*(3), 1–4.

Thompson, J. L. (1999). A strategic perspective of entrepreneurship. *International Journal of Entrepreneurial Behaviour and Research, 5*(6), 279–296.

Ting, H., & Fitzgerald, M. H. (1996). Rehabilitation market segmentation and positioning of rehabilitation providers. *Journal of Rehabilitation, 62*(2), 36–44.

Ucbasaran, D., Westhead, P., & Wright, M. (2001). The focus of entrepreneurial research: Contextual and process issues. *Entrepreneurship Theory and Practice, 25*(4), 57–80.

Wadhwa, V., Aggarwal, R., Holly, K., & Salkever, A. (2009). *The anatomy of an entrepreneur: Making of a successful entrepreneur.* Retrieved January 25, 2010, from http://www.kauffman.org/uploadedFiles/making-of-a-successful-entrepreneur.pdf

Wilson, A., Averis, A., & Walsh, K. (2003). The influences on and experiences of becoming nurse entrepreneurs: A Delphi study. *International Journal of Nursing Practice, 9,* 236–245.

Wilson, F., Kickul, J., Marlino, D., Barbosa, S. D., & Griffiths, M. D. (2009). An analysis of the role of gender and self-efficacy in developing female entrepreneurial interest and behavior. *Journal of Developmental Entrepreneurship, 14*(2), 105–119.

APPENDIX 10.A. ENTREPRENEURSHIP EVIDENCE TABLE

Topic	Findings	Evidence
Entrepreneurial identity; characteristics of entrepreneurs	Distinctiveness is an inherent characteristic of a person desiring to be an entrepreneur. Distinctiveness is not always positive, however; the drive for distinction can create a sense of isolation.	Shepherd, D., & Haynie, J. M. (2009). Birds of a feather don't always flock together: Identity management in entrepreneurship. *Journal of Business Venturing, 24,* 316–337.
	Four psychological typologies are associated with the ability to grow existing businesses and initiate new ventures.	Miner, J. B. (2000). Testing a psychological typology of entrepreneurs using business founders. *Journal of Applied Behavioral Science, 36*(1), 43–69.
Education and entrepreneurship	Individuals require a minimum of 10 years of intense study in a given area of knowledge before they can make a significant contribution within that area.	Simonton, D. K. (1999). Creativity as blind variation and selective retention: Is the creative process Darwinian? *Psychological Inquiry, 10,* 309–328.
	Excessive experience and training within a field may inhibit creativity and cognitive development.	Feldman, D. H. (1999). The development of creativity. In R. J. Sternberg (Ed.), *Handbook of creativity* (pp. 169–186). Cambridge, MA: Cambridge University Press.
		McLaughlin, N. (2001). Optimal marginality: Innovation and orthodoxy in Fromm's revision of psychoanalysis. *Sociological Quarterly, 42,* 271–288.
	The age, experience, and educational attainment of entrepreneurs at the end of the 20th and beginning of the 21st centuries increased; this trend was associated with the need for technological training for business success.	Baumol, W. J., Schilling, M. A., & Wolff, E. N. (2009). The superstar inventors and entrepreneurs: How were they educated? *Journal of Economics and Management Strategy, 18,* 711–728.
Social interactions and entrepreneurship	Peer relationships and social interactions have financial (funding) and nonfinancial (social status, prestige) business benefits; social interactions affect the likelihood a person engages in entrepreneurial activities.	Bernheim, B. D. (1994). A theory of conformity. *Journal of Political Economy, 102,* 841–877.
		Giannetti, M., & Simonov, A. (2009). Social interactions and entrepreneurial activity. *Journal of Economics and Management Strategy, 18,* 665–709.
		Gompers, P. A., Lerner, J., & Scharfstein, D. S. (2005). Entrepreneurial spawning: Public corporations and the formation of new ventures, 1986–1999. *Journal of Finance, 60,* 577–614.

APPENDIX 10.A. ENTREPRENEURSHIP EVIDENCE TABLE *(cont.)*

Occupational therapy entrepreneur	There is a connection between occupational therapy entrepreneurs and the future of the profession. It is difficult to measure professional competence in occupational therapy entrepreneurs.	Foto, M. (1998). Competence and the occupational therapy entrepreneur. *American Journal of Occupational Therapy, 52,* 765–769.
	Professional competencies for emerging practice were identified.	Holmes, W. M., & Scaffa, M. E. (2009). An exploratory study of competencies for emerging practice in occupational therapy. *Journal of Allied Health, 38,* 81–90.
	Home modification is a viable potential area for entrepreneurial activity in occupational therapy.	Morris, A., Conrad-Reingold, M. J., & Sabata, D. (2006). Home modification entrepreneurs. *Home and Community Health Special Interest Section Quarterly, 13*(3), 1–3.
	Tips for pediatric private practice are provided.	Glennon, T. J. (2007). Pediatric private practice: Perks and pitfalls. *Administration and Management Special Interest Section Quarterly, 23*(2), 1–4.
	Strategies for successful implementation of a private practice are provided.	Stafford, J. E. (2004). The ABCs of beginning a private practice. *Sensory Integration Special Interest Section Quarterly, 27*(3), 1–4.
Marketing	Occupational therapists need to be more proactive in marketing their skills and services.	Finnegan, M. (1997). Marketing occupational therapy: Can we do it? *British Journal of Therapy and Rehabilitation, 4*(4), 195–199.
	Several target markets have been identified for rehabilitation providers. These are potential areas for entrepreneurial ventures.	Ting, H., & Fitzgerald, M. H. (1996). Rehabilitation market segmentation and positioning of rehabilitation providers. *Journal of Rehabilitation, 62*(2), 36–44.
Growth and profitability	Business characteristics, such as size and geographic region, influence growth and profitability in manufacturing firms.	Glancey, K. (1998). Determinants of growth and profitability in small entrepreneurial firms. *International Journal of Entrepreneurial Behaviour and Research, 4*(1), 18–27.
Gender and entrepreneurship	Several challenges are unique to women entrepreneurs, including stereotyping, training, marketing, and management of challenges.	Ganesan, R., Kaur, D., & Maheshwari, R. C. (2002). Women entrepreneurs: Problems and prospects. *Journal of Entrepreneurship, 11*(1), 75–93.
	Women entrepreneurs face unique challenges, including dual responsibilities and business visibility.	Mazzarol, T., Volery, T., Doss, N., & Thein, V. (1999). Factors influencing small business start-ups: A comparison with previous research. *International Journal of Entrepreneurial Behaviour and Research, 5*(2), 48–63.
	Entrepreneurial education improves self-efficacy for men and women; however, education directed specifically to women should be provided to encourage the continued development of women entrepreneurs.	Wilson, F., Kickul, J., Marlino, D., Barbosa, S. D., & Griffiths, M. D. (2009). An analysis of the role of gender and self-efficacy in developing female entrepreneurial interest and behavior. *Journal of Developmental Entrepreneurship, 14*(2), 105–119.
Fieldwork education	Several strategies may be helpful in increasing fieldwork opportunities in private practice settings.	Doubt, L., Paterson, M., & O'Riordan, A. (2004). Clinical education in private practice: An interdisciplinary project. *Journal of Allied Health, 33,* 47–50.

Appendix 10.B. Entrepreneurship-Related Online Resources

- **www.aota.org/Practitioners/Reimb/Pay/Private/Private.aspx:** A 2007 publication from the American Occupational Therapy Association that includes a packet on finding and obtaining resources to become a private practitioner, including reimbursement issues.

- **www.entrepreneur.com:** A resource for starting and managing small businesses.

- **www.youngentrepreneur.com:** A resource for young business owners that includes a blog, discussion board, and small business resources.

11
Proposal and Grant Writing

Lesly S. Wilson, PhD, OTR/L

❖ Key Terms and Concepts

Grant. Award provided to a grant writer with a privilege or right or a sum of money to support research or non-research-related projects.

Grant proposal. Document used to convince a funding source to support a grant writer's idea (Gitlin & Lyons, 2004) that essentially serves as an agreement between the grant writer and the grant maker (Geever, 2007).

Grant writer. Person who participates in the research and writing activities for a grant award.

Private funding sources. Organizations that promote specific areas of interest by reaching out to the communities where they operate businesses, provide services, or have special interests.

Public funding sources. Government entities that promote their mission and purpose by partnering with external organizations.

Research. "A systematic process of collecting, analyzing, and interpreting information to increase understanding of a phenomenon about which we are interested" (Leedy & Ormrod, 2010, p. 1).

Stakeholder. An individual or organization with an interest in the grant writer's proposed topic or population being served.

❖ Learning Objectives

After completing this chapter, you should be able to do the following:

- Describe the grant proposal process.
- Identify the 2 primary categories of grant funding.
- Identify at least 2 electronic databases regularly used by grant writers.

- List the 8 typical components of a grant proposal.
- Discuss 10 tips for proposal development.

> Successful careers are the result of having a plan, setting priorities, and making sure that these are not derailed by the day-to-day events.
> —Elena Plante, PhD, CCC-SLP
> (quoted in Nunez, 2008, p. 32)

Occupational therapy organizations and practitioners typically pursue grants to

- Develop and advance scientific knowledge in the field,
- Support training and research activities,
- Expand opportunities for educating students and clinicians,
- Provide support for institutional activities,
- Enhance the prestige of an institution,
- Legitimize research programs or training projects, and

- Advance the professional career of the grant writer and researcher (Gitlin & Lyons, 2004).

Grant writing provides an opportunity to develop and advance programs that can significantly improve occupational therapy academic, clinical, and community-based programing. A grant award provides additional funds or resources to assist organizations with the implementation of proposed activities.

As students, occupational therapy professionals learn the necessity and value of research for clinical practice. They learn the components of a research proposal, how to interpret studies, and how to apply results to occupational therapy services (Accreditation Council for Occupational Therapy Education® [ACOTE®], 2007a, 2007b, 2007c;

American Occupational Therapy Association, 1991). ACOTE standards for doctoral, master's, and occupational therapy assistant programs mandate the integration of research components in educational curricula so that entry-level practitioners are empowered to begin and participate in research and grant development activities.

ACOTE (2007a, 2007b) establishes a clear research standard for doctoral and master's-degree-level educational programs indicating that during and after the completion of the degree program students are able to

- Articulate the importance of research;
- Effectively locate, understand, and evaluate research;
- Use research to make evidence-based decisions;
- Select, apply, and interpret or understand statistics;
- Understand and critique the validity of research studies;
- Demonstrate skills necessary to design a research proposal; and
- Implement aspects of research.

The ACOTE standards for occupational therapy assistant educational programs (ACOTE, 2007c) specify that during and after the completion of the degree program these students are able to

- Articulate the importance of research and literature,
- Use literature to assist with making evidence-based decisions in collaboration, and
- Identify skills necessary to follow a research protocol and related data collection.

Such education and exposure during preservice educational programming establishes a strong foundation for the occupational therapy practitioner's future participation in research and grant-writing activities.

Grant proposal writing, however, is a craft that requires additional knowledge, training, and technical skill beyond this academic preview. Successful grant writing requires significant preparation and large investments of time and energy in a process that concludes with a well-drafted proposal. Grant-making institutions use such proposals as the basis for making funding decisions.

DEVELOPING AN IDEA

The initial step in proposal writing is the development of an idea. Occupational therapy practitioners within all settings are presented with daily challenges. Such challenges can be turned into opportunities when potential ideas or solutions to these problems are put into a proposal. The grant writer should have a clear interest in the idea. In addition, the idea should be aligned with the grant writer's organizational priorities and mission as well as with the funding agency's priorities and mission. Before developing a proposal, grant writers must be knowledgeable about their organization's interest, expertise, and environment; current research related to the identified problem; and the funding agency's interests (Devine, 2009). Following this self-evaluation, the grant writer further determines the complementary expertise and resources necessary to justify feasibility and fit for a proposed project to a funding agency. The solidifying of an idea for a proposal is a process that can take months; the process involves the maturing of the idea, the identification of stakeholders, and the definition of team members' roles.

Team member collaboration is extremely helpful to grant writers in all stages of career development when developing an idea. For novice grant writers, however, team membership and mentoring are critical to develop and enhance knowledge and skill necessary for success (Miner & Miner, 2009). Such collaboration helps the grant writer refine ideas, direct research efforts, and identify additional funding sources.

Strategies to consider during the idea development phase include the following:

- Identify current research on the topics related to your idea and determine the potential for future research by completing a thorough review of the literature.
- Investigate idea options using the resources of professional societies and foundations.
- Conduct interviews with experts in the field on the local, state, and national levels to help you refine your idea.

IDENTIFYING POTENTIAL FUNDING MATCHES

Once the idea has been refined, the next step is to identify potential funding sources to support the idea. Even the greatest idea will not be funded unless it matches the interests and priorities of a funding source (Gitlin & Lyons, 2004). During the grant writer's prospect research, a clear system for identifying funding matches should be developed and compiled into a database. The grant writer can sort prospects into *yes*, *maybe*, and *no* categories on the basis of the announcement or program description. The *yes* category indicates that the grant maker's program description is in line with the ideas or programs of the grant writer. The *maybe* category indicates that the grant maker's program description might potentially fit with the grant writer's ideas or programs. The *no* category indicates that the grant maker's program description is not in line with the ideas or programs of the grant writer. Use of these categories will help the grant writer develop an organized system that can be stored electronically using database or word-processing software. The development of a robust database will facilitate quick information retrieval while providing efficient tracking of grant cycles for the grant writer.

Public and private funding are the two source categories grant writers use to find a match for proposal ideas. Public funding sources include federal and state agencies, and private funding sources include private foundations, professional associations, and private business and industry. Successful grant writers are continuously scanning both public and private funding sources for opportunities to support their ideas (Devine, 2009).

Public Funding Sources

Most federal agencies offer some form of grant program to award funding to areas that support their mission and purpose. The federal government is the largest source of research and training funding (Gitlin & Lyons, 2004). Umbrella departments that contain agencies with focused interest primarily in health and human service proposals include the following:

- National Institutes of Health (NIH),
- National Science Foundation,
- Department of Health and Human Services,
- Centers for Disease Control and Prevention (CDC),
- Health Resources and Services Administration,
- Department of Education, and
- Department of Defense.

The following are some common tools for identifying specific funding programs within agencies under these departments:

- Grants.gov is the largest online clearinghouse for federal agency funding opportunities. It provides a centralized location for the funding announcements of 26 federal or public agencies that offer more than 1,000 annual programs and about $500 billion in annual awards.
- The *Catalog of Federal Domestic Assistance* is published annually with supplements published each fall.
- The *Federal Register* lists daily updates of deadlines for new grants.
- The *Commerce Business Daily* lists available contract opportunities through request for proposal (RFP) announcements or intents to procure a project.

Grant writers can use these directories and databases to narrow their prospect research and determine the best fit of individual research interest with organization. Some databases offer key word searches and opportunities to complete individualized profiles that trigger weekly electronic newsletter updates concerning indicated areas of interest or expertise.

Private Funding Sources

More than 43,000 private foundations in the United States provide over $8 billion in research funding annually (Devine, 2009). Federal law requires foundations to give away at least 5 percent of their market-value assets or interest income annually or risk losing their tax-exempt status. Some of these foundations have an Internet presence and others do not. A complete listing of state grant makers can be found through the Foundation Center at http://foundationcenter.org or through the Council on Foundations at http://www.cof.org/links. These organizations provide electronic lists of links to foundations and a comprehensive print list of Web sites to provide grant writers with a greater awareness of the available funding opportunities within their state or geographic location.

Other widely used membership-based tools for locating private or public funding sources are offered through the Community of Science (COS) and GrantSelect. The COS (n.d.) is a leading provider of information to researchers, scholars, and professionals around the globe. It has a Database of Funded Research and houses the largest compendium of information concerning available funding. The COS allows members to find funding, people, and information important to their ideas and interests. Its database offers records on public and private funding opportunities worth over $35 billion and serves more than 1,600 universities, corporations, and government agencies worldwide (COS, n.d.). Individual membership is free, and member profiles can be used to match grant-seeking interest with grant maker notifications through e-mail. GrantSelect (n.d.) provides an online database of more than 12,500 public and private funding opportunities from more than 5,800 unique sponsors. This database allows for key word searches that focus notification alerts toward the grant writer's areas of interest. There is a membership fee for GrantSelect.

After gathering the appropriate information, grant writers should thoroughly review and read the grant maker's announcement, familiarize themselves with the requested proposal components, and contact the grant maker's project officer or contact person to review intent and expectations. The following are strategies to consider during the fund matching and prospect research phase:

- Request or download an application packet, and thoroughly read the documents.
- Contact a past grantee from the grant maker's organization to review strategies for success.
- Contact a past reviewer from the grant maker's organization to review strategies for success.
- Develop a list of questions or concerns to address with the grant maker's project officer or contact and make a phone call or personal visit.

WRITING THE GRANT PROPOSAL

The grant proposal incorporates the grant writer's planning and research, outreach, and understanding of the grant maker's mission and purpose (Geever, 2007). Pazell and Jaffe (2003) cited a good rule in writing grant proposals: "Never overestimate your audience's knowledge, and never underestimate its intelligence" (p. 237). Grant makers use proposals to determine who has the best idea, who is most suited to carry out their ideas or interests, and who is the most promising investment. The proposal is what convinces the grant maker to support the grant writer's idea (Gitlin & Lyons, 2004) and essentially serves as an agreement between the grant writer and the grant maker (Geever, 2007).

Different grant-making organizations require different components within their proposal; variations in requirements are due largely to the type of organization and funding being pursued. Thus, the grant writer should thoroughly review the application packet or call for proposal directives before drafting a proposal. Gitlin and Lyons (2004) observed that all proposals provide answers to the following questions:

- What is the project about?
- Why is it important?
- What will you do?
- How will you do it?
- What will it cost?
- Why will it cost what it does?
- Why is your organization the best one to carry out the project?

The eight typical core components of a proposal address these questions:

1. Cover letter
2. Summary
3. Statement of problem or needs
4. Objectives
5. Methods
6. Evaluation
7. Budget
8. Dissemination (Annersten & Wredling, 2006; Davis, 2005; Gitlin & Lyons, 2004; Miner & Miner, 2009).

Some grant makers request a letter of intent (LOI), typically a 2- to 5-page brief query letter to convince the grant maker to give the grant writer an opportunity to submit additional information. If the grant maker is interested in the project, an invitation is extended to submit additional information through an application or proposal (Zlotnick, 2001). The LOI should include a statement about the venture or organization, a description of the needs of the project, a description of methods or interventions planned, a projection of the outcome or results desired, and a proposed budget with time frame (Pazell & Jaffe, 2003).

Cover Letter

Grant makers typically request that a proposal be accompanied by a cover letter. The cover letter introduces the grant writer to the grant maker and provides a preview of the project title and intent. Tips for writing the cover letter include the following:

- Clearly state the title of project in a way that is eye-catching and interesting to the grant maker.
- Be thorough but succinct.
- Do not exceed one full page.

The Summary

The summary, sometimes referred to as the *abstract*, introduces the grant maker to the grant writer's idea and proposed project. The summary gives a synopsis of the research study objectives, sample and size methods, duration, and evaluation methods for research projects. For non-re-search projects, it gives a brief overview of the proposed activities, the organization, the target population, timeline, and evaluation instrument. The summary section should be precise and brief—no more than 1 full page (Annersten & Wredling, 2006). Tips for writing the summary include the following:

- Provide a thorough but succinct overview of the proposed project.
- Provide a clear overview of the organization.
- Do not exceed 1 full page.
- Provide clear sustainability ideas.
- Present an evaluation plan for overall program and individual activities.

Statement of Problem or Needs

The statement of problem or needs should convince the grant maker of the problem's significance and display the grant writer's interest in and knowledge of the problem. This section should clearly describe how the proposed project will contribute to existing knowledge and why it is important (Annersten & Wredling, 2006). The importance of the problem and the grant writer's ability to address the problem should be described in detail.

The statement of problem or needs should include current facts and evidence from the literature supporting the importance of the problem. Information in this section should not be too generic or broad but rather succinct and persuasive and should include current state and national statistics, surveys, and reports (Geever, 2007). This section should place the overall significance of the problem in context, demonstrate the grant writer's knowledge of the field, and clearly reveal the grant writer's ability to offer a solution to the problem. Tips for writing the statement of problem or needs include the following:

- Demonstrate the grant writer's command of current knowledge.
- Clearly describe current efforts and how the grant writer will contribute to existing knowledge.
- Reinforce the grant writer's credibility and expertise in addressing the problem.

Objectives

The objectives section should clearly describe the intended goal, objectives, and activities of the proposed project. *Goals* are what a project will accomplish; *objectives* are statements about a project's specific outcomes that can be evaluated or measured (Gitlin & Lyons, 2004). Objectives provide the grant maker with a clear roadmap of the grant writer's intent for the funding. The description of project activities should be clear and in line with the objectives and overall goal of the project and should specify what change is anticipated as a result of implementation of the grant writer's project. Miner and Miner (2009) suggested use of the "Keep them SIMPLE" acronym for developing objectives:

S = *Specific:* Specify the grant writer's intentions to change or add to existing knowledge, policy, or practice.

I = *Immediate:* Provide a time frame in which the current problem will be addressed.

M = *Measurable:* Provide a tangible means of measuring project success.

P = *Practical:* Describe the significance of each objective and how it provides a solution to the problem.

L = *Logical:* Indicate how the objectives systematically contribute to the overall goal of the project.

E = *Evaluative:* Indicate how much change must occur for the project to be effective.

Miner and Miner (2009) pointed out that these categories are not mutually exclusive and suggested that a grant writer's objectives meet at least two or three of these six criteria.

The objectives section may also include a clearly defined research question and hypotheses. The section should clearly define *what* will be done (the next section, "Methods," details *how* the objectives will be carried out). Tips for writing the objectives section include the following:

- Clearly state any objectives, hypotheses, or questions.
- Correlate the objectives with the anticipated outcomes of the project.
- Make sure the significance and timeliness of the objectives are clear.

Methods

The methods section describes the project activities in detail and explains how objectives will be accomplished (Miner & Miner, 2009). It provides a clear picture of what will occur during the time frame, along with who (people or personnel) will be involved in which activities, where the activities will occur, and what facilities will be used. It also describes the research design of the study, including the way in which the study is organized, the variables that will be measured, and the data collection and analytic procedures that will be followed (DePoy & Gitlin, 1998). In addition, it presents the project design, sampling plan, instruments to be used, and monitoring process. The methods section should provide the grant maker with confidence that the grant writer is able to carry out the project ideas to the best interest of the funding organization. Tips for writing the methods section include the following:

- Clearly describe the project activities, population served, personnel, and environment.
- Clearly describe any instruments, evaluations, or other specific procedures to be used.
- Clearly detail budget funding related to activities, personnel, and so forth.

Evaluation

All projects should include evaluation to determine such things as the status of the project and ways to improve it. The information obtained from an evaluation can be used to better allocate resources, improve services, and strengthen overall project performance (Miner & Miner, 2009). The evaluation section should identify if and how internal or external evaluators will be used and the specific evaluation procedures. It is important to identify precisely what will be evaluated, the type of information needed to conduct the evaluation, how information will be obtained and with what instruments, and which evaluation design and analysis will be used. Evaluation components should be included in the budget. Tips for writing the evaluation section include the following:

- Clearly explain what will be evaluated, how it will be evaluated, and who will conduct the evaluation.
- Clearly outline the evaluation design and include what processes will be evaluated and how they will be analyzed.
- Clearly outline how the project budget will support the proposed evaluation.

Budget

The project budget provides funding justification for proposed activities, personnel, facility use, and evaluation. Each component should correlate appropriately with the proposed funding. An inflated budget is a signal of waste, a low budget casts doubt on the organization's planning ability, and an incomplete budget is an indicator of sloppy preparation (Miner & Miner, 2009).

The grant writer should be familiar with the grant maker's allowable budget categories and include those items in the budget; the categories typically include direct and indirect costs, along with cost sharing. Direct costs are line items in the project budget and include personnel and nonpersonnel expenditures (Miner & Miner, 2009). Indirect costs are not directly listed in the budget but are costs incurred in the project such as library use, payroll, space, and equipment (Miner & Miner, 2009). It is important that the grant writer understand his or her organization's indirect costs and cost-sharing practices; when these costs are well defined, they add greatly to the proposal and the reviewer's understanding of the project (Geever, 2007). Tips for writing the budget include the following:

- Provide a clear narrative of the budget, justifying all components.
- Ensure that all calculations are clear.
- Use appendixes to provide additional information regarding budget categories.

Dissemination

Dissemination of project results allows the project outcomes to be shared with others. It generates publicity for the grant maker and adds to the professional creditability of the grant writer. The dissemination process should be clearly described within the proposal. The grant maker wants to see specific tentative modes of dissemination listed, such as publishing in a journal, presenting at a conference or meeting, or posting on a Web site (Miner & Miner, 2009). Tips for writing the dissemination section include the following:

- Present a clear and realistic plan for dissemination.
- Identify specific names of conferences, journals, or Web sites in which information will be disseminated.
- Clearly describe the relationship between the dissemination plan and the budget.

OVERALL TIPS FOR PROPOSALS

The following are characteristics of proposals that are more likely to gain the support of foundation staff:[1]

- *The proposal describes a new approach.* Most foundations like to fund new and exciting things, not more of the same. Foundations are increasingly interested in proposed solutions that build on the best available current knowledge, that show awareness of what has been tried, that build on what works, and that replicate proved or promising ideas. The prevailing perception of innovation among foundations includes both improvements in the effectiveness of existing program approaches and completely new programs.
- *The grant writer understands the foundation's mission.* If the grant writer can demonstrate a close match between his or her organization's mission and the mission of the foundation, the proposal is more impressive than if it was generic or just thrown together.
- *The organization is determined to do the project, no matter what.* Foundations like to fund people who are committed to what they are doing, not people who will do something only if a funder gives them money to do it.
- *The organization has the know-how to successfully complete the project.* Project staff do not have to be world-famous experts in this area, but they do need to have relevant experience and enthusiasm. Information about the principle staff members involved in the project demonstrates their qualifications to conduct the project.
- *The project is being undertaken to improve the lives of people, not to make the organization bigger and richer.* Funders care about people and results more than they care about organizations.
- *The organization is working with the people it is trying to help, not doing things to them.* If the organization is trying to help children, has the grant writer involved them in putting together the pre-proposal? Foundations think it is important that the people who will be helped have

some say in the matter. Information about the organization's board of directors and related volunteer committees helps illustrate for the funder the range and types of representatives involved in leading and advising the project.

- *The organization is investing its own money in the project.* This tells foundations that the organization is committed to the project and believes it is important. It also helps convince funders that the organization will continue the project after their funding ends and commit itself to doing whatever it takes to find other funding.
- *The organization will continue the project after foundation funding ceases.* Foundations like to help projects get started that are so valuable to people that the projects will continue even after the funding ends. There is little sense in starting a project that is going to end 2 or 3 years later after foundation funding comes to an end.
- *The organization has a comprehensive approach to the problem.* No one can solve a complicated problem with a simple solution, and foundations are looking for grant writers whose answer is at least as sophisticated as the problem they are trying to solve and who link up with other organizations to work more comprehensively.
- *The organization is willing to work collaboratively with anyone who can help.* For example, foundations do not want to fund 18 different projects to help dropouts in one high school. They like to see organizations working together to improve the lives of people.
- *The organization is willing to have impartial evaluators assess its work.* Impartial evaluation helps both the organization and the foundation learn to do a better job.

SUMMARY

Entry-level occupational therapy practitioners are equipped with preservice education, understanding, and skill to begin research and grant-writing activities. A successful grant application is an exercise in communication, and it is the grant writer's responsibility to clearly communicate ideas (Devine, 2009). Occupational therapy practitioners have ideas for projects that can improve the overall quality of life for persons receiving therapy services within a variety of service delivery settings. There is much opportunity to develop these ideas in collaboration with other health care team members in academia and community-based settings.

---

[1] From *Approaching the Foundation*, by R. F. Long and J. Orosz (n.d.). Copyright © Kellogg Foundation. Reprinted with permission.

Case Examples

LEVEL I FIELDWORK

Deris, an occupational therapy assistant student, was doing her Level I fieldwork rotation in a skilled nursing facility. The supervising occupational therapist asked Deris to locate and read a peer-reviewed article concerning fall prevention programming for the geriatric population.

Deris contacted her school librarian to obtain information and access to the Web-based library. She was given a username and password to access the library and instructed on how to perform an online key word search. She was informed that key word searches allow you to narrow research to a specific term or combination of terms. Deris accessed her school's Web-based library and began searching using an online database (e.g., PubMed, CINAHL, Academic Research Premier). She selected only peer-reviewed articles to be retrieved and used the key words *fall prevention* and *programming*. She found several peer-reviewed articles related to her search and selected one to read and share with her fieldwork supervisor.

LEVEL II FIELDWORK

Lily, a master's-level occupational therapy student, was in the 6th week of her Level II fieldwork rotation in a busy university-based rehab facility. The supervising occupational therapist was involved in a research study on children with autism spectrum disorder. The supervisor asked Lily to review the current research plan and search for potential grant funders to help sustain the research study, which was supported by a grant ending in 10 months.

Lily began prospect research. She accessed such federal sources as grants.gov, the *Catalog of Federal Domestic Assistance* (www.gsa.gov/fdac/queryfdac.htm), the *Federal Register* (www.access.gpo.gov/su_docs/aces/aces140.html), and *Commerce Business Daily* (cbdnet.access.gpo.gov/ index.html). She accessed the foundation center and used the university's membership to search the Community of Science and Grantseeker databases. She used prospect sheets to identify potential funders and created a database to track grant cycles of funding sources.

FIRST-TIME MANAGER

Danielle, the new school district system manager of occupational therapy services, was asked to review last year's child outcomes statistics and develop a report detailing the child outcomes related to occupational therapy service delivery in the district.

Danielle requested the data report from the prior year from the school system administration. She looked for trends in geographic location, types of services, frequency of services, and duration of services overall by diagnosis, gender, and race. She created a full review of the data pointing to achieved outcomes of the services. Danielle then used this information as support for a grant when writing a proposal.

MANAGER

Ashlei, a doctoral-level occupational therapist and senior faculty member, found a funding source that matched her current research agenda. Several other faculty members were interested in enhancing their research skills, and Ashlei planned on involving them in this process. She contacted other faculty with similar interest and developed a grant-writing team. She shared the grant award directives and requested that all interested members carefully read through the document to determine whether the grant award was a good fit for their interest and idea. Ashlei and team members developed a list of questions to ask the grant maker contact. The responses from the grant maker contact will be used to better determine goodness of fit for team members with the grant award.

❖ Learning Activities

1. Select a topic of research interest and conduct a key word search using the www.grants.gov database to secure potential funding opportunities from public grant sources. Identify 2 potential funding opportunities, and print out grant announcements.

2. Select a topic of research interest and conduct a key word search using the Foundation Center's RFP database at http://foundationcenter.org/pnd/rfp for potential funding opportunities from private grant sources. Identify 2 potential funding opportunities, and print out grant announcements.

3. Thoroughly review 2 public source and 2 private source grant announcements. Visit the Foundation Center at http://foundationcenter.org/findfunders/wrksheet, and download the document titled "Prospect Worksheet—Institutional Funders." Then complete 4 forms using announcement information from the 2 public and 2 private grant sources to determine

the match of the funders with your organization's areas of interest.

4. Visit the Community of Science at http://www.cos.com and register at no cost. Complete a user profile indicating your research areas of interest. Print out the profile and registration confirmation e-mail. Use the site to identify 2 other registered users with similar research interests.

5. Using announcement guidelines, draft a grant proposal for 1 identified grant match. Develop a checklist of all the required components requested in the application. After drafting the grant proposal, use the checklist to determine whether all components are present in your proposal.

✓ Multiple-Choice Questions

1. Grant proposals are typically developed for what reason?
   a. To expand educational opportunities for educating students and clinicians.
   b. To legitimize research programs or training projects.
   c. To advance professional careers.
   d. All of the above.

2. The National Institutes of Health is considered which type of funding source?
   a. Private.
   b. Public.
   c. Both private and public.
   d. None of the above.

3. A corporate organization's foundation that solicits grant proposals to support health-related programs is considered which type of funding source?
   a. Private.
   b. Public.
   c. Both private and public.
   d. None of the above.

4. The grants.gov database provides grant writers with information concerning what type of funding sources?
   a. Private.
   b. Public.
   c. Both private and public.
   d. None of the above.

5. The Foundation Center is a source for finding which type of funding opportunities?
   a. Private.
   b. Public.
   c. Both private and public.
   d. None of the above.

6. The Community of Science is a source for finding which type of funding opportunities?
   a. Private.
   b. Public.
   c. Both private and public.
   d. None of the above.

7. Which resource tool is published annually with supplements published each fall?
   a. *Grants.gov:* http://grants.gov.
   b. *Catalog of Federal Domestic Assistance:* http://www.gsa.gov/fdac/queryfdac.htm.
   c. *Federal Register:* http://www.access.gpo.gov/su_docs/aces/aces140.html.
   d. *Commerce Business Daily:* http://cbdnet.access.gpo.gov/index.html.

8. Which of the following is *not* a suggested strategy for finding funding matches during the prospect research phase?
   a. Contact past grant reviewers from the grant maker's organization.
   b. Avoid calling the grant maker with questions.
   c. Thoroughly review the application packet information.
   d. Contact past grantees from the grant maker's organization.

9. Which ideas have the greatest chance of being funded?
   a. Ideas that match the interest and priorities of the funding source.
   b. Ideas with a well-developed research design and plan.
   c. Ideas that show community collaboration.
   d. Good ideas that show potential for future funding.

10. When developing an idea, it is important to do which of the following?
    a. Investigate the idea well among colleagues.
    b. Review current research on the idea or topic.
    c. Conduct interviews with experts in the topic area.
    d. All of the above.

11. Which section of the grant proposal provides the grant maker with an introduction to the idea, research objectives, sample and size methods, duration, and evaluation methods of the proposed project?
    a. Objectives.
    b. Summary.
    c. Budget.
    d. Methods.

12. Which section of the grant proposal provides the grant maker with information concerning funding justifications for proposed activities?
    a. Objectives.
    b. Summary.
    c. Budget.
    d. Methods.

13. Which section of the grant proposal clearly describes project activities, population served, evaluations, and budget funding request?
    a. Objectives.
    b. Summary.
    c. Budget.
    d. Methods.

14. Which section of the grant proposal provides the grant maker with a clear roadmap of the grant writer's intent for funding?
    a. Objectives.
    b. Summary.
    c. Budget.
    d. Methods.

15. Which section of the grant proposal provides the grant maker with hypotheses or questions that have a clear correlation with outcomes of the project?
    a. Objectives.
    b. Summary.
    c. Budget.
    d. Methods.

16. Which section of the grant proposal provides the grant maker with a convincing argument for the significance of and need for the proposed program as well as a summary of the research in the topic area?
    a. Cover letter.
    b. Problem or needs.
    c. Budget.
    d. Methods.

17. Which section of the grant proposal should be succinct and persuasive and include current state and national statistical, survey, and report information?
    a. Problem or needs.
    b. Cover letter.
    c. Budget.
    d. Methods.

18. Which section of the grant proposal should include the title and project intent but not exceed one page?
    a. Problem or needs.
    b. Cover letter.
    c. Budget.
    d. Methods.

19. Which acronym is important to remember and follow when developing objectives?
    a. FINER (feasible, interesting, novel, ethical, and relevant).
    b. SIMPLE (specific, immediate, measurable, practical, logical, and evaluative).
    c. POIC (patient, intervention, comparison, and outcome).
    d. None of the above.

20. Which federal agency offers health care–related grant awards?
    a. National Institutes of Health.
    b. Department of Defense.
    c. Department of Education.
    d. All of the above.

References

Accreditation Council for Occupational Therapy Education. (2007a). Accreditation standards for a doctoral-degree-level educational program for the occupational therapist. *American Journal of Occupational Therapy, 61*, 641–651.

Accreditation Council for Occupational Therapy Education. (2007b). Accreditation standards for a master's-degree-level educational program for the occupational therapist. *American Journal of Occupational Therapy, 61*, 652–661.

Accreditation Council for Occupational Therapy Education. (2007c). Accreditation standards for an educational program for the occupational therapy assistant. *American Journal of Occupational Therapy, 61*, 662–671.

American Occupational Therapy Association. (1991). Essentials and guidelines for an accredited educational program for the occupational therapist. *American Journal of Occupational Therapy, 45*, 1077–1084.

Annersten, M., & Wredling, R. (2006). How to write a research proposal. *European Diabetes Nursing, 3*, 102–105.

Community of Science. (n.d.). [Home page]. Retrieved May 1, 2009, from http://www.cos.com

Davis, B. (2005). *Writing a successful grant proposal* (Minnesota Council on Foundations reprint series). Retrieved May 1, 2009, from http://www.mcf.org/mcf/grant/writingagrantproposal.pdf

DePoy, E., & Gitlin, L. N. (1998). *Introduction to research: Understanding and applying multiples strategies* (2nd ed.). Toronto: Mosby.

Devine, E. B. (2009). The art of obtaining grants. *American Journal of Health-System Pharmacists, 66*, 580–587.

Geever, J. C. (2007). *The foundation center's guide to proposal writing* (5th ed.). New York: Foundation Center.

Gitlin, L. N., & Lyons, K. J. (2004). *Successful grant writing strategies for health and human service professionals* (2nd ed.). New York: Springer.

GrantSelect. (n.d.). *About GrantSelect.* Retrieved May 1, 2009, from http://www.grantselect.com/about/index.html

Leedy, P. D., & Ormrod, J. E. (2010). *Practical research* (9th ed.). Upper Saddle River, NJ: Pearson Education.

Long, R. F., & Orosz, J. (n.d.). *Approaching the foundation.* Retrieved July 21, 2010, from http://www.wkkf.org/knowledge-center/resources/2003/09/Approaching-The-Foundation.aspx

Miner, J., & Miner, L. (2009). *A guide to proposal planning and writing.* Retrieved May 1, 2009, from http://www.wm.edu/offices/grants/documents/miner.pdf

Nunez, J. B. (2008, May 27). New scientists learn lessons for success. *ASHA Leader, 13*(7), 32–33.

Pazell, S., & Jaffe, E. G. (2003). Entrepreneurial ventures. In G. L. McCormack, E. G. Jaffe, & M. Goodman-Lavey (Eds.), *The occupational therapy manager* (4th ed., pp. 219–255). Bethesda, MD: AOTA Press.

Zlotnick, C. (2001, February). *Grant writing.* Lecture given for Professional Development course, Samuel Merritt College, Oakland, CA.

Appendix 11.A. Proposal- and Grant-Writing Evidence Table

Topic	Evidence
Research	Accreditation Council for Occupational Therapy Education. (2007a). Accreditation standards for a doctoral-degree-level educational program for the occupational therapist. *American Journal of Occupational Therapy, 61,* 641–651. Accreditation Council for Occupational Therapy Education. (2007b). Accreditation standards for a master's-degree-level educational program for the occupational therapist. *American Journal of Occupational Therapy, 61,* 652–661. Accreditation Council for Occupational Therapy Education. (2007c). Accreditation standards for an educational program for the occupational therapy assistant. *American Journal of Occupational Therapy, 61,* 662–671. Leedy, P. D., & Ormrod, J. E. (2010). *Practical research* (9th ed.). Upper Saddle River, NJ: Pearson Education.
Grant proposals	Davis, B. (2005). *Writing a successful grant proposal* (Minnesota Council on Foundations reprint series). Retrieved May 1, 2009, from http://www.mcf.org/mcf/grant/writingagrantproposal.pdf Devine, E. B. (2009). The art of obtaining grants. *American Journal of Health–System Pharmacists, 66,* 580–587. Geever, J. C. (2007). *The foundation center's guide to proposal writing* (5th ed.). New York: Foundation Center. Gitlin, L. N., & Lyons, K. J. (2004). *Successful grant writing strategies for health and human service professionals* (2nd ed.). New York: Springer. Miner, J., & Miner, L. (2009). *A guide to proposal planning and writing.* Retrieved May 1, 2009, from http://www.wm.edu/offices/grants/documents/miner.pdf Nunez, J. B. (2008, May 27). New scientists learn lessons for success. *ASHA Leader, 13*(7), 32–33. Pazell, S., & Jaffe, E. G. (2003). Entrepreneurial ventures. In G. L. McCormack, E. G. Jaffe, & M. Goodman-Lavey (Eds.), *The occupational therapy manager* (4th ed., pp. 219–255). Bethesda, MD: AOTA Press. Zlotnick, C. (2001, February). *Grant writing.* Lecture given for Professional Development course, Samuel Merritt College, Oakland, CA.
Electronic database	Community of Science. (n.d.). [Home page]. Retrieved May 1, 2009, from http://www.cos.com

APPENDIX 11.B. COMMON NEW GRANT WRITER MISTAKES

Not adequately reading the grant announcement. Once a grant announcement is identified, it is important that it is carefully and thoroughly read. Carefully reading the announcement will help determine the eligibility criteria, clarify grant maker areas of interest, identify expectations of grant awardees, and determine additional questions or concerns for the grant maker contact to address for further clarification.

Suggestion: Read the grant announcement at least 2 or 3 times, have other team members read it, and discuss the requirements of each section with team members to help clarify all of its components for the best fit.

Not following the directions when completing the application. Once the grant application process begins, it is important to follow the directives provided as they are presented. Provide the information and documents that the grant maker requests. Do not add or take away from the directives unless specific guidance is provided in writing from the grant contact.

Suggestion: Carefully follow all specific word, character, and page count limitations set by the grant maker. Use the outline or sequence provided by the grant maker to present your application. Use an appendix for sharing additional information with the grant maker.

Not allotting enough time to prepare the grant application. Review deadline dates for all components of the grant as outlined in the announcement and application. Use good judgment and foresight to determine if grant application dates are feasible for the grant seeker.

Suggestion: As a grant seeker, know what are considered feasible time frames for internal approvals within your organization. Determine if a grant application that meets eligibility also meets feasibility for internal organization approval. Prepare a timeline to assist with meeting internal and external deadlines.

Not having pilot study data or previous work on which to build (especially for federal research grants). It is important to have a pilot study or baseline data to present the interest and efforts in a specific area of research. Use preexisting data or studies to build a supporting case for current research. Collaborate with other faculty, professionals, and community organizations with similar interests.

Suggestion: Show your track record or collaborations with other organizations to convince grant makers that you are the most qualified person to implement the grant.

Not matching objectives, narrative, and budget. Consistency is critical. All aspects of the grant application should support each another and be coherent to the grant maker or reader.

Suggestion: Align the objectives, narrative, and budget. Make sure the grant seeker's plan is reflected in the budget. The budget should support the plan.

Not including a clear evaluation plan. An evaluation plan should be developed and presented in the grant application. It is important to clarify how the program success will be measured.

Suggestion: Develop an evaluation plan that is realistic and doable for the grant seeker.

Appendix 11.C. Grant-Writing Online Resources

- **American Occupational Therapy Association Researcher Resources (members-only area):** http://www.aota.org/Educate/Researcher.aspx
- *Catalog of Federal Domestic Assistance:* http://www.gsa.gov/fdac/queryfdac.htm
- *Commerce Business Daily:* http://cbdnet.access.gpo.gov/index.html
- **Common Mistakes in NIH Applications:** http://www.ninds.nih.gov/funding/grantwriting_mistakes.htm
- *Federal Register:* http://www.access.gpo.gov/su_docs/aces/aces140.html
- **Grant Writing Tutorial (The Research Assistant)**: http://www.theresearchassistant.com/tutorial/index.asp
- **Grants.gov:** http://grants.gov
- *Guide for Writing a Funding Proposal (Michigan State University):* http://learnerassociates.net/proposal
- *Writing a Successful Grant Proposal (Minnesota Council on Foundations):* http://www.mcf.org/mcf/grant/writing.htm

Part III

Leading and Organizing

12
Communication in the Workplace

Brent Braveman, PhD, OTR/L, FAOTA

❖ Key Terms and Concepts

Business letters. A common form of written business communication primarily intended for external audiences to communicate specific and concrete information.

Business memos. A common form of written business communication primarily intended for internal audiences to communicate specific and concrete information.

Business plan. A formal, written document that outlines an organization's plan for a new product for which it will seek funding or a plan for a new business.

Kinesics. Body language.

Netiquette. Guidelines for effective and polite use of Web-based communication such as e-mail, listserv mailing lists, and electronic bulletin boards and forums.

Paralanguage. The nonverbal elements of communication used to modify meaning and convey emotion.

Paralinguistics. The study of nonverbal elements of communication, including kinesics.

Proxemics. The study of space, including use of personal space during communication.

❖ Learning Objectives

After completing this chapter, you should be able to do the following:

- Identify and describe the common forms of communication managers use.
- Define key terms such as *paralanguage*, *proxemics*, and *netiquette*.
- Identify advantages and disadvantages of various forms of communication media, including e-mail, business memos, business letters, and listserv mailings.
- Identify mistakes and pitfalls associated with common forms of communication.
- Identify strategies for improving the effectiveness of common forms of communication.

In today's globally connected and technologically savvy world, communication is becoming both more convenient and more complex all the time. In just a few decades, we have moved from relying primarily on face-to-face and hard-copy, written communication to a heavy reliance on electronic communication that allows us to be in two different rooms, buildings, or even countries and communicate in real time.

Communication is a well-developed field of study with considerable research and theory. Communication theories address both written and verbal interpersonal communication, communication to individuals as well as to the public and groups, communication in mass media, and intercultural communication (Braveman, 2006). Research in the area of communication occurs across multiple disciplines, including communication studies, psychology, organi-

zational development, speech–language pathology, business and marketing, computer science, and anthropology (Bauer, Kim, Mody, & Wildman, 2009).

Barker (2006) identified three levels of communication: (1) *action,* or the reason people communicate, such as influencing others with their ideas; (2) the *information* that is exchanged when people communicate; and (3) the existing *relationship* between the persons involved in the communication. Managers often focus most on action and information and sometimes do not attend adequately to the relationship between the message sender and the message receiver. Although managerial communication is not therapeutic, managers can be more effective if they pay close attention to relationships to support ongoing performance. Negative experiences with communication can have a negative influence on future relationships.

COMMUNICATION AND MANAGEMENT

Managers often think differently about communicating with peers or those they supervise than they do as occupational therapists or occupational therapy assistants communicating and interacting with clients. For example, when communicating in a therapeutic relationship, managers may attempt to remain client-centered and to minimize sharing of their own perspective so as not to overly influence the decision-making process of the client. It is more likely, however, that managers consciously want to influence the outcomes of decisions and the thinking of their peers and subordinates. There are times when managers want to remain objective to allow decisions to be made by a group that reflect a majority view, but there are many times when it is the role of the manager to set a vision or direction for the future and to communicate that to others. There are also times when managers want to directly and clearly tell someone what to do. Part of the complexity of communicating as a manager is deciding what the goal is for one's communication and how to use both the communication medium and one's sense of self to best ensure that the message one intends to send is received.

Whether at work or in their personal lives, most managers (like most people) have experienced problems with communication. For example, someone shares information with a coworker or friend, thinking that the intent behind the communication, the content of the message, and the anticipated reaction are clear, only to discover later that all three assumptions were wrong! Things also can go wrong with the context of the communication, such as inadequate time to send or receive the message, misinterpretation of information, or actions on the part of the message sender or receiver that send unintended messages. Moreover, potential causes contributing to miscommunication include inaccurate inferences by the receiver, word-meaning confusion, differing perceptions, conflicting nonverbal messages, and cultural and gender differences (Roebuck, 2006).

One key to effective communication is to make wise choices about when and how to communicate. The manager must select the appropriate communication medium, setting, and timing. Timing includes not only when the communication is initiated but also how much time should or must be devoted for the exchange of information to be constructive and effective. Much of daily communication happens quickly and without thought; although they should not obsess over every conversation, managers can improve communication overall by developing good work and communication habits that they use consistently. Becoming familiar with the most common mistakes and pitfalls can help managers avoid them. Resources to help the manager are plentiful and easily accessible on the Internet and in local bookstore in the business section.

Nonverbal Communication

Nonverbal communication is referred to as *paralanguage*. The study of nonverbal communication, called *paralinguistics*, includes *kinesics*, or what is commonly called "body language." According to Perkins (2008), one uses nonverbal language to fulfill seven functions: (1) to substitute for words, (2) to control the impressions of others, (3) to complement one's spoken words, (4) to contradict one's spoken words, (5) to confirm the messages of others, (6) to distinguish relationships between oneself and others, and (7) to maintain congruent understanding of messages in shared contexts such as a work environment. Common elements of paralanguage that can influence the message being sent and convey meaning beyond the spoken word are listed in Table 12.1.

A closely related area of study in interpersonal communication is *proxemics*, or the study of the use of space, including personal space, during a conversation. The preferred level of physical closeness or distance during face-to-face communication varies according to culture, and being too close or too far away during a conversation may make the other person feel uncomfortable or communicate disinterest. Natives of the United States tend to prefer maintaining arm's length during conversation, but in other areas of the world, such as the Middle East, much less distance is preferred during conversation (Axtell, 2007). Managers can use elements of proxemics to influence the dynamics of communication by, for example, moving out from behind a desk to speak to an employee, which can communicate openness and teamwork, or staying behind the desk during a performance assessment or progressive disciplinary action, which can communicate control and authority.

Because the messages people send are influenced by paralanguage and space, managers can be more effective if they are aware of their own facial expressions, the tone of their voice, and the distance between themselves and the other individual; each of these factors can be controlled and can influence the outcome of the communication. Two helpful strategies for learning more about how one comes across nonverbally are to be videotaped giving a presentation or running a meeting and to be observed by supportive peers or subordinates who then share their feedback. Those who watch or listen to recordings of themselves speaking often are surprised by nonverbal habits such as gestures and facial expressions or changes in tone or word emphasis that punctuate their communication without their even being aware. Some managers use this method to rehearse an important speech they must make to the staff to introduce a change in policy or organizational structure that may evoke an emotional response.

Face-to-Face and Voice Communication

Dyads

Talking face-to-face with one other person is one of the most common and important forms of communication for a manager. The most sensitive of topics, such as employee progressive discipline or work with an employee to improve his or her performance, is often carried out while sitting face-to-face. Braveman (2006) outlined the following seven strategies for effective conversations:

Table 12.1. Common Elements of Nonverbal Communication and Examples of Their Impact

Element	Example of impact
Volume	Louder volume may communicate emotion such as anger and may be used to gain or keep someone's attention. Confidence and assertiveness may be reflected in a slightly louder volume. Lower volume may be used to draw someone into a conversation.
Pitch and inflection	Lower pitch is sometimes associated with maturity and credibility. Changes in pitch or inflection may reflect charisma or energy, but too much inflection in the work setting may decrease credibility.
Tone of voice	Higher tones can communicate increased emotion and intensity and lower tones may communicate a lack of interest or passion or a sense of calmness and steadiness.
Emphasis	Emphasizing a word can change the meaning of a sentence—for example, "*Why* did you do that?" versus "Why did you do *that*?"
Silence	Silence may communicate a variety of meanings, including respect or disapproval, depending on the context.
Facial expression	Facial movements may intentionally or unwittingly communicate emotions such as anger, impatience, doubt, or surprise.
Eye contact	Sustained eye contact may convey candor and openness, and downward glances are generally associated with modesty. Higher-ups in organizations generally maintain eye contact longer than subordinates.
Gestures	Hand signals and arm or face movements are used to send an understood message, but they can be culturally misinterpreted. For example, the thumbs-up sign means "all right" or "all set" in the United States but means money in Japan and refers to certain body parts in South America (Axtell, 2007).
Body posture	Sitting upright can communicate interest, whereas slouching can communicate boredom. Crossing the arms can communicate resistance, and relaxing the arms and leaning forward can communicate openness to discussion.

1. "Ask open-ended questions to elicit informative answers and to avoid giving the impression that you have already made decisions."

2. "Ask focused questions that are not too broad to help guide listeners toward the type of information that will help them best make their point or advocate for their position while limiting extraneous information given in response."

3. "Ask for additional details, examples, and the speaker's thoughts and impressions to show genuine interest and to indicate that you are open to the speaker's message."

4. "Paraphrase or restate what you heard, remembering that the real purpose of paraphrasing is not to clarify what the other person actually meant, but to show what it meant to you."

5. "Check your perceptions of the other person's feelings by describing them, being careful to avoid any expression of approval or disapproval. Objectively state what you believe the other person seems to be feeling."

6. "Describe behavior without making accusations or generalizations about motives, attitudes, or personality traits."

7. "Clarify agreement and summarize discussions by reviewing what has been decided or agreed on and any course of action that will be taken." (p. 314)

In addition to these suggestions, whenever possible, taking a moment to consciously plan important communication can be very helpful. Although such planning is not always possible, it can be very effective, especially if a conversation may become tense or emotionally difficult. Managers even might consider putting main topics they wish to address during a particular conversation in a short bulleted list they can use as an agenda to guide the communication more systematically. Managers also should consider keeping notes of conversations held as part of an employee's personnel record in case progressive discipline becomes necessary.

Group Communication

The use of small groups, particularly interdisciplinary or intradisciplinary teams, is very common in occupational therapy practice to coordinate client intervention, plan programs, solve problems, and improve work production and efficiency. Strategies for running effective meetings can improve small group communication by providing structure for both the group leader and the group members; such strategies include starting and ending the meeting on time, having a written agenda with time frames for each topic, and providing the agenda to group members ahead of time. Some managers have a process for tracking suggestions and recording concerns that are not on topic for discussion at another time. In addition, training for teams, on issues like group decision making and ways to identify the advantages and disadvantages of each action, can be very useful. There are readily available resources for helping the manager run effective meetings and manage group dynamics in meetings and ongoing group processes (e.g., team projects); a well-known example is *The Team Handbook* (Scholtes, Joiner, Streibel, & Mann, 2003). Organizations such as the Institute for Healthcare Improvement (www.ihi.org) provide free online resources, and entering the terms "running effective meetings" in a search engine results in millions of hits!

Managing a group process, especially decision making, is a critical skill set for occupational therapy managers. Managing communication within a group such that all participants perceive that they have had a fair opportunity to voice their opinions and to influence the group decision contributes to the positive functioning of the group. Decisions can be made through either consensus or voting. Consensus takes time, but ultimately all members of the group agree to genuinely support a group action, even if it is not the action they would have taken if acting alone. Voting is a popular mode of decision making and is typically thought to be ultimately "fair"; however, it can result in a win–lose situation if the losers become disenfranchised, leading to future conflict. Managers with effective group communication skills can guide a group through a problem-solving or decision-making process without alienating group members or creating tension and hard feelings that will limit future group interaction.

Telephone Conversations

Managers can spend a tremendous amount of time on the telephone. Speaking with others via the telephone can be effective if managers develop and practice good phone habits and etiquette. An effective telephone call comprises three parts—the opening, the middle, and the end—and the following guidelines can help managers make the most of each step:

1. Although it may be popular in general to answer the phone with "hey," in professional telephone conversations, answer all calls with a salutation and state your name, even if answering your office phone. Answering with something simple and straightforward, such as, "Hello, this Brent," can reassure the caller that he or she has reached the correct person and that you are ready for the call. If placing a call, introduce yourself, state why you are calling, and check whether he or she has the time to speak with you before you proceed. The greeting on your answering machine or voicemail should include your name, perhaps your credentials, the organization or department name, and a request to leave a brief message and telephone number so you can get back to the caller.

2. The middle of the telephone call should clearly establish the reason for the call and the objectives you wish to achieve. For example, are you calling to give or obtain information, to discuss an issue, or to make a request for future action? The often-cited approach to verbal communication of "Tell them what you are going to say, tell them what you have to say, and then tell them what you said" is directly applicable to most telephone calls. For complex topics, you might consider preparing notes to help you address all issues to be covered and keep on topic.

3. Before ending a telephone call, first ensure that the person to whom you are speaking is also ready to end the call. If you have limited time, tell the other person at the outset, and during the conversation, if time is running short, make the person aware of it and arrange to call him or her back and speak again at a different time. Then confirm his or her understanding of the information that was exchanged and whether there is any additional action to be taken by either of you. Thank the person for speaking with you, and close the call with a pleasant wish, such as, "Have a good afternoon."

Written Communication

Occupational therapy students may think that by the time they graduate, they know about as much as they need to about writing and documentation. However, the expectations for writing in a business environment are very different than those for writing in an academic program. As with each of the forms of communication addressed in this chapter, the occupational therapy manager does not need to enter a first managerial position knowing everything about business writing; the following sections summarize key points about written business communication, and additional resources are listed at the end of the chapter.

Business Memos

The business memo is a short written form of communication that may be in hard copy form (i.e., on paper) or within the body of an e-mail. The purpose of a memo is typically to inform one or more persons within the organization about something specific without a lot of detail, although additional documents may be attached to or referred to in the memo. For example, a memo might be used to notify staff of a change in office supply vendors or of a new policy or procedure. It is important to choose both the memo's audience and the information it contains carefully. Only those persons who must become aware of the content should receive the memo; copying the memo to superiors or others may send unintended messages that may be perceived as negative (e.g., that one is playing office politics). As with any form of written communication, managers must be extremely careful about including confidential or highly sensitive information because once a memo is distributed, it can become public information, and senders lose control over who sees it and recipients may misinterpret its context in the future. Therefore, for sensitive content it is good practice to send a hard copy on letterhead with "confidential" printed on the envelope.

When memos are commonly used in an organization, they are typically formatted to look somewhat similar. Figure 12.1 shows a common format for a memo that includes the audience (either an individual or a group), the sender, the date, and the subject. The spelling, title, and credentials of all persons listed should be double-checked for accu-

Memo

To:	John Stafford, PhD, PT/L
	Director of Physical Therapy
From:	Brent Braveman, PhD, OTR/L, FAOTA
	Director of Professional Education
Date:	September 1, 2010
Re:	New Office Supply Vendor

I wish to inform you that as of October 1, 2009, our new vendor for office supplies will be Chicago Office Supply Corporation.

After a thorough review and negotiation with Chicago Office Supply and our current vendor, I have identified that we will save approximately 12% on office supplies in the coming fiscal year by switching vendors.

Our current vendor will make its usual delivery on the last Monday of this month, and Chicago Office Supply will begin its deliveries on the first Monday in October.

There should be no disruption in availability of supplies. Please inform your support staff of this change, and let me know if there are any questions.

Thank you.

Figure 12.1 Common memo format.

racy. The content of a memo usually fits on one page and is specific and focused on the topic in the memo header. Memos often are used to ask the receiver to take some action, even if that "action" is simply to become aware of a new or revised policy or procedure. The action should be clearly and directly stated so that there is no ambiguity about expectations; complex problems and issues should not be addressed in a memo.

Formal Business Letter

Formal business letters are generally typed on the organization's letterhead and typically are used when communicating to persons outside the organization. The level of detail and complexity addressed in a letter should be limited, although letters may be more detailed than memos. The addresses of both the sender and the person to whom the letter is addressed are included at the top of the letter, just below the date. A formal salutation is included, and it is important to double-check details such as the spelling of names, credentials, and titles. It is usually safer to be more formal at first—for example, by using the salutation "Dear Dr. Councill" rather than the more informal "Dear Mr. Councill"—when one is sure that the person's credentials call for a formal designation. Likewise, "Ms." should be used for a female recipient when one is not sure whether she is single or married. Whenever possible, an unspecific and impersonal salutation such as "To Whom It May Concern" should be avoided because it is less effective in creating a personal or professional bond with the reader.

The body of a business letter is also brief, although it may be longer than a single page. Writing in a concise style with shorter sentences is typically more effective and easily understood. A common format for a business letter is to include an opening paragraph stating the reason for the letter, one or more middle paragraphs containing the body of the message to be delivered, and a closing paragraph that makes a request, states an action to be taken, or otherwise indicates if more follow-up or correspondence is necessary. Finally, a closing statement, most commonly "Sincerely," followed by a space for the letter writer's handwritten signature and his or her typewritten name ends the business letter. If the stationery letterhead does not include the writer's mailing address or other contact information (i.e., phone number, e-mail address), this information should be provided.

One helpful strategy for novice writers is to use a business letter template that can be found easily on the Internet or in many word processing software packages. Using a template, especially at first, can cue the letter writer for details and help ensure that the letter is properly formatted and professional in appearance. Figure 12.2 shows a common format for a business letter.

Business Plans

A *business plan* is a formal, precisely written document that outlines an organization's plan for a new product for which it will seek funding or a plan for a new business. Business plans often address both strategic and operational aspects

September 1, 2009

Brent Braveman, PhD, OTR/L, FAOTA
1919 W. Taylor Street
Chicago, IL 60612

Todd J. Councill, OTR/L
President
Ellicott City Therapy, Inc.
2901 W. Ellicott Street
Ellicott, IL 60638

Dear Mr. Councill:

    The presentation you gave yesterday on documentation strategies for facilitating reimbursement was excellent. I heard numerous positive comments from staff members who noted that they learned a great deal and plan to incorporate your suggestions. The handouts you provided will be most helpful, especially to new staff members who join us in the future.

    I also wish to accept your invitation to visit your facility to gain additional information on the documentation and billing systems you have implemented. I am optimistic that these systems will work here at our facilities. I am aware that you will be out of town for most of this month and will contact you after your return to schedule a visit.

    Thank you again for such an informative presentation, and I wish you safe travels.

Sincerely,

Brent Braveman

Brent Braveman, PhD, OTR/L, FAOTA
Director, Occupational Therapy
Ellicott City General Hospital

Figure 12.2 Common business letter format.

of a proposed new venture (see Chapter 9 for more information on business plans).

    Business plans are the summary of an intensive marketing process that includes an analysis of an organization's strengths, weaknesses, opportunities, and threats; an analysis of the internal and external environments; a description of potential customers; and a thorough and specific description of the product to be developed or the new business. Business plans are typically developed as part of the process for requesting financing from a bank or other funder or for justifying the outlay of capital and resources for a new product by an existing organization. The complexity involved and the time necessary to write an effective business plan should not be underestimated. Templates to assist with formatting the plan, sample business plans, and other resources are available from organizations such as the U.S. Small Business Administration (SBA; www.sba.gov). The SBA and local Chambers of Commerce offer both online and face-to-face training. The key sections of a business plan and a short description of each are included in Table 12.2.

E-mail and Texting

The use of e-mail and text messages has exploded in the past decade since the advent of cellular technology has allowed phones to fulfill sophisticated functions. Although there is no denying the advantages of e-mail and text messages in regard to convenience, their use in the business world is fraught with potential problems. Increasing attention and controversy have accompanied the negative impact that "instant communication" has on work productivity; constant distraction by incoming e-mail or texts and the treatment of nonemergent communication as an emergency can lower performance and disrupt interpersonal relations. The abbreviated and informal content and style of these communications also can be problematic in the workplace.

    Another controversy with e-mail and texting involves the fact that electronic messages can be exchanged much more quickly than hard-copy memos or letters. This speed can be problematic if people begin to expect an immediate reply; most managers have experienced a conversation beginning, "I sent you an e-mail an hour ago, and you haven't replied!" The fact that e-mail communication takes place almost in

Table 12.2. Common Elements of a Business Plan

Element	Description
Executive summary	A concise summary of all parts of the plan, which can determine whether readers, including possible financers, continue to read beyond the first page. It is often limited to one page and is prepared last.
Organization description	A description of the organization's mission, history, current status, strategies, and plans for the future.
Management and organization	A list of key members of the management team or organizational leadership and their titles. If outside persons such as consultants are key to the project, they should be also listed and described here.
Market and competitors	A description of the market for the project or business, current and potential customers, and competitors. Factors that influence the behavior of customers and the current position of the organization in the market are included.
Product or service	A summary of critical elements and qualities of the product to be delivered, its readiness for delivery or what must be done to ready it for market, how it is like or different from competing products, and the costs of any further development.
Marketing and sales plans	A description of the market research on the product, how it will be promoted, and the means for promotion (e.g., mailings, advertising). To convince financers to invest, efforts should be made to present conservative estimates of what might be accomplished.
Financial information	Financial forecasts, including statements of cash flow and income, that are consistent with the organization's history and the other sections of the business plan. A specific request for investment stating how much money is needed, why it is needed, and how it will be used must be provided. Most importantly, projections on when the organization expects to break even and to begin to make money on the product are provided.

real time may be advantageous at times, but the manager must remember that e-mail recipients do not have access to the nonverbal and paralanguage cues that add meaning to the spoken word and easily can misconstrue meaning. For example, one may intend to communicate sarcasm or to be humorous in an e-mail, but the receiver may get the impression that one is really angry.

The term *netiquette* was coined to refer to polite behavior when communicating by e-mail or in other virtual formats such as listserv e-mail lists or electronic bulletin boards and forums. Netiquette guidelines can help prevent serious miscommunication, and there are a growing number of online sources to aid users. It is possible to incorporate some aspects of paralanguage into e-mail messages, but this must be done with great care. For example, typing in all capital letters to bring attention to words may be interpreted as shouting. Another example is the use of *emoticons*, which are symbols or combinations of punctuation used to indicate emotion. For example, the combination of letter and symbols "<G>" indicates that the sender is grinning or saying something in jest. Braveman (2006) provided the following short list of strategies to avoid common mistakes when using e-mail:

- Never write and send e-mail or text messages when you are angry.
- Do not attach unnecessary files.
- Do not overuse the high-priority option when sending e-mail.
- Do not reference earlier messages without including them as part of the "message thread."
- Proofread e-mail and text messages before sending them.
- Use the "Reply to All" feature with caution, especially on group e-mail distribution lists.
- Be sure that abbreviations and emoticons are clear and unambiguous.
- Do not copy or forward a message or attachment without permission.
- Do not use e-mail or text messages to discuss confidential information.
- Do not send or forward e-mails or text messages containing libelous, defamatory, offensive, racist, or obscene remarks.
- Use the cc: field (copying others on an e-mail) sparingly.

Text messages should be used very little in business environments and only if use of this communication medium is well established in the culture of the organization. Texting can be useful for sharing short and concrete information such as confirming an appointment time or an address. Text messages can be perceived as highly impersonal, however, and managers should be careful not to use this communication mechanism as a substitute for other, more personal modes such as a telephone call or walking down the hallway to see a colleague face to face.

Listserv Mailing Lists and Electronic Bulletin Boards and Forums
"Listservs" got their name from a computer program called Listserv; this and similar programs allow people to create, manage, and control electronic mailing lists of recipients

who share an interest in a certain topic. Some lists are public, and anyone with an e-mail account can subscribe to the list. Some lists are private or confidential, in which case the list's owner can decide who may join the list (Indiana University Information Technology Services, 2008). An electronic bulletin board or forum discussion group is a similar mechanism in which persons who join a group or who are granted posting privileges may debate and exchange ideas, make announcements, or seek information and advice.

Listserv mailing lists and electronic bulletin boards and forums are useful tools for sharing and obtaining information, and they have proliferated widely in the professional world. An advantage of this communication mechanism is that one can communicate relatively easily and at low cost with professionals all over the world and make new contacts with persons sharing similar interests whom one might not otherwise have encountered. Communication also can be convenient because one can read messages and post when one has the time to do so. Many lists allow one to forward messages directly to an e-mail account or access them when visiting the associated Web site.

As with any form of written communication, caution is required in using these technologies. When one posts online, one no longer controls who will receive the message. Others may forward the message to persons who are not subscribed or may quote the message out of context. Some services are searchable on the Internet, and what one thought was a private communication may become a very public record of the communication. Others will draw conclusions about occupational therapy managers and form an image of the type of professional they are on the basis of how they conduct themselves in using these communication mechanisms.

Web Conferencing and Social Media

Meeting face-to-face is not always convenient or possible, especially with the high cost of travel. However, with the advent of new software platforms and networks such as Web conferencing and social media sites such as Facebook, MySpace, or OT Connections, effective alternatives now exist. Using a Web conferencing system can allow managers to meet with their colleagues online and collaborate in real time over long distances. Meeting attendees can deliver a presentation, kick off a project, brainstorm ideas, edit files, collaborate on whiteboards, and negotiate deals from their personal computer at a fraction of the cost of a face-to-face meeting and without the hassle and time required with travel. To hold a Web conference, the organization sponsoring the conference must subscribe to a service. Participants in the conference call a toll-free number and log in to a Web site using a link provided to them. The moderator of the conference runs the meeting much as if it were being held in person. There are typically mechanisms for participants to indicate that they wish to speak, and questions may be submitted to the moderator in writing electronically to be answered by the moderator or another participant.

Web conferencing can be a successful alternative to meeting face-to-face, but naturally it has limitations. As the number of participants grows, it may be increasingly difficult to manage conversation or questions. In addition, although one can hear the voice of participants when they speak, one cannot see them, so one has access only to certain elements of paralanguage, increasing the risk of misunderstandings.

Social media sites combine several forms of electronic communication, such as bulletin boards or forums for threaded discussions, blogs, groups for persons sharing common interests, the ability to post pictures, and status posting for participants to let others know what they are doing. These sites have many advantages. Most are free of charge and easily accessible. They facilitate sharing information with people located across the globe and can make it easy for someone to get answers to questions or information from others very quickly.

However, those using these sites must use caution. Because communication can be informal, some of the same warnings for e-mail must be heeded. For example, some persons have lost their jobs when pictures or information have been posted that employers deemed inappropriate. It is also easy to insult others without being aware that you have done so. Finally, many users do not consider the permanence of information that they post; once you post something, you lose control of who might see it. These sites blur the lines of personal and professional communication, so they should be used with caution.

COMMUNICATION WITH THE PUBLIC

Managers often have to communicate to groups of people in the form of presentations for the purpose of educating them, as in the case of in-service education or training programs, or convincing them to take action. Sometimes these presentations are tied to the marketing and promotion of clinical programs. A description of the full marketing process, including market research, is beyond the scope of this chapter; however, the basic strategies for effective presentations apply to verbal promotion of products and services as well. Moreover, as occupational therapists work toward achieving the profession's *Centennial Vision* (American Occupational Therapy Association, 2007), presentations to the public on the value of occupational therapy will, it is hoped, become more recognized by and important to the general public. Table 12.3 includes some suggestions for questions to guide the development of effective presentations. In addition, many Web sites, books, and training courses are devoted to giving effective presentations and can be easily found with an Internet search.

CONCLUSION

This chapter has highlighted the most common forms of communication used in management, including verbal and nonverbal communication with individuals and groups. Many of the advantages and cautions associated with each

Table 12.3. Questions to Guide Effective Presentations

Presentation activity	Success strategies
Questions about your audience	• How many people will attend? • What is the background of the attendees (e.g., age, gender, education, reason for attending)? • What prior exposure to your topic will your audience members have? • What are the expectations of your audience? • Will this be your only interaction with your audience, or will you see them again?
Questions to guide presentations to inform or explain	• What does your audience need to hear to understand what the presentation is about and what they will learn in your presentation? • How can you relate new or unfamiliar information to information the audience already knows? • How can you connect with the audience to establish a rapport and increase your credibility? • What key points do you need to review to help the attendees recognize what they have learned?
Questions to guide a presentation to persuade	• How can you establish rapport with the audience and establish a common view? On what do you already agree? • What questions can you ask the audience to get them in a "yes" mode and make them more susceptible to your message? • How can you "close the deal" and ask your attendees for agreement? • What it will take to convince the audience to take action? • What can you ask your audience to commit to before they leave the presentation?

form of communication were presented, as well as strategies for making communication by the manager more effective.

In many of today's environments, there are pitfalls when managers are pressured to communicate with increasing speed and use multiple communication media. It is easy to underestimate the impact and complexity of some of these forms of communication. With good intentions, the manager may make embarrassing mistakes, create hard feelings and tension in the workplace, or appear less competent. Although it is easy to take communication for granted, it is in the best interest of the manager to develop sound habits of communication to avoid the mistakes outlined in this chapter.

Resources to guide managers in communicating effectively in all contexts and with all communication media are readily accessible. Web sites, books, software programs, and training courses are easily found with Internet searches. Communication is an underpinning of nearly everything the manager does in today's globally and technically connected world. Evolving communication platforms provide increased flexibility and options for communicating with others. However, managers must remain aware of the limitations of each form of communication and potential problems with emerging communication platforms such as social media sites.

Case Examples

LEVEL I FIELDWORK

Chandra was a Level I fieldwork student who always considered herself actively engaged in the learning process, attentive, polite, and an effective communicator. During the second week of her fieldwork experience, however, Chandra's supervisor told her that one of the teachers and a classroom assistant perceived her as bored, disinterested, and distant. She had never received similar feedback and was quite concerned because it was so clearly different than how she perceived herself. Chandra decided to contact the academic fieldwork coordinator (AFWC) at her university for assistance.

Chandra's AFWC, Becky, was not completely surprised at the feedback that Chandra received; she had made similar assumptions about Chandra in class based on her nonverbal communication (body language). In discussions with Becky, Chandra mentioned that there was a Level II fieldwork student with whom she had become friendly. Becky suggested that Chandra ask the student to observe her and provide feedback, if this felt safe and comfortable for Chandra.

Chandra asked the other student to observe her during an individualized education program meeting and the districtwide occupational therapy staff meeting. The student confirmed the feedback that Chandra had received from her supervisor and her AFWC, noting that Chandra's posture was slumped, she took several deep

(continued)

Case Examples *(cont.)*

breaths that appeared to be sighs, and she closed her eyes from time to time, which could be interpreted as disinterest. With her level of self-awareness changed, Chandra began to work on more consciously supporting her verbal messages with paralanguage that was consistent.

LEVEL II FIELDWORK

Kevin, a Level II fieldwork student in his 7th week, was preparing to complete a common assignment given to fieldwork students, which was to prepare and deliver an in-service education presentation to the staff. Kevin decided to develop a presentation on the value of membership in the American Occupational Therapy Association (AOTA) and to provide supporting materials and give the staff a tour of the AOTA Web site. Although he had been involved in numerous group project presentations in school, Kevin was nervous about presenting his first in-service program and being the sole presenter for an entire lunchtime.

As a first step, Kevin conducted an Internet search on "preparing effective presentations" and found numerous sites that ranged from free sites sponsored by universities to commercially available training programs. He quickly found that by narrowing his search to terms such as "preparing effective handouts," he could obtain helpful hints for every aspect of planning his presentation and even software templates for handouts and visual presentations.

Before beginning to work on his presentation, Kevin found out more about his audience and their current level of understanding of the benefits of AOTA membership and their familiarity with the AOTA Web site. He also verified the amount of time he had for his presentation. Using easily accessible resources, Kevin was able to develop an organized and effective presentation that reflected positively on him as a student.

FIRST-TIME MANAGER

Kavita had recently accepted her first management position after 8 years of practice as a staff therapist in a large mental health facility. Since she started work, Kavita was consistently successful and typically received positive feedback about being an effective team member and showing a high level of professionalism. Several times since she became a manager, however, Kavita sent e-mails that were received very poorly.

After some self-reflection, Kavita realized that in each case she had replied when she was busy and feeling overwhelmed. She did not spend much time reviewing her message before sending it. In one case, she realized after hitting "Send" that she had replied to everyone on the original message rather than just the sender, and her reply was quite informal and might be taken as sarcastic if one was not familiar with her sense of humor. Moreover, Kavita had had several difficult conversations in the hallway with her supervisor and other managers. She realized that when she was a staff therapist, communication was often less formal, and that although staff members were accustomed to sharing information quickly, managers seemed to be more careful in their conversations.

Kavita decided to do some problem solving. She created a simple checklist to function as a cue for her e-mail communication and scheduled specific times of the day to answer e-mail so that she did not need to rush through her messages. She also decided to approach Kim, the director of art therapy and a more experienced manager, for advice on how to communicate more effectively on the management level. Finally, Kavita spent some time on the Internet and at the local bookstore reviewing resources on professional communication and updating her netiquette skills.

MANAGER

Ava, an experienced occupational therapy manager, applied for the position of director of a rehabilitation department in the hospital where she worked. She was preparing for a series of interviews for the position and became aware that an important duty for the new director would be to plan and oversee the department's move into a new wing of the hospital. In addition to planning the typical space for clinical equipment, such as an activities of daily living room, a kitchen, mats, and private treatment rooms, Ava began to think about other recommendations she would have for the space.

The rehabilitation department currently occupied a small and crowded space in an older section of the building. In addition to limitations in technology, the physical layout of the staff offices and public spaces challenged staff and managers alike. It was sometimes impossible to find a quiet space to have a private conversation; staff members sometimes chose to go outside the department and use their cell phones because they felt they had more privacy than when they placed calls from their desks.

Ava decided to do some reading before the interviews to prepare for questions she might receive about planning the new space. As she reviewed materials, she became fascinated with the concept of *proxemics*, or the study of the use of space. She read examples of how to arrange the flow of rooms and how to choose and place furniture to create different emotional reactions. She found descriptions of strategies to plan for the flexible use of space to facilitate communication between staff and their clients in clinical spaces and between staff members in office spaces.

When Ava met with the chief operating officer (COO) as part of the interview process, the COO was impressed with Ava's explanation of proxemics and her level of understanding of how space can be used to influence communication. The COO was particularly impressed that Ava was considering both high-tech and low-tech influences on communication systems and noted that this set Ava apart from the other candidates for the position of director.

❖ Learning Activities

1. Search the Internet for the two terms among the following that interest you most:
   - Netiquette
   - Email dos and don'ts
   - Business writing
   - Nonverbal communication.

   Spend a few minutes looking at some of the resources, and bookmark any that you think would be helpful.

2. Explore the templates in the word processing software program you use at home, work, or school. Identify templates appropriate for communication in the workplace (e.g., memos) and open them. Explore how you might customize the templates—for example, by adding your name or company logo. Identify the elements of the templates you would use most often to communicate in the workplace.

3. Partner with a friend, a classmate at school, or a colleague at work. Ask the person to observe you during meetings or group functions over a 2- or 3-month period, or long enough that you become less likely to consciously alter your behavior. Have the person give you feedback on your body language and nonverbal behavior (e.g., facial expressions). Ask the person to note whether your paralanguage was consistent with your spoken communication. Also ask the person to note any behaviors that might send unwanted messages to those present.

4. Find an opportunity to practice each of the following, and use the guidelines included in this chapter or found during your Internet search (in Learning Activity 1):
   - Place a business phone call after planning the opening, middle, and end of the conversation. For example, you might call a credit card company to verify account information or a local store to get a price for a particular item. After the call, spend a few moments reflecting on what you did well and whether there is anything you would change.
   - Write a formal business letter—for example, to thank a fieldwork supervisor, to request information on a product, or to request an appointment for an informational interview or observation experience.
   - Write a message to a listserv mailing list or post a message to an electronic bulletin board or discussion group. Before hitting "Send" or "Post," review the message with a fellow student or colleague and get his or her feedback.

5. Offer to take the lead in planning a presentation at school or work. Complete each of the following steps:
   - Do an analysis of your audience.
   - Develop an outline, including objectives, for the presentation.
   - Identify the type of presentation and its primary purpose.
   - Use a template and/or an online list of dos and don'ts to assess the effectiveness of your handouts and other materials.

SUGGESTED WEB SITES

- **About.com (for e-mail netiquette):** http://email.about.com/od/emailnetiquette/tp/core_netiquette.htm
- **The Owl at Purdue—Online Writing Lab:** http://owl.english.purdue.edu/owl
- **U.S. Small Business Association (for business plans):** http://www.sba.gov/smallbusinessplanner/index.html
- **Microsoft Office Help and How-To Home Page (for help in creating presentations and handouts):** http://office.microsoft.com/en-us/help/default.aspx

✓ Multiple-Choice Questions

1. The term *paralinguistics* means the study of
   a. Use of communication by paraprofessionals.
   b. Nonverbal communication.
   c. Nontraditional communication.
   d. Virtual communication.

2. A business memo is used primarily to communicate
   a. With an internal audience.
   b. With an external audience.
   c. Only to higher-ups in the organization.
   d. Only to subordinates in the organization.

3. Which of the following is not true in regard to the use of Web conferencing?
   a. It is less expensive than meeting face-to-face.
   b. It can allow group editing of a document.
   c. It typically includes a visual presentation.
   d. It is easier to read cues based on elements of paralanguage

4. Which of the following is true as a strategy for successful e-mail?
   a. Make frequent use of the high priority option when sending e-mail so that others pay attention to it.
   b. Reply to all persons on the original mailing list to ensure transparency.
   c. Use abbreviations whenever possible to keep messages very short.
   d. Only reference earlier messages if you include them as part of the message thread.

5. The term *proxemics* means the study of
   a. Nonverbal communication.
   b. Written communication.
   c. Virtual communication.
   d. Use of space.

6. *Netiquette* is a term that most accurately refers to guidelines for
   a. Safely searching the Internet.
   b. Effective online communication.
   c. Choosing communication software.
   d. Effective telephone communication.

7. Which of the following is true in regard to the use of texting in management communication?
   a. Texting is one of the more formal modes of management communication.
   b. It is easy to become too informal in a text message.
   c. Texting is a slower form of communication.
   d. Texting has become universally accepted for management communication.

8. Which of the following is not true in regard to listserv mailing lists?
   a. All listserv mailing lists are open to the public.
   b. *Listserv* is a proprietary name for a particular product.
   c. Listserv mailing lists are often free to the participants.
   d. Listserv posts may sometimes be found in a search of the Internet.

9. According to Barker (2006), communication occurs at three levels. Which of the following is not one of those levels?
   a. Space.
   b. Relationship.
   c. Action.
   d. Information.

10. All of the following are common suggestions for facilitating effective communication in meetings except
    a. Consistently use voting to make fair decisions.
    b. Provide an agenda with time frames ahead of time.
    c. Provide participants with objectives for the meeting.
    d. Have a mechanism to track concerns that arise that are not on topic.

11. Which of the following is not a good suggestion for enhancing the effectiveness of conversations?
    a. Paraphrase or restate what you heard, remembering that the real purpose of paraphrasing is not to clarify what the other person actually meant, but to show what it meant to you.

    b. Describe behavior without making accusations or generalizations about motives.
    c. Avoid the use of open-ended questions.
    d. Ask for additional details and examples to show interest and to indicate that you are open the speaker's message.

12. Which of the following should be avoided in a successful phone call?
    a. Using prepared notes so that you sound genuine and friendly.
    b. Introducing yourself by name even when answering your own phone.
    c. Trying to end the phone call on a positive note such as thanking the other person.
    d. Clearly establishing the reason for the call and the objectives to be accomplished.

13. *Kinesics* is a term that pertains to the study of
    a. Space in communication.
    b. Movement (body language) in communication.
    c. The use of voice in communication.
    d. Mobile technology in communication.

14. Which of the following is not a common component of a business letter?
    a. The full address of the recipient.
    b. A formal opening salutation.
    c. A standard header summarizing the topic of the letter.
    d. An introductory paragraph explaining the purpose of the letter.

15. Which of the following best describes a business plan?
    a. It is a standard template associated with the use of proxemics to plan physical spaces for a business.
    b. It is a short, one-page description of a planned product or business used primarily for press announcements and promotion.
    c. It outlines an organization's plan for a new product for which it will seek funding or a plan for a new business.
    d. It is a document traditionally shared only with internal audiences; an example is budget and financial updates for staff.

References

American Occupational Therapy Association. (2007). AOTA's *Centennial Vision* and executive summary. *American Journal of Occupational Therapy, 61*, 613–614.

Axtell, R. E. (2007). *Essential do's and taboos: The complete guide to international business and leisure travel*. Hoboken, NJ: Wiley.

Barker, A. (2006). *Improve your communication skills* (2nd ed.). Philadelphia: Kogan Page.

Bauer, J. M., Kim, S., Mody, B., & Wildman, S. (2009, May). *The role of research in communications policy: Theory and evidence*. Paper presented at the meeting of the International Communication Association, New York. Retrieved January 4, 2010, from http://www.allacademic.com/meta/p_mla_apa_research_citation/0/1/4/9/6/p14962_index.html

Braveman, B. (2006). *Leading and managing occupational therapy services: An evidence-based approach*. Philadelphia: F. A. Davis.

Gabbot, M., & Hogg, G. (2001). The role of nonverbal communication in service encounters: A conceptual framework. *Journal of Marketing Management, 17*, 5–26.

Goldman, A. (1994). The central role of national culture in cross-cultural management: Proxemic conflicts in the internationalization of TQM. *Cross Cultural Management: An International Journal, 1*, 4–10.

Indiana University Information Technology Services. (2008). *What is a Listserv mailing list?* Retrieved January 4, 2010, from http://kb.iu.edu/data/afah.html

Madlock, P. E. (2008). The link between leadership style, communicator competence, and employee satisfaction. *Journal of Business Communication, 45*, 61–78.

Payne, H. J. (2005). Reconceptualizing social skills in organizations: Exploring the relationship between communication competence, job performance, and supervisory roles. *Journal of Leadership and Organizational Studies, 11*, 63–77.

Perkins, P. S. (2008). *The art and science of communication: Tools for effective communication in the workplace*. Hoboken, NJ: Wiley.

Price, L. L., Arnould, E. J., & Tierny, P. (1995). Going to extremes: Managing service encounters and assessing provider performance. *Journal of Marketing, 59*, 83–97. Roebuck, D. B. (2006). *Improving business communication skills* (4th ed.). Upper Saddle River, NJ: Pearson Prentice Hall.

Scholtes, P. R., Joiner, B. L., Streibel, B., & Mann, D. (2003). *The team handbook: How to use teams to improve quality* (3rd ed.). Madison, WI: Oriel Incorporated.

Shao-Kang, L. (2008). The nonverbal communication functions of emoticons in computer-mediated communication. *Cyber-Psychology and Behavior, 11*, 595–597.

APPENDIX 12.A. WORKPLACE COMMUNICATION EVIDENCE TABLE

Topic	Evidence
Nonverbal communication	Gabbot, M., & Hogg, G. (2001). The role of nonverbal communication in service encounters: A conceptual framework. *Journal of Marketing Management, 17,* 5–26. Shao-Kang, L. (2008). The nonverbal communication functions of emoticons in computer-mediated communication. *CyberPsychology and Behavior, 11,* 595–597.
Communication competence and leadership	Madlock, P. E. (2008). The link between leadership style, communicator competence, and employee satisfaction. *Journal of Business Communication, 45,* 61–78. Payne, H. J. (2005). Reconceptualizing social skills in organizations: Exploring the relationship between communication competence, job performance, and supervisory roles. *Journal of Leadership and Organizational Studies, 11,* 63–77.
Proxemics	Goldman, A. (1994). The central role of national culture in cross-cultural management: Proxemic conflicts in the internationalization of TQM. *Cross Cultural Management: An International Journal, 1,* 4–10. Price, L. L., Arnould, E. J., & Tierny, P. (1995). Going to extremes: Managing service encounters and assessing provider performance. *Journal of Marketing, 59,* 83–97.

13

Personnel Management

Thomas F. Fisher, PhD, OTR, CCM, FAOTA

❖ Key Terms and Concepts

Continuing competence. The ongoing education of professionals to develop and maintain knowledge, skills, and reasoning for performance in their professional roles now and in the future.

Human resources. The department responsible for oversight and interpretation of the organization's recruitment, management, and termination of employees.

Management/supervision. Application of business principles to ensure the delivery of safe, effective, legal, ethical, and competent services.

Performance review. Evaluation or assessment performed with employees to demonstrate performance (or lack thereof) in their job tasks or roles.

Regulation and credentialing. Process for ensuring that those delivering a service have the appropriate academic and practical experience to fulfill registration, certification, or licensure requirements.

❖ Learning Objectives

After completing this chapter, you should be able to do the following:

- Understand the issues involved in recruiting, retaining, and managing personnel.
- Discuss the roles and responsibilities of occupational therapists and occupational therapy assistants with respect to personnel management.

- Explain continuing competency and credentialing for occupational therapy practitioners.
- Explain the rationale for regular performance reviews.
- Describe the components and process of performance reviews.

Managing personnel has been and will continue to be a challenging skill for occupational therapy managers (Fisher, 1999; MacDonell, 2003; Peters & Waterman, 1982). Besides recruiting and retaining qualified practitioners, managers find themselves called on to meet business expectations, provide quality services, and demonstrate sustained outcomes. They need to understand all political, economic, social, and organizational influences to participate effectively in implementing and revising policies, overseeing the demands of cost containment, enforcing disciplinary actions, facilitating productivity—and the list goes on.

Occupational therapy managers and supervisors need to understand the roles and expectations involved in personnel management when they transition to a career in management. This chapter explores issues in personnel management from an occupational therapy perspective. In addition, the chapter identifies the personnel often managed by occupational therapists and describes processes for

recruiting and retaining professionals and managing employee performance In this chapter, *personnel management* is also referred to as *human resource management* (Fisher, 1999; MacDonell, 2003; Umiker, 1998).

HUMAN RESOURCES IN HEALTH AND HUMAN SERVICES

Human resource issues are the most challenging aspect of delivering quality outcomes–oriented health and human services. Supervisors, managers, and administrators are required to understand the human resources aspects of the business of delivering a health and human service, including recruitment, retention, termination, salaries, benefits, training, safety, compliance with regulations (state, federal, and other), and establishment and review of policies and procedures. It is difficult to find a balance in allocating one's energies to human resources issues versus other administrative or procedural issues. Managers, however, must attend to both managing rehabilitation services and addressing personnel issues while not losing focus on the ultimate goal—quality client care (Braveman, 2006).

In fact, because of the complexity of the processes for managing human resources, some organizations have turned to outsourcing some aspects of managing services, like payroll or billing. *Outsourcing* is a process whereby the organization contracts with another entity to provide services that might otherwise be performed by in-house employees (TriNet, 2009). Outsourcing can allow the organization to focus on the true mission (e.g., offering occupational therapy services), while others attend to the human resource details. Umiker (1998) observed that management skills for the health care supervisor are complex and require an appreciation by those who assume the role. Besides planning, organizing, and delegating to achieve greater productivity, the occupational therapy manager may need to implement organizational changes, build high-performance teams, improve safety for workers and clients, and cultivate and negotiate with professionals from other disciplines. Many management challenges and pitfalls can be changed into win–win situations, and appropriate mentoring and provision of resources (e.g., continuing education, additional graduate work) will allow practitioners to advance professionally.

CONSIDERATIONS IN MANAGING OCCUPATIONAL THERAPY PERSONNEL

The field of occupational therapy will continue to prosper in the 21st century as society continues to recognize that individuals with disabilities have a need for independence. Furthermore, it has become clear that public policy can provide resources to support their independence. The U.S. Department of Labor's Bureau of Labor Statistics (BLS) has projected that employment of occupational therapy practitioners will increase by a minimum of 27% by 2014 (American Occupational Therapy Association [AOTA], 2006; Baum, 2007; BLS, 2009; Moyers, 2007), reflecting the changing demographics of the United States and recognition of the need for rehabilitation and habilitation services (BLS, 2009). Because of the increasing competitiveness of occupational therapy educational programs, however, there is a workforce shortage that shows no signs of lessening in the near future. Workforce shortages and the rising demand for occupational therapy services will cultivate a highly desirable profession in an aging society.

AOTA's official documents define the roles and responsibilities of occupational therapy practitioners and managers; the association reviews and revises these documents as necessary every 5 years in a process initiated by the National Office and involving volunteers from among its membership. It is the professional's responsibility not only to abide by these documents, which include the *Occupational Therapy Code of Ethics and Ethics Standards* (AOTA, 2010a), but also to comply with the profession's continuing competency standards and *Standards of Practice for Occupa-*

tional Therapy (AOTA, 2010c). Each of these documents is significant and outlines a framework for the management of personnel.

According to AOTA, occupational therapy personnel are

> individuals who work in an occupational therapy program/department/unit to ensure the delivery of occupational therapy services to consumers. Occupational therapy personnel may include occupational therapists (OTs), occupational therapy assistants (OTAs), occupational therapy students (OTSs), occupational therapy assistant students (OTASs), and the OT aide. (AOTA, 2009b, p. ix)

The AOTA defines the categories of occupational therapist and occupational therapy assistant in the Association's *Reference Manual of the Official Documents of the AOTA* (AOTA, 2009d). This manual describes the credentials and levels of preparation for each category and outlines what services each professional can offer and what the role and responsibilities of each might be in certain situations. Occupational therapists are educated at the professional level and must have a master's degree or doctorate. Occupational therapy assistants are educated at the technical level and must have an associate's degree. Both levels of education are governed by standards that are developed and overseen by the Accreditation Council for Occupational Therapy Education (ACOTE, 2007a, 2007b, 2007c). Support staff (e.g., administrative assistants) are not usually regarded as occupational therapy personnel and support occupational therapy practitioners as determined by each organization. In general,

> the occupational therapist is responsible for all aspects of occupational therapy service delivery and is accountable for the safety and effectiveness of the occupational therapy service delivery process. . . . The occupational therapy assistant delivers occupational therapy services under the supervision of and in partnership with the occupational therapist. The occupational therapist and the occupational therapy assistant are responsible for collaboratively developing a plan of supervision. (AOTA, 2009b, pp. 173–174)

Managers also must understand the practice acts and the role and responsibility delineation in the state where they are employed. Such regulation may cover a wide variety of issues, including salary, payment for services, and documentation roles and responsibilities. For example, in a community-based setting in which occupational therapy is a value-added service and there is no billing or Medicare/Medicaid reimbursement, state law may allow the occupational therapist to provide services with the support of an individual who is not credentialed but is allowed to perform certain duties. In addition, state regulations may specify what support staff are allowed to do in terms of handling confidential documentation or supporting direct or indirect occupational therapy services. In addition, occupational therapists who manage services offered by other health professionals, such as physical therapists, speech–language pathologists, recreational therapists, developmental therapists, and others must understand each discipline's scope, payment, and other personnel-related issues.

The process of obtaining credentialing is becoming increasingly sophisticated in health care. Besides successfully passing the examination for licensure, occupational therapists in many special areas of practice (e.g., hand therapy, use of physical agent modalities, driver training, low vision interventions) must fulfill further credentialing requirements; a working understanding of these requirements is important for effective and competent personnel management.

The importance of credentialing and the process for establishing competency cannot be overstated. Occupational therapy managers have an obligation to know their own scope of practice, which professionals can provide which services in their state, and any other issues associated with the delivery of ethical and competent services. This obligation is not only legal, but ethical and professional as well.

RECRUITMENT

Recruiting and retaining occupational therapy practitioners have been issues of concern since the inception of the profession. As demand increases for occupational therapy services, as well as for those of other rehabilitation professionals, recruitment and retention will become increasingly important to the continued delivery of evidence-based interventions at a high quality level. In addition, managers are likely to be presented with new opportunities as a result of health reform initiatives being considered by the federal government (AOTA, 2009a). With the increasing demand for and high level of skill required in delivering occupational therapy services, attention by occupational therapy managers to attracting qualified practitioners and retaining employees who are performing up to standards will be increasingly important in providing competent quality services to clients.

The recruitment process for hiring health professionals is costly in terms of time and other human resources (Fisher, 1999; MacDonnell, 2003). The following are seven basic steps in the recruiting process:

1. *Identify the position and create or update a job description:* When the need to fill a new or existing position is identified, the job description for the position is created or reviewed as necessary. The job description describes the essential job functions of the position.
2. *Advertise the position to attract applicants:* In most cases, the position must be advertised to comply with fair wage and labor practices and ensure compliance with affirmative action laws. Depending on the position, the manager may advertise internally (within the organization) or externally (local or national media, Web site).
3. *Screen applicants:* Applicants' résumés are screened to determine whom to invite to have a phone or face-to-face interview. Typically, the manager tries to identify three or four possible applicants who meet the criteria for the position and state they can perform the essential functions of the job.
4. *Interview candidates:* Often a phone interview takes place, then a face-to-face interview if the phone interview goes well. During the interview, the manager asks specific questions that focus on the job description, compensation, and benefits. Applicants are given an opportunity to ask their questions as well.
5. *Contact references:* Once the manager is ready to make a tentative offer, he or she asks the applicant for a minimum of three professional (not personal) references. These contacts are called to request verbal or written confirmation of information the applicant has provided.
6. *Extend offer:* Once the applicant's references have confirmed his or her appropriateness for the position, the manager extends an offer specifying compensation, benefits, terms of probation, and next steps for employment (e.g., deadline for the applicant's acceptance or rejection of the offer).
7. *Follow up:* Once the candidate has confirmed his or her acceptance, the manager (or designated person) notifies the applicants not offered the position that the position has been filled and thanks them for their interest in the position.

Sometimes the manager is asked by higher management or human resources or for another reason may want to determine whether the position needs to be filled full-time or part-time or whether the responsibilities could be absorbed into someone else's job description. Benefits for full-time employees often cost approximately one-third of their salary, so such consideration could assist in decreasing the overall human resource budget; cutting a full-time position, however, may jeopardize completion of all the job tasks.

Those responsible for managing occupational therapy personnel need to use the organization's human resources department as a resource in successfully recruiting, retaining, and terminating employees. The individuals in the human resources department stay current with employment legislation and fair wage and labor practices; occupational therapy managers typically are not able to stay abreast of these areas unless it is their area of expertise or a component of their management position.

The most important component of recruitment (and of retention and termination), besides remaining fair and equitable, is to maintain accurate documentation for the human resources department's personnel files. If an employee brings legal legal action against the organization, this documentation can be revisited in examining the organization's actions; if an action was not recorded, it could be argued, it never happened.

RETENTION

A health care organization that advances today is an organization that delivers quality services at a competitive price. Because this type of organization is dependent on people to deliver these services, it is important for managers to develop strategies for retaining employees. In addition, managers strive to reduce turnover because it is costly in terms of time and money. Because qualified occupational therapy practitioners are in short supply and heavily recruited, it is important for managers to understand what factors contribute to job satisfaction so their employees are encouraged to stay with the organization. Fyock (2001) reported that when employees were asked what gave them satisfaction on the job, they identified good communication as their top choice. So from the beginning of their employment experience, employees need to know what the performance expectations are (the job advertisement and job description should spell them out), and the process for determining how their performance will be evaluated and how they are meeting those standards will be a contributing factor in their remaining employed with the organization.

Regular performance reviews are a key aspect of this communication. Performance reviews help employees understand how they are performing, what they need to do to continue their employment, and any changes they may need to make to remain an employee. Performance reviews promote the employee's continuing competence; "[c]ontinuing competence is a process involving the examination of current competencies and the development of capacity for the future" (AOTA, 2010b). As health professionals, occupational therapy practitioners are required to demonstrate their competency through a variety of activities in order to renew their certification with the National Board for Certification in Occupational Therapy and to be credentialed (licensed) in the state where they practice.

Herzberg (1987) recognized the importance of motivators—for example, the desire to be a supervisor, conduct research, or represent the organization to outside audiences—in promoting employees' job satisfaction and retention. The challenge for managers is to identify what those motivators are and provide the resources and opportunities for employees to pursue them. Drucker (2005) supported this notion and suggested that managers use an information-based style of management as opposed to a command-and-control style. When employees understand what the issues are and are provided the necessary information to address them successfully, they are motivated to come to work, and their job satisfaction is increased. Drucker also suggested making the performance review two-way by developing collaborative action plans during the review.

Typically, an employee should expect a performance review after the probationary period (usually 90 days for professionals), again at the 1-year anniversary, and annually thereafter. Regardless of how the review process is conducted at a given organization, employees need to be familiar with the process and provided clarification when requested. Many occupational therapy managers have employees do a self-assessment of their performance as the starting point for the review. During the review, the employee and manager discuss both the self-assessment and the manager's performance review and then develop an action plan for accomplishing the employee's and manager's goals for the employee during the next year. This process, sometimes referred to as *management by objectives with a professional development plan,* is always a collaborative discussion between the employee and the manager. At each subsequent review, the two reflect on this action plan and then evaluate the employee's progress in meeting his or her goals. This process contributes to job satisfaction and thus retention of the employee.

Managing employees who are not meeting performance expectations requires an investment of time and resources. Because of the recruitment problems discussed earlier in this chapter, managers should attempt to retain those employees who show the potential to improve their performance. The organization has invested time and resources in hiring these individuals; therefore, termination is a lose–lose situation. Whenever possible, the manager should try to support, mentor, and develop personnel for a win–win outcome.

Sometimes, however, employee terminations are unavoidable. Grounds for immediate dismissal include fraudulent billing, unsafe client practices, false documentation, stealing, and ethical misconduct. Other terminations involve progressive disciplinary action following an established human resource process. In either case, the documentation of incidents and poor work performance becomes critical when an employee does not meet expectations. Performance reviews and action plans provide the documentation to support the manager's efforts to manage the employee. Ongoing communication and documentation are essential in this process.

CONCLUSION

Organizations that provide health and rehabilitation services need competent professionals who can deliver such services. Occupational therapy managers must understand the issues, policies, and laws related to personnel management. Good managers understand not only the business of providing services but also the clinical issues related to those business practices. This chapter introduced the key personnel management concepts of credentialing, competency, recruitment, and retention. Performance reviews that are timely, collaborative, and used as a competency development tool promote job satisfaction and reduce employee turnover. The occupational therapy manager needs to be flexible, creative, and aware of the organization's political, social, economic, and other environments as they influence employees.

Case Examples

LEVEL I FIELDWORK

Sarah was placed at an adult day program with an activities director for exposure to the mentally retarded/developmentally disabled population. She observed the director interacting with clients and the two aides. She later heard the two aides discussing the director and the feedback she had given them on the activities they had chosen earlier. They were pleased she had complimented them on their selection, given the functioning of the group. Sarah made a mental note to compliment those she supervised in the future.

LEVEL II FIELDWORK

Jennifer was at midterm on her first Level II experience. Her fieldwork educator informed her that during the second part of her experience, she would be expected to supervise an aide while her supervisor was on vacation. There was another occupational therapist at the facility, but the fieldwork educator believed this would be a good managerial experience for Sarah. She was told that if any issue came up that she could not handle, she should consult with the other occupational therapist. Sarah at first was intimidated by this expectation but then realized this was an important learning opportunity in her training as an occupational therapist.

FIRST-TIME MANAGER

Kayden, a new graduate occupational therapist, accepted a position with a long-term-care facility. He was to supervise two occupational therapy assistants, one physical therapy assistant, and a part-time speech–language pathologist. Within the first month of his employment, he met with them to ask them what their expectations of him were and to share what he had been told to expect from them. The meeting went well, and he set up appointments to meet with each of them individually to discuss their professional development plans.

MANAGER

Bella had been a manager for 3 years at an outpatient pediatric facility and was managing a staff of four occupational therapists. One of the therapists was not meeting expectations. She was consistently late for her appointments and with her documentation because of poor time management skills. She was, however, a competent therapist. Children and families constantly complimented her on her interventions and the progress they saw. Bella decided to begin the disciplinary action process. When she met with the therapist, she shared her concern and ended with a positive statement about the outcomes of the therapist's interventions (client progress and client and family satisfaction). Bella helped the therapist develop a plan of action and scheduled a review of the plan for 3 months later.

❖ Learning Activities

1. A basic job description states what is expected and the necessary requirements of the position. Performance standards inform employees how well they must do their work. List the uses of performance standards.
2. Review the job description in a place where you work or want to work, and provide 3 measurable performances required for the position on the basis of the job description.
3. Imagine that you are a manager of a physical rehabilitation program and you have an opening for an occupational therapy assistant. Prepare a list of 20 questions for the job candidates. Include items that help to determine competency, teamwork, managing stress, and a caring attitude.
4. You are scheduled to meet with your supervisor to discuss the need for an occupational therapist who specializes in hands. You are not familiar with the credentialing process or qualifications for hand therapists. Discuss the options for this position. How will you prepare for the meeting? What documents are important to review prior to the meeting? Considering the legislative and regulatory issues as well as the billing considerations. What else should you consider?
5. An inexperienced coordinator of a mental health rehabilitation program has asked whether occupational therapy students or an occupational therapy assistant can provide direct services to clients on the (inpatient) behavioral health unit. What are the issues and resources you can identify for the coordinator?

✓ Multiple-Choice Questions

1. When addressing management issues related to occupational therapy services, the manager needs to
   a. Understand the principles of the payment systems they are under
   b. Understand all environments (e.g., political, economic, social) affecting employees
   c. Understand the AOTA resources available
   d. All the above

2. Health care management in today's market is
   a. Complex
   b. Simple (you either have insurance or you don't)
   c. Evolving into a process that no one understands
   d. Dependent on physician referrals

3. The process in which human resource services are provided by professionals who are not in-house staff is called
   a. Marketing
   b. Outsourcing
   c. Non-in-house services
   d. Continuous quality improvement

4. In AOTA documents, occupational therapy practitioners include
   a. Occupational therapists
   b. Occupational therapy assistants
   c. Both occupational therapists and occupational therapy assistants
   d. Those who work in long-term-care settings

5. The responsibilities of those who oversee personnel management, especially the securing of professional staff, include
   a. Recruitment, retention, and termination
   b. Advertising, marketing, and termination
   c. Training
   d. Recruitment and termination

6. The recruitment process for health professionals consists of how many basic steps?
   a. Two
   b. Seven
   c. Three
   d. Five

7. The key to successful personnel management is
   a. Increasing paid time off for staff
   b. Autocratic supervision
   c. Effective communication
   d. Good salaries and benefits

8. Education for an occupational therapy practitioner is
   a. Technical (associate's degree) or professional (postbaccalaureate degree)
   b. Undefined
   c. Professional
   d. Technical

9. Occupational therapy education is overseen by the
   a. American Occupational Therapy Association
   b. National Board for the Certification of Occupational Therapists
   c. Accreditation Council for Occupational Therapy Education
   d. American Occupational Therapy Political Action Committee

10. Performance appraisals are
    a. Optional, depending on the organization
    b. Necessary only when attempting to terminate an employee
    c. An effective tool for keeping employees aware of expectations and performance
    d. The only way to measure productivity

11. The professional body for the oversight of initial certification in occupational therapy is
    a. Accreditation Council for Occupational Therapy Education
    b. American Occupational Therapy Association
    c. National Board for the Certification of Occupational Therapists
    d. American Occupational Therapy Foundation

12. When an employee who has potential is not performing as expected, the manager should
    a. Develop a plan of action
    b. Terminate the employee
    c. Suspend the employee
    d. Ignore the behavior, as it might change

13. In today's market, managers need to be
    a. Rigid and structured
    b. Flexible and creative
    c. Focused only on productivity
    d. Determined to make every employee work out as a success

14. Managers need to understand that employees want to be
    a. Satisfied on the job
    b. Challenged
    c. Supervised closely
    d. Their peer

15. A process for demonstrating competencies and development of capacity for the future is referred to as
    a. Good management
    b. Continuing competence
    c. Specialization
    d. Attaining an advance degree

16. One method for reducing turnover and retaining employees is
    a. Paying higher salaries
    b. Providing more vacation time
    c. Providing regular performance reviews
    d. Hiring the right employees

17. Professional occupational therapy education results in
    a. An associate's degree
    b. A master's degree
    c. A doctoral degree
    d. Either a master's or doctoral degree
18. The manager must understand
    a. State laws governing the employees they are supervising
    b. Trends in the hiring practices of health professionals
    c. Issues related to specialization for the future
    d. Anticipated changes in ordering supplies and equipment
19. Technical education of occupational therapy practitioners is at the
    a. Bachelor's-degree level
    b. Associate's-degree level
    c. On-the-job training level
    d. Certificate level
20. The biggest challenge for the manager of rehabilitation professionals is
    a. Recruiting and retaining competent staff
    b. Meeting productivity standards
    c. Keeping up with payment changes
    d. Understanding documentation requirements

References

Accreditation Council for Occupational Therapy Education. (2007a). Accreditation standards for a doctoral-degree-level educational program for the occupational therapist. *American Journal of Occupational Therapy, 61*, 641–651.

Accreditation Council for Occupational Therapy Education. (2007b). Accreditation standards for a master's-degree-level educational program for the occupational therapist. *American Journal of Occupational Therapy, 61*, 652–661.

Accreditation Council for Occupational Therapy Education. (2007c). Accreditation standards for an educational program for the occupational therapy assistant. *American Journal of Occupational Therapy, 61*, 662–671.

American Occupational Therapy Association. (2010a). Occupational therapy code of ethics. *American Journal of Occupational Therapy, 64*.

American Occupational Therapy Association. (2010b). Standards for continuing competence. *American Journal of Occupational Therapy, 64*.

American Occupational Therapy Association. (2010c). Standards of practice for occupational therapy. *American Journal of Occupational Therapy, 64*.

American Occupational Therapy Association. (2006). *Occupational therapy workforce and compensation report.* Bethesda, MD: AOTA Press.

American Occupational Therapy Association. (2009a). *AOTA legislative action center.* Retrieved February 19, 2009, from http://vocusgr.vocus.com/GRSPACE2/WebPublish/controller.aspx?SiteName=AOTA&Definition=Home&SV_Section=Home

American Occupational Therapy Association. (2009b). Categories of occupational therapy personnel. In *Reference manual of the official documents of the AOTA, Inc.* (14th ed.). Bethesda, MD: AOTA Press.

American Occupational Therapy Association. (2009c). Guidelines for supervision, roles, and responsibilities during the delivery of occupational therapy services. *American Journal of Occupational Therapy, 63*, 797–803.

American Occupational Therapy Association. (2009d). *Reference manual of the official documents of the AOTA, Inc.* (14th ed.). Bethesda, MD: AOTA Press.

Baum, M. C. (2007). Achieving our potential. *American Journal of Occupational Therapy, 61*, 615–621.

Braveman, B. (2006). *Leading and managing occupational therapy services: An evidence-based approach.* Philadelphia: F. A. Davis.

Drucker, P. (2005, November 28). The man who invented management. *Business Week.* Retrieved March 31, 2009, from http://www.businessweek.com/magazine/content/05_48/b3961001.htm

Fisher, T. F. (1999). Managing our limited resource: Practitioners. In K. Jacobs & M. K. Logigian (Eds.), *Functions of a manager in occupational therapy* (3rd ed., pp. 81–91). Thorofare, NJ: Slack.

Fyock, C. D. (2001). *Retention tactics that work* (White paper). Alexandria, VA: Society for Human Resources Management.

Herzberg, F. (1987). One more time: How do you motivate employees? *Harvard Business Review, 65*, 109–120.

MacDonell, C. M. (2003). Personnel management: Measuring performance, creating success. In G. L. McCormack, E. G. Jaffe, & M. Goodman-Lavey (Eds.), *The occupational therapy manager* (4th ed., pp. 309–314). Bethesda, MD: AOTA Press.

Moyers, P. A. (2007). A legacy of leadership: Achieving our *Centennial Vision. American Journal of Occupational Therapy, 61*, 622–628.

Peters, T. J., & Waterman, R. H. (1982). *In search of excellence: Lessons from America's best-run companies.* New York: Harper & Row.

TriNet. (2009). *Discover the return on investment in outsourcing your human resource function.* Retrieved March 2, 2009, from www.trinet.com/hr_outsourcing

Umiker, W. (1998). *Management skills for the new health care supervisor* (3rd ed.). Gaithersburg, MD: Aspen.

U.S. Bureau of Labor Statistics. (2009). *Occupational outlook handbook.* Retrieved February 4, 2009, from http://www.bls.gov/oco

APPENDIX 13.A. PERSONNEL MANAGEMENT EVIDENCE TABLE

Topic	Subtopics	Evidence
Occupational therapy personnel	Occupational therapist Occupational therapy assistant Occupational therapy student Occupational therapy aide	American Occupational Therapy Association. (2009b). Categories of occupational therapy personnel. In *Reference manual of the official documents of the AOTA, Inc.* (14th ed., p. ix). Bethesda, MD: AOTA Press. American Occupational Therapy Association. (2009c). Guidelines for supervision, roles, and responsibilities during the delivery of occupational therapy services. *American Journal of Occupational Therapy, 63,* 797–803.
Credentialing	Registration Certification Licensure	American Occupational Therapy Association. (2006). *Occupational therapy workforce and compensation report.* Bethesda, MD: AOTA Press.
Continuing competency	Standards for continuing competency in occupational therapy	American Occupational Therapy Association. (2010b). Standards for continuing competence. *American Journal of Occupational Therapy, 64.*

14
Conflict Resolution

Shawn Phipps, MS, OTR/L

 ## Key Terms and Concepts

Collectivistic culture. A culture that focuses on ensuring that group needs are met.

Conflict. A disagreement or clash between ideas, principles, or people.

Conflict resolution. Reduction or resolution of a conflict.

Emotional intelligence. The ability to monitor one's own or others' emotions.

Individualistic culture. A culture that focuses on ensuring that individual needs are met.

Negotiation. The process of determining a compromise between competing ideas.

Learning Objectives

After completing this chapter, you should be able to do the following:

- Define *conflict* and *conflict resolution*.
- Identify 2 core principles of conflict resolution.
- Identify the difference between individualistic and collectivistic cultural perspectives on conflict resolution.

- Identify 11 strategies for effective conflict resolution.
- Develop conflict resolution strategies using 4 case examples.

Conflict is a disagreement or clash between ideas, principles, or people (Almost, 2006). Conflict is unavoidable and can result from value clashes, distressed relationships, discrimination, poor communication, or the possibility of personal gain (Harmer, 2006). Conflict can occur during interactions with clients, caregivers, colleagues, and organizations (Lask, 2003; Nield-Anderson et al., 1999; Orr, 2001; Rotarius & Liberman, 2000). Ambiguity, role conflict, and the leader's affinity for conflict can also be contributing factors to conflict in the workplace (Porter-O'Grady, 2004). For example, the manager or clinician who uses a more aggressive or passive–aggressive leadership approach may encounter greater levels of conflict in the workplace. Unresolved conflict can lead to job dissatisfaction, absenteeism, and turnover (J. Kelly, 2006). One study found that in a hospital setting, interpersonal conflict could be linked to 67% of adverse events, 58% of compromised patient safety, and 28% of patient mortality (Mantone, 2006). Unresolved conflict, whether between an employee and employer or a practitioner and client, creates ripple effects in costly litigation felt throughout the health care system (Miller &

Wax, 1999). Premiums and legal costs are passed on to consumers, furthering client dissatisfaction with the health care system (Skjørshammer, 2001).

Conflict resolution focuses on strategically reducing or resolving conflicts that arise in the context of occupational therapy practice. Effective conflict resolution promotes staff retention, work satisfaction, and quality client care (Pettrey, 2003). This chapter discusses the principles of conflict resolution and effective strategies for resolving conflict. In the language of the *Centennial Vision*, this chapter incorporates the concept of becoming more "powerful" as an occupational therapy profession through effective conflict resolution strategies that build the collective united "power" of the profession (American Occupational Therapy Association [AOTA], 2007). In terms of the *Occupational Therapy Practice Framework*, this chapter incorporates the organizational structures of departmental relationships, leadership, and management as client factors influencing the conflict resolution process (AOTA, 2008). In addition, social demands (social environment and cultural contexts) are also incorporated as conflict resolution strategies and may be incorporated into the occupational therapy process as an activity demand.

PRINCIPLES OF CONFLICT RESOLUTION

Negotiation research shows that mutual problem solving encourages resolution of a conflict (De Dreu, Wingart, & Kwon, 2000). In contrast, standing firm on one's proposals or making threats encourages failure to reach resolution. Conceding makes agreement more likely in the short term but favors the other party's interest and may not always effectively resolve the conflict, as it may manifest in greater conflict at a future point in time.

Research has shown that during the negotiation process, the party who makes the first offer tends to achieve greater benefits than the other party (Pruitt & Carnevale, 1993). In addition, viewing a compromise as a loss can limit the effectiveness of a resolution. Focusing on one's own goals can limit the successful resolution of conflict; in contrast, focusing on mutually beneficial goals can improve the outcome of conflict resolution.

Individualistic Western cultures tend to take a more contentious approach to conflict resolution by using a more direct approach to confronting conflicts in the workplace (Bercovitch & Houston, 2000). In contrast, collectivistic Eastern cultures tend to value the maintenance of positive working relationships by minimizing confrontation. When working with a client, caregiver, or colleague, it is important to be cognizant of cultural factors that influence the strategies one takes in resolving conflict.

STRATEGIES FOR EFFECTIVE CONFLICT RESOLUTION

Eleven strategies outline evidence-based solutions for resolving conflict effectively:

1. *Foster active communication.* Research shows that the first step in bridging the communication process is to initiate dialogue with the client, colleague, or organization you are experiencing conflict with. Although you may be tempted to hope that the conflict resolves on its own or to use an avoidance strategy, the conflict is more likely to fester into a greater conflict without open dialogue and communication (Baker, 1995). If the conflict is resulting in aggressive or unproductive dialogue, however, pursue open communication at a time when there has been some distance between the parties so that communication is solution based with a focus on resolving the conflict (DelBel, 2003). In addition, the delivery of a sincere apology can be a productive means of opening up active communication. Many people struggle with the idea of apologizing in the belief that it makes them appear vulnerable. However, research indicates that apologies are considered to be a sign of strength and can serve as a key conflict resolution strategy (Porter, 2005).

2. *Discuss your needs using "I" statements.* Communicate your needs to the party you are in conflict with using "I" statements, rather than "you" statements. Blame, often communicated covertly or overtly in "you" statements, is not a productive means of resolving conflict. You should not expect the other party to accept responsibility. Instead, you should discuss your perspective and needs using "I" statements that center the discussion around your needs rather than how the other party has violated those needs. It is also important not to refer to or involve persons who are not directly involved in the conflict (Baltimore, 2006).

3. *Use authentic listening.* In addition to communicating your own needs, you should also maintain an authentic focus on understanding the other party's perspective and needs (Fontaine & Gerardi, 2005). Active listening should be the central focus with this strategy so that the other party feels that his or her perspective is valued and understood as you proceed to reach a compromise in resolving the conflict (Hendel, Fish, & Galon, 2005). Summarizing what the other person has said is also an effective active listening strategy for conflict resolution as it assures the other party that you have listened intently to his or her perspective and builds trust (Saulo & Wagner, 2000).

4. *Engage in mutual problem solving.* Once you have identified the problems resulting in the conflict, advance to active problem solving by summarizing the problems and proposing potential solutions to them (Briles, 2005). Active problem solving requires the mutual determination of a solution that works for both parties. For example, a fieldwork supervisor and student may agree to enter a clearly stated commitment to resolve a conflict over the most appropriate intervention for a particular client. Although both disagree about the best treatment options for a particular client, they have agreed to discuss the case in depth, pulling from multiple frames of reference to arrive at the best possible intervention for the client.

5. *Strive for a win–win resolution.* In resolving conflict, you should aim for a win–win solution. The result should be to agree on a mutually satisfying alternative rather than to impose the goal of one person or organization at the expense of the other (Herzog, 2000; Payne, Shook, & Voges, 2005).

6. *Remain positive.* Conflict can create stress and negative morale in the workplace. To manage conflict proactively, it is important to maintain a positive, can-do attitude toward resolving the conflict. You should emphasize mutual respect and solidarity as you engage with the other party in a collaborative approach to resolving the conflict (Jameson, 2004). Workplace gossip should also be avoided as a means to deal with conflict, as it often creates negative staff morale.

7. *Control emotions.* Emotional control and emotional intelligence (i.e., the ability to monitor one's own or others' emotions) are critical components in conflict resolution (Jordan & Troth, 2002). Although conflict

often negatively affects one's emotional state, it is critical to remain focused on the problem rather than on the person or situation that is the perceived cause of the conflict (Andrew, 1999; Desivilya & Dana, 2005). Effective communication supports control of emotional responses, the search for understanding, exploration of common needs and interests, and identification of mutual benefits (Pettrey, 2003).

8. *Respond to the ideas, not the person.* The old adage of being hard on problems and not on people applies to the conflict resolution process. Those involved in the resolution of a conflict must focus on the ideas and solutions that are generated rather than the person bringing those ideas forward to reach an effective compromise (Haraway & Haraway, 2005).

9. *Aim for resolution.* Sometimes individuals or organizations go through the motions of conflict resolution without a genuine intent to resolve the conflict. To achieve effective conflict resolution, the parties must give due consideration to all perspectives rather than merely giving the appearance of interfacing (Jormsri, 2004).

10. *Discuss one specific topic at a time.* During the conflict resolution process, discussion should concentrate on one specific topic at a time, avoiding straying into other problem areas before the topic at hand is resolved. Conflict is often complex, and if it is not dealt with effectively, it can easily overflow into areas of discussion that are not pertinent to the goal of resolving the conflict (Lachman, 1999). Discussing one specific topic and person at a time can help avoid confusion and an escalation of the conflict.

11. *Observe nonverbal communication.* During direct conflict resolution discussion, it is important to pay close attention to nonverbal communication. In fact, research shows that the majority of our communication is nonverbal (Friedman & Miller-Herringer, 1992). Nonverbal communication, or *body language*, includes our facial expressions, gestures, eye contact, and posture.

Nonverbal communication can provide important insights into the other party's readiness to resolve the conflict. Strategies can be implemented to ensure that all parties have an opportunity to voice their concerns, opinions, and proposed solutions (A. E. Kelly, 2005). To facilitate improved direct communication, an inviting, safe, and nonjudgmental setting should be created to improve communication with clients and staff through the facilitation of active listening, the validation of understanding, and the matching of nonverbal and verbal messages.

Summary

The occupational therapy practitioner, whether in a management or clinician role, is challenged to use conflict resolution strategies that focus on reducing or resolving conflicts that arise in the context of occupational therapy practice. This chapter reviewed the principles of conflict resolution and 11 effective strategies for resolving conflict in the workplace, including fostering active communication, discussing needs using "I" statements, using authentic listening, engaging in mutual problem solving, striving for a win–win resolution, remaining positive, controlling emotions, responding to ideas instead of people, aiming for resolution, discussing one topic at a time, and observing nonverbal communication.

Case Examples

Level I Fieldwork

Jane was a Level I occupational therapy fieldwork student on an acute rehabilitation unit. On her first day of fieldwork, she experienced conflict with her fieldwork supervisor, who provided the feedback that Jane's dress was unprofessional for the setting. Jane reacted defensively and explained that whether dress is professional is a matter of interpretation. Jane felt that her fieldwork supervisor was purposely trying to find deficits in her performance.

Rather than focusing on her need for improvement with professional dress during fieldwork, Jane instead reacted defensively. However, after reflecting on the feedback that was provided, Jane decided to approach her fieldwork supervisor the next day. After examining potential strategies for effective conflict resolution, Jane decided to engage in active communication with her fieldwork supervisor the next day by using "I" state-

ments, listening to her fieldwork supervisor's perspective on professional dress, asking to review the organization's dress policy in writing, remaining positive, and committing to complete her Level I fieldwork by abiding by the organization's dress policy. Jane successfully passed her Level I fieldwork rotation. She also learned that each organization may have rules and expectations that are not congruent with her own values and beliefs, but that as an intern for this organization, it was critical to understand and respect the dress policy that is in place. Instead of remaining defensive, Jane found a productive use of her energy to resolve the conflict with her fieldwork supervisor.

Level II Fieldwork

Tom was in his 10th week as a Level II occupational therapy fieldwork student in an outpatient pediatric

(continued)

Case Examples *(cont.)*

clinic. Tom was working with his client, a young woman with autism, on sensory integrative strategies for her poor social skills. The client's mother was upset that her daughter was being treated by an intern and expressed dissatisfaction with Tom's effectiveness. Tom was unsure how to approach the client's mother, as he was fearful that if he addressed the conflict or informed his supervisor, he might not pass his fieldwork.

After accepting that a definitive conflict existed with his client's mother, Tom decided to approach his Level II fieldwork supervisor to identify strategies for effective conflict resolution. Before meeting with his fieldwork supervisor, he formulated some evidence-based strategies for effectively communicating with his client's mother while minimizing conflict. Tom presented his supervisor with several strategies, including authentic listening with his client's mother to understand her concerns, an acknowledgment that his client's mother does not trust his level of skill, mutual problem solving with the parent and the fieldwork supervisor to discuss strategies for increasing the parent's level of trust during therapeutic intervention, aiming for a win–win outcome, remaining calm, responding to the ideas presented by the parent instead of her personal attacks, and closely monitoring the mother's nonverbal communication. The fieldwork supervisor decided to co-treat with the intern during the first few occupational therapy sessions and subsequently move into the background as the intern developed the parent's trust.

FIRST-TIME MANAGER

Sally had been an occupational therapy practitioner for over 20 years in a large school-based practice and had developed long and enduring relationships with her coworkers and the school staff. Sally had recently been promoted to a management position in which she supervised her former coworkers directly. She was beginning to change the productivity requirements in her department and was dealing with emerging conflict with staff members who were resisting the change. Sally felt an internal conflict between her desire to maintain good relationships with the staff she had previously worked alongside and her realization that the department would be best served when the children received timely, high-quality services.

Recognizing the challenge of change and accountability in leadership, particularly when your colleague is promoted to a higher supervisory position, Sally decided to proactively foster positive communication and team building with her staff. She used authentic listening and active communication during a staff meeting to hear her staff's concerns with the change in productivity requirements. While mutually problem solving, everyone realized that they could increase their efficiency through more effective use of group therapy for children who would benefit from therapeutic intervention in a social context with peers of their own developmental age. Together, the new supervisor and her staff engaged in program development activities to enact a more effective ues of resources while increasing overall staff productivity.

MANAGER

Roger was the director of a large occupational therapy department in an acute care hospital setting. He had served in various management roles over the past 10 years. He recently assumed responsibility for the physical therapy and speech therapy departments, as the hospital was attempting to reduce costs by integrating all rehabilitation disciplines under one department. Roger experienced conflict with the physical therapy and speech therapy staff, who resisted the idea of a merged department under the direction of someone from another discipline. In trying to appease his new direct reports, he began to focus his energy on the needs of the other departments, leaving his former occupational therapy department feeling abandoned in the midst of change.

Roger decided to actively resist defensively reacting to the employees, but committed to having a more informed understanding of their concerns and needs during the organizational transition. He developed several small focus groups representing a cross-section of the department to obtain objective feedback regarding specific areas of concern. He actively and authentically listened to the employees' concerns; remained positive about his vision, goals, and what additional resources he would advocate for to strengthen the department; and asked all employees to get involved in shaping the change they wanted to see in the department. However, he also made it clear that change was inevitable and that maintaining the status quo was not an option. Although some employees responded inappropriately and aggressively, Roger controlled his emotions and focused on the ideas, suggestions, and concerns rather than the persons providing the feedback. He discussed one topic at a time, related to the employees' areas of concern, observed nonverbal communication, and encouraged those who may not have had the courage to speak to engage in the problem-solving dialogue. All ideas were then strategically considered for inclusion in the department's strategic plan, which was shared with all employees within a month of the focus groups, demonstrating Roger's commitment to inclusiveness and resolution of conflict.

❖ Learning Activities

1. Identify a conflict you have had in your personal life or in the workplace. What strategies did you use to resolve the conflict? What specific strategies could you have used to resolve this conflict more effectively?

2. Are you more individualistic or collectivistic in your approach to resolving conflicts? What strategies would you implement to balance your approach to more effectively resolve conflict?

3. How authentic is your listening strategy? What strategies could you implement to be a more effective listener?

4. How effective are you at compromising? Identify a current or potential conflict in your work setting. How could you modify your expectations to achieve a win–win resolution?

5. Have you avoided discussion of a potential conflict in your personal or professional life? What strategies could you use to increase your confidence in resolving the conflict through active communication?

✓ Multiple-Choice Questions

1. Conflict is
   a. Unavoidable.
   b. A result of value clashes.
   c. Stressful.
   d. All of the above.

2. Conflict resolution is
   a. Avoiding conflict.
   b. A competition.
   c. An attempt to resolve a problem.
   d. None of the above.

3. Individualistic cultures tend to resolve conflict by
   a. Ensuring that each individual's needs are met.
   b. Sharing responsibility.
   c. Agreeing to disagree.
   d. All of the above.

4. Collectivistic cultures tend to resolve conflict by
   a. Ensuring interpersonal harmony.
   b. Avoiding direct communication.
   c. Maintaining the relationship.
   d. All of the above.

5. Unresolved conflict can lead to
   a. An organization moving forward with its strategic plan.
   b. Job dissatisfaction.
   c. Turnover.
   d. B and C.

6. During conflict, which active communication strategy can facilitate resolution?
   a. Engaging in dialogue with a person who is emotional.
   b. Avoiding addressing the conflict.
   c. Planning a meeting to discuss the problem.
   d. Using "you" statements.

7. "I" statements are an effective strategy for
   a. Engaging in assertive communication.
   b. Resolving conflict.
   c. Ensuring your needs are communicated directly.
   d. All of the above.

8. Authentic listening includes
   a. Summarizing.
   b. Pretending to listen.
   c. Using "I" statements.
   d. Apologizing.

9. Nonverbal communication accounts for
   a. 25% of communication.
   b. 45% of communication.
   c. The majority of communication.
   d. None of the above.

10. Strategies for controlling emotions during a conflict include
    a. Avoiding.
    b. Arguing.
    c. Seeking understanding.
    d. Reacting to the person.

11. A win–win resolution to conflict includes
    a. Achieving a double victory in favor of a person.
    b. Agreeing to disagree.
    c. Finding a mutually beneficial solution.
    d. Giving in to the other person.

12. Reaching an effective compromise requires
    a. Meeting for the intellectual exercise.
    b. Passively listening to the other party.
    c. Exploring ideas for resolution.
    d. Giving in to the other party.

13. Unresolved conflict can lead to
    a. Costly litigation.
    b. An exchange of ideas.
    c. Quality therapist–client communication.
    d. None of the above.

14. Conflict in the hospital setting can contribute to
    a. Adverse events.
    b. Compromised patient safety.
    c. Patient mortality.
    d. All of the above.

15. Conflict resolution can be impeded by
    a. Making the first offer.
    b. Seeing a compromise as a loss.
    c. Finding mutually beneficial goals.
    d. Flexibility.
16. Which of the following occupational therapy roles requires effective conflict resolution skills?
    a. Occupational therapy student.
    b. Occupational therapy practitioner.
    c. Manager.
    d. All of the above.
17. Effective conflict resolution can lead to
    a. Staff retention.
    b. Work satisfaction.
    c. Quality client care.
    d. All of the above.

18. Which of the following is not an example of effective conflict resolution?
    a. Aiming for resolution.
    b. Remaining skeptical.
    c. Engaging in authentic listening.
    d. None of the above.
19. Effective negotiation can lead to
    a. Compromise.
    b. A winner.
    c. Hostility.
    d. Future conflict.
20. Effective occupational therapy managers demonstrate
    a. An avoidance of conflict.
    b. A timely resolution to conflict.
    c. A focus on productivity.
    d. Rigidity.

References

Almost, J. (2006). Conflict within nursing work environments. *Journal of Advanced Nursing, 53,* 444–453.

American Occupational Therapy Association. (2007). AOTA's *Centennial Vision* and executive summary. *American Journal of Occupational Therapy, 61,* 613–614.

American Occupational Therapy Association. (2008). Occupational therapy practice framework: Domain and process (2nd ed.). *American Journal of Occupational Therapy, 62,* 625–683.

Andrew, L. B. (1999). Conflict management, prevention, and resolution in medical settings. *Physician Executive, 25,* 38–46.

Baker, K. M. (1995). Improving staff nurse conflict resolution skills. *Nursing Economics, 13,* 295–317.

Baltimore, J. J. (2006). Fact or fiction? *Nursing Management, 37,* 28–36.

Bercovitch, J., & Houston, A. (2000). Why do they do it like this? An analysis of the factors influencing mediation behavior in international conflicts. *Journal of Conflict Resolution, 44,* 170–202.

Briles, J. (2005). Zapping conflict builds better teams. *Nursing, 35,* 32.

De Dreu, C. K. W., Wingart, L. R., & Kwon, S. (2000). Influence of social motives on integrative negotiation: A meta-analytic review and test of two theories. *Journal of Personality and Social Psychology, 78,* 889–905.

DelBel, J. C. (2003). Conflict management, special part 1: Deescalating workplace aggression. *Nursing Management, 34,* 31–34.

Desivilya, H. S., & Dana, Y. (2005). The role of emotions in conflict management: The case of work teams. *Conflict Management, 16,* 55–69.

Fontaine, D., & Gerardi, D. (2005). Healthier hospitals? *Nursing Management, 36,* 34–44.

Friedman, H. S., & Miller-Herringer, T. (1992). Nonverbal display of emotion in public and in private: Self-monitoring, personality, and expressive cues. *Journal of Personality and Social Psychology, 61,* 766–775.

Haraway, D. L., & Haraway, W. M., III. (2005). Analysis of the effect of conflict-management and resolution training on employee stress at a healthcare organization. *Hospital Topics, 83,* 11–17.

Harmer, B. M. (2006). Do not go gentle: Intractable value differences in hospice. *Journal of Healthcare Management, 51,* 86–93.

Hendel, T., Fish, M., & Galon, V. (2005). Leadership style and choice of strategy in conflict management among Israeli nurse managers in general hospitals. *Nursing Management, 13,* 137–146.

Herzog, A. C. (2000). Conflict resolution in a nutshell: Tips for everyday nursing. *Spinal Cord Injury Nursing, 17,* 162–166.

Jameson, J. K. (2004). Negotiating autonomy and connection through politeness: A dialectical approach to organizational conflict management. *Western Journal of Communication, 68,* 257–277.

Jordan, P., & Troth, A. (2002). Emotional intelligence and conflict resolution in nursing. *Contemporary Nurse, 13,* 94–100.

Jormsri, P. (2004). Moral conflict and collaborative mode as moral conflict resolution in healthcare. *Nursing Health Science, 6,* 217–221.

Kelly, A. E. (2005). Relationships in emergency care: Communication and impact. *Topics in Emergency Medicine, 27,* 192–197.

Kelly, J. (2006). An overview of conflict. *Dimensions of Critical Care Nursing, 25,* 22–28.

Lachman, V. D. (1999). Breaking the quality barrier: Critical thinking and conflict resolution. *Nursing Case Manager, 4,* 224–227.

Lask, B. (2003). Patient–clinician conflict: Causes and compromises. *Journal of Cystic Fibrosis, 2,* 42–45.

Mantone, J. (2006). The cost of bad behavior in OR. *Modern Healthcare, 36,* 21.

Miller, M., & Wax, D. (1999). Instilling a mediation-based conflict resolution culture. *Physician Executive, 25,* 45–51.

Morten, S. (2001). Conflict management in a hospital: Designing processing structures and intervention methods. *Journal of Management in Medicine, 15,* 156.

Nield-Anderson, L., Minarik, P. A., Dilworth, J. M., Jones, J., Nash, P. K., O'Donnell, K. L., et al. (1999). Responding to difficult patients. *American Journal of Nursing, 99,* 26–34.

Orr, R. D. (2001). Methods of conflict resolution at the bedside. *American Journal of Bioethics, 1,* 45–46.

Payne, G. T., Shook, C. L., & Voges, K. E. (2005). The "what" in top management group conflict: The effects of organizational issue interpretation on conflict among hospital decision makers. *Journal of Managerial Issues, 17,* 162.

Pettrey, L. (2003). Who let the dogs out? Managing conflict with courage and skill. *Critical Care Nurse, 23,* 21–24.

Porter, S. E. (2005). Apologizing: Trying to get it right. *Journal of Psychosocial Nursing and Mental Health Services, 43,* 8.

Porter-O'Grady, T. (2004). Embracing conflict: Building a healthy community. *Healthcare Management Review, 29,* 181–187.

Pruitt, D. G., & Carnevale, P. J. (1993). *Negotiation in social conflict.* Buckingham, UK: Open University Press.

Rotarius, T., & Liberman, A. (2000). Healthcare alliances and alternative dispute resolution: Managing trust and conflict. *Health Care Manager, 18,* 25–31.

Saulo, M., & Wagner, R. J. (2000). Mediation training enhances conflict management by healthcare personnel. *American Journal of Managed Care, 6,* 473–483.

Skjørshammer, M. (2001). Conflict management in a hospital: Designing processing structures and intervention methods. *Journal of Management in Medicine, 15,* 156–166.

APPENDIX 14.A. CONFLICT RESOLUTION EVIDENCE TABLE

Topic	Evidence
Negotiation	De Dreu, C. K. W., Wingart, L. R., & Kwon, S. (2000). Influence of social motives on integrative negotiation: A meta-analytic review and test of two theories. *Journal of Personality and Social Psychology, 78,* 889–905. Miller, M., & Wax, D. (1999). Instilling a mediation-based conflict resolution culture. *Physician Executive, 25,* 45–51. Morten, S. (2001). Conflict management in a hospital: Designing processing structures and intervention methods. *Journal of Management in Medicine, 15,* 156. Orr, R. D. (2001). Methods of conflict resolution at the bedside. *American Journal of Bioethics, 1,* 45–46. Payne, G. T., Shook, C. L., & Voges, K. E. (2005). The "what" in top management group conflict: The effects of organizational issue interpretation on conflict among hospital decision makers. *Journal of Managerial Issues, 17,* 162. Pruitt, D. G., & Carnevale, P. J. (1993). *Negotiation in social conflict.* Buckingham, UK: Open University Press. Rotarius, T., & Liberman, A. (2000). Healthcare alliances and alternative dispute resolution: Managing trust and conflict. *Health Care Manager, 18,* 25–31. Saulo, M., & Wagner, R. J. (2000). Mediation training enhances conflict management by healthcare personnel. *American Journal of Managed Care, 6,* 473–483.
Cultural differences	Bercovitch, J., & Houston, A. (2000). Why do they do it like this? An analysis of the factors influencing mediation behavior in international conflicts. *Journal of Conflict Resolution, 44,* 170–202.
Active communication	Baker, K. M. (1995). Improving staff nurse conflict resolution skills. *Nursing Economics, 13,* 295–317. DelBel, J. C. (2003). Conflict management, special part 1: Deescalating workplace aggression. *Nursing Management, 34,* 31–34.
Direct assertive communication	Baltimore, J. J. (2006). Fact or fiction? *Nursing Management, 37,* 28–36. Lachman, V. D. (1999). Breaking the quality barrier: Critical thinking and conflict resolution. *Nursing Case Manager, 4,* 224–227. Porter, S. E. (2005). Apologizing: Trying to get it right. *Journal of Psychosocial Nursing and Mental Health Services, 43,* 8. Porter-O'Grady, T. (2004). Embracing conflict: Building a healthy community. *Healthcare Management Review, 29,* 181–187.
Authentic listening	Fontaine, D., & Gerardi, D. (2005). Healthier hospitals? *Nursing Management, 36,* 34–44. Hendel, T., Fish, M., & Galon, V. (2005). Leadership style and choice of strategy in conflict management among Israeli nurse managers in general hospitals. *Nursing Management, 13,* 137–146.
Mutual problem solving	Briles, J. (2005). Zapping conflict builds better teams. *Nursing, 35,* 32.
Win–win resolutions	Herzog, A. C. (2000). Conflict resolution in a nutshell: Tips for everyday nursing. *Spinal Cord Injury Nursing, 17,* 162–166.
Positive communication	Jameson, J. K. (2004). Negotiating autonomy and connection through politeness: A dialectical approach to organizational conflict management. *Western Journal of Communication, 68,* 257–277.
Emotional intelligence	Andrew, L. B. (1999). Conflict management, prevention, and resolution in medical settings. *Physician Executive, 25,* 38–46. Desivilya, H. S., & Dana, Y. (2005). The role of emotions in conflict management: The case of work teams. *Conflict Management, 16,* 55–69. Jordan, P., & Troth, A. (2002). Emotional intelligence and conflict resolution in nursing. *Contemporary Nurse, 13,* 94–100. Pettrey, L. (2003). Who let the dogs out? Managing conflict with courage and skill. *Critical Care Nurse, 23,* 21–24.
Compromise	Haraway, D. L., & Haraway, W. M., III. (2005). Analysis of the effect of conflict-management and resolution training on employee stress at a healthcare organization. *Hospital Topics, 83,* 11–17. Jormsri, P. (2004). Moral conflict and collaborative mode as moral conflict resolution in healthcare. *Nursing Health Science, 6,* 217–221. Lask, B. (2003). Patient–clinician conflict: Causes and compromises. *Journal of Cystic Fibrosis, 2,* 42–45.
Nonverbal communication	Friedman, H. S., & Miller-Herringer, T. (1992). Nonverbal display of emotion in public and in private: Self-monitoring, personality, and expressive cues. *Journal of Personality and Social Psychology, 61,* 766–775. Kelly, A. E. (2005). Relationships in emergency care: Communication and impact. *Topics in Emergency Medicine, 27,* 192–197.

APPENDIX 14.B. CONFLICT RESOLUTION ONLINE RESOURCES

- **Association for Conflict Resolution:** http://www.acrnet.org
  A professional organization made up of mediators, arbitrators, educators, and other conflict resolution practitioners.
- **Conflict Resolution Network:** http://www.crnhq.org
  Offers many conflict resolution and communication training materials that can be freely downloaded from the Web site.
- **Conflict Resolution Information Source:** http://www.crinfo.org
  Allows simple and advanced searches of conflict resolution–related resources, browsing options, and online courses.

15
Motivating Employees

Shawn Phipps, MS, OTR/L

❖ Key Terms and Concepts

Extrinsic motivation. Motivation that is driven by factors that are external to the employee (e.g., compensation).

Intrinsic motivation. Motivation that is driven by factors that are internal to the employee (e.g., pride in delivering effective occupational therapy interventions to clients).

Mentoring. Provision of ongoing formal and informal support for another's professional development.

Motivation. The act of inspiring others to move toward goal-directed action.

Team building. Use of structured and unstructured methods to build cohesion and solidarity among group members in pursuit of an organization's mission.

❖ Learning Objectives

After completing this chapter, you should be able to do the following:

- Identify 3 key concepts related to motivation in the occupational therapy workplace.
- Understand how motivation is influenced by generational differences.
- Describe the main differences between intrinsic and extrinsic motivational factors.

- Identify 5 key strategies for motivating employees.
- Describe how to incorporate motivational strategies into effective supervision, mentoring, and team building.

Occupational therapy managers are challenged to motivate employees in achieving high standards of performance. Employee motivation is a critical element in attaining organizational goals, yet understanding how to effectively motivate employees presents one of the greatest challenges for occupational therapy managers and supervisors (Nohria, Groysberg, & Lee, 2008). This chapter describes the critical leadership skills required to motivate employees and build successful working teams in occupational therapy practice.

This chapter incorporates the concept of becoming more "powerful" collectively as an occupational therapy profession through effective motivational and team-building strategies (American Occupational Therapy Association [AOTA], 2007). The chapter also addresses the organizational structures of departmental relationships, leadership, and management as client factors influencing an employee's motivation (AOTA, 2008). In addition, social demands (social environment and cultural contexts) are addressed, as motivational strategies may be incorpo-

rated into occupational therapy intervention as an activity demand.

Although this chapter primarily focuses on motivating employees from an occupational therapy management perspective, the motivational strategies presented equally apply to clients engaged in the occupational therapy process and occupational therapy students in the academic or fieldwork education context. In the clinical setting, a client achieves better functional outcomes when engaged in meaningful and intrinsically motivating occupational performance activities. Similarly, occupational therapy students best learn and develop when motivated to pursue higher levels of achievement under the supervision of an effective occupational therapy educator or clinical instructor (Kumpikaite & Alas, 2009).

GENERATIONAL CONSIDERATIONS IN EFFECTIVELY MOTIVATING EMPLOYEES

Generational differences in the work setting challenge the occupational therapy manager to incorporate innovative motivational strategies to leadership and supervision. Research indicates that differences in attitudes, preferences, and dispositions exist among various generational groups. These differences create rich organizational diversity and challenge managers to use various approaches when motivating employees across generations (Arsenault, 2004). For example, *Baby Boomers* (born between 1946 and 1964) tend to enjoy setting and achieving shared goals, value loyalty to the organization, and balance work with caring for children and aging parents (Frandsen, 2009). *Generation X* workers (those born between 1965 and 1980) typically value autonomy, independence, and immediate results (Wieck, 2007). *Generation Y* workers (those born between 1981 and 2000), also known as the *millennial generation*, are team-oriented, technologically savvy and extremely effective with multitasking. Those in this age group typically value flexible schedules and work that contributes to a socially responsible goal (Hershatter & Epstein, 2010).

Although these generational descriptions are broad, they have implications for occupational therapy managers who must relate to each group by identifying what they value and finding creative strategies to motivate workers to achieve the highest level of organizational productivity and effectiveness (Frandsen, 2009). As generations work together, conflicts may arise because these employees may approach their work from different perspectives. The occupational therapy manager is challenged to blend these perspectives into a leadership approach that motivates the team toward a shared vision.

UNDERSTANDING MOTIVATION

In personnel management, *motivation* is the act of inspiring others to move toward goal-directed action (Ambrose & Kulik, 1999). Motivation can be influenced by intrinsic factors, from sources internal to a person, such as pride in one's work, a strong work ethic, or a need to contribute to an organization or society. Employees who are intrinsically motivated are able to achieve a sense of intensive purpose and passion for their work and demonstrate a higher level of creativity, goal persistency, and perceived self-efficacy (Wang, 2007). Intrinsic motivation can be influenced by a desire to learn, grow, accomplish, and experience new challenges. Research also shows that intrinsic motivation is significantly correlated with well-being indicators, such as self-actualization and life satisfaction (Nohria et al., 2008).

Motivation also can be influenced by extrinsic factors, or sources external to the person, such as salary, bonuses, honors, awards, and management threats to name a few. Although extrinsic motivational factors are important for managers to consider, a purely extrinsic focus can harm the integrity, health, and long-term vitality of the work environment. Research also has suggested that compensation alone does not lead to overall job satisfaction (Hekman, Steensma, Bigley, & Hereford, 2009). Because each individual is motivated by a different set of factors, the occupational therapy manager is challenged to balance intrinsic

and extrinsic motivational factors in mentoring occupational therapy practitioners toward a higher standard of achievement. Understanding what motivates an employee both intrinsically and extrinsically can help the manager maximize that employee's performance. Likewise, a clear understanding of what contributes to a lack of motivation can help the manager avoid potential leadership pitfalls (Farrell & Stamm, 1988).

One way to identify intrinsic and extrinsic motivational factors is to ask employees what their professional and personal goals are in the organization (Egan, 2005). At the beginning of employment and at regular intervals, the manager can ask employees to state their goals for advancing their professional and personal development (Klein, Wesson, Hollenbeck, & Alge, 1999). Formal performance reviews are another opportunity for the manager and employee to discuss goals and objectives as the manager can capitalize on the employee's goals to promote maximum employee output. Motivational factors also can be identified through observation of the employee while engaged in occupational therapy practice. Determining what motivates an employee can help the manager understand the intrinsic and extrinsic factors that can contribute to a higher level of performance and lower rates of turnover and absenteeism.

STRATEGIES FOR EFFECTIVE MOTIVATION

Once the occupational therapy manager has identified an employee's intrinsic and extrinsic motivational factors, the manager can maximize employee performance through the use of evidence-based motivational strategies, which include feedback, fairness, active listening, effective delegation, inclusiveness in decision making and employee participation, team building, mentoring, and employee rewards. Each of these strategies is discussed in turn in the sections that follow.

Providing Effective Feedback to Enhance Motivation

Positive reinforcement can drive an employee to higher levels of achievement (Kling, 1995). When the employee engages in a desired behavior, the occupational therapy manager should take the time to provide positive feedback using verbal or written methodologies, whether through spontaneous recognition or during the employee's performance review (Cravens, Oliver, & Stewart, 2010). Positive feedback reinforces the desired behavior, encouraging the employee to engage in it with greater frequency (Shalley, 1991). Praise should be sincere, timely, and related to specific accomplishments that contribute significantly to the success of the program. If feedback is necessary to correct a behavior, the feedback should be honest, objective, constructive, specific, clear, and communicated with an emphasis on how the employee can turn a mistake into an opportunity for goal achievement (Cawley, Keeping, & Levy, 1998). Feedback promotes constructive communication, collaboration, and cooperation, and creates a work environment that fosters goal-oriented behavior and a focus on the multitude of opportunities to engage in satisfying work (Zacher, Heusner, Schmitz, Zwierzanska, & Frese, 2010). For example, an occupational therapy manager observed an employee demonstrating unprofessional behaviors with clients and staff. The manager scheduled a time to privately meet with the employee to discuss the unprofessional behaviors. The manager offered constructive feedback on the employee's performance. The employee indicated that he was not aware of the problematic behaviors and requested support and feedback to develop a plan of correction. Together, the manager and employee set a mutually agreed-upon goal for achieving a higher level of professional behavior with clients and staff, providing a platform for ongoing support, feedback, and motivation toward a shared goal.

Fairness Practices to Increase Motivation

Employees should feel that the implementation of departmental policies is conducted in a fair and judicious manner. When all employees are treated fairly and given equal opportunity for achievement, they are more likely to contribute to the success of the organization (Locke & Latham, 1990). Alternatively, if employees do not trust that the manager is implementing a policy fairly, their motivation may wane over time. For example, a new graduate distrusted a clinical supervisor who she believed focused on her clinical flaws. Instead of feeling free to contribute to the success of the occupational therapy department, the new employee reluctantly took a passive role in the organization. After the supervisor recognized the employee's disengagement, a meeting was scheduled to discuss the new graduate's performance. The employee revealed that she did not feel that she was being fairly treated, indicating that she felt the supervisor was overly critical of her work. Together, the supervisor and employee developed a plan for supported mentorship that created a safe platform for exchange of ideas and problem solving without making the employee feel singled out from the other staff.

Effective Communication Through Active Listening

Effective communication fosters empowerment, personal growth, and organizational trust in a supervisory relationship. A critical component of effective communication is *active listening*, which is the multifaceted skill of directing full attention, concentration, and effort to the employee while remaining nonjudgmental. Through active listening, the occupational therapy manager establishes trust and demonstrates respect for the concerns of the employee (Nyhan, 2000). The manager can motivate employees by listening to their concerns regarding challenges in the workplace and engaging in active problem solving (Latham & Pinder, 2005). Often, employees have creative suggestions for how to resolve a problem or concern, and having those suggestions taken seriously can motivate them to take decisive action. For example, an employee became increasingly concerned with the productivity demands of the

organization. The employee approached her manager, articulating her concerns that quality patient care was being compromised due to unrealistic productivity expectations. The manager actively listened to the employee's concerns and asked her to share her ideas for ensuring a high level of productivity that would not compromise high-quality patient care. The employee offered to lead an innovative group therapy program development project that could maximize productivity and provide better patient care. Through active listening, the manager encouraged active problem solving and creative solutions for achieving a mutually satisfying goal.

Effective Employee Empowerment Through Effective Delegation

Delegating responsibilities to employees contributes to their professional development by providing unique opportunities to build new skills and develop new competencies (Reinhard & Dickhauser, 2009). Delegation also can provide the added benefit of motivating employees toward action, as they become the drivers of change through engagement in work responsibilities that have meaning (Honold, 1997). Empowering leadership has been shown to positively affect psychological empowerment, which influences higher levels of intrinsic motivation and creative process engagement (Zhang & Bartol, 2010).

Delegation is the act of transferring some tasks and authority to an employee. It is a leadership skill that requires an astute understanding of which tasks will challenge the employee and provide him or her with an opportunity to engage fully in shaping the future of the organization. By delegating, the manager can effectively empower the employee to develop greater confidence and self-efficacy that contribute to future-oriented organizational goals (Bandura & Locke, 2003). Delegation also allows for supportive autonomy, where the employee has an opportunity to define how a delegated task is accomplished. For example, an occupational therapist was supervising an occupational therapy assistant who demonstrated a high level of creativity and potential for contributing to the department. The occupational therapist delegated a program development opportunity to the occupational therapy assistant that allowed her to use her creativity to develop a program flyer and presentation promoting occupational therapy for distribution to physicians and the public.

Inclusiveness in Decision Making and Employee Participation

Regularly communicating the organization or department's mission, values, and vision can motivate employees toward a higher level of participation (Mathieu & Zajac, 1990). When employees feel they are an important part of the larger organization and know that their contribution is valued, they are more likely to take action to help the organization meet its goals and objectives (Brown, 1996; Wagner, 1994). Occupational therapy managers and staff should create team goals through a strategic planning process that promotes full inclusion of all staff members (Cotton, Vollrath, Froggatt, Lengnick-Hall, & Jennings, 1988). Strategic initiatives should be bold, clear, and measurable to ensure that employees are motivated to achieve the objectives of the program (Glew, O'Leary-Kelly, Griffin, & Van Fleet, 1995; see Chapter 6 of this volume). The manager motivates individual occupational therapy practitioners to implement those goals by capitalizing on the strengths of each (Doucouliagos, 1995). For example, an occupational therapy manager decided to develop a new mission, values, and vision statement for the department. Rather than working on this project in isolation, the occupational therapy manager brought the entire team together and divided responsibilities for developing a shared direction for the department. The staff commented that they felt a greater level of motivation for achieving the department's goals because they were included in the development of the department's vision.

Team Building

Team-building activities have been shown to effectively lead employees toward the successful accomplishment of organizational goals and objectives (O'Leary-Kelly, Martocchio, & Frink, 1994). Team building can occur in the context of committees, staff meetings, and occupational therapy month celebration activities, to name a few. Building solid teams working in partnership can maximize productivity, interpersonal harmony, and measurable goal achievement as it facilitates the integration of an individual's goals into a larger focus on the organization's needs (Lumsdon, 1995). Effective teams are composed of an interdependent group of individuals who are organized around the organization's core mission, values, and vision for the future. Team building also infuses mutual accountability for achieving the organization's goals when work is conducted in a collaborative environment in which each member of the team has a clear sense of his or her roles and responsibilities for realizing the shared vision for the organization's success. Team building also can facilitate enthusiasm, passion, and drive toward the achievement of the program's vision and mission. Employees who typically underachieve will be motivated by the norm expectations of success from the group at large, problem solving and collective decision making are optimized with the inclusion of multiple perspectives, individual strengths are capitalized on as the group identifies lead persons to carry out specific tasks, and the collective strength of the group creates opportunities for improved productivity, quality, and optimum employee performance. During Occupational Therapy Month, the occupational therapy team developed several innovative strategies for promoting occupational therapy, including an awards ceremony and lunchtime presentations for the interdisciplinary team on the value of occupational therapy. Following the various Occupational Therapy Month celebratory activities, the team reported feeling more cohesive and more motivated to strive for excellence in their everyday work.

Mentoring

Mentoring in occupational therapy involves pairing an experienced leader with an employee who has identified a particular goal in the organization that relates to the mentor's strengths. Mentoring provides training opportunities to develop new skills and can be an effective means of motivating employees (Benson & Dundis, 2003). The mentoring process can provide the necessary support to motivate an employee toward action as accountability and mutual problem solving are established in the mentoring relationship. The occupational therapy manager can effectively motivate employees through guidance, feedback, clinical skills training, and career advancement as part of the mentoring process. For example, a new graduate and an experienced occupational therapy practitioner were paired up to provide opportunities for cotreatment, mutual problem solving, feedback, and other clinical education opportunities that enhanced the new practitioner's ability to integrate his theoretical knowledge into practice through the ongoing support of a mentor relationship.

Employee Rewards

One key to keeping employees motivated is to reward them for work well done (Jenkins, Mitra, Gupta, & Shaw, 1998). Often a simple "thank you" is all it takes to make an employee want to continue working hard. Likewise, public acknowledgment by a peer can effectively motivate employees toward higher levels of achievement. However, sometimes it is prudent to reward employees in a different way. Any reward system should be designed and implemented in consultation with employees and should reflect the values of the organization (DeMatteo, Eby, & Sundstrom, 1998).

Many options are available for rewards, but a few guidelines should be followed: The reward should be matched specifically to the person and to the achievement, and it should be bestowed in a timely and authentic manner (Perry, Mesch, & Paarlberg, 2006). Employees should feel that their reward is meant for them and that thought went into ensuring its specialness. To find out what rewards employees might like, managers should ask them, either face to face or via an interest survey, what they value or what they enjoy doing during their off time. No two people are alike, and therefore rewards should not be the same across the board. Individualizing rewards shows employees that they are cared about and respected. For example, a manager recognized a member of the occupational therapy team for his work in successfully preparing the department for a hospital accreditation survey. The manager collaborated with the team on a special recognition lunch to congratulate the employee's efforts, with attendance from key hospital administrative staff. Each team member prepared a brief statement of congratulations. This recognition was deeply effective for the employee and served as a motivator for continued levels of excellence.

Additional suggestions for providing concrete rewards for exceptional performance to motivate employees include raises and bonuses, increased paid time off, promotions, or a title change (Baltes, Briggs, Huff, Wright, & Neuman, 1999). All behavior or activity that is rewarded should be above ordinary productivity or expectations; frivolous rewards will set a precedent in which employees expect all behavior to be rewarded, which could be costly (Bucklin & Dickinson, 2001). It also should be noted that managers should not promise a reward unless they can actually deliver it (Honeywell-Johnson & Dickinson, 1999); failing to deliver on the promise devalues the employee and his or her contribution.

MOTIVATING EMPLOYEES IN CHALLENGING TIMES

Motivating employees during challenging times, whether due to a bad economy or rapid organizational change, can present the occupational therapy manager with opportunities for innovative leadership approaches to motivation.

An effective leader consistently prepares employees for inevitable change (Nohria et al., 2008). Leaders must ensure that employees understand why a change is necessary. Employees also need to feel that their ideas are valued as part of the solution to organizational challenges. Effective leaders inspire employees toward a more optimistic future by actively engaging the employee in solution-driven activity, despite the threat of layoffs and budgetary cutbacks. High morale, employee satisfaction, and the achievement of high levels of motivation are possible during challenging times if employees view their team's work as ultimately contributing to making others' lives more fulfilling.

CONCLUSION

Changing an occupational therapy workplace into a dynamic, creative environment with motivated employees can be a daunting task. By understanding the concept of motivation and strategies for increasing motivation in the workplace, it is possible to move employees toward a higher purpose that engages them in contributing to the success of the organization.

Case Examples

LEVEL I FIELDWORK

Angela, an occupational therapy student interested in pediatrics, was assigned to Level I fieldwork in a nursing home setting; the fieldwork coordinator used a lottery system for fieldwork placement. Angela was having difficulty finding the motivation to give her best effort to a fieldwork experience that did not match her professional interests. The fieldwork supervisor recognized Angela's lack of motivation in the geriatric setting and decided to provide Angela with various hands-on mentoring opportunities with clinical specialists to help her appreciate the role of the occupational therapy practitioner in skilled nursing. Angela then was provided with an opportunity to develop treatment plan for a client who reminded her of her grandmother. The fieldwork supervisor recognized this connection and assisted Angela with developing a mindful appreciation of the importance of occupational therapy for older clients.

LEVEL II FIELDWORK

David was a Level II occupational therapy fieldwork student in an acute rehabilitation setting. He was having difficulty motivating his 81-year-old client with a stroke to participate in the rehabilitation process. As with employees, using motivational strategies that are centered on the clients' most valued priorities and interests can be effective in motivating patients to engage in the thera-

peutic process. David used a client-centered and occupation-based approach to obtaining the client's goals and preferences. During an interview, the client stated that her primary goals were to return home to independently tend to her garden and prepare meals. Using active listening and effective communication, David was able to establish a rapport with the client and incorporate her primary concerns into her occupational therapy treatment program.

FIRST-TIME MANAGER

Mary, the first-time manager of a small occupational therapy department, supervised an occupational therapy practitioner with 30 years of clinical experience. This employee had had a high level of performance early in her career, but for the past 5 years she had appeared unmotivated; she also indicated that she did not plan on retiring for another 5 years.

Recognizing the challenge of motivating the practitioner with 30 years of clinical experience, Mary decided to meet with the occupational therapy practitioner to determine which professional development activities were motivating for the staff member. The experienced occupational therapy practitioner mentioned that she had been involved with mentoring new staff to develop their clinical skills, but she was removed from this duty

(continued)

Case Examples *(cont.)*

approximately 10 years ago. Still, she stated that she enjoyed teaching. Mary decided to capitalize on the employee's rich experience and asked her to conduct a series of educational in-services to the staff and to take on a primary role of mentoring all new staff in the department. The employee demonstrated a greater level of motivation following her engagement in teaching and mentoring activities.

MANAGER

Thomas was a regional manager for two outpatient hand clinics. One clinic consistently demonstrated a high level of achievement, staff productivity, and job satisfaction, but the other struggled with meeting productivity requirements, and employees had a low level of job satisfaction. Recognizing that one clinic was performing at a higher level than the other, Thomas decided to conduct regional meetings with the clinics together to share experiences and to collaborate on the development of unifying standards of practice throughout the region. Thomas also asked the higher-performing clinic to provide mentoring to the lower-performing clinic to serve as a team-building effort. It also provided an opportunity for the lower-functioning clinic to learn from their peers at the higher-functioning clinic.

❖ Learning Activities

1. Describe a work experience during which you experienced a high degree of job satisfaction. What intrinsic and extrinsic motivational factors contributed to your success?
2. Describe a leader, mentor, supervisor, or manager who has had a significant effect on your professional and personal development. Which motivational strategies did he or she use?
3. Describe a work or volunteer experience in which you had a low level of motivation. What were the contributing factors to your low motivation?
4. Identify one team-building activity you could implement in your work setting to increase the motivation of your staff.
5. Choose one person in your life whom you would like to mentor. What strategies would you use to ensure the highest level of motivation during the mentoring process?

MOTIVATION WEB SITES

- **Employee motivation "how-to" guides:** www.inc.com/guides/hr/20776.html
- **Motivation management library:** www.managementhelp.org/guiding/motivate/basics.htm
- **Motivation and retention:** www.entrepreneur.com/managingemployees/motivationandretention/archive143978.html

✓ Multiple-Choice Questions

1. Motivation is
   a. Moving others toward goal-directed action
   b. Happiness
   c. Fulfillment
   d. All of the above
2. Intrinsic motivation is
   a. External drive to achieve success
   b. Motivation driven by internal factors
   c. Moving others toward goal-directed action
   d. None of the above
3. Extrinsic motivation is
   a. Motivation driven by external factors
   b. Internal drive to achieve success
   c. Moving others toward goal-directed action
   d. Both a and c
4. An example of an intrinsic motivator is
   a. Salary
   b. Reward
   c. Need to contribute to society
   d. Honors
5. An example of an extrinsic motivator is
   a. Salary
   b. Honors
   c. Awards
   d. All of the above
6. Mentoring is
   a. Formal method of facilitating professional development
   b. Informal method of facilitating professional development

c. Driven by extrinsic factors

d. Both a and b

7. Team building is

    a. Building cohesion in pursuit of an organization's mission

    b. Building extrinsic motivation

    c. Holding a staff meeting each week

    d. None of the above

8. Which of the following is *not* a principle of rewarding employees successfully?

    a. Matching the reward to the person

    b. 3% match on the retirement plan

    c. Timeliness

    d. Authenticity

9. Mentoring can

    a. Motivate an employee toward action

    b. Produce accountability

    c. Promote mutual problem solving

    d. All of the above

10. Which of the following is not an outcome of team building?

    a. Poor morale

    b. Increased productivity

    c. Interpersonal harmony

    d. Goal achievement

11. Inclusiveness and participation effectively improve employee motivation because

    a. Employees feel they are an important part of the larger organization

    b. Employees know that their contribution to the success of a strategic plan is valued

    c. Employees are more likely to take action toward helping the organization meet its goals and objectives

    d. All of the above

12. Delegation is an effective strategy for building employee motivation because

    a. Delegation takes the workload off the manager

    b. Delegation builds morale

    c. Delegation builds new skills and develops new competencies

    d. All of the above

13. Active listening

    a. Builds trust

    b. Encourages creative problem solving

    c. Builds mutual respect

    d. All of the above

14. Fairness can contribute to employee motivation because

    a. When all employees are treated fairly and given equal opportunity for achievement, they are more likely to contribute to the success of the organization

    b. Employees do not like change

    c. Employees feel empowered

    d. None of the above

15. When providing positive feedback, praise should be

    a. Delayed

    b. Minimized

    c. Related to specific accomplishments that contribute significantly to the success of the program

    d. None of the above

16. Motivational factors can be identified through

    a. Observation

    b. Tone of voice

    c. Annual performance evaluation

    d. Both a and c

References

Ambrose, M. L., & Kulik, C. T. (1999). Old friends, new faces: Motivation research in the 1990s. *Journal of Management, 25,* 231–292.

American Occupational Therapy Association. (2007). AOTA *Centennial Vision* and executive summary. *American Journal of Occupational Therapy, 61,* 613–614.

American Occupational Therapy Association. (2008). Occupational therapy practice framework: Domain and process (2nd ed.). *American Journal of Occupational Therapy, 62,* 625–683.

Arsenault, P. M. (2004). Validating generational differences: A legitimate diversity and leadership issue. *Leadership and Organization Development Journal, 25,* 124–141.

Baltes, B. B., Briggs, T. E., Huff, J. W., Wright, J. A., & Neuman, G. A. (1999). Flexible and compressed workweek schedules: A meta-analysis of their effects on work-related criteria. *Journal of Applied Psychology, 84,* 496–513.

Bandura, A., & Locke, E. (2003). Negative self-efficacy and goal effects revisited. *Journal of Applied Psychology, 88,* 87–99.

Benson, S. G., & Dundis, S. P. (2003). Understanding and motivating health employees: Integrating Maslow's hierarchy of needs, training, and technology. *Journal of Nursing Management, 11,* 315–320.

Brown, S. P. (1996). A meta-analysis and review of organizational research on job involvement. *Psychological Bulletin, 120,* 235–255.

Bucklin, B. R., & Dickinson, A. M. (2001). Individual monetary incentives: A review of different types of arrangements between performance and pay. *Journal of Organizational Behavior Management, 21,* 45–137.

Cawley, B. D., Keeping, L. M., & Levy, P. E. (1998). Participation in the performance appraisal process and employee reactions: A meta-analytic review of field investigations. *Journal of Applied Psychology, 83,* 615–633.

Cotton, J. L., Vollrath, D. A., Froggatt, K. L., Lengnick-Hall, M. L., & Jennings, K. R. (1988). Employee participation: Diverse forms and different outcomes. *Academy of Management Review, 13*, 8–22.

Cravens, K. S., Oliver, E. G., & Stewart, J. S. (2010). Can a positive approach to performance evaluation help accomplish your goals? *Business Horizons, 53*, 269.

DeMatteo, J. S., Eby, L. T., & Sundstrom, E. (1998). Team-based rewards: Current empirical evidence and directions for future research. *Research in Organizational Behavior, 20*, 141–183.

Doucouliagos, C. (1995). Worker participation and productivity in labor-managed and participatory capitalist firms: A meta-analysis. *Industrial and Labor Relations Review, 49*, 58–77.

Egan, T. M. (2005). Factors influencing individual creativity in the workplace: An examination of quantitative empirical research. *Advances in Developing Human Resources, 7*, 160–181.

Glew, D. J., O'Leary-Kelly, A. M., Griffin, R. W., & Van Fleet, D. D. (1995). Participation in organizations: A preview of issues and proposed framework for future analysis. *Journal of Management, 21*, 395–421.

Farrell, D., & Stamm, C. L. (1988). Meta-analysis of the correlates of employee absence. *Human Relations, 41*, 211–227.

Frandsen, B. M. (2009). Leading by recognizing generational differences. *Long-Term Living, 58*, 34–35.

Hekman, D., Steensma, H., Bigley, G., & Hereford, J. (2009). Effects of organizational and professional identification on the relationship between administrators' social influence and professional employees' adoption of new work behavior. *Journal of Applied Psychology, 94*(5), 1325.

Hershatter, A., & Epstein, M. (2010). Millennials and the world of work: An organization and management perspective. *Journal of Business Psychology, 25*, 211–223.

Honeywell-Johnson, J. A., & Dickinson, A. M. (1999). Small group incentives: A review of the literature. *Journal of Organizational Behavior Management, 19*, 89–120.

Honold, L. (1997). A review of the literature on employee empowerment. *Empowerment in Organizations, 5*, 202–212.

Jenkins, G. D., Mitra, A., Gupta, N., & Shaw, J. D. (1998). Are financial incentives related to performance? A meta-analytic review of empirical research. *Journal of Applied Psychology, 83*, 777–787.

Klein, H. J., Wesson, M. J., Hollenbeck, J. R., & Alge, B. J. (1999). Goal commitment and the goal-setting process: Conceptual clarification and empirical synthesis. *Journal of Applied Psychology, 84*, 885–896.

Kling, J. (1995). High performance work systems and firm performance. *Monthly Labor Review, 118*, 29–36.

Kumpikaite, V., & Alas, R. (2009). Students' attitudes to work and studies: Practical case. *Economics and Management, 14*, 582–588.

Latham, G. P., & Pinder, C. C. (2005). Work motivation theory and research at the dawn of the twenty-first century. *Annual Review of Psychology, 56*, 485–516.

Locke, E. A., & Latham, G. P. (1990). Work motivation and satisfaction: Light at the end of the tunnel. *Psychological Science, 1*, 240–246.

Lumsdon, K. (1995). Why executive teams fail and what to do. *Hospital and Health Networks, 69*, 24.

Mathieu, J. E., & Zajac, D. M. (1990). A review and meta-analysis of the antecedents, correlates, and consequences of organizational commitment. *Psychological Bulletin, 108*, 171–194.

Nohria, N., Groysberg, B., & Lee, L. (2008). Employee motivation: A powerful new model. *Harvard Business Review, 86*, 78–84.

Nyhan, R. C. (2000). Changing the paradigm: Trust and its role in public sector organizations. *American Review of Public Administration, 30*, 87–109.

O'Leary-Kelly, A. M., Martocchio, J. J., & Frink, D. D. (1994). A review of the influence of group goals on group performance. *Academy of Management Journal, 37*, 1285–1301.

Perry, J. L., Mesch, D., & Paarlberg, L. (2006). Motivating employees in a new governance era: The performance paradigm revisited. *Public Administration Review, 66*, 505–514.

Reinhard, M., & Dickhauser, O. (2009). Need for cognition, task difficulty, and the formation of performance expectancies. *Journal of Personality and Social Psychology, 96*, 1062–1076.

Shalley, C. E. (1991). Effects of productivity goals, creative goals, and personal discretion on individual creativity. *Journal of Applied Psychology, 76*, 179–185.

Wagner, J. A. (1994). Participation effects on performance and satisfaction: A reconsideration of research evidence. *Academy of Management Review, 19*, 312–330.

Wang, L. (2007). Sources of leadership self-efficacy: Follower feedback and group performance outcomes. *International Journal of Business Research, 7*, 140–148.

Wieck, K. L. (2007). Motivating an intergenerational workforce: Scenarios for success. *Orthopaedic Nursing, 26*, 366–371.

Zacher, H., Heusner, S., Schmitz, M., Zwierzanska, M. M., & Frese, M. (2010). Focus on opportunities as a mediator of the relationships between age, job complexity, and work performance. *Journal of Vocational Behavior, 76*, 374.

Zhang, X., & Bartol, K. M. (2010). Linking empowering leadership and employee creativity: The influence of psychological empowerment, intrinsic motivation, and creative process engagement. *Academy of Management Journal, 53*, 107.

Appendix 15.A. Motivation Evidence Table

Topic	Evidence
Motivation and self-efficacy	Ambrose, M. L., & Kulik, C. T. (1999). Old friends, new faces: Motivation research in the 1990s. *Journal of Management, 25,* 231–292. Bandura, A. & Locke, E. (2003). Negative self-efficacy and goal effects revisited. *Journal of Applied Psychology, 88,* 87–99. Egan, T. M. (2005). Factors influencing individual creativity in the workplace: An examination of quantitative empirical research. *Advances in Developing Human Resources, 7,* 160–181. Farrell, D., & Stamm, C. L. (1988). Meta-analysis of the correlates of employee absence. *Human Relations, 41,* 211–227. Hekman, D., Steensma, H., Bigley, G., & Hereford, J. (2009). Effects of organizational and professional identification on the relationship between administrators' social influence and professional employees' adoption of new work behavior. *Journal of Applied Psychology, 94*(5), 1325. Latham, G. P., & Pinder, C. C. (2005). Work motivation theory and research at the dawn of the twenty-first century. *Annual Review of Psychology, 56,* 485–516. Locke, E. A., & Latham, G. P. (1990). Work motivation and satisfaction: Light at the end of the tunnel. *Psychological Science, 1,* 240–246. Nohria, N., Groysberg, B., & Lee, L. (2008). Employee motivation: A powerful new model. *Harvard Business Review, 86,* 78–84. Wang, L. (2007). Sources of leadership self-efficacy: Follower feedback and group performance outcomes. *International Journal of Business Research, 7,* 140–148.
Generational considerations in effectively motivating employees	Arsenault, P. M. (2004). Validating generational differences: A legitimate diversity and leadership issue. *Leadership and Organization Development Journal, 25,* 124–141. Frandsen, B. M. (2009). Leading by recognizing generational differences. *Long-Term Living, 58,* 34–35. Hershatter, A., & Epstein, M. (2010). Millennials and the world of work: An organization and management perspective. *Journal of Business Psychology, 25,* 211–223. Wieck, K. L. (2007). Motivating an intergenerational workforce: Scenarios for success. *Orthopaedic Nursing, 26,* 366–371.
Providing effective feedback to enhance motivation	Cawley, B. D., Keeping, L. M., & Levy, P. E. (1998). Participation in the performance appraisal process and employee reactions: A meta-analytic review of field investigations. *Journal of Applied Psychology, 83,* 615–633. Cravens, K. S., Oliver, E. G., & Stewart, J. S. (2010). Can a positive approach to performance evaluation help accomplish your goals? *Business Horizons, 53,* 269. Klein, H. J., Wesson, M. J., Hollenbeck, J. R., & Alge, B. J. (1999). Goal commitment and the goal-setting process: Conceptual clarification and empirical synthesis. *Journal of Applied Psychology, 84,* 885–896. Kling, J. (1995). High performance work systems and firm performance. *Monthly Labor Review, 118,* 29–36. Shalley, C. E. (1991). Effects of productivity goals, creative goals, and personal discretion on individual creativity. *Journal of Applied Psychology, 76,* 179–185.
Employee empowerment through effective delegation	Honold, L. (1997). A review of the literature on employee empowerment. *Empowerment in Organizations, 5,* 202–212. Reinhard, M., & Dickhauser, O. (2009). Need for cognition, task difficulty, and the formation of performance expectancies. *Journal of Personality and Social Psychology, 96,* 1062–1076. Zacher, H., Heusner, S., Schmitz, M., Zwierzanska, M. M., & Frese, M. (2010). Focus on opportunities as a mediator of the relationships between age, job complexity, and work performance. *Journal of Vocational Behavior, 76,* 374. Zhang, X., & Bartol, K. M. (2010). Linking empowering leadership and employee creativity: The influence of psychological empowerment, intrinsic motivation, and creative process engagement. *Academy of Management Journal, 53,* 107.

(continued)

APPENDIX 15.A. MOTIVATION EVIDENCE TABLE *(cont.)*

Topic	Evidence
Inclusiveness in decision making and employee participation	Brown, S. P. (1996). A meta-analysis and review of organizational research on job involvement. *Psychological Bulletin, 120,* 235–255. Cotton, J. L., Vollrath, D. A., Froggatt, K. L., Lengnick-Hall, M. L., & Jennings, K. R. (1988). Employee participation: Diverse forms and different outcomes. *Academy of Management Review, 13,* 8–22. Doucouliagos, C. (1995). Worker participation and productivity in labor-managed and participator capitalist firms: A meta-analysis. *Industrial and Labor Relations Review, 49,* 58–77. Glew, D. J., O'Leary-Kelly, A. M., Griffin, R. W., & Van Fleet, D. D. (1995). Participation in organizations: A preview of issues and proposed framework for future analysis. *Journal of Management, 21,* 395–421. Mathieu, J. E., & Zajac, D. M. (1990). A review and meta-analysis of the antecedents, correlates, and consequences of organizational commitment. *Psychological Bulletin, 108,* 171–194. Wagner, J. A. (1994). Participation effects on performance and satisfaction: A reconsideration of research evidence. *Academy of Management Review, 19,* 312–330.
Team building	Lumsdon, K. (1995). Why executive teams fail and what to do. *Hospital and Health Networks, 69,* 24. O'Leary-Kelly, A. M., Martocchio, J. J., & Frink, D. D. (1994). A review of the influence of group goals on group performance. *Academy of Management Journal, 37,* 1285–1301.
Mentoring and training	Benson, S. G., & Dundis, S. P. (2003). Understanding and motivating health employees: Integrating Maslow's hierarchy of needs, training, and technology. *Journal of Nursing Management, 11,* 315–320. Kumpikaite, V., & Alas, R. (2009). Students' attitudes to work and studies: Practical case. *Economics and Management, 14,* 582–588.
Rewarding employees	Baltes, B. B., Briggs, T. E., Huff, J. W., Wright, J. A., & Neuman, G. A. (1999). Flexible and compressed workweek schedules: A meta-analysis of their effects on work-related criteria. *Journal of Applied Psychology, 84,* 496–513. Bucklin, B. R., & Dickinson, A. M. (2001). Individual monetary incentives: A review of different types of arrangements between performance and pay. *Journal of Organizational Behavior Management, 21,* 45–137. DeMatteo, J. S., Eby, L. T., & Sundstrom, E. (1998). Team-based rewards: Current empirical evidence and directions for future research. *Research in Organizational Behavior, 20,* 141–183. Honeywell-Johnson, J. A., & Dickinson, A. M. (1999). Small group incentives: A review of the literature. *Journal of Organizational Behavior Management, 19,* 89–120. Jenkins, G. D., Mitra, A., Gupta, N., & Shaw, J. D. (1998). Are financial incentives related to performance? A meta-analytic review of empirical research. *Journal of Applied Psychology, 83,* 777–787. Perry, J. L., Mesch, D., & Paarlberg, L. (2006). Motivating employees in a new governance era: The performance paradigm revisited. *Public Administration Review, 66,* 505–514.

16
Mentoring and Professional Development

Joanne J. Foss, PhD, OTR/L

❖ Key Terms and Concepts

Formal mentorships. Programs in which mentors and mentees are assigned to one another by the management of the organization in pursuit of increased productivity, job success, worker loyalty, or job satisfaction.

Informal mentorships. Naturally occurring pairings that focus on goals set by arrangement between the mentee and the mentor.

Mentoring. A developmental partnership that has as its primary focus professional or career development and personal growth. Not all types of mentoring focus on career advancement; this chapter will present mentoring in primarily this type of context.

Mentoring culture. Environment that values mentoring as a key process for the organization's professional development programs, resulting in the formation and facilitation of formal and informal mentorship programs.

Outcome measures. In mentorship, behavioral objectives that quantify change and transition and identify the behaviors that illustrate successful professional development and the purposes of the mentorship program.

Professional development. Growth in skills, knowledge, and personal attributes. Individual therapists identify goals that reflect the key skills they need to develop and the competencies they need to gain or strengthen.

Virtual mentoring. Computer- and Internet-assisted mentoring; also referred to in the literature as *e-mentoring*, *telementoring*, or *cybermentoring*.

❖ Learning Objectives

After completing this chapter, you should be able to do the following:

- Describe formal and informal mentoring.
- Describe the benefits of mentoring to the mentor, the mentee, and the organization.
- Examine the value of virtual mentorships.
- Describe the characteristics of mentors and mentees.
- Identify key elements needed to develop a mentoring culture.

Mentoring has long been recommended as a way of helping professionals learn and develop throughout their career (Scandura, 1992). Mentors orient occupational therapists who are at the beginning of their career to professional practice and behavioral expectations. Classroom and fieldwork experiences are often designed to help students form the mentoring relationships with instructors and clinical educators that provide support and guidance as they adapt to the culture of the profession.

Professional growth begins at the entry level and continues throughout the span of a professional career. After graduation from an academic program, continued development and guidance for learning and growth throughout the career span is less defined, and strategic planning for lifelong learning is left up to the individual. The profession expects practitioners to form a plan to update and build their skills along the paths their career takes. The American Occupational Therapy Association (AOTA, 2010) *Code of Ethics and Ethics Standards* holds each practitioner responsible for maintaining competence in practice, education, and research and participating in professional development and educational activities. Although licensure and certification requirements demand the amount, and sometimes the content, of continuing education, the design and progression of an individualized professional development program is not specifically defined, and the profession has promoted autonomy in the definition of career goals and direction (Robertson & Savio, 2003).

A new graduate, an experienced clinician, a clinical or academic educator, and an occupational therapy manager all have potential needs for a mentoring relationship. Lifelong learning is necessary to sustain growth in the professional's knowledge, skills, and attitudes spanning the length of a career. Goals and plans might be altered, replaced, or redefined over time, but learning and growth should continue.

A critical element of professional development is interpersonal relationships with mentors. Authors in many disciplines have written about the importance of the guidance, encouragement, and inspiration of mentors (Gillette, 2008; Ragins & Kram, 2007; Schrubbe, 2004), and research has shown the positive impact of mentors on the career trajectory of their mentees (Dreher & Ash, 1990; Fagenson-Eland, Marks, & Amendola, 1997; Ragins & Scandura, 1999). This chapter discusses the role mentoring relationships play in professional development.

Mentoring and Professional Development Research

In the 1980s, there was increased research on the value of mentoring relationships (Kram, 2004). Studies defined the roles of mentors, the range of relationship functions, and the benefits of mentoring relationships for individuals and organizations. The focus of research was on the factors that generally contributed to successful relationships and the more specific factors required by an increasing workforce of women and minorities (Kram, 2004). On the basis of these studies' findings, human resource professionals and other organizational leaders sought to establish an environmental context that fostered mentoring relationships through formal or informal mentoring programs (Chao, Waltz, & Gardner, 1992).

More recent research has found a drastic change in the context and structure of work environments, leading researchers to reconceptualize and redefine mentoring relationships. Kram (2004) discussed the challenges of the rapid development of new technologies, instability in the workplace, and the globalization of commerce. As traditional, stable, and hierarchical contexts give way to more complex working environments, the traditional long-term relationship between one wiser, more experienced mentor and a novice mentee still exists but may evolve into a network of relationships focused on specific aspects of professional development. In today's health care environments, some aspects of mentoring relationships have expanded from the traditional one-to-one relationship to a network of multiple relationships mirroring the team approaches of health care delivery (Grossman, 2007).

In the past, staff therapists might have served an extended apprenticeship with a manager or administrator ap-proaching retirement. In today's evolving environment, a therapist who desires to move into a rehabilitation director position may be guided in the acquisition of organizational cultural knowledge by a seasoned health care administrator but may rely on an experienced occupational therapy manager to expand supervision skills. Both relationships would be shorter than the traditional one-to-one relationship, but the learning curve is also shorter, and the added information from outside the department strengthens the relationship for the future (Perrone, 2003). Nevertheless, these relationships, despite possibly being shorter or less intensive, have similar structures and benefits, and the people involved have similar roles.

Mentoring and Professional Development Defined

Mentoring is defined as a developmental partnership that has as its primary focus professional, career development or personal growth. Regardless of years of experience, it is important for every health professional to plan for continuing competence. *Professional development* advances professional growth and development, knowledge, and attributes. Therefore, occupational therapy practitioners must recognize needed skills and knowledge and seek guidance for this development process. The defining feature of mentoring is the dedication of the mentor to the career advancement and psychosocial support of another—the mentee (Ragins & Kram, 2007). Often the need for mentoring results from a transition, or the need for the development or strengthening in key areas. For example, mentees are nurtured or directed toward a change in performance or capacity, knowledge level, or position. Mentors can facilitate the development of "self-confidence, job satisfaction, upward mobility, and decision making/problem solving in a protégée" (Schrubbe, 2004, p. 324).

Typically, *mentorship* and *supervision* are defined as distinctly different roles. The manager oversees and directs task performance toward the accomplishment of outcomes dictated by a specific job or social context, whereas the support and guidance of a mentor foster individual outcomes leading to personal and professional development. Mentoring relationships are more flexible than supervision and can be adapted to the context and needs of the relationship (Urish, 2004). Unlike a supervisor, the mentor may not be employed by the same organization and may not even be of the same profession.

Can a supervisor or manager be a mentor? Although supervisors often perform some of the functions of a mentor, Clutterbuck (2004) postulated that there is a different dynamic when one member of the relationship has decision-making or evaluative influence over the other. The reported benefits of mentees with supervisory mentors are mixed. On one hand, mentees reported receiving more career mentoring and less social support and role modeling (Chao et al., 1992; Ragins & Cotton, 1999). On the other hand, another study reported both greater career mentoring and social support and less role modeling (Fagenson-Eland et al., 1997). Later sections of this chapter discuss the types of relationship and the variety of functions that make up a mentoring relationship in attempting to answer this question and define the parameters of supervisor mentoring relationships.

The Mentor

As Schrubbe (2004) observed, "Mentors have the ability to inspire confidence in others, push them to their limits, and continue to develop them to their greatest potential. How is this accomplished?" (p. 324). Often mentors have the ability to recognize potential that mentees fail to see in themselves. Scholars of mentoring have been interested in the characteristics of mentors and the mentor competencies that lead to successful mentorships. They have found that for success, mentors must share guidance, knowledge, wisdom, and organizational cultural skills and that mentees must be committed, self-motivated, and open to change. However, there also must be relationship attractors to make the relationship work and the two individuals compatible. Whether this attraction is termed *fit*, *style*, or *chemistry*, it is necessary for a mentoring pair to work well together (Schrubbe, 2004). No matter what this attraction is called, potential mentoring pairs need to have similar philosophies, compatible professional interests, and complementary interpersonal communication styles (Kram, 1985).

Wellington (2001) stated that talent draws a mentor to a mentee, whereas accomplishment and power draw a mentee. Mentors do not need to be in positions of authority, but they must have the power to represent mentees' accomplishments and be politically savvy enough to enhance mentees' career advancement. As well, mentees need the potential to be worthy of their mentor's commitment of time and investment of energy on their behalf.

Not all managers have the capacity to be good mentors. Some managers may not have the time to devote to mentoring. Cultivating and sustaining a developmental relationship can be intense, and potential mentors vary in their possession of the social skills needed. The range of social skills studied includes self-awareness, self-regulation, empathy, and relationship-building skills (Kram, 2004). Effective mentors should possess patience, enthusiasm, wisdom, and knowledge in the areas needed by the mentee. The nursing literature identifies characteristics that seem essential for mentors; these include flexibility, acceptance, optimism and hope, social skill role modeling, and communication skills (Grossman, 2007). The flexibility of the mentor allows the mentee the freedom to think freely and follow his or her own ideas. Mentors need to know when not to interfere and to empower mentees to figure things out on their own. They need to fight the temptation to take over mentees' problems and to give solutions or advice without encouraging the process of reflection and problem solving.

Effective mentors identify the developmental needs of their mentees and provide a vision for change. Guiding mentees' reflection on their experiences and recognizing their learning potential and merit are key responsibilities of the mentor (Robertson & Savio, 2003). Discussions with mentors assist mentees in thinking critically, problem solving, identifying strategies, and seeking the guidance that enhances their ability to incorporate and learn from past experiences. Mentors need to have wide-ranging skills, knowledge, and attitudes to be effective; Exhibit 16.1 lists the characteristics of effective mentors.

The Mentee

Research reveals that for a mentee to attract a good mentor, he or she must be a person that the mentor wants to associate with (Schrubbe, 2004). Wellington (2001) reported that mentors want to associate with winners, and that employees with high levels of confidence, commitment, and competence are more likely to attract mentors. For example, it was found that "rising stars," or employees who are generally acknowledged to possess the potential of reaching a high level of career success, were more likely to obtain mentors. Ragins and Kram (2007) suggested that mentors select their mentees on the basis of their perceptions of the mentees' aspirations, potential, and competency. Potential mentors appear to be attracted to mentees who show the

EXHIBIT 16.1. CHARACTERISTICS OF AN EFFECTIVE MENTOR

Knowledge
- Legal and ethical issues
- Professional expertise and basic leadership skills
- Stress and conflict management
- Goal clarification and outcome identification and measurement
- Role definition or the differences among managing, advising, supervising, and mentoring
- Cultural awareness and cultural competency
- Awareness of organizational resources
- Range of cognitive and learning styles

Skills
- Active listening and communication
- Feedback and constructive criticism
- Relationship building

Attributes
- Self-awareness, including self-regulation
- Patience and empathy
- Flexibility and acceptance
- Political astuteness
- Enthusiasm and commitment

EXHIBIT 16.2. CHARACTERISTICS OF AN EFFECTIVE MENTEE

Knowledge
- Personal learning and communication styles
- Discipline-specific knowledge

Skills
- Listening
- Articulate communication
- Collaboration and negotiation
- Self-expression and communication
- Social interaction

Attributes
- Ambition, initiation, and goal orientation
- Potential for advancement
- Willingness to be a responsible self-learner
- Cognitive flexibility
- Emotional stability
- Reflection and introspection
- Willingness to take risks
- Ability to receive feedback and take direction

---

qualities of willingness and self-reflection and who take responsibility for their own learning. In addition, Grossman (2007) identified emotional stability and cognitive flexibility as being critical to benefiting from feedback, reacting favorably to change, and gaining confidence with success, and Robertson and Savio (2003) highlighted self-initiation, realistic expectations, and the expectation of success. Exhibit 16.2 lists the characteristics of a good mentee.

COMPONENTS OF THE MENTORING RELATIONSHIP

Studies of childhood development indicate that learning results through relationships with other people, including parents, teachers, siblings, and peers. These relationships can often constitute early mentoring. Similar developmental mentoring relationships appear to continue throughout adulthood, guiding mentees toward their learning potential. According to Kathy Kram (1985), a key author and researcher in mentoring relationships since the early 1980s, mentoring relationships can serve two key functions. The first of these is the *career development* function. Mentors guide mentees in learning a range of organizational behaviors that can assist them in adapting to the organizational culture and preparing for advancement. Mentors can accomplish this guidance through a variety of methods. They can provide behavioral coaching and motivational challenge while increasing the mentee's visibility and exposure in the organization (Ragins & Kram, 2007). Kram (1985) identified sponsorship, coaching, protection, challenging assignments, and exposure as mentor roles in career devel-

opment. A mentor can expose a mentee to professional experiences both inside the organization (social activities and committees) and outside it (professional conferences and meetings), introduce the mentee to important colleagues, and arrange for challenging tasks and duties (Robertson & Savio, 2003).

The second relationship function Kram (1985) labeled the *psychosocial function*. The mentor provides support on a personal level that enhances the mentee's sense of professional self and intrapersonal growth and builds self-esteem and self-efficacy. This support is accomplished through nurturing, counseling, and friendship (Kram, 1985; Ragins & Kram, 2007). Robertson and Savio (2003) suggested that psychosocial mentoring should target self-concept and motivation through nurturing, accepting, and confirming.

Subsequent research has suggested a third function, *role modeling* (Scandura & Ragins, 1993), in which the mentor demonstrates professional behaviors by engaging in the activities and mirroring the behaviors the mentee needs to develop. Examples of role modeling include scholarly activities in an academic environment (Schrubbe, 2004) and therapeutic use of self with clients in a clinic setting (Robertson & Savio, 2003).

Allen, Eby, Poteet, Lentz, and Lima (2004) reported that career and psychosocial functions predicted mentees' ultimate career and job satisfaction. However, this research also revealed that the two functions predicted different outcomes: Career functions were a strong predictor of compensation and advancement, whereas relationships high in psychosocial functions predicted an enhanced sense of competence, self-efficacy, and personal development (Fagenson-Eland et al., 1997).

As in any relationship, there is a range of mentor behaviors and considerable variation in the degree that one or both functions are provided (Ragins & Kram, 2007). Not all relationships provide both career and psychosocial functions, and others provide a high degree of one function and less of the other (Ragins & Cotton, 1999). In part, this range of behaviors can be a reflection of the current needs of the mentee, the capacity of the mentor, and the context or environment. It important to note that other relationships or individuals in a person's life can provide some of these functions as well. A manager or colleague can serve as a role model and "adopt" a new employee to show him or her the organizational ropes without being perceived as a mentor. As well, managers often recognize the professional development needs of their supervisees and can assist them in identifying possible mentors. Even a traditional mentoring relationship offering the full range of functions develops over time; therefore, the degree and range of components can also change over the course of the relationship.

Kram (1985) suggested that there are several phases of mentoring relationships—initiation, cultivation, and separation or redefinition—and that as the relationship moves through these phases, the functions evolve as well. Understanding these phases can help mentors and mentees expect or anticipate the benefits and the trials of the relationship. During the first phase, *initiation,* the mentor and the mentee decide whether they want to work together and define expectations. They often explore the chemistry or fit of the relationship and build rapport. Grossman (2007) termed this the "getting to know each other" time. The goals of initiation include establishing a comfortable rapport and identifying a common ground of need and interests (Clutterbuck, 2004; Kram, 1985). As in all new relationships, this is a phase of negotiating mutual expectations and beginning the task of recognizing a path toward the desired outcomes.

Some career functions may be present during the initiation phase, but both career and psychosocial functions peak during the *cultivation* stage (Ragins & Kram, 2007). During this phase, the dynamic of the relationship changes to one of mutual commitment in a certain direction. The difficult work of supporting (psychosocial functions) and challenging (career functions) takes place during this time. Kram (1985) emphasized that the cultivation phase should be characterized by a strong emotional bond and feelings of reciprocity. The relationship centers on clarifying what the mentee hopes to achieve, and communication is devoted to assessing where the mentee is now and where he or she would like to be in the future. Possible activities are identified. Goals and outcomes are established, and the steps needed to promote desired change and growth are identified. The mentee and mentor select options for change and follow through on a plan. Clutterbuck (2004) suggested that the cultivation stage sets the direction of the relationship and involves a progression of achievement in change and growth. Throughout this stage, the mentee grows professionally and personally, gaining new skills and knowledge along with boosts in self-esteem and self-knowledge.

The cultivation stage ends when the mentee's outcomes have been achieved or the relationship is terminated because of changes that render the relationship unsustainable (Ragins & Kram, 2007). Organizational change or psychosocial issues may disrupt the commitment from either the mentee's or the mentor's perspective. The mentee may outgrow the relationship and become more independent, or the mentor's expertise may no longer meet his or her needs. At this point, either the intensity of the relationship decreases during a *separation* phase, or strong relationships enter a *redefinition* phase in which new directions are established or the relationship is redefined as a peer relationship or a collegial friendship (Ragins & Kram, 2007).

Benefits of Mentoring Relationships in Professional Development

The experiences provided through a mentoring relationship have been strongly associated with a wide array of positive outcomes for the mentee. Higher levels of performance, job satisfaction, and organizational success have been reported in vocational and organization management research. Mentees received more promotions and increased income, had more career mobility, and reported higher levels of career satisfaction and skill development (Baptiste, 2001; Ragins & Cotton, 1999). Mentoring has also been found to encourage more effective organizational socialization and reduced turnover (Scandura, 1992). Social and political skills and a strong professional identity are benefits that are less materially obvious in the short term but critical for long-term successful development.

Serving as a mentor is rewarding as well and can be viewed as an important part of the mentor's professional growth (Dolan, 2004). Dolan advocated that potential mentors seek mentees with different backgrounds (racial, ethnic, professional, gender, or generational) to enhance their own learning and development. Research has found that the professional development of mentors is enhanced as their mentoring skills increase with experience and that their enthusiasm for their own work increases (Ragins & Scandura, 1999). Mentors report feeling respected and needed and can experience strong feelings of satisfaction through the achievements of their mentee. Mentees can offer a fresh perspective to the mentor's work and increase mentor job performance (Fagenson-Eland et al., 1997). Another potential benefit is recognition by colleagues of the mentor's efforts to develop and prepare future leaders (Dolan, 2004); many mentors are motivated in this way to contribute to the legacy of their profession.

Types of Mentoring Relationships

Recognizing that mentoring relationships are advantageous on many levels, organizations have become interested in establishing programs that replicate or facilitate such relationships. In health care environments, workers are expected to produce outcomes that are measurable and cost-effective and that add value to the organization. Some organizations assign a skilled worker to a less skilled worker as part of a formal program designed to encourage the sharing of expertise and experience to directly benefit that organization. Others form teams of workers to facilitate networking connections, laying the basis for the spontaneous formation of relationships. Occupational therapy managers maybe asked to direct formal mentoring programs in their department or may recognize the potential benefits of organizing such a program among the department's employees.

Formal and Informal Mentoring

Mentoring relationships can be formed under different structures and levels of independence. Most can be defined as formal or informal. In formal mentoring programs, mentors and mentees are assigned to one another by the management of the organization in pursuit of increased productivity, job success, worker loyalty, or satisfaction. In general, these customized relationships appear to be more short-lived and less intense than informal relationships, which are naturally occurring pairings that focus on goals set by arrangement between the mentee and the mentor.

Informal relationships are viewed as more long term and productive. Some research has indicated that formal or assigned mentorships are more superficial; less comfortable; and less motivating, open, and supportive (Chao et al., 1992; Ragins & Cotton, 1999). Other research, however, has suggested that relationship structure and the levels of mentee and mentor experience rather than who initiated the relationship influence the individual's perceptions of the relationship's value (Gaskill, 1993; Scandura, 1992).

Shea (1999) suggested a continuum of mentor relationships. At one end are the formal relationships that result from a structured program assigning mentors and mentees to each other designed to benefit the organization. In the middle are informal interpersonal relationships, initiated and or negotiated by individuals and formed to meet the long-term needs of the mentee. At the opposite end are situational relationships, which are short-term, advising interactions that meet a mentee's immediate or acute need. An example of a situational mentorship might be the tutelage of an occupational therapist to transfer a specific skill set to a colleague.

Ragins and Cotton (1999) compared the characteristics and benefits of informal and formal mentoring relationships. They found that mentees with informal mentors received more benefits and perceived that their mentors provided more career development and psychosocial support. Mentees in informal mentoring relationships reported more relationship satisfaction and earned higher salaries. The authors explained these results as reflecting the characteristics of formal relationships, which tend to shorter in duration and to provide less comfort and motivation (psychological functions). Ragins and Cotton suggested that formal relationships may be more useful for immediate performance benefits, such as on-the-job training or the socialization of new workers. Occupational therapy managers might find that assigning short-term formal or situational mentors would prove beneficial for the orientation of new or novice therapists, for the remediation of an individual's acute developmental need, or for facilitation of adaptation to change. There is a need for more focused research on mentoring relationships; at present, long-term professional and career development relationships appear to be best left to the serendipity of human interactions.

Group Mentoring

Mentoring relationships can vary from the traditional one-to-one models. For reasons such as a lack of available or qualified potential mentors, group mentoring can be an alternative. *Group mentoring* promotes diverse perspectives, expertise, and experiences while simultaneously encouraging workplace relationships and connections (Zachary, 2005). Other advantages of a group model are the collective wisdom available for problem solving and strategizing to improve efficiencies and practice.

In facilitated group or team mentoring, a group of occupational therapists might meet on a scheduled basis with a designated and more experienced therapist to engage in a dialogue about their practice (Zachary, 2005). The experienced mentor might share his or her expertise and experience while also acting as a facilitator and taking responsibility for the give-and-take of the discussion. Another form of group mentoring can take the form of a team of individuals who pursue a specific set of learning objectives. A single mentor, or several mentors, provides guidance through the process of achieving team-focused outcomes. The team learns from the experience and perspectives of other team members while being guided and supported by the mentor (Zachary, 2005).

Peer mentoring consists of a small group, or a pair of individuals, with similar needs or interests. Because the group members are of equal status the relationship provides a supportive environment to test ideas and express opinions. The group provides an opportunity to share collective expertise and provide a sounding board for each member's ideas and concerns. This group might invite an outside guest to assist in exploring a specific topic, but the group is self-directed and self-managed (Zachary, 2005). Regional groups of occupational therapists that share like interests in specific practice or research areas often engage in peer mentoring by forming forums, Special Interest Sections, or journal clubs.

Coaching and the Mentor Relationship

The terms *mentoring* and *coaching* are often used to refer to a similar process. In fact, some publications refer to "coaching–mentoring." Are these terms synonymous? Foster-Turner (2006) wrote that coaching and mentoring are founded on common beliefs. She compared the concept of coaching–mentoring to the relationship between coach and athlete. Once performance goals are identified, the coach facilitates the development of the player by honing skills, directing practice, and motivating for peak performance. Although the person being coached (mentee) is responsible for setting personal goals, the coach (mentor) sets up the learning environment or the process to achieve that performance. The roles of mentor and coach both include responsibility for the development of another. However, the key goals of a coaching relationship are to improve performance or skill (sport), and the process consists of precise direction by the coach with a heavy emphasis on immediate performance feedback.

Foster-Turner (2006) asserted that coaching is a more direct approach to improving performance in the short term, whereas mentoring has a larger and longer-term focus on professional career development. In addition, mentoring can be considered a partnership journey (Clutterbuck, 2001), whereas coaching can be considered a more systematic skill-focused process (Parslow & Wray, 2000). Novice managers might benefit from a coaching relationship to focus on the skills needed to make the initial transition to management and a mentor relationship to prepare for a career in health care leadership. When coached by a more experienced therapist, a newly graduated occupational therapist making the transition from student to professional might gain role socialization skills, whereas a more long-term mentoring relationship might assist with a plan to gain more advanced or specialized clinical skills.

Virtual Mentorships

Although face-to-face meetings are the most common form of mentoring communication, the expansion of interactive technology is changing this dynamic. Virtual or online mentoring is computer and Internet generated. Virtual mentoring is also referred to as *e-mentoring, telementoring,* or *cybermentoring* (Fagenson-Eland & Lu, 2004). According to Muller (2000), the many benefits of virtual mentoring include cost-effectiveness, convenience in scheduling, and ability to communicate across time zones and large distances. Even when distance is not a barrier, scheduling face-to-face time around busy workloads and personal and professional obligations is often problematic, and virtual mentoring provides the capacity to communicate at more convenient times (Fagenson-Eland & Lu, 2004). Technology vastly increases the number and possible expertise of potential mentors. Global relationships are possible, as virtual mentoring provides face-to-face communication without ever being in the same physical environment.

E-mail, Internet blogs, chat rooms, and organizational listservs offer opportunities for individuals to seek a potential mentor or communicate with a network or group of mentors. Interactive technology can provide both opportunities for informal and formal mentoring with individuals and virtual forums for networking with other professionals (Bierema & Merriam, 2002). The use of technology greatly expands the list of potential mentors and broadens the types of communication and learning activities available for the mentorship pair. One example of virtual mentoring is provided through OT Connections, a Web-based social network that connects AOTA members to forums, groups, and blogs that answer a large variety of professional interests. This site can facilitate networks, provide professional knowledge and advice, and encourage advocacy (Schell, 2009). Programs such as Basecamp, Skype,™ Microsoft® Meeting, and software sharing through Google facilitate opportunities for communication that transcend boundaries created by time and distance.

Using high-level and low-level technology, mentors and mentees can use the telephone for weekly "face-to-face" discussions. Skype and other similar software facilitate computer-generated phone calls, organize simultaneous discussions, and allow the use of a camera or video. Mentorship pairs can use e-mail to arrange meeting times, exchange documents, or allow the mentee to ask questions or clarify previous discussions. Articles and other resource documents can also be exchanged by e-mail, and documents can be edited using programs such as document exchange software. However, distance mentorships require increased communication concerning expectations,

time commitment, and confidentiality (Zachary, 2005). Not everyone has the same comfort level for all types of technology, and not all types of technology fit everyone's communication style. In addition, the truncated communication style of chat rooms, instant messaging, and e-mail can cause misunderstandings. However, regular communication between the pair builds trust and familiarity with individual communication styles.

Distance technology can accommodate a wide range of mentoring relationships, and appears to assist in sustaining long-term mentoring relationships despite job changes or relocation. As is true of many new applications of technology, research concerning the effectiveness and benefits of virtual mentoring has not kept up with the rapid development of the technology (Bierema & Merriam, 2002). This area of scholarship is ripe for study and discussion.

MAINTAINING AN EFFECTIVE MENTOR–MENTEE RELATIONSHIP

A mentorship pair should begin by establishing a vision with clear goals for the relationship. The goals must be mutually satisfying and build on the strengths and resources of both the mentee and mentor. A contract should be negotiated that contains the parameters of the commitment, including the specific time commitment, meeting frequency, expected roles, and methods of communication.

In addition, the contract should identify the professional development outcomes that will guide the focus of the activities to be engaged in and be used to evaluate the effectiveness of the mentorship. Outcomes are behaviors that demonstrate role integration and increased competence and are different for each therapist based on his or her professional and personal situation, interests, and goals. Typical outcomes might include enhancing the therapist's perception of self-efficacy and self-confidence, feelings of empowerment and optimism, and ability to deal well with uncertainty. Defining these outcomes in writing will help the mentorship pair identify when the mentee has accomplished the objectives of the relationship. Outcome measures can quantify change and transition and can be designed as long- and short-term behavioral goals and objectives.

RELATED PROFESSIONAL DEVELOPMENT ISSUES
Self-Reflection and Self-Assessment

Regardless of years of experience, every professional is in need of further growth and development in skill, knowledge, and personal attributes (Urish & Schell, 2009). Individual therapists must identify the skills they wish to gain and weaknesses they wish to overcome and then choose someone who possesses the capacities to guide them in this process. Relationships with others are key to strengthening competencies and realizing potential. Before embarking on a search for an appropriate mentor, however, therapists should engage in self-reflection and self-assessment, which are critical to the successful initiation of the relationship and ultimately to successful outcomes. Reflecting on the following series of questions can be useful in the initial phase of professional development:

- What are my career aspirations? What are my goals for the next 2 years? 5 years? 10 years?
- At the peak of my career, what do I envision myself doing?
- Is there anything that would indicate that I need improvement in my approach to my job (attributes)?
- What competencies do I need to develop? What do I need to know more about (knowledge)? What do I need to get better at doing (skills)?
- What do I need to do to achieve my goals and reach my potential?
- What opportunities are available to help me achieve my goals and reach my potential?

Professional Portfolios

A trend in professional development is the professional portfolio, an organized and selective representation of professional accomplishments. It showcases the occupational therapist's essential knowledge, skills, and performance and can serve as documentation for promotions and employment searches. A portfolio can be used to provide structure for a developing mentoring relationship and documentation to evaluate the outcomes of the relationship. It can also serve as a tool to guide professional development. The Professional Development Tool (AOTA, 2003), located on the AOTA Web site, guides occupational therapists through a reflection process similar to the one described in the preceding section and helps them identify the resources and support they need to meet their developmental needs.

DEVELOPING A MENTORING CULTURE IN THE WORKPLACE

An organization that values and facilitates mentoring can benefit from employee retention, improved morale, organizational commitment and vitality, and transference of organizational knowledge, as well as accelerated professional and leadership development (Zachary, 2005). Lois Zachary, author and consultant on the creation of organizational mentoring cultures, states that mentoring programs cannot survive if they are not sufficiently "embedded in a supportive culture that values learning and development" (p. 23).

Organizational mentoring programs establish specific organizational goals, strategies, and developmental activities that match less experienced with more experienced employees. Perrone (2003) suggested several steps to ensure a meaningful mentoring experience and to garner support for the establishment of a mentoring program. First, he suggested that the organization make a clear case for the value of mentoring. By connecting mentoring to the goals of the organization and tying the contributions of mentoring to retention and professional development, a strong

"business case" for mentoring is built. A strong alignment between the organization's mentoring and business goals is necessary to establish program and cultural congruence. The organization's values, mission, and reward incentives must reflect a strong commitment to mentoring relationships and professional development (Zachary, 2005). Next, the organization needs to establish a committee to define program objectives and design an implementation strategy.

The third step is to arrange potential mentee and mentor partnerships; Perrone (2003) stressed that both groups must willingly and voluntarily enter the program. The fourth step is to provide training. Mentors often need formal training to develop their knowledge and skills to sustain a relationship, and mentees need assistance to effectively communicate their needs. Next, the mentorship pair initiates contact by negotiating a formal agreement or contract that defines the expectations of both individuals. The final step is to evaluate program outcomes that benefit both the organization and the individuals. Perrone (2003) noted that the establishment of an organization-wide culture of mentoring is more important than the success of a formal program. The expectation that the organizational leadership will encourage and support professional development and learning will foster both formal and informal mentorships. Zachary (2005) warned that establishing and maintaining an effective mentoring culture is a journey that requires evaluation and oversight and adaptation to changing business conditions and personnel.

A culture of mentoring requires a personal commitment on the part of organizational leaders (Gaskill, 1993). Those leaders can show a commitment to professional development and lifelong learning by modeling these behaviors themselves. Providing educational inservices, training, and continuing education on the need for and process of mentoring promotes a culture that fosters mentoring. Information can be provided to promote relationship building, identification of professional development needs, acquisition of job transition skills, and improvements in social environments. Forums to discuss good and bad experiences and problem solve issues with communication or outcome identification can support mentors. These efforts on the part of organization leaders can provide the supportive environment, the knowledge, and the experiences that are known to be critical for successful mentoring.

CONCLUSION

The literature has suggested that effective mentor relationships have positive outcomes for all involved (Baptiste, 2001; Ragins & Scandura, 1999). Mentoring has been found to encourage more effective organizational socialization and reduced turnover (Scandura, 1992). Multiple studies in nursing have supported the benefits of mentoring programs; mentees experienced improvements in skills and knowledge and in retention and recruitment (Greene & Puetzer, 2002), as well as increased self-confidence, critical thinking skills, and commitment to the profession (Pinkerton, 2003).

Expecting occupational therapists to engage in mentoring for professional development may do more to advance the career development of the profession than almost any other activity. Whether mentoring is an informal relationship generated by the individuals involved or a formal program designed by the manager or the administration of the organization, it clearly provides benefits to the mentee, the mentor, and the organization. Obviously, there are successful people who have never been mentored, but most experienced leaders reflecting back on their career discuss the role that mentors have played in their professional development (Gillette, 2008).

Health care environments today are uncertain and unpredictable. Changing expectations and increased pressures challenge occupational therapists to make fast decisions and solve ethical dilemmas and to develop new and improved competencies. Mentors can facilitate and guide this developmental process in both the short and the long term. Professional development strengthens the individual therapist and ensures the viability of the profession's future.

Case Examples

LEVEL I FIELDWORK

Jane was a clinical fieldwork educator in a pediatric outpatient clinic. She had 5 years of clinical experience, but today she met her first fieldwork I student. By evening, Jane was on the phone with Elle, the student's university's academic fieldwork coordinator, with a list of problems.

Because the student arrived late, Jane delayed her first intervention session to orient her to the facility, arrange for her name tag, and brief her concerning the children scheduled. After the second session, the student comfortably sat on a mat with the child. However, the parent pulled Jane aside and stated that he was very uncomfortable with the student's dress. Her short shirt and low-rise pants exposed areas of her body that should be covered in a professional environment. Jane was embarrassed because she had noticed the potential dress issues but had decided to discuss them with her student at the end of the day. During a staff meeting, issues continued to arise as the student focused on her iPhone, answering e-mail and text messaging. At the end of the day, Jane confronted the student about her behavior and dress. The student burst into tears, stating that Jane just didn't understand younger students, and fled the facility. Jane was at a loss as to how to salvage this experience.

During the phone call, Elle asked Jane to reflect about how the rest of the day had gone. Jane reported that the student had shown genuine interest and related well to the children. She had also asked some excellent questions and appeared familiar with the therapeutic process. Together, Elle and Jane explored Jane's expectations for Level I students and reviewed the school's student learning objectives.

Elle asked Jane to consider how to restart this experience and influence the student's attitudes and behaviors. They composed an e-mail message to send to the student. It included precise information about time and dress, and informed her of a morning meeting to make a fresh start.

Elle directed Jane to the university's Web site and fieldwork link. There, Jane found a description of the student preparation prior to Level I fieldwork, references for writing student learning objectives, and a copy of the *Occupational Therapy Attribute Scale* (OTAS; Hubbard, Beck, Stutz-Tanenbaum, & Battaglia, 2007). OTAS assesses a range of behavioral items, such as punctuality, dress, time use, and supervision roles. By phone, Jane and Elle reviewed the items on the scale and wrote sample measureable behavioral objectives. They discussed how the morning meeting might go and practiced how Jane could convey her expectations in a nonjudgmental way. They also agreed to talk the following evening to review the day.

Elle continued to guide Jane in a series of activities to increase her knowledge about fieldwork expectations and supervision and reviewed the literature about the characteristics of the millennial generation. She also invited Jane to attend a panel discussion of faculty, students, and fieldwork educators at a state conference.

LEVEL II FIELDWORK

Tom was an occupational therapist in an inpatient rehabilitation facility where occupational therapists, physical therapists, and speech–language pathologists often cotreated clients. His fieldwork II student seemed well prepared, and everything was going well. To his surprise, he was approached by a physical therapist who complained about the student's behavior during cotreatment sessions. The therapist stated that the student was uncooperative, making inappropriate comments about physical therapy to clients. Tom realized that although he had regularly observed or treated clients with his student, he had not observed a cotreatment session.

(continued)

Case Examples *(cont.)*

The following morning Tom observed the student during a cotreatment session. He discovered that the student was short and defensive with the physical therapist; she appeared to want to take over and was reluctant to negotiate her role. She refused to share fine-motor test results, stating "You don't need to know it; that's not PT." After the observation, Tom was very upset with the student and with himself. He wondered why he hadn't been aware of this behavior and felt that maybe he was not cut out to be a clinical educator.

For assistance Tom approached Alex, the facility's student education coordinator. Alex had a lot of experience in student supervision, and Tom thought that she might be able to help him understand where he had gone wrong. Tom realized that he needed some mentoring concerning how to handle this conflict and to explore whether he had what it takes to be an effective fieldwork educator.

Alex listened to Tom's description of the troubling behavior and his feelings about when he realized that there was a problem with the student's performance. As they talked, she asked him to reflect on his ability to deal with conflict and why this particular incident had made him question his commitment to students. After listening, Alex asked Tom how he envisioned a meeting with the student proceeding. She guided Tom to discuss his beliefs and values about interdisciplinary treatment and to distill the topic into talking points. They role played to increase Tom's comfort and self-confidence.

During subsequent meetings, they discussed supervision issues that went well or didn't go well and identified what Tom learned about his ability to manage conflict. They also reflected on how Tom would approach his next student.

Over the following month, Tom and Alex reviewed student learning objectives concerning expectations of interdisciplinary intervention, professional relationships, and communication. They made certain the objectives were clear and understandable for future students. They also identified the behaviors that would indicate when Tom's current student's behavioral objectives had been met.

Alex assisted Tom in identifying sources concerning student supervision and conflict resolution. He compiled a list of courses available locally and through the hospital human resources office, as well as literature concerning student supervision on AOTA's Web site. Alex encouraged Tom to attend a fieldwork supervision certification course and to consider writing an article about student training for cotreatment for *OT Practice* magazine or an AOTA *Special Interest Section Quarterly* newsletter.

FIRST-TIME MANAGER

Karen was the new director of occupational therapy in an academic health science center. As part of a formal mentoring program organized through the vice president's office, she was paired with Tory, the director of rehabilitation. In the first of their weekly meetings, Tory and Karen established initial outcomes that included

- Increasing Karen's awareness of the organizational culture and politics,
- Introducing Karen personally to the people at the center who would be important to her (e.g., other department heads, physicians), and
- Identifying resources and contacts for assistance (e.g., human resources, quality management, marketing).

Tory generated a list of important people who she believed would complement Karen's strengths, help her build political support and strength, and potentially extend occupational therapy's sphere of influence in the center. As Karen scheduled meetings with the people from Tory's list, she and Tory met to review each person's job responsibilities and personal interaction styles. They also role played how the meetings might proceed and reviewed possible topics of conversation or information Karen might need.

Soon, Tory arranged for Karen to serve on the search committee for the new director of physical therapy. This opportunity allowed Karen input into filling the position of her counterpart and the ability to form a relationship by assisting with the new director's orientation. After getting to know Karen better, Tory realized that Karen's particular strengths might help resolve a conflict between two departments. To showcase Karen's potential assets to the facility, Tory lobbied for Karen to head a task force on the issue. Karen's success with this task was rewarded just months later with a productivity bonus.

An experienced mentor, Tory listened as Karen described the issues she faced. Tory was her advocate and pushed her to reflect and communicate effectively. She guided Karen in reflecting on who in the organization might assist her. Sometimes Karen was certain Tory knew how to solve a problem and could give her advice, but instead of providing the answer, Tory helped her problem solve. When the vice president asked Karen to evaluate the mentoring program, she referred to the trust and respect she had for Tory and that Tory appeared to have for her. She described her meetings with Tory as a safe environment where she was motivated and challenged.

MANAGER

Dee, an experienced occupational therapy manager for a community health organization, conducted a needs assessment of the surrounding community that revealed the need for a women's health clinic specializing in weight management and lifestyle change. Dee's organization supported the idea and requested that Dee propose a plan to establish the clinic. With no experience in lifestyle coaching and weight management, Dee sought a mentor who could facilitate her development in this practice area. She contacted listservs, blogs, and Special Interest Sections through *OT Connections* to find other occupational therapists with similar interests or already engaged in similar programs. She established her presence in a network of occupational therapists interested in the area, and between the information from *OTConnection* and a thorough search of the literature, she collected a list of persons who were experts in these practice areas and considered them as possible mentors. Dee then e-mailed the people on the list and contacted them by phone if their response to her e-mail indicated an interest in forming a mentoring relationship.

Margaret, a recently retired occupational therapist, responded to Dee. After several phone conversations, their relationship seemed like a good fit, and Margaret seemed to share Dee's passion for the development of this new service. Margaret lived on the other side of the country. Using cloud computing through the Internet, they agreed to meet virtually as mentor and mentee. Their virtual relationship solved the distance and time barriers. They used Skype peer-to-peer software to conference and communicate and Google Docs to manage document preparation, including the formal program proposal.

Margaret and Dee began to develop the new program by prioritizing its goals. The two brainstormed the professional development needs of the current staff. Through discussion, Dee recognized that despite the excitement of this new opportunity, it was important not to spread the therapists in her already busy department too thin. They compiled a list of training resources to retrain and retain them.

Margaret and Dee created a program proposal for the clinic. Passing the document back and forth through Google Docs facilitated their ability to work on it simultaneously. By phone conferencing, Margaret helped Dee reflect on the issues she encountered and solve an array of problems centered on reimbursement and the identification and establishment of referral sources.

As they developed a marketing plan for the proposal, Dee recognized her discomfort around "selling" the program. She complained, "No one ever taught me marketing, and I am not a salesperson." Margaret helped Dee recognize that she had been an advocate for occupational therapy services many times in the past and that she was not a total novice at selling occupational therapy. To increase her comfort and confidence levels, Dee enrolled in some continuing education marketing courses available locally. Future goals for the relationship included working together to help Dee identify potential community agency partners and develop marketing outcomes and materials.

❖❖ Learning Activities

1. Describe where you would like to be and what you would like to be doing exactly 5 years from today.
   a. What personal values do these goals reflect?
   b. What steps could you take to make progress on your goals over the next 6 months? The next year?
   c. How will you know you have achieved your goals? What outcomes will you recognize?
2. Identify a fictional character (movie role or book character) who you think would be your perfect mentor.
   a. What traits does this character have that would be valuable to your psychosocial development? To your career development?
   b. What personality traits does this character have that would help you achieve your professional goals?
   c. What expertise does this character have that would help you achieve your professional goals?
3. Imagine that you are mentoring a high school student who is interested in becoming an occupational therapist.
   a. What psychosocial outcomes might you assume your mentee will achieve as a result of your relationship before he or she enters college?
   b. What career outcomes might your mentee achieve as a result of your relationship before he or she enters college?
   c. If you were to help this student form a network of mentors, who else would you suggest the student form a relationship with? What expertise would these professionals add to the student's network?

4. Answer the following question by drawing a picture of the environment you see yourself in: At the peak of my career, what do I envision myself doing?

5. Use Exhibit 16.1 or 16.2 to reflect on your ability to be an effective mentor or mentee.

✓ Multiple-Choice Questions

1. The 2010 AOTA *Code of Ethics and Ethics Standards* states that professional development must be supported through mentoring relationships—true or false?
   a. True.
   b. False.
   c. The code specifies that occupational therapists must have mentors but does not specify how.
   d. Professional development is not addressed in the *Code of Ethics and Ethics Standards*.

2. Which of the following is the defining feature of mentoring?
   a. The supervisory role of the mentor.
   b. Dedication to the advancement of the mentee.
   c. The benefits earned by the mentor.
   d. The sacrifices of the mentor.

3. Kram (1985) defined *psychosocial functions* as
   a. Organizational behaviors.
   b. Interpersonal growth and professional role development.
   c. Predictors of advancement and increased salary.
   d. Mental health intervention.

4. All mentoring relationships provide the same degree of both psychosocial and career development functions—True or false?
   a. True.
   b. False; relationships provide varying degrees of both.
   c. False; mentors do not provide career functions.
   d. False; both of these functions are provided by others in the mentee's life.

5. An occupational therapy manager who begins an advanced degree program is providing which of the following mentoring functions for the novice therapist in his department?
   a. Coaching.
   b. Learning.
   c. Role modeling.
   d. Psychosocial.

6. The initiation phase of a mentoring relationship involves which of the following?
   a. Negotiation and goal setting.
   b. Assessment of outcomes.
   c. Increased autonomy for the mentee.
   d. Mentor and mentee friendship.

7. Self-assessment of experiences and their learning value is called
   a. Feedback.
   b. Reflection.
   c. Managing stress anxiety.
   d. Validation.

8. When the outcomes or goals of the mentoring relationship are achieved, what stage does the relationship enter?
   a. Dissolution or termination.
   b. Separation or redefinition.
   c. Discharge.
   d. Unemployment.

9. According to the research, mentors benefit in which of the following ways from a mentorship relationship?
   a. Advancement.
   b. Increased compensation.
   c. Increased job enthusiasm and job satisfaction.
   d. Power and status.

10. Based on the research, mentees are reported to receive which of the following?
    a. Increased work tasks.
    b. Productivity awards.
    c. Ability to follow direction and less self-initiative.
    d. Increased promotions and compensation.

11. In general, research has revealed that formal mentoring relationships are which of the following?
    a. Less able to fulfill psychosocial functions.
    b. More effective than informal relationships.
    c. Shorter but more satisfying than informal relationships.
    d. Not significantly better than no relationship.

12. An occupational therapist's supervisor advises her to be more efficient so that she is able to meet the expected levels of productivity. Which of the following is this supervisor's role?
    a. Manager.
    b. Mentor.
    c. Supervisory mentor.
    d. Mentee.

13. An occupational therapist recruited a more experienced peer to help him get better organized and manage his time better. He also found his supervisor to be intimidating and asked his peer to help him learn to

communicate with her better. The peer's role is which of the following?

a. Manager.

b. Mentor.

c. Supervisory mentor.

d. Mentee.

14. Coaching is different from mentoring for which of the following reasons?

a. It involves only athletics.

b. The coach (mentor) sets the goals for the mentee.

c. Mentoring is a more direct approach.

d. Coaching is more systematic and process oriented.

15. The focus of mentoring research changed recently for which of the following reasons?

a. The context and complexity of work environments changed.

b. There was a dearth of research on the roles and benefits of successful mentoring relationships.

c. Extended apprenticeships were more the norm.

d. The workforce was younger and more diverse, so mentoring became obsolete.

16. A group of occupational therapists practicing in a rural area agree to meet once a month to network and discuss a previously agreed-upon research article. What type of group mentoring is this?

a. Facilitated-group mentoring.

b. Team mentoring.

c. Supervised mentoring.

d. Peer-group mentoring.

17. A supervisor recognized that a new occupational therapist was capable of self-reflection, open to constructive feedback, and well regarded in her organization. These characteristics are signs of which of the following?

a. Potentially good mentee.

b. Person not in need of mentoring.

c. Someone with potential and competency.

d. A and C.

18. Barriers to mentoring such as time, distance, and cost can be efficiently overcome by which of the following?

a. Telephone conversations.

b. Communication through the postal service.

c. Virtual mentoring.

d. Traditional mentoring.

19. Organizational leaders can develop a mentoring culture by doing which of the following?

a. Serving as mentor role models.

b. Providing training in mentoring processes.

c. Recognizing the time commitments of mentors.

d. All of the above.

20. Outcome measures are designed to answer which of the following questions?

a. What do I need to know more about?

b. What opportunities are available to me?

c. How will I know when I have accomplished my goals?

d. What indicates I need to make some changes?

References

Allen, T., Eby, L., Poteet, M., Lentz, E., & Lima, L. (2004). Career benefits associated with mentoring for protégés: A meta-analysis. *Journal of Applied Psychology, 89,* 127–136.

American Occupational Therapy Association. (2003). *Professional development tool.* Retrieved March 25, 2009, from http://www.aota.org/pdt

American Occupational Therapy Association. (2010). Occupational therapy code of ethics and ethics standards. *American Journal of Occupational Therapy, 64.*

Baptiste, S. (2001). *Mentoring and supervision: Creating relationships for fostering professional development.* Ottawa: Canadian Association for Occupational Therapy.

Bierema, L., & Merriam, S. (2002). E-mentoring: Using computer-mediated communication to enhance the mentoring process. *Innovations in Higher Education, 26,* 211–227.

Chao, G., Walz, P., & Gardner, P. (1992). Formal and informal mentorships. *Personnel Psychology, 45,* 619–636.

Clutterbuck, D. (2001). *Everyone needs a mentor.* London: Chartered Institute of Personnel and Development.

Clutterbuck, D. (2004). Mentor competencies: A field perspective. In D. Clutterbuck & G. Lane (Eds.), *The situational mentor: An international review of competencies and capabilities in mentoring* (pp. 42–56). Burlington, VT: Gower.

Dolan, T. (2004, September/October). Mentoring at every level: Mentoring others—and being mentored—enhances growth at every career stage. *Healthcare Executive,* pp. 6–7.

Dreher, G., & Ash, R. (1990). A comparative study of mentoring among men and women in managerial, professional, and technical positions. *Journal of Applied Psychology, 75,* 539–546.

Fagenson-Eland, E., & Lu, R. (2004). Virtual mentoring. In D. Clutterbuck & G. Lane (Eds.), *The situational mentor: An international review of competencies and capabilities in mentoring* (pp. 148–159). Burlington, VT: Gower.

Fagenson-Eland, E., Marks, M., & Amendola, K. (1997). Perceptions of mentoring relationships. *Journal of Vocational Behavior, 51,* 29–42.

Foster-Turner, J. (2006). *Coaching and mentoring in health care and social care: The essentials of practice for professionals and organisation.* Oxford, UK: Radcliffe.

Gaskill, L. (1993). A conceptual framework for the development, implementation, and evaluation of formal mentoring programs. *Journal of Career Development, 20,* 147–160.

Gillette, N. (2008). Mentors I have known (and loved). *American Journal of Occupational Therapy, 62,* 487–490.

Greene, M., & Puetzer, M. (2002). The value of mentoring: A strategic approach to retention and recruitment. *Journal of Nursing Care Quality, 17,* 63–70.

Grossman, S. (2007). *Mentoring in nursing: A dynamic and collaborative process.* New York: Springer.

Hubbard, S., Beck, A., Stutz-Tanenbaum, P., & Battaglia, C. (2007). Reliability and validity of the Occupational Therapy Attribute Scale. *Journal of Allied Health.* Retrieved July 27, 2010, from http://findarticles.com/p/articles/mi_qa4040/is_200712/ai_n21186150/?tag=content;col1

Kram, K. (1985). *Mentoring at work.* Glenview, IL: Scott Foresman.

Kram, K. (2004). Foreword: The making of a mentor. In D. Clutterbuck & G. Lane (Eds.), *The situational mentor: An international review of competencies and capabilities in mentoring* (pp. xi–xiv). Burlington, VT: Gower.

Muller, C. B. (2000). *The potential of e-mentoring as a retention strategy for women in science and engineering.* San Francisco: Blue Sky Consulting.

Parslow, E., & Wray, M. (2000). *Coaching and mentoring: Practical methods to improve learning.* London: Kogan Page.

Perrone, J. (2003). Creating a mentoring culture. *Healthcare Executive, 18*(3), 84–85.

Pinkerton, S. (2003). Mentoring new graduates. *Nursing Economics, 21,* 202–203.

Ragins, B., & Cotton, J. (1999). Mentor functions and outcomes: A comparison of men and women in formal and informal mentoring relationships. *Journal of Applied Psychology, 84,* 529–550.

Ragins, B., & Kram, K. (2007). The roots and meaning of mentoring. In K. E. Kram (Ed.), *The handbook of mentoring at work: Theory, research, and practice* (pp. 3–15). Los Angeles: Sage.

Ragins, B., & Scandura, T. (1999). Burden or blessing? Expected costs and benefits of being a mentor. *Journal of Organizational Behavior, 20,* 493–509.

Robertson, S., & Savio, M. (2003, November 17). Mentoring as professional development. *OT Practice, 8,* 12–16.

Scandura, T. (1992). Mentorship and career mobility: An empirical investigation. *Journal of Organizational Behavior, 13,* 169–174.

Scandura, T., & Ragins, B. (1993). The effects of gender and role orientation on mentorships in male-dominated occupations. *Journal of Vocational Behavior, 43,* 251–265.

Schell, B. (2009, April 6). OT Connections: A new network for professional development. *OT Practice, 14*(6), 20.

Schrubbe, K. (2004). Mentorship: A critical component for professional growth and academic success. *Journal of Dental Education, 68,* 324–328.

Shea, G. (1999). *Making the most of being mentored.* Menlo Park, CA: Crisp Learning.

Urish, C. (2004, February 9). Ongoing competence through mentoring. *OT Practice,* p. 10.

Urish, C., & Schell, B. (2009, February 2). If not now, when? *OT Practice,* p. 19.

Wellington, S. (2001). Find a mentor/be a mentor. In S. Wellington (Ed.), *Be your own mentor* (pp. 160–177). New York: Random House.

Zachary, L. (2005). *Creating a mentoring culture: The organization's guide.* San Francisco: Jossey-Bass.

Appendix 16.A. Mentoring and Professional Development Evidence Table

Topic	Evidence
Benefits of being a mentor	Ragins, B., & Scandura, T. (1999). Burden or blessing? Expected costs and benefits of being a mentor. *Journal of Organizational Behavior, 20,* 493–509.
Benefits of being a mentee	Allen, T., Eby, L., Poteet, M., Lentz, E., & Lima, L. (2004). Career benefits associated with mentoring for protégés: A meta-analysis. *Journal of Applied Psychology, 89,* 127–136.
Types of mentorships	Ragins, B., & Cotton, J. (1999). Mentor functions and outcomes: A comparison of men and women in formal and informal mentoring relationships. *Journal of Applied Psychology, 84,* 529–550.
Virtual mentoring	Bierema, L., & Merriam, S. (2002). E-mentoring: Using computer-mediated communication to enhance the mentoring process. *Innovations in Higher Education, 26,* 211–227.
Creation of a mentoring culture	Greene, M., & Puetzer, M. (2002). The value of mentoring: A strategic approach to retention and recruitment. *Journal of Nursing Care Quality, 17,* 63–70.

17

Global Perspectives in Occupational Therapy Practice

Allison Kabel, PhD, and Amy Paul-Ward, PhD, OT

❖ Key Terms and Concepts

Culturally competent practice. The capacity to effectively work with people from various ethnic, cultural, political, economic, and religious backgrounds.

Disability studies. Seeking to understand disability in all its forms and raise awareness of the disability experience in sociocultural, political, and economic contexts.

Ethnography. The core research method for cultural anthropology, which involves data collected through participant observation and interview.

Global perspective. Taking a broad yet critical look at the factors influencing various circumstances around the world.

Globalization. The process of integrating world economies; sometimes used as a synonym for *Westernization*.

Internationalization. Planning products and services so they can be translated or adapted for other cultures and languages.

Intersections. In reference to intersections of occupational therapy with social science, the point at which two or more disciplines intersect, meet, cross, or share a common area.

Multicultural practice. Strategies for working with clients of diverse backgrounds.

Palliative care settings. Places where palliative care is being given and received.

Occupational apartheid. Occurs when individuals or groups of people are deprived of meaningful activity through some sort of segregation, often due to ethnicity or religion.

Occupational deprivation. A state in which individuals or groups are prevented from occupational engagement.

Occupational justice. The process of trying to fix, remedy, or call attention to disparities people face in the pursuit of everyday occupations.

Occupational science. The study of people as occupational beings and the relationship among occupation, health, and well-being.

Social justice. Support of human rights and equality.

❖ Learning Objectives

After completing this chapter, you should be able to do the following:

- Cite examples of occupational therapy practitioners working in international practice settings.
- Identify intersections of occupational therapy and the social sciences.

- Examine the concept of meaningful engagement in diverse contexts.
- Explain the significance of occupational justice within a global context.

In an ever-changing world with shifting communities and persistent social problems related to economic instability and political conflict, it is important for occupational therapy managers, educators, researchers, and practitioners to take an interdisciplinary approach in training new therapists, researching new questions, and conducting individual

practices. In reacting to the multicultural health environment, occupational therapists are going beyond their traditional boundaries, undertaking new research directions to reveal an understanding of humans as occupational beings (Frank & Zemke, 2005) and recognizing that variables such as culture, economics, and politics must be taken into account when thinking about the therapeutic process. Moreover, it is increasingly clear that these variables must be studied and understood in both local and global contexts to allow for greater visibility of the profession and the development of new opportunities for practice. We are medical anthropologists with appointments in departments of occupational therapy and experience conducting internationally situated research, and in this chapter we comment on the expanding interdisciplinary intersections and global opportunities for occupational therapy and the social sciences in the areas of research, teaching, and practice.

Over the past several years, a growing number of researchers and educators have been exploring the benefits of combining anthropology, disability studies, occupational science, and occupational therapy for the purpose of knowledge expansion. The intersections among these disciplines are directly affecting not only research but also the ways new therapists are educated and trained and ultimately how occupational therapy will be practiced in the future. In particular, examining these intersections is relevant and necessary to ensure that occupational therapists are practicing in a manner that recognizes the influences that culture has on the therapeutic process—that is, that they are engaging in culturally competent practice. In this chapter we discuss how these intersections are being incorporated into occupational therapy programs, the meaning of these intersections, the value of a global perspective for all occupational therapists, and the increasing significance of occupational justice.

EDUCATING THE NEXT GENERATION OF OCCUPATIONAL THERAPISTS

The Accreditation Council for Occupational Therapy Education® (ACOTE®), the profession's accrediting body, has recognized that students should be provided with opportunities to explore the relationship among the cultural, socioeconomic, and political variables that influence occupational therapy interventions. The most current ACOTE standards reflect the expectation that new practitioners will be able to demonstrate knowledge of human behavior as it relates to the behavioral and social sciences. In particular, the standards clearly articulate the necessity for new practitioners to demonstrate both "knowledge and appreciation of the role of sociocultural, socioeconomic, and diversity factors and lifestyle choices in contemporary society" (ACOTE, 2007). Departments of occupational therapy have some flexibility as to how they incorporate interdisciplinary topics and cultural issues in their curricula. Some have designed and implemented new courses to provide students with opportunities to explore issues of internationalization, globalization, and multiculturalism. Other departments have embedded these issues into already existing courses. Whatever the approach, the long-term outcome will greatly influence the profession as new students are exposed to new ways of thinking about the clients they serve, their families, and the larger community.

INTERSECTIONS BETWEEN OCCUPATIONAL THERAPY AND THE SOCIAL SCIENCES

Over the past several years, a growing number of researchers and educators have been exploring the benefits of combining anthropology, disability studies, occupational science, and occupational therapy for the purposes of cross-training and knowledge expansion (Lysack, Komanecky, Kabel, Cross, & Neufeld, 2007; Mattingly, 1998; Perkinson, 2008). A significant example of this effort is the creation of an interdisciplinary working group, the Occupational Therapy and Occupational Science Interdisciplinary Special Interest Group (OT–SIG), within the National Association of Practicing Anthropologists (NAPA) in 2006. Through the efforts of its founding members, the NAPA OT–SIG identified several long-term goals, including building alliances and collaborations among anthropology, occupational therapy, and occupational science. One of the group's short-term goals is to develop awareness and institutional links to bring doctorate- and master's-level anthropologists into the occupational therapy profession to assume faculty roles and expand emerging forms of practice (Paul-Ward & Frank, 2009). The following paragraphs provide a brief overview of several NAPA OT–SIG initiatives and projects.

Because the members of the NAPA OT–SIG are located both in the United States and abroad, it was important to have a mechanism for keeping members abreast of ongoing projects and happenings that are related to their interests. Therefore, to facilitate communication among its members and other interested individuals, the NAPA OT–SIG created a moderated listserv (napaotos@yahoogroups.com). The listserv is used to inform members of upcoming conferences, calls for papers to special issues of journals, and conference sessions, as well as to provide a forum for members to get feedback from others on research ideas and projects. The group is open to anyone with an interest in health, rehabilitation, disability, culture, and related topics. Individuals interested in participating in the NAPA OT–SIG can join by sending an e-mail to devva@earthlink.net.

In the area of cross training, the most significant accomplishment of this group to date is the July 2009 launching of the NAPA Occupational Therapy Field School in Antigua, Guatemala. The goal of this 6-week program is to bring anthropologists and occupational therapists together to study, practice, and learn in an international setting with a focus on social justice. In its inaugural session, occupational therapy students completing Level II fieldwork requirements and anthropology graduate students engaged in research and hands-on practice in local institutional contexts focused on child development, services to older adults, and community-based disability studies and disability rights efforts.

In another facet of promoting opportunities for cross-training, several NAPA OT–SIG members are exploring the feasibility of developing graduate-level training programs that will enable students to pursue a doctoral degree in anthropology while also pursuing a clinical degree in occupational therapy. This undertaking is significant in that there are currently more occupational therapy faculty positions than qualified individuals to fill them. Importantly, many anthropology students are already actively engaging in meaningful research on issues that are fundamental to occupational science and occupational therapy (e.g., phenomenological accounts of the disability experience; socioeconomic, political, and cultural influences of occupation and well-being). By providing opportunities for students with broad interests to pursue degrees in both occupational therapy and anthropology, there is a greater likelihood that occupational therapy departments will be able to find well-trained faculty who are able both to teach clinical courses and to enhance the curricula in the areas of internationalism, globalism, and multicultural practice. Examples of topics with ongoing collaborations include the effect of gender on disability, clinical processes that hinder or facilitate cooperation, intersections of technology and accessibility, contributions of ethnography or "thick description" to clinical practice, and organization of rehabilitation services that respect familial, cultural, and spiritual dimensions of being (Paul-Ward & Frank, 2009).

To increase visibility and encourage greater collaboration, OT–SIG has organized more than 25 sessions at various anthropology conferences during the past 4 years. In addition to organizing these sessions, which by design brought together scholars whose work highlights the intersections of anthropology and occupational therapy, this ongoing partnership has been recognized in some very significant ways. For example, in her address to members of the Society for Medical Anthropology, Marcia Inhorn (2007) identified occupational therapy as one of the 10 most promising areas of intersection with anthropology. Also, in September 2009, Gelya Frank (2009) gave a plenary presentation at the Society for Medical Anthropology conference, whose theme was "Medical Anthropology at the Intersections: Celebrating 50 Years of Interdisciplinarity." In her talk, titled "Occupational Science and Medical Anthropology: Intersections for Critical Praxis," Frank presented a brief history of occupational science and its relationship to occupational therapy and anthropology. She also discussed how work and the organization of physical and social space affects people's lives and well-being and how occupational science was developing in ways that could address these issues (Society for Medical Anthropology, 2009).

It is clear that the intersection among occupational therapy, occupational science, and anthropology has the potential to dramatically shape both the body of knowledge on occupation and the practice of occupational therapy in the future. In the next section, we explore examples of occupational therapists in international practice settings.

AN INTERNATIONAL PERSPECTIVE ON OCCUPATIONAL THERAPY IN PALLIATIVE CARE

While conducting research on hospice care in the United Kingdom (birthplace of the modern hospice movement), the authors interviewed an occupational therapist working in a British hospice facility. Because it is somewhat less common to see an occupational therapy presence in palliative settings in the United States, the interview was an opportunity to learn about this practice setting within another culture.

Matthew (not his real name) worked with inpatients at the hospice, as well as day therapy patients who participated in a unique outpatient program. Day therapy patients, unlike those residing in the inpatient units, were not at the very end stages of life and were able to participate in the social world to a greater extent than those further along the illness trajectory. The success of day therapy was thought to rest with the ability of its staff members (nurses, occupational therapists, physical therapists, and social workers) to create a space where those attending could avoid feeling as if their status as patients was more important than any other aspect of their lives (Langley-Evans & Payne, 1997; Payne, 2006; Thompson, 1990).

Matthew's responsibilities in the facility included evaluation of all occupational therapy needs in the 36-bed inpatient facility and in the day therapy unit (up to 60 patients) and working with the multidisciplinary team to provide care and discharge planning. When asked how his training as an occupational therapist fit with the hospice mission (to help people live with their illnesses), he commented that the goals of occupational therapy and hospice fit very well together, but they might seem "incongruent" to someone on the outside, because the patients he sees are not anticipating a cure or a positive rehabilitative outcome. Expanding on this notion, Matthew explained that things like goal setting and meaningful occupation are still important to people facing life-threatening illnesses. The goals were as straightforward as teaching a relaxation technique or stress management or as nebulous as helping the person manage life skills such as tying up loose ends (e.g., creating a will, accomplishing things they had always wanted to do). He provided an example of a client who dreamed of seeing his favorite soccer team play in the local stadium; the hospice staff members facilitated that process. Overall, he was confident that his role in his particular practice setting contributed to the clients' quality of life and sense of well-being, even as they faced the challenges brought about by serious illness.

Matthew acknowledged that clients who were unsettled by the stigma of hospice as a "place to die" would most likely never come through the door; therefore, he would not have the opportunity to serve them. Other clients, however, came reluctantly after being referred by a trusted provider, and Matthew had seen the breaking down of barriers in these clients. Patients confided to him that they were initially nervous about receiving care at a hospice facility but quickly came to appreciate what he and the multidisciplinary team had to offer and were pleased with the care they received.

Other barriers were more municipal in nature. Matthew discussed the process of obtaining reimbursement for adaptive equipment. The hospice, located in a large city, treated patients from up to six social services authorities. The local authorities had different resource levels, resulting in varying levels of care. The challenge for Matthew was to do the best for each patient within the boundaries put forth by forces out of his control, not unlike U.S. occupational therapists working with public- and private-sector insurance plans.

Because occupational therapy places high value on the importance of an individual's routine and habits, one might wonder how one can be an effective occupational therapist in an end-of-life institutional care setting, especially given that institutions in general have been known to have a homogenizing effect on patients and "encompassing tendencies" (Goffman, 1961, p.4). One would expect individual routines and preferences to fall by the wayside in a 36-bed facility like the one that employed Matthew. He explained how he worked around the institutional barriers and implemented as much flexibility and autonomy as possible with both his inpatient and outpatient clients. This flexibility could include modifying an activity or arranging for a particular patient to be washed and dressed at a time that he or she found more suitable, modifications that can go a long way toward helping patients avoid institutional homogenization and supporting meaningful engagement.

The example of Matthew illustrates how a practice setting shapes the ways in which an occupational therapist can creatively use his or her skills. Although palliative care settings might not be the first example to come to mind when thinking about opportunities for U.S. occupational therapists, they are well known on the international scene and serve as a reminder that looking abroad for ideas and inspiration can open a gateway to future collaborations and opportunities.

VALUE OF GLOBAL PERSPECTIVES

Global perspectives are valuable and helpful resources that lead to increased opportunities for the field of occupational therapy. As perspectives broaden, so do opportunities for greater visibility and recognition in multiple contexts. Just as collaborations across disciplines are becoming increasingly important in obtaining funding for research or in advancing theory and practice (Perkinson & Briller, 2009), the broadening of cultural perspectives is becoming increasingly essential in the rapidly changing world.

Globalization takes place when economic and political systems collaborate, typically in the form of trade for economic growth but often at the expense of disadvantaged people around the world. One major effect of globalization is migration, arguably a defining global issue of the early 21st century. According to the International Organization for Migration (n.d.), about 3% of the world's population—approximately 192 million people—live outside their place birth.

Increased migration is one consequence of globalization that directly and indirectly affects the health sciences. Implementing a *global consciousness* (i.e., awareness of global issues) in one's local work and ensuring that it is part of program development and implementation are the responsibility of managers, which can be accomplished by requiring adherence to the American Occupational Therapy Association's (AOTA's) *Occupational Therapy Code of Ethics and Ethics Standards* (2010). For example, the principle of *beneficence*, which promotes well-being, requires occupational therapists to provide interventions tailored to the needs of the specific client, including clients from diverse backgrounds (AOTA, 2010). Managers can facilitate this process by prioritizing cultural competence and creating a work environment that encourages the type of necessary self-reflection and examination of personal biases (McCormack, Jaffe, & Frey, 2003).

Fluctuations in the world economy, international conflict, and diplomacy profoundly affect on local practice as a result of changes in immigration patterns (Zhang Liu, 2001). For example, opening U.S. diplomatic relations with China in the 1970s changed the demographic profile of Chinese immigrants living in the United States. Prior to the establishment of formal diplomatic relations that allowed immigration from mainland China, Taiwanese students from upper-class families living in the United States were a key demographic. These young, affluent people had different health-related needs and expectations than those rural and working-class immigrants arriving later from mainland China to the United States. Unlike the Taiwanese immigrants, these new immigrants were unfamiliar with the notion of mainstreaming children with disabilities in schools and might expect specialized vocational training and traditional Chinese medicine in rehabilitation settings (Zhang Liu, 2001). Over the years, many excellent international examples of occupational therapy–oriented research have explored the importance of occupation and meaningful engagement in diverse contexts.

One specific area of this internationally focused work is the growing call for the discipline to incorporate a global social justice perspective into research on occupation. Even with the best of intensions, occupational therapy as part of the rehabilitation services field has been criticized for not doing enough to prevent, and in some cases "unwittingly collude with social oppression" (Kielhofner, 2005, p. 492). Kielhofner asks "should therapists include as part of their services efforts to empower disabled clients to engage in self-advocacy and to combat discrimination? Will these be considered reimbursable services?" (Kielhofner, 2005, p. 492). Research has shown that occupational therapists often fail to grasp the full impact of social and environmental barriers on client progress, for example, bureaucratic, economic, and political issues that become "invisible" barriers (Abberley, 1995). Cultural competency and global awareness are perhaps the first steps toward helping clients remove these invisible barriers.

One of the most vivid examples is the publication of *Occupational Therapy Without Borders: Learning From the*

Spirit of Survivors (Kronenberg, Algado, & Pollard, 2005). Throughout this book, the authors provide impassioned discussions of the theoretical issues related to social justice and persuasive arguments for a more politically and socially engaged occupational therapy approach. Their ideas resonate with the profession's documented emphasis on the importance of meaningful participation for all members of any given society (e.g., AOTA, 2008). However, the ongoing professional discourse on social justice indicates that more work in this area is needed to sufficiently address the larger societal issues that ultimately affect occupational therapy practitioners' ability to effect positive change for their clients.

Recognizing that social justice is an interdisciplinary movement, occupational therapy has offered its own unique contributions to the discussion of justice-related issues, including "occupational justice," "occupational apartheid," and "occupational deprivation." Within occupational therapy, *occupational justice* is viewed as related to the "rights, responsibilities, and liberties of enablement" (Townsend & Wilcock, 2004, cited in Urbanowski, 2005). The concept of occupational justice expands on the idea of *social justice* to include issues relevant to occupational therapy (e.g., participation, empowerment, meaningful activity). Kronenberg and Pollard (2005) suggested that *occupational apartheid* is different from *social injustice* in that the latter covers a broader range of issues. They argued that occupational apartheid is based on the notion that society judges some individuals as having a different economic and social value than others. This distinction results in some groups being pushed to the periphery of mainstream society, ultimately affecting their social and occupational participation (Kronenberg & Pollard, 2005). *Occupational deprivation* was originally defined as "the influence of an external circumstance that keeps a person from acquiring, using, or enjoying something" (Wilcock, 1998, p. 145).

Whiteford (2000) expanded on the occupational deprivation concept to include some of the challenges facing vulnerable populations brought about by civil and economic unrest. Whiteford's expanded definition of *occupational deprivation* is "a state of preclusion from engagement in occupations of necessity and/or meaning due to factors that stand outside the immediate control of the individual" (p. 201). The price people pay for occupational deprivation can include marginalization and isolation. This concern applies to populations as diverse as prison inmates, ethnic or religious minority groups, and people with refugee status (Whiteford, 1997). In such circumstances, the need for occupational therapy and occupational science expertise is salient and may call for participation in advocacy work as it sheds light on the ever-broadening perspectives (Thibeault, 2005).

One recent example of how these concepts have been applied to occupational therapy is the work of Smith and Hilton (2008), who examined empowerment as the key to addressing issues of marginalization and deprivation among female domestic violence survivors with disabilities. Abuse in all its forms disrupts the meaningful occupations of women with disabilities but has only recently begun to be examined in the literature. Another recent example is research examining the relationship between health and meaningful occupation among rural South African women (Schatz, 2009). Schatz's work is helping to fill the gaps in knowledge about the contributing factors to health and well-being in the developing world. The women she studied were raising their grandchildren who had been orphaned by AIDS and HIV. The lived experiences of the women in these caregiving roles were shaped by sociocultural factors. Documenting these factors contributed to the evidence base of multiple disciplines, including occupational therapy and occupational science (Schatz, 2009).

The last example we present is based on ongoing work conducted by one of the authors addressing the needs of transitioning foster care youths (see Paul-Ward, 2008, 2009). Using both a social and occupational justice framework to better understand the needs of marginalized individuals with visible and invisible disabilities, Paul-Ward's work recognized that numerous barriers must be taken into consideration during the development of interventions to enable targeted individuals to gain the skills they need to successfully participate in society. As a critical medical anthropologist and occupational therapy researcher, Paul-Ward highlighted both the individual and collective responsibility to use the knowledge obtained from population-focused research efforts to effect positive social change for individuals and groups. She argued that adolescents transitioning out of foster care are the victims of social and occupational injustice. Specifically, she argued that

> by design, the foster care system tends to marginalize its "members" by labeling them as different from other children. Moreover, the system disrupts occupation as children are moved from placement to placement. Finally, many of the factors associated with foster care lead to underdevelopment in the areas of exploration and mastery of independent living skills that are seen with children in stable environments. (Paul-Ward, 2009, p. 83)

The short-term, micro-level goal of Paul-Ward's work was to both identify the needs of this marginalized group and to develop and implement occupation-based services that would assist adolescents transitioning out of foster care in developing the skills they need to be successful independent adults. The desired long-term outcome of this work, which she hopes will lead to macro-level changes, is seeing young adults develop into socially conscious adults who feel empowered to effect positive system changes for themselves and others coming through the foster care system.

INTERNATIONAL FIELDWORK AND RESIDENCY PROGRAMS

As the occupational therapy profession embraces global perspectives, more students are expressing interest in pursuing international fieldwork opportunities. In many programs, it is the responsibility of the fieldwork coordinator to assist the student in identifying appropriate international fieldwork opportunities in locations with therapists accredited by the World Federation of Occupational Therapists (WFOT). However, this phenomenon in not one-sided; therapists from other parts of the world are exhibiting interest in coming to the United States to enhance their training. For therapists enrolled in degree programs, clinical fieldwork opportunities are provided through partnering relationships with various clinics, hospitals, and other practice settings. For therapists not enrolled in an academic program, finding clinical opportunities becomes more challenging due to immigration and labor law restrictions. Therefore, managers who receive requests for clinical internships from therapists outside the United States must familiarize themselves with the federal restrictions.

In addition to clinical fieldwork, collaborations can be established in other countries in sensitive or relevant ways through research and ethnographic fieldwork. Fieldwork seeking to shed light on the day-to-day realities of people in the path of globalization could be used to advocate for them and give voice to those most likely to be exploited, displaced, or occupationally deprived. Establishing a collaboration of this sort can be accomplished through the formation of an interdisciplinary work group, such as the NAPA OT–SIG mentioned earlier.

CONCLUSION

Globalization has affected most facets of life, especially in the past few decades. The consequences of globalization's effect on health include migration, human trafficking, spread of disease, and environmental devastation. Globalization's effect on world health has many trade-offs, affecting the environment, culture, political systems, economic development and prosperity, and people's physical well-being (Levin Institute, n.d.). In this chapter, we explored a small sample of the expanding roles of occupational therapy and occupational science in research on the global scene. We identified the numerous intersections of occupational therapy and the social sciences and provided examples of occupational therapists working in international practice settings. Finally, we examined the concept of meaningful engagement in diverse contexts and the significance of occupational justice.

Case Examples

FIELDWORK I

Anna, an eager, conscientious student who moved to Miami from the Midwest to complete the professional master's program in occupational therapy, learned that her Level I fieldwork was to take place in a skilled nursing facility. Knowing that she enjoys working with the geriatric population, Anna was excited for her first fieldwork experience, which involved observation as well as participation that was closely monitored by the fieldwork educator. During the week, Anna met Ramon, an 84-year-old Latino man who was receiving therapy after a recent hip fracture and subsequent hemianthroplasty. After informing Ramon of the weight-bearing restrictions and hip precautions to prevent hip dislocation, the occupational therapist instructed Ramon's wife on how to assist Ramon with dressing and foot care. Although Anna recognized that occupational therapists typically provide family and caregiver education, she wondered why Ramon's wife was performing his ADLs for him. Anna did some research on cultural and generational issues that could explain the behavior she observed.

FIELDWORK II

Upon completion of his coursework for the professional master's in occupational therapy program, Daniel decided he would like to travel to Antigua, Guatemala, to complete his Level II fieldwork at the NAPA–OT field school. To prepare for the trip, Daniel tried to learn what types of occupational therapy services were currently available to the residents of Antigua. He also tried to learn as much as possible about what protections, if any, were generally afforded to individuals with disabilities in Guatemala and, specifically, in the local community. Daniel knew that he still needed to understand several aspects of life in the local community to maximize developing his clinical skills through this international training experience. He completed some background reading (i.e., published ethnographic studies) on the local culture and spoke with locals to understand the challenges people face when engaging in occupations, identifying possible barriers to participation.

(continued)

Case Examples *(cont.)*

FIRST-TIME MANAGER

After graduating from an occupational therapy program and working in the small city in which she grew up for several years, Sarah decided she was ready for adventure and new challenges. She began to look for a job in New York that would allow her to supervise other therapists and was excited when she was offered a position as a supervisor in an outpatient clinic providing occupational and physical therapy to an ethnically diverse community. Although she had worked with a fairly homogenous group of clients in her previous practice setting, she knew from her training the importance of being culturally competent to develop effective therapeutic relationships with her clients.

During her first few weeks in her role as supervisor, Sarah realized that many of the clinic staff did not take into consideration cultural differences when developing treatment plans and working with clients. To ensure that the therapy staff provided the most client-centered and culturally appropriate services, Sarah had the staff review the 14 National Standards on Culturally and Linguistically Appropriate Services (U.S. Department of Health and Human Services, 2007). Next, she encouraged staff members to familiarize themselves with the cultural background of their clients and provided the names and URLs of online tools for working with diverse clientele. Finally, Sarah organized an inservice training on cross-cultural communication and techniques such as "teach back" (having clients repeat instructions to ensure their understanding) to help therapists and clients navigate cultural barriers.

MANAGER

Jessica was a manager in an outpatient clinic in a large children's hospital. One of the occupational therapists came to her with concern about one of the clients in her caseload. The client's parents had recently mentioned that they were having difficulty paying out-of-pocket for their child's occupational therapy. The therapist knew from her conversations with the parents that the father had recently lost his job as a construction worker and the mother had always been a homemaker, taking care of the house and the children as well as her elderly parents. As an advocate for occupational and social justice, Jessica encouraged the therapist to research the state and local resources available to help her client.

❖ Learning Activities

1. Think about how you participate in the global economy. Look at the labels on the items in your home and workplace (especially food items). Make a list of the items and their national origin, and then find these places on a map.
2. Imagine practicing occupational therapy in a hospice or other palliative care setting. What types of challenges would you expect to encounter? How could you modify activities for clients who are facing life-threatening illnesses? What are your expectations for bereavement and grief among clients from non-Western cultures?
3. Perform this group activity: Play a card came using only nonverbal communication to explain the rules and conduct the game. All participants must use only nonverbal skills.
4. Think about invisible disabilities and list those that come to mind. What skills might be targeted and which intervention strategies could you could use to help people living with these disabilities?
5. Examine any standard evaluation tool and modify it for use with a client from another cultural background. What would you change? What assumptions about daily life are built into the premodified tool?

✓ Multiple-Choice Questions

1. In recent years, occupational therapy has intersected with which of the following other disciplines?
   a. Anthropology.
   b. Disability studies.
   c. Occupational science.
   d. All of the above.

2. Is occupational therapy appropriate for people receiving palliative end-of-life care?
   a. Yes, because occupational therapists help people get the most out of life, even if they are facing life-threatening illnesses.
   b. No, because occupational therapists have nothing to offer people at the end of life.

3. What do we call occupational therapy's contribution to justice-related issues?
   a. Social justice.
   b. Occupational justice.
   c. Occupational science.
   d. None of the above.

4. Why do issues such as empowerment among marginalized female domestic violence survivors with disabilities intersect with occupational therapy?
   a. Because marginalization itself disrupts meaningful engagement and participation.
   b. Because abuse in all its forms disrupts the meaningful occupations of women with disabilities.
   c. All of the above.
   d. None of the above.

5. What are some of the challenges associated with adolescents transitioning out of foster care?
   a. Adolescents transitioning out of foster care are often the victims of social and occupational injustice.
   b. The system disrupts occupation as children are moved from placement to placement.
   c. Many of the factors associated with foster care lead to underdevelopment in the areas of exploration and mastery of independent living skills.
   d. All of the above.

6. What do we call an overlap, crossing, or coming together of two or more disciplines?
   a. An intersection.
   b. Redundancy.
   c. Occupational apartheid.
   d. None of the above.

7. This chapter discussed an example of an occupational therapist working in a palliative care setting in which country?
   a. Canada.
   b. Mexico.
   c. England.
   d. Iceland.

8. Knowing how to appropriately work with a diverse clientele falls under the category of
   a. Globalization.
   b. Ethnography.
   c. Culturally competent practice.
   d. All of the above.

9. Understanding the disability experience in multiple contexts is called
   a. Disability studies.
   b. Global perspective.
   c. Social justice.
   d. Multicultural practice.

10. The method of research frequently conducted by anthropologists is called
    a. Social justice.
    b. Ethnography.
    c. Internalization.
    d. None of the above.

11. Taking a critical look at the factors shaping things like living, economic, and social conditions around the world is called
    a. Global perspective.
    b. Internationalization.
    c. Social justice.
    d. Ethnography.

12. A term often interchangeably used with *Westernization* is
    a. Occupational science.
    b. Globalization.
    c. Internationalization.
    d. Intersection.

13. Occupational justice work
    a. Is needed to sufficiently address the larger societal issues that affect occupational therapy practitioners' ability to effect positive change for their clients.
    b. Is not part of occupational therapy.
    c. Is not important.
    d. Does not contribute to health and well-being.

14. Occupational apartheid
    a. Doesn't happen in the modern world.
    b. Still takes place.
    c. Only happens in developing countries.
    d. None of the above.

15. When people are prevented from taking part in meaningful activities, we call that
    a. Globalization.
    b. Palliative care.
    c. Occupational deprivation.
    d. Ethnography.

16. This chapter discusses research examining the relationship between health and meaningful occupation

among rural South African women. What does this research have to do with occupational therapy?

a. This work is helping to fill the gaps in knowledge about the contributing factors to health and well-being in the developing world.

b. Documenting the lived experiences of these women contributes to the evidence base of multiple disciplines, including occupational therapy and occupational science.

c. All of the above.

d. None of the above.

17. Social justice is

a. Only a concern in the developing world.

b. An issue everywhere.

c. Never involves people with disabilities.

d. All of the above.

18. In this chapter, we discuss the reasons adolescents transitioning out of foster care are the victims of social and occupational injustice. These reasons are:

a. By design, the foster care system tends to marginalize its "members" by labeling them as different from other children.

b. The system disrupts occupation as children are moved from placement to placement.

c. Many of the factors associated with foster care lead to underdevelopment in the areas of exploration and mastery of independent living skills that are seen with children in stable environments.

d. All of the above.

19. Global perspectives are valuable and helpful resources because

a. Global perspectives lead to increased opportunities for the field of occupational therapy.

b. Global perspectives create opportunities for greater visibility and recognition of occupational therapy in multiple contexts.

c. The broadening of cultural perspectives is becoming increasingly essential in the rapidly changing world.

d. All of the above.

20. In this chapter, we explored which of the following:

a. A small sample of the expanding roles of occupational therapy and occupational science in research on the global scene.

b. Numerous intersections of occupational therapy and the social sciences, providing examples of occupational therapists working in international practice settings.

c. The concept of meaningful engagement in diverse contexts and the significance of occupational justice.

d. All of the above.

References

Abberley, P. (1995). Disabling ideology in health and welfare: The case of occupational therapy. *Disability and Society, 10,* 221–232.

Accreditation Council for Occupational Therapy Education. (2007). *Accreditation standards for a master's-degree-level education program from the occupational therapist. American Journal of Occupational Therapy, 61,* 652–661.

American Occupational Therapy Association. (2008). Occupational therapy practice framework: Domain and process (2nd ed.). *American Journal of Occupational Therapy, 62,* 625–683.

American Occupational Therapy Association. (2010). Occupational therapy code of ethics and ethics standards. *American Journal of Occupational Therapy, 64.*

Frank, G. (2009, September). *Occupational science and medical anthropology: Intersections for critical praxis.* Plenary lecture given at the meeting of the Society for Medical Anthropology, New Haven, CT.

Frank, G., & Zemke, R. (2005, April). *What is occupational science and what will it become?* Paper presented at the meeting of the Society for Applied Anthropology and Society for Medical Anthropology, Vancouver, BC.

Goffman, E. (1961). *Asylums.* Garden City, NY: Doubleday.

Inhorn, M. (2007). *Medical anthropology at the intersections* [Presidential address]. Retrieved January 28, 2010, from http://www.medanthro.net/maq/backissues/v21_3.html

International Organization for Migration. (n.d.). *Global estimates and trends.* Retrieved June 23, 2010, from http://www.iom.int/jahia/Jahia/about-migration/facts-and-figures/global-estimates-andtrends

Kielhofner, G. (2005). Rethinking disability and what to do about it: Disability studies and its implications for occupational therapy. *American Journal of Occupational Therapy, 59*(5) 487–496.

Kronenberg, F., Algado, S., & Pollard, N. (2005). *Occupational therapy without borders: Learning from the spirit of survivors.* London: Elsevier.

Kronenberg, F., & Pollard, N. (2005) Overcoming occupational apartheid: A preliminary exploration of the political nature of occupational therapy. In F. Kronenberg, S. Algado, & N. Pollard (Eds.), *Occupational therapy without borders: Learning from the spirit of survivors* (pp. 58–86). New York: Elsevier Churchill Livingstone.

Langley-Evans, A., & Payne, S. (1997). Light-hearted death talk in a palliative day care context. *Journal of Advanced Nursing, 26,* 1091–1097.

Levin Institute. (n.d.). *Globalization 101.* Retrieved June 23, 2010, from www.globalization101.org/

Lysack, C., Komanecky, M., Kabel, A., Cross, K., & Neufeld, S. (2007). Environmental factors and their role in community integration after spinal cord injury. *Canadian Journal of Occupational Therapy, 74*(Suppl. 1), 243–254.

Mattingly, C. (1998). Healing dramas and clinical plots: The narrative structure of experience. Cambridge: Cambridge University Press.

McCormack, G., Jaffe, E., & Frey, W. (2003). New organizational perspectives. In G. McCormack, E. Jaffe, & M. Goodman-Lavey (Eds.), *The occupational therapy manager* (4th ed., pp. 85–126). Bethesda, MD: AOTA Press.

Paul-Ward, A. (2008). Intersecting disciplinary frameworks to improve foster care transitions. *Practicing Anthropology, 30*(3), 15–19.

Paul-Ward, A. (2009). Social and occupational justice barriers in the transition from foster care to independent adulthood. *American Journal of Occupational Therapy, 63*, 81–88.

Paul-Ward, A., & Frank, G. (2009). Linkages and bridges. *NAPA e-Newsletter*. Retrieved August 5, 2010, from http://practicinganthropology.org/category/newsletter/

Payne, M. (2006). Social objectives in cancer care: The example of palliative day care. *European Journal of Cancer Care, 15*, 440–447.

Perkinson, M. (2008). Negotiating disciplines: Developing a dementia exercise program. *Practicing Anthropology, 30*(3), 10–14.

Perkinson, M., & Briller, S. (2009). Connecting the anthropology of aging and occupational therapy/occupational science. *Anthropology and Aging Quarterly, 3*(2), 25–26.

Perkinson, M., & Rockemann, D. (1996). Older women living in a continuing care retirement community: Marital status and friendship formation. *Journal of Women and Aging, 8*(3–4), 159–177.

Schatz, E. (2009). Daily occupations among elderly South Africans. *Anthropology and Aging Quarterly, 3*(2), 27.

Smith, D., & Hilton, C. (2008). An occupational justice perspective of domestic violence against women with disabilities. *Journal of Occupational Science, 15*, 166–172.

Society for Medical Anthropology. (2009). [Conference program]. Arlington, VA: Author.

Thibeault, R. (2005). Connecting health and social justice: A Lebanese experience. In F. Kronenberg, S. S. Algado, & N. Pollard (Eds.), *Occupational therapy without borders: Learning from the spirit of survivors* (pp. 232–244). London: Elsevier.

Thompson, B. (1990). Hospice day care. *American Journal of Hospice Care, 7*, 28–30.

Townsend, E., & Wilcock, A. A. (2004). Occupational justice and client-centered practice: A dialogue in practice. *Canadian Journal of Occupational Therapy, 71*, 75–87.

Urbanowski, R. (2005). Transcending practice borders through perspective transformation. In F. Kronenberg, S. S. Algado, & N. Pollard (Eds.), *Occupational therapy without borders: Learning from the spirit of survivors* (pp. 302–312). London: Elsevier.

U.S. Department of Health and Human Services. (2007). *National standards on linguistically and culturally appropriate services*. Retrieved August 5, 2010, from http://minorityhealth.hhs.gov/templates/browse.aspx?lvl=2&lvlID=15

Whiteford, G. (1997). Occupational deprivation and incarceration. *Journal of Occupational Science: Australia, 4*(3), 126–130.

Whiteford, G. (2000). Occupational deprivation: Global challenge in the new millennium. *British Journal of Occupational Therapy, 63*, 200–204.

Wilcock, A. (1998). *An occupational perspective of health.* Thorofare, NJ: Slack.

Zhang Liu, G. (2001). *Chinese culture and disabilities: Information for U.S. service providers.* Retrieved June 23, 2010, from http://cirrie.buffalo.edu/monographs/china.php

APPENDIX 17A. GLOBAL PERSPECTIVES IN OCCUPATIONAL THERAPY PRACTICE EVIDENCE TABLE

Topic	Evidence
Intersections between occupational therapy and the social sciences	Lysack, C., Komanecky, M., Kabel, A., Cross, K., & Neufeld, S. (2007). Environmental factors and their role in community integration after spinal cord injury. *Canadian Journal of Occupatioinal Therapy, 74*(Suppl. 1), 243–254. Mattingly, C. (1998). *Healing dramas and clinical plots: The narrative structure of experience.* Cambridge: Cambridge University Press. Paul-Ward, A. (2008). Intersecting disciplinary frameworks to improve foster care transitions. *Practicing Anthropology, 30*(3), 15–19. Perkinson, M., & Briller, S. (2009). Connecting the anthropology of aging and occupational therapy/occupational science. *Anthropology and Aging Quarterly, 3*(2), 25–26.
Occupational justice, occupational apartheid, and occupational deprivation	Thibeault, R. (2005). Connecting health and social justice: A Lebanese experience. In F. Kronenberg, S. S. Algado, & N. Pollard (Eds.), *Occupational therapy without borders: Learning from the spirit of survivors* (pp. 232–244). London: Elsevier. Thompson, B. (1990). Hospice day care. *American Journal of Hospice Care, 7,* 28–30. Urbanowski, R. (2005). Transcending practice borders through perspective transformation. In F. Kronenberg, S. S. Algado, & N. Pollard (Eds.), *Occupational therapy without borders: Learning from the spirit of survivors* (pp. 302–312). London: Elsevier. Whiteford, G. (1997). Occupational deprivation and incarceration. *Journal of Occupational Science: Australia, 4*(3), 126–130. Whiteford, G. (2000). Occupational deprivation: Global challenge in the new millennium. *British Journal of Occupational Therapy, 63,* 200–204. Wilcock, A. (1998). *An occupational perspective of health.* Thorofare, NJ: Slack.
Expanding roles of occupational therapy and occupational science in research on the global scene	Perkinson, M., & Rockemann, D. (1996). Older women living in a continuing care retirement community: Marital status and friendship formation. *Journal of Women and Aging, 8*(3–4) 159–177. Schatz, E. (2009). Daily occupations among elderly South Africans. *Anthropology and Aging Quarterly, 3*(2), 27. Smith, D., & Hilton, C. (2008). An occupational justice perspective of domestic violence against women with disabilities. *Journal of Occupational Science, 15,* 166–172.

APPENDIX 17.B. GLOBALIZATION RESOURCES

Organizations that provide guidance on efforts to address global perspectives:

- **International Organization for Migration:** http://www.iom.int/jahia/Jahia/about-migration/facts-and-figures
  Provides a global account of contemporary trends, issues, and challenges in the field of international migration.
- **Kaiser Family Foundation:** http://www.kff.org/globalhealth/index2.cfm
  Provides information on the U.S. role in global health.
- **World Federation of Occupational Therapists (WFOT):** http://www.wfot.org/
  Provides information on global issues affecting occupational therapy as well as opportunities to participate in international work, volunteering, and research.

International organizations offering opportunities for occupational therapy practitioners:

- **Agency for International Development:** http://www.usaid.gov
- **Carter Center:** http://www.cartercenter.org/homepage.html
- **International Justice Mission:** http://www.ijm.org
- **Peace Corps:** http://www.peacecorps.gov
- **UNICEF:** http://www.unicef.org
- **World Health Organization:** http://www.who.int/en

18
Leadership Development

Jeff Snodgrass, PhD, MPH, OTR/L

❖ Key Terms and Concepts

360-degree leadership assessment. A process of leader assessment that includes a self-evaluation as well as evaluations by colleagues, subordinates, and superiors.

Leadership. Process of motivating people to perform to their full potential with a focus on effectiveness—that is, doing the right things—to achieve the good of the individual, department, organization, profession, or society.

Management. Supervision of employees with a focus on efficiency—that is, doing things right—which includes maintaining stability by focusing on strategy, structure, and systems.

Transactional leadership. Leadership style in which leaders clarify role and task requirements and provide followers with positive and negative rewards contingent on successful performance. Transactional leadership is an essential prerequisite to effective leadership.

Transformational leadership. Leadership style in which the leader creates a connection with others that raises the level of motivation in both the leader and the follower. The transformational leader is attentive to the needs and motives of followers and tries to help followers reach their fullest potential.

❖ Learning Objectives

After completing this chapter, you should be able to do the following:

- Compare and contrast the characteristics and responsibilities of manager and leaders.
- Explain the importance of developing leadership skills while developing management skills.
- Identify and describe the 2 main types of leadership style: transformational and transactional.

- Identify similarities and emerging themes in the evidence on leadership in health care and rehabilitation.
- Identify tools and strategies for evaluating and assessing leadership development.
- Discuss best practices for developing leadership skills.

The concept of leadership has been studied extensively over the past century. Leadership is a complex, multidimensional phenomenon (Levey, Hill, & Greene, 2002). The definition of leadership is constantly changing and has comprised numerous concepts, such as individual traits, leader behaviors, influence, and interaction (Longest, Rakich, & Darr, 2000). In essence, leaders motivate people to perform to their full potential over time, either for the good of the individual and leader or for the collective good of the department, organization, profession, or society (Avolio & Bass, 2004).

Leadership opportunities abound for occupational therapy managers and practitioners. Traditional, emerging, and underserved practice areas all are fertile ground for leadership development. Many occupational therapy practitioners enter management positions within their first few years of professional practice, but they are typically ill prepared to take on leadership roles, their strengths being their technical skills and clinical ability (Atkinson, 1997; Snodgrass, Douthitt, Ellis, Wade, & Plemons, 2008). New occupational therapy managers who experience a "leadership vacuum" must seek outside training opportunities to develop their leadership traits and qualities and to be competent in their jobs.

Researchers in leadership and leader effectiveness assert that a supervisor's leadership style has a significant influence on employee effectiveness, satisfaction, and production (Avolio & Bass, 2004). It is critical, therefore, that the leadership skills of current and future occupational therapy practitioners are fully developed to enable them to successfully lead the profession toward the *Centennial Vision* for the 21st century: "We envision that occupational therapy is a powerful, widely recognized, science-driven, and evidence-based profession with a globally connected and diverse workforce meeting society's occupational needs" (American Occupational Therapy Association [AOTA], 2007, p. 613). As the profession's demand to lead increases, so does its practitioners' responsibility. It is the collective leadership ability of occupational therapy managers that will ultimately determine the success and effectiveness of the profession.

This chapter explores the complex phenomenon of leadership by comparing and contrasting management and leadership and discussing leadership styles. The contemporary evidence on leadership in health care and occupational therapy is used as a foundation for identifying tools and developing strategies for assessing leadership skills. The chapter concludes with an exploration of best practices for developing and refining leadership skills.

From Management to Leadership

According to Bass (1990), "Leaders manage and managers lead, but the two activities are not synonymous" (p. 383). There is indeed a major difference between managing and leading people, departments, organizations, or professions. Leadership and management are complementary processes, however, and both are necessary to create and promote well-functioning departments and organizations.

Managers typically recognize what their employees want to get from their work and try to see that they get it if their performance so warrants. They exchange rewards and promises of rewards for sufficient levels of effort and respond to the needs and desires of employees as long as they are getting the job done. In contrast, leaders typically raise employees' desire to achieve important outcomes and awareness of the process for achieving them. They encourage employees to move beyond their self-interest for the sake of the team, department, or organization. Leaders facilitate employees' reaching higher levels in such areas as autonomy, achievement, and affiliation (Bass, 1985; Burns, 1978).

In the past, either leadership was viewed as part of management, or the two were viewed as entirely separate concepts. More contemporary views, however, conceptualize leadership and management as complementary roles (Hunt, 2004). For the purposes of this chapter, leadership and management are viewed as complementary processes, but the art and science of leadership are seen as skills that need to be explored separately. Furthermore, this author agrees with the position of many authors of leadership theory that leadership is not simply a position but rather a willingness to make a significant difference and have a lasting impact on those around the leader.

Leadership Styles

The literature describes several styles of leadership. According to Rowitz (2009), "*Leadership styles* generally refers to the way a leader provides direction to his or her organization, how plans and programs get implemented, and how staff are motivated to do their work" (p. 19). Two primary and commonly accepted styles of leadership are *transformational* and *transactional* leadership.

In 1985, Bass argued that transformational leadership accounts for a greater share of the difference in organizational outcomes than more traditional, transactional approaches to leadership. Bass proposed an original thesis that led to one of the most widely accepted and researched leadership approaches of the late 20th century and early 21st century: the full-range leadership theory (FRLT). Numerous studies have examined the FRLT and the impact of transformational and transactional leadership styles in diverse organizational settings, including education, politics, health care, business, and the military (Avolio, Bass, & Jung, 1999; Dumdum, Lowe, & Avolio, 2002; Kark & Shamir, 2002; Snodgrass & Shachar, 2008). The sections that follow provide brief descriptions and examinations of transformational and transactional leadership styles.

Transformational Leadership

According to the FRLT, transformational leaders inspire, energize, and intellectually stimulate their followers. *Transformational leadership* occurs when leaders broaden and elevate the interests of their employees beyond self-interest to focus on the purpose and mission of the group (Bass & Bass, 2008). Avolio and Bass (2004) pointed out that transformational leaders use charisma to inspire and excite others with the notion that much can be accomplished with extra effort. They also provide intellectual stimulation by showing that difficult problems can be resolved with rational solutions. Five constructs make up the transformational leadership style:

1. *Idealized influence (attributes).* The leader is admired, respected, and trusted; followers identify with and want to emulate the leader; and the leader considers followers' needs.
2. *Idealized influence (behaviors).* The leader shares risks with followers and is consistent in his or her conduct according to underlying ethics, principles, and values.
3. *Inspirational motivation.* Leaders inspire and motivate followers to reach ambitious goals, raise followers' expectations, and communicate confidence that followers can achieve lofty goals.
4. *Intellectual stimulation.* The leader questions the status quo, appeals to followers' intellect, and invites innovative and creative solutions to problems.
5. *Individual consideration.* The leader considers the needs of each individual for achievement and growth and acts as a coach and mentor; the leader creates new learning opportunities and a supportive climate in which to grow and recognizes individual needs and differences (Antonakis & House, 2002).

Transactional Leadership

Transactional leadership in its constructive form is characterized by working with individuals and groups, establishing contracts to achieve work objectives, determining individuals' capabilities, and setting up a compensation and rewards system. In its corrective form, transactional leadership is characterized by waiting for mistakes to occur before acting (*passive*) and monitoring for the occurrence of mistakes (*active*), and the leader intervenes only when procedures and standards for accomplishing tasks are not being met (called *passive management by exception*). Transactional leaders use the promise of rewards or avoidance of penalties as their approach to leadership. This approach often proves to be ineffective either because leaders have no control over rewards or penalties or because if they do, employees may not want the rewards or may not fear the penalties. Frequently, pay increases or promotions depend on seniority or qualifications, policies over which the leader has little control. Many transactional leaders find their ability to make changes limited by contract provisions, organizational politics, or inadequate resources.

The constructs that make up the transactional leadership style are as follows:

- *Contingent reward.* The leader clarifies role requirements and rewards and praises desired outcomes; this factor is based on economic and emotional exchanges.
- *Management by exception (active and passive).* The leader establishes the criteria for compliance and noncompliance and closely monitors for deviances, mistakes, and errors. The leader may punish followers for noncompliance and takes corrective action as quickly as possible (Antonakis & House, 2002).
- One nonleadership factor described within the FRLT is referred to as *laissez-faire*. The laissez-faire leader is described as "laid back"; he or she avoids making decisions and getting involved in important issues and delays responding to urgent issues.

REVIEW OF THE EVIDENCE ON LEADERSHIP

Research evidence is important not just to inform and support clinical practice but also to promote the development of leadership skills. The subject of leadership has been discussed extensively for decades among the leaders of the occupational therapy profession, but leadership research in occupational therapy has been sparse (Dudek-Shriber, 1997; Snodgrass & Shachar, 2008). It was not until the 1980s that leadership within the profession was researched in earnest (Broiller, 1985a, 1985b). This section presents recent evidence of the impact of leaders' behaviors and styles on outcomes in occupational therapy and allied health settings. This review is not intended to be exhaustive but rather to provide a sampling of the best available and most applicable contemporary evidence. The appendix lists contemporary research examining leadership and organizational effectiveness in occupational therapy and allied health care.

From the evidence examining leadership in occupational therapy and allied health care emerges recurring themes and commonalities. The evidence indicates that transformational leadership augments transactional leadership in predicting effects on followers' perceptions of leader effectiveness (Antonakis, 2001; Dumdum et al., 2002). Empirical and meta-analytic studies have found that transformational leadership accounts for a positive and unique variance in ratings of performance beyond that accounted for by active transactional leadership in health care settings (Gellis, 2001; Leach, 2005; Snodgrass et al., 2008). Extensive research on the impact of leadership has shown that "transformational leaders differ from a transactional one by not merely recognizing associates' needs, but by attempting to develop those needs from lower to higher levels of maturity" (Avolio & Bass, 2004, p. 7). Transformational leaders encourage the growth and development of others beyond ordinary expectations. Thus, leaders displaying transformational leadership styles tend to have a greater influence and generate higher levels of employee satisfaction, extra effort, and motivation when compared to leaders exhibiting transactional leadership styles (Antonakis, 2001; Bass, Avolio, Jung, & Berson, 2003; Chen, 2004).

The evidence suggests that the most effective leaders

- Assume a goal-oriented approach to work tasks;
- Are respectful of their associates and employees and are effective communicators;
- Possess planning skills that include time management, prioritization of work tasks, and establishment of goals for work teams;
- Demonstrate a full range of leadership styles that combine transformational constructs and the transactional construct of contingent rewards as described by Avolio and Bass (2004);
- Exhibit five key leadership practices (as described by Kouzes & Posner, 2007), including (1) challenge the process, (2) inspire a shared vision, (3) enable others to act, (4) model the way, and (5) encourage the heart; and
- Recognize the need to continue their own professional development to help improve their role in leadership.

INSTRUMENTS FOR MEASURING LEADERSHIP

Exactly how a leader creates change or influences others has been the subject of much examination and debate. To better understand leadership as a complex, multidimensional phenomenon (Levey et al., 2002), one needs to be able to measure its components (Kroeck, Lowe, & Brown, 2004). Interest in using a comprehensive assessment of leadership skills has been growing over the past 15 years (Kouzes & Posner, 2007). Because of the complexity of the leadership construct, no single measure of it exists. However, many instruments are available that evaluate specific components of leadership (Kroeck et al., 2004; Rowitz, 2009).

When considering leadership assessment, the role of the rater must be considered (Kroeck et al., 2004). Researchers have found that leaders tend to rate themselves higher than they are rated by their followers, coworkers, or colleagues (Avolio & Bass, 2004; Reiss, 2000) and that therefore the leader's effectiveness must be considered within the context of his or her followers perceptions' (Avolio & Bass, 2004; Kouzes & Posner, 2007). Leader assessment thus should include both a self-evaluation and evaluations by subordinates, peers, supervisors, and perhaps even clients; this type of assessment is called a *360-degree leadership assessment.* One doesn't need to be in a formal position of leadership to benefit from this type of assessment; organizations have leaders at every level. According to Maxwell (2007), good leaders are adept at leading not only their followers but also their superiors and peers. Therefore, a true measure of leadership can be obtained only by having those around one evaluate one's leadership skills. Table 18.1 presents a list of commonly used leadership evaluation instruments and a brief description of each.

LEADERSHIP DEVELOPMENT

There is no shortage of opportunities to do great things in the profession of occupational therapy. In fact, the profes-

Table 18.1. Leadership Assessment Instruments

Instrument	Purpose	Description	Reference
Leadership Practices Inventory (LPI)	Helps leaders assess the extent to which they actually use best leadership practices	The LPI is a questionnaire comprising 30 behavioral statements with 6 questions for each of the 5 leadership practices; it takes 10–20 minutes to complete.	Kouzes, J. M., & Posner, B. Z. (2003). *Leadership Practices Inventory* (3rd ed.). San Francisco: Pfeiffer.
Student Leadership Practices Inventory (S–LPI)	Is designed specifically to help students and young adults measure leadership competencies and to guide them through the process of applying best leadership practices	This inventory is similar to the standard LPI, as described above.	Kouzes, J. M., & Posner, B. Z. (2006). *Student Leadership Practices Inventory: Facilitator's guide* (2nd ed.). San Francisco: Jossey-Bass.
Benchmarks Assessment	Offers an in-depth look at one's leadership development by assessing skills developed from previous leadership experiences, identifying what lessons still need to be learned, and helping the individual determine what specific work experiences to seek out to develop critical skills for success	The Benchmarks Assessment measures 16 skills and perspectives critical for success, as well as 5 possible factors that can derail a manager's career.	Center for Creative Leadership. (2007). *Benchmarks assessment.* Available online at http://www.ccl.org/leadership/index.aspx.
360-Degree Leader Assessment	Allows leaders to identify and enhance what they are already doing right and pinpoint areas for both short- and long-term development	Leaders compare their self-perceptions on specific leadership criteria with the perceptions of those who work with them, such as bosses, peers, and direct and indirect reports.	Maxwell, J. C. (n.d.). *The 360-Degree Leader Assessment.* Available online at http://www.injoy.com.
Multifactor Leadership Questionnaire (MLQ)	Helps individuals identify the characteristics and behaviors of a transformational leader and discover how they measure up in their own eyes and in the eyes of those with whom they work	The MLQ measures 9 different leadership styles; 5 are related to transformational leadership, 3 to transactional leadership, and 1 to nonleadership (laissez-faire). In addition, the MLQ measures 3 leadership outcomes—effectiveness, satisfaction, and extra effort.	Bass, B. M., & Avolio, B. J. (2004). *Multifactor Leadership Questionnaire.* Available online at http://www.mindgarden.com/index.htm.

sion is in dire need of individuals willing to step up and take "the leadership challenge" (Kouzes & Posner, 2007). One can become an effective leader, but one must first recognize that it is a process that can't be accomplished overnight.

Are leaders born or made? Bennis (2003) noted that "everyone has the capacity for leadership . . . but not everyone will become a leader" (p. xxxii), implying that leaders are not born but rather develop, improve, and hone their skills over time. Leadership development is a very deliberate and intentional process. Just as becoming a seasoned clinician requires years of education, practice, and experience, developing into a competent leader is an ongoing process that is a result of self-discipline, motivation, and perseverance. As noted author and leadership expert John Maxwell (2007) explained, "Leadership develops daily, not in a day" (p. 23).

Core Leadership Competencies

For the occupational therapy profession to continue to flourish and grow in an increasingly competitive and volatile health care environment, practitioners must focus on building and developing the profession's leadership capacity. Building this capacity first requires the identification of the core leadership competencies most applicable to the profession. This author proposes four broad competencies largely drawn from the work of the National Public Health Leadership Development Network (Wright et al., 2000). The proposed competencies are congruent with the values of the profession of occupational therapy as articulated in AOTA's *Centennial Vision* (AOTA, 2007). To accomplish this bold vision, as Clark (n.d.) observed, "occupational therapy practitioners will need to hold leadership roles in health care delivery systems, to be active in policymaking, and to utilize technology to provide services."

The Public Health Leadership Competency Framework, developed by the National Public Health Leadership Network (Wright et al., 2000), identified four types of leadership competencies: transformational leadership competencies, political competencies, inter- and intraorganizational competencies, and team-building competencies. This framework can serve as a guide both for occupational therapy practitioners desiring to build their leadership capacity and for health care organizations and participants in the political and policy-making process. These leadership competencies presuppose that individuals already possess the knowledge, skills, and abilities required for basic management functions (e.g., budgeting, planning, directing, controlling, organizing, staffing).

Transformational Leadership Competencies

Individuals in leadership positions should be able to do the following:

- *Display visionary leadership.* Create and articulate future scenarios relative to alternatives for change, develop and articulate a vision, and participate in the organization's and professional association's strategic decision making

- *Possess a sense of mission.* Model core professional values, attitudes, and ethics; facilitate mission development and adaptation of mission to vision; understand and articulate the purpose and value of vision and mission statements; and effectively communicate the mission and vision

- *Become an effective change agent.* Enhance creative capacities to enhance learning, critical thinking, and clinical reasoning skills; model active learning; integrate cultural competence; develop and implement outcome measurement management systems; and build organizational capacity to envision and select strategies to address short-term and long-term issues that affect access, cost, and quality of services.

Political Competencies

Individuals in leadership positions should be able to do the following:

- *Participate in political processes*: Identify, communicate, and act on political processes operating at the federal, state, and local levels
- *Direct and refine strategic planning*: Participate in and facilitate changes at the policy, professional association, management, and operational levels
- *Advocate for the profession and client/consumer*: Develop, implement, and evaluate community outreach/education and marketing strategies to achieve organizational, local, state, and national goals and objectives
- *Evaluate and leverage political resources*: Develop and implement collaborative strategies to guide appropriate political action and translate policy decisions at the organizational and community levels related to structure, programs, and services.

Inter- and Intraorganizational Competencies

Individuals in leadership positions should be able to do the following:

- *Understand organizational dynamics.* Evaluate organizational environment, needs, assets, resources, and opportunities with respect to policy development and implementation
- *Participate in interorganizational collaboration.* Identify key stakeholders and partners in collaborative ventures and develop partnering strategies, including task force, coalition, and consortium development
- *Participate in forecasting.* Identify and interpret emerging trends, create predictions and scenarios, and communicate predictions and scenarios by providing analysis and interpretation to interorganizational partners.

Team-Building Competencies

Individuals in leadership positions should be able to do the following:

- *Develop team-oriented structures and systems.* Encourage entrepreneurial spirit within team structures and develop team structures to address quality improvement and evaluate clinical and organizational outcomes

- *Develop teams and groups.* Facilitate group process, including development and use of problem-solving, conflict resolution, and decision-making skills; empower and motivate teams to accomplish objectives; create incentives and rewards; celebrate accomplishments; encourage risk-taking behavior; and facilitate the development of servant–leadership capacity (i.e., leading by serving others)
- *Serve as a positive and effective team member.* Model positive group process behavior, including listening, dialoguing, negotiating, rewarding, and encouraging, and model effective team leadership traits, including integrity, credibility, enthusiasm, commitment, honesty, caring, and trust.

Self-Assessment of Leadership Development Needs

Leadership development is a process that should begin with a thorough assessment of one's leadership skills (see Table 18.1). Once the occupational therapist has conducted a self-assessment of his or her leadership development needs and established a personal leadership plan, he or she needs to begin working intentionally and daily on developing leadership skills. The next section outlines ways to develop these skills.

Methods of Leadership Education and Training

According to Bennis (2003), "Managers wear square hats and learn through training. Leaders wear sombreros and opt for education" (p. 40). Management development is typically oriented toward training to acquire the specific knowledge, skills, and abilities needed in the traditional management functions of budgeting, planning, directing, controlling, organizing, and staffing. These traditional management functions pertain to specific, well-defined positions within an organization (Avolio & Bass, 2004). Leadership development, however, is focused more on cultivating the individual's ability to influence others, establish credibility and trust, build relationships and team cohesiveness, and engage in leadership roles and processes, regardless of title or position (Hunt, 2004; Kouzes & Posner, 2007).

A specific formula or recipe for leadership success does not exist. Rather, the methods chosen for leadership training should reflect the context of the organization as well as the content of the participant's character, values, and preferred learning styles. In other words, leaders must choose the leadership development methods that are most relevant to their own needs based on their unique talents, strengths, and experiences. Regardless of training method, the manner in which leaders and potential leaders pursue training should be action oriented by reflecting the participant's working conditions (Bass & Bass, 2008).

Leadership training can be obtained through numerous informal and formal means, including on-the-job training, book reading, mentoring, and workshops. Unfortunately, very few leadership development programs have undergone sufficient scrutiny to objectively evaluate their impact (Bass & Bass, 2008). Nevertheless, the potential pros and cons of several well-established methods of leadership education and training are briefly reviewed in Table 18.2.

FIVE PRACTICES FOR DEVELOPING LEADERSHIP SKILLS

Leadership is a set of skills that can be learned by occupational therapy practitioners who wish to influence the profession. Most people already possess leadership traits and skills gained through past experiences, such as team sports or a group or club. This section reviews five practices for developing leadership skills that are based on the work of Kouzes and Posner (2007), who referred to them collectively as *the leadership challenge.*

Modeling the Way

Mark Twain once quipped, "Action speaks louder than words but not nearly as often." Others won't follow unless one has proved oneself to be worthy of following. Leaders must lead by example, thus modeling the way others ought to act. To become a leader, one must look internally and find one's voice, use that authentic voice to identify and articulate common values with others, and then model the way by demonstrating congruency between one's actions and those shared values (Kouzes & Posner, 2007).

Leaders are expected to stand up for what they believe, and thus they need to know what it is, in fact, that they believe. Leaders are unique in having firm beliefs and in being willing to go against the prevailing winds to fight for those beliefs. Leaders can't force their beliefs and values on others, however. They must build consensus by first engaging others in common interests, desires, hopes, and aspirations. Leaders set an example through ordinary tasks and by doing so help build commitment and loyalty among their followers. Thus, developing into an effective leader is a daily, iterative process (Kouzes & Posner, 2007).

Inspiring a Shared Vision

Managers steer the ship; leaders chart the course. Leaders have an unflagging sense of what they would like the future to hold and a burning desire to make it happen. They also share the vision with others and inspire them to become part of that vision. To understand their followers, leaders must build meaningful, authentic relationships. Organizations don't lead; only individuals lead through their relationships with others (Kouzes & Posner, 2007).

Challenging the Process

To challenge the process, a leader must be willing to experiment and take risks by creating small wins (e.g., a rehabilitation department meets its monthly productivity goal), celebrating those small wins, and learning from mistakes (Kouzes & Posner, 2007). True leaders are not

Table 18.2. Potential Pros and Cons of Common Leadership Education and Training Methods

Training Method	Pros	Cons
Didactic methods— lectures and workshops	Are engaging, inspirational, and informational and stimulate thinking Generally make use of master lecturers and standardized training and evaluation methods	Allow for only limited interaction, particularly in large programs (i.e., 25 or more participants) May lack instruction in actual skill development Often lack small group interactions with guided discussion
Online training	Is convenient May give the opportunity to connect and network with people from different geographic locations May provide the opportunity to analyze scenarios, situations, and behaviors and formulate responses May promote lifelong learning	May lack opportunities for personal contact with the instructor/presenter May require more self-discipline and motivation to participate and complete than traditional face-to-face lectures and workshops
Self-paced books and other literature	Are self-directed and empower the individual to develop his or her own skills May promote self-discipline and an appreciation for self-directed lifelong learning Allow the individual to pick and choose material that is the most relevant to his or her situation and interests	May lack opportunities for formal interaction or relationship with leaders or other mentors Require high degree of motivation and self-discipline Involve difficulty in selecting the most appropriate book or other materials given the large amount of commercially available literature on leadership
On-the-job education and development, coaching and mentoring	Focus on the individual with one-on-one learning, role playing, learning from challenging assignments or experience, and rotation of jobs or tasks Often give trainees the opportunity to practice what they will eventually have to do Are often focused on doing rather than the theory of leadership Coaching and mentoring provide highly individualized instruction, guidance, and feedback; on-the-job training and mentoring may lead to more career opportunities, promotions, security, and recognition for those who receive them	May be of limited effectiveness if not applied to solving real-world issues that demand effective leadership Depend on the organizational culture to encourage or discourage leadership development Involve job rotation, which supervisors may view as a burden because of the need to train newcomers Mentoring relies heavily on the skills and competence of the mentor, who may or may not be the best match for the mentee; coaching requires that the coach provide good modeling and create an atmosphere of openness and honesty
Networking	Helps individuals connect to others in similar or different functions and areas Promotes socialization, sense of connection, relationship building, camaraderie, and problem solving	May provide limited skill development Requires the individual to be self-motivated and persistent May be very time-consuming May be focused more on exploring future opportunities and collaborations than on development of leadership skills
Formal education	Uses a structured, standardized curriculum often taught by experienced professionals with advanced degrees May offer graduate certificates or master's or doctoral degrees in leadership May be required, or at least very useful, when applying for competitive employment or seeking to move up in an organization Often leads to a higher position and salary May be available via distance-based learning to accommodate nontraditional or working professionals	Is expensive and time-consuming May not reflect the specific needs of the learner May be inconvenient, particularly for professionals working full-time while pursuing formal education

afraid of failure. When fear of failure prevents people from challenging the process, the status quo and mediocrity are reinforced (Kouzes & Posner, 2007). Leaders view mistakes as a natural part of the process that ultimately leads to better outcomes. It is in times of great challenges that leaders have the opportunity to achieve great things. Winston Churchill once said, "A pessimist sees the difficulty in every opportunity; an optimist sees the opportunity in every difficulty." Leaders are eternal optimists and believe that the bigger the challenge, the greater the opportunity.

Enabling Others to Act

Enabling others to act requires consensus leadership. Arguably, leaders can lead others through fear and intimidation or a sense of obligation. But a leader who uses these strategies is not a true leader and will have only limited, if any, short-term success. Effective leaders understand the value of building consensus. Accomplishing extraordinary things with a team or within an organization can be accomplished only by the work of many. Vince Lombardi, the Hall of Fame football coach, articulated this concept well when he said, "Coaches who can outline plays on a blackboard are a dime a dozen. The ones who win get inside their player and motivate."

Leaders must figure out how to get individual commitment to a group effort. One can't force people to do very much for very long. People have to believe that they are working on tasks and activities that are vital to the success of the organization. People need to be given the tools, autonomy, and discretion to carry out their work and to know that their hard work and dedication are recognized and appreciated. It is therefore the responsibility of the leader to build consensus by setting cooperative goals, building trust, and empowering others by freely giving away the requisite power and discretion for others to do their job (Kouzes & Posner, 2007).

Encouraging the Heart

Arguably the most important skill a leader possesses is what Kouzes and Posner (2007) described as *encouraging the heart*. As Maxwell (2007) observed, "You can't move people to action unless you first move them with emotion. . . . The heart comes before the head" (p. 115). People are more likely to buy into a leader's vision if they first have an emotional connection to the leader. The best strategy for connecting emotionally with people is to recognize individual contributions to the shared vision and express sincere gratitude for and satisfaction with the accomplishments of each individual. A leader must also be willing to communicate that those they lead have value and to encourage and support a sense of community (Kouzes & Posner, 2007).

Summary

The profession of occupational therapy has always needed and benefited from effective leaders, but leadership is not reserved for the chosen few. Rather, it is reserved for individuals willing to step up and take the leadership challenge. As the profession moves closer to realizing its *Centennial Vision* (AOTA, 2007), the need to build its collective leadership capacity has never been more pressing. To become "a powerful, widely recognized, science-driven, and evidence-based profession with a globally connected and diverse workforce meeting society's occupational needs," a groundswell of individuals willing to lead effectively will be necessary.

In this chapter, the characteristics and responsibilities of managers and leaders were compared and contrasted. Although management and leadership are indeed complementary processes, leadership as a concept and set of skills needs to be explored and developed separately. Furthermore, leadership is not a position; rather, leadership is about the leader's willingness to make a significant difference and to have a lasting impact on those around him or her.

Recurring themes and commonalities emerged from the evidence examining leadership in occupational therapy and allied health care. The evidence provides a window into what it takes to be an effective leader, which includes setting goals and priorities; respecting colleagues, associates, and employees; communicating frequently and clearly; prioritizing work tasks; displaying transformational leadership; and using the five key leadership practices. In addition, the evidence clearly reveals that leaders displaying transformational leadership styles tend to have a greater influence and generate higher levels of employee satisfaction, extra effort, and motivation when compared to leaders exhibiting a primarily transactional leadership style.

Those who wish to increase their leadership capacity must first recognize the need to develop and improve their leadership skills. Tools and strategies were presented for evaluating leadership ability, including a 360-degree leadership assessment process that highlighted the importance of obtaining feedback from followers, peers, and superiors. Best practices for developing leadership skills were offered, as was the observation that leadership development is intentional, daily, and requires desire and self-discipline.

Occupational therapists have many opportunities to develop leadership skills and become effective leaders. Just as they have developed and honed their clinical skills to become seasoned clinicians, those who want to become effective leaders can also develop and hone their leadership skills. The future of occupational therapy depends on individuals willing come forward and lead the profession.

Case Examples

LEVEL I FIELDWORK

Kirk was completing a Level I fieldwork experience in a regional health care system. The director of rehabilitation asked Kirk to lead an interdisciplinary team in developing and implementing an injury prevention program focusing on work-related musculoskeletal injuries among nursing staff. The team included representatives from the nursing, physical therapy, and risk management/quality assurance departments.

Kirk had been reading about leadership, and he had attended a 2-day workshop on developing leadership skills. In preparation for the first team meeting, Kirk considered strategies for effective leadership and team building. He decided that he needed to consider his current competency in team building, so he did a self-assessment of his strengths, weaknesses, areas for improvement, and strategies for improving his competency (see Exhibit 18.1).

After reflecting on his past leadership experience and completing a leadership development plan, Kirk identified the following competencies and strategies as ones that he needed to develop to lead his team effectively:

- *Engage in team building.* Kirk would seek to facilitate the group process by promoting and encouraging problem solving and by recognizing and resolving any conflict within the group through consensus-building and decision-making skills.

- *Model effective team leadership traits.* Kirk would model the leadership traits of integrity, credibility, enthusiasm, commitment, honesty, caring, and trust.
- *Encourage an entrepreneurial spirit.* Kirk would work to create a team environment and culture that encouraged and rewarded creative thinking and unique alternatives through group brainstorming and discussion.
- *Assess clinical and organizational outcomes.* Kirk would provide the team with a brief overview of the importance of assessing outcomes to measure the success of the injury prevention program, and he began to select appropriate strategies and tools for collecting clinical and organizational outcomes.

LEVEL II FIELDWORK

Susan was an occupational therapy assistant student on an 8-week Level II fieldwork rotation at a large, integrated health care system in a densely populated metropolitan area. As part of her fieldwork requirements, she was required to complete a project demonstrating advanced clinical skills and/or leadership skills.

In a course on management and leadership, Susan had learned about the importance of understanding organizational structure and function and of working within and between organizations. For her Level II fieldwork project, Susan decided to form a consortium of occu-

(continued)

EXHIBIT 18.1. PERSONAL LEADERSHIP DEVELOPMENT PLAN

Leadership Competency	Strengths and Opportunities	Areas for Improvement	Action Planning	Timelines	Resources
Transformational leadership					
Political competencies					
Inter- and intraorganizational competencies					
Team-building competencies					

Case Examples *(cont.)*

pational therapy and occupational therapy assistant students who were also completing Level II fieldwork rotations in the metropolitan area. Her goal was to establish a way for students to come together to learn, study, socialize, and ultimately support one another. She began by contacting occupational therapy students in the health care system in which she was completing her rotation as well as five other health care organizations that sponsored Level II fieldwork students.

Susan was very nervous about forming this consortium and decided to reflect on her current leadership skills and ways to further develop them. Susan conducted a self-assessment of her leadership strengths and weaknesses using the Student Leadership Practices Inventory (Kouzes & Posner, 2006), which helped her measure her leadership competencies and identify best leadership practices. Susan then identified the two leadership practices with which she was most comfortable: model the way and encourage the heart. She also identified the two leadership practices with which she was least comfortable—inspire a shared vision and challenge the process—and listed the following priorities and actions to help her engage in these practices more often:

1. *Inspire a shared vision* by imagining possibilities for collaboration among occupational therapy students and practitioners. Susan planned to use regular consortium meetings to develop the consortium's strategic plan, which she planned to submit as a final product for her project.
2. *Challenge the process* by seeking innovative strategies for bridging academic and clinical practice. Susan planned to begin this process by inviting her academic fieldwork coordinator and clinical fieldwork supervisor to the next consortium meeting to solicit their feedback and input.

First-Time Manager

After 10 years of practice in a variety of pediatric settings, 6 months ago Shelly accepted her first position as an occupational therapy supervisor for a contract company providing services in a rural school system. She had recently completed a graduate certificate in health care administration that incorporated class work on leadership. Shelly faced the following significant leadership challenges in her new position:

- The personnel in her department were dispersed across a large geographic area in multiple schools.
- The occupational therapy department did not function as a cohesive team and lacked a sense of vision, mission, and commitment to addressing pressing issues related to cost and access to services.

- Shelly needed to further develop and refine her own leadership skills to effectively lead her department.

After reviewing the leadership material from her graduate coursework, which included the full-range leadership theory (Avolio & Bass, 2004) and a leadership self-assessment using the Multifactor Leadership Questionnaire (MLQ), Shelly decided to conduct a 360-degree leadership assessment. She asked her department personnel and immediate supervisor to anonymously rate her leadership ability and skills with the MLQ. The results of their assessments suggested that those around Shelly perceived her as displaying more of a transactional than a transformational leadership style. She scored in the 80th percentile for overall transactional leadership style but only in the 25th percentile for overall transformational leadership style as compared to the normative data (Avolio & Bass, 2004).

Shelly understood that the most effective leaders tend to display more of a transformational leadership style than a transactional leadership style (Antonakis, 2001; Bass et al., 2003; Chen, 2004). Therefore, she decided to create an action plan to further develop and enhance her transformational leadership capacity as follows:

- *Facilitate vision and mission development.* Shelly decided to begin holding monthly meetings with all occupational therapy personnel to work on developing the department's vision and mission.
- *Create and articulate future scenarios.* Through monthly staff meetings and regular face-to-face interactions with individual staff, Shelly decided to engage the occupational therapy department in strategic planning to address short-term and long-term issues that affect access, cost, and quality of services.
- *Enhance creative capacities.* Shelly decided to promote interdepartmental interaction and foster a culture of lifelong learning among her staff by securing fiscal resources to support their continued development and sponsoring quarterly education meetings in which occupational therapy staff and other disciplines within her company (i.e., physical therapy, speech–language pathology) would present case studies and various other clinical topics.
- *Develop and implement an outcome measurement management system.* Shelly proposed to her company's president that they form an interdisciplinary ad hoc committee of representatives from each key department to develop an outcome measurement system that would allow the company to collect, analyze, and report on clinical and organizational outcomes.

Manager

Clayton had been an occupational therapist for 15 years and had risen through the ranks of a large, for-profit company that provided in-house rehabilitation services to

Case Examples *(cont.)*

more than 25 skilled nursing facilities in 4 different states. Clayton was recently promoted from regional director of rehabilitation services to vice president (VP) of strategic operations and chief operating officer (COO). The company had faced significant fiscal challenges over the past several years because of ongoing declines in reimbursement for services provided to clients covered by Medicare. One of Clayton's priorities as the new VP and COO was to advocate at the state and federal level for his company and the profession of occupational therapy regarding Medicare reimbursement policy.

Clayton had been a member of AOTA for his entire career and contributed regularly to AOTA's Political Action Committee (AOTPAC), but he had not been actively involved at the state or federal level with policy-related issues. In preparing for his involvement, he considered his current political competencies and ways he could become an agent of change, as follows:

• *Participate in political processes.* Clayton informed himself about the political process as it relates to

Medicare at the federal level. He decided to regularly check AOTA's Legislative Action Center to keep up to date with legislative and regulatory developments in Washington that are important to the profession. Specifically, Clayton learned that the federal agency that administers Medicare—the Centers for Medicare and Medicaid Services—was proposing another round of across-the-board reductions in Medicare spending, which might directly affect the reimbursement levels of his company. He contacted the members of Congress representing his state to express his concern about these proposed cuts in Medicare spending and how they would affect the delivery of occupational therapy and rehabilitation services to their constituents.

• *Evaluate and leverage political resources.* Clayton partnered his organization with his state's hospital association to participate in the development and implementation of collaborative strategies to guide appropriate political action and translate policy decisions related to structure, program, and services to the organizational and community levels.

❖ Learning Activities

1. Complete the personal leadership development plan using the format in Exhibit 18.1, prepare a written plan or presentation, and present the plan to your class or a small group of colleagues.

2. Lead a group in completing the Student Leadership Practices Inventory (S–LPI; Kouzes & Posner, 2006) as part of an in-depth exploration of how group members can develop their leadership skills. The S–LPI and a facilitator's packet with all of the necessary resources to set up this assignment can be ordered at http://www.leadershipchallenge.com.

3. Ask several students or colleagues to formulate a 2- to 3-sentence consensus definition of leadership. Identify

and discuss the themes in the definition of leadership you develop, and be prepared to dispel myths and misconceptions about leadership.

4. Answer the question, Are leaders born or made? Support your assertions with evidence from the literature.

5. Imagine yourself in the role of an occupational therapist interviewing for a full-time position. Prepare a list of your previous leadership experiences (e.g., as a student, volunteer, employee, church member), and formulate a concise summary of your leadership style that you can share with the interviewer.

✓ Multiple-Choice Questions

1. Which of the following statements is true?
   a. Leadership is a characteristic of a position within an organization.
   b. Leadership and management are synonymous.
   c. Leadership is everyone's business.
   d. Only those who possess knowledge and intelligence can be leaders.

2. Which of the following statements is true about managers as compared to leaders?
   a. Managers do the right things.
   b. Managers focus on people and relationships.
   c. Managers challenge the status quo.
   d. Managers maintain a short-range view.

3. Leaders typically do which of the following?
   a. Raise employees' desire to achieve important outcomes and awareness of the process to achieve them.
   b. Encourage employees to move beyond their self-interest for the sake of the team, department, or organization.
   c. Facilitate employees' needs to rise to higher levels in such areas as autonomy, achievement, and affiliation.
   d. All of the above.

4. A director of rehabilitation leading a group of department managers is displaying which of the following leadership attributes when she considers her followers' needs and engages her followers in the process by sharing risks?
   a. Idealized influence.
   b. Intellectual stimulation.
   c. Individual consideration.
   d. Management by exception (active).

5. An occupational therapy assistant who devotes the first meeting of a new committee to establishing role requirements for each member and a financial reward system for superior performance is displaying which of the following leadership attributes?
   a. Inspiration motivation.
   b. Contingent reward.
   c. Management by exception (passive).
   d. Laissez-faire.

6. A comprehensive assessment of leadership skills that includes both a self-evaluation and evaluations by coworkers is referred to as a
   a. 360-degree leadership assessment.
   b. Multidimensional skill assessment.
   c. Panoramic assessment.
   d. Leader-behavior assessment.

7. Which of the following leadership assessments is the most valid measure of students' leadership ability?

   a. Multifactor Leadership Questionnaire.
   b. Leader Behavior Questionnaire.
   c. Benchmarks Assessment.
   d. Leadership Practices Inventory.

8. An occupational therapy supervisor wants to evaluate his own leadership skills and his effectiveness as a leader as perceived by his followers and colleagues. The best leadership assessment to evaluate both is the
   a. Multifactor Leadership Questionnaire.
   b. Leader Behavior Questionnaire.
   c. Benchmarks Assessment.
   d. Leadership Practices Inventory.

9. To prepare for the leadership challenge of forming a quality improvement task force at each of multiple facilities, a new occupational therapy supervisor should initially focus on which of the following leadership competencies?
   a. Transformational.
   b. Political.
   c. Interorganizational.
   d. Intraorganizational.

10. Basic management functions include all of the following except
    a. Budgeting.
    b. Planning.
    c. Staffing.
    d. Influencing.

11. Although Karyn doesn't hold a formal title or position of leadership, she has pushed herself and her colleagues to become more efficient and effective by redesigning the department's processes. According to Kouzes and Posner (2007), Karyn is engaging in which of the following leadership practices?
    a. Encouraging the heart.
    b. Challenging the process.
    c. Enabling others.
    d. Inspiring a shared vision.

12. The contemporary evidence on leadership in occupational therapy suggests that the most effective leaders focus on
    a. Future planning.
    b. Short-term activities.
    c. The bottom line.
    d. Systems and processes.

13. Over the past 20 years, which of the following leadership styles has been empirically proved to generate greater follower effectiveness and satisfaction?
    a. Laissez-faire.
    b. Situational.
    c. Transactional.
    d. Transformational.

References

Adamson, B., Cant, R., & Hummell, J. (2001, April). What managerial skills do newly graduated occupational therapists need? A view from their managers. *British Journal of Occupational Therapy, 64,* 184–192.

American Occupational Therapy Association. (2007). AOTA's *Centennial Vision* and executive summary. *American Journal of Occupational Therapy, 61,* 613–614.

Antonakis, J. (2001). The validity of the transformational, transactional, and laissez-faire leadership model as measured by the Multifactor Leadership Questionnaire (MLQ–5X). Doctoral dissertation, Walden University, Baltimore. *ProQuest Digital Dissertations,* AAT 3000380.

Antonakis, J., & House, R. J. (2002). The full-range leadership theory: The way forward. In B. J. Avolio & F. J. Yammarino (Eds.), *Transformational and charismatic leadership: The road ahead* (Vol. 2, pp. 3–33). Oxford, England: Elsevier Science.

Atkinson, D. E. (1997). Rehabilitation management and leadership competencies. *Journal of Rehabilitation Administration, 21,* 249–260.

Avolio, B. J., & Bass, B. M. (2004). *Multifactor Leadership Questionnaire* (Manual and sampler set, 3rd ed.). Palo Alto, CA: Mind Garden.

Avolio, B. J., Bass, B. M., & Jung, D. I. (1999). Re-examining the components of transformational and transactional leadership using the Multifactor Leadership Questionnaire. *Journal of Occupational and Organizational Psychology, 72,* 441–462.

Bass, B. M. (1985). *Leadership and performance beyond expectation.* New York: Free Press.

Bass, B. M. (1990). *Bass and Stogdill's handbook of leadership* (3rd ed.). New York: Free Press.

Bass, B. M., & Avolio, B. J. (2004). *Multifactor Leadership Questionnaire.* Available online at http://www.mindgarden.com/index.htm

Bass, B. M., Avolio, B. J., Jung, D. I., & Berson, Y. (2003). Predicting unit performance by assessing transformational and transactional leadership. *Journal of Applied Psychology, 88,* 207–218.

Bass, B. M., & Bass, R. (2008). *The Bass handbook of leadership* (4th ed.). New York: Free Press.

Bennis, W. (2003). *On becoming a leader.* New York: Basic Books.

Broiller, C. (1985a). Managerial leadership and staff OTR job satisfaction. *Occupational Therapy Journal of Research, 5,* 170–184.

Broiller, C. (1985b). Occupational therapy management and job performance of staff. *American Journal of Occupational Therapy, 39,* 649–654.

Burns, J. M. (1978). *Leadership.* New York: Harper & Row.

Caruana, E. (2008). Review summaries: Evidence for nursing practice. Comprehensive systematic review of evidence on developing and sustaining nursing leadership that fosters a healthy work environment in health care. *Journal of Advanced Nursing, 62,* 653–654.

Center for Creative Leadership. (2007). *Benchmarks Assessment.* Available online at http://www.ccl.org/leadership/index.aspx

Chen, L. Y. (2004). Examining the effect of organization culture and leadership behaviors on organizational commitment, job satisfaction, and job performance at small and middle-sized firms of Taiwan. *Journal of American Academy of Business, 5*(1/2), 432–438.

Clark, F. (n.d.). *AOTA's Centennial Vision: What it is, why it's right* (Annotated presentation). Bethesda, MD: American Occupational Therapy Association. Retrieved February 6, 2009, from http://www.aota.org/News/Centennial/Updates.aspx

Corrigan, P. W., Lickey, S. E., Campion, J., & Rashid, F. (2000). A short course in leadership skills for the rehabilitation team. *Journal of Rehabilitation, 66*(2), 56.

Cosgrove, J. R. (2003). Faculty perceptions of occupational therapy program director leader behavior: Impact upon faculty job satisfaction. Doctoral dissertation, University of Bridgeport, Bridgeport, CT. *ProQuest Digital Dissertations,* AAT 3079366.

Dudek-Shriber, L. (1997). Leadership qualities of occupational therapy program directors and the organizational health of their departments. *American Journal of Occupational Therapy, 51,* 369–377.

Dumdum, U. R., Lowe, K. B., & Avolio, B. J. (2002). A meta-analysis of transformational and transactional leadership correlates of effectiveness and satisfaction: An update and extension. In B. J. Avolio & F. J. Yammarino (Eds.), *Transformational and charismatic leadership: The road ahead* (Vol. 2, pp. 35–66). Oxford, UK: Elsevier Science.

Gellis, Z. D. (2001). Social work perceptions of transformational and transactional leadership in health care. *Social Work Research, 25,* 17–25.

Hunt, J. G. (2004). What is leadership? In J. Antonakis, A. T. Cianciolo, & R. J. Sternberg (Eds.), *The nature of leadership* (pp. 19–47). Thousand Oaks, CA: Sage.

Kark, R., & Shamir, B. (2002). The dual effect of transformational leadership: Priming relational and collective selves and further effects on followers. In B. J. Avolio & F. J. Yammarino (Eds.), *Transformational and charismatic leadership: The road ahead* (Vol. 2, pp. 67–91). Oxford, UK: Elsevier Science.

Kleinman, C. (2004). The relationship between managerial leadership behaviors and staff nurse retention. *Hospital Topics: Research and Perspectives on Healthcare, 82*(4), 2–9.

Kouzes, J. M., & Posner, B. Z. (2003). *Leadership Practices Inventory* (3rd ed.). San Francisco: Pfeiffer.

Kouzes, J. M., & Posner, B. Z. (2006). *Student Leadership Practices Inventory: Facilitator's guide* (2nd ed.). San Francisco: Jossey-Bass.

Kouzes, J. M., & Posner, B. Z. (2007). *The leadership challenge* (4th ed.). San Francisco: Jossey-Bass.

Kroeck, K. G., Lowe, K. B., & Brown, K. W. (2004). The assessment of leadership. In J. Antonakis, A. T. Cianciolo, & R. J. Sternberg (Eds.), *The nature of leadership* (pp. 71–97). Thousand Oaks, CA: Sage.

Leach, L. S. (2005). Nurse executive transformational leadership and organizational commitment. *Journal of Nursing Administration, 35,* 228–237.

Levey, S., Hill, J., & Greene, B. (2002). Leadership in health care and the leadership literature. *Journal of Ambulatory Care Management, 25*(2), 68–74.

Longest, B. B., Rakich, J. S., & Darr, K. (2000). Leadership. In *Managing health services organizations and systems* (4th ed., pp. 735–769). Baltimore: Health Professions Press.

Maxwell, J. (2007). *The 21 irrefutable laws of leadership* (10th anniversary ed.). Nashville, TN: Thomas Nelson.

Maxwell, J. C. (n.d.). *The 360-Degree Leader Assessment.* Available online at http://www.injoy.com

Miller, P. A. (1998). Directors/chairpersons of occupational therapy professional programs: A study of leadership in higher education. Doctoral dissertation, Columbia University Teachers College, New York. *ProQuest Digital Dissertations*, AAT 9822230.

Reiss, R. G. (2000). A comparison of leadership styles of occupational therapy education program directors and clinic administrators. Doctoral dissertation, University of North Texas, Denton. *ProQuest Digital Dissertations*, AAT 3041922.

Rowitz, L. (2009). *Public health leadership: Putting principles into practice* (2nd ed.). Sudbury, MA: Jones & Bartlett.

Skinner, C., & Spurgeon, P. (2005). Valuing empathy and emotional intelligence in health leadership: A study of empathy, leadership behavior and outcome effectiveness. *Health Services Management Research, 18*(1), 1–12.

Snodgrass, J., Douthitt, S., Ellis, R., Wade, S., & Plemons, J. (2008). Occupational therapy practitioners' perceptions of rehabilitation managers' leadership styles and the outcomes of leadership. *Journal of Allied Health, 37*, 40–46.

Snodgrass, J., & Shachar, M. (2008). Faculty perceptions of occupational therapy program directors' leadership styles and the outcomes of leadership. *Journal of Allied Health, 37*, 225–235.

Wilson, L. S. (2004). The leadership practices of occupational therapy managers. Doctoral dissertation, Capella University, Minneapolis, MN. *ProQuest Digital Dissertations*, AAT 3127215.

Wright, K., Rowitz, L., Merkle, A., Reid, W. M., Robinson, G., Herzog, B., et al. (2000). Competency development in public health leadership. *American Journal of Public Health, 90*, 1202–1207.

Appendix 18.A. Leadership Development Evidence Table

Authors	Topic	Major Findings
Adamson, Cant, & Hummell (2001)	Managerial skills for new graduates in occupational therapy	The set of skills perceived to be the most important was related to future planning, including time management, prioritizing work tasks, and planning goals for a work team.
Caruana (2008)	Nursing leadership	The evidence revealed that collaboration in health care teams can improve outcomes for nursing staff and patients and result in a healthier work environment. The review of the evidence also suggested that leaders should continue with their own professional development to help improve their role in leadership
Corrigan, Lickey, Campion, & Rashid (2000)	Transformational leadership training for rehabilitation team leaders	Results revealed significant improvements in MLQ factors related to transformational individualized consideration and transactional management by exception.
Cosgrove (2003)	Leadership behaviors of occupational therapy program directors and faculty job satisfaction	Faculty perceived directors' leadership as low; faculty perceptions of directors' leadership behaviors were significantly and positively related to faculty job satisfaction.
Dudek-Shriber (1997)	Leadership of occupational therapy program directors, organizational health of their departments	Strong positive associations were found between leadership of program directors and organizational health; faculty rated overall leadership of directors as average.
Gellis (2001)	Transformational and transactional leadership in social work	Significant positive correlations were found between transformational leadership, transactional contingent reward, and leadership outcomes.
Kleinman (2004)	Nurse manager leadership behaviors and nurse staff turnover rates	Transactional management by exception leadership behavior was the only specific leadership behavior to show a significant correlation with staff nurse turnover; influence on staff retention was negative.
Leach (2005)	Nurse executive leadership and organizational commitment	Significant positive relationship was found between nurse executive leadership and organizational commitment among nurses.
Miller (1998)	Occupational therapy program directors' self-perception of leadership	Directors used all four leadership frames; human resource was used most and structural least.
Reiss (2000)	Leadership styles of academic and clinical program directors	Leadership positions in different institutional contexts were related to leadership behaviors and effectiveness; significant positive correlations were found between transformational leadership and outcomes of leadership.
Skinner & Spurgeon (2005)	Health department managers' leadership and empathy, work satisfaction, and outcomes	Significant positive correlations were found between transformational leadership and empathy displayed by managers.
Snodgrass, Douthitt, Ellis, Wade, & Plemons (2008)	Rehabilitation managers' leadership styles and outcomes of leadership	Transformational leadership styles had a positive association with leadership outcomes. Transactional leadership styles had a significant negative association with leadership outcomes, except for contingent reward, which had a positive association with the leadership outcomes.
Snodgrass & Shachar (2008)	Leadership styles of academic program directors and outcomes of leadership as perceived by faculty	Transformational leadership had a significant positive predictive relationship with leadership outcomes, whereas transactional leadership had a significant negative predictive relationship with leadership outcomes; demographic and institutional characteristics did not have a significant influence on perceived leadership styles and leadership outcomes.
Wilson (2004)	Leadership practices of occupational therapy managers	The majority of occupational therapy managers were ranked in the 70th percentile or greater in model the way, inspire a shared vision, enable others to act, and encourage the heart.

Note. MLQ = Multifactor Leadership Questionnaire (Avolio & Bass, 2004).

19

Passion = Energy = Quality: Leading Others to Love Their Work

Lynne Cord Barnes, OT, MA, FACHE, FAOTA

❖ Key Terms and Concepts

Accountability. Emphasizes keeping agreements and performing tasks in a respectful manner (Harber & Ball, 2003).

Active mentoring. Is always available, leads the protégé into independently discovering possible solutions to problems, asks reflective questions, models the learning cycle, provides feedback that is specific and evidence based, encourages the protégé to try to new things, and has an in depth understanding of the subject being learned (ASSIST Project, 2006).

Authority. The legitimate power that one person or a group holds over another, which depends on the acceptance by subordinates of the right of those above them to give them orders or directives (Giddens, 1997).

Flow. The mental state of operation in which a person in an activity is fully immersed in a feeling of energized focus, full involvement, and success in the process of the activity (Csíkszentmihályi, 1996).

Leadership. Creating a way for people to contribute to making something extraordinary happen (Kouzes & Posner, 2007).

Passive mentoring. The indirect learning from an influential person. Knowledge is acquired through readings and teachings, not from the mentor himself or herself (Burns, 2008).

❖ Learning Objectives

After completing this chapter, you should be able to do the following:

- Describe the prerequisites for leadership.
- Identify the key elements necessary for leadership that inspires others.
- Identify practical philosophies that promote employee satisfaction and quality work.

- Provide examples of servant–leadership in a manager role.
- Discuss the difference between active and passive mentoring and the role of each.

The mediocre teacher tells. The good teacher explains. The superior teacher demonstrates. The great teacher inspires.
—William Arthur Ward (Komarnicki, 2005, p. 58)

The intent of this chapter is to inform but mostly to inspire. Clients and patients served by rehabilitation personnel benefit from occupational therapy practitioners in leadership positions because the intrinsic values of the occupational therapy profession are consistent with those of leaders with enduring success. Although this chapter describes several leadership characteristics, it is most practical for the reader to choose two of these ideas and determine to implement them. Change usually comes in increments, and only rarely

wholesale. Be willing to reflect on your own strengths and weaknesses as you read on.

DETERMINING YOUR CAPACITY TO LEAD

Not everyone is born a natural leader, nor does everyone want to be a leader. Leadership requires a mixture of skill and desire. Determining one's capacity and interest in leading others is an essential part of growth and development as a professional. Leaders aren't necessarily the obvious outspoken, gregarious, and commanding individuals. True leaders are people who can turn ideas into action. They make a difference daily through their passion, their

281

energy, and their attention to the details. A leader must be willing to commit to having an unyielding passion, never-ending energy, and a proclivity for detail.

If you are reading this book and this chapter, you are likely an occupational therapy practitioner or studying to be one. That alone gives you an advantage in the area of leadership. Occupational therapy practitioners are uniquely positioned to serve as leaders. Characteristically, occupational therapy practitioners are intrinsically motivated to serve others and, through their service, to add meaning to others' lives. Why do occupational therapy practitioners have this edge? Consider the definition of occupational therapy: "Occupational therapy is skilled treatment that helps individuals achieve independence in all facets of their lives. Occupational therapy assists people in developing the 'skills for the job of living' necessary for independent and satisfying lives" (American Occupational Therapy Association, n.d.) Occupational therapy is a service profession; leadership is a service profession as well. The finest leadership demands a constant and consistent commitment to serving others. For leaders, this motivation to serve ignites a passion that brings the necessary energy every day to set a vision and to coach and encourage others toward that vision. Effectively allocating that energy may likely be the greatest challenge of leadership. Attention to quality outcomes is the capstone of effective leadership and ensures success for the organization and for employees as individuals.

Why Is Leadership So Important?
Without leadership, the world would be in disarray. Think of typical examples of leaders: generals, admirals, chiefs, team captains, chief executive officers (CEOs), presidents, senators, directors, managers, supervisors, and coordinators. Where would we be without these key individuals? The list of names for leaders goes on and on in our lexicon. According to Tichy (1997), leaders are critical for three reasons: They help manage through change, they make things happen, and they understand reality in a way that allows them to mobilize the right resources to address issues. Tichy went on to say, "The only thing that never changes is that everything changes" (p. 24), and that is precisely why leaders are crucial. In addition, as Silver (2008) noted,

> The one professional relationship that has the most impact on our experience of work is the relationship with our immediate supervisors. Research from numerous sources has demonstrated conclusively that the quality of interaction with one's boss is the single most important factor behind voluntary turnover, employee engagement, morale, work-related stress, our views of corporate culture, and even our performance. (p. 2)

Leadership matters!

Are You Willing?
Having one of the titles mentioned earlier may sound glamorous and exciting and could mean an increase in pay. So why not? Simple—leadership is a tough calling and not for the faint of heart. The more you advance in any organization, the more of a servant you become, and to more people. Leadership is a high calling, which means that a leader's needs are secondary to the needs of those led. For example, an occupational therapy manager has arranged a weekend coverage schedule for the rehab unit. One of the therapists calls in sick, and the back-up list has been exhausted. Who works the needed hours? In many cases, the manager may be expected to do so.

In another example, the week has been crazy in the clinic, and everyone, including the occupational therapy manager, has been working 10- to 12-hour days to meet the demand. One of the physicians has four tickets to a popular concert and wants to offer them to thank the group for stepping up. The band happens to be one of the manager's all-time favorites. Who gets the tickets? The manager holds a drawing for those interested and does not include herself. That is what leaders do: Effective leaders understand the importance of rewarding and encouraging those they lead, often at a cost to themselves.

One more example: There is an opportunity to present a new quality measurement tool used in the department, developed by one of the staff members, to the quality board. Being aware of the excellent work on quality in the occupational therapy department, the CEO of the hospital asks the manager to present at the meeting, stating it would be a great opportunity for the manager to interact with the board. Instead, the manager asks the CEO if it would be appropriate to have the therapist who was primarily responsible for the program present at the board meeting. The CEO is surprised, yet pleased, and agrees to this plan. This is another example of leadership—offering others the limelight.

OVERRIDING ELEMENTS OF LEADERSHIP
The following paragraphs discuss the three overriding elements necessary for successful leadership: passion, energy, and a focus on quality.

Passion
Passion is "a strong feeling or emotion, something that is desired intensely, a great enthusiasm for some thing" (Webster's Online Dictionary, n.d.). Passion is absolutely required for leadership as no leader can successfully motivate others to follow in any direction without it. Passionate behavior usually results in a keen desire to produce optimum results as well as the tenacity to achieve them. According to the Harvard Business Review (2005),

> If you are looking for leaders, how can you identify people who are motivated by the drive to achieve rather than by external rewards? The first sign is a

passion for the work itself—such people seek out creative challenges, love to learn, and take great pride in a job well done. They also display an unflagging energy to do things better and are forever raising the performance bar. (p. 87)

Because everyone obviously cannot be a leader on every issue, it is passion for particular work or subject matter, more than intelligence, that paves the way to identifying great leaders. When passion and its characteristics are applied to an ethical vision for the greater good, people follow. Excitement begets excitement.

Energy

Energy is born out of passion—the combination of desire and tenacity to continue to produce results despite barriers. Think back to your childhood and identify a time when there was an activity you were passionate about and could not wait to do; your parents may have said to you, "You can do [this particular activity] as soon as you clean your room." Your response was likely full of energy; you cleaned as furiously as you could so you could pursue your interest as soon as possible. It is easy to see that energy is fueled by passion. Drucker (1996) said, as he described entrepreneurs,

I am always struck by the fact that the leaders have so much energy and manage to transmit that energy to their subordinates. It is an energy born out of strong personal convictions, which motivates the entrepreneur and builds excitement in others. Such people often literally breathe life into the organization; hence we should use a term like *animator* to describe this kind of leader. (p. 61)

An entrepreneurial-spirited occupational therapy practitioner or "animator" can make a significant difference for an organization, a group of individuals, the people they serve, and the profession of occupational therapy.

Energetic leadership must be supported through physical preparedness. Adequate sleep, good nutrition, and exercise are important elements allowing leaders to bring their best each day. Not often discussed in many leadership books, physical preparedness can't be ignored as a contributing factor to effective leadership. As Sarah Bernhardt observed long ago, "Life begets life. Energy begets energy. It is by spending oneself that one becomes rich (Brainyquote.com, n.d.). A leader's best days are days when he or she feels "spent."

Self-awareness and self-management are important skills for any energetic leader. An individual with much energy must monitor and be aware of how he or she is being perceived by others. Energetic leaders don't often go unnoticed and consequently have a greater responsibility to closely monitor their actions and words because of the import and influence they often transmit, sometimes unknowingly. A keen self-awareness keeps the visual and auditory blinders off and allows for a careful noting of others' reactions. Self-management ensures appropriate reactions and responses to what is noted and allows those being led to have their spoken and unspoken issues, questions, and concerns addressed.

Focus on Quality

Bennis (1997) alluded to the close connection among passion, energy, and quality: "Closely linked to the concept of quality is that of dedication to, even love of, our work. This dedication is evoked by quality and is the force that energizes high performing systems" (p. 12). Regardless of the nature of the work, the keys to quality results are effective use of evidenced-based practices, attention to detail, and personal monitoring of the work and work products. In the area of health care, the quality of services rendered can alter lives, so the emphasis on quality can't be minimized.

PRACTICAL PHILOSOPHIES FOR EVERY DAY

The following paragraphs discuss concepts and practices that are central to leadership effectiveness. This list is not exhaustive, and adding to it can be the work of any leader. The principles are worth reading again and again; they help keep one focused on what is important and can promote joy in both managers and those they lead and serve.

Establish Priorities, and Consider Them Each Day

Operating with a set of reiterated priorities encourages you to self-monitor your daily actions and reactions and measure your accomplishments within that context. It is like a "megaconscious" guiding your steps as your day progresses. Review your top three or four priorities in the shower each day or as you make your way to work. Or write them out and post them on your bulletin board at work. Make them your screen saver. Put them in your digital agenda as a repeating appointment with yourself. These priorities provide context for all your attitudes and actions.

Assume That People Like You

Maybe not all individuals appreciate or like you, but don't consider this at all during the course of your day. This possibility should not be on your radar screen during interactions. The belief that others' actions and reactions toward you are motivated purely and for the greater good will help you remain more open to new ideas and growth opportunities and truly enjoy other people. Disregard skepticism. When you assume others like and appreciate you, you avoid defensive feelings and reactions. Criticism becomes a growth opportunity in the context of acceptance.

Acknowledge and Affirm Others

Acknowledging and affirming others is a critical element in creating a positive culture at work. Consistently take the time to acknowledge and affirm others in areas small and large. People relish and remember the times they are meaningfully appreciated. Acknowledgment and affirmation are more than saying "Nice tie!" or "Great talk!" Well-delivered compliments are meaningfully stated, in person or by note, and include specifics about the nature of the individual and the action. The following is an example of an effective note of praise:

> John, I just wanted you to know that your presentation was well done. I could tell by the reaction of the team they were motivated to make changes. I really appreciate the effort you put into this. I think it will make a difference for the patients.

That compliment is one that John will remember and be motivated by in his future performance; what gets noticed and rewarded by leaders will be replicated. Never think that everyone does not need or enjoy a great compliment. Even the CEO benefits from a well-stated compliment. Everyone needs encouragement to keep performing at the highest levels, which patients deserve.

Expect the Best From Yourself and Others

"You get what you expect" is a statement that is often true. Leaders must believe in followers' ability and desire to achieve and produce unless the belief is clearly disputed by repeated fact. There will be times of failure, and mistakes will be made by even the best of employees; in fact, some of life's best lessons are learned through error. However, leaders who are in tune with their employees easily separate the mistakes made because of a lack of interest and energy from those made because of a lack of knowledge or experience. To the latter, leaders respond through teaching, and to the former they respond with exit or immediate improvement strategies.

The standards leaders hold themselves to are often replicated in staff members' behaviors. Leaders, more than staff, are constantly being watched: their every move, every word, and every deed. A leader is held to a higher standard simply because of the past accomplishments that have led to greater authority earned. Authority is earned—never given.

Allow Conflict to Bring Out the Best in You

Leaders deal with numerous conflicts on a daily basis. Conflict arises when a stated or unstated expectation is not met, and the ramifications can be small or significant. Examples of typical situations that provoke conflict include the following:

- An employee is repeatedly late for work.
- One employee performs incomplete work, forcing another to do his or her job as well as the other's own.
- A report is late.
- A misunderstanding arises between department leaders as to who was doing what and who would follow up.
- The leader's boss always is late to or cancels meetings for which the leader has carefully prepared.

- A patient is upset about his or her therapy bill and feels the services weren't worth the price.
- A patient's mother is upset about the care her child received from the pediatric therapist, claiming that the therapist wasn't prepared and the child didn't respond well.

Too often, a leader's response can be measured in an increased heart rate, faster respirations, and higher blood pressure. Conflicts, however, are opportunities to make a closer friend, a stronger work tie, or a more loyal employee or customer. How a leader manages conflict is critical to effective leadership. One of the most important factors in managing conflict is preparing for the follow-up conversation. In many cases, leaders have foreknowledge of the circumstances and time to prepare for an interaction. The following are elements of a well-managed follow-up discussion:

- Be prepared; think through what you will say and when.
- Consider what you could have done differently, and be quick to apologize meaningfully.
- Avoid using the words *you* and *should*.
- Move quickly from what happened to what can be done to make the situation better in the future.

Straighten Up

Posture and eye contact are important elements in providing a perception of energy, confidence, and intelligence. Posture and eye contact are important not only for leaders but for anyone performing work that is visible or audible to the customer. Although perception is not reality, perception is fact until corrected by reality. Substance matters, but first impressions lay the groundwork for all future interactions. It is important for leaders to exude self-confidence to instill confidence in coworkers and lead them to higher levels of performance. Posture and eye contact *do* make a difference.

Envision Your Day and Your Interactions

All leaders face insecurities, regardless of how experienced they are or how high up in the organization they are promoted. A technique not called on often enough is visualization. Before a difficult meeting or challenging presentation, a run-through of the best possible scenario or circumstances in your mind can help the outcome be closer to what you hope and plan for. Envisioning the best result can increase its probability of occurring.

Control Your Language

It is no secret that effective leaders use the tools of optimism and positive approaches to manage problems and people. Positivity and good happenings are all around, despite the difficulty one may have sometimes in seeing them. It is easy to focus on what is negative, because this is what gets talked about and what gets the attention. Just as broadcast news and newspapers make an effort to tell the "good" news, leaders who focus on all that works well encourage both themselves and others. How can a growing leader further develop an optimistic attitude and skills needed to provide positive leadership?

Perry (1997), in his book *The Road to Optimism: Change Your Language—Change Your Life,* observed that most adults focus on what is not, as opposed to what is. He described a way of speech he called the *language inclusion process,* defining it as

> a mental state of optimism achieved by understanding the special impact words can have on your brain. Since what you say influences what you think, then speaking about inclusion, what's there right in front of you, is a most powerful method for guaranteeing optimism and real output in your life. (p. 13)

Table 19.1 lists a few examples of negative language restated in positive terms that can make a daily difference in working with and leading others.

Look for Flow

For example, flow occurs when someone sees you rushing in the door with your arms loaded and hurries over to hold the door. It happens when an occupational therapist works late to provide family education to a family who could not come until after work to make sure that a rehab patient is able to go home safely the next day. You observe it when you are walking the halls of the hospital heading to that next patient and you see a family surrounding a loved one's bed, providing comfort and encouragement. People are amazing, but you have to watch for it and expect it!

Table 19.1. Examples of Exclusionary (Negative) and Inclusionary (Positive) Language

Exclusionary Examples (negative)	Inclusionary Examples (positive)
Not bad.	That's good.
I can't argue with that.	I'm inclined to agree with you.
I can't complain.	I think it's OK.
I'm not ignoring that.	I'm aware that is a consideration.
It won't hurt.	Here is what will happen.
It's not as bad as it looks.	It's better than it looks.
If nothing gets in our way.	If everything goes as planned.
No problem. It was nothing at all.	It was my pleasure!
No littering.	Keep this area clean.
Why don't I send that to you?	I will send that to you.
Why don't you quit smoking?	What are your thoughts about quitting smoking?

Surprise Others With Your Own Accountability

Leaders, more than anyone, need to astound those whom they serve with their own personal accountability (Silver, 2008). The leader's level of self-imposed accountability sets an example for employees to follow. Leaders should err on the side of being overly responsive to staff, such as by responding to their e-mails, questions, and voicemails as if each issue was a very important one (it may be, to them!). Leaders should keep their commitments, deliver results on or ahead of time, and be clear and sincere in what they say.

Pay Attention to Detail

It is a common misperception that the greater responsibility one has, the less mired in the details one has to be. This misperception is likely related to the fact that greater responsibility often results in a broader scope of oversight, thus disallowing involvement in every detail. *Being involved* in the details, however, is not synonymous with *paying attention* to the details. The scope and responsibility levels of a military general, for example, are considerable. Yet he or she is aware of the exact plan for battle, the number of troops involved, and the exact location and time of each movement. The CEO of a large manufacturing or technology firm likewise knows each month's production numbers, profitability, and key issues related to positive or negative performance. Most leaders can quote from memory key performance elements.

Leaders need to know the key metrics and exactly why they are or are not achieving their goals. Even though they strive to hire, train, and retain the right people, leaders must measure and audit those people's work. The pursuit of quality is measurable and transparent. Someone needs to be examining quality, and that someone is the leader.

Focus on the Positive

You may not agree with the following conjecture, but at least consider it: There are two types of interactions, positive and negative. Certainly there are degrees of positivity and negativity, but can you describe a neutral interaction? It doesn't exist. As you pass by a coworker and he or she looks either directly at you or downward, you have an impression. As you look around the room in a meeting and see someone nodding off and another person actively engaging, you form an impression of each. When you make rounds on the floor and speak to nurses or therapists and ask questions, each response will leave you thinking about the interaction as being some degree of positive or negative.

One way to think of yourself is as a pinball from an old-fashioned pinball machine; out you go in the morning, pinging on people all day, experiencing maybe 100 or even 200 interactions each day! According to Segui (2007),

> Research indicates that the average person talks to himself or herself about 50,000 times a day. According to psychological researchers, it is 80% negative;

things such as should have said that . . . they don't like me . . . I don't like the way my hair looks today . . . I can't dance . . . I'll never be a good skater . . . I'm not a speaker . . . I'll never lose this weight . . . I can't ever seem to get organized . . . I'm always late.

Leaders have the opportunity to help change others' thought patterns to an increasingly positive percentage through interactions focused on positive support of every individual they make contact with. It can be as simple as going out of your way to hold the door for someone, enthusiastically greeting an individual or noticing something positive about him or her, and sharing a meaningful compliment. Why not leave folks on the plus side?

Surround Yourself With the Right Influences

What many parents tell their teenagers is true! Be careful whom you associate with, because you may become like them. Do not waste your precious moments with people who communicate negative mental states. Surround yourself with people who encourage you, lift you up, and have a strong commitment to their work. Leaders cannot afford to become discouraged. A discouraged leader loses his or her passion, energy, and effectiveness in leading a quality business. If you believe you are experiencing discouragement, immediately seek out an encourager for counsel and guidance.

Hold a Brag Fest With Yourself on the Way Home

Reflect every day on your successes and what was positive about your day, and encourage others to do the same. The technique is to intentionally and systematically remember and think about all the good things about your day. Don't brag to others; just give yourself credit for what you did that was good! The talk inside your head will help you keep it up the next day. Practice making it positive.

Lead With a Sense of Urgency

The world is fast paced, like it or not. With e-mail and social networking, our communication world is almost overwhelming. Expectations for responsiveness have risen at an exponential rate as compared even to the post–World War II era. It used to be that a good day's work for a secretary was typing half a dozen letters and answering the phone! Now we deal with thousands of bits of information every day.

Leaders must take in and respond to a great deal of information during the day. A typical leader in the complicated world of health care is likely to receive 100 to 150 e-mails per day for which an answer is expected, usually within 48 hours. Organizations must be nimble in responding to change to survive. Nimble leaders know when it is okay to "ready, fire, aim" to keep things moving in a positive and change-oriented direction, not for the purpose of change alone but to improve quality efficiently. An effective leader cannot wait for the "perfect" solution. The best organizations have leaders capable not only of speed, but also of facilitating efficiency and effectiveness in every area of operations.

Remain Humble and Teachable

As you achieve more in life, it is easy to lose sight of your humble beginnings and of the people who helped you along the way. A leader can manifest humility in the following ways:

- Adopt an attitude of ongoing servitude that is reflected in the words you use.
- Avoid using the word *my* to describe any employee. "My" denotes ownership, when leaders obviously don't own employees.
- Avoid sharing your aspirations with staff. Be settled, and "bloom where you are planted." If you speak of your desire to land that next promotion, you will not appear to be fully invested in your current position.
- Always be ready to say "I'm sorry." An apology, whether you are in the wrong or not, can be beneficial. An apology can denote sorrow for how another person is feeling, express regret for wrongdoing (intentional or not), and acknowledge teachability.

Remaining teachable throughout your career helps you maintain an open mind, encourages your creativity, and above all signifies a humble spirit. In fact, trust and give authority only to individuals who are committed to lifelong learning.

Bring It On . . . Joy, That Is

Having work you are passionate about certainly adds to your joy, but leaders and staff must bring their own intrinsic happiness to the work environment. Leaders who display positivity and seek joy in their surroundings are leaders whom others want to follow. Happiness and joy are contagious. Looking for the best in others and believing in them is another characteristic of leaders who bring joy to work. It is prudent and productive to avoid the extreme of naïveté but to err on the side of expecting the best.

Be Consistent

Consistency in a leader is critical. Employees need to know what to expect day in and day out from their supervisors to perform at their best. Steadiness is an underrated quality. Change is around every corner, especially in health care. Consistency in leadership helps staff weather this change. Consistency of behavior is possible when you have an internal set of guiding principles to which you strongly adhere. You must know your core values and allow them to guide your every move. You cannot afford to walk differently than you talk.

Earn Your Title

Respect and authority must be earned; use of authority and a title will not gain a leader respect. Leaders earn the respect of followers in several ways:

- They cultivate transparency in behavior, communication, and agenda. A transparent and "readable" leader is seen as approachable and real.
- They are willing to do any task.
- They always exhibit basic manners. Consistent use of manners promotes an atmosphere of respect.

These actions and ways of being facilitate leadership and inspire employees to follow because they want to, not because they have to.

Cast Balance to the Wind

An important question for a leader to ask himself or herself is, "Am I happy?" If you are, you are in a good place, and you can relax about balance. It does not matter. According to Hammonds (2004),

> Life is about setting priorities and making trade-offs; that's what grown-ups do. But in our all-or-nothing culture, resorting to those sorts of decisions is too often seen as a kind of failure. Seeking balance, we strive for achievement everywhere—and we feel guilty and stressed out when, inevitably, we fall short. (p. 68)

Hammonds posited that we live in an unbalanced world and therefore will always lead unbalanced lives! Instead of working for balance, he proposed, people should seek ways to successfully manage all that they love and truly want to do. He suggested several specific strategies for managing time:

- "Rethink the mission." Do not seek balance as a goal; seek a prioritized life.
- "Design a life of chapters." There are many aspects to your life, so accept those aspects as the many parts that make up the whole. Prioritize, and organize your life based on the prioritization.
- "Within each chapter, do what you're good at." Prioritize around your strengths. If you are not good at it, allow someone else to do it.
- "Redesign continuously." Every day, revisit your priorities and adjust them as you need and as you are needed. Your priorities are a continuous work in progress, and it is important to stay flexible as the days, weeks, and years go by.
- "Switch and link." Successful leaders are able to quickly connect and disconnect to change their focus. This way, they can take advantage of interactions and opportunities that make them happy and that support their various priorities.
- "Pick your spots." Often stated as "take the high road" or "don't sweat the small stuff," this strategy means being able to move along positively when things do not go as planned to reduce anxiety and waste less time. There is never any point in "stewing."
- "Lower your standards." Perfectionism does not pay. Most times, "good enough" is just fine. Usually nobody cares about the 10% of difference between a good-enough result and a perfect one.

Be Mentored and Mentor Others, Actively and Passively

Receiving and providing mentoring are important roles for all leaders. Mentoring occurs actively (intentionally) and passively (unintentionally). Active mentoring includes intentional opportunities for coaching, advocacy, challenges, redirection, career guidance, and—above all—listening. Active mentoring requires the mentor to give of himself or herself in both a professional and personal manner; it takes passion and energy for the protégé to truly benefit. Unintentional or passive mentoring, also instrumental in the development of leaders, occurs when an aspiring leader seeks out the best in every supervisor and learns from each positive characteristic. At the same time, the aspiring leader must be aware of what does not work and determine to not make the same mistakes.

Maintaining a keen awareness of both easily observable and subtle behaviors will help you develop your leadership skills. The key is to successfully sort out the admirable behaviors from those less desirable.

Use the Four Es of Communication

The Institute for Healthcare Communication® is an organization dedicated to improving communication between health care providers and patients. This organization's training workshops include communication tools that are not only good for the provider–client relationship, but also helpful in interactions between leaders and staff. One workshop depicts the "Four Es," which can help leaders seeking to influence employees' behavior (Institute for Healthcare Communication, 2006):

1. *Engaging with the employee.* Engagement is a connection between clinician and client that continues throughout the encounter. It is person-to-person interaction; the parties are relating professionally as partners.
2. *Empathizing with the employee.* Empathy is achieved when the employee feels seen, heard, understood, and accepted as a person by the leader.
3. *Educating the employee.* Education involves cognitive, behavioral, and affective elements. The goal is to promote employee empowerment through greater knowledge and understanding, increased capacity and skills, and decreased anxiety.
4. *Enlisting the employee.* The leader invites the employee to collaborate in planning and setting goals for coaching.

CONCLUSION

You want to make a difference in this life. One way among many is through effective and meaningful leadership. Leadership is effective when it prompts change for the greater good—when it inspires people to put themselves second and others first. Leadership is meaningful when those led change permanently for the better because of you. Be that kind of leader. Do not pass up an opportunity to make a significant difference. When occupational therapy leaders create better health care through their leadership, they cre-

ate a better community. As Sister Mary Lauretta, a nun and science teacher, said, "To be successful the first thing you do is fall in love with your work" (Quote Mountain, n.d.).

Case Examples

LEVEL I FIELDWORK

Anita was one of several students doing her Level I fieldwork placement at a large training site. Another student, Claire, repeatedly sought out Anita for lunch breaks, and Anita was glad to have the opportunity to debrief with someone about the training experience. Claire, however, was not enjoying her experience and thought her supervisor was "out to get her"; she advised Anita to watch out for this supervisor and others. Claire was consistently negative about the experience and the people around her. Anita noticed that over time, she too began to feel negative about the experience and the people she was working with. She was losing her enthusiasm for learning.

Anita resolved to spend less time with Claire and even shared with Claire her concerns. Claire was unmoved, however. Anita regained her positive spirit when she began spending time with several other students who weren't negative and who were focused on getting the most from the training.

LEVEL II FIELDWORK

Jeanine was a Level II fieldwork student doing her pediatric internship at a public grade school. Near the end of her training, she provided a series of therapy treatments and was to meet with parents under the supervision of her fieldwork supervisor. Just after the therapy sessions were completed and before the parent meetings began, however, Jeanine's supervisor became ill and had to go home.

Before leaving, her supervisor quickly reviewed the agendas for the various parent meetings and asked Jeanine to complete them. As soon as Jeanine's supervisor left, another occupational therapist came in and asked Jeanine if she wanted to review any of the agendas or notes with her, as she had a few spare minutes due to a cancellation. Also, the principal came by and offered to sit in and assist if Jeanine wanted her to. Finally, a teacher stopped by and offered to be a "runner" for Jeanine to make it easier for her to prepare for the next set of parents. Jeanine was thankful for all who helped make a successful series of parent meetings possible. That was flow . . . and simple teamwork.

FIRST-TIME MANAGER

Diane had recently been promoted to supervisor of inpatient acute therapy in a 500-bed hospital. She had 40 full-time equivalents reporting to her; they provided occupational, physical, and speech therapy. Diane was an exceptional occupational therapist who had worked well with her patients in achieving good outcomes and high productivity. Although her supervisor thought she was a natural leader, Diane was unsure if she wanted the job. Her manager, however, had convinced her that this position was a perfect opportunity. Diane was well prepared for her first meeting, but during her discourse she looked down at her notes most of the time and sat hunched over with insecurity. When she requested volunteers for a new initiative, no one raised their hand. It was clear from her posture that Diane was unsure of herself, and no one was interested in following her. Diane was disappointed in the response from her group. Then, following the meeting, one of her staff approached her and shared that she wanted to volunteer but hesitated because Diane didn't seem that enthused about the new initiative herself. Diane clarified her position, and the employee willingly volunteered.

MANAGER

Elizabeth was the manager of a moderate-sized occupational therapy practice. She led a busy and successful hand therapy business with more than 20 full-time equivalents, including both occupational therapists and occupational therapy assistants. Elizabeth oversaw 4 locations, each of which was adjacent to an orthopedic or plastic surgery group practice owned by the hospital for which she worked. Recently, there was a downturn in business related to increasing unemployment in the area. Elizabeth was faced with the need to reduce staff hours to control expenses. Elizabeth was passionate about her work, brought energy to the office every day, and enjoyed her employees. She felt bad about having to reduce work hours for her staff.

She devised a plan. On Monday following her decision to reduce hours, she called the staff together for a

(continued)

Case Examples *(cont.)*

meeting. After explaining the issues, she stated that some hours would have to be reduced. She opened the floor to suggestions and listened as staff focused mainly on ideas for growing the business. Elizabeth agreed that many of these ideas were doable, and together they developed a plan to try to increase business.

Slowly, however, the group thought returned to methods of reducing costs, and Elizabeth led them to a decision of sharing the impact by having each staff member reduce his or her hours by 5 per week. Elizabeth stated that they would implement this plan for the next 3 months and monitor productivity weekly. In addition, Elizabeth said she would focus on supporting each of them, sharing the workload if they needed help, implementing the marketing ideas, and keeping them posted about the impact of the work-hour reduction and growth projections.

Elizabeth took on the marketing plan with vigor and checked in frequently with staff to see how they were faring with the reduction in hours. She knew them well enough to know who had the biggest worries related to a reduction in salary. For those individuals, she made time to sit with each of them to listen and offer help where she could. Elizabeth also offered each of them access to the employee assistance program and helped them identify ways in which they could work additional hours in other parts of the system. Elizabeth provided detailed reports on how the business was doing from a productivity and cost-efficiency perspective. The staff were encouraged when they saw their referrals increasing.

About 4 weeks into the reduction of hours, a recruiter contacted one of the individuals who had been particularly challenged by the cut in pay. There was a similar job opening about 1 hour away for a full-time occupational therapist offering similar pay. The therapist was not interested in the job, despite the opportunity for more secure work and an increase in pay related to more hours. Why? Because she realized that Elizabeth was helping the group manage through change and that she understood the reality of the environment, knew what it would take to address the change, and was rallying the resources to make it happen. Elizabeth was the kind of leader this occupational therapist wanted to work for: She had the passion, the energy, and the will to stay focused on quality, for the patients and for the employees she served. Even an offer of more consistent hours and more money couldn't lure this staff member away because of the loyalty that Elizabeth's leadership invoked.

❖ Learning Activities

1. Write a 500-word essay describing an individual in your life who mentored you and the specific characteristics you sought to emulate.
2. Divide the class or work group into groups of 5 persons and ask them to describe scenarios in which, as leaders, they may be required to make a choice between promoting themselves and promoting one of their subordinates.
3. After reading a selection from a book on the Recommended Reading list, add 5–10 practical philosophies to the list provided in this chapter.
4. Prepare and present a 5-minute speech about a time when you experienced a passion that inspired energy in others and resulted in leadership.
5. Administer a short personality test to the class or work group, calculate the results, and ask group members to talk about how characteristics in their personality will assist them in leadership.

✓ Multiple-Choice Questions

1. An occupational therapy manager needs to accomplish an important task, and the deadline is quickly approaching. Which option displays the best example of leadership?
   a. The manager tells employees that if the deadline is not met, each person will have consequences to face.
   b. The manager hopes that the normal workflow of the employees will allow sufficient productivity to meet the deadline.
   c. The manager informs the employees of the situation and the importance of meeting the deadline while being encouraging and helpful.
   d. The manager hovers over each employee, making sure that everyone is spending every second working on meeting the deadline.

2. Why do occupational therapists have an edge in leadership?
   a. Occupational therapy assists people in developing the life skills necessary to lead independent and satisfying lives.
   b. Occupational therapy is a service profession.
   c. Outstanding leadership demands a constant and consistent commitment to serving others.
   d. All of the above.

3. According to this chapter, what is the greatest challenge of leadership?
   a. Maintaining productivity levels.
   b. Watching what every employee is doing at all times.
   c. Effectively allocating necessary energy.
   d. None of the above.

4. What is one of the three reasons that leaders are crucial?
   a. Leaders are people who can take the blame when things go wrong.
   b. Leaders help manage through times of change.
   c. Leaders always have an extremely high level of education.
   d. Leaders always follow popular views.

5. What factor is the most influential in employee satisfaction and loyalty?
   a. Amount of money in paycheck.
   b. Flexibility of hours.
   c. Available benefits.
   d. Quality leadership.

6. An employee experiences a death in the family, and extra coverage is needed for 3 days. The department has already been working overtime, and when the manager requests volunteers for coverage, no one is able. Which action will show the best-quality leadership?
   a. The manager steps in and covers open shifts, despite having previous plans.
   b. The manager forces employees to take the open shifts, even though they are already working overtime.
   c. The manager leaves the shifts open and informs the employees already working that they will just have to make do.
   d. The manager calls patients and tries to reschedule the appointments.

7. According to this chapter, which characteristic is the most important for a leader to possess?
   a. Timeliness.
   b. Intelligence.
   c. Aggressiveness.
   d. Passion.

8. Being in a leadership position means which of the following?
   a. Being able to do what you desire without regard to others' perceptions of you.
   b. Having to be especially aware of your actions and statements at all times.
   c. Having to be aware of yourself when around your superiors.
   d. All of the above.

9. For a leader to produce high quality, he or she must do which of the following?
   a. Do all the work himself or herself to ensure quality.
   b. Combine passion and energy to help produce quality.
   c. Leave the employees to do the work and have little interaction with them.
   d. Choose only tasks that are not challenging.

10. Which of the following would be the most appropriate comment for a leader to make?
    a. "Hey, nice job today."
    b. Encouraging comments are not necessary; employees are motivated by their paycheck.
    c. "I really wanted to congratulate you on the outstanding performance you have been giving. Your contributions make a difference and are appreciated."
    d. "I know you have been working a lot, but this really is not enough. We need to step it up a notch."

11. A person is hired in a leadership role. In regard to authority, they can expect which of the following?
    a. To have to earn the right to authority.
    b. To be given the right to authority the first day of work.
    c. To not have to worry about having authority.
    d. None of the above.

12. A leader should deal with conflict by doing which of the following?
    a. Not allowing the other party to have any input.
    b. Using words such as *you* and *should*.
    c. Using language that shows insincerity and sarcasm.
    d. None of the above.
13. A newly promoted leader is in a department head meeting. The leader, whose work history was highly valued before the promotion, prepared a captivating presentation full of hard-hitting facts and new ideas. While giving the presentation, the leader almost always looks at the computer screen, is hunched over, or fidgets. What did everyone take away from the presentation?
    a. It was a great idea to promote this particular employee.
    b. The ideas presented are going to help the department increase productivity and efficiency.
    c. The presentation was exceptionally well put together.
    d. The person did not stop looking at the computer screen and was hunched over and fidgeting.
14. To use the Language Inclusion Process effectively, a leader would change the statement "Why don't you quit smoking?" into which of the following?
    a. What are your thoughts about quitting smoking?
    b. What would help you to quit smoking?
    c. What benefits do you perceive in quitting smoking?
    d. All of the above.
15. Leaders should be accountable for which of the following?
    a. Their own individual projects, not those of their employees.
    b. The actions of every person within the company, regardless of department or job status.
    c. Their own actions and the actions of the people within their department.
    d. Nothing; a leader does not have to hold any accountability.
16. Which of the following statements is true in regard to the leader's responsibility for detail?

    a. The leader leaves detail to the employees; the leader handles details only if a problem arises.
    b. The leader needs to be aware of the key components of the details and must pay attention to them.
    c. The leader should be obsessed with each and every fact and with everything that happens, who did what, and why.
    d. None of the above.
17. What percentage of people's self-talk is believed to be negative?
    a. 40%.
    b. 60%.
    c. 10%.
    d. 80%.
18. When faced with a challenging situation, a leader should do which of the following?
    a. Make the best choice possible at that time and not wait for a perfect solution.
    b. Spend a lot of time searching for the perfect solution.
    c. Wait and do nothing until someone else steps up to fix the problem.
    d. Pick the easiest solution to the problem at the time.
19. Employees who reach the managerial level can now do which of the following?
    a. Feel confident that they no longer need to be educated.
    b. Always look for ways to increase their knowledge and learn new things.
    c. Only become educated in an area when they feel it is absolutely necessary.
    d. Skim the needed information and not worry about fully understanding the new material they are expected to learn.
20. The Four *E*s of communication are which of the following?
    a. Engaging, entitling, empathizing, and educating.
    b. Enlisting, educating, entitling, and enlightening.
    c. Engaging, empathizing, educating, and enlisting.
    d. Enlightening, enrolling, empathizing, and excelling.

References

American Occupational Therapy Association. (n.d.). *What is occupational therapy?* Retrieved March 28, 2009, from http://www.aota.org/Consumers/WhatisOT.aspx

ASSIST Project. (2006). *Active mentor rubric.* Retrieved July 19, 2010, from http://assist.educ.msu.edu/ASSIST/classroom/mentoring/activementor.htm

Bennis, W. (1997). *Why leaders can't lead.* San Francisco: Jossey-Bass.

Brainyquote.com. (n.d.). *Sarah Bernhardt.* Retrieved July 20, 2010, from http://www.brainyquote.com/quotes/authors/s/sarah_bernhardt.html

Burns, J. (2008). *Mentoring.* Retrieved July 19, 2010, from http://www.simplyyouthministry.com/jims-thoughts-12.html

Csíkszentmihályi, M. (1996), *Creativity: Flow and the psychology of discovery and invention.* New York: HarperPerennial.

Drucker, P. (1996). *The leader of the future.* San Francisco: Jossey-Bass.

Giddens, A. (1997). *Sociology.* London: Polity Press.

Hammonds, K. H. (2004, October 1). Balance is bunk! *Fast Company,* pp. 68–76. Retrieved June 9, 2010, from http://www.fastcompany.com/magazine/87/balance-1.html

Harber, B., & Ball, T. (2003, November). From the blame game to accountability in healthcare. *Policy Options,* 49–54.

Harvard Business Review (Eds.). (2005). *Harvard Business Review on the mind of the leader.* Boston: Harvard Business School Press.

Institute for Healthcare Communication. (2006). *Clinician-patient communication to enhance health outcomes* [Workshop presentation]. New Haven, CT: Author.

Komarnicki, J. W. (2005). *How to teach toward character development.* West Conshohocken, PA: Infinity Publishing.

Kouzes, J., & Posner, B. (2007). *The leadership challenge.* San Francisco: Jossey-Bass.

Perry, J. M. (1997). *The road to optimism: Change your language—Change your life.* San Ramon, CA: Manfit Press.

Quote Mountain. (n.d.). *Sister Mary Lauretta famous quotes.* Retrieved June 15, 2010, from http://www.quotemountain.com/famous_quote_author/sister_mary_lauretta_famous_quotations/

Segui, E. (2007, June 21). *Four steps to transforming your negative self-talk into an inner coach.* Retrieved April 13, 2009, from http://www.articlesbase.com/leadership-articles/4-steps-to-transforming-your-negative-selftalk-into-an-inner-coach-168527.html

Silver, S. R. (2008, December). Transforming professional relationships. *Training and Development, 62,* 1–4. Retrieved June 9, 2010, from http://silverconsultinginc.com/silver/tand_article_wc.pdf

Tichy, N. M. (1997). *The leadership engine.* New York: HarperCollins.

Webster's Online Dictionary. (n.d.). Passion. Retrieved March 29, 2009, from http://www.websters-online-dictionary.org/definition/passion

Recommended Reading

Covey, S. R. (1991). *Principle-centered leadership.* New York: Simon & Schuster.

Goleman, D. (1995). *Emotional intelligence.* New York: Bantam Books.

O'Toole, J. (1996). *Leading change.* New York: Ballantine Books.

Appendix 19.A. Leading Others to Love Their Work Evidence Table

Topic	Evidence
Impact of leadership	American Occupational Therapy Association. (n.d.). *What is occupational therapy?* Retrieved March 28, 2009, from http://www.aota.org/Consumers/WhatisOT.aspx
Importance of leadership	Silver, S. R. (2008, December). Transforming professional relationships. *Training and Development, 62,* 1–4. Retrieved June 9, 2010, from http://silverconsultinginc.com/silver/tand_article_wc.pdf Tichy, N. M. (1997). *The leadership engine.* New York: HarperCollins.
Passion in leadership	Harvard Business Review (Eds.). (2005). *Harvard Business Review on the mind of the leader.* Boston: Harvard Business School Press.
Energy in leadership	Drucker, P. (1996). *The leader of the future.* San Francisco: Jossey-Bass.
Focus on quality in leadership	Bennis, W. (1997). *Why leaders can't lead.* San Francisco: Jossey-Bass.
Language in leadership	Perry, J. M. (1997). *The road to optimism: Change your language—Change your life.* San Ramon, CA: Manfit Press.
Accountability in leadership	Silver, S. R. (2008, December). Transforming professional relationships. *Training and Development, 62,* 1–4. Retrieved June 9, 2010, from http://silverconsultinginc.com/silver/tand_article_wc.pdf
Positive and negative language	Segui, E. (2007, June 21). *Fours steps to transforming your negative self-talk into an inner coach.* Retrieved April 13, 2009, from http://www.articlesbase.com/leadership-articles/4-steps-to-transforming-your-negative-selftalk-into-an-inner-coach-168527.html
Balance in leadership	Hammonds, K. H. (2004, October 1). Balance is bunk! *Fast Company,* pp. 68–76.
Four *E*s of communication	Institute for Healthcare Communication. (2006). *Clinician–patient communication to enhance health outcomes* [Workshop presentation]. New Haven, CT: Author.

20

A Legacy of Leadership: Transforming the Occupational Therapy Profession

Thomas H. Dillon, EdD, OTR/L

❖ Key Terms and Concepts

Courage in leadership. Willingness to assume responsibility; serve the needs of others or organizations; appropriately challenge assumptions; participate in transformation; and recognize when it is time to leave, move on, or retire (Hackman & Johnson, 2009).

Leadership. "Leadership is human (symbolic) communication which modifies the attitudes and behaviors of others in order to meet shared group goals and needs" (Hackman & Johnson, 2009, p. 11).

Servant leaders. Leaders who focus on the needs of others and have a true concern for the welfare of others on the basis of a sense of stewardship, equity of justice, mutual indebtedness, and a clear self-understanding that includes knowing one's own attitudes and values (Greenleaf, 2002).

Transformational leaders. People who attempt to bring about self-actualization (optimal functional levels), including increased performance and higher levels of motivation and morality, for both individuals and organizations (Spinelli, 2006).

❖ Learning Objectives

After completing this chapter, you should be able to do the following:

- Analyze the principles of leadership and their relationship to various occupational therapy practice settings.
- Demonstrate the use of critical thinking to examine the role of occupational therapy practitioners as leaders.
- Discuss two leadership strategies or models an occupational therapy practitioner may use to demonstrate leadership effectiveness.

- Evaluate the contributions of past occupational therapy leaders as servant and transformational leaders and the impact of their contributions on the overall direction of the profession.
- Evaluate your progress as a leader and consider your own future leadership development goals and responsibilities.

It is important for occupational therapy practitioners to learn more about the profession through the individual stories of leaders who made significant contributions in the past. A historian may find in the occupational therapy literature information about the history of the field itself and its procedures, techniques, and theories. Yet little has been written specifically about the individual practitioners, educators, and researchers who collectively made those important contributions to the development of the profession. Developing an understanding of their stories may help today's practitioners and leaders contextualize the usefulness of leadership in their own practice when facing contemporary professional issues, many of which remain remarkably similar.

Developing an awareness of the significance of this historical information helps create a sense of meaningfulness for those who become familiar with these stories. Dillon (2001) suggested that one way to shape reality is through storytelling and that leaders help themselves and others understand the world and solve problems more effectively when they use stories to supplement traditional leadership models and techniques. In 1994, Mattingly and Fleming suggested that narrative reasoning helps practitioners see problems, develop

The author acknowledges the contributions of the following graduates of the master of occupational therapy program at the University of Findlay, Findlay, OH: **K. Boots, J. Boylen, J. Bruskotter, M. B. Dillon, J. Giffen, J. Harlan, S. Kraus, C. Lee, T. Leto, N. Miller, J. Renner, C. Salazar, B. Sarver, K. Schroeder, A. Shaw, M. Sissel, D. Slentz, J. Sloan, L. Thomas, H. Van Dyke,** and **K. Vicars.**

solutions, and envision the future informed by the past. It is hoped that the narratives provided in this chapter will help today's practitioners meaningfully connect with these universally acknowledged contributors to the field of occupational therapy. Their contributions have stood the test of time and may serve as a guide as we face the challenges that lie ahead for us, both individually and collectively.

INTERVIEWS WITH HISTORICALLY SIGNIFICANT LEADERS IN OCCUPATIONAL THERAPY

Nedra Gillette, former director of research for the American Occupational Therapy Foundation (AOTF), conducted a series of interviews, from the late 1970s through the early 1990s, with occupational therapists whom she believed were historically significant contributors to the field. She sensed the need to capture the stories of these individuals to supplement historically significant milestones for the occupational therapy profession. She audiotaped these interviews but reportedly did not have a specific purpose for the interviews at the time other than recognizing that it was important to collect this information while it was still possible. The tapes of these interviews remained with Gillette at AOTF until 2002, when she offered them to me and graduate students at the University of Findlay in Findlay, Ohio, to be used as the basis for a historical leadership study that subsequently began in 2003 and was completed in early 2009. About 35 taped interviews were transcribed at the University of Findlay (some of the tapes had deteriorated before the transcriptions were completed), resulting in more than 2,800 pages of interview transcriptions. Because of the deterioration of some of the tapes, some interviews proved to be minimally useful, but 21 of the interviews were sufficiently useable for this leadership study.

During the 6 years of this study, about 20 graduate students assisted in transcribing the interviews and analyzing the data. Because Gillette did not originally complete the interviews with a leadership study in mind, the research group used a set of about 30 questions to systematically review each interview from a leadership perspective to produce initial results in a consistent and chronological manner. The group then thematically analyzed the results for broad categories related to leadership and triangulated the analysis of this data by having multiple individuals review the interviews for thematic consistency.

The 21 women included in this analysis had similar styles of leadership, and many were friends, mentors, and colleagues of other women who were interviewed. Transformational and servant leadership styles emerged as the primary connections to the leadership literature and fit well with these women, who began their work in occupational therapy to serve the needs of others yet went on to help change the face of the profession and guide it through periods of substantial growth and development.

Transformational leadership occurs when the leader attempts to inspire followers to put aside their own interests for a greater collective purpose. The transformational leader aims to satisfy the basic needs of the followers and, once satisfied, to move toward higher-order needs, including self-esteem needs and self-actualization (Pielstick, 1998).

Servant leaders typically see the big picture and attempt to lead by ensuring that the needs of the followers are met (Crippen, 2004). Once followers' needs are met, they can productively contribute to the goal and mission of the organization. The focus on followers' needs rather than the needs and contributions of the leader make this perspective unique. The leader using this approach ensures organizational goals are met by focusing on his or her constituents rather than a need for recognition and acclaim (Greenleaf, 2002).

We found that most of the women included in this project experienced expectations by a significant family member that they would be successful and follow a nontraditional course of having a career at a time when most women worked in their homes. The majority of these women were driven to advance the profession and acknowledged their contributions to the field, but typically in a humble manner. Many of these women attained positions of great power and influence, yet they viewed their power as an increased responsibility to help foster further growth in others and in the profession.

To be an effective leader, it is often noted in the literature, leaders must have a vision; act to accomplish the goals that are embedded in that vision; and motivate, inspire, and encourage others to believe in that vision (Hayes, 2008). It is clear that these 21 women all had a vision for themselves and the profession. Even though their visions and contributions differed from one another, all these women had a significant impact on the profession of occupational therapy.

The 21 leaders included in this study were Jean Ayres, Louise Clifford, Marion Crampton, Florence Cromwell, Elizabeth Upham Davis, Gail Fidler, Marjorie Fish, Mary Louise Franciscus, Sue Hurt, Alice Jantzen, Jerry Johnson, Lela Llorens, Ruth Robinson, Mildred Schwagmeyer, Marion Spear, Clare Spackman, Caroline Thompson, Frannie Vanderkooi, Beatrice Wade, Carlotta Welles, and Wilma West. This chapter draws especially on the interviews with five of these women: Jean Ayres, Marion Crampton, Gail Fidler, Ruth Robinson, and Jerry Johnson. These women practiced occupational therapy from the early 1930s through the 1990s and were responsible for developing and implementing many significant aspects of the profession. These included assisting in the development of national policies and regulations, developing occupational therapy assistant educational programs, contributing to the professional literature, advocating for graduate-level professional education, and promoting the profession to important constituent groups and others.

EXEMPLARS OF LEADERS IN VARIOUS ROLES

In the leadership literature, many models such as traits approaches; functional theories; situational and contingency models; task vs. interpersonal skills approaches; and servant, transformational, and charismatic approaches attempt to explain and quantify leadership effectiveness, yet there is little consensus. Within that literature, a set of generally accepted leadership qualities has been outlined that seems to be evident across the spectrum of leadership models (Findley, 2008). First, leaders have *interpersonal qualities* that include self-confidence, good communication skills, emotional stability, sensitivity, and trustworthiness. Examples of *cognitive factors* or mental capabilities associated with leadership include intelligence and problem-solving, decision-making, and critical-thinking skills. Finally, *administrative factors* that are most often associated with leadership effectiveness include being well organized and having good planning skills and knowledge of specific management methods, procedures, and techniques. These administrative skills demonstrate to others that the individual leader behaves in a manner that is consistent with a common perception of leadership effectiveness (Hackman & Johnson, 2009).

Although having these skills is an important aspect of leadership effectiveness, simply having all these skills does not automatically mean that individuals will be successful leaders. The individuals who are the most successful leaders demonstrate a sense of artfulness in their efforts and are often noted to be quite different from successful managers. Such artfulness extends beyond knowing the requirements, to anticipating how others will respond and having a sense of all aspects of a situation beyond the immediate issues at hand or what is overtly discussed. In fact, Hackman and Johnson (2009) noted that successful managers implement processes and procedures, whereas effective leaders lead people. It is the ability of leaders to engage followers in a movement toward a vision and shared goals that often differentiates effective leadership from management. Hackman and Johnson suggested that one may find successful managers who are ineffective leaders, but all successful leaders are effective managers, at least at some level.

The stories of the women studied in this project provide an opportunity to consider leadership within a variety of roles and contexts. Rather than attempting to briefly summarize each of the 21 women's extensive stories, this chapter frames several significant stories around important leadership roles to provide examples of the different ways these women served and helped transform the profession of occupational therapy. These stories should help today's practitioners understand how these women's efforts in very different professional and leadership activities contributed to the greater good of the occupational therapy profession.

Occupational Therapist as Researcher: Jean Ayres

Jean Ayres was a driven individual who believed that the only right way to answer questions about her clients' ability to engage in meaningful daily occupations was to answer those questions scientifically through research. She was also known to seek out others who had the information she was looking for until she was satisfied that she had collected all of the information available.

She strongly believed and impressed on those she worked with that if occupational therapy were ever truly to be a profession that was respected by the medical world, occupational therapists needed to be well educated beyond the bachelor's-degree level. From early in her career, Ayres believed that entry-level occupational therapists needed to have a master's degree. She also believed at the time she began her occupational therapy career that occupational therapy was not a legitimate profession because it lacked professional-quality people. She thought that raising the requirement for entry-level occupational therapy to the master's degree would elevate the quality of those entering the profession.

Ayres believed research was important to occupational therapy because it would provide the profession with more credibility and acceptance as a true professional health care discipline. Physical therapy was more respected and better known at that time, she thought, because physical therapists chose to focus on one specific area of human functioning, researched that area extensively, and became experts in that area. Conversely, occupational therapists tended to be generalists, with less expertise or extensive research in one given area to support their practice.

Ayres led through her excellence in clinical research and her dedication to improving the knowledge base of occupational therapy. Ayres's belief that scientific research could guide occupational therapy practice might be seen as transformational leadership. She seemed to firmly believe that her work in sensory integration could transform the way occupational therapy practitioners provided services for children with a variety of learning disabilities. Ayres's research in sensory integration was more extensive than most research done in the field of occupational therapy at that time. The majority of her adult life was devoted to developing usable tests to assess a child's areas of sensory dysfunction. Many people were intrigued by her passion and dedication to her vision, but many more were wary of her ideas. Her ideas were, and continue to be, the topic of a great deal of discussion and controversy. Her model of sensory integration focused on areas of human functioning that were abstract and difficult to scientifically prove or understand at that time, and many of the tenets of sensory integration continue to be questioned. However, Ayres remained undeterred as she continued to search for scientific evidence to support her claims about the utility of sensory integration. Leading through her belief that research should guide clinical practice, Ayres transformed the profession, devoting her life to developing her vision of the importance of scientifically understanding sensory integrative processes and functioning in children.

Many of Ayres' personality characteristics identified in the interview led her to achieve at such a high level. First, she was very determined in her quest to prove the validity of sensory integration, and she continually searched for opportunities to satisfy her need for knowledge and to more thoroughly understand the central nervous system. Even her personal life was second to the development of sensory integration. She stated that for many years she had frequently neglected her family as she finished up the final aspects of her research. Second, Ayres was not afraid to step out of the accepted boundaries and challenge the commonly recognized beliefs of the times. Finally, Ayres was not deterred by the criticisms of her peers, and she was able to push forward even though she initially received minimal support from the occupational therapy profession and the medical world.

Ayres had no scholars in her field to model. In the 1960s and 1970s, few occupational therapists were engaged in research at such a comprehensive level, but Ayres led by example, demonstrating the power of research to support clinical practice at a time when other practitioners were not. Her efforts remain an example for those seeking to lead in occupational therapy via the less common path of research.

Ayres's vision for occupational therapy was acceptance of the profession by other professionals and the creation of a better knowledge base to assist with the ongoing development of the profession. The mark she left on the field has been a model for subsequent occupational therapy practitioners who wish to emulate her efforts as a scholar. In addition, she developed a group of followers who believed in sensory integration based on the merits of the model itself, often in spite of her focused and less personable style.

Ayres may not initially appear to be a leader because of the way she worked with others, which was task oriented rather than people oriented. However, it is nearly impossible to say that she was not a leader just because she was not a people person. While transformational for the profession, Ayres was more focused on the task than many occupational therapy leaders who tend to be more people oriented, and this fits with the task and interpersonal leadership approaches. Her research results and accomplishments speak for themselves, and though some felt Ayres was difficult to work with, she still was able to attract followers to assist her with her research because of her ability to develop her vision and remain focused on her research efforts. She was not deterred by the negative thoughts or comments of her colleagues.

Because of Ayres's influence, sensory integration has become a commonly used assessment and intervention model in pediatric occupational therapy practice. Although her research and work were not as appreciated or accepted while she was living as they are today, her contributions to occupational therapy will be recognized for decades to come and are an example of one particular type of effective leadership.

Leader as Teacher: Marion Crampton

Marion Crampton was a leader in mental health occupational therapy and occupational therapy assistant education as well as an American Occupational Therapy Association (AOTA) and AOTF member who believed in the profession and wanted to help fill the shortage of personnel following World War II to ensure that occupational therapy would survive as a profession and gain the respect of other professions. Her efforts led her to start occupational therapy assistant programs within the states' departments of mental health in the late 1950s that were dedicated to mental health practice in state hospital settings. She felt that by preparing occupational therapy staff at an assistant level the profession would continue to grow and reach the level of acceptance that was part of her vision.

After Crampton established occupational therapy assistant programs in the state mental health hospitals, she was appointed by then AOTA President Colonel Ruth Robinson to a committee to establish guidelines for occupational therapy assistant educational programs in all areas of clinical practice. Crampton elicited help from her coworkers and peers to develop appropriate curriculum standards for use by all new assistant programs. She used curricula from the nursing and social work professions and collaborated with others to ensure that the assistant program standards would be sufficient. Crampton had to convince many powerful constituent groups that these programs would be successful as there were many who were skeptical about adding an additional level of practitioner to the field. She recalled that although these efforts were essential for the future of the occupational therapy workforce, working through all the steps necessary to complete this process was not easy.

Crampton's commitment to developing occupational therapy assistants was, in part, a response to what she viewed as a lack of forward thinking by many in the profession about education and workforce needs. She worked during an era of extreme shortage of occupational therapists, and she watched many occupational therapists and programs go unmanaged as a result of this shortage. She did not think that occupational therapy educators were ready to deliver occupational therapy assistant–level educational programs, but she believed that such an effort was essential to the future of the profession.

To Crampton, leadership was not about the leaders themselves taking care of issues; it was about leaders leading followers. She mentioned that at the core of leadership is the relationship that exists between the leader and the followers. Crampton contended that she was not a leader and believed that a list of leadership traits could get very long very quickly, making it difficult to determine the connection between a particular trait and leadership success. She understood the core purpose and goals of the occupational therapy profession at that time and had a working awareness of the structures, procedures, and operations of the profession, as well as the characteristics of the organizational relationship. In addition, Crampton considered herself to be proactive and forward thinking.

Crampton's involvement with occupational therapy organizations helped her realize that a master's degree was desirable for entry-level occupational therapy practice. The reconfiguration of the occupational therapy entry-level guidelines is consistent with her beliefs about the profession, which surfaced many years ago. In the early 1950s, she made formal recommendations to the AOTA Delegate Assembly that entry-level occupational therapy positions should require a master's degree. Occupational therapy was just beginning to reap the benefits of occupational therapy assistant programs in mental health settings at that time, and Crampton believed that if occupational therapy assistants were to be trained at junior college programs, the training for occupational therapists should be significantly higher than that of occupational therapy assistants.

Crampton always saw herself as a contributor to the profession who supported its growth. She believed she accomplished an immense task by initiating occupational therapy assistants but mentioned that these efforts were the result of the contributions of many others as well. She seemed to be a humble individual, and her genuine approach to people authenticated her leadership abilities. She viewed herself as effective in her goals and her profession but not as a powerful person. Her humility exemplifies her leadership style as one of example and modest perseverance. Though her work focused primarily on creating occupational therapy assistant educational programs in mental health settings and later in general practice, the effects of her accomplishments continue to be an important part of contemporary educational practice.

Leader as Practitioner: Gail Fidler

Gail Fidler was known to many as a highly engaged and creative occupational therapy practitioner who contributed to the profession in numerous ways. She served in leadership positions at AOTA and in educational programs later in her career, yet it is her involvement in helping to formalize the practice of occupational therapy in mental health settings that gives Fidler a prominent place in occupational therapy history. Her enthusiasm for her work in occupational therapy is evident in the following quote:

> I believe that anything that you do in life should be more fun than not, and when the equation goes the other way, it is time to take a second look and do something about it. A person should not continue be engaged in any kind of a relationship or activity that is not satisfying or pleasurable. I have always tried to live my life that way, and most of the things I have done in my life, including my work in occupational therapy, have been fun.

Fidler's work as an advocate for occupational therapy in mental health culminated in a well-known book, *Occupational Therapy: A Communication Process in Psychiatry*, written in 1963 together with her husband Jay, a psychiatrist. This book focused on the role of occupational therapy with individuals who have mental illness. She developed and formalized the occupational therapy process from initial assessment through the entire treatment process. Her ef-

forts were based on many years of experience in a variety of work settings that included numerous mental health facilities, a stint at Walter Reed Army Hospital during World War II, and work at a southern Veterans Administration (VA) hospital.

Fidler was an extrovert and was known to speak her mind throughout her career. According to Fidler, her style of communication was both a hindrance and an asset to her career and to the growth of the profession, as her assertiveness and advocacy led to many positive outcomes yet at times offended others. Furthermore, her style of working with others was both task oriented and people oriented, depending on what the situation required. Fidler's love of people and her desire to surround herself with other, similar professionals were evidence of her people-oriented approach. Yet it was her ability to repeatedly lead occupational therapy departments in various hospitals that were barely surviving and turn them around in short periods of time that demonstrated her ability to focus on important projects when necessary.

Fidler's broader vision for occupational therapy was that some day the profession would grow to become widely recognized and understood and that it would be a diverse profession that mirrors the demographics of the society it serves. Her vision for occupational therapy in mental health was for the profession to demonstrate the true value of occupational therapy to other mental health professionals. As part of this vision, Fidler wanted to develop a specific master's degree in psychiatric occupational therapy, and she felt that the association needed to recognize and promote this area of practice. Fidler felt that too few occupational therapists went into mental health because they did not feel validated as true professionals in that practice area as they did in other practice areas. Reflecting back on her career, Fidler believed that she truly provided opportunities for occupational therapists in mental health practice, but she was concerned that subsequent leaders in the profession would not continue efforts to support this work.

Gail Fidler was one of the most recognized leaders in occupational therapy history. Her ideas for occupational therapy were ahead of her time, yet she was able to put many of them into action with the ease and precision of a highly skilled leader. Her vision, commitment, and motivation provide today's practitioners with an important model for their own efforts to provide leadership at the local, state, and national levels.

Leader as Professional: Ruth Robinson

Ruth Robinson contributed to occupational therapy in many ways, most notably in her service in the U. S. Army and with AOTA as both a volunteer and an elected officer. At the core of her success were her determination and her enthusiasm for her work in occupational therapy. Among numerous priorities, she believed that the Army Medical Corps needed to develop many new clinical facilities to accommodate the increased number of injured soldiers following World War II, and her term as president of AOTA helped refocus the efforts of the national office.

As president-elect of AOTA, Robinson initiated studies of group dynamics, many of which were published in the "Nationally Speaking" section of the *American Journal of Occupational Therapy* (*AJOT*). She also wrote numerous *AJOT* articles during her time in the army that discussed the importance of listening, working successfully in groups, and developing effective communication skills.

During her time as AOTA president from 1955 to 1958, Robinson advocated for the distribution of grants to universities to further occupational therapy education and research. She also worked closely with other leaders (including Crampton) to develop and implement occupational therapy assistant–level practitioners. Another of the many contributions she made to the profession during her years at Walter Reed was helping to write the history of occupational therapy in general and in the U. S. Army.

During the development of occupational therapy assistant guidelines, one of the primary issues was how to differentiate between the responsibilities of the therapist and those of the assistant. At that time, many in the field were having difficulty expressing the basic philosophy and purpose of occupational therapy. Some wondered if occupational therapy assistants could be added to the profession when occupational therapists themselves could not readily explain or define the profession. Many occupational therapists were afraid of losing their jobs to assistants.

Robinson had a democratic communication style as evidenced by her willingness to listen to other people's ideas and concerns. Although she was quick to state her own opinion on certain matters, she was open to the thoughts of others. During her years as AOTA president, she saw her role as being more of a facilitator than anything else. Robinson remembers having many long meetings during her presidency in which participants would "massage every word 'til the last degree." Her skill at open leadership through communication was demonstrated by the emphasis she placed on seeking her followers' input on decisions and allowing them to set group goals rather than enforcing her own personal goals. This skill made her a great democratic leader.

Robinson was more of a person-oriented leader when working in groups; however, she displayed some task-oriented characteristics as well. Being in the military, she acquired the task-oriented qualities of focusing more on the facts and information related to the task. She was known for being abrupt and stating her opinions no matter how they came across; however, she also exuded a person-oriented style through her openness to other people's ideas and her ability to stress the importance of listening to and working with others.

It was Robinson's assertiveness, vision, perseverance, and ambition, in collaboration with Crampton, that brought about the establishment of occupational therapy assistant programs, thereby furthering the profession. Throughout the controversies that surrounded the development of the occupational therapy assistant, Robinson held her ground and fought for what she believed. An effective leader is one who strives to carry out his or her vision to further the profession (Hackman & Johnson, 2009), and Robinson met this criterion throughout her career as evidenced by her identification of the need for occupational therapy assistants early on in her career and subsequent fulfillment of her vision.

Looking back on her contributions to the profession, Robinson felt she was an effective leader. During her presidency, she believed her role was more of a facilitator; however, she still considered herself a leader. "I see myself as an idealist," she noted, as reflected below:

> I would say this would sum up my philosophy about [leadership]: I think you're not in competition with your staff. Your responsibility is to try and develop them as a group and as individuals to their maximum capacity. And like parents, supervisors have a responsibility not to be jealous and to hope that at least a few will do far better than they [did]. If your supervisees don't learn more, do more, and grow more, then you haven't contributed very much [as a leader].

Leader as Visionary: Jerry Johnson

Jerry Johnson was a prominent leader in occupational therapy for many decades, and the focus of her contributions was on developing creative solutions to important issues of the day, such as creating innovative graduate education programs, changing standards of practice, and increasing governmental regulations. She preferred to take a broad look at the needs of the profession and regularly considered how multiple issues were connected and how solutions could build on one another.

Johnson had been an occupational therapist for 6 years when she began a wider search for administrative knowledge. She sought both formal and informal knowledge in the area and investigated a formal education in administration. After a college search for programs, she applied and was accepted into Harvard Business School. The year was 1959, when few occupational therapists recognized administration as an area of need, and few occupational therapy education programs included it. Johnson recalled,

> The greatest thing that I had gotten out of Harvard Business School was the way of thinking, the way of analyzing, the way of developing options and alternatives and making your decision based on some of those things, a thought process that allows you to make decisions in terms of the goal and the visions that you have. I wanted to be able to do that because I thought, to deal with the challenges that confronted occupational therapists, they needed to have this thought process.

From then on, Johnson used her grant-writing skills to add the resources she needed to enhance her efforts to lead various educational and clinical programs. At Boston University, she focused on developing an advanced master's program with further plans for the department to develop an entry-level master's program. Boston University had one of only three graduate programs for occupational therapy in the country at that time. The entry-level master's program met some resistance. The program also initiated a novel approach to clinical education in the graduate program, and Johnson proposed and implemented other strategies in academia that had not been attempted before.

Johnson went on to direct several occupational therapy programs at other institutions, each with their own institutional culture and challenges. She continued to develop innovative ideas for student recruitment to the profession, fieldwork development, community service programs, and graduate programs in occupational therapy.

Johnson was actively involved in being a leader in the occupational therapy profession through committee work at the local and national levels beginning in 1964. She served as AOTA president from 1973 to 1978, and her committee work included the position of chairman of the Council on Standards. The major issues the Council faced included issues of education, to which she brought considerable experience and expertise as a strong supporter of graduate occupational therapy programs. She did not support housing occupational therapy programs in schools of allied health because of her belief that allying with the medical model was an obstacle to making and maintaining connections with disciplines such as psychology and sociology. This struggle continues today, of course, and occupational therapy's alliance with allied health continues to promote a lack of understanding from external agencies at times. Her perception of this arrangement was that

> As a discipline, occupational therapy put itself as "second-class citizens" in the universities and colleges. The standards for faculty were lower, with separate expectations for tenure, professional publications, and research. There is an automatic downplay of our significance by our connection to the allied health identity. Growth in educational programs occurred quickly without a thought of our identity or our potential. We did not stop to look at why we were doing what we were doing.

Johnson became AOTA president during a time of considerable external pressures on and change within the organization. Her efforts during her term in office were centered on including AOTA members in the decision-making process and moving entry into the profession to the graduate level. Johnson saw that the organization had grown from a small business to one with a budget exceeding $1 million but no structure in place to become a full-fledged professional organization. Government grants became available, the number of schools had multiplied, certification issues had become a primary concern, and the numbers of occupational therapists and occupational therapy assistants had grown. Looking back, Johnson stated, "Our national office was basically set up to deal with educational programs. There were few membership benefits at that time. It was primarily a support for accreditation and certification." She began the process of helping the organization reflect on its goals and continually realign itself with its mission. The seeds planted during her presidency are still bearing fruit; ideas about and solutions to issues continue to evolve.

Johnson was passionate about occupational therapy to such an extent that it was the core of her life and her learning. She was committed to occupational therapy through her active involvement in important committees, her dedication to ideals she believed were in the best interest of the profession, and her ability to develop opportunities for occupational therapy beyond her immediate position. Johnson could be viewed as both a transformational and servant leader. Some of her most visionary and important ideas about graduate education in occupational therapy were the precursors to broad-based graduate education in occupational therapy. She also seemed to demonstrate qualities of servant leadership by putting the needs of the profession and her fellow practitioners ahead of her own needs by serving as a leader in many capacities and giving up her primary clinical interest in occupational therapy practice. She had some regrets:

> I have some sense of failure that some of the things I had wanted to have happen did not happen, and I had spent my political capital on the things that needed to happen for the profession. I recognize that in a sense there was a success in that.

She also regretted that her career had become so focused on administration that she was not seen as truly a clinician in any of her academic positions. In addition, she wished she had been able to do more in the area of prevention. After reflection, she decided she never experienced complete failure as long as she learned something new. She observed the following:

> I would like to be remembered for truly having cared about the profession to the point of having made personal sacrifices. I think sometimes I have been perceived as disrupting things more than contributing. I guess sometimes I have. I would like for people to know what I have done has been out of commitment and caring about the potential I think our profession has and out of frustration that sometimes we haven't developed that potential in the way we could or perhaps should. I would like to be remembered for being creative as well as for being caring and compassionate. I hope that I've had vision, foresight, and I hope I have motivated people and inspired people. I hope

that sometimes the risks I have taken will inspire others to take the risks that they see as necessary for the good of the profession.

DISCUSSION

How individuals lead others has been studied for centuries and is an important part of human existence. Leaders make a difference and influence groups and their members (Hackman & Johnson, 2009). Effective leadership, through communication with others, transforms viewpoints and actions to achieve shared group needs and objectives (Hackman & Johnson, 2009).

Leadership is a fundamental need in society. Most definitions of leadership describe a leader demonstrating various skills, abilities, and qualities to engage followers in moving toward a common goal in a specific organizational context (Hackman & Johnson, 2009). Leaders must often change the attitudes and behaviors of followers to reach a common goal. Of the various styles of leadership, many can be effective. Discovering what traits or characteristics are prominent in the leaders who have made an impact in the profession of occupational therapy may help support further growth of the profession and empower today's members to become tomorrow's leaders.

In the field of occupational therapy, most leaders have been women. The interviews showed that most of these women viewed their power as an increased responsibility to help foster the growth of others and the profession. In addition, they each had a vision, and to accomplish the goals embedded in their vision, they were able to motivate, inspire, and encourage others to believe in that vision (Greenleaf, 2002). Even though the basis and method of their visions varied from leader to leader, all of these women had a significant impact on the profession through visionary thinking.

These occupational therapy leaders used various leadership styles in directing their followers to make significant impacts on the profession that positively influenced their careers and occupational therapy's prominence and respect within the health care and education communities. These women defied traditional gender stereotypes of women of their era and advanced their careers often to the detriment of their personal lives. These leaders of occupational therapy came from similar backgrounds in terms of exposure to illness, respect for education, interest in occupational therapy organizational leadership, progression of occupational therapy degree levels, introduction to the career, and personality characteristics. Overall, these women had similar experiences that steered them in similar directions that advanced the overall growth and development of the profession.

Without the persistence and determination of these leaders, occupational therapy would not have evolved into the successful profession it is today. Many of their ideas and concerns reflect not only changes that subsequently oc-curred in occupational therapy but also issues that continue to be important.

This study provided many interesting findings about the leadership styles of these occupational therapy leaders. Of the many styles of leadership that were examined in the literature review process, we found that two styles were prominent in the transcripts: transformational and servant leadership.

Transformational Leadership in Occupational Therapy

Some leaders favored transformational over servant leadership. For example, of the 36 quotes in Gail Fidler's transcript, 25 supported transformational leadership and 11 supported servant leadership. Any given quote was as brief as one sentence or as expansive as a long paragraph, depending on how long it took the leader to convey the specific idea or concept. Each identified quote was triangulated by at least three readers of the data. As a result, we concluded that Fidler was a transformational leader. Jean Ayres particularly favored this style; of 63 quotes, 62 were categorized as transformational and only one as servant leadership. The transformational leader's goal is to help followers achieve self-actualization, as described in Maslow's hierarchy of needs (Hackman & Johnson, 2009), and the following statement by Ayres reflects this aspect of transformational leadership: "I'll have to grow at my rate; occupational therapy will have to grow at its rate. And people do not grow at the same rate." She sought actualization for herself, for others as growing professionals, and for the profession as a whole.

The women we found to be transformational leaders were creative, interactive, visionary, empowering, and passionate (Hackman & Johnson, 2009). They were accountable for their actions, honest, and direct, and they were willing to do what they thought was right regardless of personal interest. They encouraged others to receive recognition for their accomplishments, were forward thinkers, and consistently tried to better the profession. They wanted the medical community to have more respect for the profession of occupational therapy, they empowered others to share in their dreams for the profession, and they displayed exceptional written and verbal communication skills.

The theory of transformational leadership includes five common characteristics that clarify a complex motivational appeal (Hackman & Johnson, 2009). *Creativity* involves the willingness to try new things. *Passion* requires a high level of caring about the profession. *Interaction skills* enable the leader to work well with others. *Vision* allows the transformational leader to communicate and direct followers. *Empowerment of others* through encouragement is essential in transformational leadership.

The literature review also revealed a strong connection between transformational leadership and emotional intelligence. *Emotional intelligence* is a leader's capacity to manage personal and social complex dynamics (Barbuto & Wheeler, 2002). Barbuto and Wheeler identified five factors in emotional intelligence: empathic response, mood regulation, interpersonal skill, internal motivation, and self-awareness. The transcripts from leaders in occupational therapy supported this correlation. For example, a quote from Carlotta Welles—"You had to be prepared for yourself and for those people you were responsible for"—exemplifies key components of emotional intelligence; "prepared for yourself" reflects self-awareness and internal motivation, and the portion "and for those people you were responsible for" reflects interpersonal skill and mood regulation.

Servant Leadership in Occupational Therapy

Of the 49 quotes by Marion Crampton, 38 fit the criteria for a servant leader and 11 fit the category of a transformational leader; thus, we concluded that she favored servant leadership. Servant leaders put the needs of others and their profession before their own needs (Greenleaf, 2002). Most of the occupational therapy leaders were servant leaders who often sacrificed their personal lives for the sake of the profession and consequently the well-being of recipients of occupational therapy services. Some of these women empowered students to learn and, as a result, learned a great deal from their students. Others felt indebted to the profession even after retirement and continued to present at workshops and educate others about various aspects of occupational therapy education and practice. Most of these women were humble about their accomplishments.

Servant leaders value personal growth and strive to strengthen their positive characteristics and attributes. Five principles serve as the foundation for servant leadership: concern for people, stewardship, equity or justice, indebtedness, and self-understanding (Herman & Marlowe, 2005). Servant leaders believe in caring for their followers, whom they trust to carry out their responsibilities, and in reaching their goals through serving others. Servant leaders make an effort to ensure fair treatment. When both leaders and followers believe they owe each other for their responsibilities, a sense of indebtedness serves as a motivator. Servant leaders strive to be ethical and seek out opportunities for personal growth (Howatson-Jones, 2004). The following quote by Marion Crampton provides evidence that she followed the servant model of leadership:

> I got some of what I thought were our best occupational therapists together, and we must have met for 2 years planning about the content and standards for occupational therapy assistant educational programs. We hammered out what we would teach, like a theory, for the depressed, the hyperactive, the schizophrenic. We had it all figured out, and we tried to analyze activities that would be appropriate so that we really had something to offer [students].

In this quote, Crampton shows her concern for the students and program development. She acknowledges indebtedness to the community and profession as well as the pursuit of quality in education. It also shows Crampton's self-understanding of the demands required to be successful, with an emphasis on her desire to serve others.

Other Leadership Styles in Occupational Therapy

Leaders using a democratic leadership style engage in supportive communication that facilitates interaction between leaders and followers (Popper, Amit, Gal, Mishkal-Sinai, & Lisak, 2004). Many of the occupational therapy leaders displayed democratic leadership characteristics as they worked in conjunction with groups of people and praised other health care staff and occupational therapists for their contributions toward a common goal. These leaders encouraged others to become involved in various aspects of the occupational therapy profession while fostering effective communication among various constituent groups.

Leaders using an authoritarian style tend to set goals themselves; personally direct the completion of tasks; and engage primarily in one-way, downward communication (Spinelli, 2006). At times, some of these occupational therapy leaders were so determined that they seized direct control over situations, distancing themselves from their followers but leading with confidence to meet their goals.

ISSUES FOR FURTHER STUDY

Some leaders mentioned the struggle they experienced in their personal lives as everything, including families and relationships, took a back seat to their careers. Throughout their careers, these women fought against popular opinion and expectations, hoping to achieve their goals for the profession. Further description of the personal sacrifices they made might not only shed light on their times but also help identify the extent to which conditions have improved for current occupational therapy leaders and how current leaders can learn from past occupational therapy leaders by knowing their stories.

Another issue related to leadership and gender is the fact that all 21 of the women in this study were leaders at a time when men dominated leadership positions. Further research is needed to examine differences in leadership styles between men and women in occupational therapy. Several leaders expressed their thoughts and feelings on the desirability of having more men work in the field of occupational therapy. For example, Lela Llorens commented as follows:

> I think men are welcome in occupational therapy, but I think the nurturing part of occupational therapy as a profession is not comfortable for many men. The men who choose to become part of the profession, I think, are probably more comfortable with that part of the role. That's why I think it is important to recruit men not just for the sake of having more men, but to keep the profession the way that it is and let men join us if they choose to and be a part of what the profession is.

Jean Ayres noted that men might contribute to occupational therapy leadership by taking on more assertive and aggressive roles:

> It would help a great deal if there were several hundred men in occupational therapy all with very aggressive personalities who could tackle some of the interprofessional problems that arise and tackle legislatures and government and agencies. I think part of occupational therapy's problem is that we all tend to be of a less aggressive type, a more caring type than a fighting type.

Further research could also be conducted to compare these women's leadership styles with the most prominent leadership styles used today. Such an examination might help reveal which styles are likely to be most beneficial to future leaders of the profession.

CONCLUSION

The findings of this study show that the prominent occupational therapy leaders of the mid-20th century achieved success primarily through a transformational leadership style, by helping the followers self-actualize, or through a servant leadership style, by empowering their followers and the profession. One could argue that the profession built its foundation in servant leadership and grew through transformational leadership.

Today's occupational therapy professionals can learn from these women and their stories. The interviews provide a strong base of historical knowledge with the potential to motivate and inspire contemporary occupational therapy practitioners as they strive to achieve the *Centennial Vision* (Moyers, 2007). Carlotta Welles noted, "I feel that we must develop our competence in our traditional ways of serving patients and broaden practice into the community. We should be concerned with maintaining health, not just treating the sick." Although this statement was made many years ago, contemporary leaders in occupational therapy continue to echo it.

As the profession grows and evolves, leaders and others members of the profession should likewise enhance their abilities to influence others. Strong leadership is imperative for the continued growth and development of occupational therapy. By learning about the history of occupational therapy and its leaders, occupational therapy professionals will be better prepared to contribute to this influential and dynamic profession.

Case Examples

LEVEL I FIELDWORK

Mary did her Level I fieldwork with an occupational therapist in a school district. Up until now, the district has been receiving occupational therapy services on a contract basis from a large therapy provider. The special education program director had great expectations for Mary, and one of the reasons she was hired is that she was from this town originally and people know her and her family

To prepare, Mary tried to find out as much as possible about the school setting prior her scheduled first day. She reviewed relevant course materials and texts to refresh her knowledge related to working with children in school settings. In addition, Mary ensured she used good interpersonal skills upon her arrival to engage the fieldwork educator in an appropriate professional relationship. These skills included good communication, exuding self-confidence, and showing sensitivity to the students' needs. The fieldwork educator was impressed. Mary's professional manner and preparedness indicated that she had a sense of self-leadership.

LEVEL II FIELDWORK

John was nearing the end of his Level II fieldwork placement in a local inpatient rehabilitation center. He felt comfortable in the setting, and the staff had readily accepted him. Near the end of the fieldwork experience, he was approached by the occupational therapy supervisor and asked to consider accepting a position at the rehabilitation center upon completion of the fieldwork experience.

John wanted to accept the position at the rehabilitation center, but he was concerned that others would continue to view him as a student rather than a colleague, should he return to the center as a member of the staff. John decided to proactively address the issue with the occupational therapy supervisor. By addressing any specific concerns ahead of time, John developed the foundation for a good leader–follower relationship that would exist in the future with his supervisor. John realized that the specific issues that concerned John (i.e., being treated as a student rather than colleague) were not as important as being assertive and having his issues and concerns addressed prior to accepting the position. John's supervisor viewed him as an even more desirable new employee due to John demonstrating that he had the skills of an exemplary follower who is willing develop good solutions to address his concerns. His supervisor interpreted this professionalism as effective self-leadership.

(continued)

Case Examples *(cont.)*

FIRST-TIME MANAGER

Arlene was the recently hired manager of a small occupational therapy department in a private outpatient practice that previously offered physical therapy services exclusively. The practice included two clinics, 40 minutes apart, and provided outpatient services, home therapy services, and contract services for the state prison. Arlene wanted to establish herself as a manager and the role of occupational therapy in these contexts. How would you go about establishing yourself and the role of occupational therapy? What would you do specifically? What leadership initiatives would you take?

To meet the needs of the current staff and to develop an occupational therapy program, Arlene first got to know the physical therapy staff and programs offered, seeking their perspectives about adding occupational therapy services. Arlene demonstrated the characteristics of transformational leadership. She announced that she had a plan to add occupational therapy services and that some of her ideas would differ from the current marketing plan, but she also informed the staff that she was open to suggestions and valued their input. Throughout these important activities, Arlene showed her enthusiasm for occupational therapy and opportunities for her new employer. As the therapy practice prepared to undergo a significant change by adding occupational therapy services, Arlene's efforts reflected creativity, being interactive, being a visionary, empowering others, and her passion for occupational therapy and the opportunities ahead for this outpatient practice.

MANAGER

Betty, an occupational therapy manager with experience at two different institutions, was hired to establish an occupational therapy program for a 30-bed inpatient psychiatric unit in a large metropolitan medical center. She reported to the unit director, a psychiatrist, for supervision and to an administrator for budget purposes. Betty contemplated what leadership strategies would be most useful as she attempts to establish occupational therapy services on the psychiatric unit.

Although excited about the opportunity to take on this new professional opportunity, Betty was aware that there could be a few challenges to overcome as she established new occupational therapy on the psychiatric unit, such as possible resistance from staff members from other disciplines. She would have to carefully navigate the political issues that could arise despite her best interpersonal and professional efforts.

Betty decided that the best approach was to spend some time getting to know the programs and the rest of the staff to develop an occupational therapy program most likely to complement and enhance current programming and clinical outcomes. Next, she developed a strategic plan for implementing occupational therapy programs that included individual and group therapy programs; equipment, budget and space needs; and potential revenues to be generated by occupational therapy. She then shared this information with the team and said that she was open for input and suggestions from others before finalizing the occupational therapy plans with the administrators. Betty identified where she was willing to compromise and where her professional experiences told her she needed to hold her ground.

Such a leadership approach could be identified as democratic because Betty sought input from others, or interpersonally oriented if she focused more on staff interactions and program development. However, her efforts could also be viewed as servant leadership because her goals included setting up a new program and doing so in a collegial and professional manner. Betty recognized that others may have some concerns about the new services, so she acknowledged those concerns by engaging others in the planning process. Specifically, she showed concern for others, equity of justice, and good self-understanding that was reflected in her knowledge of current standards of practice, program development, and how to work effectively with others. Servant leaders lead by putting the needs of others or the organization ahead of their own while working to achieve acceptable outcomes.

❖ Learning Activities

1. Conduct several interviews with individuals whom you believe to be effective leaders in their work, volunteer, or service roles. Develop a set of specific questions beforehand, determine if you are able to validate your initial assumptions about this person's leadership effectiveness, and, if you are able, determine the leadership model that would best describe this individual. Did the interview result match your preinterview assumptions? Why or why not?

2. Write two paragraphs each about the most and least effective leaders you have encountered to date in your work, personal, or volunteer activities. What qualities or factors set these individuals apart from others in either a positive or negative way? What impact have these

individuals had on your understanding of leadership effectiveness? How can you learn from both of these individuals as you move forward with your professional career?

3. Complete a personal reflective leadership chronology to help you develop a better sense of your own leadership development to date. Effective leaders are often noted for having good self-understanding, and one way to begin this process is to think about your leadership development pragmatically. What people, events, and life milestones have shaped you into the person you are today? What meanings can you derive from these life events, and your subsequent leadership development, by examining these events through a "leadership lens"?

4. Develop your own leadership model as a way to create a meaningful working understanding of the leadership principles you see as most important. Many of us favor certain psychological or occupational therapy models to explain how and why individuals behave in certain ways and engage in daily occupations. Your own leadership model can serve as a guide for you in both your daily practice and in current and future leadership positions.

5. Identify one thing you can do today, this month, or this year that would move you one step closer to making a leadership contribution in occupational therapy. When will you do that one thing to begin your personal leadership journey?

✓ Multiple-Choice Questions

1. Hackman and Johnson (2009) defined leadership as
   a. Doing the right thing.
   b. Communicating in a way that modifies the attitudes and behaviors of others.
   c. Focusing on the emotional needs of followers.
   d. Standing up for what you believe in.

2. Leadership narratives can help practitioners and leaders learn how to do which of the following?
   a. See problems, develop solutions, and envision the future.
   b. Understand the needs of others more effectively.
   c. Learn more about people from the stories they tell.
   d. Provide connections to the past.

3. Effective leaders most often use which of the following to help accomplish their goals?
   a. Power.
   b. Judgment.
   c. Influence.
   d. Rewards.

4. One specific leadership trait that causes others to follow that leader is
   a. Making promises.
   b. Getting the task at hand completed.
   c. Providing job security.
   d. Being a visionary.

5. The basic premise of transformational leadership is that leaders attempt to do which of the following?
   a. Promote individual or organizational self-actualization.
   b. Create change, hoping things will improve.
   c. Reassure followers that the leader is aware of their needs.
   d. Support organizational needs above all else.

6. Transformational leadership theory is based on which of the following?
   a. Watson's behavioral reinforcement.
   b. Freud's psychosexual stages of development.
   c. Frankl's ideas on personal meaningfulness.
   d. Maslow's hierarchy of needs.

7. The principles of emotional intelligence correlate best with which leadership style?
   a. Authoritarian.
   b. Transformational.
   c. Laissez-faire.
   d. Situational.

8. The essence of emotional intelligence includes the leader's capacity to understand which of the following?
   a. What followers want from their leaders.
   b. How social skills affect leadership.
   c. Complex personal and social dynamics.
   d. How their own emotions affect others.

9. Servant leaders lead by
   a. Managing others fairly and equitably.
   b. Letting followers know how they feel about the issues at hand.
   c. Putting the needs of the organization and others before their own.
   d. Creating a healthy dialogue that focuses on getting the job done.

10. Which of the following is one of the 5 basic principles of servant leadership?
    a. Putting organizational needs first.
    b. Letting followers know what is expected of them.
    c. Letting followers do as they see fit with minimal direction.
    d. Fostering a sense of mutual indebtedness.

11. Servant leaders are often seen as effective leaders by others because they do which of the following?
    a. Treat others in a professional manner.
    b. Always get the job done in a timely fashion.
    c. Have good self-awareness and self-understanding.
    d. Care more about their own leadership needs and effectiveness.

12. Democratic leaders generally use communication techniques that
    a. Create good one-way communication to identify follower expectations.
    b. Increase followers' understanding of the leader's expectations.
    c. Create interaction between the leader and followers.
    d. Decrease the chances for mutual collaboration on goals.

13. Authoritarian leaders generally use which kind of communication?
    a. Collaborative and inclusive.
    b. Private but understanding.
    c. Focused on emotions, not tasks.
    d. One-way and downward.

14. Many of the leaders in this study
    a. Were from the same region of the country.
    b. Went to the same occupational therapy program.
    c. Had similar backgrounds and experiences.
    d. Believed in all of the same issues.

15. Which sacrifice did these leaders make to achieve their vision?
    a. They put their professional work before their personal lives.
    b. They focused more on what others were doing at that time.
    c. They fought for changes without regard for the needs of others.
    d. They accepted lower paying jobs for the good of the entire profession.

16. One leader encouraged occupational therapists to become advocates to accomplish which of the following goals?
    a. Meet the needs of their clients above all else.
    b. Help clients have better access to occupational therapy services.
    c. Increase the salaries of all occupational therapists.
    d. Advance the profession and influence society.

17. Courageous leaders do which of the following?
    a. Make sure their own needs are met.
    b. Serve others and challenge assumptions.
    c. Ensure that others feel comfortable with all decisions.
    d. Serve others and are satisfied with the status quo.

18. Which of the following are generally valued interpersonal leadership qualities?
    a. Good planning skills.
    b. Self-confidence and emotional stability.
    c. Being well organized.
    d. Intelligence and problem-solving skills.

19. Which of the following are generally valued administrative leadership qualities?
    a. Decision making and critical thinking.
    b. Sensitivity and trustworthiness.
    c. Effective planning and organizational skills.
    d. Good communication skills.

20. Which of the following are generally valued cognitive leadership qualities?
    a. Intelligence and critical thinking skills.
    b. Knowledge of procedures and techniques.
    c. Good organizational skills.
    d. Self-confidence and emotional stability.

References

Barbuto, J. E. (1997). Taking the charisma out of transformational leadership. *Journal of Social Behavior and Personality, 12,* 689–697.

Barbuto, J. E., & Wheeler, D. W. (2002). Becoming a servant leader: Do you have what it takes? *Nebraska Cooperative Extension.* Retrieved June 13, 2005, from http://ianpubs.unl.edu-misc/g1481.htm

Bell, C. (2000). Wearing the mantle: Healthcare leaders are demonstrating compromise and grace. *Modern Healthcare, 30,* 26.

Burke, J. P., & DePoy, E. (1991). An emerging view of mastery, excellence, and leadership in occupational therapy practice. *American Journal of Occupational Therapy, 45,* 1027–1032.

Crippen, C. (2004). Servant–leadership as an effective model for educational leadership and management: First to serve, then to lead. *Management in Education, 18*(5), 11–16.

Dillon, T. H. (2001). Authenticity in occupational therapy leadership: A case study of a servant leader. *American Journal of Occupational Therapy, 55,* 441–448.

Dudek-Schriber, L. (1997). Leadership qualities of occupational therapy department program directors and the organizational health of their departments. *American Journal of Occupational Therapy, 51,* 369–377.

Fidler, G. S., & Fidler, J. W. (1963). *Occupational therapy: A communication process in psychiatry.* New York: Macmillan.

Findley, B. (2008). Traits and virtues: Establishing exercise physiologists as leaders. *Professionalization of Exercise Physiology, 5*(5), 1.

Frick, D. M., & Spears, L. C. (Eds). (1996). *The private writings of Robert K. Greenleaf: On becoming a servant leader.* San Francisco: Jossey-Bass.

Gellis, Z. D. (2001). Social work perceptions of transformational and transactional leadership in healthcare. *Social Work Research, 25*(1), 17–25.

Gersh, M. (2006). Servant–leadership: A philosophical foundation for professionalism in physical therapy. *Journal of Physical Therapy Education, 20*(2), 12–16.

Gilfoyle, E. M. (1989). Leadership in occupational therapy. *American Journal of Occupational Therapy, 43,* 567–570.

Greenleaf, R. K. (2002). *Servant leadership: A journey into the nature of legitimate power and greatness* (rev. ed.). Mahwah, NJ: Paulist Press.

Hackman, M. Z., & Johnson, C. E. (2009). *Leadership: A communication perspective* (5th ed.). Prospect Heights, IL: Waveland Press.

Hayes, J. M. (2008). Teacher as servant: Applications of Greenleaf's servant leadership in higher education. *Journal of Global Business Issues, 2*(1), 113–134.

Herman, D., & Marlowe, M. (2005). Modeling meaning in life: The teacher as servant leader. *Reclaiming Children and Youth, 14,* 175–178.

Howatson-Jones, L. I. (2004). The servant leader. *Nursing Management, 11*(3), 20–24.

Hunter, J. C. (1998). *The servant: A simple story about the true essence of leadership.* Roseville, CA: Prima Publishing.

Lindholm, M., Sivberg, B., & Uden, G. (2000). Leadership styles among nurse managers in changing organizations. *Journal of Nursing Management, 8,* 327–335.

Mattingly, C., & Fleming, M. H. (1994). *Clinical reasoning: Forms of inquiry in a therapeutic practice.* Philadelphia: F. A. Davis.

Miller, R. J. (1992). Interwoven threads: Occupational therapy, feminism, and holistic health. *American Journal of Occupational Therapy, 46,* 1013–1019.

Moyers, P. (2007). A legacy of leadership: Achieving our *Centennial Vision. American Journal of Occupational Therapy, 61,* 622–628.

Pielstick, C. (1998). The transformational leader: A meta-ethnographic analysis. *Community College Review, 26*(3), 15–34.

Politis, J. D. (2004). Transformational and transactional leadership predictors of stimulant determinants to creativity in organizational work environments. *Electronic Journal of Knowledge Management, 2*(2), 23–34.

Popper, M., Amit, K., Gal, R., Mishkal-Sinai, M., & Lisak, A. (2004). The capacity to lead: Major psychological differences between leaders and nonleaders. *Military Psychology, 16,* 245–263.

Purnanova, R. K., Bono, J. E., & Dzieweczynski, J. (2006). Transformational leadership, job characteristics, and organizational citizenship performance. *Human Performance, 19*(1), 1–22.

Scott, W. E. (1985). Variables that contribute to leadership among female occupational therapists. *American Journal of Occupational Therapy, 39,* 379–385.

Skinner, C., & Spurgeon, P. (2005). Valuing empathy and emotional intelligence in health leadership: A study of empathy, leadership behavior, and outcome effectiveness. *Health Services Management Research, 18,* 1–12.

Spears, L. C. (Ed.). (1998). *The power of servant leadership.* San Francisco: Berrett-Koehler.

Spinelli, R. J. (2006). The applicability of Bass's model of transformational, transactional, and laissez-faire leadership in the hospital administrative environment. *Hospital Topics: Research and Perspectives on Healthcare, 84*(2), 11–18.

Strack, G., & Fottler, M. D. (2002). Spiritualism and effective leadership in healthcare: Is there a connection? *Frontiers in Health Services Management, 18*(4), 3–18.

Swearingen, S., & Leberman, A. (2004). Nursing leadership: Serving those who serve others. *Health Care Manager, 23*(2), 100–109.

Terry, R. W. (1993). *Authentic leadership: Courage in action.* Jossey-Bass.

APPENDIX 20.A. A LEGACY OF LEADERSHIP EVIDENCE TABLE

Topic	Evidence
Leadership styles	Burke, J. P., & DePoy, E. (1991). An emerging view of mastery, excellence, and leadership in occupational therapy practice. *American Journal of Occupational Therapy, 45,* 1027–1032. Gilfoyle, E. M. (1989). Leadership in occupational therapy. *American Journal of Occupational Therapy, 43,* 567–570. Hackman, M. Z., & Johnson, C. E. (2009). *Leadership: A communication perspective* (5th ed.). Prospect Heights, IL: Waveland Press. Lindholm, M., Sivberg, B., & Uden, G. (2000). Leadership styles among nurse managers in changing organizations. *Journal of Nursing Management, 8,* 327–335.
Leadership qualities	Bell, C. (2000). Wearing the mantle: Healthcare leaders are demonstrating compromise and grace. *Modern Healthcare, 30,* 26. Dudek-Schriber, L. (1997). Leadership qualities of occupational therapy department program directors and the organizational health of their departments. *American Journal of Occupational Therapy, 51,* 369–377. Miller, R. J. (1992). Interwoven threads: Occupational therapy, feminism, and holistic health. *American Journal of Occupational Therapy, 46,* 1013–1019. Scott, W. E. (1985). Variables that contribute to leadership among female occupational therapists. *American Journal of Occupational Therapy, 39,* 379–385. Skinner, C., & Spurgeon, P. (2005). Valuing empathy and emotional intelligence in health leadership: A study of empathy, leadership behavior, and outcome effectiveness. *Health Services Management Research, 18,* 1–12. Strack, G., & Fottler, M. D. (2002). Spiritualism and effective leadership in healthcare: Is there a connection? *Frontiers in Health Services Management, 18*(4), 3–18. Terry, R. W. (1993). *Authentic leadership: Courage in action.* Jossey-Bass.
Servant leadership	Crippen, C. (2004). Servant–leadership as an effective model for educational leadership and management: First to serve, then to lead. *Management in Education, 18*(5), 11–16. Dillon, T. H. (2001). Authenticity in occupational therapy leadership: A case study of a servant leader. *American Journal of Occupational Therapy, 55,* 441–448. Frick, D. M., & Spears, L. C. (Eds.). (1996). *The private writings of Robert K. Greenleaf: On becoming a servant leader.* San Francisco: Jossey-Bass. Gersh, M. (2006). Servant–leadership: A philosophical foundation for professionalism in physical therapy. *Journal of Physical Therapy Education, 20*(2), 12–16. Greenleaf, R. K. (2002). *Servant leadership: A journey into the nature of legitimate power and greatness* (rev. ed.). Mahwah, NJ: Paulist Press. Hunter, J. C. (1998). *The servant: A simple story about the true essence of leadership.* Roseville, CA: Prima Publishing. Spears, L. C. (Ed.). (1998). *The power of servant leadership.* San Francisco: Berrett-Koehler. Swearingen, S., & Leberman, A. (2004). Nursing leadership: Serving those who serve others. *Health Care Manager, 23*(2), 100–109.
Transformational leadership	Barbuto, J. E. (1997). Taking the charisma out of transformational leadership. *Journal of Social Behavior and Personality, 12*(3), 689–697. Gellis, Z. D. (2001). Social work perceptions of transformational and transactional leadership in healthcare. *Social Work Research, 25*(1), 17–25. Pielstick, C. (1998). The transformational leader: A meta-ethnographic analysis. *Community College Review, 26*(3), 15–34. Politis, J. D. (2004). Transformational and transactional leadership predictors of stimulant determinants to creativity in organizational work environments. *Electronic Journal of Knowledge Management, 2*(2), 23–34. Purnanova, R. K., Bono, J. E., & Dzieweczynski, J. (2006). Transformational leadership, job characteristics, and organizational citizenship performance. *Human Performance, 19*(1), 1–22.

21
Managing Programs in Emerging Practice Areas

Marjorie E. Scaffa, PhD, OTR, FAOTA;
Joy Doll, OTD, OTR/L; Rebecca Estes, PhD, OTR, ATP;
and Wendy Holmes, PhD, OTR/L

❖ Key Terms and Concepts

Community-based practice. Occupational therapy practice in the community as a setting or location. Community-based practice occurs in homes, in schools, on playgrounds, in day care centers, at work sites, and at senior centers, among other locations.

Consultation. "An interactive process of helping others solve existing or potential problems by identifying and analyzing issues, developing strategies to address problems, and preventing future problems from occurring" (Epstein & Jaffe, 2003, p. 260).

Corporate infusion. Introduction of new services or programs from outside of a business in an effort to make them permanent features of the corporate entity (Loukas, 2000).

Emerging practice. Development and provision of a new type of occupational therapy service either in a traditional service context or in an environment where services have not traditionally been available or well established.

Innovation. Introduction of something new or different and the means by which entrepreneurs "exploit change as

an opportunity for a different business or a different service" (Drucker, 1985, p. 19).

Intrapreneurship. Harnessing the "resources within an organization to develop, improve, promote, extend, or enhance a new or existing program" (Pazell & Jaffe, 2003, p. 223).

Needs assessment. Process by which problems, needs, gaps, and issues are identified for the purpose of developing strategies or programs to address the concerns of a community or population.

Partnership. "A relationship of individuals or groups marked by mutual cooperation and responsibility" (*American Heritage College Dictionary*, 1997, p. 997).

Stakeholders. "Persons who may or may not directly benefit from being involved in a potential program and who may also "have a stake in the program's outcome and often the ability to influence that outcome" (Scaffa, Reitz, & Pizzi, 2010, p. 204).

❖ Learning Objectives

After completing this chapter, you should be able to do the following:

- Identify emerging areas of practice in the 6 practice areas described by the American Occupational Therapy Association.
- Identify competencies needed for management in emerging practices.
- Apply the SWOT (*strengths, weaknesses, opportunities, and threats*) approach to developing emerging practice ideas.

- Apply the PRECEDE–PROCEED model to the development of emerging practices.
- Compare and contrast management functions in traditional and emerging practice areas.

The concept of *emerging practice* as part of the profession of occupational therapy is not new. Occupational therapists have repeatedly sought to provide needed services in new and emerging areas in response to changes in the health care system. Ellie Gilfoyle (1986), in her 1986 presidential address at the American Occupational Therapy Association (AOTA) Annual Conference & Expo, spoke of the entrepreneurial society and the profession's imperative to make new and creative partnerships in a challenging environment. The need to address societal and health care changes through unique practice approaches continued to be addressed through the turn of the millennium in articles on topics such as application of the consultation model (Dudgeon & Greenberg, 1998) and entrepreneurship (Foto, 1998). In the early 21st century, occupational therapy students are being exposed to emerging practice areas during fieldwork experiences (Johnson, Koenig, Piersol, Santalucia, & Wachter-Schutz, 2006), and therapists continue to explore practice options in community-based settings (Estes, Fette, & Scaffa, 2005; Fette & Estes, 2009; Glennon, 2007), public school consultation (Kiss, 2007), and ergonomics (O'Connor, 2000).

As the occupational therapy profession continues to face challenges and opportunities brought about by changes in the health care system and other external demands, the context for service provision must continue to support traditional facility-based environments, such as rehabilitation programs, hospitals, and outpatient and community programs. However, new collaborations and initiatives, including those inspired by AOTA's *Centennial Vision* (AOTA, 2007), in areas such as aging in place, driving and transportation, and caregiver issues also need to be explored (Baum, 2006). Although many examples of emerging practice roles and settings are offered in the professional literature (Baum, 2000; Jacobs, 2002a, 2002b; Scaffa, 2001; Stancliff, 1997), a cohesive definition of emerging practice does not exist. For the purposes of this chapter, *emerging practice* is defined as the development and provision of a new type of occupational therapy service either in a traditional service context or in an environment where services have not traditionally been available or well established.

The term *community-based practice* refers to occupational therapy practice that takes place in the community as a setting or location. Community-based practice occurs in homes, in schools, on playgrounds, in day care centers, at work sites, and at senior centers, among other locations. The provision of occupational therapy services in community-based settings is an essential emerging practice area; however, other settings also offer opportunities for innovative service delivery. In both emerging practice and community-based practice, the client may be an individual, a family, an organization, a community, or a population. *Emerging practice* is a broader, more inclusive, term than *community-based practice;* both involve not only new venues for practice but also innovative ways of practicing occupational therapy.

HISTORICAL CONTEXT

Changes in health care delivery and related changes in occupational therapy practice are driven by the interplay of multiple variables. Growth in health care expenditures is one of the variables affecting health care and occupational therapy service delivery. Sandstrom, Lohman, and Bramble (2003) identified three interacting factors influencing the growth in health care expenditures. First, economic factors, which include general and medical inflation and the protective role of health insurance, influence the health care market. Second, societal demographics are changing in the United States; for example, the number of persons over the age of 64, who typically have greater health care needs, is increasing. Third, system factors include the high cost of health care technology, inefficiencies in the provision of services, and the practice of defensive medicine.

Philosophical shifts and subsequent policy decisions are also contributors to the changing face of health care delivery. A shift in the focus of health care away from the medical model to alternative models of care is one example; this shift is away from an institution-centered model toward a community-based model with the intention of planning, or managing, health care delivery to lower health care costs overall (Baum, 2000; Scaffa, 2001).

Accompanying the development of alternative and managed models of care is a stronger emphasis on wellness and disease prevention (Baum, 2000). For example, since the 1970s, policy development at the national level shifted attention toward a prevention and wellness agenda for the nation's population. Healthy People 2010, a comprehensive prevention agenda for the nation, was implemented to improve the health status and quality of life of the nation's citizens while also decreasing or eliminating health disparities (U.S. Department of Health and Human Services, 2000). Healthy People 2020 is the most recent update on Healthy People 2010, and the intention is to develop and implement an updated plan every 10 years (U.S. Department of Health and Human Services, 2009). The health care needs of an aging population, coupled with the increasing availability of medical treatment for chronic diseases, are expected to continue to contribute to increasing health care expenditures in the near future (Koenig, Siegel, Dobson, Hearle, & Rudowitz, 2003).

The occupational therapy profession faces ongoing, evolving challenges and opportunities brought about by these changes in the health care system and other external demands. Inherent in the profession's transitions is a shift away from the medical model to alternative models of care.

EMERGING PRACTICE VS. TRADITIONAL PRACTICE

As a consequence of the health care delivery changes, the context for occupational therapy service provision continues to expand beyond traditional settings into ever-evolving emerging practice areas (Baum, 2006; Baum & Law, 1998; Brachtesende, 2005; Scaffa, 2001). Emerging practice is a multifaceted concept and encompasses multiple professional roles (e.g., consultant, entrepreneur, manager) in a variety of contexts for the provision of services, as well as the development of innovative businesses or models of practice.

As part of the 2017 *Centennial Vision,* AOTA reorganized and prioritized occupational therapy practice, both traditional and emerging, into six overarching areas: (1) mental health; (2) productive aging; (3) children and youth; (4) health and wellness; (5) work and industry; and (6) rehabilitation, disability, and participation (AOTA, 2009b). Each overarching practice area comprises a multiplicity of treatment settings, populations, and conditions, as well as subspecialty areas of practice encompassing both traditional and emerging areas of practice. Additionally, within five of these overarching practice areas, AOTA has identified some emerging areas of practice and provided links to resources for interested practitioners (AOTA, 2009a).

In the overarching area of children and youth, emerging practice areas have been identified relating to the psychosocial needs of children and youth; resources available currently focus on occupational therapy practice related to autism, stress and stress disorders, and violence in the schools. In the area of productive aging, emerging practice areas such as driver rehabilitation and training, assistance for seniors who desire to continue driving, and low vision interventions have been identified. The health and wellness emerging practice areas include consulting in the areas of ergonomics and injury prevention, elder wellness, environmental design, accessibility and home modifications, and assistive devices. Entrepreneurship, the opening of new businesses and private practices in community health service, is also identified as an emerging practice in health and wellness. The overarching area of work and industry includes emerging practice areas related to return-to-work interventions for individuals with disabilities and ergonomics. The last area, rehabilitation, disability, and participation, includes the emerging practice areas of technology and assistive device development and consulting and virtual reality interventions. Clearly, these emerging practice areas require occupational therapists to examine their roles, skills, and management needs to meet the unique demands of the varied settings and approaches each entails.

MODELS OF EMERGING PRACTICE

Several models of emerging practice can be conceptualized, including entrepreneurship, intrapreneurship, corporate infusion, organizational or agency infusion, and policy infusion. The entrepreneurial model includes exploration of market trends and creation of new products, services, or programs based on SWOT (*s*trengths, *w*eaknesses, *o*pportunities, and *t*hreats) analysis and needs assessment data. This is the business or private practice model with which therapists are most familiar. It involves risk to the

entrepreneur and the development of a new business entity (Loukas, 2000). *Intrapreneurship* involves harnessing the "resources within an organization to develop, improve, promote, extend, or enhance a new or existing program" (Pazell & Jaffe, 2003, p. 223). Examples include adding a driving rehabilitation program or lymphedema management service to an existing occupational therapy department in a rehabilitation hospital. Organizations vary in their ability to manifest intrapreneurship. Intrapreneurs who are not nurtured within their organizations often leave to establish their own ventures.

Corporate infusion (Loukas, 2000) involves the introduction of new services or programs from outside a business in an effort to make them permanent features of the corporate entity. Examples of this approach include ergonomics consultation within manufacturing plants and injury prevention programs in work sites. Organizational or agency infusion is essentially the same concept as corporate infusion, but the services or programs are typically infused into a nonprofit organization or government agency. Examples of organizational infusion are providing daily living skills services in homeless shelters, adapting leisure activities to meet the needs of persons with disabilities in community recreation programs, and assessing accessibility for a housing development agency. In each of these infusion approaches, therapists frequently provide the new services or programs as independent contractors or consultants. Policy infusion is a social action strategy to mandate the provision of certain services or programs in designated organizations and sites through legislative or policy actions, such as the Individuals with Disabilities Education Act (IDEA) and Ticket to Work initiatives.

OCCUPATIONAL THERAPY ROLES IN EMERGING PRACTICE

AOTA workforce surveys provide information about where occupational therapists work and allow comparison of current trends with past trends. Traditionally, occupational therapy is a female-dominated profession, with 95% of the workforce being women (AOTA, 2006). As with the general population, workers are aging, with the median age of occupational therapists now 42 years as compared to 36 years in 1990, supporting concern about future shortages of practitioners. The majority of occupational therapists work for a single employer, with only about 12% listing themselves as entirely self-employed or paid contractually, and an additional 13% list themselves as partially self-employed or contractual. However, the survey indicated that the number of occupational therapists involved in self-employment or contractual work is increasing. When the percentages of occupational therapists both completely and partially engaged in self-employment or contractual work are combined, the resulting number is close to 25% of all occupational therapists possibly working in emerging practices and/or unique roles.

Current standards for accredited occupational therapy educational programs (e.g., Accreditation Council for Occupational Therapy Education, 2007) call for the entry-level occupational therapist to receive preparation in the application of and ongoing currency with evidence-based professional practice. Additionally, the *Standards* specifically require educational curricula to prepare students for both current practice settings and emerging practice areas, with a strong focus on the role of occupation in promoting health, well-being, and quality of life and preventing disease and injury.

As emerging practice in occupational therapy continues to evolve, the required professional competencies and optimal strategies for their achievement will continue to be developed and refined. A survey of occupational therapists by Holmes and Scaffa (2009) generated a list of competencies needed in emerging practice (see Table 21.1). The range of roles and duties assumed by occupational therapy managers in community-based practice settings is more diverse than the roles of occupational therapy personnel in medical settings (Braveman, 2006). The literature provides opportunities to learn about the varied roles for therapists interested in entering emerging practice areas—for example, entre-

preneurship (Foto, 1998; Glennon, 2007; Pattison, 2006), consultation (Kiss, 2007; van Zwet-de Savornin Lohman, 1999), and management (Schell & Slater, 1998).

Occupational therapists may enter emerging practice areas to start and manage businesses, provide services to persons who are homeless, initiate community-based programs, provide consultation services, or address challenges proposed in the *Centennial Vision* (Baum, 2006). In addition to typical management functions, therapists in emerging practice need to demonstrate innovation, leadership, entrepreneurship, and consultation skills.

Innovation

Emerging practice can be considered innovative, or unconventional, within the profession (Jacobs, 2002a). According to Drucker (1985), *innovation* is the introduction of something new or different and is the means by which entrepreneurs "exploit change as an opportunity for a different business or a different service" (p. 19). Therapists engaging in innovative practices exhibit the characteristics of innovators or of those who adopt others' recent innovations. Rogers (2003) described innovators as follows: "The

Table 21.1. Competencies Needed for Emerging Practice Areas

Type of competency	Examples
Knowledge	Principles of client-centered practice Program development Community systems Public health and practice-specific principles and practice models
Critical reasoning	Holistic reasoning Translation of theory to practice Problem solving "Outside-the-box" thinking
Interpersonal abilities	Active listening Communication of occupational therapy concepts to a variety of audiences Establishment of relationships with key stakeholders and leaders Effective networking with other professionals Effective negotiation Demonstration of cultural competence Understanding and use of language and terms of other professions
Performance skills	Envisioning of occupational therapy roles and service possibilities Implementation of client-centered practices Assessment, evaluation, and provision of intervention Consultation Collaborative work Identification of and access to available resources
Ethical reasoning	Self-assessment of strengths and needs for ongoing professional development Principles of occupational and social justice
Traits, qualities, and characteristics of the individual	Self-starter, self-directed Adaptable to new situations Able to step outside the medical model Self-confident Persevering, determined, and persistent Able to challenge the status quo Flexible

Source. Holmes and Scaffa (2008). Used with permission.

salient value of the innovator is venturesomeness, due to a desire for the rash, the daring, and the risky" (p. 283). Early adopters, he noted, are more conservative than innovators and yet serve as leaders and role models by embracing the innovation; "In one sense, early adopters put their stamp of approval on a new idea by adopting it" (p. 283).

Innovators and early adopters of innovations also function as change agents and in so doing demonstrate effective communication of the vision and the ability to motivate and influence others, attributes shared by both leaders and therapists entering emerging practice areas. Innovative professional roles require a diverse blend of competencies, including skills in management and leadership, to effect success (Fazio, 2001).

Leadership

Fazio (2001) noted that in developing new programs, the occupational therapist must acquire the skill sets of both a leader and a manager. The leadership skills are needed to start a new programming venture in the community, and managerial skills are needed to develop and manage the new program.

Intrinsically, the leadership process offers ethical challenges because of the potential for misuse of authority and power. The *Occupational Therapy Code of Ethics and Ethics Standards* (AOTA, 2010) provides a guide to professional behavior by defining and describing six principles of ethical responsibility: (1) beneficence; (2) nonmaleficence; (3) autonomy, confidentiality; (4) social justice; (5) procedural justice; and (6) veracity. These principles guide occupational therapists toward ethical practice in all professional roles and therefore apply to the conduct of the therapist as leader in the emerging practice role.

Grady (2003) proposed the leadership practices developed by Kouzes and Posner (2003) as a framework for leadership in the profession of occupational therapy. This framework is also supported by AOTA and the American Occupational Therapy Foundation (2009) through a mentoring program for developing leaders in the profession. The first practice, "modeling the way" (Kouzes & Posner, 2003), identifies how colleagues should be treated and creates standards of excellence that are established as examples for others to follow. "Inspiring the vision" is a leadership practice that involves imagining the future and establishing a goal. Grady proposed that occupational therapists demonstrate this leadership practice as they work together with clients and families to "create a shared vision for the journey" (p. 334). When "challenging the process," leaders seek ways to change the routine and find creative ways to improve the program, services, or facility (Kouzes & Posner, 2003). Grady noted that this leadership practice offers therapists opportunities to advocate for changes in services systems and for community inclusion of persons with disabilities. "Enabling others to act" as a leader involves including others in the process and working in partnerships. It also involves ensuring that the work environment is characterized by trust and dignity and that others are empowered to act. The last leadership practice, "encouraging the heart," involves encouraging others by acknowledging and celebrating their endeavors (Kouzes & Posner, 2003). Grady suggested that occupational therapists implement this practice at multiple levels as they recognize the accomplishment of clients and colleagues alike.

Flexibility and adaptability are other qualities of effective managers of emerging practices. Silverthorne and Wang (2001) studied situational leadership style as a predictor of success and productivity. They used cross-sectional questionnaires and surveyed 79 managers and 234 subordinates among Taiwanese business organizations. They found that the more adaptive the leader was in style, the more productive the organization was.

Entrepreneurship

Therapists who take on the role of *entrepreneur* have been described in the literature using personal attributes such as innovativeness, resourcefulness, and vision (Wilson, Averis, & Walsh, 2003); using role descriptions such as "resource architects" who build effective organizations (Smilor & Sexton, 1996); and using descriptions of their ability to start new ventures or organizations (Gartner, 1985; Mort, Weerawardena, & Carnegie, 2002). *Opportunity recognition*, or the ability to identify an existing opportunity for development, is an important element of the entrepreneurial process. Successful entrepreneurs or entrepreneurial organizations not only recognize opportunities but capably take advantage of them for the eventual attainment of their goals (see Chapter 10 in this volume).

Thompson (2002) suggested that entrepreneurs recognize a need and an opportunity and are able to follow through with a vision and plan to address the need. They demonstrate the ability to enlist others to the cause and understand the value of networking. Additionally, as risk is inherent in entrepreneurial processes, all entrepreneurs overcome barriers and challenges to secure the necessary resources to launch new ventures or enterprises (Thompson, 2002). The delivery of occupational therapy services in community-based settings or other emerging practice areas requires these entrepreneurial skills to identify and address unmet needs through new practice methods (Fazio, 2001; Jacobs, 2002a; Scaffa, 2001).

Thus, among the multiple skills required of an entrepreneur, the ability to effectively lead the creation, transformation, and promotion of a new venture or service is critical to success. Educational programs need to provide future occupational therapists with a foundation of skills for management, marketing, research, and leadership in preparation for varied roles in diverse settings.

Consultation

Consultation is "an interactive process of helping others solve existing or potential problems by identifying and analyzing issues, developing strategies to address problems, and preventing future problems from occurring" (Epstein & Jaffe, 2003, p. 260; see Chapter 33 in this volume). Three types of consultation have been identified: task oriented, process oriented, and outcome based. In *task-oriented consultation*, the consultant is hired to complete a specific task as outlined in the consultation contract. An example of a task-oriented consultation is completing an accessibility survey of a facility or training long-term care staff in dementia management. In a *process-oriented consultation*, the consultant is hired to facilitate a process, usually for an organization—for example, strategic planning. In an *outcome-based consultation*, the consultant is hired to produce a specific outcome and is paid based on achieving this outcome. An outcome-based consultation might be writing a grant for program funding or assisting a facility in achieving accreditation.

Consultation is always client centered. Clients may be individuals, staff members, administrators, programs, or organizations. Dutton (1986) described three main issues in the development of a consultation contract: sponsorship, needs assessment, and outcome measures. The contract should identify the sponsor of the consultation, the limits of the sponsor's authority, and available facility support. In addition, a needs assessment should be conducted to determine the specific tasks and responsibilities required of each party and to incorporate these tasks and responsibilities into the contract. Identifying and agreeing on the type of consultation is critical to effectiveness. Finally, outcome measures should be specified at the outset after the goals for the consultation are established.

Consultation can serve several functions. One function is *prescriptive*—that is, the consultant provides advice or instructions based on his or her area of expertise. Another function is *informative*, when the consultant imparts new knowledge, instruction, or training to the consultee. A third function is *catalytic*, in which the consultant provides an incentive to enact change or address problems. An additional function is *confrontative*—that is, the consultant is critical and/or directive and challenges the status quo. Consultations often serve more than one function.

Consultations typically occur in stages. The first stage, or initiating the consultation, consists of preparing, identifying stakeholders, establishing rapport, and identifying the reasons for the consultation. *Stakeholders* are persons who have a vested interest in the problem or concern. They often have relevant information to share and can affect the success of a consultation or the development of a new program (Scaffa et al., 2010). The second stage consists of gathering background information, exploring the issues and problems, and analyzing the context. The third stage involves building the relationship and focusing on the client's needs, desires, and goals. The fourth stage is attending to the structure and function of the consultation, making the structure overt, and managing the process and flow of the work. The fifth stage involves providing the correct type and amount of information, achieving a shared understanding of the problem and potential solutions, and sharing decision making. The sixth stage is planning and implementing an action strategy. The final stage, or termination, includes evaluation of the consultation, a plan for follow-up if necessary, and achievement of a sense of closure for participants.

BASIC MANAGEMENT FUNCTIONS IN EMERGING PRACTICES

To analyze a prospective practice setting, occupational therapy managers must gain knowledge of the challenges and opportunities of an emerging practice area. They may use multiple strategies to develop ideas and programs, analyze outcomes, and garner resources to sustain the program. The following sections discuss four important strategies: identifying opportunities, doing strategic planning, garnering resources, and establishing partnerships. The specific services offered, the setting, and the unique role responsibilities required will determine the managerial skills needed to implement a successful program.

Identifying Opportunities

Identifying opportunities, or finding a niche, in an emerging practice area market may evolve through a variety of mechanisms.

Brainstorming

The occupational therapy practitioner may engage in a process that involves exploring ideas, services, and programs. *Brainstorming* is a key strategy for formulating an idea and can be done either formally or informally. In some cases, brainstorming may involve a structured process of determining ways to implement ideas (Baumgartner, 2003; Bond, Belensky, & Weinstock, 2000). In other cases, brainstorming occurs as a natural part of a discussion among peers, or one individual may act as a facilitator who can help direct the session and assist the group in formalizing ideas (Baumgartner, 2003; Fazio, 2008). A successful brainstorming group may include 8–12 people who can bring diverse ideas to the table. A brainstorming session may last 25–30 minutes, and all ideas are accepted without criticism. A leader who is informed about the brainstorming topic issues may be appointed to facilitate the group. The leader should be prepared to help the group formulate and document the ideas they generate (Baumgartner, 2003). The occupational therapy practitioner may lead the brainstorming group or may choose to have a neutral consultant lead the session. Brainstorming may also be used to engage in future planning or resolve challenges that arise.

Needs Assessment

Once ideas or foci of service provision in the emerging practice area are identified, the therapist assesses the viability of beginning the practice. A common approach to exploring viability of service provision in emerging practice areas is to conduct a *needs assessment*. A needs assessment is a process

Strengths	Weaknesses
External Factors: • Strong support from local psychiatrists • Substantiated need, large numbers of persons with mental disorders not receiving treatment • Support from mayor's office Internal Factors: • Committed leadership • Adequate business savvy • Previous history of providing day treatment services	External Factors: • Limited dollars available because of economic recession • Minimal experience of local psychiatrists with occupational therapy services Internal Factors: • Lack of adequate planning time • Limited financial and legal expertise • Minimal experience with establishing nonprofit organizations
Opportunities	Threats
External Factors: • Mental Health Parity Act of 1996 • Recent news stories about the needs of persons with mental disorders • State psychiatric hospital census over capacity Internal Factors: • Organizational growth potential • Expansion of existing services into new venues	External Factors: • Competition from a well-established mental health program that wants a monopoly on local services • Community concerns and resistance regarding location of program Internal Factors: • Lack of consensus among stakeholders • Inadequate start-up capital

Figure 21.1. SWOT analysis for the potential development of an occupational therapy–based community mental health day treatment center.

by which problems, needs, gaps, and issues are identified for the purpose of developing strategies or a program to address the concerns of a community or population (Issel, 2004). In a clinical setting, occupational therapists conduct needs assessments every day on individual clients through the evaluation process. A program needs assessment is conducted systematically following established procedures that allow the therapist to identify and explore needs and gaps in services as well as resources available in a given population (Brownson, 2001; Timmreck, 2003). Needs assessments, like brainstorming, may be completed either formally or informally. Techniques for assessing needs and capacities may include reviewing current literature; exploring demographics and area statistics; and conducting town hall meetings, focus groups, surveys, or interviews. The purpose of the needs assessment is to gather data regarding the feasibility of the idea and to explore the area of service provision or program as an appropriate fit for the context. The needs assessment results help frame a program to address the needs and capacities of a specific population in a specific context.

SWOT Analysis

A SWOT analysis is another approach that may be used initially to explore the value of an idea. A *SWOT analysis* is a formal analysis of a program's or idea's strengths, weaknesses, opportunities, and threats on multiple levels. The analysis first reviews the aspects of the internal environment that provide support (strengths) for the program and that inhibit (weaken) the program. Additionally, internal circumstances are reviewed to evaluate those that may provide growth (opportunities) or that may hold back (threats)

a program or idea implementation. After the internal environment and circumstances are evaluated, the analysis proceeds to the external environment and circumstances, including competition on a local, state, or national level and the impact of national policies and societal trends. According to Pazell and Jaffe (2003), a business owner must prepare for the unknown, and they identified five areas to consider: regulatory events, technological events, societal events, economic events, and competitive events. Although these events may be relatively unpredictable, the authors strongly suggested that occupational therapy entrepreneurs proactively consider the threats and identify strategies for responding to each. A SWOT analysis (see Figure 21.1 for an example) is a flexible approach to exploring what opportunities or challenges the occupational therapy practitioner will face. The analysis can be conducted at any time in a program to aid in initial strategic planning or ongoing program management.

Strategic Planning

Once a niche has been identified and viability of service provision has been established, a manager may engage in *strategic planning*, a systematic process of setting long-term organizational goals and priorities, identifying organizational activities, and predicting potential outcomes. Strategic planning aids an organization in defining its direction for the next 3–5 years and in identifying appropriate tactics for attaining the identified goals of a program (McNamara, 2008; see Chapter 6 in this volume). A strategic plan includes the priorities of the therapist or team, measurable goals, and a timeline for completion of activities. An effective plan is flexible enough to allow response to changes, making it an appropriate approach for emerging practice areas, which may be unpredictable (Foundation for Community Association Research, 2001).

Organization Type

One decision that needs to be made early in the process is whether the venture will be incorporated as a for-profit or nonprofit organization. There are many misconceptions about what it means to be a nonprofit organization. One misconception is that nonprofit organizations are prohibited from making a profit. This is entirely untrue. Well-managed nonprofits can and should make a profit to allow them to grow and deliver more and better services. The difference between for-profit and nonprofit organizations is where the profits go. In a nonprofit organization, the profits must be reinvested to enhance the organization and its programs. This may take the form of expanding facilities, purchasing equipment, adding staff, and starting new services. In a for-profit business, the profits are distributed among the shareholders. Most entrepreneurial ventures are set up as for-profit businesses, allowing business owners to use the profits in whatever way they desire.

Starting a nonprofit corporation often involves applying for grant funds, whereas for-profit businesses typically use small business or personal loans for start-up funds. The majority of funding available through federal, state, and foundation grants is restricted to nonprofit organizations that serve a community need. In addition to salary, nonprofit organizations can provide most, if not all, of the same benefits to employees as for-profit businesses. These benefits may include health insurance, financial support for professional travel, and retirement programs, among others. Nonprofit organizations are exempt from many of the usual taxes that for-profit businesses are required to pay, including taxes on profits and on goods that are purchased (Braveman, 2006).

Nonprofit status must be applied for and approved by the U.S. Internal Revenue Service. There are many advantages and disadvantages to both for-profit businesses and nonprofit organizations. The decision about incorporation as a for-profit or nonprofit should be based on a number of factors, including the mission or purpose of the business or organization and the desired outcomes. In health care, some facilities are nonprofit while others are for-profit. Many hospitals and home health care and hospice agencies are incorporated as nonprofit organizations, whereas private practices and investor-owned nursing homes and rehabilitation facilities are often set up as for-profit businesses.

Evaluation

How the program or services will be evaluated is another consideration during strategic planning (see Chapter 26 in this volume). The therapist should be able evaluate the effectiveness of the approach. In developing an evaluation plan, it is important to consider the design being used and the data to be collected. Evaluation plans demonstrate the outcomes of a program or approach and should be designed to target the outcomes. Plans also help the therapist be aware of the program's progress and impact. This information allows the manager to modify goals and objectives that are not being reached appropriately or in a timely manner. Evaluation planning should be done consistently to obtain ongoing feedback.

An evaluation plan outlines the who, what, when, where, and how of evaluating a program's outcomes. Evaluation data can be collected using a variety of methods, depending on the program, including sign-in sheets, surveys, focus groups, town hall meetings, or interviews. The manager is accountable for collecting the data required for analysis by both internal actors, such as the board of directors, and by external sources, such as grant funders. Furthermore, the manager must help identify who will collect the data and when the data will be collected. An evaluation plan can be developed as part of the strategic plan.

Garnering Resources

One goal of a manager in an emerging practice area may be to garner resources to support a program or organization. Resources include the financial and person power needed to achieve the goals of the program or organization. Managers are responsible for obtaining the resources needed to be successful. The previous strategies discussed, such as brainstorming, SWOT analysis, and strategic planning, help a manager identify the resources required for a program to be successful. A manager should be aware of the resources needed to sustain and grow an organization or program. Resources include not only dollars but also in-kind donations, staff, and volunteers. Identifying the availability and sources of resources often depends on the creativity and know-how of the manager. For example, financial support can be garnered from revenue, grants, corporate donations or sponsorships, and donations.

Revenue and Corporate Sponsorships

If an organization is for-profit, the manager should consider revenue and corporate sponsorships. Corporations often sponsor programs or organizations that fit with their mission and philosophy. The manager should network and develop relationships with corporations that typically provide sponsorship. In the case of revenue, the manager must develop a business model that allows for sufficient income to cover services and other expenses. Research should be completed comparing similar services, and a market rate should be established. The manager will need to develop a budget identifying expenses and expected income. Business expertise and savvy aid in ensuring that a program is successful.

Grants

Emerging practice areas may also be supported by *grants*, which provide financial support to an organization to implement a proposed program (see Chapter 11 in this volume).

Grants are usually available only to nonprofit organizations. Grant writing requires a unique skill set, and a manager may recruit a writer with this expertise to assist with complex grant applications. Some foundations, especially local ones, may have relatively simple applications or may provide funds because they believe in the mission of the organization. In this case, the manager should not hesitate to apply for funds.

Donations

Donations may be monetary or nonmonetary. Nonmonetary donations, often called "in-kind donations," include equipment, such as office machines, and services, such as a financial audit. In-kind donations support a program but are not financial in nature. Nonmonetary donations also include the donation of time. An organization may be more efficient if volunteers are used to help with program implementation. The manager may develop a volunteer job description and actively recruit volunteers. In some cases, a volunteer coordinator may be employed to recruit and train volunteers, develop a volunteer manual, and provide training. Volunteers should have liability insurance provided by the agency or program, and many organizations require volunteers to complete a background check. Managing volunteers can be challenging, as volunteers do not always perform in a volunteer position as responsibly as they do in a job.

Establishing Partnerships

In addition to the traditional team approach, managers should also consider partnership as a way to explore and develop emerging practice areas. A *partnership* is "a relationship of individuals or groups marked by mutual cooperation and responsibility" (*American Heritage College Dictionary*, 1997, p. 997). In a partnership, all parties come to the table with something to offer, and all parties benefit. In a partnership model, the manager and the partner collaborate on identifying needs and on developing and implementing the program. According to Suarez-Balcazar et al. (2005), maintaining a partnership requires seven principles: "(a) developing a relationship based on trust and mutual respect, (b) establishing a reciprocal learning style, (c) developing open lines of communication, (d) maximizing resources, (e) using a multi-methods approach, (f) respecting diversity and building cultural competence, and (g) sharing accountability" (p. 51). This list is neither sequential nor hierarchical; all principles are necessary in a successful partnership. Partnerships require commitment and time to develop and maintain, yet they can provide a forum for maximizing resources and impact.

One type of partnership is an *academic–community partnership* (also called *community–campus partnership*; Bringle & Hatcher, 2002; Suarez-Balcazar et al., 2005). Academic–community partnerships exist when an academic institution and a community or community agency work together to address a community need (Benoit, Jansson, Millar, & Phillips, 2005; Erwin, Blumenthal, Chapel, & Allwood, 2004).

Academic–community partnerships have a variety of models and structures. In most cases, academic institutions aid communities by conducting research or implementing important programs, while communities aid academic institutions by providing "real-world" data or learning experiences for students. Some partnerships are framed to focus on research, and others follow a service-learning model. In the service-learning model, the community receives services from students while allowing them to address learning objectives from didactic courses through community immersion. Examples include health screenings in which the student learns to administer the screening and the community member receives the needed screening free of charge or for a reduced fee. A manager should consider the resources an academic institution can offer to a program, such as student time or academic expertise.

Program Development

Although multiple program development models exist, this section explores one model that is well suited to programs in emerging practice areas. The PRECEDE (*Predisposing, Reinforcing, and Enabling Constructs in Educational Diagnosis and Evaluation*)–PROCEED (*Policy, Regulatory, and Organizational Constructs in Educational and Environmental Development*) model uses an approach that entails "a process of assessment and planning before putting a program in place (PRECEDE), followed by implementation and evaluation of the program (PROCEED)" (Edberg, 2007, p. 80). Green and Kreuter (1999) developed this ecological model to explain health behaviors and to provide a structured framework for program development and implementation. The purpose of the model is to help understand the complexity of a health problem and to provide focus in addressing a targeted need. The PRECEDE–PROCEED model occurs in phases that move from a broad focus to a narrow focus.

The purpose of *Phase 1, social assessment and situational analysis,* is to identify the need or problem. The goal of this phase is to explore quality of life and social factors affecting a health problem in a community. The role of health and its relationship to social factors is explored and discovered in this phase. There are multiple approaches to collecting the information for this phase, including talking to community leaders, holding focus groups, exploring public health data, and mapping assets. The manager can lead a team in gathering this information or assign roles and responsibilities for specific team members (Green & Kreuter, 1999).

Phase 2, epidemiological assessment, focuses on the extent of the health problem in the community. In this stage, a health condition is investigated by identifying who is affected by the health condition, how extensively the health condition permeates the community or population, and what trends surround the health condition (Edberg, 2007). Types of epidemiological data collected during this phase include prevalence, incidence, and mortality data. The manager can direct which health conditions are examined and what approaches are used to gather information.

In *Phase 3, behavioral and environmental assessment,* risk factors are identified related to both behavior and environment. *Behavioral risk factors* relate specifically to people, and *environmental risk factors* relate to the conditions that surround them.

Phase 4, educational and ecological assessment, involves exploration and analysis of what approaches can best be used to promote behavior change. Green and Kreuter (1999) identified several important factors to be assessed in this phase, including predisposing factors, enabling factors, and reinforcing factors. *Predisposing factors* are a group's knowledge, attitudes, beliefs, values, and perceptions. *Enabling factors* are the skills, resources, and barriers that facilitate or inhibit a behavior. *Reinforcing factors* are the rewards people receive for engaging in a particular behavior (Green & Kreuter, 1999).

Phase 5, administrative and policy assessment, is an exploration of the supports and infrastructure required to make the program a success. Supports and infrastructure include funding, established policies and procedures, and community involvement. In this phase, the focus is on budget, space, a timeline, and personnel. This phase is very practical and detailed; the manager delineates roles and identifies what components need to be completed and by whom. The manager needs to ensure that all the program components are developed and matched with assessment results (Green & Kreuter, 1999).

In *Phase 6, implementation,* the manager is responsible for program implementation and oversees the processes and procedures developed in Phase 5. The manager should maintain records to ensure that financials and program outcomes are appropriate and accurately documented.

Phases 7 through 9 are grouped together because they all focus on program evaluation. *Phase 7, process evaluation,* identifies if the program was implemented as planned, if goals were met, and if the need was addressed. In other words, this phase looks at the quality of the program and whether the program met established goals. *Phase 8, impact evaluation,* explores the short-term impact or changes made by the program—for example, changes in knowledge about a particular health topic. *Phase 9, outcome evaluation,* explores the long-term impact of the program to identify behavior change, improved quality of life, and impact on the community need (Green & Kreuter, 1999).

The PRECEDE–PROCEED model provides a comprehensive ecological approach to program development that occupational therapy practitioners can use in emerging practice areas and community practice settings to develop an efficient and effective health program. The model identifies specific phases for the development, implementation, and evaluation of a program; provides specific steps and roles in program implementation and evaluation; and guides managers in ensuring that a program is not missing a critical component required for success.

CONCLUSION

Managing emerging practice programs involves many of the same skills and actions as managing programs in other areas. For example, planning, organizing, coordinating, and supervising are required skills, in addition to communicating, decision making, negotiating, and leading. Management is typically less formal in style in emerging practice areas, however. Managers in such areas often use a more interactive approach that promotes open communication, feedback, and collaboration than managers in more traditional, institutionally driven medical settings. In traditional medical settings, there is more structure and hierarchy and a corresponding need for more clearly defined policies and standardized procedures.

Managers of emerging practice programs must be able to effectively communicate with a wide range of stakeholders and constituencies, many of whom are outside the traditional health care disciplines. Negotiation, collaboration, and the ability to effectively interact with and direct systems are also essential management skills in emerging practice areas.

Management of emerging practice programs is an evolving process. As more occupational therapists venture into these areas, the most promising management strategies will become more evident. For now, however, managers need to be adaptable and flexible in the application of management principles and practices in these new arenas. Just as is true in all areas of occupational therapy practice, management of programs in emerging practice areas should be based on the best available evidence. Effective managers find and evaluate data, information, and other forms of evidence to determine the best course of action in a specific situation (Braveman, 2006). Translating evidence into everyday practice is challenging, particularly in new service arenas.

Case Examples

LEVEL I FIELDWORK

Cassie was a Level I fieldwork student in an emerging practice early intervention program for children in a community-based setting. She noticed that the occupational therapy manager's approach was much different from the approaches of managers she had observed in medical settings. The manager was involved in various meetings and activities with program participants, parents, teachers, and community agencies. Cassie noticed that much of what the occupational therapy manager did was indirect-service provision and coordination of services. The manager asked Cassie to investigate funding options for the program. Using the Internet, Cassie identified several potential sources of financial support. She also found some organizations willing to donate materials and supplies for the program.

Cassie realized that much of the manager's time was spent in program maintenance activities while the occupational therapists and occupational therapy assistants under her supervision provided direct services to the children. The manager told Cassie that although she does not work directly with the children, she gets her satisfaction from seeing them and their families receive services to meet their needs, which sometimes requires referral to other programs and agencies.

The occupational therapy manager had a notebook of community resources, and she asked Cassie to verify that the agencies still existed and to locate any additional community resources. This enabled Cassie to learn more about the services offered in her community.

LEVEL II FIELDWORK

Ron, a Level II fieldwork student in an outpatient occupational therapy clinic, was asked to participate in the development of a needs assessment and SWOT analysis for a new lymphedema program. With the assistance of the occupational therapy manager, Ron identified several strategies for the needs assessment. He investigated other lymphedema services in the community and gathered statistics on the prevalence of lymphedema from the local hospital and community physicians. Ron also met with key informants, including lympedema practitioners and referring physicians. He noted that the practitioners sometimes had difficulty receiving reimbursement and that physicians often were unaware that lymphedema services were available in the community.

Ron presented his SWOT analysis to the occupational therapy staff and to the owners of the outpatient clinic. He stated that his investigation revealed a need for additional lymphedema services in the community, arguing that marketing to local physicians would be critically important to the success of the venture. Ron pointed out that the clinic currently had only one practitioner certified in lympedema, which he saw as a weakness. He suggested investing in training at least one additional occupational therapist. The clinic also had strengths: name recognition, a good reputation in the community, and already-established relationships with third-party payers. However, after much discussion, the group decided they needed more information about why other practitioners were having difficulty with reimbursement for lymphedema services.

FIRST-TIME MANAGER

A recently hired occupational therapy manager in an inpatient rehabilitation setting, Chris, was asked to assess the department and facility resources and make recommendations for how services might be expanded or developed to augment the services currently provided. Although initially overwhelmed by the assignment, Chris decided to start by gathering information from past and current patients. Chris conducted telephone interviews of patients who had been discharged in the past year and asked them what services they had needed in the hospital or after discharge that they did not receive. For current patients, he created a form for patients to complete prior to discharge on which they indicated what services they wished had been available at the rehabilitation facility and what services they thought they might need after they returned home. Some of the ideas generated from this strategy included driver training for persons with disabilities, transition back-to-work services for injured workers, and low vision services.

The rehabilitation facility was a member of the local Chamber of Commerce, so Chris decided to attend some of the meetings. He was surprised to hear that many local companies were having a difficult time obtaining work-hardening services for their employees. In addition, one chief executive officer of a large chain of discount stores expressed concerns about the number of injuries his employees were sustaining on the job and wondered how the injuries might have been prevented.

Chris learned that one occupational therapist and one physical therapist in the rehabilitation division had advanced training in ergonomics and work hardening. He met with these therapists and gathered information from the literature about ergonomics and work hardening. At a meeting with his supervisor, the manager of the rehabilitation division, Chris suggested quickly adding a transition-to-work component to their existing therapy services to meet the needs of a current subset

(continued)

Case Examples *(cont.)*

of patients who wanted or needed to return to work. In addition, he recommended that the rehabilitation division initiate contracts with local businesses to provide ergonomics consultation to prevent work injuries. Chris stated that in the long-term, it could be beneficial to develop a work-hardening program at the facility or in a community site in the city's industrial park.

MANAGER

Annette, an occupational therapist who had had manager roles for 12 years, wished to establish her own occupational therapy private practice to meet a community need. Several newspaper articles had recently appeared regarding the unmet needs of older adults in her community, indicating a demand for aging-in-place services. Annette began by reviewing models for aging services that had demonstrated effectiveness through research studies. She was particularly interested in the Lifestyle

Redesign services provided by the occupational therapy department at the University of Southern California in Los Angeles. Using the PRECEDE–PROCEED planning model, she conducted social, epidemiological, and environmental assessments to determine the factors affecting the health of older adults in her city. She identified predisposing, reinforcing, and enabling factors and began to design her program on the basis of these factors and the principles of the Lifestyle Redesign program.

Annette met with key informants and stakeholders, including the city's mayor and town council, as well as local and state agencies that provide services to the elderly. She was told the local community foundation had a request for proposals for a home modification program for elderly and disabled citizens. With this new information, she began to read the professional literature on home modifications to identify evidence-based practices. Annette knew that if she was going to apply for this funding, she needed to be sure that what she proposed was based on the best possible research findings.

❖ Learning Activities

1. Interview an occupational therapist who is working in an emerging practice area. Ask him or her which competencies are necessary to succeed in emerging practice. What differences does he or she see between managing a traditional, medical-model occupational therapy service in comparison to managing an emerging-practice occupational therapy service?
2. Read your local newspaper for 1 week, and identify, unmet needs in your community that occupational therapy might address.
3. Investigate the opportunities and potential sites (e.g.,

homeless shelter, substance abuse treatment program) in your community for developing an emerging practice program in each of the 6 practice areas identified by AOTA (2009a).
4. Pick one of the opportunities or sites identified in Learning Activity 3, and apply SWOT analysis to explore the feasibility of your emerging practice idea.
5. Interview an occupational therapy or non–occupational therapy manager of a community-based service. Ask him or her about the challenges and rewards of community-based work.

✔ Multiple-Choice Questions

1. The American Occupational Therapy Association (AOTA) reorganized and prioritized occupational therapy practice, both traditional and emerging, into which of the following 6 overarching areas?
   a. Mental health; productive aging; children and youth; health and wellness; work and industry; and rehabilitation, disability, and participation.
   b. Psychosocial, lifespan, development, health and wellness, work and industry, and rehabilitation.
   c. Psychiatry, aging in place, children and youth, wellness, work, and disability and participation.
   d. Mental health; aging in place; development; health

   promotion; work and industry; and rehabilitation, disability, and participation.
2. The practitioner best suited to practice in emerging areas demonstrates qualities and characteristics such as which of the following?
   a. Self-starter, self-directed, adaptable to new situations.
   b. Able to step outside of the medical model and to challenge the status quo.
   c. Self-confident, persevering, determined, persistent, and flexible.
   d. All of the above.

3. Emerging practice areas in occupational therapy include which of the following?
   a. New offerings of services in traditional settings.
   b. Services provided in nontraditional settings.
   c. Services in community-based settings.
   d. All of the above.
4. Professional competencies and optimal strategies identify knowledge as an important component for working in an emerging practice in occupational therapy. Such knowledge includes which of the following?
   a. Principles of client-centered practice, program development, community systems, and public health and practice-specific principles and practice models.
   b. Holistic reasoning, translation of theory to practice, problem solving, and "outside-the-box" thinking.
   c. Envisioning of occupational therapy roles and service possibilities; implementation of client-centered practices; assessment, evaluation, and provision of intervention; consultation; collaborative work; and identification of and access to available resources.
   d. Self-assessment of strengths and needs for ongoing professional development and principles of occupational and social justice.
5. Professional competencies and optimal strategies identify critical reasoning as an important component for working in an emerging practice in occupational therapy. Critical reasoning includes which of the following?
   a. Holistic reasoning, translation of theory to practice, problem solving, and "outside-the-box" thinking.
   b. Active listening, communication of occupational therapy concepts to a variety of audiences, establishment of relationships with key stakeholders and leaders, effective networking with other professionals, effective negotiation, demonstration of cultural competence, and understanding and use of language and terms of other professions.
   c. Envisioning of occupational therapy roles and service possibilities; implementation of client-centered practices; assessment, evaluation, and provision of intervention; consultation; collaborative work; and identification of and access to available resources.
   d. Self-assessment of strengths and needs for ongoing professional development and principles of occupational and social justice.
6. Professional competencies and optimal strategies identify interpersonal abilities as an important component for working in an emerging practice in occupational therapy. Interpersonal abilities include which of the following?
   a. Principles of client-centered practice, program development, community systems, and public health and practice-specific principles and practice models.
   b. Active listening, communication of occupational therapy concepts to a variety of audiences, establishment of relationships with key stakeholders and leaders, effective networking with other professionals, effective negotiation, demonstration of cultural competence, and understanding and use of language and terms of other professions.
   c. Envisioning of occupational therapy roles and service possibilities; implementation of client-centered practices; assessment, evaluation, and provision of intervention; consultation; collaborative work; and identification of and access to available resources.
   d. Self-assessment of strengths and needs for ongoing professional development and principles of occupational and social justice.
7. Professional competencies and optimal strategies identify performance skills as an important component for working in an emerging practice in occupational therapy. Performance skills include which of the following?
   a. Principles of client-centered practice, program development, community systems, and public health and practice-specific principles and practice models.
   b. Holistic reasoning, translation of theory to practice, problem solving, and "outside-the-box" thinking.
   c. Self-assessment of strengths and needs for ongoing professional development and principles of occupational and social justice.
   d. Envisioning of occupational therapy roles and service possibilities; implementation of client-centered practices; assessment, evaluation, and provision of intervention; consultation; collaborative work; and identification of and access to available resources.
8. Professional competencies and optimal strategies identify ethical reasoning as an important component for working in an emerging practice in occupational therapy. Ethical reasoning includes which of the following?
   a. Holistic reasoning, translation of theory to practice, problem solving, and "outside-the-box" thinking.
   b. Active listening, communication of occupational therapy concepts to a variety of audiences, establishment of relationships with key stakeholders and leaders, effective networking with other professionals, effective negotiation, demonstration of cultural competence, and understanding and use of language and terms of other professions.
   c. Self-assessment of strengths and needs for ongoing professional development and principles of occupational and social justice.

d. Envisioning of occupational therapy roles and service possibilities; implementation of client-centered practices; assessment, evaluation, and provision of intervention; consultation; collaborative work; and identification of and access to available resources.

9. The concept of needs assessment in emerging practice areas is similar to which concept in medical-model practice?
   a. Intervention.
   b. Intervention planning.
   c. Initial evaluation.
   d. Reevaluation.

10. *Intrapreneurship* refers to
    a. Creating a new business entity.
    b. Initiating a nonprofit organization.
    c. Creating a new service within an existing program.
    d. Analyzing the cost-effectiveness of an intervention.

11. Which of the following is *not* a factor influencing the growth of health care expenditures?
    a. Changing demographics in the United States.
    b. Infant mortality.
    c. Economic factors such as medical inflation.
    d. Inefficient provision of services.

12. All of the following are models of emerging practice *except*
    a. Intrapreneurship.
    b. Organization infusion.
    c. Corporate infusion.
    d. Corporate mergers.

13. The range of roles and responsibilities of managers in medical-model settings is more diverse than in community-based practice settings.
    a. True; managers in medical-model settings have many more responsibilities.
    b. True; managers in emerging practice settings are limited by their formal job descriptions.
    c. False; managers in medical-model settings have many fewer responsibilities.
    d. False; managing an emerging practice encompasses multiple professional roles and responsibilities.

14. Kouzes and Posner (2003) outlined all of the following practices of leadership *except*
    a. Delegating effectively.
    b. Modeling the way.
    c. Encouraging the heart.
    d. Inspiring the vision.

15. Facilitating a strategic planning session for the board of directors of a newly formed nonprofit organization is an example of which type of consultation?
    a. Task-oriented.
    b. Process-oriented.
    c. Outcome-based.
    d. Prescriptive.

16. The goals of strategic planning include all of the following *except*
    a. Setting priorities.
    b. Predicting potential outcomes.
    c. Identifying program and organization activities.
    d. Determining cost-effectiveness.

17. Which of the following is a difference between for-profit and nonprofit corporations?
    a. One has a board of directors, and the other does not.
    b. One can receive donations, and the other cannot.
    c. One pays dividends to stockholders, and the other does not.
    d. One can provide employee benefits, and the other cannot.

18. All of the following are considered in-kind donations *except* donation of
    a. Equipment.
    b. Services.
    c. Cash.
    d. Products.

19. Three functions of consultation are
    a. Adaptation, enhancement, and timeliness.
    b. Prescriptive, informative, and catalytic.
    c. Formative, summative, and evaluative.
    d. Contributory, relevant, and timely.

20. Which of the following is *not* true regarding the PRECEDE–PROCEDE model?
    a. The model uses an ecological framework.
    b. The purpose of the model is to provide focus in addressing a targeted need.
    c. The model occurs in stages moving from a narrow focus to a broad focus.
    d. The model addresses quality of life and social factors that affect health.

References

Accreditation Council for Occupational Therapy Education. (2007). Accreditation standards for a master's-degree-level educational program for the occupational therapist. *American Journal of Occupational Therapy, 61,* 652–661.

Amat, S. W. (2008). *Cultivating innovation: The role of mentoring in the innovation process.* Unpublished doctoral dissertation, University of Miami. Retrieved January 8, 2010, from http://etd.library.miami.edu/theses/available/etd-06252008-075516/

American heritage college dictionary (3rd ed.). (1997). Boston: Houghton Mifflin.

American Occupational Therapy Association. (2006). 2006 AOTA workforce and compensation survey: Occupational therapy salaries and job opportunities continue to improve [Electronic version]. *OT Practice, 11*(17), 10–12.

American Occupational Therapy Association. (2007). AOTA's *Centennial Vision* and executive summary. *American Journal of Occupational Therapy, 61,* 613–614.

American Occupational Therapy Association. (2009a). *Emerging practice areas.* Retrieved August 18, 2010, from http://www.aota.org/Practitioners/PracticeAreas/Emerging.aspx

American Occupational Therapy Association. (2009b). *Occupational therapy practice areas for the 21st century.* Retrieved August 18, 2010, from http://www.aota.org/Practitioners/PracticeAreas.aspx

American Occupational Therapy Foundation. (2009). *Leadership fellows program.* Retrieved August 18, 2010, from http://www.aotf.org/programspartnerships/jointinitiativeswithaota/leadershipfellowsprogram.aspx

American Occupational Therapy Association. (2010). Occupational therapy code of ethics and ethics standards (2010). *American Journal of Occupational Therapy, 64.*

Baum, C. M. (2000, January 3). Occupation-based practice: Reinventing ourselves for the new millennium. *OT Practice,* pp. 12–15.

Baum, C. M. (2006). Centennial challenges, millennium opportunities [Presidential Address]. *American Journal of Occupational Therapy, 60,* 609–616.

Baum, C., & Law, M. (1998). Nationally Speaking—Community health: A responsibility, an opportunity, and a fit for occupational therapy. *American Journal of Occupational Therapy, 52,* 7–10.

Baumgartner, J. (2003). *The step-by-step guide to brainstorming.* Retrieved August 18, 2010, from http://www.jpb.com/creative/brainstorming.php

Benoit, C., Jansson, M., Millar, A., & Phillips, R. (2005). Community–academic research on hard-to-reach populations: Benefits and challenges. *Qualitative Health Research, 15,* 263–282.

Berwick, D. M. (2003). Disseminating innovations in health care. *JAMA, 289,* 1969–1975.

Bond, L. A., Belensky, M. F., & Weinstock, J. S. (2000). The Listening Partners Program: An initiative toward feminist community psychology in action. *American Journal of Community Psychology, 28,* 697–730.

Brachtesende, A. (2005). The turnaround is here! *OT Practice, 23*(1), 13–19.

Braveman, B. (2006). *Leading and managing occupational therapy services: An evidence-based approach.* Philadelphia: F. A. Davis.

Bringle, R. G., & Hatcher, J. A. (2002). University–community partnerships: The terms of engagement. *Journal of Social Issues, 58,* 503–516.

Brownson, C. A. (2001). Program development: Planning, implementation, and evaluation strategies. In M. Scaffa (Ed.), *Occupational therapy in community-based practice settings* (pp. 95–118). Philadelphia: F. A. Davis.

Drucker, P. F. (1985). *Innovation and entrepreneurship: Practice and principles.* New York: Harper & Row.

Dudgeon, B. J., & Greenberg, S. L. (1998). Preparing students for consultation roles in systems. *American Journal of Occupational Therapy, 52,* 801–809.

Dutton, R. (1986). Procedures for designing an occupational therapy consultation contract. *American Journal of Occupational Therapy, 40,* 160–166.

Edberg, M. (2007). *Essentials of health behavior: Social and behavioral theory in public health.* Boston: Jones & Bartlett.

Epstein, C. F., & Jaffe, E. G. (2003). Consultation: Collaborative interventions for change. In G. L. McCormack, E. G. Jaffe, & M. Goodman-Lavey (Eds.), *The occupational therapy manager* (4th ed., pp. 259–286). Bethesda, MD: AOTA Press.

Erwin, K., Blumenthal, D. S., Chapel, T., & Allwood, L. V. (2004). Building an academic–community partnership for increasing the representation of minorities in the health professions. *Journal of the Poor and Underserved, 15,* 589–602.

Estes, R. I., Fette, C., & Scaffa, M. E. (2005). Effecting successful community re-entry: Systems of Care community-based mental health services. *Residential Treatment for Children and Youth, 23*(1–2), 133–150.

Fazio, L. S. (2001). *Developing occupation-centered programs for the community: A workbook for students and professionals.* Upper Saddle River, NJ: Prentice Hall.

Fazio, L. (2008). *Developing occupation-centered programs for the community* (2nd ed.). Upper Saddle River, NJ: Prentice Hall.

Fette, C. V., & Estes, R. I. (2009). Community participation needs of families with children with behavioral disorders: A systems of care approach. *Occupational Therapy in Mental Health, 25*(1), 44–61.

Foto, M. (1998). Competence and the occupational therapy entrepreneur. *American Journal of Occupational Therapy, 52,* 765–769.

Foundation for Community Association Research. (2001). *Best practices: Strategic planning.* Alexandria, VA: Foundation for Community Association Research.

Gartner, W. B. (1985). A conceptual framework for describing the phenomenon of new venture creation [Electronic version]. *Academy of Management Review, 10,* 698–708.

Gilfoyle, E. M. (1986). Professional directions: Management in action. *American Journal of Occupational Therapy, 40,* 593–596.

Glennon, T. J. (2007). Putting on your business hat [Electronic version]. *OT Practice, 12*(3), 23–25.

Grady, A. P. (2003). From management to leadership. In G. L. McCormack, E. G. Jaffe, & M. Goodman-Lavey (Eds.), *The occupational therapy manager* (4th ed., pp. 331–347). Bethesda, MD: AOTA Press.

Green, L. W., & Kreuter, M. W. (1999). *Health promotion planning: An educational and ecological approach.* Palo Alto, CA: Mayfield Publishing.

Holmes, W., & Scaffa, M. (2009). An exploratory study of competencies for emerging practice in occupational therapy. *Journal of Allied Health, 38,* 81–90.

Individuals with Disabilities Education Act of 1990, Pub. L. 101-476, 20 U.S.C. 33.

Issel, L. M. (2004). *Health program planning and evaluation: A practical, systematic approach for community health.* Boston: Jones & Bartlett.

Jacobs, K. (2002a, June 24). Navigating the road ahead. *OT Practice,* 24–30.

Jacobs, K. (2002b). OT and AOTA: Moving with our cheese. *American Journal of Occupational Therapy, 56,* 9–18.

Johnson, C. R., Koenig, K. P., Piersol, C. V., Santalucia, S. E., & Wachter-Schutz, W. (2006). Level I fieldwork today: A study of contexts and perceptions. *American Journal of Occupational Therapy, 60,* 275–287.

Kiss, D. (2007, August 13). Handwriting consultation in elementary schools. *OT Practice,* pp. 11–14.

Koenig, L., Siegel, J. M., Dobson, A., Hearle, K., & Rudowitz, R. (2003, June). Drivers of health care expenditures associated with physician's services [Electronic version]. *American Journal of Managed Care,* Spec. No. 1, SP34–42.

Kouzes, J. M., & Posner, B. Z. (2003). *Leadership practices inventory.* San Francisco: Pfeiffer.

Loukas, K. M. (2000, July 3). Emerging models of innovative community-based occupational therapy practice: The vision continues. *OT Practice, 5,* 9–11.

McNamara, C. (2008). *Strategic planning.* Retrieved August 18, 2010, from http://www.managementhelp.org/plan_dec/str_plan/str_plan.htm

Mental Health Parity Law of 1996, Pub. L. 104–204.

Miron, E., Erez, M., & Naveh, E. (2004). Do personal characteristics and cultural values that promote innovation, quality and efficiency compete or complement each other? *Journal of Organizational Behavior, 25,* 175–199.

Mort, G. S., Weerawardena, J., & Carnegie, K. (2002, July). Social entrepreneurship: Towards conceptualization [Electronic version]. *International Journal of Nonprofit and Voluntary Sector Marketing, 8*(1), 76–88.

O'Connor, S. M. (2000, May 8). OTs and office ergonomics consultation. *OT Practice,* 12–17.

Pattison, M. (2006). WFOT Congress—OT outstanding talent: An entrepreneurial approach to practice. *Australian Occupational Therapy Journal, 53,* 166–172.

Pazell, S., & Jaffe, E. G. (2003). Entrepreneurial ventures. In G. L. McCormack, E. G. Jaffe, & M. Goodman-Levy (Eds.), *The occupational therapy manager* (4th ed., pp. 219–255). Bethesda, MD: AOTA Press.

Rogers, E. M. (2003). *Diffusion of innovations* (5th ed.). New York: Free Press.

Sandstrom, R. W., Lohman, H. L., & Bramble, J. D. (2003). *Health services: Policy and systems for therapists.* Upper Saddle River, NJ: Prentice Hall.

Scaffa, M. (2001). *Occupational therapy in community-based practice settings.* Philadelphia: F. A. Davis.

Scaffa, M. E., Reitz, S. M. & Pizzi, M. A. (2010). *Occupational therapy in the promotion of health and wellness.* Philadelphia: F. A. Davis.

Schell, B. A. B., & Slater, D. Y. (1998). Management competencies required of administrative and clinical practitioners in the new millennium. *American Journal of Occupational Therapy, 52,* 744–750.

Silverthorne, C., & Wang, T. H. (2001). Situational leadership style as a predictor of success and productivity among Taiwanese business organizations. *Journal of Psychology, 135,* 399–412.

Smilor, R. W., & Sexton, D. L. (Eds.). (1996). *Leadership and entrepreneurship: Personal and organizational development in entrepreneurial ventures.* Westport, CT: Quorum Books.

Somech, A. (2006). The effects of leadership style and team process on performance and innovation in functionally heterogeneous teams. *Journal of Management, 32,* 132–157.

Stancliff, B. L. (1997). Emerging practice areas: Going where no OT practitioner has gone before. *OT Practice, 2*(7), 16–23.

Suarez-Balcazar, Y., Hammel, J., Helfrich, C., Thomas, J., Wilson, T., & Head-Ball, D. (2005). A model of university–community partnerships for occupational therapy scholarship and practice. *Occupational Therapy in Health Care, 19*(1/2), 47–70.

Thompson, J. L. (2002). The world of the social entrepreneur [Electronic version]. *International Journal of Public Sector Management, 15,* 412–431.

Ticket to Work and Work Incentives Improvement Act of 1999, Pub. L. 106–170.

Timmreck, T. C. (2003). *Planning, program development and evaluation* (2nd ed.). Boston: Jones & Bartlett.

U.S. Department of Health and Human Services. (2000). *Healthy People 2010: Understanding and improving health* (2nd ed.). Washington, DC: U.S. Government Printing Office.

U.S. Department of Health and Human Services. (2009). *Healthy people 2020: The road ahead.* Retrieved from http://www.healthypeople.gov/HP2020

van Zwet-de Savornin Lohman, H. H. J. (1999). A protocol for occupational therapists: Consultant for adaptations and technical aids. *Technology and Disability, 11,* 65–69.

West, M. A., Borrill, C. S., Dawson, J. F., Brodbeck, F., Shapiro, D. A., & Haward, B. (2003). Leadership clarity and team innovation in health care. *Leadership Quarterly, 14,* 393–410.

Wilson, A., Averis, A., & Walsh, K. (2003). The influences on and experiences of becoming nurse entrepreneurs: A Delphi study. *International Journal of Nursing Practice, 9,* 236–245.

Appendix 21.1. Emerging Practice Areas Evidence Table

Topic	Evidence
Leadership style	West, M. A., Borrill, C. S., Dawson, J. F., Brodbeck, F., Shapiro, D. A., & Haward, B. (2003). Leadership clarity and team innovation in health care. *Leadership Quarterly, 14,* 393–410.
Team process	Somech, A. (2006). The effects of leadership style and team process on performance and innovation in functionally heterogeneous teams. *Journal of Management, 32,* 132–157.
Work culture	Miron, E., Erez, M., & Naveh, E. (2004). Do personal characteristics and cultural values that promote innovation, quality, and efficiency compete or complement each other? *Journal of Organizational Behavior, 25,* 175–199.
Mentoring	Amat, S. W. (2008). *Cultivating innovation: The role of mentoring in the innovation process.* Unpublished doctoral dissertation, University of Miami. Retrieved January 8, 2010, from http://etd.library.miami.edu/theses/available/etd-06252008-075516/
Strategies for diffusion	Berwick, D. M. (2003). Disseminating innovations in health care. *JAMA, 289,* 1969–1975.

Part IV

Controlling Outcomes

22

Evidence-Based Practice

Beatriz C. Abreu, PhD, OTR, FAOTA, and Pei-Fen J. Chang, PhD, OTR

❖ Key Terms and Concepts

Evidence-based decisions. The process of coming to a conclusion or making a judgment that combines clinical expertise, patient concerns, and evidence gathered from scientific literature to arrive at best-practice recommendations.

Evidence-based practice. The formal gathering and synthesis of information from research findings through systematic research review to determine best clinical practice.

Management. The oganizational process that includes strategic planning, setting objectives, managing resources,

deploying the human and financial assets needed to achieve desired objectives, and measuring results.

Professional literature. The body of literary work, worldwide or relating to a specific culture, suitable for a skilled practitioner or an expert.

Research utilization. Summarizing and using research findings to address a practice problem.

❖ Learning Objectives

After completing this chapter, you should be able to do the following:

- Define *evidence-based practice (EBP)*.
- Describe the 5 steps to follow in using EBP.
- Describe the value and criticism of EBP.
- Outline management strategies that are useful for optimal implementation of EBP.

- Describe the research design hierarchy and the characteristics of quantitative and qualitative research design used for EBP.

To meet today's increasing demand for quality- and efficiency-driven health care, a highly competent workforce is vital for achieving good managerial results. Teaching staff to become more competent problem solvers has developed into an essential skill for occupational therapy managers, and evidence-based practice (EBP) is one way to create and sustain competency in the workplace. Managers use evidence and data to inform their decision making in order to develop and support effective clinical programs and efficient evaluation and intervention procedures (Bailey,

Bornstein, & Ryan, 2007; Braveman, 2006; Kleiser & Cox, 2008; Tickle-Degnen, 2008). Not all decisions made by a manager can be evidence based; managers' decisions are also based on consensus, expert opinion, and their own experience in the organization. In addition, clinical decisions must be made on a case-by-case basis, taking into account the client's personal and social environments. This chapter contains practical and simplified information that managers in occupational therapy can use to support and guide problem-solving decisions.

The authors acknowledge **Kenneth J. Ottenbacher, PhD, OTR, FAOTA,** for his numerous writings and his help as a resource person offering guidelines for analysis and critique of data interpretation even before EBP emerged. We are grateful to **Renee Pearcy** for her research support. This project was partially supported by Moody Endowment #2008-25.

What Is EBP?

EBP is the formal gathering and synthesis of information from research findings through systematic research review to determine best clinical practice. This method is derived from evidence-based medicine (Law & MacDermid, 2008; Sackett, Straus, Richardson, Rosenberg, & Haynes, 2000). EBP is an evolving process. It has its roots in medical outcomes, transformed to evidence-based medicine, expanded into EBP, and more recently further expanded to the broad area of evidence-based health care.

EBP assists occupational therapists and occupational therapy assistants in providing sufficient evidence to third-party payers to establish the effect of occupational therapy services on health outcomes and demonstrate that occupational therapy interventions are effective, beneficial, and cost-effective. Every practitioner in the field is responsible for the validation of occupational therapy services. The best outcomes provide the best evidence for practice. The best practice provides occupational therapists and occupational therapy assistants—whether they are providing services or managing—with the opportunity to render better client care and more optimal program evaluation and quality improvement systems.

Value and Criticism of EBP

The *Centennial Vision* of the American Occupational Therapy Association (AOTA, 2007) has challenged the profession to produce research evidence that demonstrates effectiveness in all areas of practice (Gutman, 2008). The ability to incorporate research findings into practice is the expectation and demand on the occupational therapy profession and the institutions where occupational therapists and occupational therapy assistants are employed (Holm, 2000; Johnston & Case-Smith, 2009; Ottenbacher & Hinderer, 2001). However, the manager faces the challenge of searching through, sorting out, and transferring knowledge from a dramatically expanding body of information, which includes impressive research advances beyond the realm of the occupational therapy literature. In addition, resistance to and criticism of EBP are emerging based on tensions and contradictions between the recommendations of EBP and those of client-centered practice (Isaac & Franceschi, 2008; Jutel, 2008).

Many traditional evidence hierarchies rate the findings of randomized controlled trials and systematic reviews as the gold standard and arguably minimize the evidence contributions from the client's values and practitioners' expertise perspective (Reagon, Bellin, & Boniface, 2008). An occupational therapy manager needs to develop strategies for translating and implementing the knowledge from peer-reviewed articles to daily practice (Caldwell, Whitehead, Fleming, & Moes, 2008; Ketelaar, Russell, & Gorter, 2008; Kleiser & Cox, 2008). In addition, the manager has a critical role in emphasizing the plurality of evidence, which includes the institution's clinical expertise and clients' values and preferences, to facilitate the use of EBP. Managers should ensure that resources are available to empower occupational therapy practitioners to be accountable for evidence-based outcomes.

Five Steps to Follow in EBP

A complete description of the EBP process for managers is beyond the scope of this chapter. Readers are referred Sackett et al. (2000) and Law and MacDermid (2008) for a more in-depth examination. This chapter describes five critical steps for managers to use in implementing EBP in clinical reasoning and problem solving. These steps include (1) formulate the question, (2) search and sort the evidence, (3) critically appraise the evidence, (4) apply to practice, and (5) self-assess. This section identifies examples, strengths, and limitations of these steps and their research and educational implications.

1. Formulate the Question

The first step, formulating the question, is to turn the clinical problem into a question. In occupational therapy, questions arise from everyday practice and occupation-based queries that stimulate the need to examine the research literature evidence. The questions can be in any topic or area related to (1) therapy/prevention, (2) etiology/harm, (3) prognosis, (4) diagnosis, and (5) economic analysis (Sackett et al., 2000). Law and MacDermid (2008) suggested a sample format for an appropriate question that can yield good results: "For persons with condition *A*, will treatment *X* be more effective than treatment *Y* in leading to outcome *P* or increasing function in outcome *P*?" (p. 190).

The therapist can frame evidence-based searching related to client care questions in many ways. For example, two types of treatment questions have to do with effectiveness and efficacy. *Effectiveness* of treatment refers to the steps the practitioner takes to ensure that occupational therapy interventions produce changes in the client's performance during his or her stay in the client's discharge environment (Ottenbacher & Hinderer, 2001). Effectiveness evidence is provided by positive findings in outcome research, including the use of outcome measures, such as the Functional Independence Measure (*Guide for the Uniform Data Set for Medical Rehabilitation*, 1997) to study the results of rehabilitation (McKenna et al., 2002) and the Community Integration Questionnaire (Willer, Rosenthal, Kreutzer, Gordon, & Rempel, 1994) to study participation results after rehabilitation (Zhang et al., 2002). Effectiveness studies answer the questions, Did the clients improve after receiving occupational therapy? and How much did they improve?

Treatment *efficacy* examines the relationship of a particular treatment intervention and outcome measures under very controlled or optimal conditions (Clark et al., 1997; Ottenbacher & Hinderer, 2001) and answers the question, Which treatment made the clients better? Evidence of treatment efficacy is more difficult to obtain in occupational therapy. Efficacy research uses controlled experiments with two or more groups of participants—one group receives the treatment under investigation, and a second group receives a standard treatment or a placebo intervention (i.e., a treatment with no known therapeutic value). Another control measure used in high-quality efficacy studies such as clinical trials involves the allocation of the client to a group in a fashion that guarantees no selection bias (i.e., randomization). The single-blind method controls for participants' awareness of the type of treatment they are receiving. Controlling for both participants' and investigators' awareness of the treatment they are receiving or providing is called *double-blinding* and adds another layer of quality control and rigor to the investigation.

Efficacy evidence requires the use of the most rigorous experimental research design, called the *randomized controlled trial (RCT)*. A properly controlled clinical trial is valued as having the most powerful experimental design and providing the most evidence for evaluating the effectiveness of a particular intervention. A *clinical trial* has been defined as a prospective (followed forward) study comparing the value and the effect of an occupational therapy intervention group against a control group that does not receive treatment. An elegant clinical trial in occupational therapy published in *JAMA* supported the benefits of occupational therapy as a preventive health program for independent living in older adults (Clark et al., 1997). An occupational therapy group, a social activity group, and a no-treatment control group were compared after 9 months of treatment. The findings showed significant health, function, and quality-of-life benefits attributable to preventive occupational therapy services.

Efficacy questions sometimes cannot be answered fully because of methodological barriers, such as the ethical issues surrounding clinical trials. Some of these ethical issues involve flaws in the research design. One example is when pharmaceutical companies provide financial incentives for primary investigators to recruit participants for the study. Rao (1999) observed that financial gain for recruiting research participants is unethical because it makes RCTs lucrative and may compromise the care of clients who are not in the trial. The ethics of withholding the best treatment from a control group has also been questioned in studies where the intervention that is withheld can save lives. Some trials provide the treatment to the control group as well after the study has been completed. RCTs are expensive and time-consuming and place high demands on people resources. They are also difficult to implement in clinical practice, and their value can be compromised if they are driven by the researcher's interest rather than the needs of the client.

Johnston and Case-Smith (2009) suggested guidelines for RCTs in occupational therapy to promote the development, refinement, and testing of occupational therapy interventions. They advocated the use of a systematic approach for creating intervention evidence, including (1) specifying the intervention; (2) blinding participants, therapists, and evaluators; and (3) identifying objective but client-centered interventions. In addition, they suggested a typology of research development for occupational therapy (based on pharmaceutical RCT development) that includes the following phases:

- The *pre-RCT research phase* includes development of tools, theories, and measures to understand function, activities, occupations, environments, beliefs, and needs of clients.
- *RCT Phase I* includes preliminary and exploratory intervention studies.
- *RCT Phase II* includes small or other well-controlled efficacy studies.
- *RCT Phase III* includes rigorous control, blinding of evaluators, and adequate statistical power; the treatment intervention is clearly defined and treatment fidelity measured.
- *Phase IV* includes treatment use in practice and outcome measurement to evaluate the possibility of generalization to other populations, settings, and treatment variations that occur in clinical and community practice.

Readers are referred to Johnston and Case-Smith (2009) for further detail.

Other questions can be formulated that go beyond occupational therapy treatment and relate to the managerial issue of quality improvement. These questions explore areas that support a continuous drive to improve service delivery performance, reduction of costs for services, and elimination of errors (Byers & Beaudin, 2002; Morahan, 2002). For example, the occupational therapy manager may use EBP to facilitate a change in policy in the workplace that will improve the quality of the health care process. A *policy* is a plan of action or statement of ideas proposed and adopted by a government, institution, or profession. Policies come in many forms, including those that determine funding in health care; public health policies; and clinical policies such as pathways, protocols, clinical standards, expert recommendations, and decision analyses that state what should be done in practice (*Oxford English Dictionary*, 1995). Muir Gray, Haynes, Sackett, Cook, and Guyatt (1997) noted that the best policy and decisions are built on sound evidence.

2. Search and Sort the Evidence

The second step in EBP is searching and sorting the current best evidence. Traditional textbooks are not acceptable sources of evidence because they cannot stay current, are lightly referenced, and many times do not provide a sufficient level of support for the statements made in the book (Sackett et al., 2000). In the future, evidence-based Internet textbooks may be developed that will be continually updated. Identifying, selecting, and summarizing evidence is a complex and labor-intensive process. Lack of time, computer availability, and Internet access challenge therapists and managers. Access to certain databases requires user codes, which are readily available to college students and faculty but less accessible to practitioners. One free public-access database is PubMed (http://www.ncbi.nlm.nih.gov/pubmed/), which, in addition to citations, has links to other related Web resources. OTseeker is another free online database available to members of AOTA for the systematic evaluation of evidence for occupational therapy (www.otseeker.com). For example, the reader can review the results of an OTseeker search about the quantity and quality of interventions for stroke rehabilitation (Hoffman et al., 2008). Because occupational therapy evaluation and intervention approaches include performance skills, managers can also thoroughly explore another source, the Physiotherapy Evidence Database (PEDro; http://www.pedro.org.au).

Regardless of the database used, searches for evidence yield two major types of research: primary and secondary. Primary studies report original analytical research and can be experimental or observational. Secondary studies, also called *systematic reviews,* are integrative studies that summarize and draw conclusions from primary research or previously published or unpublished studies (McKibbon, Eady, & Marks, 1999).

A useful resource for locating high-quality evidence from primary and secondary publications is the Cochrane Collaboration (www.cochrane.org). This worldwide network is named in honor of Archibald Leman Cochrane, a British obstetrician and epidemiologist. The Cochrane Library is an electronic-format collection of information, available from university libraries on the Internet and in CD-ROM format, to carry out the goal of helping people make informed decisions about health care.

Good topics for occupational therapy managers to search include continuous quality improvement systems; analysis of work processes; and staff and client involvement in the monitoring, measurement, and analysis of good outcomes. If readers have access, he or she can use a college or university library's database search engine (e.g., Ovid) to access the Cochrane Library, the American College of Physicians's ACP Journal Club, or the Database of Abstracts and Reviews of Effects (DARE) and then type in *occupational therapy* AND *dementia.* At the time of this writing, this search yielded 21 citations of clinical trials in the Cochrane Library. Because the Cochrane Library is updated quarterly, however, readers will likely find more results. It is important that the manager and staff specify the database, key words, phrases, and date of search because any variation in those inputs affects the quantity, quality, and type of evidence found.

3. Critically Appraise the Evidence

The third phase in developing research is critical appraisal or formal evaluation of the evidence to determine its soundness, magnitude, and usefulness to practice. RCTs provide the highest level of evidence, followed by cohort studies, case control studies, and case reports (see Figure 22.1). Levels and grading guidelines for evidence vary, reflecting the complexity of the research design used during the investigation (Geyman, Deyo, & Ramsey, 2000; McKibbon et al., 1999; Sackett et al., 2000). The level of evidence in primary research was originally ranked by Sackett et al. (2000) using numerical indexes from I to V or letter indexes from A to D, where I or A represents the most controlled, deliberate, nonbiased placement of study participants in groups (see Table 22.1). The numerical and alphabetical levels of evidence have been modified in a variety of ways, and readers are referred to Evans (2003) and Owens et al. (2010) for more detailed appraisal criteria for interventions.

Evidence is ranked on the basis of research design used, number of study participants, and level of external and internal validity. *Internal validity* is the extent to which the study results can be attributed to the intervention rather than to flaws in the research design, and *external validity* is the extent to which the findings of the study are relevant to participants and settings beyond those in the study. The best and most powerful evidence is based on a foundation of support from high-quality randomized clinical trials, ideally with controlled double-blinding, predetermined outcome measures, and a sample size calculated on the basis of a power analysis.

Another approach to classification by the degree of evidence strength is a system cited by Owens et al. (2010). Used in the Cochrane Library, this system consists of four degrees of strength: strong evidence, moderate evidence, limited evidence, or no evidence. Strong evidence is provided by generally consistent findings in multiple high-quality RCTs. Moderate evidence is provided by generally consistent findings in one high-quality RCT and multiple low-quality RCTs. Limited evidence is provided by generally consistent findings in one or more lower-quality RCTs. No evidence indicates that there were either no RCTs or the results were conflicting.

There is also a hierarchy of evidence in secondary publications, as shown in Figure 22.1. Secondary publications include meta-analyses, systematic reviews, non-systematic reviews, and other publications such as editorials and practice guidelines. EBP draws only from meta-analyses and systematic reviews. The level of evidence is dependent on the thoroughness and quality of the evidence provided by the primary research studies included in the secondary source.

Meta-analysis of multiple RCTs provides the most certain evidence, as this type of analysis includes a wide array of the strongest, most objective evidence. The traditional narrative review of the literature is prone to bias and error it does not follow the guidelines and rules of meta-analysis. Meta-analysis is more objective than other types of literature review procedures, given that single studies may produce errors and can guide the practitioner erroneously (Egger & Smith, 1997). Examples of meta-analytic

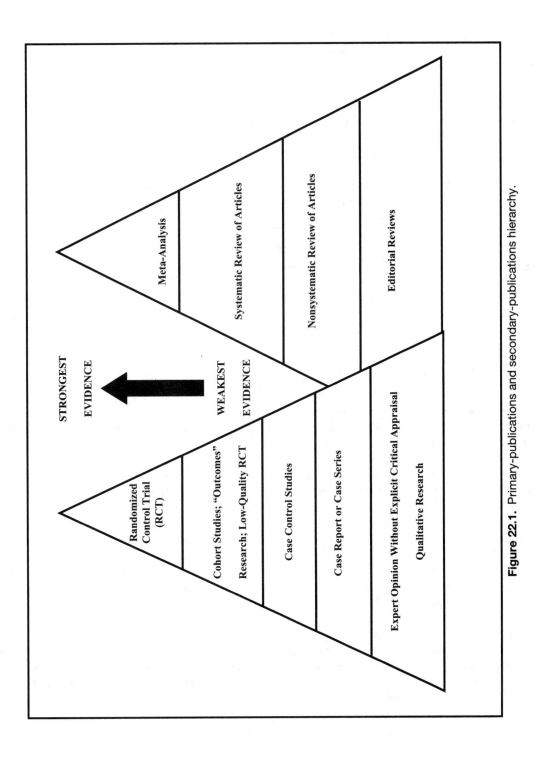

Figure 22.1. Primary-publications and secondary-publications hierarchy.

Table 22.1 Two Classifications of Evidence in Research Studies: Level and Grade

Research Design	Description	Level	Grade (levels of rigor)
Randomized controlled trials (RCTs)	Participants in the study are assigned to either the control or treatment group in an unbiased manner. In a double-blind study, the participants and researchers in the study do not know which participants are receiving the treatment under study. In a single-blind study, only the participants are blinded.	I	A (1a, 1b, 1c)
Cohort studies	A group of people are followed over time to find out what will happen to them (prospective study) or what happened to them (retrospective study).	II	B (2a, 2b, 2c)
	Outcome research, low-quality RCTs		
Case control studies	The effects of a treatment intervention are compared for a group with a particular condition (case) and a group without the condition (control). The "case" may be an individual, a group, an event, or a society.	III	C (3a, 3b)
Case report or case series	The effects of treatment of a single or several persons, cases, or events are compared from initial baseline to after treatment.	IV	D
	Poor-quality cohort and case controls		
Other	Expert opinion without explicit critical appraisal	V	E
	Qualitative research		

reviews are present in occupational therapy journals as well as in evidence-based databases. In 1996, Carlson, Fanchiang, Zemke, and Clark published a meta-analysis of the effectiveness of occupational therapy for older persons, concluding that occupational therapy represents a worthwhile treatment option for older persons. Meta-analyses generally include enough information to guide managers in using the intervention with individuals beyond the populations used in the studies. Whether the intervention can be generalized depends greatly on how different or similar one's clients are compared to the study treatment groups.

Meta-analyses appraise individual studies using appropriate techniques for statistical analysis and synthesis. Techniques typically include synthesizing the treatment effect magnitude (proportion of clients who show positive effect, difference between the groups in outcomes, number of clients needed to be treated to achieve a good outcome), confidence limits (the uncertainty of the measure), and test of significance (size of the probability that the treatment effects are not due to chance alone; Ottenbacher, Heyn, & Abreu, 2006). Potential sources of error include biases in statistical analysis, interpretation of results, and reporting of results. In addition, meta-analysis is susceptible to potential Type I (falsely concluding that there is a treatment effect) and Type II (falsely concluding that there is no treatment effect) errors (Maxwell & Delaney, 2000).

The systematic review is a new type of review article found in the evidence-based health care literature that examines the evidence on a particular topic (McKibbon et al., 1999). A systematic review uses objective and orderly methods to avoid bias in the report and synthesis of the research studies (Egger & Smith, 1997).

Meta-analysis synthesizes findings from quantitative research, but comparable methodology is not available for qualitative research (D. Davies & Dodd, 2002; Stevens, Abrams, Brazier, Fitzpatrick, & Lilford, 2001; Whittemore, Chase, & Mandle, 2001). Although there are examples of qualitative meta-analyses that synthesize findings into one description model or theory (Paterson, Thorne, Canam, & Jillings, 2001; Stern & Harris, 1985), this method is not highly valued in the EBP literature, which is based on a medical model. Qualitative research methods explore and describe social phenomena and look beyond statistics, offering access and insight into the health care process (Giacomini, 2001). Occupational therapy has embraced qualitative methodologies in search of a better understanding of the social and personal aspects of heath care (Clark, 1993; Krefting & Krefting, 1991). Although there is a lack of agreement regarding how to evaluate the quality and usefulness of qualitative studies for EBP (Marks, 1999), many occupational therapists and scientists encourage the use and application of these methods to practice (Clark, 1993; Krefting & Krefting, 1991). Readers are referred to the McMaster University Occupational Therapy Evidence-Based Practice Research Group guidelines form for a critical review of qualitative studies on the Internet (http://www.srs.mcmaster/Portals/20/pdf/ebp/qualguidelines_version2.0.pdf).

Practitioners traditionally combine the art and science of occupational therapy to determine the quality of clinical care. This integrative perspective requires the use of qualitative studies to improve professionals' understanding of occupational therapy and occupational science. Qualitative methods best address questions about social meaning, whereas quantitative research best addresses questions dealing with biomedical and causal questions (Giacomini, 2001). Both methodologies have contributed to occupational therapy evidence and can enhance client and caretaker empowerment and the quality of occupational therapy.

4. Apply to Practice

The fourth step of EBP is the application of scientific research findings to practice. This step is the culmination of the search process. The evidence is integrated into practice on the basis of its compatibility with client factors, institution factors, and staff expertise. Decision making on integration is based largely on the quality of quantitative research design, including the statistical power of the study, the use of randomization techniques, and the clinical significance of the results.

Statistical Power

The *statistical power* of a study is an index used to determine the probability that changes are due to the treatment rather than to chance. Statistical significance measures the size of the probability that the treatment effects are not due to chance alone. The optimal statistical significance of research studies is generally set at 95% likelihood that a particular effect is related to a particular treatment, with a 5% likelihood that the effect is related to chance alone. For example, Ottenbacher and Maas (1999), after examining 30 studies on the effectiveness of occupational therapy treatment intervention (outcome), found that the majority of the studies were of low power because of their small sample size. To demonstrate occupational therapy effectiveness, studies must include appropriate numbers of participants to enable the detection of statistically significant changes due to the treatment provided. Practitioners should not reject a treatment because a study provided insufficient evidence of a treatment effect, however; if the study methodology was limited, it will not provide the statistical power to conclude that the intervention was either effective or ineffective.

Randomization

Randomization refers to the procedure used to determine the assignment of treatment to participants so that the chances of assignment to a particular treatment are the same for all participants in the study. Random assignment to a treatment group is considered the best way to avoid factors that will distort findings addressing the causal relationship between the intervention and the results of treatment. In occupational therapy research studies, randomization is often difficult (e.g., financial restraints), unfeasible (e.g., small pool of participants), or unethical (e.g., no treatment provided to the control group). In occupational therapy, these constraints do not argue against using randomization in research studies; instead, they support a more flexible research design that enables problem-focused research versus methodology-focused research (Ottenbacher, 1992).

Clinical Significance

Clinical significance gives the practitioner an idea of the practical meaning of the study results. Clinical significance is unrelated to statistical significance, but both measures of significance are important (Ottenbacher & Barrett, 1989). Studies using a single-subject or group comparison design will not allow tests of statistical significance but can support clinical significance (Ottenbacher & Barrett, 1989). Occupational therapy managers should remember that EBP is only one way of obtaining evidence. Clinical significance, which takes into account the expertise of practitioners and their practice settings, as well as clients' preferences, also needs to be taken into consideration.

5. Self-evaluate

The fifth step in the implementation of EBP is to self-assess. This step, not always included in the evidence-based guidelines, includes an appraisal of the procedures undertaken in Steps 1 through 4 and a reflection on the way the occupational therapist or occupational therapy assistant formulated the question, tracked down the evidence, critically evaluated the evidence, and integrated the evidence into practice (McKibbon et al., 1999; Sackett et al., 2000). This step is necessary to determine the value of using this process within occupational therapy practice.

EVIDENCE-BASED PROCESS AND OCCUPATIONAL THERAPY PRACTICE

Once one starts using EBP, the amount of available information can become overwhelming. Therefore, managers and staff must share this methodology with each other for support and validation. This process requires time and effort to achieve strategies for efficient use of information. The commitment to continuous questioning of clinical practice can become an institutional and personal pledge (Dawes et al., 1999).

EBP is not a simple or single solution, and although EBP can promote knowledge and solutions, there are other implications for occupational therapy practice. Strong evidence has powerful merits when used to enhance problem solving. All of these merits notwithstanding, occupational therapy investigators must address, through multiple methods of inquiry, those aspects of practice that fall outside the scope of problem solving to include the therapeutic relationship, cultural differences, and institutional philosophies and visions. Occupational therapists and occupational therapy assistants must consider client-centered evidence alongside evidence generated from population-based research (Egan, Dubouloz, von Zweck, & Vallerand, 1998). Even the most rigorous research must be considered within a holistic context to produce sound interventions (Straus, 1999). A broad-based inquiry beyond EBP is needed to integrate the art and science of occupational therapy practice.

Although there is a proliferation of textbooks, articles, and courses at the local, national, and international levels in EBP, the evidence generated from occupational therapy practice is limited (Law & Baum, 1998; Law & MacDermid, 2008; Taylor, 1997; Tickle-Degnen, 1998). The process of imparting and acquiring knowledge about EBP in occupational therapy practice is in its early stages. Many organizations lack the time necessary to develop a research culture because of the heavy direct care service commitments in the practice setting or heavy teaching responsibilities in the academic setting. In addition, a limited number of role models are teaching and applying EBP. As a result, attention to investigating and disseminating evidence of relevant studies is limited. As occupational therapy moves toward a postbaccalaureate level, research will be more integrated in educational institutions.

Managers, direct care practitioners, and educators need to overcome barriers to teaching, learning, and implementing EBP. For health care professionals, four factors have been identified that interfere with teaching and learning EBP: time factors, rudimentary research skills, the limited high-quality research evidence available, and doubts about the authenticity of this approach (P. Davies, 1999).

Three studies published in the *American Journal of Occupational Therapy* investigated occupational therapists' and occupational therapy students' perceptions of EBP. The investigators in the first study used semistructured interviews to explore respondents' perception of EBP and found that respondents believed EBP was a research process of looking for understanding and viewed it as a threat to practice (Dubouloz et al., 1999). The second investigation used a single-subject design to analyze three therapists' experiences attempting to use a Cochrane review and concluded that promoting and improving access to summaries of evidence and educating practitioners are needed to encourage the use of EBP. In the third study, Dysart and Tomlin (2002) used a survey research methodology to examine the way occupational therapists in the United States accessed and used evidence. They found that therapists were engaging in a modest amount of EBP and that the therapists considered research to have poor applicability to clinical practice. More recently, through qualitative case methodology and focus group interviews, Stube and Jedlicka (2007) found that EBP is a relevant process in students' fieldwork experience. Identifying barriers to the use of EBP and expanding and clarifying the benefits of using this methodology will continue to challenge managers and occupational therapy practitioners alike.

Occupational therapy managers must ensure that they are competent in research to contribute to the development of better practice in practitioners, to promote the profession, and to advance the organization within which the manager practices (Abreu, Peloquin, & Ottenbacher, 1998).

Occupational therapy managers—both clinical and academic—are well positioned to lead and drive evidence-based changes in the workplace (McCluskey & Cusick, 2002). The following sections highlight practical strategies for managers to be key players in this process.

Staff Consultation and Planning

Careful staff consultation and adequate planning for using EBP in the workplace can increase the likelihood of successful implementation of the EBP process (McCluskey & Cusick, 2002). Mandating EBP change may seem to be a simple course of action, but change is most likely to occur when managers identify the value of research for themselves, their staff, and the institution. Managers need to evaluate both perceived and real barriers to implement change in this process. Staff educational training, motivation, and desire for EBP will vary and therefore identification of key staff members who can promote an evidence-based culture is beneficial. A reasonable timeline in order to accomplish specific training for individual and group skills is also required in the planning stage. In addition, McCluskey and Cusick (2002) recommended conducting a specialized analysis with the staff of the workplace called strengths, weaknesses, opportunities, and threats (SWOT) to introduce EBP. *SWOT analysis* is a strategic planning method that identifies and evaluates the internal strengths and weaknesses of a person or organization, and opportunities and threats external to a person or organization that are involved in undertaking a new project. SWOT analysis is frequently used when change is being considered within an organization, and its use by managers can facilitate the implementation of EBP.

Using EBP as Part of Clinical Competence

Using EBP as part of clinical competence is another management strategy that can be implemented in various ways. The manager can designate educational time for competence in EBP. This time allocation can enhance the total commitment to the EBP process. For example, assigning 1 hour per week for clinical searches at work (or offsite if computer and Internet access are limited) and assigning 1 hour per month to inservice training in EBP is an effective and motivating method of enhancing competency (Abreu & Chang, 2002). Managers can establish connections with researchers in the workplace or at an affiliated university to collaborate in the development of a strategic approach to the use of research and management of data. For example, managers can invite faculty and the doctoral student body to disseminate their occupational therapy research findings through inservice trainings to the staff (Abreu & Chang, 2002).

Another strategy to increase clinical competence in EBP is to support staff requests to attend particular continuing education courses and conferences, and provide research articles and evidence related to the topic. Sometimes, newly supported evaluation and intervention methods are presented at conference prior to publication. Attendance at such conferences can allow the staff to gain cutting-edge information and improve the quality of occupational therapy services.

Systematic Reviews

Searching and reporting on systematic reviews supporting intervention techniques and other areas of practice, such as prognosis and prevention related to the center's specific populations and specialization, is another beneficial strategy for staff development. Searching national and international journals and schools of occupational therapy, the Cochrane Library, and PubMed databases for systematic reviews and research are all excellent sources of data for EBP. For example, a search performed in the Cochrane library database using the term *systematic reviews* at the time of this writing yielded 78 reviews on dementia, 25 on head injury, and 125 on stroke, to name just a few.

Systematic reviews and other research evidence literature can be presented and discussed in journal club meetings. Such meetings can be an effective adult education format for learning how to do EBP critical appraisals and for promotion of effective health care strategies (Seelig, 1991; Sidorov, 1995). Managers can run more effective journal club meetings if they adhere to the suggestions of McLeod, Steinert, Boudreau, Snell, & Wiseman (2010), which include determining the meetings' value, goals, and frequency; promoting a broadly balanced group member representation with the ideal number of participants; and varying group leadership. In addition, the manager needs to determine the number of articles to be discussed in each meeting, the articles' selection criteria, and guidelines for discussion. Finally, the manager should encourage participants to disseminate the meeting results through publication or presentation. Some centers hold their meetings at lunch, and the administration sponsors a lunch to encourage an informal learning environment.

Using Practice Guidelines

Another EBP strategy is for managers to help the staff develop, implement, and adapt existing published clinical practice guidelines (Stergiou-Kita, 2010). These guidelines offer instructions on which diagnostic or evaluation tests to use, how to provide services, how to determine duration of services, and other details of clinical practice. Clinical practice guidelines are usually developed by a multidisciplinary expert panel sponsored by an organization in order to reduce cost of services and variations in current practice patterns. They are based on the most comprehensive review of the evidence for effectiveness of services and improving patients' quality of life (Stason, Bergstrom, Duncan, Laouri, & Johnston, 1997). Clinical practice guidelines stimulate self-evaluation by rehabilitation professionals and provide a critical focus for discussing priorities for the research needed to fill existing gaps in knowledge.

Managers and staff need to learn to search for and locate guidelines applicable to their practice, adapt the guidelines to their institutional client base, measure the effectiveness of care following these guidelines, and discuss recommendations with their clients (Stergiou-Kita, 2010). There are multiple clinical practice guidelines in health-related literature and homegrown protocols as a result of quality improvement programs. For example, a popular clinical practice guideline is the *Occupational Therapy Concise*

Guideline for Stroke Rehabilitation and Recovery (National Stroke Foundation, 2008), and AOTA published *Occupational Therapy Practice Guidelines for Adults With Stroke* (Sabari, 2008). Bedard, Purden, Sauve-Larose, Certosini, and Schein (2006) provided and evaluated the use of clinical practice guidelines of pain, describing a labor-intensive process that required time and training. These guidelines resulted in a strong collaborative and interdisciplinary EBP environment. They provided clear quality improvement guidelines required by the institution's accreditation organizations by using research evidence, clinical expertise, and client input.

EBP as Quality Improvement

Managers can reframe EBP as a quality improvement process by using two complementary strategies described in an article by Chiu and Tickle-Degnen (2002) on occupational therapy home-based services. The first strategy involved evaluating the occupational therapy services outcomes by (1) identifying effective services and (2) highlighting areas for improvement at the impairment, activity, and participation level. The second strategy involved collecting and analyzing the results of client satisfaction surveys that documented the approval for continuing practice or the need for change. Managers can also survey therapists on a periodic basis to determine their opinions of the effectiveness of EBP. They can then use the results to implement changes when warranted. The surveys will also provide managers with feedback on effectiveness of EBP as part of the quality improvement process.

Cost-effectiveness

Without evidence, managers face an increased risk of reduced payment and approval for occupational therapy services, so researching, identifying, and using cost-effectiveness is another management strategy for implementing best practice. EBP is critical to the profession's continued credibility and value (Mallinson & Fischer, 2010). Hay and colleagues (2002) quantified and reported the cost-effectiveness of occupational therapy for a preventive occupational therapy well-elderly intervention in conjunction with a trend toward decreased medical expenditures. However, there is a paucity of cost-effectiveness studies. Although health care providers have a clear ethical mandate to use EBP, defining ethical practice in the absence of strong evidence and in the presence of low rigorous methodological designs remains unclear (Malec, 2009).

Sometimes interventions that are supported by evidence are not used in the clinic; at other times interventions are widely used even though there is minimal or no research evidence to support them. For example, despite the evidence for efficacy of constraint-induced movement therapy (CIMT), a reimbursable impairment-level technique used by rehabilitation therapists, CIMT is not widely implemented by occupational therapists (Walker & Pink, 2009). Many factors contribute to the discrepancy between evidence research findings and practice. Some practitioners suggest that CIMT may be difficult to implement because of the demanding contact time and expense and clients' lack of compliance and interest (Page, Levine, & Hill, 2007). Others suggest lack of education about the intervention (Walker & Pink, 2009) as a determining factor. Many clients with a hemiplegic hand are also ineligible for CIMT and other modified CIMT programs because severe hand motor recovery leaves them unable to perform active wrist and finger extension, which is a required entry criterion for the programs (Page et al., 2007).

Managers can facilitate effective techniques using the most recent evidence in the occupational therapy literature (Hayner, Gibson, & Giles, 2010). Conversely, managers encounter wide use of hand splints and shoulder slings in persons with hemiplegia, even though these interventions have minimal or no evidence research support for these clients (Gustafsson & Yates, 2009; Lannin, Cusick, McCluskey, & Herbert, 2007). More research is required to understand why the discrepancy between clinical practice and evidence continues to exist in health-related fields, including occupational therapy. Managers can encourage researchers to work with the practitioners to confirm the results of these findings.

Evidence-based decision making is always evolving. Systematic reviews and clinical trials are the gold standards needed to provide a synthesis of current research on interventions for clinical application. However, some interventions do not have enough evidence of effect because of lack of information, low-powered research designs, or inconclusive research studies that recommend further research. Managers inspire others to make decisions guided by evidence, including clinical reasoning, which embraces the expertise of the organization and therapists as well as the client's preferences as part of the decision-making process.

Conclusion

As is evident from the discussion in this chapter, occupational therapy managers who wish to base their practice decisions on evidence-based research must be familiar with research design, methodology, and inferential or descriptive statistics to become accurate appraisers of the evidence. Although research design familiarity is a practice responsibility, statistical appraisal is not a required practice competence for occupational therapists and occupational therapy assistants. The responsibility for using sound principles of research design rests on the practitioners, managers, and faculty conducting the research. Evidence-based databanks supply summary reviews that provide statistical appraisals of the articles, thus easing some of the responsibility on the occupational therapist. As occupational therapy continues to develop at higher academic levels, including a postbaccalaureate level and an expansion of clinical doctoral studies, the competencies and ease of use of statistical appraisal will continue to evolve. EBP should become the priority of every occupational therapy practitioner. Every practitioner needs to find some way to be part of the EBP process, and that is what occupational therapy managers can inspire every practitioner to do.

Case Examples

Level I Fieldwork

Jill was a Level I fieldwork student in a stroke rehabilitation clinic. Her manager asked her to find evidence supporting the benefit of occupational therapy for clients with stroke. Jill did a search of systematic reviews and found one systematic review that included 9 RCT studies and 1,258 clients. This review provided evidence that occupational therapy interventions for persons after stroke reduced the chances of a poor outcome in terms of deterioration in ability to perform activities of daily living and improved patients' ability to perform personal activities of daily living and extended activities of daily living (Legg et al., 2007).

Level II Fieldwork

Les was a Level II fieldwork student in a nursing home. His manager, who recognized that meta-synthesis of qualitative research can promote the inclusion of clients' preferences and values in EBP, formulated the following question: "For persons with stroke, is qualitative evidence beneficial?" Les did a search in a database and found 1 qualitative meta-synthesis of 9 qualitative studies. The meta-synthesis identified 5 interrelated themes: (1) change, transition, and transformation; (2) loss; (3) uncertainty; (4) social isolation; and (5) adaptation and reconciliation. The synthesis also noted that after stroke most clients moved forward through adaptation toward recovery. Les concluded that yes, qualitative research can benefit practice with persons with stroke.

First-Time Manager

June, who was recently promoted to occupational therapy manager, questioned her clinical supervisor about exploring a community-based occupational therapy program. The supervisor recommended a search of the

(continued)

Case Examples *(cont.)*

Cochrane Library, a collection of databases published quarterly and distributed on a subscription basis, and formulated a question about persons with dementia: "Will a community-based occupational therapy intervention be more effective in increasing function than no treatment at all?" June conducted a search in the Cochrane Library database and found that yes, there was evidence that community-based occupational therapy programs should be advocated for both dementia clients and their caregivers, because they improve clients' mood, quality of life, and health status and caregivers' sense of control of life (Graff et al., 2007).

MANAGER

Chris, an occupational therapy manager, asked a cost-related question of her staff: "For persons with dementia, is community-based occupational therapy cost-effective?" The staff did a search using the terms *occupational therapy* AND *dementia* in the Cochrane Library database and found 21 evidence-based clinical trial articles. After they identified, downloaded, and sorted the articles, they realized that not all of the articles addressed the topic in the way they needed and that not all would be helpful in tracking evidence. They targeted the searching and sorting process to the manager's focus of interest and found that, yes, there was evidence that community occupational therapy for both dementia clients and their caregivers is successful and cost-effective (Graff et al., 2008).

❖ Learning Activities

1. Read 1 systematic review in occupational therapy that is cited in 1 of the 2 reviews on the McMaster University Web page (http://www.srs.mcmaster/ca/Default.aspx?tabid=630). Outline what the authors tell you about how they conducted the literature search, what rules they used to decide if studies were relevant to the hypothesis, and what rules they used to decide if cumulative relations existed.

2. Read 1 meta-analysis in the occupational therapy literature. Identify how the authors of the meta-analysis formulated the problem, collected the data from each individual study, evaluated the quality of each individual study, analyzed and interpreted the data, and presented the final results. It is not necessary to understand the statistical rules, only the steps of the meta-analysis.

3. Read 1 overview of the occupational therapy literature. Identify the amount of personal opinion in the article, and compare the article with the systematic review and the meta-analysis articles you reviewed.

4. Search for at least 3 evidence-based articles by occupational therapists in an area of interest having to do with therapy/prevention, etiology/harm, prognosis, diagnosis, or economic analysis.

5. Present the results of Learning Activity 4 in a 12-slide presentation following the 5 steps of formulating the question, searching and sorting the evidence, critically appraising the evidence, applying the evidence to practice, and self-evaluating. Reflect on the presence or lack of evidence in the area you investigated.

✔ Multiple-Choice Questions

1. Three criteria for a randomized clinical trial are
   a. Random sample, comparison group, and controls to internal validity.
   b. Random sample, large number of participants, and signed consent form.
   c. Random sample, same age, and heterogeneity of sample.
   d. None of the above.

2. *EBP* refers to
   a. The use of knowledge from research findings to guide competent clinical practice.
   b. The use of information from textbooks to guide competent clinical practice.
   c. Elimination of clinical expertise and clients' values and preferences.
   d. Elimination of clinical mentorship.

3. Which of the following is true of EBP?
   a. EBP provides support to establish the effectiveness of occupational therapy services.
   b. EBP is the responsibility of every practitioner.
   c. EBP provides support that occupational therapy services are cost-effective.
   d. All of the above.

4. A manager's role in EBP requires which of the following?
   a. Having some research knowledge.
   b. Guarding against minimizing practitioners' and centers' expertise over research evidence.
   c. Ensuring transfer of research knowledge to clinical practice.
   d. All of the above.

5. An EBP system includes which of the following steps?
   a. Formulate a question, and search and sort for evidence.
   b. Critically appraise the evidence, and apply to practice.
   c. Self-assess regarding the EBP process.
   d. All of the above.

6. Best occupational therapy practice means which of the following?
   a. Better client care.
   b. Optimal program evaluation.
   c. Quality improvement systems.
   d. All of the above.

7. Effectiveness studies answer which of the following questions?
   a. Did the clients receiving occupational therapy improve?
   b. How much did the clients improve?
   c. Which treatment made the clients better?
   d. A and B.

8. Treatment efficacy studies answer which of the following questions?
   a. Did the clients receiving occupational therapy improve?
   b. How much did the clients improve?
   c. Which treatment made the clients better?
   d. A and B.

9. Which of the following is true of randomized clinical trials?
   a. RCTs are studies comparing the value and effect of an occupational therapy intervention against a control group not receiving treatment.
   b. RCTs may present the ethical issue of withholding treatment from clients in the study.
   c. RCTs may not control for selection bias.
   d. A and B.

10. What is the Cochrane Library (www.cochrane.org)?
    a. A collection of databases published quarterly and distributed on a subscription basis.
    b. A commercial database that focuses primarily on allied health topics.
    c. A bibliographic database that contains health care literature.
    d. None of the above.

11. A database search should be reproducible by another therapist unless
    a. The search is done 3 months later.
    b. The search is done in a different database.
    c. The key words used are different.
    d. All of the above.

12. The third EBP step includes
    a. A formal evaluation of the evidence.
    b. An analysis of research flaws.
    c. Relevancy to clients and centers beyond the study.
    d. All of the above.

13. The term *primary publication* refers to a
    a. Report of an original research study.
    b. Textbook.
    c. Meta-analysis.
    d. Systematic review study.

14. The term *secondary publication* refers to a/an
    a. Report of an original research study.
    b. Meta-analysis.
    c. Original opinion article.
    d. Original handout.

15. The term *meta-analysis* refers to
    a. A quantitative study that summarizes a group of studies.
    b. A qualitative study that summarizes a group of studies.
    c. A quantitative study that summarizes a group of studies and does statistical analyses and synthesis.
    d. All of the above.

16. A *Type I error* in a study refers to
    a. Falsely concluding that the occupational therapy treatment had a positive effect.
    b. Falsely concluding that there was no occupational therapy treatment effect.

c. Falsely concluding that the treatment effect was due to chance.

d. All of the above.

17. What is the role of qualitative evidence in EBP?

a. It looks beyond statistics exploring and describing social phenomena.

b. There is a lack of agreement on how to assess its methodological rigor.

c. There is a lack of agreement on its usefulness.

d. All of the above.

18. Which degrees of evidence strength are the strongest?

a. Level I; Grade A.

b. Level V; Grade E.

c. Cohort studies.

d. Case control studies.

19. *Clinical significance* means

a. Random assignment.

b. A statistic related to the size of probability of treatment effects.

c. The degree of practical meaning in the data.

d. Type I error.

20. Phase IV randomized clinical trials include which of the following?

a. Preliminary and exploratory studies.

b. Well-controlled efficacy studies.

c. High treatment fidelity, blinding of evaluators, and statistical power.

d. Evaluation of generalization to other populations and settings.

References

Abreu, B. C., & Chang, P.-F. (2002). Getting started in evidence-based practice. *OT Practice, 7*(18), CE1–CE8.

Abreu, B. C., Peloquin, S. M., & Ottenbacher, K. (1998). Competence in scientific inquiry and research. *American Journal of Occupational Therapy, 52*, 751–759.

American Occupational Therapy Association. (2007). AOTA's *Centennial Vision* and executive summary. *American Journal of Occupational Therapy, 61*, 613–614.

Bailey, D. M., Bornstein, J., & Ryan, S. (2007). A case report of evidence-based practice: From academia to clinic. *American Journal of Occupational Therapy, 61*, 85–91.

Bedard, D., Purden, M. A., Sauve-Larose, N., Certosini, C., & Schein, C. (2006). The pain experience of postsurgical patients following the implementation of an evidence-based approach. *Pain Management Nursing, 7*(3), 80–92.

Braveman, B. (2006). *Leading and managing occupational therapy services: An evidence-based approach*. Philadelphia: F. A. Davis.

Byers, J. F., & Beaudin, C. L. (2002). The relationship between continuous quality improvement and research. *Journal of Healthcare Quality, 24*(1), 4–8.

Caldwell, E., Whitehead, M., Fleming, J., & Moes, L. (2008). Evidence-based practice in everyday clinical practice: Strategies for change in a tertiary occupational therapy department. *Australian Occupational Therapy Journal, 55*(2), 79–84.

Carlson, M., Fanchiang, S.-P., Zemke, R., & Clark, F. (1996). A meta-analysis of the effectiveness of occupational therapy in older persons. *American Journal of Occupational Therapy, 50*, 89–98.

Chiu, T., & Tickle-Degnen, L. (2002). Learning from evidence: Service outcomes and client satisfaction with occupational therapy home-based services. *American Journal of Occupational Therapy, 56*, 217–220.

Clark, F. (1993). Occupation embedded in a real life: Interweaving occupational science and occupational therapy [Eleanor Clarke Slagle Lecture]. *American Journal of Occupational Therapy, 47*, 1067–1078.

Clark, F., Azen, S. P., Zemki, R., Jackson, J., Carlson, M., Mandel, D., et al. (1997). Occupational therapy for independent-living older adults: A randomized controlled trial. *JAMA, 278*, 1321–1326.

Davies, D., & Dodd, J. (2002). Qualitative research and the question of rigor. *Qualitative Health Research, 12*, 279–289.

Davies, P. (1999). Teaching evidence-based health care. In M. Dawes, P. Davies, A. Gray, J. Mant, K. Seers, & R. Snowball (Eds.), *Evidence-based practice: A primer for health care professionals* (pp. 223–242). New York: Churchill Livingstone.

Dawes, M., Davies, P., Gray, A., Mant, J., Seers, K., & Snowball, R. (Eds.). (1999). *Evidence-based practice: A primer for health care professionals*. New York: Churchill Livingstone.

Dubouloz, C.-J., Egan, M., Vallerand, J., & von Zweck, C. (1999). Occupational therapists' receptions of evidence-based practice. *American Journal of Occupational Therapy, 53*, 445–453.

Dysart, A. M., & Tomlin, G. S. (2002). Factors related to evidence-based practice among U.S. occupational therapy clinicians. *American Journal of Occupational Therapy, 56*, 275–284.

Egan, M., Dubouloz, C.-J., von Zweck, C., & Vallerand, J. (1998). The client-centered evidence-based practice of occupational therapy. *Canadian Journal of Occupational Therapy, 65*, 136–143.

Egger, M., & Smith, G. D. (1997). Meta-analysis: Potentials and promise. *British Medical Journal, 315*, 1371–1374.

Evans, D. (2003). Hierarchy of evidence: A framework for ranking evidence evaluating health care interventions. *Journal of Clinical Nursing, 12*(1), 77–84.

Geyman, J. P., Deyo, R. A., & Ramsey, S. D. (Eds.). (2000). *Evidence-based clinical practice: Concepts and approaches*. Boston: Butterworth-Heinemann.

Giacomini, M. K. (2001). The rocky road: Qualitative research as evidence. *ACP Journal Club, 134*(1), A11–A13.

Graff, M. J. L., Adang, E. M. M., Vernooij-Dassen, M. J. M., Dekker, J., Jonsson, L., Thijssen, M., et al. (2008). Community occupational therapy for older patients with dementia and their care givers: Cost effectiveness study. *British Medical Journal, 336*, 134–138.

Graff, M. J. L., Vernooij-Dassen, M. J. M., Thijssen, M., Dekker, J., Hoefnagels, W. H. L., & Olde Rikkert, M. G. M. (2007). Effects of community occupational therapy on quality of life, mood, and health status in dementia patients and their caregivers: A randomized controlled trial. *Journal of Gerontology: A. Biological Sciences and Medical Sciences, 62*, 1002–1009.

Guide for the Uniform Data Set for Medical Rehabilitation (including the FIM instrument) (version 5.1). (1997). Buffalo: State University of New York.

Gustafsson, L., & Yates, K. (2009). Are we applying interventions with research evidence when targeting secondary complications of the stroke-affected upper limb? *Australian Occupational Therapy Journal, 56*(6), 428–435.

Gutman, S. A. (2008). Research priorities of the profession. *American Journal of Occupational Therapy, 62*, 499–501.

Hay, J., LaBree, L., Luo, R., Clark, F., Carlson, M., Mandel, D., et al. (2002). Cost-effectiveness of preventive occupational therapy for independent-living older adults. *Journal of the American Geriatrics Society, 50*(8), 1381–1388.

Hayner, K., Gibson, G., & Giles, G. M. (2010). Comparison of constraint-induced movement therapy and bilateral treatment of equal intensity in people with chronic upper-extremity dysfunction after cerebrovascular accident. *American Journal of Occupational Therapy, 64*(4), 528–539.

Hoffmann, T., Bennett, S., McKenna, K., Green-Hill, J., McCluskey, A., & Tooth, L. (2008). Interventions for stroke rehabilitation: Analysis of the research contained in the OTseeker evidence database. *Topics in Stroke Rehabilitation, 15*, 341–350.

Holm, H. A. (2000). Our mandate for the new millennium: Evidence-based practice [Eleanor Clarke Slagle Lecture]. *American Journal of Occupational Therapy, 54*, 575–585.

Isaac, C. A., & Franceschi, A. (2008). EBM: Evidence to practice and practice to evidence. *Journal of Clinical Practice, 14*, 656–659.

Johnston, M. V., & Case-Smith, J. (2009). Development and testing of interventions in occupational therapy: Toward a new generation of research in occupational therapy. *OTJR: Occupation, Participation and Health, 29*(1), 4–13.

Jutel, A. (2008). Beyond evidence-based nursing: Tools for practice. *Journal of Nursing Management, 16*, 417–421.

Ketelaar, M., Russell, D. J., & Gorter, J. W. (2008). The challenge of moving evidence-based measures into clinical practice: Lessons in knowledge translation. *Physical and Occupational Therapy in Pediatrics, 28*, 191–206.

Kleiser, H., & Cox, D. L. (2008). The integration of clinical and managerial supervision: A critical literature review. *British Journal of Occupational Therapy, 71*(1), 2–12.

Krefting, L., & Krefting, D. (1991). Leisure activities after a stroke: An ethnographic approach. *American Journal of Occupational Therapy, 45*, 429–436.

Lannin, N. A., Cusick, A., McCluskey, A., & Herbert, R. D. (2007). Effects of splinting on wrist contracture after stroke: A randomized controlled trial. *Stroke, 38*(1), 111–116.

Law, M., & Baum, C. (1998). Evidence-based occupational therapy. *Canadian Journal of Occupational Therapy, 65*, 131–135.

Law, M., & MacDermid, J. (Eds.). (2008). *Evidence-based rehabilitation: A guide to practice* (2nd ed.). Thorofare, NJ: Slack.

Legg, L., Drummond, A., Leonardi-Bee, J., Gladman, J. R. F., Corr, S., Donkervoort, M., et al. (2007). Occupational therapy for patients with problems in personal activities of daily living after stroke: Systematic review of randomised trials. *British Medical Journal, 335*, 922–925.

Malec, J. F. (2009). Ethical and evidence-based practice in brain injury rehabilitation. *Neuropsychological Rehabilitation, 19*(6), 790–806.

Mallinson, T., & Fischer, H. (2010). *Centennial Vision*: Rehabilitation research. *American Journal of Occupational Therapy, 64*, 506–514.

Marks, S. (1999). Qualitative studies. In A. McKibbon, A. Eady, & S. Marks (Eds.), *PDQ evidence-based principles and practice* (pp. 187–204). Hamilton, Ontario: B. C. Decker.

Maxwell, S. E., & Delaney, H. D. (2000). *Designing experiments and analyzing data.* Mahwah, NJ: Erlbaum.

McCluskey, A., & Cusick, A. (2002). Strategies for introducing evidence-based practice and changing clinician behaviour: A manager's toolbox. *Australian Occupational Therapy Journal, 49*(2), 63–70.

McKenna, K., Tooth, L., Strong, J., Ottenbacher, K. J., Connell, J., & Cleary, M. (2002). Predicting discharge outcomes for stroke patients in Australia. *American Journal of Physical Medicine and Rehabilitation, 81*, 47–56.

McKibbon, A., Eady, A., & Marks, S. (1999). *PDQ evidence-based principles and practice.* Hamilton, Ontario: B. C. Decker.

McLeod, P., Steinert, Y., Boudreau, D., Snell, L., & Wiseman, J. (2010). Twelve tips for conducting a medical education journal club. *Medical Teacher, 32*(5), 368–370.

Morahan, S. (2002). Wide application of CQI in home care. *Journal of Nursing Care Quality, 16*(3), 36–49.

Morrell, K. (2008). The narrative of "evidence based" management: A polemic. *Journal of Management Studies, 43*, 613–635.

Muir Gray, J. A., Haynes, R. B., Sackett, D. L., Cook, D. J., & Guyatt, G. H. (1997). Transferring evidence from research into practice: 3. Developing evidence-based clinical policy. *ACP Journal Club, 126*, A14.

National Stroke Foundation. (2008). *Occupational therapy concise guideline for stroke rehabilitation and recovery.* Retrieved July 2, 2010, from http://www.guideline.gov/summary/summary.aspx?doc_id=12934

Ottenbacher, K. J. (1992). Statistical conclusion validity and Type IV errors in rehabilitation research. *Archives of Physical Medicine and Rehabilitation, 73*, 121–125.

Ottenbacher, K. J., & Barrett, K. A. (1989). Measures of effect size in rehabilitation research. *American Journal of Physical Medicine and Rehabilitation, 68*, 52–58.

Ottenbacher, K. J., Heyn, P., & Abreu, B. C. (2006). Meta-analysis. In G. Kielhofner (Ed.), *Research in occupational therapy: Methods of inquiry for enhancing practice* (pp. 281–325). Philadelphia: F. A. Davis.

Ottenbacher, K. J., & Hinderer, S. R. (2001). Evidence-based practice: Methods to evaluate individual patient improvement. *American Journal of Physical Medicine and Rehabilitation, 80*, 786–796.

Ottenbacher, K. J., & Maas, F. (1999). How to detect effects: Statistical power and evidence-based practice in occupational therapy research. *American Journal of Occupational Therapy, 53*, 181–188.

Owens, D. K., Lohr, K. N., Atkins, D., Treadwell, J. R., Reston, J. T., Bass, E. B., et al. (2010). Grading the strength of a body of evidence when comparing medical interventions: Agency for Healthcare Research and Quality and the Effective Health Care Program. *Journal of Clinical Epidemiology, 63*(5), 513–523.

Oxford English Dictionary (5th ed.). (1995). Oxford, UK: Oxford University Press.

Page, S. J., Levine, P., & Hill, V. (2007). Mental practice as a gateway to modified constraint-induced movement therapy: A promising combination to improve function. *American Journal of Occupational Therapy, 61*, 321–327.

Paterson, B. L., Thorne, S. E., Canam, C., & Jillings, C. (2001). *Meta-study of qualitative health research: A practical guide to meta-analysis and meta-synthesis* (Vol. 3). Thousand Oaks, CA: Sage.

Rao, J. N. (1999). Clinical trials in primary care: Paying doctors for clinical trials is unethical [Letter]. *British Medical Journal, 318,* 1485.

Reagon, C., Bellin, W., & Boniface, G. (2008). Reconfiguring evidence-based practice for occupational therapists. *International Journal of Therapy and Rehabilitation, 15,* 428–436.

Sabari, J. S. (2008). *Occupational therapy practice guidelines for adults with stroke.* Bethesda, MD: AOTA Press.

Sackett, D. L., Straus, S. E., Richardson, W. S., Rosenberg, W., & Haynes, R. B. (2000). *Evidence-based medicine: How to practice and teach EBM* (2nd ed.). New York: Churchill Livingstone.

Seelig, C. B. (1991). Affecting residents' literature reading attitudes, behaviors, and knowledge through a journal club intervention. *Journal of General Internal Medicine,* 6(4), 330–334.

Sidorov, J. (1995). How are internal medicine residency journal clubs organized, and what makes them successful. *Archives of Internal Medicine, 155*(11), 1193–1197.

Stason, W. B., Bergstrom, N., Duncan, P. W., Laouri, M., & Johnston, M. V. (1997). Can clinical practice guidelines increase the cost-effectiveness of geriatric rehabilitation? *Medical Care, 35*(6), JS68–JS89.

Stergiou-Kita, M. (2010). Implementing clinical practice guidelines in occupational therapy practice: Recommendations from the research evidence. *Australian Occupational Therapy Journal, 57*(2), 76–87.

Stern, P., & Harris, C. (1985). Women's health and the self-care paradox: A model to guide self-care readiness—Clash between client and nurse. *Health Care for Women International, 6,* 151–163.

Stevens, A., Abrams, K., Brazier, J., Fitzpatrick, R., & Lilford, R. (Eds.). (2001). *The advanced handbook of methods in evidence-based healthcare.* Thousand Oaks, CA: Sage.

Straus, S. E. (1999). Evidence-based medicine: Bringing evidence to the point of care. *ACP Journal Club, 4,* 70–71.

Stube, J. E., & Jedlicka, J. S. (2007). The acquisition and integration of evidence-based practice concepts by occupational therapy students. *American Journal of Occupational Therapy, 61,* 53–61.

Taylor, M. C. (1997). What is evidence-based practice? *British Journal of Occupational Therapy, 60,* 470–473.

Tickle-Degnen, L. (1998). Using research evidence in planning treatment for the individual client. *Canadian Journal of Occupational Therapy, 65,* 152–159.

Tickle-Degnen, L. (2008). Communicating evidence to clients, managers, and families. In M. Law & J. MacDermid (Eds.), *Evidence-based rehabilitation: A guide to practice* (2nd ed., pp. 263–295). Thorofare, NJ: Slack.

Walker, J., & Pink, M. J. (2009). Occupational therapists and the use of constraint-induced movement therapy in neurological practice. *Australian Occupational Therapy Journal, 56*(6), 436–437.

Whittemore, R., Chase, S. K., & Mandle, C. L. (2001). Validity in qualitative research. *Qualitative Health Research, 11,* 522–537.

Willer, B., Rosenthal, M., Kreutzer, J., Gordon, W., & Rempel, R. (1994). *Community Integration Questionnaire.* St. Catharine's, Ontario: Ontario Brain Injury Association.

Zhang, L., Abreu, B. C., Gonzales, V. A., Seale, G., Masel, B., & Ottenbacher, K. J. (2002). Comparison of the Community Integration Questionnaire, the Craig Handicap Assessment Reporting Technique, and the Disability Rating Scale in traumatic brain injury. *Journal of Head Trauma Rehabilitation, 17*(6), 497–509.

APPENDIX 22.A. EVIDENCE-BASED PRACTICE EVIDENCE TABLE

Topic	Subtopic	Evidence
Application to practice	Application to practice, cost-effectiveness	Chiu, T., & Tickle-Degnen, L. (2002). Learning from evidence: Service outcomes and client satisfaction with occupational therapy home-based services. *American Journal of Occupational Therapy, 56*, 217–220. Graff, M. J. L., Adang, E. M. M., Vernooij-Dassen, M. J. M., Dekker, J., Jonsson, L., Thijssen, M., et al. (2008). Community occupational therapy for older patients with dementia and their care givers: Cost effectiveness study. *British Medical Journal, 336*, 134–138. Hay, J., LaBree, L., Luo, R., Clark, F., Carlson, M., Mandel, D., et al. (2002). Cost-effectiveness of preventive occupational therapy for independent-living older adults. *Journal of the American Geriatrics Society, 50*(8), 1381–1388.
Clinical guidelines	Application to practice, cost-effectiveness	Bedard, D., Purden, M. A., Sauve-Larose, N., Certosini, C., & Schein, C. (2006). The pain experience of post surgical patients following the implementation of an evidence-based approach. *Pain Management Nursing, 7*(3), 80–92. National Stroke Foundation. (2008). *Occupational therapy concise guideline for stroke rehabilitation and recovery.* Retrieved July 2, 2010, from http://www.guideline.gov/summary/summary.aspx?doc_id=12934 Sabari, J. S. (2008). *Occupational therapy practice guidelines for adults with stroke.* Bethesda, MD: AOTA Press. Stason, W. B., Bergstrom, N., Duncan, P. W., Laouri, M., & Johnston, M. V. (1997). Can clinical practice guidelines increase the cost-effectiveness of geriatric rehabilitation? *Medical Care, 35*(6), JS68–JS89. Stergiou-Kita, M. (2010). Implementing clinical practice guidelines in occupational therapy practice: Recommendations from the research evidence. *Australian Occupational Therapy Journal, 57*(2), 76–87.
Randomized controlled trials	Application to practice	Clark, F., Azen, S. P., Zemki, R., Jackson, J., Carlson, M., Mandel, D., et al. (1997). Occupational therapy for independent-living older adults: A randomized controlled trial. *JAMA, 278*, 1321–1326. Graff, M. J. L., Vernooij-Dassen, M. J. M., Thijssen, M., Dekker, J., Hoefnagels, W. H. L., & Olde Rikkert, M. G. M. (2007). Effects of community occupational therapy on quality of life, mood, and health status in dementia patients and their caregivers: A randomized controlled trial. *Journal of Gerontology: A. Biological Sciences and Medical Sciences, 62*, 1002–1009. Lannin, N. A., Cusick, A., McCluskey, A., & Herbert, R. D. (2007). Effects of splinting on wrist contracture after stroke : A randomized controlled trial. *Stroke, 38*(1), 111–116.
Qualitative research	Application to practice	Davies, D., & Dodd, J. (2002). Qualitative research and the question of rigor. *Qualitative Health Research, 12*, 279–289. Giacomini, M. K. (2001). The rocky road: Qualitative research as evidence. *ACP Journal Club, 134*(1), A11–A13. Krefting, L., & Krefting, D. (1991). Leisure activities after a stroke: An ethnographic approach. *American Journal of Occupational Therapy, 45*, 429–436. Whittemore, R., Chase, S. K., & Mandle, C. L. (2001). Validity in qualitative research. *Qualitative Health Research, 11*, 522–537.
Meta-analysis	Application to practice	Carlson, M., Fanchiang, S.-P., Zemke, R., & Clark, F. (1996). A meta-analysis of the effectiveness of occupational therapy in older persons. *American Journal of Occupational Therapy, 50*, 89–98. Ottenbacher, K. J., Heyn, P., & Abreu, B. C. (2006). Meta-analysis. In G. Kielhofner (Ed.), *Research in occupational therapy: Methods of inquiry for enhancing practice* (pp. 281–325). Philadelphia: F. A. Davis
Outcome research	Application to practice	Hayner, K., Gibson, G., & Giles, G. M. (2010). Comparison of constraint-induced movement therapy and bilateral treatment of equal intensity in people with chronic upper-extremity dysfunction after cerebrovascular accident. *American Journal of Occupational Therapy, 64*(4), 528–539.

APPENDIX 22.A. EVIDENCE-BASED PRACTICE EVIDENCE TABLE *(cont.)*

Topic	Subtopic	Evidence
Systematic review	Application to practice	Legg, L., Drummond, A., Leonardi-Bee, J., Gladman, J. R. F., Corr, S., Donkervoort, M., et al. (2007). Occupational therapy for patients with problems in personal activities of daily living after stroke: Systematic review of randomised trials. *British Medical Journal, 335*, 922–925.
Evidence-based practice process	Management	Law, M., & MacDermid, J. (Eds.). (2008). *Evidence-based rehabilitation: A guide to practice* (2nd ed.). Thorofare, NJ: Slack. McCluskey, A., & Cusick, A. (2002). Strategies for introducing evidence-based practice and changing clinician behaviour: A manager's toolbox. *Australian Occupational Therapy Journal, 49*(2), 63–70. Morrell, K. (2008). The narrative of "evidence based" management: A polemic. *Journal of Management Studies, 43*, 613–635. Sackett, D. L., Straus, S. E., Richardson, W. S., Rosenberg, W., & Haynes, R. B. (2000). *Evidence-based medicine: How to practice and teach EBM* (2nd ed.). New York: Churchill Livingstone. Stevens, A., Abrams, K., Brazier, J., Fitzpatrick, R., & Lilford, R. (Eds.). (2001). *The advanced handbook of methods in evidence-based healthcare.* Thousand Oaks, CA: Sage.
Journal clubs	Application to practice	McLeod, P., Steinert, Y., Boudreau, D., Snell, L., & Wiseman, J. (2010). Twelve tips for conducting a medical education journal club. *Medical Teacher, 32*(5), 368–370. Seelig, C. B. (1991). Affecting residents' literature reading attitudes, behaviors, and knowledge through a journal club intervention. *Journal of General Internal Medicine, 6*(4), 330–334. Sidorov, J. (1995). How are internal medicine residency journal clubs organized, and what makes them successful? *Archives of Internal Medicine, 155*(11), 1193–1197.

23
Evidence-Based Occupational Therapy Management

Steven C. Eyler, MS, OTR/L, and
Kristie Horner Kapusta, MS, OT/L

❖ Key Terms and Concepts

Attitude of inquiry. The regular use of skills, such as reflecting, predicting, questioning, and hypothesizing, to deepen understanding.

Chosen accountability. The recognition of one's own responsibility for choices, personal involvement in creating expectations, and active role in defining purpose and intent. This type of accountability implies a more internal locus of control as opposed to an external locus of control (e.g., meeting someone else's expectations).

Complex adaptive systems. Systems that have the ability to evolve, self-organize, and adapt to a changing environment. Examples of adaptive systems are living organisms, the immune system, health care organizations, and the economy.

Connection precedes content. A principle that stresses that learning is enhanced when there is a developed relationship with those from whom one is learning.

Multiple points of entry. The multiple portals for developing the skills and understanding that contribute to evidence-based practice.

❖ Learning Objectives

After completing this chapter, you should be able to do the following:

- Describe the importance of and methods for promoting a sense of ownership, accountability, engagement, and commitment.
- Identify examples of research-based management approaches.
- Identify resources available to facilitate evidence-based management practice.

- Discuss the implications of a management approach based on a machine metaphor versus a naturally adaptive systems metaphor.
- Describe methods for measuring the effect of evidence-based practice.

This chapter describes the role of management in creating a work environment that fosters and supports evidence-based practice (EBP). Sackett, Straus, Richardson, Rosenberg, and Haynes (2000) defined *EBP* as "the integration of best research evidence with clinical expertise and patient values" (p. 1). This chapter addresses the following leadership themes that influence EBP:

- How to prepare clinicians to better serve clients in a world of expanding knowledge and rapid change

- How to implement change in a culture
- How to create an invitation to urge others to join in EBP
- How to create a sense of ownership
- How to build an infrastructure that supports EBP
- How to foster the commitment to both initiate and sustain a context and culture of EBP
- How to deal with the dilemma that it is seemingly impossible for a single individual to read, recall, and apply the large volume of clinically relevant scientific literature

- How to create an element of trust for the expression of doubts and reservations regarding evidence-based practice.

The intent of this chapter is to describe methods for encouraging, enhancing, and sustaining a culture of EBP. The supporting evidence for these methods is drawn from the health care, business, and leadership literature. Throughout the chapter, true–false questions are presented as a way to illustrate for occupational therapy practitioners the empirical foundation and validity of the evidence-based leadership approaches.

ROLE OF LEADERSHIP

The implementation of EBP requires an authentic commitment from the occupational therapy manager, other leaders, and practitioners. The ability to respond to the challenges of acquiring, analyzing, and applying knowledge in a manner that is scientifically rigorous demands a disciplined approach to therapeutic interventions. Knowledge of scientific reasoning and skills in critical thinking are essential. This section discusses the concepts of *mandated versus chosen authority* and *connection precedes content* in guiding practitioners toward EBP.

MANDATED ACCOUNTABILITY VS. CHOSEN ACCOUNTABILITY

The term *mandated accountability* refers to the dominant view of accountability, which attempts to hold individuals responsible through tighter controls and policies (Block, 2008). The methods of traditional mandated accountability seem inadequate for the task of promoting a culture of EBP. This approach to accountability attempts to force compliance. An occupational therapy manager taking this approach tends to unilaterally define and control the methods, measures, and consequences of the implementation of EBP.

By contrast, *chosen accountability* emphasizes the personal commitment that occurs when an individual chooses to care for the well-being of the whole (Block, 2008). This approach to accountability fosters the willingness of each practitioner to take personal responsibility to contribute to the future state of EBP in his or her workplace and among the profession as a whole. Chosen accountability emphasizes shared responsibility for the further development of occupational therapy as a science-driven, evidence-based profession. To promote chosen accountability, the manager needs to lead and facilitate a collaborative process that allows practitioners to be directly involved in creating goals, plans, and measurements. The desired outcome is to develop a culture in the workplace in which practitioners are consistently mindful of EBP. In this environment, they will question themselves and colleagues critically for the greater good of sharing information and promoting the science of occupational therapy.

The first step required of an occupational therapy manager or leader who is seeking to engage others in a mean-

ingful inquiry or conversation about EBP is to issue an invitation that defines the debate and invites others to join in. An invitation in the sense we are using it here is not to gain "buy in" or to "roll out" an initiative but rather to offer a possibility for change and urge others to participate as partners in contributing ideas and forming workable solutions (Block, 2008). The topic of EBP offers rich opportunities to deepen accountability and commitment in areas that many professionals find meaningful. Such meaningful conversations may result in outcomes such as expanding or enhancing services to clients; identifying meaningful ways to apply and integrate new technologies; and enhancing learning, teamwork, and networking skills.

For example, both occupational therapists and physical therapists use ultrasound as an intervention. In a setting that lacks an evidence-based policy regarding the application of ultrasound, the occupational therapy manager could issue an invitation to both departments to join an ultrasound working group. The memo might read as follows:

> This is an invitation for you to participate in an evidence-based practice group to establish treatment standards and guidelines for the use of ultrasound. This discussion will require some time commitment both during working hours and outside of work. You will be encouraged to participate in an open dialogue about available research, and you should be able to support your decisions and conclusions through logical thinking and evidence.
>
> Participation in this project is voluntary. We realize that there are many demands on your time, and if you choose not to participate, we will assume you have a good reason. The goal of the discussion group is to develop an action plan, written guidelines, and/or policy based on the best available evidence and best practices.
>
> Please let me know within the next 2 weeks if you are interested in being a member of this group.

Constructing an authentic invitation for engagement in EBP requires the manager to name the possibility, allow room for refusal, explicitly state the requirements, and clearly define the request (Block, 2008). This invitation could be a collaborative effort between the occupational therapy manager and the physical therapy manager and could be delivered in person, by phone, or by e-mail.

CONNECTION PRECEDES CONTENT

To be successfully engaged in EBP, a practitioner needs to experience a sense of belonging to a community of like-minded practitioners. The large-scale effects and transformations possible through EBP are the result of the continual accumulation of knowledge and incremental progress over time. Individual efforts become connected to group efforts. Group efforts then become connected to the larger community of occupational therapy. Through this sequence of connections, the future of the profession is shaped and transformed. Scientific method and theory, statistical analysis, and the analysis of available research all provide challenging material for intellectual discourse.

Personal connections that create the experience of belonging to a community of evidence-based practitioners can overcome feelings of isolation and make a difficult, complex task seem doable. An extensive study of employee satisfaction surveys provided evidence for the importance of a personal connection with those in the workplace (Buckingham & Coffman, 1999). The Gallup Organization identified 12 key questions that correlated with the important business indicators of productivity, employee turnover, profitability, and customer satisfaction. For example, agreement with the statement "I have a best friend at work" positively correlated with customer satisfaction and productivity. Agreement with the statement "My supervisor, or someone at work, seems to care about me as a person" positively correlated with all four indicators (Buckingham & Coffman, 1999). This study provides evidence that the most effective performance occurs when employees establish a personal connection with each other. Group support and personal connections facilitate shared values, optimism, willingness to act, and commitment to persevere.

Strengthening work relationships and personal connections among employees thus enhances participation, engagement, and a sense of community in the organization. Appreciating relatedness and communal possibility is integral to promoting EBP within an occupational therapy practice and the wider profession. Managers can encourage personal connections during meetings and presentations by asking a series of connecting questions. A sample exercise using connecting questions would proceed as follows:

- Help participants connect to their self by asking them to reflect on a personal question: How present are you at this moment? Describe to what extent you are here by choice. Questions like these highlight that each person has his or her own answer and that each one is right. These questions are designed to invite inquiry and exploration.
- Help participants connect to another by sharing the answers to a question with a partner: What would it take for you to be fully present? How much do you plan to participate in this meeting? Questions like this carry the implication of individual accountability and responsibility.
- Help participants connect with a group by discussing their answers in a small group of 3–4 individuals. A small group discussion allows participants to discover that even if others do not agree with them, they can at least understand what they are thinking. The sense of belonging is also fostered by the experience that their own concerns are shared by others.
- Help participants connect to the whole room (community) by asking for volunteers to share with the whole room something that struck them during the group conversation. By connecting with the larger group, participants are reminded of what they have in common with the group, as well as of the diversity of points of view represented in the room.

This exercise encourages active participation in the process of EBP and can be used as a warm-up in a gathering of any size. This method engages people even if their expectation is to sit and listen. Active participation establishes the primacy of connection, increases the overall focus and engagement of participants, and is a small-scale example of the larger process for promoting EBP within our profession.

Presenting choices, convening authentic conversations, and using an approach that values relatedness are the fundamental starting points for the role of leadership in creating a culture of EBP. This process engenders EBP by encouraging practitioners to make a personal commitment in choosing to contribute to EBP. This approach also helps occupational therapy practitioners acknowledge that the future of occupational therapy as an evidence-based profession is built on the collective contributions of practitioners at all levels.

PROMOTING EVIDENCE-BASED PRACTICE IN THE CLINICAL SETTING

The following are three key principles for a leader to incorporate when promoting EBP:

1. *Attitude of inquiry:* Encourage practitioners to apply scientific reasoning to their practice. For example, ask critical questions about their approaches and outcomes, and help them generate hypotheses about their clinical observations and find and appraise the research evidence to explain their observations.
2. *Ownership and accountability:* Help practitioners recognize their own contribution to the current condition and their freedom to create the future and to see themselves as a locus of change.
3. *Participation:* Empower others to actively engage in any aspect of the EBP process.

These three principles can be effectively and powerfully taught by example, and they provide guidance for approaching and structuring group efforts toward incorporating EBP. Each principle is discussed in more detail in the sections that follow.

Attitude of Inquiry

An attitude of inquiry is a key attribute of a scientific approach to therapy practice. This approach includes carefully observing and evaluating the impact of one's interventions, using evidence to guide what one does, and reviewing and appraising relevant research (Holm, 2000). Humans are intensely curious, but they may not recognize their inherent interest or curiosity until they have been confronted by a challenge to their knowledge or memory. In one study (Gilbert, 2007), volunteers were asked to take a short geography quiz and then offered a choice of two rewards: the answers to the quiz or a candy bar. Volunteers who were asked to select their reward before taking the quiz preferred the candy bar. Those who were asked after taking the quiz preferred the answers. Finally, a third group of volunteers was asked to predict which reward they would choose if the offer was made before or after taking the quiz. This last group predicted that they would prefer the candy bar regardless of when the offer was made, revealing a tendency to underestimate the power of curiosity.

For the occupational therapy manager, studies like this indicate that regular attempts to tap into and foster scientific curiosity can be an effective strategy even for practitioners who initially seem disinterested in EBP. The manager promotes EBP whenever he or she asks interesting questions, generates hypotheses, or engages in critical analysis. The following are some general questions directly related to EBP:

- In what ways did the client demonstrate improved performance?
- Which intervention allowed the client to improve?
- Does a particular intervention produce better outcomes than another intervention?
- What are alternative interventions?
- What would the outcome be if no intervention was provided?
- How do practitioners translate knowledge or theory into clinical practice?

Another way to generate interest in reviewing current literature and research is to present colleagues with a true–false quiz on clinically interesting topics. Managers can ask their colleagues to answer the following three true–false statements:

1. External memory aids are a very effective compensatory strategy for individuals with memory impairment.
2. Daily stretching routines prevent the development of contractures.
3. The risk of falls in elderly clients is related more to decreased speed of movement than to decreased strength.

According to Fielding (2002) and based on research, the answers are as follows: Statement 1 is false, Statement 2 is true, and Statement 3 is true. The manager can ask these true–false questions as part of an initial effort to stimulate interest in EBP, as an introduction to an inservice sharing of research results from a literature review or conference, or as a warm-up activity to generate ideas for clinical questions of interest. The manager may also note that although evidence exists for each of these items, the evidence may be of varying strength and may even be contradicted by more recent research.

Ownership and Accountability

Ownership is one's decision to become the author of one's own experience (Block, 2008). Ownership hinges on the context leaders create to promote inclusiveness and on the nature of the questions they use to engage people. *Accountability* is the willingness to take personal responsibility to contribute to the future state of EBP in one's workplace and among the profession as a whole. The following are key questions leaders can ask to foster practitioners' reflection on ownership and accountability:

- What is the nature of the crossroads we are facing?
- How participative do you plan to be?
- How invested are you in the future of the profession?

These questions can be used with staff at all levels to encourage conversations that foster ownership and accountability for their actions. By creating a consistent expectation of staff participation and by allowing diverse opinions to be expressed, the occupational therapy manager can overcome any initial resistance to this kind of activity. These questions share the following characteristics: There is no single answer, they are personal in nature, and they carry the implication that each individual is responsible to some degree for creating the circumstances at work or the situation he or she experiences in daily life (Block, 2008).

Participation

Participation is defined in this chapter as active engagement and empowerment of staff in implementing EBP. Participation is broad in the sense that all practitioners are encouraged to be actively engaged in at least some aspect of EBP. Broad participation is a strategy that promotes EBP, given the reality that practitioners often have limited time within their workday to read, retain meaning, and make informed decisions on the basis of the best available research. The growth of the scientific medical literature far outpaces the capacity of any individual clinician to remain up-to-date. The tactic of having many therapists engaged in EBP assists in accomplishing key objectives and staying abreast of new information. Broad participation ensures that the workload can be distributed among many therapists, thereby helping a practice keep pace with current research and advances. Additionally, such participation helps ensure that one is exposed to a broader frame of reference in which alternate hypotheses and possibilities can be entertained, resulting in a thorough and holistic approach to problem solving and decision making about clinical challenges. Practitioners who perform therapy every day in the trenches can benefit from a collective effort of scientific inquiry and sound decision making. This process forces them to consider varied frames of reference from the widest possible number of resources.

Another true–false question the manager can ask colleagues is as follows: In small groups, diversity of opinion is the single factor that best ensures the group will benefit from face-to-face discussion as opposed to a less direct and representative communication: true or false? This statement is true. In fact, this statement is true even when minority points of view lack evidence and merit. Studies of jury decisions indicate that confrontation with a dissenting view forces the majority of participants to stand back and reflect on their own positions more critically, thus producing more rigorous and sound decisions (Surowiecki, 2004).

Managers should consider multiple points of entry into a topic in seeking to encourage participation in EBP. For example, there are many possible starting points for generating a group discussion, including completing an article search, reading and discussing an article in a journal club, brainstorming about clinical questions, sharing a case study, or brainstorming alternative treatment ideas. The main point is to begin the process in several ways. For instance, the group can start with an issue of *OT Practice*, and each member can choose an article and take a position or form an argument for or against the thesis of the article. Some advanced groups use journals from neuroscience to find evidence that is more specific. In the 2007 Eleanor Clarke Slagle Lecture, Hinojosa stated that occupational therapists cannot afford to "wait and see" in this era of "hyperchange." Rather, they need to work to develop and provide theory-based interventions. Establishing and facilitating multiple points of entry can encourage broad participation and promote EBP by pooling the collective knowledge of the group.

Another method for facilitating participation in EBP is to include in the rules for the meeting the requirement that everyone's voice will be heard during the meeting. To assist group members in getting used to the expectation of broad participation, the leader can ask a question that requires an individual response from all who are present. The leader can start with simple questions, such as "Let's go around the table and give one word that you would use to describe EBP." The group can then progress to more challenging questions, such as "Think about what you do that prevents a more timely response from the department in translating research evidence into clinical practice" or "What can you do to improve your participation in EBP?"

In reinforcing the requirement to hear from everyone, the manager can still provide a choice to pass on a particular question, but he or she should make it an active choice and not a passive response. Simply requiring that an individual state "pass" loud enough for everyone to hear accomplishes this objective. Active responses provide the baseline expectation that everyone participates and can begin to increase participants' sense of safety by not imposing negative consequences for dissent. This activity can be used in almost any group setting. When used consistently, it can be an effective method for establishing the expectation of active participation. Individuals who are not inclined to speak up are often able to find their voice in this type of activity.

Broad and active participation in the context of meetings or work groups is also an expectation of a professional group. Both work groups and professional groups enable members to recognize that their knowledge is never complete and that EBP is a never-ending process. In the workplace, EBP can take a lower priority when staff are busy and the workload increases. EBP takes an ongoing commitment, and the task of promoting it should never be crossed off the to-do list. EBP is a commitment to continuing education and lifelong learning. All scientific knowledge is provisional; research knowledge changes continuously as more evidence is accumulated. Staff members may be involved in different activities at different times to keep the process alive. One group may start a critical article review while another group constructs a clinical question to address the problem based on the best available evidence. Through the application of EBP, clinical practice is enhanced by the expansion of the occupational therapy practitioner's body of knowledge.

MOVING THE MEAN

Moving the mean refers to increasing, on average, clinicians' use of treatment approaches that are supported by the best available research evidence. The manager's objective is to "move the mean" so that client treatments are based increasingly on science and evidence rather than on habit and techniques that lack adequate research support. This concept does not suggest that all therapists provide identical treatments. The studies that support occupational therapy practice are open to interpretation; the variables embodied in each individual client may limit the applicability of available small-sample research. As a profession, occupational therapists and occupational therapy assistants strive to make choices and decisions within the scope of practice, the *Occupational Therapy Practice Framework: Domain and Process* (American Occupational Therapy Association [AOTA], 2008), and a context of the best available evidence. EBP allows individual practitioners to draw different conclusions from the available research and through critical reasoning to arrive at a decision. EBP is a process that evolves over time and does not allow for a refusal to expand one's knowledge of the evidence. The objective is to be more effective, to use better interventions today than yesterday, and to move the mean of practice to elevate the decision-making process in the direction of best practice.

The occupational therapy manager can promote EBP not only through promoting broad participation but also by setting an example and by acknowledging those who participate rather than dwelling on those who are resistant. It is possible to move the mean of the unit's practice without 100% participation. As with any change, some people take to change right away, many are "fence sitters," and a small minority resist or even try to sabotage the process. More progress can be made by focusing time, attention, and encouragement on the practitioners who are not actively opposed to the philosophy of EBP. The beginning steps to establish a culture of EBP are more encouraging of behavioral change in resistors than supervisory pressure or coercion. Successful projects and meetings focus on those who *choose* to show up rather than those who are not mentally and philosophically present.

One final argument for an approach that relies on broad participation rather than directive leadership is the evidence found in the literature that groups are often smarter than the most intelligent individual in the group. Numerous studies of the performance of chief operating officers have found that strong leadership alone is often not enough when coming up with solutions to problems. According to Surowiecki (2004), who reviewed numerous studies of executive decision making, aggregate group knowledge tends to be better than the knowledge even of the smartest individual in the group. He found surprisingly little evidence that single individuals can consistently make superior forecasts or strategic decisions. There are, however, conditions that tend to make group decision making more intelligent: breadth of information, diversity of membership, and independence of analysis. Findings also indicate that individuals with local knowledge are often best positioned to identify problems and come up with workable solutions.

RESOURCES

Contemporary occupational therapists and occupational therapy assistants are fortunate to have relatively easy electronic access to evidence for clinical practice. A few keystrokes thrust one into the world of databases and search engines. The abundance of EBP information can, in fact, be overwhelming. This section highlights resources that can best be used to access, analyze, and appraise the evidence before putting it into practice.

Many resources have been developed to measure the quality of the evidence and assist in critically appraising the research. AOTA has organized an *Evidence-Based Practice Resource Directory* that serves as a link to evidence in many practice domains. This resource is available to AOTA members through the AOTA Web site and provides links to many resources, including *American Journal of Occupational Therapy* articles, *OT Practice* articles, *Special Interest Section Quarterly* articles, critically appraised topics, critically appraised papers, evidence briefs, evidence perks, and evidence bytes. In addition, the Physiotherapy Evidence Database (PEDro) provides access to the PEDro scale, a tool that measures the methodological quality of randomized controlled trials (Centre for Evidence-Based Physiotherapy, n.d.). This scale comprises 11 yes–no questions for evaluating an article; answers are used to compile a score that reflects the quality of the evidence.

The Article Analysis Format introduced by Holm (2000) highlights pertinent information within an article. The Article Analysis Format includes relevant findings, interventions provided, and a description of the independent and dependent variables. Holm's uses a qualitative format, as compared to the quantitative format of the PEDro scale. In addition, Trombly and Ma (2002) developed the Levels of Evidence grading scale. The research design, sample size, and internal and external validity are included in this scale.

Occupational therapy managers can use these resources to increase their familiarity with research language and their level of comfort in critically appraising the evidence. The PEDro scale, Holm's (2000) Article Analysis Format, and Trombly and Ma's (2002) Levels of Evidence grading scale provide in-depth assessments of a research article. Reading and drawing conclusions from the abstract alone, however, do not take full advantage of the evidence and can lead practitioners to make clinical decisions without all of the necessary information. Dropout rate, inclusion and exclusion criteria, and demographic characteristics are also of clinical importance. True evidence can be revealed only with a more thorough review of the research article using tools such as Holm's methodology as a guide.

COMMON BARRIERS TO OVERCOME IN PROMOTING EBP

How does an occupational therapy manager discuss the barriers to a cultural shift toward EBP openly with staff? The manager may anticipate some barriers, which usually include a lack of awareness of available resources, lack of skill in searching the literature, lack of time, and fear of losing clinical judgment. These issues are addressed individually in the sections that follow.

Availability of Resources

As discussed earlier, authentic commitment from leaders and practitioners alike is necessary to promote a culture of EBP, and that commitment is reflected in the investment of funds to expose practitioners to available resources and of time to allow open discussion among all levels of staff to share knowledge concerning best practices. There are many ways to promote EBP without large investments of funds or time, however. The occupational therapy manager can devote one staff meeting per month (or more, if possible) to a critical article review, with practitioners selecting articles relevant to their practice setting. In addition, new or recent occupational therapy graduates may be considered available resources: Because their instruction in the research process is more recent, they may be familiar with the most current research terminology, online sources, and publications in traditional journals. Some health care institutions have an existing reference library and designated staff to provide education on resources to promote EBP. If funds are available, a position can be created for a clinical research educator with responsibilities to "evaluate and develop evidence-based clinical practice and multidisciplinary programs for staff and the community . . . [and] serve as a resource for outcomes-based practice and direct research and education to improve patient outcomes" (Reid, Lawrence, & Orest, 2008, p. 32).

Development of Skills in EBP

The occupational therapy manager can help colleagues increase their skill in reading and interpreting the literature. For example, monthly journal clubs provide a forum to help staff familiarize themselves with the process of critically appraising research articles and become comfortable with research terminology. The manager can have a staff member with expertise in EBP lead the process; this person could be a supervisor, a clinical research educator, a new graduate, or simply an interested staff member. Project management, adult learning, and group dynamics are helpful areas of expertise (Reid et al., 2008).

Availability of Time

Lack of time is a concern for most health care providers. Constructing a flexible timeline is essential in creating a cultural shift toward EBP. A timeline provides a structured, goal-oriented method for organizing time. It also steps up the level of commitment to a systematic approach to EBP discussions. Assignments can be due on a specific date that is agreed on ahead of time by the practitioners involved. Colleagues making timeline commitments to each other supports the notion of chosen accountability and helps keep the process moving. An added value of implementing time-sensitive schedules is that it makes EBP part of the job responsibility and provides a forum for continuing competency. The perceived lack of time is often related to an inability to see an end point because the search for and analysis of research could continue indefinitely. By creating timelines, the occupational therapy manager clarifies the scope of the task and defines the time commitment required of participants. Lastly, a structured format, such as a project development worksheet, can help the group organize the most pertinent information needed to begin and keep track of progress; a sample format is provided in Exhibit 23.1.

Improvement in Clinical Judgment

Sackett et al.'s (2000) definition of EBP explicitly includes the use of "clinical skills and past experience . . . to rapidly identify benefits of potential interventions." (p. 1) Clinical judgment is thus an integral part of the EBP equation and should be considered a resource rather than something to be squelched. In addition, as Case-Smith (2004) observed, "applying research studies to one's work does not necessarily mean changing intervention strategies. It may mean providing more specific, detailed, and up-to-date information to your clients about the efficacy and expected outcomes of the approaches used" (p. 7). As previously stated, clients are subject to unique combinations of variables, and not all protocols or research regimens will necessarily apply. Pertinent findings can be extracted from the evidence to apply as appropriate; clinical reasoning is used to determine and judge which treatment elements to use with which clients.

CHALLENGES OF COMPLEX SYSTEMS

In implementing the approach to fostering EBP outlined in this chapter, the occupational therapy manager may need to overcome some significant hurdles. Common hurdles include the following:

- How does one manage the complex and potentially confusing process of both encouraging multiple points of entry and asking people to follow their individual interests and passions?
- How does one avoid creating a chaotic mess while responding to competing priorities and conflicts?
- How does one design an EBP system that is sustainable, innovative, and responsive to changing conditions in health care?

EXHIBIT 23.1. SAMPLE PROJECT DEVELOPMENT WORKSHEET FORMAT FOR STRATEGIC PERFORMANCE IMPROVEMENT

Project Title

- Opportunities, challenges, and barriers:
- Problem statement, formatted as follows:

Condition	Stem + Key Verb	Purpose	Situation Parameters
"Because . . . ,"	"how might we . . .?" "in what ways might we . . .?"	"in order to . . ." "so that . . ."	"if," "after," "in," "before," "within," "given," "when"

For example, "Because some rehab clients present with complex conditions and behaviors, how might we provide adequate supervision so that clients are safe when they are with volunteers and the volunteers can have a positive experience after an appropriate orientation?"

- Solution ideas:
- Desired results, impact on key areas (what is to be *accomplished*, not what is to be *done*):
- Resources required (financial, personnel, technical, organizational):
- Accountability criteria (how results will be measured):
- Action plan (plan/do/study/act phases, include timelines and responsible person):
- Membership:
- Administrative support:

A *system* can be defined as the combination of many parts and interconnections to fulfill a purpose (Institute of Medicine, Committee on Quality Health Care in America, 2001). When managers think about designing a system, they typically think of a mechanical approach or a machine metaphor. A common mechanical example is a building's heating system, which includes interconnected thermostats, ducts, furnace, and vents. Mechanical or engineering systems are designed to provide a predictable response to particular circumstances or environmental stimuli. A mechanical systems approach is frequently used to manage human organizations and behaviors. Managers decide what they want the system to do and then define all the parts and connections. Complex tasks are broken down into component parts with the intent of achieving increased control over how the system responds.

In contrast, complex adaptive systems are those whose parts are able to respond to stimuli in many different and fundamentally unpredictable ways. These systems are

- Complex in terms of the number and diversity of connections among a wide variety of elements,
- Adaptive in their the ability to alter and change in response to changing conditions, and
- Systems in that a set of connected and interdependent parts work to perform certain tasks in an organizational setting.

Examples of complex adaptive systems include living and social systems, such as those in the human body, the health care system in the United States, an ecosystem, and the practice of occupational therapy as a whole. Complex adaptive systems provide for the possibility of emergent, surprising, and creative behavior. Such behaviors can be for better or for worse; that is, they can manifest as either innovation or a source of error. For example, the top-down management or engineering approach to designing a mechanical system is linear and does not provide the most helpful paradigm for designing a complex process, such as the incorporation of a culture of EBP. An alternative approach to the mechanical/engineering frame of reference is based on complexity theory, as described by Paul Plsek, an author on creativity (Institute of Medicine, 2001).

As discussed in Chapter 4 of this volume, an understanding of systems theory can help the occupational therapy manager understand approaches to change management. An understanding of complex adaptive systems provides a framework for shifting a practice toward a culture of EBP. The first step is to recognize that a culture of EBP has more in common with the characteristics of an ecological or naturally adaptive system than a reductionist or mechanical system.

Mechanical Systems vs. Naturally Adaptive Systems

Both mechanical and naturally adaptive systems can be extremely complex. The distinction lies in the actions and predictability of the parts. Each part in a mechanical system responds to any particular condition or stimulus, is defined in great detail, and is highly predictable. In naturally adaptive systems, the individual components have the ability to respond to conditions in unique, creative, and therefore unpredictable ways. Creativity, innovation, and diversity of responses are valued in a naturally adaptive system. In a mechanical system, on the other hand, too much diversity can be a source of error and failure. For instance, in a lawn mower motor, the internal combustion engine depends on fuel, oil to lubricate parts, and cog wheels to rotate the blade that cuts grass. The parts of the mower have a direct mechanical dependency that articulates in this system to cut grass.

By contrast, a complex adaptive system has more flexibility, and diversity becomes the source of adaptability and sustainability. A complex adaptive system is characterized by rich interconnections and the ability to self-organize (Institute of Medicine, 2001). For instance, the immune system in the human body interacts and adjusts to environmental stimuli such as pathogens, steps up its activities, and receives feedback from the endocrine and nervous systems in response to stress. Although the behavior of a mechanical system is defined by precise mechanical laws of physics, the complex behavior of a naturally adaptive system can emerge from a few simple rules that are applied consistently by the individual components of the system. The coherence and order of a complex adaptive system emerge when individuals within the system both have the autonomy to behave independently and follow a set of shared agreements or simple rules.

For example, a bird who is at the head of a flock does not engineer the behavior of the flock. Instead, the flock is a group of independent entities following a shared set of simple yet adaptable rules (Institute of Medicine, 2001, p. 315). Computer simulations have demonstrated that the rules for flocking of birds are to avoid collisions, to match speed with neighbors, and to move toward the center of the mass. Similarly, to nurture a complex adaptive system that allows its members to take a creative, adaptable, sustainable, and self-organized approach to EBP and avoids the challenges listed at the beginning of this section, the manager needs to develop an effective list of simple rules. One possible list is as follows:

- Everyone is involved in some EBP activity.
- Everyone is knowledgeable about common tools for finding and assessing evidence.
- Everyone shares a common definition of EBP (Exhibit 23.2).

Managers can ask their colleagues the following true–false question: Incorporating a story line about literacy into a popular soap opera produced dramatic results in previously intractable literacy rates in Mexico—true or false? This statement is true. Patterson, Grenny, Maxfield, McMillan, and Switzler (2008) provided extensive examples of significant measurable behavior change among both

EXHIBIT 23.2. DEFINITION OF *EVIDENCE-BASED PRACTICE*

Statement of Purpose

Our desire is that the Rehabilitation Therapies administration, clinicians, and clients work together to design and develop therapeutic processes in accordance with the principles of evidence-based decision making. We will create systems that enable clinicians to continuously improve service to clients in a world of expanding knowledge and rapid change.

Principles

- EBP is the integration of best research evidence with clinical expertise and client values.
- EBP involves the timely translation of knowledge into practice.
- The task is not to treat all situations alike but to understand when specifications and standardization are appropriate and when they are not.

Definitions

Best research evidence: Clinically relevant research on the efficacy and safety of therapeutic rehabilitative and preventive interventions and regimens.

Client values: The unique preferences, concerns, and expectations that each client brings to a clinical encounter and that must be integrated into clinical decisions if they are to serve the client.

Clinical expertise: The ability to use clinical skills and past experience for timely identification of each client's unique health state and condition, individual risks and benefits of potential interventions, and personal values and expectations.

Effectiveness: The degree to which systematically acquired evidence indicates that an intervention produces better outcomes than the alternatives, including the alternative of doing nothing.

Relationship to Outcomes

Outcomes research refers to the use of measures that make it possible to understand the degree to which performance is consistent with best practices and clients are being helped.

Note. Developed by the Rehabilitation Therapies management team at Fletcher Allen Health Care, Burlington, VT, to provide a position statement and staff education tool regarding evidence-based practice. Used with permission.

individuals and large groups of people. These changes were the result of a focus on a few vital behaviors or simple rules.

Mechanical systems require high control and predictable outcomes to function properly. A mechanical system depends on control, or it quickly breaks down. Complex adaptive systems need to constantly adjust to changing conditions, including the addition of new information. The decreased control and predictability characteristic of adaptive systems allow for flexibility under rapidly changing conditions and provide the opportunity for responses that are novel, creative, and innovative. For a system that needs to adapt, too much control can be as damaging to the outcomes as not enough control. The occupational therapy manager should take all of these factors into account in formulating guiding principles for implementing and sustaining a culture of EBP.

Complex Systems and Occupational Therapy Practice

The occupational therapy manager needs to skillfully balance the amount of control he or she exerts over the processes of EBP. Too little control can result in chaos, and too much control can stifle the innovation and creativity practitioners need to be successful. Progress within complex adaptive systems is evolutionary. These processes are expected to generate variation; useful variations can be encouraged while harmful variations are discouraged. Evolutionary adaptation involves constant tension and rebalancing. Evolutionary growth occurs best in an environment that includes opportunities to try lots of alternatives, keep what works, and weed out what does not work. Novelty, uncertainty, tension, and anxiety are all considered healthy traits in an evolving complex adaptive system.

An occupational therapy practice needs to function on multiple interdependent levels. The practice needs to be able to adapt to constantly changing conditions and to incorporate new learning. Finally, an occupational therapy practice needs to have a balance of success on multiple levels, including successful patient outcomes, financial viability, and employee satisfaction.

The study of complex adaptive systems provides a science-based metaphor for the management of complex endeavors, such as therapy practice or a culture of EBP. This frame of reference provides a more complete picture than a simple machine metaphor. Health care endeavors have a high interest in sustainability, adaptability, and innovation. A complexity framework provides insights into how management and leadership can be structured to facilitate these desired outcomes (Zimmerman, Lindberg, & Plsek, 1998).

DOUBTS AND RESERVATIONS ABOUT EBP

EBP does not produce absolute knowledge but rather helps practitioners know more today than they knew yesterday. A commitment to EBP requires that one be open to new evidence that may support, modify, or refute previously held beliefs. Answer these true–false questions: The earth is flat—true or false? The earth is a sphere—true or false? Both of these statements are false. The earth's shape approximates a sphere, but scientific evidence tells us that in fact the diameter from pole to pole is shorter than the diameter at the equator. Although both statements are false, the second is more true than the first. Likewise, clinical research does not provide final answers, but each advance in knowledge provides a closer approximation of reality.

Provisional Nature of Scientific Knowledge

All it takes to overturn accepted scientific knowledge is proof of a counterexample. Based on his keen observations, Charles Darwin concluded that all white cats with blue eyes are deaf. This observation appears to be true but will be immediately refuted if anyone ever finds a white cat with blue eyes that is not deaf (Patten, 2004, p. 40). The opportunity to disprove previously held ideas occurs every day. The scientific process itself requires researchers who are seeking the truth and an intellectual openness to challenging currently held beliefs and the expression of alternative viewpoints. It is important for occupational therapy practitioners to recognize that, as part of a science-driven profession, they will continually encounter new information that simultaneously enhances their knowledge and often contradicts previous understanding. The knowledge base that informs clinical practice is subject to constant revision.

Importance of Dissent Conversations in EBP

Sometimes dissent is viewed as a barrier to change. Dissent, however, is a healthy component of the scientific process, and it is also a component in facilitating a commitment to EBP. To effectively implement and encourage an environment of EBP, an occupational therapy manager needs to tolerate and even facilitate dissent conversations. Managers should not fear open discussions with those espousing active positions of dissent. Dissent conversations can be constructive because they bring doubts into the open; if everyone seems to think alike, there is little stimulus for change (Surowiecki, 2004). Hearing the dissent directly allows the manager to acknowledge, examine, and respond to concerns that may impede progress.

The dissent conversation is also the beginning of the process of commitment. If practitioners are prohibited or limited in their ability to say no, then saying yes means little (Block, 2003). Dissent conversations strengthen the commitment to a search for the truth and use critical reasoning as the primary tool for analyzing and solving problems.

The manager has the responsibility to encourage open discussion and move the group toward understanding. Because the effective facilitation of EBP encourages the accumulation of knowledge to make informed decisions, the manager can model the search for and acquisition of scientific truth by questioning unsupported beliefs, actively seeking alternative explanations, and changing beliefs when confronted with new evidence.

In general, leaders' tolerance of the expression of doubts and reservations is more important than the specific responses they make. The public expression of doubts is a key component of shifting a culture and building commitment and accountability. For any endeavor that really matters, the essential investment that is needed is personal commitment to knowledge (Block 2003). Table 23.1 lists potential objections and appropriate responses managers can make.

Evidence of the Successful Implementation of EBP

One particular doubt that may be raised is the following: What is the evidence that EBP is an effective approach to managing an occupational therapy practice? The initial answer is the self-evident response that if clients are being provided with interventions that are proved to be more effective, then one is clearly providing a better service. A more thorough response includes considering some measurable indicators. The effectiveness of any particular management approach to implementing EBP can be measured in a variety of ways.

For example, practitioners at an inpatient rehabilitation center used an approach focused on patient functional outcome benchmarks to redesign their spinal cord injury program. The redesign led to a significant long-lasting change in interdisciplinary clinical practice. Measurable patient improvements included favorable results on all 11 measures of a 90-day postdischarge follow-up survey (Lawrence, Eyler, & Orest, 2007). Using evidence-based functional outcome benchmarks can be a driver for both significant improvement in client outcomes and sustainable quality improvements. When practitioners find evidence such as this, they are obligated to share this information so others can benefit.

Client Outcome Measures

Client outcome measures provide one primary source of information regarding the quality of service being provided. Depending on the practice setting, outcome measures may include

- Functional scores on standardized tests,
- Postdischarge measures of pain,
- Postdischarge record of falls,
- Frequency of postdischarge hospitalization,
- Scores on quality-of-life assessments,
- Satisfaction with community participation,
- Goal attainment satisfaction, and
- Average length of stay in the hospital or rehabilitation unit.

Employee Satisfaction

In addition to client measures, staff satisfaction measures can provide a measure of the climate and success of a manager's approach. Standardized employee satisfaction surveys can provide a measure that can be compared both over time and across occupational therapy practitioners

Table 23.1. Responding to Practitioners' Dissent Regarding Evidence-Based Practice

Practitioner's Statement	Manager's Response
We will have too many projects going on, and we will end up completing nothing.	We are interested in finding new ideas. Initially, we want to create variety and diversity. There does eventually need to be a weeding-out process, but if it occurs too soon, we will prevent some of the best ideas from emerging.
We will create a confusing mess.	Maybe so; evolution can be messy, but complexity theory demonstrates that systems can develop an inherent order without central control. The point is to encourage staff to be players, not spectators.
It will take too much time.	It is often true that authentic change takes much longer than we ever imagine; however, a thorough and successful change process can still be more efficient than continuing with an ineffective process or struggling through multiple failed change efforts.
We will not be able to measure some things.	There are indeed valuable qualities that seem to defy measurement, such as creativity and imagination. However, as a scientific endeavor, evidence-based practice (EBP) requires that we identify objective measures of the things we are studying. The task of defining measures can be an intellectual challenge in and of itself. Sometimes the search can be facilitated by shifting the focus from "How do we measure it?" to "What measurements would have meaning to me?"
We will never get everybody to participate. What will the consequences be for those who do not?	This is another way of saying, "What does not get rewarded does not get done. What does not get punished continues." Behaviorists demonstrated this with rats and pigeons. As occupational therapists, we understand that meaning is a more powerful driver of human behavior than reward and compensation.
Thirty percent of providers will not change their behavior.	That means that 70% may change their behavior. Peer influence is a much stronger catalyst for change than management directives.
Everyone is entitled to his or her opinion.	Although individuals are entitled to their own opinion in matters of personal taste and preference, for the purposes of participating in the scientific practice of occupational therapy, individuals are entitled to their own opinion only to the extent that they are entitled to generate their own hypotheses and cite evidence and arguments in support of these hypotheses. Conversely, they have the right to generate evidence and arguments that refute alternative hypotheses. The right to your own opinion does not oblige others to agree with you when you are unable to support it with evidence, nor are others obliged to refrain from confronting you with evidence or logical arguments that refute your opinion (Whyte, 2005).
All we seem to do is find that things we used to know are not true. The more EBP we do, the less I know.	Scientific knowledge is cumulative and evolutionary. Pruning away previously held beliefs or practices that are disproved by research is as important as adding new facts and better interventions.
EBP slows productivity.	Productivity is one of the balancing tasks of the manager. In evaluating productivity, managers tend to focus on the amount of service being delivered to clients. The time and effort required in direct delivery of service, however, needs to be in balance with that required in ensuring that the interventions being delivered are effective. An overemphasis on billable time makes economics the highest priority. Managers need to understand and consider the economics of how their staff spend their time, but they should not allow economics to dominate decisions regarding how service is delivered.

and other health care providers. Research conducted by the Gallup Organization identified 13 core factors of employee satisfaction that correlate with the key business indicators of turnover, productivity, profitability, and customer satisfaction (Buckingham & Coffman, 1999). By measuring staff agreement with the following statements, an occupational therapy manager can reliably determine the business impact of creating a culture of EBP:

1. Overall satisfaction: On a 5-point scale in which *5* is *extremely satisfied* and *1* is *extremely dissatisfied*, how satisfied are you with [name of company] as a place to work?
2. I know what is expected of me at work.
3. I have the materials and equipment I need to do my work right.
4. At work, I have the opportunity to do what I do best every day.
5. In the past 7 days, I have received recognition or praise for doing good work.
6. My supervisor, or someone at work, seems to care about me as a person.

7. There is someone at work who encourages my development.
8. At work, my opinions seem to count.
9. The mission or purpose of my company makes me feel my job is important.
10. My fellow employees are committed to doing quality work.
11. I have a best friend at work.
12. In the past 6 months, someone at work has talked to me about my progress.
13. This past year, I have had opportunities at work to learn and grow. (Buckingham & Coffman, 1999, pp. 255–256)

Increased Body of Knowledge

Finally, one of the aims of EBP is to contribute to the professional body of knowledge. Managers can track the number of times that members of their practice make a significant contribution, such as publishing in national or peer-reviewed journals, presenting at national or statewide conferences, and completing quality improvement projects that show measurable results.

CONCLUSION

Successful occupational therapy practice requires that the actions and decisions of managers have both a theoretical and an empirical foundation. In the process of developing this foundation, managers will improve their own management approaches and techniques. As managers' capacity to incorporate EBP into their clinical and leadership methods grows, they will continue to strengthen the value and impact of occupational therapy. A culture of EBP will not result from one single defining action or from one grand stroke of leadership or transformational presentation. Instead, creating a culture of EBP begins with a clear vision and purpose, and the needed commitment, attitudes, personnel engagement, tools, skills, flexible work processes, and knowledge to begin participation build momentum. As participation increases, incremental gains will result in breakthrough benefits for the profession and, most importantly, for occupational therapy clients.

Case Examples

LEVEL I FIELDWORK

Tiffany, a Level I fieldwork student working at a skilled nursing facility, used the AOTA Web site to find evidence to develop her treatment plan. Tiffany's goal was to promote participation in an exercise group for people with cognitive decline due to Alzheimer's disease. First, Tiffany used AOTA's *Evidence-Based Practice Resource Directory* to find evidence-based treatment ideas. She reviewed AOTA's Critically Appraised Papers and Topics, which provide synopses of articles selected for focused-question literature reviews and summaries of selected individual papers. Next, she accessed the Evidence Briefs Series, which are easy-to-read summaries or abstracts of articles that are selected from the scientific literature and that provide ratings of level of evidence. Using the system of evidence suggested by Abreu (Chapter 22, this volume), Tiffany reviewed Level I, II, and III articles for the best available evidence.

Tiffany noticed several articles addressing the effect of music on Alzheimer's clients. One article, "Emotional and Behavioural Responses to Music in People With Dementia: An Observational Study" (Sherratt, Thornton, & Hatton, 2004), provided Level III evidence to support the use of carefully selected music (live and recorded) as a background auditory stimulus to increase participation in meaningful occupations. Another article, "Effects of Music on Alzheimer Patients" (Lord & Garner, 1993), was rated Level IA2b and found that music from earlier eras may improve recall, social interaction, and mood compared to puzzle/pegboard and television/paint/draw activities. Tiffany used these findings to develop a treatment plan centered on music that was relevant to individuals with Alzheimer's dementia to be used during an exercise activity with the intended outcome of increasing participation.

LEVEL II FIELDWORK

John, a Level II fieldwork student working in an outpatient rehabilitation clinic, was required to present an inservice during his fieldwork. John wanted to gather information on standardized assessments that could be used for clients with right upper-extremity hemiplegia.

John logged onto the AOTA Web site; accessed the *Evidence-Based Practice Resource Directory;* selected Rehabilitation, Disability, and Participation Evidence-Based Practice Resources; and searched the topics. He then selected the link to the StrokEngine-Assess Web site, part of the Canadian Stroke Network, which provides names of assessments, in-depth summaries, descriptions of psychometric properties, and a summary table rating each of the assessments. The Web site also provides contact information to purchase copies of the standardized assessments. John compared and contrasted the Fugl-Meyer (Fugl-Meyer, Jaasko, Leyman, Olsson, & Steglind, 1975) and the Chedoke Arm and

(continued)

Case Examples *(cont.)*

Hand Activity Inventory (Barreca, Stratford, Lambert, Masters, & Streiner, 2005) to determine which was best suited for the project. He acquired copies of the tests, studied how to administer them, and presented his findings to staff in completion of the inservice requirement.

First-Time Manager

Joan, a first-time manager, worked with a staff of 6 occupational therapists and 2 occupational therapy assistants in a small acute rehabilitation hospital. The occupational therapy staff mutually agreed on the following clinical question: "Do adult clients with shoulder subluxation and a diagnosis of acute cerebrovascular accident benefit from management of their shoulder subluxation?" (Horner, Lawrence, & Restucci, 2007). Thirty minutes of weekly meeting time was spent reviewing the evidence. The EBP project progressed as follows:

- Joan devoted 3 months to educate staff on conducting a literature search, using various scales to weigh the evidence, and understanding research terminology.
- With the occupational therapy staff, Joan created a reasonable timeline for each step of the process and developed a mutually agreed-on clinical question using the Patient Intervention Comparison Outcome (PICO) format (Sackett et al., 2000). The acronym *PICO* stands for the *patient* or *problem*, the *intervention* of interest, *comparison*, and *outcome*. The PICO format is used to create clinical questions and is useful in identifying solutions to patient or diagnostic-specific problems. Group

members conducted a review of the current literature and found 12 appropriate articles. The staff broke into pairs, and each pair critically read 2 or 3 articles and presented the articles to the whole group at an assigned weekly meeting.

- The group reviewed an article once a week for 12 weeks using at least two scales (i.e., PEDro [Centre for Evidence-Based Physiotherapy, n.d.], Holm's [2000] Article Analysis Format, and Trombly and Ma's [2002] Levels of Evidence). The group tracked pertinent data from each article using a table that Joan organized and maintained.

After the 12 weeks of critical article reviews, Joan led a group decision on whether to make a practice change based on findings. If the group had agreed that a practice change was not indicated, the project would have been terminated. However, group members felt that a practice change was indicated, and Joan helped her group move forward with the next phase of drafting a treatment protocol and guidelines.

Manager

Jill, an experienced manager, supervised 25 occupational therapists at an inpatient rehabilitation facility and three outpatient sites. Jill led a project group composed of 5 occupational therapy practitioners. The objective of the group was to improve the department's ability to convey EBP in its clinical documentation. Using the change strategy matrix described by Patterson et al. (2008), the group created a staff development session designed to reflect six sources of influence (Table 23.2).

Table 23.2. Six Sources of Influence to Promote Evidence-Based Practice

	Motivation (This is worth doing)	Ability (I can do this)
Personal	To encourage practitioners to make a personal connection to EBP, the following multiple-choice question was presented to generate discussion: If you or a loved one needed occupational therapy services, which of the following therapists would you choose? A. This therapist has 10 years of experience and will select a treatment plan on the basis of what she has tried before and she believes has been effective with other patients. B. This therapist has 10 years of experience and will select a treatment plan on the basis of what has been effective with other patients as demonstrated by documented data on standardized assessments. C. This therapist has 10 years of experience and will select a treatment plan on the basis of what has been effective with other patients as demonstrated by documented data on standardized assessments. She will have considered which treatment options are supported by current research evidence.	Each practitioner was asked to pledge to take one small step to improve her documentation of EBP, such as • More consistent use of standardized tests • Refer to norms • Read a research article on neuroplasticity for patients with cerebrovascular accident.

(continued)

Case Examples *(cont.)*

Table 23.2. Six Sources of Influence to Promote Evidence-Based Practice *(cont.)*

	Motivation (This is worth doing)	Ability (I can do this)
Social	Practitioners were reminded that EBP is what the best practitioners in the occupational therapy field do. Everyone was asked to consider mentors, teachers, and colleagues who were role models for EBP, and then answer the question, Who is your EBP hero?	By reviewing the significant number of national presentations and publications the department produced in the past 3 years, practitioners were reminded how small items add up.
Structural	To demonstrate that documentation of EBP will be noticed and rewarded, volunteers were requested to serve on a task group to design a recognition ladder for EBP mastery. The intent was to create a tiered system for recognizing staff accomplishments in the area of EBP. The ladder was designed as a progression through levels of mastery in understanding, application, and promotion of EBP.	An EBP resources folder was created that could be emailed to practitioners with instructions on how to copy the folder to their Windows desktop. The folder contained the following links: • Cochrane Collaboration (systematic reviews of the effects of health care interventions) • UVM Library Tips and Tutorials (helpful suggestions for literature searches) AOTA • Evidence Briefs Series (easy-to-read summaries of Level I and II studies) • Critically Appraised Topics and Papers (at-a-glance synthesis of findings, limitations, and practice implications) • Evidence Bytes (1-minute updates on EBP in occupational therapy) • Evidence Perks (quarterly column designed to address day-to-day evidence needs of occupational therapy practitioners).

Note. AOTA = American Occupational Therapy Association; EBP = evidence-based practice.

❖ Learning Activities

1. Discuss with a group of students or colleagues whether scientific knowledge is certain and known to be absolutely true for all times and all places or whether there is always the possibility that a future observation or experiment will contradict what is currently known.

2. Discuss the practical consequences of the application of complexity principles to health care, including the following:
   - Describe one tradition in health care that seems counter to these principles.
   - Tell one story from your past that illustrates these principles (positively or negatively).
   - Discuss a current issue and how you might approach it with these principles in mind.
   - Discuss the contrast between a top-down engineering approach and a lower-control, high-experimentation approach.
   - Identify situations that require creativity and adaptability and illustrate how complexity principles apply.

3. Write an authentic invitation to ask others to join you in a project or an initiative. The invitation should contain the following components:
   - *The possibility:* Tell recipients in simple, direct language why you are calling them together.
   - *The requirements:* Describe what will be required of them if they choose to participate, including what sacrifices they may need to make.
   - *The right of refusal:* Stress that participation is voluntary and that refusal is perfectly acceptable.

4. Try leading the connection sequence activity described in this chapter's first case example. Start with a question that is ambiguous and personal and that evokes accountability. Allow time for individual reflection, then connecting with another, and finally connecting with the entire room. When connecting with the entire room, questions like "What struck you about your small-group conversation?" tend to generate more interest than simply asking for a recap.

5. While leading a group or meeting, pay attention to the nonparticipants and identify ways to include them. Initially, identify some simple, low-threat questions to which everyone can respond. Clarify and model the expectation that you want input from everyone. Acknowledge the importance and value of diverse points of view.

✓ Multiple-Choice Questions

1. Which of the following statements does *not* apply to the concept of broad participation?
   a. The workload of analyzing and implementing current evidence is shared.
   b. More rigorous decision making can be achieved.
   c. All practitioners use the exact same approach.
   d. 100% participation is not required.

2. Which of the following does AOTA's *Evidence-Based Practice Research Directory* include?
   a. Critically Appraised Papers.
   b. Evidence Briefs.
   c. PEDro scores.
   d. Education research links.

3. The concept of *multiple points of entry* includes which of the following activities?
   a. Using the Levels of Evidence grading scale by Trombly and Ma (2002) to analyze an article.
   b. Starting a treatment with a purposeful activity rather than a preparatory method.
   c. Starting a monthly journal club.
   d. A and C.

4. Which tool, when completed, assigns a numeric score to a research article?
   a. PEDro scale.
   b. Holm's (2000) Article Analysis Format.
   c. Critically Appraised Topics.
   d. Trombly and Ma's (2002) Levels of Evidence grading scale.

5. All of the following are helpful in developing and researching a clinical question except
   a. Using the Patient Intervention Comparison Outcome (PICO) format.
   b. Developing a question that everyone cares about.
   c. Following a timeline to keep staff on track.
   d. Reading abstracts rather than the whole article to save time.

6. One of the goals of using evidence to support practice is to
   a. Educate clients about the expected outcomes of occupational therapy treatment.
   b. Help reduce the burden of using clinical reasoning.
   c. Develop strict protocols to be used for specific diagnostic groups regardless of a client's individual presentation.
   d. Limit treatment options.

7. Which of the following should a leader avoid when promoting broad participation?
   a. Allowing room for dissent.
   b. Discussing barriers openly.
   c. Mandating accountability.
   d. Supporting multiple projects at once.

8. How can a manager ensure success for a group involved in a research project?
   a. Use a timeline developed by staff to help meet goals.
   b. Use a tracking table to help organize pertinent information from each article.
   c. Acquire administrative support ahead of time.
   d. All of the above.

9. Which of the following statements is true of evidence-based practice?
   a. EBP is a finite process.
   b. EBP helps practitioners apply current treatment options.
   c. EBP takes precedence over clinical judgment and a client's priorities.
   d. EBP is optional.

10. Which of the following is the least effective method for identifying a quality research article?
    a. Reading the abstract.
    b. Completing the PEDro scale.
    c. Using Holm's (2000) Article Analysis Format.
    d. Completing Trombly and Ma's (2002) Levels of Evidence grading scale.

11. Summaries of articles that include research findings and limitations of a study can be found in AOTA's
    a. Critically Appraised Topics.
    b. Critically Appraised Papers.
    c. Evidence Briefs.
    d. *Evidence-Based Practice Research Directory.*

12. Which of the following is a characteristic of *mandated accountability*?
    a. It is designed to reflect purpose.
    b. Goals and plans are set collectively.
    c. The leader is responsible for solving problems identified by others.
    d. It encourages the public expression of doubt.

13. According to a study by the Gallup Organization (Buckingham & Coffman, 1999), all of the following employee satisfaction items are correlated with key business indicators except
    a. At work, I have the opportunity to do what I do best every day.
    b. The pay and benefits structure is equitable.
    c. I have a best friend at work.
    d. My supervisor, or someone at work, seems to care about me as a person.

14. According to research on jury decisions, what is the single factor that best ensures that a group decision-making process will benefit from face-to-face discussion?
    a. Diversity of opinion.
    b. A skilled facilitator.
    c. A member who is a professional scientist.
    d. Expertise in the subject matter.

15. Which of the following is *not* an example of a complex adaptive system?
    a. The heating, cooling, and ventilation system of a large office building.
    b. A therapy clinic.
    c. An ant colony.
    d. A surgical team.

16. Which of the following is *not* a desired outcome of a culture of EBP?
    a. The ability to question critically.
    b. Shared responsibility for promoting occupational therapy as a science.
    c. An attitude of caring about the objective evidence related to therapy interventions.
    d. Increased supervisory control over treatment decisions.

17. To best allow for flexibility in a system, it should function in which of the following environments?
    a. High control and planning.
    b. Zone of complexity between order and chaos.
    c. Low control over and low certainty of outcomes.
    d. Support through detailed policies and procedures.

18. Which of the following is a characteristic of evolutionary progress?
    a. Steady, predictable progress.
    b. Unlimited growth and expansion.
    c. Constant tension and rebalancing.
    d. Consensus before experimenting with options.

19. Which of the following is *not* a client outcome measure?
    a. Responses to a quality-of-life satisfaction survey.
    b. Rate of rehospitalization.
    c. Number of falls.
    d. Amount of client education materials received.

20. Which of the following is a measure of contribution to the occupational therapy body of knowledge?
    a. Number of years of experience as an occupational therapist.
    b. Number of conferences attended.
    c. Number of conference presentations made.
    d. Promotion to a higher health care administrative position.

References

American Occupational Therapy Association. (2008). Occupational therapy practice framework: Domain and process (2nd ed.). *American Journal of Occupational Therapy, 62,* 625–683.

Barreca, S., Stratford, P., Lambert, C., Masters, L., & Streiner, D. (2005). Test–retest reliability, validity, and sensitivity of the Chedoke Arm and Hand Activity Inventory: A new measure of upper-limb function for survivors of stroke. *Archives of Physical Medicine and Rehabilitation, 86,* 1616–1622.

Block, P. (2003). *The answer to how is yes: Acting on what matters.* San Francisco: Berrett-Koehler.

Block, P. (2008). *Community: The structure of belonging.* San Francisco: Berrett-Koehler.

Buckingham, M., & Coffman, C. (1999). *First break all the rules.* New York: Simon & Schuster.

Case-Smith, J. (2004). Continuing competence and evidence-based practice. *OT Practice, 9,* 7–8.

Centre for Evidence-Based Physiotherapy. (n.d.). *PEDro scale.* Retrieved February 8, 2006, from http://www.pedro.org.au/

Collins, J. (2001). *Good to great.* New York: HarperCollins.

Fielding, R. A. (2002, November). *Training muscle power in mobility-limited elders.* Paper presented at the annual assembly of the American Academy of Physical Medicine and Rehabilitation, Orlando, FL.

Fugl-Meyer, A. R., Jaasko, L., Leyman, I., Olsson, S., & Steglind, S. (1975). The post-stroke hemiplegic patient, I: A method for evaluation of physical performance. *Scandinavian Journal of Rehabilitation Medicine, 7,* 13–31.

Gilbert, D. (2007). *Stumbling on happiness.* New York: Vintage.

Hinojosa, J. (2007). Becoming innovators in an era of hyperchange [Eleanor Clarke Slagle Lecture]. *American Journal of Occupational Therapy, 61,* 629–637.

Holm, M. B. (2000). Our mandate for the new millennium: Evidence-based practice [Eleanor Clarke Slagle Lecture]. *American Journal of Occupational Therapy, 54,* 575–585.

Horner, K., Lawrence, S., & Restucci, J. (2007). Evidence-based practice in a busy clinical setting. *OT Practice, 12,* 9–11.

Institute of Medicine, Committee on Quality Health Care in America. (2001). *Crossing the quality chasm: A new health system for the 21st century.* Washington, DC: National Academy Press.

Lawrence, S., Eyler, S., & Orest, M. (2007). Redesigning a spinal cord injury program. *PT Magazine, 15*(6), 62–72.

Lord, T. R., & Garner, J. E. (1993). Effects of music on Alzheimer patients. *Perceptual–Motor Skills, 76*(2), 451–455.

Patten, B. (2004). *Truth, knowledge, or just plain bull: How to tell the difference.* New York: Prometheus.

Patterson, K., Grenny, J., Maxfield, D., McMillan, R., & Switzler, A. (2008). *Influencer: The power to change anything.* New York: McGraw-Hill.

Reid, S., Lawrence, S., & Orest, M. (2008). Promoting a culture of evidence-based practice. *PT Magazine, 16*(7), 25–32.

Sackett, D. L., Straus, S. E., Richardson, W. S., Rosenberg, W., & Haynes, R. B. (2000). *Evidence-based medicine: How to practice and teach EBM* (2nd ed.). Edinburgh, UK: Churchill Livingstone.

Sherratt, K., Thornton, A., & Hatton, C. (2004). Emotional and behavioural responses to music in people with dementia: An observational study. *Aging and Mental Health, 8*(3), 233–241.

Surowiecki, J. (2004). *The wisdom of crowds.* New York: Doubleday.

Trombly, C., & Ma, H. (2002). A synthesis of the effects of occupational therapy for persons with stroke: Part I. Restoration of roles, tasks, and activities. *American Journal of Occupational Therapy, 56,* 250–259.

Whyte, J. (2005). *Crimes against logic.* New York: McGraw-Hill.

Zimmerman, B., Lindberg, C., & Plsek, P. (1998). *Edgeware: Insights from complexity science for healthcare leaders.* Dallas, TX: VHA Publishing.

APPENDIX 23.A. EVIDENCE-BASED OCCUPATIONAL THERAPY MANAGEMENT EVIDENCE TABLE

Topic	Evidence
Connection precedes content	Buckingham, M., & Coffman, C. (1999). *First break all the rules.* New York: Simon & Schuster.
Attitude of inquiry	Gilbert, D. (2007). *Stumbling on happiness.* New York: Vintage.
Broad participation	Surowiecki, J. (2004). *The wisdom of crowds.* New York: Doubleday.
Simple rules	Patterson, K., Grenny, J., Maxfield, D., McMillan, R., & Switzler, A. (2008). *Influencer: The power to change anything.* New York: McGraw-Hill.
Evidence-based benchmarks	Buckingham, M., & Coffman, C. (1999). *First break all the rules.* New York: Simon & Schuster. Collins, J. (2001). *Good to great.* New York: HarperCollins.

24

Documentation of Occupational Therapy

Marie J. Morreale, OTR/L, CHT

❖ Key Terms and Concepts

Long-term goal. A desired, measurable outcome to be attained within a specific time period, such as the end of a course of therapy or a school year.

Short-term goal. An incremental step toward accomplishing a long-term goal or desired outcome; also called an *objective*.

Skilled occupational therapy. Services regarded by Medicare as reasonable and necessary for a client's situation and requiring supervision by and the expertise of a qualified occupational therapist and implementation by a qualified occupational therapy practitioner (Centers for Medicare and

Medicaid Services [CMS], 2006a, 2008b). Documentation justifies that these services are warranted and validates the care provided.

SOAP note. A specific four-part documentation format: *S*ubjective, *O*bjective, *A*ssessment, and *P*lan.

Third-party payer. An entity other than the client or service provider, such as an insurance company, Medicaid, or Medicare, that provides payment for a client's health services. Documentation must meet requirements delineated by the payer.

❖ Learning Objectives

After completing this chapter, you should be able to do the following:

- Describe the purpose of documentation as it relates to clinical practice and reimbursement.
- Identify and describe 7 types of documentation reports used in occupational therapy practice.
- Discuss the legal, professional, and ethical issues that influence documentation.

- Understand the importance of documenting services as skilled occupational therapy.
- Describe the process of establishing appropriate occupational therapy goals and interventions for desired client outcomes.

Clinical documentation serves many functions and is an important aspect of occupational therapy practice for both the occupational therapist and the occupational therapy assistant. Entries in a client's health record detail the standards and scope of care that occupational therapy practitioners provide. Occupational therapy documentation primarily focuses on three elements: (1) the client's ability to participate in desired roles and occupations, (2) the internal and external factors that impede or facilitate performance, and (3) the specific interventions implemented or recommended to attain desired outcomes. The occupational therapy assistant can assist with the development of

the plan, but the occupational therapist has the ultimate responsibility for planning, implementing, and documenting occupational therapy services (American Occupational Therapy Association [AOTA], 2009, 2010c). However, with the occupational therapist's supervision and partnership, the occupational therapy assistant can also provide care and contribute to documentation throughout the treatment continuum, as long as this is in accordance with regulatory guidelines (AOTA, 2009, 2010c). Practitioners supervising occupational therapy or occupational therapy assistant students must also adhere to stringent rules regarding the care and documentation that students may provide, particularly for clients with Medicare but always in accordance with state laws (CMS, 2006b).

Each phase of the occupational therapy process (evaluation, intervention, and outcomes) requires distinct reports that encompass specific methods and content (AOTA, 2008a, 2008b). Different practice settings may vary in their individual procedures, formats, requirements, and frequency for documentation (and have discrete audiences), but all must comply with state and federal mandates and fulfill standards established by payers and accrediting bodies (Borcherding & Morreale, 2007). It is important to realize that protocols, regulations, and public policy may be periodically modified or new rules enacted. Therefore, it is essential that occupational therapy managers and practitioners keep current with facility or agency policies, state laws, and federal statutes regarding professional issues affecting occupational therapy practice and documentation such as licensure, privacy protocols (i.e., the Health Insurance Portability and Accountability Act of 1996 [HIPAA]), referral requirements, health records management, supervision, and scope of practice.

The *Guidelines for Documentation of Occupational Therapy* (AOTA, 2008a) delineates the typical documentation reports used in occupational therapy practice. An initial client contact for the purpose of gathering information and determining the need for occupational therapy intervention will generate an *evaluation* or *screening report*. Another type of evaluation report is a *reevaluation report,* written at subsequent periodic intervals to document changes in the client's status or situation and to modify goals and client care. Following evaluation, the occupational therapist establishes an *intervention plan* to determine desired client outcomes, the time frame to achieve those outcomes, and the discharge plan. As part of the intervention plan, *long-term goals* and *short-term goals* (objectives) are established, along with the specific interventions or approaches to treatment that will be used to achieve those goals. Additional documentation reports during the intervention process may include *occupational therapy service contacts*, *progress reports,* and *transition plans* (AOTA, 2008a). When occupational therapy is no longer indicated or ceases, a *discharge/discontinuation report* describing outcomes is written.

Purposes of Documentation

Health record documentation is an essential means to chronicle a client's medical, psychological, social, or educational history and to delineate current problematic areas and strengths. By using the record, team members can expediently convey and integrate information about the client and systematically track and measure progress. This communication allows each discipline to establish relevant objectives and implement appropriate interventions for the client's condition. Dissemination of information in the health record helps facilitate continuity of care among the client's health care team, especially beneficial when a client transitions from one setting to another, such as from a hospital to home care or from early intervention to school-based services. Occupational therapy documentation should reflect a client-centered and holistic approach centering on the client's ability to effectively participate in meaningful and essential life tasks (AOTA, 2008b).

Documentation encompasses other significant purposes, such as meeting legal, ethical, and public health requirements, and it also serves as an important tool for quality improvement activities, accreditation, utilization review, evidence-based practice, and research (Borcherding & Morreale, 2007). Furthermore, because Medicare and other third-party payers have strict guidelines for reimbursement, documentation is a means to justify that occupational therapy services were warranted and to validate the actual care provided (CMS, 2008a). According to Medicare, the only occupational therapy services eligible for reimbursement are those deemed *skilled,* meaning the services not only are reasonable and necessary for the client's situation but also require the professional training, clinical judgment, and expertise of a qualified occupational therapist (CMS, 2006a, 2008b). Medicare regulations delineate that a qualified occupational therapy assistant can provide services only under the supervision of an occupational therapist who directs the skilled care and documentation (CMS, 2006a, 2008b). These regulations also include the expectation that the client will make reasonable progress; repetitive or routine tasks to simply maintain, rather than improve, function are not considered reimbursable, although the clinician may establish a home exercise program for caregivers to implement (CMS, 2006a). Many third-party payers have guidelines similar to Medicare. Therefore, occupational therapy documentation for each client must clearly reflect how the unique and skilled services that occupational therapy practitioners provide meet the strict criteria for effective and safe care (CMS, 2008a).

Occupational therapy practitioners must also realize that health records, including occupational therapy notes, are considered legal documents. In certain instances, such as personal injury or malpractice lawsuits, situations of physical or emotional abuse, or suspected billing irregularities or fraud, notes may be subpoenaed and used as evidence, sometimes even years after the client has been discharged (Borcherding & Morreale, 2007). Occupational therapy practitioners should keep this fact in mind when recording information to help ensure that that notations are timely, objective, pertinent, truthful, and complete (Borcherding & Morreale, 2007). In addition, clients have the right to access their medical records, including their therapy information. Occupational therapy managers and practitioners must familiarize themselves with the specific policies and procedures that facilities typically have in place to handle such requests.

Professional Standards and Ethics in Documentation

First and foremost, the occupational therapy manager and practitioner must always consider current laws, professional standards, and ethical issues affecting clinical practice and documentation. Important factors include honesty, confidentiality, and nondiscrimination. Tenets of honesty or veracity include accurately representing one's credentials and documenting occupational therapy services objectively and factually (AOTA, 2010a). Documentation must be signed clearly with the practitioner's name and the appropriate professional designation signifying his or her credentials to deliver that service. In situations where a cosignature is required, the supervising practitioner should never blindly cosign notes; the cosignature is really verification that the cosigner has overseen the treatment rendered and provided the appropriate supervision. The cosigner is responsible for the outcomes if the plan should be harmful or inappropriate.

Professional signatures certify that the necessary standards have been followed to meet legal guidelines and criteria for reimbursement. For example, it would be unethical if an occupational therapy aide rendered a client treatment, such as helping the client dress or eat breakfast, and the occupational therapist then wrote and signed a note describing it as an activities of daily living (ADLs) instructional session and billed Medicare for occupational therapy services. Medicare guidelines clearly state that a qualified occupational therapy practitioner, not an aide, must provide the actual skilled care (CMS, 2008b). The *Guidelines for Supervision, Roles, and Responsibilities During the Delivery of Occupational Therapy Services* (AOTA, 2009) also affirms that an aide cannot provide skilled occupational therapy but should perform only selected routine or supportive tasks that do not require any clinical judgment on the part of the aide. Therefore, documentation must always reflect the appropriate standards of skilled service provision when depicting services as occupation-based practice. Although it may be appropriate in some instances to make notations about pertinent ancillary services or the help provided by unskilled personnel, those services should *not* be represented as occupational therapy if they do not meet the criteria for skilled care.

In a related example, if an occupational therapy practitioner took a minute to replace a client's lost buttonhook without providing any further instruction or intervention, this brief client contact could certainly be documented to indicate that a replacement buttonhook was provided (and a charge submitted for the new buttonhook if appropriate for that setting). It would be unethical, however, to depict this activity in the medical record as skilled occupational therapy and bill the insurance company for a full ADL session. Because an aide could have handed the client a new buttonhook, this encounter does not meet the standard of a skilled occupational therapy session and cannot be represented as such.

The occupational therapy practitioner must always ensure that health record notations accurately and truthfully represent the client's situation and care when recording information and submitting claims to third-party payers.

"Fudging" the facts or documenting and billing for services that were unnecessary, embellished, provided by an unqualified person, or not actually rendered may result in legal and professional sanctions, as they may be considered fraud, a serious infraction. Therefore, information must never be deceptive, exaggerated, or dishonest in any way (AOTA, 2010a).

Another guideline is that the occupational therapy practitioner should avoid using disparaging or defamatory remarks when writing about coworkers, clients, or students, as these types of comments are subjective and unprofessional. For instance, rather than recording, "The client is tired because the PT [physical therapist] overworked him in therapy," it would be preferable to objectively state, "The client reported feeling tired following the PT session." Unlike the first statement, the second statement does not express any judgment or negativity about the physical therapist but merely reports a fact.

The issue of client confidentiality is a fundamental principle by which health care workers and all others associated with client care must abide. In addition to being a basic right of clients (AOTA, 2010a), privacy is addressed in HIPAA, which delineates standards to guard the confidentiality of protected health information. HIPAA directly pertains to information recorded in the health record along with the various methods of disseminating client information (e.g., electronically) for billing and client care purposes. Confidentiality can very easily be breached by careless acts such as accidentally leaving notes on the fax machine or copier, forgetting to turn off the computer, or keeping charts lying open in a treatment area. Double-checking that a fax number or e-mail address is correct and entered accurately before sending any confidential documentation will help ensure that the information is properly sent to the intended recipient. Occupational therapy managers and practitioners have a professional obligation to properly safeguard client information, follow facility or agency policy, and adhere to HIPAA guidelines at all times.

In clinical practice or a working environment, situations sometimes occur that cause personal uneasiness or ethical questioning. Professional documentation should not express the occupational therapy practitioner's personal beliefs or value judgments. Clients come from all kinds of ethnic, cultural, and socioeconomic backgrounds and may have lifestyles, values, and beliefs that differ from or are directly opposed to those of the clinician. Clear laws prohibit discrimination on the basis of factors such as age, race, gender, religion, and sexual orientation. The *Occupational Therapy Practice Framework: Domain and Process, 2nd Edition* (AOTA, 2008b) maintains that those factors are part of what makes an individual unique and are integral to developing an occupational profile. Furthermore, the *Occupational Therapy Code of Ethics and Ethics Standards* (AOTA, 2010a) asserts that occupational therapy practitioners must treat each client equally and prudently and recognize the value of cultural diversity and cultural competence. Thus, documentation (and treatment) should not reflect any prejudice or bias on the part of the clinician when describing the client or recording his or her behaviors. The intervention plan and treatment notes should objectively reflect what is relevant and important to the client and consider the outcomes that the client values or desires (obviously, as long as those factors are not unlawful or a danger to the client or others). The clinician does not have to condone a particular behavior or lifestyle but must demonstrate respect, tolerance, and impartiality.

USEFUL RESOURCES FOR DOCUMENTATION

The World Health Organization (WHO) established the *International Classification of Functioning, Disability and Health (ICF)*, a health and disability framework officially endorsed by WHO members in 2001 (WHO, 2001). *ICF* contains universal, standard language to classify, describe, and measure how health conditions influence capacities, performance of life activities, and participation in society (WHO, 2002). *ICF* applies to individuals, institutions, society, and public policy, and it includes domains of body functions and structures, activity and participation considerations, and a delineation of environmental factors (WHO, 2001, 2002). *ICF* language and tenets are reflected in the *Framework–II* (AOTA, 2008b) and are used in documentation to describe capacities and limitations.

To help guide the occupational therapy practitioner in the arena of documentation and clinical practice, AOTA has produced many useful resources. The following documents provide a basis for consistent professional language and delineate the breadth of occupational therapy practice and professional standards and ethics, which are ultimately reflected in the clinician's notations:

- *Framework–II* (AOTA, 2008b)
- *Guidelines for Documentation of Occupational Therapy* (AOTA, 2008a)
- *Occupational Therapy Services in the Promotion of Health and the Prevention of Disease and Disability* (AOTA, 2008c)
- *Occupational Therapy Code of Ethics and Ethics Standards* (AOTA, 2005a)
- *Standards of Practice for Occupational Therapy* (AOTA, 2010c)
- *Guidelines for Supervision, Roles, and Responsibilities During the Delivery of Occupational Therapy Services* (AOTA, 2009)
- *Scope of Practice* (AOTA, 2010b).

In addition, further information regarding professional documentation can be found at the following Web sites:

- *American Health Information Management Association:* www.ahima.org

- *American Occupational Therapy Association:* www.aota.org
- *Centers for Medicare and Medicaid Services:* www.cms.hhs.gov
- *Centers for Medicare and Medicaid Services forms:* www.cms.hhs.gov/CMSforms.

As clinical practice evolves, treatment protocols and professional standards and terminology sometimes change. Documents from AOTA and other sources may also be periodically revised or eventually replaced. Thus, occupational therapists and occupational therapy assistants must stay abreast of pertinent changes that affect health care, documentation, and reimbursement, as well as the profession of occupational therapy in general.

Additional occupational therapy resources are widely available for various documentation topics, such as how and what to document, examples of specific methods or forms used to document client data, treatment planning, and efficacy of specific assessments or interventions. However, the body of scientific studies critiquing occupational therapy clinical documentation quality or documentation methods and formats is limited, because many resources are anecdotal or informative rather than evidence based. The appendix lists some useful evidence-based resources.

HEALTH RECORD FUNDAMENTALS

Occupational therapists and occupational therapy assistants must be familiar with the fundamentals of health care record keeping, including basic elements of documentation, organizational formats, and the use of electronic health records.

Basic Elements of Documentation

At times it is truly a balancing act for the occupational therapy manager to oversee and the occupational therapy practitioner to adeptly and completely document the necessary information while being concise. There is often little time available in the practitioner's day to devote to documentation. However, practitioners should always make particular effort to communicate legibly, professionally, and accurately. In addition to causing possible harm to the client, carelessness and mistakes in documentation or gross deficiencies in spelling and grammar will reflect poorly on the clinician and may cause others to question the clinician's competence. Clinical documentation also entails certain protocols that the manager must instill and the practitioner must follow (AOTA, 2008a). As previously indicated, each notation in the health record requires an appropriate signature and professional designation (and cosignature as required). Every page in the health record should also specify the facility or agency along with the client's identifying information (e.g., full name and health record number). The manager should make sure that every occupational therapy entry is clearly identified as occupational therapy so that it can be located easily and so that no one can confuse it with another discipline such as physical therapy or nursing.

Once information is entered in the health record, it must not be erased, deleted, or altered with correction fluid. Recordings should always denote the date of service or client communication, and some facilities and third-party payers also require notation of the total minutes of occupational therapy provided for each session and/or the time of day service was rendered. The occupational therapy manager may use these time notations for billing purposes and to track sequence of care or worker productivity. It is also important to adhere to proper procedures for storage and disposal of client information along with any additional directives or protocols that the particular setting requires.

Organizational Formats

The occupational therapy manager and practitioner may see a variety of formats that are unique to the unit or facility. Health records can be organized in various ways, and each method has benefits and limitations. The actual format used depends on the type of practice setting and facility policy. Facilities and agencies commonly use a *source-oriented* format, which divides the medical record into distinct sections for each discipline (Kuehn, 2006). For example, there may be separate sections for nursing notes, lab and diagnostic test results, social work intervention, and notes by each rehabilitation discipline, including occupational therapy. Because professionals from each discipline record clinical notes chronologically in their individual section, it is easy for team members to find specific information or track a discipline's progress, but this format creates difficulty in determining overall status (Kuehn, 2006). Another organizational method is an *integrated* format, which is interdisciplinary and strictly chronological (Kuehn, 2006). Thus, occupational therapy notes might immediately precede or follow a notation from nursing, social work, physical therapy, or another discipline on the very same page. This format enables team members to easily check a client's overall status at any point (Kuehn, 2006). However, with the integrated format it is more laborious to locate a particular item or track a problem or discipline over a period of time, such as when gathering information to write an occupational therapy discharge note or to determine how many occupational therapy sessions were provided in a given time period.

In the 1960s, physician Lawrence Weed created a unique format called the *problem-oriented medical record*, which consists of four parts: the collection of client data, a list of problems ascertained from the data, a plan to address each specific problem, and progress notes addressing treatment for particular problems (Kuehn, 2006). Those progress notes use a distinct four-part format designated SOAP: *S*ubjective, *O*bjective, *A*ssessment, and *P*lan. Nowadays, some facilities combine parts of the source-oriented, integrated, and SOAP organizational methods or use various adaptations of the SOAP format that incorporate other components or are called a different name or acronym (Borcherding & Morreale, 2007).

Facilities or agencies normally furnish all the disciplines with the required paperwork or forms to be used for the health record, and these are often unique to that setting. The paperwork may include specific structured or semistructured occupational therapy forms that the occupational therapist, with assistance from the occupational therapy assistant, fills out for evaluation, reevaluation, progress reports, or discharge reports. Formats may include checklists, fill-in-the-blank items, designated categories, numerical scales, narrative responses, grids, menus of problems or goals, or a combination of these. Often, additional specialized forms are used for selected occupational therapy assessments such as a standardized cognitive, visual–motor, or coordination test; pain diagram; range of motion (ROM) measures; or leisure or play checklist. Forms for treatment notes are typically less structured or detailed and might simply be a lined sheet with the facility's identifying information preprinted at the top or bottom. Depending on facility guidelines, the occupational therapy practitioner may use a narrative or SOAP note format to record the interventions implemented or, instead, might fill out a basic flow sheet or attendance log for each session.

Use of Electronic Health Records

In recent years, there has been an increasing trend for health care providers to use electronic health records as a means to improve client care and lower costs. President George W. Bush even announced a goal for most Americans to have access to electronic medical records by the year 2014 (U.S. Department of Health and Human Services [USDHHS], 2008). Although special effort is essential to secure sites and ensure privacy, there are many benefits to electronic records. Computerized health records take up much less storage space than traditional paper records. Electronic notes are typewritten so errors due to mistakes in penmanship or poor handwriting are minimized (although the risk of errors due to poor typing or incorrect entry remains). They streamline procedures, enable better access and faster communication among health care providers and clients, and help to reduce medical errors and redundancy (USDHHS, 2008). Electronic health records can be especially useful for health care workers providing care in remote sites such as a client's home or satellite clinic. In addition to being able to submit client data immediately, health care providers can easily access pertinent client information from the main facility or agency or from other health team members. Electronic documentation helps to organize and standardize documentation and can be a timesaver for the occupational therapy practitioner. Specialized software is available for different areas of occupational therapy practice.

TYPES OF OCCUPATIONAL THERAPY DOCUMENTATION

The *Guidelines for Documentation of Occupational Therapy* (AOTA, 2008a) describes the different reports used for evaluation, intervention, and outcomes and offers suggestions for the basic information to be included. As previously indicated, requirements vary based on the particular practice setting and managerial directives.

Evaluation and Intervention Plan

The first step in the occupational therapy process is an evaluation to determine the client's ability to engage in meaningful occupations (AOTA, 2008b). The occupational therapy manager oversees the occupational therapist, who may also be delegating tasks to the occupational therapy assistant to ensure that they obtain pertinent information about the client. Next, the occupational therapist interprets that information to consider desired outcomes and appropriate interventions and documents the evaluation results and intervention plan (AOTA, 2009, 2010c). Occupational therapy evaluations encompass a variety of client-centered methods such as observation, chart review, interview, and administration of specific standardized evaluations and assessments. Key to this process is development of an occupational profile, which identifies and prioritizes the client's desired occupations, relevant roles, and performance patterns and considers influential factors such as contexts and the client's values, interests, and life experiences (AOTA, 2008a, 2008b). The client's occupational performance status is then analyzed through the use of evaluations and assessments to determine and document which client factors, performance skills, contexts, activity demands, and so forth are assets or hindrances in the present situation (AOTA, 2008a, 2008b).

After those steps are completed, formulation of an intervention plan can commence. At periodic intervals, reevaluations are performed to update the occupational profile, analyze and compare data regarding the client's present condition and situation, and revise the intervention plan (AOTA, 2008a). Occupational therapy managers and practitioners must ensure that evaluation results, intervention plans, and subsequent reevaluations are documented on appropriate forms and properly entered into the client's chart according to facility or agency guidelines and timeframes.

When gathering information during the evaluation process, it may be insufficient to simply note that an area of occupation is problematic. The occupational therapist should delve into the specific reasons for the client's difficulty through further interview or other types of assessment to determine and document whether and how occupational therapy might specifically intervene in that area. For example, there are numerous reasons why a client may report difficulty with rest and sleep. Clients with mental health issues may not sleep well because of a manic episode, severe stress and anxiety, or hallucinations that create paranoid behavior. Conversely, a client may sleep excessively due to depression or the side effects of medication. Clients with physical conditions may have poor sleep patterns due to pain from recent surgery or a pinched nerve. An elderly client with prostate cancer may need to get up several times

a night to urinate, and a mother with a newborn will have erratic sleep patterns for a very different reason. Poor sleep can even be due to a purely environmental contextual issue, such as whether the client's home is located adjacent to railroad tracks. Occupational therapy practitioners must precisely organize and document relevant information so that members of the treatment team can understand the client's problems, progress, and situation.

The occupational therapy manager in conjunction with the practitioner determines whether occupational therapy is appropriate for the circumstances and what interventions or recommendations may be helpful. Those interventions, recommendations, and desired outcomes are documented in the occupational therapy intervention plan. In the case of a client with stress and anxiety, the occupational therapist's approach might be to provide relaxation techniques, coping mechanisms, exploration of leisure tasks, and physical exercise recommendations, all in collaboration with other team members. For the client with prostate cancer, although he should be advised to see his doctor for further medical management, the occupational therapist may determine that there are also significant safety concerns with the client getting up at night, particularly if he has poor vision and impaired balance. Thus, it may be appropriate to make recommendations for a bedside commode, grab bars, better lighting, or removal of throw rugs in addition to working on safe transfer skills. If poor sleep is caused by pain, the occupational therapist can consider positioning aids or other methods such as physical agent modalities or splinting. Regarding the client whose home is next to railroad tracks, if poor sleep secondary to noise is the client's only functional limitation, occupational therapy is certainly not warranted. However, the occupational therapist may offer suggestions such as the use of earplugs or a white noise machine.

The occupational therapist also fully takes into account and documents the client's necessary or desired roles, particular performance patterns, activity demands, and any pertinent contextual issues. A 30-year-old mother with three toddlers, a full-time job, and a large house to maintain will obviously have a very different slate of daily activities, time constraints, and responsibilities than a 75-year-old retiree living in an assisted living facility. Then, the occupational therapist carefully considers individual client factors (such as cognition, emotional stability, ROM, strength, skin integrity, and cardiovascular and respiratory functions), astutely observes, and assesses relevant performance skills such as ability to safely transfer, plan a meal, ask for directions, manipulate grooming implements, select the correct items to bring to class, and carry a laundry basket (AOTA, 2008b). The practitioner systematically organizes, analyzes, and appropriately documents all the information gathered in the evaluation report using the format and procedures established by that facility or agency.

Following evaluation, the next step in the occupational therapy process is an intervention plan, established by the occupational therapist and implemented with the assistance of the occupational therapy assistant (AOTA, 2008b, 2009). The intervention plan is entered in the chart and becomes a blueprint to address the precise problems or limitations ascertained from the evaluation and to establish appropriate and realistic desired outcomes. Although the intervention plan expressly focuses on improving occupational engagement, it also designates specific approaches to improve or remediate individual client factors and performance skills that influence function (AOTA, 2008b). The plan may also recommend modification of specific task procedures or the environment to enable task performance or to ensure safety.

The intervention plan specifies long- and short-term goals and the specific course of therapy to be implemented, including frequency and duration of therapy, types of interventions, recommendations or approaches to treatment, and anticipated discharge plan (AOTA, 2008a). The focus of the intervention plan should be on realistic and attainable client outcomes such as participation in desired occupations, role competence, quality of life, and health and wellness (AOTA, 2008b). Long-term goals are the desired ultimate outcomes to be attained by the end of a specified time period, such as by the end of a course of therapy or of a school year. Objectives (short-term goals) are the incremental steps toward accomplishing a long-term goal or ultimate desired outcome. Exhibit 24.1 shows sample goals and objectives for a client with a wrist fracture.

Clearly documented goals should delineate reasonable and necessary functional changes that the client can realistically attain within a given time frame based on the client's status, rehabilitation potential, and expected environment. Goals must also include measurable or objective criteria (e.g., specific assist level, necessary adaptive devices, number of trials completed, time factors), and the focus of goals varies according to the practice setting and payment source (Borcherding & Morreale, 2007). For example, objectives in school-based settings must relate to educationally related tasks such as handwriting, changing for gym, scissors use, carrying books, or mobility. Elderly clients with Medicare in a home care or outpatient setting require goals that reflect functional outcomes such as the ability to safely transfer, bathe, dress, or prepare a meal.

Intervention: Contact Notes

Treatment notes, also called "contact notes," are recorded following intervention or after pertinent communication with the client, caregiver, or others (AOTA, 2008a). Practitioners in some settings use either SOAP notes or narrative formats for all contacts, whereas those in other settings may use checklists, grids, attendance logs, or flow sheets for daily contacts and later write formal progress notes at specific intervals such as weekly, every 2 weeks, or monthly (Borcherding & Morreale, 2007). Occupational therapy practitioners working in some settings, such as acute care or home care, normally write a formal treatment note after

each client contact as part of the client's medical record. However, an occupational therapist or occupational therapy assistant working in a school system might keep an informal log following each session. The format and specific criteria for documentation vary considerably in different settings.

SOAP notes are a useful format for contact notes. SOAP notes, which consist of the following four components (Borcherding & Morreale, 2007), should directly relate to implementation of the intervention plan and include any pertinent issues that affect treatment or outcomes.

1. *Subjective:* Information the client (or, in certain instances, the family or caregiver) tells the clinician that is pertinent to his or her condition
2. *Objective:* Description of intervention implemented, client's behaviors and response to treatment, and data or information obtained during the session
3. *Assessment:* The occupational therapy practitioner's clinical reasoning and judgment about what transpired during the session, relating it to the client's progress or problems affecting desired outcomes
4. *Plan:* Intervention or follow-up to be implemented in the next session or in the near future.

SOAP notes can provide an accurate and objective account of what occurred during the treatment session and enable other team members to know what is happening with the client in occupational therapy. The notes also help the occupational therapy practitioner determine whether the client is making progress toward the goals established in the intervention plan. Exhibit 24.2 shows sample case notes using the SOAP format from a client who underwent a total hip replacement. Occupational therapy practitioners vary in their style of writing or may use a narrative format instead of a SOAP note format. However, the basic elements and necessary client information should always be present in the contact note.

Intervention: Progress Reports and Transition Plans

The purpose of progress reports is to provide a timely update of the client's status. Progress reports are written at specific intervals (e.g., weekly, every 2 weeks, or monthly) to summarize the treatment implemented and address progress the client has made toward achieving goals (AOTA, 2008a). In the progress report, the occupational therapist makes recommendations to update goals, modify the course of therapy as needed, or discontinue services. The specific time frames for progress notes, reevaluations, and recertifications are typically mandated by payers such as Medicare and managed care programs.

A transition plan is indicated when a client goes from one type of setting to another within a system of care (e.g., when a student transitions from a special education program to supported employment; AOTA, 2008a). The transition plan identifies the client's problems and strengths and current occupational performance abilities. Also in-

Exhibit 24.1. Sample Documentation of Client Goals

Kimberly is a 50-year-old woman who sustained a right Colles fracture 6 weeks previously after falling in her driveway. She was referred to occupational therapy after removal of her cast. The occupational therapy evaluation indicated that Kimberly had range of motion (ROM) deficits and decreased strength in her right hand and wrist. She was unable to return to her bookkeeping job because of difficulty with writing, holding objects, and using a computer keyboard. She also could not manage clothing fastenings with her dominant right hand and had difficulty with meal preparation tasks (e.g., cutting and peeling vegetables, opening jars and packages).

The following are some examples of functional long- and short-term goals for Kimberly that focus on different areas of occupation. These goals are pertinent to the client's desired roles and occupations and can realistically be attained based on her diagnosis and present condition.

Area of Occupation	Long-Term Goal	Short-Term Goal
Basic activities of daily living	Client will demonstrate ability to manage all clothing fastenings independently within 3 weeks.	Client will be able to button and unbutton her shirt independently using a large-handle buttonhook within 4 days.
Instrumental activities of daily living	Client will be able to perform all meal preparation tasks independently within 4 weeks.	Client will be able to peel vegetables independently with use of a large-handle vegetable peeler within 2 weeks.
Work	Client will demonstrate ability to perform all work-related tasks to enable return to her job within 4 weeks.	Client will demonstrate ability to use computer keyboard to type at 50% of prior word per minute rate within 2 weeks.

Although occupational therapy practitioners often develop a general repertoire of goals for use in documentation, goals must always specifically relate to each client's unique situation and be appropriate to the practice setting. Listed in the chart below are some examples of how a common goal for "independent bathing" can be individually tailored for different client situations to address or emphasize specific client factors, performance skills, performance patterns, or activity demands.

Occupational Therapy Domain	Example of Goal
Client factor: ROM	Client will increase right shoulder internal and external rotation by 30 degrees in order to bathe independently within 4 weeks.
Client factor: Strength	To bathe independently, client will demonstrate increased bilateral upper–extremity strength from fair to good within 4 weeks.
Cognitive performance skills	Client will demonstrate ability to organize and gather all necessary items needed to bathe independently within 4 weeks. Client will demonstrate ability to properly sequence all steps required to bathe independently within 4 weeks.
Motor performance skills	Client will be able to adequately hold and manipulate soap and washcloth to bathe independently within 4 weeks. Client will demonstrate good dynamic balance sitting on tub seat 15 minutes to bathe independently within 4 weeks.
Performance patterns	Within 4 weeks, client will demonstrate good time management for independent bathing by using a timer to complete task within 20 minutes. Within 4 weeks, client will independently remember to take a shower 5/5 days before going to work.
Activity modification	Within 4 weeks, client will be able to bathe independently using a wash mitt and soap/shampoo dispenser while seated on a shower chair. While seated at sink, client will be able to bathe self independently within 4 weeks.

Although all the goals are represented as compartmentalized, the occupational therapy practitioner considers the entire process to be dynamic and intertwined with all other aspects of the occupational therapy domain (AOTA, 2008b). Client behaviors and function are influenced by a complex combination of internal and external factors, and occupational therapy intervention often consists of a variety of methods.

EXHIBIT 24.2. SAMPLE CONTACT NOTE

John was a 68-year-old man who underwent a right total hip replacement. After transfer to a rehabilitation hospital 5 days' postsurgery, he was evaluated by the occupational therapist. The occupational therapy intervention plan indicated that John would receive occupational therapy 5 days a week until his expected discharge date in 2 weeks. The plan was for John to attain independence in all basic activities of daily living (BADL) so that he could return home to his apartment, where he lived alone.

The second occupational therapy session consisted of reviewing total hip precautions, providing John with assistive devices for dressing, and instructing him in the use of equipment and adapted dressing techniques. The occupational therapist recorded the following occupational therapy treatment note using a SOAP note format:

TLC Rehab Hospital

Rehabilitation Department

Occupational Therapy Contact Note

Name: Doe, John

Medical Record #: 24681012

Date: January 20, 2010

Time: 8:45 a.m.

Subjective:

Client stated, "I need to be able to take care of myself so I can go back home."

Objective:

A 30-minute OT session was administered in client's hospital room. Client accurately recalled 3/3 total hip precautions and was issued a reacher, long-handle shoehorn, and sock assist. Client was then instructed in use of devices and compensatory methods for lower body dressing. While sitting on edge of bed, client donned underwear and pants over affected lower extremity with moderate assistance and over unaffected leg with minimum assistance using reacher and dressing stick. Client also required minimum assistance to don socks using sock aid and to don loafers using long-handle shoehorn. Contact guard and use of walker were required for client to stand and pull up clothing. Client demonstrated good endurance and ability to safely adhere to total hip precautions throughout session.

Assessment:

Excellent potential for BADL independence is evident in client's good endurance and ability to understand and follow instructions. Continued OT is recommended to maximize client's self-care abilities and safety for return home.

Plan:

Continue OT 5 times weekly for skilled instruction in lower–body dressing, bathing, and transfers. Next session instruct client in use of transfer tub bench and assistive devices for bathing.

[Signed]Emma Empathy, OTR/L

cluded in the plan are time frames, methods for facilitating the transition, and specific recommendations such as necessary modifications, assistive technology, special accommodations, and any other required supportive services, including occupational therapy (AOTA, 2008a).

Outcomes: Discharge or Discontinuation Reports

An occupational therapy discharge or discontinuation report describes outcomes and is written when therapy stops or is no longer indicated. The reason for cessation of therapy should be indicated in the report—for example, the client attained all occupational therapy goals, maximized progress, was discharged from the facility, graduated, or moved. The report summarizes the course of therapy, such as the time frame and number of sessions provided, kinds of interventions implemented (including home programs, modifications, or adaptive equipment), and progress or changes from initial to current status. Any need for follow-up, referrals, or further recommendations is also indicated in the report. The occupational therapist, with input from the occupational therapy assistant, uses clinical judgment to determine when the client should be discharged from therapy (AOTA, 2010c).

REQUIREMENTS FOR DIFFERENT PRACTICE SETTINGS

Documentation requirements for occupational therapy vary according to the practice setting. In addition to the typical occupational therapy reports, there may be additional documentation that the practitioner can contribute. For example, CMS requires that skilled nursing facilities use a structured, interdisciplinary approach to identifying and addressing a client's problems through a process called the Resident Assessment Instrument, or RAI (CMS, 2002a). The RAI consists of a holistic and comprehensive assessment tool called the Minimum Data Set (MDS). Multiple disciplines, including occupational therapy, are assigned relevant sections of the MDS to complete and document (CMS, 2002b). Client problems, called *triggers*, are then identified from the MDS, and an interdisciplinary care plan is formulated to improve the resident's function and quality of life. Subsequent documentation from all disciplines must reflect that this care plan is being implemented.

Adult clients who have Medicare and Medicaid in home care settings (with some exceptions) must receive a comprehensive functional assessment called the OASIS, which is an acronym for Outcome and Assessment Information Set (CMS, 2008c). This assessment is used to determine the client's eligibility for home care and the specific services and care needed for the client's situation. According to CMS regulations, an occupational therapist cannot complete the initial OASIS assessment for clients with Medicare but is allowed to complete the OASIS recertification assessment in certain instances (CMS, 2008d). However, OASIS guidelines state that in specific situations where occupational therapy establishes program eligibility for non-Medicare payers, the initial OASIS assessment can be completed by the occupational therapist (CMS, 2008d). Occupational therapy documentation in home care typically focuses on the client's ability to perform functional tasks and safety. Complete forms and requirements for both the OASIS and the MDS can be found at www.cms. hhs.gov/CMSForms.

Occupational therapy practitioners in mental health settings often contribute to a multidisciplinary evaluation and treatment plan, with some settings incorporating critical care pathways or computer-generated plans for more common conditions (Borcherding & Morreale, 2007). Documentation in mental health primarily focuses on factors affecting the client's role competence and psychosocial well-being, such as emotional regulation skills, interpersonal abilities, task behaviors, coping mechanisms, thought processes, self-esteem, and ability to engage in desired and necessary life tasks.

In a school system, occupational therapy is provided to students classified as having special needs. The specific services a student requires are delineated in the individualized education program (IEP), which is an annual report compiled by all the disciplines working with that student. The occupational therapist directs and documents the occupational therapy evaluation and specifies the occupational therapy objectives and intervention to be implemented during the school year. Objectives and services in the IEP must relate to the student's functional performance in school-related tasks.

Programs requiring particular expertise, such as hand therapy, neonatal intensive care, low vision rehabilitation, dysphagia programs, and driver rehabilitation, normally have specialized assessments, forms, and protocols pertinent to that specialized practice area. In addition, occupational therapy managers, assisted by occupational therapy practitioners, may be responsible for other types of documentation that do not involve direct client contact but are nevertheless pertinent to the overall needs of the department. Examples include developing informative materials to market occupational therapy (e.g., brochures, letters to physicians or payers), creating forms or client information handouts, developing or revising policy and procedure manuals, managing student programs, documenting quality improvement activities, filing accreditation reports, appealing insurance denials, writing staff evaluations and budget requests, and completing professional development activities or program review and development. All these tasks are essential to effectively manage a department and maintain clinical standards.

CONCLUSION

Documentation is an integral component of occupational therapy practice and has different audiences and obligations depending on the particular setting. The frequency and focus of occupational therapy notes, specific requirements, and organizational structure all vary according to the practice setting, regulatory directives, and payment source. The occupational therapy practitioner must carefully meet ethical, professional, and legal standards while fulfilling specific criteria for reimbursement. Different types of occupational therapy reports are written for the process areas of evaluation, intervention, and outcomes. Recordings should reflect the specific and unique skilled services that occupational therapy practitioners provide as they relate to the client's role performance and ability to participate in meaningful occupations.

Case Examples

LEVEL I FIELDWORK

Ben, a Level I fieldwork student, was sitting in the rehabilitation office and happened to notice his favorite professor's name on the physical therapy schedule. He did not know why the professor was admitted nor the severity of her problem. Ben became curious and concerned, and he knew it would be very easy to quickly peek at his professor's chart at lunchtime to find out information. Although tempted, Ben ultimately did not look at the chart because he realized it would be a severe violation of privacy laws, facility policy, and the *Occupational Therapy Code of Ethics and Ethics Standards* (AOTA, 2010a). He understood that the professor was not his client and that only those involved in her care may access her chart. He also realized that it would be inappropriate to ask the physical therapist about the professor, because the therapist could not ethically divulge any confidential information.

LEVEL II FIELDWORK

Laura, a Level II fieldwork student, had just started fieldwork in a hospital located in an urban area far from her very rural and conservative hometown. The client population was culturally and ethnically diverse, and Laura observed that some clients dressed in strict religious attire and that others had multiple tattoos, body piercings, and brightly colored hair. Some of the occupational therapy clients identified themselves as lesbian, gay, or transgender. Several clients were admitted because of gunshot wounds from gang activity or had been diagnosed with AIDS from intravenous drug use. One client had even talked about her recent third abortion.

This was Laura's first time living in a big city and interacting with a diverse population. She was taken aback by lifestyles that were so different from hers; some client activities and ways of life went against her deep religious beliefs. She knew she would have to interview and develop an intervention plan for clients whose lifestyles and beliefs contrasted greatly with hers.

Despite her initial personal uneasiness, Laura strived to adhere to the *Occupational Therapy Code of Ethics and Ethics Standards* (AOTA, 2010a) and provide the best care possible for all her clients. She spoke to her fieldwork supervisor and academic fieldwork coordinator about her unfamiliarity with such a diverse environment and expressed a strong desire to better understand her clients' values, beliefs, contexts, and environments. She obtained information to improve her comfort level and cultural competence. She reflected on the many discussions and readings in her occupational therapy classes that confirmed her belief in the equality, worth, and dignity of each individual and the importance of the occupation-based practice.

Laura made a conscious effort to objectively and effectively interact with all her clients throughout the occupational therapy process. She used appropriate documentation formats for each client's situation and completed documentation without any expression of personal bias or judgment. Under the occupational therapist's supervision, Laura also appropriately established, implemented, and documented intervention plans and treatment that met the needs of each unique individual.

FIRST-TIME MANAGER

Allison, a first-time manager, worked at a skilled nursing facility. She evaluated Estelle, a 68-year-old woman with Medicare who recently underwent a right total knee replacement. A brief segment of Allison's evaluation report, highlighting Estelle's problem areas and assets, is given below.

Basic activities of daily living (BADLs):

- *Dressing:* Client requires moderate assistance to don/doff right sock and shoe and minimal assistance to stand and adjust slacks and underwear.
- *Bathing:* Client requires a tub seat for safety and moderate assistance only to wash and dry right foot.
- *Transfers:* Client requires minimum assistance when transferring to all surfaces with use of a walker.

Instrumental activities of daily living (IADLs):

- Moderate assistance is needed for household chores (i.e. cooking, laundry) because of client's right knee pain when standing with walker more than 1 minute and difficulty with transfers and functional mobility.

Client factors:

- *Cognition:* Client is alert and oriented and demonstrates good long- and short-term memory, ability to follow directions, and safety awareness.
- *Range of motion:* Bilateral active range of motion is within normal limits. Client lacks 30 degrees of right knee extension and can only flex right knee to 75 degrees, limiting occupational performance.
- *Strength:* Bilateral upper extremities within normal limits.

Estelle received daily occupational therapy, physical therapy, and skilled nursing services with the goal to return home to her tri-level townhouse. She made excellent progress in occupational therapy and regained independence in all BADLs, including transfers to all surfaces. Allison also wrote the following as part of a treatment note:

(continued)

Case Examples *(cont.)*

Client demonstrated independence in IADL tasks, which included light stovetop meal preparation and cleanup and laundry. During those tasks, client safely used a quad cane for functional mobility and transfers and a rolling cart to transport large or heavy items more easily. Client also demonstrated good activity tolerance by standing for 30 minutes.

The physical therapy documentation indicated that although Estelle had good endurance for ambulation, she still required use of a quad cane and had limitations in right knee flexion and extension and difficulty with stair climbing. The occupational therapist wanted to discharge Estelle from occupational therapy, but the nursing home administrator wondered whether Estelle should continue to receive occupational therapy for another week so that the care level remained the same for reimbursement purposes. Together, they reviewed the occupational therapy documentation.

The documentation clearly indicated that Estelle was safe and functional in BADLs and IADLs and had met all her occupational therapy goals. Although there were some residual limitations in knee range of motion and stair climbing, those deficits were already being addressed in physical therapy. The occupational therapist and administrator realized that it would not be appropriate to duplicate the services that physical therapy was providing and that, because Estelle's present status no longer required the expertise of an occupational therapy practitio-ner, continued services would be routine and unnecessary and would not adhere to Medicare guidelines. Estelle was therefore discharged from occupational therapy.

Manager

Amanda, an experienced manager, had a new job at a skilled nursing facility. She supervised Joe, an occupational therapy assistant. Amanda soon realized that although Joe was great with clients, he had difficulty completing his documentation in a timely manner. His notes sometimes appeared rushed and incomplete, and he did not always submit his paperwork by the end of the workday as required. Amanda quickly decided to discuss this issue in a nonconfrontational manner with Joe. Joe stated that he always had problems with organization and that he sometimes wrote slowly owing to spelling difficulties. Amanda reviewed facility policies with Joe regarding documentation quality and time frames. Together they worked on creating some practical solutions. Considering his caseload, Amanda helped Joe rearrange his schedule to set aside specific time daily for note writing. Amanda also delegated routine tasks to the rehabilitation aide, such as transporting clients and putting charts away, to allow more time for Joe's note writing. Amanda also suggested that Joe use a pocket-sized, electronic spell-checking device, which helped Joe immensely. Amanda provided positive reinforcement to Joe as his time management improved and he met expectations for documentation and time frames.

❖Learning Activities

1. Gather blank occupational therapy initial evaluation, discharge, and other forms from a variety of facilities and different practice settings. Compare and contrast the organizational formats, terminology, and information asked on the forms and consider the following:
   - In addition to occupational therapy practitioners, who are the expected readers of each form?
   - Do the forms reflect terminology from the *Occupational Therapy Practice Framework*?
   - What categories or sections are similar for a pediatric form versus a form for adult rehabilitation or mental health? What categories or sections are different? How do forms vary within the same type of practice setting?
   - What are the pros and cons of each form (e.g., which form is easier or clearer, more comprehensive, or better organized than the others)?
   - Is any information redundant or not necessary?
   - Is any important information missing?
   - How can each form be made better?
   - Which form do you like best or least, and why?

2. In a group discussion, ask one student or colleague to pretend to be an occupational therapy practitioner and another a client with a designated disability. Pretend the "client" has been receiving occupational therapy for several weeks and just arrived for today's session. The "practitioner" greets and briefly chats with the client before initiating treatment. On the basis of their observations of this exchange, group members should write the Subjective (*S*) part of the SOAP note that is pertinent to the client's diagnosis and treatment. They can then compare the different ways and styles in which they each have recorded similar information (e.g., use of direct quotes vs. paraphrasing).

3. In a group setting, watch a 5-minute video clip of a person with a disability performing a particular

activity such as a transfer, self-care task, or leisure activity. If the video clip is not an actual occupational therapy treatment demonstration, group members can simply pretend that what they are observing is part of an occupational therapy treatment session. Using appropriate terminology and format, group members should document the Objective (O) part of the SOAP note. They should note the setting (e.g., client's home, occupational therapy clinic, classroom) and the skilled occupational therapy service provided (e.g., cooking assessment, education in safe transfers, instruction in compensatory techniques for upper-body dressing). In addition, the note should include pertinent information regarding the client's ability to perform the task, such as level of assistance required, performance skills, and client factors. The note should clearly contain specific reasons for the client's difficulty or increased time requirements, such as left neglect, poor standing balance, spasticity, or decreased attention.

4. Watch a video clip of a person with a disability performing a particular activity such as a transfer, self-care task, or leisure activity. Using terminology from the *Occupational Therapy Practice Framework* (AOTA, 2008b), brainstorm with the group a problem list of the client's deficits that are observed in the video.

Determine which of the deficits are appropriate for occupational therapy. Then, for each of those deficits, list 5 specific occupational therapy treatment activities.

5. Create a brief client scenario, including age; diagnosis; and general level of physical, cognitive, sensory, or social ability. Assign a different performance skill, area of occupation, or general ADL task to each group member. Group members can create several specific short-term goals that are appropriate to address their assigned category or client task or occupation. For example, if the scenario is a 9-year-old child with autism, educationally related goals can be assigned for general tasks such as hygiene (e.g., washing hands after toileting, using tissues as appropriate), eating in the cafeteria (e.g., ordering food, properly discarding containers), and social interaction (e.g., sharing art supplies, taking turns). Another suggested example can be a scenario involving an 80-year-old woman with a total hip replacement. Categories can be assigned for standing tolerance, safety, lower-body dressing, tub transfers, light homemaking, and functional mobility. Group members should use proper goal format and terminology. The goals should be functional and should incorporate any compensatory techniques, adaptive devices, ambulation aids, or level of assist required.

❖❖ Multiple-Choice Questions

1. The *P* in *SOAP note* stands for
   a. Prognosis.
   b. Patient.
   c. Plan.
   d. Program.
2. Useful AOTA resources for documentation include which of the following?
   a. *Scope of Practice* (AOTA, 2010b).
   b. *Guidelines for Documentation of Occupational Therapy* (AOTA, 2008a).
   c. *Occupational Therapy Practice Framework: Domain and Process* (AOTA, 2008b).
   d. All of the above.
3. Test results and actual treatment provided should be included in which section of a SOAP note?
   a. Subjective.
   b. Objective.
   c. Assessment.
   d. Plan.
4. Long- and short-term goals are included in which of the following?
   a. Assessment.
   b. Evaluation.
   c. Referral.
   d. Intervention plan.
5. Which of the following does *not* indicate the immediate need for an occupational therapy discharge report?
   a. The client returned home following hospitalization.
   b. All occupational therapy goals were met.
   c. The client requires only maintenance therapy.
   d. The client's present status necessitates update and revision of goals.
6. Which type of occupational therapy documentation is appropriate when a child who receives occupational therapy progresses from preschool to elementary school in the same district?
   a. Transition plan.
   b. Contact note.
   c. No documentation is necessary.
   d. IDEA.
7. Which of the following is a reason for documentation?
   a. To determine efficacy of treatment.
   b. To meet legal requirements.
   c. To facilitate health team communication.
   d. All of the above.

8. Medicare requires that occupational therapy treatment is
   a. Reasonable and necessary for the condition.
   b. Provided only by an occupational therapist.
   c. Provided only if physical therapy is also indicated.
   d. Provided at least twice weekly.

9. Who can complete the OASIS initial assessment for a client with Medicare?
   a. Occupational therapists.
   b. Occupational therapy assistants.
   c. Nurses.
   d. All of the above.

10. *IEP* stands for
    a. Intervention for elementary school patients.
    b. Individualized excellence plan.
    c. Intervention for early programming.
    d. Individualized education program.

11. Who can write an occupational therapy contact note?
    a. Occupational therapists and physical therapists.
    b. Only occupational therapists.
    c. Occupational therapists and occupational therapy assistants.
    d. Occupational therapists, occupational therapy assistants, and occupational therapy rehab aides.

12. When a client arrives in the rehabilitation department, he tells the occupational therapist that he hasn't worn his splint because he forgot to put it on. This should be recorded in which section of the SOAP note?
    a. Subjective.
    b. Objective.
    c. Assessment.
    d. Plan.

13. The Minimum Data Set is used in
    a. Home care settings.
    b. Skilled nursing facilities.
    c. School systems.
    d. None of the above.

14. Which of the following is it *not* necessary to include on each piece of occupational therapy documentation?
    a. Client name.
    b. Client identification number.

c. Type of note.
d. Charge for that therapy session.

15. The process areas for occupational therapy documentation include all of the following *except*
    a. Evaluation.
    b. Ethics.
    c. Outcomes.
    d. Intervention.

16. Which of the following is considered a third-party payer?
    a. Client.
    b. Facility supplying the care.
    c. Occupational therapy practitioner.
    d. Managed care company.

17. HIPAA guidelines pertain to which of the following types of communication?
    a. Fax.
    b. E-mail.
    c. Oral.
    d. All of the above.

18. Which of the following is appropriate to document and bill as occupational therapy services?
    a. An occupational therapy assistant modifying a client's transfer technique for safety.
    b. An occupational therapy aide instructing a client in adaptive equipment use.
    c. A session consisting only of a hot pack treatment.
    d. An occupational therapy practitioner giving a client a brochure about transfers and body mechanics.

19. Another term for *short-term goal* is
    a. Long-term goal.
    b. Objective.
    c. Intervention.
    d. Skilled service.

20. Goals should include all of the following *except*
    a. Measurable criteria.
    b. Time frame.
    c. Client behavior or function.
    d. Minutes of therapy.

References

American Occupational Therapy Association. (2008a). Guidelines for documentation of occupational therapy. *American Journal of Occupational Therapy, 62,* 684–690.

American Occupational Therapy Association. (2008b). Occupational therapy practice framework: Domain and process (2nd ed.). *American Journal of Occupational Therapy, 62,* 625–683.

American Occupational Therapy Association. (2008c). Occupational therapy services in the promotion of health and the prevention of disease and disability. *American Journal of Occupational Therapy, 62,* 694–703.

American Occupational Therapy Association. (2009). Guidelines for supervision, roles, and responsibilities during the delivery of occupational therapy services. *American Journal of Occupational Therapy, 63,* 797–803.

American Occupational Therapy Association. (2010a). Occupational therapy code of ethics and ethics standards. *American Journal of Occupational Therapy, 64.*

American Occupational Therapy Association. (2010b). Scope of practice. *American Journal of Occupational Therapy, 64.*

American Occupational Therapy Association. (2010c). Standards of practice for occupational therapy. *American Journal of Occupational Therapy, 64.*

Anderson, R. E. (2008). The art of caring in the computer age: Perceptions of home care occupational therapy practitioners. *Home and Community Health Special Interest Section Quarterly, 15*(2), 1–4.

Backman, A., Kåwe, K., & Bjorklund, A. (2008). Relevance and focal view point in occupational therapists' documentation in patient case records. *Scandinavian Journal of Occupational Therapy, 15,* 212–220.

Borcherding, S., & Morreale, M. J. (2007). *The OTA's guide to writing SOAP notes* (2nd ed.). Thorofare, NJ: Slack.

Carroll, A. E., Tarczy-Hornoch, P., O'Reilly, E., & Christakis, D. A. (2004). The effect of point-of-care personal digital assistant use on resident documentation discrepancies. *Pediatrics, 113,* 450–454.

Cederfeldt, M., Lundgren, P. B., & Sadlo, G. (2003). Occupational status as documented in records for stroke inpatients in Sweden. *Scandinavian Journal of Occupational Therapy, 10,* 81–87.

Centers for Medicare and Medicaid Services. (2002a). *RAI version 2.0 manual* (Ch. 1, Section 1.1). Baltimore: Author. Retrieved January 16, 2009, from http://www.cms.hhs.gov/NursingHomeQualityInits/20_NHQIMDS20.asp#TopOfPage

Centers for Medicare and Medicaid Services. (2002b). *RAI version 2.0 manual* (Ch. 1, Section 1.12). Baltimore: Author. Retrieved January 16, 2009, from http://www.cms.hhs.gov/NursingHomeQualityInits/20_NHQIMDS20.asp#TopOfPage

Centers for Medicare and Medicaid Services. (2006a). *Medicare benefit policy manual* (Ch. 15, Section 220.2). Baltimore: Author. Retrieved January 8, 2009, from http://www.cms.hhs.gov/manuals/Downloads/bp102c15.pdf

Centers for Medicare and Medicaid Services. (2006b). *Medicare benefit policy manual* (Ch. 15, Section 230). Baltimore: Author. Retrieved January 8, 2009, from http://www.cms.hhs.gov/manuals/Downloads/bp102c15.pdf

Centers for Medicare and Medicaid Services. (2008a). *Medicare benefit policy manual* (Ch. 15, Section 220.3). Baltimore: Author. Retrieved January 8, 2009, from http://www.cms.hhs.gov/manuals/Downloads/bp102c15.pdf

Centers for Medicare and Medicaid Services. (2008b). *Medicare benefit policy manual* (Ch. 15, Section 230.2). Baltimore: Author. Retrieved January 8, 2009, from http://www.cms.hhs.gov/manuals/Downloads/bp102c15.pdf

Centers for Medicare and Medicaid Services. (2008c). *OASIS implementation manual* (Ch. 2, page 2.1). Baltimore: Author. Retrieved January 16, 2009, from http://www.cms.hhs.gov/HomeHealthQualityInits/14_HHQIOASISUserManual.asp#TopOfPage

Centers for Medicare and Medicaid Services. (2008d). *OASIS implementation manual* (Ch. 2, page 2.3). Baltimore: Author. Retrieved January 16, 2009, from http://www.cms.hhs.gov/HomeHealthQualityInits/14_HHQIOASISUserManual.asp#TopOfPage

Davis, J., Zayat, E., Urton, M., Belgum, A., & Hill, M. (2008). Communicating evidence in clinical documentation. *Australian Occupational Therapy Journal, 55,* 249–255.

Donaldson, N., McDermott, A., Hollands, K., Copley, J., & Davidson, B. (2004). Clinical reporting by occupational therapists and speech pathologists: Therapists' intentions and parental satisfaction. *Advances in Speech–Language Pathology, 6,* 23–38.

Dosa, D., Bowers, B., & Gifford, D. R.(2006). Critical review of resident assessment protocols. *Journal of the American Geriatrics Society, 54,* 659–666.

Erhart, A., Delehanty, L. M., Morley, N. E., Pickens, D., & Greene, D. (2005). Consistency between documented occupational therapy services and billing in a skilled nursing facility: A pilot study. *Physical and Occupational Therapy in Geriatrics, 24,* 53–62.

Garcia-Castillo, D., & Fetters, M. D. (2007). Quality in medical translations: A review. *Journal of Health Care for the Poor and Underserved, 18,* 74–84.

Health Insurance Portability and Accountability Act of 1996, Pub. L. 104–191.

Hedberg-Kristensson, E., & Iwarsson, S. (2003). Documentation quality in occupational therapy patient records: Focusing on the technical aid prescription process. *Scandinavian Journal of Occupational Therapy, 10,* 72–80.

Hoffman, T., McKenna, K., Herd, C., & Wearing, S. (2007). Written education materials for stroke patients and their carers: Perspectives and practices of health professionals. *Topics in Stroke Rehabilitation, 14,* 88–97.

Kuehn, L. (2006). *CPT/HCPCS coding and reimbursement for physician services.* Chicago: American Health Information Management Association. Retrieved January 6, 2009, from http://library.ahima.org/xpedio/groups/public/documents/ahima/bok1_015859.pdf#page%3D14

Montero-Odasso, M., Levinson, P., Gore, B., Epid, D., Tremblay, L., & Bergman, H. (2007). A flowchart system to improve fall data documentation in a long-term care institution: A pilot study. *Journal of the American Medical Directors Association, 8,* 300–306.

Salvatori, P., Simonavicius, N., Moore, J., Rimmer, G., & Patterson, M. (2008). Meeting the challenge of assessing clinical competence of occupational therapists within a program management environment. *Canadian Journal of Occupational Therapy, 75,* 51–60.

Schnelle, J., Osterweil, D., & Simmons, S. (2005). Improving quality of nursing home care and medical-record accuracy with direct observational technologies. *Gerontologist, 45,* 576–582.

Stengel, D., Bauwens, K., Walter, M., Kopfer, T., & Ekkernkamp, A. (2004). Comparison of handheld, computer-assisted, and conventional paper chart documentation of medical records: A randomized, controlled trial. *Journal of Bone and Joint Surgery, 86,* 553–560.

Taunton, R. L., Swagerty, D. L., Smith, B., Lasseter, J. A., & Lee, R. H. (2004). Care planning for nursing home residents: Incorporating the Minimum Data Set requirements into practice. *Journal of Gerontological Nursing, 30,* 40–49.

Thomson, C., & Black, L. (2008). An exploratory study of the differences between unidisciplinary and multidisciplinary goal setting in acute therapy services. *British Journal of Occupational Therapy, 71,* 422–426.

U.S. Department of Health and Human Services. (2008). *Electronic health records: Advancing 21st century medicine.* Washington, DC: Author. Retrieved January 14, 2009, from http://www.hhs.gov/news/facts/20080131c.html

Vreeman, D. J., Taggard, S. J., Rhine, M. D., & Worrell, T. W. (2006). Evidence for electronic health record systems in physical therapy [Invited commentary, author response]. *Physical Therapy, 86,* 434–449.

Welch, A., & Forster, S. (2003). A clinical audit of the outcome of occupational therapy assessment and negotiated patient goals in the acute setting. *British Journal of Occupational Therapy, 66,* 363–368.

World Health Organization. (2001). *International classification of functioning, disability and health (ICF).* Geneva: Author.

World Health Organization. (2002). *Towards a common language for functioning, disability and health: ICF.* Retrieved June 16, 2010, from http://www.who.int/classifications/icf/training/icfbeginnersguide.pdf

Appendix 24.A. Documentation Evidence Table

Topic	Subtopic	Evidence
Documentation quality	Goals	Thomson, C., & Black, L. (2008). An exploratory study of the differences between unidisciplinary and multidisciplinary goal setting in acute therapy services. *British Journal of Occupational Therapy, 71,* 422–426. Welch, A., & Forster, S. (2003). A clinical audit of the outcome of occupational therapy assessment and negotiated patient goals in the acute setting. *British Journal of Occupational Therapy, 66,* 363–368.
	Peer or caregiver review	Donaldson, N., McDermott, A., Hollands, K., Copley, J., & Davidson, B. (2004). Clinical reporting by occupational therapists and speech pathologists: Therapists' intentions and parental satisfaction. *Advances in Speech–Language Pathology, 6,* 23–38. Salvatori, P., Simonavicius, N., Moore, J., Rimmer, G., & Patterson, M. (2008). Meeting the challenge of assessing clinical competence of occupational therapists within a program management environment. *Canadian Journal of Occupational Therapy, 75,* 51–60.
	Occupational therapy domain terminology	Backman, A., Kåwe, K., & Bjorklund, A. (2008). Relevance and focal view point in occupational therapists' documentation in patient case records. *Scandinavian Journal of Occupational Therapy, 15,* 212–220. Cederfeldt, M., Lundgren, P. B., & Sadlo, G. (2003). Occupational status as documented in records for stroke inpatients in Sweden. *Scandinavian Journal of Occupational Therapy, 10,* 81–87.
	Documentation protocols	Hedberg-Kristensson, E., & Iwarsson, S. (2003). Documentation quality in occupational therapy patient records: Focusing on the technical aid prescription process. *Scandinavian Journal of Occupational Therapy, 10,* 72–80. Hoffman, T., McKenna, K., Herd, C., & Wearing, S. (2007). Written education materials for stroke patients and their carers: Perspectives and practices of health professionals. *Topics in Stroke Rehabilitation, 14,* 88–97.
	Accuracy	Garcia-Castillo, D., & Fetters, M. D. (2007). Quality in medical translations: A review. *Journal of Health Care for the Poor and Underserved, 18,* 74–84. Schnelle, J., Osterweil, D., & Simmons, S. (2005). Improving quality of nursing home care and medical-record accuracy with direct observational technologies. *Gerontologist, 45,* 576–582.
Methods	Electronic documentation	Anderson, R. E. (2008). The art of caring in the computer age: Perceptions of home care occupational therapy practitioners. *Home and Community Health Special Interest Section Quarterly, 15*(2), 1–4. Carroll, A. E., Tarczy-Hornoch, P., O'Reilly, E., & Christakis, D. (2004). The effect of point-of-care personal digital assistant use on resident documentation discrepancies. *Pediatrics, 113,* 450–454. Stengel, D., Bauwens, K., Walter, M., Kopfer, T., & Ekkernkamp, A. (2004). Comparison of handheld, computer-assisted, and conventional paper-chart documentation of medical records: A randomized, controlled trial. *Journal of Bone and Joint Surgery, 86,* 553–560. Vreeman, D. J., Taggard, S. J., Rhine, M. D., & Worrell, T. W. (2006). Evidence for electronic health record systems in physical therapy [Invited commentary, author response]. *Physical Therapy, 86,* 434–449.
	Formats	Montero-Odasso, M., Levinson, P., Gore, B., Epid, D., Tremblay, L., & Bergman, H. (2007). A flowchart system to improve fall data documentation in a long-term care institution: A pilot study. *Journal of the American Medical Directors Association, 8,* 300–306.
	Resident assessment instrument	Dosa, D., Bowers, B., & Gifford, D. R. (2006). Critical review of resident assessment protocols. *Journal of the American Geriatrics Society, 54,* 659–666. Taunton, R. L., Swagerty, D. L., Smith, B., Lasseter, J. A., & Lee, R. H. (2004). Care planning for nursing home residents: Incorporating the Minimum Data Set requirements into practice. *Journal of Gerontological Nursing, 30,* 40–49.

(continued)

APPENDIX 24. DOCUMENTATION EVIDENCE TABLE *(cont.)*

Topic	Subtopic	Evidence
Reimbursement		Davis, J., Zayat, E., Urton, M., Belgum, A., & Hill, M. (2008). Communicating evidence in clinical documentation. *Australian Occupational Therapy Journal, 55,* 249–255. Erhart, A., Delehanty, L. M., Morley, N. E., Pickens, D., & Greene, D. (2005). Consistency between documented occupational therapy services and billing in a skilled nursing facility: A pilot study. *Physical and Occupational Therapy in Geriatrics, 24,* 53–62.

25

Reimbursement

V. Judith Thomas

❖ Key Terms and Concepts

Assignment. In Medicare Part B, agreement by a private practitioner to accept the Medicare fee as full payment. The beneficiary is still responsible for any coinsurance or deductible.

Benefits. The range of services provided by a health care insurance plan.

Bundled rate. A payment for a group of related health care services, often over a specific period (e.g., a rehabilitation hospital stay, 60 days of home health care).

Case management. A process by which a health care practitioner monitors and directs the utilization of health care services by a single member of a health plan.

Centers for Medicare and Medicaid Services (CMS). The federal agency that administers the Medicare program and works with states to run Medicaid and the State Children's Health Insurance Programs (SCHIP).

Claim. A written or electronic statement to an insurance company requesting payment of an amount due under the terms of the policy.

Coinsurance, copayment. A fixed dollar amount that an individual or secondary insurance company pays for each medical service received. Coinsurance pays a percentage of the cost of the service.

Comprehensive outpatient rehabilitation facility (CORF). A facility that provides a variety of outpatient services, including occupational therapy, medical, and social or psychological services.

Covered services. Services or benefits for which the health plan makes either partial or full payment.

Diagnosis code(s). The code or codes that must be included on a bill to describe the health condition for which a person received services. The *ICD–9–CM* coding system, which is scheduled to be replaced by the *ICD–10–CM* in 2013, is the standard set of codes in the United States (National Center for Health Statistics & Centers for Medicare and Medicaid Services, 2000).

Durable medical equipment, prosthetics, orthotics, and supplies (DMEPOS). Under the Medicare definition, DMEPOS includes medical equipment and other items that are ordered by a qualified health care practitioner for use in the home. Orthotics, both custom fabricated and prefabricated, are classified as DMEPOS and are billed separately from occupational therapy interventions.

Early and periodic screening, diagnosis, and treatment (EPSDT). A required comprehensive Medicaid benefit package for children up to 21 years of age that covers screening and diagnostic services to determine physical or mental impairments, as well as necessary health care interventions to correct or improve any condition.

Employee Retirement Income Security Act (ERISA). A federal statute that sets the minimum standards under which employee benefit plans are established and maintained by private-sector employers, employee organizations, or jointly by one or more private-sector employers and an employee organization.

Exclusions. Items or services that a plan does not cover and for which it will not pay.

Fee schedule. A list of fees used by health plans to pay providers. The Medicare Physicians Payment System is an example of a fee schedule.

Fraud and abuse. *Fraud:* The act of purposely misrepresenting items or services on a bill (e.g., billing for services not provided, billing an inflated amount for an item). *Abuse:* The act of incorrectly billing for items or services but without fraudulent intent.

Health care provider. Any health care practitioner (e.g., physician, occupational therapist) or facility (e.g., hospital, nursing home) or organization that is licensed to provide health care services.

Health Insurance Portability and Accessibility Act (HIPAA). A law, also known as the Kennedy–Kassebaum Act (P.L. 104–191), that includes rules governing the use

The author acknowledges the assistance of Boston University occupational therapy student **Miranda Hellman** in developing the multiple-choice questions used in this chapter.

of standards and administrative code sets for the electronic exchange of health care data; requires the use of national identification systems for health care patients, providers, payers (or plans), and employers (or sponsors); and specifies the types of measures required to protect the security and privacy of personally identifiable health care information.

Incident to a physician. Rendered to beneficiaries in a physician's office or in a physician-directed clinic; outpatient occupational therapy services are covered under Medicare (Part B) as incidental to a physician's services. Occupational therapy services must be directly related to the condition for which the physician is treating the patient, the physician must be in the office suite, and services must be included on the physician's bill to Medicare.

Managed care plan. Health insurance plan that generally provides comprehensive health services to its members and offers financial incentives for patients to use the providers that belong to the plan. Examples include health maintenance organizations (HMOs), preferred provider organizations (PPOs), exclusive provider organizations (EPOs), and point-of-service plans (POSs).

Medicare Administrative Contractor (MAC). A private insurance company that contracts with CMS to pay bills submitted by physicians, nonphysician practitioners, and suppliers under Parts A and B of Medicare.

Medicare Part D. A Medicare benefit enacted in 2003 to help beneficiaries with expenses for prescription drugs (Medicare Prescription Drug, Improvement, and Modernization Act of 2003 [P.L. 108-173], also called Medicare Modernization Act or MMA).

Minimum Data Set (MDS). Assessment data routinely collected by nursing homes on residents via the Resident Assessment Instrument (RAI) at specified intervals to assess residents' physical, mental, cognitive, and clinical conditions and abilities, as well as preferences and life care wishes. These assessment data have been used to develop a quality measure.

National Provider Identifier (NPI). The Administrative Simplification provisions of HIPAA mandated the adoption of standard unique identifiers for health care providers and health plans. All health care providers and practitioners must obtain an NPI to bill for services.

Network. A group of health care practitioners, hospitals, pharmacies, and other health care organizations that are under contract to a health plan to provide services to its members.

Out-of-network provider. A health care practitioner or facility that does not participate in a specific patient's health plan. An insurance company may not pay for care or may pay a lower percentage for services provided by an out-of-network provider.

Out-of-pocket expenses. Health care costs that are not covered by a plan and for which an individual is responsible.

Per diem payment. An amount paid for a group of services provided in a single day.

Prospective payment system (PPS). A method of paying for predefined health care services. Sometimes a PPS is for a specific illness, injury, or patient profile over a specific duration of time (e.g., per episode, per day).

Regulation. A rule or order interpreting a law; regulations are promulgated by a part of the executive branch of the government (e.g., Centers for Medicare and Medicaid Services, U.S. Department of Defense).

Secondary payer. An insurance policy or plan that pays after an individual's primary insurance has paid.

Third-party payer. Any payer for health care services (e.g., insurance company, worker's compensation) other than the individual receiving care.

Note. These definitions were derived from multiple sources, including the Centers for Medicare and Medicaid Services (http://cms.hhs.gov), the U.S. Office of Personnel Management (http://www.opm.gov), and the Bureau of Labor Statistics (http://www.bls.gov/ncs/ebs/sp/healthterms.pdf). This glossary describes terms used in the Medicare and other health care systems, but it is *not* a legal document. Refer to relevant laws, regulations, and rulings for official definitions and explanations.

❖ Learning Objectives

After completing this chapter, you should be able to do the following:

- Identify the provisions of the Health Insurance Portability and Accountability Act of 1996, and discuss how they affect the health care system and occupational therapy practice.
- Describe 3 different health care programs or plan structures and how each affects access to care.
- Identify the settings in which occupational therapy practitioners work where services are paid by the Medicare program and discuss differences in payment methodologies.
- List 3 health care programs that are administered by states.

In the United States, access to and payment for health care are controlled by an ever-changing equation that includes federal and state regulation, private insurance company policies, employer choice, provider rules, and consumer choice. All of these variable factors and their relative importance in the equation affect practitioner delivery of services. Therefore, occupational therapy practitioners and other health care professionals must understand these influences to effectively treat and advocate for their clients.

This chapter examines third-party payers, payment systems, and policies that affect occupational therapy decision making and care management. It provides insight into the various payment methodologies incorporated into the array of benefits under the Medicare program, which is the largest payer in the country. Additionally, the chapter discusses the ways recent and projected changes to the health care system may affect service delivery options, as well as the need for occupational therapy practitioners to be proactive in protecting their scope of practice and the rights of consumers to optimum care.

Overview of Health Care Financing

Health care in the United States is funded by federal, state, or local programs; is paid for by private insurance plans under contracts with employers, other organizations, and individuals; or is paid entirely by those receiving care. Table 25.1 shows the distribution of the U.S. population with public or private health insurance and with no insurance.

Although concern about access to health care in the United States has focused on the approximately 47 million uninsured persons, there are also more than 25 million people who are underinsured (Mitka, 2008). Underinsured adults are those with limited health coverage that does not adequately protect against high medical expenses or pay for all services. Therefore, access to occupational therapy is limited not only for the uninsured population but also for the many people with insurance plans that do not recognize specific occupational therapy interventions, do not cover occupational therapy for specific populations or conditions, or severely limit access.

Public funding for health care is typically available through programs such as Medicare, Medicaid, the Indian Health Service, and workers' compensation or grant-funded programs. These programs are administered in a variety of ways by federal, state, or local organizations. Each insurance program has structured guidelines specifying which services are covered, in what settings, and by whom. Payment mechanisms and amounts differ from payer to payer and within payer programs depending on site of service, scope of benefits, and other factors.

Private insurance companies, either proprietary or nonprofit, provide health care benefits under a wide variety of plans with differing benefits and restrictions. Insurers primarily contract with employers and other organizations to cover employees (or members) and their dependents for a specific array of benefits. Employers may pay all or part of the cost (i.e., premium) of health insurance. Additionally, the employee, or policyholder, may be responsible for partial payment of premiums, out-of-pocket copayments, and deductibles. Other types of groups (e.g., professional associations) and individuals also may purchase health care coverage from private insurers. Total expenditures for health care in the United States in 2008 were about $2.3 trillion. Figure 25.1 shows the proportions of personal health care spending through public programs (e.g., Medicare, Medicaid, State Children's Health Insurance Programs), private health insurance payers, and consumer out-of-pocket expenditures.

Occupational therapists also play a fundamental role in "nonmedical" community-based or social programs, including adult day programs, adaptations for older drivers, home modification, and lifestyle redesign or life care management, that enhance overall living skills. These programs may receive financial support through funding by public agencies, private foundations, or corporations. Federally funded programs include the Individuals with Disabilities Education

Table 25.1. Health Insurance Coverage in the United States, 2006–2007: Percentage of People Covered, by Health Plan Type

Health plan type	%
Medicare	12.1
Medicaid	13.2
Military (including TRICARE)	3.6
Employer-based	59.3
Any private plan	67.5
Uninsured	15.3

Note. Percentages do not add to 100 due to dual coverage.

Source. U.S. Census Bureau (2008).

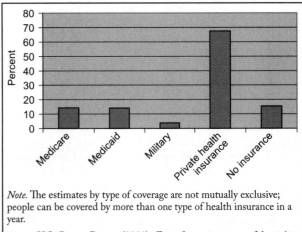

Note. The estimates by type of coverage are not mutually exclusive; people can be covered by more than one type of health insurance in a year.

Source. U.S. Census Bureau (2008). For information on confidentiality protection, sampling error, nonsampling error, and definitions, see http://www.census.gov/apsd/techdoc/cps/cpsmar09.pdf.

Figure 25.1. Health care coverage by type of insurance (2008).

Act (1990, P.L. 191-476); the Community Mental Health Act (1963, P.L. 88-164); the Older Americans Act (1965, P.L. 89-73); and Social Security Title XX, the Social Services Block Grant Program, which is part of the Omnibus Budget Reconciliation Act of 1981 (P.L. 97-35). Additionally, occupational therapy is often provided to individuals who pay out-of-pocket fees for preventive and other services that are not reimbursed by third-party payers.

Historically, most federal laws have limited application to private and employer self-funded health insurers. State regulation has been primary. However, a broader application of federal law was achieved with the passage of the Health Insurance Portability and Accountability Act of 1996 (HIPAA; P.L. 104-191). One of its amendments, the Mental Health Parity Act of 1996 (MHPA; P.L. 104-204), and the Mental Health Parity and Addiction Equity Act of 2008 (P.L. 110-343) also affect public health programs, such as Medicare and Medicaid, and some employment-related group health plans. The provisions of these laws laid the path for additional legislation with national implications, especially the landmark Patient Protection and Affordable Care Act of 2010 (PPACA; P.L. 111-148).

HIPAA is a broad law consisting of many components, each with its own set of policies and implementation deadlines. The concepts included in sections of this law provided, for the first time, a structure for collecting, tracking, and analyzing health care data across all health care plans, providers, and consumers. A key goal in the passage of HIPAA was to "promote standardization and efficiency in the health care industry" (Centers for Medicare and Medicaid Services [CMS], 2003). The availability of aggregated comparison data on health plans and providers will help consumers and practitioners make more informed health care choices.

Of particular interest to occupational therapy practitioners are the requirements set forth under the Administration Simplification provisions (CMS, 2010d). These provisions require the U.S. Department of Health and Human Services to establish national standards for electronic health care transactions and national identifiers for providers, health plans, and employers. It also addressed the security and privacy of health data. These regulations apply to all health plans, health care clearinghouses, and those health care providers who conduct certain financial and administrative transactions electronically (e.g., eligibility, referral authorizations, claims submissions). Table 25.2 identifies those provisions of particular interest to occupational therapy practitioners and the federal agency responsible for implementation.

Table 25.2. HIPAA Standards of Interest to Occupational Therapy Practitioners

HIPAA standard	Enforcement authority and resource
National Provider Identifier (NPI)—Requires that a unique 10-digit identification number be obtained by all health care providers and practitioners that bill for medical services. As of May 23, 2009, the NPI is required for all HIPAA standard electronic transactions.	Centers for Medicare and Medicaid Services (http://www.cms. hhs.gov/NationalProvIdentStand/03_apply.asp#TopOfPage)
Electronic health care transaction and code sets—Requires the establishment of standard data elements, codes, and formats for submitting electronic claims and other health care transactions. In 2013, HHS will adopt the *International Classification of Diseases, 10th Revision, Clinical Modification (ICD–10–CM)* for diagnosis coding and the *International Classification of Diseases, 10th Revision, Procedural Coding System (ICD–10–PCS)* for inpatient hospital procedure coding.	Centers for Medicare and Medicaid Services (http://www.cms.hhs.gov/TransactionCodeSetsStands/02_TransactionsandCodeSetsRegulations.asp#TopOfPage)
Health information privacy—Requires protection of the confidentiality of individually identifiable health information. The rule limits the use and disclosure of certain individually identifiable health information; gives patients the right to access their medical records; restricts most disclosure of health information to the minimum needed for the intended purpose; and establishes safeguards and restrictions regarding the use and disclosure of records for certain public responsibilities, such as public health, research, and law enforcement	Office for Civil Rights (http://www.hhs.gov/ocr/privacy/hipaa/administrative/privacyrule/index.html)
Security—Requires protection of electronic health information systems from improper access or alteration. Under the security standards, covered entities must protect the confidentiality, integrity, and availability of electronic protected health information. The rule requires covered entities to implement administrative, physical, and technical safeguards to protect the information in their care.	Centers for Medicare and Medicaid Services (http://www.cms.hhs.gov/ocr/privacy/hipaa/administrative/securityrule/techsafeguards.pdf)

Note. HIPAA = Health Insurance Portability and Accessibility Act of 1996 (P. L. 104-191).

The MHPA is a federal law that affects large self-funded group health plans and large employment-related group health plans. Only specific types of health plans are subject to this law. For example, MHPA does not apply to small group health plans (<50 workers) or to individual (non-employment-related) plans. For plans to which MHPA applies (i.e., those that have mental health benefits), the law requires that benefits not be more restrictive in terms of dollar limitations than benefits for medical and surgical coverage. Effective after October 3, 2009, the Mental Health Parity and Addiction Equity Act of 2008 expands the provisions of the MHPA to require additional parity with medical and surgical benefits in financial (e.g., deductibles and copayments) and treatment limitations (e.g., number of visits, number of treatments; CMS, 2010b). Despite these laws, many health insurance plans are not subject to the requirements, and no health plan is required to include mental health in its benefit package. Some states have additional requirements regarding mental health benefits that apply to health insurers selling policies in those states.

FEDERAL HEALTH CARE PAYMENT SYSTEMS
Medicare
Medicare, established by Congress in 1965 as Title XIII of the Social Security Act amendments (P.L. 89-97), provides health care coverage for people older than age 65, people with disabilities, and people with end-stage renal disease. Benefits are covered under four sections of the act: the Hospital Insurance Program (Part A), the Supplementary Medical Insurance Program (Part B), the Medicare Advantage Program (Managed Care; Part C), and the Prescription Drug Program (Part D). The agency that administers Medicare and Medicaid, CMS, is the largest single payer of health care services in the United States. Its payment and coverage policies affect virtually every practice setting in which occupational therapy practitioners work and are a major influence on the policies and administration of other systems, including military health care systems and most private insurance plans. Because Medicare pays for so much of occupational therapy and Medicare policy is often followed by other third-party payers, a basic understanding of Medicare law, regulations, and policy is essential for occupational therapy managers and practitioners.

Occupational therapy services are subject to coverage and payment policies under Medicare Part A (Hospital Insurance Program) and Part B (Supplementary Medical Insurance Program), which together are generally referred to as the "traditional" or "original" Medicare program, and Part C (Managed Care), commonly referred to as Medicare Advantage Plans. To obtain full coverage for all health care services covered by traditional Medicare (except prescription drugs), a Medicare beneficiary must participate in either a combination of Parts A and B (the later is optional) or in one of a variety of Advantage Plans (Part C). Choosing an Advantage Plan is also optional. All of these

Medicare programs are described in more detail in later parts of this section.

CMS provides interpretation of legislative requirements through regulations, which have the force of law, and what are called "manual instructions," which are further interpretations of regulations. The federal regulatory process requires that before new rules can be implemented, the government proposes changes and allows for public comment. During this comment period, providers, practitioners, and other interested parties have the opportunity to challenge policies and recommend changes, which the federal agency must consider but is not obligated to adopt. This process is important as it allows occupational therapists to participate in the development of policies that will affect their practice. The American Occupational Therapy Association (AOTA) provides opportunities for occupational therapy educators, researchers, and practitioners to assist in responding to Medicare and other payer policy proposals.

In addition to regulations, CMS disseminates instructions on Medicare requirements through manual transmittals and program instructions. This information provides guidance on national coverage criteria, billing, and documentation required for a claim to be paid.

Generally, occupational therapy is considered a Medicare-covered service under certain circumstances. Services must be

- Prescribed by a physician and furnished according to a written plan of care approved by the physician
- Performed by a qualified occupational therapist or by an occupational therapy assistant under the supervision of an occupational therapist
- Require the skills of a therapist or assistant
- Reasonable and necessary for the treatment of the person's illness or injury.

Under the traditional Medicare program, CMS contracts with various insurance companies to process Medicare claims, make payments, and perform medical review services in accordance with policies promulgated by CMS. At the end of a major change in the structure of these contractors begun in 2008, there will be 23 Medicare Administration Contractors (MACs) nationally to process Medicare claims under Parts A and B (Fletcher, 2008). Of these, 4 process home health agency and hospice claims exclusively, and 4 focus on claims for durable medical equipment, prosthetics, orthotics, and supplies (DMEPOS). The other 15 process claims for all the remaining Part A and Part B providers, including hospitals, skilled nursing facilities (SNFs), comprehensive outpatient rehabilitation facilities (CORFs), rehabilitation agencies, and physician and therapy (including occupational therapy) private practices.

Medicare contractors have the authority to develop local coverage determinations, which provide additional interpretation and instruction to providers and practitioners in claims submission and documentation. Individual contractors can be accessed through the CMS Web site (http://www.cms.gov/DeterminationProcess/04_LCDs.asp).

Medicare benefits include inpatient and outpatient occupational therapy services when they are provided to eligible beneficiaries by all types of "institutional" providers (i.e., hospitals, SNFs, home health agencies, rehabilitation agencies, CORFs, and hospices). Additionally, Medicare beneficiaries may receive outpatient services from occupational therapists who are in private practice or working for physicians. The general coverage guidelines apply to all settings. Criteria for payment as well as additional coverage, billing, coding, and documentation requirements vary from setting to setting and from plan to plan; this variation affects how therapists must provide and document services.

Medicare Part A Benefits

Hospitals. Individual hospitals determine the mix of services that is appropriate for each acute care inpatient, and occupational therapy services "if provided, must be provided by staff who meet the qualifications specified by the medical staff, consistent with State law" (42 CFR 482.56). Since October 1983, acute care inpatient hospital services have been paid under a prospective payment system (PPS) based on the range of services expected to be provided to each patient on the basis of established diagnosis-related groups. This per case or per episode rate covers all inpatient services, including occupational therapy.

Inpatient rehabilitation facility (IRF) or hospital unit stays. An IRF is a type of hospital or unit that treats rehabilitation patients. To be classified as an IRF, a specific percentage of the facility's inpatient population must have one of the following specific conditions (future regulations may amend the specific conditions and/or required patient percentage):

- Stroke
- Spinal cord injury
- Congenital deformity
- Amputation
- Major multiple trauma
- Fracture of femur (hip fracture)
- Brain injury
- Neurological disorder
- Burns
- Arthritis-related medical condition (3 types specified in the rule)
- Knee or hip joint replacement, or both, during an acute hospitalization immediately preceding the IRF stay when one or more of the following criteria are met: (1) the procedure was bilateral, (2) the patient's body mass index is at least 50 at the time of admission to the IRF, or (3) the patient was 85 or older at the time of admission to the IRF.

For eligibility for IRF-level care, regulations also require that a patient "need the active and ongoing therapeutic intervention of at least two therapy disciplines (physical therapy, occupational therapy, speech–language pathology, or prosthetics/orthotics therapy), one of which must be physical or occupational therapy" (CMS, 2009b). The Balanced Budget Act of 1997 (P.L. 105-33) authorized the implementation of a per discharge PPS for inpatient rehabilitation hospitals and rehabilitation units. The IRF PPS, effective beginning January 2002, uses information from a patient assessment instrument to classify patients into distinct groups based on clinical characteristics and expected resource needs. Separate payments are calculated for each group.

Psychiatric hospital stays. For discharges beginning on or after January 1, 2005, inpatient psychiatric facilities (IPF), including distinct psychiatric units of acute care hospitals and critical access hospitals, are paid under an IPF PPS (42 CFR 412, Subpart N) for treatment of their patients. This system, required under the Medicare, Medicaid, and SCHIP (Balanced Budget Refinement Act of 1999, P.L. 106-33), includes a per diem rate and a "patient classification system that reflects the differences in patient resource use and costs among psychiatric hospitals and psychiatric units" (CMS, n.d.).

SNF inpatient stays. Medicare covers occupational therapy in a SNF as a Part A benefit for 100 days of skilled nursing and therapy care, provided the patient needs any combination of skilled nursing, occupational therapy, physical therapy, and speech–language pathology services daily (defined in Medicare policy as at least 5 days per week). In those cases, Medicare pays for the cost of room and board and nursing services at the SNF in addition to the needed occupational and physical therapy and speech–language pathology.

The Balanced Budget Act of 1997 mandated the implementation of a per diem PPS for SNFs covering all costs (routine, ancillary, and capital) related to services furnished to beneficiaries under Part A of the Medicare program effective July 1, 1998. A patient's need for services and the prospective per diem rate are established by a Resident Assessment Instrument (RAI), which classifies patients into resource utilization groups. The RAI consists of the Minimum Data Set (MDS; a core set of screening, clinical, and functional status assessment elements), the resident assessment protocols, and utilization guidelines (CMS, 2010c). The therapy resource utilization groups are based on the number of minutes of therapy per week required by the patient. Use of the RAI and comparison of data have led to the development of quality indicators that focus on outcomes for SNFs rather than process of care (Liu, Taghavi, & Cornelius, 1992).

Home health agency (HHA) services. To qualify under the Medicare home health benefit, a homebound patient must need intermittent skilled nursing care, physical therapy, or speech–language therapy. Occupational therapy is a covered service only after the client qualifies for the home health benefit. However, Medicare patients may continue to be qualified if the need to receive occupational therapy after their need for skilled nursing, physical therapy, or speech–language therapy ends. HHAs classify patients using a standard system, the Outcome and Assessment Information Set (OASIS). An HHA is paid a single rate for each 60-day episode of care that is based on the information about individual patient needs described in the OASIS. A higher payment is provided if the need for a specific level of therapy is projected and provided.

Hospice care. Hospice care is a special Part A benefit for eligible Medicare beneficiaries whom a physician has certified as *terminally ill*, defined in the regulations as having a medical prognosis of fewer than 6 months to live. A patient who elects to receive hospice benefits must waive all other inpatient Medicare benefits during the election period. Occupational therapy may be provided only to control a patient's symptoms or to enable a patient to maintain activities of daily living and basic functional skills. Hospice benefits are paid on a prospective basis. The rates, which are updated annually, are based on four primary levels of care that correspond to the degree of illness and the amount of care required.

Medicare Part B Benefits

Outpatient occupational therapy. Occupational therapy is covered as a Part B outpatient service when furnished by or under contractual arrangements with any Medicare-certified provider (i.e., comprehensive outpatient rehabilitation facility, rehabilitation agency, clinic, hospital outpatient department, home health agencies, occupational therapists in private practice, physicians). An occupational therapy practitioner working under the auspices of any Medicare provider may furnish outpatient occupational therapy services to a beneficiary in the home or in the provider's outpatient facility or, under certain circumstances, to a beneficiary who is an inpatient in another institution. Payment for individual outpatient therapy services (i.e., occupational therapy, physical therapy, and speech–language pathology) is computed within the Medicare Physician Fee Schedule (MPFS), which is based on *Current Procedural Terminology (CPT)* code description (see *"Current Procedural Terminology"* section). Medicare pays a provider 80% of the fee schedule amount after the beneficiary has paid a yearly deductible for all Medicare Part B services. All outpatient therapy services except those performed in hospital outpatient settings are subject to a dollar limitation per beneficiary per calendar year, or "cap," although this policy currently allows for exceptions to go over the cap. In addition, there are several specific documentation requirements and local contractor policies with which therapists must comply when outpatient services are rendered and billed.

Occupational therapist in private practice and physicians. Outpatient occupational therapy (Part B) may be furnished to Medicare beneficiaries by an occupational therapist working incident to a physician in the physician's office suite, in private practice in an office setting, or in a patient's home (including in some cases in a non-Medicare certified institution). Therapists in private practice enroll in the Medicare program as participating practitioners through their assigned MAC in much the same way that physicians enroll.

DMEPOS. Expenses incurred by a beneficiary for the rental or purchase of durable medical equipment (e.g., wheelchair, walker) are reimbursable under Medicare Part B if the equipment is used in the patient's home and is necessary and reasonable to treat an illness or an injury. Medicare defines *durable medical equipment* as that which can withstand repeated use, is primarily and customarily used to serve a medical purpose, and generally is not useful to a person in the absence of illness or injury. Reachers, bathtub grab bars, and most types of adaptive equipment are generally not covered at this time because they are not considered medically necessary.

Orthotic devices are defined in regulations as "leg, arm, back and neck braces" and require a prescription and certificate of medical necessity signed by a physician. Medicare covers all orthotic management services provided by occupational therapy practitioners, including assessment, fabrication, fitting, and training, in inpatient and outpatient settings.

All medical equipment companies, private practitioners, and providers that bill for equipment must apply to become Medicare suppliers. All items classified as durable medical equipment are paid under a separate durable medical equipment fee schedule which uses Level II Healthcare Common Procedure Coding System (HCPCS) codes (see "Procedure Codes" section later in this chapter). Orthotics also are covered items that are billed in the same manner as durable medical equipment to DME MACs by some outpatient suppliers and private practitioners. Other providers (e.g., SNFs, hospitals) bill orthotics to their local MAC. To protect the public interest, recent policy proposals have included additional certification requirements for DMEPOS suppliers. To date, occupational therapists have been exempted from most of these additional requirements.

Medigap Policies

The traditional Medicare plan (i.e., Parts A and B) does not pay 100% of the cost of most services but requires that the beneficiary be responsible for deductibles and coinsurance amounts. To cover the out-of-pocket cost differences, or "gaps," many Medicare beneficiaries purchase secondary insurance. The Medicare program must approve Medigap policies, which provide a standardized group of basic benefits identified by letters A through L. These policies are sold by several different organizations that may provide coverage for items and services not covered by Medicare. Bills must be submitted to Medicare before the secondary insurance policy will pay.

Medicare Advantage Plans (Part C)

Medicare Advantage Plans are health plan options that are approved by Medicare but run by private insurance companies. They are part of the Medicare program and are sometimes referred to as Part C. Different types of Medicare Advantage plans are available either locally or regionally. Medicare Advantage plans must cover all Medicare Part A and Part B services, but plans have differing guidelines for coverage. Plans may offer additional services not covered by traditional Medicare or other incentives. They may charge a supplemental premium in addition to the Medicare Part B premium, and all plans must offer an option that includes the Part D drug benefit. Regional plans must be preferred provider organizations and serve one of 26 regions established by CMS. All types of plans may not be available in all parts of the country (Medicare Payment Advisory Commission, 2007).

Federal Employees Health Benefit Program

The Federal Employees Health Benefits Program (FEHBP), which currently covers 8 million active and retired federal employees (including members of Congress) and their dependents, is the nation's largest employer-sponsored health insurance plan. The FEHBP, administered by the Office of Personnel Management under Part 890 of Title 5 and Chapter 16 of Title 48 of the *Code of Federal Regulations* (U.S. Government Printing Office, 2010), offers more than 350 health plans across the United States. The program has been touted by some as a national model for health care reform because of the range of options available in those plans to federal employees. However, although some plans are available nationwide, others are available only to employees who are in specific areas or working for specific government agencies (U.S. Office of Personnel Management, 2002).

Although federal law and regulations mandate a minimum range of benefits that must be offered, coverage of individual types of service such as occupational therapy, the settings in which they may be provided, out-of-pocket expenses, and limitations on coverage are determined by each of the private plans with which the government contracts to administer health care services. For example, many of the FEHBP plans have visit or treatment day limitations on occupational therapy services or all therapies (i.e., occupational therapy, physical therapy, and speech–language pathology) combined (American Federation of Government Employees, 2009).

U.S. Department of Defense Health Care Programs

The Military Health System (MHS), under the auspices of the U.S. Department of Defense, consists of the Office of the Assistant Secretary of Defense for Health Affairs; the medical departments of the Army, Navy, Marine Corps, Air Force, Coast Guard, and Joint Chiefs of Staff; the Combatant Command surgeons; and TRICARE providers (including private-sector health care providers, hospitals, and pharmacies). The MHS covers all military personnel and their families, whether on active duty or retired; however, eligibility varies for some specialized programs.

Veterans Programs

In 2007, more than 23 million veterans received health care coverage from the U.S. Department of Veteran Affairs (2009a). Veterans Affairs is required by law to provide health care benefits to all men and women who were on active military service in the Army, Navy, Air Force, Marines, or Coast Guard (or Merchant Marines during World War II) and discharged under other than dishonorable conditions. Coverage includes treatment, procedures, supplies, and services under a standard benefit package.

In addition to the usual inpatient and outpatient services, the Veterans Affairs health plan covers additional needs for some veterans, including readjustment counseling, home improvements and structural alterations, alcohol and drug dependence treatment, orthotics, prosthetics, and sensory aids. Eligibility and specific out-of-pocket liability for different benefits vary depending on the veteran's status and disability level. Additional information can be found on the Web sites for each Veterans Affairs medical center (U.S. Department of Veterans Affairs, 2009b).

Occupational therapy interventions play a valuable role not only in providing rehabilitation services to veterans with service-related physical, mental, and psychosocial disabilities but also in maximizing the quality of life of the growing number of aging veterans (Thalheimer, 1991). In a statement to the House Committee on Veterans Affairs for the hearing *Examine VA's Long-Term Care Programs* (2007), AOTA testified that "Occupational therapy practitioners can provide a unique and valuable service in supporting veterans in long-term care programs, in their occupations and activities of daily living, and in their efforts to remain independent and to successfully age in place" (p. 2).

TRICARE Program

TRICARE is a major component of the MHS, serving active-duty service members, National Guard and Reserve members, retirees, their families, survivors, and certain former spouses. As of 2006, about 9.5 million members were enrolled in TRICARE plans receiving service from military and nonmilitary providers (TRICARE, n.d.). TRICARE offers eight different plans through six regions in the United States and abroad. Eligibility for these plans depends on such factors as the status of the sponsor (i.e., person connected to the military), proximity to military health care facilities, and whether age 65 or older. In some plans, members must receive services at military facilities; others use private health care providers or provider networks.

Most health care services are fully paid under the TRICARE plans, but coverage may differ. Occupational therapy is generally covered "to improve, restore, or maintain function, or to minimize or prevent deterioration of function of a patient when prescribed and supervised by a physician" (TRICARE, 2009). However, regional contractors may exclude specific occupational therapy services.

PUBLIC HEALTH CARE PROGRAMS MANAGED BY STATE AGENCIES

Public programs that are funded, administered, or regulated at the state or local level (or both) pay for health care costs for many individuals younger than 65 years of age. State programs also pay for health care and social services excluded from Medicare for the over-65 population. This section describes the major types of publicly funded (federal or state) health care programs that are regulated or administered by state·agencies.

Program of All-Inclusive Care for the Elderly

The Program of All-Inclusive Care for the Elderly (PACE) is a managed care program serving participants who are ages 55 or older, are eligible for both Medicare and Medicaid, need a nursing facility level of care, and live in a PACE organization service area. Each PACE benefit package includes, but is not limited to, all Medicare and Medicaid services. Services that must be provided through PACE include primary care services, social services, restorative therapies (i.e., occupational therapy, physical therapy, speech–language pathology, rehabilitation therapy), personal care and supportive services, nutritional counseling, drugs, recreational therapy, and meals.

PACE organizations receive prospective, capitated monthly payments for each Medicare beneficiary. Because a capitated system program receives a set amount, the PACE provider assumes some financial risk, because the program must provide all Medicare covered services for the set amount. Under the Medicaid program, the monthly capitation rate is negotiated between the PACE provider and the state Medicaid agency and is specified in the contract between them. The capitation rate is fixed during the contract year regardless of changes in the participant's health status.

Medicaid

Medicaid, Title XIX of the Social Security Act (originally enacted in the Social Security Amendments of 1965), is a federal–state matching entitlement program that provides health and rehabilitation services to people with limited incomes and resources who also meet specific additional state requirements (42 USC § 1396). The federal government pays a share of the "medical assistance" expenditures under each state's Medicaid program. That share—known as the Federal Medical Assistance Percentage—is determined annually by a formula that compares the state's average per capita income level with the national income average.

States with higher per capita income levels are reimbursed a smaller share of their costs (Work World, 2009).

Within broad federal guidelines that require some services to be provided and certain individuals to be covered, each state establishes its own eligibility standards; determines the type, amount, duration, and scope of services; and sets the rate of payment for services. In fiscal year (FY) 2001, Medicaid provided assistance to more than 46 million persons. In FY 2003, direct payments to providers were $197.3 billion, and total outlays for the program (federal and state) were $278.3 billion. Medicaid-covered services fall into two categories: mandatory and optional. Mandatory services are ones that a state must provide to qualify for federal matching funds. They include

- Inpatient and outpatient hospital services
- Physician services
- Early and periodic screening, diagnosis, and treatment (EPSDT) for people younger than 21 years of age (which includes access to occupational therapy)
- Laboratory work and X-ray services
- Nursing facility services (ages 21 years or older), including occupational therapy
- Pregnancy-related services, nurse–midwife services, pediatric and family nurse–practitioner services, family planning services and supplies, and vaccines for children
- Rural health clinic services.

In addition, states may provide optional services for some or all of their Medicaid enrollees with CMS approval of their state plan. The following are some of the most common of these services:

- Rehabilitation, including occupational therapy services
- Diagnostic services
- Orthotics and prosthetics
- Drugs
- Home and community-based care for persons with chronic conditions
- Transportation services
- Optometrist services and eyeglasses
- Hospice care (Hoffman, Klees, & Curtis, 2008).

Occupational therapy provided as an outpatient discipline is considered an optional service for adults. In 2006, 56% of states and the District of Columbia provided outpatient occupational therapy as an optional service. Many of these plans limited the scope or amount of occupational therapy provided by limiting Medicaid group eligibility, number of units or visits per time period, and types of conditions (e.g., acute, posttrauma). The majority of states pay a fee-for-service rate for outpatient occupational therapy; that is, the state establishes a maximum payment amount for a particular service or uses the maximum applicable to the Medicare program for the service and pays the lesser of the provider's charge or this amount. Often the payment is capped by an estimate of cost. Some states cover outpatient occupational therapy services but do not support billing by other than institutional providers (e.g., hospitals), effectively eliminating private practitioners from Medicaid payment (Kaiser Family Foundation, 2006).

The state must submit a plan and receive approval from CMS to receive federalfunding (42 USC § 1396). In addition, states may expand their Medicaid programs by applying to the federal government for waivers under Section 1115 Research and Demonstration Projects, Section 1915(b) Managed Care/Freedom of Choice Waivers, 1915(c) Home and Community Based Services Waivers, and Combined 1915(b)/(c) Waivers Section 1915(b), all of which allow states flexibility in types of services provided and delivery methods (CMS, 2005). Section 1915(b) of the Social Security Act allows a state to implement managed care restrictions and is often limited to selected geographic regions within a state. A Section 1115 waiver is a more extensive research-and-demonstration option that is usually granted for 5 years but may be extended for up to 3 additional years under a 1997 Balanced Budget Act (P.L. 105-33) amendment. Under Section 1115, states are allowed to test major changes in how Medicaid services are delivered. Under most Section 1115 waivers, the existing benefit packages, including occupational therapy benefits that were available before the waiver was approved, continue to be available through a managed care plan contractor. However, the risk of having services limited is increased when authority for case management, coverage decisions, and utilization review is transferred from the state government to a managed care plan.

Medicaid Nursing Facility Care

One of the largest Medicaid health care expenses is for care for elderly or disabled persons in state-licensed inpatient facilities that provide medical, nursing, and rehabilitation services. Although the generic term *nursing home* is often used, nursing facilities provide both postacute care and services for longer-term residents. The Omnibus Budget Reconciliation Act of 1987 (OBRA 87; P.L. 100-203) merged Medicare and Medicaid standards and survey and certification processes for nursing facilities into a single system that reflects the higher standards of federal law at that time. Previously, states separately and inconsistently set certification standards for what were then designated intermediate care facilities. OBRA 87 was also important because it established additional quality of life and patients' rights standards.

Another improvement of OBRA 87 required nursing homes to use a uniform Resident Assessment Instrument for all residents. As discussed in the Medicare SNF section, the RAI and Minimum Data Set (MDS) elements provide necessary data on resident need for treatment, progress, and outcomes (Wiener, Freiman, & Brown, 2007). Many state Medicaid programs required use of the RAI and MDS even before its requirement under Medicare rules, and these data have been used to improve systems in some states.

Occupational therapists work with nursing home residents at many levels of care. If a person originally eligible for a skilled nursing level of care uses up his or her limited number of Medicare days or is otherwise found ineligible for SNF Part A coverage, he or she may be eligible for Medicare Part B skilled occupational therapy services in the nursing facility even when Medicaid may pay for nursing and other services. A person who no longer qualifies for the SNF level of care from Medicare or Medicaid may still be able to receive some occupational therapy services as a resident of the facility under either program. Each individual state regulates the methods determining eligibility, levels of care, and payment amounts.

State Children's Health Insurance Programs

The Balanced Budget Act of 1997 established the State Children's Health Insurance Program as Title XXI of the Social Security Act. The SCHIP provides federal funding for states to expand health care coverage to uninsured, low-income children and pregnant women who do not meet the Medicaid eligibility requirements (Medicare, Medicaid, and SCHIP Benefits Improvement and Protection Act of 1999, P.L. 106-113). On February 4, 2009, President Obama signed into law the Children's Health Insurance Program Reauthorization Act of 2009 (CHIPRA), which renews and expands coverage of the Children's Health Insurance Program (CHIP) from 7 million children to 11 million children (Families USA, 2009). Within federal guidelines, each state determines the design of its individual CHIP program, including eligibility parameters, benefit packages, payment levels for coverage, and administrative procedures (CMS, 2009a). Two major expansions of coverage in CHIPRA are mandatory dental coverage and mental health parity. In effect, states are required to provide mental health coverage to the same extent they provide other health coverage.

Individuals with Disabilities Education Act (IDEA)

The Education for All Handicapped Children Act of 1975, reenacted as the Individuals with Disabilities Education Act (IDEA) in 1990 and in 1997 with subsequent reauthorizations to date, provides federal funds to states to "assure that all children with disabilities have available to them . . . a free appropriate public education which emphasizes special education and related services designed to meet their individual needs." This statute has been amended over the years to include preschool-age children and additional services such as assistive technology and transition planning. Infants and toddlers with disabilities (ages 0–2) and their families receive early intervention services under IDEA Part C. Children and youths (ages 3–21) receive special education and related services under IDEA Part B. Under both parts, occupational therapy is considered a "related service" (CMS, 2003) and must be provided according to an individualized education plan (IEP) or an individualized family service plan (IFSP) by a qualified therapist.

In 1988, Congress approved the Medicare Catastrophic Coverage Act (P.L. 100-360) to allow school systems to bill Medicaid for certain related services, including occupational therapy, provided to children in schools. Therefore, services may also be provided by occupational therapists employed by or under contract to school districts for Medicaid beneficiaries whose IEP or IFSP includes the services. However, although some services are covered as a medical benefit and may be paid by the state Medicaid program, other services within the scope of IDEA are funded as educational services. Medicaid covers services included in an IEP under the following conditions:

- The services are medically necessary and included in a Medicaid-covered category (e.g., occupational therapy, speech–language pathology);
- All other federal and state Medicaid regulations are followed, including those for provider qualifications; comparability of services; and amount, duration, and scope of services; and
- The services are included in the state's plan as an optional service or available because of the EPSDT requirement (CMS, 2003).

Occupational therapy in the schools should be paid from Medicaid or education funding. Occupational therapists working within school districts should investigate how funding is provided in their states and the specific requirements for payment for services in schools.

WORKERS' COMPENSATION HEALTH CARE

Workers' compensation laws provide wage replacement benefits, medical treatment, vocational rehabilitation, and other benefits to federal, state, and private industry workers who sustain job-related injuries or acquire occupational diseases. The focus of this section is on the policies that apply to the medical benefits extended to workers.

Most workers' compensation programs are financed jointly by individual employers or groups of employers and state governments (Burton, 2007). Each state has a workers' compensation governing board or commission that develops policies regulating whether an employer is required to participate, what the financial responsibility of the employer is, what benefits are provided, which workers are covered, and how the insurance is administered. Workers' compensation insurance may be administered through private insurance plans under contract with the state or through individual employers or groups of employers that administer their own programs (a practice known as *self-insuring*). In addition, federal employees' workers' compensation laws are administered by the U.S. Department of Labor under one of the following programs: the Energy Employees Occupational Illness Compensation Program, the Federal Employees' Compensation Program, the Longshore and Harbor Workers' Compensation Program, and the Black Lung Benefits Program.

The National Council on Compensation Insurance (NCCI) manages the nation's largest database of workers' compensation insurance information. NCCI analyzes industry trends, prepares workers' compensation insurance rate recommendations, determines the cost of proposed legislation, and provides a variety of services and tools to maintain a healthy workers' compensation system. According to NCCI, about 9 out of 10 people in the nation's workforce are protected by workers' compensation insurance. Medical care costs in the workers' compensation system accounted for 59%, or $25.4 billion, of total workers' compensation claim costs in 2007, compared with 41% for lost income payments, or $19.8 billion (Mont, Burton, Reno, & Thompson, 2001). In 1987, the medical component represented only 46% of total costs. Since that time, medical claim costs have risen by more than 200% due to increased claim severity rather than frequency of use (Insurance Information Institute, 2009).

Many states have adopted various measures to control medical costs. Use of treatment guidelines that specify covered treatments and diagnostic tests for specific injuries such as low back and certain types of upper-extremity injuries are becoming more prevalent. Practice guidelines have been developed by individual state workers' compensation boards or commercial entities, such as the *Official Disability Guidelines Treatment* (Work Loss Data Institute, 2010), the *Medical Disability Advisor* (Reed Group, 2009), and the *Occupational Medicine Practice Guidelines* (American College of Occupational and Environmental Medicine, 2004) and are used at the discretion of each state. Moreover, states are showing increased interest in the role of rehabilitation therapies, including occupational therapy, in the recovery and return-to-work potential of workers' compensation recipients (Kaskutas & Snodgrass, 2009).

Additional cost containment strategies include use of provider networks and fee schedules that set maximum payment amounts to doctors for certain types of care. Fee schedules vary according to which services are included; what coding scheme is required; what formulas are used to calculate the actual dollar amounts; and which state entity develops and controls the use, as well as the updating, of fee schedules. A relative value system is used in many jurisdictions, but wide state-to-state variations exist in the amount of compensation for individual procedures. Along with providing interventions to promote return-to-work goals, occupational therapy practitioners can play a key role in assisting employers with adopting ergonomically efficient and safe workplaces to prevent accidents and illnesses (although this would be paid for by employers, not the state).

PRIVATE HEALTH INSURANCE GROUP AND INDIVIDUAL PLANS

Although about 170 million people in the United States currently have private health care insurance (U.S. Census Bureau, 2008) , there are wide ranges in types of services covered, amount of care, cost, restrictions, and exclusions.

Each insurance company markets a variety of products, including managed care options, often negotiating unique benefits for one specific employer. For example, there are 39 local Blue Cross Blue Shield plans in the United States, with multiple benefit packages that are sold to individuals, employers, or other groups (Vachon, 2007).

With the passage of the Patient Protection and Affordable Care Act of 2010 and the Health Care and Education Reconciliation Act of 2010 (P.L. 111-152), private insurance companies will be subject to federal restrictions (see section "Looking Toward the Future"). In addition, each state can determine the extent of control that it wants to impose on the insurance companies operating within its jurisdiction. Requirements for insurance companies are generally found in the state's insurance regulations. Employers that choose to self-insure health care benefits (fund their own "insurance" plan) are excluded from state requirements but must comply with the Employee Retirement Income Security Act of 1974 (ERISA). Requirements for self-insured plans also will be affected by PPACA.

Private insurance and ERISA self-insured plans use management strategies for lowering their risk and costs that are similar to those used by public programs. Employers have multiple options in choosing whether employees are required to use network providers to receive covered services (see Table 25.3). Plans also vary as to level of patient out-of-pocket expenses for copays and deductibles, definitions of occupational therapy scope of practice, amounts of therapy covered, payment methodologies, and exclusions based on diagnoses. In addition, many plans incorporate administrative techniques to better manage cost and quality of services.

PRACTITIONER MANAGEMENT AND FISCAL RESPONSIBILITY

Whether in private practice or as employees, occupational therapy practitioners should develop good fiscal management skills, as well as clinical expertise; they should have a basic understanding of federal regulations, health care coding systems, and reimbursement policies of their clients' public and private insurers. The following sections introduce some important regulations and policies that affect the ability of practitioners to receive payment, regardless of payer type.

Payment for Occupational Therapy Services: Practical Considerations

Individual third-party payers may structure their health care plans in many different ways and reimburse for services under a variety of payment methods. Often, when occupational therapy is provided in a facility or for a large organization that provides many types of health care services, these services are not paid for separately but are included as part of a bundled rate, such as a per diem or case amount. In hospitals, clinics, and other large facilities, the business office generally determines insurance coverage be-

Table 25.3. Examples of Health Care Plan Structures

Type of plan	General description
Fee-for-service Indemnity plan	Plan members may visit any health care provider. The health plan will either pay the medical provider directly or reimburse members after an insurance claim is filed for each covered medical expense. Consumers are usually responsible for out-of-pocket deductible and coinsurance charges.
Health maintenance organization (HMO) Exclusive provider organization (EPO)	These health plans provide care through a network of contracted physicians and hospitals in particular geographic or service areas. Members must use network providers for the HMO or EPO to pay for services. Out-of-pocket costs are reduced; usually there is a copayment amount for outpatient visits and no deductibles for inpatient stays. The plan may require referrals from a primary care physician. No payment is made to providers outside the network, except for an emergency. EPOs generally have a smaller provider network.
Individual practice association (IPA) HMO Physician–hospital organization (PHO)	IPAs are a type of health care provider organization composed of a group of independent practicing physicians who maintain their own offices and band together for the purpose of contracting their services to HMOs or employers. An IPA may contract with and provide services to both HMO and non-HMO plan participants. PHOs are alliances between physicians and hospitals that sell their services to managed care organizations or directly to employers.
Point-of-service (POS) option to HMO	Some HMOs contain an option that allows members to use out-of-network providers for an additional cost in copays and/or deductibles. Premiums for POS plans are generally higher than for straight HMO plans.
High-deductible health plan (HDHP)	Members pay a specified high deductible with an annual out-of-pocket amount (including deductibles and copayments) cap. HDHPs may provide 100% coverage for preventive care and have higher out-of-pocket copayments and coinsurance for services received from nonnetwork providers.
Health savings account (HSA)	An HSA allows individuals to pay for current health expenses and save for future qualified medical expenses on a pretax basis. HSAs are subject to several rules and limitations established by the U.S. Department of Treasury.

Sources. Medicare Options Compare (n.d.), U.S. Office of Personnel Management (2002), and U.S. Bureau of Labor Statistics (n.d.).

fore the occupational therapist treats the patient. Although the therapist should ascertain the payer's requirements to provide services in a way consistent with both the patient's and the payer's needs, the therapist's income generally does not depend on claim approval.

In contrast, private practitioners must develop a system to determine each payer's coverage requirements and payment amount. For example, if an occupational therapist is not in the payer's network, the patient may receive a lower level of reimbursement or be responsible for the total bill as an out-of-pocket expense. Third-party payers generally pay private practitioners according to a fee schedule the third-party payer has predetermined based on type of procedure performed. Types and rates of payment to providers are generally negotiated between providers seeking to become part of a network or plan with health plans. Rates may be based on the types of individual services (e.g., identified by *CPT* code), bundled (groups of) services (e.g., older driver program), or factors such as the number of persons in a geographic area.

Health Care Plan Policies and Options

Under most public health programs and private insurance plans, consumers and/or employers can choose specific plan options that affect access to and costs of care. Table 25.3 provides general definitions of how specific types of plans are structured and affect a person's coverage and access to care. Not all insurance companies, programs, or employers offer all of these options, nor are they all available in every area of the country. Payers may have hybrid systems with additional rules and restrictions. It is important to know the coverage definitions and payment limitations of client plans before treatment begins.

Whether private or public, health insurance programs and plans pay for services by practitioners or providers under specific agreements that are made between the payer and individual providers. That is, the health care program or plan maintains policies that specify the type, amount, and limitations on specific services. They also determine types and rates of payment for providers and practitioners based on relationship to the plan (e.g., whether the practitioner is in the network). CMS administers the Medicare program and develops coverage and payment rules in accordance with federal legislation (Social Security Act) and regulations. Medicaid and workers' compensation plans must adhere to federal and state laws and regulations in developing policies. Private payers, such as Blue Cross Blue Shield and Aetna, have greater latitude in writing plan policies and may offer multiple levels of coverage at different premium and payment rates (Aetna, n.d.). Health insurance companies are subject to limited rules set out by individual State Insurance Commissions, which may mandate coverage of certain services as part of regulations that control sale of health insurance products. For many private plans, payment rates often are negotiated on a provider-by-provider basis.

Occupational therapists should understand the provisions that may affect their decision to affiliate with a specific plan or network or provide service to a client with a specific insurance plan. Payers often incorporate features into their rules to manage the cost, use, and quality of the health care services group members receive; the following examples of such features may affect occupational therapy practice and decision making:

- Restrictive definitions of the scope of occupational therapy
- Specific credentialing requirements
- Precertification or preauthorization of services before treatment can begin
- Limitations (or "caps") on the number of visits, the sites at which services may be received, or the yearly costs incurred for occupational therapy services or for all service received
- Requirement that the occupational therapist be a member of a specific network of providers and accept certain rates
- Requirement of case management services for some conditions
- Reimbursement system that bundles the payment for occupational therapy into a group of services (e.g., a set amount for all inpatient services) rather than paying a fee for service
- Out-of-pocket copayments, deductibles, or other expenses that may affect access to occupational therapy services.

Submitting Claims

Practitioner and provider claims may be submitted electronically using claim implementation guides adopted as national standards under HIPAA or through paper claims when a provider qualifies for a waiver under the Administrative Simplification provisions. The National Uniform Claim Committee (NUCC) is responsible for the design and maintenance of the CMS-1500 Health Insurance Claim Form, the standard claim form used by freestanding outpatient providers (e.g., occupational therapist in private practice or physician's office) and suppliers to bill Medicare Part B Medicare Administrative Contractors and other health care payers for outpatient services. The UB-04 (CMS-1450) form is used by institutional providers (e.g., hospitals, SNFs) to bill for both inpatient and outpatient services. Submission of complete and accurate claim forms is essential to receiving correct payment, as electronic systems are programmed to identify specific information that is critical to coverage.

Diagnosis Codes

Diagnosis and procedure codes are key items on claim forms; they describe the patient's condition (diagnosis) and what treatment the therapist provided. Certain coding requirements are common to most claims submissions, regardless of payer. Under HIPAA, uniform coding systems were adopted for diagnoses and procedures. At this time, the *International Classification of Diseases, Ninth Revision, Clinical Modification* (ICD–9–CM; National Center for Health Statistics & CMS, 2000) is used in billing to describe the patient's condition or the medical reason for the patient's requiring services. (Beginning in 2013, the *International Classification of Diseases, 10th Revision, Clinical Modification* will be the standardized diagnosis coding system for the United States; this system has already been adopted in many other countries, including the United Kingdom, France, and Canada.) Under both the *ICD–9–CM* and *ICD–10–CM* coding system, diseases are categorized primarily by anatomical systems. However, *ICD–10–CM* will present a radical change for providers and billing companies, as it has almost four times the number of codes and a different coding scheme. Among other goals, *ICD–10–CM* is intended to incorporate greater specificity and clinical information into the claims processing system; include updated medical terminology and classification of diseases; and provide better data for such activities as conducting research, designing payment systems, measuring care furnished to patients, clinical decision making, and identifying fraud and abuse. An additional volume (*ICD–10–PCS*) contains surgical and medical procedures, which are mainly used to code inpatient hospital services. The *Diagnostic and Statistical Manual of Mental Disorders, 4th Edition, Text Revision* (American Psychiatric Association, 2000), currently under revision, groups mental health disorders into 16 major diagnostic classes and will be incorporated as part of *ICD–10–CM* when implemented.

Another diagnostic coding system of considerable interest to occupational therapy practitioners is the *International Classification of Functioning, Disability and Health* (ICF; World Health Organization, 2001). Although this system is not used in the United States for claim processing at present, its concepts are especially significant to occupational therapy practice and are echoed in the *Occupational Therapy Practice Framework: Domain and Process, 2nd Edition* (AOTA, 2008). The *ICF* is structured around the following broad components:

- Body functions and structures
- Activities (related to tasks and actions by an individual) and participation (involvement in a life situation)
- Additional information on severity and environmental factors.

Procedure Codes

Under the HIPAA transaction and code set standards, in addition to using a standardized diagnosis code set, occupational therapy practitioners (along with all other professionals billing health care claims) also must report standard clinical procedures using the Healthcare Common Procedure Coding System (HCPCS) *Level I Current Proce-*

dural Terminology–4th edition[1] (*CPT–4*) codes (American Medical Association [AMA], 2008a). The HCPCS system comprises Level I codes, used to define medical and rehabilitation treatment, and Level II codes, used by Medicare, Medicaid, and some other payers to describe DMEPOS.

Current Procedural Terminology

The *CPT* coding system, owned and maintained by the American Medical Association (AMA), was developed in 1966 and is updated annually. It is available in book form, which is a critical resource to all practitioners. Its purpose "is to provide a uniform language that will accurately describe medical, surgical, and diagnostic services and will thereby provide an effective means for reliable nationwide communication among physicians [and nonphysician practitioners], patients, and third parties" (AMA, 2008a). Proposals for new and revised codes are submitted each year by medical societies, individual practitioners, and others to the AMA's *CPT* Editorial Panel, a 17-member panel of physicians and nonphysician practitioners appointed to revise, update, or modify *CPT*. These members represent medical specialty societies, the Blue Cross Blue Shield Associations, America's Health Insurance Plans, the CMS, the American Hospital Association, managed care, and the *CPT* Health Care Professionals Advisory Committee (HCPAC; AMA, 2008b). AOTA has been a member of the HCPAC since its inception in 1993. The HCPAC represents nonphysician practitioners (through their national associations) and annually advises the *CPT* Editorial Panel on codes and issues affecting nonphysician practitioner services.

The *CPT* system includes five-digit codes grouped into six sections: Evaluation and Management, Anesthesiology, Surgery, Radiology, Pathology and Laboratory, and Medicine. Occupational therapy practitioners most often use codes in the Physical Medicine and Rehabilitation subsection of the Medicine section; however, under AMA guidelines, physicians and nonphysician practitioners may select any codes that most accurately identify the services performed and that are within their scope of practice. Therefore, other codes (e.g., relating to central nervous system assessments and swallowing evaluation and treatment) also are appropriate for occupational therapy reporting. The existence of a code in the *CPT* book does not imply coverage by any insurer; individual payers determine their own rules for coding and billing, which may limit the number and range of codes that a specialty may use to bill services.

Common procedure codes and modifiers used for correct coding and billing are commonly referred to as Category I *CPT*. The *CPT* book also includes other categories of procedure codes and appendixes. CMS tracks performance

[1] *CPT*™ is a trademark of the AMA. *CPT* five-digit codes, two-digit codes, modifiers, and descriptions only are copyrighted © (2008) by the AMA. All rights reserved.

measures (AMA, 2008a, Appendix H) as part of a quality effort involving use of Category II codes. Another section (Category III) contains temporary codes for emerging technology, services, and procedures.

Level II HCPCS Codes

CMS develops alphanumeric codes, referred to as Level II HCPCS, for billing durable medical equipment, drugs, prosthetics, orthotics, and supplies to the Medicare program. This system also is used to identify Medicare procedures for which no Level I *CPT* code exists. Medicaid programs often incorporate some of these codes into their payment systems, and some private insurers also may use them for billing purposes. Of most interest to occupational therapists are HCPCS Level II codes that describe orthotics and some prosthetics that may be billed as rehabilitation services (CMS, 2010a).

LOOKING TOWARD THE FUTURE

Health care policy and direction in the United States change over time depending on the priorities placed on this issue by the congress and the administration in Washington, DC. Sweeping changes to the health care system occurred shortly before publication of this chapter. On March 23, 2010, President Obama signed PPACA into law. Many of the provisions of this law, which are either now in place or scheduled to be implemented over the next few years, are intended to increase health care consumer choices, improve health care system quality, and create incentives for coverage of individuals by insurance companies (Kaiser Family Foundation, 2010). PPACA is a national, comprehensive reform law, containing multiple changes to coverage and payment policies affecting public and private health care programs nationwide. As individual provisions are phased in, occupational therapists should monitor these changes to determine how they may affect their clients and the provision of therapy services.

Synopses of some of the important health care provisions of this act are included in Table 25.4. However, the importance and effectiveness of these provisions in changing the direction of U.S. health care policy will only be seen as they are interpreted by regulation and implementing instructions, and some provisions may be modified by future legislation.

Expect future government and private payer policies to stress the continued importance of high-quality care, institute various ways to ensure effective and efficient patterns of care, and continue to better define health care outcome expectations. There will be inevitable conflicts among competing interests, such as the need for administrative simplicity and increased use of health information technology, demands for privacy and security, and the desire to curb fraud and abuse. Public and private insurers want assurance that they are paying only for necessary services that result in good outcomes. At the same time, payers and providers want less administrative burden on operations and more emphasis on client care. Clients are concerned with the privacy of their health care information, access to quality care, and the ability to make informed choices regarding coverage. With all of these pressing issues, occupational therapy practitioners can expect new laws, regulations, and policies aimed at maintaining a balance among these competing interests for the foreseeable future.

SUMMARY

Medicare is the single largest payer of health care services in the United States, and other payers often adopt its policies. Recent proposals for changes in payment policies for many types of Medicare benefits, including SNF and outpatient therapy services, are directly related to year-to-year increases in costs and utilization of therapy services. The implementation of health care reform provisions that expand health care coverage will require corresponding policies that further control expenditures for all health care services, including therapy.

An understanding of third-party payers' rules and coding terminology is essential to obtaining reimbursement. Although most occupational therapists do not personally bill insurance companies for interventions, they play an important role in ensuring that services are properly coded and documented to avoid unnecessary denials and misconceptions about the scope of occupational therapy practice.

HIPAA foreshadowed larger change in U.S. health care policy, encouraging greater standardization and data exchange by requiring uniform coding and the use of a national identification system for health care patients, providers, payers, and employers. With the passage of PPACA and more scrutiny by public and private payers, the coverage and financing of all health care services, including occupational therapy procedures will change significantly over the next decade. Occupational therapy practitioners should look for opportunities to influence how these new laws affecting coverage and payment policies are implemented to ensure clients' continued access to high-quality occupational therapy services.

Occupational therapy practitioners, whether working for medical facilities, in private practice, or in community programs, must challenge themselves to discover new ways for occupational therapy to fit into an increasingly technologically based, managed health care system. It is the occupational therapy practitioner's responsibility not only to deliver high-quality care but also to provide patients with options for therapy within the structure of their health care coverage. The differences among third-party health care plans and payment systems may lessen as national health care reform guidelines are implemented but advocacy with government officials, health care plans, employers, and patients will continue to be critical to assuring continued access to high-quality occupational therapy services.

Table 25.4. Patient Protection and Affordable Care Act: Highlights and Timetable

Issue	Requirements of law	Effective date (if applicable)
Access to health insurance	Individuals: • All citizens (with some exceptions) must have qualifying health coverage. Employers: • 50 or more employees: must offer coverage • With more than 200 employees must automatically enroll employees in health plans (with opt-out option for employee). Access is improved through establishment of state "exchanges" through which individuals can buy insurance.	2014 (with phased in penalties for individual noncompliance)
Employer incentives	Provide small employers with no more than 25 employees with tax credits to provide health insurance. Create a temporary reinsurance program for employers providing health insurance coverage to retirees over 55 years of age who are not eligible for Medicare.	2010 (phased in) 2010–2014
Insurance reforms and plan options	Prohibit preexisting-condition exclusions for children (effective 6 months following enactment). Create government- and nonprofit-run, state-based "exchanges" that provide information about and access to health care coverage options for individuals and small businesses. Prohibit coverage exclusions on the basis of preexisting condition or health status. Prohibit health care plans from discriminating against a plan provider who is providing services within his or her scope of practice (does not mean plans must contract with any willing provider). Authorize an appropriation to give small businesses access to comprehensive workplace wellness programs. Require plans to allow enrollees to select their primary care providers (PCPs) from a list of all available participating PCPs.	2010 2014 2014
Mandatory benefit package	Large employer plans must include rehabilitation and habilitation services and devices; mental health and substance use disorders; hospitalization, ambulance, and emergency services; maternity and newborn care; prescription drugs and preventative and wellness services; and pediatric services, including oral and vision care.	2014
Medicare	Create an independent Medicare advisory board to control per capita Medicare spending. Create a new Medicare and Medicaid innovation center to test innovative payment and service delivery models. Provide a $250 rebate to Medicare beneficiaries who reach the Part D coverage gap in 2010 and gradually eliminate the coverage gap by 2020. Reduce Medicare payments to specific provider types (various formulas and dates). Extends payments under the Physicians' Quality Reporting Initiative, which includes occupational therapists, through 2014. Eliminate cost-sharing for some Medicare-covered preventive services. Provide Medicare beneficiaries with a comprehensive health risk assessment and incentives to complete behavior modification programs.	 2010–2020 2010–2014 2011 2011
Medicaid	Expand eligibility and provide increased federal funding to states to cover additional costs through 2016. Create additional state coverage options for specific populations (e.g., childless adults, family planning services). Establish the Community First Choice Option to provide community-based attendant support services to some individuals with disabilities. Offer incentive payment to states that provide Medicaid coverage of some preventive services with no cost-sharing.	2010 2010 2011 2011

Sources. Kaiser Family Foundation (2010) and AOTA (n.d.).

❖ Learning Activities

1. Look up the names of the Medicare Administrative Contractors for your state, find a local coverage determination that applies to occupational therapy, and prepare a chart highlighting its major provisions.
2. Pick one provision of the Patient Protection and Affordable Care Act, and describe how it could affect occupational therapy clients and access to occupational therapy services.
3. Select 5 *CPT* codes that you think are highly applicable to reporting occupational therapy interventions. By creating 5 case examples, describe the types of patients for whom these services would likely be provided.
4. Select 3 case studies developed in Learning Activity 3, and determine possible diagnoses that could be reported for these patients using either the *ICD–9–CM* or *ICD–10–CM* coding systems.
5. Shadow a local occupational therapist in any setting (e.g., hospital outpatient, skilled nursing facility, private practice), and do a time study of the therapist's activities during that day. Record how much time is spent with patients and the types of patients, and time spent with other activities (e.g., documentation, meetings).

✓ Multiple-Choice Questions

1. Which of the following describes the Health Insurance Portability and Accountability Act of 1996 (HIPAA)?
   a. It contains requirements relating to national health care reform.
   b. It contains requirements relating to privacy and electronic health care transaction and code sets.
   c. It requires health care practitioners to report Medicare fraud.
   d. It is a Medicare-only law.
2. Occupational therapists should apply for a National Provider Identification (NPI) number under which of the following conditions?
   a. They plan to bill Medicare.
   b. They plan to bill any governmental health care payer.
   c. They plan to bill private insurance companies.
   d. All of the above.
3. What government agency is the single largest payer of health care services in the United States?
   a. Veterans Administration.
   b. Centers for Medicare and Medicaid Services.
   c. Food and Drug Administration.
   d. Office of Personnel Management.
4. Which of the following Medicare programs *does not* pay for occupational therapy services?
   a. Hospital Insurance Program (Part A).
   b. Supplementary Medical Insurance Program (Part B).
   c. Medicare Advantage Program (Managed Care) (Part C).
   d. Prescription Drug Program (Part D).
5. *Per diem payment* refers to
   a. An amount paid per diagnostic test given.
   b. An amount paid for a group of services provided in a single day.
   c. An amount paid per episode of illness.
   d. An amount paid for a group of services provided in a week.
6. In 2007, most personal health care spending (spending for clinical and professional services received by patients) was paid for by
   a. Private health insurance.
   b. Out-of-pocket expenses.
   c. Medicare.
   d. Medicaid and SCHIP.
7. The American Medical Association (AMA) has which committee that annually advises the *CPT* Editorial Panel on codes and issues affecting non-physician practitioner services?
   a. American Association of Non-Physicians (AANP).
   b. Non-Physician Health Care Advisory Committee (NPHCAC).
   c. Health Care Professionals Advisory Committee (HCPAC).
   d. Physicians for Non-Physician Health Care Committee (PFNPHCC).
8. Under the point of service (POS) option to HMOs, a member
   a. Pays the same co-pay amount for in-network and out-of-network providers.
   b. Pays nothing to see an out of network provider.
   c. Pays the entire cost of a visit with an out-of-network provider.
   d. May see an out-of-network provider but will pay an increased co-pay amount.

9. Most worker's compensation programs are jointly financed by
   a. Employers and state governments.
   b. Employers and the federal government.
   c. State governments and the federal government.
   d. Employers and private insurance companies.

10. Which of the following describes the Individuals with Disabilities Education Act (IDEA)?
    a. A free public program that emphasizes children being placed in the same classrooms and learning the same lessons, regardless of disability.
    b. Ensures that all children with disabilities have available to them a free appropriate public education that emphasizes special education and related services designed to meet their individual needs.
    c. Ensures that all children with disabilities have special education and related services provided to them with a minimal fee.
    d. Mandates that all children with disabilities attend school year-round until they are 22 years of age.

11. All of the following are mandatory Medicaid-covered services *except*
    a. Inpatient and outpatient hospital services.
    b. Pregnancy-related services.
    c. Orthotics and prosthetics.
    d. Laboratory work and X-ray services.

12. How does Medicare pay for Program of All-Inclusive Care for the Elderly (PACE)?
    a. Fee-for-service payments.
    b. Per-diem payments.
    c. Capitated monthly payments.
    d. PACE is not covered under Medicare.

13. Which of the following health care programs is publicly funded (either at the federal or state level)?
    a. Medicaid health care programs.
    b. State children's health insurance programs.
    c. Individuals with Disabilities Education Act.
    d. All of the above.

14. Who is covered under the TRICARE program?
    a. Active-duty service members, National Guard members, and reserve members.
    b. People who live in a tri-city area.
    c. Families with 3 or more children.
    d. Anyone 65 years of age or older.

15. Clients would purchase a Medigap Policy to
    a. Insure them from the time they retire to when they turn 65 years of age.
    b. Cover the out-of-pocket deductibles and co-insurance amounts required by the traditional Medicare plan.
    c. Cover dental and vision appointments.
    d. Insure them when they travel out of state.

16. Hospice care is a benefit of which part of Medicare?
    a. Medicare Part A.
    b. Medicare Part B.
    c. Medicare Part C.
    d. Medicare Part D.

17. Which of the following patients *would not* be covered by Medicare?
    a. DJ, a 75-year-old male with heart disease.
    b. Justin, a 20-year-old male with a spinal cord injury who is receiving Social Security benefits.
    c. Daniel, a 50 year-old-male with end-stage renal disease.
    d. Alexandra, a 30-year-old female who is pregnant.

18. The Mental Health Parity and Addiction Equity Act of 2008 requires that large self-funded group health plans and large employment-related health plans
    a. Include mental health benefits for an additional cost of no more than $100.
    b. Include mental health benefits for children who have experienced trauma.
    c. Provide mental health benefits that are no more restrictive in terms of dollar limitations and treatment limitations than benefits for medical and surgical coverage.
    d. Offer add-on packages that pay for mental health services.

19. Occupational therapists should understand federal, state, and private health insurance policy requirements to
    a. Be able to help patients choose health insurance plans.
    b. Be able to provide patients with options for therapy within the structure of their health care coverage.
    c. Be able to limit therapy, so the patient never pays out of pocket.
    d. Ensure they get paid for everything they do.

20. People who are underinsured
    a. Acquire their health insurance under their parents or spouses plans.
    b. Have insurance, but coverage does not adequately protect against high medical expenses or pay for all services.
    c. Do not pay much for their insurance plan.
    d. Have insurance that covers all medical expenses but does not cover dental or vision expenses.

References

Aetna. (n.d.). *Health reimbursement arrangements (HRAs).* Retrieved May 11, 2009, from http://www.aetna.com/about/aoti/aetna_perspective/health_reimb_arrangmnts.html

American College of Occupational and Environmental Medicine. (2004). *Occupational medicine practice guidelines* (2nd ed.). Beverly Farms, MA: OEM Press.

American Federation of Government Employees. (2009). *Federal Employees Health Benefits Program.* Retrieved May 12, 2009, from http://www.afge.org/index.cfm?page=2009ConferenceIssuePapers&Fuse=Content&ContentID

American Medical Association. (2008a). *Physicians' Current Procedural Terminology.* Chicago: Author.

American Medical Association. (2008b). *RVS update process.* Chicago: Author.

American Nurses Association. (2008). *Health system reform agenda.* Retrieved May 12, 2009, from http://www.nursingworld.org/MainMenuCategories/HealthcareandPolicyIssues/HealthSystemReform/Agenda/Principles/ANAsHealthSystemReformAgenda.aspx

American Occupational Therapy Association. (2007). *Examine VA's long-term care programs: Statement of the American Occupational Therapy Association submitted to the Subcommittee on Health, of the U.S. House of Representatives Committee on Veterans,* 110th Cong. (2007). Retrieved February 7, 2010, from http://www.aota.org/Practitioners/Advocacy/Federal/Testimony/2007/40385.aspx

American Occupational Therapy Association. (2008). Occupational therapy practice framework: Domain and process (2nd ed.). *American Journal of Occupational Therapy, 62,* 625–638.

American Occupational Therapy Association. (n.d.). *Health care reform: An OT perspective.* Retrieved August 10, 2010, from http://www.aota.org/Practitioners/Advocacy/Federal/Highlights/Reform.aspx

American Psychiatric Association. (2000). *Diagnostic and statistical manual of mental disorders* (4th ed., text rev.). Washington, DC: Author.

Balanced Budget Act of 1997, Pub. L. 105-33.

Balanced Budget Refinement Act of 1999, Pub. L. 106-113.

Burton, J. F., Jr. (2007, May/June). An introduction to workers' compensation. *Workers' Compensation Policy Review, 7*(3).

Centers for Medicare and Medicaid Services. (2003). *Medicaid school-based administrative claiming guide.* Baltimore: Author. Retrieved March 2, 2009, from http://www.cms.hhs.gov/MedicaidBudgetExpendSystem/Downloads/Schoolhealthsvcs.pdf

Centers for Medicare and Medicaid Services. (2005). *Medicaid State Waiver Program demonstration projects—General information.* Retrieved May 11, 2009, from http://www.cms.hhs.gov/MedicaidStWaivProgDemoPGI/01_Overview.asp

Centers for Medicare and Medicaid Services. (2009a). *The Children's Health Insurance Program (CHIP).* Retrieved May 11, 2009, from http://www.cms.hhs.gov/lowcosthealthinsfamchild

Centers for Medicare and Medicaid Services. (2009b). Medicare Program; Inpatient Rehabilitation Facility Prospective Payment System for Federal Fiscal Year 2010; Final Rule. 72 FR 39793, August 7, 2009.

Centers for Medicare and Medicaid Services. (2010a). *HPCPS codes.* Retrieved July 22, 2010, from http://www.icd9data.com/HCPS/default.htm

Centers for Medicare and Medicaid Services. (2010b). *The Mental Health Parity and Addiction Equity Act.* Retrieved February 7, 2010, from http://www.cms.hhs.gov/healthinsreformforconsume/04_thementalhealthparityact.asp

Centers for Medicare and Medicaid Services. (2010c). *Minimum Data Sets 2.0.* Retrieved August 11, 2010, from http://www.cms.gov/MinimumDataSets20

Centers for Medicare and Medicaid Services. (2010d). *Overview* [Administrative Simplification provisions]. Retrieved February 7, 2010, from http://www.cms.hhs.gov/hipaaGenInfo/

Centers for Medicare and Medicaid Services. (n.d.). *CMS Internet-only manuals.* Medicare Benefit Policy Manual Pub. 100-02, Chapter 2.

Children's Health Insurance Program Reauthorization Act of 2009, Pub. L. 111-3.

Community Mental Health Act of 1963, Pub. L. 88-164.

Education of for All Handicapped Children Act of 1975, Pub. L. 94-142.

Employee Retirement Income Security Act of 1974, Pub. L. 93-406, 88 Stat. 829.

Families USA. (2009). *CHIPRA 101: Overview of the CHIP reauthorization legislation.* Washington, DC: Author. Retrieved May 11, 2009, from http://www.familiesusa.org/assets/pdfs/chipra/chipra-101-overview.pdf

Fletcher, K. (2008, June 16). 23 new Medicare administrative contractors replace Medicare's current contracts. *California Medicare News.* Retrieved July 9, 2009, from http://www.cahealthadvocates.org/news/basics/2008/23new.html

Health Care and Education Reconciliation Act of 2010, Pub. L. 111-152.

Health Insurance Portability and Accountability Act of 1996, Pub. L. 104-191.

Hoffman, E., Klees, B., & Curtis, C. (2008). *Brief summaries of Medicare and Medicaid.* Retrieved February 6, 2010, from http://www.cms.hhs.gov/MedicareProgramRatesStats/downloads/MedicareMedicaidSummaries2008.pdf

Individuals with Disabilities Education Act Amendments of 1997, Pub. L. 105-17, 20 USC § 1400 *et seq.*

Individuals with Disabilities Education Act of 1990, Pub. L. 191-476, 20 USC Ch. 33.

Insurance Information Institute. (2009). *Issues updates.* Retrieved May 12, 2009, from http://www.iii.org/media/hottopics/insurance/workerscomp

Kaiser Family Foundation. (2006). *Medicaid benefits: Online database.* Retrieved January 5, 2009, from http://medicaidbenefits.kff.org

Kaiser Family Foundation. (2010). *Health reform implementation timeline.* Retrieved August 5, 2010, from http://www.kff.org/healthreform/8060.cfm

Kaskutas, V., & Snodgrass, J. (2009). *Occupational therapy practice guidelines for individuals with work-related injuries and illnesses.* Bethesda, MD: AOTA Press.

Liu, K., Taghavi, L., & Cornelius, E. (1992). Changes in Medicaid nursing home beds and residents: Medicare and Medicaid statistical supplement. *Health Care Financing Review Annual Supplement*, pp. 303–310.

Lumpkin, J. R. (2009, March). *Improving quality in a time of change*. Paper presented at the Physician Consortium for Performance Improvement, American Medical Association, Chicago.

Medicare Catastrophic Coverage Act of 1988, Pub. L. 100-360.

Medicare, Medicaid, and SCHIP Benefits Improvement and Protection Act of 1999, Pub. L. 106-113.

Medicare Options Compare. (n.d.). *How Medicare plans work.* Retrieved August 11, 2010, from http://www.medicare.gov/MPPF/Static/TabHelp.asp?language=English&version=default&activeTab=3&planType=MA

Medicare Payment Advisory Commission. (2007). *Medicare Advantage Program payment system*. Washington, DC: Author.

Medicare Prescription Drug, Improvement, and Modernization Act of 2003, Pub. L. 108-173, 117 Stat. 2066.

Mental Health Parity Act of 1996, Pub. L. 104-204.

Mental Health Parity and Addiction Equity Act of 2008, Pub. L. 110-343.

Mitka, M. (2008). Health insurance costs remain a burden for employers and working families. *JAMA, 300*, 1863–1868.

Mont, D., Burton, J., Reno, V., & Thompson, C. (2001). *Workers' compensation: Benefits, coverage, and costs: 1999 new estimates and 1996–1998 revisions*. Washington, DC: National Academy of Social Insurance.

National Center for Health Statistics, & Centers for Medicare and Medicaid Services. (2000). *International classification of diseases, ninth revision, clinical modification* (6th ed.). Washington DC: U.S. Department of Health and Human Services.

National Venture Capital Association. (2008). *NVCA health reform priorities*. Retrieved May 12, 2009, from http://www.nvca.org/index.php?option=com_docman&task=doc_download&gid=243&Itemid=93

Older Americans Act of 1965, Pub. L. 89-73, 79 Stat. 218, as amended.

Omnibus Budget Reconciliation Act of 1981, Pub. L. 97-35, 95 Stat. 357.

Omnibus Budget Reconciliation Act of 1987, Pub. L. 100-203, 42 USC § 4211.

Patient Protection and Affordable Care Act of 2010, Pub. L. 111-148.

Reed Group. (2009). *Medical disability advisor* (6th ed.). Westminster, CO: Reed Group.

Rosenstein, A., O'Daniel, M., White, S., & Taylor K. (2009). Medicare's value-based payment initiatives: Impact on and implications for improving physician documentation and coding. *American Journal of Medical Quality, 24*, 250–258.

Sakowski, J. A., Kahn, J. G., Kronick, R. G., Newman, J. M., & Luft, H. S. (2009, May 14). Peering into the black box: Billing and insurance activities in a medical group. *Health Affairs*, pp. 544–554.

Shortell, S. M., & Peck, W. A. (2006). Enhancing the potential of quality improvement organizations to improve quality of care. *Annals of Internal Medicine, 145*, 388–389.

Social Security Amendments of 1965, Title XVIII, Medicare, Pub. L. 89-97, 79 Stat. 286, as amended.

Thalheimer, L. B. (1991). Occupational therapy in the Department of Veterans Affairs: Focus on health care of the elderly veteran. *American Journal of Occupational Therapy, 45*, 613–620.

TRICARE. (2009). *Covered services: Occupational therapy.* Retrieved February 6, 2010, from http://www.tricare.mil/mybenefit/jsp/Medical/IsItCovered.do?kw=Occupational+Therapy&x=14&y=8

TRICARE. (n.d.). *TRICARE facts and figures.* Retrieved February 6, 2010, from http://www.tricare.mil/pressroom/press_facts.aspx

U.S. Bureau of Labor Statistics. (n.d.). *Definitions of health insurance terms.* Retrieved August 11, 2010, from http://www.bls.gov/ncs/ebs/sp/healthterms.pdf

U.S. Census Bureau. (2008). *Income, poverty, and health insurance coverage in the United States: 2007.* Retrieved August 9, 2010, from http://www.census.gov/prod/2008pubs/p60-235.pdf

U.S. Department of Veterans Affairs. (2009a). *Demographics: Veterans population 2007.* Retrieved February 6, 2010, from http://www1.va.gov/vetdata/page.cfm?pg=15

U.S. Department of Veterans Affairs. (2009b). *Federal benefits for veterans, dependents and survivors: Chapter 1 VA health care.* Retrieved February 6, 2010, from http://www1.va.gov/opa/Is1/1.asp

U.S. Government Printing Office. (2010). *Code of federal regulations*. Author.

U.S. Office of Personnel Management. (2002). *Federal Employees Health Benefits (FEHB) Program.* Retrieved May 22, 2009, from http://www.opm.gov/insure/health/

Vachon, J. (2007, July). *Blues update: Building the future.* Paper presented at the Labor Healthcare Forum, National Labor Office. Retrieved on August 8, 2010, from www.bcbs.com/coverage/nlo/serota-vachon.ppt

Wiener, J., Freiman, M., & Brown, D. (2007). *Nursing home quality 20 years after the Omnibus Budget Reconciliation Act of 1987*. Washington, DC: Henry J. Kaiser Family Foundation.

Work Loss Data Institute. (2010). *Official disability guidelines.* Encinitas, CA: Author

Work World. (2009). *Medicaid: Payment for services.* Retrieved May 12, 2009, from http://www.workworld.org/wwwebhelp/medicaid_payment_for_services.htm

World Health Organization. (2001). *International classification of functioning, disability and health (ICF)*. Geneva: Author.

APPENDIX 25.A. REIMBURSEMENT EVIDENCE TABLE

Topic	Subtopic	Evidence
Health care reform	Accessing health care	Mitka, M. (2008). Health insurance costs remain a burden for employers and working families. *JAMA, 300,* 1863–1868.
	Position statements	American Nurses Association. (2008). *Health system reform agenda.* Retrieved May 12, 2009, from http://www.nursingworld.org/MainMenuCategories/HealthcareandPolicyIssues/HealthSystemReform/Agenda/Principles/ANAsHealthSystemReformAgenda.aspx National Venture Capital Association. (2008). *NVCA health reform priorities.* Retrieved May 12, 2009, from http://www.nvca.org/index.php?option=com_docman&task=doc_download&gid=243&Itemid=93
Practice administration	Costs	Sakowski, J. A., Kahn, J. G., Kronick, R. G., Newman, J. M., & Luft, H. S. (2009, May 14). Peering into the black box: Billing and insurance activities in a medical group. *Health Affairs,* pp. 544–554.
Quality	Physicians	Lumpkin, J. R. (2009, March). *Improving quality in a time of change.* Paper presented at the Physician Consortium for Performance Improvement, American Medical Association, Chicago.
	Medicare	Rosenstein, A., O'Daniel, M., White, S., & Taylor K. (2009). Medicare's value-based payment initiatives: Impact on and implications for improving physician documentation and coding. *American Journal of Medical Quality, 24,* 250–258. Shortell, S. M., & Peck, W. A. (2006). Enhancing the potential of quality improvement organizations to improve quality of care. *Annals of Internal Medicine, 145,* 388–389.

APPENDIX 25.B. ONLINE REIMBURSEMENT RESOURCES

- **American Occupational Therapy Association:** http://www.aota.org
- **Blue Cross Blue Shield Association:** http://www.bluecares.com
- **Centers for Medicare and Medicaid Services:** http://cms.hhs.gov
- **Insurance Information Institute:** http://www.iii.org/media/hottopics/insurance/workerscomp

26

Evaluating Occupational Therapy Services

Pat Precin, MS, OTR/L, LP

❖ Terms and Concepts

Efficacy studies. Research studies that measure the effectiveness of a program or intervention with regard to specified treatment outcomes, cost-effectiveness, client satisfaction, and safety.

Outcomes. Health-related dimensions, including satisfaction with care, perceptions of health, and functional capacity that result from intervention (American Occupational Therapy Association, 2008).

Psychometric integrity. Degree to which assessment data are valuable in providing an understanding the par-

ticipants and program; components include sample size, demographics, reliability and validity of the assessment, and standard of error in measurement.

Randomized controlled trial. Research design with a high degree of experimental rigor that includes randomization of participants into treatment and control groups.

Research bias. Factor not part of the research design that influences and contaminates outcomes; biases need to be controlled for or eliminated.

❖ Learning Objectives

After completing this chapter, you should be able to do the following:

- Articulate the importance of occupational therapy services evaluation to your program and to the clients the program serves.
- List biases common to rehabilitation research.
- State 4 research questions addressed by efficacy studies.

- Describe the 8 steps in evaluating occupational services, and apply them to your program.
- Discuss elements necessary to include in a research publication, and apply them to your study of evidence-based practice and composition.

In an American Occupational Therapy Association (AOTA) member survey, respondents identified skills in outcomes management as one of the essential knowledge, skills, and attributes of a competent occupational therapy manager (Bondoc, Kroll, & Herz, 2008a, 2008b). *Program evaluation* defines and reviews outcomes of care to monitor systems that affect all services related to the client (Commission on Accreditation of Rehabilitation Facilities [CARF], 1999). According to the second edition of *Occupational Therapy Practice Framework: Domain and Process* (AOTA, 2008), the term *clients* has been expanded from its original reference to people to include organizations and populations within communities. Thus, occupational therapy practitioners should provide assessment, program

planning, intervention, and documentation of outcomes for organizations and community populations as well as for individual clients.

Evaluation of occupational therapy services supports occupational therapy intervention and helps market the skills of occupational therapy practitioners as administrators, clinicians, and consultants. Program evaluation examines the therapeutic process and forms the basis for program improvements such as the adjustment or establishment of intervention techniques, strategies, clinical decisions, intervention time frames, protocols, and discharge criteria (Prabst-Hunt, 2002). It can explain different treatment outcomes and provide program justification. It generates practice-based evidence through publication and program reproduction and can expand areas of practice into nontraditional health care markets (Ellenberg, 1996; Fazio, 2001; Scaffa, 2001). Funding agencies, both government and private, require periodic reports from grantees demonstrating use of their funds and resultant outcomes, which can become the basis for further financial support after start-up funds extinguish. Evaluation of occupational therapy services is integral in obtaining new and maintaining current third-party reimbursers.

TYPES OF EVALUATION

There are many methods for evaluating occupational therapy services. Regulatory agencies such as the Joint Commission and CARF International evaluate health organizations so that the organization can obtain or continue its ability to provide services and make improvements. The Joint Commission (2000) has required program evaluation, utilization review, and quality assurance since 1988. Government agencies may also regulate and evaluate standards of care and delivery of services. Internally, health care organizations participate in continuous quality improvement by identifying root problems and implementing solutions through team effort. Programs are often evaluated using a logic model (Letts et al., 1999; Millar, Simeone, & Carnevale, 2001; Stewart, Law, Russell, & Hanna, 2004) or cost–benefit analysis (Rogers, Sciarappa, MacDonald-Wilson, & Danley, 1995; Watson, 2000; Watson & Mathews, 2000). Even training of health care professionals is evaluated using standardized methods such as regional accreditation of learning institutions. This chapter focuses on the evaluation of occupational therapy services and programs through efficacy studies.

Efficacy studies are research investigations that examine the effectiveness, cost, safety, and duration of and client satisfaction with services and programs (Sussman, Valente, Rohrbach, Skara, & Pentz, 2006). The need to examine the efficacy of occupational therapy intervention has been present throughout the profession's lifespan. Emphasis on documenting efficacy was initially driven by health care's responsibility and contract to provide safe and effective services to society (Jette & Keysor, 2002). Later on, managed care companies began denying payment for interventions that lacked proof of efficacy, driving the need for evidence-based practice (Sung et al., 2003) to ensure accountability and cost containment. AOTA's (2007) *Centennial Vision* calls on occupational therapists to measure the efficacy of occupational therapy services in all areas of practice. The *American Journal of Occupational Therapy* encourages submission of scholarly efficacy studies (Gutman, 2008) in support of the *Centennial Vision*. In addition, scholars have encouraged rigorous efficacy research to support practice (Case-Smith & Powell, 2008; Holm, 2000; Kielhofner, Hammel, Finlayson, Helfrich, & Taylor, 2004). Costa (2009) published a call for research on fieldwork education in the recognition that fieldwork can be considered an intervention that requires investigation.

In the evaluation of occupational therapy services, the manager may benefit from applying Gutman's (2008) research questions pertaining to efficacy studies to the bigger picture of service outcomes: (1) "Is this clinical intervention effective—in other words, does it provide the health benefits it purports to for a majority of clients?" (2) "Is this clinical intervention safe—can therapists be certain that the provision of the clinical intervention will not cause harm?" (3) "Is this clinical intervention the most effective for the least amount of cost and time required?" and (4) "Is this clinical intervention acceptable to clients—is it tolerable to clients and congruent with client health care goals?" (p. 499). Efficacy studies also provide suggestions for further research with greater experimental rigor, as well as important information necessary to refine clinical practice.

STEPS TO EVALUATE AN OCCUPATIONAL THERAPY PROGRAM OR INTERVENTION

Evaluation of occupational therapy programs must be guided by investigators' client-centered clinical reasoning, which includes skills and knowledge, available evidence, theories, and frames of reference (AOTA, 2008). Investigators need to carefully consider what to investigate, reasons for investigating, client and program needs, and the cost, time, and staff involved before they begin the eight steps of evaluation, discussed in the sections that follow.

1. Describe Service Recipients

Step 1 is to identify service recipients through demographics, diagnoses, symptoms, role participation and restrictions, routine activities and limitations, body functional and structural capacities and impairments, goals, and other characteristics important to the study. This information is relevant to occupational therapy programs because it adds to the knowledge and understanding of its own client base as well as allowing or disallowing comparison among clients in other programs and in the literature.

2. Describe the Service or Intervention

In Step 2, investigators fully describe the particular service, intervention, or program to be studied. Even factors that will not be studied are included in the description so that readers are able to compare the results to those of other programs.

3. Identify the Outcomes

Occupational therapy outcomes are health-related dimensions, including satisfaction with care, perceptions of health, and functional capacity, that result from occupational therapy intervention (AOTA, 2008). They include but are not limited to occupational performance, adaptation, health and wellness, participation, prevention, quality of life, role competence, self-advocacy, and occupational justice, and they focus on health, participation, and engagement in occupation (AOTA, 2008). Outcomes are measured in research studies to help describe how occupational therapy intervention helps clients (AOTA, 2008).

4. Select Assessments

Assessments that are standardized, reliable, and valid should be used whenever possible. An assessment is *standardized* if it has specific guidelines for administration and data analysis so that participants being evaluated have consistent testing experiences and results can be compared. There are three types of standardized test: normative, criterion referenced, and procedurally standardized. *Normative assessments* are based on research using specific populations ("normal" or with a specific disability) and provide data investigators can compare with their own results. *Criterion-referenced assessments* test for mastery of a certain area. *Procedurally standardized assessments* are standardized only with respect to their procedures (interviews and observation-based evaluations).

Reliability (intrarater, interrater, and internal) indicates how well an assessment produces consistent scores over time and across raters. Reliability coefficients range from 0 to 1.0; for an assessment to be sufficiently reliable, a coefficient of greater than or equal to .70 is required. A rating of greater than .80 is considered high reliability. *Validity* (content, convergent, discriminant, and construct) is the degree to which an assessment measures what it states it measures. There is no single coefficient to assess validity. Crist (2005) provided in-depth information on reliability and validity.

Investigators should choose assessments on the basis of participants' disability status, culture, and situational variables related to the individual and context to avoid biasing assessment results. Assessments should be appropriate to the outcomes selected and sensitive enough to measure change in occupational performance (AOTA, 2008).

Table 26.1 provides a list and descriptions of selected standardized, reliable, and valid occupational therapy assessments, data collection tools, and other resources whose data can be examined relative to overall program evaluation (Prabst-Hunt, 2002). A more detailed review of these and additional assessment tools is available through the Education Testing Service Web site (http://ets.org/tests), the Mental Measurement Yearbook Web site (http://www.unl.edu/buros), and Asher's (2007) *Occupational Therapy Assessment Tools: An Annotated Index, 3rd Edition*. Clifton (2005) provided information on how to locate additional sources of disability-related data.

5. Choose an Experimental Design

To evaluate occupational therapy services or programs, an appropriate experimental design must be chosen. Although an occupational therapist may be using an evidence-based intervention, additional evaluation may be necessary, such as when multiple interventions are used. For example, recently housed, previously homeless clients may be receiving training in substance misuse, money management, and vocational rehabilitation for them to keep their apartments. Managing money and the stress of work are often triggers for drug relapse, which could result in homelessness. Evidence may exist that suggests that each of these interventions could individually aid in preventing homelessness, but the combination may or may not be effective. Intervention and programming for clients involve particular demographics and take place within context within a certain culture or milieu over time, all of which can affect best practices unless all these variables are perfectly matched. In certain clinical programs, "perfect matching" is not always possible. Thus, an appropriate research design that best meets the needs of clients and the program, has the most rigor, and best fits the research question should be chosen.

Examples of research questions in the context of evaluating a program could include

1. Is the program cost-effective compared to other programs that treat the same population?
2. Are the interventions effective?
3. What is the level of client satisfaction and staff job satisfaction?

To address the first question, a manager of a housing agency may calculate the daily cost per client in his or her own program and then compare it to the daily cost for a control group of participants not housed through the agency using a randomized-controlled trial design. To test the efficacy of the same housing program, the manager may compare the two groups on outcomes such as the number of days homeless, number of psychiatric hospitalizations, the severity of substance misuse, and number of days employed. To examine client satisfaction with the housing program, the manager could use a before-and-after, within-subjects design in which he or she performs a quality of life assessment on the first day of the program then after completion of a year in the program. Staff satisfaction could be ascertained through a cross-sectional study using descriptive statistics after administering a one-time satisfaction questionnaire that uses a Likert scale and produces numerical values. This section describes these and other types of research designs most commonly used in rehabilitation.

Several classification systems evaluate the rigor of research designs. AOTA's Evidence-Based Literature Review Project (Lieberman & Scheer, 2002) classified a randomized controlled trial (RCT) as Level I (most rigorous), cohort designs and case control studies as Level II, before–after designs with no control or randomization as Level III, and single-case designs and case studies as Level IV (least rigorous). To be able to state that one variable caused changes in another, the design must be randomized and controlled and include the manipulation of a variable (Portney & Watkins, 2000).

In an RCT, participants are recruited and randomly assigned to either an experimental (receives treatment) or a control (no treatment) group. Randomization helps ensure that comparisons between the two groups are meaningful by minimizing confounding variables. An RCT is often chosen to measure the effectiveness of an intervention or a program or to compare different types of intervention. A standardized, well-developed assessment tool and easily quantifiable

Table 26.1. Data Collection Tools and Resources

Tool or resource	Description	Source
Agency for Healthcare Research and Quality	Source of health care goals and databases related to outcomes	http://www.ahrq.gov
Canadian Occupational Performance Measure	Self-report measure of change in occupational performance over time	Law, Baptiste, Carswell, McColl, Polatajko, and Pollock (2005) http://www.caot.ca/copm
Cognitive Performance Test	Assessment of cognitive status in terms of memory, executive function, and level of consciousness	Burns, Mortimer, and Merchak (1994).
Dexter System and Treatment Outcome Program	Software tracking program that assesses the efficacy of intervention for the upper and lower extremities and the spine	Cederon Medical (1993)
The FIM™	Direct assessment of functional skills necessary to evaluate rehabilitation outcomes	Uniform Data Systems for Medical Rehabilitation (1993)
Functional Assessment Scale	Simple, uniform method of rating the level of self-care in institutionalized clients and can be used for within- or between-subjects research designs	Breines (1988)
Functional Status Questionnaire	Assessment of psychological, social, physical, and role function in ambulatory individuals	Jette, Davies, and Cleary (1986)
Level of Rehabilitation Scale	National database for rehabilitation outcome, comparisons, and program evaluations	Velozo, Magalhaes, Pan, and Leiter (1995)
Medicare Outcome and Assessment Information Set for Home Health Care (OASIS)	Measure of outcomes in home health care	Higgins (1997) http://www.cms.gov/oasis
National Institute on Disability and Rehabilitation Research	Disability databases via the National Rehabilitation Information Clearinghouse	http://www.2ed.gov/programs/nidrr/index.html
National Institutes of Health	Database of resources for health information	http://www.nih.gov
Nottingham Health Profile	General health status questionnaire	Hunt, McKenna, McEwan, Williams, and Papp (1981)
Occupational Therapy Functional Assessment Compilation Tool (OT FACT)	Reporting system that compiles occupational therapy intervention over time	Smith (1995) http://www.execpc.com/~dgtldesn/otfact.htm
ORCA	Software application for assessment of the hand and upper extremity, compatible with a digital assistant and designed to meet the needs of managed care	Innocente and Stickland (2000)
Patient Evaluation and Conference System	Reporting system for rehabilitation from admission to discharge	Harvey, Hollis, & Jellinek (1981)
SF–36	Measure of health-related quality of life	Ware (2000); Ware and Sherbourne (1992) http://www.sf-36.com
Uniform Data System for Medical Rehabilitation	Database that documents rehabilitative efficacy; includes performance measures for adults and pediatric clients in hospital, long-term care facility, behavioral health care, and ambulatory settings	http://www.udsmr.org
U.S. Department of Health and Human Services	Source of databases and statistics on outcomes	http://www.hhs.gov
WeeFIM System	Measure of functional performance in cognition, mobility, and activities of daily living in infants to 21 years of age; its database provides outcomes from outpatient, inpatient, and community settings	Uniform Data System for Medical Rehabilitation (1993) http://www.info@weefim.org

outcomes are necessary for this experimental design. Disadvantages of an RCT design are that it is expensive, that large sample sizes are required, and that it may be unethical to withhold treatment from the control group.

In a cohort design (also called a *prospective study*), a group of participants who have been exposed to a similar situation, such as a disease, diagnosis, or program, are observed over time beginning at the point at which participants were identified for the study. Because a cohort design is not randomized, it has more rigor if it includes a control group of participants who were not exposed to the identified situation but match the cohort group in other important variables such as demographics. Inability to perfectly match groups introduces confounding factors that may affect outcomes. To increase certainty that outcomes are due to treatment exposure, investigators may use statistical corrections to equalize groups. Cohort studies are usually less expensive and time consuming than RCTs.

A single-case design (*n* of 1 study, before–after trial with the same participant, or single-case series) involves one or a small number of participants evaluated on outcomes of interest over time, usually before (baseline) and after intervention. Each participant is compared to himself or herself, serving as his or her own control. Because there is no control group or randomization, it is difficult to state that the intervention was solely responsible for the change in outcomes (other potential influences include disease progression, environmental changes, and medication use). This design can be easily replicated with more participants and is often used as a pilot study to justify funding or further research. A before–after design measures the change in outcomes within a group of participants (or one participant, as in the single-case design) after an intervention as compared to before the intervention. This design is useful when intervention cannot be withheld because no control group is used, but lack of a control group introduces confounding factors.

A case control design (case comparison study or retrospective study) is used in studies of what makes a group of participants different. Participants are selected on the basis of a situation such as involvement in a certain type of intervention. The original group is compared to a control group without the situation but with similar characteristics to determine the difference between the groups. A case-control design is performed retrospectively and therefore can use data from large national databases. To decrease the large error introduced by this design, a large number of participants (i.e., hundreds to thousands) is required.

A cross-sectional design involves evaluating a group of participants once, not over time. It is used when little is known about an outcome to explore what factors may have influenced it. Examples include questionnaires, interviews, and surveys. It is difficult to conclude a cause-and-effect relationship from the results of these studies.

A case study design (descriptive study) generates descriptive data regarding the relationship between a particular intervention and an outcome. No control group is used.

This design is helpful for exploring an intervention or topic about which little is known. Results cannot be generalized; they describe only a certain situation but can be used to support further examination of the topic.

The experimental designs described in this section are for the most part quantitative in nature, meaning they provide numerical outcomes using standardized, valid, and reliable assessments or questionnaires (except for the case study design, which can be either qualitative or quantitative). Yet there are research designs that are qualitative in nature in that they produce outcomes in textual form through participant observation, interviews, and life histories. A research project may contain both qualitative and quantitative designs, in which case it is termed a *mixed-methods study*.

6. Analyze and Interpret Data

Psychometric integrity is the degree to which assessment data are valuable in providing an understanding of the participants and program; components of psychometric integrity include sample size, demographics, reliability and validity of the assessment, and the standard of error in measurement (Cohen, Hinojosa, & Kramer, 2005). Psychometric integrity can be affected by a number of different biases that may affect outcomes in either direction. It is important to eliminate as many biases as possible while designing the methodology. Biases that cannot be eliminated need to be identified as limitations to the study. Table 26.2 provides a list of common biases in rehabilitation research and likely direction of bias; occupational therapists must develop their analytic reasoning skills to be able to recognize these biases in the research they read and publish. (Using the correct statistical methods to analyze data is imperative yet beyond the scope of this chapter.)

7. Plan for Improvement

According to the Accreditation Council for Occupational Therapy Education's (2006) Standard B.7.8, it is the responsibility and role of occupational therapists to address changes in service delivery policies and to effect changes in the system. A plan for service improvement is similar to an intervention plan; it identifies areas of strength or occupation and problems or deficits on the basis of the program or client assessment and contains an action plan to address each problem constructed by the client with involved staff members. After the plan is implemented, its effectiveness is measured and results are disseminated to staff and members of the program, if appropriate. If identified outcomes were not achieved, a modified plan for service improvement is constructed, implemented, and measured.

8. Disseminate Evaluation Results

There are many ways to disseminate the results of an evaluation. One of the most professional and effective ways is to publish in a peer-reviewed journal. Although some journals have differences in styles, most occupational therapy journals follow the *Publication Manual of the American Psychological Association* (American Psychological Association, 2009).

Table 26.2. Biases Common in Rehabilitation Research

Type of bias	Description
Sample or selection biases	
Volunteer or referral bias	People who volunteer to participate in a study or who are referred to a study may be different than nonvolunteers or nonreferrals. This bias usually, but not always, favors the treatment group, as volunteers tend to be more motivated and concerned about their health.
Seasonal bias	If all participants are recruited, are evaluated, and receive treatment at one time, the results may be influenced by the timing of selection and intervention. For example, elders tend to be healthier in the summer than in the winter, so the results may be more positive if the study takes place only in the summer. This bias could work in either direction, depending on the time of year.
Attention bias	People who are evaluated as part of a study are usually aware of the purpose of the study and, as a result of the attention, give more favorable responses or perform better than people who are unaware of the study's intent. Some studies use an "attention control" group to assess whether this bias is present; the people in the control group receive the same amount of attention as the people in the treatment group, although they do not receive the same treatment.
Measurement and detection biases	
Number of outcome measures used	If only one outcome measure is used, there can be a bias in the way that the measure itself evaluated the outcome. For example, one activities of daily living measure considers dressing, eating, and toileting but does not include personal hygiene and grooming or meal preparation. This bias can influence the results in either direction; it can favor the control group if important elements of the outcome that would have responded to the treatment were missed. Bias can also be introduced if there are too many outcome measures for the sample size, an issue involving statistics that usually favors the control group, because the large number of statistical calculations reduces the ability to find a significant difference between the treatment and control groups.
Lack of "masked" or "independent" evaluation	If the evaluators are aware of which group a participant was allocated to or which treatment a person received, it is possible for the evaluator to influence the results by giving the person or group of people a more or less favorable evaluation. Usually the treatment group is favored. This bias should be considered when the evaluator is part of the research or treatment team.
Recall or memory bias	This bias can be a problem if outcomes are measured using self-report tools, surveys, or interviews that require the person to recall past events. Often people recall fond or positive memories better than negative ones, which may influence the answers of people being questioned about an issue or receiving treatment.
Intervention or performance biases	
Contamination	Contamination occurs when members of the control group inadvertently receive treatment; the difference in outcomes between the two groups may thus be reduced. This bias favors the control group.
Cointervention	If participants receive another form of treatment at the same time as the study treatment, cointervention can influence the results in either direction. For example, taking medication while receiving or not receiving treatment could favor the results for people in either group. The reader must consider whether the other or additional treatment could have a positive or negative influence on the results.
Timing of intervention	If treatment of children is provided over an extended period, maturation alone could be a factor in improvements seen. If treatment is very short in duration, there may be insufficient time for a noticeable effect on the outcomes of interest, favoring the control group.
Site of treatment	Where treatment takes place can influence the results—for example, providing a treatment program in a person's home may result in a higher level of satisfaction that favors the treatment group. The site of treatment should be consistent among all groups.
Different therapists	If different therapists are involved in providing the treatments under study to the different groups of clients, the results could be influenced in one direction—for example, one therapist could be more motivating or positive than another, hence the group that she worked with could demonstrate more favorable outcomes. Therapist involvement should be equal and consistent among all treatment groups.

Source. From *Evidence-based rehabilitation: A guide to practice* (pp. 335–346), by M. Law & J. MacDermid, 2008, Thorofare, NJ: Slack. Copyright © 2008, by Mary Law. Adapted with permission.

Table 26.3 provides a summary of what must be included in a research article. Other methods for dissemination include congress proceedings, conference presentations, seminars, and use of the Internet. Providing feedback to team or program members can provide positive reinforcement for services well rendered and motivate change in necessary areas.

SUMMARY

Evaluation of occupational therapy services is an integral part of the continuation and growth of programs and services provided to clients. Experimentally rigorous efficacy studies that examine the cost, effectiveness, safety, and duration of and client satisfaction with services and programs provide evidence-based research to guide and expand clinical intervention. The evaluation process is multistepped and includes selection of standardized, reliable, and valid assessments whenever possible to measure selected outcomes through well-constructed research designs. Knowledge of this process is necessary for interns, practitioners, and managers of occupational therapy.

Table 26.3. Sections of a Research Article

Section	Contents
Title	Major variables in the study and the population
Abstract	About 150 words Purpose, methods, results, and conclusions
Introduction	Nature and scope of problem presented Rationale, need, and importance of the study described Clear statement of the purpose of the study, including how it addresses the clinical need or professional direction
Research questions	Clearly articulated research questions
Definitions	Definitions of all independent and dependent variables Operationalization of appropriate definitions
Literature review	Exhaustive discussion of related studies Relevant and up-to-date citations Clear description of what the study will uniquely contribute to the literature
Methodology	Clear statement of research design Description of research design's appropriateness to the research question Adequate description of instruments Adequate description of participant selection Adequate description of setting Adequate description of procedures and methods Adequate description of data collection Validity and reliability of data collection addressed Strategies used to ensure validity (trustworthiness) Adequate description of data analysis Methodology written clearly enough to be replicated
Results	Agreement between data presented in text and in figures and tables Relevant statistical analysis (if quantitative design) Clear and accurate description of analysis Description of themes that emerged from the findings (if qualitative design) Objective and clear presentation of results
Discussion	Relationship of findings to the problem statement and to the research questions Relationship of findings to the work of others (described in the literature review) Discussion that expands on and interprets results Discussion of limitations of study Absence of claims or generalizations that the findings cannot support
Directions for future research	Suggestions for further research or the next step of this study
References	Pertinent and current citations Presented in American Psychological Association (2009) style Reference citations corresponding to all text citations
Figures and tables	Information that complements, not duplicates, text Clear labels and understandable content

Source. From "Full Manuscript Submission Report to Editor," by the American Occupational Therapy Association (2009). Adapted with permission.

Case Examples

LEVEL I FIELDWORK

Arthur, a Level I fieldwork student at an inpatient physical disabilities rehabilitation unit, was asked to complete an evaluation of his fieldwork site and experience before receiving his final evaluation from his supervisor. Arthur felt uncomfortable being completely honest in his responses because he feared his statements might influence his grades from the site. The site director assured him that his supervisor would not see his comments until she had completed evaluation of Arthur. After this reassurance, Arthur completed the survey in approximately 30 minutes with the hopes that his suggestions would be used to make improvements for incoming interns.

After completing this Level I fieldwork site, Arthur received a letter from the site director that included a summary of student feedback submitted over the past year and a plan of action that the site would use to improve certain issues that more than one student experienced as problematic. He saw from the descriptive data that he was not the only Level I student who wished to gain more experience with hands-on manual muscle testing. In fact, out of the 7 students that completed a Level I affiliation there, 56% of them wanted more experience. Arthur was happy to read that the site's corrective action plan included the production of a short video demonstration of manual muscle testing of the upper extremities for new students to watch prior to conducting this evaluation with a client.

From his participation in this study focused on improving the quality of student training through compilation and analysis of survey data, Arthur better understood how the program used his and other students' comments to generate positive change. Arthur wished to make positive changes in himself, so using a similar research design, he examined all four of his Level I evaluations for areas that more than one supervisor recommended changing and developed a plan of action to better prepare himself for Level II fieldwork.

LEVEL II FIELDWORK

Terri, an occupational therapy intern, wanted to select a Level II occupational therapy fieldwork project that would help her clients with dual diagnoses (mental illness and substance misuse) more fully participate in therapeutic groups because she noticed that some were more easily engaged than others. She also wished to choose a study that could be published in order to help others in outpatient dual diagnosis clinics. Her supervisor had several research projects in mind, but she had not had time to implement them herself. She described each one to Terri, who chose to study cognitive impairments in clients with dual diagnoses (chronic psychotic disorders and substance abuse) and considerations for treatment (Harrison & Precin, 1996).

According to the eight steps of evaluation mentioned in this chapter, Terri and her supervisor's investigation proceeded as follows. In Step 1, describing the population, Terri collected demographic data (e.g., age, gender, ethnicity, education, psychiatric diagnoses, substance use) for 27 clients from her outpatient dual diagnosis clinic. This information helped Terri better understand her client population with relationship to cognitive functioning because cognitive impairments had already been noted in individuals singly diagnosed with alcoholism and schizophrenia. Demographic information would also inform staff of other dual diagnosis clinics whether or not this study's population resembled their own for comparison.

In Step 2, describing the service, Terri described this 18-month dual diagnosis outpatient clinic as providing case management, living skills training, medical services, prevocational training, substance misuse intervention, and psychiatric services by a multidisciplinary staff to approximately 50 individuals.

In Step 3, identifying outcomes, Terri determined that outcomes for this study would be scores on the following components of cognition: orientation, attention, comprehension, repetition, naming, construction, memory, calculation, similarities, and judgment.

In Step 4, selecting assessments, outcomes were measured via the Neurobehavioral Cognitive Status Examination (NCSE; Kiernan, Mueller, Langston, & Van Dyke, 1987).

In Step 5, choosing an experimental design, Terri made a statistical comparison of mean, standard deviation, and z scores for each subtest of the NCSE between a normative group and a group of psychiatric clients from another study to test the level of significant difference between each group at the $p < .01$ level.

In Step 6, analyzing and interpreting data, two-thirds of the dual diagnosis sample had cognitive impairments, with 37% having impairments in 3 or more of the 10 subtests. There was great variation among dual diagnosis subjects, but most deficits appeared in the areas of memory and judgment. Dual diagnosis clients had greater cognitive deficits than the normative and psychiatric groups.

In Step 7, plan for improvement, Terri and her supervisor realized cognitive screening of every client in this dual diagnosis program was necessary because so much variation in cognitive functioning between dual diagnosis clients was found; no one cognitive profile could be identified for this population. After obtaining the results of each client in the program, clients would be regrouped into therapeutic groups according to the type of cognitive impairment. For example, those with comprehension difficulty would be grouped together and the group leader would use methods to enhance comprehension while discussing the topic of the group.

In Step 8, disseminating results, Terri was able to finish her study within the 3 months of her Level II fieldwork. She presented the results to the dual diagnosis staff during an in-service. Case managers gave participants feedback on their results. The study was published in *Occupational Therapy International* (Harrison & Precin, 1996).

FIRST-TIME MANAGER

As a new manager, Rich, who directed a welfare-to-work program that helped disabled welfare recipients find and keep gainful employment, wanted to make sure that his occupational therapy program was working effectively. He decided to use the eight steps in program evaluation to construct a plan to evaluate the program. As a result, he was able to prioritize the outcomes that were most important to him and the organization.

Rich's 8 steps of program evaluation were as follows. For Step 1, describe the subjects, Rich had kept demographic data on all of his clients, so he already knew that most of them had multiple physical disabilities, predominantly back injuries; diabetes; and heart conditions. Most did not have a high school diploma or a general educational development (GED) certificate. Rich's program did a thorough assessment of incoming individuals daily. From this data, Rich already knew that most of his clients spoke English as a second language, had sporadic work histories or had never been employed, had no résumé, and were reluctant to work for fear they would lose their benefits and have no income.

In Step 2, describe the service or intervention, Rich described the program as providing assessment (physical, psychological, vocational, contextual); life skills training; case management; work hardening; Social Security income support; English-as-a-second-language, adult basic education, and GED classes; job search assistance; and job retention services to over 2,000 individuals per year to help them secure and keep gainful employment.

For Step 3, identifying outcomes, Rich already knew that out of all the clients that got jobs, only 10% of them remained employed after 180 days. He wanted to find out why. Not only was retention important to clients, but Rich's program received its funding on the basis of client performance, and one of the performance measures was job retention. Rich limited his investigation to the operation of the retention department.

In Step 4, selecting assessments, Rich created questionnaires that included open-ended questions and checklists directed at discovering why a client was no longer working at a particular site. He made one for clients and one for supervisors to get a broad perspective. He constructed his own assessments instead of using a valid and reliable one from the literature because he could not find one that was sensitive enough to his clients' issues.

In Step 5, choosing an experimental design, Rich chose a mixed-methods (qualitative and quantitative) survey study for his investigation.

In Step 6, analyze and interpret data, Rich's study used descriptive statistics to identify reasons for job termination. For the qualitative aspect of the study, clients' and supervisors' answers to open-ended questions were analyzed for themes and the frequencies of these themes were reported in percentages. Results indicated that most of the jobs were lost during the first week of employment because of clients' lack of communication. They often felt that they were given more work than they could accomplish or that they did not understand exactly what to do or how to do it, but they did not ask for help. Supervisors were usually confused as to why clients did not return to work.

In Step 7, plan for improvement, Rich used these results to assign a job coach to each newly placed client for the first week of employment. In no case was the presence of the job coach counter indicated or disallowed by the job site. The job coach's mission was to help the client verbalize problems, attempt to solve them himself or herself, and, if not solvable, to bring the issue to his or her supervisor. This intervention may have been responsible for a 50% increase in job retention.

MANAGER

As the director of an occupational therapy program that provided physical rehabilitation to 150 individuals with Parkinson's disease, Sarah was notified that she must cut 10% of her next year's budget to comply with the program's overall budget reduction plan.

Sarah examined her budget. She realized she could not cut any supplies or equipment without jeopardizing client care. In fact, the only budget item that seemed logical was to lay off one staff member. However, from supervising her staff, she knew that everyone was spending at least 80% of their time in direct client care. Sarah held a meeting with her staff and told them of the 10% cutback. She also told them not to worry because she wanted to avoid any layoffs, but she said needed their help to come up with a way to save money.

Sarah guided her staff in finding a solution by asking each member to describe what a typical day entailed. It turned out that all of the occupational therapists were

(continued)

Case Examples *(cont.)*

spending 10–15 minutes of each treatment session discussing psychosocial issues such as depression from loss of functioning, fear of falling, and sleep hygiene. These issues were just as important as physical rehabilitation, but unlike the physical rehabilitation that the occupational therapists were providing, they could be addressed in a group setting. Sarah asked a member of the occupational therapy staff to volunteer to run a once-per-week psychosocial group directed at psychosocial issues relevant to people with Parkinson's disease. She encouraged her occupational therapists to make referrals to this group when clients began to discuss psychosocial issues during or after their physical rehabilitation sessions. This new plan allowed each occupational therapist to treat more clients per day, generating more revenue for the program. Therefore, instead of cutting 10% from her budget, Sarah kept her budget intact by generating more income.

❖ Learning Activities

1. Using Table 26.3, "Sections of a Research Article," critique a research article that evaluates an occupational therapy program or service.
2. Using Table 26.2, "Biases Common in Rehabilitation Research," examine the same research article for biases and list all you can identify.
3. Request an institutional review board form from your institution, and review the difference between exempt, expedited, and full reviews.
4. Online certification in the protection of human subjects ensures that a professional understands ethical guidelines in practice, the history of ethics of research, informed consent, and the proper review process of a research proposal. There are many such certification programs; the Collaborative Institutional Training Initiative is one and can be found at http://www.citiprogram.org.
5. Investigate one of the assessment tools in Table 26.1, "Data Collection Tools and Resources," and answer the following questions.
   a. What are the reliability coefficients?
   b. Is the assessment valid?
   c. Does it have a norm reference or criterion reference?
   d. Is it standardized?
   e. What populations has it been used for, and what are the sample sizes for each population?

✓ Multiple–Choice Questions

1. Evaluation of occupational therapy services is important in which of the following efforts?
   a. Marketing occupational therapy skills.
   b. Identifying program improvements.
   c. Securing grants.
   d. All of the above.
2. The most rigorous research design is which of the following?
   a. Cohort design.
   b. Case control study.
   c. Randomized controlled trial.
   d. Single-case design.
3. To claim causality, a research study must have which of the following characteristics?
   a. Randomization.
   b. Control group.
   c. Manipulation of a variable.
   d. All of the above.
4. Psychometric integrity cannot be evaluated without knowledge of which of the following factors?
   a. Sample size.
   b. Demographics.
   c. Validity and reliability.
   d. All of the above.
5. According to the standards of the Accreditation Council for Occupational Therapy Education (2006), which of the following persons or entities is responsible for addressing changes in service delivery policies and effecting changes in the system?
   a. Program director.
   b. Grantor.

c. Managed care delivery service.

d. Occupational therapist.

6. Recruiting participants for a research study by asking for volunteers is an example of a _____ bias and tends to favor _____.

a. Measurement/the treatment group.

b. Selection/the treatment group.

c. Measurement/the control group.

d. Selection/the control group.

7. Using interviews, self-report tools, or surveys that require participants to recall past events is an example of which kind of bias?

a. Measurement.

b. Intervention.

c. Attention.

d. Timing.

8. If a participant in a control group inadvertently receives treatment, a _____ bias has been introduced in favor of the _____.

a. Cointervention/treatment group.

b. Contamination/treatment group.

c. Cointervention/control group.

d. Contamination/control group.

9. If a participant receives another form of treatment at the same time as the research investigation, a _____ bias has been introduced in favor of _____.

a. Cointervention/the treatment group.

b. Cointervention/the control group.

c. Cointervention/either group.

d. Contamination/treatment group.

10. An occupational therapist wants to measure the efficacy of her stress management group for psychiatric clients at her long-term outpatient clinic. Her ongoing stress management group runs for 10 sessions and then repeats with different clients, as most of her clients could benefit from stress management training. The best research design for her would be which of the following?

a. Randomized controlled trial.

b. Cohort design.

c. Before–after design.

d. Cross-sectional design.

11. An occupational therapist in an outpatient diabetes management clinic wants to perform a research investigation in which he studies client characteristics over the next 6 months and compares them to a group of age-matched participants without diabetes. The best research design for him would be which of the following?

a. Case-control design.

b. Cohort design.

c. Single-case design.

d. Before–after design.

12. An occupational therapist is interested in correlating the number of foster care placements foster care children have had with their grade point average. She does not have access to a population of foster children, but she does have access to a national database that stores confidential information about thousands of foster children. She plans to examine the database once to gather data for her research. The best research design for her to use is which of the following?

a. Case study design.

b. Randomized controlled trial.

c. Cross-sectional design.

d. Case control design.

13. Efficacy research studies may examine which of the following?

a. Effectiveness.

b. Cost.

c. Patient satisfaction.

d. All of the above.

14. Which is *not* a type of validity?

a. Contaminant.

b. Content.

c. Convergent.

d. Construct.

15. To claim reliability, an assessment tool must have a coefficient of at least

a. .10.

b. .90.

c. .70.

d. .005.

16. The research design must be clearly stated in which section of a research article?

a. Introduction.

b. Literature review.

c. Methodology.

d. Results.

17. The discussion section of a research article does not include

a. Limitations of the study.

b. Generalizations not supported by the research design.

c. A relationship of findings to the work of others.

d. A relationship of findings to the problem statement and research question.

18. The publication manual most frequently used by professional occupational therapy journals is published by the

a. Accreditation Council for Occupational Therapy Education.

b. National Board for Certification in Occupational Therapy.

c. American Psychological Association.

d. American Occupational Therapy Association.

19. A client is being examined by an occupational therapist to determine if he has memory loss and, if so, how extensive it is. The best type of assessment for this purpose would have which of the following characteristics?
    a. Norm-referenced standardized test scores.
    b. Criterion-referenced standardized test scores.
    c. A reliability coefficient of .70 or less.
    d. None of the above.

20. Health-related dimensions, including satisfaction with care, perceptions of health, and functional capacity, that result from occupational therapy intervention are what is meant by which of the following terms?
    a. Criterion referenced.
    b. Outcomes.
    c. Assessments.
    d. Biases.

References

Accreditation Council for Occupational Therapy Education. (2006). *Accreditation Council for Occupational Therapy Education (ACOTE) educational standards and interpretive guidelines.* Bethesda, MD: Author.

American Occupational Therapy Association. (2007). AOTA's *Centennial Vision* and executive summary. *American Journal of Occupational Therapy, 61,* 613–614.

American Occupational Therapy Association. (2008). Occupational therapy practice framework: Domain and process (2nd ed.). *American Journal of Occupational Therapy, 62,* 625–683.

American Occupational Therapy Association. (2009). *Full manuscript submission report to editor.* Retrieved July 14, 2010, from http://www.aota.org/DocumentVault/AJOT/full-report.aspx

American Psychological Association. (2009). *Publication manual of the American Psychological Association* (6th ed.). Washington, DC: Author.

Asher, I. E. (2007). *Occupational therapy assessment tools: An annotated index* (3rd ed.). Bethesda, MD: AOTA Press.

Bondoc, S., Kroll, C., & Herz, N. (2008a). Managerial competencies for the occupational therapy practitioner: Part I. *Administration and Management Special Interest Section Quarterly, 24*(3), 1–4.

Bondoc, S., Kroll, C., & Herz, N. (2008b). Managerial competencies for the occupational therapy practitioner: Part II. *Administration and Management Special Interest Section Quarterly, 24*(4), 1–4.

Breines, E. (1988). The Functional Assessment Scale as an instrument for measuring changes in levels of function for nursing home residents following occupational therapy. *Canadian Journal of Occupational Therapy, 55,* 135–140.

Burns, T., Mortimer, J. A., & Merchak, P. (1994). Cognitive Performance Test: A new approach to functional assessment in Alzheimer's disease. *Journal of Geriatric Psychiatry and Neurology, 7,* 46–54.

Case-Smith, J., & Powell, C. A. (2008). Research literature in occupation therapy, 2001–2005. *American Journal of Occupational Therapy, 62,* 480–486.

Cederon Medical. (1993). *Dexter evaluation and therapy systems. User's manual.* Davis, CA: Author.

Clifton, D. W., Jr. (2005). How to locate sources of disability-related data. In D. W. Clifton, Jr. (Ed.), *Physical rehabilitation's role in disability management: Unique perspectives for success* (pp. 229–238). St. Louis, MO: Elsevier/Saunders.

Cohen, M. E., Hinojosa, J., & Kramer, P. (2005). Administration of evaluation and assessments. In J. Hinojosa, P. Kramer, & P. Crist (Eds.), *Evaluation: Obtaining and interpreting data* (pp. 81–99). Bethesda, MD: AOTA Press.

Commission on Accreditation of Rehabilitation Facilities. (1999). *Standards manual for organizations serving people with disabilities.* Tucson, AZ: Author.

Costa, D. M. (2009, March 23). Call for research on fieldwork education. *OT Practice,* p. 21.

Crist, P. (2005). Reliability and validity: The psychometrics of standardized assessments. In J. Hinojosa, P. Kramer, & P. Crist (Eds.), *Evaluation: Obtaining and interpreting data* (pp. 175–194). Bethesda, MD: AOTA Press.

Ellenberg, D. B. (1996). Outcomes research: The history, debate, and implications for the field of occupational therapy. *American Journal of Occupational Therapy, 50,* 435–441.

Fazio, L. S. (2001). *Developing occupation-centered programs for the community: A workbook for students and professionals.* Upper Saddle River, NJ: Prentice Hall.

Gutman, S. A. (2008). Research priorities of the profession. *American Journal of Occupational Therapy, 62,* 499–501.

Harrison, T. S., & Precin, P. (1996). Cognitive impairments in clients with dual diagnosis (chronic psychotic disorders and substance abuse): Considerations for treatment. *Occupational Therapy International, 3*(2), 122–141.

Harvey, R. F., Hollis, M., & Jellinek, M. (1981). Functional Performance assessment: A program approach. *Archives of Physical Medicine and Rehabilitation, 62,* 456–461.

Higgins, C. A. (1997). Outcomes measurement in home health. *American Journal of Occupational Therapy, 51,* 458–459.

Hinojosa, J., Kramer, P., & Crist, P. (Eds.). (2005). *Evaluation: Obtaining and interpreting data.* Bethesda, MD: AOTA Press.

Holm, M. B. (2000). Our mandate for the new millennium: Evidence-based practice [Eleanor Clarke Slagle Lecture]. *American Journal of Occupational Therapy, 54,* 575–585.

Hunt, S. M., McKenna, S. P., McEwan, J., Williams, J., & Papp, E. (1981). The Nottingham Health Profile: Subjective health status and medical consultations. *Social Science Medicine, 15*(A), 221–229.

Innocente, V., & Stickland, D. (2000). *The design, implementation, and deployment of functional prototype 00 reconstruction software for CMS: The ORCA project. Proceedings of CHEP 2000, Padova, Italy.* Retrieved on June 28, 2010, from http://cmsdoc.cern.ch/ORCA

Jette, A. M., Davies, A., & Cleary, P. (1986). The Functional Status Questionnaire (FSQ): Reliability and validity when used in primary care. *Journal of General Internal Medicine, 1,* 143–149.

Jette, A. M., & Keysor, J. H. (2002). Uses of evidence in disability outcomes and effectiveness research. *Milbank Quarterly, 80,* 325–345.

Joint Commission on Accreditation of Healthcare Organizations. (2000). *The quality assurance guide.* Chicago: Author.

Kielhofner, G., Hammel, J., Finlayson, M., Helfrich, C., & Taylor, R. (2004). Documenting outcomes of occupational therapy: The Center for Outcomes Research and Education. *American Journal of Occupation Therapy, 58,* 15–23.

Kiernan, R., Mueller, J., Langston, J., & Van Dyke, C. (1987). The neurobehavioral cognitive status examination: A brief but differentiated approach to cognitive assessment. *Annals of Internal Medicine, 107,* 481–485.

Law, M., Baptiste, S., Carswell, A., McColl, M. A., Polatajko, H., & Pollock, N. (2005). *The Canadian Occupational Performance Measure* (4th ed.). Ottowa, ON: Canadian Association of Occupational Therapists.

Law, M., & MacDermid, J. (2008). *Evidence-based rehabilitation: A guide to practice.* Thorofare, NJ: Slack.

Letts, L., Law, M., Pollock, N., Stewart, D., Westmorland, M., Philpot, A., et al. (1999). *A programme evaluation workbook for occupational therapists: An evidence-based practice tool.* Ottawa, Ontario: Canadian Association of Occupational Therapists.

Lieberman, D., & Scheer, J. (2002). AOTA's Evidence-Based Literature Review Project: An overview. *American Journal of Occupational Therapy, 56,* 344–349.

Millar, A., Simeone, R. S., & Carnevale, J. T. (2001). Logic models: A systems tool for performance management. *Evaluation and Program Planning, 24,* 73–81.

Portney, L. G., & Watkins, M. P. (2000). *Foundations of clinical research: Applications to practice.* Englewood Cliffs, NJ: Prentice Hall.

Prabst-Hunt, W. (2002). *Occupational therapy administration manual.* Albany, NY: Delmar.

Rogers, E. S., Sciarappa, K., MacDonald-Wilson, K., & Danley, K. (1995). A benefit–cost analysis of a supported employment model for persons with psychiatric disabilities. *Evaluation and Program Planning, 18,* 105–115.

Scaffa, M. (Ed.). (2001). *Occupational therapy in community-based practice settings.* Philadelphia: F. A. Davis.

Smith, R. O. (1995). *OT FACT software system for integrating and reporting occupational therapy assessment, version 2.03* [computer software and manual]. Rockville, MD: American Occupational Therapy Association.

Stewart, D., Law, M., Russell, D., & Hanna, S. (2004). Evaluating children's rehabilitation services: An application of a programme logic model. *Child: Care, Health and Development, 30,* 453–462.

Sung, N. S., Crowely, W. F., Genel, M., Salber, P., Sandy, L., Sherwood, I. M., et al. (2003). Central challenges facing the national clinical research enterprise. *JAMA, 289,* 1278–1287.

Sussman, S., Valente, T. W., Rohrbach, L. A., Skara, S., & Pentz, M. A. (2006). Translation in the health professions: Converting science into action. *Evaluation and the Health Professions, 29.* Retrieved March 29, 2009, from http://ehp.sagepub.com/ci/content/abstract/29/1/7

Uniform Data System for Medical Rehabilitation. (1993). *Guide for the uniform data set for medical rehabilitation for children (WeeFIM™, Version 4.0).* Buffalo: State University of New York.

Uniform Data System for Medical Rehabilitation. (1997). *Guide for the uniform data set for medical rehabilitation (Adult FIM™, Version 5.1).* Buffalo: State University of New York.

Velozo, C. A., Magalhaes, L., Pan, A., & Leiter, P. (1995). Differences in functional scale discrimination at admission and discharge: Rasch analysis of the Level of Rehabilitation Scale–II (LORS–III). *Archives of Physical Medicine and Rehabilitation, 76,* 705–712.

Ware, J. E. (2000). SF–36 Health Survey update. *Spine, 25,* 3130–3139.

Ware, J. E., & Sherbourne. (1992). *SF–36 Health Survey.* Boston: Health Institute.

Watson, D. E. (2000). Cost–consequence and cost-effectiveness analysis. In D. E. Watson (Ed.), *Evaluating costs and outcomes: Demonstrating the value of rehabilitation services* (pp. 41–51). Bethesda, MD: AOTA Press.

Watson, D. E., & Mathews, M. (2000). Cost–utility and cost–benefit analysis. In D. E. Watson (Ed.), *Evaluating costs and outcomes: Demonstrating the value of rehabilitation services* (pp. 53–62). Bethesda, MD: AOTA Press.

APPENDIX 26.A. EVALUATING OCCUPATIONAL THERAPY PROGRAMS EVIDENCE TABLE

Topic	Evidence
Importance of evaluating occupational therapy programs, types of evaluations	American Occupational Therapy Association. (2008). Occupational therapy practice framework: Domain and process (2nd ed.). *American Journal of Occupational Therapy, 62,* 625–683.
Importance of evaluating occupational therapy programs, areas of practice in need of efficacy studies	American Occupational Therapy Association. (2007). AOTA's *Centennial Vision* and executive summary. *American Journal of Occupational Therapy, 61,* 613–614.
Importance of evaluating occupational therapy programs	Case-Smith, J., & Powell, C. A. (2008). Research literature in occupation therapy, 2001–2005. *American Journal of Occupational Therapy, 62,* 480–486.
Importance of evaluating occupational therapy programs, reliability and validity of assessments	Gutman, S. A. (2008). Research priorities of the profession. *American Journal of Occupational Therapy, 62,* 499–501.
Importance of evaluating occupational therapy programs, types of evaluations, steps to evaluate programs, experimental designs, assessments, ethics, philosophy of evaluation	Hinojosa, J., Kramer, P., & Crist, P. (Eds.). (2005). *Evaluation: Obtaining and interpreting data.* Bethesda, MD: AOTA Press.
Importance of evaluating occupational therapy programs, outcome studies, efficacy studies	Jette, A. M., & Keysor, J. H. (2002). Uses of evidence in disability outcomes and effectiveness research. *Milbank Quarterly, 80,* 325–345.
Importance of evaluating occupational therapy programs, outcome studies	Kielhofner, G., Hammel, J., Finlayson, M., Helfrich, C., & Taylor, R. (2004). Documenting outcomes of occupational therapy: The Center for Outcomes Research and Education. *American Journal of Occupation Therapy, 58,* 15–23.

Appendix 26.B. Online Resources Related to Evaluation

- **Cochrane Collaboration:** http://www.cochrane.org
  An international, not-for-profit organization in which contributors produce systematic reviews of health care interventions, called *Cochrane reviews*, which are published online in The Cochrane Library.
- **Medical Outcomes Trust:** http://www.outcomes-trust.org
  A not-for-profit organization that aims to achieve universal adoption of health outcomes assessment in health care to improve the value of health care services. Contains lists and descriptions of assessments approved by its Scientific Advisory Committee.

27

Managing Organizational Change

Jeffrey D. Loveland, OTD, OTR/L,
and Jon M. Thompson, PhD

❖ Key Terms and Concepts

Benchmark. A method of setting standards of performance based on the characteristics of organizations that have a high degree of success.

Change. To make different; to alter.

Dashboard report. Report used to assess performance; usually includes quick reference indicators of cost, revenue, customer satisfaction, and quality outcomes for a given time period.

External forces. Dynamics that can affect an organization from the outside, including technological, economic, legal, political, social, cultural, and competitive elements.

Internal forces. Factors that can affect an organization that exist within its walls, including organizational culture and values; management; and employee job performance, skill, and morale.

Line of supervision. Established organizational personnel structure that identifies one's administrative and subordinate reporting and supervisory responsibilities.

❖ Learning Objectives

After completing this chapter, you should be able to do the following:

- Identify technological, economic, legal, political, social, cultural, and competitive factors that have influenced change in occupational therapy practice.
- Recognize changes that the profession of occupational therapy has experienced during its evolution and understand the implications of those changes.
- Understand and discuss why managing change is one of modern health care's critical competencies for health care managers.

- Analyze and discuss the 4 interrelated steps in the organizational change process.
- Identify the major barriers to change in an organization, and analyze how they can be minimized.
- Identify and discuss the roles of an occupational therapy manager in planning for, implementing, and evaluating change.

Failure is not fatal, but failure to change might be.
—John Wooden (Jamison & Wooden, 1997, p. 96)

In March 1917, six people, all identified as reformers or "change agents" (Hanson & Honey, 2008), met at Consolation House in Clifton Springs, New York, and approved a constitution and signed incorporation papers. This group was individually and collectively dedicated to founding a holistic and humanistic discipline that would effectively

combine with existing scientific and medical approaches to client treatment (Quiroga, 1995). As a result, occupational therapy was born, and the landscape of traditional and contemporary care in health, educational, and community-based settings was forever changed.

When individuals decide to pursue a career in a health and human services profession, they need to realize that encountering the forces of change will be a dynamic they will face daily. This tide of reorganization, readjustment, and refinement is a constant challenge to all practitioners, regardless of their level of expertise and place of employment. As occupational beings, each person constantly adjusts and adapts his or her performance in areas of occupation based on response to intrinsic and extrinsic feedback.

CHANGE: A DAILY EVENT

People of all ages daily confront shifts from the anticipated norm that demand flexibility, skill, and support to react effectively. These events occur regularly and are sometimes taken for granted because response to change can appear so trouble- and stress-free. A developing child takes his first steps and realizes a new sense of mobility and autonomy. A preschooler is asked to smoothly transition between playing with toys to an art activity that does not look like as much fun. A kindergarten student steps off the bus that she has ridden for the first time and begins to slowly approach her school building for her first day of school. A new middle school student arrives for his first day of class but has to successfully use the correct combination to open his locker. A high school senior meets with recruiters from prospective colleges but does not know if she wants to go away to college or stay closer to home.

A college graduate celebrates during his commencement ceremony but is unsure if he will be able to find a job in the area of his major. A young couple from the East Coast decide to get married and plan to move out west shortly thereafter. A 53-year-old automotive supply worker has lost his job and doubts if he will be able to afford the mortgage to his home and assist his children with college expenses. A librarian retires from her position after 35 years and worries whether she and her husband will enjoy their postemployment period. A 76-year-old man returns home from his wife's funeral and wonders what the future holds and if he can live without his partner of 55 years. As these examples indicate, the need to change as life unfolds sometimes occurs without warning and sometimes can be planned for and scheduled.

Although occupational therapy practitioners provide evaluation and intervention to clients who confront developmental or traumatic changes in their lives, clinical and academic practice is often affected by change that is brought about by external forces. Reimbursement, regulatory, and accreditation issues are examples of external factors that can influence occupational therapy practice and training. These extrinsic influences can be viewed as positive (e.g., bonus for a state employee due to a budget surplus) or negative (e.g., increased costs for clinical supplies). Outside pressures can also be looked at from a neutral perspective because the effect or outcomes of impending change can be difficult to assess or predict (e.g., the impact of health care reform on occupational therapy). On March 23, 2010, President Barack Obama signed the Patient Protection and Affordable Care Act (PPACA). This law will be progressively implemented over the course of the next several years. The American Occupational Therapy Association's (AOTA's) Federal Affairs staff diligently worked throughout this process to review parallel legislation from the House of Representatives and Senate while also lobbying to include occupational therapy in newly designed health care plans (Nanof, 2009). PPACA has identified that key improvements be made in preventative care, coordinated care, diversity and cultural competency, increasing the number of health care providers for underserved communities, ending insurance discrimination, and ensuring affordable insurance coverage (U.S. Department of Health & Human Services [DHHS], 2010). One aspect of the PPACA Act is the Preexisting Condition Insurance Plan (PCIP), which will provide access to health care to individuals who have previously been denied by private insurance companies due to a previous health condition (DHHS, 2010). Although how the recent changes in health care accessibility and delivery will affect occupational therapy is not completely known, occupational therapy practitioners will need to stay informed by AOTA leadership while simultaneously advocating for the profession so that this transition is as smooth as possible.

CHANGES IN OCCUPATIONAL THERAPY

Specific changes that can affect an occupational therapy practitioner are numerous and extensive and begin during the academic and clinical training process. The Accreditation Council for Occupational Therapy Education (ACOTE) established educational standards for the occupational therapist and occupational therapy assistant and regularly reviews and revises them as determined by the results of evaluative measures (see, e.g., ACOTE, 2007b). Current standards for both technical and professional educational programs were adopted in December 2006 and became effective on January 1, 2008. Entry-level undergraduate occupational therapy educational programs also had to shift their degree level to postbaccalaureate by January 1, 2007, as a result of mandates by ACOTE and AOTA. Once students graduate, the National Board for Certification of Occupational Therapy (NBCOT) exam is their next challenge, and this test has recently been modified to include clinical simulation questions. The final step for a graduate, which occurs before or during job seeking and acquisition, is obtaining a license from the state regulatory body. Procedures to obtain a license to practice can vary significantly from state to state and require patience, planning, and flexibility on the part of the entry-level practitioner.

Any occupational therapy practitioner employed in a management position for an extended time can attest that the knowledge, skills, and abilities required for clinical or academic practice never remain static. The boundaries of the profession continue to grow as occupational therapy moves into emerging areas of practice, is recognized for providing evidence-based interventions, and gains increased respect as a science (see Figure 27.1). The populations served by occupational therapy professionals are changing; they are becoming more culturally diverse, are less fit at an earlier age, and are living longer due to medical advances. Occupational therapy theories, frames of reference, and models of practice continually evolve and influence the established process that a practitioner uses to engage clients in the evaluation and intervention processes.

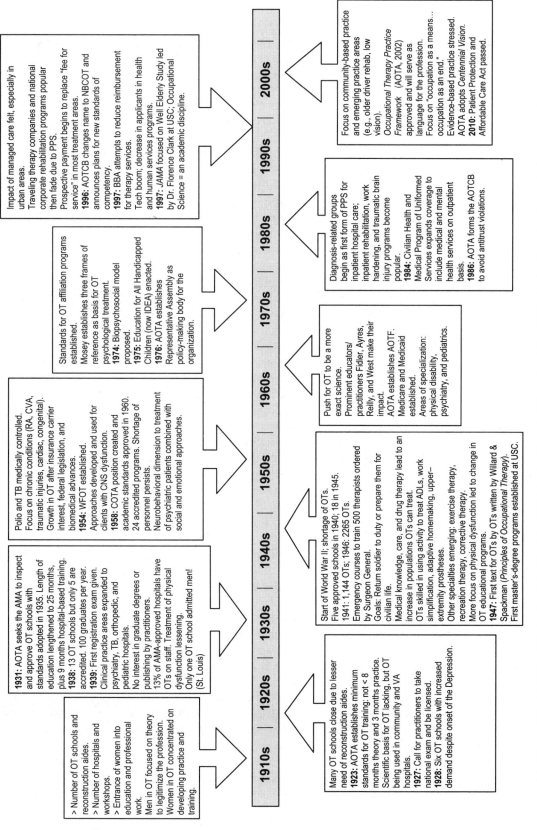

Figure 27.1. Chronological record of change in occupational therapy.

Note. ADLs = activities of daily living; AMA = American Medical Association; AOTA = American Occupational Therapy Association; AOTCB = American Occupational Therapy Certification Board; AOTF = American Occupational Therapy Foundation; BBA = Balanced Budget Act; CNS = central nervous system; COTA = certified occupational therapy assistant; CVA = cardiovascular accident; IDEA = Individuals With Disabilities Education Act; NBCOT = National Board for Certification in Occupational Therapy; OT = occupational therapy, or occupational therapist; PPS = prospective payment system; RA = rheumatoid arthritis; TB = tuberculosis; USC = University of Southern California; VA = Veterans Affairs; WFOT = World Federation of Occupational Therapists.

Technology has revolutionized both traditional and emerging health care practice and has had a great influence on employee recruitment, documentation, billing and reimbursement, communication, management, and research. All of the transition and reform occupational therapy personnel face throughout the sum total of their careers give validity to a statement attributed to inventor Charles F. Kettering: "The world hates change, yet it is the only thing that has brought about progress" (as quoted in Mackenzie, 2007, p. 10).

On the occasion of occupational therapy's 50th anniversary, Eleanor Clarke Slagle lecturer Wilma West (1968) considered the responsibilities of the practitioner to himself or herself, the profession, and the professional organization during a period of sweeping transition. She identified the need for comprehensive health care that would include an emphasis on health, prevention of illness and disability, maintenance and promotion of well-being, and continuity of care. She stressed the importance of professional unity among AOTA members during a period when specialization was increasingly being recognized. She encouraged practitioners to become leaders so they could influence the quality of service provision and the development of future practice arenas. At the end of her lecture, she shared the following viewpoint, which reflects the reason this chapter would be written 42 years later:

I do not suppose any of us knows, with any degree of certainty, the ideal future course for our profession. We do, however, see many signs that it must keep changing if it is to stay abreast of the larger world of which it is a part. Change is seldom easy or comfortable. Yet there is little about the world in which we live today that is more characteristic of it than the continual and fast-moving changes which transcend every aspect of our lives. Although each of us makes the necessary adaptation to these changes as they affect our personal concerns and activities, we are slower as a group to adjust our professional directions and developments to that which is new. We are often, in fact, resistant to the suggested need for change and all that it implies in the necessity for new learning and the establishment of new roles and functions. We are also reluctant to explore new potentials, to experiment, to take an occasional risk. (p. 15)

ROLE OF OCCUPATIONAL THERAPY MANAGERS IN IDENTIFYING AND OVERSEEING CHANGE

Organizational change is necessary in managing health services organizations, and the occupational therapy manager has a difficult but pivotal role in ensuring that services are provided effectively and efficiently. Managers deal with a variety of external and internal issues that challenge their ability to lead their units to high levels of performance. The *Occupational Therapy Code of Ethics and Ethics Standards*

(AOTA, 2010) and *Guidelines for Supervision, Roles, and Responsibilities During the Delivery of Occupational Therapy Services* (AOTA, 2009) address several complex concepts necessary to effectively supervise others and to understand the supervisory process of occupational therapy and non–occupational therapy personnel. An essential focus of being an effective occupational therapy manager and working with and supervising others is the willingness and ability to make changes that will have positive impacts on staff, the delivery of services, and the clients being served.

Role of Occupational Therapy Managers in Health Services Organizations

The delivery of health services occurs primarily through formal organizations that are designed and operated to provide a variety of appropriate, effective, and efficient health services. There are a number of different types of health services organizations in the United States that provide a range of inpatient and ambulatory services, including diagnostic, treatment, and rehabilitation services. These organizations, including hospitals, nursing homes, rehabilitation centers, and schools, may employ occupational therapy practitioners to provide one clinical service among many that are provided. Structured organizations are needed in health services because patient care requires the expertise of many clinical and nonclinical professionals working together to make sure that patient needs are met. A single individual clinician does not have the skills and expertise to provide more than his or her area of specialized care. As a result, occupational therapists and occupational therapy assistants work with other therapists, including speech therapists and physical therapists, to serve clients. They may also work with nursing and other clinical staff in developing and implementing a care plan for the client. Organizational theory suggests that health services organizations are an efficient and effective way to structure and provide care to patients and that the specific organizational design allows for the completion of organizational goals through the integration and coordination of care (Borkowski, 2009).

The role of the occupational therapy manager is critical to the delivery of services in these organizations. Organizations typically use one of several design structures to allow for the delineation and grouping of work and a clear line of supervision and communication. These structural models are typically known as *functional structures, matrix models,* and *service line models* (Buchbinder & Thompson, 2010). Occupational therapy managers are placed in positions of authority within these structures to manage the delivery of occupational therapy services and, in some cases, of other rehabilitation services such as speech therapy and physical therapy. In this role, they are responsible for leadership and supervision of others, resource management, and overall delivery of care. Managing change within their unit or division is a critical component of the role of occupational therapy managers. These changes can be either micro or macro changes. Whitlock (2009) defined these types of changes as *transitional change,* or making small changes to a process, and *transformational change,* or making major or radical changes in the organization, such as major restructuring. As defined by Maxwell (2009), such changes can be either planned (discretionary changes are brought about by management) or unplanned changes (unexpected issues create a need for sudden action). The occupational therapy manager must identify the need for change and design a specific desired change either alone or through interactive and participatory methods with staff occupational therapy professionals and others. Managing change has been identified as one of the critical competencies of health care managers (Guo, 2009; Stefl, 2008), and in many ways, managers have increasingly been charged with being change agents because the complexity and extent of forces affecting organizations and delivery of care has been accelerating in recent years.

Occupational Therapy Managers as Change Agents

Why do managers need to be change agents? Managers face a variety of internal and external forces that create a need to change the way things are done. Organizational theory suggests that organizational management teams must identify these forces and adapt to these pressures so as to better align their organizations with their environments, both external and internal. Adaptations can be either proactive or reactive, and a good manager is proactive as much as possible. Most changes are either structural changes or process changes (Longest, Rakich, & Darr, 2000).

For example, the push for widespread use of electronic health records will create significant challenges for occupational therapy practitioners in documenting their clinical client notes and represents a significant departure from paper records (Alexander, 2007). Occupational therapy managers will be instrumental in designing a system that will meet the needs of the organization and the occupational therapy staff. Another illustration of change is in staffing. Because of difficulties in recruiting rehabilitation staff, occupational therapy managers may consider and make adjustments to staffing schedules and offer financial incentives to staff to work a new schedule. In these examples, change is necessary to help improve the way the work is carried out and care is provided. In some cases, the change is at the manager's discretion, and in other cases the change is necessary to comply with external mandates, such as insurance, accreditation, or safety requirements.

Recent observers have suggested that organizations need to be more agile, flexible, innovative, and change oriented (Lawler & Worley, 2009). Alignment of the organization with the intention to preserve the status quo is not consistent with success in the current turbulent time of health services organizations.

Managing Change and Managing Performance

One of the occupational therapy manager's key concerns is the performance of his or her unit, division, or clinical service. Managers use a wide variety of indicators or measures to assess the performance of their areas and to monitor trends in performance over time. Typical measures include volume of clients, number of therapies, revenue per visit or discharge, and expense per visit or discharge. In addition, quality and customer service measures are widely used to describe the outcomes of services and changes in functional performance and client satisfaction. Managers frequently use these measures in benchmark (i.e., compared to successful organizations) or dashboard (i.e., use of selected indicators) reports, developed to document how their unit or service is performing during a specified time period and how that performance compares to earlier reporting periods. Such reports are used to inform change but also to report on effects of change. For example, a manager's dashboard report may reveal that expenses are higher than expected compared to a prior reporting period, indicating the need to cut back on expenses. The manager would then determine a specific strategy for reducing costs to regain balance within the budget.

Performance can be improved through structural and process changes within occupational therapy services. These changes can reflect the way occupational therapy services are organized (e.g., use of teams, number of staff, allocation of tasks and responsibilities) as well as the way things are done (e.g., allocation of financial resources, process of care delivery, use of new therapeutic modalities). Managers need to continuously think of ways to change for the better so that performance can be improved.

A FRAMEWORK FOR MANAGING CHANGE

Now that the importance of managers being change agents in their organizations has been discussed, it is helpful to review a framework for managing change in the organization. As noted earlier, engaging in change first requires the recognition of the need to change. Longest, Rakich, and Darr (2000) noted four interrelated steps in the organizational change process: (1) identifying the need for change, (2) planning for implementing the change, (3) implementing the change, and (4) evaluating the change (see Figure 27.2).

Identify the Need for Change

First, managers realize that a change is needed when they recognize that organizational performance is not optimal or falls below expected targets. For example, a manager may determine from reviewing documentation that client information is not being appropriately recorded, or he or she may decide that staff scheduling needs to be modified to accommodate more flexible staffing arrangements. An identified change can be either planned (e.g., developing a more flexible staff scheduling arrangement in advance) or unplanned (e.g., responding to new information, regulations, or requirements). A critical component of this first step is to identify the specific change to be made.

Plan for Implementation of the Change

The second step is planning the implementation of the change. In this step, alternatives for addressing the problem or need are identified and evaluated. The manager determines

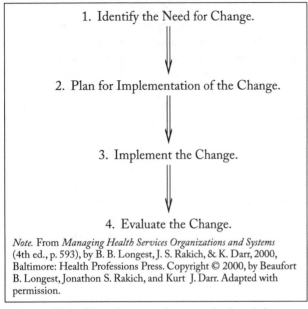

1. Identify the Need for Change.

2. Plan for Implementation of the Change.

3. Implement the Change.

4. Evaluate the Change.

Note. From *Managing Health Services Organizations and Systems* (4th ed., p. 593), by B. B. Longest, J. S. Rakich, & K. Darr, 2000, Baltimore: Health Professions Press. Copyright © 2000, by Beaufort B. Longest, Jonathon S. Rakich, and Kurt J. Darr. Adapted with permission.

Figure 27.2. Steps in managing organizational change.

the best options and designs an implementation strategy that includes increasing support for and decreasing resistance to the change (Maxwell, 2009). Campbell (2008) noted that organizational change is psychological as well as situational; individual employees are greatly affected by organizational changes, and it is therefore critical to explain the basis for the change to increase support and decrease resistance. Specific managerial strategies for addressing resistance to and support for change are addressed in the next section.

Implement the Change

The third step is implementing the change. During this step, the change is introduced and incorporated into actual day-to-day operations and activities. The change becomes the norm for a specific behavior or process being modified (Longest et al., 2000). The objective of this step is to translate the change from innovation to an accepted way of completing work (Whitlock, 2009). As the change is accepted, it is institutionalized within the organization (Whitlock, 2009).

Evaluate the Change

The final step involves evaluating the net results of the change. This step is necessary so that results can be compared with expectations and the basis for any variations identified. Findings from an evaluation of the change can also be used to adjust the specific change that has been made and will be helpful to inform future needed organizational changes.

Summary

Occupational therapy managers can use this framework to address any organizational change—planned or unplanned, micro or macro—that they are facing. As noted earlier, managers can use a directive or participatory managerial style to effect the change depending its nature, scope, and importance.

Managing Support and Resistance to Change

Charles Darwin is credited with the acknowledgment that the species that is most adaptable to change is more apt to survive rather than the one that is strongest or most intelligent. This view may also be applied to the longevity of organizations, as well as of senior, middle, and lower-level managers. In 2009 alone, newspaper groups, automobile manufacturers, and banking institutions experienced drastic reform that could be attributed to a reluctance to favorably respond to external and internal forces. What allows different organizations and their leaders to anticipate, develop a plan for, and adapt to change more effectively than others? There are many answers to this question.

The process of change is fraught with complexity and potential barriers, which health care organizations and their leaders need to be constantly aware of. Any prospective modification should be viewed as a challenge and not as a threat to enable a successful outcome (Marquis & Huston, 2003). Change can endanger corporate culture and the environment that defines an employee, with innovative (or unfamiliar) change being more threatening and anxiety provoking than the adaptive (familiar) type (Mackenzie, 2007). Leaders involved in planning change must be optimistic, open, insightful, decisive, and communicative (Hanson & Honey, 2008) and need to fully invest in the planning and conversion process. Mackenzie (2007) identified employee needs, organizational culture, board or shareholder interests, and a manager's own continued personal employment status or position as vying factors confronting leaders during periods of significant job revision. Individuals involved in management can intentionally or unknowingly create roadblocks to transition; they may share the same uneasiness regarding job upheaval as the employees they direct. The pull to adhere to the status quo is forceful and can come from any level of a company's organizational chart when change is proposed.

Kantor, Kram, and Sala (2008) described the characteristics of adaptability, a trait that all assured, logical, and effective leaders should possess. This trait has two components—courage and curiosity. Courageous leaders are consistent and can convey their thoughts and opinions even when circumstances make it difficult to do so. They boldly forge committed relationships with both coworkers and their organization and can make difficult decisions based on what is best for their employer. Courageous leaders tolerate peril, uncertainty, apprehension, and constructive criticism, and they acknowledge and learn from their mistakes. Curious leaders are driven to learn from everyone and everything in their environment. They ask questions, love to learn, and show consistent interest in how processes both large and small operate. Leaders who have this inquisitive style are open to the suggestions of others, are not afraid to make adjustments when necessary, and value diverse opinions. Kantor et al. proposed four contrasting styles of leadership: (1) the *good citizen* (low courage and low curiosity), (2) the *steadfast visionary* (low curiosity and high courage), (3) the *creative accommodator* (low courage and high curiosity), and (4) the *pioneer* (high courage and high curiosity); the pioneer style is favored by the leaders who are the most prepared for and adaptable to change (see Figure 27.3).

There are many dynamics within a health care organization relevant to staff-level employees that can delay or defeat the implementation of change proposed by management. Mackenzie (2007) cited the following factors as barriers to change:

- Distrust of senior managers
- Inadequate employee preparation for the specific change
- Perception that the proposed change will disrupt employee culture
- Lack of employee involvement in the change process
- Disproportionate management focus on the change rather than the needs of employees
- Poor employee coping capacity or feelings of insecurity
- Inadequate communication while planning and implementing change
- Poor work relationships
- Low employee motivation and initiative
- Insufficient skill or experience
- Harm to perceived employee competence due to technology shifts.

Employees at every level of an organization need to work together to understand, accept, prepare for, and implement change. Recruiting key members across a facility's organizational chart to participate in the process of reform empowers them to take ownership of whatever the outcome may be. Achieving employee buy-in for change requires clear explanation of what benefits will result from the proposed change and how identified benefits will outweigh any disadvantages or drawbacks.

QUALITY ENHANCEMENT PROGRAMS

Two quality enhancement programs—continuous quality improvement (the Deming management method) and Six Sigma (SSA & Company) strategic process management—are popular training methods that are currently used, together with evidence-based practice, in health care settings to facilitate change.

Continuous Quality Improvement

Continuous quality improvement (CQI), developed by W. Edwards Deming (1900–1993), is a management process that evaluates the arrangement of people, equipment, and procedures in a series of tasks intended to repeatedly produce a desired end result (Joint Commission, 2004). Products and services are the outputs of processes, and all quality problems occur because something went wrong in a particular process. The more complex the process, the greater the chance for errors. Well-defined, -established and -disciplined processes do the "right thing" more often than those that are less effective and rehearsed (Walton, 1986). A research-based model within the CQI approach that is frequently used in health care to identify and correct problem areas is FOCUS–PDCA. This is an acronym that defines a nine-step process that can yield higher quality performance in a timely manner (Joint Commission, 2004):

1. *Find* a process that requires improvement.
2. *Organize* a working group that understands what needs to be improved.
3. *Clarify* the issues surrounding the process by asking "who, what, when, and where."
4. *Understand* the factors that are causing inconsistency in performance by asking "why."

	Low Curiosity	High Curiosity
High Courage	**The Steadfast Visionary** + Intelligent, results oriented, enthusiastic, confident − Inflexible, stubborn, not open to suggestions about change	**The Pioneer** + Inquisitive, constant learner, pragmatic, insightful, continuously seeks change to improve service, adaptable, challenges the status quo, key problem solver − May not be a good fit in companies that maintain the status quo
Low Courage	**The Good Citizen** + Stickler for detail, results oriented, good people skills, good with mature organizations in stable marketplace − Lacks skill in anticipating marketplace changes and ability to adapt, relies on doing things the same way	**The Creative Accommodator** + Flexible, precise, adventurous, efficient − A builder but not a sustainer, difficulty holding people accountable, does not adapt as needs change

+ = strengths, − = weaknesses.

Source. From "Change Factor: Making the Case for Executive Adaptability," by S. Kantor, K. E., Kram, and F. Sala, 2008, *Leadership in Action*, 27(6), 8–12.

Figure 27.3. Matrix showing four contrasting styles of leadership on the basis of level of courage and curiosity.

5. *Select* a solution that has been identified to improve the process. This is the step in which errors can be made by hurrying to select an intervention strategy that may not improve the outcomes of the process being examined.

6. *Plan* to improve the process being analyzed. Brainstorming, diagramming, goal setting, and action planning for data collection are performed.

7. *Implement* identified improvement measures on a small scale while closely monitoring the process.

8. *Check* to assess if the plan for improvement to the process was effectively implemented and to examine the effects of the change vs. what was predicted. If results are less than desired, then a review of FOCUS–PDCA steps is in order. If results are satisfactory and process improvement is noted, then proceed to the last step.

9. *Act* to ensure that improvements are maintained and to improve the team performance during the FOCUS–PDCA cycle.

Six Sigma Strategic Process Management

Six Sigma was created by Bill Smith at the Motorola Corporation in 1986 (Snee & Hoerl, 2003). This system, originally designed to enhance manufacturing practices and eliminate mistakes, has been extended into health care settings. Statistical methods are used to eradicate defects, defined as any occurrence that could lead to customer dissatisfaction. Six Sigma leaders in an organization receive extensive training, and decision making is heavily influenced by facts and hard data rather than subjective impressions (Anthony, 2008). The Six Sigma process has a cycle that resembles the CQI–PDCA model that is identified as the "DMAIC approach" (*d*efine, *m*easure, *a*nalyze, *im*prove, *c*ontrol; Snee & Hoerl, 2003).

Evidence-Based Practice

The evidence-based practice process can also facilitate change. Once the manager defines a clinical question and locates and critically evaluates the evidence he or she can then implement change effectively (Plastow, 2006). Ilott (2003) recommended an additional step in the evidence-based practice process that allows for evaluating the outcomes of change implementation using evidence that has been rigorously analyzed. Outcomes that can be measured in occupational therapy practice include client performance, cost of service delivery, quality of life, and therapist effectiveness (Cohen & Kearney, 2005). There are many advantages in staying abreast of current guidelines for evidence-based practice and incorporating this information into everyday best clinical practice (Taylor, 1997).

Cultivation of an attitude of learning can strengthen an organization's ability to effect ongoing change; as workers acquire more knowledge and skill, change becomes less difficult to experience. To achieve desired outcomes as change occurs, managers need to demonstrate skill in conveying information, eliminating obstacles, and making sound decisions (Greenwood, 1997).

Participants involved in the change process also need to be keenly aware of forces external to their organization. These outside constraints can hinder the effectiveness of planned corporate, service, or departmental reform. Technological, economic, legal, political, cultural, and competitive factors all can influence organizational change (Mackenzie, 2007). For example, prospective payment is an external force that has had a profound impact on occupational therapy practice; it started in 1983 in acute inpatient hospital settings through the implementation of diagnosis-related groups. This reimbursement system capped inpatient hospital revenues, so health care managers across the country shifted resources into nonacute settings, which included outpatient services, home health care, inpatient rehabilitation, and skilled nursing facilities. As a result, phenomenal growth resulted for occupational therapy in a variety of new and existing service areas. Similarly, the Education for All Handicapped Children Act of 1975 (renamed the Individuals with Disabilities Education Act in 1990) first paved the way for occupational therapy services to be offered in school-based settings (Swinth, 2003). Occupational therapy managers are strongly encouraged to monitor external forces that can influence both regulatory policy and their employment settings through organized professional or legislative forums that allow for dialogue so their interests can be heard. AOTA members can readily access such forms at www.aota.org.

IMPLICATIONS FOR OCCUPATIONAL THERAPY MANAGEMENT

This chapter has addressed the important role of occupational therapy managers in managing change in their organizations. As we have described, change in the structure and delivery of health services is constant and challenging, yet necessary. Managers must play a key role in anticipating and making needed changes. Above all, they must be change oriented, advocates of change, and change agents in their organizations for the improvement of occupational therapy services. The following sections identify several key implications for occupational therapy managers.

Identify and Implement Change as Needed

Recognize that identifying the need for change and making change happen is part of your position as an occupational therapy manager. Managers face many external and internal factors that influence their ability to manage their units effectively and efficiently. Examples of external factors include legislation and regulation that affect occupational therapy practice, competitive environments that affect recruitment and retention of staff, and the increased demand for occupational therapy services by older populations. As a result, managers must continuously monitor their external environments, stay abreast of the issues and trends that exist, and anticipate needed changes within their organizations.

Internal factors include staff relationships, resource constraints, the mandate to incorporate evidenced-based practices, and pressure to provide quality outcomes and customer service. Occupational therapy managers should draw on the experiences of colleagues and mentors who have developed effective strategies for being change agents and who have been effective in managing change. Managers should work with others in the organization and draw knowledge and support from them and their ability to successfully manage change with their own staff.

Use a Change Management Process

Use a change management process for any change, large or small, planned or unplanned. Regardless of the nature and scope of the change being made, the occupational therapy manager must use a structured process to manage change within their organization. The four-step framework for managing change discussed in this chapter (see Figure 27.2) provides a rational, structured guideline for addressing and communicating change. It is an integrated, problem-solving approach that occupational therapy staff can relate to and provides the necessary structure for the manager to address needed changes within the organization. Although implementation of a change process presents a significant challenge to the manager, it is critical to the effectiveness of the manager's role (Buchbinder & Thompson, 2010).

Anticipate the Needs of Staff

Be aware that change is difficult, and it will create both resistance and support on the part of staff. Change evokes strong feelings in management and staff; few people like change. To address positive and negative feelings about impending or likely changes, occupational therapy managers must be able to convincingly point to the need for and benefits of the change and specify how the benefits will outweigh any short- or long-term drawbacks. This process requires forthright and continuous communication and may include time-paced announcements (MacPhee, 2007). In addition, gaining buy-in from staff requires the manager's openness to thoughts and suggestions from staff and other managers regarding effective ways to implement the change.

Acknowledge That Change Will Always Be Necessary

Recognize that change is necessary to make the organization innovative, competitive, and successful in the long term. Few organizations that preserve the status quo end up being high performers and highly regarded organizations. Occupational therapy managers who are content in doing business as usual or operating as it has "always been done" will not be providing the leadership necessary to make their services effective and efficient in the long run. To the contrary, effective occupational therapy management requires changes to demonstrate and incorporate innovative, state-of-the-art services that draw on the latest knowledge and successful industry experiences. These changes must be based on sound organizational learning.

Hone Your Leadership Skills

Are leaders born or made? According to Kantor et al. (2008), some experts believe that adaptability is a fixed personality trait rather than an attainable skill but that it can be improved if an individual has the motivation to do so. All leaders require accurate self-appraisal, meaningful constructive input on their virtues and limitations, challenging performance experiences, and an opportunity to exercise their growing competencies.

CONCLUSION

This chapter identifies the contemporary challenges involving the topic of organizational change that can confront occupational therapy managers. To be successful as a manager in today's health care arena, occupational therapy practitioners need to possess a skill set that is decidedly different from that of their predecessors (Ritchie, 2007). Today's managers are typically outgoing, communicative, flexible, and confident and are keenly aware of their strengths and weaknesses. They demonstrate appeal in their ability to reach out to both consumers and stakeholders, who are each important to the success of their service. They value their coworkers and subordinates, understand how to maximize performance by having the right people in the right positions, and are not afraid to make key decisions or use their authority. The modern manager responds favorably to the challenges presented by continuous change and is a model for the people who report to him or her.

AOTA's (2007) *Centennial Vision* states the following: "We envision that occupational therapy is a powerful, widely recognized, science-driven, and evidence-based profession with a globally connected and diverse workforce meeting society's occupational needs" (p. 613). As part of the vision, the AOTA identified six barriers that could interfere with its goals being realized; barrier number 1 was "rigid adherence to the status quo." This identified barrier sends a message to all practicing occupational therapy practitioners and students that change is essential for both personal and professional growth and for the profession of occupational therapy to move forward.

Case Examples

LEVEL I FIELDWORK

Joan was a 38-year-old occupational therapy assistant student performing her second Level I fieldwork experience at an inpatient adult rehabilitation unit, which she attended 1 full day a week. Her first fieldwork experience was at a state psychiatric facility, where she was able to observe and participate in client assessment and intervention. At her current placement, Joan observed that occupational therapy assistants did not participate with occupational therapists in client evaluation but were used extensively to provide intervention. She was unsure why occupational therapy assistants were used in the evaluation process at her previous placement but not at her current site. Joan was trying to understand why these differences exist

Joan discussed her interest to more actively participate in the evaluation process with Beth, her supervisor who was an occupational therapist. Joan indicated that she was trained to gather and share data during the screening and evaluation process at her occupational therapy assistant education program. Beth told Joan that she supported having her responsibilities increased during the evaluation process, but she said that she would have to talk with her director because her organization had a philosophy in which occupational therapists performed all screening and evaluation duties. Beth spoke to her director, Elaine, and the two of them decided to call Joan's academic fieldwork coordinator, Robin, to further discuss this issue. Robin reviewed the *Accreditation Standards for an Educational Program for the Occupational Therapy Assistant* (ACOTE, 2007a) with Beth and Elaine, indicating that Joan possessed the knowledge, technical training, and degree of readiness necessary to participate in the evaluation process under the supervision of an occupational therapist. Elaine communicated to the entire occupational therapy staff that department procedures would be revised to allow occupational therapy assistants to begin involvement in selected client evaluations. Evaluative processes for the occupational therapist assistant were discussed with all members of the occupational therapy department, and Joan was able to gain experience in performing specific assessment tools during the last 4 weeks of her Level I fieldwork experience.

LEVEL II FIELDWORK

Laura was a Level II fieldwork student who was scheduled to spend 12 weeks in a hospital-based outpatient adult rehabilitation program. She felt very fortunate to have been assigned this placement, because this particular service had an outstanding reputation for providing excellent care. She was able to meet her clinical fieldwork supervisor in advance and had a great working relationship with her.

Wendy was also a Level II fieldwork student at the same facility but from a different university than Laura. Wendy was assigned to the inpatient traumatic brain injury (TBI) unit. The midterm point of Laura's and Wendy's experience arrived, and their performance was very different. Laura excelled in her placement, while Wendy struggled. Laura was very organized and effective with her clients, while Wendy had a limited caseload, needed much more structure, and reported that her clinical fieldwork supervisor was "too intense" and did not give her the space she would have liked to treat clients on her own.

After receiving her midterm evaluation, Wendy announced that she wanted to switch clinical sites and supervisors with Laura by indicating that work with individuals with acute brain injury was "too overwhelming" for her. The clinical supervisors met to discuss this idea and approved it, although Laura's supervisor was lukewarm in endorsing this plan. As a result, Laura would now transfer to the inpatient brain injury unit at the start of the week. She was stunned by this turn of events since she had chosen this fieldwork site specifically for an experience in the outpatient program. Laura would have to adjust to a new supervisor about whom Wendy had voiced several concerns. Laura did not think this was fair and called her academic fieldwork coordinator (AFWC) to report what had happened.

Laura called her AFWC, Elizabeth, to discuss the plans of this abrupt, undesired change. Elizabeth allowed Laura ample time to explain the situation from her point of view and to express frustration about it. Elizabeth agreed with Laura that the change was unanticipated and very sudden, but her upcoming career as an occupational therapist was going to be full of unplanned shifts and surprises. Having this change occur during a Level II placement was a great challenge and opportunity for her. Elizabeth encouraged Laura to further process her situation with her supervisor and to call her back in 2 days to allow time for Elizabeth to contact Laura's fieldwork supervisor and to gather more information about the situation.

After speaking with Laura's supervisor, Elizabeth was reassured that Laura was well respected by all members in the occupational therapy department and would perform well as a full-time Level II fieldwork student on the inpatient TBI unit. Wendy's difficulties on the acute TBI unit were discussed as being more due to difficulties in planning evaluation and interventions for profoundly impaired clients rather than as a result of a supervisory conflict. A plan was developed in which Elizabeth would do a site visit and meet with Laura and both of her clinical fieldwork supervisors on her first day on the acute TBI unit.

As planned, Laura called Elizabeth back 2 days after their initial contact and was much more open to the change but still nervous about it. Elizabeth explained to her that all members in the department respected the knowledge, skill, and dedication that she had thus far demonstrated and that they felt she would do a great job on the acute TBI unit. Elizabeth explained that she had planned to visit her on her first day on her new unit and would meet with both of her supervisors. Laura felt very confident and encouraged by this plan and now looked forward to this new experience.

FIRST-TIME MANAGER

John was a first-time manager who had been promoted from within at a children's rehabilitation hospital, where he had worked for 5 years. Two of his coworkers also applied for the occupational therapy department manager position, and, after an extensive interview process, John was selected. He was to manage a department that included 6 occupational therapists, 2 certified occupational therapy assistants, and 1 office manager.

During the interview process, John had discussed with the managers of physical therapy and speech therapy his interest in participating in the development of interdisciplinary group treatment programs. He received enthusiastic endorsement of this idea from everyone he had interacted with in his interview. After beginning his new role, John met individually with all occupational therapy personnel in his department, along with the office manager. He shared his plans for developing group treatment activities in combination with other rehabilitation disciplines, but most occupational therapy staff members voiced more concerns about John's ideas than support. John now realized that a concept that he thought would be warmly embraced by occupational therapy department staff members was going to take much more communication, promotion, and effort to eventually implement than he had anticipated.

John decided to discuss his ideas for group treatment with other rehabilitation department directors during a regularly scheduled meeting. All leaders were enthusiastic about initiating group treatment because it was identified that group intervention activities were already successfully being used at a number of competing rehabilitation programs in the area. All directors pointed out that enthusiasm among members of their department to develop and implement interdisciplinary group intervention programs was currently very inconsistent. John decided to arrange visits with two of these facilities as well as with the directors of physical therapy and speech–language pathology.

Group activities were observed and therapy staff members involved in providing these interventions had discussions with John and his two colleagues about their views on group treatment. Feedback received identified interdisciplinary group treatment as valuable for both clients and therapists, but it required significant planning and flexibility before and after the groups were implemented. Therapists anecdotally noted that clients received a psychosocial boost from group treatment because they could identify skills and interests they didn't think they possessed and could get to know fellow clients better. It was also mentioned that providing group activities allowed therapists more time to complete their documentation requirements compared to consistently seeing clients on a one-to-one basis. John and his rehabilitation team cohorts were impressed by what they saw and heard and were eager to get back and discuss their findings with members of their departments. John now realized that he needed to better sell the idea of interdisciplinary group treatment to his staff by pointing out the distinct advantages of group intervention that he witnessed and heard about during his two facility tours.

MANAGER

Steve was manager of an occupational therapy department at a 130-bed metropolitan hospital that provided services to inpatient (rehabilitation and acute care), outpatient, home health, and skilled nursing programs. He discussed schedules for coverage of these occupational therapy service areas, and the occupational therapy staff unanimously agreed that they would like to remain on a rotating assignment calendar. The therapists indicated to Steve that they enjoyed switching job assignments every 3 months as it provided them with job variety and challenged their skills and abilities in different contexts.

Several weeks after therapists in the occupational therapy department reaffirmed their desire to stay on a rotating schedule, Dr. Maguire, the medical director of the hospital's rehabilitation unit, abruptly asked to speak to Steve in a small private office. Dr. McGuire told Steve, "Bonnie, one of your occupational therapists on my rehabilitation unit, is not any good, and I want you to replace her. I want her to be replaced by Megan, and I would like to have her stay on the unit permanently. I also think that your four best therapists should be on my unit, since it is one of the top money makers for the hospital."

Steve was surprised by Dr. McGuire's sudden request, because professionals from all other disciplines had complimented Bonnie's work. Steve responded to Dr.

Case Examples (cont.)

McGuire's request by saying, "With all due respect, sir, I cannot meet your request. Occupational therapists in the department have unanimously indicated that they want to continue rotating through all programs, and I need to honor this because I am concerned about staff retention. Surely you recognize that if our more skilled and experienced therapists are not heard in this regard, we both could lose key members of our team. If you have concerns about Bonnie's performance, I would be glad to meet with you to discuss them so we can develop a performance enhancement plan for her." As Steve spoke to Dr. McGuire, he did so confidently and maintained eye contact with him. Judging by Dr. McGuire's reaction, he was sure that this was not what he wanted to hear.

Because staff retention was an important human resources issue for all clinical departments, Steve was very tuned in to what members of his department desired from their jobs from a professional development and challenge standpoint. He realized that assertively communicating the needs of staff members in the occupational therapy department to Dr. McGuire was contrary to what he was strongly instructed to do. Hearing that Dr. McGuire had vague concerns about Bonnie's work performance, Steve decided to discuss it with Marilyn, who was the lead occupational therapist on the rehabilitation unit. Marilyn confided that Bonnie had indicated that her mother was recently diagnosed with breast cancer. Bonnie was not sleeping as well and, as a result, was more distracted at work. Bonnie needed to have more organization with her reports in team meetings but otherwise was performing her job well.

Steve and Marilyn met with Bonnie and suggested that she visit human resources and seek out support from the hospital's Employee Assistance Program (EAP) due to the stress that her mother's illness was causing. Marilyn also met with Bonnie on two occasions to discuss how to better organize her client reports for team meetings, and she improved. Bonnie also benefitted from consultation that she received through the EAP referral program. Two months after his abrupt meeting with Steve, Dr. McGuire briefly met with him again and indicated that Bonnie's work performance had improved and that he was glad that she was still a part of "his" rehabilitation unit.

❖ Learning Activities

1. Identify personal and professional changes that have occurred in your life in all areas of occupation as outlined by the *Occupational Therapy Practice Framework: Domain and Process, 2nd Edition* (AOTA, 2008): activities of daily living, instrumental activities of daily living, rest and sleep, education, work, play, leisure, and social participation. Discuss changes that have evolved within the past 3 months, 6 months, 1 year, and 2 years. Identify whether these changes were due to internal or external circumstances. Discuss your transition in adapting to these changes.

2. Assume the role of occupational therapy manager. You have witnessed inefficiencies and staff frustration with documentation in client records and have concluded that an electronic documentation and record system is needed. Develop a statement of rationale to communicate with staff why such a system is needed; include 3 statements of likely support for the system and 3 statements that reflect likely resistance to the system. Be sure to outline a process for overcoming the issues of resistance you have identified.

3. Define, compare, and contrast the following types of change: micro and macro, planned and unplanned, transitional and transformational. Give an example of each type of change, and discuss why each is important in the role of occupational therapy manager.

4. Identify 3 different organizational settings for the practice of occupional therapy. For each setting, identify 2 external and 2 internal forces that create the need for organizational change, and identify and discuss a specific change in the structure or process of occupational therapy services for each of the forces you have identified. Which of these forces is the most important, and why?

5. You recently started in a position as manager of a large occupational therapy department in a rehabilitation hospital. During your job interview, the administrator had indicated that an assignment for the newly hired manager would be to discontinue paid overtime for occupational therapy personnel 2 months after the new manager's start date. During those 2 months, you had occupational therapy staff complete time utilization studies, which reflect no increases in productivity despite the longer schedules. Several therapists indicated that they preferred to complete all of their daily documentation toward the end of their shift and enjoyed the extra compensated time they were allowed. There is a waiting list of names for outpatient occupational therapy services, but staff members indicate they are too busy to add an outpatient to their caseload. Your concern is that this practice is driving up salary expenses in your department but not bringing in any extra revenue. You know that you are going to have to address this issue very soon. What strategies can you use to discuss the discontinuation of overtime with occupational therapy staff members?

✓ Multiple-Choice Questions

1. All educational programs for the occupational therapist were required to be at the post-baccalaureate level by which date?
   a. January 1, 2006.
   b. January 1, 2007.
   c. January 1, 2008.
   d. January 1, 2009.

2. Which element from an organization's external environment has revolutionized health care practice?
   a. Cultural influences.
   b. Technological influences.
   c. Political influences.
   d. Economic influences.

3. Which well-known occupational therapist delivered the 1967 Eleanor Clarke Slagle lecture titled Professional Responsibility in Times of Change?
   a. Mary Reilly.
   b. Gail Fidler.
   c. Anne Mosey.
   d. Wilma West.

4. A transformational change is synonymous with which kind of change?
   a. Micro change.
   b. Unplanned change.
   c. Macro change.
   d. Contextual change.

5. A discretionary change by management is referred to as which of the following?
   a. Planned change.
   b. Unplanned change.
   c. Micro change.
   d. Macro change.

6. A health care system that is forced to suddenly downsize due to lower than projected revenues, incurs which type of change?
   a. Micro change.
   b. Planned change.
   c. Unplanned change.
   d. Scheduled change.

7. A major university that is restructuring academic programs into a new college alignment incurs which type of change?
   a. Micro change.
   b. Transformational change.
   c. Unplanned change.
   d. Traditional change.

8. Planning, developing, and building new space for an occupational therapy department to use for client evaluation and intervention are an example of which type of change?
   a. Unplanned change.
   b. Process change.
   c. Micro change.
   d. Structural change.

9. Newly introduced therapeutic activities that occur within newly developed space by an occupational therapy department are an example of which type of change?
   a. Transformational change.
   b. Process change.
   c. Unplanned change.
   d. Structural change.

10. The important first step for a manager in the change process is
   a. Assessing to see if financial resources exist to make the change.
   b. Assessing to see if there is administrative support to make the change.
   c. Communicating the change to occupational therapy staff.
   d. Realizing that a change is needed.

11. Identifying and evaluating alternatives for addressing a problem or need and increasing support for a proposed change are consistent with which step in the organizational change process?
   a. Step 1: Identification of the need for change.
   b. Step 2: Planning for implementing the change.
   c. Step 3: Implementing the change.
   d. Step 4: Evaluating the change.

12. Examining the net results of an implemented change is consistent with which step in the organizational change process?
   a. Step 1: Identification of the need for change.
   b. Step 2: Planning for implementing the change.
   c. Step 3: Implementing the change.
   d. Step 4: Evaluating the change.

13. Incorporating a change into actual day-to-day operations is consistent with which step in the organizational change process?
   a. Step 1: Identification of the need for change.
   b. Step 2: Planning for implementing the change.
   c. Step 3: Implementing the change.
   d. Step 4: Evaluating the change.

14. Which competing internal force can compromise a manager's drive for reform in an organization?
   a. Corporate cultural forces.
   b. Competitive forces.
   c. Economic forces.
   d. Political forces.

15. According to Kantor et al.'s (2008) discussion of leadership adaptability, which of the following are important characteristics for successful leaders to possess?
   a. Courage and charm.
   b. Organization and curiosity.
   c. Courage and curiosity.
   d. Popularity and curiosity.

16. According to Kantor et al.'s (2008) discussion of leadership adaptability, which style of leadership is the most effective during periods of constant change?
    a. The pioneer.
    b. The good citizen.
    c. The steadfast visionary.
    d. The creative accommodator.
17. The Balanced Budget Act (BBA) of 1997 has had a tremendous impact on the practice of occupational therapy. The BBA is an example of what type of external force?
    a. Legal.
    b. Political.
    c. Cultural.
    d. Competitive.
18. The first form of prospective payment system occurred in 1983 and had a significant influence on reimbursement and the development of programs that now employ many occupational therapists and occupational therapy assistants. That system is called
    a. Fee for service.
    b. Managed care.
    c. Diagnosis-related groups.
    d. Retrospective payment.
19. The AOTA noted that which of the following barriers can interfere with the success of the *Centennial Vision* statement?
    a. Continuation of the Medicare cap on outpatient services.
    b. Consumer confusion between occupational therapy and physical therapy.
    c. A rigid adherence to the status quo.
    d. Limited knowledge and use of technology by occupational therapy practitioners.
20. Which of the following reports used by managers to assess performance of therapy program services usually includes quick reference indicators of cost, revenue, client satisfaction, and quality outcomes for a given time period?
    a. Benchmark.
    b. Dashboard.
    c. Quality assurance.
    d. Productivity.

References

Accreditation Council for Occupational Therapy Education. (2007a). Accreditation standards for an educational program for the occupational therapy assistant. *American Journal of Occupational Therapy, 61,* 662–671.

Accreditation Council for Occupational Therapy Education. (2007b). Accreditation standards for a master's-degree-level educational program for the occupational therapist. *American Journal of Occupational Therapy, 61,* 652–661.

Alexander, I. (2007). Electronic medical records for the orthopaedic practice. *Clinical Orthopaedics and Related Research, 457,* 114–119.

American Occupational Therapy Association. (2002). Occupational therapy practice framework: Domain and process. *American Journal of Occupational Therapy, 56,* 609–639.

American Occupational Therapy Association. (2009). Guidelines for supervision, roles, and responsibilities during the delivery of occupational therapy services. *American Journal of Occupational Therapy, 63,* 797–803.

American Occupational Therapy Association. (2010). Occupational therapy code of ethics and ethics standards (2010). *American Journal of Occupational Therapy, 64.*

American Occupational Therapy Association. (2007). AOTA's *Centennial Vision* and executive summary. *American Journal of Occupational Therapy, 61,* 613–614.

American Occupational Therapy Association. (2008). Occupational therapy practice framework: Domain and process (2nd ed.). *American Journal of Occupational Therapy, 62,* 625–683.

Anthony, J. (2008). *Pros and cons of Six Sigma: An academic perspective.* Retrieved July 30, 2009, from http://www.improvement and innovation.com/features/articles/pros-and-cons-six-sigma-academic-perspective

Balanced Budget Act of 1997, Pub. L. 105-33, 111 Stat. 251.

Borkowski, N. (2009). Overview and history of organizational theory. In N. Borkowski (Ed.), *Organizational behavior, theory, and design in health care* (pp. 387–405). Sudbury, MA: Jones & Bartlett.

Buchbinder, S. B., & Thompson, J. M. (2010). *Career opportunities in health care management: Perspectives from the field.* Sudbury, MA: Jones & Bartlett.

Campbell, R. J. (2008). Change management in health care. *Health Care Manager, 27*(1), 23–39.

Cohen, M. E., & Kearney, P. J. (2005). Use of evaluation data to support evidence-based practice. In J. Hinojosa, P. Kramer, & P. Crist (Eds.), *Evaluation: Obtaining and interpreting data* (2nd ed., pp. 263–281). Bethesda, MD: AOTA Press.

Education for All Handicapped Children Act of 1975, Pub. L. 94-142, 20 U.S.C. § 1400 *et seq.*

Greenwood, A. (1997). Leadership for change. *Nursing Standard, 11*(19), 22–24.

Guo, K. L. (2009). Core competencies of the entrepreneurial leader in health care organizations. *Health Care Manager, 28*(1), 19–29.

Hanson, Y., & Honey, S. (2008). Essential steps to safe, clean care: The process of managing change. *British Journal of Infection Control, 9*(6), 10–14.

Ilott, I. (2003). Challenging the rhetoric and reality: Only an individual and systematic approach will work for evidence-based occupational therapy. *American Journal of Occupational Therapy, 57,* 351–354.

Individuals with Disabilities Education Act of 1990, Pub. L. 101-476, 20 U.S.C. 33.

Jamison, S., & Wooden, J. (1997). *Wooden: A lifetime of observations and reflections on and off the court.* New York: McGraw-Hill Books.

Joint Commission. (2004). *Cost-effective performance improvement in hospitals.* Oakbrook Terrace, IL: Joint Commission Resources.

Kantor, S., Kram, K. E., & Sala, F. (2008). Change factor: Making the case for executive adaptability. *Leadership in Action, 27*(6), 8–12.

Lawler, E. E., & Worley, C. G. (2009). Designing organizations that are built to change. In F. Hesselbein & M. Goldsmith (Eds.), *The organization of the future 2* (pp. 188–202). San Francisco: Jossey-Bass.

Longest, B. B., Rakich, J. S., & Darr, K. (2000). *Managing health services organizations and systems* (4th ed.). Baltimore: Health Professions Press.

Mackenzie, M. L. (2007). Leadership in the Information Age: A culture of continual change. *Bulletin of the American Society for Information Science and Technology, 33*(4), 10–13.

MacPhee, M. (2007). Strategies and tools for managing change. *Journal of Nursing Administration, 37*(9), 405–413.

Marquis, B. L., & Huston, C. J. (2003). *Leadership roles and management functions in nursing—Theory and application* (4th ed.). Philadelphia: Lippincott Williams & Wilkins.

Maxwell, P. D. (2009). Resistance to change and change management. In N. Borkowski (Ed.), *Organizational behavior, theory, and design in health care* (pp. 355–382). Sudbury, MA: Jones & Bartlett.

Nanof, T. (2009). Keeping the habilitation in and out of rehabilitation. *OT Practice, 14*(21), 6.

Patient Protection and Affordable Care Act of 2010, Pub. L. 111-148.

Plastow, N. A. (2006). Implementing evidence-based practice: A model for change. *International Journal of Therapy and Rehabilitation, 13*, 464-469.

Quiroga, V. A. M. (1995). *Occupational therapy: The first 30 years—1900 to 1930.* Bethesda, MD: American Occupational Therapy Association.

Ritchie, J. (2007). The health-care climate: Managing the change. *International Journal of Therapy and Rehabilitation, 14*(8), 342.

Snee, R. O., & Hoerl, R. W. (2003). *Leading Six Sigma: A step-by-step guide based on experience with GE and other Six Sigma companies.* Upper Saddle River, NJ: Pearson Education.

Stefl, M. E. (2008). Common competencies for all healthcare managers: The healthcare leadership alliance model. *Journal of Healthcare Management, 53*, 360–374.

Swinth, Y. L. (2003). Educational activities. In E. B. Crepeau, E. S. Cohn, & B. A. B. Schell (Eds.), *Willard and Spackman's occupational therapy* (10th ed., pp. 347–354). Philadelphia: Lippincott Williams & Wilkins.

Taylor, M. C. (1997). What is evidence-based practice? *British Journal of Occupational Therapy, 60*, 470–474.

U.S. Department of Health and Human Services. (2010). *Understanding the Affordable Care Act.* Retrieved July 22, 2010, from http://www.healthcare.gov/law/introduction/index.html

Walton, M. (1986). *The Deming management method.* New York: Dodd, Mead.

West, W. (1968). Professional responsibility in times of change (Eleanor Clarke Slagle Lecture). *American Journal of Occupational Therapy, 22*, 9–15.

Whitlock, J. (2009). Transformational change and development. In J. A. Johnson (Ed.), *Health organizations: Theory, behavior, and development* (pp. 291–310). Sudbury, MA: Jones & Bartlett.

Willard, H. S., & Spackman, C. S. (1947). *Principles of occupational therapy.* Philadelphia: J. B. Lippincott.

APPENDIX 27.A. MANAGING ORGANIZATIONAL CHANGE EVIDENCE TABLE

Topic	Evidence
Common management competencies	Stefl, M. E. (2008). Common competencies for all healthcare managers: The healthcare leadership alliance model. *Journal of Healthcare Management, 53,* 360–374.
Core competencies for entrepreneurial leadership	Guo, K. L. (2009). Core competencies of the entrepreneurial leader in health care organizations. *Health Care Manager, 28*(1), 19–29.
Executive adaptability	Kantor, S., Kram, K. E., & Sala, F. (2008). Change factor: Making the case for executive adaptability. *Leadership in Action, 27*(6), 8–12.
Health care climate and change	Ritchie, J. (2007). The health-care climate: Managing the change. *International Journal of Therapy and Rehabilitation, 14*(8), 342.
Resistance to change	Maxwell, P. D. (2009). Resistance to change and change management. In N. Borkowski (Ed.), *Organizational behavior, theory, and design in health care* (pp. 355–382). Sudbury, MA: Jones & Bartlett.

Part V

Public Policy, Professional Standards, and Collaboration

28

Federal Legislative Advocacy

Amy Lamb, OTD, OTR/L; Melissa Meier, OTD, OTR; and Christina Metzler

❖ Key Terms and Concepts

Advocacy. The act of speaking up, or pleading the case of another.

Amendment. A change or a proposed change to the text of a bill or law.

Appropriation. The provision of funds through an annual appropriations act or a permanent law for federal agencies to make payments out of the Treasury for specified purposes.

Authorization. A law that establishes or continues one or more federal agencies or programs, sets the terms and conditions under which they operate, authorizes the enactment of appropriations, and specifies how appropriated funds can be used.

Bill. A proposed law that addresses either matters of general interest (**public bill**) or narrow interest (**private bill**), such as individual immigration cases or private claims against the federal government.

Budget resolution. A concurrent resolution that sets forth the congressional budget, which establishes various budget totals, divides spending totals into functional categories, and may include reconciliation instructions to designated House or Senate committees.

Caucus. An informal organization of senators or representatives created to discuss issues of mutual concern. Caucuses can be organized based on regional, political or ideological, ethnic, or economic issues.

Cloture. A procedure by which the Senate can vote to limit debate in order to move to a vote. It is used to overcome a filibuster. Under cloture, the Senate may limit consideration of a pending matter to 30 additional hours if three-fifths of the full Senate (normally 60 votes) concurs.

Committees. Subsidiary organizations of the House and the Senate established for the purpose of considering legislation, conducting hearings and investigations, or carrying out other assignments as instructed by the House or Senate.

Conference committee. A committee that is established with members of both chambers specifically named to work out differences between same-subject bills passed by both

chambers. Any compromise reached must be approved by the full Senate and House.

Continuing resolution. A joint resolution enacted by Congress to provide budget authority for federal agencies and programs to continue in operation until the regular appropriations acts are enacted.

Earmark. A specific section added to a bill or law (usually an appropriations bill or law) by a member of Congress to specify funds for a particular purpose, bypassing Executive Branch merit-based or competitive allocation processes or otherwise limiting the ability of the Executive Branch to manage aspects of funds allocation.

Expenditures. The actual spending of money (rather than the permission to spend given in appropriation bills). The executive branch makes expenditures; Congress votes appropriations. The two are rarely identical in any fiscal year, because expenditures often represent money appropriated in previous years.

Filibuster. An informal term used in the Senate to describe an attempt to block or delay action on a bill or other matter by lengthy debate, numerous procedural motions, or other obstructive actions. It can be stopped only by a three-fifths cloture vote of the senators present and voting.

Hold. An informal practice used in the Senate by which a senator informs his or her floor leader that he or she does not wish a particular bill or other measure to reach the floor for consideration. The majority leader need not follow the senator's wishes but understands that the opposing senator could filibuster any motion to consider the measure.

Joint committee. Permanently established committees that include members from both chambers of Congress. Joint committees usually are established with narrow jurisdictions and normally lack authority to report legislation but rather provide a forum for discussion of particular issues. Chairmanship usually alternates between the House and Senate members from Congress to Congress.

Majority leader. The leader of the majority party in either the House or the Senate. In the House, the Majority Leader is second in command to the Speaker. In the Senate, the Majority Leader and Minority Leader serve as the chief representatives for their parties and manage and schedule the legislative and executive business of the Senate.

Mark up. The process by which congressional committees and subcommittees debate, amend, and rewrite proposed legislation in a section-by-section review.

Minority leader. The leader of the minority party in either the House or the Senate. In the Senate, the Majority Leader and Minority Leader serve as the chief speakers for their parties and manage and schedule the legislative and executive business of the Senate.

Oversight. Committee review of the activities of a federal agency or program.

Ranking member. Member of the majority party on a committee who ranks first in seniority after the chairman or chairwoman.

Ranking minority member. Member of a committee who has the highest rank on the minority party's side.

Report. A committee's written record of its actions and views on a bill. Committee reports discuss and explain the purpose of measures and contain other related information. The term also may refer to the action taken by a committee to submit its recommendations to the House or the Senate.

Resolution. A formal statement of a decision or opinion by the House or Senate or both. A **simple resolution** is made by one chamber and generally deals with that chamber's rules or prerogatives. A **concurrent resolution** is presented in both chambers and usually expresses a congressional view on a matter not within congressional jurisdiction. A **joint**

resolution requires approval in both chambers and goes to the president for approval. Simple and concurrent resolutions do not go to the president.

Roll-call vote. Senators vote as their names are called by the clerk. Representatives electronically record their votes. Each House member has a card to insert at voting stations and a running count of votes is displayed. Roll-call votes and recorded teller votes are the only votes for which a public record is made of how individual members of Congress voted.

Speaker of the House of Representatives. The individual elected by the House to preside over the House of Representatives. Each party usually puts forward a candidate for Speaker for the vote before the entire House. No member is obligated to vote for any candidate. Typically, the majority party's candidate wins in a House vote. The person who holds this post is third in line of succession to the U.S. presidency after the Vice President.

Table. A motion that seeks to put aside a bill and remove it from consideration. Adopting a motion to table eliminates any possibility a bill will be enacted.

Veto. A President's refusal to approve a bill or joint resolution, preventing its enactment into law. A veto can be overturned only by a two-thirds vote in both the Senate and the House.

Whip. Assistants to the floor leaders who are elected by their party conferences. The Majority Whip and Minority Whip (and their assistants) are responsible for mobilizing votes within their parties on major issues. In the absence of a party floor leader, the whip often serves as acting floor leader.

❖ Learning Objectives

After completing this chapter, you should be able to do the following:

- Articulate the role of the policy process in occupational therapy practice.
- Identify ways an occupational therapy manager can

encourage and foster a policy-aware environment with staff therapists.
- Develop an advocacy action plan.

Political ability is the ability to foretell what is going to happen tomorrow, next week, next month, and next year. And to have the ability afterwards to explain why it didn't happen.

—Winston Churchill (1874–1965, as cited in Giuliani, 2003)

Management brings with it a variety of hats for occupational therapy practitioners to wear. This chapter focuses

on the advocacy hat and identifies ways that occupational therapy managers can facilitate advocacy within the department, facility, or program in an effort to affect clients, the program itself, and the entire occupational therapy profession. While the focus of this chapter is on occupational therapy mangers, many of the principles described will be applicable for rehabilitation department or program managers who are overseeing multiple disciplines as part of their role.

WHAT IS POLICY?

Policy expressed in federal, state, and local law in many ways drives the health care system, the education system, and other social systems. Policy affects access to services, the quality of care we receive, and how much we will pay to receive care (Weissert & Weissert, 2002). All of this ultimately affects the state of society's health and, in the long run, people's lifespan and quality of life.

Health care and education policies have answered the following questions:

- Who is and is not eligible for government subsidized services?
- If an individual is eligible for government subsidies, what share does he or she pay, and what is paid by government?
- Which types of services and procedures are covered?
- Who can deliver care and receive reimbursement for service delivery?
- What happens when a person needs care but does not have the money to pay for it?
- Who receives financial assistance with medical training?
- What can and cannot health care professionals do for patients?
- How wide does a doorway on a hospital bathroom need to be?
- Can children with disabilities obtain a free, appropriate public education?

Each question has been answered by laws and the regulations that stipulate how those laws are carried out. From this list it is easy to see why it is important for occupational therapy practitioners to speak up and weigh in on these important issues, as they directly affect practice and clients.

THE POLICY PROCESS

In the policy process, there are a multitude of players weighing in on the issues and of targets of advocacy efforts for occupational therapy. At the federal level, the three primary entities are Congress, the President, and special interest groups. Executive Branch agencies are also involved in the policy process.

U.S. Congress

The U.S. Congress is a bicameral system (consisting of two separate chambers) important for policy making, as it allows for checks and balances as well as distinct opportunities for advocacy. Congress is made up of the House of Representatives and the Senate. The House of Representatives has 435 members. The membership number in the House is stable, but distribution is in flux among states, with each state's delegation being based on population numbers from the most recent Census of the Population. The Senate has 100 members and also is a stable membership number; each of the 50 states has 2 senators regardless of population.

Congress is organized by political parties and has its own internal leadership. The majority party selects the Speaker of the House and the Majority Leader of the Senate, who then proceed to make the decisions on the process of each chamber, such as what bills will have hearings, the schedule of those hearings, committee membership, which committees hear what bills, who sits on conference committees to resolve differences between House and Senate legislation, and more. The House of Representatives leadership is composed of the Speaker of the House, the Majority Leader, the Minority Leader, and party whips. The Senate leadership consists of the Majority Leader, the Minority Leader, and party whips. In general, the *whips* in both the House and Senate mobilize party members behind legislative positions that the leadership has decided are in the party's best interest and track counts of members' positions prior to the vote (Weissert & Weissert, 2002). The Vice President of the United States, under the Constitution, presides over the Senate, but usually senators sit in as President of the Senate.

Congress can function largely because of committees, the workhorses that hold hearings, make recommendations and amendments, and support their product on the floor (see Exhibit 28.1). The House and Senate have separate committees that hold hearings and vote on legislation within their jurisdiction, marking up bills to allow them to proceed to a full vote on the House or Senate floor. After a piece of legislation has passed both the House and Senate, if there are differences in the bills, a conference committee is appointed to work out the differences and come to consensus on one piece of legislation to be approved by both chambers and be forwarded to the President for signature (see Exhibit 28.2).

President and Executive Branch

The President has two roles in policy making: first in setting the agenda and second in letting Congress know what he or she would like to see passed into law. He or she also takes the initiatives public to get constituent support. Finally, the President uses his or her political capital (e.g., stature, accomplishments, popularity with the public) to put pressure on Congress via their constituents to ac-

EXHIBIT. 28.1. KEY CONGRESSIONAL COMMITTEES FOR OCCUPATIONAL THERAPY

- Senate Committee on Finance
- House Ways and Means Committee
- House Education and Labor Committee
- Senate Committee on Health, Education, Labor and Pensions
- House Energy and Commerce Committee
- Senate Committee on Appropriations
- House Appropriations Committee
- Senate Committee on the Budget
- House Budget Committee
- House Rules Committee

EXHIBIT 28.2. HOW A BILL BECOMES A LAW

Any Member of Congress can introduce a piece of legislation, and many ideas come from constituents in the districts they represent (Reich, 1988).

Members in the House of Representatives introduce legislation by giving a copy of the intended legislation to the Clerk of the House. Senators must gain recognition of the presiding officer to announce the introduction of a bill. After introduction in either house, a bill is assigned a number (e.g., H.R. 1111, S. 1), is labeled with the sponsors' names, and is sent to the U.S. Government Printing office for copying.

After introduction, the bill is referred to the committee with jurisdiction. This committee may request information from government agencies or others regarding the bill, can assign bills to a subcommittee, and can hold hearings. After a subcommittee reports their findings and "marks" a version of the bill to the full committee, there is a full committee vote. A committee can hold a "mark-up" session during which they can make revisions and additions (i.e., putting their "mark" on the bill).

After a committee approves a bill, it is sent to the appropriate chamber and placed on the legislative calendar. In the House, bills are placed on one of the four House calendars. The Speaker of the House and the Majority Leader decide what will reach the floor and when. In the Senate, legislation is placed on the legislative calendar, and the scheduling of legislation is the job of the Majority Leader. After a bill is advanced from the calendar it goes to the floor for debate. In the House, debate is limited by the rules formulated in the Rules Committee. Debate on the floor is guided by the committee with jurisdiction, and time is divided equally between proponents and opponents. The committee with jurisdiction decides how much time to allot to each person. After debate, the bill is reported back to the House and voted on. A quorum of members (218) must be present to hold a final vote.

In the Senate, debate is unlimited unless *cloture*—a vote by two-thirds to finalize debate on a bill—is invoked. Members may speak as long as they want. Entire bills can be offered as amendments to other bills in most circumstances. Unless cloture is invoked, Senators can use a filibuster to defeat a measure.

Once the floor vote occurs, whether in the House or the Senate, if passed the bill is then sent to the other chamber. If neither chamber passes the bill, then it dies at the end of each two-year Congress. If the House and Senate pass the same bill, it advances to the President.

If the House and Senate pass different bills, as is the case with most major legislation, the bills are sent to a conference committee formed for that particular legislation. In conference committee, members from each chamber meet to work out the differences. The committee is usually made up of senior members who are usually appointed by the leaders of the committees that originally handled the bill. If the committee reaches a compromise, it prepares a written report that is submitted to each chamber and must be approved by both. After passage by both chambers, the bill is then sent to the President for review.

A bill becomes a law when signed by the President. The President also can veto a bill and send it back to Congress. A bill may become law if the President does not veto and does not sign the bill within 10 days and Congress remains in session during that time. If Congress adjourns before the 10 days and the President has not formally vetoed or signed the bill, the bill does not become law (a *pocket veto*).

Note. For an engaging (and pop-culture) overview of how a bill becomes a law, see Frishberg (1975).

complish the items on the agenda. The President also directs the federal agencies—the Executive Branch of the government—such as the U.S. Department of Education (DoE), the U.S. Department Health and Human Services (DHHS), and the U.S. Department of Justice.

Regulatory agencies in the Executive Branch have public administrators and presidential appointees who have a large impact on policy development. They are responsible for implementation of what Congress directs in the language of a law and often are responsible for taking vague laws passed by Congress and establishing the rules and regulations to make them into programs that run (Weissert & Weissert, 2002).

In the federal government, the primary and most commonly known health agency is the DHHS, which encompasses numerous subagencies that coordinate, plan, implement, and oversee health policy in the United States. Many of these agencies have a direct impact on occupational therapy practice, including the

- Centers for Medicare and Medicaid Services (CMS), whose rules and regulations provide guidelines for Medicare reimbursement, Medicaid programs, and more; CMS originated the diagnostic-related groups (DRGs) in the 1980s to increase efficiency in Medicare payments to acute hospitals;

- National Institutes of Health (NIH), which has 28 institutes, centers, and offices within it and is a key agency for evidence-based practice and research in health care quality and effectiveness;
- Agency for Healthcare Research and Quality (AHRQ), which is the lead federal agency charged with improving the quality, safety, efficiency, and effectiveness of health care in the United States; and
- DoE, which develops rules for programs such as those under the Individuals with Disabilities Education Improvement Act (IDEA, P.L. 101-476).

Special Interest Groups and Political Actions Committees

Special interest groups play a large role in policy making. Insurance companies, physicians, pharmaceutical companies, nurses, and occupational therapy practitioners weigh in on the issues with Congress and mobilize their memberships to share their views with their Members of Congress to accomplish their agenda. Special interest groups often employ lobbyists to represent the group on a daily basis and also use grassroots advocacy to get a message to their members, who in turn share their opinions with Members of Congress.

In conjunction with lobbyists and grassroots advocacy comes *political action committees (PACs)*, which are groups formed (as by an industry or an issue-oriented organization) to raise and contribute money to the campaigns of candidates likely to advance a particular group's interests ("Political Action Committee," n.d.).

Public policies emerge from the public demand for action or for inaction. In many cases, Members of Congress gauge the demand for an issue on the basis of the level of advocacy. As more and more groups advocate for an issue, the discussions throughout the halls of Congress reflect this. For example, physicians advocate for increased payment through the Medicare system to be able to appropriately manage the complex conditions of the elderly population. Their demand is reflected in their direct advocacy efforts and their support for candidates who support their position. Likewise, occupational therapy professionals advocate for their profession and their clients in the same way to demonstrate the demand for occupational therapy services and to show the value that occupational therapy brings to society. To help prevent negative policy consequences, such as the outpatient therapy cap (see below), it is important that experts in health care, education, and research, including occupational therapy practitioners, speak up and be heard when such a policy is being debated.

Why Is Advocacy Important for Occupational Therapy Practice?

Although occupational therapy is an integral part of the ever-changing health care system, occupational therapists and occupational therapy assistants are consistently challenged as a profession to maintain an existence. Occupational therapy is constantly under the microscope of the reimbursement system, which is always examining the effectiveness of services to determine if payment is justified. Occupational therapy managers and practitioners often are placed in a position of advocating for clients as well as the profession to ensure the continued survival of occupational therapy's role in health care, education, and other systems.

Occupational therapy is a science-driven, evidence-based profession that enables people of all ages to live life to its fullest by helping them promote health and prevent—or live better with—illness, injury, or disability (AOTA, 2009). Without occupational therapy intervention, countless clients would not be as independent and successful in their daily lives as they are today. Now, more than ever in the dynamic U.S. social care system, occupational therapy must make advocacy a focal point to ensure that future generations of clients and colleagues will have access to occupational therapy.

LANDMARK LEGISLATION AFFECTING OCCUPATIONAL THERAPY PRACTICE

Much of occupational therapy exists today only as a result of the advocacy efforts throughout the profession's history. Certain pieces of legislation, discussed below, have been very influential in the practice of occupational therapy as well as in the rights of our clients to receive our services.

Education for All Handicapped Children Act of 1975 and Individuals with Disabilities Education Act

In 1975, Congress passed the Education for All Handicapped Children Act (P.L. 94-142), which required all public schools accepting federal funds to provide equal access to education for children with physical and mental disabilities. Public schools were required to evaluate students with disabilities and create an educational plan with parent input that would emulate as closely as possible the educational experience of students without disabilities. This landmark legislation made a place for occupational therapy in the school and assisted in the reimbursement for such services.

This act was a precursor to IDEA of 1990, which expanded the reach of "special education" beyond children ages 3 to 21 to ensure the availability of occupational therapy services for infants, toddlers, and preschool children (Jackson, 2007). IDEA, which was the impetus for occupational therapy's role in education, is continually evolving, as is the practice of occupational therapy for children and families with disabilities.

Medicare Part B

Medicare has undergone many changes since its inception in 1965. Perhaps one of the most notable in recent years was the 1987 provision to cover occupational therapy as a free-standing service under Medicare Part B. This provision led to a demand for occupational therapy professionals in various rehabilitation settings (Institute of Medicine,

1989). The ability to access Medicare Part B reimbursement for occupational therapy services transformed practice over the years, particularly as occupational therapy services were provided in skilled nursing facilities (SNFs) to residents in long-term care. This change also allowed for the establishment of occupational therapy private practices, providing more independence and economic flexibility to the profession.

Americans with Disabilities Act of 1990

The Americans with Disabilities Act of 1990 (ADA, P.L. 101-336) was a landmark law changing the way in which society viewed people with disabilities. The ADA was the first comprehensive civil rights law for individuals with disabilities. Social attitudes about health, disease, and disability have, as a result of the ADA, dramatically changed. This legislation has affected the profession of occupational therapy and its clients by requiring attention to accessibility of facilities and programs, by promoting accommodations to enable employment, and by increasing supports for independent living.

Health Insurance Portability and Accountability Act of 1996

The Health Insurance Portability and Accountability Act of 1996 (HIPAA, P.L. 104-191) protects health insurance coverage for workers and their families when they change or lose their jobs. It also required the establishment of national standards for electronic health care transactions and national identifiers for health providers, insurance plans, and employers. The perhaps better-known piece of HIPAA addresses the security and privacy of health data (Green & Bowie, 2007). As health information technology has grown, the standards set forth by HIPAA have improved the security, efficiency, and effectiveness of the nation's health care system by promoting protections of privacy, especially as usage of an electronic data interchange has became more common.

Balanced Budget Act of 1997

The Balanced Budget Act of 1997 (BBA, P.L. 105-133) made significant changes to the Medicare program and to occupational therapy practice. With the BBA, Medicare adopted a new approach to payment for therapy services. Until that time, only private practitioner services were paid on the Medicare physician fee schedule (PFS) for Part B Medicare services. The congressional logic was that a fee schedule determined "prospectively," or ahead of time, what would be paid for therapy services. The coding system using *Current Procedural Terminology (CPT®;* see American Medical Association, 2010) also helped solve another problem: *CPT* codes allowed for identification of the services that were provided.

However, another "prospective" payment system also was instituted in this law and implemented in 1999: the skilled nursing home prospective payment system (SNF PPS). This system provided SNFs with payment based on the evaluation of patients and categorization of things such as need for therapy. SNFs were paid based on those patient characteristics. Previously, SNFs had been paid directly for the services they provided, incentivizing some overutilization.

A third change in the 1997 law became a notorious policy: the cap on outpatient therapy. Under this system, outpatient rehabilitation services—occupational therapy, physical therapy, and speech therapy—were limited by an annual monetary cap. A mandatory limit was set for $1,500 for physical and speech therapy and a separate $1,500 for occupational therapy. The cap became a rallying cry for change because it had a direct impact on beneficiaries. Over the years, advocacy efforts by professional associations, patient groups, and grassroots activities have been successful in preventing full implementation of the cap. In 2010, an exception process is still in place while several studies supported by the CMS are developing alternatives to assure the provision of appropriate therapy as well as manage costs.

Patient Protection and Affordable Care Act of 2010

The recently enacted Patient Protection and Affordable Care Act (P.L. 111-148, "health care reform," 2010) will guide the development of the health care service system for many years and will provide many new opportunities for occupational therapy while addressing some of the profession's long-standing challenges.

Mandatory Rehabilitation and Habilitation Benefits

The act explicitly includes both rehabilitation and habilitation services in the mandatory benefits package under the reformed health care system. This inclusion recognizes the importance of these services, including occupational therapy, and will reduce historic denials of coverage for occupational therapy deemed habilitative.

Occupational Therapy Workforce Provisions

Occupational therapy is specifically listed in all workforce sections of the bill, providing occupational therapy practitioners with elevated recognition. This inclusion allows occupational therapy practitioners to compete for new training and education grant programs to be developed by the federal government to address future health care workforce issues.

Physician Quality Reporting Initiative

The act extends through 2014 payments under the Physician Quality Reporting Initiative (PQRI) program, which provides incentives to providers, including occupational therapists, who report quality data to Medicare. The act creates appeals and feedback processes for participating professionals in PQRI. Beginning in 2014, physicians and other eligible providers who do not submit measures to PQRI will have their Medicare payments reduced.

Insurance Market Reforms

Starting in 2010 and ending by 2014, states must establish health insurance exchanges through which individuals or employers, who are required to have health coverage by that time, can purchase health insurance through a regulated system intended to increase availability to people currently uninsured and keep costs under control. The reforms include other important insurance-related provisions such as the elimination of discrimination based on health status, a prohibition on exclusions on the basis of preexisting conditions (including an implementation of an immediate ban on exclusions for children), establishment of high-risk pools, guaranteed issue and renewal requirements, elimination of rescission of benefits except in the case of fraud or misrepresentation, and elimination of annual and lifetime caps.

Medicare Post-Acute Care Bundling Pilot

A pilot program of methods to address rehospitalization rates within a 30-day period following an acute hospital stay will be established.

Community Living Assistance Services and Supports

The act includes the Community Living Assistance Services and Supports (CLASS), a new actuarially sound, premium-based, optional national long-term services insurance program to help adults with severe functional impairments remain independent, employed, and a part of their communities, without having to impoverish themselves to become eligible for Medicaid. Individuals may voluntarily opt out of this program.

Wellness

The act establishes an annual wellness visit under Medicare, which would identify prevention needs of beneficiaries and make referrals to needed services. Medicare copayments for preventive services have been eliminated. The act authorizes an appropriation to give employees of small businesses access to comprehensive workplace wellness programs that are evidence-based and consistent with best practices.

Patient Protections

The act includes patient protections requiring plans to allow enrollees to select their primary care provider from any available participating primary care provider (e.g., pediatrician, gerontologist), as well as precludes the need for prior authorization or increased cost-sharing for emergency services, whether provided by in-network or out-of-network providers. The law also includes provider nondiscrimination language to prevent health plans from restricting practice.

System Redesign

The law includes options and pilot programs to be established and tested under Medicare or Medicaid to improve the response of the health care system to the need for more appropriate, better-monitored care, including chronic care coordination, the establishment of accountable care organizations, and an Independence at Home project to provide primary care in the home.

Community Health Centers

A total of $15 billion of increased funding from the Public Health Trust fund has been given for 1,200 community health centers across all 50 states and territories.

Mental Health Coverage

The law includes mental health and substance abuse services under the required benefits category for all new health plans under the reformed system.

Preventive Health Coverage

The act requires all existing and future health care plans to cover preventive services and immunizations recommended by the U.S. Preventive Services Task Force and the Centers for Disease Control and Prevention, as well as certain child preventive services recommended by the Health Resources and Services Administration, without any cost-sharing.

Expanded Medicaid Eligibility

Medicaid eligibility has been expanded to 133% of the federal poverty level. The act also provides increased federal funding to states to cover the additional costs through 2016, with a gradual return to state responsibility after that. Mandatory coverage has been expanded to childless adults under the specified poverty level for the first time. The act extends Early, Periodic, Screening, Diagnosis, and Treatment (EPSDT) mandates to all children on Medicaid, including those in managed care. EPSDT mandates Medicaid coverage of services to address developmental disabilities and delays and includes occupational therapy services.

Independent Medicare Advisory Board

The law creates an independent board to control per capita Medicare spending. This 15-member panel, appointed by the President with the advice and consent of the Senate, would be tasked with recommending reductions in spending to reach target growth rates during its 6-year term. The board's recommendations would be binding unless Congress enacted legislation to restrict their implementation.

Medicare and Medicaid Innovation Center

The act creates a new Center for Medicare and Medicaid Innovation (CMI) under the CMS. The purpose of the CMI is to test innovative payment and service delivery models to reduce program expenditure under the applicable titles while preserving or enhancing the quality of care. This CMI will have authority to conduct a study of the impact of direct access to outpatient services on costs, quality, and access. Occupational therapy is eligible for this study.

Comparative Effectiveness Research
A federal coordinating council will be responsible for the annual funding of comparative effectiveness research. A patient-centered outcomes research institute will develop national comparative effectiveness research priorities and will conduct clinical outcomes research.

Health Information Technology
The act creates health information technology enrollment standards and protocols and provides funding for implementation of these protocols.

Summary

The effects of three policy changes—the Medicare fee schedule, the SNF PPS, and the therapy cap—are perhaps the most recent examples of how legislation affects occupational practice. SNFs, rehabilitation agencies, and hospitals reduced therapy staff, changed service protocols, and cut expenditures during 1998 to be ready for the changes that were implemented in 1999. However, by the early 2000s, occupational therapy jobs increased and salaries rose. According to AOTA's 2006 *Workforce and Compensation Survey,* occupational therapist salaries in SNFs went from $50,000 in 1997 to $46,000 in 2000 and up to $58,000 by 2006. Salaries have continued to increase, and by 2009, the median salary for occupational therapists was $64,700 (AOTA, 2010).

Occupational therapy managers and practitioners should be able to articulate how Medicare, the BBA, IDEA, or health care reform has and will affect their practice, their clients, and the profession. It is because of this intimate link between policy and practice that occupational therapy practitioners must develop their advocacy abilities and become confident leaders in the development of legislation and policy. Of equal importance is for the managers of occupational therapy departments to understand how to facilitate such skills and abilities and promote involvement among their staff and occupational therapy students affiliated with their facility.

OCCUPATIONAL THERAPY ADVOCATES

Many practitioners do not see themselves as advocates but as people who simply want to help others establish, increase, regain, or maintain independence in their daily lives. In today's health care or education systems, this independence often includes helping clients identify ways to advocate for themselves and their needs, with practitioners often advocating on behalf of clients. Occupational therapy practitioners do not always see the link between this type of advocacy and advocacy for legislation with state and federal governments. Exhibit 28.3 offers a series of true-or-false questions to use to evaluate one's capacity to be a policy advocate.

Instilling passion in occupational therapy practitioners regarding policy often is as simple as demonstrating how they and their clients can be or are affected by proposed or

EXHIBIT 28.3. CAN YOU BE A POLICY ADVOCATE?

- Have you ever disagreed with a rule or policy?
- Are you willing to take a risk for change?
- Do you believe actions speak louder than words?
- Do you vent frustrations to coworker?
- Do you frequently find yourself explaining occupational therapy?

A "true" response to any of these questions means you have what it takes to serve as an advocate for occupational therapy.

new legislation. The key is to provide multiple ways to be involved in advocacy efforts (Schein, 2004; see also Exhibit 28.4).

Encouraging Participation

How do occupational therapy managers encourage participation among staff in advocacy efforts? Many people are of the mindset that one person cannot make a difference in politics or policy. Recent elections have disproved that theory, as a handful of votes often can decide a local election and just 1 percentage point or less has decided recent congressional races, several of which have ended in legal challenges to the results.

Using a variety of methods to engage in advocacy is helpful to promote participation. Advocacy is not one size fits all, and different people will be comfortable with different levels of involvement at different times (Showalter, 2008). While this is not a comprehensive list of ways to encourage involvement, it provides a starting point in identifying strategies that will work for a particular department or staff person.

Policymakers listen to constituents more than paid representatives. They know that lobbyists are paid to put forth a particular position, but constituents taking time off from work or out of their busy lives to visit the office or call shows the importance of an issue to the Member of Congress. In-person visits and letters are doubled in their effectiveness when a follow-up phone call is made to the office, which stresses further the weight of an issue.

Being an AOTA member and a member of a state association is important, because those connections help people stay informed and maintain ownership in the profession. In addition, AOTA leadership and members periodically visit Capitol Hill to let Congress know of the profession's views, and they have provided examples of research to illustrate the effectiveness of the profession.

Providing testimony on issues relevant to areas of occupational therapy practice also is important, as occupational therapy practitioners are the experts in the practice of occupational therapy. Speaking before Congress may seem

Exhibit 28.4. Advocacy Dos and Don'ts

When getting involved in advocacy, occupational therapy managers can remember the following to increase their effectiveness as advocates for occupational therapy:

Do Establish Relationships—

Developing relationships with elected officials and their staff allows you to provide information on local or national issues and demonstrate your reputation for reliability as a knowledgeable person within the health care, education, or other system. Your provision of information builds a foundation for the Representative to be able to assist you in solving a problem, such as obtaining special grant funding, or signing on to a particular bill.

The first step is to call, e-mail, or visit the office of your Member of Congress and ask to speak with the person in charge of health, research, or education issues. From there introduce yourself, state that you are an occupational therapy professional from the district, and thank them for their public service. You can indicate that you have an interest in a current issue or that you just want to be made aware of the Member's activities in health care.

Your next call may include a request to support a particular issue. Or you may receive a call from the staff person to ask for information about a problem in the district or state.

As you continue on with your advocacy, you will talk to this staff member again, become known to him or her as a credible and authoritative source, and continue to expand the topics that you discuss. Such relationships are foundational to long-term advocacy success.

Some employers may restrict employee advocacy communication, but often you can, as a citizen, use your home as your base for advocacy. Check your employer's rules for advocacy if there is any question.

Do Know the Facts, and Be Specific—

Be specific about why you are contacting the Representative or staff, and know your facts. AOTA provides its members with brief fact sheets on the AOTA Legislative Action Center that discuss legislative issues of key importance to occupational therapy. Provide these fact sheets to the individuals you are meeting with, and focus your meeting on one or two topics, not every area of occupational therapy practice. It is important to communicate consistent messages so Members of Congress and their staff know the occupational therapy profession is well prepared, is knowledgeable, and can make a contribution to society.

Do Request Specific Action—

Your advocacy success is increased when you request specific action. Requesting specific action helps makes it clear what you are looking for and gives the Member or staff something to work from. Again, AOTA can be a great resource to practitioners to know what action to request.

Do Follow Up—

Thanking those with whom you met for their time is essential. Always exchange business cards and get the contact information for your follow-up call or e-mail. You also may consider inviting them to visit your facility on their next trip to the district. (Be sure to work first with the appropriate people in your facility.) Extending an invitation helps you open the door for the next opportunity for advocacy.

Do Not Assume Anything—

You cannot assume the individuals you are meeting with are familiar with your issues or even occupational therapy. Some of our issues, such as the Medicare therapy cap, have been around for quite some time and are known as a problem. However, other issues, such as occupational therapy's role in prevention and wellness, are not as well known. You can be the one to explain occupational therapy's role in those and other areas because you are the expert in your profession.

Do Not Say Too Much—

You also must avoid the urge to overload the Member of Congress and staff with written material or a large number of issues. Starting with the basic facts and then following up with additional documentation as requested is appropriate. Remember that your's will be one of many meetings on a variety of issues throughout the day. AOTA has identified priorities for legislative advocacy to help practitioners focus their opportunities.

Do Not Bluff—

Do not make up a response if you do not know an answer to a question. If you are wrong, it will only damage the credibility that you have worked so hard to establish. Instead, say that the question is important and that you will check into the answer and get back to them. Then do so.

intimidating in light of the high-profile hearings shown on television, but Members of Congress and legislators do listen to what occupational therapy professionals have to say in both their offices and in committee hearings. Even assisting the national or state association in drafting and reviewing testimony is helpful to paint the most accurate picture of occupational therapy practice.

Writing letters or sending e-mails to state and federal representatives about health or education issues, and relating them to their home district or state with examples, also is effective in advocating a perspective and can be done via the AOTA Legislative Action Center (see http://www .aota.org/Practitioners/Advocacy/Tools.aspx for more information).

Finally, keep up the communication. Tell staff and elected officials when you see something in the local paper or about special events or concerns in your community. The more you communicate, the more often you will come to mind when they have questions on health, education, or other issues.

Participating in PACs

Participating in PACs is another avenue for helping ensure that the profession has support to help move its policy agenda forward. However, PACs often are misunderstood and painted as part of the negative side of American politics. In reality, PACs are highly regulated and limited by federal and state laws, which cover daily operations and public reporting of funds collected and dispersed.

A PAC such as the American Occupational Therapy Association Political Action Committee (AOTPAC) can seize the opportunity to help elect the candidates who are supportive of occupational therapy's public policy agenda, which has been set by the association's members and elected leadership. AOTPAC has documented procedures that enable PAC board members to make carefully studied and well-informed decisions on which candidates to support and thus play an important role in protecting the interests of the organization.

Another benefit of PACs is that they can serve as important educational tools for elected officials. When candidates and incumbents appeal for money from, for example, AOTPAC, it means they want to learn more about the occupational therapy profession and those whom it serves.

Role Modeling Advocacy

The most effective strategy for encouraging participation in advocacy efforts is to be a role model (Flynn & Verma, 2008). For managers, a great way to do this is to invite your Member of Congress or his or her staff to visit your workplace when home on recess. Have him or her tour the department, meet your staff and the clients, and see occupational therapy firsthand. Be sure to get the support of the facility management, unless you own the business. This visit will be a win–win for you, your department, your facility, your profession, and the visiting officials.

CONCLUSION

Advocacy for occupational therapy is vital to the existence of the profession and essential to ensure that clients have access to occupational therapy services. Elected representatives enter office wanting to do what is right for their constituents. The profession must remember that it is generally up to occupational therapy practitioners to speak up about our own profession, what we offer to society, and how our services assist in increasing quality of life and reducing costs.

❖ Learning Activities

1. Create a 1-year advocacy plan. For example,
   - *January to March:* Examine overall legislation affecting occupational therapy practice.
     a. Become a member of AOTA and of your state association.
     b. Explore AOTA's Web site regarding specific legislative issues.
     c. Listen to podcasts by AOTA lobbyists at the Legislative Action Center.
   - *April to June:* Analyze 1 piece of current legislation affecting occupational therapy.
     a. Identify pros and cons for passage of the bill in relation to occupational therapy.
     b. Produce a fact sheet on an issue, and disseminate to local practitioners who would be affected by the legislation.
   - *July to September:* Integrate an advocacy component into your student occupational therapy organization or your workplace.
     a. Brainstorm advocacy ideas to be implemented into your organization or workplace.
     b. Implement a trial advocacy project into your organization or workplace during the upcoming year (e.g., AOTPAC fundraiser, campus occupational therapy promotion project).
   - *October to December:* Plan and organize a meeting with Members of Congress or local representatives.
     a. Compose a letter to a Member of Congress or local representative.
     b. Outline key issues to be discussed, and use evidence-based practice to support specific arguments.

2. Prepare a definition of occupational therapy for the following audiences, and provide specific examples of how occupational therapy can benefit them and the clients they serve.
   - Optometrists/ophthalmologists
   - Teachers/principals
   - Physicians
   - Physical therapists
   - Speech–language pathologists
   - Case managers
   - Nurses
   - Patients
   - Mental health practitioners
   - Legislators
   - Children and parents
   - Insurance companies
   - Various community sites (e.g., homeless shelter)
   - Various associations (e.g., American Heart Association, Alzheimer's Association).

3. Investigate specific legislation (e.g., BBA, IDEA), and identify how it directly affects occupational therapy. Write a persuasive paper, prepare a presentation, or develop a handout informing occupational therapy practitioners about one of the following issues:
   - Medicare Home Health Flexibility Act (H.R. 1094, 111th Congress)
   - Medicare Access to Rehabilitation Services Act (S.46/H.R 43, 111th Congress)
   - Medicare Independent Living Act (H.R. 3184, 111th Congress) of 2009
   - Medicare Telehealth Enhancement Act of 2009 (H.R. 2068, 111th Congress)
   - Mental Health Parity.

   (*Note.* Bill numbers change from one Congress to the next.)

4. Contact a Member of Congress about an issue affecting occupational therapy and its clients.
   Example:
   As a constituent and an occupational therapist, I am asking you to support inclusion of the purpose of H.R. 1094, to allow occupational therapy more opportunities in home health under Medicare, in the Manager's Amendment of health care reform as it moves to the floor in September. I understand action is needed immediately and hope you will express your support to the Chairs and Ranking Members of the appropriate Committees and to the House Leadership.

   The bill has no cost, has no opposition, and will help home health agencies in every district. The bill will allow occupational therapists to open home health cases and conduct initial assessments for Medicare home health patients. The provision is supported by the National Association for Home Care and Hospice, the American Occupational Therapy Association, the American Physical Therapy Association, and the American Speech–Language Hearing Association.

   Please express your support for the inclusion of this provision today.
   Sincerely,
   [Insert Name]

5. Prepare an agenda for an effective lobby visit with an elected representative or his or her staff (adapted from http://www.aota.org/Students/Advocate/HillDay/40498.aspx).
   Example:
   Target: 30 minutes maximum
   a. *Introductions of all present*—Briefly give your name, where you live, and where you work. State that you are a representative for AOTA and a constituent.
   b. *Statement of issues*—Mention what overall issue you wish to discuss (e.g., health care reform, education). Tell why it is important to you (e.g., what kind of work you do, the type of individuals you work with, the situation as you see it). State why it is important to your audience (e.g., what impact it has in his or her district).
   c. *Highlight particular issues*—Detail 2 or 3 (at most) critical issues you think he or she may be interested in or in which you have expertise or experience. Make your arguments with personal stories, which helps an audience understand the personal side of an issue.
   d. *Ask for your audience's position on the issue*—Determine their views, and ask if they can support AOTA's position.
   e. *Thank everyone for their time*—Tell them that you would like to continue a dialogue on the issue; ask if you may write or call on the issue in the future. Ask to be on their mailing list for health, education, or other events in the district or state. Leave them the packet of information.

✓ Multiple-Choice Questions

1. Which question has been answered by health care policy?
   a. What can and cannot health care professionals do for patients?
   b. Who is and is not eligible for subsidized care?
   c. What share does an individual pay?
   d. All of the above.
2. The Senate has how many members?
   a. 50.
   b. 100.

    c.   435.
    d.   425.

3. The House has how many members?
    a.   50.
    b.   100.
    c.   435.
    d.   425.

4. Congress is organized by
    a.   Geographic zones.
    b.   The President.
    c.   The Vice President.
    d.   Political parties.

5. The Speaker of the House is selected by the
    a.   Majority party.
    b.   President.
    c.   Entire House of Representatives.
    d.   Minority party.

6. The Vice President presides over
    a.   The House of Representatives.
    b.   The Senate.
    c.   Congress.
    d.   All of the above.

7. The role of congressional committees is to
    a.   Hold hearings.
    b.   Make recommendations and amendments.
    c.   Support their product on the floor.
    d.   All of the above.

8. The President's role in policy making includes
    a.   Setting the agenda.
    b.   Holding hearings on the issues.
    c.   Employing lobbyists to advocate for special interest groups.
    d.   All of the above.

9. The Individuals with Disabilities Education Act
    a.   Expanded the availability of occupational therapy services for infants, toddlers, and preschool children and maintained services for students up to age 21.
    b.   Made significant changes to the Medicare program.
    c.   Is the first comprehensive civil rights law for individuals with disabilities.
    d.   All of the above.

10. The Americans with Disabilities Act
    a.   Helped ensure the availability of occupational therapy services for infants, toddlers, and preschool children.
    b.   Made significant changes to the Medicare program.
    c.   Was the first comprehensive civil rights law for individuals with disabilities.
    d.   All of the above.

11. The Balanced Budget Act
    a.   Helped ensure the availability of occupational therapy services for infants, toddlers, and preschool children.

    b.   Made significant changes to the Medicare program.
    c.   Was the first comprehensive civil rights law for individuals with disabilities.
    d.   All of the above.

12. Occupational therapy practitioners should participate in advocacy because
    a.   Their job depends on it.
    b.   Policymakers listen to constituents.
    c.   Appropriate policies protect consumers' access to services.
    d.   All of the above.

13. Advocacy can occur
    a.   By writing letters and e-mails.
    b.   By in-person visits in the district office or in Washington, DC.
    c.   Over the phone.
    d.   All of the above.

14. A group formed (as by an industry or an issue-oriented organization) to raise and contribute money to the campaigns of candidates likely to advance the group's interests is more commonly known as a
    a.   Congressional committee.
    b.   Political action committee.
    c.   Professional association.
    d.   Presidential forum.

15. When meeting with Members of Congress
    a.   Talk about as much as possible in 15 minutes.
    b.   Bring a binder of information.
    c.   Provide a fact sheet on 1–2 issues.
    d.   Say that if he or she does not support you, you will not vote for him or her.

16. Advocacy dos include
    a.   Establish credibility.
    b.   Request specific action.
    c.   Follow up.
    d.   All of the above.

17. All Members of Congress and their staff know about
    a.   Medicare Home Health Flexibility Act (H.R. 1094).
    b.   Medicare Access to Rehabilitation Services Act (S. 46/H.R. 43).
    c.   Medicare Independent Living Act (H.R. 3184) of 2009.
    d.   Do not assume they know about your issues.

18. Regulatory agencies
    a.   Propose budgets.
    b.   Interpret laws.
    c.   Supervise implementation of laws.
    d.   All of the above.

19. Special interest groups include
    a.   The American Occupational Therapy Association.
    b.   Congress.
    c.   The President.
    d.   All of the above.

20. The purpose of a bicameral design in Congress is to
    a. Have more people in office.
    b. Ensure representation of states as well as individuals.
    c. Create interesting discussion.
    d. All of the above.

References

American Medical Association. (2010). *Current procedural terminology (CPT)*. Chicago: Author.

American Occupational Therapy Association. (2006). *2006 AOTA workforce and compensation survey*. Bethesda, MD: AOTA Press.

American Occupational Therapy Association. (2009). *Occupational therapy: Living life to its fullest™* [brochure]. Bethesda, MD: Author. Available online at http://www.aota.org/Brand/Toolbox/Brand-Material/Brochure_1/Brochure.aspx

Americans with Disabilities Act of 1990, Pub. L. 101-336, 104 Stat. 327.

Balanced Budget Act of 1997, Pub. L. 105-133, 111 Stat. 1501.

Dressler, J., & MacRae, A. (1998). Advocacy, partnerships, and client-centered practice in California. *Occupational Therapy in Mental Health, 14*(1), 35–43.

Education for All Handicapped Children Act, Pub. L. 94-142, 89 Stat. 773 (1975).

Flynn, L., & Verma, S. (2008). Fundamental components of a curriculum for residents in health advocacy. *Medical Teacher, 30*(7), 178–183.

Frishberg, D. (1975). *I'm just a bill* [Schoolhouse Rock video]. Retrieved April 11, 2010, from www.youtube.com/watch?v=mEJL2Uuv-oQ

Gallew, H. A., Haltiwanger, E., Sowers, J., & van den Heever, N. (2004). Political action and critical analysis: Mental health parity. *Occupational Therapy in Mental Health, 20*(1), 1–25.

Green, M., & Bowie, M. (2007). *Essentials of health information management*. Florence, KY: Delmar/Cengage Learning.

Giuliani, R. (2003). *Leadership through the ages*. New York: Mirimax Books.

Health Insurance Portability and Accountability Act of 1996, Pub. L. 104-191, 110 Stat. 2021–2031.

Individuals with Disabilities Education Act, Pub. L. 101-476, 104 Stat. 1142 (1990).

Institute of Medicine. (1989). *Allied health services: Avoiding crises*. Washington, DC: National Academies Press.

Jackson, L. (Ed.). (2007). *Occupational therapy services for children and youth under IDEA* (3rd ed.). Bethesda, MD: AOTA Press.

Merryman, B. M. (2002, May 13). Networking as an entree to paid community practice. *OT Practice*, pp. 10–13.

Patient Protection and Affordable Care Act, Pub. L. 111-148, 124 Stat. 119 (2010).

Political action committee. (n.d.). *Merriam-Webster's Online Dictionary*. Retrieved August, 17, 2009, from http://www.merriam-webster.com/netdict/political%20action%20committee

Reich, R. (1988). *The power of public ideas*. Cambridge, MA: Harvard University Press.

Schein, E. (2004). *Organizational culture and leadership* (3rd ed.). San Francisco: Jossey-Bass.

Showalter, A. (2007). *How to build a grassroots network*. Retrieved August 30, 2010, from http://www.showaltergroup.com/downloads/HowtoBuildGrassrootsNetwork.pdf

Showalter, A. (2008). *The habits of effective advocacy groups*. Retrieved May 15, 2009, from http://www.showaltergroup.com/grassroots/free_articles.htm

Weissert, C. S., & Weissert, W. G. (2002). *Governing health: The politics of health policy* (2nd ed.). Baltimore: John Hopkins University Press.

Appendix 28.A. Advocacy Evidence Table

Topic	Evidence
Patient advocacy	Dressler, J., & MacRae, A. (1998). Advocacy, partnerships, and client-centered practice in California. *Occupational Therapy in Mental Health, 14*(1), 35–43.
Legislative advocacy	Gallew, H. A., Haltiwanger, E., Sowers, J., & van den Heever, N. (2004). Political action and critical analysis: Mental health parity. *Occupational Therapy in Mental Health, 20*(1), 1–25.
Grassroots advocacy	Showalter, A. (2007). *How to build a grassroots network.* Retrieved August 30, 2010, from http://www.showaltergroup.com/downloads/HowtoBuildGrassrootsNetwork.pdf
Networking	Merryman, B. M. (2002, May 13). Networking as an entree to paid community practice. *OT Practice,* pp. 10–13.

29

State Regulation of Occupational Therapists and Occupational Therapy Assistants

Chuck Willmarth

❖ Key Terms and Concepts

Certification. The process by which an agency grants a person permission to use a certain title if that person has attained entry-level competence; may also be nongovernmental.

Certification by NBCOT. Recognition by the National Board for Certification in Occupational Therapy, Inc. (NBCOT), that an occupational therapist or occupational therapy assistant has met certain professional requirements and is authorized to use NBCOT's registered certification marks Occupational Therapist Registered (OTR®) or Certified Occupational Therapy Assistant (COTA®).

Credentialing. The process of assessing and validating the qualifications of a practitioner according to a predetermined set of standards such as current license, education, training, experience, competence, and professional judgment (O'Leary, 1994, pp. 169–170).

Legislation. The making of laws, specifically, the exercise of the power and function of making rules that have the force of authority by virtue of their promulgation by an official organ of the state (*Merriam-Webster's Dictionary of Law*, 1996).

Licensure. "The process by which an agency of government grants permission to an individual to engage in a given occupation upon finding that the applicant has attained the minimal degree of competence required to ensure that the public health, safety, and welfare will be reasonably well protected" (U.S. Department of Health, Education, and Welfare, 1977, p. 17).

Registration. A formal process by which qualified individuals are listed on an official roster or registry maintained by a government or nongovernmental agency, enabling these people to use a particular title and attesting to employing agencies and individuals that minimum qualifications have been met and maintained (O'Leary, 1994).

Regulation. 1. The act of regulating or state of being regulated. 2. A rule or order issued by a government agency and often having the force of law. An agency often is delegated the power to issue regulations by the legislation that created it. Regulations must be made in accordance with prescribed procedures such as those set out in the federal or a state administrative procedure (*Merriam-Webster's Dictionary of Law*, 1996).

Scope of practice. "The activities that an individual health care practitioner is permitted to perform within a specific profession. Those activities should be based on appropriate education, training, and experience. Scope of practice is established by the practice act of the specific practitioner's board, and the rules adopted pursuant to that act" (Federation of State Medical Boards, 2005, p. 8).

Statute. A law enacted by the legislative branch of a government (*Merriam-Webster's Dictionary of Law*, 1996).

Sunrise law. A law requiring that a profession meet certain criteria before licensing is initiated (Young, 1987).

Sunset law. A law requiring termination of the enabling legislation by a specific date unless the legislature renews it (Young, 1987).

Title protection. The process by which an agency grants a person permission to use a certain title if that person has attained entry-level competence.

❖ Learning Objectives

After completing this chapter, you should be able to do the following:

- Explain the importance of state regulation for occupational therapists and occupational therapy assistants.
- Describe the differences among the various forms of regulation.
- Identify requirements to practice as an occupational therapist or occupational therapy assistant.
- Distinguish between the legal requirements of state law regulating occupational therapy and the requirements of private credentialing organizations, such as NBCOT.

- Identify components of an occupational therapy practice act.
- Describe roles and responsibilities of occupational therapy regulatory bodies.
- Identify key American Occupational Therapy Association documents that are used as resources by state policymakers and regulators.

Occupational therapy is regulated in all 50 American states, the District of Columbia, Puerto Rico, and Guam. Different states have various types of *regulation* that range from licensure, the strongest form of regulation, to registration, a weak form of regulation. The major purpose of regulation is to protect consumers in a state or jurisdiction from unqualified or unscrupulous practitioners. Regulation also assures a high level of professional conduct on the part of occupational therapists and occupational therapy assistants.

State laws and regulations significantly affect the practice of occupational therapy. Laws or statutes are enacted by legislators, who are elected public officials. Regulations specifically describe how the intent of the laws will be carried out. These regulations are developed by regulators, who are appointed public officials of various departments in state government. Both kinds of officials make decisions that directly and indirectly affect occupational therapy managers and practitioners. These decisions may include the setting of certain standards, coverage and reimbursement for occupational therapy services, funding for higher education, and the awarding of research grants.

In the United States, the earliest evidence of state regulation of professions was the Virginia Medical Practice Act of 1639 (American Occupational Therapy Association [AOTA], 1996). State licensure activity did not begin in earnest, however, until the late 1800s. Action by the Supreme Court had an impact on state licensure: "The most far-reaching action of the federal government related to state regulation of the health professions was the affirmation by the U.S. Supreme Court of the constitutional right of state licensing boards to require a specific educational credential in the late 19th century (*Dent v. West Virginia* 1888)" (Morrison, 1996). "By 1900 most states had licensed attorneys, dentists, pharmacists, physicians, and teachers. Between 1900 and 1960, most states also granted licensure to 20 additional groups, including accountants, nurses, real estate brokers, barbers, chiropractors, and funeral directors" (Shimberg & Roederer, 1994, pp. 1–2).

AOTA and state occupational therapy associations have successfully advocated for the state regulation of occupational therapy for more than 35 years. New York and Florida were the first states to enact occupational therapy licensure legislation in 1975.

TYPES OF REGULATION

Although licensure is by far the predominant form of regulation for occupational therapists and occupational therapy assistants, a few states use less-stringent forms of regulation such as certification and registration. As of 2010, 48 states, the District of Columbia, Guam, and Puerto Rico license occupational therapists, and 2 states (Colorado and Hawaii) have registration laws (AOTA State Affairs Group, 2010a). The form of regulation for occupational therapy assistants is often but not always the same as it is for occupational therapists in a given jurisdiction. The District of Columbia, Guam, Puerto Rico, and 46 states license occupational therapy assistants, and 2 states (Indiana and New York) have certification laws. Hawaii and Colorado do not regulate occupational therapy assistants (AOTA State Affairs Group, 2010b).

Licensure, the strongest form of state regulation, is "the process by which an agency of government grants permission to an individual to engage in a given occupation upon finding that the applicant has attained the minimal degree of competence required to ensure that the public health, safety, and welfare will be reasonably well protected" (U.S. Department of Health, Education, and Welfare, 1977, p. 17). A key feature of a *licensure law* is that it legally defines a scope of practice. A licensure law is therefore often referred to as a *practice act*, although certification laws also use that term.

Certification and *registration* are less stringent forms of state regulation than licensure and may be defined differently by individual state regulatory boards (SRBs) or councils. Certification in the context of state regulation is not the same as certification granted by the National Board for Certification in Occupational Therapy (NBCOT; see the section "Nongovernmental Certification" in this chapter). In general, certification and registration protect the public by requiring individuals who use the titles *occupational therapist* or *occupational therapy assistant* to meet specific eligibility requirements, similar to licensure. However, under some circumstances, unlike licensure, individuals who are not certified or registered are allowed to use occupational therapy techniques if they do not refer to their services as occupational therapy. Certification and registration may provide a definition of occupational therapy. However, these forms of regulation do not establish a scope of practice. For example, Hawaii, which has registration, has a definition of occupational therapy, although somewhat limited, and does not have language that restricts others from performing some of those services.

Title protection provides the least amount of protection to consumers. As the name implies, this form of regulation protects the titles used (occupational therapist or occupational therapy assistant) but not specific occupational therapy interventions and techniques. States with title protection do not designate scope of practice. Therefore, others without qualifications to practice occupational therapy can claim that they can provide those services. With the enactment of the registration law for occupational therapists in Colorado in 2008, no states have title control or trademark laws for occupational therapists or occupational therapy assistants (AOTA State Affairs Group, 2010a, 2010b).

Generally—unlike certification, registration, and title protection laws—a *licensure law* defines a lawful scope of practice for occupational therapists and for occupational therapy assistants under the supervision of occupational therapists. Defining a scope of practice legally articulates the domain of occupational therapy practice and provides guidance to facilities, providers, consumers, and major public and private health and education facilities about the appropriate use of occupational therapy services and practitioners. Defining the appropriate scope of occupational therapy practice can further ensure important patient protections, particularly in the investigation and resolution of consumer complaints involving fraudulent or negligent delivery of occupational therapy services. A clearly articulated scope of practice also protects occupational therapy from another profession that may challenge the qualifications of practitioners to provide certain services or that may encroach on occupational therapy's scope of practice through unqualified expansion of its practice.

REGULATORY OR ADVISORY BOARDS FOR REGULATED JURISDICTIONS

In the health care professions, the agency of government granting the permission under the various types of regulation is typically the state department of health. Under a licensure system, that department usually delegates its authority to administer regulations to a board that consists of members of the profession (who are regulated); consumers or public members; and, in some cases, representatives

of related professions. SRBs operate on a continuum from full autonomy to a strictly advisory role to no board at all but only a centralized agency responsible for administration (Shimberg & Roederer, 1994). Most SRBs have the authority to establish the procedures for licensure, investigate violations of the practice act, and promulgate rules to regulate the profession.

In some states, appointed practitioners serve as part of an occupational therapy advisory council. Councils perform many of the same tasks as an occupational therapy SRB but are less autonomous and serve to advise the administration's staff on the regulation of occupational therapists and occupational therapy assistants. Some states combine occupational therapy SRBs or advisory councils with other professions such as physical therapy or athletic training. A handful of states have no occupational therapy SRB or advisory council and rely on administrative officials to promulgate and enforce regulations for the profession. Several states have placed regulation of occupational therapists and occupational therapy assistants under the state's medical board. In these states, a group made up of occupational therapists and, in some cases, occupational therapy assistants advises the medical board on occupational therapy regulatory issues, but this group has far less power and autonomy than a board (AOTA, 2001).

No matter what type of regulatory structure is in place in the state, occupational therapy managers, practitioners, entrepreneurs, and consultants as well as state occupational therapy association leaders need to monitor the activities of the occupational therapy SRB, medical board, or administrative officials who are responsible for regulating occupational therapy and to maintain an ongoing dialogue on professional issues. Occupational therapy SRBs may discuss the need to amend state occupational therapy practice acts or regulations to keep them up-to-date with current practice. This updating process may entail making additions or revisions to scope of practice, continuing competence, supervision, reentry to the profession, or references to certification bodies or education program accreditation institutions.

Occupational therapists and occupational therapy assistants can give input into these processes in a variety of ways. State occupational therapy associations or individuals can propose changes in the practice act or statutes through legislative amendments. They also can attend hearings and comment on amendments to regulations that are proposed by the SRB or advisory council and work with them to initiate needed changes (AOTA, 2001).

State associations leaders should be on the mailing list of the occupational therapy SRB or the advisory council to receive meeting announcements and minutes, and one or more representatives of the associations should regularly attend public occupational therapy SRB or council meetings. The positive relationships that state associations can develop with SRB or council members will enhance the work of both entities and help ensure competent practice by occupational therapists and occupational therapy assistants. In states where practitioners are regulated by a state agency or a medical board, occupational therapists and especially occupational therapy managers should follow medical board activities and meetings as well as regulations proposed by the agency with jurisdiction over health professions. State legislatures are generally the most active from January through May. Activity levels of boards and agencies do not follow this trend; they make important policy decisions year round (AOTA, 2001).

COMPONENTS OF AN OCCUPATIONAL THERAPY PRACTICE ACT

Practice acts refer to laws passed by state legislators that establish regulation for health care professions. The purpose of regulating occupational therapy practice is to

- Safeguard the public health, safety, and welfare;
- Protect the public from incompetent, unethical, or unauthorized persons;
- Assure a high level of professional conduct on the part of occupational therapists and occupational therapy assistants; and
- Assure the availability of high-quality occupational therapy services to people in need of those services (AOTA, 2000).

The practice act provides consumers and others with important information about minimum qualifications for practitioners, protects the titles of practitioners, and defines an appropriate scope of practice. Most practice acts or licensure laws have similar components, including requirements for licensure, renewal, supervision, and referral as well as a defined scope of practice, code of ethics, and disciplinary provisions.

SCOPE OF PRACTICE

Most states include a definition of occupational therapy or occupational therapy practice in their practice acts. Defining a scope of practice legally articulates the domain of occupational therapy practice and provides guidance to facilities, providers, consumers, and major public and private health and education facilities on the appropriate use of occupational therapy services and practitioners. Most practice acts have specific language that prohibits the unauthorized practice of occupational therapy by individuals who are not qualified occupational therapists or occupational therapy assistants and that allows for prosecution of those individuals.

The scope of practice of a profession should be directly related to the standards for education, training, and clinical application within that profession. Some elements of the scopes of practice for different professions may appropriately overlap, but a practice act should also delineate unique aspects of that scope. For example, although both the occupational therapy and physical therapy practice acts in a given state may authorize the use of physical agent modalities, the occupational therapy practice act might use the wording "application of physical agent modalities as an adjunct to or in

preparation for engagement in occupations" to distinguish the unique focus of occupational therapy on occupation, not on the modality. Exhibit 29.1 presents AOTA's Definition of Occupational Therapy Practice for State Regulation (AOTA, 2004). States often adopt this model language related to scope of practice because it reflects the current appropriate scope of practice as articulated by the standard-setting body of the profession. All managers, private practice owners, and practitioners need to be aware of their state's or their jurisdiction's scope of practice and need to ensure that practitioners under their supervision are not performing services that are outside their legal scope of practice.

REQUIREMENTS FOR LICENSURE OR OTHER FORMS OF REGULATION

Requirements for licensure or other forms of regulation generally include demonstration by the applicant that he or she has successfully completed the academic and fieldwork requirements of an educational program for occupational therapists or occupational therapy assistants that is accredited by AOTA's Accreditation Council for Occupational Therapy Education® (ACOTE®) and has passed an examination approved by the occupational therapy board (typically, the NBCOT entry-level certification examination). States may have additional requirements for internationally trained therapists to ensure that their education and training are equivalent to the standards in the United States and that their English proficiency is adequate. It is important to note that internationally trained therapists must have an education that is considered to be comparable to an entry-level post-baccalaureate degree in occupational therapy from an ACOTE accredited program to sit for the NBCOT exam. NBCOT's Occupational Therapist Eligibility Determination (OTED®) process "allows occupational therapists without entry-level post-baccalaureate degrees from U.S.-accredited programs to be considered for exam eligibility" (NBCOT, 2010b). States may have less complicated requirements for licensure by endorsement for practitioners who are currently licensed or regulated in another state or jurisdiction.

ADDITIONAL REQUIREMENTS FOR CERTAIN INTERVENTIONS AND SETTINGS

Occupational therapy practitioners should be aware that several states have created additional education and experience requirements to provide certain interventions and or work in certain settings. For example, several states have established requirements for practitioners to use physical agent modalities. Other states have created requirements for other interventions. For example, the California Occupational Therapy Practice Act requires "occupational therapists offering services in hand therapy, physical agent modalities, and/or swallowing assessment, evaluation or intervention to demonstrate, through post-professional education and training, that they are competent to do so" (California Board of Occupational Therapy, 2010).

EXHIBIT 29.1. DEFINITION OF OCCUPATIONAL THERAPY PRACTICE FOR STATE REGULATION

The *practice of occupational therapy* means the therapeutic use of everyday life activities (occupations) with individuals or groups for the purpose of participation in roles and situations in home, school, workplace, community, and other settings. Occupational therapy services are provided for the purpose of promoting health and wellness and to those who have or are at risk for developing an illness, injury, disease, disorder, condition, impairment, disability, activity limitation, or participation restriction. Occupational therapy addresses the physical, cognitive, psychosocial, sensory, and other aspects of performance in a variety of contexts to support engagement in everyday life activities that affect health, well-being, and quality of life.

The practice of occupational therapy includes:

A. Methods or strategies selected to direct the process of interventions such as:
   1. Establishment, remediation, or restoration of a skill or ability that has not yet developed or is impaired.
   2. Compensation, modification, or adaptation of activity or environment to enhance performance.
   3. Maintenance and enhancement of capabilities without which performance in everyday life activities would decline.
   4. Health promotion and wellness to enable or enhance performance in everyday life activities.
   5. Prevention of barriers to performance, including disability prevention.

B. Evaluation of factors affecting activities of daily living (ADLs), instrumental activities of daily living (IADLs), education, work, play, leisure, and social participation, including:
   1. Client factors, including body functions (such as neuromuscular, sensory, visual, perceptual, cognitive) and body structures (such as cardiovascular, digestive, integumentary, genitourinary systems).
   2. Habits, routines, roles, and behavior patterns.
   3. Cultural, physical, environmental, social, and spiritual contexts and activity demands that affect performance.
   4. Performance skills, including motor, process, and communication/interaction skills.

C. Interventions and procedures to promote or enhance safety and performance in activities of daily living (ADLs), instrumental activities of daily living (IADLs), education, work, play, leisure, and social participation, including:
   1. Therapeutic use of occupations, exercises, and activities.
   2. Training in self-care, self-management, home management, and community/work reintegration.
   3. Development, remediation, or compensation of physical, cognitive, neuromuscular, sensory functions, and behavioral skills.
   4. Therapeutic use of self, including one's personality, insights, perceptions, and judgments, as part of the therapeutic process.
   5. Education and training of individuals, including family members, caregivers, and others.
   6. Care coordination, case management, and transition services.
   7. Consultative services to groups, programs, organizations, or communities.
   8. Modification of environments (home, work, school, or community) and adaptation of processes, including the application of ergonomic principles.
   9. Assessment, design, fabrication, application, fitting, and training in assistive technology, adaptive devices, and orthotic devices, and training in the use of prosthetic devices.
   10. Assessment, recommendation, and training in techniques to enhance functional mobility, including wheelchair management.
   11. Driver rehabilitation and community mobility.
   12. Management of feeding, eating, and swallowing to enable eating and feeding performance.
   13. Application of physical agent modalities, and use of a range of specific therapeutic procedures (such as wound care management; techniques to enhance sensory, perceptual, and cognitive processing; manual therapy techniques) to enhance performance skills.

Source. American Occupational Therapy Association. (2004). Policy 5.3.1: Definition of occupational therapy practice for state regulation. *American Journal of Occupational Therapy, 58,* 694–695.

Several states have created additional requirements for occupational therapy practitioners to be credentialed to provide services through state early intervention programs. For example,

> occupational therapy practitioners in Illinois must fulfill extensive requirements in addition to licensure, including a background check, EI [early intervention] system training, and documentation of the completion of educational experience that includes at least two college semester hours or the equivalent of 30 continuing education units in several core content areas. These areas include the development of typical and atypical young children, working with families of young children with disabilities, intervention strategies for young children with special needs, and assessing young children with special needs. (Kohl, 2008)

LICENSURE RENEWAL REQUIREMENTS

States also require renewal of licensure, certification, or registration at specific intervals. For most states, this renewal is required every 1 or 2 years. In New York, the renewal period is 3 years. Increasingly, states are requiring not only a fee and completion of the renewal application but also completion of a specific amount of continuing competence activities.

An important role of SRBs is to protect the public from incompetent practitioners. State regulators are mandating continuing competence requirements in an attempt to ensure that practitioners who are licensed or regulated in their state maintain competence. Some SRBs limit acceptable continuing competence activities to those activities directly related to clinical practice. Others recognize the importance of an individual maintaining competence in the varied roles and responsibilities related to occupational therapy throughout his or her career and the important ways that these roles directly and indirectly affect competent practice.

As of January 2010, 43 states, the District of Columbia, and Puerto Rico had continuing competence or continuing education requirements (AOTA State Affairs Group, 2009). Forces both internal and external to the profession are encouraging states to adopt continuing competence requirements, and the expectation is that the number of states with these requirements will continue to grow. Accrediting organizations such as the CARF International and The Joint Commission address competence-related activities in their standards. In their accreditation reviews, The Joint Commission and CARF International look to see that organizations develop competencies needed by their staff members to perform their duties, that a mechanism is in place to measure the level of competency, and that the required competencies are assessed annually. In addition, the organizations must make opportunities available to improve the competencies of staff members.

Acceptable activities vary in states or jurisdictions and range from attending or presenting courses to supervising fieldwork

> **EXHIBIT 29.2. STATE REGULATION WEB RESOURCES**
>
> - **AOTA Licensure Page:** http://www.aota.org/Practitioners/Licensure.aspx
> - **Director of State Licensure Boards:** http://www1.aota.org/state_law/reglist.asp
> - **State Continuing Competence Requirements:** http://www.aota.org/Practitioners/Licensure/StateRegs/ContComp.aspx
> - **NBCOT:** http://www.nbcot.org

students or participating in research. The number of required points or contact hours of continuing education activity also varies widely from state to state, ranging from an average of 6 hours per year to 20 hours per year. AOTA maintains a compilation of state requirements on the licensure page of its Web site (see Exhibit 29.2 for a list of suggested Web resources). For the most up-to-date information on specific state requirements, contact the individual SRB or agency.

RE-ENTRY TO THE PROFESSION

Occupational therapy practitioners who leave the profession for a period of time need to understand provisions in their state's practice act and regulations that establish requirements to re-enter the profession. States have a variety of requirements to regain licensure, from requiring the completion of continuing competence activities to requiring applicants to re-take the NBCOT examination (Kohl, 2007). Some states include a provision that requires that the applicant complete a period of supervised work experience. In many states, the number of years that the person has been out of practice dictates the specific requirements that must be met to re-enter the profession.

Although intended to keep consumers safe, these guidelines can discourage practitioners from returning to practice. Not only are the provisions daunting, but compliance could involve a significant amount of time and money. Occupational therapy managers should be aware of such provisions to be sure that any supervised work experience at their place of employment complies with state and federal laws.

To address this concern, some states have included inactive status stipulations in either statute or regulation. In many instances, inactive status allows a practitioner to leave active practice without losing his or her license. States that offer inactive status provide practitioners with a much smoother transition back to active licensure. More than 15 states currently allow this option (Kohl, 2007). The provisions regarding inactive status typically require the practitioner to complete continuing competence activities during the period of inactive status.

REFERRAL REQUIREMENTS

Several state occupational therapy practice acts include *referral requirements,* which state that for occupational therapists to evaluate or treat a client, they must first receive an order from another health professional, typically a physician. Most state referral requirements include a broad range of referral sources such as physicians, physician assistants, nurse practitioners, podiatrists, optometrists, and others. The laws also include exemptions from the referral requirements for occupational therapy services that are provided in nonmedical settings or for prevention, education, or wellness. It is important for occupational therapy managers to note that payers may have their own referral requirements for reimbursement purposes.

SUPERVISION AND ROLE DELINEATION OF OCCUPATIONAL THERAPY ASSISTANTS AND AIDES

SRBs address supervision and role delineation of occupational therapy assistants and aides in different ways. Supervision requirements may be included in the definitions of occupational therapy assistant or in the definitions of types or levels of supervision allowed in that state. In many states or jurisdictions, specific subsections in the regulations address the role and supervision of occupational therapy assistants and aides. Most states look to AOTA's professional standards on supervision such as the *Guidelines for Supervision, Roles, and Responsibilities During the Delivery of Occupational Therapy Services* (AOTA, 2009) as well as the *Model State Regulations for Supervision, Roles, and Responsibilities During the Delivery of Occupational Therapy Services* (AOTA, 2005) to reflect current best practice in the profession.

When promulgating state regulations, SRBs consider problems or issues that arise in their state with respect to the supervision of occupational therapy assistants in specific settings and address workplace issues. Some states have established ratios for the number of occupational therapy assistants and aides that a therapist may supervision. At least one state, New Hampshire, has included a provision in its practice act that prohibits coercing occupational therapists or occupational therapy assistants into compromising patient safety by requiring them to delegate treatment inappropriately.

Many SRBs also address supervision of unregulated support personnel such as aides. Aides who provide supportive services to occupational therapists or occupational therapy assistants are considered nonlicensed or unregulated personnel. Many states do not mention this level of personnel in their statutes or regulations. However, some states have incorporated regulations about the use and supervision of nonlicensed personnel or aides under rules or regulations that outline the responsibilities of occupational therapists or occupational therapy assistants who supervise these people. The regulations also may list types of activities that aides can and cannot do under the supervision of occupational therapists and occupational therapy assistants. This list is often consistent with AOTA's *Guidelines for Supervi-*

sion, Roles, and Responsibilities During the Delivery of Occupational Therapy Services (AOTA, 2009), which states that

> An *aide,* as used in occupational therapy practice, is an individual who provides supportive services to the occupational therapist and the occupational therapy assistant. Aides do not provide skilled occupational therapy services. An aide is trained by an occupational therapist or an occupational therapy assistant to perform specifically delegated tasks. The occupational therapist is responsible for the overall use and actions of the aide. An aide first must demonstrate competency to be able to perform the assigned, delegated client and non-client tasks. (p. 801)

Managers, consultants, entrepreneurs, and practitioners who supervise occupational therapy assistants and aides must be familiar with their individual state's or jurisdiction's requirements for supervision because they do vary. Some states may require documentation of supervisory sessions in a supervision log or may limit the number of personnel that an occupational therapist may supervise. The amount and type of supervision also varies from jurisdiction to jurisdiction. Many occupational therapists are not fully aware of an important concept: They are legally responsible for the patient care rendered by occupational therapy assistants and aides under their supervision.

DISCIPLINARY ACTION

Boards protect the public by providing consumer information, monitoring regulated practitioners, and investigating complaints. They have the power to discipline practitioners through a variety of sanctions that range from reprimand to revocation of license (or certificate or registration). Revocation removes the practitioner's right to practice in that state and, thus, is used only in extreme cases. Less harsh actions may require peer review of records; educational meetings; supervision with or without a mentor; continuing education; payment of a fine; and suspension of a license, a certificate, or registered status (AOTA, 1996). Reports of disciplinary actions taken by SRBs, NBCOT's Disciplinary Action Committee, or AOTA's Ethics Commission are frequently shared among those three bodies and also may be reported to the National Practitioner Data Bank (see http://www.npdb-hipdb.hrsa.gov).

Boards also may adopt a code of ethics that articulates the expected behaviors of those who are regulated by the board. They often adopt AOTA's *Occupational Therapy Code of Ethics and Ethics Standards* (AOTA, 2010a) in whole or in part. AOTA's code is a public statement of the common set of values and principles used to promote and maintain high standards of behavior in occupational therapy. The code is a set of principles that applies to occupational therapy personnel at all levels. These principles to which occupational therapists and occupational therapy assistants aspire are part of a lifelong effort to act in an ethical manner. The various roles of practitioner (occupational therapist and occupational therapy assistant), educator, fieldwork educator, clinical supervisor, manager, administrator, consultant, fieldwork coordinator, faculty program director, researcher–scholar, private practice owner, entrepreneur, and student are included in the code's scope (AOTA, 2010a).

FUTURE OF STATE REGULATION

Some have viewed state regulation of health care professionals critically, believing that more can be done to strengthen the state regulatory framework. Reform has occurred through the appointment of public members to licensing boards, the creation of umbrella agencies to oversee licensing boards, the passing of sunrise and sunset laws, and rulings by the Federal Trade Commission on the anticompetitive aspects of some licensing laws (Young, 1987). Some critics have proposed a system that would encourage consumers to rely on information and on their own judgment with respect to the preparation of health care professionals. Others have proposed programs to modify the state regulatory structure.

In 1994, the Pew Health Professions Commission (1995) assembled the Taskforce on Health Care Workforce Regulation to identify how regulation protects the public's health and to propose recommendations with respect to regulation of the health care workforce that might better serve the public's interest. The task force identified many issues that were crucial elements in regulating health professions to best serve the public's interest, including

- Setting requirements for entry to practice,
- Ensuring continuing professional competence,
- Standardizing regulatory terms and language, and
- Evaluating regulatory effectiveness.

The task force called for a system that would be standardized when appropriate; accountable to the public; flexible, to support optimal access to a competent workforce; and effective and efficient in protecting and promoting the public's health, safety, and welfare (Gragnola & Stone, 1997).

The report sparked much debate and comment from professions and other stakeholders. Many were supportive of the report's message that regulatory reform was needed but thought that it did not provide adequate information on how to finance and carry out reform (Gragnola & Stone, 1997). In its fourth and final report, the Pew Health Professions Commission (1998) urged health professionals to continually reconsider how they may best add value to the delivery of health services. The commission cited public representation in the regulatory process, demonstration of continuing competence, and flexibility to practice in those domains of demonstrated competence as the most important elements to consider in the needed restructuring of health care regulation. Some of these recommendations appear to be taking hold within the occupational therapy profession because several SRBs have increased the number of consumer members on their boards and many boards have added continuing competence requirements over the past 10 years.

In 2000, the governors of Minnesota and Florida proposed budget cuts to streamline government. These cuts included deregulation of occupational therapy along with several other professions in their states. Both of these initiatives were defeated because the occupational therapy practitioners in those states, led by their state associations, strongly objected to the proposed deregulation. They were able to provide information that countered the state's rationale for deregulation and made a strong case for licensure as a way to protect consumers from unqualified practitioners.

NONGOVERNMENTAL CERTIFICATION

Nongovernmental credentialing organizations such as NBCOT recognize through the mechanism of certification those individuals who have attained entry-level competence in broad areas of responsibility within their profession. A person completing this nongovernmental certification process is granted a certificate and also is entitled to use a special designation such as "certified" or "registered" with his or her name. (Chapter 31 on continuing competency discusses advanced certification, which is a different type of nongovernmental certification that recognizes advanced training or experience in specific areas.)

ENTRY-LEVEL CERTIFICATION

In the mid-1930s, AOTA initiated a program of nongovernmental certification for occupational therapists, which it then administered for more than 50 years. In the early years, AOTA called the program for occupational therapists *registration* and granted the designation *registered* to applicants who successfully completed the education, fieldwork, and examination requirements. The association introduced a similar program for occupational therapy assistants in the 1960s. In 1986, AOTA created an independent organization, the American Occupational Therapy Certification Board (AOTCB), and transferred the certification program from AOTA to AOTCB. In 1996, AOTCB changed its name to the National Board for Certification in Occupational Therapy, Inc., or NBCOT (AOTA, 1996).

NBCOT is a private, not-for-profit credentialing organization that oversees and administers the entry-level certification examination for occupational therapists and occupational therapy assistants. This examination is what the SRBs use as one of the criteria for licensure (or other forms of regulation). NBCOT uses the examination as one of the criteria for initial NBCOT certification (AOTA, 2006).

NBCOT certifies eligible individuals as Occupational Therapist Registered (OTR®) or Certified Occupational Therapy Assistant (COTA®). The OTR and COTA credentials are registered certification marks owned by NBCOT. Certification by NBCOT indicates to the public that the OTR or the COTA has met all of NBCOT's educational, fieldwork, and examination requirements (AOTA, 2006).

Entry-Level Certification Examination

NBCOT certifies occupational therapy practitioners on the basis of separate examinations for therapists and assistants.

The OTR and COTA examinations are constructed based on the results of practice analysis studies. The studies identify the domains, tasks, knowledge, and skills required for occupational therapy practice relative to the respective credential. The ultimate goal of a practice analysis study is to ensure that there is a representative linkage of examination content to practice. The periodic performance of practice analysis studies assists NBCOT with evaluating the validity of the test specifications that guide content distribution of the credentialing examinations. (NBCOT, 2010a)

The examinations consist of the following: OTR: 3 Simulation Test Items and 170 Multiple Choice Test Items and COTA: 200 Multiple Choice Items only (NBCOT, 2010a).

Requirements for Eligibility to Take the Examination

Eligibility requirements for NBCOT certification examinations vary depending on the candidate's educational background and the type of certification sought. The requirements must be met before a candidate can take an examination. Certification candidates should obtain the latest *Certification Examination Handbook* from NBCOT at http://www.nbcot.org.

NBCOT Certification Renewal

NBCOT created a certification renewal program in 1997 and added Phase II to the program in 2002 that includes a professional development requirement (Smith & Willmarth, 2003, p. 452). Maintaining NBCOT certification entitles individuals to the continued use of NBCOT's registered certification marks OTR® or COTA®. Individuals who choose not to renew this certification are required by NBCOT to no longer use its certification marks. State licensure or jurisdiction laws (or other forms of state regulation) generally authorize practitioners who meet their licensure requirements to use a wide variety of professional designations, including OT (occupational therapist), OTA (occupational therapy assistant), OT/L (occupational therapist/licensed), and OTA/L (occupational therapy assistant/licensed), among others. Certification renewal candidates should obtain the latest *Certification Renewal Handbook* from NBCOT at http://www.nbcot.org.

RELATIONSHIP OF NONGOVERNMENTAL CERTIFICATION TO STATE REGULATION, PRIVATE OR PUBLIC EMPLOYMENT, AND THIRD-PARTY REIMBURSEMENT

States or jurisdictions commonly require occupational therapists and occupational therapy assistants to be initially certified (i.e., pass the NBCOT entry-level certification exam) before they can qualify for a license. Most states or jurisdictions, however, do not require practitioners to renew this certification to maintain their licenses to practice.

NBCOT recertification is not a legal requirement to practice occupational therapy unless a state mandates it as a condition of licensure, certification, or registration. Certification renewal status does not affect the ability to be reimbursed by Medicare, Medicaid, or other third-party payers. Additionally, The Joint Commission and CARF International do not independently require in their standards that occupational therapists and occupational therapy assistants employed by facilities renew their certification with NBCOT.

DISCIPLINARY ACTION BY NBCOT

NBCOT undertakes disciplinary action against OTRs, COTAs, and examination candidates who are incompetent, unethical, or impaired (e.g., by substance abuse). The disciplinary action program makes it possible to identify, discipline, and require improvements of those who demonstrate incompetent, unethical, or impaired behavior. Individuals who are not exam candidates or who are not currently certified by NBCOT would not be subject to discipline by NBCOT. However, all occupational therapists and occupational therapy assistants who are regulated by a state are subject to discipline by their state regulatory body, and all members of AOTA are subject to discipline by AOTA's Ethics Commission.

CONCLUSION

Occupational therapy is regulated in all 50 states, the District of Columbia, Puerto Rico, and Guam. The type of regulation may differ from licensure, the strongest form of regulation, to title protection, the weakest form of regulation. The purpose of regulation is to protect consumers of that state or jurisdiction from unqualified or unscrupulous practitioners.

State laws and regulations significantly affect the profession of occupational therapy, including setting of professional standards, coverage and reimbursement for occupational therapy services, funding for higher education, and awarding of research grants. Most licensure laws or practice acts have similar components, including requirements for licensure and renewal and a defined scope of practice. Each individual is responsible for being aware of and compliant with all statutes and regulations governing the occupational therapy practitioners and practice of occupational therapy.

Authority to administer regulations is generally delegated to an SRB that provides consumer information, monitors regulated practitioners, investigates complaints, and disciplines practitioners. Practitioners, managers, entrepreneurs, consultants, and state association leaders can take an active part in shaping appropriate state regulation of occupational therapy practice. Occupational therapy managers need to be aware of the state regulatory framework to ensure compliance with state laws as well as to participate in the process to develop and refine the laws and regulations that affect practice.

❖ Learning Activities

1. Determine the definition of occupational therapy in your home state, and compare and contrast it with AOTA's *Definition of Occupational Therapy Practice for State Regulation* as used in this chapter.
2. Explore which scope of practice issues recently have come up in your home state.
3. Report on the licensure process in your home state.
4. Provide detailed information about licensure renewal requirements, including the development of a plan to secure any necessary continuing competence activities needed for licensure renewal.
5. Identify AOTA documents, professional literature, and information about occupational therapy education that can be used to support AOTA's *Definition of Occupational Therapy Practice for State Regulation* as used in this chapter.

✓ Multiple-Choice Questions

1. Which of the following is *not* a typical state licensure requirement for occupational therapy practitioners?
   a. Pass the entry-level examination administered by NBCOT.
   b. Graduation from an accredited OT or OTA school.
   c. Complete fieldwork requirements.
   d. Certification as an orthotist by American Board for Certification in Orthotics, Prosthetics, and Pedorthics.
2. The purpose of state regulation of occupational therapy practice is to
   a. Safeguard the public health, safety, and welfare.
   b. Protect the public from incompetent, unethical, or unauthorized persons.
   c. Assure a high level of professional conduct on the part of occupational therapists and occupational therapy assistants.
   d. All of the above.
3. Which AOTA body publishes the standards for accredited occupational therapy and occupational therapy assistant educational programs?
   a. NBCOT.
   b. ACOTE.
   c. AOTA Commission on Practice.
   d. AOTA Commission on Standards and Ethics.
4. Which of the following is *not* a typical component of an occupational therapy practice act?
   a. Licensure requirements.
   b. Definition of *occupational therapy practice.*
   c. Reimbursement rates for occupational therapy services.
   d. Disciplinary procedures.
5. A key feature of an occupational therapy licensure law is that it
   a. Creates a legally defined scope of practice.
   b. Allows occupational therapy practitioners to perform surgery.
   c. Mandates insurance coverage for occupational therapy.
   d. Allows occupational therapy practitioners to practice in multiple states.
6. The weakest form of state regulation for occupational therapy practitioners is
   a. Licensure.
   b. Title protection.
   c. State certification.
   d. Registration.
7. Which entity typically develops rules or regulations to implement the occupational therapy practice act?
   a. Occupational therapy SRB.
   b. Governor's office.
   c. Centers for Medicare and Medicaid Services.
   d. State department of labor.
8. Which of the following AOTA documents is used as a resource to define the occupational therapy scope of practice in state law?
   a. *Definition of Occupational Therapy Practice for State Regulation.*
   b. *Occupational Therapy Code of Ethics and Ethics Standards.*
   c. *Standards of Practice for Occupational Therapy.*
   d. *Guidelines for Supervision, Roles, and Responsibilities During the Delivery of Occupational Therapy Services.*
9. Occupational therapy SRBs often adopt or incorporate by reference which following document?
   a. *Occupational Therapy Code of Ethics and Ethics Standards.*
   b. Hippocratic Oath.
   c. Patient's Bill of Rights.
   d. Medicare Physician Fee Schedule.
10. Occupational therapy practitioners should become familiar with which aspects of the state's occupational therapy practice act and regulations?
    a. Definition of *occupational therapy practice.*

b. Supervision requirements for occupational therapy assistants.

c. Continuing competence requirements.

d. All of the above.

11. The roles and responsibilities of occupational therapy SRBs do *not* include

a. Investigating violations of the practice act.

b. Issuing licenses to occupational therapists and occupational therapy assistants that meet licensure requirements.

c. Promulgating rules to regulate the profession.

d. Advocating for the profession on reimbursement issues.

12. Which of the following are types of regulatory structures that are used by state governments to regulate the occupational therapy profession?

a. Occupational therapy SRB.

b. State agency administrator.

c. Occupational therapy advisory committee under medical board.

d. All of the above.

13. NBCOT owns which of the following registered marks?

a. OTR and COTA.

b. OT and OTA.

c. OT/L and OTA/L.

d. LOT and LOTA.

14. Disciplinary action may be taken against occupational therapy practitioners by the following entity

a. AOTA Ethics Commission.

b. NBCOT.

c. Occupational therapy SRB.

d. All of the above.

15. Licensure renewal requirements for occupational therapy practitioners often require

a. Retaking the NBCOT examination.

b. Completion of acceptable continuing competence activities.

c. Demonstration of completing fieldwork education.

d. Graduation from a post-professional occupational therapy education program.

16. Which entity administered the registration program for occupational therapists for more than 50 years?

a. AOTA.

b. NBCOT.

c. AOTCB.

d. AOTF.

17. Many SRBs have created additional education and experience requirements beyond entry-level for occupational therapy practitioners that use which of the following interventions

a. Use of physical agent modalities.

b. Therapeutic exercise.

c. Training in activities of daily living.

d. Training in techniques to enhance functional mobility.

18. State occupational therapy practice acts and regulations recognize the entry-level examination for occupational therapists and occupational therapy assistants is administered by

a. AOTA.

b. NBCOT.

c. ACOTE.

d. JCAHO.

19. Which of the following states has a title protection law for occupational therapists and occupational therapy assistants?

a. California.

b. Colorado.

c. Virginia.

d. None of the above.

20. The AOTA document *Guidelines for Supervision, Roles, and Responsibilities During the Delivery of Occupational Therapy Services* asserts the following about aides

a. Minutes of therapy provided by aides in skilled nursing facilities may be counted on the Minimum Data Set.

b. Aides may be supervised by physical therapists.

c. Aides may work as occupational therapy assistants with 6 months of on-the-job training.

d. Aides do not provide skilled occupational therapy services.

References

American Occupational Therapy Association. (1996). *The occupational therapy manager* (rev. ed.). Bethesda, MD: Author.

American Occupational Therapy Association. (2000). *Model occupational therapy practice act*. Bethesda, MD: Author.

American Occupational Therapy Association. (2001, October/November). Building relationships. *AOTA State Affairs Group News*, p. 3.

American Occupational Therapy Association. (2002). Policy 5.3: Licensure Policy. *American Journal of Occupational Therapy, 56,* 670–671.

American Occupational Therapy Association. (2004). Policy 5.3.1: Definition of occupational therapy practice for state regulation. *American Journal of Occupational Therapy, 58,* 694–695.

American Occupational Therapy Association. (2005). *Model state regulation for supervision, roles, and responsibilities during the delivery of occupational therapy services.* Retrieved August 10, 2010, from http://www.aota.org/Practitioners/Advocacy/State/Resources/Supervision/36447.aspx (AOTA Members only).

American Occupational Therapy Association. (2006). *Continuing competence in the occupational therapy profession* [Fact Sheet].

Retrieved February 1, 2010, from http://www.aota.org/Practitioners/Advocacy/State/Resources/ContComp/36433.aspx (AOTA Members only).

American Occupational Therapy Association. (2007). *Model occupational therapy practice act.* Retrieved February 1, 2010, from http://www.aota.org/Practitioners/Advocacy/State/Resources/PracticeAct/36445.aspx (AOTA Members only).

American Occupational Therapy Association. (2008). Occupational therapy practice framework: Domain and process (2nd ed.). *American Journal of Occupational Therapy, 63,* 625–683.

American Occupational Therapy Association. (2009). Guidelines for supervision, roles, and responsibilities during the delivery of occupational therapy services. *American Journal of Occupational Therapy, 63,* 797–803.

American Occupational Therapy Association. (2010a). Occupational therapy code of ethics and ethics standards (2010). *American Journal of Occupational Therapy, 64.*

American Occupational Therapy Association. (2010b). Scope of practice. *American Journal of Occupational Therapy, 64.*

American Occupational Therapy Association, State Affairs Group. (2009). *Occupational therapy: Continuing competence requirements—Summary chart.* Bethesda, MD: Author.

American Occupational Therapy Association, State Affairs Group. (2010a). *Jurisdictions regulating occupational therapists (OTs)* [Fact Sheet]. Bethesda, MD: Author.

American Occupational Therapy Association, State Affairs Group. (2010b). *Jurisdictions regulating occupational therapy assistants (OTAs)* [Fact Sheet]. Bethesda, MD: Author.

California Board of Occupational Therapy. (2010). *Advanced practice.* Retrieved February 1, 2010, from http://www.bot.ca.gov/licensees/advanced.shtml

Gragnola, C. M., & Stone, E. (1997). *Considering the future of health care workforce regulation.* San Francisco: University of California–San Francisco Center for Health Professions.

Federation of State Medical Boards. (2005). *Assessing scope of practice in health care delivery: Critical questions in assuring public access and safety.* Dallas, TX: Author.

Institute of Medicine. (2001). *Crossing the quality chasm: A new health system for the 21st century.* Washington, DC: National Academy Press.

Kohl, R. (2007, December 24). Re-entering the profession—State regulatory considerations [Capital Briefing]. *OT Practice,* p. 6.

Kohl, R. (2008, October 6). OT and early intervention [Capital Briefing]. *OT Practice,* p. 6

Merriam-Webster's dictionary of law. (1996). Regulation. Retrieved February 1, 2010, from http://dictionary.lp.findlaw.com/scripts/results.pl?co=dictionary.lp.findlaw.com&topic=2a/2a88f11f6e30ed88e457de11d9e5e127

Morrison, R. (1996). *Webs of affiliation: The organizational context of health professional regulation.* Last accessed February 1, 2010, at http://www.clearhq.org/resources/morrison_brief.htm

National Board for Certification in Occupational Therapy. (2010a). *Certification examination handbook 2010.* Retrieved August 10, 2010, from http://www.nbcot.org/pdf/Cert-Exam-Handbook.pdf

National Board for Certification in Occupational Therapy. (2010b). *The occupational therapist eligibility determination (OTED®).* Retrieved February 1, 2010, from http://www.nbcot.org/index.php?option=com_content&view=article&id=88&Itemid=117

O'Leary, M. (1994). *Lexikon: Dictionary of health care terms, organizations, and acronyms for the era of reform.* Oakbrook, IL: Joint Commission on Accreditation of Healthcare Organizations.

Pew Health Professions Commission. (1998). *Recreating health professional practice for a new century.* San Francisco: University of California–San Francisco Center for Health Professions. Retrieved August 10, 2010, from http://futurehealth.ucsf.edu/Content/29/1998-12_Recreating_Health_Professional_Practice_for_a_New_Century_The_Fourth_Report_of_the_Pew_Health_Professions_Commission.pdf

Pew Health Professions Commission, Taskforce on Healthcare Workforce Regulation. (1995). *Reforming healthcare workforce regulation: Policy considerations for the 21st century.* Washington, DC: Author.

Pew Health Professions Commission, Taskforce on Healthcare Workforce Regulation. (1998). *Strengthening consumer protection: Priorities for health care workforce regulation.* Washington, DC: Author.

Schmitt, K., & Shimberg, B. (1996). *Demystifying occupational and professional regulation: Answers to questions you may have been afraid to ask.* Lexington, KY: Council on Licensure, Enforcement and Regulation.

Shimberg, B. (1982). *Occupational licensing: A public perspective.* Princeton, NJ: Educational Testing Service.

Shimberg, B., & Roederer, D. (1994). *Questions a legislator should ask* (2nd ed.). Lexington, KY: Council on Licensure, Enforcement, and Regulation.

U.S. Department of Health, Education, and Welfare. (1976). *A proposal for credentialing health manpower.* Washington, DC: U.S. Government Printing Office.

U.S. Department of Health, Education, and Welfare. (1977). *Credentialing health manpower* (Pub. No. OS-77-50057). Bethesda, MD: Author.

Smith, K., & Willmarth, C. (2003). State regulation of occupational therapists and occupational therapy assistants. In G. L. McCormack, E. G. Jaffe, & M. Goodman-Lavey (Eds.), *The occupational therapy manager* (4th ed., pp. 439–459). Bethesda, MD: AOTA Press.

Young, S. D. (1987). *The rule of experts: Occupational licensing in America.* Washington, DC: Cato Institute.

Appendix 29.A. State Regulation Evidence Table

Topic	Subtopic	Evidence
State regulation	Health professions	Federation of State Medical Boards. (2005). *Assessing scope of practice in health care delivery: Critical questions in assuring public access and safety.* Dallas, TX: Author. Institute of Medicine. (2001). *Crossing the quality chasm: A new health system for the 21st century.* Washington, DC: National Academy Press. Morrison, R. (1996). *Webs of affiliation: The organizational context of health professional regulation.* Last accessed February 1, 2010, at http://www.clearhq.org/resources/morrison_brief.htm Pew Health Professions Commission, Taskforce on Healthcare Workforce Regulation. (1995). *Reforming healthcare workforce regulation: Policy considerations for the 21st century.* Washington, DC: Author. Pew Health Professions Commission, Taskforce on Healthcare Workforce Regulation. (1998). *Strengthening consumer protection: Priorities for health care workforce regulation.* Washington, DC: Author. Schmitt, K., & Shimberg, B. (1996). *Demystifying occupational and professional regulations: Answers to questions you may have been afraid to ask.* Lexington, KY: Council on Licensure, Enforcement and Regulation. Shimberg, B. (1982). *Occupational licensing: A public perspective.* Princeton, NJ: Educational Testing Service. U.S. Department of Health, Education, and Welfare. (1976). *A proposal for credentialing health manpower.* Washington, DC: U.S. Government Printing Office.
Occupational therapy	Scope of practice	American Occupational Therapy Association. (2004). Policy 5.3.1: Definition of occupational therapy practice for state regulation. *American Journal of Occupational Therapy, 58,* 694–695. American Occupational Therapy Association. (2008). Occupational therapy practice framework: Domain and process (2nd ed.). *American Journal of Occupational Therapy, 63,* 625–683. American Occupational Therapy Association. (2010a). Occupational therapy code of ethics and ethics standards (2010). *American Journal of Occupational Therapy, 64.* American Occupational Therapy Association. (2010b). Scope of practice. *American Journal of Occupational Therapy, 64.*
Occupational therapy	State regulation	American Occupational Therapy Association. (2002). Policy 5.3: Licensure Policy. *American Journal of Occupational Therapy, 56,* 670–671. American Occupational Therapy Association. (2007). *Model occupational therapy practice act.* Retrieved February 1, 2010, at http://www.aota.org/Practitioners/Advocacy/State/Resources/PracticeAct/36445.aspx (AOTA Members only). American Occupational Therapy Association, State Affairs Group. (2010a). *Jurisdictions regulating occupational therapists (OTs)* [Fact Sheet]. Bethesda, MD: Author. American Occupational Therapy Association, State Affairs Group. (2010b). *Jurisdictions regulating occupational therapy assistants (OTAs)* [Fact Sheet]. Bethesda, MD: Author.

30
Ethical Dimensions of Occupational Therapy

Lea Cheyney Brandt, OTD, OTR/L, and
Deborah Yarett Slater, MS, OT/L, FAOTA

❖ Key Terms and Concepts

Ethical dilemma. A conflict that involves two (or more) morally correct courses of action that cannot both (or all) be followed (Purtilo, 2005).

Ethics. A systematic view of rules of conduct that is grounded in philosophical principles and theory; character and customs of societal values and norms that are assumed in a given cultural, professional, or institutional setting as ways of determining right and wrong (Slater, 2008).

Moral (ethical) distress. The painful feelings and psychological disequilibrium that result from a moral conflict in which one knows the correct action to take, but constraints prevent implementation of the action (Jameton, 1984).

Morality. Personal beliefs regarding values, rules, and principles of what is right or wrong; may be culture-based or culture-driven (Slater, 2008).

Organizational ethics. The ideals and mechanisms that comprise the ethical climate of a health care organization and its impact on associated stakeholders (Mills, Spencer, & Werhane, 2001).

❖ Learning Objectives

After completing this chapter, you should be able to do the following:

- Differentiate between *morality* and *ethics,* and appropriately apply concepts to ethical analysis in clinical occupational therapy practice, including use of a framework for decision making.
- Become familiar with the most prevalent ethics principles addressed in the occupational therapy profession, and identify how they are linked to management responsibilities.
- Understand the relationship among ethical reasoning, the profession's *Occupational Therapy Code of Ethics and*

Ethics Standards (Code and Ethics Standards; American Occupational Therapy Association [AOTA], 2010) and ethical delivery of occupational therapy services.
- Recognize how evolving organizational ethics issues may affect the provision of occupational therapy services.
- Identify barriers occupational therapy managers may encounter in facilitating professional integrity and ethical practice and strategies to address them.

The time is always right to do what is right.
—Martin Luther King, Jr., civil rights leader and minister
(1929–1968; brainyquote.com, n.d.)

The management of occupational therapy services and personnel is a complex enterprise marked by market pressures to "do more with less" in a pluralistic society. Due to the complexity of the current and proposed future health care system, occupational therapy managers and practitioners alike may find it difficult to adhere to the ethics standards that traditionally have defined and molded clinical practice. As a consequence, "the skills of recognizing, defining, and examining ethical tensions become necessary components of managerial decision-making" (Opacich, 2003, p. 494). This chapter outlines the ethical responsibilities and challenges facing occupational therapy managers and provides resources to address them in the context of today's health care environment.

ETHICS FOUNDATIONS

Most health care professionals practice ethics every day and may not even realize they are applying the concepts of *right* and *wrong* to choices in their daily lives. However, it is important to recognize that the study of ethics is systematic in nature and is grounded in philosophical principles and theory. To apply ethical reasoning in management, it is necessary to be able to differentiate among ethics, morality, and the law.

Ethics and Morality

Often health care professionals assume that *ethics* refers to how individuals feel morally, in other words, shared beliefs about right and wrong conduct in a society (Fletcher, Lombardo, Marshall, & Miller, 1997). While this may reflect concepts of common *morality, ethics* is more accurately defined as a practical discipline that provides rules or guidance for how one should act in consideration of others and not necessarily how one feels or believes (Pojman, 2006). Given the complexity and diversity of the environments in which occupational therapy services are provided, it is important to appropriately apply ethical reasoning and refrain from making decisions solely based on value-laden judgments.

Ethical Issue, Distress, or Dilemma

There is no replacement for careful deliberation regarding the ethical implications of an action. Often one is unaware of how to proceed when encountering an ethical issue, ethical distress, or ethical dilemma. The first step is to be able to differentiate among these varying situations. According to ethicist Ruth Purtilo (2005), an *ethical issue* is any situation that one believes may "have important moral challenges embedded in it that [one wants] to identify" (p. 16). An ethical issue is a conflict that may occur frequently with many clients or is a concern for the profession as a whole. For example, an ethical issue common to occupational therapy practice is the demand to increase the productivity standard beyond what appears to be reasonable and the potential negative impact on the quality and benefit of services to a patient (Lopez, Vanner, Cowan, Samuel, & Shepherd, 2008). This issue often results in ethical challenges for the practitioner and manager. In addition, unrealistic productivity expectations may result in poor communication, fragmentation of care, pressure to fraudulently document and bill, and decreased job satisfaction for the provider. Not only can an emphasis on market pressures negatively affect care provision, but ongoing ethics issues also may ultimately result in moral distress (Slater & Brandt, 2009).

Ethical distress relates to the painful feelings and psychological disequilibrium that result from a moral conflict in which one knows the correct action to take, but constraints prevent implementation of the action (Jameton, 1984). Ethical distress is often called *moral distress* because practitioners feel like they may have to compromise their values when providing treatment. Ethical distress, therefore, can result from organizational ethics issues related to the pressure to do more with less and increasing profit as a goal instead of respecting the autonomous clinical decision making of professionals whose focus is to provide client-centered care.

An *ethical dilemma* occurs when one is confronted with a "common type of problem that involves two (or more) morally correct courses of action that cannot both be followed" (Purtilo, 2005, p. 39). Ethical dilemmas also can occur when a practitioner is required to make a decision and must act, but all courses of action violate an ethical principle. For example, an occupational therapy manager may encounter an ethical dilemma when service recipients request clinical interventions that have not been proven to result in benefit; providing that intervention will violate the principle of beneficence (see below). In contrast, refraining from provision of the requested interventions may violate principles of autonomy (see below).

When encountering an ethical dilemma, health care professionals often are inclined to engage in the problematic response of collapsing moral dilemmas into medical or legal questions. To avoid conflict, difficult dialogue, or necessary deliberation, occupational therapy practitioners and managers may respond by attempting to defer ethical decision making to those with expertise in the law or medicine. Again, while it is important to clarify clinical and legal implications to engage in diligent ethical analysis, ethical dilemmas should not be collapsed into medical or legal questions.

The Law and Ethics

The *law* and *ethics* are similar in the sense that a situation is analyzed to decide if it is legal or illegal, ethical or unethical. However, these concepts are not the same. "This is to say that finding out what the law permits or requires is not necessarily to find out what is morally right" (Callahan, 1988, p. 11). Because something is legal does not mean it is ethical; similarly, if something is illegal, it is not always unethical. Although legal information may be relevant and needed for deliberation in making an ethical decision, the law often does not dictate what should be done in any given situation. Instead, the law provides a framework within which decisions should be made.

Ethics and Clinical Expertise

The other common mistake made by practitioners is to generalize expertise in the clinical health care arena to ethics. In the area of medicine, physicians often are assumed to have expertise in ethical aspects of decision making on the basis of their expertise about the technical facts (Fletcher et al., 1997). Occupational therapy practitioners and managers often make the mistake of defaulting to the physician's recommendation with regard to ethical decisions. It is important to recognize that all members of the treating team must be involved in the ethical-reasoning process, including occupational therapy practitioners. In cases in which conflict exists among members of the clinical team, occupational therapy managers may have to step in to resolve it because they may be able to communicate with physicians and other health care professionals in a way that minimizes power imbalances (Brandt, 2007).

Ethical Approaches

In addition to the differentiation between ethics and morality, ethics and the law, and ethics and clinical expertise, ethicists commonly distinguish between approaches used in ethical deliberation. Some approaches to ethical analysis include descriptive ethics, metaethics, and normative ethics.

Descriptive ethics is a fact-based examination of different societies or cultures using scientific inquiry to identify how people reason and act (Beauchamp & Childress, 2009). In descriptive ethics, the scientist is examining a society's perception of right and wrong without judging whether that society has the "correct" ethical principles.

When engaging in *metaethics*, philosophers ask questions about the meaning of moral judgments and principles, how moral knowledge might be possible, and the reasons for cultural beliefs. Metaethics "involves analysis of the language, concepts, and methods of reasoning in normative ethics" to factually identify what is occurring, not what ethically should occur (Beauchamp & Childress, 2009, p. 2). Like descriptive ethics, metaethics rarely enters into health care ethics discussions, as it does not provide guidance as to the direction to take when faced with an ethical issue, distress, or dilemma.

Normative ethics is the practice of putting forward the correct moral principles and rules (Beauchamp & Childress, 2009). However, debate exists as to what the correct moral view may be. This lack of consensus has resulted in the introduction of several normative theories that have been utilized as frameworks to guide ethical decision making in clinical practice (Purtilo, 2005).

ETHICAL THEORIES

To determine the most ethical course of action, normative ethical theories focus on analyzing human acts or human character. Normative ethics generally focuses on the day-to-day deliberations about the right thing to do. Normative theories focusing on acts are epitomized by two major categories, *teleological theories* and *deontological theories* (Callahan, 1988). Contrasting these two major categories are *virtue ethics,* which focuses on human character, and *ethics of care,* which emphasizes intimacy, caring, and relationship building (Rachels & Rachels, 2007). Although certain theories may be more applicable to certain situations, all have strengths and weaknesses in addressing ethical issues arising in daily practice.

Virtue Ethics

Virtue ethicists seek to ascertain the correct virtues that those of strong moral character should have. *Virtue ethics* uses the *moral agent,* the person engaging in the action, as the indicator for whether an action is ethical in nature. Those ethicists who support virtue ethics believe that virtuous individuals will make ethical decisions. Therefore, to determine if an action is ethical or unethical, one only need look at the character of a person who is executing the action. Using virtue ethics, one could argue that an occupational therapy practitioner who chooses the profession for altruistic reasons and has high moral character can be depended on to make ethical decisions. The circular logic of this theory, which "holds the right and the good to be what the virtuous person takes them to be while defining the virtuous person as the one who is and does what is right and good," poses a distinct challenge to the use of virtue ethics as a normative theory (Pellegrino, 2001, p. 114). For example, most can envision a situation in which a typically virtuous person will act in an immoral way when there is a conflict of interest. Conversely, a typically immoral individual may do what is considered ethically right. Compounding the issue is the application of this theory in a pluralistic society. In addition to relying on the character as the basis for moral judgment, the desirability of virtues may vary across cultures, which leads to critiques of subjectivism (Rachels & Rachels, 2007).

Ethics of Care

The ethics of care theory has been criticized for its inability to provide a normative standard for resolution of ethical conflict (Hekman, 1995). *Ethics of care* is a feminist approach to ethical reasoning that focuses on the relationships of the actors in the case (Gilligan, 1982). Ethical action is determined on the basis of the facilitation of solidarity, community, and caring. Ethics of care is arguably the best-suited ethical approach for fostering interpersonal relationships with recipients of health care services by ensuring treatment of the whole person (Purtilo, 2005). However, due to the imprecise nature of using character and relationships as a means to evaluate ethical behavior of professionals, theories that focus on the action versus personal qualities have been used predominantly in the health care arena.

Teleological Theory and Utilitarianism

Teleological theories hold that the rightness of an action depends exclusively on it producing certain kinds of good consequences. In fact "the term *teleological* comes from the Greek *telos,* meaning 'end' or 'goal'" (Callahan, 1988, p. 19; italics added). Teleological theories focus on the outcomes of a proposed action. Teleologists will defend ethical action based on the result. The most recognized version of teleological theory is utilitarianism.

Utilitarianism, which stems from work done by 19th-century British philosophers Jeremy Bentham and John

Stuart Mill (Rachels & Rachels, 2007), states that an act is right if it brings about the greatest happiness for the greatest number, but numerous variations exist on this basic idea among different proponents of utilitarianism. Consider a simple, contrived example. Suppose one is in a situation in which he or she is facing a choice among variable alternative courses of action. He or she could go to the movies, babysit a neighbor's children, or volunteer at a pro bono occupational therapy clinic. Watching television would bring some personal amusement and perhaps education, watching the neighbor's children may make the parents happy and ensure that the children have safe child care, and providing occupational therapy intervention would result in improved occupational performance for several clients and their families. If one determines which situation would bring the most happiness overall in terms of total happiness for all people affected, one might determine that providing occupational therapy services at no cost would bring the greatest amount of happiness (especially to the clients and their families), and a utilitarian would say that this choice would be the right thing to do.

In health care contexts, the appeal of utilitarianism becomes evident in discussions about allocating resources. With only a finite amount of money to spend on health care, where should it be spent? For the same amount of money, should an occupational therapy manger use capital funds to enhance a pediatric clinic, or should the manager support use of funds for pro bono pediatric services for uninsured families? Utilitarianism would advocate doing that which brought the most overall good, or happiness, to the most people.

Although the appeal is evident in this context, all theories are fallible if universally applied. One critique of teleological theory is that there may be unfair consequences for the minority. In addition, some argue that decisions should not be based solely on the potential outcome, as one can never truly be sure of the result until the action is executed.

Deontological Theory

While an individual making a teleological argument might say "the ends justify the means," by contrast, a deontologist would say "the ends *never* justify the means." *Deontological theory* is a common ethics approach that does not emphasize the consequence of one's actions but rather the action itself. The name stems from the Greek word *deon*, meaning "duty" (Callahan, 1988). As opposed to teleological theory, deontology emphasizes the importance of moral duties, obligations, and principles, not consequences. The rightness or wrongness of an act may depend on other situations, such as whether it aligns with or is done for the sake of certain moral rules or principles. In other words, it is not just the consequence of the action; it also is the path to the consequence that matters. While deontologists may agree that ethical reasoning should be based on certain moral principles or duties, they often disagree on which

ethical principles to apply and whether those principles can conflict.

Eighteenth-century German philosopher Immanuel Kant thought that the rightness of an action was predicated on certain universal rules or duties. These universal rules are "derived from a principle that every rational person must accept: The Categorical Imperative" (Rachels & Rachels, 2007, p. 121). The basis of this imperative is that actions must follow certain principles, and one can identify what those principles are by universally applying them to all other people in similar situations. If in willing that everyone follow that principle certain kinds of contradictions present, then according to Kant that principle is not a legitimate moral principle or universal law. So, to use one of Kant's examples, if we take as a moral principle that everyone should be allowed to tell a lie when it is convenient, and it is willed that everyone follow that principle, then one could argue that the whole institution of truth-telling would break down. People could not trust each other if the principle to tell a lie when convenient were followed, and telling a lie would be meaningless. Therefore, Kantians would argue that "it is ethical to tell a lie" is not a legitimate moral principle.

Although general application of Kant's theory is ethically sound, there are several situations in which legitimate moral principles may conflict and Kantian ethics oppose common-sense morality (Rachels & Rachels, 2007). For example, Kant would argue that it would be unethical to lie even for a compelling reason such as saving a life.

In response to flaws in Kant's absolute application of deontological arguments, other deontologists, such as 20th-century Scottish philosopher W. D. Ross, have tried to list general principles in more moderate terms. "Ross held that we have a variety of general duties which arise from our positions and relations in the world, including duties to avoid doing harm, to prevent harm, to repair harm done, to do good, to be loyal, to be truthful, to be grateful, to improve ourselves, to be just" (Callahan, 1988, p. 20). Ross also acknowledges that these duties may conflict. Therefore, he believed that true moral behavior was based on one's ability to identify which duty would take precedence based on the situation in which the conflict occurred.

Many of the principles identified by Ross continue to be applied in the health care environment through ongoing application by bioethicists and through professional codes of ethics such as the Code and Ethics Standards. Duty-based or deontological theories are arguably those that are most used in the health care arena. In addition to those theories developed by Kant and Ross, duty-based theories have evolved in the work completed by ethicists Tom Beauchamp and James Childress. Most codes of ethics used by various health care professions also take a principles-based approach to promoting ethical behavior. Understanding these principles and their application to professional decision making provides a foundation for addressing ethical issues and dilemmas in the health care arena.

PRINCIPLES OF BIOMEDICAL ETHICS

Arguably the most commonly used ethical approach in health care is a principle-driven model framed by Beauchamp and Childress. This model stems from concepts developed through classical deontological ethical theories and is reinforced in *The Belmont Report* (National Institutes of Health, 2009), which focuses on four principles:

1. Respect for autonomy (respect for the freedom of persons),
2. Nonmaleficence (do no harm),
3. Beneficence (do good), and
4. Justice (fairness).

Autonomy

Autonomy refers to an individual's right to self-determination and one's ability to independently act on one's decision for one's own well-being (Beauchamp & Childress, 2009). In other words, to respect autonomy is to respect a person's freedom to make decisions that control his or her life. In health care, most agree that patients deserve to have their autonomy respected, in that they should be presented with the clinical situation, advised of the options and their expected outcomes and risks, and ultimately have the freedom to make decisions about their treatment. To facilitate autonomous choice, clients should not only have the opportunity to make an informed choice but should also not be coerced or misled in this process.

The principle of autonomy often overshadows other ethical obligations, especially in the American health care system. There are limits to a person's autonomy. Although clients and their families may have the ethical right to decline services, they do not have an ethical right under the principle of autonomy to demand services that are not clinically indicated. Often providers and their managers are placed in difficult situations in which clients demand services that the provider believes to be either harmful or nonbeneficial. This example demonstrates a common ethical conflict between the principle of autonomy and two other principles: nonmaleficence and beneficence.

Nonmaleficence

Nonmaleficence is a principle of ethics widely held inside and outside the context of health care that each person has the obligation to refrain from harming another person, unless extraordinary circumstances exist. For example, most would support self-defense but agree that harming an innocent person is morally wrong. In health care, this principle means that clinicians have an obligation not to harm patients without an intended benefit. Temporary pain and discomfort caused by tests, procedures, or other treatment interventions should be balanced with the intended therapeutic benefit. For example, working on range of motion for some patients may be painful, but occupational therapy providers are ethically supported in providing this intervention as long as it is clinically indicated in producing the intended outcome (i.e., increased ability to engage in meaningful occupations, decreased risk for pressure sores, improved function).

Beneficence

The principle of *beneficence* closely relates to nonmaleficence and also is recognized outside of health care, stating that everyone has a general moral obligation to do good for one another. There are, however, limits, in that no other person has a right to demand charity. Examples of beneficence include protecting and defending the rights of others, preventing harm from occurring to others, removing conditions that will cause harm to others, helping persons with disabilities, and rescuing persons in danger (Beauchamp & Childress, 2009).

In health care, the principle of beneficence plays a key role, as recipients of service expect that health care providers will work for their benefit and provide the best possible care. This is based on the fiduciary nature (trust) that characterizes the provider–patient relationship and that is particularly important given the vulnerability of patients in care.

Justice

In health care, the principle of *justice* generally is applied in the context of resource and time allocation. Justice can be interpreted as "fair, equitable, and appropriate treatment in light of what is due or owed to persons" (Beauchamp & Childress, 2009, p. 241). However, the application of this principle is not always clear, as differing interpretations exist of what *fairness* means—equality, based on merit or need. Beauchamp and Childress examine several theories of justice, including utilitarian, libertarian, communitarian, and egalitarian approaches. All identify fair allocation of resources in varying ways.

Although occupational therapy personnel have a vested interest in "addressing unjust inequities that limit opportunities for participation in society" (Braveman & Bass-Haugen, 2009, p. 7), the profession has not developed a definitive approach to just allocation of resources or services. Relevant health care–based discussions often focus primarily on *distributive justice,* which "refers to the fair, equitable and appropriate distribution of resources" (AOTA, 2010). The Code and Ethics Standards also addresses issues related to procedural justice which is the assurance that "processes are organized in a fair manner" (Slater, 2008, p. 172).

The Code and Ethics Standards are predicated on work done by Beauchamp and Childress (Opacich, 2003). In addition, other principles and guidelines are incorporated into this document to assist occupational therapy personnel in the ethical decision-making process and to provide a "guide to professional conduct when ethical issues arise" (AOTA, 2010).

OCCUPATIONAL THERAPY CODE OF ETHICS AND ETHICS STANDARDS (2010)

The hallmark of a profession is the development of ethics standards that make a statement to the public about the values the profession considers important. These standards also inform the public about the conduct to expect from members of that profession. The existence of a code of ethics and other related documents supports the autonomy and greater privilege the public grants to professionals, because they are presumed to answer to a higher standard. There also is an assumption that a breach of those ethical standards will be subject to action by enforcement procedures carried out within the profession.

The Code and Ethics Standards have gone through multiple revisions. Throughout these revisions, the Ethics Standards have been comprised of as many as three documents: the *Occupational Therapy Code of Ethics*, the *Guidelines to the Occupational Therapy Code of Ethics*, and the *Core Values and Attitudes of Occupational Therapy Practice*. The Code was initially adopted by the AOTA Representative Assembly in 1977 and has been revised six times, most recently in 2010 (AOTA, 2010). The *Guidelines*, originally published in 1998, were designed to provide greater specificity and descriptive detail to the broader concepts in the *Code* (AOTA, 2006) Finally, the *Core Values*, developed in 1993, identify timeless values and beliefs to which individuals in the profession are committed (AOTA, 1993). These values and attitudes should drive the interactions occupational therapy practitioners have with those they serve and interact.

According to the AOTA Ethics Commission's *Standard Operating Procedures* (AOTA, Ethics Commission, 2009), the Code is on a 5-year review cycle, as are most of the association's official documents, but can be revised more frequently should important ethical trends arise. It is comprised of 7 principles, many of which also can be found in the ethics codes of other disciplines, as they represent universally accepted professional values. Although the Code may appear to be focused on clinical situations, in fact the language is broad enough in many cases to apply to educational and research settings. In nearly all cases, the principles apply to managers in their personal conduct and the way they operate their areas of responsibility or business and certainly to the values that guide the policies, procedures, and culture of their departments.

Although these documents were developed at different times, they are intended to collectively support ethical conduct and decision-making in all roles in which occupational therapists, occupational therapy assistants, and occupational therapy students may serve. The most recent revision of the Ethics Standards has integrated the three documents into one to more clearly demonstrate their relationship to each other and to facilitate ease in day-to-day use among practitioners, educators, researchers, and students.

The principles of the Code reinforce the duties or responsibilities that occupational therapy personnel can and should apply to resolving ethical issues in their areas of practice (including education). Managers can play an important role in making the Code and Ethics Standards available and visible, both tangibly by placement on the department's bookshelf or intranet and by articulating how they guide development of policies and procedures and support an ethical culture within the department and, ideally, the larger organization.

ORGANIZATIONAL ETHICS

Some of the top ethical issues facing occupational therapy managers today stem from conflicts related to organizational ethics, such as

- Unrealistic productivity expectations that ignore client needs, leading to potentially fraudulent documentation and billing;
- Pressure to provide intervention beyond a practitioner's competency or the profession's scope of practice; and
- Inadequate supervision and use of unqualified personnel to provide skilled services.

Organizational ethics and clinical ethics differ in that *organizational ethics* issues relate to business practices that include marketing, billing, managed care, and institutional policies, whereas *clinical ethics* primarily focus on patient care and rights (Fletcher et al., 1997). Ethical issues related to organizational behavior have become more evident in recent years with the emergence of a more explicit market approach to medicine (American Society for Bioethics and Humanities, 1998). The underlying conflicts between health care provision and market systems have resulted in a push toward the integration of organizational ethics into the health care environment.

In recent years, organizational ethics has emerged as one of the most prevalent concerns for occupational therapy practitioners due to the business environment in which therapy often is provided (Slater & Brandt, 2009). In addition, clinical ethics issues continue to persist in occupational therapy practice. In fact, clinical decisions by occupational therapy personnel are often strongly influenced by and subject to organizational directives that include the pressure to do more with fewer resources. This example demonstrates that while organizational and clinical ethics are distinct subsets of ethics, they are not mutually exclusive and can be highly interrelated. An emphasis on reimbursement-driven decision making can threaten to override the traditional autonomy clinicians have had in evaluating and developing individualized plans of care and implementing service delivery based on a patient's unique clinical needs. Therefore, many clinical ethics issues cannot be resolved without considering the organizational context.

With this integration has been speculation on whether business ethics and clinical ethics can coexist within the infrastructure of the health care institution. However, an organization's attention to ethical issues does not have to detract from a business-based agenda. In addition, decisions focusing on financial gains in place of quality indicators can undermine the public's view of the organization, longitudinally leading to financial insolvency marked by decreased market share. If a facility has a strong reputation in the community as a health advocate and ethical organization, the number of self-referrals potentially can increase, as well as the degree of market power wielded by the organization (Weeks & Bagian, 2003; Weeks & Mills, 2003).

Public relations expenses are one cost implication associated with ethical conflicts (Nelson & Campfield, 2008). In fact, a more comprehensive approach to ethics management has been shown to "reduce the occurrence of ethical conflicts along with many kinds of associated economic costs and negative operational intangibles" (MacLeod, 2008, p. 52). Therefore, integrating ethics into practice can lead to improved patient satisfaction, employee morale, and loyalty; to fewer lawsuits and unwanted and wasteful treatments; and to enhanced efficiency, productivity, and professionalism, thereby also benefitting the organization (Veterans Health Administration [VHA], 2009c). For example, following adverse events in the health care setting, fewer lawsuits were reported when practitioners provided full, honest explanations and apologies and did not treat patients as "neurotic" (Vincent, Young, & Phillips, 1994).

Integrated ethics programs (IEPs) refocus "an organization's approach to ethics in health care from a reactive, case-based endeavor in which various aspects of ethics (e.g., clinical, organizational, professional, research, business, government) are handled in a disjointed fashion, into a proactive, systems-oriented, comprehensive approach" (VHA, 2009b, p. 12). Truly integrated ethics programming will move ethics toward organizational collaboration, which "emphasizes that rules-oriented compliance approaches and values-oriented integrity approaches *both* play vital roles in the ethical life of organizations" (VHA, 2009b, p. 12). Through an IEP, policies and procedures are proactively established to promote an explicitly ethical system of health care delivery. Instead of attempting to resolve an ethical dilemma related to a specific case, an IEP should ask, "What organizational policies, procedures, or structures contributed to the moral dilemma or distress? [And] what alternatives might have alleviated or prevented such a problem?" (Goold, Kamil, Cohan, & Stefansky, 2000, p. 72). This type of analysis also is relevant in providing guidance to occupational therapy managers as they seek to replicate an ethical culture within their own areas of responsibility and among their staff.

Even though development of proactive policies and procedures can lead to fewer ethical conflicts, ethical dilemmas in health care will inevitably continue to arise. When they do, individual clinicians as well as organizations must be aware of their ethical obligations and responsibilities. Ethics programming that promotes systems-level analysis will encourage accountability throughout the organization. However, without an established ethical culture, it is unfair to assume that professionals are aware of their ethical obligations. Similarly, if ethics are not promoted at an administrative level, it is difficult to hold practitioners accountable for their actions. Lack of a consistent ethical culture throughout the organization also can present a barrier to the occupational therapy manager as the procedures, values, and expectations that he or she wish to enforce within their department may be contradicted by what actually occurs in the greater institution, putting practitioners and the manager himself or herself in an ethical conflict.

CREATING AN ETHICAL CULTURE THROUGH ETHICAL LEADERSHIP

Occupational therapy practice and, specifically, management of occupational therapy service provision is and will continue to be influenced by organizational pressures. Occupational therapy managers, as with many in middle management, may face particular challenges as they seek to create an ethical culture that is clearly demonstrated by their words, reasoning, actions, and expectations but that may or may not mirror that culture at the highest organizational levels. Managers must acquire tools to effectively address organizational ethics issues and their impact on delivery of clinical services if there is no system-wide program. But principles of an integrated ethics system as previously described for organizations also can be adopted within the departments for which the manager has responsibility.

In addition, the VHA (2009a) has worked to develop leadership tools for ethics management and promoting an ethical work environment. Managers can play an influential role in assisting occupational therapy personnel and other health care professionals in adhering to ethical principles in practice. Conversely as is relayed in the following examples, managers can inadvertently encourage unethical behavior.

The VHA's (2009a) National Center for Ethics outlines four ways in which health care leaders and managers can influence unethical behavior:

1. Failing to link performance incentives to ethical practice,
2. Overemphasizing compliance with legal standards,
3. Setting unrealistic expectations of performance, and
4. Blaming individuals inappropriately.

Failing to Link Performance Incentives to Ethical Practice

Failing to link performance incentives to ethical practice occurs "when leaders create strong incentives to perform in certain areas without creating equally strong incentives to adhere to ethical practice in achieving the desired goals" (VHA, 2009a, p. 18). This can occur in occupational therapy practice when, for example, compensation is tied to productivity. This is especially problematic when monetary incentives are linked to the quantity of billable services without implementation of associated quality safeguards. For example, practitioners should not be directed to provide group therapy yet document and charge as if individual therapy had been rendered. Practitioners should not be monetarily incentivized for increasing productivity through such means.

Overemphasizing Compliance With Legal Standards

Although compliance with legal standards is linked to the ethical principle of procedural justice in the Code and Ethics Standards, overemphasis on legal compliance may still result in unethical practice. While "employees must know, understand, and adhere to law and regulation, and policy…studies have shown that an organizational culture that emphasizes obedience to authority and following rules is associated with more unethical behavior than a culture that emphasizes" values-based accountability (VHA, 2009a, p. 18).

In the occupational therapy profession, there may be instances in which a practitioner may act in a way that he or she believes to be in accordance with the law or policy, knowing that it is not in the patient's best interest or in line with professional values. For example, there has been much speculation with regard to truth-telling and transparency in the health care environment. Although studies continue to demonstrate that it is in the organization's best interests to disclose medical errors, many organizations continue to have policies that prohibit or limit disclosure of error to patients. Although prudence is always encouraged, there may be situations in which *veracity*, or the duty to tell the truth, outweighs the duty to adhere to procedural justice principles. Values of the profession that promote altruism and justice may assist providers and managers in making these very difficult decisions. Support in both the department and the organization for such values will reinforce appropriate priorities in providing care and avoid placing employees in situations of ethical conflict.

Setting Unrealistic Expectations of Performance

The pitfall of setting unrealistic expectations for performance can "invite employees to game the system or misrepresent results" (VHA, 2009a, p. 19). With market pressures to remain financially viable or capture a profit in an environment with significant limitations on reimbursement, managers may be directed by higher level administrators (or may be tempted by their own financial incentives or goals) to raise productivity standards to an unrealistic level. The goal to serve more clients with fewer staff may appear reasonable, and there may be realistic financial considerations that force managers to assess staff numbers and levels of personnel in their departments to serve a fixed number of clients.

However, it is the manager's ethical responsibility to ensure that the clinical needs and benefit of patients are the first priorities and are not ultimately compromised. When occupational therapy providers are working hard to meet patient needs in a complex health care system with many barriers to care provision, they may become cynical and frustrated when management does not seem to hear their concerns. Setting unrealistic productivity standards may indicate to employees that management goals are strictly

based on improving profit margin and not on providing quality of care or a providing a healthy work environment for employees who are producing those profits. This can be at odds with public statements from administration about the values of the organization and can put managers and employees in a challenging position.

Blaming Individuals Inappropriately

Managers have a responsibility to hold employees accountable for their actions. However, when managers inappropriately blame individuals for outcomes out of their control, it "sends a message that ethics doesn't matter much" (VHA 2009a, p. 19). Picture, for example, during a particularly tight staffing day, one of the department occupational therapists states that she has injured her back during a transfer, has gone to employee health, and will be on medical leave pending her worker's compensation medical evaluation. The department will be short-staffed for up to 12 weeks, and a worker's compensation claim will have a negative impact on the budget. Although difficult, it is especially important in this situation to refrain from blaming the employee. A flawed organizational process may have contributed to this injury rather than personal irresponsibility. Managers who focus on process improvement, such as increasing access to mechanical lifts, increasing practitioner awareness of the impact of the increasing weight of patient populations, and putting policies in place that support employee safety, set a tone that fosters ethical practice standards within the department. Although this may be more difficult in some organizations than in others, when leaders consistently adhere to ethical standards in management, they have an opportunity to influence the culture of the organization as a whole.

Creating an Ethical Culture

Managers also have a responsibility to create a workplace culture based on integrity, accountability, fairness, and respect. They can empower and support employees to "do the right thing." Creating an ethical culture will benefit employee morale and, ultimately, productivity and customer relations. In addition, it also will likely increase quality of care by reinforcing the altruism that led employees to choose occupational therapy as a profession and the importance of respecting patient autonomy related to care decisions.

Leadership always begins by example and is reinforced when a manager's actions mirror his or her words. Setting aspirational goals and mirroring exemplary behavioral expectations, for example, what one *should do* versus what one *must do*, is a good start to developing an ethical culture within the department. Others include promoting competency in ethical reasoning through providing access to continuing education; raising awareness of or promoting available resources (see Exhibit 30.1); and, most important, assisting employees in applying a framework for ethical decision making (see below) to analyze clinical situations that may pose ethical dilemmas.

Continuing education through a variety of means that is related to aspects of clinical practice is important, as each

Exhibit 30.1. Ethics Resources

- **The Hastings Center:** www.thehastingscenter.org
  - o The Hastings Center, founded in 1969 and located in Garrison, NY, is a nonprofit bioethics research-based institute, whose mission is "to address fundamental ethical issues in the areas of health, medicine, and the environment as they affect individuals, communities, and societies."
- **Kennedy Institute of Ethics:** http://kennedy institute.georgetown.edu
  - o The Kennedy Institute of Ethics, founded at Georgetown University in 1971, is a world-renowned comprehensive center for bioethics, which includes an extensive research library.
- *American Journal of Bioethics:* http://www .bioethics.net/journal
  - o This comprehensive bioethics Web site contains everything from journal articles to news briefs and job postings.
- **Center for Practical Bioethics:** http://www .practicalbioethics.org/
  - o The Center for Practical Bioethics, in Kansas City, MO, is an independent, nonprofit organization recognized as a resource for health care professionals, patients and their families, policymakers, and corporations attempting to resolve ethics-based issues in medicine and research.
- **National Bioethics Advisory Commission:** http:// www.bioethics.gov
  - o This Web site links users to information regarding The Presidential Commission for the Study of Bioethical Issues, which acts as an advisory board to the President of the United States addressing bioethical issues related to areas of science and technology.
- **AOTA:** ethics@aota.org
  - o E-mailbox for member questions and consultation on ethical issues.

productivity or "efficiency" but also to maximize the billing codes that can be charged. Given the limited timeframe, it may not be possible to evaluate patients with neurological diagnoses, those who are more elderly, or those who have complex medical issues adequately to identify problems needed to develop an appropriate plan of care and goals. In addition, a focus on identifying occupational performance deficits that is the philosophical basis of the profession requires some time in discussion with patients or clients to determine meaningful activities with which they are having difficulty. This may not lend itself to a cursory evaluation, followed by a treatment session of routine exercises. Principle 1B of the Code and Ethics Standards emphasizes the need for appropriate evaluation and plan of care as the basis for providing specific services (AOTA, 2010).

An important component of a manager's job is developing staffing and service delivery models. In health care, salaries (with benefits) may be one of the largest budgetary expenses. There inevitably will be pressure to utilize different levels of personnel to save money and continue to provide billable services to as many patients as possible. This can incentivize the manager to limit the number of occupational therapists, use them largely to perform evaluations, or utilize occupational therapy assistants and even aides to provide much of the clinical services. While this may meet budgetary constraints, it is the manager's responsibility to understand the legal and ethical parameters related to the use of all levels of personnel and the services they provide. The manager must clearly be aware of and comply with state licensure laws related to scope of practice for occupational therapy assistants and aides, if they can be legally used at all. In addition, managers must comply with applicable payer regulations for providing skilled services.

From an ethical perspective, managers must support their clinicians in decisions about the most appropriate type (e.g., group, individual), duration, and frequency of therapy based on client need and benefit provided that those decisions accurately reflect the clinical data that is obtained and documented. They also have a responsibility to ensure that occupational therapy assistants and aides have appropriate (to meet state licensure laws and professional standards of practice) supervision with delegated aspects of care so that patients or clients are safe and receive beneficial services to meet their goals.

On the other hand, managers have accountability for contributing to the financial viability of the organization and for operating a service that utilizes personnel as productively and efficiently as possible so that patients move through the system without undue delay. This can create an ethical conflict for managers who may feel caught in the middle, answering to both their senior administration and their direct-report staff from whom they need respect and collaboration. Managers must expect to be creative and flexible in balancing priorities arising from the needs of both groups. In the past, traditional therapy often used a 1:1 model, hour-long intervention by an occupational therapist. However, a skilled manager who analyzes the caseload, diagnostic mix, staff clinical skill sets, and setting can match different levels of all occupational therapy

ethical dilemma may be unique. Therefore, developing reasoning skills in this area is more helpful than rules that may not be applicable to every situation. Departmental inservices using case examples for analysis with the Ethics Standards and other relevant ethics literature can promote development of ethical reasoning.

In addition, managers should analyze systemic situations that seem to cause the most frequent ethical angst to staff. Proactive policies, procedures, and educational efforts can focus on addressing them preventively rather than taking a reactive approach. An example of such a situation could be pressure to schedule patients for 20-minute evaluation slots, with the last 10 minutes being treatment. This may be an effort to maximize personnel (e.g., occupational therapists, occupational therapy assistants, aides) with varied service delivery methods (e.g., individual, group, concurrent) to effectively meet the needs of a variety of patients, some of whom need more intensive or individualized intervention than others.

The key is to know the laws, regulations, and ethical tenets that guide practice and always focus on what will benefit the patient. Transparent communication that is supported by objective data may be effective in convincing upper management that adequate and competent staff and clinically driven decisions can result in better, more cost-effective outcomes and have a positive impact on length of stay and the bottom line while decreasing moral distress (Slater & Brandt, 2009).

In addition, limitations in insurance coverage may pose a challenge for clients who need ongoing services and have no alternate payment sources. This can create an ethical dilemma for clinicians who feel that the client's needs exceed the allowable therapy visits. Managers should be aware that occupational therapy practitioners may exhibit moral sensitivity that may manifest as moral distress in situations of ethical conflict resulting from organizational ethics constraints. Because many clinicians seek out the occupational therapy profession for altruistic purposes, when practitioners feel constrained in providing clinically indicated services, negative outcomes associated with moral distress may surface (Slater & Brandt, 2009). In this situation, a manager may reduce the factors contributing to moral distress by being aware of institutional policies related to reduced-fee, free care, or other alternate methods that may be available to cover needed therapy. The manager also should problem solve with the clinician about strategies to enable clients to achieve their goals when therapy sessions may be limited.

PROFESSIONAL OVERSIGHT AND DISCIPLINARY ACTION

Despite the best efforts to develop and support an ethical culture, violations or unprofessional conduct can occur. This reflects poorly on those within the profession and of course has the potential to inflict harm on clients, violating a basic ethical tenet. Three agencies oversee the occupational therapy profession: AOTA, state licensure boards, and the National Board for Certification in Occupational Therapy. Each has specific jurisdictional oversight and procedures for filing complaints, as well as varied disciplinary sanctions depending on the gravity of the offense. Managers must understand the differences between these agencies and their potential actions should they need to report unethical or unprofessional conduct or advise others (for more information, see Chapter 29 on state regulation).

FRAMEWORK FOR ETHICAL DECISION MAKING

While many models for addressing ethical dilemmas exist, most have common key components:

- What is the nature of the perceived problem (e.g., ethical distress, ethical dilemma), and what is the specific problem (i.e., "name and frame" the problem)?

- Who are the players—not just those immediately involved but others who may be influenced by the situation or any decision that is made?
- What information is known, and what additional information is needed to thoroughly evaluate the situation and formulate options?
- What resources are available to assist?
- What are the options and likely consequences of each option?
- How are values prioritized (e.g., prioritize moral values, despite potential negative personal repercussions, to act on best decision)? Good intentions do not always bring about good deeds (Kanny & Slater, 2008).
- What action is being taken, and is it defensible?
- Was the outcome expected? Would one make a different decision if confronted with a similiar situation in the future?

While a framework provides a systematic method of working through an ethically challenging situation, the benefits of utilizing external or additional resources are important. Managers must be aware of available resources and facilitate access to them by their staff. In an organization with an integrated ethics program, this will be easier, as systems will be designed to support education and transparency with a goal of open communication to address ethical challenges at all levels of the institution. In other facilities, an Ethics Committee of knowledgeable and competent members can provide valuable assistance in clarifying issues and potential actions for a patient-specific issue with the health care team so there is consensus and consistency. An Ethics Committee also can advise managers about relevant literature and other educational materials that can assist them in formulating departmental policies and procedures supporting an ethical culture. Librarians may assist with literature searches on aspects of ethics related to organizational cultures. AOTA also offers a variety of educational resources (in addition to the Code and Ethics Standards and *Reference Guide to the Occupational Therapy Code and Ethics Standards,* Slater, 2010), an ethics mailbox (ethics@aota.org) for answering questions, and individualized consultation to managers who want to ensure that they develop systems to support ethical practice operations and staff policies.

CONCLUSION

Occupational therapy managers play a critical role in developing and maintaining an ethical culture in their departments as well as promoting systems and policies that support ethical conduct within their organizations. Knowledge of basic ethics theories and resources, as well as a commitment to competence in ethical reasoning, are important skills for managers to develop and model for their employees and colleagues at all levels. Effective managers need to understand organizational and environmental forces that affect the provision of services within institutional systems and how to balance these with their ultimate responsibility to oversee high-quality care that complies with the Ethics Standards of the occupational therapy profession.

Case Examples

Everything you do sends a message about who you are and what you value.
—Michael Josephson, founder of Character Counts and the Josephson Institute (Forcharacter.com, n.d.)

FIELDWORK I

While shadowing his clinical supervisor, an occupational therapy assistant student observes his supervisor providing substandard care to patients who are receiving financial assistance through a charity care fund set up for indigent patients. The supervisor also makes inappropriate comments about the patients, stating "these people are a drain on society."

Guiding Questions—

- What principles in the Code and Ethics Standards have been violated in this scenario?
- What are some possible actions and their results?
- What is the best action to take, and why?

FIELDWORK II

An occupational therapy student is asked to work with a patient who has been diagnosed with pancreatic cancer and is asking for palliative care. The patient consistently refuses occupational therapy intervention and has stated that she does not want to work toward goals related to rehabilitation. The physician and family are pressuring the patient and student to work toward goals to increase independence with activities of daily living no longer valued by the patient. When the student discusses the issues with her clinical supervisor, the supervisor informs her that because the physician and family are both in agreement that the patient should continue to receive occupational therapy services, intervention must be provided consistent with their wishes.

Guiding Questions—

- What principles of the Code and Ethics Standards may be violated here?
- Who are the involved parties?
- Whose rights should prevail, and why?
- What actions might be taken to address this situation?

FIRST-TIME MANAGER

An occupational therapist discharges a patient from services, as the patient is no longer making progress toward goals. The patient complains to his physician, who writes another referral for occupational therapy services 3x/week for 12 weeks. The physician calls the manager to complain about the discharge, which was done without the physician's knowledge. The physician states that if any employee discharges one of his patients without conferring with him first, he will no longer refer patients to the clinic. To complicate the situation, last week the director said she was concerned about the recent decline in outpatient referrals for therapy services. As a result, a target of increasing referrals by 3% in the next 6 months was added to the manager's performance goals, which will adversely affect the manager's annual raise if not met by the end of the fiscal year.

Guiding Questions—

- What are the ethical issues?
- What possible actions can be taken?
- Which is the best option, and why?

MANAGER

The occupational therapy manager is told by administration that all outpatient pediatric programming will be eliminated, as it is not revenue generating. The manager feels that this action will result in patient abandonment, as her employees provide care in the neonatal intensive care unit and will not be able to follow through with treatment interventions if outpatient programming is cut. In addition, all outpatient-based pediatric practices in the area have closed due to financial insolvency.

Guiding Questions—

- What are the ethical issues?
- Who are the stakeholders affected by this decision?
- What additional information may be helpful in developing potential options?
- Are there strategies that the manager can take to address or reverse this decision?
- Which is the best strategy, and why?

❖ Learning Activities

1. Who or what have been the three most important influences on your understanding of right and wrong?
2. What three things do you value most, and why?
3. Name three qualities or "virtues" that you think are essential in living a moral life.
4. Think about a situation in fiedwork or in your job that created moral distress and how you handled it, if at all, and how you would handle it having read this chapter.

5. Complete an ethical analysis of either a case or ethical issue relevant to occupational therapy practice. Utilize Ethics Commission advisory opinions as a framework for paper development. Review *OT Practice* articles, the AOTA Web site, relevant issues in the media/newspapers, and so forth to identify possible topics for the assignment. Use the Framework for Ethical Decision Making in this chapter for the analysis.

✓ Multiple-Choice Questions

1. Carey has researched the best techniques in scar management. Because Carey believes that no other interventions are comparable to the one he has chosen, he does not explain the options or ask patients what outcomes they expect or desire. Carey is not upholding the ethical principle of
   a. Beneficence.
   b. Confidentiality.
   c. Nonmaleficence.
   d. Autonomy.
2. Dr. Smith is lecturing about the concepts of providing therapeutic interventions based on the clinical needs of the client and utilizing techniques that have demonstrated therapeutic benefit. He is talking primarily about aspects of the concept of
   a. Fidelity.
   b. Beneficence.
   c. Justice.
   d. Morality.
3. Lauren and Stuart, occupational therapy students, are discussing nonmaleficence and conclude that the best description of the concept involves taking responsibility for
   a. Protecting privileged confidential information and forms for all clients.
   b. Advocating for recipients to obtain needed services through available means.
   c. Being familiar with all laws and policies that apply to occupational therapy.
   d. Addressing personal problems that may impair professional judgment.
4. Wanda and Joe are trying to differentiate among deontological, teleological, and virtue-based ethical theories. Teleological ethics would be best described as
   a. Theory related to the idea that the outcome justifies the actions taken.
   b. Theory that bases concepts of right and wrong on the character of the actors.

   c. Theory that examines the societal perspectives of right and wrong.
   d. Theory of ethics based on the concept of duty.
5. To differentiate between morality and ethics, Juan and Carol conclude that morality is most often expressed in a
   a. Code followed by a professional organization.
   b. Discipline of study based on philosophical principles.
   c. Theory of cultural behavior in the western hemisphere.
   d. Shared belief system about right and wrong conduct in society.
6. Fergie, an occupational therapy manager, hears from a colleague that Bessy, a staff occupational therapy assistant, is sleeping in the break room instead of seeing patients. Because Bessy has always been a dedicated employee, instead of believing the accusations, Fergie opts to speak directly to Bessy to get an explanation for her out-of-character behavior. Which ethical theory is Fergie using to shape her actions?
   a. Teleology.
   b. Virtue ethics.
   c. Deontology.
   d. Principle-driven ethics.
7. Which of the following is not an important function of a code of ethics?
   a. Identify and describe the values supported by the occupational therapy profession.
   b. Socialize occupational therapy personnel new to the profession to expected standards of conduct.
   c. Enhance the visibility and profitability of the occupational therapy profession.
   d. Educate the general public and members about established principles of professional conduct for which occupational therapy personnel are accountable.
8. The Code and Ethics Standards apply to the following individuals
   a. Occupational therapists.
   b. Occupational therapy assistants.

c. Occupational therapists, occupational therapy assistants, and students.

d. Occupational therapists, occupational therapy assistants, and their employers.

9. Sarah is an occupational therapy manager is an outpatient pediatric clinic. After ongoing discussions with a family who has not kept 10 out of the last 12 scheduled visits, she decides to encourage the treating occupational therapist to discharge the child, as there is an extensive waiting list for the clinic's services. Which of the following ethical theories may be guiding Sarah's decision?

a. Virtue ethics.

b. Utilitarianism.

c. Ethics of care.

d. Beneficence.

10. John is a manager for an inpatient rehabilitation unit. Barry, an occupational therapist, tells him that he observed Beth, the physical therapist, inappropriately yelling at a patient during her morning session. He also asks John to please not tell Beth that he was the person who disclosed this information. John tells Barry that he appreciates having the information brought to his attention, and he will talk to Beth. However, if Beth asks how he knows about the incident, he will have to disclose that Barry brought it to his attention. Which ethical approach is John applying to the situation?

a. Teleological.

b. Virtue ethics.

c. Ethics of care.

d. Kantian.

11. Once facing an ethical dilemma, the next step is to

a. Determine your risk or impact on your future career.

b. Check if your malpractice insurance is up to date.

c. Identify additional information needed and collect it.

d. Report the individual's behavior to all state and national agencies.

12. Rowena owns a durable medical equipment business in addition to her occupational therapy private practice. She frequently makes recommendations to her patients about equipment and only provides one recommendation for purchase, which is from her own business. Her behavior may be an example of

a. Professionalism.

b. Conflict of commitment.

c. Conflict of interest.

d. Violation of universal moral laws.

13. Which of the following is not applicable to analyzing or resolving ethical dilemmas?

a. Framework for decision making.

b. Ethics Committee.

c. AOTA Code and Ethics Standards.

d. Consulting a lawyer.

14. Competent managers reflect on their management duties

a. Annually, during their performance evaluations.

b. Each time the Code of Ethics is revised.

c. Daily.

d. When they believe they have an ethical dilemma or have committed a medical error.

15. Characteristics of an integrated ethics system include all but which of the following:

a. Systemwide ethics policies.

b. Policy of nondisclosure of medical errors.

c. Promoting values-based decision making.

d. Identified accountability.

16. Sue is accused by her employer of violating facility policy by failing to post a bedside sign with the wearing schedule for her patient's splint. The patient has diabetes, has fragile skin, and developed a pressure sore when the splint was left on for 24 hours without removal. The facility is taking action against Sue. Which agency would *not* be appropriate to consider in filing a complaint?

a. AOTA Ethics Commission.

b. State occupational therapy association.

c. National Board for Certification in Occupational Therapy.

d. State licensure board.

17. Competency in ethical reasoning can be developed through all of the following except

a. Continuing education on ethics.

b. Increasing familiarity with a framework for ethical decision making.

c. Attending a course on physical agent modalities.

d. Reading the Code and Ethics Standards.

18. Name one way in which managers can promote ethical behavior.

a. Linking performance incentives to ethical practice.

b. Overemphasizing compliance with legal standards.

c. Setting unrealistic expectations for performance.

d. Inappropriately blaming individuals.

19. All of the following are possible benefits of an integrated ethics program except:

a. Improved employee morale.

b. Eradication of moral distress.

c. Fewer lawsuits.

d. Enhanced ethical decision making.

20. To meet productivity standards in his skilled nursing facility, Gabe could engage in all of the following except

a. Charging for individual treatment while treating multiple patients in a group.

b. Using an occupational therapy assistant where appropriate to maximize access to treatment.

c. Using rehabilitation aides, if appropriate, to transport patients to the treatment site and increase efficiency.

d. Using support staff to create transportable, occupation-based "kits" to decrease set-up time for intervention sessions.

References

American Occupational Therapy Association. (1993). Core values and attitudes of occupational therapy practice. *American Journal of Occupational Therapy, 47*, 1085–1086.

American Occupational Therapy Association. (2006). Guidelines to the occupational therapy code of ethics. *American Journal of Occupational Therapy, 60*, 652–658.

American Occupational Therapy Association. (2010). Occupational therapy code of ethics and ethics standards (2010). *American Journal of Occupational Therapy, 64*.

American Occupational Therapy Association, Ethics Commission. (2007). *Everyday ethics: Core knowledge for practitioners and educators* [CEonCD]. Bethesda, MD: Author.

American Occupational Therapy Association, Ethics Commission. (2009). *American Occupational Therapy Association's Ethics Commission standard operating procedures*. Bethesda, MD: Author.

American Society for Bioethics and Humanities. (1998). *Core competencies for health care ethics consultation*. Glenview, IL: Author.

Beauchamp, T. L., & Childress, J. F. (2009). *Principles of biomedical ethics* (6th ed.). New York: Oxford University Press.

Brainyquote.com. (n.d.). *Martin Luther King, Jr. quotes*. Retrieved August 12, 2010, from http://www.brainyquote.com/quotes/authors/m/martin_luther_king_jr_5.html

Brandt, L. C. (2007, November 26). Organizational ethics. *OT Practice*, pp. 15–19.

Brandt, L. C. (2009a). *Moral distress: Surviving clinical chaos* [CEonCD]. Bethesda, MD: American Occupational Therapy Association.

Brandt, L. C. (2009b). *Organizational ethics* [CEonCD]. Bethesda, MD: American Occupational Therapy Association.

Braveman, B., & Bass-Haugen, J. D. (2009). From the Desks of the Guest Editors—Social justice and health disparities: An evolving discourse in occupational therapy research and intervention. *American Journal of Occupational Therapy, 63*, 7–12.

Callahan, J. C. (1988). *Ethical issues in professional life*. New York: Oxford University Press.

Fletcher, J. C., Lombardo, P. A., Marshall, M. F., & Miller, F. G. (1997). *Introduction to clinical ethics*. Hagerstown, MD: University Publishing Group.

Forcharacter.com. (n.d.). *Quotations discussion guide*. Retrieved August 12, 2010, from http://www.forcharacter.com/quotationguide.htm

Gilligan, C. (1982). *In a different voice*. Cambridge, MA: Harvard University Press.

Goold, S., Kamil, L., Cohan, N., & Sefansky, S. (2000). Outline of a process for organizational ethics consultation. *HEC Forum, 12*(1), 69–77.

Hekman, S. J. (1995). *Moral voices, moral selves*. University Park, PA: Pennsylvania State University Press.

Jameton, A. (1984). *Nursing practice: The ethical issues*. Englewood Cliffs, NJ: Prentice Hall.

Kanny, E. M., and Slater, D. Y. (2008). Ethical Reasoning. In B. A. Boyt Schell and J. W. Schell (Eds.), *Clinical and professional reasoning in occupational therapy* (pp. 188–208). Philadelphia: Wolters Kluwer/Lippincott Williams & Wilkins.

Lopez, A., Vanner, E. A., Cowan, A. M., Samuel, A. P., & Shepherd, D. L. (2008). Intervention planning facets—Four facets of occupational therapy intervention planning: Economics, ethics, professional judgment, and evidence-based practice. *American Journal of Occupational Therapy, 62*, 87–96.

MacLeod, L. (2008). The organizational costs of ethical conflicts: Practitioner application. *Journal of Healthcare Management, 53*(1), 52–53.

Mills, A. E., Spencer, E. M., & Werhane, P. H. (2001). *Developing organization ethics in health care: A case-based approach to policy, practice, and compliance*. Hagerstown, MD: University Publishing Group.

National Institutes of Health. (2009). *The Belmont Report: Ethical principles and guidelines for the protection of human subjects of research*. Retrieved July 1, 2009, from http://ohsr.od.nih.gov/guidelines/belmont.html

Nelson, W. A., & Campfield, J. M. (2008). The organizational costs of ethical conflicts. *Journal of Healthcare Management, 53*(1), 41–52.

Opacich, K. (2003). Ethical dimensions of occupational therapy management. In G. L. McCormack, E. G. Jaffe, & M. Goodman-Lavey (Eds.), *The occupational therapy manager* (4th ed., pp. 491–511). Bethesda, MD: AOTA Press.

Pellegrino, E. (2001). *Physician philosopher: The philosophical foundation of medicine: Essays by Dr. Edmund Pellegrino*. Charlottesville, VA: Carden Jennings.

Pojman, L. P. (2006). *Ethics: Discovering right and wrong* (5th ed.). Belmont, CA: Thomson Wadsworth.

Purtilo, R. (2005). *Ethical dimensions in the health professions* (4th ed.). Philadelphia: Elsevier/Saunders.

Rachels, J., & Rachels, S. (2007). *The elements of moral philosophy* (5th ed.). Boston: McGraw Hill.

Slater, D. Y. (Ed.). (2010). *Reference guide to the occupational therapy ethics standards* (2010 ed.). Bethesda, MD: AOTA Press.

Slater, D. Y., & Brandt, L. C. (2009, February 2). Combating moral distress. *OT Practice*, pp. 13–18.

Veterans Health Administration. (2009a). *Ethical leadership: Fostering an ethical environment and culture*. Retrieved June 10, 2009, from http://www.ethics.va.gov/docs/integratedethics/Ethical_Leadership_Fostering_an_EthicalEnvironment_and_Culture_20070808.pdf

Veterans Health Administration. (2009b). *Integrated ethics: Improving ethics quality in health care*. Retrieved June 10, 2009, from http://www.ethics.va.gov/docs/integratedethics/IntegratedEthics_monograph--20070808.pdf

Veterans Health Administration. (2009c). *Preventive ethics toolkit: A manual for the preventive ethics coordinator*. Retrieved June 10, 2009, from http://www.ethics.va.gov/docs/integratedethics/Preventive_Ethics_Toolkit--20070228.pdf

Vincent, C., Young, M., & Phillips, A. (1994). Why do people sue doctors? A study of patients and relatives taking legal action. *Lancet, 343*(8913), 1609–1613.

Weeks, W. B., & Bagian, J. P. (2003). Making a business case for patient safety. *Joint Commission Journal on Quality and Safety, 29*(1), 51–54.

Weeks, W. B., & Mills, P. D. (2003). Reduction in patient enrollment in the Veterans Healthcare Administration after media coverage of adverse medical events. *Joint Commission Journal on Quality and Safety, 29*(12), 652–658.

APPENDIX 30.A. ETHICS EVIDENCE TABLE

Topic	Evidence
Ethics standards	American Occupational Therapy Association. (2010). Occupational therapy code of ethics and ethics standards (2010). *American Journal of Occupational Therapy, 64.* Slater, D. Y. (2010). *Reference guide to the occupational therapy ethics standard* (2010 ed.). Bethesda, MD: AOTA Press.
Organizational ethics	Brandt, L. C. (2009b). *Organizational ethics* [CEonCD]. Bethesda, MD: American Occupational Therapy Association.
Clinical application	American Occupational Therapy Association, Ethics Commission. (2007). *Everyday ethics: Core knowledge for practitioners and educators* [CEonCD]. Bethesda, MD: Author.
Moral distress	Brandt, L. C. (2009a). *Moral distress: Surviving clinical chaos* [CEonCD]. Bethesda, MD: American Occupational Therapy Association.

31

Continuing Competence and Competency

Penelope A. Moyers Cleveland, EdD, OTR/L, BCMH, FAOTA, and Jim Hinojosa, PhD, OT, FAOTA

❖ Key Terms and Concepts

Competence. "An individual's capacity to perform job responsibilities" (McConnell, 2001, p. 14).

Competencies. Explicit statements that define specific areas of expertise and are related to effective or superior performance in a job (Spencer & Spencer, 1993).

Competency. "An individual's actual performance in a particular situation" (McConnell, 2001, p. 14). Competency implies a determination of whether one is competent.

Competent. Successful in performing a behavior or task as measured according to a specific criterion (Hinojosa et al., 2000b).

Continuing competence. Development of capacity and competency characteristics needed for the future. Continuing competence is a component of ongoing professional development or lifelong learning.

Continuing professional development. Focus on one's career development in terms of achieving excellence or independent practitioner and expert role status and assuming new, more complex roles and responsibilities; may include a program of continuing competence.

❖ Learning Objectives

After completing this chapter, you should be able to do the following:

- Define *competence, competency, continuing professional development*, and the elements of a professional development plan.
- Discuss the self-directed learning process to ensure competent practices.
- Identify personal responsibilities and relationships with state regulatory boards, the American Occupational Therapy Association, the National Board for Certification in Occupational Therapy, and other accreditation agencies.

- Describe the purpose and the design of the American Occupational Therapy Association's Continuing Competence Plan for Professional Development.
- Discuss the importance of selecting the most effective learning activities given the learning need.
- Describe the impact of continued professional development on the organizational system and the importance of establishing a learning culture.

Managers and leaders in occupational therapy are facing mounting pressure to ensure that occupational therapy practitioners and other personnel whom they supervise are competent, have ongoing learning plans to continuously develop competency, and are developing themselves for potential career opportunities. The competency of managers is reflected not only in their own supervisory and management competencies, but also in the competency of their staff in providing services. In addition, managers are interested in the long-term development of staff as a method of ensuring the legacy of the organization or business that otherwise could be challenged when current leaders retire or take other positions. The organizational risks incurred as a result of poorly performing direct service providers are quite high and may include client harm, reduction in business volume, payment denials, legal difficulties, loss of status as a reimbursable or fundable provider, decline in reputation, inability to attract outstanding staff, and loss of facility accreditation.

This chapter provides the occupational therapy manager or leader a foundation for understanding the competency, continuing competence, and professional development of staff. Useful strategies are discussed that can help managers guide individual practitioners in their efforts to remain updated; however, the manager or leader must take a wider view of competence that goes beyond a focus on the individual practitioner to a focus on the staff as a whole. The manager must adopt an attitude of shared responsibility (i.e., between employees and employer) for competency and continuing competence that considers overall system flexibility in supporting change. The competency process is a team effort and a collaborative one in which the manager and staff members participate to ensure competence. Therefore, the manager must have a broader understanding of how practitioners learn and apply new learning to their practice on an ongoing basis given the larger social systems in which they live and work. Learning methods for achieving competency are reviewed with a particular emphasis on addressing system issues so that the learning is more likely to change practice and ultimately to improve client service outcomes.

UNDERSTANDING COMPETENCY, CONTINUING COMPETENCE, AND PROFESSIONAL DEVELOPMENT

The manager of occupational therapy services must have confidence in a staff member's competency, which is "an individual's actual performance in a particular situation" (McConnell, 2001, p. 14); whether one is currently competent to perform a behavior or task is measured against a specific criterion (Hinojosa et al., 2000b). Competent occupational therapy practitioners have particular skills that authorize them to perform restricted activities within their professional scope in a skillful manner that will result in defined client outcomes. A restricted activity is one that only someone licensed or trained in a given profession or technical trade may perform. Competency is closely associated with scope of practice, which refers to the procedures, actions, and processes characteristic of a profession (Wise, 2008). In occupational therapy, the scope of practice involves the processes of evaluation, intervention planning and implementation, and outcome measurement as they relate to the occupational performance and daily participation (American Occupational Therapy Association [AOTA], 2008) of persons, populations, and organizations. Occupational therapy practitioners are competent when they have the prerequisite knowledge, skills, and attitudes to effectively implement and measure the effectiveness of these processes within their scope of practice.

Continuing competence is slightly different in that this term refers to ongoing learning so that "an individual's capacity to perform job [professional] responsibilities" (McConnell,

2001, p. 14) is always expanding. Lately, the differentiation among competency and continuing competence is less important as there is a growing preference for the phrase "continuing professional development" to encompass all of the learning that takes place in one's professional life (Council of Medical Specialty Societies, 2002), including when there is a change in jobs, roles, and responsibilities as one matures in one's career. Learning characterized as professional development is typically self-directed, although to be effective, the practitioner must have additional understanding of how organizational and system factors may deter, support, or modify application to practice, thereby affecting client outcomes (Davis, Barnes, & Fox, 2003). This expanded understanding of professional development as pursuit of continuous high-quality involves a strong connection between the practitioner's learning, application to practice, and data-driven feedback that occurs throughout one's career.

Another factor important in understanding continuing professional development is that there is not a linear relationship between learning and improved practice performance. Instead, there may be periods when there is either no improvement or even a slight decrease in performance. These periods of little change then may be followed by sudden jumps in practice performance (Handfield-Jones et al., 2002). Because most of practice is based on cognitively complex tasks, learning typically requires cognitive reorganization that may involve abandonment of previously held ideas and principles. Therefore, the impact of learning on practice appears to occur in sudden leaps rather than through continuous and gradual change. Consequently, although practice performance improves in some areas, it may simultaneously deteriorate in others.

IMPORTANCE OF CONTINUING PROFESSIONAL DEVELOPMENT

Although it is true that all health professionals must continue to acquire new information at an increasing rate, studies still indicate that professionals may not implement this new information in practice (National Center for Health Statistics, 2002). Unfortunately, difficulty in transferring new knowledge into practice occurs simultaneously with the changing definition of harm (Moyers & Hinojosa, 2003); harm is no longer limited to the prevention of serious injury to clients (whether a person, population, or organization) during implementation of services due to practitioner neglect or malpractice or due to poor risk management. Harm may also occur due to ineffective intervention or intervention that is not as effective as an alternative method in improving occupational performance and participation in daily life. At least four negative outcomes have been associated with ineffective services:

1. Intervention continuing over a longer duration than expected
2. Additional burden for caregiving resulting from reduced performance in activities of daily living

3. Loss of the worker role to support daily living
4. Possible reduction in the economic viability of the community if a large population or organization is negatively affected by ineffective programming.

Third-party payers, grant funders, and clients are increasingly aware of expected outcomes and thus unwilling to pay for outcomes that do not meet benchmarks. Efforts designed to reduce costs associated with poor quality of care include pay-for-performance reimbursement methodologies implemented for medical model settings (Sautter et al., 2007) and more stringent requirements from grant funders or business and industry to demonstrate effectiveness of community-based or organization-based programs.

An occupational therapy professional who does not maintain competency or engage in continuing competence will have difficulty achieving job promotion, may lose his or her job, or may have difficulty being hired for other jobs. In extreme cases of provider incompetence resulting in harm, clients may sue for malpractice or negligence, and the occupational therapy practitioner could lose the state license or certification needed to practice in a given jurisdiction. The practitioner could lose National Board for Certification in Occupational Therapy (NBCOT) certification and membership in AOTA as well. Loss of license or certification in one state and loss of NBCOT certification are reported to other state licensure boards or jurisdictions in which occupational therapy practitioners may relocate, thereby preventing or making it more difficult to practice in the new location.

STAKEHOLDERS IN CONTINUING PROFESSIONAL DEVELOPMENT

Basic competency in occupational therapy is established upon completing formal academic education normally from a program accredited by the Accreditation Council for Occupational Therapy Education® (ACOTE®) or its precursor, successfully finishing all required fieldwork experiences, and passing the NBCOT initial certification examination or its precursor. As a result of establishing this basic competency, the occupational therapy practitioner obtains a state license or certification qualifying him or her to perform selected restricted activities as defined by the profession's scope of practice (e.g., the occupational therapy assistant practices in collaboration with and under the supervision of the occupational therapist).

State Regulatory Boards

State regulatory boards (SRBs) are public bodies created by state legislatures to protect the public from potential harm caused by incompetent or unqualified health care practitioners. SRBs have the legal authority to determine whether occupational therapists and occupational therapy assistants have the necessary requirements to practice in a given legal jurisdiction. Typically, the requirements to initially obtain a state license or certification include evidence of passing the NBCOT initial certification examination, a diploma from an accredited occupational therapy educational program, completion of the required fieldwork, and payment of a state fee.

Most jurisdictions require the state license or certification to be renewed annually or biennially. In an attempt to ensure that practitioners maintain competence, the licensure renewal process in 41 states also includes submission of evidence, typically in the form of contact hours or continuing education units (CEUs), showing that the applicant has participated in professional development activities. Most states require approximately 20–30 contact hours biennially.

In those states allowing a variety of learning activities as evidence of continuing competency, there is often a delineation of how many contact hours may be obtained in each type of learning activity, with most of the contact hours given for continuing education programming. The continuing education contact hours typically must be obtained through state licensure board–approved programs, such as those offered by the state occupational therapy association, AOTA, other professional organizations, and universities. If an occupational therapy practitioner obtains continuing education from a provider not included in the state's list of approved providers, the onus is usually on the practitioner to seek regulatory board approval for acceptance of the course. Recognized learning activities often include the following:

- Publication of books, articles, chapters, film, or video
- Presentations, including workshops, seminars, and inservice training
- Self-study, including article review
- Research grants
- Work as a research assistant or teaching assistant
- Fieldwork supervision
- Mentoring
- Original design of new occupational therapy equipment (presented or published)
- Professional meetings and activities
- Specialty certification
- Graduate or undergraduate coursework
- Term in state or national office in a professional organization.

Although many licensure boards recognize the importance of maintaining competence in the varied roles and responsibilities related to occupational therapy, some state licensure laws limit acceptable continuing competence to learning activities that are directly related to practice. Some licensure boards specifically require a certain portion of contact hours to be obtained in general occupational therapy practice as opposed to specialized practice areas. There may also be mandatory topics, including HIV, ethics, medical error detection, and jurisprudence. Certain exceptions from meeting the continuing education requirements may be made, such as military service, financial hardship, or illness or disability.

States often require the occupational therapy practitioner to maintain records and to submit on renewal some minimal evidence of continuing competence. Evidence of continuing education includes a copy of the program title and content; a description of the program sponsor, presenter, or author; a certificate of completion or some other verification of course participation, such as a university transcript; location and attendance dates; number of contact hours; and affirmation that the continuing education information is true or correct. Some licensure boards periodically audit the practitioner's documented continuing professional development. If the practitioner does not cooperate with the audit, this may be considered an attempt to obtain a license through misrepresentation, creating grounds for revoking the license to practice in the given jurisdiction. A negative audit may be appealed, with potential decisions including removal of the state license or certification, reversal of the audit decision, and modification of the audit decision. Most states allow the occupational therapy practitioner time to correct problems found in the audit before proceeding with disciplinary action.

National Board for Certification in Occupational Therapy

NBCOT is a private credentialing body that, like SRBs, has a mission to protect the public. NBCOT is not a membership organization but rather is responsible for developing, updating, and administering the initial certification examination used by SRBs in determining whether to initially allow occupational therapy practitioners to practice in a given jurisdiction. NBCOT uses the examination as one of the criteria for initial NBCOT certification, thereby legally allowing occupational therapists to use the initials OTR and the occupational therapy assistant to use the initials COTA. The OTR and COTA credentials are registered certification marks owned by NBCOT. There are renewal requirements for maintaining NBCOT certification, which is voluntary; most SRBs do not require certification to maintain one's license, and the federal government does not require the practitioner to hold it to receive Medicare or Medicaid reimbursement for the delivery of occupational therapy services. NBCOT requires that individuals who choose not to renew this certification no longer use its certification marks.

To renew NBCOT certification, practitioners must obtain 36 professional development units (PDUs) during a 3-year renewal cycle (NBCOT, 2010). Learning activities that can be counted as PDUs are classified as performing professional service; attending workshops, classes, or independent learning; presenting; providing fieldwork supervision; and publishing. Additionally, PDUs may be collected in general practice or in a declared area of practice emphasis, such as administration or management, mental health, pediatrics, education or research, work and industry, rehabilitation, geriatrics, or orthopedics. Occupational therapy practitioners may earn one PDU for completing the NBCOT online self-assessment tool or a similar self-assessment tool and one PDU for using the results to develop goals relating to competence and skills development. Each year, NBCOT selects a random sample of occupational therapy practitioners and audits the documentation of their PDUs to determine whether requirements for what constitutes an acceptable PDU have been met. NBCOT places practitioners who fail to meet the renewal requirements on noncompliant–inactive status.

Organizational Accreditors

Health care and other service organizations often must go through an organizational accreditation process to qualify for payment or funding from third parties and to represent the organization as a high-quality service provider. Two such organizational accrediting bodies include The Joint Commission and CARF International (see Chapter 35). A primary area of focus for The Joint Commission (2008) is to ensure that the organization determines the qualifications and competencies for all staff positions. The Joint Commission stresses the following areas to determine competency: preemployment (qualifications), job requirements, job preparation (orientation plan guided by baseline assessment of performance), performance appraisal (comparison of demonstrated job skills with expected standard), and response to appraisal (action plan to bring performance up to the expected level).

Competence assessment occurs before staff may perform their assigned job duties independently upon hiring, assignment of a new responsibility or technology, or implementation of a new standard of performance. The organization must comply with Joint Commission standards related to staff development, staff competency, orientation, inservice education, and job descriptions and ensure that staff members are addressing population-specific needs (Currie & Roberts, 2008). *Population-specific needs* in these standards refer to the particular issues experienced by persons with various diseases, conditions, or ages. Organizations must collect data to systematically assess staff competency, including performance evaluations, performance improvement, aggregate data on competency, and assessments of learning needs.

Employers

Employers expect occupational therapy practitioners beginning a job to be competent in managing multiple responsibilities. Of particular concern to employers is how practitioners translate their basic competencies into a specific work context after meeting NBCOT and state licensure requirements. Each work setting is unique because of its specific client base and corresponding customer expectations, unique set of institutional policies and protocols for assessment and intervention, physical environment consisting of limited space and equipment, and prescribed methods for delegating roles and tasks to employees. Entry-level NBCOT certification and initial state license or certification establish only that an occupational therapy practitioner is competent for general practice at that point in time. After initial entry-level certification, the profession does not have an agreed-on standard process for ensuring competency over time and for promoting the process of continuing competence (Lysaght & Altschuld, 2000). Therefore, employers must identify competencies required for successful implementation of the duties of a particular job. Competencies are explicit statements that define specific areas of expertise and are causally related to effective job performance (Decker, 1999). To delineate the competencies that lead to an expected level of expertise, the employer needs to determine the required knowledge, the set of complex skills, and the criteria for skillful performance. Expert knowledge and skills involve particular behaviors or activities and have discrete performance criteria.

Within a work setting, according to Decker and Strader (1997), there are four types of competencies: those that are generic across all jobs in an organization, those that are related to management or supervision roles, those that are threshold or that are the minimum requirements of a job, and those that are specific to a job. Depending on the organization, *generic competencies* for all employees might involve showing respect for clients, being accountable for completion of one's job tasks with minimal supervision, using decision-making and problem-solving skills, supporting the organization's values and goals, and demonstrating a customer service orientation (Decker, 1999). *Management competencies* relate to administering budgets; directing client programs; hiring, supervising, and training personnel; assigning work and managing workflow through flexible staffing; and assessing program outcomes and quality to inform changes in program processes. The manager must competently implement a variety of service or business models, comprehend market-driven standards, use communication technologies, and interface with large systems (Schell & Slater, 1998).

Threshold or minimum requirements arise from the license or scope of practice and from the entry-level education required to fulfill the demands of the position. It is expected that occupational therapists can implement and that assistants can support the occupational therapy process of referral and screening, evaluation, intervention planning, intervention implementation, discharge planning, termination of therapy services, and outcome measurement, all of which are appropriately focused on the domain of occupational therapy (i.e., facilitating and supporting engagement in occupations and participation within relevant social and physical contexts; Moyers & Dale, 2007). In terms of *job-specific competencies*, the threshold requirements are modified by the precise nature of the job. For example, the occupational therapist in an elementary school setting might need to be proficient in competencies addressing the occupational performance needs of children with learning disabilities who demonstrate perceptual–motor problems that interfere with learning.

Within each of the four general categories of competencies, an unlimited number of specific competencies can be generated. The goal is for the employer to select, in consultation with the occupational therapy practitioner, only those competencies that result in superior client outcomes. What constitutes a superior client outcome is driven partly by the profession in terms of benchmarks, standards, and evidence and partly by client satisfaction indicating the level of success in meeting client needs (Decker & Strader, 1997). Often, key areas from which competencies are derived involve reduction of "high-risk" behaviors that routinely result in poor client outcomes (e.g., implementing an often-used evaluation or intervention incorrectly) or an increase in "low-volume" behaviors that, when occurring infrequently, lead to poor client outcomes (e.g., infrequent assessment of pain). The employer must work with its occupational therapy practitioners to determine the criteria to judge performance on the work-related competencies generated from an understanding of client outcomes.

Validation of competence is a process in which the employer ascertains whether the occupational therapy practitioner performs the behavior according to standard. Validation may involve the supervisor directly observing the performance of the employee and may also include simulation, paper-and-pencil tests, client satisfaction surveys, medical record audits, skills checklists, client case conferences or rounds, or peer reviews. It is not possible to determine an exact point at which an error in performance means the employee is incompetent; ultimately, determination of competence or incompetence is subjective and depends on the supervisor's tolerance for error in an employee's performance of job tasks (Sharpless & Barber, 2009). The difficulty in determining incompetence is that the supervisor must balance protection of the client's safety with fair treatment of the occupational therapy practitioner in the competency validation process. In some cases, any evidence of missing threshold competencies represents such significant risk to the client that there can be little tolerance for error.

The supervisor must remember that error-free performance is not consistently possible from all employees. Instead, the manager must create strategies for modeling learning when errors in daily work occur (Bauer & Mulder, 2007). If the supervisor judges the occupational therapy practitioner to be incompetent in most of the delineated competencies, the employee would immediately be suspended from his or her duties until remedial learning led to corrected performance. If the occupational therapy practitioner is unable to correct the performance problem, then the supervisor has no choice but to begin disciplinary action, which could lead to firing and a report of the concern to the SRB and to NBCOT.

American Occupational Therapy Association

Recall that competency is a comparison of current performance with standards. AOTA sets the standards for competence not only when it accredits entry-level educational programs for the occupational therapist and the occupational therapy assistant, but also through formulating official documents such as the *Standards of Practice for Occupational Therapy* (AOTA, 2010c); the *Occupational Therapy Code of Ethics and Ethics Standards* (AOTA, 2010a); *Guidelines for Supervision, Roles, and Responsibilities During the Delivery of Occupational Therapy Services* (AOTA, 2009); *The Guide to Occupational Therapy Practice* (Moyers & Dale, 2007; not an "officcial document" but widely read); *Occupational Therapy Practice Framework: Domain and Process, 2nd Edition* (AOTA, 2008), and various practice guidelines.

AOTA has also implemented portfolio-based board and specialty certification programs. The specialty certifications can be obtained after 2 years of experience by both occupational therapists and occupational therapy assistants in the areas of eating, feeding, and swallowing; driving and community mobility; environmental modification; and low vision. Board certifications are an advanced-practice designation given after 5 years of experience. Occupational therapists may obtain board certification in the areas of gerontology, mental health, pediatrics, and physical rehabilitation. Both board and specialty certifications require the occupational therapy practitioner to produce evidence of a variety of learning methods demonstrating achievement of the specified competencies, to reflect on this evidence in terms of impact on client outcomes, and to develop a plan for continued learning.

Individual Professionals

Even though the employer of occupational therapy practitioners is concerned about the competency of its employees, the *Occupational Therapy Code of Ethics and Ethics Standards* (AOTA, 2010a) clearly states that it is the individual practitioner's personal responsibility to ensure that he or she is competent to practice. Therefore, occupational therapy practitioners are required by the profession's code of ethics to engage in a lifelong process of self-directed learning to make certain that they are competent to practice occupational therapy (Moyers, 2005).

However, a practitioner's ability to enact a competency may depend not only on his or her skills and knowledge but also on several other factors, including motivation to change performance, tendency to respond in a consistent manner, positive self-concept or self-image, or certain attitudes or values (Decker, 1999). Competency is determined by the person's unique personality, ethics, philosophy, social conscience, intellectual ability, and mental and physical state. Most organizational accrediting bodies, such as The Joint Commission, limit discussion of competency to knowledge, psychomotor skills, critical thinking, and interpersonal skills (Decker & Strader, 1997). These taxonomies do not include the more hidden determinants

of competency involving motives, traits, and self-concept. Epstein and Hundert (2002) identified the dimensions of professional competence as cognitive (e.g., core knowledge and recognition of gaps in knowledge), technical (e.g., procedural skills), integrative (e.g., judgment and clinical reasoning), context (e.g., clinical setting and use of time), relationship (e.g., communication and handling conflict), affective/moral (e.g., tolerance of ambiguity, respect), and habits of mind (e.g., attentiveness and critical curiosity). Knowledge and skill competencies can be developed through training, whereas motives and traits are more difficult to assess and influence through training. Instead, occupational therapy managers may need to make sure the hiring process specifically examines candidate qualifications in terms of all the competencies needed, not just in terms of knowledge and skills.

AOTA CONTINUING COMPETENCE PLAN FOR PROFESSIONAL DEVELOPMENT

AOTA's Continuing Competence Plan for Professional Development (Hinojosa et al., 2000a) is a self-initiated approach that encourages each occupational therapist and occupational therapy assistant to develop an individualized plan to meet his or her competency and continuing competence learning needs (see Figure 31.1). This plan consists of eight components that together form a dynamic continuum: (1) use triggers to determine need for self-assessment, (2) examine responsibilities, (3) perform a self-assessment, (4) identify needs in light of the *Standards for Continuing Competence* (AOTA, 2010b), (5) develop a plan for continuing competence, (6) implement the continuing competence plan, (7) document continuing competence and changes in performance, and (8) implement changes and demonstrate continuing competence. An occupational therapy practitioner can start in the continuum for professional development at any point in the schema and continue with the process from there.

Use Triggers to Determine Need for Self-Assessment

Triggers are events or circumstances that prompt a person to examine his or her knowledge, skills, or attitudes as they are applied to his or her job. Triggers can come from many sources, including changes in a performance appraisal or competency assessment, government regulations, the marketplace, or the profession itself. Triggers can be gradual or sudden and can be the result of a planned (e.g., personnel evaluation period) or unplanned event (e.g., client dissatisfaction). They can be significant events or minor changes in the system or the external environment. Triggers are often changes beyond the person's control that affect the person's ability to carry out his or her job responsibilities in an efficient and competent manner. Hinojosa et al. (2000a) identified the following common triggers:

(a) return to clinical practice after years of absence,
(b) practice in isolation without a professional sup-

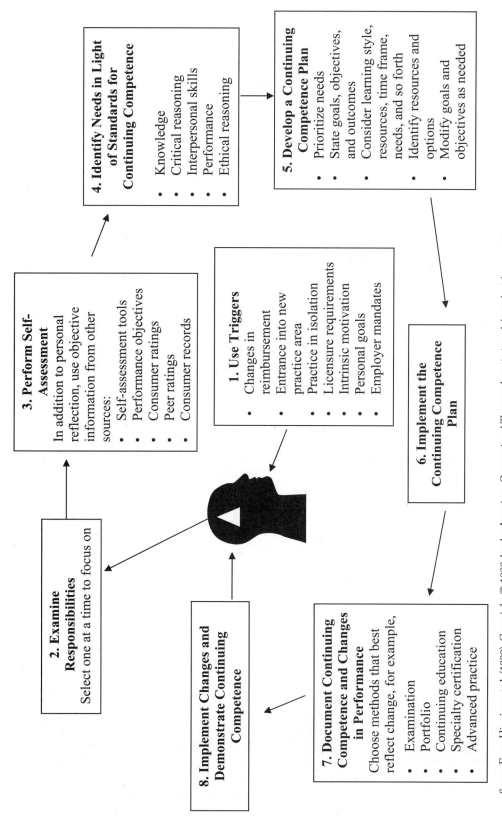

4. Identify Needs in Light of Standards for Continuing Competence

- Knowledge
- Critical reasoning
- Interpersonal skills
- Performance
- Ethical reasoning

5. Develop a Continuing Competence Plan

- Prioritize needs
- State goals, objectives, and outcomes
- Consider learning style, resources, time frame, needs, and so forth
- Identify resources and options
- Modify goals and objectives as needed

3. Perform Self-Assessment

In addition to personal reflection, use objective information from other sources:

- Self-assessment tools
- Performance objectives
- Consumer ratings
- Peer ratings
- Consumer records

1. Use Triggers

- Changes in reimbursement
- Entrance into new practice area
- Practice in isolation
- Licensure requirements
- Intrinsic motivation
- Personal goals
- Employer mandates

2. Examine Responsibilities

Select one at a time to focus on

6. Implement the Continuing Competence Plan

8. Implement Changes and Demonstrate Continuing Competence

7. Document Continuing Competence and Changes in Performance

Choose methods that best reflect change, for example,

- Examination
- Portfolio
- Continuing education
- Specialty certification
- Advanced practice

Source. From Hinojosa et al. (1999). Copyright © 1999, by the American Occupational Therapy Association. Adapted with permission.

Figure 31.1. AOTA's Continuing Competence Plan for Professional Development.

port system, (c) employer-mandated productivity that may endanger delivery of safe and effective consumer services, (d) multiple job-site assignments within a short period, (e) an unsatisfactory job performance rating, and (f) personal objectives that may require changes in roles and responsibilities. (p. CE2)

Examine Responsibilities

At this point in the competence process, the occupational therapy practitioner, along with his or her supervisor, must reflect on the responsibilities and expertise the practitioner needs to skillfully produce the desired outcomes or performances. This examination of responsibilities begins when the occupational therapy practitioner reflects on practice and asks several questions:

- What are the expectations of the position or role?
- What are the responsibilities and requirements of the situation?
- What knowledge, interpersonal and performance skills, and types of critical and ethical reasoning are needed?
- What expectations do others have?
- Are there changes in technology, consumer expectations, employer demands, systems, the community, or my personal life that may affect performance?

For example, if an occupational therapist was asked to assume responsibilities for supervising occupational therapy students, he or she would have to answer each of these questions in terms of the new responsibilities that would be added to his or her job related to student learning and supervision of entry-level occupational therapists or occupational therapy assistants.

Maintaining competence also requires that occupational therapy practitioners continually refine and update their knowledge, skills, and attitudes in the areas that make up the core of occupational therapy. In examining their responsibilities, practitioners should consider the unique occupational therapy knowledge of occupations, human activities, and their impact on human performance and the unique occupational therapy skills in the areas of activity analysis, activity synthesis, and critical problem solving about occupational performance and community participation. Occupational therapy practitioners share a worldview of persons as occupational beings who seek to engage and participate in meaningful and purposeful activities, and continuing competence efforts must be consistent with this worldview.

Perform a Self-Assessment

Self-assessment provides occupational therapy practitioners with a baseline for developing goals and plans for professional growth, reassessing current goals, assessing performance on defined competencies, analyzing demands and resources of the work environment, and interpreting information about clients' outcomes. To develop a continuing competence plan, an occupational therapy practitioner should engage in formalized methods of self-assessment, which may include any of the following (Sharpless & Barber, 2009):

- Self-assessment tools (Cowan, Wilson-Barnett, Norman, & Murrells, 2008)
- Reflective portfolios (Gustafsson & Fagerberg, 2004; Tillema, 2001; Wilkinson et al., 2002)
- Performance observation of actual or simulated client interventions (Rethans et al., 2002)
- Computer-based simulation assessments
- Client and peer ratings
- Client outcomes
- Audits of client records (Salvatori, Simonavicius, Moore, Rimmer, & Patterson, 2008).

Multisource feedback improves the validity of self-assessment and involves a 360° approach (i.e., from all around the practitioner) in which the practitioner receives feedback from colleagues (persons in the same profession), coworkers (all persons with whom the practitioner works), supervisors, and clients (Violato, Lockyer, & Fidler, 2008). Self-assessment tends to be ineffective when the practitioner does not incorporate external sources of data and instead relies on his or her own assessment or self-ratings of performance (Davis et al., 2006). The occupational therapy practitioner synthesizes the data and reflects on his or her own assets and limitations in performing the expected responsibilities or competencies.

The annual performance evaluation is a natural trigger for conducting a self-assessment to inform the development of a continuing competence plan. The annual evaluation provides an opportunity for the practitioner to review his or her responsibilities, skills, and expertise within the context of the institutional goals and expectations. A review of the prior year's plan can validate the existing plan and provide valuable information to the individual and his or her supervisor about the effectiveness of selected activities in pursuing competence. Other triggers, however, may necessitate that the plan be updated before the yearly performance evaluation.

Identify Needs in Light of Standards for Continuing Competence

The *Standards for Continuing Competence* (AOTA, 2010b) outline five standards practitioners can use in determining their focus of learning (Exhibit 31.1). After defining the responsibilities of his or her primary roles in a given employment setting, the occupational therapy practitioner reflects on current performance in each area of responsibility or defined competency as measured against each of the standards. For instance, if the practitioner identifies a learning need related to improving his or her competency in evaluating the occupational performance of older adults after a cerebrovascular accident, he or she can use the standards to analyze whether the need is a result of lack of knowledge or of problems in applying knowledge during the critical reasoning process. While reflecting on each

Exhibit 31.1 AOTA's Standards for Continuing Competence

Standard 1. Knowledge

Occupational therapists and occupational therapy assistants shall demonstrate understanding and comprehension of the information required for the multiple roles and responsibilities they assume. The individual must demonstrate

- Mastery of the core of occupational therapy as it is applied in the multiple responsibilities assumed;
- Expertise associated with primary responsibilities;
- Integration of relevant evidence, literature, and epidemiological data related to primary responsibilities and to the consumer population(s) served;
- Integration of current AOTA documents and legislative, legal, and regulatory issues into practice; and
- The ability to anticipate how new knowledge is necessary to meet client needs.

Standard 2. Critical Reasoning

Occupational therapists and occupational therapy assistants shall employ reasoning processes to make sound judgments and decisions. The individual must demonstrate

- Deductive and inductive reasoning in making decisions specific to roles and responsibilities;
- Problem-solving skills necessary to carry out responsibilities;
- The ability to analyze occupational performance as influenced by environmental factors;
- The ability to reflect on one's own practice;
- Management and synthesis of information from a variety of sources in support of making decisions;
- Application of evidence, research findings, and outcome data in making decisions; and
- The ability to assess previous assumptions against new evidence and revise decision-making process.

Standard 3. Interpersonal Abilities

Occupational therapists and occupational therapy assistants shall develop and maintain their professional relationships with others within the context of their roles and responsibilities. The individual must demonstrate

- Use of effective communication methods that match the abilities, personal factors, learning styles, and therapeutic needs of consumers and others;

- Effective interaction with people from diverse backgrounds;
- Use of feedback from consumers, families, supervisors, and colleagues to modify one's professional behavior;
- Collaboration with consumers, families, and professionals to attain optimal consumer outcomes; and
- The ability to develop and sustain team relationships to meet identified outcomes.

Standard 4. Performance Skills

Occupational therapists and occupational therapy assistants shall demonstrate the expertise, aptitudes, proficiencies, and abilities to competently fulfill their roles and responsibilities. The individual must demonstrate expertise in

- Practice grounded in the core of occupational therapy;
- The therapeutic use of self, the therapeutic use of occupations and activities, the consultation process, and the education process to bring about change;
- Integrating current practice techniques and technologies;
- Updating performance based on current evidence-based literature with consideration given to client desires and practitioner judgment; and
- Quality improvement processes that prevent practice error and maximize client outcomes.

Standard 5. Ethical Reasoning

Occupational therapists and occupational therapy assistants shall identify, analyze, and clarify ethical issues or dilemmas to make responsible decisions within the changing context of their roles and responsibilities. The individual must demonstrate

- Understanding and adherence to the profession's *Code of Ethics and Ethics Standards (2010)*, other relevant codes of ethics, and applicable laws and regulations;
- The use of ethical principles and the profession's core values to understand complex situations;
- The integrity to make and defend decisions based on ethical reasoning; and
- Integration of varying perspectives in the ethics of clinical practice.

From the *American Journal of Occupational Therapy, 64.* Copyright © 2010, by the American Occupational Therapy Association.

standard, the occupational therapy practitioner creates a list of job performance areas or competencies where his or her knowledge, critical and ethical reasoning, and interpersonal and performance skills do not match what is required in the professional role. Additionally, the practitioner may create a list of areas for growth in his or her career.

Develop a Continuing Competence Plan

Developing a continuing competence plan involves four steps (Hinojosa et al., 2000a): (1) prioritizing learning needs based on the self-assessment and the *Standards for Continuing Competence* (AOTA, 2010b); (2) reviewing current goals and objectives or developing goals and objectives (expected outcomes); (3) identifying resources and options; and (4) modifying goals and objectives in view of resources, individual learning style, and personal needs.

In selecting resources and options for learning (Step 3), the practitioner must ensure that the learning strategy incorporates not only evidence-based content but also learning strategies that have been shown to improve client outcomes (Bloom, 2005). Learning is more likely to translate into a change in practice when interactive components are included, such as role-playing, case discussions, or opportunities to practice skills (Forsetlund et al., 2009). Rather than relying on the traditional continuing education experience (i.e., workshops, lectures, and conferences), practitioners should use multiple learning activities selected specifically to target particular learning needs (Robertson, Umble, & Cervero, 2003) and engage in regularly spaced or ongoing education (Cleland, Fritz, Brennan, & Magel, 2009; Kerfoot, Kearney, Connelly, & Ritchey, 2009). Single learning strategies have little or no effect on translating knowledge into practice (Forsetlund et al., 2009).

The learning method chosen should be appropriate to the content required. For example, role-playing and video feedback might be more appropriate for improving interpersonal abilities, whereas a self-study program of completing readings or e-learning might be more appropriate for knowledge acquisition (Hugenholtz, de Croon, Smits, van Dijk, & Nieuwenhuijsen, 2008). Critical and ethical reasoning might best be fostered through case studies and discussions, Web-based clinical simulations (Kowlowitz, Davenport, & Palmer, 2009), reflective writing, work with a mentor, participation in educational outreach visits (O'Brien et al., 2007), collaborative learning groups (Welch & Dawson, 2006), or peer teaching (Clark, Cabana, Kaciroti, Gong, & Sleeman, 2008). Likewise, practice and demonstration to a rater who judges performance against a criterion may be more appropriate for performance skill development.

Implement the Continuing Competence Plan

To be implemented successfully, a continuing competence plan must be based on desired and realistic outcomes. Further, the plan must be administratively feasible, publicly credible, professionally acceptable, legally defensible, and economically feasible. An important aspect of the continu-

ing competence plan is identification of the most appropriate methods for assessing and documenting outcomes for each of the specific self-competence goals. AOTA's Continuing Competence Plan for Professional Development (Hinojosa et al., 2000a) recommends three methods for assessing outcomes of learning: (1) examination (multiple choice, computer adaptive testing, case simulation), (2) reflective portfolio, and (3) outcome-based education (academic, continuing education). This implementation component need not be rigid—any plan should allow for modification or changes in the learning need or competencies to be addressed; the focus upon knowledge, skills, or reasoning; the learning outcomes; and the learning strategies.

Document Continuing Competence and Change in Performance

The documentation of the continuing competence plan is important to allow ongoing evaluation of competence and to enable the individual to meet advanced or specialized certification, renewal certification, and licensure requirements. There are many ways to document a continuing competency plan, including keeping a written log or jounal. A highly recommended method of documenting continuing competence is use of a reflective portfolio. In a *reflective portfolio*, the occupational therapy practitioner collects evidence that supports his or her competence. The *traditional portfolio* contains the practitioner's curriculum vita documenting his or her academic record, involvement in professional activities, committee appointments and positions, awards, and honors; performance evaluations; client satisfaction reports; documentation of professional accomplishments (e.g., papers, videotapes, articles); and complete listing of continuing education activities. A reflective portfolio is more effective than a traditional portfolio in that it goes beyond simply documenting learning and learning outcomes. A reflective portfolio begins the process of determining whether learning needs remain and how best to resolve them. Consider the reflective portfolio as a careful analysis of a practitioner's career development, making the portfolio highly individualized and well-connected to the practitioner's continuing competence plan. Many credentialing agencies and licensure boards recognize portfolios as an effective method for establishing a person's professional competence.

Implement Changes and Demonstrate Continuing Competence

Once a continuing competency plan has been developed, refined, and recorded, a practitioner has the challenge of implementation. Implementation involves obtaining and using knowledge and skills to improve performance. Examining performance relative to a continuing competency plan requires that a practitioner evaluate the changes. Thus, the practitioner continually evaluates the impact or success of the continuing competency plan. A practitioner should self-evaluate daily practices and the outcomes of the plan.

The practitioner should also continue to assess the success or effectiveness of what he or she is doing to identify potential areas for growth. After reflecting on the how one's learning affects practice, particularly focusing on change in client outcomes, the occupational therapy practitioner reviews the learning goals and decides if the goals have been met. If more learning is needed, the goal may need revision and the resources re-examined. The practitioner should perhaps select other types of learning methods. Talking to the manager is important to determine whether there are system issues that prevented the application (or the proper application) of the new learning to practice.

System Factors Influencing Continuing Professional Development

Ultimately, an occupational therapy practitioner engages in continuing competence activities to ensure that his or her competent practice translates into improved client outcomes. However, many factors influence the outcome of any continuing competence plan. Consequently, changing practice patterns or behaviors is complex and is best accomplished through a multidimensional management or leadership approach that targets entire teams of employees. Creating a learning organization culture that integrates the change efforts of teams of personnel produces high levels of competence beyond what can be accomplished when an organization focuses efforts on the individualized plans of single occupational therapy practitioners (McWilliam, 2007). A change in practice as the result of a continuing competence plan depends on the following factors:

- Employer recognition of the effect of social systems on change efforts (Sebrant, 2008)
- Agreement among employees and employers on the nature of change and its enactment within the organization
- Participation of occupational therapy practitioners in the design and implementation of practice changes
- Flexibility of administrative rules (e.g., institutional policies and procedures, standards from organizational accrediting bodies, state licensure renewal processes, or voluntary certification renewals; Townsend, Sheffield, Stadnyk, & Beagan, 2006)
- Quality of feedback on the attempts of occupational therapy practitioners to alter practice
- Relationship of financial incentives (e.g., promotions, bonuses, awards and recognition, career ladders) to demonstration of competency and continuing competence efforts (Nelson & Cook, 2008).

The ability to problem solve and perform is complex and is influenced by multiple variables, as well as the interaction among those variables. Competency is not always located solely in the person and may arise as an interaction between the person's competency and a combination of factors within the environment or the organization in which he or she works. For instance, multiple health care professionals working together on the same case affect outcomes differently, especially when not all team members are delivering the same level of quality of care. Whether employee learning as a part of improving client outcomes is valued is also organization specific and can be ascertained by examining the organization's financial support of its employees' professional development activities and leaders' support for the application of employees' learning to change systems. Finally, some competency programs may be heavily influenced by the latest management or health care issue rather than by a focus on systematic change. For example, the generation of multiple nationally sponsored practice guidelines may cause problems when organizational change and new competency expectations are based solely on this type of expert recommendation without determining which competencies would be most relevant to and consistent with the organization's mission, would most likely be supported within the specific organizational context, and would therefore be most likely to improve client outcomes.

Continuing education is now being informed by theories of quality improvement in delivering more effective care, theories of organizational change, and theories of knowledge translation from research to application (Price, 2005). Clinical educators are using these theories, with the support of administrators, not only to help individual practitioners but also to change the practice of teams of health professionals. Changing team practice typically involves educational interventions that focus on areas of high variability in outcomes. First, a needs assessment identifies performance gaps within the organization, as well as barriers and motivations for change. The educators and practitioners then analyze successful practice and review the evidence to determine what knowledge is to be transferred. The educational methods selected typically involve interactive approaches and realistic and meaningful case-based scenarios. Practitioners and leaders make a commitment to change the organization, and planning for the implementation of the new learning includes removal of organizational barriers and use of organizational facilitators. Once evaluation of the impact of the education indicates where further training is needed and where unforeseen barriers to implementation occur, follow-up education is provided. This cycle is ongoing until the desired client outcomes are achieved.

Conclusion

Assessing and maintaining one's competency to practice as an occupational therapist or occupational therapy assistant is gaining increasing importance. Competency is somewhat dependent on supportive attitudes and motivations toward change. Professional development and promotion of continuing competence should begin within the academic portion of the occupational therapy entry-level curriculum and should be modeled not only by faculty but also by fieldwork supervisors. It is vital for employers to support learning through development of a learning organizational culture where the process for professional development is integrated throughout all aspects of the workday.

Effective continuing competence management is based on an understanding of how a change in employees' practice patterns best occurs. Changing practice patterns or behaviors is complex and is best accomplished through a multidimensional approach. Thus, competency and continuing competence depend on the interaction among the individual involved, the nature of the learning needs in terms of influencing client outcomes, the type of learning methods selected, the change process involved when incorporating learning into practice, and the way the change in behavior is supported over time.

Case Examples

LEVEL I FIELDWORK

For his Level I fieldwork, Donald was assigned to an adult day care center for persons with chronic mental illness who had socioeconomic challenges. He had just completed a class on evaluation and intervention for persons with mental illness. In discussing his learning needs with the occupational therapist supervisor at the day care center, Donald shared with her that he would like to have an opportunity to administer a cognitive-based occupational performance assessment. To make his supervisor more comfortable with his ability, he suggested that he practice administering the assessment tool on her first before working with a client. Donald's supervisor agreed but wanted him to bring in materials so she could familiarize herself with the instrument before the practice assessment. Donald practiced the assessment with his supervisor and then benefited from feedback. His supervisor also stated that she enjoyed learning about an assessment tool with which she had not been familiar. Donald then successfully implemented the assessment tool with the client, and he worked with his supervisor to carefully interpret the results before documenting them in the medical record.

LEVEL II FIELDWORK

Luisa did her Level II fieldwork in an outpatient orthopedic center working with occupational therapists specializing in upper-extremity rehabilitation. On her first day, her supervisor stated that Luisa would be completing some computer-based competency education with supervisor checkoff of the skills taught before she could begin to see clients. The competency training was part of The Joint Commission requirements and involved measuring range of motion, manual muscle testing, heat and cold modalities, infection control, and the electronic medical record. Luisa decided that to reread her textbooks and notes from her coursework on these topics prior to completing the computer-based education. Then, after she successfully completed the computer-based education, she practiced what she had learned with other Level II fieldwork students who were also working on these competencies. After her hard work, her supervisor was impressed with her skill performance during the check-off assessment of competency.

FIRST-TIME MANAGER

Jo was the manager of a multidisciplinary stroke rehabilitation team in a freestanding rehabilitation hospital. One of her goals was to make sure the team determined whether the treatment approach reflected the latest practice guidelines on stroke. Jo was aware that several team members were skeptical about the need for change just because of new practice guidelines. Jo considered the possibility that their skepticism might be appropriate, so she decided that the first step would be to analyze ADL outcomes data and compare them to appropriate benchmarks. Jo's analysis of outcomes data and comparison to benchmarks confirmed her concern about the stroke rehabilitation team needing to learn about the latest practice guidelines. She convened a meeting with the team to present the outcomes and show them the benchmarks. At the conclusion of the meeting, the team reviewed the practice guidelines and decided to schedule a series of meetings to discuss how the guidelines should be implemented and to identify the system issues that might prevent implementation of the practice changes. The goal was to develop a solid plan for training team members in the new procedures to ensure competency.

MANAGER

Randi was an owner of a pediatric practice that employed 50 therapists, including occupational and physical therapists, speech and language pathologists, and clinical psychologists. In her market outreach, she discovered that the practice could substantially increase referrals if it developed programming for children with Tourette's syndrome with comorbidities of either obsessive–compulsive disorder (OCD) or attention-deficit disorder (ADD). None of the occupational therapists or clinical psychologists currently on staff had expertise with Tourette's syndrome, but some had experience with OCD and ADD. Randi and the team of therapists worked together to develop an intervention program complete with an outcome measurement process and a competency training program for the therapists who would be working with each type of client. Randi and her team collaboratively developed a plan for obtaining the knowledge, skills, and attitudes needed to provide an effective intervention program for children with Tourette syndrome with the identified comborbidities. The competency training program included distributing reading material, holding discussion groups, interacting with experts to answer questions, observing demonstrations of the new procedures, practicing techniques and receiving feedback, and implementing procedures with clients with follow-up discussions of the process to make modifications. Client outcomes were examined at mid-intervention, postintervention, and at 6-month follow-up to determine further training needs.

❖ Learning Activities

1. Spend time reflecting about your career goals 5 years from now. Identify generally what you would need to learn to achieve these goals, the resources you would need, and how you would obtain these resources.
2. Suggest some ways you could incorporate self-assessment to determine how well you are learning in a particular class.
3. For a colleague who states she never has time to read about occupational therapy, develop an explanation of how this is an ethical dilemma, and provide suggestions to address this situation.
4. Explore some learning methods most likely to lead to a change in critical reasoning in terms of interpreting the results of client assessments, and select several to engage in.
5. If you were a manager of a service line in a hospital, such as services for people with a head injury, describe how you would create a learning environment for the team members who implement the service.

✓ Multiple-Choice Questions

1. Which of the following correctly explains the difference between *competence* and *competency*?
   a. *Competence* refers to capacity, or one's development for future performance in one's professional roles, and *competency* refers to actual performance measured against standards.
   b. *Competency* refers to capacity, or one's development for future performance in one's professional roles, and *competence* refers to actual performance against standards.
   c. *Competency* is the singular of *competencies*, and *competence* refers to either current or future performance within one's professional roles.
   d. There is no difference between the two terms.
2. Professional development is differentiated from both continuing competence and competency. Which of the following is true?
   a. *Professional development* is focused on learning for future professional roles, and *continuing competence* and *competency* are focused on learning for current professional roles.
   b. All purposes of learning are focused on both current and future professional roles.
   c. *Professional development* is the umbrella term that includes both *continuing competence* and *competency*, as well as learning for future professional roles.
   d. *Professional development* is a term that is no longer used.
3. Given that the practice environment supports application of learning to practice, the relationship between learning and improved practice performance is nonlinear because
   a. It takes time for one to remember all that one has learned.
   b. The content of what one has to learn is complex and requires in-depth study.
   c. Learning requires cognitive complexity; previous knowledge must be reorganized to incorporate new knowledge and may necessitate abandonment of old ways of approaching problems.
   d. All of the above.
4. Self-assessment as a part of continuing competence and competency and professional development is an important way to do which of the following?
   a. Connect learning with practice performance.
   b. Prepare for employer performance evaluations.
   c. Obtain a license to practice.
   d. Determine whether one has attended the best continuing education programs.
5. Self-assessment involves all the following *except*
   a. Analysis of one's job responsibilities or future responsibilities.
   b. Analysis of client outcomes.
   c. Comparison of one's performance or skills with standards, practice guidelines, research, expert judgment, and so forth.
   d. Judgment of whether one is competent to practice.
6. Examples of self-assessment methods include all of the following *except*
   a. Reflection on practice.
   b. Knowledge tests.

c. Portfolios.

d. Peer evaluations of performance.

7. Which is an example of a threshold competency?

a. The evaluation should include an interpretation of the client's occupational areas requiring improvement.

b. The dysphagia evaluation should include the underlying factors impeding the tasks related to feeding, eating, and swallowing.

c. The low vision evaluation of the child should include the assistive technology needed for improving occupational performance in the occupational area of education.

d. The administrator should select the best method for evaluating the job performance of the different types of professional, aide-level, and office staff of the multidisciplinary service.

8. Learning needs are determined from which of the following?

a. Any discrepancy between the results of the self-assessment and specific criteria.

b. Convenient continuing education programs that may have relevance to one's job or professional roles.

c. A large-enough discrepancy between the results of the self-assessment and specific criteria.

d. What the employer believes is important for quality improvement.

9. Examples of external motivators for learning include all of the following *except*

a. Employer expectations.

b. Desire to be a virtuous or "good" practitioner.

c. Licensure renewal requirements.

d. NBCOT certification renewal requirements.

10. Which is an example of an internal motivator for learning?

a. To develop expertise in a specific practice area as a personal goal.

b. To receive professional recognition.

c. To obtain more referrals.

d. To see improvement in clients' occupational performance.

11. Certain basic abilities in learning to change one's practice performance may not be amenable to training. Which of the following abilities *is* amenable to training?

a. Cognitive ability.

b. Relational ability.

c. Emotional ability.

d. Knowledge.

12. A learning plan includes

a. Learning goals.

b. Resources.

c. Learning methods.

d. All of the above.

13. Which learning method may not be the best strategy for improving interpersonal skills?

a. Role-playing how to give positive feedback.

b. Watching an expert give positive feedback.

c. Reading about how to give positive feedback.

d. Videotaping oneself giving positive feedback.

14. In today's complex world of practice, which might not be the best method for learning how to more effectively solve client problems?

a. Attending a lecture.

b. Discussing a case study with a small group of learners.

c. Shadowing an expert.

d. Reflecting on a current client situation.

15. Which of the following statements best describes a professional portfolio?

a. A collection of continuing education certificates.

b. A carefully appraised set of evidence showing achievement of the goals articulated within a learning plan developed from a thorough self-assessment.

c. A type of scrapbook of one's professional career.

d. Proof that one is competent to practice.

16. Which example of portfolio evidence would best indicate that one has successfully applied the new learning regularly in practice?

a. Improved client outcomes.

b. Demonstration of the steps of a procedure to one's supervisor.

c. Verbalization of the steps of a procedure to one's peers.

d. Successful completion of a knowledge test.

17. Reliable and valid portfolios depend upon which of the following factors?

a. Type of self-assessment tools used.

b. Training in the use of portfolios to change client outcomes.

c. Feedback about the quality of one's portfolio.

d. All of the above.

18. Stakeholders who have a primary interest in the professional development of an occupational therapy practitioner include all but which of the following?

a. The practitioner.

b. The employer.

c. The licensure board.

d. A professional organization.

19. Stakeholders who have a primary interest in competency include all but which of the following?

a. The public.

b. Clients.

c. The professional organization.

d. The licensure board.

20. What role do employers play in continuing competence and competency?

a. Employers help interpret client outcomes in terms of learning needs.

b. Employers provide resources for engagement in learning.

c. Employers remove barriers to and provide facilitators for the application of learning to practice.

d. All of the above.

References

American Occupational Therapy Association. (2008). Occupational therapy practice framework: Domain and process (2nd ed.). *American Journal of Occupational Therapy, 62,* 625–683.

American Occupational Therapy Association. (2009). Guidelines for supervision, roles, and responsibilities during the delivery of occupational therapy services. *American Journal of Occupational Therapy, 63,* 797–803.

American Occupational Therapy Association. (2010a). Occupational therapy code of ethics and ethics standards (2010). *American Journal of Occupational Therapy, 64.*

American Occupational Therapy Association. (2010b). Standards for continuing competence. *American Journal of Occupational Therapy, 64.*

American Occupational Therapy Association. (2010c). Standards of practice for occupational therapy. *American Journal of Occupational Therapy, 64.*

Bauer, J., & Mulder, R. (2007). Modelling learning from errors in daily work. *Learning in Health and Social Care, 6,* 121–133.

Bloom, B. S. (2005). Effects of continuing medical education on improving physician clinical care and patient health: A review of systematic reviews. *International Journal of Technological Assessment in Health Care, 21,* 380–385.

Clark, N. M., Cabana, M., Kaciroti, N., Gong, M., & Sleeman, K. (2008). Long-term outcomes of physician peer teaching. *Clinical Pediatrics, 47,* 883–890.

Cleland, J. A., Fritz, J. M., Brennan, G. P., & Magel, J. (2009). Does continuing education improve physical therapists' effectiveness in treating neck pain? A randomized clinical trial. *Physical Therapy, 89,* 38–47.

Council of Medical Specialty Societies. (2002). *Repositioning for the future of continuing medical education.* Lake Bluff, IL: Author.

Cowan, D. T., Wilson-Barnett, D. J., Norman, I. J., & Murrells, T. (2008). Measuring nursing competence: Development of a self-assessment tool for general nurses across Europe. *International Journal of Nursing Studies, 45,* 902–913.

Currie, M. K., & Roberts, P. (2008). Staff competence: A Joint Commission perspective. *OT Practice, 13,* 31–32.

Davis, D. A., Barnes, B. E., & Fox, R. (2003). *The continuing professional development of physicians.* Chicago: AMA Press.

Davis, D. A., Mazmanian, P. E., Fordis, M., Van Harrison, R., Thorpe, K. E., & Perrier, L. (2006). Accuracy of physician self-assessment compared with observed measures of competence: A systematic review. *JAMA, 296,* 1094–1102.

Decker, P. J. (1999). The hidden competencies of healthcare: Why self-esteem, accountability, and professionalism may affect hospital customer satisfaction scores. *Hospital Topics, 77*(1), 14.

Decker, P. J., & Strader M. K. (1997). Beyond JCAHO: Using competency models to improve healthcare organizations, Part 1. *Hopital Topics, 75*(1), 23.

Epstein, R. M., & Hundert, E. M. (2002). Defining and assessing professional competence. *JAMA, 287,* 226–235.

Forsetlund, L., Bjorndal, A., Rashidian, A., Jamtvedt, G., O'Brien, M. A., Wolf, F., et al. (2009). Continuing education meetings and workshops: Effects on professional practice and health care outcomes (Art. No. CD003030). *Cochrane Database of Systematic Reviews,* Issue 2.

Gustafsson, C., & Fagerberg, I. (2004). Reflection, the way to professional development? *Journal of Clinical Nursing, 13,* 271–280.

Handfield-Jones, R. S., Mann, K. V., Challis, M. E., Hobma, S. O., Klass, D. F., McManus, I. C., et al. (2002). Linking assessment to learning: A new route to quality assurance in medical practice. *Medical Education, 36,* 949–958.

Happell, B., & Martin, T. (2004). Exploring the impact of the implementation of a nursing clinical development unit program: What outcomes are evident? *International Journal of Mental Health Nursing, 13,* 177–184.

Hicks, C., & Hennessy, D. (2000). An alternative technique for evaluating the effectiveness of continuing professional development courses for health care professionals: A pilot study with practice nurses. *Journal of Nursing Management, 9,* 39–49.

Hinojosa J., Bowen, R., Case-Smith, J., Epstein, C., Schwope, C., Moyers, P. et al. (1999). *Professional development for continuing competency.* Bethesda, MD: American Occupational Therapy Association.

Hinojosa, J., Bowen, R., Case-Smith, J., Epstein, C. F., Moyers, P., & Schwope, C. (2000a). Self-initiated continuing competence. *OT Practice, 5*(24), CE1–CE8.

Hinojosa, J., Bowen, R., Case-Smith, J., Epstein, C. F., Moyers, P., & Schwope, C. (2000b). Self-Study—Standards for continuing competence for occupational therapy practitioners. *OT Practice, 5*(20), CE1–CE8.

Hugenholtz, N. I. R., de Croon, E. M., Smits, P. B., van Dijk, F. J. H., & Nieuwenhuijsen, K. (2008). Effectiveness of e-learning in continuing medical education for occupational physicians. *Occupational Medicine, 58,* 370–372.

The Joint Commission. (2008). *Comprehensive accreditation manual for hospitals.* Oakbrook Terrace, IL: Joint Commission Resources.

Keim, K. S., Johnson, C. A., & Gates, G. E. (2001). Learning needs and continuing professional education activities of professional development portfolio participants. *Journal of the American Dietetic Association, 101,* 692–713.

Kerfoot, B. P., Kearney, M. C., Connelly, D., & Ritchey, M. L. (2009). Interactive spaced education to assess and improve knowledge of clinical practice guidelines: A randomized controlled trial. *Annals of Surgery, 249,* 744–749.

Khomeiran, R. T., Yekta, Z. P., Kiger, A. M., & Ahmadi, F. (2006). Professional competence: Factors described by nurses as influencing their development. *International Nursing Review, 53,* 66–72.

Kowlowitz, V., Davenport, C. S., & Palmer, M. H. (2009). Development and dissemination of web-based clinical simulation for continuing geriatric nursing education. *Journal of Gerontological Nursing, 35,* 37–43.

Lysaght, R. M., & Altschuld, J. W. (2000). Beyond initial certification: The assessment and maintenance of competency in professions. *Evaluation and Program Planning, 23,* 95–104.

McConnell, E. A. (2001). Competence vs. competency. *Nursing Management, 32*(5), 14.

McWilliam, C. L. (2007). Continuing education at the cutting edge: Promoting transformative knowledge translation. *Journal of Continuing Education in the Health Professions, 27,* 72–79.

Meretoja, R., & Leino-Kilpi, H. (2003). Comparison of competence assessments made by nurse managers and practicing nurses. *Journal of Nursing Management, 11,* 404–409.

Moyers, P. A. (2005). The ethics of competence. In R. B. Purtilo, G. M. Jensen, & C. B. Royeen (Eds.), *Educating for moral action: A sourcebook in health and rehabilitation ethics* (pp. 21–30). Philadelphia: F. A. Davis.

Moyers, P. A., & Dale, L. M. (2007). *The guide to occupational therapy practice* (2nd ed.). Bethesda, MD: AOTA Press.

Moyers, P. A., & Hinojosa, J. (2003). Continuing competency. In G. McCormack, E. Jaffe, & M. Goodman-Lavey (Eds.), *The occupational therapy manager* (4th ed., pp. 463–489). Bethesda, MD: AOTA Press.

National Board for Certification in Occupational Therapy. (2010). *Certification renewal handbook 2010.* Gaithersburg, MD: Author.

National Center for Health Statistics. (2002). *Health, United States, 2002, with chartbook on trends in the health of Americans: Table 117.* Hyattsville, MD: Author.

Nelson, J. M., & Cook, P. F. (2008). Evaluation of a career ladder program in an ambulatory care environment. *Nursing Economics, 26,* 353–360.

Nylenna, M., & Aasland, O. G. (2000). Primary care physicians and their information-seeking behaviour. *Scandinavian Journal of Primary Health Care, 18,* 9–13.

O'Brien, M. A., Rogers, S., Jamtvedt, G., Oxman, A. D., Odgaard-Jensen, J., Kristoffersen, D. T., et al. (2007). Educational outreach visits: Effects on professional practice and health care outcomes (Art. No. CD000409). *Cochrane Database of Systematic Reviews,* Issue 4.

Parks, J., Hyde, C., Deeks, J., & Milne, R. (2001). Teaching critical appraisal skills in health care settings (Art. No. CD001270). *Cochrane Database of Systematic Reviews,* Issue 3.

Price, B. (2005). Understanding clinical learning. *Nursing Standard, 19*(18), 89–90.

Rappolt, S., Pearce, K., McEwen, S., & Polatajko, H. J. (2005). Exploring organizational characteristics associated with practice changes following a mentored online educational module. *Journal of Continuing Education in the Health Professions, 25,* 116–124.

Rethans, J.-J., Norcini, J. J., Barón-Maldonado, M., Blackmore, D., Jolly, B. C., LaDuca, T., et al. (2002). The relationship between competence and performance: Implications for assessing practice performance. *Medical Education, 36,* 901–909.

Robertson, M. K., Umble, K. E., & Cervero, R. M. (2003). Impact studies in continuing education for health professions: Update. *Journal of Continuing Education in the Health Professions, 23,* 146–156.

Salvatori, P., Simonavicius, N., Moore, J., Rimmer, G., & Patterson, M. (2008). Meeting the challenge of assessing clinical competence of occupational therapists within a program management environment. *Canadian Journal of Occupational Therapy, 75,* 51–61.

Sautter, K. M., Bokhour, B. C., White, B., Young, G. J., Burgess, J. F., Berlowitz, D., et al. (2007). The early experience of a hospital-based pay-for-performance program. *Journal of Healthcare Management, 52*(2), 95–107.

Schell, B. B., & Slater, D. Y. (1998). Management competencies required of administrative and clinical practitioners in the new millennium. *American Journal of Occupational Therapy, 52,* 744–750.

Sebrant, U. (2008). The impact of emotion and power relations on workplace learning. *Studies in the Education of Adults, 40,* 192–206.

Sharpless, B. A., & Barber, J. P. (2009). A conceptual and empirical review of the meaning, measurement, development, and teaching of intervention competence in clinical psychology. *Clinical Psychology Review, 29,* 47–56.

Smith, K., & Tillema, H. H. (2001). Long-term influences of portfolios on professional development. *Scandinavian Journal of Educational Research, 45*(2), 183–203.

Sparrow, J., Ashford, R., & Heel, D. (2005). A methodology to identify workplace features that can facilitate or impede reflective practice: A National Health Service UK study. *Reflective Practice, 6,* 189–197.

Spencer, L. M., & Spencer, S. M. (1993). *Competence at work.* New York: Wiley.

Tillema, H. H. (2001). Portfolios as developmental assessment tools. *International Journal of Training and Development, 5*(2), 1360–1376.

Townsend, E., Sheffield, S. L, Stadnyk, R., & Beagan, B. (2006). Effects of workplace policy on continuing professional development: The case of occupational therapy in Nova Scotia, Canada. *Canadian Journal of Occupational Therapy, 73,* 98–108.

Violato, C., Lockyer, J. M., & Fidler, H. (2008). Assessment of psychiatrists in practice through multisource feedback. *Canadian Journal of Psychiatry, 53,* 525–533.

Welch, A., & Dawson, P. (2006). Closing the gap: Collaborative learning as a strategy to embed evidence within occupational therapy practice. *Journal of Evaluation in Clinical Practice, 12,* 227–238.

Wilkinson, T. J., Challis, M., Hobma, S. O., Newble, D. I., Parboosingh, J. T., Sibbald, R. G., et al. (2002). The use of portfolios for assessment of the competence and performance of doctors in practice. *Medical Education, 36,* 918–924.

Wise, E. H. (2008). Competence and scope of practice: Ethics and professional development. *Journal of Clinical Psychology, 64,* 626–637.

Appendix 31.A. Continuing Competence and Competency Evidence Table

Topic	Evidence
Self-assessment	Hicks, C., & Hennessy, D. (2000). An alternative technique for evaluating the effectiveness of continuing professional development courses for health care professionals: A pilot study with practice nurses. *Journal of Nursing Management, 9,* 39–49. Meretoja, R., & Leino-Kilpi, H. (2003). Comparison of competence assessments made by nurse managers and practicing nurses. *Journal of Nursing Management, 11,* 404–409. Rethans, J.-J., Norcini, J. J., Barón-Maldonado, M., Blackmore, D., Jolly, B. C., LaDuca, T., et al. (2002). The relationship between competence and performance: Implications for assessing practice performance. *Medical Education, 36,* 901–909. Wilkinson, T. J., Challis, M., Hobma, S. O., Newble, D. I., Parboosingh, J. T., Sibbald, R. G., et al. (2002). The use of portfolios for assessment of the competence and performance of doctors in practice. *Medical Education, 36,* 918–924.
Portfolios	Keim, K. S., Johnson, C. A., & Gates, G. E. (2001). Learning needs and continuing professional education activities of professional development portfolio participants. *Journal of the American Dietetic Association, 101,* 692–713. Smith, K., & Tillema, H. H. (2001). Long-term influences of portfolios on professional development. *Scandinavian Journal of Educational Research, 45*(2), 183–203. Tillema, H. H. (2001). Portfolios as developmental assessment tools. *International Journal of Training and Development, 5*(2), 1360–1376. Wilkinson, T. J., Challis, M., Hobma, S. O., Newble, D. I., Parboosingh, J. T., Sibbald, R. G. (2002). The use of portfolios for assessment of the competence and performance of doctors in practice. *Medical Education, 36,* 918–924.
Learning methods	Gustafsson, C., & Fagerberg, I. (2004). Reflection, the way to professional development? *Journal of Clinical Nursing, 13,* 271–280. Happell, B., & Martin, T. (2004). Exploring the impact of the implementation of a nursing clinical development unit program: What outcomes are evident? *International Journal of Mental Health Nursing, 13,* 177–184. Hicks, C., & Hennessy, D. (2000). An alternative technique for evaluating the effectiveness of continuing professional development courses for health care professionals: A pilot study with practice nurses. *Journal of Nursing Management, 9,* 39–49. Khomeiran, R. T., Yekta, Z. P., Kiger, A. M., & Ahmadi, F. (2006). Professional competence: Factors described by nurses as influencing their development. *International Nursing Review, 53,* 66–72. Welch, A., & Dawson, P. (2006). Closing the gap: Collaborative learning as a strategy to embed evidence within occupational therapy practice. *Journal of Evaluation in Clinical Practice, 12,* 227–238.
System barriers and facilitators	Nylenna, M., & Aasland, O. G. (2000). Primary care physicians and their information-seeking behaviour. *Scandinavian Journal of Primary Health Care, 18,* 9–13. Parks, J., Hyde, C., Deeks, J., & Milne, R. (2001). Teaching critical appraisal skills in health care settings (Art. No. CD001270). *Cochrane Database of Systematic Reviews,* Issue 3. Rappolt, S., Pearce, K., McEwen, S., & Polatajko, H. J. (2005). Exploring organizational characteristics associated with practice changes following a mentored online educational module. *Journal of Continuing Education in the Health Professions, 25,* 116–124. Sparrow, J., Ashford, R., & Heel, D. (2005). A methodology to identify workplace features that can facilitate or impede reflective practice: A National Health Service UK study. *Reflective Practice, 6,* 189–197.

32

Legal Dimensions of Occupational Therapy Practice

Barbara L. Kornblau, JD, OTR, FAOTA,
and Richard Y. Cheng, JD, OTR

❖ Key Terms and Concepts

Assault. An intentional tort that occurs when a person perceives a threat that another person will engage in an offensive touch or cause immediate harm (Keeton, Dobbs, Keeton, & Owens, 2004).

Battery. Occurs when a person intentionally comes in physical contact with another person without that person's permission, resulting in a harmful consequence (Keeton et al., 2004).

Confidentiality. Implies a trust in private communications. When a patient makes a disclosure to an occupational therapy practitioner, the practitioner must not disclose the information to others (AOTA, 2010a). Confidentiality refers to information or data about the patient (Beauchamp & Childress, 1994).

Copyright. Protects authors of published and unpublished works from infringement by others. Authors of "original works of authorship," including literary, dramatic, musical, artistic, and certain intellectual works in the occupational therapy world (e.g., this book, an occupational therapy assessment; 17 USC §101), hold the exclusive right to reproduce and otherwise derive income from their work (17 USC §106).

Fair use. A limited exception to copyright protection that allows use of copyrighted materials in limited circumstances such as teaching, scholarship, research, or book reviews in which the use meets certain criteria specified in the law (17 USC §107).

Informed consent. The "rational and informed decision about undertaking a particular treatment or undergoing a particular surgical procedure" on the basis of knowledge of the "significant potential risks involved in the proposed treatment or surgery" (*Johnson v. Kokemoor*, 1996).

Law. "A binding custom or practice of a community; a rule of conduct or action prescribed or formally recognized as binding or enforced by a controlling authority" (*Merriam-Webster*, 2010).

Negligence. The failure to exercise the standard of care a reasonable, prudent person would exercise in a similar situation (Garner, 2004; The Joint Commission, 2006).

Malpractice. The "improper or unethical conduct or unreasonable lack of skill by a holder of a professional or official position. Often applied to physicians, dentists, lawyers, and public officers to denote negligent or unskillful performance of duties when professional skills are obligatory" (The Joint Commission, 2006).

Policy. "Whatever governments choose to do or not to do" (Dye, 2002, p. 2). For example, public policies may regulate behavior, organize government agencies, or require licenses or fees.

Privacy. The right of patients "to be left alone," free from intrusion, and to choose whether or not to share one's self (*Olmstead v. United States*, 277 U.S. 438, 1928). *Privacy* concerns information about the patient (Beauchamp & Childress, 1994).

Tort. An intentional or negligent harm or wrong against another that results in damages for which one party may be liable (Keeton et al., 2004)

Vicarious liability. Indirect legal responsibility such the liability of an employer for the acts of an employee (Keeton et al., 2004)

❖ Learning Objectives

After completing this chapter, you should be able to do the following:

- Identify areas of concern to occupational therapy managers and practitioners that present potential legal ramifications in clinical practice.
- Explain sources of law or regulations that affect occupational therapy practice.
- List actions managers and occupational therapy practitioners can take to avoid legal problems in practice.
- Describe and discuss the standard of care expected of occupational therapy practitioners.

- Analyze how federal legislation can affect current occupational therapy practice and reimbursement.
- Articulate the legal significance of proper supervision of subordinates, competent practice, staying current, and use of good documentation.
- Analyze when to seek legal advice to address occupational therapy practice and related legal issues.

Occupational therapy managers work within a structure of seemingly complicated rules and policies. Some rules or policies come from laws or regulations; others stem from reimbursement requirements. Accrediting bodies such as The Joint Commission or CARF International promulgate rules and policies that affect occupational therapy management and practice. No one expects occupational therapy managers to be attorneys, but they need to familiarize themselves with the basic legal issues that affect what they do, especially as health care becomes increasingly complicated.

This chapter looks at some of the key laws and regulations affecting occupational therapy practice and management, highlighting issues that may present legal problems and providing guidance so you know when to ask questions or seek advice. Like prevention's role in health care, prevention plays an important role helping people avoid potential legal issues and their consequences. This chapter also provides tips for occupational therapy managers, suggesting ways to lessen the risk that such problems will occur. After discussing the sources of law and regulation in occupational therapy, the chapter discusses legal issues in hiring and firing employees, copyright issues in occupational therapy, privacy and confidentiality, liability issues (including negligence and malpractice), and fraud and abuse in reimbursement.

SOURCES OF LAW

Legal requirements that impose policy come from a variety of sources. Such requirements may take the form of a law passed by a federal, state, or local legislative body. For example, the Medicare program, which began in 1965 and is amended periodically, is governed by a federal law (42 USC §1395 et seq., 2009). Federal laws apply across the country, whereas licensure laws are state laws that can vary from state to state (e.g., West Virginia Occupational Therapy Practice Act, Article 28 §30-28-16(e), 2009). A law that specifies the size of the sign a practice may post outside its clinic is probably a local law or ordinance, which typically varies from town to town. Laws can also result from case law, or judge-made law based upon the prec-

edent established in previous cases (i.e., common law, or laws established by court decisions instead of statutes).

Regulations, the rules that implement laws on a state or national basis, also provide a foundation for public policy, and occupational therapy managers must follow them. Occupational therapy policy can also come from the following sources:

- Consensus statements (e.g., American Academy of Pain Medicine and American Pain Society, 1997; Wallis, 1992; Wang et al., 2007);
- Practice guidelines (e.g., Agency for Healthcare Research and Quality, 1992; Joint Commission on Accreditation of Healthcare Organizations, 1999; Phillips, 2000; Sabari, 2008; Tomchek & Case-Smith, 2009); and
- State regulations that incorporate these factors to form the standards of care, the ethical obligations, and/or the weight of law (Federation of State Medical Boards of the United States, 1998).

Policymakers also may look to research-derived evidence to develop policy (Hall et al., 2008; see also Chapter 29, this volume).

Policy affects how occupational therapy managers make clinical and business decisions. For example, policy determines how occupational therapists obtain reimbursement through Medicare and Medicaid and the parameters of the federal payment system (Marron, 2006; see also Chapter 25, this volume). Policymakers on a state level, through legislation and licensure requirements, decide scope of practice issues, such as those that influence practice and management decisions regarding occupational therapy versus physical therapy. The federal government addresses the payment aspect of this issue through health care financing policy under Medicare laws and regulations.

A combination of state and federal policy and judicial decisions determines who can practice and where they can practice (e.g., Florida Administrative Code, Minimum Standards for Home Health Agencies, ch. 59A-8.0095(8), 2006) and establishes legal requirements for supervision.

Policy determines the degree of training needed to treat patients. Policy determines whom occupational therapists and occupational therapy assistants may treat—for example, adults, children, immigrants—and where they can treat them—for example, in the rehabilitation clinic or in the home, office, or hospital setting.

State policymakers determine continuing education requirements in licensure laws or in the implementing regulations of these laws. State regulatory boards determine the proper behavior of occupational therapists and occupational therapy assistants and determine sanctions for deviating from these standards. Because these requirements are determined on a state-by-state basis, they often vary from one state to another, and occupational therapy managers and practitioners should read their state practice acts to familiarize themselves with their legal obligations. Membership in the American Occupational Therapy Association (AOTA) and individual state occupational therapy professional organizations helps occupational therapy managers and practitioners stay abreast of changes to practice acts and other laws and regulations on national and state levels, ultimately helping them stay current with their legal obligations as professionals.

LEGAL ISSUES WITH EMPLOYEES AND INDEPENDENT CONTRACTORS

Among the functions a manager performs is hiring and firing of employees or other staff. Managers should familiarize themselves with their employer's policies on hiring and firing. Several laws govern hiring and firing practices; this section provides an overview of some of the applicable laws and policies.

The overriding principle behind hiring an employee involves a match between the candidate's skills and abilities and the job's requirements. Under federal law one may not consider any of the following in making a hiring decision, because these factors do not affect the candidate's ability to perform the job requirements: race, creed, sex, age if age 40 or older (U.S. Equal Employment Opportunity Commission [EEOC], 2008), religion, national origin, military status, pregnancy (EEOC, 2009), union membership, or disability. Federal law also prohibits inquiries about a candidate's arrest record (*Gregory v. Litton Systems*, 316 F. Supp. 401, 2 EPD ¶10,264 [C.D. Cal. 1970], modified on other grounds, 472 F.2d 631, 5 EPD ¶8089, 1972; *Schware v. Board of Bar Examiners*, 353 U.S. 232, 241, 1957; EEOC, 1990). State and local laws may add other factors, such as sexual orientation or marital status (e.g., California Non-Discrimination Law, Cal Gov Code §12920; Cal Civ Code §51, 2001; State of Maryland, Department of Budget and Management, Office of the Statewide EEO Coordinator, 2009). The following is a list of questions one should not ask as part of the hiring process (the protected group is specified in parentheses following each question; HR World Editors, 2007):

- What does your husband do? (marital status)
- Where were you born? (national origin)

- When did you graduate from high school? (age)
- What kind of accent is that? (national origin)
- Which church do you attend? (religion)
- Do you have any children? (marital status)
- Are you planning to have children? (sex)
- How do you feel about being supervised by a man [or woman]? (sex)
- Have you ever been arrested? (general civil rights)
- Are you a member of the National Guard? (military status)
- Have you ever filed a claim for workers' compensation? (disability)
- Do you have any physical disabilities that may affect your job performance? (disability).

In sum, occupational therapy managers should not ask questions that will reveal any information regarding these factors or that may lead to information that may disproportionately exclude members of protected groups. The exception is when the employer can show that the inquiry is job related and consistent with business necessity (EEOC, 2000). In this case, the interviewer can show applicants a job description and ask if they can perform specific job tasks, arrive at work on time, or work weekends if required to perform the job.

Just as occupational therapy managers cannot ask certain questions in the hiring process, they cannot use discriminatory or other illegal reasons to terminate employees. Certain federal laws protect employees from termination for specific reasons, and some states add to those protections. For example, the Family Medical Leave Act of 1993 (P.L. 103-3; see, 29 CFR §825.101, 2009) allows employees who meet certain criteria to take 12 weeks off of work for specific health- and family-related issues. These reasons include, among others, to treat a serious health condition; to give birth or to care for a newborn; to care for a newly adopted or placed foster child; to care for a sick child, spouse, or parent (but not parent-in-law); or to support a family member as part of an impending military deployment. An occupational therapy manager cannot terminate employees for exercising their right under the law to take family medical leave.

Occupational therapy managers also need to be familiar with the Americans with Disabilities Act (ADA) of 1990 (as amended P.L. 100-325, 42 USC 12101 *et seq.*, 2009). Some occupational therapists and occupational therapy assistants involve themselves with the ADA clinically, such as when performing job analysis and creating workplace accommodations. Occupational therapy managers must realize that some of their employees and fieldwork students may be individuals with disabilities. They must follow the ADA's requirements to make requested reasonable accommodations in the workplace for occupational therapy practitioners and fieldwork students with disabilities. They must also make reasonable modifications to their policies and practices to make the programs and services they offer, including fieldwork programs, accessible to individuals with disabilities (28 CFR §36.302).

According to the ADA, reasonable accommodations in the workplace include changes to the work environment or to the way the worker performs the work to enable individuals with disabilities to perform their work (29 CFR §1630.2(o)). For example, an occupational therapist working in a clinic who uses a wheelchair may need to work from a sitting position and may request to stay in the hand clinic instead of rotating through the spinal cord unit, where heavy lifting is required. If considered a reasonable accommodation in light of all the circumstances, the occupational therapy manager must make this accommodation of allowing the employee to remain in the hand clinic.

The requirement to provide reasonable modifications to policies, practices, or procedures and to provide auxiliary aids and services to make programs and services accessible is analogous to the reasonable accommodation requirement in the workplace. For example, a fieldwork student with a learning disability might ask to use a tape recorder during supervisory sessions while completing the fieldwork program. The occupational therapy manager might need to ensure that students can use the requested auxiliary aids that will allow them to benefit from the fieldwork program (28 CFR §36.302).

Other laws and rules are related to hiring. For example, when hiring foreign-trained therapists, managers need to address the complicated immigration issues involved and will probably want to engage the services of human resources and of an attorney who specializes in immigration law as set forth in the Immigration and Nationality Act (8 USC 1101 *et seq.*, 2005).

Managers should know if they are hiring an employee or making a contract with an independent contractor. In practice, some act as if the decision is up to the facility or company. In reality, the law dictates who is an independent contractor and may require repayment of employment taxes for employers who violate the law by declaring independent contractors "employees" (Internal Revenue Service [IRS], 2009a). IRS rules include a series of factors, particularly the nature of the behavioral and financial control the business exerts over the worker and the relationship between the parties (IRS, 2009b). If in doubt about whether an occupational therapy practitioner is in fact an independent contractor, managers should seek counsel from competent attorneys who are familiar with labor law.

COPYRIGHT ISSUES IN OCCUPATIONAL THERAPY

The frequently updated U.S. copyright laws (see Title 17, USC §101 *et seq.,* as amended 2009) protects authors of published and unpublished works from infringement by others. Authors of "original works of authorship," including literary, dramatic, musical, artistic, and certain intellectual works in the occupational therapy world (e.g., this book, an occupational therapy assessment; 17 USC §101;

laws often cited in publishing and usage issues are the 1998 Digital Millennium Copyright Act, P.L. 105-304, and later amendments), hold the exclusive right to reproduce and otherwise derive income from their work (17 USC §106). If others imitate or copy these works and present them to the public without the express consent (i.e., verbal or, as is often required, written permission) of the original author, they violate copyright laws and infringe on the owner's copyright (17 USC §106–122; §501). One can acquire copyright for original works only within a concrete "medium of expression," which in the occupational therapy world would include a literary work, a motion picture or audiovisual work, and a pictorial and graphic work, among others (17 USC §103(a)).

Some limited exceptions exist under these exclusivity provisions for "fair use," such as teaching, scholarship, research, or book reviews. Whether use of copyrighted material is considered fair use depends on the following four factors (17 USC §107):

1. The purpose and character of the use, including whether such use is of a commercial nature or is for nonprofit educational purposes;
2. The nature of the copyrighted work;
3. The amount and substantiality of the portion used in relation to the copyrighted work as a whole; and
4. The effect of the use on the potential market for or value of the copyrighted work.

Fair use can appear ambiguous and may vary in interpretation. Generally, uses that advance public interests, such as criticism, education, or scholarship, are favored, particularly if the work is seldom copied or is copied only to a limited degree (17 USC §107). Uses that generate income or interfere with the copyright owner's income are not considered fair use. Fairness also means that users must credit the original artists or authors. For example, an occupational therapy student who photocopies this chapter instead of purchasing this book interferes with the income of the copyright owner and therefore is doing something illegal—violating the owner's copyright. Occupational therapists and occupational therapy assistants who photocopy, without credit, another institution's assessment materials also violate the owner's copyright.

Occupational therapists and occupational therapy assistants encounter a multitude of potential copyright concerns or pitfalls. Managers and directors of facilities work with many different examples of intellectual property that neither they nor their staff created, such as standardized assessments, evaluations, measuring tools, and intervention materials. Managers provide these materials to staff to enable them to assess their patients, develop occupational profiles, and conduct their interventions. If staff members copy these materials internally instead of purchasing additional copies, they infringe on the owner's copyright. Therapists who make copies for later use at another facility also violate the copyright law.

Managers should ensure that professionals use assessment tools and intervention materials in a way that protects both the employer and the authors of the materials from copyright infringement. They should ensure that staff do not treat a modified tool as their own work or distribute work created by another. Occupational therapy practitioners should obtain express permission to use materials in all professional capacities, including photocopying; typical ways to secure this permission include applying through a publisher or author's Web site or through the Copyright Clearance Center (a clearinghouse for many scholarly and professional works at www.copyright.com). Unless they guard against illegal and unethical behavior in the copyright arena, managers may find their facilities open to potential lawsuits.

PRIVACY AND CONFIDENTIALITY

Long before the passage of the Health Insurance Portability and Accountability Act (HIPAA) of 1996 (P.L. 104-191), occupational therapists had an obligation to preserve patients' privacy and keep patient information confidential (Gleave, 1963). That tradition continues and stands embedded in AOTA's (2010a) *Occupational Therapy Code of Ethics and Ethics Standards*, which mandates that occupational practitioners keep written communication confidential and maintain the privacy of their patients.

Privacy implies the right of patients "to be left alone," free from intrusion, and to choose whether or not to share one's self (*Olmstead v. United States*, 277 U.S. 438, 1928). In the health care context, *confidentiality* implies a trust in private communications; when a patient makes a disclosure to an occupational therapy practitioner, the practitioner must not disclose the information to others (AOTA, 2010a). *Privacy* concerns information about the patient, whereas *confidentiality* refers to information or data about the patient (Beauchamp & Childress, 1994).

Some licensure laws specifically incorporate the *Occupational Therapy Code of Ethics and Ethics Standards* by reference, giving its aspirational guidelines for privacy and confidentiality the full weight of law. (e.g., "Louisiana Occupational Therapy Practice Act, Louisiana Revised Statutes Title 37, ch. 39 §3001 *et seq.*, 2009). Other licensure laws specifically mandate patient confidentiality and/or privacy (e.g., Pennsylvania Occupational Therapy Practice Act, 63 PS §§ 1501–1519, 2010). Occupational therapy practitioners need to familiarize themselves with their licensure laws and adjust their behavior accordingly.

HIPAA and its implementing regulations, or "Privacy Rule," went a step further and codified patient privacy and confidentiality requirements into law, attempting to weave together all of the local, state, and federal privacy and confidentiality laws and rules into one. HIPAA sets forth requirements to protect the privacy of patient health information. The privacy standards address the circumstances under which private patient information (called *protected health information,* or *PHI*) may be used and distributed and the actions organizations and others that are subject to the privacy rule (called *covered entities*) must take to protect the privacy of the PHI (45 CFR §164.102 *et seq.*, 2007). Covered entities include health plans; all health care providers who electronically transmit health information, directly or through a third party (e.g., claims, benefit eligibility inquiries, referral authorization requests); and health care clearinghouses, such as billing services (45 CFR §162, 2007).

The purpose of the HIPAA Privacy Rule is to define and limit the use and disclosure of individuals' PHI. Under the rules, a covered entity cannot use or disclose PHI unless the Privacy Rule allows or requires the disclosure or the individual or his or her personal representative authorizes the release in writing (45 CFR §164.502(a), 2007).

Because they are health care providers or work for health care providers, occupational therapists and occupational therapy assistants must abide by the HIPAA Privacy Rule. Most facilities provide their own HIPAA training with their own interpretation of the law. HIPAA regulations change from time to time as technology changes (see, e.g., American Recovery and Reinvestment Act of 2009, P.L. 111-5 [ARRA], also called the "stimulus package"), so managers should make sure their staff members maintain current knowledge and practice of HIPAA requirements to avoid significant penalties to their institution or their own practices.

The federal government can bring criminal charges against covered entities and other responsible corporate parties that knowingly violate HIPAA's privacy rules (General Counsel Department of Health and Human Services & Senior Counsel to the Deputy General, 2005). ARRA established a tiered civil penalty structure for HIPAA violations that allows the Secretary of Health and Human Services to impose civil penalties if HIPAA violations go uncorrected for 30 days, unless the violation is a case of willful neglect. The HITECH Act of 2009 (42 USC §1320d-5), part of ARRA, authorizes state attorneys general to pursue criminal actions for HIPAA violations that adversely affect citizens of their states.

Although HIPAA provides for civil and criminal penalties (42 USC §1320d-6, 2000), it does not create a private cause of action for individuals whose protected health information is disclosed (65 Fed. Reg. 82566, 2000). In other words, the patient whose protected health information is disclosed by an occupational therapist cannot sue the occupational therapist or the hospital/employer for violating HIPAA (*Acara v. Banks*, 470 F.3d 569, 2006). However, the law provides other remedies for aggrieved patients and penalties for therapists who disclose protected health information. Therapists may be subject to individual liability for breach of confidentiality or invasion of privacy, a civil lawsuit, or disciplinary action from state licensure boards.

The disclosure of some categories of medical information can result in drastic consequences for patients, and special laws provide specific protection in such cases. For example, discrimination based on the results of genetic tests is specifically prohibited by the Genetic Information Non-discrimination Act of 2008 (P. L. 110-233). For example, a medical record contains genetic test results for a heart condition. The same test also indicates the patient's genetic profile, indicating that he is at high risk to get Alzheimer's disease (Mayo Clinic Staff, 2008). Disclosure of this information may risk job loss or loss of health insurance, so an occupational therapist may not disclose this information without the patient's permission; not only would disclosure violate legal requirements for confidentiality, privacy, and HIPAA, it may also threaten the patient in other significant ways Similarly, some states treat HIV status and/or HIV testing in a special manner, with specific requirements for privacy and notification in the event of an exposure (e.g., HIV Testing, Fla. Stat. 381.004, 2009). Occupational therapy practitioners who may come in contact with blood-borne pathogens should familiarize themselves with their facility's infection control procedures and the state's requirements.

Some exceptions to the obligation to protect the privacy of medical information exist. For example, professionals in all 50 states have a legal obligation to report child abuse and neglect (Child Abuse Prevention and Treatment Act as amended, 42 USC 5101 *et seq.*,1996), and some states require reporting of elder abuse (Illinois's Elder Abuse and Neglect Act, 320 ILCS 20, from ch. 23, par. 6601, 2010). Some of these laws obligate occupational therapy practitioners to report abuse to the proper authorities, and some waive confidentiality requirements to protect occupational therapy practitioners who do report child abuse (Pennsylvania Occupational Therapy Practice Act, 63 P.S. §§1501–1519, 2010).

Some states recognize that mental health professionals have a duty to warn potential victims when a patient communicates to the therapist a credible threat to another individual (*Tarasoff v. Regents of University of California,* 17 Cal. 3d 425, 551 P.2d 334, 131 Cal. Rptr. 14, 1976). However, few states consider occupational therapists to be mental health professionals, and courts have not yet applied *Tarasoff* to occupational therapy. Managers may want to seek legal advice should a patient make a threat in their clinic.

Although they do not necessarily require it, some states permit occupational therapists to report impaired drivers on the basis of information obtained in an occupational therapy assessment (Louisiana Occupational Therapy Practice Act, Louisiana Revised Statutes Title 37, ch. 39 §3001 *et seq.*, 2009). Occupational therapy managers should familiarize themselves with reporting obligations—whether required or permitted—to protect their patients and avoid possible criminal or civil penalties for failing to report.

Liability Issues

Occupational therapists are responsible for performing accurate assessments; developing sound plans of care; delivering proper clinical interventions; and, above all, doing no harm. Managers must understand and try to prevent legal claims against occupational therapy practitioners or occupational therapy departments in cases where therapists fails to properly perform their duties.

Legal claims fall into two main categories—civil and criminal. Civil claims, unlike criminal claims or charges, do not threaten therapists with jail time or a criminal record. Civil liability or responsibility is concerned with either money damages or "injunctive relief" (or prevention of a future occurrence or event). This section focuses on the civil aspect of legal actions, and tort actions in particular.

Most lawsuits filed against occupational therapy practitioners for harm fall under the umbrella of tort law (Ranke & Moriarty, 1997). *Tort law* covers intentional or negligent harm or wrong against another that results in damages for which one party may be liable (Keeton et al., 2004). Virtually all the diverse forms of activities of daily living (ADLs) or other occupations in people's lives—driving, working, writing, owning, using real or personal property, having sexual intercourse—may cause harm. That harm may lead to a potential civil tort claim or civil lawsuit. Various forms of liability can arise from occupational therapy intervention in ADLs and in other occupations, depending on the circumstances.

The legal system categorizes various types of torts. This section addresses some of these categories, including battery and assault, false imprisonment, intentional infliction of emotional distress, negligence, and malpractice.

Battery and Assault

Battery and assault are "intentional" torts or harms, meaning that the person doing the harm has the intention to do something that ultimately causes harm to another (Keeton et al., 2004). *Battery* occurs when a person intentionally comes in physical contact with another person without that person's permission, resulting in a harmful consequence (Keeton et al., 2004). The person who makes a claim for a battery must prove that a touching occurred, that the person who did the touching intended to do it, and that the touching harmed the person touched. In this context, "person" includes both one's body and the things closely connected to it (e.g., a reacher, wheelchair; Keeton et al., 2004).

Like battery, assault is an intentional tort. An *assault* occurs when a person apprehends a threat that the other will engage in an offensive touch or cause immediate harm (Keeton et al., 2004). The court will inquire as to whether a reasonable person would apprehend an offensive touch or immediate harm. It must appear the threat is imminent, coupled with obvious intent to carry it out. Words alone, however strong, do not constitute an assault. There are circumstances when an act itself may appear innocuous or harmless (e.g., crossing one's arms), but the words that accompany it create the required apprehension. If the court finds that a reasonable person would not perceive an immediate danger, the threatening gestures probably will not constitute an assault.

Assault and battery in health care settings generally occur because practitioners perform acts or procedures without informed consent. *Informed consent* implies "a rational and informed decision about undertaking a particular treatment or undergoing a particular surgical procedure" on the basis of knowledge of the "significant potential risks involved in the proposed treatment or surgery" (*Johnson v. Kokemoor*, 1996). Battery may occur if patients do not agree to an intervention or would not have agreed had the occupational therapy practitioner informed them about it. For example, if an occupational therapy assistant wishes to assist an adult with autism and sensory defensiveness to put on a shirt, before assisting the patient he or she should inform the patient of the objectives of the task and the role the occupational therapy assistant will play in the task and obtain the patient's consent. If the occupational therapy assistant fails to obtain informed consent, reaching forward while communicating the intent to provide assistance could be considered assault, and actually touching the patient and providing hands-on assistance could be considered battery. In some states, failure to obtain informed consent in itself may provide its own independent basis for malpractice.

False Imprisonment

False imprisonment occurs when someone violates another's basic personal right to freedom from wrongful confinement (Keeton et al., 2004). The focus is on the mental harm caused by the knowledge of confinement. False imprisonment could occur if therapists confine patients, with the intent to confine them, within certain boundaries: The "imprisoned" person must know of no reasonable or safe avenue of escape (merely blocking his or her path in one direction or exerting moral or social pressure does not constitute false imprisonment), and the person must know of the confinement.

In health care, a patient who has not been lawfully committed to an appropriate facility has no obligation to stay, and physical or coercive efforts to restrict movement may constitute false imprisonment. The Nursing Home Reform Act (in the Omnibus Budget Reconciliation Act [OBRA] of 1987, P.L. 100-203) requires nursing homes to take certain steps to avoid unnecessarily restraining its residents. If the restraint is not in patients' care plans, tying nursing home residents to a wheelchair to prevent them from wandering might constitute false imprisonment. If a patient who voluntarily admits herself to a psychiatric setting decides to leave a few days later, the occupational therapist and nursing staff cannot coerce her to stay by threatening to have her committed should she leave; a court could determine that this threat meets enough of the basic elements to bring a case of false imprisonment (Kazin, 1989; *Metropolitan Life Ins. Co. v. McCarson*, 1985).

Intentional Infliction of Emotional Distress

In health care, patients may claim they experienced intentionally inflicted emotional distress while in a facility or with a provider such as an occupational therapist. *Intentional infliction of emotional distress* occurs when, through extreme and outrageous conduct, someone intentionally causes severe emotional or mental distress, such as grief or anguish, to another person (Keeton et al., 2004; Prosser, 1971). The person's conduct must be "so outrageous in character, and so extreme in degree, as to go beyond all possible bounds of decency" (*Metropolitan Life Ins. Co. v. McCarson*, 1985). Insulting, profane, abusive, annoying, or even threatening conduct is not enough to meet this criterion unless the offending person knows of some special sensitivity of the person being subjected to harm. The person filing a claim must suffer severe emotional damages; a brief episode of unhappiness, humiliation, or mild despondence or a few restless nights do not amount to severe emotional distress. If the emotional anguish is great and prolonged, however, it may form the basis of a successful claim for intentional infliction of emotional distress (Keeton et al., 2004).

Sometimes a bystander who witnesses another's injury may seek remedies as the party who suffered severe emotional distress. The distress to the bystander must represent a foreseeable consequence of the alleged conduct to constitute intentional infliction of emotional distress (Keeton et al., 2004).

For example, an outpatient clinic provides occupational therapy treatment for a patient's carpal tunnel syndrome. The patient told his therapist that he was undergoing treatment for depression, and she noted his antidepressant medications in his medical record. When the patient arrives late to an extremely busy outpatient clinic for his third visit, the occupational therapist screamed and swore at him for showing up late. The therapist told the patient that he was a "worthless patient" and insisted that he leave the outpatient clinic. Under these circumstances, the court would probably find a valid claim for intentional infliction of emotional distress (a similar situation occurred in *Anderson v. Prease*, 445 A.2d, 612, D.C., 1982).

Negligence

In addition to actions for intentional acts of assault, battery, false imprisonment, and intentional infliction of emotional distress, malpractice actions often rest on theories of negligence. Ordinary *negligence* is the failure to exercise the standard of care a reasonable, prudent person would exercise in a similar situation (Garner, 2004; Joint Commission, 2006). Negligence does not involve intentional or reckless actions; it involves carelessness. The person's state of mind is not considered; only his or her actions.

Ordinary negligence applies to everyday people in everyday situations. It can result from something one does—for example, rear-ending a car that brakes suddenly to avoid a squirrel—or something one fails to do—for example, not placing a "wet floor" sign on a recently washed floor (Keeton et al., 2004). To establish the claim of negligence, one must prove four elements: (1) a duty to act in a particular way, (2) a breach of that duty, (3) actual harm or damages, and (4) a causal connection or "proximate cause" between the breach of the duty and the harm or damages (Keeton et al., 2004).

For example, while Mary is driving down the road to do a home evaluation, she drops her cell phone, reaches down to get it, and crashes into a car stopped at a light. Mary might be found negligent on the basis of each of the four elements in negligence (assuming her state does not follow "no-fault" insurance laws):

1. *Duty to act in a particular way:* In exchange for the privilege of driving, Mary had a duty to other drivers to drive carefully, keeping her eyes on the road and watching for other cars to avoid a collision.
2. *Breach of that duty:* Mary breached her duty to drive carefully when she took her eyes off the road to reach for her cell phone.
3. *Actual harm or damage:* Mary crashed into a car and caused damage to the car and harm to the passenger.
4. *Causal connection or proximate cause between the breach of the duty and the actual harm:* Mary's failure to drive carefully—taking her eyes off the road—was the proximate or direct cause of the car accident.

Malpractice

The Joint Commission (2006) defined *malpractice* as

improper or unethical conduct or unreasonable lack of skill by a holder of a professional or official position; often applied to physicians, dentists, lawyers, and public officers to denote negligent or unskillful performance of duties when professional skills are obligatory.

The legal system holds health care professionals to a higher standard than avoiding ordinary carelessness because of their training and the expectations the public ascribes to them. The therapist–patient relationship creates a legal duty to the patient. In most cases, the health care provider has a duty to obtain informed consent before providing intervention. The provider of occupational therapy services has a duty to provide those services according to the standard of care of the profession. When patients enter into a relationship with an occupational therapist or occupational therapy assistant, they have an expectation that the professional will perform using the specialized skills, knowledge, and abilities of a reasonable and prudent occupational therapist or occupational therapy assistant; this expectation includes, among other things, accurate assessments, sound plans of care, and proper and safe interventions.

To constitute the tort of malpractice, the patient has to show that the occupational therapist's or occupational therapy assistant's action or inaction fell below the professional standard of care and injured the patient. The action or inaction must be contrary to the standards of the profession (AOTA, 2008, 2010b). The occupational therapy practitioner must do something, or fail to do something, that a reasonable, prudent therapist in the same situation would do and that caused unnecessary harm to a patient.

State laws govern damages in malpractice cases. There are generally two types of damages: compensatory and punitive. *Compensatory* damages compensate an injured party harmed through the willful or reckless conduct of a practitioner, usually through monetary relief. Successful plaintiffs in medical malpractice cases can usually recover out-of-pocket losses (medical bills and future medical expenses); loss of income and temporary or permanent impairment of earning capacity; and incidental expenses and money to fairly represent the pain, suffering, and mental distress experienced (Keeton et al., 2004). *Punitive damages* are damages meant to punish the party who caused the harm (Keeton et al., 2004). Some states limit the amount of punitive damages courts may award.

In the legal context, occupational therapists and occupational therapy assistants need not provide superior care. Rather, they must stay within the standard of care. Occupational therapists' failure to follow the standard of care resulting in harm or injury to patients may constitute professional malpractice. The following are examples of possible malpractice in occupational therapy settings:

- Improperly transferring a patient, resulting in a fall
- Failing to supervise a patient during an activity, resulting in an overuse injury
- Forgetting to tell the nurse of the patient's complaints of chest pain during occupational therapy intervention, resulting in a heart attack and subsequent death
- Improperly maneuvering a wheelchair in preparation for a transfer, causing the chair to fall backward and the patient's head to hit the floor, resulting in a subdural hematoma
- Failing to ensure that a fieldwork student was competent to perform a patient transfer before allowing him or her to do so, causing a patient injury
- Failing to secure sharp instruments properly in the occupational therapy clinic of a locked psychiatric unit
- Failing to lock the wheelchair during a transfer
- Causing burns from a hot pack (Ranke & Moriarty, 1997)
- Engaging in sexual misconduct with a patient (Ranke & Moriarty, 1997)
- Failing to evaluate patient safety
- Ignoring seizure precautions for a child during spinning activities for a sensory integration intervention, causing a seizure
- Improperly instructing a patient in the use of a splint or other device
- Failing to refer the patient to another therapist more competent to treat the patient.

Vicarious Liability

Occupational therapists, occupational therapy assistants, and occupational therapy managers may find themselves vicariously liable or responsible for the negligence of others under the doctrine of "*respondeat superior*," Latin for "let the master answer" from the historical master–servant relationship. This doctrine holds the employer or supervisor liable or responsible for the actions of employees or subordinates that occur in the course of employment. It implies that the superior may be liable for the acts of the subordinate, even if the superior is without fault (Keeton et al., 2004).

Negligent Supervision

Another basis for a malpractice action is negligent supervision. Whereas *respondeat superior* holds employers liable for actions of others that were not their fault, under negligent supervision, supervisors are held liable for their own actions in hiring incompetent employees, failing to train them, or failing to properly supervise them (New Jersey Jury Verdict Review and Analysis, 2010; *Smith, etc. v. Archbishop of St. Louis*, 632 S.W. 2d 516, 1982). Occupational therapy practitioners must know and fulfill their professional responsibilities for supervision. In addition to a civil lawsuit, negligent supervision could lead to loss of license (Centers for Medicare and Medicaid Services [CMS], 2009).

Victims of malpractice in the therapeutic relationship may suffer in a multitude of areas, physically, mentally, and emotionally. Because laws related to medical malpractice vary from state to state, it is important for managers to familiarize themselves with the laws that govern malpractice in their own state and take steps to prevent malpractice among their staff. Department in-services can keep occupational therapy practitioners current in relevant areas of practice. Encouraging and promoting continuing education opportunities directly related to practice help keep people competent. Peer reviewing other practitioners' practices can give them insight into their own needs, their strengths and weaknesses, and ways to improve their own interventions.

Accurate, timely, and detailed documentation can help protect occupational therapy practitioners from lawsuits. Conversely, documentation that does not specify what the intervention was and how the patient responded to it can hurt practitioners. As the profession makes the change to electronic medical records, issues in documentation should be reviewed periodically. Once something is in a client's record, there is no erasing it. Similarly, failing to record something in the medical or health record means it never happened; it cannot be added to the record later.

Simple steps such as clear communication with patients and being nice to patients help prevent lawsuits. Research shows that the relationship between actual negligence and the number of malpractice claims is weak (Localio et al., 1991), whereas good communication with patients de-

creases the incidence of malpractice lawsuits (Levinson, 1997). Managers can play a key role in lowering the risk of malpractice by fostering good communication and good customer service with patients and ensuring that staff members practice within the boundaries of their practice act, standard of practice, and code of ethics (AOTA, 2010a, 2010b; Oklahoma Occupational Therapy Practice Act, Title 59, O.S. §888.1–888.16, 2004).

FRAUD AND ABUSE IN REIMBURSEMENT

The heath care reform debate of 2009 and 2010 highlighted the rising costs of health care and the increasing incidence of fraud and abuse in Medicare (U.S. Department of Health and Human Services & U.S. Department of Justice, 2010). The federal government has special fraud and abuse teams across the country that arrest perpetrators and prosecute offenses (Federal Bureau of Investigation, 2009). Because of the increasing number and complexity of laws, regulations, and other rules governing federal reimbursement programs and other health care programs, occupational therapy practitioners, as well as durable medical equipment (DME) vendors, hospitals, clinics, nursing homes, hospices, rehabilitation facilities, physician practices, and home health agencies, all face increased scrutiny in what they do and what they bill for.

This section samples some of the relevant laws governing federal programs. It discusses Medicare fraud and abuse, the antikickback statute, the Stark Law (self-referrals by physicians), and the False Claims Act. Therapists who violate these laws can lose their license, be barred from ever billing Medicare, incur large fines, or go to jail.

Medicare Fraud and Abuse

Under Medicare's rules, "fraud is the intentional deception or misrepresentation that an individual knows to be false or does not believe to be true and makes, knowing that the deception could result in some unauthorized benefit to himself/herself or some other person" (CMS, 2009). Most Medicare fraud stems from false statements or misrepresentations that are directly related to Medicare entitlement or payment and that are made by health care providers or their employees; a Medicare beneficiary; or a business entity, such as a rehabilitation agency or home care agency. Among the most common examples of fraud in occupational therapy are billing for occupational therapy services not provided; misrepresenting the patient's diagnosis to justify the occupational therapy services; and "upcoding," or billing for interventions that reimburse at higher amounts (e.g., charging an ADL code [97535] instead of a therapeutic exercises code [97110], which reimburses at a lower rate; American Medical Association, 2010; Becker, Kessler, & McClellan, 2005).

Medicare rules define *abuse* as incidents or provider practices that are inconsistent with accepted sound medical practice (CMS, 2009). Whereas Medicare fraud may or may not involve the provision of health care services such as occupational therapy, Medicare abuse usually occurs when providers give too much or unnecessary care (Becker et al., 2005). Abuse adds unnecessary cost to the Medicare program and may involve improper reimbursement for services not medically necessary or not within professionally recognized standards of care. Overutilization is the most common form of abuse, and in certain circumstances, a practice initially categorized as abuse can develop into fraud (CMS, 2009). Typical examples of fraud in occupational therapy include performing occupational therapy assessments every 2 weeks, charging Medicare patients higher rates than non-Medicare patients, and performing ADL interventions on patients who are in a coma.

Several different laws prohibit Medicare fraud and abuse and impose a variety of penalties for these behaviors. The following sections discuss some representative Medicare-related statutes and provide examples of what not to do.

Antikickback Statute

The purpose of the antikickback statute is to limit the influence of financial incentives on medical care. The statute is intentionally broad to cover any activity that could affect referrals, and it ascribes criminal and civil liability to parties on both sides of a kickback transaction (Medicare and Medicaid Patient Protection Act of 1987, as amended, 42 USC §1320a–7b, 2009). The antikickback statute, set forth at §1128B of the Social Security Act, makes it a criminal offense to knowingly and willfully offer, pay, solicit, or receive any remuneration to induce or reward referrals of items or services reimbursable by a federal health care program. For purposes of the antikickback statute, *remuneration* includes the transfer of anything of value, directly or indirectly, overtly or covertly, in cash or in kind. When someone purposely pays to induce or reward referrals of items or services payable by a federal health care program, they violate the antikickback statute (*United States v. Greber*, 760 F.2d 68, 71 (3rd Cir.), cert. denied, 474 U.S. 988, 1985). Such activity includes bribes and rebates, as well as kickbacks.

The penalties for violating the antikickback statute are serious. If found guilty, occupational therapy practitioners face criminal felony convictions and fines of up to $25,000, imprisonment for up to 5 years, or both (Medicare and Medicaid Patient Protection Act, of 1987, as amended, 42 USC. §1320a–7b, 2009). Criminal conviction also means automatic exclusion from reimbursement from all federally funded health care programs, including Medicare and Medicaid. Civil penalties up to $50,000 and "treble damages" (i.e., damages three times the amount of the kickback) are also available against those who violate the antikickback statute (42 USC §1320a–7a(a)).

Violation of the antikickback statute sometimes happens in occupational therapy when a therapist or program is offered an arrangement that is too good to be true. For example, a doctor may offer to refer all of her patients to an occupational therapy practice if the practice will pay her

20% of all Medicare and Medicaid payments it receives. At first blush, the practice might be tempted by an increase in referrals and new patients, but the plan looks like remuneration for referrals or a kickback and is impermissible.

Occupational therapy programs and practices should not pay anyone or accept payment from anyone if they intend the payment to generate money from Medicare or Medicaid. This rule includes money for both services and goods, such as reimbursable DME. However, there are some exceptions to the law. Because the statute was written so broadly, health care providers raised concerns that it might prohibit even beneficial or innocent transactions. Congress responded to these concerns over time by implementing specific "safe harbors" for various allowable business arrangements that would escape prosecution under the antikickback statute (Office of Inspector General, 1999). The safe harbor provisions are reviewed regularly and updated based on public comments (Office of Inspector General, 2009). Rather than risk fines, prison, and permanent exclusion from federal health program reimbursement, occupational therapy managers should check with a knowledgeable health care attorney before entering into agreements that involve remuneration of any kind.

Stark Law

The Physician Self-Referral Prohibition Statute, commonly referred to as the "Stark Law" (Social Security Act, 42 USC §1395nn, "Limitation on certain physician referrals," 2009) prohibits physicians from referring Medicare patients for certain "designated health services" (DHS) to an entity with which the physician (or an immediate family member) has a financial relationship, unless an exception applies. It also prohibits an entity from submitting claims to anyone for a DHS provided that resulted from the prohibited referral. DHS include, among others, physical therapy, occupational therapy, and speech–language pathology services; DME and supplies; orthotic and prosthetic devices and supplies; home health services; and inpatient and outpatient hospital services.

Violations of the statute are punishable by denial of payment for all DHS claims, refund of amounts collected for DHS claims, exclusion from all federal health care programs, and substantial civil monetary penalties of up to $100,000 for knowing violations of the prohibition (42 USC §1320a-7a(a)). Occupational therapy practitioners who want to collaborate with physicians should seek advice from a competent health care attorney who can advise them as to whether their financial relationship with the physician is legal under the Stark Law or constitutes one of the safe harbors provided under the law.

False Claims Act

The False Claims Act (31 USC §§3729(a)-3733, 2009), also called the "Lincoln Law" or the "Whistleblower Law," imposes liability on anyone who knowingly submits a false claim to the federal government. The act defines *knowingly* to include (1) actual knowledge of the false claim, (2) action in deliberate ignorance of the truth or falsity of the claim, or (3) action in reckless disregard of the truth or falsity of the claim. Anyone who knowingly submits false claims to the government is liable for damages up to three times the amount of the erroneous payment plus mandatory penalties between $5,500 and $11,000 for each false claim submitted. In larger health care settings, where providers submit thousands of claims annually, damages and penalties can turn into large expenses quickly.

False Claims Act violations occur in occupational therapy when occupational therapy practitioners or their employers bill Medicare for services they knew were neither performed nor covered. For example, a rehabilitation department that submits bills to Medicare for recreational therapy services but labels them as occupational therapy is filing false claims, because recreational therapy is not a covered service under Medicare.

The False Claims Act encourages people who discover a false claim (called *relators*) to report it by giving them a share of the proceeds from the action or settlement (31 USC 3730(b)). An occupational therapy practitioner who discovers that his or her employer is billing recreational therapy as occupational therapy, for example, could report the employer, who would face fines and penalties for each claim made for recreational therapy.

Occupational therapy managers need to know whether their state has enacted its own false claims act (e.g., Hawaii False Claims Act, Haw. Rev. Stat. §§661-21 *et seq.*, 2001; Massachusetts False Claims Act, Mass. Gen. Laws Ann. ch. 12 §§5(A) *et seq.*, 2001). Violations of the federal law can also trigger prosecution under the state's version of the False Claims Act.

Professional Consequences of Fraud and Abuse Violations

In addition to the other civil and criminal penalties, the Health and Human Services Office of Inspector General (OIG) can permanently exclude individuals who have participated or engaged in certain impermissible, inappropri-
ate, or illegal conduct with federal health care programs from participation in Medicare, Medicaid, and all other federal health care programs (CMS, 2009). Entities that participate in or bill a federal health care program generally may not employ or contract with excluded or "debarred" individuals or entities. Federal health care programs may not make any payments for any items or services furnished, ordered, or prescribed, directly or indirectly, by an excluded or debarred individual or entity. Federal health care programs include Medicare, Medicaid, and all other plans and programs that provide health benefits funded directly or indirectly by the U.S. government (other than the Federal Employees Health Benefits Plan; CMS, 2009). The OIG provides information on all individuals and entities currently excluded from participation in federal health care programs at http://www.oig.hhs.gov/fraud/exclusions.asp (U.S Department of Health and Human Services, Office of Inspector General, 2010).

Managers are ultimately accountable for the fiscal oversight of their departments. Those who participate in billing schemes, even tangentially or unknowingly, could find themselves involved in serious criminal matters and subject to civil penalties or criminal charges. Managers must be diligent with their oversight and make sure that their department's policies and procedures ensure that employees bill for actual services provided according to all of the rules.

CONCLUSION

The U.S. health care system is becoming more complicated every day with the many changing laws and regulations that affect practice. Occupational therapy managers need to continually educate themselves regarding the legal issues that affect occupational therapy practice. They need to encourage and lead their staff members in practicing occupational therapy as competent practitioners within the boundaries of the law and the standards of the profession. Occupational therapy professionals at all levels must follow the standards of the profession, their practice acts, and the applicable laws and regulations that govern the practice of occupational therapy.

Case Examples

LEVEL I FIELDWORK

Maria, a Level I fieldwork student, is observing and assisting with treatment of a new patient, a 62-year-old man who had a mild stroke. He looks familiar to her and she discovers that he is the lead singer of a rock-and-roll band of her parents' era. He tells her some stories about life on the road and how badly he feels now that he is old. He is in the hospital under an assumed name to keep his fans and the tabloids away.

That evening she asks her parents if they knew who he was and tells them that she is treating their teen idol. She tells the whole story to another Level I fieldwork student the next day in the elevator on their way to the occupational therapy clinic.

Maria has violated the patient's privacy right by telling her parents about her patient and by discussing the patient with another student where others could overhear her on the elevator. She violated patient confidentiality by disclosing information the patient obviously intended to be private because he was in the hospital under an assumed name to keep the information confidential. If she disclosed her patient's diagnosis to her parents and fellow student, then she also violated HIPAA. The facility would face fines for the HIPAA violation and could even be sued for the breach of privacy or confidentiality if damages to the patient resulted from Maria's action. Maria would possibly fail her fieldwork assignment and could face expulsion from her academic program.

LEVEL II FIELDWORK

Octavia, an occupational therapist in a rehabilitation facility, evaluated Mildred, a client recovering from a crushed ankle. She noted in the medical record that the external fixator on Mildred's right ankle was fragile and she was non–weight bearing on her left leg secondary to morbid obesity, fatiguing easily, and was unable to support the leg with the external fixator during transfers. Octavia assigned Mildred to Oliver, a Level II fieldwork student.

Three days later, a nurse asked Oliver to help transfer Mildred to a bedside chair. During the transfer, Mildred's right leg fell to the floor, breaking the external fixator. Oliver had never read Octavia's initial evaluation with all of the precautions specified. Under the doctrine of *respondeat superior*, Octavia could have been liable for Oliver's negligence. Octavia's actions could have resulted in direct liability for negligent supervision, had she failed to provide appropriate oversight of Oliver, failed to make sure he knew how to transfer a patient with an external fixator, or told him not to worry when he called to find out what to do when the patient hit her leg on the floor. Octavia's manager could also be liable, as well as the next person in the chain of command.

FIRST TIME MANAGER

Ray is a young and ambitious occupational therapist working at a medical center in a small town. Most residents of Small Town, a rural community, work at the Tire Company (TTC). The medical center assigns Ray to develop a PowerPoint presentation for the employees of a tire manufacturer in the town that would teach them how to prevent back and upper-extremity injuries while lifting large tractor tires. Ray decided also to develop a companion assessment tool on company time to evaluate workers' stability and flexibility following his presentation. He worked diligently during the next 4 weeks to develop both the PowerPoint presentation and the assessment tool. The presentation and assessment tool were an instant success. Other companies approached the medical center to implement the program and use the assessment tool Ray created.

Seeing the potential of the injury prevention program, Ray resigns to become manager of his own clinic and hires two former coworkers. He markets "his" presentation and assessment tool to other companies and trains the two people who now work for him to do the presentations. The medical center where Ray worked immediately sought legal remedies against him. Ray did not own the copyright to his creation because he created it on company time. The copyright law does not consider Ray the author of his PowerPoint presentation and assessment tool; they were considered "work made for hire," and the medical center was considered the author of the works. Ray's use of the tools he had developed on company time constituted copyright infringement, and the medical center would be entitled to legal remedies if Ray or his employees used them in his new clinic.

MANAGER

Bill, an occupational therapy manager with extensive experience, took a new position supervising 12 occupational and physical therapy employees in a comprehensive rehabilitation center. During Bill's first week, Terry, a 50-year-old, 350-pound man, came in for an assessment. The occupational therapist assigned to Terry gave him a history form, which he filled out. The therapist looked over the completed form and engaged the patient in a lifting test. During the test, Terry clutched his chest; he was having a heart attack.

Bill filled out an incident report. Concerned about the potential for legal consequences from Terry's treatment, Bill reviewed the clinic's written procedures and identified areas of weakness. He consulted with risk management, who sent in-house counsel to meet with the staff to discuss what had happened and use Terry's case as an example to prevent further such incidents, explaining that although no legal action had been brought, Terry's case might have exposed the program to legal action. They also told staff not to discuss the incident outside of this meeting with the center's attorney.

In the meeting, in-house counsel reviewed the four principles of negligence—a duty to act in a particular way, a breach of that duty, occurrence of actual harm or damages, and a causal connection between the breach of the duty and the harm or damages (Keeton et al., 2004). Bill explained to the staff and in-house counsel that he understood that the occupational therapist attending Terry owed him a duty to do no harm and to engage in competent practice. According to the program's written procedures, the occupational therapist should have taken the client's blood pressure before engaging him in a lifting test. By failing to do so, the occupational therapist's conduct fell below the standard of practice.

Although the extent of harm to Terry was unclear, Bill addressed the question of whether the occupational therapist's actions had caused the heart attack. Like ordinary negligence, causation is a necessary element of malpractice. In-house counsel explained that if the facility is sued, an expert witness might testify that Terry might not have had a heart attack "but for" the lifting test. Had the occupational therapist taken Terry's blood pressure before the lifting task, she might have realized that the task was contraindicated. In addition, had she instructed Terry not to hold his breath during the task, avoiding the *val salva* maneuver, Terry's blood pressure might not have increased during the task.

In-house counsel explained to the staff that for Terry to sue them, he had to have suffered permanent damages. He also explained to the staff the various types of damages available in their state should Terry sue them. He encouraged Bill to review the licensure law and AOTA *Code of Ethics and Ethics Standards* (AOTA, 2010a) with all the staff.

❖ Learning Activities

1. Interview an attorney who handles malpractice cases. Ask the attorney about the kinds of things that often trigger malpractice cases. How can you avoid those triggers in your practice?

2. Visit your local courthouse, and sit in on a trial. Is it a criminal trial or a civil trial? What are the issues in the case?

3. Attend a meeting of your state's licensure board. What kinds of disciplinary issues come before it? How can you prevent encountering those issues in your practice?

4. Talk to a Department of Health investigator in your state. Ask him or her about the kinds of problems encountered in long-term care facilities in your state. What kind of compliance issues are of concern? Describe the kinds of things you can do to prevent or avoid them in your practice.

5. Think about the kinds of things you have seen people copying that are not permissible to copy. What will you do next time you see this happening?

✓ Multiple-Choice Questions

1. If a therapist performs an intervention and bills the patient for a different intervention that reimburses at a higher rate, this is an example of
   a. Malpractice.
   b. Vicarious liability.
   c. Fraud.
   d. Battery.

2. An occupational therapy manager could lose his or her license for which of the following
   a. Billing for services not performed.
   b. "Upcoding."
   c. Paying money in exchange for referrals.
   d. All of the above.

3. Mrs. Smith, age 85, is in a coma and nonresponsive. The therapist goes to her room twice per day for occupational therapy services. The therapist tries to stimulate her with sensory intervention but gets no response. After 8 weeks, the therapist decides to stop seeing Mrs. Smith because the patient census goes up. Mrs. Smith's status remains the same. The therapist may have committed
   a. Medicare fraud.
   b. Medicare abuse.

c. HIPAA violations.

d. Breach of confidentiality.

4. A physician offers the occupational therapy department a deal. He will refer all of his hand patients to the clinic and in return the clinic will give the physician 10% of the money paid for occupational therapy services. Which of the following is true about this arrangement?

a. It will increase referrals and makes good business sense.

b. It may be a form of malpractice in some states that cover this behavior.

c. It is probably prohibited by the antikickback statute.

d. All of the above.

5. To increase revenues, an occupational therapy manager in a rehabilitation center is told to bill recreational therapy as occupational therapy for all the Medicare and Medicaid patients. Which of the following is true?

a. It will increase referrals and makes good business sense.

b. It probably violates the False Claims Act.

c. It is an example of the antikickback law.

d. It is a good example of false imprisonment.

6. An occupational therapist is filling in for maternity leave in a hospital. She has worked for 3 months full-time and side-by-side the other occupational therapists performing the same work with the hospital's materials. Which of the following is true?

a. If the therapist has a signed contract to perform the work, she is an independent contractor.

b. The occupational therapist is an employee.

c. There are many factors one must consider to determine whether someone is an employee.

d. The key is whether hospitals exert the same control over this occupational therapist as employees.

7. Research shows that practitioners can avoid claims for malpractice by

a. Discussing patients with your friends to get feedback.

b. Being nice to your patients.

c. Carefully planning your treatment sessions.

d. None of the above.

8. Eric, a Level II occupational therapy fieldwork student, decides to copy some assessment tools so he can use them in his practice after he passes the certification exam. He plans to open his own practice, and copying the assessments will save him some money. Which of the following is true?

a. Eric may copy the assessments if he only makes 1 copy for now.

b. Eric is probably violating the copyright for the publisher or author.

c. Eric has no problem as long as he doesn't make additional copies of the assessment tools after he passes the certification exam.

d. Eric can make these copies because they fall under the fair use exception.

9. You work in a pediatric occupational therapy program and notice some strange marks on a child's arm. The child confides in you that his father sometimes burns him with cigarettes. Which of the following is true?

a. You are required to keep this information confidential because the child confided in you.

b. HIPAA mandates that you keep the information confidential.

c. You must report this child abuse if your state has a mandatory reporting law.

d. Privacy and confidentiality require that you keep the information confidential.

10. Failure to obtain informed consent can lead to

a. An action for malpractice in some states.

b. A lawsuit against you for assaults.

c. A lawsuit against you for battery.

d. All of the above.

11. All of the following could lead to a claim for malpractice from harm to the patient *except*

a. Leaving a patient alone during an activity resulting in an overuse syndrome.

b. Forgetting to lock the wheelchair during a transfer.

c. Having sexual relations with a patient.

d. None of the above.

12. An occupational therapy manager can be found liable even if he or she did not treat a patient

a. Under the doctrine of false imprisonment.

b. Under the doctrine of *respondeat superior*.

c. If the therapist was incompetent.

d. All of the above.

13. An occupational therapist manager who supervises other occupational therapy practitioners is responsible for

a. Assuring they are properly trained to perform the assigned work.

b. Making sure they lock the wheelchair before each transfer.

c. Reminding them to renew their license.

d. Following seizure precautions for each patient.

14. Which of the following are steps occupational therapists can take to avoid malpractice?

a. Renew their license in a timely manner.

b. Only bill for occupational therapy services actually performed.

c. Be nice to patients.

d. All of the above.

15. Which of the following questions is permissible during a job interview?

a. The job requires handling money and billing. Have you ever been arrested?

b. How do you feel being supervised by a woman?

c. The job requires working weekends. Can you do that?

d. Do you have any physical disabilities that may affect your job performance?

16. Which of the following impose legal requirements that occupational therapy managers must follow?
    a. Laws.
    b. Regulations.
    c. Practice guidelines.
    d. All of the above.

17. As a manager, you are very inconvenienced by Peter's absence following the birth of his child. He took off 9 weeks from work, returned to work, and then took another 3 weeks off when his baby needed surgery. You really want to terminate him because you feel he is not a responsible employee. You consult with human resources and they tell you
    a. You can't terminate Peter because he is protected by the Family Medical Leave Act.
    b. You can terminate Peter because he is *not* protected by the Family Medical Leave Act.
    c. You can't terminate Peter because he is protected by the Americans with Disabilities Act.
    d. You can terminate Peter because he is *not* protected by the Americans with Disabilities Act.

18. You manage an occupational therapy department in a large long-term care facility. One of the occupational therapists calls to your attention the treatment of the patients with dementia on the afternoon shift. It seems that patients are being restrained by being tied to their wheelchairs. None of the patients who receive occupational therapy and are restrained have a care plan that includes the restraints. You are concerned that the facility
    a. May be committing elder abuse.
    b. May be involved in false imprisonment.
    c. May be violating OBRA.
    d. All of the above.

19. Which of the following is *not* true about licensure laws?
    a. They are the same in every state.
    b. They may incorporate the AOTA *Occupational Therapy Code of Ethics and Ethics Standards*.
    c. They can impose criminal and civil penalties on violators.
    d. All of the above.

20. Occupational therapy managers must ensure that their staff practice according to requirements of
    a. Their state's licensure law.
    b. AOTA's *Occupational Therapy Code of Ethics and Ethics Standards*.
    c. Applicable practice guidelines.
    d. All of the above.

References

Acara v. Banks, 470 F.3d 569 (5th Cir. 2006).

Agency for Healthcare Research and Quality. (1992). *Acute pain management: Operative or medical procedures and trauma* (Clinical Practice Guideline; AHCPR Publication No. 92-0032). Rockville, MD: Agency for Health Care Policy and Research, Public Health Service, U.S. Department of Health and Human Services. Retrieved January 10, 2009, from http://www.ahrq.gov/clinic/medtep/acute.htm

American Academy of Pain Medicine & American Pain Society. (1997). *The use of opioids for the treatment of chronic pain: A consensus statement.* Glenview, IL: Authors.

American Medical Association. (2010). *CPT® 2010 professional edition.* Chicago: Author

American Occupational Therapy Association. (2008). Occupational therapy practice framework: Domain and process (2nd ed.). *American Journal of Occupational Therapy, 63,* 625–683.

American Occupational Therapy Association. (2010a). Occupational therapy code of ethics and ethics standards (2010). *American Journal of Occupational Theapy, 64.*

American Occupational Therapy Association. (2010b). Standards of practice for occupational therapy. *American Journal of Occupational Therapy, 64.*

American Recovery and Reinvestment Act of 2009, Pub. L. 111–5.

Americans with Disabilities Act of 1990, Pub. L. 110–325, 42 U.S.C. § 12101 *et seq.,* as amended (2008).

Americans with Disabilities Act, Title II Regulations, 29 CFR §1630.2(o), "Modifications in policies, practices, or procedures" (2009). Retrieved February 16, 2009, from http://ecfr.gpoaccess.gov/cgi/t/text/text-idx?c=ecfr&sid=91397326d026acd8d58b364349c3a698&rgn=div8&view=text&node=29:4.1.4.1.20.0.26.2&idno=29

Americans with Disabilities Act, Title III Regulations, 28 CFR §36.302, "Modifications in policies, practices, or procedures" (2009). Available online from http://ecfr.gpoaccess.gov/cgi/t/text/textidx?c=ecfr;sid=ce90c0423d641fe2176bebf05b9a230c;rgn=div5;view=text;node=28%3A1.0.1.1.37;idno=28;cc=ecfr#28:1.0.1.1.37.3.32.2.

Anderson v. Prease, 445 A.2d 612 (D.C. 1982).

Beauchamp, T., & Childress, T. (1994). *Principles of biomedical ethics.* New York: Oxford University Press.

Becker, D., Kessler, D., & McClellan, M. (2005). Detecting Medicare abuse. *Journal of Health Economics, 24,* 189–210.

California Non-Discrimination Law, Cal. Gov't Code §12920; Cal. Civil Code §51 (2001).

Centers for Medicare and Medicaid Services. (2009). Medicare A/B reference manual: Chapter 21—Benefit integrity and program safeguard contractors. *CMS Medicare Manuals.* Retrieved February 21, 2010, from https://www.highmarkmedicareservices.com/refman/chapter-21.html

Centers for Medicare and Medicaid Services, Medicare Learning Network. (2009, January). *Medicare fraud and abuse fact sheet.* Washington, DC: Author. Retrieved from http://cms.hhs.gov/MLNProducts/downloads/110107_Medicare_Fraud_and_Abuse_brochure.pdf

Child Abuse Prevention and Treatment Act, 42 U.S.C. §5101 *et seq.*, as amended (1996).

Digital Millennium Copyright Act, Pub. L. No. 105-304, 112 Stat. 2860, 2887 (Title IV amending §108, §112, §114, ch. 7 and ch. 8, Title 17, USC, 1998).

Dye, T., (2002). *Understanding public policy* (10th ed). Upper Saddle River, NJ: Prentice Hall.

Elder Abuse and Neglect Act, 320 ILCS 20, ch. 23, para. 6601 (Illinois, 2010).

False Claims Act, 31 U.S.C. §§3729(a)–3733 (2009).

Family Medical Leave Act, 29 CFR §825.101 (2009).

Federal Bureau of Investigation. (2009, December 15). *Medicare fraud strike force expands operations into Brooklyn, New York; Tampa, Florida; and Baton Rouge, Louisiana* (Press release). Retrieved February 21, 2010, from http://www.hhs.gov/news/press/2009pres/12/20091215a.html

Federation of State Medical Boards of the United States. (1998). *Model guideline for the use of controlled substances for the treatment of pain.* Dallas, TX: Author.

Florida Administrative Code. (2006). *Minimum standards for home health agencies* (ch. 59A-8.0095(8)). Tallahassee: Florida Department of State. Retrieved July 11, 2010, from https://www.flrules.org/gateway/ChapterHome.asp?Chapter=59A-8

Garner, B. A. (2004). *Black's law dictionary* (8th ed.). St. Paul, MN: West.

General Counsel Department of Health and Human Services, & Senior Counsel to the Deputy General. (2005). *Scope of criminal enforcement under 42 U.S.C. § 1320d-6: Memorandum opinion.* Retrieved February 21, 2010, from http://www.justice.gov/olc/hipaa_final.htm

Genetic Information Nondiscrimination Act of 2008, Pub. L. 110–233.

Gleave, G. M. (1963). Organization and administration of occupational therapy departments. In H. S. Willard & C. S. Spackman (Eds.), *Occupational therapy* (3rd ed.). Philadelphia: Lippincott.

Gregory v. Litton Systems, 316 F. Supp. 401, 2 EPD ¶10,264 (C.D. Cal. 1970), modified on other grounds, 472 F.2d 631, 5 EPD ¶8089 (9th Cir. 1972).

Hall, A. J., Logan, J. E., Toblin, R. L., Kaplan, J. A., Kramer, J. C., Bixler, D., et al. (2008). Patterns of abuse among unintentional pharmaceutical overdose fatalities. *JAMA, 300,* 2613–2620.

Hawaii False Claims Act, Haw. Rev. Stat. §§661–21 *et seq.* (2001).

Health Insurance Portability and Accountability Act, Pub. L. 104–191 (1996).

Health Insurance Portability and Accountability Act, 42 USC §1320d-6 (2000).

Health Insurance Portability and Accountability Act, 65 Fed. Reg. 82566 (2000).

Health Insurance Portability and Acountability Act, Privacy Rules, 45 CFR §164.102 *et seq.* (2007).

Health Insurance Portability and Acountability Act, Privacy Rules, 45 CFR §164.502(a). (2007).

Health Insurance Portability and Acountability Act, Transactions Rule at 45 CFR Pt. 162 (2007).

HITECH Act, 42 USC §1320d-5 (2009).

HIV Testing, Fla. Stat. 381.004 (2009).

HR World Editors. (2007). *30 interview questions you can't ask and 30 sneaky, legal alternatives to get the same info.* Retrieved April 4, 2009, from http://www.hrworld.com/features/30interview-questions-111507/

Immigration and Nationality Act, 8 USC §1101 *et seq.* (2005).

Internal Revenue Service. (2009a, June 15). *Independent contractor (self-employed) or employee?* Retrieved February 24, 2010, from http://www.irs.gov/businesses/small/article/0,,id=99921,00.html

Internal Revenue Service. (2009b, December 18). *Topic 762—Independent contractor vs. employee.* Retrieved February 24, 2010, from http://www.irs.gov/taxtopics/tc762.html

Johnson v. Kokemoor, 199 Wis.2d 615, 630 (1996).

The Joint Commission. (2006, January 26). *Sentinel event glossary of terms.* Retrieved February 18, 2010, from http://www.jointcommission.org/SentinelEvents/se_glossary.htm

Joint Commission on Accreditation of Healthcare Organizations. (1999). *Comprehensive accreditation manual for hospitals: Official handbook.* Oakbrook, IL: Author.

Kazin, C. (1989). "Nowhere to go and chose to stay": Using the tort of false imprisonment to redress involuntary confinement of the elderly in nursing homes and hospitals [Comment]. *University of Pennsylvania Law Review, 137,* 903–927.

Keeton, W., Dobbs, D., Keeton, R., & Owens, D. (2004). *Prosser and Keeton on torts* (5th ed). St. Paul, MN: West Group.

Levinson, W. (1997). Physician–patient communication: The relationship with malpractice claims among primary care physicians and surgeons. *JAMA, 277,* 553–559.

Localio, A., Lawthers, A., Brennan, T., Laird, N., Hebert, L., Peterson, L., et al. (1991). Relation between malpractice claims and adverse events due to negligence: Results of the Harvard Medical Practice Study III. *New England Journal of Medicine, 325,* 245–251.

Louisiana Occupational Therapy Practice Act, La. Rev. Stat. Title 37, ch. 39, §3001 *et seq.* (2009).

Marron, D. B. (2006, July 26). *Medicare's physician payment rates and the sustainable growth rate.* Retrieved January 10, 2009, from http://www.cbo.gov/doc.cfm?index=7425

Massachusetts False Claims Act, Mass. Gen. Laws Ann. ch. 12 §§ 5(A) *et seq.* (2001).

Mayo Clinic Staff. (2008). *Alzheimer's: Is it in your genes?* Retrieved February 22, 2010, from http://www.mayoclinic.com/health/alzheimers-genes/AZ00047

Medicare and Medicaid Patient Protection Act of 1987. 42 USC §1320a–7b, as amended (2009).

Merriam-Webster Online Dictionary. (2010). *Law.* Retrieved August 21, 2010, from http://www.merriam-webster.com/dictionary/law

Metropolitan Life Ins. Co. v. McCarson, 467 So. 2d 277, 278, 279 (Fla. 1985).

New Jersey Jury Verdict Review and Analysis. (2010). *Verdict—Unlicensed physical therapy aide treats plaintiff following rotator cuff surgery* (41805). Retrieved February 21, 2010, from http://www.juryverdictreview.com/Verdict_Trak/article.aspx?id=41805

Nursing Home Reform Act of 1987, in Omnibus Budget Reconciliation Act (OBRA), P.L. 100-203, 42 CFR pt. 483 (1987).

Office of Inspector General. (1999, August 18). *Federal antikickback laws and regulatory safe harbors fact sheet.* Retrieved February 24, 2010, from http://oig.hhs.gov/fraud/docs/safeharbor regulations/safefs.htm

Office of Inspector General. (2009, December 29). *Proposed rules: Notice of intent to develop regulations.* 74 Fed. Reg.(Federal Register document E9-30560). Retrieved February 24,

2010, from http://www.thefederalregister.com/d.p/2009-12-29-E9-30560

Oklahoma Occupational Therapy Practice Act, Title 59 O.S. §§888.1–888.16 (2004).

Olmstead v. United States, 277 U.S. 438, Justice Brandeis's dissent (1928).

Pennsylvania Occupational Therapy Practice Act, 63 P.S. §§1501–1519 (2010).

Phillips, D. M. (2000). JCAHO pain management standards are unveiled. *JAMA, 284,* 726–733.

Physician Self-Referral Prohibition Statute (Stark Law), 42 USC §1395nn (2009).

Prosser, W. L. (1971). *Law of torts* (4th ed.). St. Paul, MN: West.

Ranke, B. A., & Moriarty, M. P. (1997). An overview of professional liability in occupational therapy. *American Journal of Occupational Therapy, 51,* 671–680.

Sabari, J. (2008). *Occupational therapy practice guidelines for adults with stroke.* Bethesda, MD: AOTA Press.

Schware v. Board of Bar Examiners, 353 U.S. 232, 241 (1957).

Smith, etc. v. Archbishop of St. Louis, 632 S.W.2d 516 (Mo. App. E.D. 1982).

Social Security Act, 42 USC §1395nn, "Limitation on certain physician referrals" (2009).

State of Maryland, Department of Budget and Management, Office of the Statewide EEO Coordinator. (2009, September 21). *Marital status discrimination: Protections for state employees* [Brochure]. Retrieved September 25, 2009, from http://dbm.maryland.gov/eeo/documents/eeobrochures/maritalstatusrev.pdf

Tarasoff v. Regents of University of California, 17 Cal. 3d 425, 551 P.2d 334, 131 Cal. Rptr. 14 (1976).

Title 17 (copyright) U.S.C. § 101 *et seq.,* as amended (2009).

Tomchek, S. D., & Case-Smith, J. (2009). *Occupational therapy practice guidelines for children and adolescents with autism.* Bethesda, MD: AOTA Press.

United States v. Greber, 760 F.2d 68, 71 (3rd Cir.), cert. denied, 474 U.S. 988 (1985).

U.S. Department of Health and Human Services, Office of Inspector General. (2010). *Exclusions program.* Retrieved February 21, 2010, from http://www.oig.hhs.gov/fraud/exclusions.asp

U.S. Department of Health and Human Services, & U.S. Department of Justice. (2010). *Health Care Fraud Prevention and Enforcement Action Team (HEAT) successes.* Retrieved February 21, 2010, from http://www.stopmedicarefraud.gov/heat-success/index.html

U.S. Equal Employment Opportunity Commission. (1990, August 23). *Policy guidance on the consideration of arrest records in employment decisions under Title VII of the Civil Rights Act of 1964, as amended, 42 U.S.C. $2000e et seq. (1982).* Retrieved April 4, 2009, from http://www.eeoc.gov/policy/docs/arrest_records.html

U.S. Equal Employment Opportunity Commission. (2000, March 24). *EEOC enforcement guidance on disability-related inquiries and medical examinations of employees under the Americans with Disabilities Act (ADA).* Retrieved April 4, 2009, from http://www.eeoc.gov/policy/docs/guidance-inquiries.html

U.S. Equal Employment Opportunity Commission. (2008, September 8). *Facts about age discrimination.* Retrieved April 4, 2009, from http://www.eeoc.gov/facts/age.html

U.S. Equal Employment Opportunity Commission. (2009, March 31). Britthaven to pay $300,000 to settle pregnancy discrimination [Press release]. Retrieved April 4, 2009, from http://www.eeoc.gov/eeoc/newsroom/release/3-31-09a.cfm

Wallis, G. (1992). Occupational therapy and mental disorders consensus statement by the Royal College of Psychiatrists and the College of Occupational Therapy. *Psychiatric Bulletin, 16,* 180–183.

Wang, C. H., Finkel, R. S., Bertini, E. S., Schroth, M., Simonds, A., Wong, B., et al. (2007). Consensus statement for standard of care in spinal muscular atrophy. *Journal of Child Neurology, 22,* 1027–1049.

West Virginia Occupational Therapy Practice Act, Art. 28 §30-28-16(e) (2009).

Appendix 32.A. Legal Dimensions Evidence Table

Topic	Subtopic	Evidence
Employee and independent contractors	Hiring issues	*Gregory v. Litton Systems*, 316 F. Supp. 401, 2 EPD ¶10,264 (C.D. Cal. 1970), modified on other grounds, 472 F.2d 631, 5 EPD ¶8089, 1972. HR World Editors. (2007). *30 interview questions you can't ask and 30 sneaky, legal alternatives to get the same info.* Retrieved April 4, 2009, from http://www.hrworld.com/features/30-interview-questions-111507/ *Schware v. Board of Bar Examiners*, 353 U.S. 232, 241, 1957. U.S. Equal Employment Opportunity Commission. (1990, August 23). *Policy guidance on the consideration of arrest records in employment decisions under Title VII of the Civil Rights Act of 1964, as amended, 42 U.S.C. §2000e et seq. (1982).* Retrieved April 4, 2009, from http://www.eeoc.gov/policy/docs/arrest_records.html U.S. Equal Employment Opportunity Commission. (2008, September 8). *Facts about age discrimination.* Retrieved April 4, 2009, from http://www.eeoc.gov/facts/age.html U.S. Equal Employment Opportunity Commission. (2009, March 31). *Britthaven to pay $300,000 to settle pregnancy discrimination* [Press release]. Retrieved April 4, 2009, from http://www.eeoc.gov/eeoc/newsroom/release/3-31-09a.cfm
	Employee vs. independent contractor	Internal Revenue Service. (2009a, June 15). *Independent contractor (self-employed) or employee?* Retrieved February 24, 2010, from http://www.irs.gov/businesses/small/article/0,,id=99921,00.html Internal Revenue Service. (2009b, December 18). *Topic 762—Independent contractor vs. employee.* Retrieved February 24, 2010, from http://www.irs.gov/taxtopics/tc762.html
Reimbursement	Fraud and abuse	False Claims Act, 31 U.S.C. §§3729(a)–3733 (2009). Federal Bureau of Investigation. (2009, December 15). *Medicare fraud strike force expands operations into Brooklyn, New York; Tampa, Florida; and Baton Rouge, Louisiana* (Press release). Retrieved February 21, 2010, from http://www.hhs.gov/news/press/2009pres/12/20091215a.html U.S. Department of Health and Human Services, & U.S. Department of Justice. (2010). *Health Care Fraud Prevention and Enforcement Action Team (HEAT) successes.* Retrieved February 21, 2010, from http://www.stopmedicarefraud.gov/heatsuccess/index.html Hawaii False Claims Act, Haw. Rev. Stat. §§661–21 *et seq.* (2001). Massachusetts False Claims Act, Mass. Gen. Laws Ann. ch. 12 §§ 5(A) *et seq.* (2001). Becker, D., Kessler, D., & McClellan, M. (2005). Detecting Medicare abuse. *Journal of Health Economics, 24,* 189–210.
	Prohibition on physician self-referral Antikickback laws	Social Security Act, 42 USC §1395nn, "Limitation on certain physician referrals" (2009). Office of Inspector General. (1999, August 18). *Federal antikickback laws and regulatory safe harbors fact sheet.* Retrieved February 24, 2010, from http://oig.hhs.gov/fraud/docs/safeharborregulations/safefs.htm
Privacy and confidentiality		Health Insurance Portability and Acountability Act, Privacy Rules, 45 CFR §164.102 *et seq.* (2007). HITECH Act, 42 USC §1320d-5 (2009). West Virginia Occupational Therapy Practice Act, Art. 28 §30-28-16(e) (2009).
Copyright		Title 17 (copyright) U.S.C. § 101 *et seq.,* as amended (2009).
Malpractice, professional liability, and torts		Keeton, W., Dobbs, D., Keeton, R., & Owens, D. (2004). *Prosser and Keton on torts* (5th ed.). St. Paul, MN: West Group. Prosser, W. L. (1971). *Law of torts* (4th ed.). St. Paul, MN: West. Ranke, B. A., & Moriarty, M. P. (1997). An overview of professional liability in occupational therapy. *American Journal of Occupational Therapy, 51,* 671–680.

33

Consultation: Collaborative Interventions for Change

Evelyn G. Jaffe, MPH, OTR/L, FAOTA,
and Cynthia F. Epstein, MA, OTR, FAOTA

❖ Key Terms and Concepts

Client. The person or the system seeking help.

Consultant role. A set of behaviors a consultant performs in the course of a consultation. Primary consultant roles include adviser, helper, facilitator, outsider, change agent, evaluator–diagnostician, clarifier, trainer, planner, and advocate.

Consultation. The interactive process of helping others solve existing or potential problems by identifying and analyzing issues, developing strategies to address problems, and preventing future problems from occurring.

Consultation process. A facilitative process in which a client receives help from a consultant through an interactive, egalitarian relationship based on mutual respect.

Levels of consultation. A conceptualization of consultation as occurring on three possible levels: *case centered* (targeted on a specific person), *educational* (targeted on a specific client group), and *program or administrative* (targeted on a specific system).

Models of consultation. A conceptualization of consultation as having 9 possible foci, each calling for different strategies on the part of the consultant: clinical or intervention model, collegial or professional model, behavioral model, educational model, organizational development model, process management model, program development model, social action model, and systems model.

❖ Learning Objectives

After completing this chapter, you should be able to do the following:

- Define the essence of consultation.
- Describe the 9 theoretical models of consultation that determine the various consultative approaches.
- Describe the levels of consultation that form the foundation of consultation activities, including the target, goal, and preventive outcomes of each level.
- Describe the consultation process, including the stages and basic steps of consultation.
- Identify emerging consultation practice arenas for occupational therapy practitioners relative to changes in occupational therapy practice.

> I have found the best way to give advice to your children is to find out what they want and then advise them to do it.
> —Harry S. Truman (wisdomquote.com, n.d.)

Consultation is an important component of the occupational therapy intervention process (American Occupational Therapy Association [AOTA], 2008), and it is essential that occupational therapy practitioners understand the basic principles and process of establishing consultation activities in their practice. Every practitioner may provide consultation within the context of his or her job. Those possessing particular expertise may provide consultation as their primary role and source of employment. Whether consultation is a secondary or primary role, occupational therapy practitioners must understand how to use principles of consultation to meet client needs. This chapter describes the theoretical framework on which consultation activities are based, focusing on the particular knowledge, skills, and techniques necessary to develop consultation approaches in an occupational therapy practice. Additionally, new and emerging areas for consultation are discussed.

DEFINITION AND OVERVIEW

Consultation is the interactive process of helping others, including individuals, organizations, or populations, solve existing or potential problems by identifying and analyzing issues, developing strategies to address problems, and preventing future problems from occurring. Key elements in consultation, in addition to occupational therapy expertise, include an understanding of (1) systems, (2) organizational development, (3) behavior, and (4) principles of prevention. The consultant must have the ability to listen and effectively communicate, as well as the capacity to diagnose and facilitate resolution of existing or potential problems (Yerxa, 1980). In AOTA's *Occupational Therapy Practice Framework, 2nd Edition* (*Framework–II*; AOTA, 2008), the consultation process is described as

> a type of intervention in which occupational therapy practitioners use their knowledge and expertise to collaborate with the client. The collaborative process involves identifying the problem, creating possible solutions, trying solutions, and altering them as necessary for greater effectiveness. When providing consultation, the practitioner is not directly responsible for the outcome of the intervention. (p. 653)

The consultation process is considered an essential component of entry-level occupational therapy education. The American Council for Occupational Therapy Association Educational Standards (2007) standards require academic programs for master's-degree-level students to include consultation skills and process in the curriculum (Standards B.5.22, B.5.23).

Occupational therapy consultants provide services in varied settings. These include such traditional environments as hospitals, long-term care facilities, and schools (including colleges and universities) and the growing arenas of industry, community programs, regulatory agencies, professional organizations, and international health programs. Consultant services may be requested by individuals, departments, or entire systems, and may involve a brief intervention or an extended relationship. Services are delivered using a client-centered approach that emphasizes an interactive relationship between consultant and client (AOTA, 2002).

A consultant may be from a private practice or from another type of organization, such as an academic setting, that is outside the system requesting help. Alternatively, a consultant may be an employee of the organization that is seeking consultation; an occupational therapy practitioner might receive a request to provide consultation to a department or staff of his or her organization or to the family or caretaker of a particular client. The *client* is the individual, population, organization, or system seeking help,

and a client or combination of clients use consultation to improve planning, participation, and interaction with colleagues, consumers, or employees. The consultant helps the client mobilize internal and external resources that will facilitate change and lead to problem resolution (Lippitt & Lippitt, 1986; Ulschak & SnowAntle, 1990). In the course of consultation, the consultant offers the client suggestions for new or revised processes, including information, concepts, perspectives, values, attitudes, and skills. The consultant views problems from a broad, client-centered perspective, with systems, theoretical models, and environmental contexts as an integral part of the decision-making process (AOTA, 2001, 2007; Dunn, Brown, & McGuigan, 1994; Jaffe & Epstein, 1992b). This process is shown in case examples at the end of this chapter.

Inherent in occupational therapy practice is enablement of the client through occupation. Engagement in occupation supports client participation in the many contexts in which daily life activities occur. Client and practitioner collaboratively work to design and implement required interventions (AOTA, 2002, 2007). Similarly, occupational therapy consultation requires collaboration between client and consultant. The goal of consultation is to enable the client. The consultant's task is to identify or collaboratively develop enhanced environments in which positive change can take place, thereby leading to improved client performance. The collaborative approach to resolving client problems expands the potential for successful client outcomes.

MODELS OF CONSULTATION

Consultation is a multidimensional, highly complex, and dynamic activity. Successful consultation results from the practitioner's grounding in the theoretical foundations of the activity. Before undertaking consultation, a prospective consultant should have a thorough knowledge of the concepts that provide a theoretical framework for consultation.

Jaffe and Epstein (1992b) propose a theoretical model of consultation that "integrates occupational therapy and consultation concepts within an ecological framework" (p. 709). *Ecology*, in this context, is the global environment in which the consultation occurs, including the entire system or organization. The model relates the principles, philosophical assumptions, and theoretical premises of occupational therapy to those of consultation. It recognizes ecological contexts as a critical factor in goal achievement for both occupational therapy and consultation, and the *Framework–II* (AOTA, 2008) supports this perspective. Jaffe and Epstein's model incorporates and acknowledges "The synergetic relationship between occupational therapy, human ecology and consultation" (1992b, p. 677). Concepts of prevention are basic to this model because the ultimate goal of consultation is to help the client develop skills to prevent future problems. Consultation, therefore, enables the client to assume a proactive stance, and thus anticipate and forestall situations that could lead to further problems or dysfunction.

Table 33.1. Theoretical Models of Consultation

Model	Description
Clinical or intervention model	Patient- or client-focused model based on diagnosis and recommendations for intervention, frequently in a specific case; often considered case consultation
Collegial or professional model	Peer-centered model based on egalitarian, problem-solving relationships with professional colleagues; considered collaborative consultation
Behavioral model	Behavior-focused model based on control, adaptation, modification, or change of learned behavior
Educational model	Information-centered model with consultant acting as educator and trainer to enhance the staff's knowledge and skills that can support desired consultation outcomes
Organizational development model	Management-focused model based on examination of organizational structure, leadership styles, and interpersonal communication and relationships
Process management model	Group-based model focused on process dynamics of client, with consultant acting as a catalyst for staff development and the building of group skills to mange organizational process more effectively
Program development model	Service-centered model focused on development of new programs or modification of existing programs to improve services; involves assessment, design, implementation, and evaluation
Social action model	Social reform model focused on social values and policies, with consultant acting as advocate to foster social change
Systems model	Overall system-centered model based on specific values and culture of client; focused on understanding the system's mission and goals to effect change in system

Note. From "Theoretical Concepts of Consultation," by E. G. Jaffe, in *Occupational Therapy Consultation: Theory, Principles, and Practice* (pp. 44–46, Table 2.1), edited by E. G. Jaffe and C. F. Epstein, 1992, St. Louis, MO: Mosby/YearBook. Copyright © 1992, by Mosby/YearBrook. Adapted with permission.

Jaffe and Epstein (1992b) identified nine theoretical models, as shown in Table 33.1, and three levels of consultation activity. In most situations, consultants are asked to address complex issues that require multiple models and levels of consultation. Figure 33.1 illustrates the fluid nature of consultation when levels and models are applied during the consultation process. They provide an organizing framework for analyzing, planning, and implementing any given consultative experience.

- *Level I: Case-centered consultation*
  a. *Target:* specific client
  b. *Goal:* to achieve appropriate behavior or physical change
  c. *Outcome:* tertiary preventive change
- *Level II: Educational consultation*
  a. *Target:* specific client, group, or population
  b. *Goal:* to improve functioning, efficiency, and ability
  c. *Outcome:* secondary preventive change
- *Level III: Program or administrative consultation*
  a. *Target:* specific system, organization, or population
  b. *Goal:* to promote institutional change
  c. *Outcome:* primary preventive change.

In most situations, consultants are asked to address complex issues that require multiple models or approaches and levels of consultation. (The case examples at the end of this chapter illustrate the interrelationship of these models and levels.)

ENVIRONMENT AND SYSTEMS ANALYSIS

A *systems analysis* is the identification and determination of the state of the system under review. It includes study and evaluation of all internal and external environmental

factors influencing that system as well as a complex of internal and external factors, on both macro-environmental and micro-environmental levels, that influence individual or community behavior and organizational structure (McCormack, Jaffe, & Frey, 2003). *Environment* is "the external physical and social environments that surround the client and in which the client's daily life occupations occur" (AOTA, 2008, p. 645).

Successful consultation outcomes begin with careful analysis and planning, and an environment and systems analysis is an important preliminary step. The systems in which occupational therapy consultation may take place include health care facilities, schools, social agencies, prisons, the community, industry, regulatory agencies, and political arenas. The analysis should ascertain the state of the system and the particular social and physical environment of the client. A thorough study and evaluation of all influential internal and external environmental factors will help determine the consultation frame (or frames) of reference and the consultation goals and strategies.

The *social environment* is the client's relationship with individuals, groups, and organizations (AOTA, 2008). The *macro-environment* consists of forces in the external environment surrounding the client system. These external factors or conditions include local or national legislative acts and regulatory policies; local or national economic concerns; the political climate; and the social structure, cultural mores, customs, attitudes, and values that shape occupational life. The *micro-environment* consists of forces close to the client system. These forces include the context or interrelated conditions that surround the client,

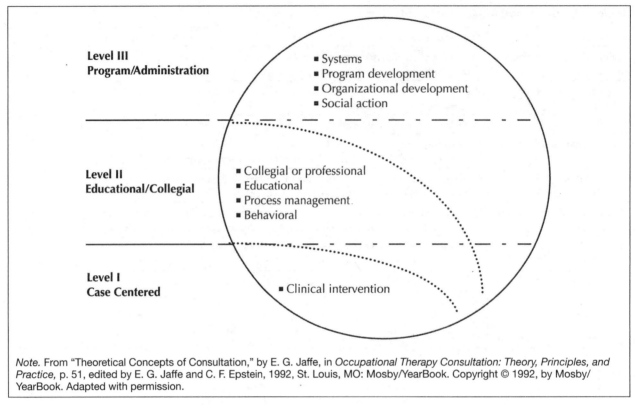

Level III
Program/Administration

- Systems
- Program development
- Organizational development
- Social action

Level II
Educational/Collegial

- Collegial or professional
- Educational
- Process management
- Behavioral

Level I
Case Centered

- Clinical intervention

Note. From "Theoretical Concepts of Consultation," by E. G. Jaffe, in *Occupational Therapy Consultation: Theory, Principles, and Practice,* p. 51, edited by E. G. Jaffe and C. F. Epstein, 1992, St. Louis, MO: Mosby/YearBook. Copyright © 1992, by Mosby/YearBook. Adapted with permission.

Figure 33.1. Levels and models of consultation.

including administrative policies and procedures of the organization; internal resources of funds, personnel, and supplies; the corporate culture; and the mission and goals of the organization.

Within the macro- and micro-environments, the consultant considers each of the following environments:

- The *human environment* includes the individuals who may influence the program or organization, including patients, administrators, staff, families, teachers, health professionals, and others.
- The *social environment* refers to the client's relationships with individuals, groups, and organizations (AOTA, 2008).
- The *natural environment* consists of the particular settings in which the managerial, entrepreneurial, or consultation activities occurs, including community agencies, schools, workplace settings, and health care facilities.
- The *physical environment* includes the external factors or conditions that influence the managerial, entrepreneurial, or consultation activities, including space, architecture, accessibility, and physical structure (McCormack et al., 2003).

All these factors influence behavior, organizational structure, and occupational performance, and "examining the environments and contexts in which occupational performance can or does occur provides insights into overarching, underlying, and embedded influences on engagement"

(AOTA, 2008, p. 651). In these currently difficult economic and political times, an analysis of these factors is especially crucial. In addition, this analysis helps determine the consultant's specific role and relationship in any given setting.

CONSULTANT ROLES AND RELATIONSHIPS

Natural role shifts occur at various stages of occupational therapy intervention as relationships develop, new information becomes available, and change is implemented. The consultant frequently assumes multiple roles as the consultation progresses, providing a variety of services depending on the needs and the setting of the client. What role the consultant plays and when also depends on whether the consultant is internal or external to the system.

An *internal consultant* is an employee of the client system who is asked to provide consultation services within the organization. An *external consultant* is an independent agent, outside the organization, with whom the client contracts to provide consultation services.

The consultant's behavior, identified frames of reference, and role choice are directly related to the consultant's relationship with the system. The internal consultant, an employee, is an integral part of the system, with knowledge of the corporate culture and the strengths and the weaknesses of the organization. This may or may not be considered an advantage, depending on the organization's needs. The external consultant, as an outsider, may have a fresh, objective perspective, but he or she must dedicate time and

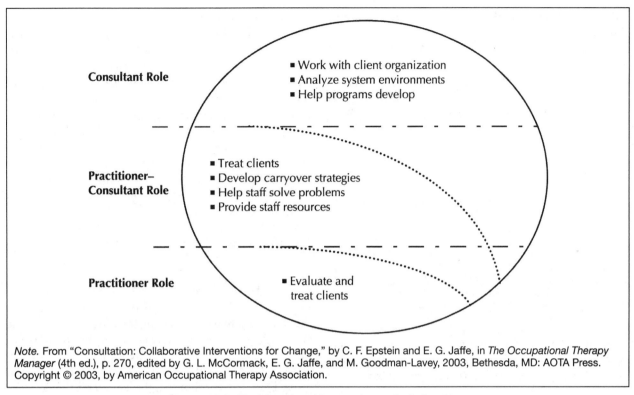

Consultant Role
- Work with client organization
- Analyze system environments
- Help programs develop

Practitioner–
Consultant Role
- Treat clients
- Develop carryover strategies
- Help staff solve problems
- Provide staff resources

Practitioner Role
- Evaluate and treat clients

Note. From "Consultation: Collaborative Interventions for Change," by C. F. Epstein and E. G. Jaffe, in *The Occupational Therapy Manager* (4th ed.), p. 270, edited by G. L. McCormack, E. G. Jaffe, and M. Goodman-Lavey, 2003, Bethesda, MD: AOTA Press. Copyright © 2003, by American Occupational Therapy Association.

Figure 33.2. Evolving practitioner roles and relationships.

effort to system analysis. Because each type of consultant has advantages and disadvantages, the client should consider specific system problems and needs before deciding whether to use an internal or external consultant (Jaffe & Epstein, 1992b).

MOVING FROM PRACTITIONER TO CONSULTANT

Consultation approaches are embedded in the practitioner role, and intervention typically shifts from a direct to an indirect perspective as occupational therapy practitioners consider the human and nonhuman factors required to support the client's functional outcomes. As practitioner–consultant roles evolve, direct-client intervention may continue, but indirect intervention becomes increasingly important as the intervention shifts to client support systems, organizations, and populations. The practitioner–consultant roles change to those of trainer, collegial collaborator, problem solver, information specialist, and clarifier (Lippitt & Lippitt, 1986). The consultant's role differs from that of a mentor or coach in regard to the ranking or level of the relationship. The roles of mentor or coach are more hierarchical in that the mentor or coach makes suggestions that are traditionally expected to be followed by the person receiving the mentoring and coaching, whereas the consultant–client relationship should be egalitarian, collaborative, or collegial. The client may or may not accept the suggestions and advice of the consultant, and the final decision making is up to the client, not the consultant (see Chapter 16 for

more information on mentoring). Figure 33.2 illustrates the evolution from the practitioner's direct intervention role to the indirect consultant role. Activities at each role level are depicted and the roles and activities of consultant and practitioner are described as a fluid relationship during a given client intervention.

CONSULTATION PROCESS

Occupational therapy consultation is a facilitative process through which a client receives help in an interactive, egalitarian relationship based on mutual respect. Problem solving, a key component, involves identification and analysis of issues and joint resolution of problems, with the client making the final decision. Consultants use a systems perspective to develop an environmental analysis, identify available internal and external resources, and foster interactive communication.

The consultation process includes four stages: (1) initiation and clarification, (2) assessment and planning, (3) interactive problem resolution, and (4) evaluation and termination. Within these stages are eight basic steps, shown in Table 33.2.

Initiation and Clarification

In some settings, the initial identification of a need or problem may precipitate a request for consultation services. In other settings, the consultant may see a need within a particular system and present a proposal. In early meetings with the client, the consultant delineates his or her knowledge and experience. The client presents an overview of the system and

Table 33.2. Stages and Basic Steps in the Consultation Process

Stage of Process	Step in Process
1. Initiation and clarification	1. Entry into system 2. Negotiation of contract
2. Assessment and planning	3. Diagnostic analysis leading to problem identification 4. Goal setting and planning through establishment of trust
3. Interactive problem resolution	5. Maintenance phase of intervention and feedback
4. Evaluation and termination	6. Evaluation 7. Termination 8. Possible renegotiation

Note. From "The Process of Consultation", by E. G. Jaffe, in *Occupational Therapy Consultation: Theory, Principles, and Practice* (p. 136), edited by E. G. Jaffe and C. F. Epstein, 1992, St. Louis, MO: Mosby/Year Book. Copyright 1992 by Mosby/Year Book. Adapted with permission.

enumerates the desired outcomes of the consultation. During these interactions, there is opportunity to clarify roles, expectations, and goals that can lead to a formal contract.

Entry Into the System

Entry into the system or the organization may develop in one of four ways (Jaffe & Epstein, 1992b):

1. *Planned entry*: The potential consultant develops a strategy and presents a proposal.
2. *Opportunistic entry*: The situation arises spontaneously, and the potential consultant seizes the moment.
3. *Uninvited entry*: The potential consultant perceives a need and attempts to enter the system.
4. *Invited entry*: The potential consultant is invited because of his or her specific skills.

In planned, opportunistic, and uninvited entry, the consultant obtains a foothold for the formalized consultation process by helping the client appreciate the benefits that can be derived through the consultation process. Unless the consultant ultimately is invited into the system, however, the consultation is unlikely to reach completion. During the entry step, the consultant considers the potential for a mutual relationship, makes an initial assessment of needs, evaluates the client's readiness for change, and proposes possible consultation activities.

Negotiation of a Contract

Clear communication and understanding are essential in establishing a collaborative relationship. The *contract* is a formal document that defines the purpose of the consultation; describes the qualifications of the consultant; identifies the obligations and the expectations of both parties; and delineates procedures, time constraints, and the method and the amount of compensation. This stage culminates in the contract, which both parties sign.

Assessment and Planning

Once the consultant has entered the system and formalized a contract, assessment of the problem begins. The consultant draws on professional knowledge, experience, and resources in conjunction with an in-depth study of the client's competence, knowledge, and willingness to participate in a cooperative, collaborative relationship. Special terminology, policies and procedures, and cultural values and attitudes particular to the setting are identified and noted to ensure effective communication and accurate identification of client problems and needs. Additionally, the consultant considers any external sources of power such as regulatory agencies, funding sources, legislative imperatives, and community advocacy and consumer groups that may have a direct influence on the system and the issues for which consultation has been requested.

Diagnostic Analysis Leading to Problem Identification

Preliminary diagnostic work in the entry phase prepares the consultant to perform a more intensive diagnosis of the system. A systems analysis reveals the organizational structure; the internal and external trends and resources that affect the system; and the corporate culture, mission, and goals. During data collection, the consultant should identify forces that impede movement and forces that facilitate progress (Lewin, 1951).

Goal Setting and Planning Through Establishment of Trust

In addition to helping the consultant identify the needs and the problems of the system, the diagnostic process provides the framework for the next step in consultation: collaborative goal setting and planning. This step aids the consultant in establishing the mutual respect necessary for a successful consultation. The consultant must develop a good working relationship with the client to identify the desired outcomes of the consultation. Knowledge of formal and informal lines of communication, including listening skills, system politics, key power figures, and the ways in which decision making occurs in the system, will enhance the planning phase and collegial relationships.

Interactive Problem Resolution

After thoroughly studying the situation and carefully analyzing gathered data, the consultant begins the process of interactive problem resolution, which demonstrates the consultant's commitment to helping the client change through collaborative strategy development. First, the consultant and client share data. Then, through participative decision making, the consultant helps the client identify multiple strategies for consideration. Decisions remain the province of the client.

The success of this step depends on the ability of the consultant and the client to build a relationship of mutual trust and respect, establishing an open environment that enables the client to consider changing strategies and feel confident in using the perspective and the suggestions offered by the consultant. In addition, the client has responsibilities in the consultative process, including providing access to information, willingness to participate in the development of strategies, and the ability to assume the responsibility for the final decisions. Additionally, the consultant must demonstrate a commitment to confidentiality and an adherence to professional ethics (see Chapter 30, this volume).

In the maintenance phase of the consultation, while the client is putting into effect the decisions that emerged from the problem resolution phase, the consultant must remain aware of the needs of the people working in the system and of the difficulties they face as the system changes. The consultant should develop a communication network to gather feedback, observations, perceptions, and progress reports. This network should include a variety of people who are concerned with the issues, including key power individuals in the system (e.g., administrators, managers, directors) and general staff. Interviews and meetings with these individuals provide opportunities to observe the system in action, identify potential problems, and consider possible solutions.

Especially if the consultant is an outsider, he or she will depend on this network to report perceptions and interpretations of actions and information from within the system. The network enables the consultant not only to verify information and data using various analysis techniques, including interviews, surveys, group discussions, and documentation, but also to promote a greater understanding and appreciation of the consultant's occupational performance perspective.

Evaluation and Termination

The final stage of the consultation process is evaluation and termination. Approximately 2 weeks prior to the previously negotiated scheduled completion of the consultation, the client is given a suggested plan of final activities for the consultant and client. Consultant and client then usually hold an exit or summary conference to provide an opportunity for clarification, feedback, evaluation of both the consultation strategies and the consultant's performance, and discussion of any remaining areas of concern. The consultant prepares a final report containing dates of service, individuals and departments involved, and a final update summarizing all activities and responsibilities. This summary includes initial data-gathering methodology, findings, assessments, collaborative strategy development, and recommendations or a plan of action for both the consultant and client once the consultation is completed, including possible follow-up to allow an avenue for further communication as needed. When the client receives this report, he or she has the option to terminate the consultation or renegotiate the contract.

Evaluation

Throughout the consultation activities, the consultant monitors and evaluates the outcomes of the intervention. There must be ongoing interaction among evaluation, intervention, and outcomes throughout the consultation

process (AOTA, 2008, p. 648), and the evaluation process provides the data necessary "to clarify goals, refine or revise intervention strategies, and develop future plans" (Jaffe & Epstein, 1992b, pp. 147–148).

Like the data gathering performed during the diagnostic phase, evaluation includes both formal and informal methods of assessment. Informal evaluation occurs during the consultant's periodic observations of and feedback from the client. Formal evaluation tools must be appropriate to the specific situation and "the specific outcome objectives desired from the consultation" (Jaffe & Epstein, 1992b, p. 149). The evaluation of a consultation experience is similar to an analysis of occupational performance and contributes to evidence-based practice.

The following structure can be used for evaluating a specific consultation experience:

- Target or client
- Issue or problem statement
- Environment and systems analysis findings
- Intervention plan
- Targeted outcomes
- Final report
- References.

Termination

The consultant and the client should prepare for termination during development of the initial contract by preparing a tentative timeline for completion of the consultation when preliminary goals and time frames are established. Termination may occur at any time during the consultation, either when the consultant and client mutually agree that goals have been achieved or when further intervention is no longer appropriate. Termination of the consultation may be an informal decision by one or both parties, or a formal document stating completion or end of the consultation.

Possible Renegotiation

Contracts may include the possibility of renegotiation at any time in the consultation process to allow for changes in or expansion of the goals of the consultation. After termination of the original contract, the parties may decide to renegotiate an extension of the contract if the client requests additional help.

PREVENTION AND PREVENTIVE OUTCOMES

The ultimate goal of consultation is to help clients assume a proactive stance to anticipate or forestall problems that otherwise could lead to dysfunction. Prevention is therefore inherent in all consultation (Grossman, 1977; Jaffe, 1986; Jaffe & Epstein, 1992b; Scaffa, 2001; West, 1969).

1. *Primary prevention* consists of activities undertaken before the onset of a problem to avoid the occurrence of malfunction or disability in a population potentially at risk. Program or administrative (Level III) consultation involves transformation, institutional, and system change

through program development, management, and organizational restructuring and is the most appropriate consultation level for primary prevention initiatives.

2. *Secondary prevention* involves early diagnosis, identification, and detection of at-risk populations to prevent chronic dysfunction or permanent disability. Educational (Level II) consultation activities are the most appropriate to bring about client behavior modification through skill development.

3. *Tertiary prevention* consists of rehabilitation and remediation of a problem or illness to prevent further problems, loss, or disability. Case-centered (Level I) consultation activities are the most appropriate to bring about client behavior modification through remediation or maintenance activities.

Preventive outcomes are the results (outcomes) achieved through consultation activities. Preventive outcomes are defined by Jaffe and Epstein (1992b) in terms of their potential for social, organizational, and health preventive programming and are directly related to the three levels of consultation. As the consultant addresses specific issues, consultation strategies are based on the levels at which the consultation activities occur. The consultant considers the preventive outcome that he or she can expect at that level. Merging the concepts of prevention with occupational therapy consultation practice at various levels ensures appropriate outcome expectations and fosters proactive approaches by both clients and consultants that acknowledge the important relationship among client, consultant, and the environment. Examples of these three levels of preventive outcomes are provided in the case examples at the end of this chapter.

- *Tertiary Preventive Outcome*—Modification of the specific client behavior occurs as a result of remediation or maintenance activities at Level I: case-centered consultation (see Case Examples 1–2).
- *Secondary Preventive Outcome*—Modification of behavior through skill development occurs as a result of consultation activities at Level II: educational consultation (see Case Examples 1–4).
- *Primary preventive outcome*—Transformation, institutional, and system change occur as the result of program development, management, and organizational restructuring at Level III: program or administrative consultation (see Case Examples 2–4).

SKILLS AND KNOWLEDGE

The occupational therapy philosophy of helping others do for themselves naturally carries over into consultation. Knowledge and professional competence in occupational therapy practice and an understanding of professional ethics and behavior help provide a sound foundation for developing consultation skills and that ensure safe and effective service delivery (AOTA, 2010; Doherty, 2009; Moyers & Dale, 2007; Scott, 2009).

Numerous authors have identified areas of knowledge critical in consultation. These areas include systems theory and behavioral sciences; developmental theory as it applies to individuals, groups, organizations, and communities; education and training methodologies, including problem solving and role playing; human occupation and personality, attitude formation, adaptation, and change; and self-knowledge (Dunn, 2000; Kielhofner & Forsyth, 2002; Jaffe & Epstein, 1992b; Scaffa, 2001). Key skills that the consultant must possess are (1) communicating; (2) educating; (3) diagnosing; (4) linking; (5) establishing effective interpersonal relationships; and (6) maintaining key attitudes and attributes, such as flexibility, creativity, maturity, and self-confidence.

Communicating

Communicating is a primary consultation skill. It encompasses more than verbal and written abilities; body language, role modeling, use of analogies, reflection, and confrontation are also included. Listening skills are of the utmost importance. What the client says or does not say and how it is communicated provide valuable insight into the attitudes, potential behavior, and working relationships between client and consultant. For example, in our very visual world, a popular way for consultants to introduce themselves and their service is a slideshow presentation. This communication tool helps the consultant reinforce concepts and build clients' understanding of what to expect in the consultation process. Figure 33.3 is an example of a key slide in such a presentation; it illustrates the consultant's multiple roles and varied functions. Its design helps the speaker demonstrate how the level of control shifts from the consultant to the client and support systems. In addition to visually communicating and providing reinforcement, the figure can be used to solicit active communication between the audience and the consultant.

In any consultation setting, the consultant's written and oral communication convey a particular message to the recipient, and the consultant must use communication in the most effective way. In a school setting, industry program, or day care center, for example, the consultant should be familiar with the special terms and jargon used in that setting and should use them as part of the communication process. As outsiders, consultants unfamiliar with this language initially may have trouble establishing meaningful dialogue. Consultants must define their terms from the client's perspective, using the client's language where possible.

Educating

Training and educating are basic components of consultation. A consultant may choose from among a variety of methods to help broaden client skills and develop client abilities to effect independent change. Designing and leading workshops is one such method (Epstein & Gardner, 2007; Jaffe & Epstein, 1992b) that allows the consultant

Clinician	Problem Solver	Trainer/ Mentor	Resource Person	Program Developer	Consultant
Evaluates client within identified occupational performance settings. Analyzes environment and context issues limiting functional performance in setting. Provides report and intervention plan with identified outcomes.	Involves client and support teams in collaborative identification and creation of strategies and plans required to determine course of action.	Uses expert knowledge and skills to provide mentorship and formal and informal training for client and circles of support to enable client success within identified contexts and environments.	Uses knowledge and expertise to provide related resources, proactive and advocacy-oriented information, and referrals as appropriate.	Advises and collaborates with client, supports, and larger system to create new or revised programs as appropriate and as requested.	Upon request, uses expertise in collaborative manner to help define problem areas. Raises questions for reflection. Considers alternatives.

PRACTITIONER

CLIENT AND CIRCLE OF SUPPORT

Consultant Role Emphasis

← Direct   Indirect →

Note. Developed by Occupational Therapy Consultants, Inc., Somerset, NJ. Used with permission.

Figure 33.3. Occupational therapy consultant roles and functions.

to present new material as the client participates actively through experiential learning. Specialized materials and instructional programs may be used, allowing the client to proceed at a comfortable pace with built-in opportunities for feedback and discussion. The consultant chooses materials that are clearly presented and relevant for the client.

Diagnosing

Occupational therapy practitioners are most familiar with assessment technology as it pertains to diagnosis and direct intervention on behalf of individuals referred for services. Consultation calls for a more global perspective. Moving into a dysfunctional system, the consultant gathers data from a variety of sources in collaboration with the client. As the consultant reviews and assesses data, he or she requests feedback to verify and clarify issues before reaching a final diagnosis or conclusion. To diagnose problems, the consultant must locate sources of help, power, and influence; understand the client's values and culture; and determine the client's readiness for change (Epstein & Gardner, 2007; Jaffe & Epstein, 1992b; Lippitt & Lippitt, 1986).

Linking

Linking is a skill that comes naturally to occupational therapy practitioners. The consultant links the client to appropriate resources both within and outside the consultation environment. As proponents of occupational adaptation (Schkade & Schultz, 2003; Schultz, 2009), consultants constantly identify resources and alternative methods to help achieve a particular goal. For example, a consultant may learn about new and competitive sources of equipment and supplies when consulting with one organization; he or she may then link another client to these resources, when appropriate.

Establishing Effective Relationships

To help client stakeholders establish effective interpersonal relationships, the consultant must develop an understanding of the client's value system and attitudes and the external and internal pressures on the system. Community practice especially requires recognition of the complex, variable, and important stakeholders who are unique to the person, organization, or population with whom the consultant works. Epstein and Gardner (2007) used the metaphor of pick-up sticks, each stick representing one of a client's relationship supports, to illustrate how moving or removing a support could cause disruption of the whole system and endanger the effectiveness of all supports. The pick-up stick metaphor helped staff in the program understand the importance of each and every community stakeholder—the community organizations, health care services and transportation, family and friends, state and local interested agencies, and so forth—in planning for client job placement in the community.

Each consultation experience brings its own challenges in the development of effective collaborative relationships. The consultant must analyze each situation to identify the most appropriate strategy and implementation plan.

Maintaining Key Attitudes and Attributes

Consultation requires a high degree of self-direction, comfort with taking risks, and ease in working without a formalized support system. Satisfaction for a job well done comes through success achieved by the client. This indirect type of gratification necessitates a strong sense of security and self-confidence on the part of the consultant. In addition, maturity, flexibility, a sense of humor, and a sense of timing are important. At times, a crisis may shunt the original consultation problem aside. The consultant may come prepared to deal with one problem and find the system's priority to be quite different. At such a moment, staff may be reluctant to consider other issues, and the consultant must help resolve the more pressing problem. The consultant must make a realistic appraisal of his or her limitations and abilities, however. When additional skills are required, the consultant should have the confidence to acknowledge this and to suggest that the client tap other resources.

ESTABLISHING A CONSULTATION BUSINESS

It is an exciting and rewarding experience to be in business for oneself. Although there are many risks, numerous frustrations, and extensive commitments, this model of practice is attracting increasing numbers of practitioners (Scott, 2009). The satisfaction of building a business, the opportunities offered in new markets, and the freedom of self-direction are among the many dividends.

A decision to own and operate a business is a significant step for any practitioner. The considerations and the complexities of entrepreneurship require major commitments of time, energy, and money. Self-education, risk-taking abilities, and organization and management skills are important prerequisites (Biech, 2007; Jaffe & Epstein, 1992b; Weiss, 2009). Fortunately, a broad array of books, periodicals, organizations, and the Internet are available to practitioners contemplating this step.

When developing a consulting practice, occupational therapy practitioners should follow the Boy Scout motto: "Be prepared." They prepare by creating a marketing plan based on careful study of economic factors and appropriately developing and using resources. The business of being in business can then become a reality.

Consultation Business Plan

The *business plan* provides an overall framework for the consultation practice and a basis for decision making. It includes an assessment of the target market, a statement of mission and goals, a business concept, and an organizational plan (see Chapter 9, this volume). The aspiring consultant entrepreneur should seek guidance from financial and legal advisers, whose knowledge is critical in making effective decisions regarding the issue of self-employment versus partnership or incorporation and the development of contract formats for use with potential clients.

Marketing of Consultation Services

Consultation is a service product. It is intangible and directly related to the consultant providing the service. As such, it is also inseparable from the consultant's perspective and his or her interactions with the client. Consultant services are perishable. If a limited or fluctuating market exists, the consultant can be without work. Therefore, marketing must be a continuous process. Indeed, the consultant must integrate consistent and meaningful marketing into his or her management of the consultation practice. The consultant must dedicate time, energy, and money to this important aspect of business (Biech, 2007; Epstein, 1992b; Scaffa, 2001; Weiss, 2009; see Chapter 8, this volume, for more detail on marketing).

A successful marketing effort begins with an in-depth analysis of both the target market and the ability of the business to respond to the needs of this market. To establish an effective marketing mix that is persuasive to potential clients, the consultant identifies a needed consultation service (a product) in a particular market, prices services competitively, and uses creative promotional strategies to build a referral base.

The promotion plan specifies the activities occupational therapists will undertake to generate referrals or recommended clients (Epstein, 1992b; Richmond, 2003). Examples include the following:

- Promoting services through such tools as Web site, professional brochures, letters, business cards, and telephone listings
- Networking with fellow practitioners, professionals in allied fields, and former clients and agency personnel who are advocates for the consultant's competence
- Researching health planning reports, economic indicators of growing health services, local health classified ads, and state health department listings of potential user agencies and organizations.

One effective marketing activity is to contribute time and energy to community activities that focus on health concerns. A consultant can heighten his or her visibility by educating potential client organizations and the populations they serve about the benefits of consultation. By providing free lectures; assisting in planning and running special programs; and participating on committees, boards, electronic forums, and social networking sites, the consultant keeps current and shares perspectives with potential clientele. In addition, involvement with advocacy organizations whose mission and vision are congruent with those of the consultant offers an avenue of information and visibility and an opportunity to expand the consultant's knowledge base and resource network. The consultant might offer free information on a subject of interest to potential clients as a sales promotion technique, such as providing current information on new rulings pertaining to the recent amendments to the Americans with Disabilities Act (ADA, 2008). Public relations strategies, another marketing tool, include distributing news releases, publishing articles, and giving lectures at meetings at which potential clients gather.

Development and Use of Resources

An important aspect of effective consultation services is the development and use of resources, including people, organizations, literature, and educational experiences. Experience alone will not expand the consultant's knowledge base for consultation activities. Meeting other professionals within and outside occupational therapy and networking with local and national professional organizations broaden the consultant's perspective and heighten awareness of important trends. Additionally, networking can alert the consultant to changes affecting health care practice and build a natural support system. These affiliations help the consultant develop a roster of experts who can provide needed information, advice, or direction on a specific problem. Field visits stimulate information sharing and networking and help provide broader perspectives on geographic and socioeconomic differences that influence the responses of a given system.

Reading and continuing education help keep the consultant abreast of trends, changes, new information, and emerging issues affecting the health care market. Consultants should regularly review the professional and related literature and attend occupational therapy and other multidisciplinary conferences and workshops. The Internet offers a variety of important sources of information, including listservs, electronic newsletters, and social networking and communication vehicles such as Facebook and Twitter. Additionally, continuing education is required of all practitioners to maintain and improve competence and can increase the consultant's familiarity with differences in language usage and terminology in a given system, thus enhancing communication skills.

Additionally, the consultant should stay up-to-date with publications and special newsletters on economics and politics, which play major roles in shaping the delivery of health care. Newly enacted legislation, changes in reimbursement methodologies, and revised guidelines for service provision all have significant implications. Judicious use of resources helps consultants maintain a broad and well-rounded knowledge base. A well-informed perspective and extensive support system hone the consultant's creativity and flexibility. Ultimately, making a commitment to the continued development of resources allows both the consultant and his or her clients to draw from a comprehensive and current pool of information.

EXPANDING CONSULTATION SERVICES AMID CHANGE

The changing nature of health and human service delivery has created challenges for all occupational therapy practitioners, and the current economic downturn may have serious implications for practice and the need for consultation. Limited available funds, stringent criteria for approval of services, time-limited appropriations, fixed payments, and increasing cross-discipline competition for funding require practitioners who are knowledgeable, skilled, creative, and responsive. They must be able to diagnose an individual's functional problems while concurrently considering system, organizational, population, and process problems that affect intervention outcomes. Organizations and facilities may chose to provide indirect occupational therapy services on a less frequent basis and have expert consultants train (lesser paid) staff to carry out the direct intervention under supervision, which would include occupational therapy assistants, thereby decreasing some (higher paid) professional costs. School systems, concerned with the cost of weekly direct intervention services, may encourage their educational teams and the occupational therapy practitioners to develop monthly consultations as a less expensive option for intervention.

In times of significant change, consultation opportunities arise with greater frequency as individuals, organizations, and populations seek expertise and guidance to move forward. Occupational therapy's *Centennial Vision* (AOTA, 2007) and the publication of the *Framework–II* (AOTA, 2008) challenged the profession to expand consultation services using our occupational perspective. As the 21st century's first decade drew to a close, populations in the United States and worldwide experienced shifting economic tides, changing cultural perspectives, and social and technological innovations, as well as financial and health care uncertainty.

Termed "The Great Recession" by the media (Andersen, 2009), unemployment escalated; many businesses failed; and local, regional, state, and national programs and services supporting health care faced downsizing or closure. Provisions in the American Recovery and Reinvestment Act of 2009 supported the needs of organizations and populations served by occupational therapy (AOTA, 2009). For example, the National Institute of Mental Health (NIMH, 2009), reported that some funds would create "NIH Challenge Grants" supporting studies to address scientific and health research gaps. Occupational therapy consultants in the NIMH community then had opportunities to participate with colleagues to help develop or implement such grants. Other important funding with potential consultation opportunities included Medicaid, special education under the Individuals with Disabilities Education Improvement Act (2004), and health information technology.

As national, state, and local legislative priorities shifted, indirect consultation opportunities to address the needs of systems and populations rather than direct client-focused (i.e., person-focused) occupational therapy services, took on greater priority. To facilitate client engagement in occupation related to health and participation, varied direct and indirect interventions are considered, and the role of practitioner evolves to one of a consultant.

OPPORTUNITIES FOR CONSULTATION

Occupational therapy practitioners have ongoing opportunities to hone their consultation skills. At an entry level, consultation skills are a critical support to clinically driven client needs. They can help clientele identify and resolve their specific occupational needs as they face complex and multifaceted change. Frequently, individual clients, their families, circles of support, and the system benefit when the occupational therapy intervention incorporates an indirect collaborative consultation approach (AOTA, 2008; Epstein & Gardner, 2007). For example, a person whose parent has early Alzheimer's disease needs to bring that parent to live with him or her. Should the new home environment need adaptation to support successful transition, an opportunity for consultation services arises (Siebert, 2005).

Successful individual outcomes often lead occupational therapy practitioners toward consultation. As the practitioner matures and his or her expertise expands, consultation may concentrate on client organizational and population needs in community settings (Brachtesende, 2005). Important resources and expertise are then available to the disability community and those at risk. The consultant analyzes and pinpoints trends to identify areas where consultative knowledge, skills, and abilities can help address needed change. The emphasis and perspective becomes one of helper and collaborative facilitator.

Growing community-based consultation services requires the development of a marketing plan and creation of direct and indirect marketing tools (Epstein, 1992a; Epstein & Gardner, 2007; Richmond, 2003). As practitioners evolve their practice roles, links are forged with community-based organizations and services. By drawing on prior practitioner experiences and the communication opportunities such experiences provide, the consultant can network with and educate targeted community professionals and the environments they serve. This helps lay the foundation for potential consultation services (Scott, 2009).

As a result of the recent economic instability, communities face increasing numbers of individuals with disabilities and projections indicate this will continue to grow (U.S. Census Bureau, 2008). Traditional funding streams have shrunk or been eliminated. Community planners, health professionals, and legislators are seeking preventive initiatives to help reduce disabling conditions.

Occupational therapy consultants can help organizations and populations address these needs, but they must be aware of and conversant with such national initiatives as Healthy People 2020 (Fielding, 2009) and growing health issues, as was reported to the Senate Committee on Aging in the Alzheimer Study Report of 2009 (Medical News Today, 2009). For example, the study report recommended creation of the Alzheimer's Solutions Project to focus on delaying onset and on prevention of the disease. Consultants will be needed to participate in these important efforts that affect so many older Americans and their families.

Many in the aging Baby Boomer cohorts have critical functional limitations placing them at risk of losing community independence. The need for community-based occupational therapy consultation services for the older adult, particularly those 80 years of age and older, will continue to grow as consultants are sought to develop programs, provide case consultation, and train families and others providing support (AOTA, 2007; Maddox, 2001).

On the other side of the developmental spectrum, the number and types of children diagnosed with an autism spectrum disorder (ASD) continue to expand (Centers for Disease Control and Prevention, 2009), resulting in increased funding for autism research (Autism Speaks, 2008).

Federal mandates, including IDEA and the 2008 revisions to ADA, also exemplify funding that targets disability and community concerns across the developmental spectrum. Recent ADA revisions emphasizing expanded requirements for reasonable accommodations have created innumerable opportunities for occupational therapy consultation to industries, private and public businesses, and corporations.

Growing assistive technology has created new and exciting options for persons with disabilities. Children, adults, and older adults who may be challenged with physical and intellectual disabilities require assistive technology and strategic adaptations to achieve greater independence and productivity (Morris, 2009). Technology consultation addressing problems in seating, positioning, and mobility is readily understood but often difficult to fund. The expert consultant may then be asked to identify appropriate equipment and funding for needs such as environmental controls and communication devices (Bender & Davidson, 2002; Mann 2001).

The consultant is often found at the leading edge of practice, initiating occupational therapy services in new markets. When the Ticket to Work and Work Incentives Improvement Act of 1999 was revised to help individuals with disabilities seek and select services necessary to obtain and retain employment (Long-Bellil & Henry, 2009; Silverstein, 2002), it provided case consultation opportunities for the consultant to evaluate an individual's potential for vocational training. Work center staff can then collaborate with the consultant to develop a training plan, using recommended adaptive strategies. Consultation opportunities frequently expand when training program staff requires consulting services to assist with job configuration for the needs of other clients.

City planners, developers, architects, and others involved in designing living space need consultation services, as do employers and lawyers concerned with employment of persons with disabilities. The occupational therapy consultant is uniquely qualified to identify job performance accommodations; conduct work capacity evaluations; and collaborate with contractors or builders to further successful outcomes for disabled individuals (Hoelscher & Taylor, 2000).

Schools and early intervention programs constitute a large practice setting for occupational therapists and the second largest for occupational therapy assistants. Consultants with expertise in pediatrics and knowledge of educational systems are in demand to develop educationally related programs for children with special needs (Hanft & Shepherd, 2008; Swinth, 2004). In 2008, many school districts faced budget reductions due to the recession, but educationally relevant services were still required to meet the mandates of IDEA. In-class support and inclusion services have become the model of choice, which requires understanding and use of a consultative approach. The practitioner–consultant applies consultation principles and expertise within classroom settings (Dunn, 2000; Rainville, Cermak & Murray 1996; Swinth & Mailloux, 2002). The consultant establishes a supportive milieu for collaborative problem solving using a collegial model of consultation. The combined expertise of teacher and consultant benefits the student with special needs as well as peers within the classroom (Dettmer, Dyck, & Thurston, 1999).

In concert with the *Centennial Vision* (AOTA, 2007) and the *Framework–II* (AOTA, 2008; Roley & Delany, 2009), societal inequities that influence opportunities for occupational performance and participation have become important concerns (Braveman & Bass-Haugen 2009; Wilcock & Townsend, 2009). In today's community-based practice, the consultant must recognize and consider social justice issues that may affect the development and implementation of the planned consultation initiative (Gupta & Walloch, 2006). Krongenberg, Algado, and Pollard (2005) vividly illustrate this in their work with populations affected by ravages of war and displacement around the world. In working with residents in Letcher County, Kentucky, Blakeney and Marshall (2009) and their Eastern Kentucky University students helped pinpoint the damaging effect of water-related diseases in this rural county. Their study confirmed that pollution from coal-mining practices had contaminated the water used by residents, creating "occupational injustice" (Townsend & Wilcock, 2003) where significant health problems resulted for all who resided in this area of Appalachia. In this study, students and faculty used a consultant role as they worked with individual families, concerned county representatives, and local social justice organizations.

Occupational therapy educators can contribute to the growth of consultation services. Using community settings as the laboratory, students and professor implement programs with a consultation focus. One such program targeted mental health clients participating in a vocationally oriented reentry program. Students and their professor collaborated with community center staff to develop and implement a program targeting important self-sufficiency skills required to enter the center's employment training program (Diffendal, 2000).

Changes in health care delivery models, combined with younger and older populations that are rapidly increasing as a result of life-sustaining technology, will continue to expand consultation opportunities. Emerging areas of occupational therapy practice include opportunities in case management, driver rehabilitation, ergonomics, wellness, health promotion, forensics and low vision rehabilitation, and cognitive decline—all of which have a consultation component (Best, Noblitt, Synold, & Hughes, 2001; Christiansen, 2007).

Conclusion

Consultation is a rapidly expanding area of occupational therapy practice, helping to keep occupational therapy in a strong position in diverse health environments. Occupational therapy professionals at all levels can use consultation skills to help consumers, families, employers, and communities assess needs, identify strengths, and develop and coordinate resources (Jaffe, 1996). Consultation services have assumed a more prominent role in occupational therapy service delivery, especially as major changes in the political, economic, and social environments increase the need for community-based practice. Practitioners at every level should develop and apply consultation skills and embed the principles of effective consultation in all areas of practice.

Regardless of the setting, the four stages and eight basic steps in the consultation process provide the foundation for all consultation. As practitioners gain experience, they can attempt more complex consultation tasks and increase their repertoire of consultation approaches on the basis of the nine theoretical models and three levels described in this chapter. And, because the ultimate goal of any consultation is to help the client or client system prevent further problems, the consultant should understand and use prevention principles to achieve appropriate preventive outcomes.

The fast-paced and continuously evolving health care environment requires consultants with expertise to help planners, managers, and consumers move successfully through the process of change. The principles and concepts of consultation will help prepare the practitioners of today and tomorrow effectively function in this world of rapid change.

Case Examples[1]

CASE EXAMPLE 1. CASE-CENTERED CONSULTATION: LIFESTYLE ADAPTATIONS FOR DISABLED WIDOW

Models: Clinical or treatment, educational, behavioral models

Levels: Level I, case centered; Level II, educational or collegial

a. *Target:* Widow and son
b. *Goal:* Independence in home
c. *Preventive outcome:* Tertiary.

Laurie, an occupational therapy consultant specializing in community case management services, was referred by a colleague to the home of a disabled 55-year-old widow, Debbie. Debbie's husband, Ralph, had suddenly died, leaving Debbie without a caregiver. Debbie's relationship with her high school–aged son, 17-year-old Mark, was strained, and he was an unwilling participant in her care needs. One month after Ralph's death, Debbie acknowledged that she needed someone to help guide her and Mark so that they could develop a plan for life "after Ralph."

Laurie's initial consultation took place at Level I, *case-centered consultation*. She used her first visit with Debbie and Mark to initiate a collaborative relationship, assess the home environment, identify a time for Debbie's occupational therapy evaluation, and arrange a time to separately meet with Mark. During this initial meeting, Debbie shared her unusual case history. She had a rare form of Tay-Sachs disease, which gradually affected her ability to speak clearly, walk independently, and perform other vital daily living tasks. She crawled up and down the flight of stairs to her bedroom once per day. She had a walker and wheelchair available to her on both levels. Debbie had not driven for several years but still maintained her driver's license. During this first month since Ralph's death, responsibility for food shopping had been shared among members of Debbie's family and Mark. Debbie and Mark shared responsibility for household management tasks (e.g., cooking, cleaning). Finances were tight, limiting what could be allocated for consultation services and any necessary home adaptations.

It was agreed that Laurie would analyze all information gathered during the assessment process and put an initial report together so that all three of them could review and discuss it. She would meet separately with Debbie and Mark to discuss personal aspects of the report prior to discussing them in relation to any suggested family plan.

Laurie's analysis and initial recommendations were as follows:

• Bring Debbie's bedroom down to first floor, preferably use dining room space.
• Enlarge first-floor bathroom by adding a shower for Debbie.
• Create wheelchair-height work space in kitchen.
• Enroll Mark in school driver-education program, and arrange driver insurance coverage.
• Refer a professional tailor knowledgeable in clothing adaptation to work with Debbie.
• Present and review safe driver criteria to consider Debbie's abilities and safety.
• Develop weekly schedule of tasks Mark could assume to support family living needs.

Debbie, Mark, and Laurie reviewed these recommendations. Laurie referred three builders experienced in home modifications to meet with Debbie, and she selected one whose bid fit her budget. The modified bathroom allowed her to transform the dining room into her new bedroom. Kitchen modifications were put into a "Phase 2" category, as funds were low. Using a limited budget, clothing adaptations were accomplished by the tailor.

Driving was a central concern. Laurie drew upon her skills at Level II, *educational consultation*, to address Debbie's behavioral issues and desire to continue driving. Debbie acknowledged that she did not meet all criteria for safe driving, but she wanted to continue to drive. Ethically, Laurie could not support this decision and counseled Debbie to accept alternative means of transportation that were available in the community, arranging for Debbie to become enrolled in these community transportation programs. Debbie chose to stop further driving discussions with Laurie and ended the case consultation services after the home modifications had been accomplished.

CASE EXAMPLE 2. COMMUNITY CONSULTATION AND COLLABORATION: SCOUTING IN THE COMMUNITY

Models: Educational, collegial, process management, program development, systems

Levels: Level I, case centered; Level II, educational or collegial; Level III, program and administrative

a. *Targets:* Scout troop with special needs; county recreation department and staff; community-dwelling, at-risk older adults
b. *Goals:* Increased physical activity and socialization, expanded public awareness and use of county recreational environment
c. *Preventive outcomes:* Tertiary, secondary, and primary.

---

[1]The case examples in this chapter have been designed to reflect the consultation process.

Cathy, an occupational therapy consultant specializing in pediatric services, was asked by Mary, leader of the community junior scout troop for girls with special needs in grades 4–6, to help develop a scout community project. A new county park system had just been established, and Mary wanted the girls to create a community project that would help publicize the new park. She wanted the project to provide opportunities for more physical activity because obesity was a growing concern with these girls.

Cathy was glad to volunteer her time and expertise for this cause. She had recently attended an occupational therapy conference in which a presentation was given about a group walking program for individuals with mental health disabilities. The program encouraged walkers to take photographs of environments that appealed to them, write or record why they chose that spot, and describe what it meant to them. Some photographs were framed and displayed at a local coffee house. Concurrently, participant exercise levels increased and their awareness of local environments was enhanced.

The scouts in Mary's troop could participate in a similar program, and pictures could be part of the publicity campaign now under way at the recreation department. Cathy had worked with the county recreation and parks planner during another consultation and knew he was interested in supporting populations with special needs. Mary came up with a name for the program, Walking in Our New Park: A Picture-Perfect Opportunity for All. Cathy listened as Mary discussed the proposed project with her troop members and their parents. Although the project proposal was enthusiastically received by all concerned, a number of parents questioned how Mary would handle safety and physical endurance challenges that might occur. A parent committee was formed to consider these issues, and Cathy was identified as their resource.

Cathy provided an in-service for the parents, drawing from both case-centered and educational models of consultation. At the educational level, she shared detailed information regarding the park's safe design. At the case-centered level, she advised parents to consult with their family physicians to determine their daughters' physical capacity for park walks of up to a half-mile. The physician note would become part of the scout's back-up information that would be shared with the adults covering each session, should one of the girls need special attention.

One very concerned parent kept disrupting the meeting, claiming that such a project could endanger her daughter. Cathy used her process management skills to help the group calm the parent. It was suggested that the parent become one of the "helping parents" for the walking program. Participation in this role satisfied the parent's concerns. Once parent support and commit-

ment was ensured, Mary and Cathy met with staff at the recreation and parks department. The project proposal submitted was at Level III, program or administration consultation.

The project proposal included

- Scouts to be provided with pedometers, cameras, and recorders while walking once per week at park
- Funds to be provided for above equipment and picture prints
- Scouts to develop increased awareness of park environments, demonstrated in pictures and shared thoughts
- Scouts' safety and well-being planned in design of project.

The proposal outlined target outcomes, including

- Greater public visibility for the new park and its enjoyable environments
- Scout contribution to community service
- Public relations enhanced using scout photographs and narratives
- Scouts increase their physical fitness and well-being
- Increased scout awareness and advocacy for public support of new park.

This collaborative consultation effort was launched in early spring and culminated at the end of the school year with a showing of scout photographs and accompanying narratives at the central parks and recreation county office. Its success resulted in continuation of the scout walking program as part of the park and recreation department's annual calendar. The very positive results achieved by the scout program generated a new program targeting older adults called Leisurely Walks With Your Camera, offered by the parks and recreation department as part of its community adult education programming.

This time-limited community consultation shows tertiary, secondary, and primary preventive outcomes. Tertiary outcomes are noted with student weight loss and endurance for activity. Secondary outcomes were achieved when scouts and parents committed to continuation of the walking program as part of the park's annual calendar. A primary outcome to consider is the park's offer of a new walking program for older adults living in the community seeking out such programs to address physical exercise needs.

Case Example 3. High School Student Transition to Community: Secondary Prevention Consultation

Models: Clinical, educational, collegial, behavioral, program development, social action, and systems

(continued)

Case Examples *(cont.)*

Levels: Level I, case centered; Level III, program and administrative

a. *Target:* Student, education team, job coach, parents, community worksite staff
b. *Goal:* Student assessment followed by education of school team and parents; move into community programming as secondary prevention efforts
c. *Preventive outcomes:* Tertiary and secondary.

Jimmy, a student in special education with significant disabilities, was in his last year of high school. He would soon transition from a supportive and familiar high school to a complex and variable inner-city community environment. Occupational therapy intervention services had been provided during Jimmy's elementary educational program. When the individualized educational plan preliminary team met at the beginning of his senior year of high school, the team learned that a new service was available. An occupational therapy consultant had been assigned at the school to help support team transition efforts for students with significant disabilities.

Jimmy was referred for occupational therapy assessment at Level I, case-centered consultation. This student's significant disabilities included Down syndrome and impairments in coordination, communication, motor skills, social skills, organization, and task completion. The goal of the transition plan was placement in a work-training program or a sheltered workshop. Using the clinical model, the consultant assessed Jimmy's problems as they related to transition needs. Performance of school prevocational activities and job sample tasks taken from the community work-training program as well as the related physical and social environments and performance contexts were considered. Recommendations to the team focused on Jimmy's need for structure, materials organization, visual cues, and use of adaptations to facilitate correct sequencing of tasks. To help implement assessment recommendations and move to Level II, educational or collegial services, the consultant provided a slide presentation for the team and parents of transitioning students. Her goal was to build acceptance for the more limited indirect service model and its greater involvement with community programming and placement of transitioning students.

The presentation included a graphic that illustrated the multiple roles and functions of occupational therapy and delineated varied services and activities available to the team and student (i.e., client; see Figure 33.3). The interactive discussion that followed this presentation helped build support for the consultant's active participation as a helper and facilitator on Jimmy's team.

The consultant's initial role on the team was to develop problem-solving strategies when Jimmy's organizational difficulties impeded his productivity in simulated work activities. Through the consultant's analysis and collaboration with the trainer on site, adaptive strategies using a picture exchange communication (PEC) task sequence and cut-out jig section shapes resolved the problem.

As trainer or mentor to Jimmy's job coach, the consultant prepared and modeled a protocol for his community training that included giving him structured, predictable activities and opportunities for practicing work-related social skills (e.g., hand shake, morning greeting). In the community training site, difficulties arose when Jimmy continuously took tools or supplies from neighboring workers. Negative staff attitudes arose, causing difficulties for both the student and the job coach. The consultant did an environmental and work context analysis and found that individual work stations were crowded and poorly defined. Materials needed for assemblies were not separated by station, and structure for assembly of units was not in place. The consultant, job coach, and worksite manager then met and established station modifications to improve productivity and task organization. These strategies also helped extinguish staff behaviors that had contributed to negativity in the work environment.

Level III, program and administration consultation, came into play as actual community transition approached. The reality of limited occupational placement options became clear for the educational team, parents, and Jimmy's circle of support. The consultant used principles of social action to help the team develop advocacy-oriented approaches to further the establishment of community work-training programs. The consultant shared program development examples from other areas of the state and successful strategies used to support these programs to generate their thinking and help develop strategies for system change.

As his graduation date approached, Jimmy was gaining the skill sets necessary for employment at a structured work site. However, limited openings and decreased funding prevented placement. Jimmy was entered on the state's worksite waiting list. Placement became a profound concern for Jimmy's parents, who decided to use the program development information provided by the consultant as part of their advocacy plan. To support this advocacy effort in collaboration with the parents, the consultant gathered the following information to share with the team and parents:

- Federal, state, local funding information for potential qualification for work-training programs
- Resources to obtain information and regulations governing establishment of sites

- Community sites that had previously accepted student workers with severe disabilities
- Identification of advocacy-oriented community groups speaking out on this issue
- State and national Web sites discussing the need for such programs
- Opportunities for students with severe disabilities in community volunteer roles
- State agency contact to call regarding placement of Jimmy
- Points to stress when communicating with state agencies.

The advocacy efforts of the consultant, educational team, parents, and circle of support concluded with Jimmy's assignment at a work-training site 1 month after he was placed on the state waiting list. His parents had been told such placement might take an entire year to accomplish.

This case example illustrates the importance of the consultant's knowledge and understanding of regulations and laws related to the consultation case. In this situation, although the education law mandates transition services, there is no mandate for post-secondary programming in the community. Occupational therapy was an integral part of Jimmy's transition from high school to post-secondary occupational placement. In Jimmy's case, the placement was work related, but the same process would be appropriate for other community-based organizations. Additionally, this case example illustrates a targeted outcome at the secondary level of preventive outcomes, based on teacher, parent, and community education.

CASE EXAMPLE 4. SYSTEM-WIDE COMMUNITY PRIMARY PREVENTION CONSULTATION

Models: Educational, collegial, behavioral, process management, program development, organizational development, social action, and systems
Levels: Level II, educational; Level III, program and administrative

a. *Target:* Program director, volunteers, children, principal, school district administrators, and community agency planners
b. *Goal:* Initially to reduce disruptive behavior at school; progressed to develop school and community primary prevention programs
c. *Preventive outcomes:* Secondary and primary.

Two occupational therapy consultants, who were members of a community mental health school consultation team, were asked to assess a problem in a local elementary school resulting from overcrowding in classrooms and tensions on the playground at recess. An influx of new residents in the neighborhood had recently arrived to work in a nearby factory. Children from these

families were enrolled in the school that previously had been populated by predominately White, middle-class families, mainly with academic jobs at a nearby university. The new families were predominately Black, from a lower socioeconomic and educational level and in blue-collar jobs. The integration of these new children into the school resulted in severe overcrowding—an immediate problem for the teachers. In addition, tensions had built up between the adults in the two groups of residents, which then spilled over to relationships among the children. Considerable fighting, name-calling, shoving, and general chaos occurred on the playground at recess.

One woman was hired to coordinate volunteers to help in the lunchroom, another site of tensions, and on the playground. The volunteers were mostly mothers from the community, with no particular training in organization or working with groups. The coordinator and the volunteers were having little success in stemming the escalating altercations among the children.

The occupational therapy consultants initially were asked to provide in-service training regarding skill building and understanding of group behaviors, using a Level III, educational model of consultation, but it became apparent the entire environment, including the community neighborhood with its changing social context and new cultural values and mores, needed to be analyzed. Consultants reviewed the situation in the school system and the effect the disruptive behaviors were having on the teachers, lunchroom staff, and the children.

The occupational therapy consultants were external to the school system and initially regarded with some skepticism and even hostility by some of the school personnel. As "outsiders" to the system, the occupational therapists attempted to gain the trust and respect of the staff by volunteering to help at lunch and on the playground, distributing milk cartons at the children's lunch period, and organizing games at recess. Over time, the consultants developed a strong collegial relationship with the coordinator of the volunteers, the volunteer mothers, and the school staff.

The teachers were overwhelmed by the hyperactivity and distractibility of the children when they came in from the chaotic recess period. The consultants realized that the children needed more structure to ease the free-floating anxieties that had built up. Recess activities were planned with the volunteers that included both outdoor active games and quiet, indoor activities. Children rotated among the activities every other day, choosing what they wanted to do for recess. Suggestions also were made to physically reorganize the classrooms from the experimental "open classroom without walls," which was conducive to the children distractively wandering about the room, to individual "cubbies" where the children could retreat

(continued)

Case Examples *(cont.)*

peacefully to do their schoolwork. Structured, age-appropriate activities and changes in the classroom had an amazingly quieting effect for children and staff alike. The teachers and parents were very supportive of the changes and the children seemed happier, with friendly relationships beginning between the old and new children. The consultants had progressed from the initial educational model to a collegial model that allowed behavioral and process management models to develop. The activities and changes suggested by the consultants were based on their professional beliefs in the power of occupations, as stated in the *Framework–II*: "Occupational therapy is founded on an understanding that engaging in occupations structures everyday life and contributes to health and well-being" (AOTA, 2008, p. 628).

A new parent–teacher committee was formed, with one of the more vocal, "take charge" mothers from the new neighborhood members elected as president. The occupational therapy consultants were asked to help develop another ongoing activity program for an after-school program. The consultants engaged the children in suggesting ideas for activities, and the program expanded to include arts and crafts, cooking, a reading program in the school library, and team games at recess and after school. The program became so successful that the principal of the new elementary school being built to accommodate the population increase asked the consultants to work with him to develop a similar program for his school.

The neighborhood gradually came together as a cohesive yet diversified community. Community leaders appreciated the program planning in the schools and saw a need to develop some community-wide activities to address issues of common interest. The occupational therapy consultants were asked to help with the organization and development of a community program for adults and teens that included educational, recreational, and skill development activities such as housing and relocation information, career advancement information, financial advice, a Boys and Girls Club, a babysitting skills class, prevocational classes, and several recreational activities for all levels and ages. The consultants involved

occupational therapy students doing their mental health fieldwork to help coordinate some of the recreational and skill development activities. These community activities reflected the cultural values and interests of this population and provided the necessary structure to living harmoniously in a culturally, economically, and educationally diverse neighborhood.

The occupational therapy consultants had been instrumental in gaining the support of the school board and district superintendent, the community leaders, local social agencies, and professors in the school of education and department of psychology at the nearby university. This community effort even received positive feedback from the local media.

The initial consultation progressed to a social action model in which the consultants were advocates to facilitate social change in the community. Eventually, the consultation progressed to the overall system-centered model on the basis of the specific values and culture of this population, and the main focus of the consultation shifted to primary prevention. Additionally, concepts of occupational justice, diversity, and advocacy were important components of the occupational therapy consultants' involvement in what became a 5-year community and system-wide project. The *Framework–II* (AOTA, 2008) reinforces the work of these consultants:

> Occupational therapy practitioners recognize that health is supported and maintained when clients are able to engage in occupations and activities that allow desired or needed participation in home, school, workplace, and community life. Thus, occupational therapy practitioners are concerned not only with occupations but also the complexity of factors that empower and make possible clients' engagement and participation in positive health-promoting occupations. (p. 629)

This system-wide, community primary prevention consultation exemplifies how occupational therapy practitioners using consultation concepts and the development of collaborative relationships built on mutual trust could effect positive, health promoting change in the entire community.

❖ Learning Activities

The teacher of the concepts and process of consultation should allow two sessions of 2–3 hours each to cover the material in this chapter. If students are doing independent projects, especially community-based projects, they could chose to form consultation activity groups of 3–5 people, based on their project groups, for the exercises below.

The student groups can complete the following activities in approximately 20 minutes each, with time allowed for feedback from each group to the whole class. If students do not have any projects of their own suitable for the activities, the teacher could develop some hypothetical cases, assign them to groups of 3–5 students, and each group can report back to the class.

Examples of hypothetical cases:

Group A: Acute care
A facility is downsizing and administration is reassessing its service-delivery patterns, including the need for continued occupational therapy and physical therapy services.

Group B: Long-term care
A facility has had a recent influx of younger people with traumatic brain injury.

Group C: Local school
Students with special needs, previously in one school, are now to be placed in schools closest to their homes, and emphasis is to be on inclusion.

Group D: Industry
A large shipping company has had a significant increase in extended worker sick leave due to recent employee back and hand injuries.

Group E: Community agency program
A community agency program has recently received funding for employment and training of young adults recovering from substance abuse dependency.

Group F: School system
A school district is opening a new program for children with multiple disabilities to attend classes part of the day and spend the other part in self-contained classrooms.

Group G: Rehabilitation
A private rehabilitation clinic is restructuring the business to include hand therapy and must consider adding more therapists to handle increased client load.

1. **Experiential Group Exercise: Environmental and Systems Analysis**
   Purpose: To demonstrate the importance of the environmental and systems analysis and practice performing one.
   Use assigned case descriptions, or choose your own project.
   Small group assignment: Choose a recorder and a reporter from the group. (Allow 20 minutes to complete the exercise.)

   - Develop a case scenario based on your project or hypothetical setting.
   - Perform an *environment and systems analysis* of the consultative system.
   - Identify the *internal* and *external* factors that affect the system using the environmental and systems analysis with the 5 different environments described in the chapter.
   - Report back (2 minutes for each group):
     - Program description (scenario group develops)

   - Describe the environmental effects of the consultation experience, including the 5 environments (i.e., human, micro, macro, natural, physical).

2. **Experiential Group Exercise: Consultation Approaches**
   Purpose: To simulate consultation experiences that emphasize the basic concepts of consultation.
   Use assigned case descriptions, or choose your own project.
   Small group assignment: Choose a recorder and a reporter from the group. (Allow 20 minutes to complete the exercise.)

   - Describe a case scenario on the basis of your setting (use scenario developed in Learning Activity 1).
   - Determine the consultative approach(s) based on the theoretical models.
   - Determine the level(s) of consultation and levels of preventive outcomes.
   - Report back (2 minutes for each group):
     - Program description (scenario group developed)
     - Model(s) of consultation chosen
     - Level(s) of consultation and levels of preventive outcomes desired.

3. **Experiential Group Exercise: Role of the Consultant**
   Purpose: To enhance understanding of the role of the consultant, including whether the consultant is internal or external to the organization.
   Use hypothetical case descriptions or students' own group projects (continue the scenario developed in Learning Activity 1).
   Small group assignment: Choose a recorder and a reporter from the group. (Allow 20 minutes to complete the exercise.)

   - Use the case scenario previously developed and build on it as necessary.
   - Identify the role(s) of the consultant appropriate for your system.
   - Discuss the functions of this consultant's role within your organization.
   - Determine whether the consultant is *internal* or *external* to the organization.
   - Determine the advantages and disadvantages to the consultant's role on the basis of whether the consultant is internal or external to the organization.
   - Report back (2 minutes for each group):
     - Briefly review the scenario developed and expanded by group.
     - Identify the role(s) of the consultant.
     - Discuss the advantages or disadvantages of the role in your organization.

4. **Experiential Group Exercise: Consultation Process**
   Purpose: To enhance understanding of the consultation process regardless of setting, emphasizing the basic steps and process of consultation.
   Use hypothetical case descriptions or students' own group projects (expand the scenario developed in Learning Activity 1).

Small group assignment: Choose a recorder and a reporter from the group. (Allow 20 minutes to complete the exercise.)

- Use the case scenario previously developed and build on it as necessary.
- Identify the type of *entry* appropriate for your system.
- Discuss the *establishment of trust* within your client system.
- Determine the data collection methodology, evaluation techniques, and feedback strategies.
- Determine when and if *termination* is appropriate and how the consultant terminates.
- Report back to the class (allow 2 minutes for each group):
  - Review briefly the scenario developed and expanded by group.
  - Identify the type of entry.
  - Discuss the establishment of trust.
  - Present the data collection, evaluation methodology, feedback strategies.
  - Discuss the issue of termination.

5. Experiential Group Exercise: Emerging Roles

Purpose: To enhance understanding of the potential for consultation activities in new or expanded occupational therapy practice settings. AOTA's *Centennial Vision* (AOTA, 2007) emphasizes emerging roles in the profession, and many are especially conducive to consultation approaches.

Students develop hypothetical case descriptions that reflect the emerging practice arenas, especially in community-based settings.

Small group assignment: Choose a recorder and a reporter from the group. (Allow 20 minutes to complete the exercise.)

- Build a case scenario that has a potential for consultation activities.
- Develop a brief "statement of intent" that could be used for the prospective consultation proposal.
- Discuss the advantages of a consultation approach to this setting and identify the specific models of consultation that might be used.
- Determine how the evaluation report will reinforce evidence-based practice.
- Report back to the class (allow 2 minutes for each group):
  - Briefly review the scenario developed by the group.
  - Identify the advantages of a consultation approach in this setting.
  - Discuss how a proposal could be presented to the prospective client (e.g., initial statement of intent, followed by a full proposal or business plan).
  - Discuss the issue of evaluation and evidence-based practice in consultation.

Note. Learning activities created by Evelyn Jaffe and Cynthia Epstein for classroom and workshop use. Copyright © 2010. Used with permission.

✓ Multiple-Choice Questions

1. Which of the following statements is true regarding the client in a consultation?
   a. The client is the person who gives the consulting.
   b. The client is the recipient of the consultation.
   c. The client is responsible for helping the consultant.
   d. B and C.
2. The consultant is responsible for doing which of the following?
   a. Developing the intervention plan.
   b. Solving the issue or problem.
   c. Evaluating the consultation intervention.
   d. A and C.
3. *Consultation* may best be defined as
   a. An indirect intervention to help solve a problem.
   b. The act of preventing future problems.
   c. A facilitative process.
   d. All of the above.
4. Which of the following is an essential component of consultation?
   a. Developing mutual trust.
   b. Creating a secret bond.
   c. Finding solutions.
   d. All of the above.

5. Which of the following statements is true of an environment and systems analysis?
   a. It is the responsibility of the client.
   b. It helps define the consultation frame of reference.
   c. It is controlled by the Environmental Protection Agency.
   d. A and B.
6. Analysis of the structure and policies of the organization is an example of which type of occupational therapy consultation?
   a. Administrative model of consultation.
   b. Systems model of consultation.
   c. Organizational development model of consultation.
   d. All of the above.
7. Which level of consultation does the consultant analyzing organizational structure and policies provide?
   a. Level I.
   b. Level II.
   c. Level III.
   d. B and C.
8. Which level of preventive outcomes can be expected from an analysis of organizational structure and policies?
   a. Primary.
   b. Secondary.

c. Tertiary.

d. B and C.

9. Which component do the roles of administrator, manager, supervisor, and consultant have in common?

a. They all have responsibility for decision making.

b. They all have ultimate authority.

c. They all are an indirect service.

d. All of the above.

10. The *ecological perspective* of consultation refers to

a. The impact on earth, air, and water.

b. The respect for the dignity and rights of plants and animals.

c. The holistic approach taking into account all environmental influences.

d. All of the above.

11. The consultant may assume many roles during the course of the consultation, including which of the following?

a. Trainer.

b. Decision maker.

c. Problem solver.

d. All of the above.

12. Which of the following is 1 of the 8 steps in the process of consultation?

a. Negotiating a contract.

b. Marketing services.

c. Setting up the practice.

d. All of the above.

13. In the course of the consultation process, the consultant must do which of the following?

a. Provide constant feedback.

b. Determine evaluation procedures.

c. Provide resolution of the issue.

d. A and B.

14. Which of the following is true of the external consultant?

a. He or she is an employee outside of the department in which he or she is consulting.

b. He or she is an independent, contracted agent.

c. He or she brings a fresh, objective perspective.

d. B and C.

15. Which of the following is true of the internal consultant?

a. He or she usually understands the organization's corporate culture.

b. He or she is an integral part of the system.

c. He or she has prior knowledge of the strengths and weaknesses of the organization.

d. All of the above.

16. To market services, consultants should do which of the following?

a. Use promotional tools.

b. Engage in networking activities.

c. Do market research.

d. All of the above.

17. Which of the following could be considered an emerging community consultation environment?

a. Insurance companies.

b. Hospital systems.

c. Architectural firms.

d. A and C.

18. To own and operate a consultation practice, the occupational therapy professional must do which of the following?

a. Hire a tax accountant.

b. Develop a business plan.

c. Obtain a bank loan.

d. All of the above.

19. Which of the following is required to establish a consultation business?

a. Tolerating risk.

b. Opening a business office.

c. Creating business cards.

d. All of the above.

20. The successful consultant must devote time, energy, and money to which of the following important activities?

a. Developing a Web site.

b. Educating potential client organizations and populations.

c. Establishing an office.

d. A and C.

References

Accreditation Council for Occupational Therapy Education. (2007). Accreditation standards for a master's-degree-level educational program for the occupational therapist. *American Journal of Occupational Therapy, 61,* 652–661.

American Occupational Therapy Association. (2001). Occupational therapy in the promotion of health and the prevention of disease and disability statement. *American Journal of Occupational Therapy, 55,* 656–660.

American Occupational Therapy Association. (2002). Occupational therapy practice framework: Domain and process. *American Journal of Occupational Therapy, 56,* 609–639.

American Occupational Therapy Association. (2007). AOTA's *Centennial Vision* and executive summary. *American Journal of Occupational Therapy, 61,* 613–614.

American Occupational Therapy Association. (2008). Occupational therapy practice framework: Domain and process (2nd ed.). *American Journal of Occupational Therapy, 62,* 625–683.

American Occupational Therapy Association. (2009). *President Obama signs the American Recovery and Reinvestment Act* [Legislative update]. Retrieved February 22, 2009, from http://capwiz.com/aota/issues/alert

American Occupational Therapy Association. (2010). Occupational therapy code of ethics and ethics standards (2010). *American Journal of Occupational Therapy, 64.*

American Recovery and Investment Act of 2009, Pub. L. 111-5.

Americans with Disabilities Act Amendment Act of 2008, Pub. L. 110–325.

Andersen, K. (2009, April 6). Essay: The reset. *TIME Magazine*, pp. 32–38.

Autism Speaks. (2008). *Science news: 2008 IMFAR shows progress in all areas of autism research.* Retrieved July 10, 2008, from http://www.autismspeaks.org/science/science_news/imfar_2008_recap.php

Bayona, C. L., McDougall, J., Tucker, M. A., Nichols, M., & Mandich, A. (2006). School-based occupational therapy for children with fine motor difficulties: Evaluating functional outcomes and fidelity of services. *Physical and Occupational Therapy in Pediatrics, 26*(3), 89–110.

Bender, M., & Davidson, D. (2002). Freedom through technology. *Technology Special Interest Section Quarterly, 12*(1), 1, 2, 4.

Best, K., Noblitt, M., Synold, S., & Hughes, B. (2001). What are you fit for? Emerging practice areas for occupational therapists. *Advance for Occupational Therapy Practitioners, 17*(15), 30–33.

Biech, E. (2007). *The business of consulting: The basics and beyond* (2nd ed.). San Francisco: Pfeiffer.

Blakeney, A. B., & Marshall, A. (2009). Water quality, health, and human occupations. *American Journal of Occupational Therapy, 63,* 46–57.

Brachtesende, A. (2005). Careers: The evolution of an enterprise. *OT Practice, 10*(1), 7–8.

Braveman, B., & Bass-Haugen, J. D. (2009). From the Desks of the Guest Editors—Social justice and health disparities: An evolving discourse in occupational therapy research and intervention. *American Journal of Occupational Therapy, 63,* 7–12.

Centers for Disease Control and Prevention. (2009). *Autism information center: Autism spectrum disorders overview.* Retrieved March 31, 2009, from http://www.cdc.gov/ncbdd/autism/overview.htm

Christiansen, C. (2007, April). *Imagine a world different than the one you now inhabit.* Paper presented at the AOTA Annual Conference & Expo, St. Louis, MO.

Dettmer, P., Dyck, N., & Thurston, L. (1999). *Consultation, collaboration, and teamwork for students with special needs* (3rd ed.). Boston: Allyn & Bacon.

Diffendal, J. (2000, August 28). Community re-entry: Blazing new trails. *Advance for Occupational Therapy Practitioners,* pp. 10–11.

Doherty, R. F. (2009). Ethical decision making in occupational therapy practice. In E. B. Crepeau, E. S. Cohn, & B. A. B. Schell (Eds.), *Willard and Spackman's occupational therapy* (11th ed., pp. 274–285). Philadelphia: Lippincott Williams & Wilkins.

Dunn, W. (2000). *Best practice occupational therapy in community service with children and families.* Thorofare, NJ: Slack.

Dunn, W. (2006). *Sensory Profile school companion.* San Antonio, TX: Harcourt Assessment.

Dunn, W., Brown, C., & McGuigan, A. (1994). The ecology of human performance: A framework for considering the effect of context. *American Journal of Occupational Therapy, 48,* 595–607.

Epstein, C. F. (1992a). Developing a consultation practice. In E. G. Jaffe & C. F. Epstein (Eds.), *Occupational therapy consultation: Theory, principles, and practice* (pp. 634–649). St. Louis, MO: Mosby/Year Book.

Epstein, C. F. (1992b). Marketing: A continuous process. In E. G. Jaffe & C. F. Epstein (Eds.), *Occupational therapy consultation: Theory, principles, and practice* (pp. 650–674). St. Louis, MO: Mosby/Year Book.

Epstein, C. F., & Gardner, C. (2007). Developmental disabilities community-based practice: Widening our focus. *OT Practice, 12*(21), CE1–CE7.

Epstein, C., Gardner, C., & Deotte, P. (2004). Adults with developmental disabilities benefit from community consultation services. *OT Practice, 9*(4), 11–15.

Epstein, C. F., & Jaffe, E.G (2003). Consultation: Collaborative interventions for change. In G. L. McCormack, E. G. Jaffe, & M. Goodman-Lavey (Eds.), *The occupational therapy manager* (4th ed., 259–286). Bethesda, MD: AOTA Press.

Fielding, J. (2009). *Report of secretary: Advisory committee on health promotion and disease prevention objectives for 2020.* Retrieved March 31, 2009, from http://www.healthypeople.gov/hp2020/default.asp

Grossman, J. (1977). Preventive health care and community programming (nationally speaking).

Gupta, J., & Walloch, C. (2006). Process of infusing social justice into the *Practice Framework:* A case study. *OT Practice, 11*(15), CE1–CE7.

Hanft, B., & Shepherd, J. (Eds.). (2008). *Collaborating for student success: A guide for school-based occupational therapy.* Bethesda, MD: AOTA Press.

Hoelscher, D., & Taylor, S. (2000). Ergonomics consultation: An opportunity for occupational therapists. *OT Practice, 5*(1), 16–18, 19.

Individuals with Disabilities Education Improvement Act of 2004, Pub. L. 108-446.

Jaffe, E. G. (1986). Prevention, "an idea whose time has come": The role of occupational therapy in disease prevention and health promotion. *American Journal of Occupational Therapy, 40,* 749–752.

Jaffe, E. G. (1989). Medical consumer education: Health promotion in the workplace. In J. A. Johnson & E. G. Jaffe (Eds.), *Occupational therapy: Program development for health promotion and preventive services.* Binghampton, NY: Haworth Press.

Jaffe, E. G. (1992a). Related theories: Challenges of the 1990s. In E. G. Jaffe & C. F. Epstein (Eds.), *Occupational therapy consultation: Theory, principles, and practice* (pp. 55–85). St. Louis, MO: Mosby/Year Book.

Jaffe, E. G. (1992b). A systems approach to community health promotion consultation: The occupational therapist as a change agent. In E. G. Jaffe & C. F. Epstein (Eds.), *Occupational therapy consultation: Theory, principles, and practice* (pp. 395–407). St. Louis, MO: Mosby/Year Book.

Jaffe, E. G. (1992c). Theoretical concepts of consultation. In E. G. Jaffe & C. F. Epstein (Eds.), *Occupational therapy consultation: Theory, principles, and practice* (pp. 15–54). St. Louis, MO: Mosby/Year Book.

Jaffe, E. G. (1996). Occupational therapy consultation in a managed care environment. *OT Practice, 1*(3), 26–31.

Jaffe, E. G., & Epstein, C. F. (1992a). Occupational therapy consultation practice: An overview. In E. G. Jaffe & C. F. Epstein (Eds.). *Occupational therapy consultation: Theory, principles, and practice* (pp. 167–187). St. Louis, MO: Mosby/Year Book.

Jaffe, E. G., & Epstein, C. F. (Eds.). (1992b). *Occupational therapy consultation: Theory, principles, and practice.* St. Louis, MO: Mosby/Year Book.

Jaffe, E. G., & Epstein, C. F. (1992c). Preparation for consultation. In E. G. Jaffe & C. F. Epstein (Eds.), *Occupational therapy consultation: Theory, principles, and practice* (pp. 118–134). St. Louis, MO: Mosby/Year Book.

Jaffe, E. G., & Epstein, C. F. (1992d). The process of consultation. In E. G. Jaffe & C. F. Epstein (Eds.), *Occupational therapy consultation: Theory, principles, and practice* (pp. 135–166). St. Louis, MO: Mosby/Year Book.

Jaffe, E. G., & Epstein, C. F. (2003). A consultative approach to occupational therapy practice. In E. B. Crepeau, E. S. Cohn, & B. A. B. Schell (Eds.), *Willard and Spackman's occupational therapy* (10th ed., pp. 937–949). Philadelphia: Lippincott Williams & Wilkins.

Johnson, J. A., & Jaffe, E. G. (Eds.). (1989). *Occupational therapy: Program development for health promotion and preventive services.* Binghampton, NY: Haworth Press.

Kielhofner, G., & Forsyth, K. (2002). Thinking with theory: A framework for therapeutic reasoning. In G. Kielhofner (Ed.), *Model of human occupation: Theory and application* (3rd ed., pp. 162–178). Baltimore: Lippincott Williams & Wilkins.

Kronenberg, F., Algado, S. S., & Pollard, N. (2005). *Occupational therapy without borders: Learning from the spirit of survivors.* Edinburgh, UK: Elsevier.

Lewin, K. (1951). *Field theory in social science.* New York: Harper & Row.

Lippitt, G., & Lippitt, R. (1986). *The consulting process in action* (2nd ed.). San Diego, CA: University Associates.

Long-Bellil, L., & Henry, A. D. (2009). Promoting employment for people with disabilities: Update on the Ticket to Work and Work Incentives Improvement Act. *OT Practice, 14*(7), CE1–CE7.

Maddox, G. L. (Ed.). (2001). *Encyclopedia of aging* (3rd ed.). New York: Springer.

Mann, W. (2001). Assistive technology and older adults. *OT Practice, 6*(10), 12–15.

McCormack, G. L., Jaffe, E. G., & Frey, W. (2003). New organizational perspectives. In G. L. McCormack, E. G. Jaffe, & M. L. Goodman-Lavey (Eds.), *The occupational therapy manager* (4th ed., pp. 85–126). Bethesda, MD: AOTA Press.

Medical News Today. (2009). *Senate Special Committee on Aging examines Alzheimer's Study Group report, hears testimony from high-profile advocates.* Retrieved March 31, 2009, from http://www.medicalnewstoday.com/articles/143927.php

Morris, A. L. (2009). Collaboration for accessibility and aging in place. *OT Practice, 14*(6), 14–17.

Moyers, P., & Dale, L. (2007). *The guide to occupational therapy practice* (2nd ed.). Bethesda, MD: AOTA Press.

National Institute of Mental Health. (2009). *NIMH and the stimulus package.* Retrieved March 3, 2009, from http:///www.nimh.nih.gov/about/director/index.shtml

Rainville, E. B., Cermak, S. A., & Murray, E. A. (1996). Supervision and consultation services for pediatric occupational therapists. *American Journal of Occupational Therapy, 50,* 725–731.

Richmond, T. (2003). Marketing. In G. L. McCormack, E. G. Jaffe, & M. Goodman-Lavey (Eds.), *The occupational therapy manager* (4th ed., pp. 177–192). Bethesda, MD: AOTA Press.

Roley, S. S., & Delany J. (2009). Improving the *Occupational Therapy Practice Framework: Domain and Process. OT Practice, 14*(2), 9–12.

Scaffa, M. E. (2001). *Occupational therapy in community-based practice settings.* Philadelphia: F. A. Davis.

Schkade, J. K., & Schultz, S. (2003). Occupational adaptation. In P. Kramer, J. Hinojosa, & C. Royeen (Eds.), *Perspectives in human occupation* (pp. 181–221). Philadelphia: Lippincott Williams & Wilkins.

Schultz, S. (2009). Theory of occupational adaptation. In E. B. Crepeau, E. S. Cohn, & B. A. B. Schell (Eds.), *Willard and Spackman's occupational therapy* (11th ed., pp. 462–475). Philadelphia: Lippincott Williams & Wilkins.

Scott, J. B. (2009). Consultation. In E. B. Crepeau, E. S. Cohn, & B. A. B. Schell (Eds.), *Willard and Spackman's occupational therapy* (11th ed., pp. 964–972). Philadelphia: Lippincott Williams & Wilkins.

Siebert, C. (2005). *Home modifications: Occupational therapy practice guidelines.* Bethesda, MD: AOTA Press.

Silverstein, R. (2002). *Final regulations implementing the Ticket to Work and Self-sufficiency Program (the Ticket to Work program).* Iowa City: Law, Health Policy & Disability Center, University of Iowa College of Law.

Swinth, Y. (Ed.). (2004). *Occupational therapy in school-based practice: Contemporary issues and trends* [Online Course]. Bethesda, MD: American Occupational Therapy Association.

Swinth, Y., & Mailloux, Z. (Eds). (2002, January 28). Addressing sensory processing in the schools. *OT Practice, 7*(2), 8–13.

Ticket to Work and Work Incentives Improvement Act of 1999, Pub. L. 106–170.

Townsend, E., & Wilcock, A. A. (2003). Occupational justice. In C. Christiansen & E. Townsend (Eds.), *Introduction to occupation: The art and science of living* (pp. 243–273). New York: Prentice Hall.

Ulschak, F. L., & SnowAntle, S. M. (1990). *Consultation skills for health care professionals.* San Francisco: Jossey-Bass.

U.S. Census Bureau. (2008). *Number of Americans with a disability reaches 54.4 million.* Retrieved December 22, 2008, from http://www.inclusiondaily.com/news/2008/red/1222a.html

Weiss, A. (2009). *Getting started in consulting* (3rd ed.). Hoboken, NJ: Wiley.

West, W. L. (1969). The growing importance of prevention. *American Journal of Occupational Therapy, 23,* 226.

Wilcock, A. A., & Townsend, E. (2009). Occupational justice. In E. B. Crepeau, E. S. Cohn, & B. A. B. Schell (Eds.), *Willard and Spackman's occupational therapy* (11th ed., pp. 192–199). Philadelphia: Lippincott Williams & Wilkins.

Wisdomquote.com. (n.d). *Advice.* Retrieved August 17, 2010, from http://www.wisdomquotes.com/topics/advice

Yerxa, E. J. (1980). Occupational therapy's role in creating a future climate of caring. *American Journal of Occupational Therapy, 34,* 529–534.

APPENDIX 33.A. CONSULTATION EVIDENCE TABLE

Topic	Subtopic	Evidence
Concepts of consultation	Levels of consultation Multiple roles Theoretical models	Epstein, C. F., & Gardner, C. (2007). Developmental disabilities community-based practice: Widening our focus. *OT Practice, 12*(21), CE1–CE7. Jaffe, E. G. (1992c). Theoretical concepts of consultation. In E. G. Jaffe & C. F. Epstein (Eds.), *Occupational therapy consultation: Theory, principles, and practice* (pp. 15–54). St. Louis, MO: Mosby/Year Book. Jaffe, E. G., & Epstein, C. F. (Eds). (1992b). *Occupational therapy consultation: Theory, principles, and practice.* St. Louis, MO: Mosby Year Book.
Process of consultation	4 stages, 8 basic steps	Bayona, C. L., McDougall, J., Tucker, M. A., Nichols, M., & Mandich, A. (2006). School-based occupational therapy for children with fine motor difficulties: Evaluating functional outcomes and fidelity of services. *Physical and Occupational Therapy in Pediatrics, 26*(3), 89–110. Epstein, C. F., & Jaffe, E. G. (2003). Consultation: Collaborative interventions for change. In G. L. McCormack, E. G. Jaffe, & M. Goodman-Lavey (Eds.), *The occupational therapy manager,* (4th ed., pp. 259–286). Bethesda, MD: AOTA Press. Jaffe, E. G., & Epstein, C.F. (1992d). The process of consultation. In E. G. Jaffe & C. F. Epstein (Eds.), *Occupational therapy consultation: Theory, principles, and practice* (pp. 135–166). St. Louis, MO: Mosby/Year Book.
Preparation for consultation	Knowledge, skills, and attributes	Epstein, C., Gardner, C., & Deotte, P. (2004) Adults with developmental disabilities benefit from community consultation services. *OT Practice, 9(4),* 11–15. Jaffe, E. G., & Epstein, C. F. (1992c). Preparation for consultation. In E. G. Jaffe & C. F. Epstein (Eds.), *Occupational therapy consultation: Theory, principles, and practice* (pp. 118–134). St. Louis, MO: Mosby/Year Book. Jaffe, E. G., & Epstein, C. F. (2003). A consultative approach to occupational therapy practice. In E. B. Crepeau, E. S. Cohn, & B. A. B. Schell (Eds.), *Willard and Spackman's occupational therapy* (10th ed., pp. 937–949). Philadelphia: Lippincott Williams & Wilkins.
Practice of consultation	Business concepts, marketing	Epstein, C. F. (1992a). Developing a consultation practice. In E. G. Jaffe & C. F. Epstein (Eds.), *Occupational therapy consultation: Theory, principles, and practice* (pp. 634–649). St. Louis, MO: Mosby/Year Book. Epstein, C. F. (1992b). Marketing: A continuous process In E. G. Jaffe & C. F. Epstein (Eds.). *Occupational therapy consultation: Theory, principles, and practice* (pp 650–674). St. Louis, MO: Mosby/Year Book. Richmond, T. (2003). Marketing. In G. L. McCormack, E. G. Jaffe, & M. Goodman-Lavey (Eds.), *The occupational therapy manager* (4th ed., pp. 177–192). Bethesda, MD: AOTA Press. Scaffa, M. E. (2001). *Occupational therapy in community-based practice settings.* Philadelphia: F. A. Davis. Scott, J. B. (2009). Consultation. In E. B. Crepeau, E. S. Cohn, & B. A. B. Schell (Eds.), *Willard and Spackman's occupational therapy* (11th ed., p. 964–972). Philadelphia: Lippincott Williams & Wilkins.

(continued)

APPENDIX 33.A. CONSULTATION EVIDENCE TABLE *(cont.)*

Topic	Subtopic	Evidence
Principles of prevention	Preventive outcomes	Jaffe, E. G. (1986). Prevention, "an idea whose time has come": The role of occupational therapy in disease prevention and health promotion. *American Journal of Occupational Therapy, 40,* 749–752. Jaffe, E. G. (1989). Medical consumer education: Health promotion in the workplace. In J. A. Johnson & E. G. Jaffe (Eds.), *Occupational therapy: Program development for health promotion and preventive services.* Binghampton, NY: Haworth Press. Jaffe, E. G., & Epstein, C. F. (1992a). Occupational therapy consultation practice: An overview. In E.G. Jaffe & C. F. Epstein (Eds.), *Occupational therapy consultation: Theory, principles, and practice* (pp. 167–187). St. Louis, MO: Mosby/Year Book. Johnson, J. A., & Jaffe, E. G. (Eds.). (1989). *Occupational therapy: Program development for health promotion and preventive services.* Binghampton, NY: Haworth Press.
Environment and systems analysis	Systems theory	American Occupational Therapy Association. (2008). Occupational therapy practice framework: Domain and process (2nd ed.). *American Journal of Occupational Therapy, 62,* 625–683. Jaffe, E. G. (1992a). Related theories: Challenges of the 1990s. In E.G. Jaffe & C. F. Epstein (Eds.), *Occupational therapy consultation: Theory, principles, and practice* (pp. 55–85). St. Louis, MO: Mosby/Year Book. Jaffe, E. G. (1992b). A systems approach to community health promotion consultation: The occupational therapist as a change agent. In E. G. Jaffe & C. F. Epstein (Eds.), *Occupational therapy consultation: Theory, principles, and practice* (pp. 395–407). St. Louis, MO: Mosby/Year Book. McCormack, G. L., Jaffe, E. G., & Frey, W. (2003). New organizational perspectives. In G. L. McCormack, E. G. Jaffe, & M. L. Goodman-Lavey (Eds.), *The occupational therapy manager* (4th ed., pp. 85–126). Bethesda, MD: AOTA Press.

34

Health Disparities in Practice and the Workplace: A Manager's Role in Ensuring Equitable Client Care

Diane L. Smith, PhD, OTR/L, FAOTA

❖ Key Terms and Concepts

Discrimination. Different treatment of others based solely on their membership in a socially distinct group or category, such as race, ethnicity, sex, religion, age, or disability.

Health disparity. Difference in the quality of health care related to race or ethnicity, gender, education or income, disability, geographic location, or sexual orientation that is not due to access-related factors or clinical needs.

Health literacy. The degree to which individuals have the capacity to obtain, process, and understand basic health information and services needed to make appropriate health decisions.

Justice. Concept that relates to issues of equity and fairness. *Deliberative justice* refers to fairness in conceptualizing and planning programs or services intended to benefit certain people. *Distributive justice* involves the allocation of property, control, or access to services.

Socioeconomic status. Location in the structure of society, typically determined by education, income, or occupational status, or some combination of these, that determine differential access to power, privilege, and desirable resources.

❖ Learning Objectives

After completing this chapter, you should be able to do the following:

- Describe the relationship of health and health care disparity to the ethical concept of justice.
- Understand the issues of health disparity and health care disparity as separate and intersecting concepts.
- Analyze the influence of health disparities and health care disparities on client care as part of the client's environmental context.

- Identify barriers to overcoming issues of health disparities and health care disparities in client care.
- Discuss strategies that occupational therapy practitioners can use to address disparity issues at the individual and community level.
- Understand the role of occupational therapy managers and practitioners as advocates for justice at the individual, local, state, and national level.

Occupational therapy managers are called on to ensure that all clients are treated in an equitable manner. Because of the focus of the profession, occupational therapists often interact with members of vulnerable populations, including those who are aging; have a disability; or are a member of a minority population based on race, ethnicity, or sexual orientation or a combination of these populations. Disparities in health and in health care access not only affect these clients' participation but also compromise their ability to obtain the occupational therapy services they need to engage in meaningful and purposeful activities important to health. To facilitate holistic intervention, it is important that managers and staff be aware of these disparities as a contextual influence on their clients' engagement. To fully understand this influence, it is first important to define *health disparity* and *health care disparity*.

DEFINITION OF HEALTH DISPARITY AND HEALTH CARE DISPARITY

Even as health systems, medical and other health professional programs, legislators, and others are paying increased attention to the problem of health disparities, no universally accepted definition of the issue exists. The Institute of Medicine has focused specifically on health care, defining *disparities* as "racial or ethnic differences in the quality of healthcare that are not due to access-related factors or clinical needs, preferences, and appropriateness of intervention" (Smedley, Stith, & Nelson, 2003, p. 31). The National Institutes of Health referred to "a population where there is significant disparity in the overall rate of disease incidence, prevalence, morbidity, mortality, or survival rates in the population as compared to the health status of the general population" (Harvard School of Public Health, Robert Wood Johnson Foundation, & ICR/International Communications Research, 2005, p. 1).

When considering health and health care disparities, one important definitional difference is whether *disparities* refers specifically to differences in health care or more broadly to differences in health. In this context, *health care* usually refers to access to or quality of services in the conventional Western medical care delivery system. *Health* refers to overall health status and outcomes related to a complex variety of influences and life experiences, including access to high-quality preventive and curative care as needed (Harvard School of Public Health et al., 2005). These two concepts are often inextricably linked, and therefore this chapter considers both.

DISPARITY AS PART OF THE ENVIRONMENTAL CONTEXT

According to the second edition of the *Occupational Therapy Practice Framework: Domain and Process* (*Framework–II;* American Occupational Therapy Association [AOTA], 2008), occupational therapists recognize that health is supported and maintained when individuals are able to engage in activities and occupations that allow desired or needed participation in home, school, workplace, and community life situations. When a client experiences a disparity in health or health care access, health is compromised both in the traditional sense of higher rates of disease but also in the broader sense of prevention of participation in meaningful and purposeful occupations. Therefore, concern regarding these disparities is within the domain of occupational therapy as engagement in occupation to support participation in context is the focus and targeted end objective of occupational therapy intervention. Finally, the issue of justice is discussed as a product of the intervention area of advocacy within the *Framework–II* (AOTA, 2008). The *Framework–II* defines advocacy as "Efforts directed toward promoting occupational justice and empowering clients to

seek and obtain resources to fully participate in their daily life occupations" (p. 654).

Occupational therapists also recognize that engagement in occupation occurs in a variety of contexts (cultural, physical, social, personal, temporal, spiritual, and virtual). They acknowledge that the individual's experience and performance cannot be understood or addressed without understanding the many contexts in which daily life occupations occur. Many of the disparities described in later sections will illustrate how context affects the experience of health disparities and health care disparities and, ultimately, participation in meaningful and purposeful occupations.

INFLUENCES ON HEALTH DISPARITIES: MODELS AND THEORIES

Ecological Model

The issue of what creates health disparities for the occupational therapy client population is complex. Describing the influences on health disparities requires examination of factors within and outside the individual that influence health behaviors and outcomes. A useful construct for such analysis is the ecological model (Meyers, 2007). Although the traditional ecological model focuses on behaviors, when applied to health disparities, this model enables an understanding of how these factors directly influence health status or outcomes themselves. Figure 34.1 illustrates the relationship among influences on health disparities: individual, interpersonal, organizations, community environment, and society/public policy.

The *individual* level includes a variety of factors that influence health, including personal characteristics that are immutable (e.g., race, age, biological gender, genetic profile) and characteristics that are potentially alterable with adequate support systems (e.g., socioeconomic factors such as education, income, wealth, and occupation; health-related behaviors; resources; and beliefs). This level represents both the individual as a whole and the characteristics of that individual that influence health.

The *interpersonal* level includes those first-line support systems for and influences on individuals, such as families, peers, and neighbors. These persons have opportunities to influence positively or negatively the potentially alterable individual characteristics that influence health and help establish community or cultural norms that influence health.

The *organizations* level includes persons in the immediate community who influence (and are influenced by) the individual and interpersonal levels, as well as the broader community environment level. These organizations may enable or discourage activities at the individual or community levels that support health.

The *community environment* level includes both the physical and the cultural characteristics of communities that

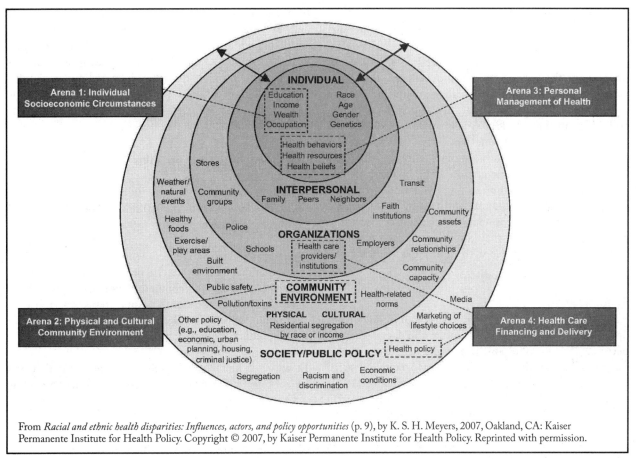

From *Racial and ethnic health disparities: Influences, actors, and policy opportunities* (p. 9), by K. S. H. Meyers, 2007, Oakland, CA: Kaiser Permanente Institute for Health Policy. Copyright © 2007, by Kaiser Permanente Institute for Health Policy. Reprinted with permission.

Figure 34.1. Landscape of influences on health disparities and arenas for policy action.

can affect the health of individuals. *Physical aspects* include factors with direct effects on health, including pollution or toxins and crime, as well as factors with indirect effects on health, such as public safety and crime, the built environment, the availability of health-supporting resources, and residential segregation. *Cultural aspects* include community relationships and capacity, economic inequality or concentration of poverty, and health-related norms and beliefs that support or discourage healthy behaviors and lifestyles.

Finally, the *social/public policy* level includes factors that influence health across multiple communities. This broad category includes policies or social circumstances that affect all of the inner circles. The focus in this model is on key policies or circumstances with broad general impact on health disparities, including health care policies, economic conditions, racism and discrimination, segregation, media, and marketing of lifestyle choices.

This chapter provides examples of all of these influences, some at multiple levels (e.g., socioeconomic status, disability). Because of the focus in occupational therapy on the whole person and contextual influences from the environment, occupational therapy services have the potential to address these influences on clients.

Occupational therapy managers need to ensure that staff are considering all of these influences. They need to be aware not only of each type of disparity but also of what influences contribute to the disparity and how they can best provide intervention.

Theories of Discrimination and Disparity

The practice of occupational therapy, with its focus on consideration of the whole person and the contexts that influence him or her, must take into consideration theories that demonstrate how clients may experience health and health care disparities, much in the same way as other theory directs practice. Three theories—simultaneous oppression, multiple other, and intersectionality theory—address how persons experience discrimination and disparities due to multiple issues. These theories focus on racism, sexism, and ableism but can be applied to all populations experiencing one or more types of discrimination. It is important to consider these theories in organizing treatment, as often the disparities that clients face are the result of multiple influences. An understanding of these theories will help occupational therapists approach evaluation, intervention, and program development.

Simultaneous Oppression

Stuart (1992) suggested that for those who are a member of a racial or ethnic minority and also have a disability, racism within disability is experienced as simultaneous oppression; the author cited the oppression that individuals of African descent experience daily in Western society, and the oppression that divides persons with disabilities from their African American able-bodied peers. Stuart identified three themes associated with simultaneous oppression: limited or no individuality and disability identity; resource discrimination (e.g., inequitable access to financial opportunities); and isolation within the African American community and family. Stuart argued that although White persons with disabilities also experience marginalization, they do so as accepted members of society. Not all people with disabilities embrace this theory, however.

Multiple Other

Vernon (1999) argued that the concept of simultaneous oppression is too simplistic to capture the day-to-day experience of those who possess multiple negatively labeled identities because it overlooks the importance of social class positioning. That is (to continue with Stuart's [1992] example), not all people with disabilities (Morris, 1991) or individuals of African descent (Miles, 1989) are in the same social class position. The author argued that the reality of being a multiple "other" results in shared alliances, as well as oppositional interests, between different groups. In other words, a person may be oppressed in one context and be the oppressor in another context. Thus, minorities with disabilities, women, gay men and lesbians, older people, and those from the working class all experience oppression singularly, multiply, and simultaneously, depending on the context (Vernon, 1996).

Intersection Theory

Intersection theory emphasizes the simultaneous production of race, class, and gender inequality, such that in any given situation, the unique contribution of one factor might be difficult to measure. This framework suggests that the content and implications of gender and race as socially constructed categories vary as a function of each other (Schultz & Mullings, 2006, p. 5).

At the micro level, advocates of this position contend that one of the pathways by which systems of inequality can influence health outcomes is through identity formation (Weber & Para-Medina, 2003). New identities (and therefore new challenges or new sets of stressors) are formed when multiple minority statuses (linked to limited resources and a different set of relationships) converge within a social space.

DISPARITY ISSUES

Several overarching issues influence the role of occupational therapy in addressing the disparities vulnerable populations face with regard to health and health care delivery—the ethical concept of beneficence, changing client demographics, and provider demographics. Awareness of these issues can help occupational therapists strategize with their clients how to best address and reduce the disparities clients experience, thus increasing engagement and participation in meaningful and purposeful activities and improving health.

Health Disparities and the Ethical Concept of Social Justice

According to the *Occupational Therapy Code of Ethics and Ethics Standards,* (AOTA, 2010), under the subsection regarding social justice, practitioners are obligated to

> provide services that reflect on understanding of how occupational therapy service delivery can be affected by factors such as economic status, age, ethnicity, race, geography, disability, marital status, sexual orientation, gender, gender identity, religion, culture, and political affiliation.

Therefore, it is managers' responsibility to ensure that staff are abiding by the professional code of ethics, providing services in an equitable manner, and therefore helping reduce disparity.

Changing Demographics of Client Populations

Because the U.S. population is becoming more diverse, it is increasingly important to address health disparities or these disparities will continue to widen. Between 1980 and 2000 the Asian American population tripled, the Hispanic population doubled, the American Indian population increased 62%, and the African American population increased 31%, while the White population remained stable (U.S. Census Bureau, 2004b). From 2000 to 2050, both the Asian American and Hispanic populations are expected to triple, and the overall U.S. population is expected to be 50% non-White (U.S. Census Bureau, 2004a). As of 2004, four states—Texas, California, New Mexico, and Hawaii—are already "minority–majority" (i.e., minority racial groups make up the majority of the population: 50%, 56%, 57%, and 77%, respectively). Currently, 100 million Americans, or 1 out of 3 individuals, are non-White.

The future demographic trends of other populations are more difficult to measure. For example, *disability* is defined differently depending on who is conducting the measurement or making the distinction. According to the American Community Survey conducted in 2005 by the U.S. Census Bureau (2007), an estimated 12.8% (22,295,000) of noninstitutionalized men and women 21 to 64 years of age, regardless of race, ethnicity, or education level, reported a disability. (Data are limited to the true numbers in the household population and exclude the population living in institutions, college dormitories, and other group quarters.) Because of the limitations in demographic measurement, it is difficult to predict future trends. Given the increasing age of the population and continued medical advances for those with health insurance, however, it can be assumed that this population with a disability will also increase in size.

The demographics of the lesbian, gay, bisexual, and transexual (LGBT) population are complicated to measure for several reasons, making projections difficult. A 1992 National Health and Social Life survey (Laumann, Gagnon, Michael, & Michaels, 1995) estimated the prevalence of homosexuality at 15% for women and 24% for men. Another major U.S. study (Sell, Wells, & Wypij, 1995) on a large representative sample ages 18 to 59 revealed that 2.8% of men and 1.4% of women reported a homosexual orientation and that 9% of men and 5% of women had had at least one homosexual experience after puberty. This is likely to be a low estimate, as barriers exist in collecting the information regarding disparities. For example, 16 states in the United States have sodomy laws, which criminalize homosexuality and are used as a means to deny jobs, child custody, or participation in the political process. As a result, gay men or women may be reluctant to self-disclose or honestly report their behaviors when seeking health care in those states (Lambda Legal Defense and Education Fund, 1999). Occupational therapists should also consider the disparities faced by an aging population. By the year 2030, 1 of every 5 Americans will be 65 years of age or older, causing a tremendous impact on health care and social systems and on occupational therapy practice. According to the Centers for Disease Control and Prevention (CDC & Merck Company Foundation, 2007), health care costs for persons in developed countries who are older than 65 years of age are three to five times greater than the costs for those who are younger.

Provider Demographics

Data on the race and ethnicity of health care providers show they are not as diverse as the populations they serve (Baicker, Chandra, & Skinner, 2005). For example, White and Asian Americans are overrepresented in the physician population. White Americans comprise 69% of the U.S. population and 74% of the physician population. Asian Americans comprise nearly 4% of the U.S. population and 15% of the physician population. Hispanics, African Americans, Native Hawaiians and Other Pacific Islanders, and American Indian/Alaska Natives are underrepresented in the U.S. physician population (Sullivan Commission on Diversity in the Healthcare Workforce, 2004).

Occupational therapists are primarily female (95%) and White (72%). AOTA looked at ethnicity among their membership in 2002 (Palmer, 2003). Out of 33,003 members, 20% did not list ethnic origin. Of those who did, 1.9% were African American, 0.2% were American Indian, 3.3% were Asian, 0.3% were Asian American, 1.5% were Hispanic/Latino/Latina, 0.2% were multiracial, 0.8% were another category, and 71.9% were White. Data regarding disability status and sexual orientation were not gathered.

A similar disconnect in patient–provider demographics exists in mental health services. Low mental health treatment rates in minority populations may be related to poor minority representation in the health care workforce (American Medical Association, 2005; Substance Abuse and Mental Health Services Administration, 2004) and even poorer representation in the mental health care workforce (Table 34.1). Disparities in patient–provider demographics also likely contribute to the inadequate representations of minorities in research, including important clinical trials. The occupational therapy workforce has not been examined for minority representation within mental health specifically; this is an important practice area for occupational therapy, and data are needed.

GROUPS VULNERABLE TO DISPARITIES

Occupational therapy clients who are members of vulnerable populations face possible health disparities and health care disparities. Because clients may belong to more than one vulnerable group, statistics on disparities are often not "clean" or linear but rather are complex. At times it is difficult to separate influences (e.g., race/ethnicity,

Table 34.1. Percentage of U.S. Mental Health Care Workforce According to Race or Ethnicity

Race	Total U.S. Population	Physicians	Psychiatrists	Psychologists	Social Workers
White	67.0	77.0	81.0	93.0	92.0
Hispanic	14.0	4.0	5.0	3.0	3.0
Black	13.0	5.0	3.0	2.0	4.0
Asian	5.0	14.0	11.0	2.0	1.0
American Indian/Alaska Native	1.5	0.1	0.1	0.3	0.2

Sources. American Medical Association (2005); Substance Abuse and Mental Health Services Administration (2004).

socioeconomic status), but occupational therapists and managers must consider the multiple disparity influences on clients. In addition, at any given time, one influence may be more important than another, as discussed in the theory section of this chapter. The list of vulnerable populations in the sections that follow is not meant to be exhaustive but rather to provide a point of departure in designing services, devoting financial resources, and improving service delivery.

Race and Ethnicity

Health Disparities

African Americans, American Indians/Alaska Natives, Asians, Hispanics, and Native Hawaiians/Pacific Islanders are disproportionately affected by the leading causes of death and disability (National Center for Health Statistics, 2005). Immunization rates are lower among minorities (excluding Asians), and minority infants have higher death rates than White infants. In addition, African Americans, American Indians, Hawaiians, and Puerto Ricans were 1.4 to 3.6 times more likely to present with advanced (Stage 4) breast cancer than non-Hispanic White Americans (Li, Malone, & Dahling, 2003).

Future health disparities may be driven in part by differential rates of obesity currently found among young minorities; associated health risks include heart disease; type 2 diabetes; high blood pressure; stroke; arthritis-related disabilities; sleep disorders; and cancers of the breast, prostate, and colon. African American and Latina women have obesity rates of 52% and 40%, respectively, compared with a rate of 32% for White women (30% of men across racial groups are obese; National Center for Health Statistics, 2005).

Mental health disparities exhibit a decidedly different pattern than do health disparities. Hispanic Americans, Asian Americans, and African Americans have fewer mental disorders than do White Americans (Alegría et al., 2007; Takeuchi et al., 2007; Williams, Haile, et al., 2007). Similarly, American Indians are at heightened risk for posttraumatic stress and alcohol dependence but at lower risk of depression (Beals et al., 2005). Although minorities have fewer psychiatric disorders than do White Americans, both African Americans and Hispanic Americans are more likely to be persistently ill (Breslau, Kendler, Su, Gaxiola-Aguilar, & Kessler, 2005). Similarly, depression is more likely to be chronic, severe, disabling, and untreated among African Americans compared to White Americans (Williams, Gonzalez, et al., 2007).

Health Care Disparities

From 2000 to 2003, the proportion of adults who received care for illness or injury as soon as they wanted decreased for White Americans but increased for African Americans (Agency for Healthcare Research and Quality [AHRQ], 2004). From 2002 to 2003, the proportion of adults who

reported communication problems with providers decreased somewhat for White Americans but even more for American Indian/Alaska Natives (AHRQ, 2004). From 2000 to 2003, the proportion of adults who had not received the recommended screening for colorectal cancer decreased for White Americans but increased for American Indian/Alaska Natives (AHRQ, 2004). From 2001 to 2003, the rate of pediatric asthma hospitalizations remained the same for White Americans but increased for Hispanics.

Members of racial and ethnic minority groups have less access to mental health services than do their White counterparts despite a higher need, are less likely to receive needed care, and are more likely to receive poor quality of care when treated. Minorities are also more likely than White Americans to delay or fail to seek mental health treatment (Miranda, McGuire, Williams, & Wang, 2008).

Socioeconomic Status

Health Disparities

Traditional socioeconomic status (SES) measures of education, income, occupation, and wealth, sometimes referred to as *social class*, can be described as "crude indicators of location in social structure" (Williams & Collins, 1995, p. 354). The health benefits of higher SES stem from several factors. First, individuals who have high incomes and are highly educated tend to smoke and drink less, exercise more, and practice healthier eating habits compared to their less privileged counterparts (Mirowsky, Ross, & Reynolds, 2000). Second, high-SES individuals generally have greater access to adequate health care and are much more likely to seek preventive medical care (Mutchler & Burr, 1991; Verbrugge, 1989). Third, high income and education typically protect individuals from financial strain and other stressors that may have negative effects on health (Mirowsky et al., 2000).

Low SES is similarly associated with a more sedentary lifestyle and lower consumption of fiber and fresh fruits and vegetables (Krebs-Smith & Cook, 1995; Pamuk, Makuc, Heck, Reuben, & Lockner, 1998). Patterns of alcohol use by socioeconomic status are more complex, as are the health risks related to alcohol. Moderate drinking does not show an SES gradient, whereas heavy drinking is more common at lower SES levels (Pamuk et al., 1998).

SES-related health effects of social environments may be even more important than those of physical environments. Isolation and lack of engagement in social networks are strong negative predictors of health. Socially isolated persons have relative risks of mortality ranging between two and five times greater than those with better social connections (Berkman & Glass, 2000). Patterns of social interaction also affect disease risk. For sexually transmitted diseases, transmission is most rapid in high-risk networks, which are often clustered in lower socioeconomic areas, thus putting lower-SES persons at greater risk for exposure.

Health Care Disparities

The quality of health care obtained can vary by socioeconomic status. In 1996, 40% of uninsured adults did not graduate from high school, and more than 60% were in low-income families (Monheit & Vistnes, 2000). Persons who lack insurance receive less medical care, including screening and treatment, than those who are covered, and they may receive poorer quality health care (Baker, Shapiro, & Schur, 2000). For example, from 2000 to 2003, the proportion of adults age 40 and over who did not receive three recommended services for diabetes decreased substantially for high-income persons but less for poor persons.

Although very poor individuals may be eligible for Medicaid and persons over age 65 for Medicare, many fail to enroll (Gross et al., 1999). States with greater income inequality and higher mortality also have fewer primary care doctors per capita (Shi, Starfield, Kennedy, & Kawachi, 1999), suggesting that access to primary care may be one pathway by which income inequality affects mortality.

Gender

Health Disparities

Gender differences in mortality and life expectancy vary by country, but in most countries, women live longer than men. In the United States, the male longevity disadvantage is approximately 5 years (75 vs. 80 years; Haub, 2007). Men have higher rates of cigarette smoking, heavy drinking, gun use, employment in hazardous occupations, and risk taking in recreation and driving, which contribute to higher death rates due to lung cancer, accidents, suicide, and homicide. Risky male behavior may be fueled by hormonal differences, biology, and culture. Research suggests that testosterone contributes to greater physical activity and aggressiveness in men; this domino effect leads to the higher death rate from accidents and homicide. As women continue to catch up in socioeconomic status with men, the gender gap is expected to decrease. In the workplace, women who achieve higher status on the job may adopt unhealthy behaviors similar to men's, such as drinking and smoking more, and may experience more job-related stress. In addition, the mortality gap is narrowing as women begin to smoke more and men to smoke less than before (Waldron, 2005).

Women experience higher rates of pain (e.g., headache, arthritis) and some respiratory conditions, including bronchitis, asthma, and lung problems not related to cancer (Case & Paxson, 2005). They are also much more likely to experience reproductive cancers, hypertension, vision problems, and depression. Men are more likely to experience hearing loss; smoking-related diseases, such as emphysema

and respiratory cancer; and circulatory problems, including cardiovascular disease and diabetes, and are more likely to die than women with these conditions.

Health Care Disparity

Although women rate their health worse than men and visit the hospital more often, from early adolescence to late middle age women are less likely than men to die at each age. This paradox can be explained at least in part by differences in the prevalence of chronic conditions in men and women (Case & Paxson, 2005).

One of the primary barriers to access is lack of insurance coverage (Brittle & Bird, 2007). Uninsured women were more likely to report that they had not visited a provider in the past year, that they had delayed care, that they were not able to see a specialist, and that they did not fill a prescription in 2004 (Salganicoff, Ranji, & Wyn, 2005). Women also tend to have lower incomes than men. Half (52%) of poor women and more than a third (38%) who were near poor (100% to 199% of the poverty level) in 2004 reported they delayed or did not get needed health care because of the cost (Salganicoff et al., 2005).

Disability

Health Disparity

Adults with disabilities have different health care needs than adults without disabilities. Persons with disabilities may be more vulnerable to acquiring health problems and may develop chronic conditions at an earlier age as a result of limitations preventing engagement in health-promoting activities such as aerobic exercise (DeJong, 1997). Likewise, diabetes, cardiovascular disease, substance abuse, and depression are all common comorbid diagnoses for persons with disabilities (Tingus et al., 2005). Acquisition of new health conditions may lead to secondary functional losses, exacerbating the individual's difficulties with completing activities of daily living.

Health Care Disparity

Compared to their contemporaries without disabilities, working-age persons with disabilities are hospitalized 12 times as many days per year and incur over seven times their health care costs per year (DeJong, 1997). Persons with a disability have been shown to utilize two to three times the number of professional health care services when compared to an individual of equal health status without a disability (McColl, 2005). Persons with disabilities may also require more prolonged and extensive treatments and, following the interventions, may require assistive technology to functionally perform daily living skills (DeJong, 1997).

Persons with poorer health status and greater disability severity often perceive more barriers to health care access and are more concerned about affordability and quality of health care services. Physical and environmental barriers include insufficient space for wheelchairs and lack of accessible medical screening equipment essential for early diagnosis of serious diseases, such as breast and cervical cancer (DeJong, 1997; Scheer, Kroll, Neri, & Beatty, 2003). Other barriers include issues of office accessibility, such as parking, entry, restrooms, waiting rooms, examination rooms, and diagnostic equipment. Transportation barriers—for example, access to public transportation, publicly funded door-to-door transportation, and taxicab services—also have an effect on the perceived accessibility of health care services (Scheer et al., 2003). Communication barriers may result from lack of alternative modalities to accommodate people with sensory impairments, such as American Sign Language interpreters for the Deaf (Iezzoni, Davis, Soukup, & O'Day, 2003). For people with learning or cognitive disabilities, obstacles to effective care may occur when long wait times are required or providers do not allow enough time to make clients feel comfortable (Scheer et al., 2003).

Several personal and cultural barriers to health care access have been documented in the literature; they include providers' negative attitudes, misperceptions, and lack of knowledge about the client's particular culture (Drainoni et al., 2006). Clients also frequently report lack of provider knowledge and lack of timeliness of service. Negative provider attitudes sometimes result in withholding of treatment or provision of inferior treatment when compared to the services provided to those of the provider's culture.

Structural barriers refer to a lack of financial coverage for all necessary services. Limited health benefit programs, whether publicly or privately funded, may not provide for services such as physical therapy and occupational therapy; high-quality, well-fitted, and functional durable medical equipment; and mental health services (Scheer et al., 2003). A considerable proportion of people with disabilities report serious problems accessing prescription drugs (32%), dental care (29%), equipment (21%), mental health services (17%), and home care (16%) because of cost (Kaiser Family Foundation, 2003).

Sexual Orientation
Health Disparities
Although extremely limited in comparison to the wealth of data documenting health disparities associated with race and ethnicity, a growing body of research points to clear disparities when lesbian, gay, bisexual, and transsexual populations are compared with the national profile. Lesbian and bisexual orientations among women are associated with tobacco use and heavy alcohol consumption (Diamant, Wold, Spritzer, & Gelberg, 2000). Morbidity and mortality are more prevalent in gay men due to HIV disease; hepatitis A, B, C, E, and G; and other sexually transmitted diseases (Ungvarski & Grossman, 1999). Gay men are also at higher risk for lung cancer and heart disease because of high rates of smoking and are at high risk

for eating disorders and athletic and gym-related injuries. Gay and bisexual men have been found to be at excess risk for anal cancer, non-Hodgkin's lymphoma, and Hodgkin's disease (Koblin et al., 1996).

With regard to mental health, especially of LBGT youths, the Minnesota Adolescent Health Survey of more than 30,000 students in Grades 7 through 12 found that homosexual boys were more likely than heterosexual boys to report poor body image, binge eating, and purging behaviors (French, Story, Remafedi, Resnick, & Blum, 1996). Whereas 10% of the general adolescent population attempt suicide, 20% to 30% of LGBT youths do so (J. A. Baker, 1993), and they account for up to 30% of completed suicides each year (Harrison, 1996).

Health Care Disparities
Important findings with regard to health care disparities for the LGBT population include the following:

- Young lesbians across all educational levels are less likely to receive Pap smears relative to young women in the general U.S. population (Diamant, Schuster, & Lever, 2000).
- A 1998 survey of physicians revealed that 22% believed they should assume heterosexuality in their patients, 41% reported thinking that it was appropriate to assume that all gay and bisexual male adolescents are HIV positive until proved otherwise, and 90% reported reservations about approaching the issue of sexual orientation (East & El Rayess, 1998).
- A 1998 survey of LGBT adolescents found that 61% did not feel safe discussing sexual orientation with their physicians, 57% were afraid that physicians would violate their confidentiality and reveal their sexuality to their parents, and 65% were not made aware of their right to confidentiality (Allen, Glicken, Beach, & Naylor, 1998).

LGBT partnerships and families often are not recognized as authentic family support networks. Insurance companies, government, hospitals, health clinics, and patients' parents often deny LGBT families the privileges granted to married heterosexual families, thus creating stress and barriers to care and prohibiting honest disclosure of identity (Albarron & Salmon, 2000; O'Hanlan, Cabaj, Schatz, Lock, & Nemrow, 1997).

Geography
Health Disparities
The influence of geographic "place" on health disparities among clients is often overlooked but can be significant. Studies have found that residents of poorer areas experience higher rates of heart disease, respiratory ailments, cancer, and overall mortality (Adler, Boyce, Chesney, Folkman, & Syme, 1993). Research also suggests that in poorer neighborhoods, mothers are prone to deliver low–birth weight babies, infants are more likely to die in their

first year of life, and children are more likely to be hospitalized (Guest, Almgren, & Hussey, 1998). Social networks may also shape norms about health-related behaviors in a neighborhood. For example, smoking or eating a high-fat diet may be more socially acceptable or of lesser concern in some neighborhoods than others (Braithwaite & Lythcott, 1989; Spence, 1993).

The most commonly discussed way in which neighborhoods influence health is through the proximity of polluting factories and toxic waste sites, which may increase people's chances of contracting cancer and other illnesses. These threats tend to be more common in low-income areas (Hamilton, 1995; Vrijheid, 2000). In addition, low-income households tend to live in older housing and older neighborhoods. The existence of lead paint in older housing and other structures has been linked to neurological damage in children under age 6, and studies have found a link between cockroach infestation and childhood asthma (Wallace & Wallace, 1990). Aging and poorly maintained environments with crumbling sidewalks, decaying stairwells, and dangerous playgrounds present the risk of accidents.

Health Care Disparities

Communities and neighborhoods positively or negatively influence health outcomes through neighborhood institutions and resources, stresses in the physical and social environments, and neighborhood-based networks and norms (Ellen, Mijanovich, & Dillman, 2001). For example, the number and quality of medical practitioners differ across neighborhoods, as does the quality of medical technology and facilities. Moreover, poor and inadequate transportation or even high crime rates can make people unable to or fearful of travel to receive services. The presence of health facilities in the neighborhood might encourage health-promoting behaviors among residents, such as exercising regularly or eating nutritious foods (McKnight, 1995; Minkler, 1997).

Age

Health Disparities

In 2002, the top three causes of death for U.S. adults ages 65 or older were heart disease, cancer, and stroke, which accounted for 61% of all deaths in this age group (CDC, National Center for Health Statistics Data Warehouse, 2006). Currently, at least 80% of older Americans are living with at least one chronic condition, and 50% have at least two. In addition, the burden of many chronic diseases and conditions, especially high blood pressure, diabetes, and cancer, varies widely by race and ethnicity (National Institute on Aging, 2006).

In 2004, falls were the leading cause of injury deaths among older adults, responsible for almost 43% of such deaths (Stevens, 2005). Stevens (2005) found that fall-related death rates rose sharply with increasing age and that the greatest increase occurred after age 79.

Health Care Disparities

By 2030, the nation's health care spending is projected to increase by 25% unless improving and preserving the health of older adults are more actively addressed (CDC, National Center for Health Statistics Data Warehouse, 2006). The Medicare program provides core health insurance to nearly all elderly Americans and reduces many financial barriers to acute and postacute care services.

The Medicare Prescription Drug Improvement and Modernization Act of 2003 has added new prescription drug and preventive benefits to Medicare and provides extra financial help to persons with low incomes. Consequently, differences in access to and quality of health care tend to be smaller among Medicare beneficiaries than among younger populations (CDC, National Center for Health Statistics Data Warehouse, 2006). However, older adults may have physical access issues similar to persons with disabilities, especially with regard to environmental barriers and transportation.

Employment

Health Disparities

In a review of evidence-based literature, Jin, Shah, and Svoboda (1995) found that most aggregate-level studies reported a positive association between unemployment rates and rates of overall mortality and mortality due to cardiovascular disease and suicide. However, the relationship between unemployment rates and motor-vehicle fatality rates may be inverse. Workers laid off due to factory closure reported more symptoms and illnesses than employed people. Unemployed people also were more likely than employed people to visit physicians, take medication, or be admitted to hospitals.

Health Care Disparities

Health care disparities related to employment are largely the result of health insurance coverage. Zuvekas and Taliaferro (2003) found that insurance coverage explained up to one-third of Hispanic–White disparities and two-fifths of Black–White disparities in having a usual source of care. The authors' analyses suggest that disparities in access to employment-related coverage for Blacks can be traced to lower employment among single Blacks and lower marriage rates. For Hispanics, the lower levels of employment among single people also reduce access to employment-related coverage. The types of jobs that both single and married Hispanics hold are much less likely to offer insurance than the types of jobs held by other ethnic groups, which further contributes to the disparities in access to health insurance (Zuvekas & Taliaferro, 2003).

In times of rising unemployment, it is estimated that for every 1% loss in employment, 1.1 million people lose their health care coverage. Loss of health insurance reduces access to services such as occupational therapy. Vulnerable populations such as those described in this chapter are disproportionately affected by unemployment. For example, between the beginning of the recession in December 2007 and December 2008, Hispanic unemployment rose to 10.9%, African American unemployment to 13.4%, and White unemployment rose to 7.3%. The resultant lack of access to health care for these populations can be expected to worsen disparities (U.S. Department of Labor, 2009).

IMPLICATIONS FOR OCCUPATIONAL THERAPY PRACTICE

Occupational therapists have a unique perspective of the client as an occupational being for whom access to and participation in meaningful and productive activities are central to health and well-being. Those who experience disparities in health and health care access may be limited in this participation, ultimately affecting their health in the broadest sense. As seen in this chapter, occupational therapy managers and practitioners must consider not only prevention of health disparities in the traditional clinical sense but also the contexts that may contribute to these disparities to develop interventions or strategies that will result in more effective reduction of these disparities. In line with outcomes outlined in the *Framework–II* (AOTA, 2008), occupational therapy practitioners can facilitate improved self-advocacy and occupational justice at the individual, group, and population levels.

What is the role of occupational therapy practitioners in crafting a climate in which health disparities associated with vulnerable populations are identified and addressed? First, occupational therapy practitioners can start with their own hearts. Examining our knowledge and feelings about these populations will help us to identify ways in which we may have inadvertently silenced a client or assumed a response. As practitioners and managers, a heightened understanding of the disparities our clients experience allows us to better direct our energies to crucial and effective intervention.

In clinical intervention, occupational therapists should take a client-centered approach not only to advocate for clients but also to empower them and their families to become their own self-advocates with regard to prevention and reduction of hazardous influences from the environment. Practitioners and clients can combine their knowledge to modify the factors that influence engagement in occupation to improve and support clients' performance in healthy lifestyles.

At the individual level, when evaluating clients, occupational therapists must consider the contextual factors contributing to the disparities experienced by clients, including societal prejudice, health literacy, and the built environment. They must discover what the client wants and needs to do and identify those factors that act as supports or barriers to performance. As a manager, support for staff to develop cultural competence and consideration of the health and health care disparities that exist and influence client health is an important strategy.

Although the most common form of service delivery within the profession involves a direct provider-to-client model, occupational therapists are beginning to serve clients at the group and population level (e.g., communities, organizations). When providing interventions other than in a one-to-one model, the occupational therapist is an agent who helps others support client engagement in occupations rather than personally providing that support. Often, education and consultation processes are the interventions implemented.

Advocacy for occupational justice at the population level involves knowledge and participation in the political process. The distinction between health disparities and health care disparities has a bearing on potential policy opportunities, including which players hold primary responsibility for making changes. If defined in the context of health care, disparities are to some extent the responsibility of the entities that make up the health care system, such as physicians, other health care providers such as occupational therapists, hospitals, nursing homes and other nonhospital care settings, academic institutions that train clinical providers, health insurance providers, and third-party payers. As a manager, potential solutions include approaches such as cultural competency training, providing access for clients to linguistically appropriate care, advocating for expansion of insurance coverage, and support for consistent delivery of known best care practices to all patients. If defined in the context of health, disparities are also connected to factors outside the health care system and require a much broader set of stakeholders to address the problem. Potential solutions include advocacy of and support to services that address individual and community-based social determinants of health, such as education, income, neighborhood safety, support for healthy lifestyles, and more.

Creation of an Environment Free of Discrimination

Incorporating the tenets of health literacy into the work environment is another important method for creating an environment free of discrimination. The Institute of Medicine (2004) defined *health literacy* as "the degree to which individuals have the capacity to obtain, process, and understand basic health information and services needed to make appropriate health decisions" (p. 32). According to a study by the Institute of Medicine (2004), nearly half of Americans, or 90 million people, have difficulty understanding and acting on health information, and more than 40 million cannot read complex text. Studies have found that racial and ethnic minority populations and older adults have decreased health literacy. Yet a great deal of health information, from insurance forms to treatment contraindications, contains complex text. To provide a supportive environment, managers need to ensure that general information and educational materials are written at a level that is understandable by clients and free from jargon, and occupational therapists should incorporate techniques such as the teach-back method to ensure that clients understand the intervention (Barrett, Puryear, & Westpheling, 2008).

Occupational therapy practitioners can play a role in health literacy in their own practice by ensuring clients understand their diagnoses and treatments and communicate in a way that clients understand to increase compliance with treatment. Furthermore, occupational therapy practitioners can also provide education on health literacy–related topics to other health care professionals and other types of facilities. Occupational therapists are uniquely qualified to assess health care facilities with regard to providing support or barriers to the client–provider relationship because the concept of health literacy considers the disparity between the skills of the client (person) and the complexity of the health care system (environment) that affects the person's ability to obtain and use health care information (occupation; Smith, Hedrick, Earhart, Galloway, & Arndt, in press).

Health Care Workforce Implications

Efforts to increase minority participation in the health care workforce (especially occupational therapy) would most likely improve disparities in health care by improving patient–provider communication through a common language. In occupational therapy, increased efforts by AOTA to increase diversity have resulted in creation of caucuses and networks to support diverse subgroups within the profession, including the Association of Asian/Pacific Occupational Therapists in America; Black Occupational Therapy Caucus; the Network for Lesbian, Gay, Bisexual, and Transgender Concerns in Occupational Therapy; Orthodox Jewish Occupational Therapy Caucus; TODOS Network of Hispanic Practitioners; Network of Native American Practitioners; and Network of Practitioners With Disabilities. More needs to be done, however, to recruit students of diverse backgrounds into the profession to promote culturally competent care for clients. In the interim, however, it is the manager's obligation to create a work environment that considers not only the diversity of the clients but also the impact that disparities may have on client outcomes.

Conclusion

This chapter provides evidence of the many health disparities and health care disparities clients face because of race or ethnicity, disability status, gender, sexual orientation, socioeconomic status, geography, and age. When clients experience disparities in one or more of these areas, participation in occupation can be affected, reducing overall quality of life and health in the broadest sense. Awareness of these disparities will provide managers and staff with a valuable context to consider when planning and developing new services or interventions for clients and their family and caregivers.

Occupational therapists' intervention plans must include not only the traditional clinical intervention but also prevention, promotion, and wellness strategies that improve the contextual influences on client participation. Therapeutic use of self must include cultural competency and sensitivity. It is incumbent on managers to ensure that staff are trained in cultural sensitivity issues to reduce negative contextual influences during evaluation and intervention from the provider himself or herself. Interventions must also include consideration of client access not only to occupational therapy services but also to other health care services they need.

Occupational therapy managers and practitioners must support and be active in political advocacy to ensure client access to occupational therapy services. The use and promotion of evidence-based interventions will assist in justifying why clients need occupational therapy services and help reduce the disparity that results from insurance plans that do not include occupational therapy services. The ultimate outcome of engagement in intervention is engagement in occupation, which cannot occur when clients experience disparities in health and health care access.

Case Examples

Level II Fieldwork

Maria was completing her Level II fieldwork at a community center for low-income older adults. Many of the participants at the community center were having difficulty negotiating their home environments and simple activities of daily living. When Maria asked her supervisor why the participants were not receiving occupational therapy services, her supervisor explained that the participants' insurance did not cover occupational therapy.

When Maria returned to her class in the occupational therapy program, she and the other students brainstormed with the instructor and decided to bring the matter to the attention of local and state legislators. The students began a letter-writing campaign and visited the offices of the appropriate legislators to inform them of the disparity in health care coverage for occupational therapy services and of the ways occupational therapy

(continued)

Case Examples *(cont.)*

interventions can increase independence in the home environment, thereby reducing the need for expensive institutional care.

LEVEL II FIELDWORK

During his mental health fieldwork (and all of his fieldwork experiences before it), Anthony observed that there was a discrepancy between the demographics of the clients seen in occupational therapy and the occupational therapists providing the services. Many clients told Anthony that because he was a man and a person of color, they felt more comfortable with him.

Anthony decided to bring this issue to the attention of his occupational therapy program. Together with the faculty, Anthony spoke at high schools and community colleges to encourage applicants from more diverse backgrounds to apply to occupational therapy educational programs.

FIRST-TIME MANAGER

Brandon had just been hired as the manager of the occupational therapy department in an inner-city hospital. At a recent staff meeting, the occupational therapists were complaining that client compliance with home programs was poor and that this poor compliance was affecting the clients' functional outcomes. The home program information materials contained occupational therapy jargon and no pictures, and the programs were not explained until clients were being discharged.

Brandon determined that his staff needed training in health literacy concepts and contracted with an expert to provide an in-service. All staff were required to attend. Following the training, home programs were rewritten at the appropriate level, using plain language and pictures. Staff were instructed to explain the home programs more than once (if possible) to clients and to use the teach-back method of having the client repeat back the instructions as a means of ensuring comprehension.

MANAGER

Lejla was the manager of several small rural occupational therapy departments. Lately, the refugee and immigrant population had increased in the area, and many clients had limited English proficiency. Communication with these clients was difficult, and the staff were concerned that lack of understanding would compromise functional outcomes. Because of the location, however, it was difficult to find a professional interpreter. Many times family and friends who spoke the client's language were used, but concern about accurate interpretation remained.

Lejla investigated the use of telehealth to provide interpretation services to the clients. Telehealth is a means of delivering medical information and health care through the use of telecommunication technologies such as videoconferencing so clients can have a live, real-time interaction with a professional. Lejla was able to work with an already established telehealth network to provide interpreters from other health care sites to translate client–therapist communication throughout therapy sessions.

❖ Learning Activities

1. List and discuss the various characteristics of the cultural groups to which you belong.
2. Determine the characteristics of population diversity in your state and the geographic pockets of potential disparities faced by those populations.
3. Identify agencies or organizations in your state or community that have as their primary goal to advocate for the populations mentioned in this chapter and determine the types of service they provide.
4. Interview at least 5 people from the various populations mentioned in this chapter, and ask them what they believe are the most important health and health care disparity issues that affect them.
5. Conduct an evaluation of the health literacy efforts of a health care site in the city or town where you live (e.g., signage, home programs).

✓ Multiple-Choice Questions

1. Which of the following is *not* a level of the ecological model?
   a. Organizational.
   b. Interpersonal.
   c. Biological.
   d. Community.

2. Which of the following describes the *simultaneous oppression* theory of discrimination or disparity?
   a. Results in shared alliances, as well as oppositional interests, between different groups of persons experiencing discrimination.
   b. Emphasizes the simultaneous production of race, class, and gender inequality, such that in any given situation, the unique contribution of one factor might be difficult to measure.
   c. Identifies 3 areas of oppression, including limited identity, resource discrimination, and isolation within the community.
   d. Involves consideration of each area of discrimination that a client is experiencing separately.

3. Which of the following describes the *multiple other* theory of discrimination or disparity?
   a. Results in shared alliances, as well as oppositional interests, between different groups of persons experiencing discrimination.
   b. Emphasizes the simultaneous production of race, class, and gender inequality, such that in any given situation, the unique contribution of one factor might be difficult to measure.
   c. Identifies 3 areas of oppression, including limited identity, resource discrimination, and isolation within the community.
   d. Involves consideration of each area of discrimination that a client is experiencing separately.

4. Which of the following describes the *intersection* theory of discrimination or disparity?
   a. Results in shared alliances, as well as oppositional interests, between different groups of persons experiencing discrimination.
   b. Emphasizes the simultaneous production of race, class, and gender inequality, such that in any given situation, the unique contribution of one factor might be difficult to measure.
   c. Identifies 3 areas of oppression, including limited identity, resource discrimination, and isolation within the community.
   d. Involves consideration of each area of discrimination that a client is experiencing separately.

5. The ethical principle of "providing services in a fair and equitable manner" falls under which area of the *Occupational Therapy Code of Ethics and Ethics Standards*?
   a. Beneficence.
   b. Justice.
   c. Nonmaleficence.
   d. Veracity.

6. Which of the following populations is *not* expected to increase by 2050?
   a. Hispanic.
   b. Asian.
   c. White.
   d. African American.

7. Which of the following populations is overrepresented in the U.S. physician population survey (compared to client demographics)?
   a. African American.
   b. American Indian.
   c. Asian.
   d. Hispanic.

8. Which of the following groups has the highest rate of obesity?
   a. Hispanic women.
   b. Asian men.
   c. African American men.
   d. American Indian women.

9. Generally, which of the following populations experiences the highest rate of psychiatric disorders?
   a. Hispanic.
   b. White.
   c. African American.
   d. Asian.

10. Socioeconomic status includes all of the following *except*
    a. Occupation (employment).
    b. Education.
    c. Race and ethnicity.
    d. Income.

11. Which of the following is *not* a reason that men tend to live shorter lives than women?
    a. Less access to health care services.
    b. Higher rates of alcohol and tobacco use.
    c. Employment in hazardous occupations.
    d. Risk taking in driving and recreation.

12. Compared to their contemporaries without disabilities, working-age persons with disabilities are hospitalized _____ times as many days per year and incur over _____ times their health care costs per year.
    a. 2, 10.
    b. 7, 12.
    c. 10, 2.
    d. 12, 7.

13. Limited health care coverage for occupational therapy services is an example of which of the following

categories of health care access barrier (as defined by Scheer et al., 2003) encountered by persons with disabilities?

a. Environmental.

b. Communication.

c. Structural.

d. Personal or cultural.

14. Negative attitudes of health care providers is an example of which of the following categories of health care access barrier (as defined by Scheer et al., 2003) encountered by persons with disabilities?

a. Environmental.

b. Communication.

c. Structural.

d. Personal or cultural.

15. Inaccessible medical screening equipment is an example of which of the following categories of health care access barrier (as defined by Scheer et al., 2003) encountered by persons with disabilities?

a. Environmental.

b. Communication.

c. Structural.

d. Personal or cultural.

16. Lack of alternative formats (e.g., American Sign Language interpreters, Braille materials) for health care information is an example of which of the following categories of health care access barrier (as defined by Scheer et al., 2003) encountered by persons with disabilities?

a. Environmental.

b. Communication.

c. Structural.

d. Personal or cultural.

17. Which of the following is *not* considered a health disparity for the lesbian, gay, bisexual, and transgender population?

a. Increased risk for suicide among adolescents.

b. Increased risk for lung cancer and heart disease among gay men.

c. Increased risk for obesity among lesbian women.

d. Increased risk for eating disorders among gay adolescent and adult men.

18. When unemployment rises, how many people lose their health care coverage for every 1% loss in employment?

a. 100,000.

b. 550,000.

c. 1.1 million.

d. 1.1 billion.

19. Which population is most affected by unemployment?

a. White Americans.

b. Hispanics.

c. African Americans.

d. Asians.

20. Which of the following terms means "the degree to which individuals have the capacity to obtain, process, and understand basic health information and services needed to make appropriate health decisions" (U.S. Department of Health and Human Services, 2000)?

a. Health education.

b. Health literacy.

c. Health promotion.

d. Wellness.

References

Adler, N. E., Boyce, W. T., Chesney, M. A., Folkman, S., & Syme, S. L. (1993). Socioeconomic inequalities in health: No easy solution. *JAMA, 269,* 3140–3145.

Agency for Healthcare Research and Quality. (2004). *National Healthcare Disparities Report.* Rockville, MD: Author.

Albarron, J. W., & Salmon, D. (2000). Lesbian, gay, and bisexual experiences with critical care nursing, 1988–1998: A survey of the literature. *International Journal of Nursing Studies, 37,* 445–455.

Alegría, M., Mulvaney-Day, N., Woo, M., Torres, M., Gao, S., & Oddo, V. (2007). Correlates of past-year mental health service use among Latinos: Results from the National Latino and Asian American Study. *American Journal of Public Health, 97,* 76–83.

Allen, L. B., Glicken, A. D., Beach, R. K., & Naylor, K. E. (1998). Adolescent health care experiences of gay, lesbian, and bisexual young adults. *Journal of Adolescent Health, 23,* 212–220.

American Medical Association. (2005). *U.S. physician data.* Chicago: Author.

American Occupational Therapy Association. (2008). Occupational therapy practice framework: Domain and process (2nd ed.). *American Journal of Occupational Therapy, 62,* 625–683.

American Occupational Therapy Association. (2010). Occupational therapy code of ethics and ethics standards (2010). *American Journal of Occupational Therapy, 64.*

Baicker, K., Chandra, A., & Skinner, J. S. (2005). Geographic variations in health care and the problem of measuring racial disparities. *Perspectives in Biological Medicine, 48*(Suppl.), S42–S53.

Baker, D. W., Shapiro, M. F., & Schur, C. L. (2000). Health insurance and access to care for symptomatic conditions. *Archives of Internal Medicine, 160,* 1269–1274.

Baker, J. A. (1993). Is homophobia hazardous to lesbian and gay health? *American Journal of Health Promotion, 7,* 255–256, 262.

Barrett, S. E., Puryear, J. S., & Westpheling, K. (2008). *Health literacy practices in primary care settings: Examples from the field.* New York: Commonwealth Fund.

Beals, J., Manson, S. M., Whitesell, N. R., Spicer, P., Novins, D. K., & Mitchell, C. M. (2005). Prevalence of *DSM–IV* disorders and attendant help-seeking in two American Indian reservation populations. *Archives of General Psychiatry, 62,* 99–108.

Berkman, L. F., & Glass, T. (2000). Social integration, social networks, social support, and health. In L. F. Berkman & I. Kawachi (Eds.), *Social epidemiology* (pp. 137–173). New York: Oxford University Press.

Braithwaite, R. L., & Lythcott, N. (1989). Community empowerment as a strategy for health promotion for Black and other minority populations. *JAMA, 261,* 282–283.

Breslau, J., Kendler, K. S., Su, M., Gaxiola-Aguilar, S., & Kessler, R. C. (2005). Lifetime risk and persistence of psychiatric disorders across ethnic groups in the United States. *Psychology in Medicine, 35,* 317–327.

Brittle, C., & Bird, C. E. (2007). *Literature review on effective sex- and gender-based systems/models of care.* Arlington, VA: Office of Women's Health, Department of Health and Human Services.

Case, A., & Paxson, C. (2005). Sex differences in morbidity and mortality. *Demography, 42,* 189–214.

Centers for Disease Control and Prevention, & Merck Company Foundation. (2007). *The state of aging and health in America 2007.* Retrieved March 4, 2009, from http://www.cdc.gov/Aging/pdf/saha_2007.pdf

Centers for Disease Control and Prevention, National Center for Health Statistics Data Warehouse. (2006). *Trends in health and aging.* Retrieved March 5, 2009, from http://www.cdc.gov/nchs/agingact.htm

DeJong, G. (1997). Primary care for persons with disabilities: An overview of the problem. *American Journal of Physical Medicine and Rehabilitation, 76,* 52–58.

Diamant, A. L., Schuster, M. A., & Lever, J. (2000). Receipt of preventive health care services by lesbians. *American Journal of Preventive Medicine, 19,* 141–148.

Diamant, A. L., Wold, C., Spritzer, B. A., & Gelberg, L. (2000). Health behaviors, health status, and access to and use of health care: A population-based study of lesbian, bisexual, and heterosexual women. *Archives of Family Medicine, 9,* 1043–1051.

Drainoni, M.-L., Lee-Hood, E., Tobias, C., Bachman, S. S., Andrew, J., & Maisels, L. (2006). Cross-disability experiences of barriers to health-care access: Consumer perspectives. *Journal of Disability Policy Studies, 17,* 101–115.

East, J. A., & El Rayess, F. (1998). Pediatricians' approach to the health care of lesbian, gay, and bisexual youth. *Journal of Adolescent Health, 23,* 191–193.

Ellen, I. G., Mijanovich, T., & Dillman, K.-N. (2001). Neighborhood effects on health: Exploring the links and assessing the evidence. *Journal of Urban Affairs, 23,* 391–408.

French, S. A., Story, M., Remafedi, G., Resnick, M., & Blum, R. (1996). Sexual orientation and prevalence of body dissatisfaction and eating disordered behaviors: A population-based study of adolescents. *International Journal of Eating Disorders, 19,* 119–126.

Gross, D. J., Alecxih, L., Gibson, M. J., Corea, J., Caplan, C., & Brangan, N. (1999). Out-of-pocket health spending by the poor and near-poor elderly Medicare beneficiaries. *Health Services Research, 34,* 241–254.

Guest, A. M., Almgren, G., & Hussey, J. M. (1998). The ecology of race and socioeconomic distress: Infant and working age mortality in Chicago. *Demography, 35,* 23–35.

Hamilton, J. T. (1995). Testing for environmental racism: Prejudice, profits, political power? *Journal of Policy Analysis and Management, 14,* 107–132.

Harrison, A. E. (1996). Primary care of lesbian and gay patients: Educating ourselves and our students. *Family Medicine, 28,* 10–20.

Harvard School of Public Health, Robert Wood Johnson Foundation, & ICR/International Communications Research. (2005). *Americans' views of disparities in health care.* Retrieved January 8, 2009, from http://www.rwjf.org/files/research/Disparities_Survey_Report.pdf

Haub, C. (2007). *2007 world population data sheet.* Washington, DC: Population Reference Bureau.

Iezzoni, L. I., Davis, R. B., Soukup, J., & O'Day, B. (2003). Quality dimensions that most concern people with physical and sensory disabilities. *Archives of Internal Medicine, 163,* 2085–2092.

Institute of Medicine. (2004). *Health literacy: A prescription to end confusion.* Washington, DC: National Academy of Science.

Jin, R. L., Shah, C. P., & Svoboda, T. J. (1995). The impact of unemployment on health: A review of the evidence. *Canadian Medical Association Journal, 153,* 529–540.

Kaiser Family Foundation. (2003). *New survey shows people with disabilities face major barriers.* Retrieved February 25, 2009, from http://www.kff.org/newsroom/Disability-Health-Coverage.cfm?RenderForPrint=1

Koblin, B. A., Hessol, N. A., Zauber, A. G., Taylor, P. E., Buchbinder, S. P., Katzh, M. H., et al. (1996). Increased incidence of cancer among homosexual men: New York City and San Francisco, 1978–1990. *American Journal of Epidemiology, 144,* 916–923.

Krebs-Smith, S. M., & Cook, A. (1995). U.S. adults' fruit and vegetable intakes, 1989–1991: A revised baseline for Healthy People 2000 objective. *American Journal of Public Health, 85,* 1623–1629.

Lambda Legal Defense and Education Fund. (1999). *State-by-state sodomy law update.* New York: Author.

Laumann, E. O., Gagnon, J. H., Michael, R. T., & Michaels, S. (1995). *National health and social life survey, 1992.* Chicago: University of Chicago and National Opinion Research Center.

Li, C. I., Malone, K. E., & Dahling, J. R. (2003). Differences in breast cancer stage, treatment, and survival by race and ethnicity. *Archives of Internal Medicine, 163,* 49–56.

McColl, M. A. (2005). Disability studies at the population level: Issues of health service utilization. *American Journal of Occupational Therapy, 59,* 516–526.

McKnight, J. (1995). *Careless society: Community and its counterfeits.* New York: Basic Books.

Medicare Prescription Drug Improvement and Modernization Act of 2003, Pub. L. 108–173.

Meyers, K. S. H. (2007). *Racial and ethnic health disparities: Influences, actors, and policy opportunities.* Oakland, CA: Kaiser Permanente Institute for Health Policy.

Miles, R. (1989). *Racism.* Philadelphia: Routledge.

Minkler, M. (1997). *Community organizing and community building for health.* New Brunswick, NJ: Rutgers University Press.

Miranda, J., McGuire, T. G., Williams, D. R., & Wang, P. (2008). Mental health in the context of health disparities. *American Journal of Psychiatry, 165,* 1102–1108.

Mirowsky, J., Ross, C., & Reynolds, J. (2000). Links between social status and health status. In C. Bird, P. Conrad, & A. Freemont (Eds.), *Handbook of medical sociology* (pp. 47–67). Upper Saddle River, NJ: Prentice Hall.

Monheit, A. C., & Vistnes, J. P. (2000). Race/ethnicity and health insurance status: 1987 and 1996. *Medical Care Research and Review, 57,* 11–35.

Morris, J. (1991). *Pride against prejudice.* London: Women's Press.

Mutchler, J., & Burr, J. (1991). Racial differences in health and health care service utilization in later life: The effect of socioeconomic status. *Journal of Health and Social Behavior, 32,* 342–356.

National Center for Health Statistics. (2005). *Health, United States: 2003 chartbook on trends in the health of Americans.* Hyattsville, MD: Author.

National Institute on Aging. (2006, March 9). *Dramatic changes in U.S. aging highlighted in new census* [Press Release]. Bethesda, MD: National Institutes of Health. Retrieved March 10, 2009, from http://www.nih.gov/news/pr/mar2006/nia-09.htm

O'Hanlan, K., Cabaj, R. B., Schatz, B., Lock, J., & Nemrow, P. (1997). A review of the medical consequences of homophobia with suggestions for resolution. *Journal of Gay and Lesbian Medical Association, 1,* 25–40.

Palmer, S. (2003). Where's the diversity? Diversifying the allied health care workforce is vital in providing quality health care for all Americans. *Allied Health Careers.* Retrieved March 12, 2009, from http://alliedhealthmag.com/features/01-08-04b.htm

Pamuk, E., Makuc, D., Heck, K., Reuben, C., & Lochner, K. (1998). *Socioeconomic status and health chartbook: Health, United States.* Hyattsville, MD: National Center for Health Statistics.

Salganicoff, A., Ranji, U. R., & Wyn, R. (2005). *Women and health care: A national profile.* Menlo Park, CA: Henry J. Kaiser Family Foundation.

Scheer, J., Kroll, T., Neri, M. T., & Beatty, P. (2003). Access barriers for persons with disabilities: The consumer's perspective. *Journal of Disability Policy Studies, 13,* 221–230.

Schultz, A. J., & Mullings, L. (Eds.). (2006). *Gender, race, class and health: Intersectional approaches.* San Francisco: Jossey-Bass.

Sell, R. L., Wells, J. A., & Wypij, D. (1995). The prevalence of homosexual behavior and attraction in the United States, the United Kingdom, and France: Results of national population-based samples. *Archives of Sexual Behavior, 24,* 235–248.

Shi, L., Starfield, B., Kennedy, B., & Kawachi, I. (1999). Income inequality, primary care, and health indicators. *Journal of Family Practice, 4,* 275–284.

Smedley, B. D., Stith, A. Y., & Nelson, A. R. (2003). *Unequal treatment: Confronting racial and ethnic disparities in health care.* Washington, DC: National Academies Press.

Smith, D. L., Hedrick, W., Earhart, H., Galloway, H., & Arndt, A. (in press). Evaluating two health care facilities' ability to meet health literacy needs: A role for occupational therapy. *Occupational Therapy in Health Care.*

Spence, L. H. (1993). Rethinking the social role of public housing. *Housing Policy Debate, 4,* 355–368.

Stevens, J. A. (2005). Falls among older adults—Risk factors and prevention strategies. In *Falls free: Promoting a national falls prevention action plan.* Washington, DC: National Council on the Aging.

Stuart, O. W. (1992). Race and disability: Just double oppression? *Disability, Handicap, and Society, 7,* 177–188.

Substance Abuse and Mental Health Services Administration. (2004). *U.S. psychologist and social worker data.* Rockville, MD: Author.

Sullivan Commission on Diversity in the Healthcare Workforce. (2004). *Missing persons: Minorities in the health professions.* Retrieved February 10, 2009, from http://minority-health.pitt.edu/archive/00000040/01/Sullivan_Final_Report_000.pdf

Takeuchi, D. T., Zane, N., Hong, S., Chae, D. H., Gong, F., Gee, G. C., et al. (2007). Immigration-related factors and mental disorder among Asian-Americans. *American Journal of Public Health, 97,* 84–90.

Tingus, S. J., Roecker, S., Lutzky, S., DeJong, G., Master, R. J., & Kronick, R. G. (2005). Plenary session on disability. *Neurorehabilitation and Neural Repair, 19*(1), 10S–14S.

Ungvarksi, P. J., & Grossman, A. H. (1999). Health problems of gay and bisexual men. *Nursing Clinics of North America, 34,* 313–331.

U.S. Census Bureau. (2004a). *More diversity, slower growth: Census Bureau projects tripling of Hispanic and Asian populations in 50 years; non-Hispanic Whites may drop to half of total population.* Retrieved January 9, 2009, from http://www.census.gov/PressRelease/www/releases/archives/population/001720.html

U.S. Census Bureau. (2004b). *U.S. interim projections by age, sex, race, and Hispanic origin.* Washington DC: Author.

U.S. Census Bureau. (2007). *American community survey.* Retrieved February 4, 2009, from: http://www.census.gov/PressRelease/www/releases/archives/population/010048.html.

U.S. Department of Health and Human Services. (2000). *Healthy People 2010: Understanding and improving health* (2nd ed.). Washington DC: U.S. Government Printing Office.

U.S. Department of Labor. (2009). *Unemployment rate statistics.* Retrieved February 10, 2009, http://www.dol.gov

Verbrugge, L. (1989). The twains meet: Empirical explanations of sex differences in health and mortality. *Journal of Health and Social Behavior, 30,* 282–304.

Vernon, A. (1996). Fighting two different battles: Unity is preferable to enmity. *Disability and Society, 11,* 285–290.

Vernon, A. (1999). The dialectics of multiple identities and the disabled people's movement. *Disability and Society, 14,* 385–398.

Vrijheid, M. (2000). Health effects of residence near hazardous waste landfill sites: A review of epidemiologic literature. *Environmental Health Perspectives, Suppl. 1,* 101–112.

Waldron, I. (2005). Gender differences in mortality—Causes and variations in different societies. In P. Conrad (Ed.), *The sociology of health and illness: Critical perspectives* (7th ed; pp. 38–55). New York: Worth/St. Martin's Press.

Wallace, R., & Wallace, D. (1990). Origins of public health collapse in New York City: The dynamics of planned shrinkage, contagious urban decay, and social disintegration. *Bulletin of the New York Academy of Medicine, 66,* 391–434.

Weber, L., & Para-Medina, D. (2003). Intersectionality and women's health: Charting a path to eliminating health disparities. *Advances in Gender Research: Gender Perspectives on Health and Medicine, 7,* 181–230.

Williams, D. R., & Collins, C. (1995). U.S. socioeconomic and racial differences in health: Patterns and explanations. *Annual Review in Sociology, 21,* 349–386.

Williams, D. R., Gonzalez, H. M., Neighbors, H., Nesse, R. L., Abelson, J. M., Sweetman, J., et al. (2007). Prevalence and distribution of major depressive disorder in African Americans, Caribbean Blacks, and non-Hispanic Whites: Results from the National Survey of American Life. *Archives of General Psychiatry, 64,* 305–315.

Williams, D. R., Haile, G., Gonzalez, H. M., Neighbors, H., Baser, R., & Jackson, J. S. (2007). The mental health of Black Caribbean immigrants: Results from the National Survey of American Life. *American Journal of Public Health, 97,* 52–59.

Zuvekas, S. H., & Taliaferro, G. S. (2003). Pathways to access: Health insurance, the health care delivery system and racial/ethnic disparities, 1996–1999. *Health Affairs, 22,* 139–155.

APPENDIX 34.A. HEALTH DISPARITIES EVIDENCE TABLE

Topic	Subtopic	Evidence
Influences on health disparities—Models and theories	Ecological model	Meyers, K. S. H. (2007). *Racial and ethnic health disparities: Influences, actors, and policy opportunities.* Oakland, CA: Kaiser Permanente Institute for Health Policy.
	Theories of discrimination	Schultz, A. J., & Mullings, L. (Eds.). (2006). *Gender, race, class, and health: Intersectional approaches.* San Francisco: Jossey-Bass. Stuart, O. W. (1992). Race and disability: Just double oppression? *Disability, Handicap, and Society, 7,* 177–188. Vernon, A. (1999). The dialectics of multiple identities and the disabled people's movement. *Disability and Society, 14,* 385–398.
Disparity issues	Race and ethnicity	Agency for Healthcare Research and Quality. (2004). *National healthcare disparities report.* Rockville, MD: Author. National Center for Health Statistics. (2005). *Health, United States: 2003 chartbook on trends in the health of Americans.* Hyattsville, MD: Author.
	Socioeconomic status	Mirowsky, J., Ross, C., & Reynolds, J. (2000). Links between social status and health status. In C. Bird, P. Conrad, & A. Freemont (Eds.), *Handbook of medical sociology* (pp. 47–67). Upper Saddle River, NJ: Prentice Hall.
	Gender	Waldron, I. (2005). Gender differences in mortality—Causes and variations in different societies. In P. Conrad (Ed.), *The sociology of health and illness: Critical perspectives* (7th ed.; pp. 38–55). New York: Worth–St. Martin's Press.
	Disability	DeJong, G. (1997). Primary care for persons with disabilities: An overview of the problem. *American Journal of Physical Medicine and Rehabilitation, 76,* 52–58. Scheer, J., Kroll, T., Neri, M. T., & Beatty, P. (2003). Access barriers for persons with disabilities: The consumer's perspective. *Journal of Disability Policy Studies, 13,* 221–230.
	Sexual orientation	Diamant, A. L., Wold, C., Spritzer, B. A., & Gelberg, L. (2000). Health behaviors, health status, and access to and use of health care: A population-based study of lesbian, bisexual, and heterosexual women. *Archives of Family Medicine, 9,* 1043–1051.
	Geography	Ellen, I. G., Mijanovich, T., & Dillman, K.-N. (2001). Neighborhood effects on health: Exploring the links and assessing the evidence. *Journal of Urban Affairs, 23,* 391–408.
	Age	Centers for Disease Control and Prevention, & Merck Company Foundation. (2007). *The state of aging and health in America 2007.* Retrieved March 4, 2009, from http://www.cdc.gov/Aging/pdf/saha_2007.pdf
	Employment	Zuvekas, S. H., & Taliaferro, G. S. (2003). Pathways to access: Health insurance, the health care delivery system and racial/ethnic disparities, 1996–1999. *Health Affairs, 22,* 139–155.
Implications for practice	Creating an environment free of discrimination	Institute of Medicine. (2004). *Health literacy: A prescription to end confusion.* Washington, DC: National Academy of Science.

APPENDIX 34.B. ONLINE RESOURCES RELATED TO HEALTH DISPARITIES

- **American Medical Association Health Literacy Resources:** http://www.ama-assn.org/ama/pub/about-ama/ama-foundation/our-programs/public-health/health-literacy-program/health-literacy-kit.shtml
- **Cornell University Disability Statistics:** http://www.ilr.cornell.edu/edi/DisabilityStatistics/
- **Network for Lesbian, Gay, Bisexual, and Transgender Concerns in Occupational Therapy:** http://www.diverseot.org/

35

Major Accrediting Organizations That Influence Occupational Therapy Practice

Guy L. McCormack, PhD, OTR/L, FAOTA

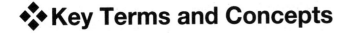

❖ Key Terms and Concepts

Accreditation. A process by which an institution or an educational organization seeks to demonstrate that it complies with generally accepted standards. Accreditation gives official recognition to sanction, authorize to certify, or guarantee meeting required standards (*American Heritage Dictionary*, 1993).

Function. A goal-directed, interrelated series of processes such as consumer assessment or human resource management.

National consensus standards. Standards based on consensus among providers, consumers, and purchasers of services. National consensus standards pertain to any occupational and health standard that is usually adopted by a nationally recognized organization (USLegal.com, n.d.).

Quality of care. The degree to which health services for individuals and populations increase the likelihood of desired health outcomes and are consistent with current professional knowledge. Dimensions of performance include consumer respect; safety within the care envi-

ronment; and accessibility, appropriateness, continuity, effectiveness, efficacy, efficiency, and timeliness of care (Donabedean, 1997).

Regulation. A law or rule prescribed by authority to regulate conduct (*Webster's American Dictionary*, 2000).

Standard. A statement that defines the performance expectations, structures, or processes that must be substantially in place in an organization to enhance the quality of care.

Standard of quality. A generally accepted, objective standard of measurement such as a rule or guideline that is supported through findings from expert consensus and that is based on evidence-based literature against which an organization's level of performance may be compared.

Survey. An onsite visit to an organization seeking accreditation during which an individual or a team assesses an organization's compliance with standards by reviewing documents; conducting interviews with the people served, the staff members, the purchasers, and other consumers; and making observations (Scalenghe, 2003).

❖ Learning Objectives

After completing this chapter, you should be able to do the following:

- Explain the importance of The Joint Commission and CARF International for occupational therapy practitioners.
- Describe how occupational therapy practitioners participate in maintaining compliance with current standards for accreditation.

- Analyze the influence of accreditation on quality of care.
- Understand the role of the occupational therapy managers and practitioners as participants in the accreditation process.
- Distinguish between regulatory requirements and accreditation standards.

In general, accreditation is used to recognize educational institutions and professional programs affiliated with those institutions for a level of performance, integrity, and quality, which entitles them to the confidence of the educational community and the public they serve (American Occupational Therapy Association [AOTA], 2007). In the United States, the recognition of accreditation is extended primarily through nongovernmental, voluntary institutional, or professional associations. These groups establish criteria, arrange site visits, and evaluate those institutions and professional programs that desire accredited status.

In most countries outside the United States, the establishment and maintenance of educational standards are the responsibility of a central government bureau. In the United States, however, public authority in education is constitutionally reserved to individual states. This system of voluntary nongovernmental evaluation, called *accreditation,* has evolved to promote both regional and national approaches to the determination of educational quality (see Chapter 36 for more information).

Although accreditation is a private, voluntary process, accrediting decisions are used as a consideration in many formal actions. The accrediting process requires institutions and programs to examine their goals, activities, and achievements; to consider the expert criticism and suggestions of a visiting team; and to determine internal procedures for action on recommendations from the accrediting agency. Because accreditation status is reviewed periodically, recognized institutions and professional programs are encouraged to maintain continuous self-study and improvement mechanisms.

It is important for occupational therapy managers to be aware of the specific accrediting bodies that are used to denote compliance in their setting. It also is important to have a basic understanding of the standards and regulations that are used to provide oversight for patient or client care and safety. The occupational therapy manager is the person on whom practitioners depend to learn about policies, procedures, regulations, and standards that are currently acceptable. Accreditation and regulatory standards act as "guideposts" for the daily operation of the occupational therapy program.

ACCREDITATION AND REGULATION

There is a sharp distinction between accreditation and regulation. *Accreditation* is the "recognition of an institution of learning as maintaining standards requisite for its graduates to gain admission to other reputable institutions of higher learning or to achieve credentials for professional practice" (U.S. Department of Education, n.d.). When a novice occupational therapy practitioner has been educated by an accredited program, he or she has been has been prepared to practice under accreditation standards in which the program's institution is accountable for the student meeting performance standards for entry-level competencies in occupational therapy.

Accountability shifts to the individual as the student graduates and becomes certified and licensed under state law. The jurisdiction falls to the state regulatory board (SRB) to determine the scope of practice within state law. Therefore, *regulation* is a law or rule prescribed by authority to regulate conduct (*Webster's American Dictionary,* 2000). Accrediting agencies are present in educational institutions, hospitals, and rehabilitation centers. Both accrediting agencies and regulatory boards are concerned with protecting the public and strive for quality assurance, maintaining the competencies of practitioners, and ethical decision making in daily practice. As occupational therapy practitioners perform within accredited health care institutions, the accountability shifts to the individual to comply with accreditation standards and the requirements of the SRB.

Ultimately, the occupational therapy practitioner is responsible to the practice requirements of state law (National Council of State Boards of Nursing, 2007). State regulations stem from statues, which begin as bills. A bill must be constitutional and go through parliamentary process to be debated and approved by the legislature. Regulations are formed and validly adopted to make sure the statue is enforced according to law.

In occupational therapy education, accreditation provides a uniform set of standards and core educational competencies. Accreditation agencies, such as The Joint Commission and CARF International, provide a voluntary, self-regulatory process by which the agencies can grant formal recognition that an institution has met quality standards that are relevant to consumers, employers, and stakeholders. Furthermore, institutional accreditation represents some degree of prestige and legitimacy that sets the institution apart from those that are not accredited.

State regulatory bodies have a more narrow scope of authority on the basis of law to ensure competency and ethical practice and to protect consumers from unnecessary harm. Because educational accreditation and state regulation are addressed in other chapters, this chapter will focus on The Joint Commission and CARF accreditation.

Accreditation standards change frequently. Therefore, this chapter provides the most current information as of press time; readers are advised to visit an accreditation agency's Web site for the most up-to-date information.

THE JOINT COMMISSION

The Joint Commission, formerly the *Joint Commission on Accreditation of Healthcare Organizations (JCAHO),* is a private sector–based, not-for-profit organization. The current mission statement is "To continuously improve health care for the public, in collaboration with other stakeholders, by evaluating health care organizations and inspiring them to excel in providing safe and effective care of the highest quality and value" (The Joint Commission, n.d.g).

The Joint Commission operates voluntary accreditation programs for hospitals and other health care organizations such as behavioral health care, home health care, laboratory services, long-term care, office-based surgery, and Medicare or Medicaid. In the United States, The Joint Commission accredits nearly 18,000 health care organizations and programs. A majority of state governments recognizes The Joint Commission accreditation as a condition of licensure and receiving Medicare reimbursement.

History

The Joint Commission is the largest and oldest private agency involved in voluntary accreditation in health care. It dates back to the 1917 formulation of minimum standards for hospitals by the American College of Surgeons and to that group's initiation of onsite inspections of hospitals in 1918. In 1951, the American College of Physicians, the American Hospital Association, the American Medical Association, and the Canadian Medical Association joined with the American College of Surgeons to create The Joint Commission on Accreditation of Hospitals as an independent, not-for-profit organization to provide voluntary accreditation for hospitals. In the 1960s, The Joint Commission expanded to include accreditation for long-term care, mental health, and other areas (Scalenghe, 2003).

The Joint Commission International (JCI) extends its mission worldwide. Through both international consultation and accreditation, JCI helps improve the quality of consumer care in public and private health care organizations and with local governments in more than 40 countries.

Accreditation Process

All health care organizations, with laboratories being the exception, are subject to a Joint Commission 3-year accreditation cycle. The Joint Commission conducts *call surveys,* site visits that usually follow published standards. The findings are made available to the public in an accreditation quality report through the Joint Commission's Quality Check listings (see The Joint Commission, 2010a).

The Joint Commission also conducts unannounced *full survey* visits as part of the accreditation process. In these visits, the organization does not receive an advance notice of its survey date. Follow-up surveys typically occur 18–39 months after the organization's previous unannounced survey (Scalenghe, 2003).

During the accreditation process, surveyors conduct document review, interviews with the organization's leaders, visits to settings that provide care for clients, function interviews, review of the organization's processes to assess competence, feedback sessions, and public information interviews. Because of the nature of functions that occur throughout an organization, surveyors cannot reach a final score on compliance until they have visited all the scheduled consumer care settings and have conducted all the other survey interviews and activities. Anyone who has information about an organization's compliance with the accreditation standards may request a public information interview (The Joint Commission, n.d.d).

It is important that a program's policies and procedures, plans, and other documents are updated, appropriately approved, and consistent with other units or programs within the organization and that they reflect actual practice. (New "E-dition" manuals have been available since December 2009. The electronic manuals cost $1,486–$2,345 for institutions [available at http://www.jointcommission.org/Standards/Manuals)]. An online version of the new *Roadmap for Hospitals* [The Joint Commission, 2010c] also is available.) For example, an occupational therapy program does not need to have separate occupational therapy policies and procedures if sufficient information is contained in the overall organizational policies and procedures. Surveyors will tour an occupational therapy setting, review clinical records, speak with or observe clients, and meet with some occupational therapy practitioners. These practitioners may be questioned about their qualifications with specific responsibilities, education and training, and continuing competency.

At the end of the onsite survey, the surveyors enter the findings into a laptop computer, print a draft copy of the report, and present it to the organization. The surveyors then send the findings electronically to The Joint Commission's central office for analysis and review. Professional staff members internally review these results, reach an accreditation decision, and define any necessary follow-up requirements for improvement. Approximately 45 days after the survey, the organization is sent the official accreditation decision and a report detailing the findings. Most accredited organizations receive recommendations (each of which requires either a visit or a progress report) and supplemental recommendations, such as unique laws and regulations, patient care models, patient care–centered communication standards, and cultural competency (The Joint Commission, n.d.e).

After being surveyed, an organization is classified into an accreditation category. As of January 1, 2010, the accreditation decision categories were

- Accreditation,
- Provisional Accreditation,
- Conditional Accreditation,
- Preliminary Denial of Accreditation,
- Denial of Accreditation, and
- Preliminary Accreditation (Joint Commission, n.d.a).

Organizations that are denied accreditation have the right to appeal before a final accreditation decision is made.

Hospital organizations do not make the details of the survey findings public information. However, they do provide the organization's accreditation decision, the date that accreditation was awarded, and any standards that were cited for improvement. Hospital organizations are deemed to be in compliance when all or most of the applicable standards are met to the satisfaction of the site visitation team. Behavioral, home health, and laboratory facilities have additional options in that they can request a scheduled appointment meeting, a scheduled onsite review to discuss the survey results, and The Joint Commission to send agents to conduct interviews about the compliance and noncompliance issues (The Joint Commission, n.d.b).

The Joint Commission currently offers a joint survey option to rehabilitation hospitals that choose to have both The Joint Commission and CARF International accreditation (see below). This optional survey is structured in a manner to coordinate many survey activities (i.e., interviews, document reviews) between both sets of surveyors.

Preparation for a Survey

Occupational therapy managers and practitioners should continuously be in compliance with The Joint Commission standards. Continuous improvement and attention to detail will limit emotional stress that can be experienced when being surveyed. In addition, continuous readiness will prepare occupational therapy practitioners for the unannounced surveys.

Occupational therapy managers and practitioners should begin formal preparation for a survey 16 months before the anticipated survey date to be able to demonstrate a 12-month track record of compliance with standards. Managers and practitioners should have access to the standards, the scoring guidelines, and the *Perspectives* newsletter (see below). To meet the standards, managers and practitioners must collaborate with consumers, their families, other disciplines, and peers.

Some typical questions the surveyor might ask include, What mechanisms are used to identify and prioritize individual needs in determining care delivery? How is education instruction presented for the consumer and the family to address the consumer's health rehabilitation needs? How is occupational therapy integrated into the organization (e.g., through strategic planning, budgeting, performance improvement)? What steps have been taken to assess the risks for consumer care and the safety of the organization's buildings, grounds, equipment, occupants, and physical systems? How have staff participated in the organization's information management needs assessment?

The survey team looks for a collaborative, interdisciplinary approach in an intervention to meet client-centered care goals and to achieve optimal outcomes. The assessment should include the client's physical, cognitive, emotional, and social status, and a written intervention plan should identify the client's rehabilitation needs such as objectives related to activities of daily living, learning, and return to work; measures and time frames for achievement of rehabilitation goals and objectives; and factors that may influence use of services or goal achievement. Long-term rehabilitation goals should be stated in functional terms and developed in collaboration with the client and family. Preparing for a Joint Commission survey can be challenging process for the hospital administration and occupational therapy managers and practitioners as well. At a minimum, hospital administrators and staff must be completely familiar with the current Joint Commission standards and examine their current processes, policies, and procedures relative to those standards and prepare to improve any areas that are not currently in compliance. Occupational therapy managers can promote improved standards compliance by reading the standards, attending related seminars and related presentations at occupational therapy conferences, and networking with other occupational therapy managers and practitioners.

Accreditation is a continuous improvement process in which all divisions and departments must participate to remain in compliance. For example, the hospital seeking accreditation for the first time must be in compliance with the standards for at least 4–6 months prior to the initial survey. Health care organizations seeking recertification must be in compliance 6–9 months prior to the site visit (The Joint Commission, 2010a). The hospital should then be in compliance with applicable standards during the entire period of accreditation, which means that survey team usually looks for a full 3 years of implementation for several standards-related issues.

The focus of the standards and the survey is on the important processes and outcomes affecting customer care and organizational performance, not on specific disciplines. Occupational therapy managers and practitioners who provide care in Joint Commission–accredited organizations will be held accountable to be knowledgeable of the standards and the strategies they can contribute to the process to meet the requirements for compliance.

National Patient Safety Goals and Universal Protocol

In recent years The Joint Commission has established the National Patient Safety Goals (NPSGs) with the purpose of identifying specific improvements in patient safety. The NPSGs highlight areas considered to be problematic in health care and provide evidence– and expert-based solutions to typical problems. The rationale for the NPSGs is to reinforce the premise that a well-coordinated system design is important to the delivery of safe, high-quality health care. For instance, The Joint Commission established a Universal Protocol to reduce surgical errors and enforces existing regulations on medication reconciliation for 2009 on the basis of feedback received during onsite surveys. Occupational therapists see patients shortly after surgery in acute care. Complications related to surgical errors need to be reported to the occupational therapy manager and appropriate personnel. In addition, occupational therapy practitioners should be aware of side effects of major drugs and patient compliance with taking medications such as blood pressure pills in a timely manner as part of the patients' daily activities (The Joint Commission, 2010e).

The *2010 National Patient Safety Goals* outlines and chapters for applicable programs have changed recently. The newest version of the NPSGs includes minor changes to Element of Performance 3 (NPSG.03.04.01) and Element of Performance 3 (NPSG.07.03.01), which became effective July 1, 2010 (The Joint Commission, 2010b).

Collaboration With Other Agencies

In keeping with its' stated mission, The Joint Commission relies on collaboration with multiple professional and health care organizations, including AOTA and occupational therapy practitioners. The Joint Commission evaluates and accredits a range of organizations, including mental health and pediatric organizations; rehabilitation hospitals; health care networks, such as health maintenance organizations (HMOs), integrated delivery networks (IDNs), and preferred provider organizations (PPOs); home care organizations; home infusion and other pharmacy services; durable medical equipment services; hospice services; nursing homes and assisted living facilities; behavioral health care organizations; ambulatory care providers; and clinical laboratories. In addition, The Joint Commission has a disease-specific care (DSC) certification designed to evaluate disease management and chronic care services. The Joint Commission also maintains a Professional and Technical Advisory Committee (PTAC) for each field, including fire safety, occupational health, hazardous waste, health care engineering, and disease specific care (The Joint Commission, n.d.c).

Occupational therapy managers who are interested in participating in the development of standards (see below), the survey process, and strategic initiatives are encouraged to communicate with the occupational therapy representatives. AOTA can provide information about the occupational therapy practitioner PTACs representing various occupational therapy fields.

Standards

For occupational therapy managers and practitioners, survey preparation begins with a knowledge of the current standards and access the standards manual (or manuals) for the health care field in which they provide services. Manuals are available electronically or in print in a "comprehensive" version (which contains accreditation policies, standards, intent statements, scoring guidelines, and aggregation rules) and in a "standards" version (which contains accreditation policies, standards, and intent statements). Every accredited organization receives a complimentary copy of the comprehensive standards manual (or manuals) that applies to its organization (for a list, see http://www.jcrinc. com/Products-and-Services/). The types of standards that most pertain to occupational therapy are in the areas of disease and specific care, primary stroke centers, obstructive pulmonary disease, supporting self-management, and performance measures. Within these categories, occupational therapy practitioners are likely to find specific language that pertains measures affecting occupational therapy practice. The *Health Care Professional Quality Report User Guide* (The Joint Commission, 2010d) can be found online and is an excellent resource.

Many of the standards are focused on performance and are structured around functions. Occupational therapy managers and practitioners can influence standards either through their AOTA PTAC representative or on an individual basis. Sharing thoughts and suggestions about the standards with AOTA is important. This can be accomplished by contacting an AOTA representative to The Joint Commission. (Current representatives are listed at http://www.aota.org/About/AboutOT/Alliances/38599. aspx.) This information might include feedback about the survey experience, in particular, whether occupational therapy services were sufficiently included in the survey and whether the surveyors had adequate knowledge to fairly survey these services. Practitioners and managers can direct standards interpretation questions to the Commission's Standards Interpretation Group by phone at 630-792-5900 or by submitting an online question form at http:// www.jointcommission.org/AboutUs/ContactUs/contact_ us_directory.htm#s.

Perspectives Newsletter

Joint Commission standards undergo frequent changes. The Joint Commission publishes *Perspectives,* a monthly newsletter that reports changes in standards, policies, and procedures and that prints a range of features to improve understanding of accreditation. At the time of the site survey, practitioners are held accountable not only for what is in the current standards manual but also for the changes, additions, and corrections noted in *Perspectives.*

CARF International

During the time of budgetary shortfalls, when the general public demands more accountability, the pressure increases for organizations to disclose information about their outcomes. Third-party payers and regulators need many ways to ensure that the organization has identified its risks and has systems in place to reduce risk and exposure to loss. Accredited providers can evaluate the results of their services and their performance by using key indicators outlined by CARF International.

CARF accreditation standards establish the framework for business, information, and measurement systems as well as the programmatic components of service delivery. Occupational therapists, providing services as part of a team in a health care, school-based practice, home health, or community wellness programs, need to demonstrate they are in compliance with these standards.

History, Mission, and Goals

CARF International, formerly the Commission on Accreditation of Rehabilitation Facilities, is a private, not-for-profit organization that accredits human services organizations with programs and services in the fields of adult day services, assisted living, mental or behavioral health, community agencies, and medical rehabilitation facilities around the world. CARF was established in 1966 to assist consumers in identifying quality rehabilitation programs and services. CARF also includes a variety of services such as occupational rehabilitation programs, respite services, criminal justice programs, adult day care services, and workforce development programs (CARF International, n.d.d).

The mission statement of CARF is to promote the quality, value, and optimal outcomes of services through a consultative accreditation process that centers on enhancing the lives of the persons served (CARF International, n.d.a). CARF's primary purpose is to

1. Develop and maintain current, field-driven standards that improve the value and responsiveness of the programs and services delivered to people in need of rehabilitation and other life enhancement services;

2. Recognize organizations that achieve accreditation through a consultative peer-review process and demonstrate their commitment to the continuous improvement of their programs and services;

3. Conduct research on accreditation process and outcomes that measure the management, common program strengths, and areas that need improvement;

4. Provide consultation, education, training, and publications that support organizations in achieving the requirements for accreditation;

5. Provide information and education to the public, consumers, and other stakeholders on the value of accreditation;

6. Seek input through a variety of resources (e.g., national leadership panels, focus groups, one-on-one interactions, surveyor interactions) for continuous improvement (CARF International, n.d.a).

CARF is governed by a board of trustees that represents the consumers who receive services, the providers, the payers, and the regulators. AOTA has been involved in the development and revision of CARF standards and its practices for more than 20 years (CARF International, n.d.b).

Performance Indicators for Rehabilitation Programs

Because of growing pressure to demonstrate services that are valued and evidence based, CARF conducted focus groups with consumers, health administrators, and health professionals to establish national standards that can be applied as a measure of quality outcomes. Thus CARF developed performance indicators to more precisely define the desired outcome through a common metric that could establish benchmarking from pooled data sets. The CARF board uses the Performance Indicators for Rehabilitation Programs, which are "qualitative expressions used to point to program quality within the area of concern". (Wilkerson, Shen, & Duhaime, 1998, p. 33). For example, if the area of concern is the client's living situation, then the performance indicator may be the degree to which the consumer experiences increased independence in his or her living environment. Indicators are expressed as degrees, rates, ratios, or percentages. In many ways, CARF's policies also reflect the values of occupational therapy; people who receive support and services in accredited organizations should have the opportunity to live fulfilling lives, or living life to its fullest (see Moyers Cleveland, 2008).

Standards

CARF develops and maintains relevant and practical standards of quality for human services organizations. The standards address good business practices, measurable outcomes of services, the process of how the services are delivered, and specific standards for particular populations and services (MacDonell, 2003). The standards are organized in several categories: financial management, risk management, human resources, physical plant, strategic planning, corporate compliance, and corporate citizenship. Standards about information and outcome management focus on performance improvement.

The site survey is based on a consultative, peer approach that provides feedback on conformance to the standards. The degree of conformance to the standards determines the accreditation outcome.

CARF develops standards using a field-driven approach. The term *field* relates to the persons served, the providers of services, the purchasers of services, and other stakeholders (i.e., people who have a vested interest in the organization). The members of the field or the committee come together with surveyors, board of trustee members, and CARF staff members to develop a proposed set of standards. The proposals then go to the field for review and comment. After careful review and revision, the board of trustees gives the final approval for the set of standards. The standards are then applied to specific programs and services, including occupational therapy.

Accreditation Process

The process of a CARF accreditation is based on an onsite review conducted by peer surveyors. The emphasis is always on those receiving services and how the provider has developed an individualized program that has achieved predicted outcomes. If those outcomes have not been achieved, then performance improvement will be analyzed so that a plan to accomplish the goal has been realized. The CARF surveyors act as collaborative partners with the organization throughout the process.

The following 10 steps outline what is involved in the process of accreditation:

1. An organization contacts the CARF office to verify which of the standards manuals it should use for accreditation.

2. An organization conducts a self-study, which is an evaluation of the organization's conformance to the standards.

3. The organization implements the CARF standards for at least 6 months. During this time, the organization can actively engage CARF staff members in phone conversations, conference calls, e-mails, and in-person meetings for technical assistance and standards interpretation.

4. The organization requests an application for the accreditation survey, which it completes and submits a minimum of 3 months before the month in which it is requesting the site visit.
5. After reviewing and approving the application, CARF sends a bill to the organization for the survey fee, which is based on the number of surveyors and days needed to evaluate the organization's programs and services.
6. CARF selects the survey team based on a match of the surveyors' areas of expertise and the organization's unique needs.
7. The onsite CARF survey is conducted by a peer survey team that evaluates conformance to the standards. The survey comprises interviews with individuals and groups, observations of the service delivery, and review of necessary documentation. Persons served are always interviewed and are an integral part of the survey.
8. CARF evaluates the survey team's findings, and the CARF Board of Trustees renders an accreditation decision from the following options: 3-year accreditation, 1-year accreditation, provisional accreditation, and non-accreditation (see below). The organization is notified of the decision and receives a written survey report about 8 weeks after the survey.
9. The organization is awarded a certificate of accreditation that lists the programs or services that have been included in the rehabilitation process.
10. Within 90 days after notification, the organization submits a quality improvement plan to CARF outlining the actions that have been taken or will be taken in response to any recommendations of the report.

The typical time frame for an organization to prepare for an initial survey is 12–16 months. Accredited organizations should be maintaining compliance to the standards at all times. Preparing for most re-surveys takes approximately 6–9 months. A quality improvement plan should be submitted within 90 days after notice of accreditation. Although an organization may not be in full compliance with every applicable standard, the accreditation decision will be based on the balance of the organization's strengths with those areas in which the organization requires improvement.

Accreditation decisions acknowledge compliance outcomes in four categories: (1) 3-year accreditation, (2) 1-year accreditation, (3) provisional accreditation, and (4) non-accreditation.

3-Year Accreditation

The organization has demonstrated that its services and practices are designed and carried out to benefit the people it serves. Services, personnel, and documentation clearly indicate that present conditions represent an established pattern of total operation and that these conditions are likely to be maintained or improved in the near future.

1-Year Accreditation

Guidelines for 1-year accreditation require the organization to meet each of the CARF accreditation conditions. Although the organization may demonstrate non-compliance with respect to the standards, the evidence shows the organization's capability and commitment to correct the deficiencies and progress toward their correction.

Provisional Accreditation

The organization is given provisional accreditation if it meets each of the CARF accreditation conditions. Although the organization may demonstrate non-compliances in relation to the standards, the evidence shows the organization's capability and commitment to correct the deficiencies and progress toward conformance.

Non-accreditation

The organization will receive a non-accreditation decision when (1) it demonstrates major non-compliances in several areas of the standards and serious questions arise as to the benefits of services or the health, welfare, or safety of its clientele; (2) the organization has failed over time to bring itself into substantial compliance with the standards; or (3) the organization has failed to meet anyone of the CARF accreditation conditions. Non-accredited organizations cannot reapply for accreditation for a minimum of 6 months.

Conclusion

This chapter has provided an overview of The Joint Commission and CARF accreditation as it pertains to occupational therapy. Both The Joint Commission and CARF are independent and not-for-profit organizations. The Joint Commission was established in 1951 and accredits approximately 18,000 organizations in the United States, and CARF was established in 1966 and is present in 17 different countries.

The accreditation process is the gate keeper for high-quality health care. It is a collaborative venture whereby the organizations develop standards that are mutually agreed upon by consumers, stakeholders, and expert health professionals so that the standards exemplify best practices. Accrediting agencies provide a stamp of approval that informs the health care consumer that the organization strives for quality care, continuous improvement, and high standards in business practices. Occupational therapy practitioners are often called upon to participate in the self-study process and be interviewed by the surveyors or site visitors. The hospital or rehabilitation center will then receive a very thorough summary of the self-study document and the site visit findings, which describe the organization's strengths and areas that need improvement. The occupational therapy manager should view the accreditation process as a positive opportunity to improve services for clients and patients.

❖ Learning Activities

1. Compare and contrast CARF International with The Joint Commission. Compose a list of 10 characteristics the two accreditation agencies have in common.
2. Describe the difference between *accreditation* and *regulation*.
3. Write a short paragraph that argues for accreditation and one that argues against it.
4. Write a short paragraph stating how CARF and The Joint Commissions benefit occupational therapy practice.
5. Describe the occupational therapy manager's role in pursuing and complying with accreditation standards.

✓ Multiple-Choice Questions

1. Which best describes *accreditation?*
   a. The process of qualifying for a business loan.
   b. The process of meeting standards.
   c. A system of recognizing organizations for meeting a level of performance, integrity, and quality.
   d. A system in which the government sends surveyors to find noncompliances that fail to meet a standard.
2. Which of the following is true?
   a. The Joint Commission was formerly called CARF.
   b. The Joint Commission was formally called JCAHO.
   c. The Joint Commission was formed to accredit educational institutions only.
   d. The Joint Commission is under the supervision of AOTA.
3. The Joint Commission improves health care for the public by doing all of the following except:
   a. Collaborating with stakeholders.
   b. Evaluating rehabilitation centers.
   c. Evaluating health care organizations.
   d. Promoting safe and effective care.
4. To prepare for a Joint Commission survey, occupational therapy practitioners must do which of the following:
   a. Memorize all of the standards, and create policies for the self-study document.
   b. Perform continuous improvement until the standards are practiced at the administrative level.
   c. Become completely familiar with the current standards, and examine current policies and procedures for conformance with the standards.
   d. Conduct a survey among staff and clients, and see if The Joint Commission accepts your survey as a substitute for their standards.
5. Which of the following provides guidelines for patient safety?
   a. Universal safety goals.
   b. National Patient Safety Goals.
   c. International Joint Commission on Safety.
   d. Error-Free Committee on Safety.
6. The Joint Commission has a monthly publication titled
   a. *OT Practice.*
   b. *Joint Commission Magazine.*
   c. *Monthly Commission.*
   d. *Perspectives.*
7. The clients' rehabilitation needs for occupational therapy on The Joint Commission survey would include all of the following area except
   a. Work and productive activities.
   b. Cognitive integration components.
   c. Activities of daily living.
   d. Wound care medication prescriptions.
8. When The Joint Commission survey team conducts a site visit, which of following is not true?
   a. The occupational therapy practitioners may be interviewed.
   b. The occupational therapy department's policies and procedures will be audited.
   c. The survey team may wish to know how occupational therapy services contribute to the organization's care of clients.
   d. The survey team may interview clients.
9. After The Joint Commission conducts its site survey, approximately how long does it take to make an official accreditation decision?
   a. 3 years.
   b. 1 week.
   c. 45 days.
   d. 24 hours.
10. Which of the following is not one of the 8 fields covered by The Joint Commission?
    a. Home care.
    b. Long-term care facilities.
    c. Clinical and pathology labs.
    d. Rehabilitation facilities.
11. Which best describes CARF accreditation?
    a. The accreditation process most commonly for small businesses.
    b. The process of meeting standards to operate skilled-nursing facilities.

c. A system of recognizing organizations for meeting a certain level of performance, integrity, and quality in rehabilitation facilities.

d. An accreditation system in which the government monitors compliance and fines those facilities that fail to meet its rigorous standards.

12. Which of the following is a true statement about CARF?
    a. It is the process of qualifying for a small business loan.
    b. It develops standards from a field-driven approach.
    c. It is a system of recognizing organizations for meeting government standards.
    d. It is a system in which the government sends surveyors to find noncompliances that fail to meet a standard.

13. Which of the following statements is true?
    a. The Joint Commission was formerly called CARF.
    b. CARF conducts a site survey as a collaborative effort.
    c. CARF was formed to accredit educational institutions only.
    d. CARF is under the supervision of AOTA.

14. CARF improves health care for the public by doing which of the following:
    a. Notifying stakeholders to invest in programs that meet standards.
    b. Evaluating rehabilitation centers.
    c. Evaluating health care organizations.
    d. Promoting safe and effective academic programs.

15. To prepare for a CARF survey, occupational therapy managers should do which of the following?
    a. Memorize all of the standards, and create policies for the self-study document.
    b. Make all of the standards into policy so that the standards are practiced at the clinical level.
    c. Become completely familiar with the current standards, and examine current policies and procedures for conformance with the standards.

d. Conduct a survey among staff and clients, and see if The Joint Commission accepts your survey as a substitute for its standards.

16. CARF developed performance indicators to
    a. Measure the cost of health care.
    b. Make accreditation more difficult to obtain.
    c. Better demonstrate services' value and basis in evidence.
    d. None of the above.

17. CARF has a 10-step process for accreditation and publishes the most recent information about it where?
    a. *OT Practice*
    b. The CARF monthly newsletter.
    c. The CARF Web site.
    d. *Perspectives.*

18. CARF's standards for an occupational therapy survey would include all of the following area except
    a. Work and productive activities.
    b. Cognitive integration components.
    c. Activities of daily living.
    d. Health care operations.

19. When CARF survey team conducts a site visit,
    a. Occupational therapy practitioners may be interviewed.
    b. The policies and procedures of the occupational therapy department will be audited.
    c. The survey team may wish to know how occupational therapy services contribute to the organization's care of clients.
    d. The survey team may interview clients.

20. Which of the following is the highest CARF category for accreditation?
    a. 2-year accreditation.
    b. 3-year accreditation.
    c. 4-year accreditation.
    d. Approximately 45 days.

References

Accreditation. (1993). *American heritage dictionary* (p. 122). London, UK: Williams & Collins.

American Occupational Therapy Association. (2007). *Introduction to accreditation.* Retrieved September 7, 2010, from http://www.aota.org/Educate/Accredit/Overview/38123.aspx

CARF International. (n.d.a). *CARF's mission, vision, core values, and purposes.* Retrieved September 2, 2010, from http://www.carf.org/About/Mission/

CARF International. (n.d.b). *Payers choose CARF to reduce risk and raise accountability.* Retrieved September 2, 2010, from http://www.carf.org/Payers/

CARF International. (n.d.c). *The public says: Accreditation matters!* Retrieved September 2, 2010, from http://www.carf.org/Public/

CARF International. (n.d.d). *Who we are.* Retrieved September 2, 2010, from http://www.carf.org/About/WhoWeAre/

CARF Internaitonal. (n.d.e). *Why does accreditation matter?* Retrieved September 2, 2010, from http://www.carf.org/Accreditation/

Donabedean, A. (1997). The quality of care: How can it be assessed? *Archives of Pathology and Laboratory Medicine, 11,* 121.

The Joint Commission. (2010a). *2010 certification handbook.* Retrieved September 2, 2010, from http://www.jointcommission.org/NR/rdonlyres/F9C16D19-98F3-4FE8-B51F-129560AD57A8/0/2010HealthCareServicesCertificationHandbook.pdf

The Joint Commission. (2010b). *2010 national safety patient goals.* Retrieved September 2, 2010, from http://www.jointcommission.org/PatientSafety/NationalPatientSafetyGoals

The Joint Commission. (2010c). *Advancing effective communication, cultural competence, and patient- and family-centered care: A roadmap for hospitals.* Retrieved September 2, 2010, from http://www.jointcommission.org/NR/rdonlyres/87C00B33-FCD0-4D37-A4EB-21791FB3969C/0/ARoadmapforHospitalsfinalversion727.pdf

The Joint Commission. (2010d). *Health care professional quality report user guide.* Retrieved September 8, 2010, from http://www.jointcommission.org/NR/rdonlyres/EE7A17FB-2AB3-4B20-A343-7D2B7CBEF9CC/0/Hospital_user_guide_2010.pdf

The Joint Commission. (2010e). *Medication reconciliation national patient safety goal to be reviewed, refined.* Retrieved September 7, 2010, from http://www.jointcommission.org/PatientSafety/NationalPatientSafetyGoals/npsg8_review.htm

The Joint Commission. (n.d.a). *Accreditation process overview.* Retrieved September 2, 2010, from http://www.jointcommission.org/AboutUs/Fact_Sheets/overview_qa.htm

The Joint Commission. (n.d.b). *Alternatives for sharing sentinel event-related information with The Joint Commission.* Retrieved September 2, 2010, from http://www.jointcommission.org/SentinelEvents/ReportingAlternatives/

The Joint Commission. (n.d.c). *Disease-specific care certification.* Retrieved September 7, 2010, form http://www.jointcommission.org/CertificationPrograms/Disease-SpecificCare/

The Joint Commission. (n.d.d). *Field reviews.* Retrieved September 2, 2010, from http://www.jointcommission.org/Standards/FieldReviews/

The Joint Commission. (n.d.e). *Hospitals, language, and culture.* Retrieved September 7, 2010, from http://www.jointcommission.org/PatientSafety/HLC/HLC_Develop_Culturally_Competent_Pt_Centered_Stds.htm

The Joint Commission. (n.d.f). *Joint Commission requirements.* Retrieved September 7, 2010, from http://www.jointcommission.org/Standards/Requirements/

The Joint Commission. (n.d.g). *Mission statement.* Retrieved September 2, 2010, at http://www.jointcommission.org/AboutUs/

MacDonell, C. M. (2003). CARF…Commission of Rehabilitation Facilities. In G. McCormack, E. G. Jaffe, & M. Goodman-Lavey (Eds.), *The occupational therapy manger* (4th ed., pp. 535–542). Bethesda, MD: AOTA Press.

Moyers Cleveland, P. (2008). Be unreasonable. Knock on the big doors. Knock loudly [Presidential address]. *American Journal of Occupational Therapy, 62,* 737–742.

National Council of State Boards of Nursing. (2007). *Why regulation matters.* Retrieved September 2, 2010, from https://www.ncsbn.org/247.htm

Regulation. (2000). *Webster's American dictionary* (p. 663). New York: Random House.

Scalenghe, R. W. (2003). Joint Commission of Healthcare Organizations. In G. McCormack, E. G. Jaffe, & M. Goodman-Lavey (Eds.), *The occupational therapy manager* (4th ed., pp. 515–534). Bethesda, MD: AOTA Press.

U.S. Department of Education. (n.d.). *Glossary.* Retrieved September 8, 2010, from http://ope.ed.gov/accreditation/Glossary.aspx

U.S.Legal.com. (n.d.). *National consensus standard law and legal definition.* Available online http://definitions.uslegal.com/n/national-consensus-standard/

Wilkerson, D., Shen, D., & Duhaime, D. (1998). *Performance indicators for rehabilitation programs.* Tucson, AZ: Rehabilitation Accreditation Commission.

APPENDIX 35.A. MAJOR ACCREDITING ORGANIZATIONS EVIDENCE TABLE

Topic	Subtopic	Evidence
Quality of care	Variables of assessment	Donabedean, A. (1997). The quality of care: How can it be assessed? *Archives of Pathology and Laboratory Medicine, 11,* 121.
Regulation	Statutes	National Council of State Boards of Nursing. (2007). *Why regulation matters.* Retrieved September 2, 2010, from https://www.ncsbn.org/247.htm
Accreditation	The Joint Commission	The Joint Commission. (n.d.f). *Joint Commission requirements.* Retrieved September 7, 2010, from http://www.jointcommission.org/Standards/Requirements/
Accreditation	CARF International	CARF International. (n.d.c). *The public says: Accreditation matters!* Retrieved September 2, 2010, from http://www.carf.org/Public/ CARF International. (n.d.e). *Why does accreditation matter?* Retrieved September 2, 2010, from http://www.carf.org/Accreditation/

36
Accreditation Related to Education

Paula Kramer, PhD, OTR/L, FAOTA,
and Neil Harvison, PhD, OTR/L

❖ Key Terms and Concepts

Accreditation. A formal process used to determine if an academic institution or program is minimally in compliance prescribed sets of standards.

Accreditation agencies. Private educational and professional associations who develop evaluation criteria and conduct peer evaluations to assess whether or not those criteria are met by an academic institution or program seeking accreditation (U.S. Department of Education, n.d.).

Occupational therapy education. An academic program usually housed at a college or university designed to prepare students to become entry-level occupational therapists or occupational therapy assistants.

Standard. Stated criteria used to judge minimal compliance (Accreditation Council for Occupational Therapy Education®, n.d.b).

❖ Learning Objectives

After completing this chapter, you should be able to do the following:

- Understand the purpose and value of institutional and specialized accreditation.
- Appreciate the history of accreditation of occupational therapy educational programs.

- Demonstrate a beginning understanding of the accreditation process for occupational therapy educational programs.
- Understand the important role of external review and recognition.

Accreditation of occupational therapy educational programs ensures the quality of the program by making certain that it meets minimal standards and by assisting the program with ongoing reflection for the purpose of continuous improvement.

(Kramer, Seitz, & Dickson, 2003, p. 549).

This chapter focuses on the accreditation processes for higher education in the United States. First, the chapter identifies the similarities and differences between institutional accreditation agencies that focus on the broader based accreditation for colleges and universities and programmatic accreditation agencies that focus on specific programs. The history, structure, process, and functions of the Accreditation Council for Occupational Therapy Education (ACOTE) are explored. The role of ACOTE as the recognized programmatic accreditor for occupational therapy education is explained.

Second, the roles of the Council for Higher Education Accreditation (CHEA) and the U.S. Department of

Education (USDE) in external recognition of accreditation agencies are outlined. The chapter concludes with an overview of the member association of specialized accreditation agencies (the Association of Specialized and Professional Accreditors, or ASPA) and processes to ensure quality and fairness in international academic and professional mobility, credentialing, and recognition (the Center for Quality Assurance in International Education, or CQAIE).

It is important that occupational therapy managers understand the accreditation and regulatory requirements affecting the educational programs that prepare occupational therapy practitioners. First, as employers of the graduates, occupational therapy managers are key stakeholders in the outcome of the educational programs. Second, all students in the academic programs complete mentored fieldwork placements in practice settings under the supervision of managers and their practitioners. An understanding of the accreditation and regulatory requirements enhances managers' ability to foster productive learning experiences.

ACCREDITATION AND EDUCATION

Accreditation is a system for recognizing educational institutions and professional programs affiliated with those institutions for a level of performance, integrity, and quality that entitles them to the confidence of the educational community and the public they serve. In most other countries, the establishment and maintenance of educational standards is the responsibility of a government bureau. In the United States, this recognition is extended primarily through nongovernmental, voluntary institutional, or professional associations. These accreditation agencies establish standards for accreditation; conduct peer reviews; arrange site visits; evaluate the qualifications or credentials of personnel, institutions, and professional programs that desire accredited status; and publicly designate those that meet their standards. In addition, the accreditation agencies provide ongoing external review on a periodic basis (USDE, n.d.).

Accrediting bodies can be divided into two general groups: (1) organizations that accredit colleges and universities as institutions and (2) organizations that accredit professional, specialized, and special-purpose programs (USDE, n.d.). Institutional accrediting agencies are responsible for endorsing or approving the university or college as a whole. The institutional accrediting agencies fall into two categories:

1. *Regional accreditors*, which are agencies that accredit public and private, mainly nonprofit and degree-granting, two-and four-year institutions, and
2. *National accreditors*, which are agencies that accredit public and private, nonprofit and for-profit institutions; frequently single-purpose institutions, including distance learning colleges and universities; private career institutions; and faith-based colleges and universities (USDE, n.d.).

The various commissions of the regional accrediting associations have accredited the colleges and universities where occupational therapy programs are located. Occupational therapy assistant programs often are housed in community colleges and career schools; these institutions are accredited by either regional or national career school accrediting agencies recognized by the USDE.

Regional Accreditation Agencies

The first regional accrediting agencies were formed in the 1880s with a focus on educational standards and admissions procedures with colleges and universities. Six regional associations currently are operating eight accreditation agencies (Commissions) within the United States (see Table 36.1). Each regional accrediting agency operates independently in decision making and application of standards. However, there are ongoing collaborations and sharing among the agencies to promote consistency in accreditation across the nation. All of the regional accrediting agencies meet the recognition criteria of both USDE and CHEA (CHEA, n.d.).

Structure

Each regional accreditation agency is governed by a board of commissioners. The commissions include individuals elected by the member colleges and universities with term limitations. At least 1 in 7 commissioners is a representative of the public interest, with the remainder being faculty

Table 36.1. Regional Accreditation Agencies Recognized by the U.S. Department of Education

Regional Accreditation Agency	Region
Middle States Association of Colleges and Schools Middle States Commission on Higher Education	Delaware, District of Columbia, Maryland, New Jersey, New York, Pennsylvania, Puerto Rico, U.S. Virgin Islands
New England Association of Schools and Colleges Commission on Institutions of Higher Education	Connecticut, Maine, Massachusetts, New Hampshire, Rhode Island, Vermont
New England Association of Schools and Colleges Commission on Technical and Career Institutions	Connecticut, Maine, Massachusetts, New Hampshire, Rhode Island, Vermont
North Central Association of Colleges and Schools The Higher Learning Commission	Arizona, Arkansas, Colorado, Iowa, Illinois, Indiana, Kansas, Michigan, Minnesota, Missouri, North Dakota, Nebraska, Ohio, Oklahoma, New Mexico, South Dakota, Wisconsin, West Virginia, Wyoming
Northwest Commission on Colleges and Universities	Alaska, Idaho, Montana, Nevada, Oregon, Utah, Washington
Southern Association of Colleges and Schools Commission on Colleges	Alabama, Florida, Georgia, Kentucky, Louisiana, Mississippi, North Carolina, South Carolina, Tennessee, Texas, Virginia
Western Association of Schools and Colleges Accrediting Commission for Community and Junior Colleges	California and Hawaii; the territories of American Samoa, Federated States of Micronesia, Guam, Republic of Palau, Commonwealth of the Northern Marianas Islands
Western Association of Schools and Colleges Accrediting Commission for Senior Colleges and Universities	California and Hawaii; the territories of American Samoa, Federated States of Micronesia, Guam, Republic of Palau, Commonwealth of the Northern Marianas Islands

and administrators from member institutions. Regional accreditation is overseen by a professional staff for each commission. Annually the work of accreditation is carried out by volunteers who serve on visiting teams and on the commissions. These volunteers include college and university presidents, academic officers, faculty, and campus experts in finance, student services, and library or technology.

Process for Accreditation

Each regional accreditation agency follows a similar process for accreditation of colleges and universities. The agencies assesses standards related to (1) formal educational activities, (2) governance structure and administration, (3) financial stability, (4) admissions and student services, (5) institutional resources, (6) student learning, (7) institutional effectiveness, and (8) relationships with stakeholders including consumers. Each institution is reviewed regularly through a process that includes the preparation of a self-evaluation (self-study) and report of the institution's compliance with the established standards. The report is reviewed by the agency, and an onsite visit is conducted to see if the facilities and resources of the institution meet the standards. The onsite visit is a peer-review process conducted by volunteers who are college and university faculty, staff, and administrators.

Following the onsite visit, a report is prepared for the commissioners who determine the accreditation status of

the institution (CHEA, n.d.). In occupational therapy accreditation, faculty and staff should be involved throughout the self-study process and onsite review. Often members of the occupational therapy department serve on committees preparing different aspects of the self-study report and onsite visit.

Council of Regional Accrediting Commissions

The regional accrediting agencies are members of the Council of Regional Accrediting Commissions (C–RAC), which meets regularly. The council is composed of the executive officers and commission chairs from each regional agency. C–RAC has developed common statements, policies, and training materials in areas such as distance learning and assessment of student learning outcomes. The professional staffs of all commissions meet biennially to share best practices and common strategic planning.

National Career School Accrediting Agencies

Like the regional accrediting agencies, the national career school accrediting agencies operate independently in decision making and for the application of standards (see Table 36.2 for a list). Occupational therapy assistant programs may be located in either a regionally accredited college or an institution accredited by a USDE-recognized national accrediting agency. Unlike the regional accrediting agencies, many of the national accrediting agencies

Table 36.2. National Accreditation Agencies Recognized by the U.S. Department of Education

National Accreditation Agency	Scope
Accrediting Commission of Career Schools and Colleges of Technology	The accreditation of private, postsecondary, non-degree-granting institutions and degree-granting institutions in the United States, including those granting associate's, bachelor's, and master's degrees, that are predominantly organized to educate students for occupational, trade, and technical careers and including institutions that offer programs via distance education.
Accrediting Council for Continuing Education and Training	The accreditation throughout the United States of institutions of higher education that offer continuing education and vocational programs that confer certificates or occupational associate degrees, including those programs offered via distance education.
Accrediting Council for Independent Colleges and Schools	The accreditation of private postsecondary institutions offering certificates or diplomas and postsecondary institutions offering associate's, bachelor's, or master's degrees in programs designed to educate students for professional, technical, or occupational careers, including those that offer those programs via distance education.
Council on Occupational Education	The accreditation and pre-accreditation ("Candidacy Status") throughout the United States of postsecondary occupational education institutions offering non-degree and applied associate-degree programs in specific career and technical education fields, including institutions that offer programs via distance education.
Distance Education and Training Council, Accrediting Commission	The accreditation of postsecondary institutions in the United States that offer degree programs primarily by the distance education method up to and including the professional doctoral degree and are specifically certified by the agency as accredited for Title IV purposes, and for the accreditation of postsecondary institutions in the United States not participating in Title IV that offer programs primarily by the distance education method up through the professional doctoral degrees.
Transnational Association of Christian Colleges and Schools Accreditation Commission	The accreditation and pre-accreditation ("Candidate" status) of postsecondary institutions in the United States that offer certificates, diplomas, and associate, baccalaureate, and graduate degrees, including institutions that offer distance education.

focus their reviews on vocational schools offering technical curricula focused on obtaining an associate's degree.

OCCUPATIONAL THERAPY EDUCATION ACCREDITATION

History

The first standards for occupational therapy education can be traced to about 1923 and appear to have been written in large part by Eleanor Clarke Slagle, one of the founders of the occupational therapy profession (Slagle, 1931). Slagle noted that, a few years after 1923, "the Council of the American Medical Association made a study of the training of workers in occupational therapy and issued a report recommending even higher standards than were in force" (p. 15). Simultaneously, several deans of training schools (as they were called at the time) also recommended that minimal requirements be increased. These changes were adopted. At this time, the accreditation of occupational therapy programs became one of the roles of the American Occupational Therapy Association (AOTA).

In 1933, AOTA requested that the American Medical Association (AMA) work in cooperation to develop and improve educational programs for occupational therapists. In 1935 the AMA House of Delegates adopted the "Essentials of an Acceptable School of Occupational Therapy" (ACOTE, n.d.a), which was the AMA's first cooperative accreditation activity.

The AOTA Accreditation Committee began approving educational programs for occupational therapy assistants in 1958. At the same time, curriculum directors began a strong movement to again study and increase the requirements for the education of occupational therapists, and they expressed concern that preparation should be more stringent academically, with less technical and medical focus. Some evidence also indicates that the curriculum directors were conflicted about the role of the AMA in regulating occupational therapy education (Colman, 1990).

The collaboration of AOTA and the AMA was officially recognized by numerous private and governmental agencies over the years, including the National Commission on Accreditation, the Federation of Regional Accrediting Commissions of Higher Education, the Council on Post-Secondary Education (COPA), and the USDE. The AMA collaboration with AOTA on accreditation continued under the aegis of AMA's Committee on Allied Health Education and Accreditation (CAHEA). CAHEA was recognized by the USDE as the accrediting body for occupational therapy education. In 1991, based on a request from AOTA, CAHEA began accrediting occupational therapy assistant programs (ACOTE, n.d.a).

The 1990s were a critical period of growth and change for occupational therapy accreditation. In 1994, the Accreditation Committee of AOTA officially changed its name to the Accreditation Council for Occupational Therapy Education and began to exercise some autonomy. After discussion with various constituency groups, ACOTE began to operate independently from CAHEA. During that same year, ACOTE was recognized by the USDE as the accrediting agency for professional programs in occupational therapy.

In 1998, ACOTE adopted a position statement indicating that, because of "the demands, complexity, and a diversity of contemporary occupational therapy practice, ACOTE's position was that the forthcoming educational standards are most likely to be achieved in post-baccalaureate degree programs" (ACOTE, 1998, p. 1). In April 1999, at the AOTA Annual Conference & Expo, the AOTA Representative Assembly passed Resolution J, which called for entry-level education for occupational therapist to be at the post-baccalaureate level (AOTA, 1999). While the Representative Assembly passed Resolution J, they left the timeline for implementation of this resolution to ACOTE.

In August 1999, ACOTE determined that professional, entry-level education programs must be offered at the post-baccalaureate entry level by January 1, 2007 to receive and maintain ACOTE accreditation status (ACOTE, 1999). Although 2007 seemed to a long time off, this date was carefully chosen to allow for all students who were currently enrolled in educational programs to complete the program that they had entered without disruption. The timeline also allowed colleges and universities to explore whether their charters allowed them to move to the master's level and gave programs time to get courses of study approved through the necessary administrative processes.

In 2003, a change in the AOTA Bylaws made ACOTE an associated body of the AOTA Board of Directors, which demonstrated that ACOTE had a degree of independence from AOTA. As ACOTE was renewing its petition with USDE in 2004, it was felt by both the leadership of ACOTE and the leadership of AOTA that there was a need for a formal understanding of the roles and responsibilities of each group and the need for autonomy of ACOTE. In collaboration, ACOTE and AOTA developed a formal memorandum of understanding (MOU), which gave ACOTE "unfettered autonomy for establishing standards for educational programs" (AOTA & ACOTE, 2005, p. 1) and budgetary autonomy, including establishing fees. This MOU was signed in January 2005. Both the MOU and the AOTA Bylaws change cemented the relationship of ACOTE to AOTA as well the need for autonomy in ACOTE's deliberations.

ACOTE Standards

Historically, ACOTE had one set of standards for accredited educational programs for occupational therapists and one set for accredited educational programs for occupational therapy assistants. This allowed ACOTE to accredit programs rather than degree levels. However, the development of new program formats led to a decision by ACOTE in August 2004 to transition from accreditation of occupational therapy educational programs to accreditation of occupational therapy program degree levels, effective January 1, 2005.

Further, as physical therapy and other professionals developed doctoral entry programs, an increased interest in such programs was discussed in the occupational therapy community. For this reason, ACOTE formed a task force to explore the need for doctoral-level standards. It was decided that there was a need for doctoral-level standards that were separate from those required for the master's degree.

Following the traditional standards review process, in August 2006, ACOTE formally adopted *Accreditation Standards for a Master's-Degree-Level Educational Program for the Occupational Therapist* (ACOTE, 2007b) and *Accreditation Standards for an Educational Program for the Occupational Therapy Assistant* (ACOTE, 2007c). In December 2006, ACOTE formally adopted *Accreditation Standards for a Doctoral-Degree-Level Educational Program for the Occupational Therapist* (ACOTE, 2007a). An effective date of January 1, 2008, was established for all of the 2006 ACOTE Standards.

All three sets of standards include two major sections with the objective of preparing entry-level practitioners at the respective degree level (i.e., doctoral occupational therapy, master's occupational therapy, or occupational therapy assistant; see ACOTE 2007a, b, and c): (1) "General Requirements for Accreditation" and (2) "Specific Requirements for Accreditation." The general requirements include standards related to (1) sponsorship and institutional accreditation, (2) academic resources, (3) students, (4) operational policies, (5) strategic plan and assessment, and (6) curriculum framework. The specific requirements for accreditation include standards related to content (knowledge) and skill requirements of a graduate of the program. Each of the standards are operationally defined and written as a measurable outcome that begins with the statement that the "student will be able to…" (ACOTE, 2007a, b, c). In addition, the specific include standards detailing the requirements for Level I and Level II fieldwork and other opportunities for experiential learning. As occupational therapy is a practice-based profession, experiential learning is essential component on any occupational therapy educational program.

ACOTE Structure

ACOTE is made up of 18 occupational therapists and occupational therapy assistants, 1 higher education administrator member, 2 public members, and 1 alternate public member. The council is responsible for setting standards for education for occupational therapists and occupational therapy assistants and for monitoring and regularly reviewing all occupational therapy educational programs.

ACOTE standards are routinely reviewed, with a formal review process instituted approximately 5 years after each set of standards is revised and accepted.

ACOTE Process for Accreditation

Programs are routinely required to engage in a self-study process to assess their compliance with the educational standards, a process that is achieved through biennial reports and comprehensive self-study documents. After the completion of a self-study document, representatives of the council conduct a comprehensive onsite visit to meet with all constituency groups involved in the educational process and to verify the information supplied in the report of self-study. Onsite visits are conducted by members of ACOTE and members of the Roster of Accreditation Evaluators (RAE), a group of occupational therapy educators and practitioners who have been trained to understand the standards and to conduct onsite visits. Onsite teams are made up of an educator and a practitioner to adhere to the USDE requirements for accreditation of a practice profession. This requirement is helpful in ensuring that the program is meeting the current standards and reflects current practice.

When a new academic program applies for ACOTE accreditation, the program must follow a three-step process. First, the program must submit an application for developing program status. This application is reviewed by 1 member of the council and 2 RAE members. The results of this review are submitted to the council and discussed. After preliminary approval, the program can continue in the self-study process and admit students.

Second, the program submits an initial, comprehensive report of self-study to the council, describing the program in detail for an initial review. In this report, programs must review and comment on all aspects of the educational process included in the standards. This process requires significant time and input from many sources on campus and can help the faculty identify the strengths and potential weaknesses of the program. Once the council has approved this review, programs have an opportunity to make improvements.

At this point, the third step in the process, the onsite visit, can take place. After an onsite visit, the council meets (twice a year) to review the report and determine the accreditation status of the program. The council report includes a detailed description of compliance with the standards, strengths of the program, suggestions for improvement, and areas of noncompliance. Programs that are cited for noncompliance are given an opportunity to correct the infractions so they can meet minimal standards. Accreditation status for new programs includes a status of accreditation or of accreditation withheld. Programs being reaccredited may receive a status of accreditation, probationary accreditation, or accreditation withheld.

Once a program has been initially accredited, it must submit biennial reports that provide ongoing information about the program and must assist in determining continuing compliance with educational standards. Accreditation is granted for a period of 5 years after the initial onsite visit and for either 7 or 10 years subsequently. Before an onsite visit can be conducted, each program must perform a complete self-study and submit the appropriate documentation (ACOTE, n.d.b).

Value of Accreditation

The accreditation process is valuable to the occupational therapy educational program, to its students, and to the community it serves. Through the development and periodic review of comprehensive standards, the occupational therapy profession can be assured that education is meeting the needs of society. As the profession and its practice grows and changes, the standards are revised to reflect those changes, thus ensuring that future practitioners will have the basic information and skill sets needed for practice. The standards ensure some degree of uniformity in the education of future occupational therapists and occupational therapy assistants and require educational programs and faculty to remain current and to reflect what is offered for study.

The universities and colleges also benefit from the accreditation process. External review helps validate the quality of the program. Specialty accreditation informs society that the institution cares about the quality of its programs and welcomes this type of review. Further, programs that receive good reviews and accreditation status are considered prestigious.

The inclusion of practitioner's or an educator's involvement in the accreditation process also provides valuable professional perspectives. Participation requires time and effort, but it also is very rewarding. As an RAE member, one can learn about the education process from a different perspective. One has an opportunity to understand the educational and accreditation processes in more depth and to have some input into the education of future practitioners. This type of service to the profession is highly valued by the association and its members. ACOTE routinely calls for new candidates for the RAE in AOTA publications such as *OT Practice*. Experienced RAE members are considered as potentially ACOTE members.

EXTERNAL REVIEW OF ACCREDITING AGENCIES

External review of accrediting agencies may be conducted by CHEA or the USDE through a process called *recognition*. Both the CHEA and USDE have published standards that must be met by an accrediting organization to be recognized. Recognition is not the same as accreditation; recognition involves acknowledging an accrediting organization for its high standards of quality performance in its work to accredit organizations and institutions. Although occupational therapy educational programs are not recognized by the external agencies, the recognition requirements do affect the standards and procedures they must meet in order to be accredited by ACOTE. Occupational therapy managers must be aware of the influence that the federal government and nongovernmental higher-education associations have on occupational therapy education through the recognition process.

Council for Higher Education Accreditation

CHEA is a private member organization that was founded in 1966 by the presidents of American universities and colleges to provide recognition of accredited organizations that support higher education (e.g., universities, colleges, schools, educational programs). CHEA's mission statement is to "serve students and their families, colleges and universities, sponsoring bodies, governments, and employers by promoting academic quality through formal recognition of higher education accreditation bodies and will coordinate and work to advance self-regulation through accreditation" (CHEA, 2006b).

For an accrediting organization to be recognized by CHEA, the organization must meet the following recognition standards: (1) advance academic quality, (2) demonstrate accountability, (3) employ appropriate and fair procedures in decision making, (4) demonstrate ongoing review of accreditation practice, and (5) possess sufficient resources (CHEA, 2006b).

CHEA Structure

The CHEA Board of Directors appoints members to the Committee on Recognition according to recommendations by the president of CHEA made in consultation with CHEA-recognized accrediting organizations. The 9-member committee is responsible for the recognition status of new and continuing accrediting organizations. Each member serves a 3-year term. The committee includes members from professional accrediting organizations, colleges and universities, and the public. Public members are people who are not directly involved with an institution or an accrediting organization.

The committee also may consult with external readers during the process of recognition. External readers are nonmembers of the committee who will read the organization's application for recognition. The committee advises the 17-member board of directors on which organizations are eligible for recognition, and the board makes the final decision (CHEA, 2006b).

CHEA Process for Recognition

Usually, the accrediting organization will undergo a recognition review every 10 years, with an interim 5-year report. However, CHEA may decide to review a recognized accrediting organization out of sequence when the organization decides to change its activities or when concerns about the organization have been documented over a period of time.

The steps in the CHEA recognition review process are as follows (CHEA, 2006b):

1. The accrediting organization sends a letter of intent to apply for recognition and an application fee to CHEA.
2. CHEA sends the accrediting organization the recognition review materials.
3. The accrediting organization returns the eligibility portion of the application to CHEA, and the committee makes a recommendation on eligibility to the board of directors for consideration.
4. The board considers the committee's recommendation and provides the accrediting organization with the opportunity to appear before the board if necessary.
5. The accrediting organization completes the self-study and sends it to CHEA; the self-study should provide evidence that the accrediting organization meets CHEA's five recognition standards.
6. If applicable, CHEA sends a site visitor to the accrediting organization. Site visits are required in any of the following three instances: (a) the accrediting organization is seeking initial recognition, (b) the committee believes that the material provided by the accrediting organization is insufficient for a fair judgment by the committee, or (c) the committee believes that third-party comments received by the committee are sufficient to raise questions that may be addressed by a site visit.
7. The accrediting organization's response, any reader and site visit reports, and any third-party comments are sent to the CHEA office. An institution's representative, an association's representative, or a member of the general public can make a third-party comment. The third-party comment must relate to the CHEA recognition standards and can be negative or positive. Many third-party comments are testimonials.
8. The accrediting organization gives a public presentation to the committee, and the committee gives a recommendation to the board of directors.
9. The accrediting organization responds to any questions the committee has about the public presentation.
10. The board of directors considers the committee's recommendation and, if necessary, provides the accrediting organization with an opportunity to appear before the board.
11. The board considers the recommendations of the committee before making its decision (which is published) and notifies accrediting organizations of the board's actions within 30 days after taking any action. If the board recognizes an accrediting organization, the notice will specify the scope of the organization's recognition (including, where indicated, the geographic area, the types of higher education institutions or programs that the organization may accredit, and the degrees and certificates awarded by higher education institutions accredited by the accrediting organization) and the recognition period.

CHEA (2006b) may withdraw recognition of an accrediting organization for any sufficient cause, including a determination that the organization no longer meets the requirements for eligibility or the standards for recognition.

U.S. Department of Education

Accreditation by an agency recognized by the USDE is one of the conditions qualifying an educational institution or program to participate in federal funding programs. Placement on the list of recognized accrediting agencies also serves consumer interests by acknowledging an accrediting body's ability to identify institutions or programs of quality. Federal legislation requires the U.S. Secretary of Education to publish a list of the accrediting agencies the Secretary recognizes as reliable authorities concerning the quality of education offered by educational institutions or programs. The criteria and procedures developed by the department for its evaluations and the list of agencies granted national recognition are published in the *Federal Register* (USDE, n.d.).

USDE Process for Recognition

The criteria and procedures are established through the negotiated rule-making process to meet the requirements stipulated in the Higher Education Opportunity Act of 2008 (P.L. 110-315). To be granted recognition by the USDE, accrediting agencies must maintain criteria or standards in specific areas: (1) student achievement, (2) curricula, (3) faculty, (4) facilities (includes equipment and supplies), (5) fiscal and administrative capacity, (6) student support services, (7) recruiting and admissions practices, (8) measures of the degree and objectives of degrees or credentials offered, (9) record of student complaints, and (10) record of compliance with program responsibilities for student aid as required by the Higher Education Act of 1965 (P.L. 89-329, Title IV), as amended.

USDE recognition review normally takes place every 5 years. The accreditation agency prepares a written report demonstrating compliance with the criteria established for recognition. USDE staff members conduct the review based on the report, communication with the accreditation agency, and site visits if needed. USDE staff members make recommendations to the National Advisory Committee on Institutional Quality and Integrity (NACIQI), an appointed group of educators and public members, to recognize or not recognize an accrediting organization. Under the Higher Education Opportunity Act, 6 members of NACIQI are appointed by the House of Representatives, 6 members by the Senate, and 6 members by the U.S. Secretary of Education. The agency appears in front of NACIQI to respond to questions regarding the report. The committee, in turn, recommends action to the Secretary. The Secretary makes the final determination on whether to grant recognition and the term of recognition.

Association of Specialized and Professional Accreditors

ASPA is the only member organization that represents only specialized accreditation agencies. ASPA was formed in the Fall of 1993 when COPA dissolved. Members of COPA, which had authority over specialized accrediting agencies in the United States, created ASPA to act as a voice for accrediting agencies and to provide policy and developmental services.

ASPA was formed under the District of Columbia Nonprofit Corporation Act for educational, scientific, research, mutual improvement, and professional purposes. ASPA's goals are to maintain and improve the quality of education and to safeguard the public. The bylaws charge the association with several tasks (ASPA, 2008):

- Promote quality and integrity in nongovernmental specialized and professional accreditation of postsecondary programs and institutions;
- Provide a forum for discussion and analysis and a mechanism for common action for those concerned with specialized and professional accreditation;
- Address accreditation issues in educational, governmental, and public policy contexts and communicate with the public about accreditation;
- Foster collaboration among programs, institutions, and accreditation organizations; and
- Provide a mechanism for individuals and organizations with accreditation responsibility to participate in continuing education.

ASPA Structure

ASPA's membership comprises accrediting agencies that adhere to the ASPA member code of good practice. According to ASPA bylaws, voting members review, approve, and amend articles of incorporation review; approve and amend bylaws; review and approve proposals for a major reorganization, reorientation, or dissolution of the association; elect a board of directors and officers; and elect the chair and members of the Committee on Nominations.

ASPA's board of directors consists of 8 members: 3 chief staff officers from agencies that hold ASPA votes; 1 chief executive or chief academic officer of an institution holding institutional or programmatic accreditation by at least one voting member of the association; 1 academic member from programs or institutions accredited by voting members of the association; 1 practitioner member from among the professions represented by voting members of the association; 1 member of the public whose vocation is outside the academic and accreditation communities; and APSA's executive director, who is ex officio and nonvoting. With the exception of the public member, all board members must have significant experience in accreditation as site visitors, commission or board members, or staff members.

What ASPA Does

ASPA provides members with a strong national voice on important issues with respect to specialized accreditation. Accrediting agencies that belong to ASPA set national educational standards for entry into approximately 40 specialized disciplines or defined professions (ASPA, n.d.b).

Any accrediting body that wants to join ASPA must demonstrate that its governing body has endorsed the ASPA member code of good practice, which states that the accrediting agency pursues its mission, goals, and objectives and conducts its operations in a trustworthy manner; maximizes service, productivity, and effectiveness in the accreditation relationship; respects and protects institutional autonomy; maintains a broad perspective as the basis for wise decision-making; focuses accreditation reviews on the development of knowledge and competence; exhibits integrity and professionalism in the conduct of its operation; and has mechanisms to ensure that expertise and experience in the application of its standards, procedures, and values are present in members of its visiting reams, commissions, and staff (ASPA, n.d.a).

To be eligible for ASPA membership, accrediting agencies must demonstrate that they meet ASPA's definition of a specialized or professional accrediting body, which is defined as "one with a national scope that accredits higher education programs or institutions that prepare individuals for entry into practice in a specialized discipline or defined profession" (ASPA, n.d.c). ASPA member agencies represent professionals in the nursing, dentistry, education, acupuncture, theater, psychology, and medical education fields.

Center for Quality Assurance in International Education

CQAIE, founded in 1991 from an offshoot of COPA and located at the National Center for Higher Education in Washington, DC, was created to deal with issues of quality and fairness in international academic and professional mobility, credentialing, and recognition (CQAIE, n.d.a).

What CQAIE Does

CQAIE's purpose is threefold: (1) to assist countries in the development or enhancement of quality assurance systems for higher education, (2) to promote the globalization of the professions, and (3) to monitor quality issues in the transnational movement of higher education. CQAIE fosters communication and collaboration among organizations responsible for quality education and practice within the world's primary professions (CQAIE, n.d.b).

CQAIE focuses on the international dimension of accreditation, helping organizations address the growing need for new technology and education about new technology, establishing common standards across borders in the globalization of professions, and handling quality issues as institutions of higher education and accrediting agencies move into other countries. CQAIE has done extensive work in countries such as Morocco, Indonesia, Japan, Bolivia, Mexico, Estonia, and Romania. It encourages accreditation in these countries by designing legislation or national policy, carrying out training, or evaluating an existing system. In regional meetings that CQAIE convenes, most if not all of the countries of the region participate in developing quality initiatives for that territory (CQAIE, n.d.b).

Because of multinational trade agreements and new technology, health care professions are expanding outside a country's borders. CQAIE helps professionals who want to move into other countries and assists professions going through the globalization process by working on quality assurance in education and competency assurance in practice (CQAIE, n.d.a). By advising member organizations on issues such as how to identify those countries in which members of a profession wish to practice and how to protect consumers while simultaneously maintaining quality in higher education and practice, CQAIE helps professions learn how to globalize (CQAIE, n.d.a).

In addition, CQAIE monitors the quality of education that crosses U.S. borders. Increasingly, U.S. universities are starting programs abroad, but also, many foreign schools are establishing campuses within the United States.

In response to the needs of these growing professional communities, CQAIE sponsors national and regional meetings. The goals of these meetings include learning about practical issues related to providing higher education in foreign countries, developing principles of good practice, and advocating international trade in education services (CQAIE, n.d.c). CQAIE often sponsors these meetings in conjunction with accrediting agencies.

Summary

This chapter has focused on accreditation's roles and processes for higher education. The chapter identified the similarities and differences between institutional and programmatic accreditation agencies and how these agencies affect occupational therapy education programs. In addition, the chapter explored the external agencies and organizations that affect educational programs through the recognition process. As the employer of the graduates of the educational programs, occupational therapy managers are key stakeholders in occupational therapy education. Managers must understand the accreditation process and how it ensures the quality of educational programs. As stakeholders, occupational therapy managers have the ability to affect this process and its outcomes.

❖ Learning Activities

1. Identify the regional or national career accrediting body for your college or university (or your alma mater if your have graduated). Identify some of the strengths and limitations of your institution. Read the summary from the most recent report from the regional accrediting body to see if it agrees with your evaluation.

2. Identify the role of the occupational therapy department or program in the last regional accreditation review. If the department or program was not an active participant, find out who was involved.

3. Discuss with your professor or program director the ACOTE self-study process for your program.

4. Identify the strengths and limitations of your educational program. Ask your professor or program director to share with you the Report of the Accreditation Council to see if your thoughts agree with that of ACOTE.

5. Accreditation relies on volunteers from the profession. ACOTE's Roster of Accreditation Evaluators is made up of volunteers from both practice and academia. Identify the requirements, including training, to be an evaluator.

✓ Multiple-Choice Questions

1. Most colleges and universities in the country are accredited by
   a. ACOTE.
   b. Regional accrediting agencies.
   c. The U.S. Department of Education.
   d. The Council for Higher Education Accreditation.

2. Accreditation is valued because it
   a. Demonstrates that the program has financial stability.
   b. Shows that students are learning effectively.

   c. Demonstrates that the institution values external evaluation.
   d. Shows that the program and institution have adequate resources.

3. Occupational therapy education accreditation began in the
   a. 1920s.
   b. 1950s.
   c. 1940s.
   d. 1930s.

4. The accreditation of the education of occupational therapy assistants
   a. Began at the same time as accreditation of occupational therapists.
   b. Is not governed by ACOTE.
   c. Was started in 1958.
   d. Has always been controlled by the American Medical Association.

5. For many years, accreditation of occupational therapy education was a joint process of AOTA with the
   a. U.S. Department of Education.
   b. American Medical Association.
   c. Council of Higher Education Accreditation.
   d. Association of Specialized and Professional Accreditors.

6. The basis for all types of accreditations is
   a. To meet the needs of society.
   b. The desire to improve the education of professionals.
   c. Concern for the students.
   d. The development of standards.

7. The purpose of all accreditations is to
   a. Ensure the quality of the educational program.
   b. Protect the public.
   c. Further develop the profession.
   d. Manage the number of programs available.

8. Resolution J, which was passed by the AOTA Representative Assembly, called for
   a. The accreditation of occupational therapy education to be independent of the American Medical Association.
   b. Increased practical skills to be included in all educational programs.
   c. Entry-level occupational therapy education to be at a post-baccalaureate level.
   d. ACOTE to separate from AOTA.

9. The relationship between ACOTE and AOTA is
   a. Complete independence of each group.
   b. ACOTE is part of AOTA.
   c. ACOTE is an associated body of the AOTA Board of Directors.
   d. AOTA has complete control over ACOTE.

10. Although the move to post-baccalaureate education was mandated in 1999, it was not enacted until 2007 because
    a. Educational programs could not make such a change in a short time.
    b. This date would give the AOTA Representative Assembly time to change its mind about such an action.
    c. Higher education requires at least 8 years to change a program level.
    d. This date would allow currently enrolled students to complete the program that they started.

11. The Council for Higher Education Accreditation was started to
    a. Provide recognition of accredited organizations that support higher education.
    b. Build another layer into the accreditation system.
    c. Provide an alternative to regional accrediting bodies.
    d. Accredit those colleges and universities that offer primarily distance programs.

12. To qualify for federal funding programs, an academic institution or program has to be accredited by
    a. An agency recognized by the Council for Higher Education Accreditation.
    b. An agency recognized by the Association of Specialized and Professional Accreditors.
    c. An agency recognized by the U.S. Department of Education.
    d. The U.S. Department of Education.

13. The Committee on Allied Health Education and Accreditation was an accrediting body under the aegis of the
    a. AOTA.
    b. American Medical Association.
    c. Council for Higher Education Accreditation.
    d. Association of Specialized and Professional Accreditors.

14. The purpose of the self-study process is to
    a. Perform a comprehensive review of the program.
    b. Determine the strengths and weakness of the program.
    c. Examine how the program meets societal needs.
    d. Assess compliance with the educational standards.

15. The purpose of the onsite visit is to
    a. Evaluate the quality of the faculty.
    b. Evaluate the competence of the students.
    c. Determine if the institution in fact meets the standards.
    d. Ensure that the self-study is truthful.

16. Currently, ACOTE accredits
    a. Programs.
    b. Degree levels.
    c. Colleges and universities.
    d. Only professional-level programs.

17. ACOTE currently accredits
    a. Master's entry-level programs and assistant programs.
    b. Master's- and doctoral entry-level programs.
    c. Master's-, doctoral-, and assistant-level programs.
    d. Only doctoral entry-level programs.

18. Recognition by the U.S. Department of Education is generally reviewed every
    a. 5 years.
    b. 3 years.
    c. 10 years.
    d. 2 years.

19. ASPA represents
    a. Professional organizations.
    b. Specialized accrediting bodies of disciplines and professions.
    c. College administrators.
    d. Governmental concerns about professions.

20. ACOTE members include
    a. Only occupational therapists.
    b. Occupational therapists and occupational therapy assistants.
    d. Occupational therapists, occupational therapy assistants, public members, and an academic administrator.
    d. Only doctoral-level occupational therapists.

References

Accreditation Council for Occupational Therapy Education. (1998). *Educational standards: Foundation for the future* [White Paper]. Bethesda, MD: Author.

Accreditation Council for Occupational Therapy Education. (1999, August 26). ACOTE sets timeline for postbaccalaureate-degree programs. *OT Week*, pp. i–ii.

Accreditation Council for Occupational Therapy Education. (2007a). Accreditation standards for a doctoral-degree-level educational program for the occupational therapist. *American Journal of Occupational Therapy, 61*, 641–651.

Accreditation Council for Occupational Therapy Education. (2007b). Accreditation standards for a master's-degree-level educational program for the occupational therapist. *American Journal of Occupational Therapy, 61*, 652–661.

Accreditation Council for Occupational Therapy Education. (2007c). Accreditation standards for an educational program for the occupational therapy assistant. *American Journal of Occupational Therapy, 61*, 662–671.

Accreditation Council for Occupational Therapy Education. (n.d.a). *Accreditation overview: ACOTE history, meetings, and members.* Retrieved July 1, 2009, from http://www.aota.org/Educate/Accredit/Overview.aspx

Accreditation Council for Occupational Therapy Education. (n.d.b.). *ACOTE manual: Policies and procedures.* Retrieved July 1, 2009, from http://www.aota.org/Educate/Accredit/Policies.aspx

American Occupational Therapy Association. (1999, April 29). RA makes history: Resolution J adopted. *OT Week*, pp. i, ii.

American Occupational Therapy Association, & Accreditation Council for Occupational Therapy Education. (2005, January 29). *Memorandum of understanding between the Accreditation Council for Occupational Therapy Education and the American Occupational Therapy Association.* Bethesda, MD: Authors.

Association of Specialized and Professional Accreditors. (2008). *Association of specialized and professional accreditors bylaws.* Chicago: Author.

Association of Specialized and Professional Accreditors. (n.d.a). *ASPA member code of good practice.* Retrieved July 1, 2009, from http://www.aspa-usa.org/documents/membercode.pdf

Association of Specialized and Professional Accreditors. (n.d.b). *ASPA role, function, and purposes.* Retrieved July 1, 2009, from http://www.aspa-usa.org/role_and_function_aspa.asp

Association of Specialized and Professional Accreditors. (n.d.c). *Membership information.* Retrieved July 1, 2009, from http://www.aspa-usa.org/membership_info_aspa.asp

Baker, S., Morrone, A., & Gable, K. (2004). Allied health deans' and program directors' perspectives of specialized accreditation effectiveness and reform. *Journal of Allied Health, 33*(4), P247–P254.

Center for Quality Assurance in International Education. (n.d.a). *Advocacy and planning in the globalization of the professions.* Retrieved July 1, 2009, from http://www.cqaie.org/globalization.htm

Center for Quality Assurance in International Education. (n.d.b). *National and institutional capacity building and training in quality assurance, accreditation, and strategic planning for quality assurance.* Retrieved July 1, 2009, from http://www.cqaie.org/assisting.htm

Center for Quality Assurance in International Education. (n.d.c). *Transnational education quality.* Retrieved July 1, 2009, from http://www.cqaie.org/transnational.htm

Colman, W. (1990). The curriculum directors: Influencing occupational therapy education, 1948–1964. *American Journal of Occupational Therapy, 44*, 357–362.

Council on Higher Education Accreditation. (2002). Specialized accreditation and assuring quality in distance education. *CHEA Monograph Series, 2002*(2).

Council on Higher Education Accreditation. (2006a). Presidential perspectives on accreditation: A report of the CHEA President's Project. *CHEA Monograph Series, 2006*(1).

Council on Higher Education Accreditation. (2006b). *Recognition of accrediting agencies: Policies and procedures.* Washington DC: Author.

Council on Higher Education Accreditation. (n.d.). *An overview of U.S. accreditation.* Retrieved July1, 2009, from http://www.chea.org/pdf/overview_US_accred_8-03.pdf

Higher Education Act of 1965, Pub. L. 89-329, 20 USC 1070, Title IV.

Higher Education Opportunity Act of 2008, Pub. L. 110-315, 20 USC 1001.

Kramer, P., Seitz, S., & Dickson, B. (2003). *The occupational therapy manager* (4th ed., pp. 549–567). Bethesda, MD: AOTA Press.

Slagle, E. C. (1931). The training of occupational therapists. *Psychiatric Quarterly, 5*, 12–20.

U.S. Department of Education. (n.d.). *Financial aid for postsecondary students: Accreditation in the United States.* Retrieved July 1, 2009, from http://www.ed.gov/admins/finaid/accred/index.html

APPENDIX 36.A. ACCREDITATION RELATED TO EDUCATION EVIDENCE TABLE

Topic	Evidence
Perceived effectiveness	Baker, S., Morrone, A., & Gable, K. (2004). Allied health deans' and program directors' perspectives of specialized accreditation effectiveness and reform. *Journal of Allied Health, 33*(4), P247–P254.
Distance education	Council on Higher Education Accreditation. (2002). Specialized accreditation and assuring quality in distance education. *CHEA Monograph Series, 2002*(2).
Institutional leadership knowledge and perceived value	Council on Higher Education Accreditation. (2006a). Presidential perspectives on accreditation: A report of the CHEA President's Project. *CHEA Monograph Series,* 2006(1).

APPENDIX 36.B. ACCREDITATION FOR EDUCATION ONLINE RESOURCES

- **Association of Specialized and Professional Accreditors (ASPA):** http://www.aspa-usa.org
- **Council on Higher Education Accreditation (CHEA):** http://www.chea.org/
- **U.S. Department of Education (USDE) Accreditation:** http://www.ed.gov/admins/finaid/accred

Part VI

Supervision

37
Management of Fieldwork Education

Donna M. Costa, DHS, OTR/L, FAOTA

❖ Key Terms and Concepts

Academic fieldwork coordinator (AFWC). The person employed by the occupational therapy or occupational therapy assistant education program who is responsible for arranging placements, securing contracts, and overseeing all of the program's fieldwork sites. Every educational program in the profession must assign a faculty member to function in this role to maintain accreditation status.

Fieldwork education. One of the two components of professional education for the occupational therapy and occupational therapy assistant student that occurs in clinical practice settings (the other is academic or classroom education).

Fieldwork educator. The person who supervises and educates entry-level students during Level I or Level II fieldwork.

❖ Learning Objectives

After completing this chapter, you should be able to do the following:

- Articulate the purpose of Level I and Level II fieldwork education.
- Describe the role competencies of the fieldwork educator and academic fieldwork coordinator.
- Explain the importance of adult learning theories and supervision models.

- Identify the major components of a fieldwork education program.
- Locate additional resources to continue professional development as a fieldwork educator.

Our students and their learning are our most important focus as educators. Their learning is our principal goal. They are our customers, our reviewers, and in the near future our colleagues.

—Dwyer & Higgs, 1999, p. 125

In recent years, a shift has occurred toward a more student-centered learning approach to occupational therapy fieldwork education, similar to the change that has occurred in health care to a more client-centered approach. To prepare fieldwork students to develop entry-level competencies, fieldwork educators need to spend time planning the necessary components for an effective fieldwork education program and then need to manage all of these components once the program is up and running. This chapter will review the essential components of fieldwork education and suggest a timeline that can be used for program development.

PURPOSE OF LEVEL I AND LEVEL II FIELDWORK

In 2009, the American Occupational Therapy Association's (AOTA's) Commission on Education published *Occupational*

Therapy Fieldwork Education: Value and Purpose, which described the purpose of fieldwork education to

> propel each generation of occupational therapy practitioners from the role of student to that of practitioner. Through the fieldwork experience, future practitioners achieve competence in applying the occupational therapy process and using evidence-based interventions to meet the occupational needs of a diverse client population. (p. 821)

Fieldwork experiences are designed to provide occupational therapy and occupational therapy assistant students with opportunities to

- "Apply theoretical and scientific principles learned from their academic programs to address actual client needs within the context of authentic practice environments"
- "Develop competency to ascertain client occupational performance needs to identify supports or barriers affecting health and participation and document interventions provided"

- "Provide opportunities for the student to develop advocacy, leadership, and managerial skills in a variety of practice settings"
- "Develop a professional identity as an occupational therapy practitioner, aligning his or her professional judgments and decisions with the . . . *Standards of Practice* [AOTA, 2005] and the *Occupational Therapy Code of Ethics [and Ethics Standards* (AOTA, 2010b)]." (p. 821)

The previously described opportunities are provided to students through a variety of learning experiences in progressively increasing levels of responsibility, with supervised intervention and professional role modeling.

> Fieldwork education is an essential bridge between academic education and authentic occupational therapy practice. Through the collaboration between academic faculty and fieldwork educators, students are given the opportunity to achieve the competencies necessary to meet the present and future occupational needs of individuals, groups, and indeed, society as a whole. (AOTA, 2009a, p. 822)

The Accreditation Council for Occupational Therapy Education® (ACOTE®) is the body that oversees the compliance of all occupational therapy education programs in the United States with a set of guidelines called *Standards*. These Standards are reviewed and revised every 5 years, reflecting trends in practice and education. One section of the Standards is specific to fieldwork education. ACOTE defines *fieldwork education* as a "crucial part of professional preparation and is best integrated as a component of the curriculum design" (ACOTE, 2007b, p. 660). Fieldwork is considered an extension of the occupational therapy or occupational therapy assistant academic program, and there must be a link between the design of the curriculum of the educational program and the fieldwork site. Fieldwork educators need to know not only what school students come from but also about the school's emphasis, philosophy, and curricular structure.

Level I fieldwork experiences usually occur concurrently with courses in the academic program and are "designed to enrich didactic coursework through directed observation and participation in selected aspects of the occupational therapy process" (ACOTE, 2007b, p. 661). Level II fieldwork experiences generally occur at or near the conclusion of the didactic phase of the academic program and are designed to develop competent, entry-level, generalist practitioners (ACOTE, 2007b). Level II fieldwork assignments feature in-depth experiences in delivering occupational therapy services to clients, focusing on the application of purposeful and meaningful occupation and evidence-based practice through exposure to a "variety of clients across the life span and to a variety of settings" (ACOTE, 2007a, p. 670; ACOTE, 2007b, p. 661). Level II fieldwork experiences for occupational therapy and occupational therapy assistant students are the same in that they both

must connect to the school's curriculum design, both must include in-depth experiences in delivering occupational therapy services to clients, and both must focus on providing purposeful and meaningful occupations. However, Level II fieldwork for the occupational therapy student also requires additional experiences in research, administration, and management of occupational therapy services.

The total amount of time devoted to Level II fieldwork is a minimum of 24 weeks of full-time experience for the occupational therapy student and a minimum of 16 weeks for the occupational therapy assistant student; in most schools, this time in divided equally into two fieldwork experiences of 12 weeks each for the occupational therapy student and 8 weeks each for the occupational therapy assistant student. Some schools require a third Level II experience of between 8 and 12 weeks, either as a "specialty" or in a third practice area. Responsibility for compliance with the ACOTE Standards is jointly shared between the academic fieldwork coordinator (AFWC) and the fieldwork site.

COMPONENTS OF FIELDWORK EDUCATION

Multiple components are involved in managing a fieldwork education program. First and foremost is the *student* whose professional education is the goal of fieldwork. A student-centered fieldwork program must include the recognition of the many ways in which students may be different and how these differences can affect their learning during fieldwork, such as generational differences, learning style preferences, previous life experiences, educational preparation, and personality.

The next component is the *fieldwork educator,* who must be a graduate of an accredited occupational therapy or occupational therapy assistant program, have successfully passed the initial National Board for Certification in Occupational Therapy (NBCOT) certification examination, has at least 1 year of work experience since passing the NBCOT exam, and "is adequately prepared to serve as a fieldwork educator." (ACOTE, 2007a, p. 670; ACOTE, 2007b, p. 661). This latter qualifier suggests that the fieldwork educator should in some way be competent to supervise students, by virtue of having taken some training, engaged in some self-learning, or participated in a mentoring relationship.

If the fieldwork site has more than one occupational therapist or occupational therapy assistant supervising students, there may be a *site director of fieldwork education,* or *fieldwork coordinator,* or *director of fieldwork education.* In some large clinical sites, this person may oversee the placement of students from multiple disciplines and schools. This individual is responsible for establishing contracts with schools, developing policies and procedures for the fieldwork education program, scheduling students, and mentoring fieldwork educators.

The *environment* of the fieldwork site refers to the aspects of the site that affect students' learning, such as the pace of the site, number of staff, level of clients' severity of illness and length of stay, structure of management, number of Medicare clients, and whether it's a teaching hospital or a private facility. The individuals who receive services from the health care facility may be called *patients, clients, consumers,* or *families;* it is the duty and obligation of the fieldwork educator to monitor the safety of these clients being treated by the student during fieldwork.

As defined at the beginning of the chapter, the *AFWC* is the individual employed by the college or university to oversee all fieldwork activities; this includes the origination of all contracts, assignment of students, site visits, and primary linkage between the fieldwork site and the school. The *academic institution* is the college or university that houses the occupational therapy or occupational therapy assistant program and confers the associate's degree, master's degree, or doctoral degree on completion of all academic and fieldwork education. Each educational program in the United States that offers an occupational therapy or occupational therapy assistant program must secure accreditation status from ACOTE and continue to maintain that accreditation through annual program reviews and periodic site visits.

COMPETENCIES

The AOTA Commission on Education has issued a document that summarizes role competencies for all academic roles, including the AFWCs and fieldwork educators: *Specialized Knowledge and Skills of Occupational Therapy Educators of the Future* (AOTA, 2009c). This document spells out the responsibilities, values, knowledge, and skills that are required and can be modified to the specific clinical practice.

These competency statements can be used to form the basis of a job description for a fieldwork educator in a particular health care facility or can be used as the basis of a professional development plan. The document addresses skills and knowledge at the novice, intermediate, and advanced levels of experience and also links the competencies to AOTA's (2007) *Centennial Vision.* "These attributes are described in the language of possibility, including the characteristics of innovator/visionary, scholar/explorer, leader, integrator, and mentor. Because the embodiment of these attributes is developmental, they are described in a continuum of experience from novice, to intermediate, and advanced practitioner" (AOTA, 2009c, p. 805).

The Self-Assessment Tool for Fieldwork Educator Competency (SAFECOM; AOTA 2009b) can be used by occupational therapy practitioners to self-assess their readiness to become a fieldwork educator. SAFECOM is available for download on the AOTA Web site at http://www.aota.org/ Educate/EdRes/Fieldwork/Supervisor/Forms/38251.aspx. The SAFECOM has 69 specific competencies, divided into the 5 categories of Professional Practice, Education, Supervision, Evaluation, and Administration. Each item is scored by the prospective fieldwork educator on a 1–5 Likert scale, ranging from low to high proficiency. The last page of the SAFECOM contains the Fieldwork Educator Professional

Development Plan, which can be used to list strengths and areas that need further development, along with recording learning strategies and target dates.

The user-friendly Fieldwork Experience Assessment Tool (FEAT; AOTA, 1995) is designed to be used by the student and fieldwork educator during a Level II fieldwork experience. Its purpose is to determine if the placement is providing the just-right challenge to the student or whether the experience is too limited or too challenging. The FEAT can facilitate a dialogue between the fieldwork educator and student as to whether the structure of the fieldwork experience is helping the student meet his or her learning goals and whether the teaching strategies being used by the fieldwork educator are effective. The FEAT also provides feedback to the student about his or her attitudes and behaviors toward learning. This tool is not an evaluation of the student or the fieldwork site but rather provides a framework to design an optimal learning experience for the student. The FEAT is available on the AOTA Web site at http://www.aota.org/ Students/Current/Fieldwork/FEAT.aspx.

An important competency for fieldwork educators is that they be skilled in providing the student with prompt, direct, specific, and constructive feedback throughout the fieldwork experience. *Feedback* is defined as "information given to indicate the level of competence that has been achieved in performance of a task. Feedback can therefore be positive or negative depending on whether the task was completed well or not" (Rose & Best, 2005, p. 63). It is a crucial motivating factor in learning, and student satisfaction with feedback is linked to the quality and timeliness of feedback received. Research (Lofmark & Wikblad, 2001; Scheidt et al., 1986; Westberg & Jason, 2001) also demonstrates that students who receive regular feedback tend to perform better in clinical practice.

Some important components of effective feedback are contained in the mnemonic *PEARLS:*

- *P* = partnership for joint problem-solving
- *E* = empathic understanding
- *A* = apology for barriers to learner's success
- *R* = respect for learner's values and choices
- *L* = legitimization for feelings and intentions
- *S* = support for efforts at correction (Milan, Parish, & Reichgott, 2006).

For feedback to be effective, it should be accurate, factual, and clear—never exaggerated. It should be specific and focus on the behavior the student displayed rather than the student himself or herself. Fieldwork educators should remember that feedback is descriptive, not evaluative, and that it should occur as close to the event or completion of the task as possible. When providing feedback to students, it is important to do so in a setting that is private—never in front of peers, other students, or colleagues.

Feedback is most effective when it is routine and also when the student seeks it. When necessary, sandwich negative feedback between positive feedback, particularly when you are aware of a particular student's sensitivity to criticism. Feedback has to be relevant to the student and should relate to his or her learning goals. When providing feedback to students, allow the student time to respond to feedback, preface feedback with "I" statements, and avoid using inflammatory language. Many helpful resources on feedback are listed in the "References" section and evidence table (Appendix 37.A) at the end of this chapter.

DEVELOPING THE FIELDWORK PROGRAM

The first step in developing a fieldwork program at a health care facility is to reach out to nearby educational institutions. Establishing contact with the occupational therapy or occupational therapy assistant academic program at a college or university is a good way to start. Most academic programs are actively looking for additional fieldwork sites, particularly during times when enrollment is increased because of demand. The AOTA Web site has a listing of all accredited occupational therapy and occupational therapy assistant programs listed alphabetically by state, with links to the program's Web site where the program director's name and e-mail address should be listed (http://www .aota.org/Educate/Schools/EntryLevelOT.aspx); the program director is the ideal person to contact to explore establishing a fieldwork contract.

The next step is to gain institutional support, which requires a written proposal to the facility administration to "sell" the idea of starting a fieldwork program. In this proposal the reasons why starting a fieldwork program should be listed, along with a description of how this can advance practice at the facility and reflect positively on the facility. Some reasons typically given for starting a fieldwork program are

- Bringing new ideas to the facility, as students usually are taught the most "cutting-edge" knowledge in their curricula;
- Increasing the skills of practitioners through teaching and mentoring students;
- Increasing the amount of services available at the facility, because students will be providing services under the supervision of staff; and
- Reflecting positively on the facility as a training site for the college or university program.

In addition, if it is difficult to fill occupational therapy vacancies as they occur, taking fieldwork students can serve as a recruitment tool, as many students often accept positions where they did their fieldwork.

The staff in the occupational therapy department will then need to "get on board" with the mission of training students. Most health care practitioners in today's world report feeling overworked, and occupational therapists and occupational therapy assistants are no exception. Their initial reactions to your request to start accepting students may be negative, based on their belief that the program will increase their workload. To address this concern, it is best to identify the benefits to taking students, or perhaps brainstorm a list of benefits at a weekly staff meeting. Some of these ideas might include

- Getting new ideas for treatment interventions;
- Increasing departmental productivity numbers, as students will be seeing clients;
- Acquiring assistance with managing the caseload once the student has achieved a certain level of competency;
- Providing professional development units (PDUs) toward NBCOT recertification; and
- Gaining benefits to the site through the incentives that some colleges and universities provide for accepting fieldwork students, such as library access, voluntary or clinical faculty status, and credits that can be used to take courses.

The most important reason, however, for taking fieldwork students is professional obligation; the only way to ensure the future success of the profession is to participate in the high-quality training of students.

Supervising students enhances the fieldwork educator's own professional development by providing exposure to current practice trends, evidence-based practice, and research. Moreover, the experience of fieldwork supervision is recognized by . . .[NBCOT] and many state regulatory boards as a legitimate venue for achieving continuing competency requirements for occupational therapy practitioners.

Another benefit to the fieldwork site for sponsoring a fieldwork education program is with the recruitment of qualified occupational therapy personnel. Through the responsibilities expected during Level II fieldwork, occupational therapy staff and administration are given opportunity for an in-depth view of a student's potential as a future employee. In turn, an active fieldwork program allows the student, as a potential employee, to view first-hand the agency's commitment to the professional growth of its occupational therapy personnel and to determine the "fit" of his or her professional goals with agency goals. The fieldwork program also creates a progressive, state-of-the-art image to the professional community, consumers, and other external audiences through its partnership with the academic programs. (AOTA, 2009a, pp. 821–822)

Once the fieldwork program has been approved by staff and administration, and academic programs have been contacted to start the contract process, the next step is to understand fieldwork education. A good place to start is with the ACOTE Standards. It is important to be familiar with Standards B.10.1–B.10.22 in particular, as they relate to fieldwork. Some Standards specify what the AFWC must do, others what the fieldwork educator is responsible for, and others that address both parties. While it is beyond the scope of this chapter to review all the Standards, there are several that should be highlighted:

- *Standard B.10.3*—"Provide fieldwork education in settings that are equipped to meet the curriculum goals, provide educational experiences applicable to the academic program, and have fieldwork educators who are able to effectively meet the learning needs of students" (ACOTE, 2007a, p. 670; 2007b, p. 660). This means that the fieldwork site must know the curricular goals for each academic program that sends students, as well as its scope and coursework. In addition, this Standard underscores the importance of fieldwork educators receiving some training in adult learning theory, principles, and strategies.
- *Standard B.10.15*—"Provide Level II fieldwork in a traditional and/or emerging setting, consistent with the curriculum design. In all settings, psychosocial factors influencing engagement in occupation must be understood and integrated for the development of client-centered, meaningful, occupation-based outcomes." (ACOTE, 2007a, p. 670; 2007b, p. 661). This is particularly important because many students across the United State no longer participate in a Level I or Level II placement in psychosocial practice, yet this is the core of the profession. The last revision of the Standards included this so that all students gain exposure to psychosocial practice skills, regardless of their assigned fieldwork settings.
- *Standards B.10.17–B.10.22* address the required qualifications of fieldwork educators; they must have at least 1 year of experience after initial NBCOT certification and must be "adequately prepared to serve as a fieldwork educator" (Standard B.10.17; ACOTE, 2007a, p. 670; 2007b, p. 661). The fieldwork site and the academic program determine what constitutes adequate preparation. Fieldwork sites must establish some procedures for documenting the effectiveness of fieldwork supervision according to Standard B.10.18; this can be done through the Student Evaluation of Fieldwork Experience (SEFWE) or other feedback tools. This Standard states that the fieldwork site must be able to document the available resources for enhancing the effectiveness of fieldwork supervision, which could include a library of supervision resources or materials from continuing education opportunities.
- *Standard B.10.20* addresses fieldwork in settings that are considered emerging areas of practice, which might be sites that do not employ occupational therapy practitioners or that offer only limited services from a part-time or consulting occupational therapy practitioner. In this case, the fieldwork educator must have at least 3 years of experience, as the supervisory skills required in these types of settings are considered advanced. This Standard also specifies that the amount of supervision provided to students in these settings must be for a minimum of 8 hours per week, that the supervisor must be available to the student at other times via phone or e-mail, and that another staff member must be available on-site to serve as the student's supervisor.

Every educational program at the occupational therapy and occupational therapy assistant level has a curriculum framework, which includes the mission of the program, its philosophy, and the design of the curriculum. Often these are found on the Web page for the school, or they can be requested from the school. While every accredited occupational therapy or occupational therapy assistant program has to follow the same set of Standards, each program has a unique emphasis, an institutional mission, a philosophy of teaching, and a sequence of coursework; it is helpful to at least understand the major emphases of each academic program.

For a fieldwork site to begin accepting students for Level I or Level II fieldwork, a contract must be established between the site and the academic institution. Sometimes called a *memorandum of understanding*, this contract is a legal document that may take many months to be approved by all parties involved. The major components of the contract are the

- Delineation of the responsibilities and obligations of the school and the fieldwork site with regard to the preparation and supervision of students,
- Limits of liability coverage,
- Confidentiality requirements, and
- Removal of students under certain conditions.

Once the contract has been reviewed by legal counsel and signed by all parties concerned, it must be kept on file and then reviewed at least every 5 years, sooner if there have been changes in governance of the fieldwork site or academic institution.

Training for fieldwork educators is an ongoing process. At least in the beginning, most fieldwork educators report feeling ill-prepared to supervise students. The Fieldwork Educator Certificate Workshops, in a train-the-trainer format, were recently developed by AOTA, in conjunction with the Commission on Education representatives and a panel of authors, reviewers, and editors (see http://www .aota.org/Educate/EdRes/Fieldwork/Workshop.aspx). Other venues to increase knowledge of fieldwork education include reading the numerous references at the end of this chapter and in the evidence table (Appendix 37.A), and attending regional continuing education workshops sponsored by area fieldwork consortia.

DESIGNING THE FIELDWORK PROGRAM

Often a new fieldwork program is set up with only one occupational therapy practitioner serving as fieldwork site coordinator and as fieldwork educator. However, as the program grows, staff roles may need to be better delineated. Depending on the size of the program, there may be someone who coordinates all of the contracts with schools, someone who schedules students and tracks paperwork, someone who handles Level I fieldwork, and someone else who coordinates Level II. The fieldwork site may have the ability to mentor new fieldwork educators by pairing them with more experienced educators. The fieldwork site coordinator also may train and supervise new fieldwork educators.

One competency listed on the SAFECOM (AOTA, 2009b) is that the fieldwork educator be able to articulate the supervision model (supervision theory to guide work with students) they use with students. Some of the models currently being used in occupational therapy fieldwork education are developmental, situational leadership, student centered, and personality type (based on the Myers–Briggs Trait Inventory). Which model is used depends on the learning and teaching style of the fieldwork educator, his or her professional practice orientation, and his or her own experiences as a fieldwork student:

> We may think we are teaching according to a widely accepted curricular or pedagogical model, only to find, on reflection, that the foundations of how we work have been laid in our autobiographies as learners. In the face of crises or ambiguities, we fall back instinctively on memories from our times as learners to guide how we respond. (Brookfield, 1998, p. 198)

The fieldwork educator also must be familiar with some of the more prominent adult learning theories. Adult learners are characterized by being self-directed in their learning, bringing their life experiences to learning, having a problem-solving focus, demonstrating a readiness to learn, seeking relevant concepts as well as relationships between concepts, and recognizing that there may be more than one correct answer. In addition, there also are several fieldwork placement models that refer to the structure of the supervision:

- *1:1*—The most frequently used model; 1 fieldwork educator is assigned to 1 student.
- *2:1*—Two fieldwork educators are assigned to 1 student, usually for training a novice fieldwork educator, because the fieldwork educator works part-time, or because a student is working between two sites or units.
- *1:2*—One fieldwork educator is assigned to 2 students.
- *Group:* One fieldwork educator is assigned to a group of 3 or more students; all of the supervision is conducted in a group setting, with only evaluations and sensitive issues being discussed in private 1:1 sessions.
- *Collaborative:* Used with a group of 2 or more students in which the fieldwork educator and students are working together to coconstruct new knowledge; the students take a more active role in their learning with this model, thus promoting more autonomy and self-directed learning.

Before students arrive at the fieldwork site, it is important to develop site-specific learning objectives that are written for each of the items on the Fieldwork Performance Evaluation forms (FWPE; available from AOTA) for the occupational therapy and occupational therapy assistant student. Because each fieldwork site is very different in terms of caseload, setting, structure, acuity, pace, and so forth, these learning objectives inform the student how their performance will be graded at midterm and final. While the prospect of creating site-specific objectives may seem like a daunting task, there are hundreds of examples listed on the AOTA Web site in the "Fieldwork Education" section, grouped by type of practice setting.

Creating a library of resources is another important step in setting up a fieldwork program, including textbooks that staff have used, continuing education workshop materials, videotapes and DVDs, and manuals. Students who come through the fieldwork site may create additional resources that can be housed in this library. It also is important to set up a workspace for students. This area does not have to be a dedicated office, but just a place they can leave their belongings, do some reading or research, or complete their required documentation. Policies and procedures are probably in place for the department or unit, and so there may need to be a policy and procedure manual for fieldwork, particularly if it is a large department with students coming from multiple schools. Having a policy and procedure manual ensures that the program has continuity. In addition, a separate student fieldwork manual needs to be developed for them to refer to during and after their orientation to the site. On the AOTA Web site in the "Fieldwork Resources" section is a list of possible items to include. Content can be added gradually over time. Some sections of the manual can come from departments within your health care facility such as infection control or medical records.

Assembling a fieldwork manual is a good student project, particularly for more advanced students. Students can be asked to add additional content to an existing manual or asked for suggestions on what resources could be included that would have been helpful to them.

Forms that will be used for fieldwork experiences need to be created or ordered. The FWPE forms are available from AOTA at a nominal fee; usually the academic program orders these and sends them out to the fieldwork site as part of the student packet. Similarly, the SEFWE is usually sent out by the academic program; it is also available on the AOTA Web site. Some fieldwork educators like to use weekly feedback forms to provide students with written feedback; samples are on the AOTA Web site.

Managing a fieldwork program means managing a continual flow of paper, much of which needs to be kept secure. This paperwork includes personal data sheets on students, information with students' names on it, previous records of former students, performance evaluations, legal contracts, correspondence from academic programs, and any incident reports or other documentation of a sensitive nature. Security procedures must be in place, including designating who locks and unlocks the filing cabinets or has passwords to electronic storage, where keys are housed, and who has access to the protected information.

CHALLENGES IN MAINTAINING FIELDWORK PROGRAMS

Reporting

Maintaining a high-quality fieldwork education program, as with maintaining any other kind of high-quality program, has its challenges. Periodically, reports detailing with the productivity of the manager should be written. Items to include in this report include

- Records of meetings, continuing education, and conferences attended;
- Number of contracts with schools and new contracts in development; and
- Number of Level I and Level II students supervised annually.

Training

The fieldwork manager has the responsibility of maintaining fieldwork educators' motivation to provide clinical education to students. This is just as important now as in 1927 when Marjorie Taylor said the following at the AOTA Conference:

> The staff workers need to have their interest in training stimulated, not only at the beginning of the students' training, but every day the students are with us. Only this way is the extra burden of training of enough interest to them to make them give the most to it. (as quoted in Privott, 1998, p. 439)

This can be accomplished through creating an environment of excellence in clinical education where students are welcomed as future colleagues; where fieldwork educators accept the challenge of supervising students out of a sense of commitment to the profession; where fieldwork education skills and knowledge constantly are being expanded and refined; and where students and fieldwork educators learn together, informing each other's practice.

Performance Issues With Students

Other challenges faced in providing fieldwork education include working with students whose performance is below acceptable standards, as well as with students whose advanced levels of performance create other kinds of challenges or students with disabilities.

Failing Students

In situations with students who may be at risk for failing their fieldwork placement, the AFWC from the student's school must be contacted; the earlier this occurs, the more support the school can provide. Failure, if it is to happen, should not come as a surprise to either the student or the school.

Usually the first step in remediation is to create a remedial learning contract, which requires that the reasons for the substandard performance be identified. Difficulties in fieldwork can include the student, the site, or the supervisor. Regardless of the reason, it is imperative to keep accurate supervision logs, weekly reviews, and copies of the student's work. The key to deciding if a student is failing is to determine whether he or she is or is not achieving the "developmental milestones" of task mastery within the expected time frames.

It is important that the fieldwork site also outline during orientation the behaviors that will lead to automatic failure. According to the AOTA FWPE, these are unethical behavior and jeopardizing patient safety. As gatekeepers of the occupational therapy profession, fieldwork educators have a responsibility to fail students who score less than a 3 on the first 3 items on the FWPE that deal with safety and ethics.

The following student difficulties are generally cause for alarm:

- Weak knowledge base,
- Underdeveloped clinical skills,
- Limited problem-solving ability,
- Trouble with organization, and
- Poor time management skills.

Other sources of student struggles include behaviors such as

- Poor motivation;
- Negative attitude;
- Over- or underconfidence;
- Being a poor team player;
- Demonstrating impolite, hostile, or rude behavior toward clients, other students, and staff (see below);
- Recurrent lateness or absences;
- Assignments not submitted in a timely manner;
- Exhibiting an argumentative style with the fieldwork educator; and
- Inappropriate grooming, dress, or hygiene for the practice setting.

Sometimes, the cause of a student's difficulty is the fieldwork educator, and if this is the case, several questions can be asked to help determine the problem:

- Has the fieldwork educator adapted his or her teaching style to match student's learning needs?
- Have expectations been made clear to the student, or does he or she understand them differently?
- Has adequate time been allocated to spend with the student, observing performance, modeling roles, and giving feedback?
- Are the personalities of the fieldwork educator and the student a mismatch?
- Is there something lacking in the fieldwork site?

Most fieldwork educators report feeling uncomfortable at the prospect of failing a student and sometimes do not fail a student whose performance is below that of entry-level performance. Some reasons reported for not doing this are

- Lack of documentation,
- Belief that failing opens up a hornets' nest,
- Feeling that failing a student is a personal failure,
- Lack of experience or support,
- Fear of the emotional issues involved,
- Having to deal with student's response,
- Waiting too long to intervene or not having enough time left in the fieldwork placement,
- Student's personal situation or circumstances, and
- Consideration of the impact of failure on finances and the student's career path.

Fieldwork educators must realize that they serve as gatekeepers of the profession. They have a responsibility to fail a student whose performance is subthreshold. Fear of how this will affect the student's life or fear of repercussions have no bearing on the assignment of a failing grade to a student (Lew, Cara, & Richardson, 2007; Marsh et al., 2004). Several excellent resources on this topic are listed in the "References" section and evidence table (Appendix 37.A).

Advanced Students

Advanced students also present a challenge to fieldwork educators. They can become bored, and their performance can deteriorate. Advanced students often finish tasks quickly and then have time on their hands. Having a "just-right challenge" is key; advanced students should not feel penalized for getting work done or achieving competencies early. Having this type of student set up learning goals at the beginning of fieldwork is good practice.

Students With Disabilities

Students with disabilities regularly present in fieldwork, and successful placement and completion of fieldwork require knowledge of the legal issues involved. Reasonable accommodation in fieldwork is defined by the same laws that govern employment: the Americans with Disabilities Act (ADA) of 1990 and Section 504 of the Rehabilitation Act of 1973. Fieldwork educators must be aware of what questions they may or may not ask a student with disabilities. Educators also must understand that the student's school cannot disclose any information to the fieldwork site without the consent of that student. Therefore, in most cases, it is up to the student to disclose to the fieldwork site the nature of his or her disability and the accommodations required. Ideally, this should occur before the student begins the fieldwork placement.

Both the fieldwork site and the fieldwork educator must carefully define the essential functions and critical tasks that a student must be able to perform to achieve entry-level competency. Reasonable accommodations must be made to enable a student to perform these critical tasks. An excellent resource for more information about accommodating students with disabilities is found in AOTA (2010a).

Conflict

Despite a fieldwork educator's best efforts, sometimes conflict develops at the fieldwork site, occurring between students, between the student and the fieldwork educator, and between a student and another staff member. Learning how to negotiate conflicts in a way that promotes resolution is an important skill to be learned.

Some of the behaviors that might be demonstrated in conflict include

- Unspoken tension between individuals,
- Negativity,
- Avoidance,
- Ignoring others' input,
- Abruptness,
- Anxiety,
- Game-playing to exert control,
- Ongoing questioning of authority, and
- Excessive display of knowledge.

Some of the potential sources of conflict include

- Different communication styles;
- Unclear expectations at outset;
- Differing values and personal beliefs;
- Environmental stressors;
- Unacknowledged learning styles;
- Differences among the generations (e.g., Baby Boomers, Generation X, Generation Y); and
- Differences in roles, status, and power.

The fieldwork educator needs to be able to model for students effective ways to resolve conflict. Fieldwork educators could discuss a conflict interaction they had with a colleague, demonstrating to the student how they professionally handled it. Also, when the fieldwork educator senses that a student does not agree with him or her, this can be an opportunity to elicit feelings so that a harmonious resolution can be achieved (see Chapter 14, this volume).

Staffing Changes

Most AFWCs try to reserve placements for their students 1–2 years in advance, which fieldwork sites may find problematic. Planning for students needs to be done well in advance, because new contract generation can take up to a year or longer to negotiate. As occupational therapy program class size is increasing, the need for more high-quality fieldwork placements is increasing. The occupational therapy department manager or clinical education coordinator at the fieldwork site will receive requests from multiple schools and will have to determine a fair system to accommodate these requests.

It may be difficult to predict future staffing patterns, so most facilities make the commitment for a fieldwork slot on the basis of their optimal staffing. When facilities find themselves in short staffing patterns, they often have to cancel the fieldwork reservation. This necessitates the AFWC having a list of active back-up sites that he or she can contact for an alternate student placement.

As the time gets closer to a student starting fieldwork, an interview can be arranged so that the facility can begin preparing the fieldwork educator. At this time it is good to remember that "We first encounter fieldwork as a requirement for becoming an occupational therapist, then revisit it again as a professional responsibility. Serving as a fieldwork educator and sharing with students our affirmation for the profession is a primary way to contribute to the profession" (Cohn & Crist, 1995, p. 105).

Medicare Reimbursement

Medicare affects the delivery of services provided by students in health care facilities. Fieldwork educators must understand the regulations, which are listed on the AOTA Web site. It is equally important that fieldwork sites that rely on Medicare reimbursement find creative ways to include students in the delivery of services without jeopardizing their reimbursement. The most recent Medicare regulations regarding the provision of therapy services by students state that Medicare Part B will only reimburse for the services of an occupational therapist. The actual ruling states, "The services provided by a student are not reimbursed even if provided under 'line of sight' supervision of the therapist; however, the presence of the student 'in the room' does not make the services unbillable" (Centers for Medicare and Medicaid Services, 2003, 100.10.1). The occupational therapy supervisor must be present in the room for the entire therapy session; the student may participate in the treatment, providing it is the occupational therapist who is directing and responsible for the treatment.

Conclusion

The future of occupational therapy practice is based on educating competent occupational therapy practitioners in high-quality fieldwork settings across the scope of occupational therapy practice. Occupational therapy managers must commit to fieldwork education and therefore must know about fieldwork education. Students add a quality dimension to fieldwork sites by stimulating occupational therapy staff through asking questions, bringing fresh new ideas into the practice setting, and providing a potential source of new hires.

Case Examples

Maryelle, OT Student

Maryelle is an occupational therapy student currently completing her Level II fieldwork in psychosocial practice in an acute inpatient psychiatric unit. She is in the 5th week of the placement in her first Level II fieldwork experience.

Maryelle described herself on the personal data sheet as a shy, hard-working student. She listed her strengths as diligence, intelligence, and tenacity. Areas of growth she identified were wanting to learn more about the role of occupational therapy in inpatient psychiatry and how to run groups. Maryelle listed painting and sketching as her special skills and interests. She wrote the following statement in response to the item asking for preferred learning style: "I learn best when I can watch someone demonstrate first and then have them coach me through it the second time with feedback." She also wrote that her preferred style of supervision was a 1:1 model.

The setting Maryelle is assigned to has a part-time occupational therapy consultant who works 8–10 hours per week, as well as 4 Level II students who are assigned from four different universities. The fieldwork educator explained the first day during orientation that she uses a collaborative model of supervision and after a brief description gave the students several articles to read about this model. The fieldwork educator spent the entire first day with the students, introducing them to staff and patients and conducting several groups that day so that students could first observe how groups are to be led in this setting. She completed all documentation with students that first day and reviewed a very detailed 12-week outline of responsibilities, readings, and assignments with them.

Maryelle was initially worried about this placement because she has a part-time job during the summer, working 30 hours per week; she did not know there would be so many assignments and readings to be completed during evenings and weekends. She has been struggling to keep up with the assignments and readings, but each week during supervision, she is unable to summarize the assigned articles when asked. Her supervisor has returned all of her written assignments with many corrections to be made.

Maryelle has written a group protocol for a stress management group that her supervisor approved. Her supervisor sits in on the first day of the group to observe and has to jump in several times to keep the conversation going and set limits with some patients. Maryelle and

(continued)

Case Examples *(cont.)*

her supervisor sit down after the group to process how the group was conducted, and after some feedback from her fieldwork educator, Maryelle blurts out that she doesn't feel she can do anything right. Her supervisor suggests she read a few articles on leading groups, and Maryelle leaves the room in tears. Can you suggest another way the fieldwork educator could have processed the group with Maryelle? Could Maryelle have said something other than "I feel I can't do anything right?" What are some effective strategies that could have been used to give the student feedback about her performance?

CASE 2. KATRINA, NEW FIELDWORK EDUCATOR

Katrina is a relatively new OTR, having graduated from a large Midwestern university last year and successfully passing the NBCOT certification exam just 12 months ago. The outpatient rehabilitation clinic where she works has an active student fieldwork program, and everyone is expected to take on Level I and Level II students. Her supervisor has just informed Katrina that she will be getting her first student in 2 months and should "start getting ready." Katrina is not sure what that means, but when asked by her supervisor if she has any questions, she doesn't know where to begin, so she replies "No."

Katrina reflects on her own Level II fieldwork experiences, recalling that one was "good" and was "bad." What made a fieldwork experience good was that the supervisor appeared to care about her as a person, always had time to discuss an issue with Katrina, and made her feel competent. The bad experience was one in which the supervisor was very busy, supervisory sessions were brief, and the only feedback Katrina received was negative. She remembers feeling that she couldn't do anything right.

Katrina begins to mentally prepare for her first student, wondering how she will manage her own patient care responsibilities and those relating to the student. She hopes the student will be competent and not need a lot of "hand-holding," and is a bit worried what will happen if the student knows more than she does. She decides to spend a lot of time with the student, scheduling daily briefings at the end of each day, and makes a mental promise to herself to have all student paperwork reviewed within 24 hours. She has not taken any classes or had any training in fieldwork education but briefly remembers a psychology class she took that explained learning theories.

Katrina's first student, Mark, is an entry-level doctoral student for whom occupational therapy is a second career, with his first career having been carpentry. He talks a great deal the first day about how he was an independent contractor and asks very few questions. When Katrina asks him why he switched to occupational therapy,

he says that he wants an "easier" job than that of being a carpenter, which took its toll on his knees. Mark tells Katrina that he expects to open a private practice after graduation.

In the third week of the fieldwork experience, Katrina is becoming overwhelmed. She has been meeting with Mark at the end of every day, which is the time previously when she completed all her documentation. She completes her notes after Mark leaves for the day and thus has been working at least an hour later each day. She takes Mark's documentation home each evening and reviews it after a quick dinner. New patients' evaluations have been late because she is explaining every step of the evaluation to Mark and then completing the report with him at the end of the day.

Katrina's supervisor has spoken to her twice since Mark began fieldwork about late documentation. Katrina would like to schedule some vacation time to "catch her breath," but her supervisor says that she will have to get a colleague to cover her student while she is away. So far none of her colleagues want to work with Mark because of what they call "his attitude of superiority." Katrina cannot imagine another 9 weeks of the situation and makes a promise to herself not to accept another student. What questions do you think Katrina could have asked her supervisor when told she was getting a new student? What strategies do you think Katrina could have used to minimize her feelings of being overwhelmed with the supervision of her student? What can new fieldwork educators do to better prepare themselves for the role of fieldwork educator?

CASE 3. ROBERTA, NEW AGENCY PROGRAM DIRECTOR

Roberta has just been hired by a community-based mental health program as a full-time director of the vocational readiness program. She graduated 4 years ago with a master's degree in occupational therapy and a bachelor's degree in psychology. During her last position as a staff therapist in a hospital, she worked with several occupational therapy and occupational therapy assistant students, providing both Level I and Level II fieldwork experiences.

Roberta's supervisor is a social worker and director of the agency. He expects that she will oversee the vocational readiness program, provide evaluations to new clients being referred, and develop a student fieldwork program. Roberta enjoys challenges but is unsure about where to start first in establishing the fieldwork program. Her supervisor would like her to submit a time line for the development of the fieldwork program within the next 2 weeks. Do you think 2 weeks is a reasonable time frame to generate a time line for the development of the fieldwork education program? What are the steps that need to be followed? How long do you think this will take, given Roberta's other assignments?

Case 4. John, OTA Student

John is an occupational therapy assistant student currently assigned to a fast-paced hand therapy clinic for a Level I fieldwork experience. Lynne is the fieldwork educator assigned to him; she is a new graduate from an occupational therapy program. Lynne tells John on his first day that he will be shadowing her; she explains that she will be making some splints today and that he can assist. He has not yet had any coursework on splinting.

She also explains to him that she will be off the following week but that he can still come in and work with the other therapists working with clients.

Lynne asks John to develop a learning contract for his 6-week placement with her. He has never heard of a learning contract and thought he was just going to be observing. John wants to take advantage of the learning opportunity but is unsure how to approach Lynne with his concerns. If you were John, how would you go about finding out what needs to be in a learning contract? What would you suggest he say to Lynne regarding his uncertainty? Where could John get an example of a learning contract?

❖ Learning Activities

1. *Experiences with supervision.* Recall a fieldwork education experience. Reflect on the type and amount of supervision you received. What did you like and dislike about the supervision you received? Contrast this to the way you currently provide supervision or how a colleague or supervisor does so. In what ways has your own experiences with supervision influenced how you supervise others? What type of training do you think your supervisor may have had to prepare him or her for the fieldwork educator role? What supervision model do you think he or she used?

2. *Strengths and weaknesses.* What qualities do you think are important for an effective fieldwork educator? What characteristics or behaviors do you think an ineffective fieldwork educator displays?

3. *Exploring biases.* Imagine that you are told by your supervisor that you are to receive a fieldwork student next week. Create a description of the ideal student you would like to have and one for the student you would least like to be assigned. Include age, gender, learning style, height and weight, academic level, ethnicity, religion, health status, interests, and so on. Organize these descriptors in a two-column table. How is Column 1

reflective of who you are, who you want to be, and the qualities you're most attracted to in others? How is Column 2 reflective of who you are, who you don't want to be, and the qualities you're least attracted to? What impact does Column 1 and Column 2 have on the way you do or would provide supervision to fieldwork students?

4. *Giving and receiving feedback.* Recall the last time someone gave you feedback on something you had done. What were the circumstances under which the feedback was given and received? Did the feedback communicate what you did right, what you did wrong, or both? At the end of the feedback, did you know what specific areas needed improvement? How did you process the feedback received?

5. *Managing a failing student.* Recall a student you supervised whose performance did not measure up to your expectations. Was the behavior a pattern or an isolated event? Did this behavior affect the student's learning? Did the behavior affect your ability to teach the student? Did the behavior affect patient care? If you have responded "no" to the previous two questions, then what else could have influenced you to react negatively to the situation?

✓ Multiple-Choice Questions

1. Your supervisor tells you that you are going to be working with an occupational therapy student for a Level II fieldwork experience who has "some sort of disability." Your first response should be to
   a. Contact the school's AFWC to request more information about the nature of the student's disability.
   b. Interview the student about the nature of the disability to determine what reasonable accommodations he or she needs.
   c. Contact the Legal Affairs Division of the hospital in which you work to find out what you can have the student do during fieldwork.
   d. Create a list of the essential functions and critical tasks that a student must be able to perform to achieve entry-level competency.

2. You complete the final evaluation for the student you have been working with during Level II fieldwork and discover that he has not scored enough points to pass this experience. What should you do?
   a. Call the student into your office and advise him that he has failed the fieldwork experience.
   b. Contact the AFWC and tell her that the student will be failing the fieldwork experience.
   c. Change some of the scores so that the total number of points adds up to the minimum passing score.
   d. Contact the AFWC and request a meeting between the three parties involved—student, yourself, and the AFWC.

3. You want to start a new fieldwork program at your health care facility. Which of the following should you do first?
   a. Contact the Legal Affairs Department and ask them to send out a standard contract to all of the occupational therapy and occupational therapy assistant schools in the area.
   b. Contact the academic programs in your area to inquire whether they need additional fieldwork sites, and set up a meeting
   c. Order FWPE forms from AOTA.
   d. Create a 12-week outline for OT students and an 8-week outline for OTA students of expectations and assignments.

4. The purpose of Level I fieldwork is to
   a. Introduce students to the concept of therapeutic use of self through learning how to interview patients.
   b. Enrich didactic coursework through directed observation and participation in selected aspects of the occupational therapy process.
   c. Provide opportunities for students to practice handling and transfer skills they are learning in the classroom.
   d. Teach students how to correctly write documentation for reimbursement in the medical record.

5. The person employed by the academic program who is responsible for all aspects of the student's clinical education is the
   a. AFWC.
   b. Program director.
   c. Fieldwork educator.
   d. Clinical education coordinator.

6. Confidentiality of a fieldwork student's records is regulated by which of the following?
   a. HIPAA
   b. IDEA
   c. ADA
   d. FERPA

7. In which of the following fieldwork placement models is there an emphasis on the fieldwork educator and students working together to coconstruct new knowledge?
   a. Group model.
   b. Situational leadership model.
   c. Collaborative model.
   d. Process model.

8. The currently preferred title in the United States for the occupational therapy practitioner who supervises and educates entry-level OT and OTA students during Level I or II fieldwork is
   a. Clinical instructor.
   b. Clinical supervisor.
   c. Fieldwork educator.
   d. Fieldwork supervisor.

9. The body responsible for developing and enforcing accreditation guidelines for fieldwork is
   a. JCAHO.
   b. COE.
   c. CARF.
   d. ACOTE.

10. The assessment that is useful for students and fieldwork educators to discuss around the time of the midterm performance evaluation is the
    a. SAFECOM.
    b. SEFWE.
    c. FEAT.
    d. FWPE.

11. In a role-emerging fieldwork placement, the fieldwork educator needs to have how many years of experience before accepting students?
    a. One.
    b. Two.
    c. Three.
    c. Four.

12. The minimum number of hours of supervision required weekly in a role-emerging practice setting is
    a. Two.
    b. Four.

c. Six.

d. Eight.

13. The two areas that can result in automatic failure for students during Level II fieldwork are
    a. Safety and documentation.
    b. Documentation and ethics.
    c. Ethics and judgment.
    d. Safety and ethics.

14. Which of the following statements are true?
    a. Students must complete a psychosocial fieldwork experience, but it may be either a Level I or Level II.
    b. ACOTE states that psychosocial fieldwork experiences can occur in either inpatient or community-based settings.
    c. Psychosocial factors about engagement in occupation must be understood and integrated for client-centered, meaningful, occupation-based outcomes in all settings.
    d. Psychosocial fieldwork is no longer required by ACOTE as a condition of accreditation.

15. The assessment that can be used by practitioners to determine their readiness for being a fieldwork educator is
    a. SAFECOM.
    b. FEAT.
    c. SEFWE.
    d. FWPE.

16. A fieldwork educator can begin supervising students
    a. As soon as they pass the NBCOT exam.
    b. As soon as they receive their state license.
    c. After 1 year of professional work experience.
    d. 1 year after initial NBCOT certification.

17. Fieldwork educators can earn which of the following for supervising students?
    a. Professional development units.
    b. Continuing education units.
    c. Advanced-degree credit.
    d. Fieldwork educators' commendations.

18. An emerging practice area is one in which all but which of the following is true?
    a. One that does not employ an occupational therapy practitioner.
    b. One that does not yet have an ACOTE contract.
    c. One that employs a part-time occupational therapy practitioner.
    d. One that has limited services of an occupational therapy consultant.

19. According to ACOTE, the contract between the academic institution and the fieldwork site must be reviewed at a minimum every
    a. 1 year.
    b. 2 years.
    c. 3 years.
    d. 5 years.

20. The rules that are created by ACOTE are called
    a. Essentials.
    b. Standards.
    c. Guidelines.
    d. Policies.

21. Reasonable accommodations given to a student with a disability during fieldwork is governed by which of the following?
    a. FERPA.
    b. Section 504.
    c. IDEA.
    d. HIPAA.

References

Accreditation Council for Occupational Therapy Education. (2007a). Accreditation standards for an educational program for the occupational therapy assistant. *American Journal of Occupational Therapy, 61,* 662–671.

Accreditation Council for Occupational Therapy Education. (2007b). Accreditation standards for a master's-degree-level educational program for the occupational therapist. *American Journal of Occupational Therapy, 61,* 652–661.

American Occupational Therapy Association. (1995). *Fieldwork Experience Assessment Tool (FEAT).* Retrieved August 12, 2010, from http://www.aota.org/Students/Current/Fieldwork/FEAT.aspx

American Occupational Therapy Association. (2005). Standards of practice for occupational therapy. *American Journal of Occupational Therapy, 59,* 663–665.

American Occupational Therapy Association. (2007). AOTA's *Centennial Vision* and executive summary. *American Journal of Occupational Therapy, 61,* 613–614.

American Occupational Therapy Association. (2009a). Occupational therapy fieldwork education: Value and purpose. *American Journal of Occupational Therapy, 63,* 821–822.

American Occupational Therapy Association. (2009b). *Self-Assessment Tool for Fieldwork Educator Competency.* Retrieved August 26, 2010, from http://www.aota.org/Educate/EdRes/Fieldwork/Supervisor/Forms/38251.aspx

American Occupational Therapy Association. (2009c). Specialized knowledge and skills of occupational therapy educators of the future. *American Journal of Occupational Therapy, 63,* 804–806.

American Occupational Therapy Association. (2010a). Ethical considerations for professional education of students with disabilities [Advisory Opinion]. In D. Y. Slater (Ed.), *Reference manual to the occupational therapy code of ethics and ethics standards* (2010 ed.). Bethesda, MD: AOTA Press.

American Occupational Therapy Association. (2010b). Occupational therapy code of ethics and ethics standards (2010). *American Journal of Occupational Therapy, 64.*

Americans With Disabilities Act of 1990, Pub. L. 101-336, 104 Stat. 327.

Brookfield, S. (1998). Critically reflective practice. *Journal of Continuing Education in the Health Professions, 18,* 197–205.

Centers for Medicare and Medicaid Services. (2003). *Medicare claims processing manual: Chapter 5—Part B outpatient rehabilitation.* Retrieved August 12, 2010, from http://www.aota.org/Educate/EdRes/Fieldwork/StuSuprvsn/35394.aspx

Cohn, E., & Crist, P. (1995). Back to the future: New approaches to fieldwork education. *American Journal of Occupational Therapy, 49,* 103–106.

Costa, D. (2007). *Clinical supervision in occupational therapy: A guide for fieldwork and practice.* Bethesda, MD: AOTA Press.

Dwyer, G., & Higgs, J. (1999). Profiling health science students. In J. Higgs & H. Edwards (Eds.), *Educating beginning practitioners: Challenges for health professional education* (pp. 125–135). Woburn, MA: Butterworth-Heineman.

Ende, J. (1983). Feedback in clinical medical education. *JAMA, 250,* 777–781.

Lew, N., Cara, E., & Richardson, P. (2007). When fieldwork takes a detour. *Occupational Therapy in Health Care, 21*(1/2), 105–122.

Lofmark, A., & Wikblad, K. (2001). Facilitating and obstructing factors for the development of learning in clinical practice: A student perspective. *Journal of Advanced Nursing, 34*(1), 43–50.

Marsh, S., Cooper, K., Jordan, G., Merrett, S., Scammell, J., & Clark, V. (2004). *Managing failing students in practice.* Retrieved September 30, 2008, from http://www.practicebasedlearning.org/resources/materials/docs/Failing%20Students

Milan, F. B., Parish, S. J., & Reichgott, M. J. (2006). A model for educational feedback based on clinical communication skills strategies: Beyond the "feedback sandwich." *Teaching and Learning in Medicine, 18,* 42–47.

Miser, W. F. (n.d.). *Giving effective feedback.* Retrieved August 25, 2010, from http://www.ohioafp.org/pdfs/members/educator_resources/GivingEffectiveFeedback.pdf

Privott, C. (1998). *The fieldwork anthology: A classic research and practice collection.* Bethesda, MD: American Occupational Therapy Association.

Rose, M., & Best, D. (Ed.). (2005). *Transforming practice through clinical education, professional supervision, and mentoring.* New York: Elsevier.

Scheidt, P., Lazoritz, S., Ebbeling, W., Figelman, A., Messner, H., & Singer, J. (1986). Evaluation of a system providing feedback to students on videotaped patient encounters. *Journal of Medical Education, 61,* 585–590.

Section 504 of the Rehabilitation Act of 1973, 29 U.S.C. 794.

Southern New Hampshire Area Health Education Center. (n.d.). *Feedback: An education module for community-based teachers.* Retrieved August 25, 2010, from http://www.snhahec.org/documents/Feedback.doc

Westberg, J., & Jason, H. (2001). *Fostering reflection and providing feedback.* New York: Springer.

Appendix 37.A. Fieldwork Education Evidence Table

Topic	Evidence
Assessment	American Occupational Therapy Association. (1995). *Fieldwork Experience Assessment Tool (FEAT)*. Retrieved August 12, 2010, from http://www.aota.org/Students/Current/Fieldwork/FEAT.aspx American Occupational Therapy Association. (2009b). *Self-Assessment Tool for Fieldwork Educator Competency*. Retrieved August 26, 2010, from http://www.aota.org/Educate/EdRes/Fieldwork/Supervisor/Forms/38251.aspx
Feedback	Ende, J. (1983). Feedback in clinical medical education. *JAMA, 250,* 777–781. Miser, W. F. (n.d.). *Giving effective feedback*. Retrieved August 25, 2010, from http://www.ohioafp.org/pdfs/members/educator_resources/GivingEffectiveFeedback.pdf Southern New Hampshire Area Health Education Center. (n.d.). *Feedback: An education module for community-based teachers*. Retrieved August 25, 2010, from http://www.snhahec.org/documents/Feedback.doc Westberg, J., & Jason, H. (2001). *Fostering reflection and providing feedback*. New York: Springer.
Placement	Preceptor Education Program (available at www.preceptor.ca)
Supervision	Costa, D. (2007). *Clinical supervision in occupational therapy: A guide for fieldwork and practice*. Bethesda, MD: AOTA Press. Rose, M., & Best, D. (Ed.). (2005). *Transforming practice through clinical education, professional supervision, and mentoring*. New York: Elsevier.

Appendix A.

Occupational Therapy Code of Ethics and Ethics Standards (2010)

Preamble

The American Occupational Therapy Association (AOTA) *Occupational Therapy Code of Ethics and Ethics Standards (2010)* ("Code and Ethics Standards") is a public statement of principles used to promote and maintain high standards of conduct within the profession. Members of AOTA are committed to promoting inclusion, diversity, independence, and safety for all recipients in various stages of life, health, and illness and to empower all beneficiaries of occupational therapy. This commitment extends beyond service recipients to include professional colleagues, students, educators, businesses, and the community.

Fundamental to the mission of the occupational therapy profession is the therapeutic use of everyday life activities (occupations) with individuals or groups for the purpose of participation in roles and situations in home, school, workplace, community, and other settings. "Occupational therapy addresses the physical, cognitive, psychosocial, sensory, and other aspects of performance in a variety of contexts to support engagement in everyday life activities that affect health, well-being, and quality of life" (AOTA, 2004, p. 694). Occupational therapy personnel have an ethical responsibility primarily to recipients of service and secondarily to society.

The *Occupational Therapy Code of Ethics and Ethics Standards (2010)* was tailored to address the most prevalent ethical concerns of the profession in education, research, and practice. The concerns of stakeholders including the public, consumers, students, colleagues, employers, research participants, researchers, educators, and practitioners were addressed in the creation of this document. A review of issues raised in ethics cases, member questions related to ethics, and content of other professional codes of ethics were utilized to ensure that the revised document is applicable to occupational therapists, occupational therapy assistants, and students in all roles.

The historical foundation of this Code and Ethics Standards is based on ethical reasoning surrounding practice and professional issues, as well as on empathic reflection regarding these interactions with others (see e.g., AOTA, 2005, 2006). This reflection resulted in the establishment of principles that guide ethical action, which goes beyond rote following of rules or application of principles. Rather, *ethical action* it is a manifestation of moral character and mindful reflection. It is a commitment to benefit others, to virtuous practice of artistry and science, to genuinely good behaviors, and to noble acts of courage.

While much has changed over the course of the profession's history, more has remained the same. The profession of occupational therapy remains grounded in seven core concepts, as identified in the *Core Values and Attitudes of Occupational Therapy Practice* (AOTA, 1993): *altruism, equality, freedom, justice, dignity, truth,* and *prudence. Altruism* is the individual's ability to place the needs of others before their own. *Equality* refers to the desire to promote fairness in interactions with others. The concept of *freedom* and personal choice is paramount in a profession in which the desires of the client must guide our interventions. Occupational therapy practitioners, educators, and researchers relate in a fair and impartial manner to individuals with whom they interact and respect and adhere to the applicable laws and standards regarding their area of practice, be it direct care, education, or research *(justice)*. Inherent in the practice of occupational therapy is the promotion and preservation of the individuality and *dignity* of the client, by assisting him or her to engage in occupations that are meaningful to him or her regardless of level of disability. In all situations, occupational therapists, occupational therapy assistants, and students must provide accurate information, both in oral and written form *(truth)*. Occupational therapy personnel use their clinical and ethical reasoning skills, sound judgment, and reflection to make decisions to direct them in their area(s) of practice *(prudence)*. These seven core values provide a foundation by which occupational therapy personnel guide their interactions with others, be they students, clients, colleagues, research participants, or communities. These values also define the ethical principles to which the profession is committed and which the public can expect.

The *Occupational Therapy Code of Ethics and Ethics Standards (2010)* is a guide to professional conduct when ethical issues arise. Ethical decision making is a process that includes awareness of how the outcome will impact occupational therapy clients in all spheres. Applications of Code and Ethics Standards Principles are considered situation-specific, and where a conflict exists, occupational therapy personnel will pursue responsible efforts for resolution. These Principles apply to occupational therapy personnel engaged in any professional role, including elected and volunteer leadership positions.

The specific purposes of the *Occupational Therapy Code of Ethics and Ethics Standards (2010)* are to

1. Identify and describe the principles supported by the occupational therapy profession.

2. Educate the general public and members regarding established principles to which occupational therapy personnel are accountable.

3. Socialize occupational therapy personnel to expected standards of conduct.

4. Assist occupational therapy personnel in recognition and resolution of ethical dilemmas.

The *Occupational Therapy Code of Ethics and Ethics Standards (2010)* define the set of principles that apply to occupational therapy personnel at all levels:

DEFINITIONS

- **Recipient of service:** Individuals or groups receiving occupational therapy.

- **Student:** A person who is enrolled in an accredited occupational therapy education program.

- **Research participant:** A prospective participant or one who has agreed to participate in an approved research project.

- **Employee:** A person who is hired by a business (facility or organization) to provide occupational therapy services.

- **Colleague:** A person who provides services in the same or different business (facility or organization) to which a professional relationship exists or may exist.

- **Public:** The community of people at large.

BENEFICENCE

Principle 1. Occupational therapy personnel shall demonstrate a concern for the well-being and safety of the recipients of their services.

Beneficence includes all forms of action intended to benefit other persons. The term *beneficence* connotes acts of mercy, kindness, and charity (Beauchamp & Childress, 2009). Forms of beneficence typically include altruism, love, and humanity. Beneficence requires taking action by helping others, in other words, by promoting good, by preventing harm, and by removing harm. Examples of beneficence include protecting and defending the rights of others, preventing harm from occurring to others, removing conditions that will cause harm to others, helping persons with disabilities, and rescuing persons in danger (Beauchamp & Childress, 2009).

Occupational therapy personnel shall

A. Respond to requests for occupational therapy services (e.g., a referral) in a timely manner as determined by law, regulation, or policy.

B. Provide appropriate evaluation and a plan of intervention for all recipients of occupational therapy services specific to their needs.

C. Reevaluate and reassess recipients of service in a timely manner to determine if goals are being achieved and whether intervention plans should be revised.

D. Avoid the inappropriate use of outdated or obsolete tests/assessments or data obtained from such tests in making intervention decisions or recommendations.

E. Provide occupational therapy services that are within each practitioner's level of competence and scope of practice (e.g., qualifications, experience, the law).

F. Use, to the extent possible, evaluation, planning, intervention techniques, and therapeutic equipment that are evidence-based and within the recognized scope of occupational therapy practice.

G. Take responsible steps (e.g., continuing education, research, supervision, training) and use careful judgment to ensure their own competence and weigh potential for client harm when generally recognized standards do not exist in emerging technology or areas of practice.

H. Terminate occupational therapy services in collaboration with the service recipient or responsible party when the needs and goals of the recipient have been met or when services no longer produce a measurable change or outcome.

I. Refer to other health care specialists solely on the basis of the needs of the client.

J. Provide occupational therapy education, continuing education, instruction, and training that are within the instructor's subject area of expertise and level of competence.

K. Provide students and employees with information about the Code and Ethics Standards, opportunities to discuss ethical conflicts, and procedures for reporting unresolved ethical conflicts.

L. Ensure that occupational therapy research is conducted in accordance with currently accepted ethical guidelines and standards for the protection of research participants and the dissemination of results.

M. Report to appropriate authorities any acts in practice, education, and research that appear unethical or illegal.

N. Take responsibility for promoting and practicing occupational therapy on the basis of current knowledge and research and for further developing the profession's body of knowledge.

NONMALEFICENCE

Principle 2. Occupational therapy personnel shall intentionally refrain from actions that cause harm.

Nonmaleficence imparts an obligation to refrain from harming others (Beauchamp & Childress, 2009). The principle of nonmaleficence is grounded in the practitioner's responsibility to refrain from causing harm, inflicting injury, or wronging others. While beneficence requires action to incur benefit, nonmaleficence requires non-action to avoid harm (Beauchamp & Childress, 2009). Nonmaleficence also includes an obligation to not impose risks of harm even if the potential risk is without malicious or harmful intent. This principle often is examined under the context of *due care*. If the standard of due care outweighs the benefit of treatment, then refraining from treatment provision would be ethically indicated (Beauchamp & Childress, 2009).

Occupational therapy personnel shall

A. Avoid inflicting harm or injury to recipients of occupational therapy services, students, research participants, or employees.

B. Make every effort to ensure continuity of services or options for transition to appropriate services to avoid abandoning the service recipient if the current provider is unavailable due to medical or other absence or loss of employment.

C. Avoid relationships that exploit the recipient of services, students, research participants, or employees physically, emotionally, psychologically, financially, socially, or in any other manner that conflicts or interferes with professional judgment and objectivity.

D. Avoid engaging in any sexual relationship or activity, whether consensual or nonconsensual, with any recipient of service, including family or significant other, student, research participant, or employee, while a relationship exists as an occupational therapy practitioner, educator, researcher, supervisor, or employer.

E. Recognize and take appropriate action to remedy personal problems and limitations that might cause harm to recipients of service, colleagues, students, research participants, or others.

F. Avoid any undue influences, such as alcohol or drugs, that may compromise the provision of occupational therapy services, education, or research.

G. Avoid situations in which a practitioner, educator, researcher, or employer is unable to maintain clear professional boundaries or objectivity to ensure the safety and well-being of recipients of service, students, research participants, and employees.

H. Maintain awareness of and adherence to the Code and Ethics Standards when participating in volunteer roles.

I. Avoid compromising client rights or well-being based on arbitrary administrative directives by exercising professional judgment and critical analysis.

J. Avoid exploiting any relationship established as an occupational therapist or occupational therapy assistant to further one's own physical, emotional, financial, political, or business interests at the expense of the best interests of recipients of services, students, research participants, employees, or colleagues.

K. Avoid participating in bartering for services because of the potential for exploitation and conflict of interest unless there are clearly no contraindications or bartering is a culturally appropriate custom.

L. Determine the proportion of risk to benefit for participants in research prior to implementing a study.

AUTONOMY, CONFIDENTIALITY

Principle 3. Occupational therapy personnel shall respect the right of the individual to self-determination.

The principle of autonomy and confidentiality expresses the concept that practitioners have a duty to treat the client according to the client's desires, within the bounds of accepted standards of care and to protect the client's confidential information. Often *autonomy* is referred to as the *self-determination* principle. However, respect for autonomy goes beyond acknowledging an individual as a mere agent and also acknowledges a "person's right to hold views, to make choices, and to take actions based on personal values and beliefs" (Beauchamp & Childress, 2009, p. 103). Autonomy has become a prominent principle in health care ethics; the right to make a determination regarding care decisions that directly impact the life of the service recipient should reside with that individual. The principle of autonomy and confidentiality also applies to students in an educational program, to participants in research studies, and to the public who seek information about occupational therapy services.

Occupational therapy personnel shall

A.   Establish a collaborative relationship with recipients of service, including families, significant others, and caregivers in setting goals and priorities throughout the intervention process. This includes full disclosure of the benefits, risks, and potential outcomes of any intervention; the personnel who will be providing the intervention(s); and/or any reasonable alternatives to the proposed intervention.

B.   Obtain consent before administering any occupational therapy service, including evaluation, and ensure that recipients of service (or their legal representatives) are kept informed of the progress in meeting goals specified in the plan of intervention/care. If the service recipient cannot give consent, the practitioner must be sure that consent has been obtained from the person who is legally responsible for that recipient.

C.   Respect the recipient of service's right to refuse occupational therapy services temporarily or permanently without negative consequences.

D.   Provide students with access to accurate information regarding educational requirements and academic policies and procedures relative to the occupational therapy program/educational institution.

E.   Obtain informed consent from participants involved in research activities, and ensure that they understand the benefits, risks, and potential outcomes as a result of their participation as research subjects.

F.   Respect research participant's right to withdraw from a research study without consequences.

G.   Ensure that confidentiality and the right to privacy are respected and maintained regarding all information obtained about recipients of service, students, research participants, colleagues, or employees. The only exceptions are when a practitioner or staff member believes that an individual is in serious foreseeable or imminent harm. Laws and regulations may require disclosure to appropriate authorities without consent.

H.   Maintain the confidentiality of all verbal, written, electronic, augmentative, and non-verbal communications, including compliance with HIPAA regulations.

I.   Take appropriate steps to facilitate meaningful communication and comprehension in cases in which the recipient of service, student, or research participant has limited ability to communicate (e.g., aphasia or differences in language, literacy, culture).

J.   Make every effort to facilitate open and collaborative dialogue with clients and/or responsible parties to facilitate comprehension of services and their potential risks/benefits.

SOCIAL JUSTICE

Principle 4. Occupational therapy personnel shall provide services in a fair and equitable manner.

Social justice, also called *distributive justice,* refers to the fair, equitable, and appropriate distribution of resources. The principle of social justice refers broadly to the distribution of all rights and responsibilities in society (Beauchamp & Childress, 2009). In general, the principle of social justice supports the concept of achieving justice in every aspect of society rather than merely the administration of law. The general idea is that individuals and groups should receive fair treatment and an impartial share of the benefits of society. Occupational therapy personnel have a vested interest in addressing unjust inequities that limit opportunities for participation in society (Braveman & Bass-Haugen, 2009). While opinions differ regarding the most ethical approach to addressing distribution of health care resources and reduction of health disparities, the issue of social justice continues to focus on limiting the impact of social inequality on health outcomes.

Occupational therapy personnel shall

A. Uphold the profession's altruistic responsibilities to help ensure the common good.

B. Take responsibility for educating the public and society about the value of occupational therapy services in promoting health and wellness and reducing the impact of disease and disability.

C. Make every effort to promote activities that benefit the health status of the community.

D. Advocate for just and fair treatment for all patients, clients, employees, and colleagues, and encourage employers and colleagues to abide by the highest standards of social justice and the ethical standards set forth by the occupational therapy profession.

E. Make efforts to advocate for recipients of occupational therapy services to obtain needed services through available means.

F. Provide services that reflect an understanding of how occupational therapy service delivery can be affected by factors such as economic status, age, ethnicity, race, geography, disability, marital status, sexual orientation, gender, gender identity, religion, culture, and political affiliation.

G. Consider offering *pro bono* ("for the good") or reduced-fee occupational therapy services for selected individuals when consistent with guidelines of the employer, third-party payer, and/or government agency.

PROCEDURAL JUSTICE

Principle 5. Occupational therapy personnel shall comply with institutional rules, local, state, federal, and international laws and AOTA documents applicable to the profession of occupational therapy.

Procedural justice is concerned with making and implementing decisions according to fair processes that ensure "fair treatment" (Maiese, 2004). Rules must be impartially followed and consistently applied to generate an unbiased decision. The principle of procedural justice is based on the concept that procedures and processes are organized in a fair manner and that policies, regulations, and laws are followed. While *the law* and *ethics* are not synonymous terms, occupational therapy personnel have an ethical responsibility to uphold current reimbursement regulations and state/territorial laws governing the profession. In addition, occupational therapy personnel are ethically bound to be aware of organizational policies and practice guidelines set forth by regulatory agencies established to protect recipients of service, research participants, and the public.

Occupational therapy personnel shall

A. Be familiar with and apply the Code and Ethics Standards to the work setting, and share them with employers, other employees, colleagues, students, and researchers.

B. Be familiar with and seek to understand and abide by institutional rules, and when those rules conflict with ethical practice, take steps to resolve the conflict.

C. Be familiar with revisions in those laws and AOTA policies that apply to the profession of occupational therapy and inform employers, employees, colleagues, students, and researchers of those changes.

D. Be familiar with established policies and procedures for handling concerns about the Code and Ethics Standards, including familiarity with national, state, local, district, and territorial procedures for handling ethics complaints as well as policies and procedures created by AOTA and certification, licensing, and regulatory agencies.

E. Hold appropriate national, state, or other requisite credentials for the occupational therapy services they provide.

F. Take responsibility for maintaining high standards and continuing competence in practice, education, and research by participating in professional development and educational activities to improve and update knowledge and skills.

G. Ensure that all duties assumed by or assigned to other occupational therapy personnel match credentials, qualifications, experience, and scope of practice.

H. Provide appropriate supervision to individuals for whom they have supervisory responsibility in accordance with AOTA official documents and local, state, and federal or national laws, rules, regulations, policies, procedures, standards, and guidelines.

I. Obtain all necessary approvals prior to initiating research activities.

J. Report all gifts and remuneration from individuals, agencies, or companies in accordance with employer policies as well as state and federal guidelines.

K. Use funds for intended purposes, and avoid misappropriation of funds.

L. Take reasonable steps to ensure that employers are aware of occupational therapy's ethical obligations as set forth in this Code and Ethics Standards and of the implications of those obligations for occupational therapy practice, education, and research.

M. Actively work with employers to prevent discrimination and unfair labor practices, and advocate for employees with disabilities to ensure the provision of reasonable accommodations.

N. Actively participate with employers in the formulation of policies and procedures to ensure legal, regulatory, and ethical compliance.

O. Collect fees legally. Fees shall be fair, reasonable, and commensurate with services delivered. Fee schedules must be available and equitable regardless of actual payer reimbursements/contracts.

P. Maintain the ethical principles and standards of the profession when participating in a business arrangement as owner, stockholder, partner, or employee, and refrain from working for or doing business with organizations that engage in illegal or unethical business practices (e.g., fraudulent billing, providing occupational therapy services beyond the scope of occupational therapy practice).

VERACITY

Principle 6. Occupational therapy personnel shall provide comprehensive, accurate, and objective information when representing the profession.

Veracity is based on the virtues of truthfulness, candor, and honesty. The principle of *veracity* in health care refers to comprehensive, accurate, and objective transmission of information and includes fostering the client's understanding of such information (Beauchamp & Childress, 2009). Veracity is based on respect owed to others. In communicating with others, occupational therapy personnel implicitly promise to speak truthfully and not deceive the listener. By entering into a relationship in care or research, the recipient of service or research participant enters into a contract that includes a right to truthful information (Beauchamp & Childress, 2009). In addition, transmission of information is incomplete without also ensuring that the recipient or participant understands the information provided. Concepts of veracity must be carefully balanced with other potentially competing ethical principles, cultural beliefs, and organizational policies. Veracity ultimately is valued as a means to establish trust and strengthen professional relationships. Therefore, adherence to the Principle also requires thoughtful analysis of how full disclosure of information may impact outcomes.

Occupational therapy personnel shall

A. Represent the credentials, qualifications, education, experience, training, roles, duties, competence, views, contributions, and findings accurately in all forms of communication about recipients of service, students, employees, research participants, and colleagues.

B. Refrain from using or participating in the use of any form of communication that contains false, fraudulent, deceptive, misleading, or unfair statements or claims.

C. Record and report in an accurate and timely manner, and in accordance with applicable regulations, all information related to professional activities.

D. Ensure that documentation for reimbursement purposes is done in accordance with applicable laws, guidelines, and regulations.

E. Accept responsibility for any action that reduces the public's trust in occupational therapy.

F. Ensure that all marketing and advertising are truthful, accurate, and carefully presented to avoid misleading recipients of service, students, research participants, or the public.

G. Describe the type and duration of occupational therapy services accurately in professional contracts, including the duties and responsibilities of all involved parties.

H. Be honest, fair, accurate, respectful, and timely in gathering and reporting fact-based information regarding employee job performance and student performance.

I. Give credit and recognition when using the work of others in written, oral, or electronic media.

J. Not plagiarize the work of others.

FIDELITY

Principle 7. Occupational therapy personnel shall treat colleagues and other professionals with respect, fairness, discretion, and integrity.

The principle of fidelity comes from the Latin root *fidelis* meaning loyal. Fidelity refers to being faithful, which includes obligations of loyalty and the keeping of promises and commitments (Veatch & Flack, 1997). In the health professions, fidelity refers to maintaining good-faith relationships between various service providers and recipients. While respecting fidelity requires occupational therapy personnel to meet the client's reasonable expectations (Purtillo, 2005), Principle 7 specifically addresses fidelity as it relates to maintaining collegial and organizational relationships. Professional relationships are greatly influenced by the complexity of the environment in which occupational therapy personnel work. Practitioners, educators, and researchers alike must consistently balance their duties to service recipients, students, research participants, and other professionals as well as to organizations that may influence decision making and professional practice.

Occupational therapy personnel shall

A. Respect the traditions, practices, competencies, and responsibilities of their own and other professions, as well as those of the institutions and agencies that constitute the working environment.

B. Preserve, respect, and safeguard private information about employees, colleagues, and students unless otherwise mandated by national, state, or local laws or permission to disclose is given by the individual.

C. Take adequate measures to discourage, prevent, expose, and correct any breaches of the Code and Ethics Standards, and report any breaches of the former to the appropriate authorities.

D. Attempt to resolve perceived institutional violations of the Code and Ethics Standards by utilizing internal resources first.

E. Avoid conflicts of interest or conflicts of commitment in employment, volunteer roles, or research.

F. Avoid using one's position (employee or volunteer) or knowledge gained from that position in such a manner that gives rise to real or perceived conflict of interest among the person, the employer, other Association members, and/or other organizations.

G. Use conflict resolution and/or alternative dispute resolution resources to resolve organizational and interpersonal conflicts.

H. Be diligent stewards of human, financial, and material resources of their employers, and refrain from exploiting these resources for personal gain.

References

American Occupational Therapy Association. (1993). Core values and attitudes of occupational therapy practice. *American Journal of Occupational Therapy, 47,* 1085–1086.

American Occupational Therapy Association. (2004). Policy 5.3.1: Definition of occupational therapy practice for state regulation. *American Journal of Occupational Therapy, 58,* 694–695.

American Occupational Therapy Association. (2005). Occupational therapy code of ethics (2005). *American Journal of Occupational Therapy, 59,* 639–642.

American Occupational Therapy Association. (2006). Guidelines to the occupational therapy code of ethics. *American Journal of Occupational Therapy, 60,* 652–658.

Beauchamp, T. L., & Childress, J. F. (2009). *Principles of biomedical ethics* (6th ed.). New York: Oxford University Press.

Braveman, B., & Bass-Haugen, J. D. (2009). Social justice and health disparities: An evolving discourse in occupational therapy research and intervention. *American Journal of Occupational Therapy, 63,* 7–12.

Maiese, M. (2004). *Procedural justice.* Retrieved July 29, 2009, from http://www.beyondintractability.org/essay/procedural_justice/

Purtillo, R. (2005). *Ethical dimensions in the health professions* (4th ed.). Philadelphia: Elsevier/Saunders.

Veatch, R. M., & Flack, H. E. (1997). *Case studies in allied health ethics.* Upper Saddle River, NJ: Prentice-Hall.

Authors

Ethics Commission (EC):

Kathlyn Reed, PhD, OTR, FAOTA, MLIS, Chairperson
Barbara Hemphill, DMin, OTR, FAOTA, FMOTA, Chair-Elect
Ann Moodey Ashe, MHS, OTR/L
Lea C. Brandt, OTD, MA, OTR/L
Joanne Estes, MS, OTR/L
Loretta Jean Foster, MS, COTA/L
Donna F. Homenko, RDH, PhD
Craig R. Jackson, JD, MSW
Deborah Yarett Slater, MS, OT/L, FAOTA, AOTA Staff Liaison

Adopted by the Representative Assembly 2010CApr17.

Note. This document replaces the following rescinded Ethics documents 2010CApril18: the Occupational *Therapy Code of Ethics (2005)* (*American Journal of Occupational Therapy, 59,* 639–642); the *Guidelines to the Occupational Therapy Code of Ethics* (*American Journal of Occupational Therapy, 60,* 652–658); and the *Core Values and Attitudes of Occupational Therapy Practice* (*American Journal of Occupational Therapy, 47,* 1085–1086).

Copyright © 2010 by the American Occupational Therapy Association, Inc. To be published in 2010 in the *American Journal of Occupational Therapy, 64* (November/December).

Appendix B.

Scope of Practice

Statement of Purpose

The purpose of this document is to

A. Define the scope of practice in occupational therapy by

1. Delineating the domain of occupational therapy practice that directs the focus and actions of services provided by occupational therapists and occupational therapy assistants;

2. Delineating the dynamic process of occupational therapy evaluation and intervention services used to achieve outcomes that support the participation of clients in their everyday life activities (occupations);

3. Describing the education and certification requirements needed to practice as an occupational therapist and occupational therapy assistant;

B. Inform consumers, health care providers, educators, the community, funding agencies, payers, referral sources, and policymakers regarding the scope of occupational therapy.

Introduction

The occupational therapy scope of practice is based on the American Occupational Therapy Association (AOTA) document *Occupational Therapy Practice Framework: Domain and Process* (AOTA, 2008) and on the *Philosophical Base of Occupational Therapy*, which states that "the understanding and use of occupations shall be at the central core of occupational therapy practice, education, and research" (AOTA, 2006b, Policy 1.11). Occupational therapy is a dynamic and evolving profession that is responsive to consumer needs and to emerging knowledge and research.

This scope of practice document is designed to support and be used in conjunction with the *Definition of Occupational Therapy Practice for the Model Practice Act* (AOTA, 2004b). While this scope of practice document helps support state laws and regulations that govern the practice of occupational therapy, it does not supersede those existing laws and other regulatory requirements. Occupational therapists and occupational therapy assistants are required to abide by statutes and regulations when providing occupational therapy services. State laws and other regulatory requirements typically include statements about educational requirements to practice occupational therapy, procedures to practice occupational therapy legally within the defined area of jurisdiction, the definition and scope of occupational therapy practice, and supervision requirements.

It is the position of AOTA that a referral is not required for the provision of occupational therapy services and that "an occupational therapist accepts and responds to referrals in compliance with state laws or other regulatory requirements"(AOTA 2005a, Standard II.1, p. 664). State laws and other regulatory requirements should be viewed as minimum criteria to practice occupational therapy. Ethical guidelines that ensure safe and effective delivery of occupational therapy services to clients always influence occupational therapy practice (AOTA, 2005b). Policies of payers such as insurance companies also must be followed.

Occupational therapy services may be provided by two levels of practitioners—the occupational therapist and the occupational therapy assistant. Occupational therapists function as autonomous practitioners and are responsible for all aspects of occupational therapy service delivery and are accountable for the safety and effectiveness of the occupational therapy service delivery process.

The occupational therapy assistant delivers occupational therapy services under the supervision of and in partnership with the occupational therapist (AOTA, 2009). When the term *occupational therapy practitioner* is used in this document, it refers to both occupational therapists and occupational therapy assistants (AOTA, 2006a).

Definition of *Occupational Therapy*

AOTA's *Definition of Occupational Therapy for the Model Practice Act* defines *occupational therapy* as

> The therapeutic use of everyday life activities (occupations) with individuals or groups for the purpose of participation in roles and situations in home, school, workplace, community, and other settings. Occupational therapy services are provided for the purpose of promoting health and wellness and to those who have or are at risk for developing an illness, injury, disease, disorder, condition, impairment, disability, activity limitation, or participation restriction. Occupational therapy addresses the physical, cognitive, psychosocial, sensory, and other aspects of performance in a variety of contexts to support engagement in everyday life activities that affect health, well-being, and quality of life. (AOTA, 2004b)

Occupational Therapy Practice

Occupational therapists and occupational therapy assistants are experts at analyzing the performance skills and patterns necessary for people to engage in their everyday activities in the contexts and environments in which those activities and occupations occur. The practice of occupational therapy includes

A. Methods or strategies selected to direct the process of interventions, such as

1. Establishment, remediation, or restoration of a skill or ability that has not yet developed or is impaired.

2. Compensation, modification, or adaptation of activity or environment to enhance performance.

3. Maintenance and enhancement of capabilities without which performance in everyday life activities would decline.

4. Health promotion and wellness to enable or enhance performance in everyday life activities.

5. Prevention of barriers to performance, including disability prevention.

B. Evaluation of factors affecting activities of daily living (ADLs), instrumental activities of daily living (IADLs), education, work, play, leisure, and social participation, including

1. Client factors, including body functions (e.g., neuromuscular, sensory, visual, perceptual, cognitive) and body structures (e.g., cardiovascular, digestive, integumentary, genitourinary systems).

2. Habits, routines, roles, and behavior patterns.

3. Cultural, physical, environmental, social, and spiritual contexts and activity demands that affect performance.

4. Performance skills, including motor, process, and communication/interaction skills.

C. Interventions and procedures to promote or enhance safety and performance in activities of daily living (ADLs), instrumental activities of daily living (IADLs), education, work, play, leisure, and social participation, including

1. Therapeutic use of occupations, exercises, and activities.

2. Training in self-care, self-management, home management, and community/work reintegration.

3. Development, remediation, or compensation of physical, cognitive, neuromuscular, sensory functions, and behavioral skills.

4. Therapeutic use of self, including one's personality, insights, perceptions, and judgments, as part of the therapeutic process.

5. Education and training of individuals, including family members, caregivers, and others.

6. Care coordination, case management, and transition services.

7. Consultative services to groups, programs, organizations, or communities.

8. Modification of environments (e.g., home, work, school, community) and adaptation of processes, including the application of ergonomic principles.

9. Assessment, design, fabrication, application, fitting, and training in assistive technology, adaptive devices, and orthotic devices, and training in the use of prosthetic devices.

10. Assessment, recommendation, and training in techniques to enhance functional mobility, including wheelchair management.

11. Driver rehabilitation and community mobility.

12. Management of feeding, eating, and swallowing to enable eating and feeding performance.

13. Application of physical agent modalities and use of a range of specific therapeutic procedures (e.g., wound care management; techniques to enhance sensory, perceptual, and cognitive processing; manual therapy techniques) to enhance performance skills (AOTA, 2004b).

Scope of Practice: Domain and Process

The scope of practice includes the domain (see Figure 1) and process (see Figure 2) of occupational therapy services. These two concepts are intertwined, with the *domain* defining the focus of occupational therapy and the *process* defining the delivery of occupational therapy (see Figure 3). The domain of occupational therapy is the everyday life activities (occupations) that people find meaningful and purposeful. Within this domain, occupational therapy services enable clients to engage (participate) in their everyday life activities in their desired roles, contexts and environments, and life situations. Clients may be individuals or persons, organizations or populations. The occupations in which clients engage occur throughout the life span and include

• ADLs (self-care activities);

• Education (activities to participate as a learner in a learning environment);

• IADLs (multistep activities to care for self and others, such as household management, financial management, and child care);

• Rest and sleep (activities relating to obtaining rest and sleep, including identifying need for rest and sleep, preparing for sleep, and participating in rest and sleep);

• Leisure (nonobligatory, discretionary, and intrinsically rewarding activities);

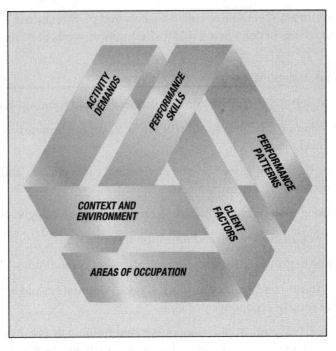

Figure 1. Occupational Therapy's Domain.
Supporting health and participation in life through engagement in
occupation (AOTA, 2008).

- Play (spontaneous and organized activities that promote pleasure, amusement, and diversion);

- Social participation (activities expected of individuals or individuals interacting with others); and

- Work (employment-related and volunteer activities).

Within their domain of practice, occupational therapists and occupational therapy assistants consider the repertoire of occupations in which the client engages the performance skills and patterns the client uses, the contexts and environments influencing engagement, the features and demands of the activity, and the client's body functions and structures. Occupational therapists and occupational therapy assistants use their knowledge and skills to help clients attain and resume daily life activities that support function and health throughout the lifespan. Participation in activities and occupations that are meaningful to the client involves emotional, psychosocial, cognitive, and physical aspects of performance. Participation in meaningful activities and occupations enhances health, well-being, and life satisfaction.

The domain of occupational therapy practice complements the World Health Organization's (WHO) conceptualization of participation and health articulated in the *International Classification of Functioning, Disability and Health* (*ICF*; WHO, 2001). Occupational therapy incorporates the basic constructs of *ICF*, including environment, participation, activities, and body structures and functions, when addressing the complexity and richness of occupations and occupational engagement.

The process of occupational therapy refers to the delivery of services and includes evaluating, intervening, and targeting outcomes. Occupation remains central to the occupational therapy process. It is client-centered, involving collaboration with the client throughout each aspect of service delivery. During the evaluation, the therapist develops an occupational profile; analyzes the client's ability to carry out everyday life activities; and determines the client's occupational needs, problems, and priorities for intervention.

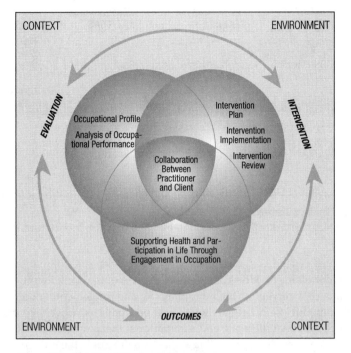

Figure 2. Occupational Therapy's Process.
Collaboration between the practitioner and the client is central to the
interactive nature of service delivery (AOTA, 2008).

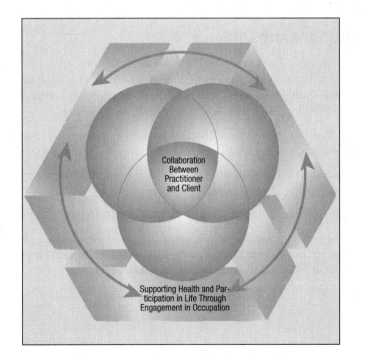

Figure 3. Occupational Therapy.
The domain and process are inextricably linked (AOTA, 2008).

Note: Mobius in figures 1 and 3 originally designed by Mark Dow. Used with permission.

AREAS OF OCCUPATION	CLIENT FACTORS	PERFORMANCE SKILLS	PERFORMANCE PATTERNS	CONTEXT AND ENVIRONMENT	ACTIVITY DEMANDS
Activities of Daily Living (ADL)*	Values, Beliefs, and Spirituality	Sensory Perceptual Skills	Habits	Cultural	Objects Used and Their Properties
Instrumental Activities of Daily Living (IADL)	Body Functions	Motor and Praxis Skills	Routines	Personal	Space Demands
Rest and Sleep	Body Structures	Emotional Regulation Skills	Roles	Physical	Social Demands
Education		Cognitive Skills	Rituals	Social	Sequencing and Timing
Work		Communication and Social Skills		Temporal	Required Actions
Play				Virtual	Required Body Functions
Leisure					Required Body Structures
Social Participation					
*Also referred to as *basic activities of daily living (BADL)* or *personal activities of daily living (PADL).*					

Figure 4. Aspects of Occupational Therapy's Domain.
All aspects of the domain transact to support engagement, participation, and health. This figure does not imply a hierarchy (AOTA, 2008).

Evaluation and intervention may address one or more aspects of the domain (see Figure 4) that influence occupational performance. Intervention includes planning and implementing occupational therapy services and involves therapeutic use of self, activities, and occupations, as well as consultation, education, and advocacy. The occupational therapist and occupational therapy assistant utilize occupation-based theories, frames of reference, evidence, and clinical reasoning to guide the intervention (AOTA, 2008).

The outcome of occupational therapy intervention is directed toward "supporting health and participation in life through engagement in occupations" (AOTA, 2008, p. 660). Outcomes of the intervention determine future actions with the client. Outcomes include the client's occupational performance, adaptation, health and wellness, participation, prevention, quality of life, role competence, self-advocacy, and occupational justice initiatives (AOTA, 2008, pp. 662–663).

Sites of Intervention and Areas of Focus

Occupational therapy services are provided to persons, organizations, and populations. People served come from all age groups. Practitioners work with individuals one to one, in organizations, or at the population level to address occupational needs and issues in mental health, work and industry, rehabilitation, disability and participation, productive aging, and health and wellness.

Along the continuum of service, occupational therapy services may be provided to clients throughout the life span in a variety of settings. The settings may include, but are not limited to, the following:

- Institutional settings (inpatient) (e.g., acute rehabilitation, psychiatric hospital, community and specialty-focused hospitals, nursing facilities, prisons)

- Outpatient settings (e.g., hospitals, clinics, medical and therapy offices)

- Home and community settings (e.g., home care, group homes, assisted living, schools, early intervention centers, day care centers, industry and business, hospice, sheltered workshops, transitional-living facilities, wellness and fitness centers, community mental health facilities)

- Research facilities.

Education and Certification Requirements

To practice as an occupational therapist, an individual

- Must have graduated from an occupational therapy program accredited by the Accreditation Council for Occupational Therapy Education (ACOTE®) or predecessor organizations,[1] and

- Must have successfully completed a period of supervised fieldwork experience required by the recognized educational institution where the applicant met the academic requirements of an educational program for occupational therapists that is accredited by ACOTE® or predecessor organization.

- Must have successfully passed the national certification examination for occupational therapists and/or met state requirements for licensure/registration.

To practice as an occupational therapy assistant, an individual

- Must have graduated from an occupational therapy assistant program accredited by ACOTE® or predecessor organizations, and

- Must have successfully completed a period of supervised fieldwork experience required by the recognized educational institution where the applicant met the academic requirements of an educational program for occupational therapy assistants that is accredited by ACOTE® or predecessor organizations.

- Must have successfully passed the national certification examination for occupational therapy assistants and/or met state requirements for licensure/registration.

AOTA supports licensure of qualified occupational therapists and occupational therapy assistants (AOTA, 2004a, Policy 5.3). State and other legislative or regulatory agencies may impose additional requirements to practice as occupational therapists and occupational therapy assistants in their area of jurisdiction.

References

Accreditation Council for Occupational Therapy Education. (2007a). Accreditation standards for a doctoral-degree-level educational program for the occupational therapist. *American Journal of Occupational Therapy, 61*, 641–651.

Accreditation Council for Occupational Therapy Education. (2007b). Accreditation standards for a master's-degree-level educational program for the occupational therapist. *American Journal of Occupational Therapy, 61*, 652–661.

Accreditation Council for Occupational Therapy Education. (2007c). Accreditation standards for an educational program for the occupational therapy assistant. *American Journal of Occupational Therapy, 61*, 662–671.

American Occupational Therapy Association. (2004a). Policy 5.3: Licensure. *Policy manual* (2008 ed., p. 64). Bethesda, MD: Author.

American Occupational Therapy Association. (2004b). Definition of occupational therapy practice for the AOTA Model Practice Act. (Available from the State Affairs Group, American Occupational Therapy Association, PO Box 31220, Bethesda, MD 20824-1220. E-mail: stpd@aota.org)

---

[1] Foreign-educated graduates of occupational therapy programs approved by the World Federation of Occupational therapy also may be eligible for certification/licensure as an occupational therapist provided that additional requirements are met.

[2] The majority of this information is taken from the *Accreditation Standards for a Doctoral-Degree-Level Educational Program for the Occupational Therapist* (ACOTE, 2007a), *Accreditation Standards for a Master's-Degree-Level Educational Program for the Occupational Therapist* (ACOTE, 2007b), and *Accreditation Standards for an Educational Program for the Occupational Therapy Assistant* (ACOTE, 2007c).

American Occupational Therapy Association. (2005a). Standards of practice for occupational therapy. *American Journal of Occupational Therapy, 59*, 663–665.

American Occupational Therapy Association. (2005b). Occupational therapy code of ethics (2005). *American Journal of Occupational Therapy, 54*, 614–616.

American Occupational Therapy Association. (2006a). Policy 1.44: Categories of occupational therapy personnel. In *Policy manual* (2008 ed., p. 10). Bethesda, MD: Author.

American Occupational Therapy Association. (2006b). Policy 1.11: The philosophical base of occupational therapy. In *Policy manual* (2008 ed., pp. 33–34). Bethesda, MD: Author.

American Occupational Therapy Association. (2008). Occupational therapy practice framework: Domain and process (2nd ed.). *American Journal of Occupational Therapy, 62*, 625–688.

American Occupational Therapy Association. (2009). Guidelines for supervision, roles, and responsibilities during the delivery of occupational therapy services. *American Journal of Occupational Therapy, 63*.

World Health Organization. (2001). *International classification of functioning, disability, and health (ICF)*. Geneva, Switzerland: Author.

Additional Reading

Moyers, P., & Dale, L. (Eds.). (2007). *The guide to occupational therapy practice* (2nd ed.). Bethesda, MD: AOTA Press.

Authors
The Commission on Practice:
Sara Jane Brayman, PhD, OTR/L, FAOTA, *Chairperson, 2002–2005*
Gloria Frolek Clark, MS, OTR/L, FAOTA
Janet V. DeLany, DEd, OTR/L
Eileen R. Garza, PhD, OTR, ATP
Mary V. Radomski, MA, OTR/L, FAOTA
Ruth Ramsey, MS, OTR/L
Carol Siebert, MS, OTR/L
Kristi Voelkerding, BS, COTA/L
Patricia D. LaVesser, PhD, OTR/L, *SIS Liaison*
Lenna Aird, *ASD Liaison*
Deborah Lieberman, MHSA, OTR/L, FAOTA, *AOTA Headquarters Liaison*

for

The Commission on Practice
Sara Jane Brayman, PhD, OTR/L FAOTA, *Chairperson*

Adopted by the Representative Assembly 2004C23

Edited by the Commission on Practice 2005

Edited by the Commission on Practice 2009

Note: This replaces the 2004 document Scope of Practice (previously published and copyrighted in 2004 by the *American Journal of Occupational Therapy 58*, 673–677).

Copyright © 2010, by the American Occupational Therapy Association. To be published in the *American Journal of Occupational Therapy, 64*(November/December).

Appendix C.
ACOTE® Standards Addressed in Each Chapter

Chapters in this edition of *The Occupational Therapy Manager* addressed the following Accreditation Council for Occupational Therapy Education® (ACOTE®) standards:

CHAPTER 1
This chapter does not contain ACOTE standards.

CHAPTER 2

B.4.5	Compare and contrast the role of the occupational therapist and occupational therapy assistant in the screening and evaluation process and the importance of and rationale for supervision and collaborative work between the occupational therapist and occupational therapy assistant in that process.
B.5.18	Effectively interact through written, oral, and nonverbal communication with the client, family, significant others, colleagues, other health providers, and the public in a professionally acceptable manner.
B.5.21	Identify and demonstrate techniques in skills of supervision and collaboration with occupational therapy assistants on therapeutic interventions.
B.5.22	Understand when and how to use the consultative process with groups, programs, organizations, or communities.
B.5.23	Refer to specialists both internal and external to the profession for consultation and intervention.
B.5.26	Organize, collect, and analyze data in a systematic manner for evaluation of practice outcomes. Report evaluation results and modify practice as needed to improve outcomes.
B.5.28	Document occupational therapy services to ensure accountability of service provision and to meet standards for reimbursement of services. Documentation must effectively communicate the need and rationale for occupational therapy services and must be appropriate to the context in which the service is delivered.
B.6.4	Articulate the role and responsibility of the practitioner to address changes in service-delivery policies, to effect changes in the system, and to identify opportunities in emerging practice areas.

CHAPTER 3

B.6.1	Differentiate among the contexts of health care, education, community, and social systems as they relate to the practice of occupational therapy.
B.6.2	Discuss the current policy issues and the social, economic, political, geographic, and demographic factors that influence the various contexts for practice of occupational therapy.
B.6.3	Describe the current social, economic, political, geographic, and demographic factors to promote policy development and the provision of occupational therapy services.
B.6.4	Articulate the role and responsibility of the practitioner to address changes in service delivery policies to effect changes in the system and to identify opportunities in emerging practice areas.
B.6.5	Articulate the trends in models of service delivery and their potential effect on the practice of occupational therapy, including, but not limited to, medical, educational, community, and social models.
B.7.1	Explain how the various practice settings (e.g., medical institutions, community practice, school systems) affect the delivery of occupational therapy services.

CHAPTER 4

B.7.0	Management of Occupational Therapy Services Management of occupational therapy services includes the application of principles of management and systems in the provision of occupational therapy services to individuals and organizations. The program must facilitate development of the performance criteria listed below. The student will be able to:
B.7.1	Explain how the various practice settings (i.e., medical institutions, community practice, school systems, etc.) affect the delivery of occupational therapy services.
B.7.2	Describe and discuss the impact of contextual factors on the management and delivery of occupational therapy services.
B.7.3	Describe the systems and structures that create federal and state legislation and regulation and their implications and effects on practice.
B.7.4	Demonstrate knowledge of applicable national requirements for credentialing and requirements for licensure, certification, or registration under state laws.
B.7.6	Describe the mechanisms, systems, and techniques needed to properly maintain, organize, and prioritize workloads and treatment environments including inventories.
B.7.7	Demonstrate the ability to plan, develop, organize, and market the delivery of services to include the determination of programmatic needs, service delivery options, and formulation and management of staffing for effective service provision.
B.7.8	Demonstrate the ability to design ongoing processes for quality improvement (such as outcome studies analysis) and develop program changes as needed to ensure quality of services and to direct administrative changes.
B.7.9	Develop strategies for effective, competency-based, legal, and ethical supervision of occupational therapy and non–occupational therapy personnel.
B.9.7	Discuss and justify the varied roles of the occupational therapist as a practitioner, educator, researcher, consultant, and entrepreneur.
B.9.8	Explain and justify the importance of supervisory roles, responsibilities, and collaborative professional relationships between the occupational therapist and the occupational therapy assistant.
B.9.9	Describe and discuss professional responsibilities and issues when providing service on a contractual basis.
B.9.10	Explain strategies for analyzing issues and making decisions in order to resolve personal and organizational ethical conflicts.
B.9.12	Describe and discuss strategies to assist the consumer in gaining access to occupational therapy services.

CHAPTER 5

B.7.2	Describe and discuss the impact of contextual factors on the management and delivery of occupational therapy services.
B.7.6	Demonstrate the mechanisms, systems, and techniques needed to properly maintain, organize, and prioritize workloads and intervention settings including inventories.
B.7.7	Demonstrate the ability to plan, develop, organize, and market the delivery of services to include the determination of programmatic needs, service delivery options, and formulation and management of staffing for effective service provision.

CHAPTER 6

B.6.1.	Differentiate among the contexts of health care, education, community, and social systems as they relate to the practice of occupational therapy.
B.6.2.	Discuss the current policy issues and the social, economic, political, geographic, and demographic factors that influence the various contexts for practice of occupational therapy.
B.6.3.	Describe the current social, economic, political, geographic, and demographic factors to promote policy development and the provision of occupational therapy services.
B.6.4.	Articulate the role and responsibility of the practitioner to address changes in service delivery policies to effect changes in the system, and to identify opportunities in emerging practice areas.
B.6.5.	Articulate the trends in models of service delivery and their potential effect on the practice of occupational therapy, including, but not limited to, medical, educational, community, and social models.
B.7.1.	Explain how the various practice settings (e.g., medical institutions, community practice, school systems) affect the delivery of occupational therapy services.
B.7.2.	Describe and discuss the impact of contextual factors on the management and delivery of occupational therapy services.

CHAPTER 7

B.5.28	Document occupational therapy services to ensure accountability of service provision and to meet standards for reimbursement of services, adhering to applicable facility, local, state, federal, and reimbursement agencies. Documentation must effectively communicate the need and rationale for occupational therapy services.
B.6.2	Discuss the current policy issues and the social, economic, political, geographic, and demographic factors that influence the various contexts for practice of occupational therapy.
B.6.3.	Describe the current social, economic, political, geographic, and demographic factors to promote policy development and the provision of occupational therapy services.
B.7.1.	Explain how the various practice settings (i.e., medical institutions, community practice, school systems, etc.) affect the delivery of occupational therapy services.
B.7.5.	Demonstrate knowledge of various reimbursement systems (e.g., federal, state, third-party, private-payer), appeals mechanisms, and documentation requirements that affect society and the practice of occupational therapy.
B.7.6.	Describe the mechanisms, systems, and techniques needed to properly maintain, organize, and prioritize workloads and intervention settings including inventories.
B.7.12	Identify and adapt existing models or develop new service provision models to respond to policy, regulatory agencies, and reimbursement and compliance standards.

CHAPTER 8

B.2.3.	Articulate to consumers, potential employers, colleagues, third-party payers, regulatory boards, policymakers, other audiences, and the general public both the unique nature of occupation as viewed by the profession of occupational therapy and the value of occupation to support participation in contexts for the client.
B.2.9.	Express support for the quality of life, well-being, and occupation of the individual, group, or population to promote physical and mental health and prevention of injury and disease considering the context (e.g., cultural, physical, social, personal, spiritual, temporal, virtual).
B.5.7.	Describe the role of the occupational therapist in care coordination, case management, and transition services in traditional and emerging practice environments.
B.5.16.	Demonstrate the ability to educate the client, caregiver, family, and significant others to facilitate skills in areas of occupation as well as prevention, health maintenance, and safety.
B.5.18	Effectively interact through written, oral, and nonverbal communication with the client, family, significant others, colleagues, other health providers, and the public in a professionally acceptable manner.
B.9.3	Promote occupational therapy by educating other professionals, service providers, consumers, third-party payers, regulatory bodies, and the public.
B.9.12	Describe and discuss strategies to assist the consumer in gaining access to occupational therapy services.

CHAPTER 9

B.2.4	Articulate the importance of balancing areas of occupation with the achievement of health and wellness.
B.6.1	Differentiate among the contexts of health care, education, community, and social systems as they relate to the practice of occupational therapy.
B.6.2	Discuss the current policy issues and the social, economic, political, geographic, and demographic factors that influence the various contexts for practice of occupational therapy.
B.6.3	Describe the current social, economic, political, geographic, and demographic factors to promote policy development and the provision of occupational therapy services.
B.6.4	Articulate the role and responsibility of the practitioner to address changes in service delivery policies to effect changes in the system and to identify opportunities in emerging practice areas.
B.6.5	Articulate the trends in models of service delivery and their potential effect on the practice of occupational therapy, including, but not limited to, medical, educational, community, and social models.
B.7.1	Explain how the various practice settings (e.g., medical institutions, community practice, school systems) affect the delivery of occupational therapy services.
B.7.2	Describe and discuss the impact of contextual factors on the management and delivery of occupational therapy services.
B.7.6	Describe the mechanisms, systems, and techniques needed to properly maintain, organize, and prioritize workloads and intervention settings including inventories.
B.7.7	Demonstrate the ability to plan, develop, organize, and market the delivery of services to include the determination of programmatic needs, service delivery options, and formulation and management of staffing for effective service provision.

CHAPTER 10

B.5.7	Describe the role of the occupational therapist in care coordination, case management, and transition services in traditional and emerging practice environments.
B.9.7	Discuss and justify the varied roles of the occupational therapist as a practitioner, educator, researcher, consultant, and entrepreneur.
B.9.9	Describe and discuss professional responsibilities and issues when providing service on a contractual basis.

CHAPTER 11

B.8.1	Articulate the importance of research, scholarly activities, and the continued development of a body of knowledge relevant to the profession of occupational therapy.
B.8.2	Effectively locate, understand, and evaluate information, including the quality of research evidence.
B.8.3	Use research literature to make evidence-based decisions.
B.8.4	Select, apply, and interpret basic descriptive, correlational, and inferential quantitative statistics and code, analyze, and synthesize qualitative data.
B.8.5	Understand and critique the validity of research studies, including designs (both quantitative and qualitative) and methodologies.
B.8.6	Demonstrate the skills necessary to design a research proposal that includes the research question, relevant literature, sample, design, measurement, and data analysis.
B.8.7	Design and implement a research study that evaluates clinical practice, service delivery, and/or professional issues.
B.8.9	Demonstrate an understanding of the process of locating and securing grants and how grants can serve as a fiscal resource for research and practice.

CHAPTER 12

B.1.1	Demonstrate oral and written communication skills.
B.8.7	Demonstrate basic skills necessary to write a research report in a format for presentation or publication.
B.9.13	Demonstrate professional advocacy by participating in organizations or agencies promoting the profession (e.g., American Occupational Therapy Association, state occupational therapy associations, advocacy organizations).

CHAPTER 13

B.5.21	Identify and demonstrate techniques in skills of supervision and collaboration with occupational therapy assistants on therapeutic interventions.
B.5.23	Refer to specialists (both internal and external to the profession) for consultation and intervention.
B.5.26	Organize, collect, and analyze data in a systematic manner for evaluation of practice outcomes. Report evaluation results and modify practice as needed to improve outcomes.
B.5.27	Terminate occupational therapy services when stated outcomes have been achieved or it has been determined that they cannot be achieved. This includes developing a summary of occupational therapy outcomes, appropriate recommendations and referrals, and discussion with the client and with appropriate others of post-discharge needs.
B.5.28	Document occupational therapy services to ensure accountability of service provision and to meet standards for reimbursement of services. Documentation must effectively communicate the need and rationale for occupational therapy services and must be appropriate to the context in which the service is delivered.
B.6.2	Discuss the current policy issues and the social, economic, political, geographic, and demographic factors that influence the various contexts for practice of occupational therapy.
B.6.3	Describe the current social, economic, political, geographic, and demographic factors to promote policy development and the provision of occupational therapy services.
B.6.4	Articulate the role and responsibility of the practitioner to address changes in service delivery policies to effect changes in the system and to identify opportunities in emerging practice areas.
B.6.5	Articulate the trends in models of service delivery and their potential effect on the practice of occupational therapy, including, but not limited to, medical, educational, community, and social models.
B.6.6	Use national and international resources in making assessment or intervention choices, and appreciate the influence of international occupational therapy contributions to education, research, and practice.
B.7.9	Develop strategies for effective, competency-based legal and ethical supervision of occupational therapy and non–occupational therapy personnel.

B.7.10	Describe the ongoing professional responsibility for providing fieldwork education and the criteria for becoming a fieldwork educator.
B.8.1	Articulate the importance of research, scholarly activities, and the continued development of a body of knowledge
B.9.1	Demonstrate a knowledge and understanding of the American Occupational Therapy Association (AOTA) *Occupational Therapy Code of Ethics, Core Values and Attitudes of Occupational Therapy Practice, and AOTA Standards of Practice* and use them as a guide for ethical decision making in professional interactions, client interventions, and employment settings.
B.9.4	Discuss strategies for ongoing professional development to ensure that practice is consistent with current and accepted standards.

Chapter 14

B.1.1	Demonstrate oral and written communication skills.
B.1.2	Employ logical thinking, critical analysis, problem solving, and creativity.
B.5.18	Effectively interact through written, oral, and nonverbal communication with the client, family, significant others, colleagues, other health providers, and the public in a professionally acceptable manner.
B.5.21	Identify and demonstrate techniques in skills of supervision and collaboration with occupational therapy assistants on therapeutic intervention.
B. 9.6	Discuss and evaluate personal and professional abilities and competencies as they relate to job responsibilities.
B.9.8	Explain and justify the importance of supervisory roles, responsibilities, and collaborative professional relationships between the occupational therapist and the occupational therapy assistant.
B.9.10	Explain strategies for analyzing issues and making decisions to resolve personal and organizational ethical conflicts.
B.9.11	Explain the variety of informal and formal ethical dispute-resolution systems that have jurisdiction over occupational therapy practice.
B.10.14	Ensure that the fieldwork experience is designed to promote clinical reasoning and reflective practice, to transmit the values and beliefs that enable ethical practice, and to develop professionalism and competence in career responsibilities.
B.10.18	Document a mechanism for evaluating the effectiveness of supervision (e.g., student evaluation of fieldwork) and for providing resources for enhancing supervision (e.g., materials on supervisory skills, continuing education opportunities, articles on theory and practice).

Chapter 15

B.1.1	Demonstrate oral and written communication skills.
B.1.2	Employ logical thinking, critical analysis, problem solving, and creativity.
B.5.18	Effectively interact through written, oral, and nonverbal communication with the client, family, significant others, colleagues, other health providers, and the public in a professionally acceptable manner.
B.5.21	Identify and demonstrate techniques in skills of supervision and collaboration with occupational therapy assistants on therapeutic intervention.
B.9.6	Discuss and evaluate personal and professional abilities and competencies as they relate to job responsibilities.
B.9.8	Explain and justify the importance of supervisory roles, responsibilities, and collaborative professional relationships between the occupational therapist and the occupational therapy assistant.
B.9.10	Explain strategies for analyzing issues and making decisions to resolve personal and organizational ethical conflicts.
B.9.11	Explain the variety of informal and formal ethical dispute-resolution systems that have jurisdiction over occupational therapy practice.
B.10.14	Ensure that the fieldwork experience is designed to promote clinical reasoning and reflective practice, to transmit the values and beliefs that enable ethical practice, and to develop professionalism and competence in career responsibilities.
B.10.18	Document a mechanism for evaluating the effectiveness of supervision (e.g., student evaluation of fieldwork) and for providing resources for enhancing supervision (e.g., materials on supervisory skills, continuing education opportunities, articles on theory and practice).

Chapter 16

B.6.3	Describe current social, economic, political, geographic and demographic factors that promote policy development and the provision of occupational therapy services.
B.6.4	Articulate the role and responsibility of the practitioner to address changes in service delivery polices, to effect changes in the system, and to identify opportunities in emerging practice areas.
B.7.9	Develop strategies for effective competency-based, legal, and ethical supervision of occupational therapy and non–occupational therapy personnel.
B.8.1	Articulate the importance of research, scholarly activities, and the continued development of a body of knowledge relevant to the profession of occupational therapy.
B.8.2	Effectively locate, understand, and evaluate information including the quality of research evidence used.
B.8.3	Use professional literature to make evidence-based practice decisions.
B.9.1	Demonstrate knowledge and understanding of the American Occupational Therapy Association (AOTA) *Code of Ethics, Core Values and Attitudes of Occupational Therapy, and AOTA Standards of Practice* and use them as a guide for ethical decision making in professional interactions, client treatment, and employment settings.
B.9.4	Acknowledge personal responsibility for planning ongoing professional development.
B.9.5	Discuss strategies for ongoing professional development to ensure that practice is consistent with current and accepted standards.
B.9.6	Discuss and evaluate personal and professional abilities and competencies as they relate to job responsibilities.
B.9.10	Explain strategies for analyzing issues and making decisions in order to resolve personal and organizational ethical conflicts.

Chapter 17

B.1.6	Demonstrate knowledge and understanding of the concepts of human behavior to include the behavioral and social sciences.
B.1.7	Demonstrate knowledge and appreciation of the role of sociocultural, socioeconomic, and diversity factors and lifestyle choices in contemporary society.
B.1.8	Articulate the influence of social conditions and the ethical context in which humans choose and engage in occupations.

Chapter 18

B.6.4	Articulate the role and responsibility of the practitioner to address changes in service-delivery polices, to effect changes in the system, and to identify opportunities in emerging practice areas.
B.9.4	Acknowledge personal responsibility for planning ongoing professional development.
B.9.6	Discuss and evaluate personal and professional abilities and competencies as they relate to job responsibilities.
B.9.7	Discuss and justify the varied roles of the occupational therapist as a practitioner, educator, researcher, and entrepreneur.

Chapter 19

This chapter does not contain ACOTE standards.

Chapter 20

B.9.7	Discuss and justify the varied roles of the occupational therapist as a practitioner, educator, researcher, consultant, and entrepreneur.
B.9.13	Demonstrate professional advocacy by participating in organizations or agencies promoting the profession (e.g., American Occupational Therapy Association, state occupational therapy associations, advocacy organizations).

CHAPTER 21

B.6.1	Differentiate among the contexts of health care, education, community, and social systems as they relate to the practice of occupational therapy.
B.6.4	Articulate the role and responsibility of the practitioner to address changes in service delivery policies to effect changes in the system, and to identify opportunities in emerging practice areas.
B.7.1	Explain how the various practice settings (e.g., medical institutions, community practice, school systems) affect the delivery of occupational therapy services.
B.7.2	Describe and discuss the impact of contextual factors on the management and delivery of occupational therapy services.
B.7.7	Demonstrate the ability to plan, develop, organize, and market the delivery of services to include the determination of programmatic needs, service delivery options, and formulation and management of staffing for effective service provision.
B.9.7	Discuss and justify the varied roles of the occupational therapist as a practitioner, educator, researcher, consultant, and entrepreneur.

CHAPTER 22

B.7.4	Demonstrate knowledge of applicable national requirements for credentialing and requirements for licensure, certification, or registration under state laws.
B.7.7	Demonstrate the ability to plan, develop, organize, and market the delivery of services to include the determination of programmatic needs, service delivery options, and formulation and management of staffing for effective service provision.
B.7.8	Demonstrate the ability to design ongoing processes for quality improvement (e.g., outcome studies analysis) and develop program changes as needed to ensure quality of services and to direct administrative changes.
B.8.1	Articulate the importance of research, scholarly activities, and the continued development of a body of knowledge relevant to the profession of occupational therapy.
B.8.2	Effectively locate, understand, and evaluate information, including the quality of research evidence.
B.8.3	Use research literature to make evidence-based decisions.
B.7.2	Identify the impact of contextual factors on the management and delivery of occupational therapy services.
B.8.1	Articulate the importance of professional research and literature and the continued development of the profession.
B.8.2	Use professional literature to make evidence-based practice decisions in collaboration with the occupational therapist that are supported by research.

CHAPTER 23

B.6.4	Articulate the role and responsibility of the practitioner to address changes in service delivery policies to effect changes in the system, and to identify opportunities in emerging practice areas.
B.6.6	Use national and international resources in making assessment or intervention choices, and appreciate the influence of international occupational therapy contributions to education, research, and practice.
B.7.2	Describe and discuss the impact of contextual factors on the management and delivery of occupational therapy services.
B.7.8	Demonstrate the ability to design ongoing processes for quality improvement (e.g., outcome studies analysis) and develop program changes as needed to ensure quality of services and to direct administrative changes.
B.8.1	Articulate the importance of research, scholarly activities, and the continued development of a body of knowledge relevant to the profession of occupational therapy.
B.8.2	Effectively locate, understand, and evaluate information, including the quality of research evidence.
B.8.3	Use research literature to make evidence-based decisions.
B.8.5	Understand and critique the validity of research studies, including designs (both quantitative and qualitative) and methodologies.

CHAPTER 24

B.1.1.	Demonstrate oral and written communication skills.
B.1.2.	Employ logical thinking, critical analysis, problem solving, and creativity.
B.2.3.	Articulate to consumers, potential employers, colleagues, third-party payers, regulatory boards, policymakers, other audiences, and the general public both the unique nature of occupation as viewed by the profession of occupational therapy and the value of occupation to support participation in context(s) for the client.
B.2.9.	Express support for the quality of life, well-being, and occupation of the individual, group, or population to promote physical and mental health and prevention of injury and disease considering the context (e.g., cultural, physical, social, personal, spiritual, temporal, virtual).
B.2.10.	Use clinical reasoning to explain the rationale for and use of compensatory strategies when desired life tasks cannot be performed.
B.4.7.	Consider factors that might bias assessment results, such as culture, disability status, and situational variables related to the individual and context.
B.4.10.	Document occupational therapy services to ensure accountability of service provision and to meet standards for reimbursement of services, adhering to applicable facility, local, state, federal, and reimbursement agencies. Documentation must effectively communicate the need and rationale for occupational therapy services.
B.5.18.	Effectively interact through written, oral, and nonverbal communication with the client, family, significant others, colleagues, other health providers, and the public in a professionally acceptable manner.
B.5.26.	Organize, collect, and analyze data in a systematic manner for evaluation of practice outcomes. Report evaluation results and modify practice as needed to improve outcomes.
B.5.27.	Terminate occupational therapy services when stated outcomes have been achieved or it has been determined that they cannot be achieved. This includes developing a summary of occupational therapy outcomes, appropriate recommendations and referrals, and discussion with the client and with appropriate others of post-discharge needs.
B.5.28.	Document occupational therapy services to ensure accountability of service provision and to meet standards for reimbursement of services. Documentation must effectively communicate the need and rationale for occupational therapy services and must be appropriate to the context in which the service is delivered.
B.7.5.	Demonstrate knowledge of various reimbursement systems (e.g., federal, state, third-party, private-payer), appeals mechanisms, and documentation requirements that affect the practice of occupational therapy.
B.9.1.	Demonstrate a knowledge and understanding of the American Occupational Therapy Association (AOTA) *Occupational Therapy Code of Ethics, Core Values and Attitudes of Occupational Therapy Practice*, and AOTA *Standards of Practice* and use them as a guide for ethical decision making in professional interactions, client interventions, and employment settings.

CHAPTER 25

B.6.0	Context of Service Delivery Context of service delivery includes the knowledge and understanding of the various contexts in which occupational therapy services are provided. The program must facilitate development of the performance criteria listed below. The student will be able to
B.6.1.	Differentiate among the contexts of health care, education, community, and social systems as they relate to the practice of occupational therapy.
B.6.2.	Discuss the current policy issues and the social, economic, political, geographic, and demographic factors that influence the various contexts for practice of occupational therapy.
B.6.3.	Describe the current social, economic, political, geographic, and demographic factors to promote policy development and the provision of occupational therapy services.
B.6.4.	Articulate the role and responsibility of the practitioner to address changes in service delivery policies to effect changes in the system, and to identify opportunities in emerging practice areas.
B.6.5.	Articulate the trends in models of service delivery and their potential effect on the practice of occupational therapy, including, but not limited to, medical, educational, community, and social models.
B.6.6.	Use national and international resources in making assessment or intervention choices, and appreciate the influence of international occupational therapy contributions to education, research, and practice.

CHAPTER 26

B.4.7	Consider factors that might bias assessment results, such as culture, disability status, and situational variables related to the individual and context.
B.4.8	Interpret the evaluation data in relation to accepted terminology of the profession and relevant theoretical frameworks.
B.5.26	Organize, collect, and analyze data in a systematic manner for evaluation of practice outcomes. Report evaluation results and modify practice as needed to improve outcomes.
B.6.4	Articulate the role and responsibility of the practitioner to address changes in service delivery policies and to effect changes in the system.
B.7.8	Demonstrate the ability to design ongoing processes for quality improvement (such as outcome studies analysis) and develop program changes as needed to ensure quality of service and to direct administrative changes.

CHAPTER 27

B.1.2	Employ logical thinking, critical analysis, problem solving, and creativity.
B.2.1	Articulate an understanding of the importance of the history and philosophical base of the profession of occupational therapy.
B.3.4	Analyze and discuss how history, theory, and the sociopolitical climate influence practice.
B.6.4	Articulate the role and responsibility of the practitioner to address changes in service delivery policies to effect changes in the system and to identify opportunities in emerging practice areas.
B.7.2	Describe and discuss the impact of contextual factors on the management and delivery of occupational therapy services.

CHAPTER 28

B.7.3	Describe the systems and structures that create federal and state legislation and regulation and their implications and effects on practice.
B.9.2	Discuss and justify how the role of a professional is enhanced by knowledge of and involvement in international, national, state, and local occupational therapy associations and related professional associations.
B.9.3	Promote occupational therapy by educating other professionals, service providers, consumers, third-party payers, regulatory bodies, and the public.
B.9.13.	Demonstrate professional advocacy by participating in organizations or agencies promoting the profession (e.g., American Occupational Therapy Association, state occupational therapy associations, advocacy organizations).

CHAPTER 29

B.2.3.	Articulate to consumers, potential employers, colleagues, third-party payers, regulatory boards, policymakers, other audiences, and the general public both the unique nature of occupation as viewed by the profession of occupational therapy and the value of occupation to support participation in context(s) for the client.
B.7.3.	Describe the systems and structures that create federal and state legislation and regulation and their implications and effects on practice.
B.7.4.	Demonstrate knowledge of applicable national requirements for credentialing and requirements for licensure, certification, or registration under state laws.

CHAPTER 30

B.90	Professional ethics, values, and responsibilities include understanding and appreciation of ethics and values of the profession of occupational therapy. The program must facilitate development of the performance criteria listed below. The student will be able to:
B.9.1	Demonstrate knowledge and understanding of the American Occupational Therapy Association (AOTA) Code of Ethics, Core Values and Attitudes of Occupational Therapy, and AOTA Standards of Practice and use them as a guide for ethical decision making in professional interactions, client treatment, and employment settings.
B.9.4	Acknowledge personal responsibility for planning ongoing professional development.
B.9.5	Discuss strategies for ongoing professional development to ensure that practice is consistent with current and accepted standards.
B.9.6	Discuss and evaluate personal and professional abilities and competencies as they relate to job responsibilities.

B.9.8	Explain and justify the importance of supervisory roles, responsibilities, and collaborative professional relationships between the occupational therapist and the occupational therapy assistant.
B.9.10	Explain strategies for analyzing issues and making decisions in order to resolve personal and organizational ethical conflicts.
B.9.11	Explain the variety of informal and formal ethical dispute resolution systems that have jurisdiction over occupational therapy practice.

CHAPTER 31

B.7.4	Demonstrate knowledge of applicable national requirements for credentialing and requirements for licensure, certification, or registration under state laws.
B.7.9	Develop strategies for effective, competency-based legal and ethical supervision of occupational therapy and non–occupational therapy personnel.
B.9.1	Demonstrate a knowledge and understanding of the American Occupational Therapy Association (AOTA) *Occupational Therapy Code of Ethics, Core Values and Attitudes of Occupational Therapy Practice*, and AOTA *Standards of Practice* and use them as a guide for ethical decision making in professional interactions, client interventions, and employment settings.
B.9.2	Discuss and justify how the role of a professional is enhanced by knowledge of and involvement in international, national, state, and local occupational therapy associations and related professional associations.
B.9.4	Discuss strategies for ongoing professional development to ensure that practice is consistent with current and accepted standards.
B.9.6	Discuss and evaluate personal and professional abilities and competencies as they relate to job responsibilities.
B.9.7	Discuss and justify the varied roles of the occupational therapist as a practitioner, educator, researcher, consultant, and entrepreneur.

CHAPTER 32

B.4.10	Document occupational therapy services to ensure accountability of service provision and to meet standards for reimbursement of services, adhering to applicable facility, local, state, federal, and reimbursement agencies. Documentation must effectively communicate the need and rationale for occupational therapy services.
B.5.28	Document occupational therapy services to ensure accountability of service provision and to meet standards for reimbursement of services. Documentation must effectively communicate the need and rationale for occupational therapy services and must be appropriate to the context in which the service is delivered.
B.6.3	Describe the current social, economic, political, geographic, and demographic factors to promote policy development and the provision of occupational therapy services.
B.7.0	Management of Occupational Therapy Services. Management of occupational therapy services includes the application of principles of management and systems in the provision of occupational therapy services to individuals and organizations.
B.7.3	Describe the systems and structures that create federal and state legislation and regulation and their implications and effects on practice.
B.7.9	Develop strategies for effective, competency-based legal and ethical supervision of occupational therapy and non–occupational therapy personnel.
B.9.1	Demonstrate a knowledge and understanding of the American Occupational Therapy Association (AOTA) *Occupational Therapy Code of Ethics, Core Values and Attitudes of Occupational Therapy Practice*, and AOTA *Standards of Practice* and use them as a guide for ethical decision making in professional interactions, client interventions, and employment settings.
B.9.4	Discuss strategies for ongoing professional development to ensure that practice is consistent with current and accepted standards.
B.9.5	Discuss professional responsibilities related to liability issues under current models of service provision.

Chapter 33

B.3.5	Apply theoretical constructs to evaluation and intervention with various types of clients and practice contexts to analyze and effect meaningful occupation.
B.5.22	Understand when and how to use the consultative process with groups, programs, organizations, or communities.
B.5.23	Refer to specialists (both internal and external to the profession) for consultation and intervention.
B.5.26	Organize, collect, and analyze data in a systematic manner for evaluation of practice outcomes. Report evaluation results and modify practice as needed to improve outcomes.
B.5.27	Terminate occupational therapy services when stated outcomes have been achieved or it has been determined that they cannot be achieved. This includes developing a summary of occupational therapy outcomes, appropriate recommendations and referrals, and discussion with the client and with appropriate others of postdischarge needs.
B.6.2	Discuss the current policy issues and the social, economic, political, geographic, and demographic factors that influence the various contexts for practice of occupational therapy.
B.7.2	Describe and discuss the impact of contextual factors on the management and delivery of occupational therapy services.
B.7.7	Demonstrate the ability to plan, develop, organize, and market the delivery of services to include the determination of programmatic needs, service delivery options, and formulation and management of staffing for effective service provision.
B.7.8	Demonstrate the ability to design ongoing processes for quality improvement (e.g., outcome studies analysis) and develop program changes as needed to ensure quality of services and to direct administrative changes.
B.9.7	Discuss and justify the varied roles of the occupational therapist as a practitioner, educator, researcher, consultant, and entrepreneur.

Chapter 34

B.6.2	Discuss current policy issues and the social, economic, political, geographic, and demographic factors that influence the various contexts for practice of occupational therapy.
B.6.3	Describe current social, economic, political, geographic, and demographic factors that promote policy development and the provision of occupational therapy services.
B.7.2	Describe and discuss the impact of contextual factors on the management and delivery of occupational therapy services.
B.9.10	Explain strategies for analyzing issues and making decisions in order to resolve personal and organizational ethical conflicts.
B.9.12	Describe and discuss strategies to assist the consumer in gaining access to occupational therapy services.

Chapter 35

B.6.2	Discuss current policy issues and the social, economic, political, geographic and demographic factors that influence the various contexts for practice of occupational therapy.
B.6.3	Describe current social, economic, political, geographic and demographic factors that promote policy development and the provision of occupational therapy services.
B.9.10	Explain strategies for analyzing issues and making decisions in order to resolve personal and organizational ethical conflicts.
B.9.12	Describe and discuss strategies to assist the consumer in gaining access to occupational therapy services.

Chapter 36

This chapter does not contain ACOTE standards.

CHAPTER 37

B.10.1.	Document the criteria and process for selecting fieldwork sites. Ensure that the fieldwork program reflects the sequence, depth, focus, and scope of content in the curriculum design.
B.10.2.	Ensure that the academic fieldwork coordinator and faculty collaborate to design fieldwork experiences that strengthen the ties between didactic and fieldwork education.
B.10.3.	Provide fieldwork education in settings that are equipped to meet the curriculum goals, provide educational experiences applicable to the academic program, and have fieldwork educators who are able to effectively meet the learning needs of the students.
B.10.4.	Ensure that the academic fieldwork coordinator is responsible for advocating the development of links between the fieldwork and didactic aspects of the curriculum, for communicating about the curriculum to fieldwork educators, and for maintaining contracts and site data related to fieldwork placements.
B.10.5.	Demonstrate that academic and fieldwork educators collaborate in establishing fieldwork objectives, identifying site requirements, and communicating with the student and fieldwork educator about progress and performance during fieldwork.
B.10.6.	Document a policy and procedure for complying with fieldwork site health requirements and maintaining student health records in a secure setting.
B.10.7.	Ensure that the ratio of fieldwork educators to student(s) enables proper supervision and the ability to provide frequent assessment of student progress in achieving stated fieldwork objectives.
B.10.8.	Ensure that fieldwork agreements are sufficient in scope and number to allow completion of graduation requirements in a timely manner in accordance with the policy adopted by the program.
B.10.9.	For programs in which the academic and fieldwork components of the curriculum are provided by two or more institutions, responsibilities of each sponsoring institution and fieldwork site must be clearly documented in a memorandum of understanding. For active Level I and Level II fieldwork sites, programs must have current fieldwork agreements or memoranda of understanding that are signed by both parties. (Electronic contracts and signatures are acceptable.)
B.10.10.	Documentation must be provided that each memorandum of understanding between institutions and active fieldwork sites is reviewed at least every 5 years by both parties. Programs must provide documentation that both parties have reviewed the contract.
B.10.11.	Ensure that Level I fieldwork is integral to the program's curriculum design and include experiences designed to enrich didactic coursework through directed observation and participation in selected aspects of the occupational therapy process.
B.10.12.	Ensure that qualified personnel supervise Level I fieldwork. Examples may include, but are not limited to, currently licensed or credentialed occupational therapists and occupational therapy assistants, psychologists, physician assistants, teachers, social workers, nurses, and physical therapists.
B.10.13.	Document all Level I fieldwork experiences that are provided to students, including mechanisms for formal evaluation of student performance. Ensure that Level I fieldwork is not substituted for any part of Level II fieldwork.
B.10.14.	Ensure that the fieldwork experience is designed to promote clinical reasoning and reflective practice, to transmit the values and beliefs that enable ethical practice, and to develop professionalism and competence in career responsibilities.
B.10.15.	Provide Level II fieldwork in traditional and/or emerging settings, consistent with the curriculum design. In all settings, psychosocial factors influencing engagement in occupation must be understood and integrated for the development of client-centered, meaningful, occupation-based outcomes. The student can complete Level II fieldwork in a minimum of one setting if it is reflective of more than one practice area, or in a maximum of four different settings.
B.10.16.	Require a minimum of 24 weeks' full-time Level II fieldwork. This may be completed on a part-time basis as defined by the fieldwork placement in accordance with the fieldwork placement's usual and customary personnel policies as long as it is at least 50% of a full-time equivalent at that site.
B.10.17.	Ensure that the student is supervised by a currently licensed or credentialed occupational therapist who has a minimum of 1 year of practice experience subsequent to initial certification, and is adequately prepared to serve as a fieldwork educator. The supervising therapist may be engaged by the fieldwork site or by the educational program.
B.10.18.	Document a mechanism for evaluating the effectiveness of supervision (e.g., student evaluation of fieldwork) and for providing resources for enhancing supervision (e.g., materials on supervisory skills, continuing education opportunities, articles on theory and practice).

B.10.19.	Ensure that supervision provides protection of consumers and opportunities for appropriate role modeling of occupational therapy practice. Initially, supervision should be direct and then decrease to less direct supervision as is appropriate for the setting, the severity of the client's condition, and the ability of the student.
B.10.20.	Ensure that supervision provided in a setting where no occupational therapy services exist includes a documented plan for provision of occupational therapy services and supervision by a currently licensed or credentialed occupational therapist with at least 3 years of professional experience. Supervision must include a minimum of 8 hours per week. Supervision must be initially direct and then may be decreased to less direct supervision as is appropriate for the setting, the client's needs, and the ability of the student. An occupational therapy supervisor must be available, via a variety of contact measures, to the student during all working hours. An on-site supervisor designee of another profession must be assigned while the occupational therapy supervisor is off site.
B.10.21.	Document mechanisms for requiring formal evaluation of student performance on Level II fieldwork (e.g., the American Occupational Therapy Association *Fieldwork Performance Evaluation for the Occupational Therapy Student* or equivalent).
B.10.22.	Ensure that students attending Level II fieldwork outside the United States are supervised by an occupational therapist who graduated from a program approved by the World Federation of Occupational Therapists and has 1 year of experience in practice. Such fieldwork must not exceed 12 weeks.

Appendix D.
Answers to Multiple-Choice Questions

CHAPTER 1
1. c
2. d
3. b
4. d
5. b
6. c
7. d
8. b
9. c
10. b
11. d
12. b
13. b
14. d
15. c
16. d
17. c
18. a
19. d
20. c

CHAPTER 2
1. d
2. c
3. a
4. b
5. d
6. b
7. c
8. c
9. d
10. c
11. b
12. d
13. c
14. c
15. d
16. b
17. c
18. d
19. c
20. c

CHAPTER 3
1. c
2. b
3. a
4. d
5. d
6. a
7. a
8. b
9. a
10. b
11. d
12. c
13. a
14. d
15. d
16. d
17. c
18. c
19. b
20. d

CHAPTER 4
1. d
2. c
3. a
4. d
5. a
6. d
7. b
8. a
9. c
10. a
11. c
12. a
13. c
14. c
15. c
16. b
17. d
18. c
19. d
20. a

CHAPTER 5
1. c
2. d
3. b
4. a
5. c
6. b
7. d
8. a
9. c
10. d
11. b
12. c
13. a
14. b
15. d
16. a
17. c
18. d
19. b
20. d

CHAPTER 6
1. c
2. b
3. d
4. a
5. d
6. b
7. a
8. d
9. b
10. c
11. b
12. b
13. d
14. c
15. a
16. d
17. b
18. d
19. c
20. c

CHAPTER 7
1. b
2. a
3. c
4. b
5. a
6. a
7. c
8. b
9. a
10. c
11. c
12. a
13. d
14. b
15. b
16. a
17. c
18. d
19. a
20. c

CHAPTER 8
1. b
2. b
3. d
4. c
5. d
6. d
7. a
8. b
9. d
10. a
11. d
12. b
13. d
14. d
15. c
16. d
17. d
18. c
19. a
20. d

CHAPTER 9
1. d
2. b
3. d
4. c
5. b
6. d
7. a
8. d
9. b

10. d
11. d
12. b
13. a
14. b
15. b
16. c
17. d
18. c
19. a
20. a

CHAPTER 10
1. d
2. d
3. d
4. d
5. a
6. b
7. c
8. a
9. b
10. a
11. d
12. c
13. b
14. a
15. b
16. d
17. d
18. b
19. d
20. a

CHAPTER 11
1. d
2. b
3. a
4. b
5. a
6. c
7. b
8. b
9. a
10. d
11. b
12. c
13. d
14. a
15. a
16. b
17. a
18. b
19. b
20. d

CHAPTER 12
1. b
2. a
3. d
4. d
5. d
6. b
7. b
8. a
9. a
10. a
11. c
12. a
13. b
14. c
15. c

CHAPTER 13
1. d
2. a
3. b
4. c
5. a
6. b
7. c
8. a
9. c
10. c
11. c
12. a
13. b
14. a
15. b
16. c
17. d
18. a
19. b
20. a

CHAPTER 14
1. d
2. c
3. a
4. d
5. d
6. c
7. d
8. a
9. c
10. c
11. c
12. c
13. a
14. d
15. b

16. d
17. d
18. b
19. a
20. b

Chapter 15

1. a
2. b
3. a
4. c
5. d
6. d
7. a
8. b
9. d
10. a
11. d
12. c
13. d
14. a
15. c
16. d

Chapter 16

1. b
2. b
3. b
4. b
5. c
6. a
7. b
8. b
9. c
10. d
11. a
12. a
13. b
14. d
15. a
16. d
17. d
18. c
19. d
20. d

Chapter 17

1. d
2. a
3. b
4. c
5. d
6. a
7. c
8. c

9. a
10. b
11. a
12. b
13. a
14. b
15. c
16. c
17. b
18. d
19. d
20. d

Chapter 18

1. c
2. d
3. d
4. a
5. b
6. a
7. d
8. a
9. c
10. d
11. b
12. a
13. d

Chapter 19

1. c
2. d
3. c
4. b
5. d
6. a
7. d
8. b
9. b
10. c
11. a
12. d
13. d
14. d
15. c
16. b
17. d
18. a
19. b
20. c

Chapter 20

1. b
2. a
3. c
4. d

5. a
6. d
7. b
8. c
9. c
10. d
11. c
12. c
13. d
14. c
15. a
16. d
17. b
18. b
19. c
20. a

Chapter 21

1. a
2. d
3. d
4. a
5. a
6. b
7. d
8. c
9. c
10. c
11. b
12. d
13. d
14. a
15. b
16. d
17. c
18. c
19. b
20. c

Chapter 22

1. a
2. a
3. d
4. d
5. d
6. d
7. d
8. c
9. d
10. a
11. d
12. a
13. a
14. b
15. c

16. a
17. d
18. a
19. c
20. d

CHAPTER 23

1. c
2. c
3. d
4. a
5. d
6. a
7. c
8. d
9. b
10. a
11. c
12. c
13. b
14. a
15. a
16. d
17. b
18. c
19. d
20. c

CHAPTER 24

1. c
2. d
3. b
4. d
5. d
6. a
7. d
8. a
9. c
10. d
11. c
12. a
13. b
14. d
15. b
16. d
17. d
18. a
19. b
20. d

CHAPTER 25

1. b
2. d
3. b
4. d
5. b

6. a
7. c
8. d
9. a
10. b
11. c
12. c
13. d
14. a
15. b
16. a
17. d
18. c
19. b
20. b

CHAPTER 26

1. d
2. c
3. d
4. d
5. d
6. b
7. a
8. d
9. c
10. c
11. b
12. c
13. d
14. a
15. c
16. c
17. b
18. c
19. a
20. b

CHAPTER 27

1. b
2. b
3. d
4. c
5. a
6. c
7. b
8. d
9. b
10. d
11. b
12. d
13. c
14. a
15. c
16. a
17. b

18. c
19. c
20. b

CHAPTER 28

1. d
2. b
3. c
4. d
5. c
6. b
7. d
8. a
9. a
10. c
11. b
12. d
13. d
14. b
15. c
16. d
17. d
18. d
19. a
20. b

CHAPTER 29

1. d
2. d
3. b
4. c
5. a
6. b
7. a
8. a
9. a
10. d
11. d
12. d
13. a
14. d
15. b
16. a
17. a
18. b
19. d
20. d

CHAPTER 30

1. d
2. b
3. d
4. a
5. c
6. b
7. c

8. c
9. b
10. d
11. c
12. c
13. d
14. c
15. b
16. b
17. c
18. a
19. b
20. a

CHAPTER 31

1. a
2. a
3. c
4. a
5. d
6. c
7. a
8. c
9. b
10. a
11. d
12. d
13. c
14. a
15. b
16. a
17. d
18. c
19. c
20. d

CHAPTER 32

1. c
2. d
3. b
4. c
5. b
6. d
7. b
8. b
9. c
10. d
11. d
12. b
13. a
14. c
15. c
16. d
17. a
18. d
19. a
20. d

CHAPTER 33

1. d
2. d
3. d
4. a
5. b
6. c
7. c
8. a
9. c
10. c
11. a
12. a
13. d
14. d
15. d
16. d
17. d
18. b
19. a
20. b

CHAPTER 34

1. c
2. c
3. a
4. b
5. a
6. c
7. c
8. d
9. b
10. c
11. a
12. d
13. c
14. d
15. a
16. b
17. c
18. c
19. c
20. b

CHAPTER 35

1. c
2. b
3. b
4. c
5. b
6. d
7. d
8. b
9. c
10. d
11. c

12. b
13. b
14. b
15. c
16. c
17. c
18. d
19. c
20. c

CHAPTER 36

1. b
2. c
3. a
4. c
5. b
6. d
7. a
8. c
9. c
10. a
11. a
12. c
13. b
14. d
15. c
16. b
17. c
18. a
19. b
20. c

CHAPTER 37

1. d
2. d
3. b
4. b
5. a
6. d
7. c
8. c
9. d
10. c
11. c
12. d
13. d
14. c
15. a
16. d
17. a
18. b
19. d
20. b
21. b

Index

Page numbers in **bold** refer to tables.
Page numbers in *italics* refer to figures and exhibits.